The **Rough Gu**

# Tanzania

written and researched by

## Jens Finke

with additional contributions from

## Henry Stedman

ROUGH
GUIDES

www.roughguides.com

# Contents

**Wild Tanzania**
colour section
following p.368

◄◄ Hippo, Serengeti National Park ◄ Carved doorway, Stone Town, Zanzibar

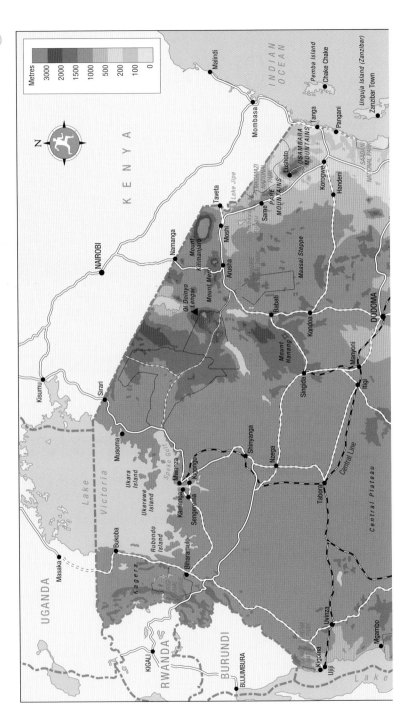

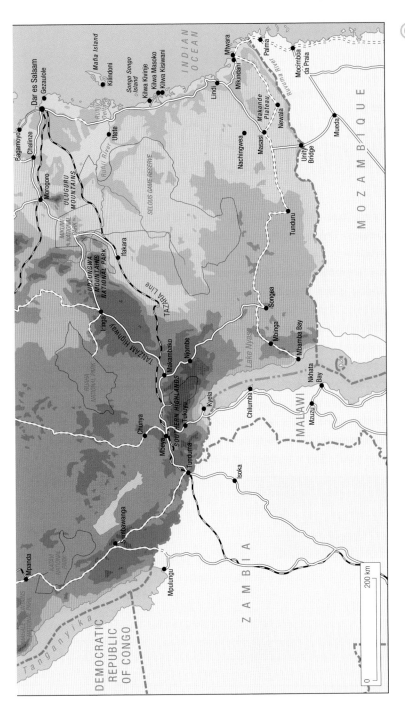

## Introduction to

# Tanzania

**Lying just south of the equator and bounded by the Indian Ocean, Tanzania, East Africa's largest country, is an endlessly fascinating place to visit. Filling the brochures are several world-famous attractions: Zanzibar, with its idyllic palm-fringed beaches, pristine coral reefs and historic Stone Town; the almost six-kilometre-high Mount Kilimanjaro, Africa's highest peak, which can be climbed in a week; and a glorious spread of wildlife sanctuaries that cover one third of the country, and include Ngorongoro Crater, and the dusty Serengeti plains – the classic Africa of elephants, antelopes, lions, leopards and cheetahs. Add to this Tanzania's rich ethnic diversity, rainforest hikes, and arguably the continent's best diving and snorkelling, and you have a holiday of a lifetime.**

For all these headline grabbers, Tanzania's richest asset is its **people**. Welcoming, unassuming and relaxed, they'll treat you with uncommon warmth and courtesy wherever you wander, and genuine friendships are easily made. Unusually for Africa, Tanzanians have a strong and peaceful sense of *dual* identity: as proud of their nation as they are of their tribe. Although most tribes ditched their traditional modes of life decades ago, a handful resist, the most famous of which are the cattle-herding **Maasai** – whose fiercely proud, red-robed spear-carrying warriors are a leitmotif for East Africa. Yet there are almost 130 other tribes, all with rich traditions, histories, customs, beliefs and music – some of which you'll be able to experience first-hand via Tanzania's award-winning cultural- tourism programmes.

# Where to go

Most visitors make a beeline for the national parks and reserves of Northern Tanzania, which includes the **Serengeti**, whose annual migration of over 2.5 million wildebeest, zebra and antelope – trailed by lions and hyenas, and picked off by crocodiles at river crossings – is an awesome spectacle. Another highlight is **Ngorongoro Crater** next door, an enormous volcanic caldera providing a year-round haven for rhinos, and plentiful predators. Ngorongoro is also the starting point for a wild hike to Tanzania's only active volcano, **Ol Doinyo Lengai**, and on to **Lake Natron**, an immense salt lake appealing to flamingos and desert fanatics alike. Less well-known parks include **Tarangire**, fantastic for elephants, whose size is amply complemented by forests of gigantic baobabs; **Lake Manyara**, in a particularly spectacular section of the Rift Valley; and **Arusha National Park**, which contains the country's second-highest mountain, **Mount Meru**. The main base for Northern Circuit safaris is **Arusha**, which also has a clutch of **cultural tourism programmes** within easy reach. East of here is snow-capped **Mount Kilimanjaro**, the week-long ascent of which is an exhausting but fulfilling challenge, while to the south are the ancient formations of the **Pare** and **Usambara mountains**, repositories of some of the world's most biologically diverse rainforests, especially at **Amani Nature Reserve** near the coast, which well deserves its nickname of "the Galápagos of Africa".

Much of Central Tanzania is dry and semi-arid woodland, at the centre of which – almost a desert – is **Dodoma**, Tanzania's administrative capital. It's mainly useful as a springboard for seeing the fabulous **prehistoric rock**

## Fact file

- Tanzania was **created in 1964** through the union of Tanganyika, on the mainland, and Zanzibar. The administrative capital is Dodoma, but Dar es Salaam is the social and economic powerhouse.

- Covering **945,203 square kilometres**, Tanzania is four times bigger than the UK, and twice the size of California. The population is 40 million.

- Tanzania is a **multi-party democracy**. Elections on the mainland give no cause for concern, but Zanzibar's separate polls (the islands are semi-autonomous) are bitterly divisive.

- Tanzania is among the world's poorest countries, and receives over $1 billion annually in aid. The average salary is $60–80 a month, but a third of the population subsist on under a **dollar a day**.

- Tanzania is among the four most **naturally diverse** nations on earth, and thirty percent of the country is protected natural habitat. Species counts include 320 types of mammals, around 1200 kinds of birds, as many butterflies, over 10,000 plant species, and hundreds of species of fish, corals and other marine life.

- With 128 officially recognized tribes and a handful more ignored by the census, Tanzania is second only to Congo for **ethnic diversity** in Africa. Unlike Congo Tanzania's ethnic melange is admirably peaceful, helped along by Kiswahili as a common **language**.

**paintings** of the Irangi Hills, the oldest of which date back at least eighteen thousand years. The town of Morogoro offers hikers access to the **Uluguru Mountains**, another place notable for high species diversity, as well as interesting local culture. Even richer are the **Udzungwa Mountains**: their eastern flanks are amazing for seeing primates, while the western side is birdwatching paradise. Safari-goers are catered for by a trio of sanctuaries: the star is the vast **Selous Game Reserve**, housing more elephants than anywhere else in the country. It's a beautiful place, too, the northern sector watered by the Rufiji River's inland delta.

Also good for wildlife is **Ruaha National Park**, en route to southern Tanzania. Ignored by mainstream tourism, the Southern Highlands are a walkers' wonderland of volcanic crater lakes, dense rainforests and craggy peaks and the flower-bedecked **Kitulo Plateau**, with over fifty species of orchid. The highlands are best explored in the company of a guide from the town of Mbeya, or from Tukuyu – Tanzania's wettest place. Further south is **Lake Nyasa**, the southernmost of the Rift Valley lakes and home to hundreds of species of colourful cichlid fish; a port-hopping trip on the weekly ferry is one of the country's classic journeys.

The other big Rift Valley lake, in Western Tanzania, is the immense **Lake Tanganyika** – the world's longest and second-deepest freshwater body, and scene of another unforgettable ferry ride, with luck aboard the vintage MV *Liemba*. The lakeshore is also the scenic setting for two remote national parks – **Mahale Mountains** and **Gombe Stream** – both of which are home to **chimpanzees**. North-western Tanzania is dominated by the shallow **Lake Victoria**, the world's second-largest freshwater lake. The views are magnificent, and the lake's southwestern corner contains the little-known **Rubondo Island National Park**, positively swarming with birds. Equally remote, and just as rewarding, is **Kagera Region** between Uganda, Rwanda and the lake, where a cultural-tourism programme from Bukoba gets you to places that few tourists have seen.

The Indian Ocean is an altogether different experience. Especially recommended is **Zanzibar**, one of Africa's most famous and enticing destinations. It comprises the islands of Unguja and Pemba, which have languorous **beaches** and multicoloured coral reefs aplenty

## Hey, Mzungu!

*Mzungu* (plural *wazungu*) is a word white travellers will hear all over East Africa – children, especially, take great delight in chanting it whenever you're around. Strictly speaking, a *mzungu* is a white European, although Afro-Europeans and Afro-Americans need not feel left out, being known as *mzungu mwafrikano* (Asian travellers will have to content themselves with *mchina*, and Indians *mhindi*). The term was first reported by nineteenth-century missionaries and explorers, who flattered themselves to think that it meant wondrous, clever or extraordinary.

The real meaning of the word is perhaps more appropriate. Stemming from *zungua*, it means to go round, to turn, to wander, to travel, or just to be tiresome. However weary you may grow of the *mzungu* tag, you should at least be grateful that the Maasai word for Europeans didn't stick: inspired by the sight of the trouser-wearing invaders from the north, they christened the newcomers *iloridaa enjekat* – those who confine their farts.

▶ Zebras, Ngorongoro Crater

(perfect for **diving and snorkelling**), ancient ruins, and – in the form of **Stone Town** – a fascinating Arabian-style labyrinth of narrow, crooked alleyways packed with nineteenth-century mansions, palaces and bazaars. On the mainland, the biggest settlement is **Dar es Salaam**, the country's former capital and still its most important city, and worth hanging around in to sample its exuberant nightlife. North of here are a series of beach resorts (**Pangani** is best), the coastal **Saadani National Park**, and several towns involved in the nineteenth-century **slave trade** – most infamously **Bagamoyo**, stuffed with buildings from the time. Tanzania's south coast is wilder: historical colour is provided by the ruins of the medieval island-state of **Kilwa**, in its heyday one of the wealthiest and most important cities in all of Africa. Offshore, the **Mafia archipelago** has its own fair share of historical ruins, plus stunning coral reefs.

▲ Locals playing bao, Stone Town, Zanzibar

# When to go

Being tropical, Tanzania lacks the four seasons of temperate zones, and instead has two rainy and two dry seasons, mostly dictated by the western Indian Ocean's monsoon winds and currents. The **long rains** (*masika*) should fall from March to May (almost certainly in April and May), but the lighter **short rains** (*mvuli*) are impossible to predict with certainty: they should, depending on the location, fall for about a month sometime between October and December, but in southern Tanzania they tend to merge with the long rains, giving just one dry season, being May or June to November. **Coastal and lakeside regions** are hot and almost always humid, making the air feel even hotter than it really is. Temperatures drop by about 6°C (11°F) for every 1000m you climb, making for very pleasant conditions in **highland regions**, although it can get chilly in June and July.

In general, **dry-season travel** – particularly June to September – is best: it's not as humid, wildlife is easier to see, and even the roughest unsurfaced roads are drivable, which isn't always the case in the rains. Try to avoid the

coast (including Zanzibar) during the rains, when the heavy humidity and insects can be intolerable. Also not the best time for Zanzibar, but with not much impact on the mainland, is the month of **Ramadan** (see dates on p.000), when most restaurants are closed, and the daytime mood, in Stone Town particularly, isn't at its brightest.

## Tanzania's temperature ranges and average rainfall

|  | Jan | Feb | Mar | Apr | May | Jun | Jul | Aug | Sep | Oct | Nov | Dec |
|---|---|---|---|---|---|---|---|---|---|---|---|---|
| **Arusha (altitude 1400m)** | | | | | | | | | | | | |
| °C | 14–28 | 14–29 | 15–28 | 16–25 | 15–23 | 13–22 | 12–22 | 13–23 | 12–25 | 14–27 | 15–27 | 14–27 |
| Rainy days/mm | 8/70 | 8/75 | 12/140 | 19/225 | 12/85 | 4/15 | 3/10 | 2/6 | 2/10 | 4/25 | 10/125 | 11/100 |
| **Dar es Salaam (sea level)** | | | | | | | | | | | | |
| °C | 23–32 | 23–32 | 23–32 | 22–31 | 21–30 | 19–29 | 18–29 | 18–29 | 18–30 | 20–31 | 21–31 | 23–32 |
| Rainy days/mm | 7/80 | 5/60 | 12/130 | 19/265 | 13/180 | 5/40 | 5/30 | 4/25 | 5/25 | 6/60 | 8/120 | 9/110 |
| **Kigoma (altitude 781m)** | | | | | | | | | | | | |
| °C | 19–28 | 19–28 | 19–28 | 20–28 | 19–29 | 17–29 | 16–29 | 17–30 | 19–30 | 20–29 | 19–28 | 19–28 |
| Rainy days/mm | 9/75 | 8/75 | 9/60 | 11/100 | 6/20 | 0/0 | 0/0 | 1/10 | 2/20 | 9/70 | 12/120 | 12/155 |
| **Mbeya (altitude 1700m)** | | | | | | | | | | | | |
| °C | 14–23 | 14–24 | 13–24 | 12–23 | 9–22 | 5–22 | 5–22 | 6–23 | 9–25 | 12–27 | 13–26 | 13–24 |
| Rainy days/mm | 20/200 | 18/170 | 18/170 | 14/110 | 4/20 | 0/1 | 0/0 | 0/0 | 1/5 | 2/15 | 7/65 | 8/180 |
| **Zanzibar (sea level)** | | | | | | | | | | | | |
| °C | 22–32 | 24–32 | 25–32 | 25–30 | 23–28 | 23–28 | 22–27 | 22–28 | 22–28 | 22–30 | 23–31 | 24–31 |
| Rainy days/mm | 5/75 | 5/60 | 8/150 | 11/350 | 10/280 | 4/55 | 2/45 | 2/40 | 3/50 | 4/90 | 9/170 | 8/145 |

# 16

## things not to miss

*It's not possible to see everything that Tanzania has to offer in one visit, and we don't suggest you try. What follows is a selective taste of the country's highlights – dramatic landscapes, idyllic beaches and awe-inspiring wildlife – arranged in five colour-coded categories. All highlights have a page reference to take you straight into the guide, where you can find out more.*

**01 Mount Kilimanjaro** Page **262** • Africa's highest mountain and the world's tallest free-standing volcano, Kilimanjaro draws hikers from all over the world – although only two thirds of them get to Uhuru Peak at the very top.

**02** **Tarangire National Park** Page **340** • In the dry season, Tarangire is the best place in all of Africa for seeing elephants – though even these mighty beasts are dwarfed by the park's huge baobab trees, many of them over a thousand years old.

**04** **Kondoa-Irangi rock paintings** Page **233** • The Irangi Hills of central Tanzania are home to a remarkable complex of painted rock shelters, the oldest dating back some 18,000 years.

**05** **Kilwa Kisiwani** Page **166** • The spectacular ruins of the island city-state of Kilwa Kisiwani are testimony to the immense riches that were made first from gold, then from ivory and slaves.

**03** **Cultural tourism** Page **54** • Often tacked on to the end of a trip as an afterthought, Tanzania's cultural-tourism programmes end up being the highlight of many a holiday.

## 06 Hiking in the Usambara and Udzungwa

**mountains** Pages **283** & **473** • Ancient rainforests, rare plant and animal species, and eyeball-to-eyeball encounters with primates; hiking in the Usambara and Udzungwa mountains is one of Tanzania's foremost pleasures.

## 07 Forodhani Gardens, Stone Town

Page **525** • Stone Town's waterfront Forodhani Gardens are a paradise for street-food enthusiasts, with a bewildering array of seafood, snacks and even roast bananas covered in melted chocolate – and all for no more than a dollar or two.

## 09 Scuba diving

Page **160** • The coral reefs off Tanzania's coast at Zanzibar and Mafia Island offer some of the world's finest scuba diving.

## 08 Chimpanzees at Gombe Stream and Mahale

**Mountains** Pages **437** & **442** • Studies of wild chimp populations at Mahale Mountains and Gombe Stream national parks have shed light on many fascinating aspects of chimp life.

## 10 Serengeti
Page **374** • The legendary Serengeti is home to Africa's highest density of plains game and the backdrop to one of the greatest wildlife spectacles on earth, when over 2.5 million animals set off on their annual migration.

## 11 Beaches, Zanzibar Page **553** • There's no better place to relax after a hot and dusty safari than on Zanzibar's beaches.

## 12 Ngorongoro Conservation Area Page **363** • An enormous caldera of an extinct volcano provides the spectacular setting for Ngorongoro's abundant plains game and their predators – close-up encounters with lions, buffaloes and rhinos are virtually guaranteed.

**13 Seafood, Zanzibar** Page **524** • Seafood features prominently in Swahili cooking, especially in Zanzibar, where fish, prawns, squid and lobster are served with subtle spices and blended with sauces.

**14 Lake ferries** Pages **434** & **496** • Each of Tanzania's great lakes has ferry services, including two classic overnight journeys: down Lake Tanganyika aboard the venerable MV *Liemba*, or alongside the uplifting Livingstone Mountains on Lake Nyasa.

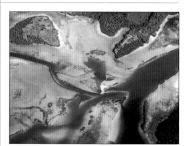

**15 Indian Ocean flights** Page **157** • Any flight from the mainland to Zanzibar or Mafia Island offers an unforgettable bird's-eye panorama of the coral reefs of the Indian Ocean.

**16 Stone Town** Page **509** • Stone Town's labyrinthine network of narrow streets is magically atmospheric, with opulent nineteenth-century palaces and poignant reminders of the slave trade at every turn.

# Basics

# Basics

# Getting there

Flying is the only practical way to reach Tanzania from outside East Africa – there are direct or one-stop flights from Europe to Dar es Salaam, Kilimanjaro (between Moshi and Arusha) and Zanzibar. Travellers from North America, Australia and New Zealand will have to change planes in Europe or South Africa. Don't worry if you can't find a direct or through flight to Zanzibar, or if it's too expensive: the twenty-minute hop from Dar can be booked on arrival or online, and there are ferries, too. If you don't want to arrange things yourself, package tours offer classic "beach and bush" combinations, being a wildlife safari followed by time on the beach, usually in Zanzibar. A more adventurous approach is overland, easiest (and safest) from southern Africa, by train or by bus. Land routes from Tanzania's immediate neighbours are also fine, but Sudan poses a likely insurmountable obstacle if you're thinking of driving down from Egypt.

## Flights from the UK and Ireland

The only direct flight **from the UK** is on British Airways thrice a week from London Heathrow to Dar (9hr; from £750 return in high season), arriving in the morning; **from Ireland** (€1150 from Dublin) and UK airports you'll need to catch a connecting flight to London. The cheapest flights are one-stop via Dubai on Emirates (15hr to Dar; from £540 return in high season). KLM has a wide choice (via Amsterdam) from various UK airports, plus Dublin and Cork, to Kilimanjaro (10hr 30min; from £950/€1140 return) and Dar (12hr 30min; from £1000/€1200), but these arrive at night. Faster, and arriving by day, are flights with KLM (9hr) and Kenya Airways (11hr) via Nairobi, with the final leg on Tanzania's Precisionair. For Zanzibar, two-stop routings, cobbled together by online agents, start at £860 return.

## Flights from the US and Canada

There are no direct flights from North America to Tanzania. The fastest one-stop routings **from the US** – and also the cheapest – are on Emirates from JFK to Dar via Dubai (21hr; from $1900 return in high season), and Northwest/KLM from JFK via Amsterdam to Dar (21hr) or Kilimanjaro (19hr), both costing $2000–2300. Slower is British Airways via London (25–28hr; $2100). Two-stop routings,

which can take over thirty hours, are not necessarily cheaper. **From Canada**, best currently is Swiss from Toronto or Montreal via Zurich and Nairobi (21hr to Dar; from Can$2200 return in high season).

## Flights from Australia, New Zealand and South Africa

There are no direct flights from the Antipodes – all require a stop in Asia, South Africa or the Middle East. The best deals **from Australia** are currently on Qatar Airways, with the first leg on Singapore Airlines (26hr 30min from Sydney to Dar, via Singapore; from Aus$2200 return in high season), or Virgin Atlantic (30hr; Aus$2300). Emirates also have good deals, and are by far the cheapest option from **New Zealand** (31hr from Auckland; from NZ$4300 return in high season).

From **South Africa**, South African Airways has daily flights to Dar, arriving after sunset, from Johannesburg (3hr 30min; from R5500 return in high season) and Cape Town (7hr; from R7650). 1Time fly Saturday mornings from Johannesburg to Zanzibar (3hr 30min; R4600 return). Air Tanzania, which used to fly daily from Johannesburg, is not currently operating.

## RTW tickets

Tanzania seldom features as an option on **Round the World (RTW) tickets**, but

Kenya's capital, Nairobi, does, and it's just a few hours away by bus. Prices range from £1500 to £2500/$2500 to $4000. The classic African RTW option is to arrive in Nairobi and make your own way overland to Johannesburg or Cape Town for the onward flight.

Many sites have online route planners, but one and all are a complete pain to use, especially as one date or airport variant can shoot up the price. It's much easier to deal with a real human. Recommended **RTW specialists** to call include the UK-based Gap Year (ⓦ www.gapyear.com), and US-based Air Treks (ⓦ www.airtreks.com). Major airline alliances also offer RTW tickets, such as ⓦ www.oneworld.com and ⓦ www.star alliance.com; the latter also offers an "Africa Airpass" (mostly South African Airways routes) that includes Dar es Salaam.

## Airlines and agents

For the best airfares, buy well in advance, even six months before travel. Shop around: the cost of the exact same seat can vary greatly.

### Airlines

The airlines listed below all fly to Tanzania; their Tanzanian offices, if any, are noted in the "Listings" sections on p.109 (Dar), p.318 (Arusha) and p.530 (Zanzibar). Local airlines are listed on p.32.

**1Time** South Africa 0861/345345, ⓦ www.1time .co.za.
**Air Malawi** South Africa ⓣ 011/390 1211, UK ⓣ 020/8933 1000, US ⓣ 1-800/537-1182; ⓦ www.airmalawi.com.
**Air Zimbabwe** UK ⓣ 020/7399 3600, US ⓣ 1-800/742-3006, Australia ⓣ 02/9221 9988; ⓦ www.airzimbabwe.com.
**British Airways** UK ⓣ 0844/493 0787, Ireland ⓣ 1890/626 747, US & Canada ⓣ 1-800/AIRWAYS, Australia ⓣ 1300/767 177, New Zealand ⓣ 09/966 9777, South Africa ⓣ 011/441 8600; ⓦ www.ba.com.
**Emirates** UK ⓣ 0844/800 2777, US & Canada ⓣ 1-800/777-3999, Australia ⓣ 1300/303 777, New Zealand ⓣ 05/0836 4728, South Africa ⓣ 0861/364 728; ⓦ www.emirates.com.
**Ethiopian Airlines** US ⓣ 1-800/445-2733, UK ⓣ 020/8987 7000; ⓦ www.ethiopianairlines.com.
**Kenya Airways** US & Canada ⓣ 1-866/536-9224, Australia ⓣ 02/9767 4310, UK ⓣ 01784/888 222,

South Africa ⓣ 0822/345 786; ⓦ www.kenya -airways.com.
**KLM** US & Canada ⓣ 1-800/225-2525 (Northwest), UK ⓣ 0870/507 4074, Ireland ⓣ 1850/747 400, Australia ⓣ 1300/392 192, New Zealand ⓣ 09/921 6040, South Africa ⓣ 0860/247 747; ⓦ www .klm.com.
**LAM** Mozambique ⓣ 800/147000 or 01/465809, South Africa ⓣ 011/616 4536 or 11/622 4889; ⓦ www.lam.co.mz.
**Precisionair** Kenya ⓣ 020/327 4747, Uganda ⓣ 077/276 0268; ⓦ www.precisionairtz.com.
**Qatar Airways** US ⓣ 1-877/777-2827, Canada ⓣ 1-888/366-5666, UK ⓣ 020/7399 2577, Australia ⓣ 1300/340 600, South Africa ⓣ 011/523 2928; ⓦ www.qatarairways.com.
**South African Airways** South Africa ⓣ 011/978 1111, US and Canada ⓣ 1-800/722-9675, UK ⓣ 0870/747 1111, Australia ⓣ 1300/435 972, New Zealand ⓣ 09/977 2237; ⓦ www.flysaa.com.
**Swiss** US & Canada ⓣ 1-877/359-7947, UK ⓣ 0845/601 0956, Ireland ⓣ 1890/200 515, Australia ⓣ 1300/724 666, New Zealand ⓣ 09/977 2238, South Africa ⓣ 0860/040 506; ⓦ www.swiss.com.

### Travel agents

The following offer reductions for **students and under-26s, and** have stores you can visit.
**North South Travel** UK ⓣ 01245/608291, ⓦ www.northsouthtravel.co.uk. Friendly and competitive agency offering discounted airfares worldwide, with the big pull being that all profits support projects in the developing world, especially sustainable tourism.
**STA Travel** UK ⓣ 0871/230 0040, US ⓣ 1-800/781-4040, Canada ⓣ 1-888/427-5639, Australia ⓣ 134 782, New Zealand ⓣ 0800/474 400, South Africa ⓣ 0861/781 781; ⓦ www.statravel.com.
**Trailfinders** UK ⓣ 0845/058 5858, ⓦ www .trailfinders.com; Ireland ⓣ 01/677 7888, ⓦ www .trailfinders.ie; Australia ⓣ 1300/780 212, ⓦ www .trailfinders.com.au.
**Travel Cuts** US ⓣ 1-800/592-2887, Canada ⓣ 1-886/246-9762; ⓦ www.travelcuts.com.

## Overland from Africa

**Visas** (see p.69) can be bought on arrival at any overland border. There are direct bus services into the country from **Uganda** (Kampala to Bukoba, or via Nairobi to Mwanza, Arusha or Dar es Salaam), **Kenya** (Nairobi to Mwanza, Arusha or Dar es Salaam; Mombasa to Tanga or Dar es

Salaam), and **Malawi** (Lusaka to Mbeya and Dar es Salaam). You'll need to change bus at the border if coming from **Mozambique**, **Burundi**, **Rwanda** or **Zambia** – the last of these has a weekly ferry connection from Mpulungu to Kigoma, and a weekly train from New Kapiri Mposhi to Dar es Salaam. Overlanding from **South Africa** is perfectly feasible, whether by road (sealed all the way), or by train via Zambia, but coming overland from **Egypt** – only feasible via northern **Sudan and Ethiopia** – is not for the faint hearted, as several stretches are known for banditry.

## Overland truck tours

If Tanzania is part of a longer trip, and you're young at heart, consider an **overland truck tour** in a converted lorry, taking three to twelve weeks from Cape Town to Tanzania (and on to Kenya), or vice versa. Given the wealth of things to see and do along the way, they can be rather hurried affairs, and are often dominated by party animals who could be on Mars for all they cared, but the trips do provide a easy way of getting a feel for Africa. The classic trans-Africa trip went from the UK to Cape Town via Morocco or Egypt, but conflict in central Africa and Sudan means most tours finish in Cameroon, continuing – one flight later – from Kampala or Nairobi. The operators listed below cover the Cape Town to Nairobi route via Tanzania. Costs vary depending on how much time you spend inside national parks: expect to pay £30–80 per day, including your contribution to the "kitty".

**Absolute Africa** UK ☎020/8742 0226, ⓦwww .absoluteafrica.com.
**African Trails** UK ☎01580/761171, ⓦwww .africantrails.co.uk.
**Drifters** South Africa ☎011/888 1160, ⓦwww .drifters.co.za.
**Exodus** See p.22.
**Guerba** UK ☎01373/826611, ⓦwww.guerba.com.
**Kumuka Worldwide** UK ☎0800/092 9595, Ireland ☎1800/946 843, US & Canada ☎1800/517 0867, Australia ☎1300/667 277, New Zealand ☎0800/440 499, South Africa ☎0800/991 503; ⓦwww.kumuka.com.

## Package tours

As far as Tanzania is concerned, most **package tours** are "beach and bush" combinations of wildlife safaris followed by spells on Zanzibar or perhaps Mafia. Whilst there are hundreds of overseas operators offering such packages, only very few run the trips themselves (and then only through subsidiaries). The rest piece together their offerings using (hopefully) carefully selected hotels, lodges and safari companies ("ground handlers"). Of course, you could do the same thing using the information in this book, but you won't get the often hefty discounts on accommodation available to agents, some of which may be passed on to you. It's also much easier to deal with just one company and pay just one overall price.

Whilst many companies offer **pre-packaged tours** with set departure dates, all claim to specialize in **tailor-made** trips. What this means is that you either take a sample itinerary and send it back marked with your preferences, or – better, but time-consuming – work out exactly what you want beforehand in terms of so many nights here or there and in what kind of accommodation, then fire it off to several operators and see what comes back. Incidentally, tours offered by UK operators can also be booked by people outside the UK, and vice versa, so don't limit yourself to companies in your own country.

The following are the cream of overseas **specialist tour operators** for Tanzania. Most demand full payment up to three months before departure. Offering the same services are **Tanzanian safari operators**: the best of them are reviewed on pp.51–53.

## Package tour operators

**Africa Travel Resource** UK ☎01306/880770, US & Canada ☎1-888/487-5418; ⓦwww .africatravelresource.com. An "outfitter" with a solid reputation for mid- to upper-range safaris, built on a superlatively comprehensive and impartial website. They don't actually run the trips, but their knowledge of the various options, especially accommodation, is unrivalled.
**African Portfolio** US ☎1-800/700-3677, ⓦwww.onsafari.com. Highly regarded US/Zimbabwe outfit offering a range of customizable packages, including birding.
**Aim 4 Africa** UK ☎0845/408 4541, ⓦwww .aim4africa.com. Responsible agent for all manner of trips and in all price ranges, including a dollop of cultural interaction and offbeat activities.

**Awaken to Africa** US ☎1-888/271-8269, ⓦwww.awakentoafrica.com. A Tanzanian/American company (registered in Tanzania, too), with excellent service and guides, responsible involvement, and a preference for smaller and more intimate lodges and camps, as well as cultural side trips.

**Baobab Travel** UK ☎0121/314 6011, ⓦwww.baobabtravel.com. Responsible and ethical agent offering tailor-made packages all over the country; Tanzanian-owned operators are preferred.

**Exodus** UK ☎020/8675 5550, Ireland ☎01/804 7153, US ☎1-800/843-4272, Canada ☎1-800/267-3347, Australia ☎1300/655 433, New Zealand ☎0800/838 747, South Africa ☎011/807 3333; ⓦwww.exodus.co.uk. Originally just focused on overlanding, Exodus now offer adventures worldwide. They have set departures to Tanzania up to mid-range level, and pay more than lip service to responsible tourism.

**Foxes African Safaris** UK ☎01452/862288, ⓦwww.tanzaniasafaris.info. British family-run company based in Tanzania; see review on p.53.

**Gane & Marshall** UK ☎01822/600 600, ⓦwww.ganeandmarshall.com. A long-established agent using ethically and environmentally sound local companies. Also offers walking and cycling in the Rift Valley, and various options in western Tanzania.

**IntoAfrica** UK ☎0114/255 5610, ⓦwww.intoafrica.co.uk. A Tanzanian-British outfit gleaning tons of highly deserved recommendations, particularly useful for veering off the beaten track. They run their own trips (the Tanzanian arm is Maasai Wanderings, ⓦwww.maasaiwanderings.com), and fully live up to their fair-trade/ethical promise.

**Naipenda Safaris** US ☎1-888/404-4499, ⓦwww.naipendasafaris.com. More a Tanzanian company with US representation, this affordable set-up offers an unusual array of custom-made trips including tribal culture, volunteering, art, and even cooking.

**Tanzania Odyssey** UK ☎020/7471 8780, US ☎1-866/356-4691; ⓦwww.tanzaniaodyssey.com. Long-established and knowledgeable specialists whose trump card is tailor-made safaris at cost, meaning their profit lies in commissions (which you'd be paying anyway if booking direct).

**Tribes** UK ☎01728/685971, ⓦwww.tribes.co.uk. A wide choice of luxurious yet adventurous trips away from the crowds, with some community involvement, inevitably with the Maasai.

# Health

If your inoculations are up to date and you're taking anti-malarials, Tanzania is unlikely to afflict you with more than an upset stomach, sunburn or perhaps heatstroke. Just as well, given the scarcity of well-equipped hospitals and clinics: the better ones are included in the "Listings" following our town accounts.

First stop before coming is your family doctor or a travel clinic, for advice, prescriptions and vaccinations: typically **recommended jabs** or boosters are for typhoid, tetanus, polio and hepatitis A. You'll also need to show a **yellow fever** vaccination certificate if your passport has a stamp from a country in an "endemic zone", which includes all of West, Central and East Africa down to Zambia, though not Malawi or Mozambique. Tanzania itself is not an endemic zone, although some other countries may think it is, so if you'll be travelling beyond Tanzania, get the shot. **Rabies** jabs can be skipped unless you'll be handling animals or travelling extensively by bicycle; the disease is treatable in any case. For advice on HIV and sexually transmitted diseases, see p.62.

## Travel clinics

The following websites list **travel clinics**, and also have general advice.

**Australia & New Zealand** Travellers' Medical and Vaccination Centre ⊛ www.tmvc.com.au.

**Canada** Public Health Agency ⊛ www.phac-aspc.gc.ca.

**Ireland** Tropical Medical Bureau ⊛ tmb.exodus.ie. Also lists centres in the UK and elsewhere.

**South Africa** Travel Doctor ⊛ www.traveldoctor.co.za.

**UK (England, Wales, Northern Ireland)** National Health Travel Network ⊛ www.nathnac.org.

**UK (Scotland)** Health Protection Scotland ⊛ www.hps.scot.nhs.uk/travel.

**US** CDC ⊛ www.cdc.gov/travel.

## General precautions

In the tropics, where heat dances with humidity, take more care than usual over minor **cuts and scrapes**, which can easily become throbbing infections should you ignore them. Tropical conditions also favour **fungal infections**, which flourish perfectly well in groins, among toes, or under thick hair. Rarely more than itchy inconveniences, fungal infections can be difficult to dispose of once firmly established, so shy away from using soap or damp or dirty towels that are not your own. After washing, dry yourself thoroughly, and, if you sweat profusely, use medicated talc to dust yourself off with. In bedrooms and bathrooms, it's best to wear (your own) sandals: you never know what fungus has taken a liking to the floor, or to the flip-flops provided by guesthouses.

Other reasons for not walking barefoot (except on sandy beaches) are **jiggers**: fly pupae that like to burrow into your toes. Less horrible than they sound, jiggers are easily disposed of by physically removing the bugs with a pin or a pair of tweezers, and repeatedly dousing the cavities with iodine or some other disinfectant until the holes close up, a few days later.

In cheap hotels, check bedsheets for tiny brown spots (**fleas** are messy eaters). Move elsewhere if you find them, as fleas can also carry diseases as well as being hell to cohabit with. That said, out of the hundreds of guesthouses so far sampled by the author, only two had fleas (he says, scratching his leg).

Finally, be sure to have a thorough **dental check-up** before leaving, and take extra care of your teeth while away: stringy meat, acidic fruit, but especially sodas can cause diabolical damage. There are reliable dentists in Arusha, Dar es Salaam and Dodoma.

### Solar protection

Tanzania lies just south of the equator, so for much of the day the sun hangs near its zenith. This means that skin that is normally vertical is less likely to get **sunburn** than in, say, Spain or Miami, but it makes the

## Medicine bag

Common medicines are widely available in Tanzania, so your **medical kit** only needs to tide you over until you reach a clinic or pharmacy: a day at most unless you're way off the beaten track, meaning you can dispense with antibiotics. Be aware that metal tubes of cream almost always spring leaks, so keep them in a box or transfer the contents into a jar. Apart from **malarial prophylactics**, **solar protection** and perhaps **insect repellent**, the following are useful to have around:

**Anti-diarrhoeal tablets** Imodium (Loperamide) does the trick; for emergency use only.

**Antihistamine cream** For insect bites. Alternatively, smear bites with toothpaste: you heard it here first…

**Antiseptic** More versatile than creams are alcohol, tea tree oil or iodine (also useful for purifying water).

**Pain relief** Aspirin also relieves inflammations.

**Tweezers** Included in Swiss Army knives.

**Wound dressing** Fabric plasters adhere best and let wounds breathe. If you'll be indulging in physically dangerous activities (such as mountaineering), also pack gauze, surgical tape and wound-closures.

---

sun a bigger hazard for shoulders, noses, tops of balding heads, even feet – in short, anything horizontal, which is why swimming or snorkelling can leave you with quite severe burns. The solution, obviously, is to use high-factor sunblock on exposed limbs and lip salve, and to wear a hat. If you're dipping underwater, however, it's best to replace sunblock with clothing: Tanzania's amazing marine life doesn't thrive on sun cream. Failing prevention, a great **sunburn remedy** is yoghurt or curdled milk (ask for *mtindi* or *maziwa mgando*), spread generously on affected areas, or use aloe vera, available in some local supermarkets.

Your eyes also need protection: shiny white beaches can cause eye-strain, and may even get you "snow-blind". UV-shielded **sunglasses** minimize the risks, but raise psychological barriers against people (no eye contact), so use them only when you really need to.

The intensity of the equatorial sun (fewer atmospheric kilometres to burn through) can also stoke **heatstroke**, a potentially dangerous condition where you stop sweating while still hot. Subsequent symptoms include fever, cramps, rapid pulse and/or vomiting, followed by mental confusion, hallucinations ensue, and eventually death. Victims should be removed to as cool a place as possible, covered in wet towels or have their clothes soaked in water,

and be given rehydration mix (p.25). More common but not dangerous are **skin rashes**, especially between November and March when the weather's particularly sultry. Oddly enough, a warm shower helps (it opens the pores), as does wearing loose cotton clothes. Lastly, if you tend to **sweat** a lot, you should keep cooler than most other people, but you'll need to eat more salt to compensate.

## Malaria

East Africa's **malaria** strain, *Plasmodium falciparum*, is transmitted by the bite of female *Anopheles* mosquitoes, and can be fatal if untreated. The disease is present throughout Tanzania, and peaks during and after the rains, though the risk decreases with altitude: negligible above 1400m, absent over 1800m. The disease is most prevalent along the coast (including Zanzibar), around lakes, and anywhere with still or stagnant water, including banana groves, as the plants hold pools of water. **Prevention** is better than cure: start a course of prophylactics before leaving home, and take precautions against bites once you arrive. Don't worry yourself sick about malaria: it's treatable if properly diagnosed. The symptoms appear anything from a few days to several weeks after infection, so if you feel poorly after returning home, tell your doctor where you've been.

## Prophylactics

Most **anti-malarial tablets** contain synthetic quinine. A doctor or travel clinic can provide personalized recommendations – especially important for children, pregnant women and those with medical conditions. Note that Proguanil and Chloroquine, widely used elsewhere, are useless as East Africa's malarial strain has acquired considerable resistance. The main drugs are:

**Malarone** Taken daily. A combination of Atovaquone and Proguanil hydrochloride, this is very effective, with few side effects compared to the rest so long as your liver and kidneys are okay. Upwards of $25/£20 a week. In Europe, it's only prescribed for trips up to three weeks duration.

**Mefloquine** Taken weekly. Better known by the brand name Lariam, this is very cheap ($3 a tablet in Tanzania), and can be taken over several months, but is beset by potential side effects – most commonly mild depression, dizziness or sleep disturbances – and is specifically warned against for scubadivers. Some travellers report minimizing side effects by taking half a tablet at four-day intervals; start two weeks before leaving home to test your reaction.

**Doxycycline** Taken daily. An antibiotic useful for those allergic to quinine. The major side effect is exaggerated sensitivity to sunlight (skin and eyes), so cover up.

## Avoiding bites

The best way to avoid malaria is to avoid getting bitten. *Anopheles* mosquitoes like to bite in the evening and at night; you can minimize bites by sleeping under **mosquito nets**, provided by virtually every hotel and guesthouse in the country, and by burning **mosquito coils**, available locally. At dusk and at night, keep your limbs covered, and consider using **insect repellent**. Most contain diethyltoluamide ("DEET"), an oily substance that corrodes many artificial materials, including plastic. If you're bringing a net, it's worth impregnating it with insecticide as well. If you don't like synthetic protection, **natural alternatives** based on pyrethrum flowers or citronella (lemon grass) are also effective.

## Symptoms and treatment

Common **symptoms** include waves of flu-like fever, shivering, headaches, or joint pain. Some people also get diarrhoea. If you suspect malaria, get a **blood test** as quickly as possible. **Treatment** essentially consists of stuffing yourself with quinine: anything but the prophylaxis you were taking. Locals use an effective brew made from the extremely bitter leaves of the neem tree (known as the *muarbaini*, or "forty tree", due to its many uses).

# Water and stomach bugs

In some towns, locals are quite happy quaffing **tap water**, but most tourists give it, and ice, a wide berth. On short trips, **bottled water** (sold throughout Tanzania) is the popular choice. More environmentally sound (no bottles) is **purifying water yourself**: in the unlikely case that the water is cloudy, filter it first through fine muslin, then boil or add iodine tincture (four drops per litre), shake and wait twenty minutes. Chlorine tablets do the same but impart a vile taste.

On short trips it makes sense to remain cautious about foods that may make you ill, but on longer trips it's best to "re-educate" your stomach: **travellers' diarrhoea**, a catch-all for all sorts of minor bugs caught from badly washed or spoiled food or contaminated water, is best weathered rather than blasted with antibiotics (which don't work on viruses anyway). The important thing is to stay hydrated. A typical **rehydration mix** consists of four heaped teaspoons of sugar and half a teaspoon of salt in a litre of water; commercial rehydration remedies are much the same. Avoid coffee, strong fruit juice and alcohol. Most upsets resolve themselves after a couple of days. If you have to travel a long way and have diarrhoea, **anti-diarrhoea** tablets are available in Tanzania: most merely slow your digestive tract, so shouldn't be overused.

Outbreaks of **cholera** (scary but actually easily treated) are rare, and tend to be limited to highly populated urban areas that lack adequate sanitation, occurring when the water supply is contaminated during periods of flooding. Also contracted through contaminated water, more frequently too, is **giardiasis**, which just makes you feel shitty whilst blessing you with horrendously smelly burps and farts. It normally clears up after three days; the definitive treatment, and for **amoebic dysentery**, is metronidazole.

## Terrestrial animals

Tanzania knows its animals, and their value: "man-eaters", those critters you pay lots of money to see, are largely confined to national parks and reserves. That said, fences are few and far between, and **lions** do sporadically terrorize some districts, especially between Dodoma and Babati, Songea and Tunduru, and the whole region east of Selous Game Reserve. Still, there's no reason to be terrified unless you're a farmer (for whom elephants are also a threat) or like camping rough, in which case you should always seek local advice. Actually, far more dangerous are **hippos** (never get between them and their water), and solitary male **buffaloes**, who may well help you reveal tree climbing skills you never knew you had. Heading down the scale, **dogs** – rarely seen, and often despised – are usually sad and skulking, posing little threat. Troops of **baboons**, however, should be treated with caution: keep food out of sight, and ideally in airtight containers.

**Snakes** are mostly harmless, and to see one at all you'd need to search stealthily; walk heavily and most species obligingly disappear. In bushy or wooded areas, wear boots and long trousers to minimize the risk of scratched "bites". If someone *is* bitten, apply a tourniquet, but open it every fifteen minutes. Victims should be hospitalized as quickly as possible (even toxic bites are survivable if treated in time). Above all, **don't panic** – shock can be just as fatal. Also, don't try to suck out the poison like you see in films: that technique was discredited many moons ago. If you're really worried, any market should have **jiwe ya punju** ("snake bite medicine stone"), which looks like a small piece of charcoal, and is applied to a wound immediately after a bite: it might actually work, as it sucks up liquid via capillary action.

Lastly, don't worry about spiders (quite harmless), and whilst **scorpions** abound, they're hardly ever seen unless you deliberately turn over rocks or logs (something baboons do purposely; scorpions are tasty snacks). While the stings are painful, they're almost never fatal: clean the wound and pack with ice to slow the spread of the venom.

## Aquatic hazards

Dar es Salaam suffered a short but deadly spate of **shark attacks** in 2000, the first in Tanzanian waters in recorded memory. There have been no attacks since, so the "freak migration from southern Africa" theory proffered at the time fits convincingly, and you can safely forget about a rerun of *Jaws*. Rather more likely is the painful annoyance of stepping on a **sea urchin**: spreading papaya pulp helps extract the spines, and dousing the wound in 50°C water reduces the pain. You might also be stung by jellyfish, for which vinegar is the miracle cure. Much more serious, but only likely to afflict incautious scuba divers, are neurotoxic darts delivered by **cone shells**: apply a non-constrictive compress and seek urgent medical attention.

**Swimming in lakes and rivers** poses far greater risks: hippos and crocodiles, obviously, but also **bilharzia** (schistosomiasis), a dangerous but curable disease caused by tiny flukes living in freshwater snails and which, as part of their life cycle, leave their hosts to multiply in mammals. The standard advice is never swim in, wash with, or even touch lake water that cannot be vouched for. The risks are higher close to river inlets and in turbid or slow-moving water, especially around vegetation. Well-maintained swimming pools are fine.

# Getting around

Chaotic it may be, but Tanzania's public transport will get you to most destinations within the same day. Buses and minibuses are the usual way around, though there are also two railway lines, and ferry services across lakes Tanganyika, Victoria and Nyasa and from Dar to Zanzibar. Air travel is a relatively affordable option for tourists, and covers much of the country.

Tanzania's **main arteries** run north to south: from the Kenyan border to Zambia and Malawi via Dar es Salaam, and behind the coast from Tanga in the north to Mtwara and beyond in the south, also via Dar. There's also an asphalt link from Morogoro to Dodoma in the centre, and – only partially complete – from Arusha to Mwanza looping around the northern national parks. Most other roads are unsurfaced, making them either dusty or muddy, and potentially impassable in the rains.

## Buses, minibuses and pick-ups

For most Tanzanians and independent tourists, buses, minibuses (called "daladalas") or pick-ups are the usual way of getting around: sometimes driven with breathtaking lack of road sense, they do reach pretty much every corner of the country, and can actually be an _enjoyable_ way of getting around, throwing you into close contact with the locals. That said, on **unsurfaced roads** especially you should be prepared for a degree of physical discomfort: vehicles tend to be stuffed to the rivets with passengers and

their bags, boxes, chickens or even goats, and rough roads aren't kind to bottoms, either, nor to heads if you're sitting on a "catapult seat" near the rear axle – hitting bumps at full speed can literally bounce you off the ceiling. Only a handful of buses have **toilets**. Instead, vehicles stop every few hours for passengers to scurry into the bush, women on one side, men on the other. You won't need to bring much **food** as there's plenty from hawkers along the way, and on long-distance trips you'll stop for lunch at a roadside restaurant.

**Buses** cover all the main routes, asphalted or not, and as such will be your primary means of transport. The better, more expensive services, such as Scandinavian Express (reservations online at ❿www .scandinaviagroup.com) don't allow standing passengers and may even benefit from slightly saner drivers, but even they have been known to speed. Minibus **daladalas** are fine for short journeys (see p.29) but best avoided for long trips as they tend to be even more badly driven. In remote areas with particularly bad roads, transport will be by **pick-up**, often a Land Rover (nicknamed "One Ten"), or an open-backed truck.

---

## Safari njema…have a safe journey!

Travelling by bus or daladala, it's all too easy to appreciate the deadly reality behind Tanzania's gruesome **road safety record**, one that would be much worse were there more surfaced roads. Driving standards are frankly abysmal, with speeding and reckless overtaking the primary culprits. As such, the "Moving on" sections throughout this guide contain recommendations for **safer companies**, and warn against the most dangerous. Nonetheless, things do change, so always seek local advice before choosing (and be clear when asking, as for some people "the best bus" means the fastest). If you're really worried, you can minimize the statistical risk of accident-caused injury by sitting in the middle of the vehicle away from windows.

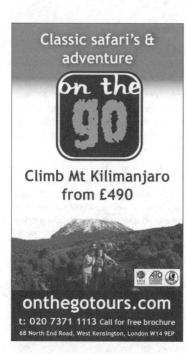

Departure times tend to be reliable (it's arrival times that vary). Most vehicles head off at 6am ("twelve o'clock" in Swahili time; see p.73 for an explanation). Departures are usually from a central **bus stand** (bus station), where you'll find ticket offices. Get there at least thirty minutes before departure, but it's best to **book ahead**: you'll not only be sure of your seat, but can choose it, too. The least uncomfortable place to sit is in the front of the vehicle away from the rear axle. Consider which side will be shadier, and remember that in the southern hemisphere the sun travels in the northern half of the sky. Public transport is prohibited from travelling between midnight and 4am, so if you're on a long-distance bus that gets delayed, expect to spend the night in your seat. **Fares** average Tsh2000 for an hour's travel. As a tourist you may be overcharged a little, but no more than a local who doesn't know the price either. Baggage charges shouldn't be levied unless you're transporting commercial goods.

## Urban transport

**Daladalas** (usually battered Toyota Hiace minivans) are the standard way of getting around large towns; fares for most journeys are just Tsh300 (around $0.25). The vehicles run along pre-determined routes, often colour-coded; destinations are marked (sometimes cryptically) on boards behind the windscreen. Daladalas have the advantage of being plentiful and quick; the downside is that they can get amazingly crowded – 25 people in a vehicle with just twelve seats is common. When boarding a vehicle at a daladala stand, choose one that's full and about to leave, or you'll have to wait. Competition is intense and touts will lie unashamedly to persuade you their vehicle is going "just now"...

More comfortable are **taxis**, which are also the only safe way of getting around at night. They lack meters, so settle on a fare before getting in. A ride around town averages Tsh4000, though drivers will invariably try for more – haggle hard and, if you get nowhere, try another. Less than half the price are **motorized rickshaws** ("bajaji"), which take their name from the Indian manufacturer, Bajaj Auto. These are tiny three-wheelers with space for two passengers, and can be found in a growing number of towns.

## Hitching

**Hitchhiking** is generally not recommended, especially for lone females, but may be unavoidable in very remote areas – in which case the risks are considerably less. Beckon the driver to stop with your whole arm, and be prepared to pay.

## Car rental

For freedom of movement, it's hard to match a **private vehicle**, though few car rental companies let tourists self-drive: the risks, given the bad roads and (lack of) local driving skills, are too great. Instead, a **driver** is included in the deal, and the price should include his accommodation and meals. It's actually no bad thing to have a driver along: he's fluent in Kiswahili, obviously, and will likely double as a wildlife guide.

The other constraint is that **4WD** (necessary for entering national parks) doesn't come cheap unless you can share the cost. The classic safari vehicles are Land Rovers or Land Cruisers, **prices** for which average $140–160 per day (with driver or self-drive), including 120km but excluding fuel; additional kilometres cost around 80¢. Cheaper are Rav 4 or Suzuki Escudo (also called Vitara), which are smaller and have lower clearance but are rugged enough for most conditions. For one of these, you'll pay $60–100 per day self-drive, with each kilometre above 120km charged at 50–60¢. Rates are always cheaper by the week, and many firms are prepared to negotiate, but be wary of VAT (twenty percent, not always included in quotes), and check whether the driver's allowance is indeed included. Expect to pay a hefty deposit roughly equivalent to the anticipated bill; that, or a credit card. Most **car rental companies** are in Dar, Arusha, Mwanza and Stone Town; we've noted the best ones in those cities and towns' "Listings" sections. As with safari companies, car rentals need a valid TALA licence if you'll be entering national parks (see p.50).

**Self-drive saloon cars**, for paved roads only, cost $50–70 a day, excluding fuel. With a driver, add $20 or so. Less hassle, if you just need an ordinary car, is to **rent a taxi,** though it'll cost about the same unless you have your bargaining hat on straight.

### Self-drive

**Self-drive** isn't cheaper than going with a company driver, as you'll have to pay insurance premiums instead. Before signing on the dotted line, check the small print for **insurance** arrangements, and always pay the daily collision damage waiver (CDW), else even a small bump could be costly. Theft protection waiver (TPW) should also be taken. Even with these, however, you'll still be up for **excess liability** (anything from $400 to $3000) if you total the car. Some companies are distinctly cagey about these matters – as a rule of thumb, excess liability over $1000 is the trademark of outfits secretly hoping their punters crash for cash.

Drivers must be between 25 and 70 years old and have held a licence for at least two years. Zanzibar additionally requires an **International Driving Permit** (available from motoring organizations), which must be endorsed by the police on arrival. If you don't have one, a temporary fifteen-day permit can be obtained on production of your national licence and $10. Car rental companies can arrange all this.

**Fuel** is available almost everywhere except along remote roads or in the smallest villages. Out of the way, it won't be delivered by pump but in plastic bottles. Fill up wherever you can. You'll get 10–14km per litre out of a Land Rover TDI, less from a Land Cruiser. In Dar es Salaam in early 2009, a litre of petrol/diesel cost around $1.10/$1.20. Fuel gets more expensive the further inland or away from a major town you get; in national parks, you'll pay almost double.

Further **advice for self-drivers** – covering checking a vehicle; buying secondhand; regulations and fines; driving hazards and etiquette; and tips on surviving loose sand or deep mud – is given online at Ⓦwww .bluegecko.org/tanzania.

### Trains

Tanzania has two passenger-carrying railways, both of them very slow but the journey is comfortable enough if you travel in a sleeper. Delays are frequent, so don't count on arriving at the scheduled time. All

## Train security

Overnight trains are obvious targets for **thieves**. If you have a compartment, keep the door and windows locked when you're asleep or outside, or ensure that there's always someone there to look after bags (Tanzanian travellers are just as wary). Be especially careful when the train pulls in at main stations, especially Dodoma and Tabora on the Central Line. You should also be wary of people looking for a spare seat in second class (genuine passengers always have numbered tickets corresponding to a particular compartment) and of passengers without bags – they may leave with yours. If you really get suspicious stay awake until the ticket inspector comes round. In third class you'll probably have to stay awake all night or else stash your valuables out of reach (in a bag under your seat hemmed in by other people's bags, for example). All this is not to say that you should be paranoid – just don't drop your guard.

trains have a dining car (which mainly sees use as a dissolute bar), but food can also be ordered from a roving waiter, and on long journeys the train stops at trackside villages whose inhabitants sell some of the best "street" food in the country.

The **Central Line** runs 1254km between Dar es Salaam and Kigoma on Lake Tanganyika, with branches to Mwanza (Lake Victoria), Singida and Mpanda. The main stretch to Kigoma was laid by the Germans just before World War I, and has been partially rehabilitated; the branch to Mwanza was added by the British in the 1920s. Trains on all routes run two or three times a week; details are given in the "Moving on" sections of this guide.

The **TAZARA Line** runs 1992km from Dar es Salaam to New Kapiri Mposhi in Zambia, passing through Mbeya. It was constructed by Chinese engineers in the 1960s to provide an outlet for Zambian copper exports without going through the racist regimes of Southern Rhodesia (Zimbabwe), South-West Africa (Namibia) and South Africa, or through the war-torn Portuguese colonies of Angola and Mozambique. Southbound services are relatively reliable, but northbound timings are a total shambles. On the positive side, the route passes through some especially beautiful landscapes, including part of Selous Game Reserve, where, by day, you might see antelopes, buffaloes or giraffes. If the train leaves in the morning, it's a very nice way of getting to the Udzungwa Mountains, too (get off at Mang'ula). Currently there are only two trains a week in either direction: the ingeniously

named "express" to Zambia, and another terminating in Mbeya.

### Schedules and tickets

Up-to-date **timetables** are difficult to come by, even in Tanzania, and unfortunately neither of the railway's websites is regularly updated (ⓦwww.trctz.com for the Central Line, and the pathetic ⓦwww.tazara.co .tz for TAZARA). More useful is ⓦwww .seat61.com.

There are four kinds of ticket. **First class** on the Central Line is in compartments with just two bunks each, ideal for couples. On the TAZARA Line they have four bunks. **Second class** is in compartments with six bunks each, segregated by sex unless you book and pay for six people. Both first- and second-class have washbasins, bed linen and blankets. Both kinds should be reserved in advance; ticket offices take bookings up to three months ahead, and for the Central Line you can also use ☏022/211 7833 or Ⓔ ccm_cserv@trctz.com. **Second-class seating** is also in compartments and can be booked. **Third class**, which is standard seating in open carriages, can be uncomfortably crowded with plenty of suitcases, boxes, baskets, chickens, children and broad-hipped *mama kubwas* ("big ladies").

Fares are priced in shillings; slipping exchange rates mean that dollar equivalents have remained stable over the last few years. For Dar to Kigoma, expect to pay around $42 in first class, $31 in a second-class bunk, and $14–17 in second-class seating or in third class.

## Flights

Tanzania has a number of reasonably priced **internal air services** and it's well worth seeing the country from above at least once: the flight from Dar es Salaam or Stone Town to Pemba, over spice and coconut plantations, reefs, sandbanks and creeks, is especially beautiful. Flight schedules are given at the end of each chapter. Except for Air Tanzania (languishing in agonizingly prolonged death throes), all can be relied on to keep more or less to schedule, at least in clear weather, although flights in remote areas can be delayed due to things like giraffes on the airstrip. The largest planes – twin-props and a jet – are owned by Precisionair. Other companies rely on **light aircraft**, frequently mono-props – worth bearing in mind if the thought of being kept aloft by just three whirring blades gives you the heebie-jeebies, though the planes are generally well-maintained. **Baggage limits** are usually 15kg, with additional weight carried at the pilot's discretion (and possibly at extra cost).

**Ticket prices** for tourists ("non-residents") are quoted in dollars but can be paid in shilling equivalent. If you've been around a while, you may be able to wangle cheaper "resident" fares on less touristy routes – it all depends on the guy or gal in the office, as resident status is not checked at the airports. Some sample non-resident fares: Arusha–Dar $230; Arusha–Mwanza $280; Dar–Zanzibar $70; Dar–Selous $150. Not included are a $6 airport tax and $1 safety tax, paid at the airport.

**Charter flights** are offered by companies in Arusha, Dar, Mwanza and Zanzibar –

see those cities' "Listings" sections. Prices depend on the destination and the type of aircraft, but you'll always pay more per person than a standard fare. They can be worth-while for short hops (say from Stone Town to Pemba; in 2009, Coastal Aviation were charging $600 for a six-passenger Cessna), but are rarely a bargain over long distances.

## Ferries

On the **coast**, there are several daily ferries between Dar es Salaam and **Zanzibar** (Stone Town), and a few each week to Pemba. There are also weekly sailings, generally cargo boats that also take passengers, between Tanga and Pemba. On **Lake Victoria**, steamers sail several times a week from Mwanza to Bukoba (see p.401), and daily to Ukerewe Island. A ferry runs weekly from Kigoma to Mpulungu in northern Zambia across **Lake Tanganyika** – if you're lucky it'll be the marvellous MV *Liemba*, a pre-World War I relic (see p.435). There are two weekly ferries on **Lake Nyasa**, both from Itungi Port in the north. The useful ones go to Mbamba Bay in the south, then cross over to Malawi (p.496).

## Dhows

**Dhow-hopping** along the Tanzanian coastline is undeniably a romantic vision, but the reality is a little different. For a start, it's potentially dangerous, and officials won't necessarily be angling for bribes when they try to discourage you: dhows do capsize, and there's little chance of being rescued should that happen. You should also be prepared for cramped conditions, diesel-fume-laced air, choppy

### Tanzanian airlines

The following operate within Tanzania. Phone numbers and offices are included throughout this book in the "Listings" sections of the towns they serve.

**Air Excel** Ⓦ www.airexcelonline.com.
**Air Tanzania** Ⓦ www.airtanzania.com (currently defunct).
**Coastal Aviation** Ⓦ www.coastal.cc.
**Precisionair** Ⓦ www.precisionairtz.com.
**Regional Air** Ⓦ www.regionaltanzania.com.
**Safari AirLink** Ⓦ www.safariaviation.info.
**Tropical Air** Ⓦ www.tropicalair.co.tz.
**ZanAir** Ⓦ www.zanair.com.

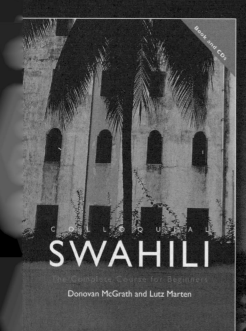

seas, the language barrier, and rudimentary toilet facilities slung over the vessel's side (it's always best to clear your bowels beforehand). All routes take at least five or six hours, and considerably longer if there are problems with motors or the weather, so take plenty of food and water. Also, know that it's *rumoured* to be illegal for tourists to catch non-motorized dhows for long-distance trips.

If all that doesn't put off, enquire with the **harbour master** or **dhow registrar** (their offices are usually inside the harbour or close by) for what ships might be heading your way, then agree a fare with the captain; anything up to $20 is reasonable for tourists. Once settled, the dhow registrar will inscribe your name on the manifest and collect the **harbour tax** (Tsh5000 at most). In theory, that's all that's needed if you're not leaving the country, but officialdom being the petty beast it is, **immigration and customs** might feel slighted if you don't drop by, so ask the harbour master whether this is necessary. Whatever happens, be sure that immigration people don't put an exit stamp in your passport, as that would nullify your visa. Lastly, catching a dhow to or from Zanzibar can be impossible during the clove harvests (Sept to Nov and around Feb), when smuggling is common, and at times of political turmoil – basically the months before and especially after elections: the next bout is at the end of 2010.

For information on recreational dhow trips, see p.58.

### Dhow harbours

To get to Zanzibar, the most useful dhow harbours are **Pangani** (for Nungwi or Mkokotoni), **Saadani** (for Mkokotoni) and **Bagamoyo** (for Kizimkazi or possibly Stone Town). The cultural tourism programmes at Pangani and Saadani can help arrange things for you; in Bagamoyo, the tourist office or *Bagamoyo Beach Resort* can be helpful.

The larger harbour at **Tanga** has dhows to Wete on **Pemba**, but Tanga's officials are obstructive so the route is more feasible in reverse. You can forget about arranging anything in **Dar es Salaam**, but things are easier at **Kisiju**, 90km south of Dar, from where you can get to **Mafia Island** or **Songo Songo Island**. With a bit of luck you'll find an onward connection from Songo Songo to **Kilwa Kivinje** (or sometimes Kilwa Kisiwani), and then on to **Lindi** or Mtwara. From **Mtwara**, dhows occasionally head on to Mozambique, but you'll need to have bought a Mozambican visa beforehand (you can do that in Dar). Catching a dhow to **Mombasa** in Kenya is virtually impossible, as the route is known for smugglers and is therefore tightly controlled.

## Cycling

Tanzania's climate, hilly terrain, and reckless drivers aren't exactly perfect for **cyclists**, but with an adventurous frame of mind, plenty of time, perhaps some decent life insurance, and a rear-view mirror bolted on to the handlebars, you can reach parts of the country that would be virtually impossible to visit by other means except walking. Pedal-powered foreigners are also still a novelty, so you'll likely be the star attraction wherever you turn up: all great fun. Bringing **your own bicycle** is no longer straightforward: contact your airline for conditions, fees and packing requirements. Easier is to **buy a bike** on arrival: basic mountain bikes can be bought in most towns for around $100.

Obviously, you'll need to be extremely cautious when **cycling on main roads**. If the pavement is broken at the edge, give yourself plenty of space and be ready to leave the road if necessary, even if it means ending up in a ditch – local cyclists wisely scatter like chickens at the approach of a bus. For more advice on cycling in Tanzania, see ⓦwww.bluegecko.org/tanzania.

# Accommodation

Tanzania's accommodation ranges from humble guesthouses charging under $10 a night to luxurious beach resorts and bush camps priced in the hundreds or even thousands. Irrespective of the price range, single travellers get a rough deal, rarely paying less than eighty percent the price of a double, as cheaper hotels tend to charge per room, whilst upmarket abodes, which like to quote their prices per person, slap on hefty "single supplements". Note that en-suite rooms are also known as "self-contained". In many places, including inside national parks and nature reserves, the cheapest – and often most enchanting – way of staying over is in your own tent, but on the mainland only, as for some reason camping is illegal on Zanzibar. Kiswahili terms for accommodation are listed on p.626.

**Booking ahead** is essential if staying in upmarket hotels, particularly in peak season (generally July–Sept, and from mid-Dec to Feb). Bookings are also necessary in Zanzibar, Stone Town in particular, at festival times: February for Sauti za Busara, and July for ZIFF. Given that a fifty percent **deposit** is usually required to confirm reservations, and full payment due ten to twelve weeks before arriving, you should rightly expect perfection. Unfortunately, in some cases, price isn't a reliable guide, so before making a reservation or letting a tour operator arrange things for you, read some recent client **reviews online**. Best for this is Ⓦwww.tripadvisor.com; also useful are Ⓦwww.virtualtourist.com, Ⓦwww.expertafrica.com, and the travellers' forums listed on p.74. In cheaper hotels and guesthouses reservations are not usually required, but if a place tickles your fancy, there's no harm in trying. You'll rarely be expected to pay a deposit, but there are no guarantees of your reservation actually being honoured: bringing along print-outs of any email correspondence might help.

Tourist seasons mainly affect prices in upmarket hotels. **High season** can be almost the entire year, with **low season** (disingenuously dubbed "green season") restricted to April and May, and perhaps a month either side, coinciding with the long rains. More reasonable hoteliers consider high season to be August, and from mid-December to January or February. Peak season supplements are charged for

## Accommodation price codes

All accommodation listed in this guide has been graded according to the **price codes** below, based on the cost of a **standard double or twin room** in high season. Abbreviations used are: BB (bed and breakfast); HB (half board); FB (full board). Where none is given, the hotel's rates are bed-only.

For dormitory accommodation, hostels and campsites, which charge per person, exact prices have been given where possible.

Most mid-range hotels, almost all upmarket accommodation, and all hotels on Zanzibar, have two tariffs: one for **"non-residents"** (tourists) priced in US dollars but payable in shillings, albeit at bad rates; the other for **"residents"** (Tanzanians and sometimes expats), usually quoted in shillings and invariably much cheaper; rates at such places vary according to the season. In our price codes, we have used the non-resident rates.

| | | |
|---|---|---|
| ❶ $10 and under | ❹ $41–70 | ❼ $151–250 |
| ❷ $11–20 | ❺ $71–100 | ❽ $251–350 |
| ❸ $21–40 | ❻ $101–150 | ❾ $351 and over |

## Mosquito nets and bug spray

Mosquitoes, and hence malaria, are prevalent in most parts of Tanzania. Virtually every guesthouse and hotel room comes with **mosquito nets** for its beds, so you don't need to bring your own. Some rooms also have wire-mesh window screens, but they don't offer one hundred percent protection on their own (mosquitoes can simply follow you in). Before signing in to a hotel, always check nets and screens for size and holes. Bringing a stapler or duct tape can be useful for quick repairs.

We've made a distinction in our hotel reviews between **round nets**, hung from a single point, and **box nets**, which are hung from four points or from a wooden frame. The latter are far preferable as they give you more room to move about in at night without touching the net. Less than perfect are the large "walk-in" nets preferred by many posher places, and the box nets with "entrance flaps" popular on Zanzibar, few of which will close up properly: for those, you'll need to check whether it's possible to tuck them in under the mattress, or be sure that nets reaching the floor really do touch the floor all the way around. Also potentially problematic are Zanzibar's four-poster *semadari* beds, as the fancy carved ends can leave plenty of gaps for mosquitoes if the net is hung outside rather than inside the frame.

Some mid-range and upmarket hotels prefer the **bug spray** approach: not wonderful, either, even ignoring potential toxicity, as the effect only lasts a few hours, and, in humid areas, the spray's perfume can become a stench over time.

---

Christmas, New Year and Easter. For **events** worth coinciding with, see p.45.

### Security

In the cheapest places, don't take **security** for granted, especially in cities. While the author of this book has never had a problem (other than losing some passion fruit to a hungry maid), obviously the more an establishment relies on its bar or on "short time" guests for income, the less secure it will be. Whilst all hotels disclaim responsibility for thefts, **leaving valuables in rooms** is usually safe enough, but don't leave stuff lying around temptingly, and if you get a bad vibe, try to take the key with you when you go out. Actually, **keys** themselves are good indicators: some are so simple that they'd open every other door in the country. If you leave valuables in your room, bury them in the bottom of your bag and use padlocks or other devices to deter temptation. You might also consider hiding stuff between a mattress and the bed frame – usually safe enough, judging by the amount of accumulated grime.

If you decide to leave things with the management, exercise caution, and ensure you get an **itemized receipt** (signed by the manager or owner, not the receptionist), including banknote serial numbers.

### Hostels and guesthouses

Nearly every town in Tanzania has at least one clean and comfortable **guesthouse**, usually a two- or three-storey building, sometimes with a bar and restaurant too. Guesthouses are usually fairly quiet themselves, but street noise, mosques, nearby bars or discos, or bus stations might keep you awake or wake you earlier than you might wish. The less reputable guesthouses, often close to markets or bus terminals, maximize their potential by admitting couples on "short time", though they're rarely too tawdry. The more puritanical display belligerent signs forbidding "women of immoral turpitude". Virtually all guesthouses have **security guards** (*askaris*) at night, whom you'll need to wake if you're staggering home after the doors or gates are locked. Similar in standards to guesthouses, but with a cloying atmosphere and often with overly narrow beds (presumably intended to hinder carnal pleasures) are **church-run hostels**. These have no membership- or faith-based requirements, but night owls should look elsewhere. There are no internally-affiliated youth hostels in Tanzania.

At a decent guesthouse, where you should get running water, toilet seats and intact nets, **room rates** average Tsh10,000–20,000 ($8–16) per night for a double room with a bathroom, or half that for shared bathrooms.

Comparable singles are rarely less than eighty percent the cost of a double. Guest-houses in Dar es Salaam and on Zanzibar are usually priced in dollars and are more expensive, with the cheapest doubles starting at $20 (around Tsh25,000), though this should be bargainable, especially in low season or if you'll be staying a few days. **Before signing in**, test the lights and fans (and electric socket if you need it), running water, toilets and the size and condition of mosquito nets. Toilet paper, soap and towels are provided in all but the humblest places, but it's a good idea to bring your own along (towels aren't always clean), as well as pillow cases and two thin cotton sheets (a *kanga* or *kitenge* will do) to replace the ubiquitous nylon ones, many of which are too small for the beds.

## Hotels

For mid-range and upmarket travellers, the mainstay in **towns** are hotels as opposed to guesthouses, where you'll get a room with private bathroom and hot water, plus satellite or cable TV, air conditioning, and breakfast included. Prices are almost always in dollars, though you can pay in shillings, albeit at bad exchange rates. For $150–200 a night and upwards, you should be getting facilities and standards of service equivalent to four- or five-star hotels worldwide. In more modest places, the majority charging between $40 and $80, price isn't always a reliable guide: some are bristlingly smart and efficient, but others can be bland, or even boozy, if there's a bar attached.

With the exception of the resorts just north of Dar es Salaam, and Kiwengwa on Zanzibar, Tanzania's **beach hotels** are almost all low-key and low-rise. Rooms are usually in **bungalows**, either individual, or containing two or more guest rooms perhaps sharing the same veranda or balcony. It's worth spending a little more to be sure of a sea view, if there is one, and for air conditioning, especially between November and March when the heat and humidity are sapping. **Costs** can be surprisingly reasonable: from $40–60 or so per night for two people on Zanzibar, though some "boutique" hotels feel justified in charging over $500.

## Wildlife lodges and luxury tented camps

At the top of the scale are the lodges and luxury tented camps in and around Tanzania's **national parks and game reserves**, which can charge pretty much what they like as demand far outstrips availability: indeed, when reserving rooms, you need a degree of flexibility regarding dates even if you book half a year in advance. The more remote of these places tend to be closed in April and May during the long rains.

The **lodges** are the mainstay of mid-range and "cheaper" upmarket safaris, and are essentially large four- and five-star hotels transported into the bush. The better ones can feel quite intimate, but by and large this is package-tour land, and they lack that wilderness feeling you might be hankering for. For that, either camp (if you're on a budget), or drain your bank account (upwards of $400 for a couple) to stay at one of an ever-growing number of **luxury tented camps** (or "tented lodges"). Accommodation in these is usually in large, walk-in tents pitched on raised wooden platforms, with a bathroom plumbed in at the back – not exactly camping in the wild. There's invariably also a thatched restaurant, bar and lounge area, and an atmosphere that tends to be neo-colonial in the extreme, dominated by "white hunter" - type wildlife guides, tall tales around evening camp fires, and minimal if any local involvement beyond the employment of menial staff and perhaps a Maasai warrior or two to lend some tribal colour. Bush walks are often possible, and should be – together with game drives – included in "all inclusive" prices.

## Camping

Camping is illegal on Zanzibar, but mainland Tanzania has enough **campsites** to make carrying a tent worthwhile. The advantages are the low cost (around $5 per person), and often gorgeous locations. In rural areas, hotels may also let you camp in their grounds. During the dry seasons you'll rarely have trouble finding wood for a fire, so a stove is optional, but don't burn more fuel than you need, and take care to put out embers completely before leaving. A torch is also useful, and a foam sleeping mat is essential.

The public campsites in Tanzania's **national parks** ($30 per person plus entrance fees) are the cheapest way of staying over, and don't require bookings. Most but not all have toilets and showers: details are given throughout this guide. The parks' "special campsites" ($50 per person) do require reservations, and as far ahead as possible as they're often block-booked by upmarket camping tours. They're generally miles away from the crowds and have no facilities at all, but can be reserved for your exclusive use: contact TANAPA in Arusha (p.307). Collecting **firewood** is not permitted in the parks; some provide it for a small fee, others insist you use gas canisters (available in Arusha and Dar es Salaam).

Unless you're with someone who knows the area well, **camping rough** is not recommended, although a decent dose of common sense should keep you safe. Wherever you are, before pitching a tent seek permission from the headman or an elder (*jumbe*) in the nearest village – else a worried delegation armed with *pangas* may turn up to see who you are. Obviously, don't pitch beside roads, in dry riverbeds or near animal trails. **Areas to be wary of** include: Loliondo district north of the Serengeti (wildlife risk, and bandits were present until a few years ago); Mara district north of Musoma (clashes between Kuria clans); the fringes of Maasai territory (cattle rustling); areas bordering Burundi and Rwanda; anywhere around Selous Game Reserve including between Masasi and Songea (lions); and between Dodoma and Kondoa (also lions). In addition, camping on any but the most deserted of beaches could be an invitation to robbers.

# Food and drink

On the Tanzanian mainland, culinary traditions are necessarily humble, but that's not to say that the food isn't tasty: venturing beyond the realm of fast food (chicken, chips and various snacks), your taste buds are in for a treat, as the relatively limited selection of ingredients in each area has fostered plenty of innovation. The classic Tanzanian meal – eaten with your hands, although as a tourist you'll usually be given cutlery – consists of several stews based on vegetables, beans or even plantain, into which you dip a small ball of rice or thick cornmeal porridge (*ugali*). Where Tanzanian cuisine really comes into its own, however, is on Zanzibar: home to an extraordinarily eclectic and delicious gastronomic tradition, as distinctive, subtle and tasty as any more internationally renowned cuisine, and making inspired use of the island's famous spices as well as fruits: fish, octopus or squid simmered in coconut sauce is a classic.

You'll find restaurants, even if only basic ones, almost everywhere. In a local **hoteli** (a restaurant, not a hotel) or **mgahawa** (even more basic), dishes are intended to fill you up as cheaply as possible, often for under Tsh2000 (around $1.60). In the most popular such places, you may find your meal arriving on a metal platter containing several hollows, one for each dish (various stews, *ugali* or rice, vegetables, and meat or fish), so you can mix things as you wish. Salads are rarely offered: where they are, they'll often be fresher in local dives, where they're made to order, than in touristic establishments.

Lunch is typically served from noon to 2pm, with dinner no later than 8pm; at other times you may have to choose from the dreaded display cabinet (pre-fried chicken or goat meat, chips or pasties). Restaurants aimed at **tourists** and well-to-do locals charge $5–15 (roughly Tsh6500–20,000) and may be open all day. They can provide all sorts of international fare, from Italian and Indian to Chinese and Japanese. For a blow-out, some big **hotels and lodges** offer eat-all-you-want buffet lunches, though you'd need to be really hungry to justify the cost: $20–40 a head.

## Street food and snacks

A fun and cheap alternative to restaurants is **street food**, which you'll find in or around most transport terminals and markets. Most vendors – known as *mama/baba lisha* (feeding women/men) offer just one or two snacks, but some provide full (and often wholesome) meals, eaten at makeshift tables – and which, at night, in the flickering light of charcoal braziers and oil lamps, can be very memorable experiences. Zanzibar has an especially regal choice of seafood. The majority of vendors, however, rely on **standard favourites**: fried chicken (*kuku choma*; often coated in bright orange masala spices; you'll want it straight off the fire), *mishkaki* (skewers of grilled meat), *chipsi mayai* (Spanish-style omelettes made with chips), and grilled corncobs (*mahindi*) or cassava (*muhogo*). The latter can be mouth-drying, but at its best is deliciously moist, especially when doused with a lemony chilli sauce.

Wherever you are, ask for local or seasonal **specialities**, as the street is often the only place you'll find such things other than in someone's home. On Pemba, for instance, you could try cockles (cooked in a tomato- and onion-based broth with potatoes) or stewed octopus. Around the great lakes, try *dagaa*, which are tiny freshwater sardines, fried and eaten whole, whilst in semi-arid Dodoma, some of the critters that make farmers' lives hell end up on hawkers' platters: field mice, say (whenever there's an invasion), or deep fried bite-sized birds.

Less squeamish **snacks**, which you'll also find in modest *mgahawa* restaurants, include *samosas* (sometimes vegetarian), *chapatis* (which, when stuffed in any of several dozen ways, are called *mantabali* or "Zanzibari pizza"), *kitumbua* (rice cakes), *kababu* (meat balls), and "*chops*" or "*cutlets*" which can be all sorts of fried things but are usually either minced meat or a whole egg wrapped in mashed potato and batter.

## Breakfast

Most mainland hotels, and virtually every hotel on Zanzibar, include **breakfast** in their rates, not that it's always worth getting up for (a slice or two of stale white bread, a smudge of plastic-tasting Blue Band margarine, another smear of jam, and a cup of weak tea). The better guest-houses include eggs and a good dose of seasonal fruit. For something different, local *mgahawa* restaurants are sure to have *andazi* – sweet, puffy, deep-fried doughnuts that are best accompanied by sweet milky *chai* (tea), which is particularly refreshing when laced with ginger (*chai tangawizi*). Bars can also be good for breakfast, and not just for dipsomaniacs: many open at dawn, and most will offer **supu**, a light broth made from bony or gristly pieces of meat, chicken or fish, or indeed boiled hooves (*supu ya makongoro*) or intestines (*supu ya utumbo*) – infinitely nicer than it sounds. Commonly accompanied by chapati, *supu* is also a matchless hangover cure (being salty, and laced with lemon and sometimes chilli or pepper). Other good and filling traditional breakfasts, often provided by street food vendors, include *uji* millet gruel, and – from Arusha westwards – a plantain stew called **mtori**.

Rocketing upmarket, **luxury hotels** and lodges lay on lavish expanses of hot and cold buffets that you can't possibly do justice to; if you're staying elsewhere, expect to pay $10–20 for the pleasure. Dropping down a few notches, most **mid-priced hotels** offer full English-style breakfasts – sausages (beef, not pork), eggs and baked beans.

## Lunch and dinner

Tanzania's main **staples** are *ugali* (a thick cornmeal porridge, which can either be stodgy, or soft and deliciously aromatic), rice, cassava, over a hundred varieties of bananas or plantain, and – especially in the form of chips – potatoes. Less common but more traditional staples are sorghum and eleusine millet. Unfortunately, giving specific names to dishes is often quite impossible, as most meals go by the names of their main ingredient(s).

The classic Tanzanian meal consists of one of the staples served with two or more **stews**, often including beans, vegetables, and perhaps a small amount of fish or meat. The vegetable stews, in particular, are worth seeking out, as they often make use of local varieties with distinct tastes, especially spinach. You may also discover vegetables you never knew existed, such as *nyanya chungu* ("bitter tomato"), a small yellow-green aubergine that makes absolutely wonderful sauces. Other meals are all-in-one stews: the marriage of potatoes, plantain and chicken innards is especially felicitous, as is the green and gloopy mess made from cassava leaves, cassava flour and cornmeal, known simply as *kisamvu* ("cassava leaves").

Eating out isn't a tradition among Tanzanians, but there's one exception; a feast of **nyama choma** (grilled beef or goat), which you'll find in most bars, along with grilled bananas or *ugali*. After roasting (order by weight), the meat is brought to your table on a wooden platter and chopped into bite-size pieces. The better places bring you a small bowl of home-made **chilli sauce** – at its best laced with tomato, onion and lemon or vinegar, where the subtlety and freshness seems to caress the kick. More humble places simply chop up a scotch bonnet chilli, varying in potency from hot to incendiary.

Over on Zanzibar, so-called **Swahili cooking** is the product of centuries of contact across the Indian Ocean, resulting in a wonderful blend of African and Asian, Indian and Arabian flavours and aromas. Drawing on ample maritime resources – prawns, octopus, squid, and dozens of varieties of fish – it can taste like heaven even at its simplest, when grilled. But where the Swahili really shine is in their brilliant use of herbs, spices, coconut milk, and even fruit (tamarind with seafood? genius). The classic dishes are fish or octopus simmered in coconut sauce (*samaki na nazi* and *pweza na nazi*), and fish encrusted in mango compote (often spelled on menus as "fish mango combat"). **Pilau**, which you'll also find in Dar, is another enduring favourite: rice flavoured with cloves, cinnamon and fresh peppercorns, and perhaps also coriander, cumin, fenugreek or aniseed.

## Fruit and nuts

**Fruit** is always a delight. Bananas and papayas provide year-round pleasure. Seasonal fruits include mango and pineapple, citrus fruits, plum, melon and jackfruit, the latter banned from some local guesthouses on account of the smell. Also look out for passion fruit (the sweeter and less acidic yellow ones are quite something), tree tomatoes, custard apples (sweetsops) and guavas – all distinctive and delicious. You may also find local fruits with no English names; rarely very sweet, they're worth trying at least once.

On the coast, roasted **cashew nuts** are popular, especially in the south where they're grown and processed, while **coconuts** are filling and nutritious, going through several satisfying changes of condition (all edible) before becoming the familiar hairy brown nuts.

## Vegetarians

The **vegetarian** ideology is an strange concept for most Tanzanians. Although the majority consume little meat, that's mostly a consequence of income: given the choice – as can be seen in *nyama choma* bars – most people would jump at the chance of meat-centred meals. So, as a vegetarian, you need to tread softly in some areas. If you're strict about your diet (no fish), the main problem is getting enough protein. In modest restaurants, beans are almost certain to feature, but in more expensive places it can be difficult avoiding omelettes (again). Indian restaurants, which you'll find in most large towns and on Zanzibar, are a good bet (various pulses and cooked cheeses), as are Chinese restaurants (bean sprouts, cashews, even tofu).

For your own supplies, supermarkets in Arusha, Moshi and Dar es Salaam stock a good range of **dairy produce**, much of it pasteurized; Tanzania's best cheese (excellent at that) is produced in the Usambara Mountains.

## Being invited to eat at home

If you're invited for a meal at someone's home, do accept – it's an honour, for the people whose home you visit as well as for you – and the food is likely to be way better than what you'll find in a restaurant. That said, it can be galling to know that the family slaughtered their last chicken just to honour you, so at the very least bring some gifts: see p.62 for ideas.

Make sure you leave a big hole in your stomach before coming: your hosts will probably make a huge play out of the fact that you're not eating enough, even if you've just gobbled up twice what anyone else has. Before eating, one of the girls or women will appear with a bowl, some soap, and a jug of hot water for you to wash your hands. Traditionally, food is eaten with the right hand from a communal bowl or plate. Never use your left hand to take or give food, as it's destined for ablutions and is considered unclean, no matter how much you've washed it.

Eating techniques vary between regions, but in general you take a small handful of *ugali* or rice and roll it in your palm to make a small ball (the messy part), which is dipped in one of the sauces before being popped into your mouth. Don't worry about making a mess: as a foreigner, you're almost expected to – and it'll give the kids something to laugh about for many moons to come!

## Non-alcoholic drinks

A legacy of colonization, East Africa's national beverage is **tea** (*chai*). Drunk mainly in the morning, it's a hyper-sweet variant on the classic British brew (lots of milk), and very reviving. Variants laced with ginger (*chai tangawizi*) or other spices (*chai masala*) are even better. Ironically for a major coffee-producer, **coffee** is often limited to a tin of instant Africafé, although the commercial acumen of Mbeya's Utengule Estate is finally changing things for the better: in touristy areas, posher hotels, cafés and restaurants are now likely to offer brews made from real beans. The best coffee though is from Moshi: if purple has a taste, Kilimanjaro's Arabica is it. For a cup of coffee on the hoof, in larger towns and cities and especially on Zanzibar, look or ask for a coffee vendor, who will charge little more than Tsh100 for a small Turkish-style cupful; double your money and you'll get some *kashata*, too: sugared cashews, peanuts, coconut or pistachios.

**Sodas** are cheap, and crates of Coke and Fanta find their way to the wildest corners of the country. Local varieties include Krest bitter lemon, and the supremely punchy Stoney Tangawizi ginger ale. Fresh **juice** is available in towns, especially on the coast. Passion fruit is excellent, but may just be watered-down concentrate. You might also find orange, pineapple, sugar cane (sometimes laced with ginger or lime), water-melon, mango, the sublimely refreshing tamarind (always mixed with water), or the delightful bungo, which tastes like a cross between mango and peach. It comes from the strychnine tree: don't worry, it's the bark and seeds that are toxic, not the pulp.

Bottled **water** can be bought everywhere but is expensive (from Tsh700/$0.50 for 1.5 litres). Most brands are merely purified tap water; the best real mineral water, almost sweet in taste, is from Ndanda, available in the southeast. Tap water, unless cloudy, is often drinkable if you're up to date with inoculations (typhoid being particularly important), but heed local advice.

## Alcoholic drinks

Mainland Tanzania has a vibrant drinking culture, and you should attract plenty of (mostly pleasant) attention in the country's bars. There are bars on Muslim Zanzibar, too, almost all of them aimed at tourists. When leaving a bar, don't take your bottle unless you've paid the deposit.

### Beer and cider

Tanzania's **beer** is good stuff as far as lagers go. A bottle costs Tsh1000–1500 in local dives, and up to Tsh4000 ($3) in hotel bars, or on Zanzibar. The main brands are Safari, Kilimanjaro and Tusker; you can also find some Pilsner-style beers, and a couple more distinctive brews: Ndovu ("Elephant"), with a very sweet aroma, and the infamously strong The Kick (seven percent alcohol). **Imported beers**, or brands brewed under licence, include Namibia's Windhoek, South Africa's Castle, the Czech Pilsner Urquell (superb), and Miller, Carlsberg and Heineken. There are also two **stouts**: a head-thumping "Export" version of Guinness which, at 7.5 percent, owes more to soya sauce than pure genius (connoisseurs mix it with Coca-Cola to soften the blow); and Castle Milk Stout (six percent), milder and far more palatable. Alternatively, try a **fake cider**: 49er or Redds Cool, both sickly-sweet concoctions that have never been near real apples.

In rural locations, and especially if you're invited to a celebration, you may come across home brew generally known as **pombe**. Often frothy and deceptively strong, *pombe* is as varied in taste and colour as its ingredients, which may include fermented sugar cane (*boha*), maize and honey (*kangara*), bananas and sorghum (*rubisi*), cashew fruit (*gongo*), bamboo juice (*ulanzi*), and barley and/or millet (*busa*). Herbs and roots may also be added, for flavouring or to initiate fermentation.

## Wine, spirits and liqueurs

**Wine** is sold at posher restaurants and bars, but is expensive at $25 and up for a bottle. South Africa's output travels best, but if you're up for adventure, track down a bottle of Tanzanian wine: the best is Sakharani Usambara, made by the Benedictine Fathers in the Usambara Mountains. Less tempting but more easily found is the output of Tanganyika Vineyards from Dodoma, who are purveyors of quite possibly the world's worst

plonk (their Chenin Blanc is the more merciful, as it knocks out your taste buds after the first sip). More enjoyable are **papaya wine** and **banana wine** – look for the latter in Moshi, Arusha and Lushoto. On the coast, lopping off a shoot at the top of a coconut palm produces a sweet and very drinkable sap which, when left to ferment (a day suffices), becomes **palm wine** (*tembo*). Despite the dominance of Islam in coastal areas, the drink is popular (headless palm trees bearing witness), even if *tembo* drinking sessions have a furtive discretion about them. When indulging, keep a Kiswahili proverb in mind: "If the maker of *tembo* is praised for his wine, he adds water to it" (*mgema akisifiwa tembo hulitia maji*).

**Spirits** are nothing to write home about, unless you're a Scotsman aghast at the local take on "whisky" (usually sold in plastic sachets called *kiroba*, as is "vodka"). You'll find plenty of imported spirits, though, and the home-grown gin-like **Konyagi**. Originally made from papaya, it's now a blend of imported spirits and mysterious "Konyagi flavour", which may be papaya, or cashew nut, or just sugar cane. It's drinkable neat, but is usually mixed with bitter lemon (Konyagi Ice being the same in bottles). Stay away from illegally distilled spirits collectively known as **chang'aa**: often deliberately contaminated with gasoline, acetone or worse (to give a kick), this routinely kills drinking parties en masse.

**Liqueurs**, where you can find them, are international brands. A couple less common ones you might find are Ghana's chocolate and coconut Afrikoko, and South Africa's Amarula, made from the eponymous fruit much loved by elephants.

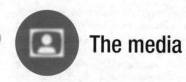

# The media

Tanzania is a nation absorbed in its press, with many lively and outspoken newspapers and magazines, mostly in Kiswahili. Local TV is rather staid but very popular: you'll find sets in even the most modest bars and restaurants. Radio is best for swotting up on the latest music craze.

## Newspapers and magazines

The leading **English-language daily** is *The Guardian*, whose independence relies on the financial clout of tycoon Reginald Mengi (currently under fire for reporting on grand corruption). The government-owned *Daily News* is strong on eastern and southern African affairs, but is spoiled by slavish bias toward the ruling CCM party. Both have good coverage of the main global stories. *The Citizen* is independent, but relies a little too much on dubious online sources for its features.

Best of the **weeklies** is *The East African*, whose relatively weighty, conservatively styled round-up of regional affairs is shot through with an admirable measure of cynicism. It also carries syndicated articles from European and American broadsheets, but these days tends to concentrate on financial matters. Better for social and political news is the *Guardian on Sunday*, with incisive columnists. Less substantial but equally impartial is *The African*, combining a combative and occasionally scurrilous editorial line with syndicated articles from Britain's *Guardian* newspaper. *The Express* is more downmarket but still entertaining.

**Tanzanian magazines** in English are limited to touristic themes. Easiest to find are the free listings booklets available in Arusha, Dar and Zanzibar. The main ones, with good articles, are the *Dar es Salaam Guide* (ⓦwww.mhgallery.net), and *Swahili Coast* (ⓦwww.swahilicoast.com). For wildlife, *Tanzania Wildlife* (an insert in the Kiswahili *Kakakuona*) carries good articles on ecology, people and conservation. If you can read a bit of Kiswahili, there are tons more to choose from, from smutty cartoons to music and Christian fundamentalist propaganda.

Of the **foreign press**, the *Daily Telegraph*, *USA Today* and *International Herald Tribune* get to all sorts of expatriate bastions a day or two late: availability largely depends on what passengers left on the plane. The UK's *The Times*, *Express*, *Daily Mail* and, occasionally, *The Guardian* can sometimes be found in Arusha or Dar. **International magazines** often available include *Time*, *The Economist*, *Newsweek*, and the BBC's *Focus on Africa*.

## Radio

The government-run **Radio Tanzania** broadcasts mainly in Kiswahili but is good for getting to know traditional music. The station competes with several **independent networks**, most of them on a diet of imported soul and home-grown "Bongo Flava". The **BBC World Service** and **Voice of America** provide newsfeeds for local FM stations, and also have their own frequencies: these, together with live streams and clips, are given on ⓦwww.bbc.co.uk/worldservice and ⓦwww.voa.gov.

## Television

Founded in 2000, the Government-run **TBC1** is the country's most popular TV station, thanks to its preference for Kiswahili, and a popular blend of political propaganda, religious material (Muslim on Friday, Christian on Sunday), interviews, local as well as Nigerian ("Nollywood") soaps, and Tanzanian music. Its main competitor is **ITV**. Both channels carry newsfeeds from CNN, the BBC and – way better for in-depth coverage – Al Jazeera. The other national stations, Channel Ten and Pulse Africa, prefer imported sitcoms. On Zanzibar, TVZ is a particularly noxious example of state control when it comes to political coverage. There are also some none-too-memorable regional stations. **Satellite or cable TV** is ubiquitous in bars, restaurants and hotels, piping up to sixty different channels, ranging from BBC World and Discovery to Iranian stations featuring Islamic clerics and sermons, plus a ton of Bollywood flicks.

### Current affairs websites

ⓦ **allafrica.com/tanzania** Collation from many sources; searchable archive.

ⓦ **www.afrika.no** Daily summaries from Africa's press; free email news service.
ⓦ **news.bbc.co.uk** Reliable coverage; searchable archive.
ⓦ **www.dailynews.co.tz** Digital edition of Tanzania's *Daily News*.
ⓦ **www.ippmedia.com** Digital edition of Tanzania's *The Guardian*.
ⓦ **www.theeastafrican.co.ke** Digital edition and archive of the leading weekly.
ⓦ **www.theexpress.com** Digital edition of the English-language weekly.

# Festivals

Compared to West Africa, East Africa is quiet for celebrations, but Tanzania still has a handful of traditional events well worth catching, and a growing number of contemporary festivals that rival Africa's finest.

The best areas for **traditional celebrations** are the country's remotest corners, including much of the south and west, plus mountainous zones, and the semi-arid and arid lands in the north. The celebrations mark virtually every stage of life, from the birth of a child and its being named (sometimes years later) to circumcision and passage into adulthood, marriage, a woman's first child, the life-giving seasons, and death... There's rarely a clear distinction between performer and spectator, so if you do chance upon an event, do join in.

Also traditional are **Islamic celebrations**, whose dates shift forward by ten or eleven days each year (see p.72 for the next few years). Like their Christian counterparts, they're national holidays, and are best experienced if you can stay with a local family. Zanzibar is the main place, though there are also sizeable Muslim communities on the mainland, especially along the coast. The big dates, other than the month-long fast of Ramadan (not the best time to be on Zanzibar, when many restaurants are closed) are **Idd al-Fitr**

(or *Idd al-Fitri*), being a two- to four-day holiday immediately after Ramadan (much feasting, merrymaking, gleeful kids, and firecrackers), and **Maulidi** (or *Maulid an-Nabi*), the Prophet Muhammad's birthday. The other big event, but a more private affair, is **Idd al-Haj** (or *Idd al-Adha*; the one-day feast of the sacrifice). At all these times hotels fill up quickly, so arrive a few days early or book ahead.

The following events are worth changing your travel plans to coincide with:

### January to May

Bullfighting Pemba Island (p.570). A very enjoyable example of Zanzibar's multicultural compote. The fights were introduced during Portuguese rule in the seventeenth century, and, as in the original, the bulls aren't killed but merely annoyed. The fights are at their most traditional in February, just before the long rains. Dec–Feb.
Sauti za Busara Festival Stone Town ⓦ www .busaramusic.org (p.529). One of Africa's best music festivals, focused on both contemporary and traditional genres from East Africa. Feb.
B-Connected Festival Dar es Salaam ⓦ www .musicmayday.org (p.105). Two days of Bongo Flava

(an easy blend of rap and R&B), plus otherwise almost impossible-to- find hip-hop. May.

## June to August

Bulabo Bujora **Mwanza (p.403).** A traditional music contest (*mashindano*) of the Sukuma tribe, coinciding with Corpus Christi, pitting rival dance societies against each another in gladiatorial-style displays of crowd-pulling prowess. June.

Via Via music festival **Arusha (p.318).** The best place for the performing arts in northern Tanzania. The festival includes theatre and acrobatic performances as well as music. June.

Mwaka Kogwa Makunduchi **Zanzibar (p.541).** Weirdly wonderful thousand-year-old celebrations to see out the Zoroastrian Year, Persian-style. July.

Zanzibari International Film Festival **Unguja** ⓦ www.ziff.or.tz **(p.529).** A major cinematic event, also with musicians from around the Indian Ocean. July.

MaKuYa Festival **Mtwara (p.186).** Traditional music and dance from the Makonde, Makua and Yao tribes of southern Tanzania. Aug.

Arusha Street Festival **Arusha (p.319).** Held along Boma Road, this combines music with a carnival atmosphere. End of Aug or early Sept.

## September to December

Bagamoyo Arts Festival **Bagamoyo (p.127).** A bit of everything; disorganized but fun. Oct.

East African Art Biennale **Dar es Salaam (p.106).** Contemporary East African art; held in odd-numbered years. Dec.

Kizimkazi Cultural Music Festival **Zanzibar (p.540).** A new Rasta-run shindig; bring a tent. Dec.

# Safaris

**Tanzania has more designated wildlife areas than any other country on earth, with one third of its surface area given over to national parks, game and forest reserves and other valuable protected spaces.**

Central to the country's wildlife crown are its fifteen **national parks**: unfenced wildlife sanctuaries with no settlements other than facilities for tourists and researchers. None have asphalt roads, and consumptive utilization of natural resources is prohibited. The classic parks such as Serengeti mostly occupy plains, and are where you'll get to see the animals you probably came to Tanzania for, albeit from inside a **vehicle** – although some parks now allow limited hiking in designated areas, usually if arranged as part of an organized tour. Getting around the more forested parks of Udzungwa Mountains, Mahale Mountains, Gombe Stream and Kitulo is done **on foot**, usually in the company of an official guide or ranger. Acting as ecological buffers around the parks are over sixty **game reserves**, which allow limited human settlement and resource use; in some, wildlife viewing can be as good as inside the parks, especially if they cover land visited during annual migrations. Forest reserves, usually in mountainous areas, are rarely visited by tourists, as few have any facilities, and getting the required permit can be awkward, too: we've given details where appropriate.

## Organized safaris

The easiest and often the cheapest way to get to know Tanzania's wild side is on an **organized safari** arranged through a safari company in Tanzania (the best of which are reviewed on pp.51–53), or via an overseas tour operator (see pp.21–22). For mid-range and upmarket trips, **booking ahead** by months rather than weeks is essential to be sure of getting the dates and accommodation you want, but at the budget level, where quality is a mercurial beast, it's fine to arrange things once you arrive, which gives you the chance to check out the company in person.

## Park regulations and guidelines

**Driving** Most national parks and game reserves have a speed limit of 50kph, with 25kph recommended to avoid throwing up too much dust or scaring animals; driving is only permitted in daylight. Keep to authorized tracks and roads: off-road driving is illegal and causes irreparable damage to fragile ecosystems via erosion-fuelled chain reactions.

**Do not disturb** So much is made of seeing the "Big Five" – elephant, lion, leopard, cheetah (or buffalo), and rhino – that at times you'll find up to a dozen vehicles converging on the same pride or pissed-off leopard up in a tree. For some species, this is just an annoyance, but for cheetahs, it's a serious problem: they only hunt by day, and it's difficult to be stealthy when surrounded by gaggles of tourists. So, let the driver know your preference. Also, be quiet while game-viewing, switch off the engine, and keep a distance of 25m.

**Do not feed animals** This leads to dependence on humans; you can see the effect on baboons and vervet monkeys, which can brazen, and even violent.

**Leave no trace** Don't pick or damage plants, and take care putting out campfires and cigarettes.

---

**Safari vehicles** tend to be Land Rovers or Land Cruisers, sometimes with roof hatches (handy for taking pictures). On a normal driving safari, you can keep costs down by sharing with other travellers; in a group of four or five, you might pay half what you would have paid in a couple. **Minibuses** are not normally recommended due to bigger group sizes: ensure at least that it has a pop-up roof or roof hatch, and that a window seat is guaranteed. When on safari, don't take too passive an **attitude**. Although some of the itinerary may be fixed, it's not all cast in stone, and daily routines may be altered to suit you and your fellow travellers – if you want to go on an early game drive, for example, don't be afraid to suggest you skip breakfast, or take sandwiches. As long as the staff know there are reasonable tips awaiting them at the end, most will go out of their way to help.

### Types of safari

The **type of safari** you take is largely determined by your budget, with accommodation being the main factor, but is never cheap. And be aware that in safari-speak, a "three-day safari" actually means two nights, and that most of the first and last days will likely be spent getting to and from the wildlife areas if you're not flying. For this reason we'd recommend at least three nights unless you're starting close by. **Prices**

should include everything except alcoholic drinks and tips.

At the lower end are so-called "budget" **camping safaris**, but which are far from cheap at around **$120–150** per person per day, and you'll be sharing with other travellers, too. Nights are usually spent in small tents, either in public campsites inside the parks, or in cheaper ones outside. Expect to muck in with the crew for some of the work, like pitching tents and washing up, and be prepared for a degree of discomfort: thin mattresses and sleeping bags, not having a shower every night, and basic food. More expensive camping trips ($150–250) feature better tents and food but are otherwise similar.

More comfortable, costing **$250–350** a day, are mid-range trips with accommodation in **safari lodges**. Some can be wonderfully intimate, but others are overrun by package tours, and lack that "in the wild" feeling you might be hankering for: read our accommodation reviews. Before booking, find out what kind of vehicle will be used, if you're on a shared safari, establish the maximum group size. Be aware that group sizes may become irrelevant if you end up being ferried around in convoys, as frequently happens with larger operators dealing with (mostly US) package tours. Much cosier but rarely offered as they need more time and effort on the

## Tanzania's wildlife areas at a glance

| National Park / Reserve | Description | Minimum costs* |
|---|---|---|
| **Amani** (see p.295) | The ancient rainforests of the East Usambara Mountains, nicknamed "Galapagos of Africa" on account of their immense biodiversity, are a delight for hikers, with many unique plant and animal species, including bright orange land crabs. | Entrance $30 (child $10)<br>Guided walk $25 (per person; optional)<br>Camping $30; Rest House approx. $7 |
| **Arusha** (see p.321) | This encloses most of Mount Meru, a dormant 4566m volcano looming over Arusha city. Hike to the top in three days, or drive or walk around the mountain's base in search of plains game. Canoeing is also possible. Wildlife includes buffaloes, elephants, monkeys and plains game. | Entrance $35 (child $10)<br>Guide (for hikes) $10<br>Porter (optional) $10–15<br>Ranger (for bush walks) $20<br>Camping or Rest House $30;<br>Mountain Hut $20 |
| **Gombe Stream** (see p.437) | A forested hillside rising from Lake Tanganyika's northern shore, made famous by Jane Goodall's long-term study of its chimpanzees – which can be visited. | Entrance $100 (child $20)<br>Guide (obligatory for chimps) $20<br>Camping or Banda $30 |
| **Katavi** (see p.455) | A remote floodplain in western Tanzania filled with hippos, buffaloes and crocodiles, among which you're welcome to walk – safe in the company of an armed ranger. | Entrance $20 (child $5)<br>Guide (for hikes) $20<br>Camping or Rest House $30 |
| **Kilimanjaro** (see p.262) | Africa's tallest mountain, and the world's highest free-standing massif, presents sturdy legs with a 5892m ice-capped challenge, best tackled over six or seven days. | Entrance $60 (child $10)<br>Guide $15–20 (obligatory)<br>Porter $10–15 (optional)<br>Camping or Mountain Hut $50 |
| **Kitulo** (see p.489) | Best visited during the rains, this highland plateau, locally dubbed "God's Garden", is a wonderland of wild flowers, especially orchids, and is also home to the extremely rare Kipunji monkey, only discovered in 2004. Driving is allowed, but hiking is far better. | Entrance $20 (child $5)<br>Guide (optional) $20<br>Camping $30 |
| **Lake Manyara** (see p.352) | At the base of a Rift Valley escarpment, Manyara's tangled shoreline is home to many species, including tree-climbing lions. The lake itself has hippos and vast flocks of pink flamingoes, drawn by algae that thrive off alkaline springs. | Entrance $35 (child $10)<br>Camping $30; Banda $20 |
| **Mahale Mountains** (see p.442) | Halfway down Lake Tanganyika, this contains even more chimpanzees than Gombe – and they're the reason to come. | Entrance $80 (child $30)<br>Camping or Banda $30 |

| | | |
|---|---|---|
| **Mikumi**<br>(see p.211) | Within easy reach of Dar es Salaam and Morogoro, this has heaps of classic plains game, including sometimes sizeable packs of endangered African hunting dogs. | Entrance $20 (child $5)<br>Camping or Rest House $60 |
| **Mkomazi**<br>(see p.282) | A new savanna park between the Pare Mountains and the Kenyan border, with a range of predators, and few, if any, tourists. | Entrance $20 (child $5)<br>Camping $30 |
| **Ngorongoro**<br>(see p.367) | The world's densest population of predators is to be found in the volcanic caldera at the heart of this conservation area, which is also the only place in Tanzania to virtually guarantee sightings of black rhino. Most visitors come on game drives, but an exciting alternative is to explore the Ngorongoro's northern highlands on foot, in the company of an armed ranger. | Entrance $50 (child $10)<br>Crater Fee $200/vehicle<br>Ranger (Crater Highlands walks) $20<br>Camping $30 |
| **Ruaha**<br>(see p.475) | The southernmost of the Rift Valley parks, watered on and off by the Great Ruaha River. All the plains game of northern Tanzania plus elephants, the usual predators and rich birdlife, but with far fewer crowds. | Entrance $20 (child $5)<br>Camping or Banda $30 |
| **Rubondo Island**<br>(see p.419) | An isolated bird-rich haven in Lake Victoria's southwest corner, but awkward (or expensive) access means it's one for dedicated twitchers only. | Entrance $20 (child $5)<br>Camping or Banda $30 |
| **Saadani**<br>(see p.130) | Bush, beach, mangroves, forest and river: Saadani's variety of habitats draws a rich selection of animals, though a recent history of poaching means that many are skittish. Activities are game drives, boat trips, snorkelling and bush walks. | Entrance $20 (child $5)<br>Activities $45 per person<br>Camping $30 |
| **Selous**<br>(see p.215) | Africa's second-largest animal sanctuary. Plenty of birds but mammals can be elusive. Activities include game drives, boat safaris and bush walks. | Entrance $65 (child $5)<br>Activities $35–100 per person<br>Camping $35 |
| **Serengeti**<br>(see p.375) | The famous "endless plains" are centre-stage for the world's biggest mammalian migration, with millions of animals including wildebeest, zebra, and ever-attentive lions. Game drives are the usual way around, though lodges can arrange short hikes, and you float over the lot in a hot-air balloon. | Entrance $50 (child $10)<br>Camping or Rest House $30 |
| **Tarangire**<br>(see p.340) | Like the Serengeti, Tarangire bushland is the turntable for a wildlife migration. A perennial river ensures good animal spotting year-round, especially elephants. The park's other giants are baobab trees. Birding is big, too, and you can go hiking in the adjacent conservation area. | Entrance $35 (child $10)<br>Camping $30 |
| **Udzungwa Mountains**<br>(see p.222) | Several types of pristine rainforest cover a wide range of elevations here, all of them rich in often unique species, including primates and birds. There are plenty of waterfalls, too, making it ideal hiking territory. | Entrance $20 (child $5)<br>Ranger (obligatory on all but one trail) $20<br>Camping $30; Guesthouse $20 |

\* Prices are per person and for 24 hours, except at Amani which has no time limit. To enter with your own vehicle, there's an additional $40/day/vehicle ($30/day with no time limit at Amani). Prices for guides and rangers are per group, except at Amani which charges per visitor. Prepayment is obligatory for Arusha, Kilimanjaro, Lake Manyara, Mkomazi, Serengeti and Tarangire: see p.54.

part of the safari company are trips using large **walk-in tents** pitched on public or special campsites; the tents are fitted with camp-beds, linen and sometimes showers and portable (chemical) toilets.

Spending **upwards of $350** a day gets you a private "tailor-made" safari including **flights** – dispensing with the dusty discomfort and time wasted getting to places by road. On such jaunts, the guiding and service should be top-notch, as should the **tented camps** you'll be staying in, some of them amazingly luxurious affairs

straight out of the pages of *Condé Nast*. Pulling out all the stops, for a blistering $1000 a day or thereabouts you can treat yourself to a Hemingwayesque "**mobile camping safari**", with fly-camps set up in the bush before your arrival each evening, champagne breakfasts (actually sparkling wine), and a rifle-toting expat as your wildlife guide. The main disadvantage to such capers is the almost total exclusion of Tanzanians from the safari and its profits – most of these outfits are owned by Europeans or South Africans.

## Choosing a reliable safari operator

The importance of taking your time in choosing a reliable and trustworthy safari company cannot be stressed highly enough. We've been extremely careful with our selections, and they should be among the most responsible, ethical, and – within reason – best priced. At the time of writing, all held TALA licences for wildlife parks. Operators also licensed for mountain climbing (Kilimanjaro and Meru) are noted, but see also our reviews of hiking companies based in and around Moshi on p.271. There are also a handful of safari companies in Mwanza (see p.402), and around Iringa for visiting Ruaha National Park (p.477), and don't forget overseas tour operators, reviewed on pp.21–22.

Given the considerable cost of safaris, and the hefty **deposit** required when booking ahead (anything from thirty to one hundred percent), always check up on companies you're interested in beforehand: standards can change quite quickly, especially as reputations are often built on the backs of just two or three driver-guides or owners. For the latest developments check out Ⓦwww.bluegecko.org/tanzania. Heeding the following advice should also help.

### Before you go

**TALA licence** In order to enter national parks with clients, safari companies need a "TALA licence", valid for one year starting July 1. The licence comes in several flavours, the most common being "Safari operator" or "Tour operator", which costs the company $5000 and should (but doesn't, in practice) guarantee that the company owns at least five vehicles. The "mountaineering" version is *only* valid for climbing Kilimanjaro or Mount Meru, and lets the company use their own guides. PDFs listing licensees are posted at Ⓦwww.tanzaniaparks.com and Ⓦwww.tanzaniatouristboard.com.

**TATO membership** Most but not all reputable safari companies belong to the Tanzania Association of Tour Operators (list on Ⓦwww.tatotz.org). There are no quality checks, but membership does at least guarantee that companies aren't so bad they got expelled.

**Internet research** There are several good travellers' forums where you can search for answers and ask advice (see p.74), but don't believe everything you read, especially multiple recommendations in bad English for previously unheard-of companies. Similarly, just because a company has a flashy website it doesn't guarantee quality, but if the blurb goes into passionate detail about non-standard options (birding off the beaten track, say, or rock art or village tourism), they're more likely to be credible.

**Who's really running the safari?** Many safari and tour companies, including overseas "specialists", don't run their own trips at all, but subcontract them to local companies ("ground handlers"). Get that company's name *before* booking,

## Safari companies in Arusha

Arusha's safari companies specialize in the "**northern circuit**", namely Ngorongoro, and the national parks of Arusha, Lake Manyara, Tarangire and Serengeti. Most also offer Crater Highlands walks, including Lake Natron and Ol Doinyo Lengai, and can tack on any of the region's many cultural tourism offerings.

### Budget

**Duma Explorer** PPF Oloirien Estate #22, Njiro ☎0787/079127, Ⓦwww.dumaexplorer.com.

A US/Tanzanian company licensed for both mountaineering and wildlife parks, and especially recommended for the former: Mount Meru hikes are a speciality.

**Easy Travel & Tours** New Safari Hotel, Boma Rd ☎027/250 3929, Ⓦwww.easytravel.co.tz. Large, reputable and well informed, with a wide range of trips, from budget camping to semi-luxury mobile camping expeditions. They also offer scheduled departures, Kilimanjaro climbs (for which they're licensed), and Zanzibar beach stays. The main office is in Dar.

**Maasai Wanderings** Block C, #11–15, Njiro (behind Abercrombie & Kent) ☎0755/984925 or

---

so you can check them out. On shared safaris, simple economics mean that most companies will farm out clients to other operators if they can't fill enough seats to make a trip worthwhile. You should be informed of this at the very least, and be given a chance to back out.

### In Tanzania

**Tourist offices** The tourist board offices in Arusha and Dar es Salaam maintain "blacklists" of particularly noxious companies, which are just collections of tattered business cards. Hardly comprehensive and often very old, the list is at least useful for comparing PO Box numbers of your choice (if not on the TALA list) against known bad eggs: such companies will change their names and phone numbers, but tend to stick to the same address. Incidentally, don't necessarily believe recommendations from the tourist offices, or the ads on their walls.

**TALA licence** If a company claims to be licensed but you can't find them on the official list (see opposite), demand to see their original licence – not a photocopy – and be sure the date and company name are correct.

**Travellers' grapevine** Fellow travellers are great sources of up-to-date advice, but remain wary of recommendations: good companies can turn bad very quickly, while even the most consistently bad company can occasionally come up trumps. In Arusha, good places to meet up include *Bamboo Café*, *Jambo's Coffee House*, *The Patisserie* and *Via Via*, as well as the *Meru House Inn* and *Arusha Backpackers* hotels. Unfortunately, there are no such travellers' focuses in Dar: closest are the clutch of hotels and the *Chef's Pride* restaurant in Kisutu area.

**Briefcase companies** If the office is just a desk and chair in a rented room, move on.

**Flycatchers** These are young men who approach tourists with offers of cheap safaris, usually for disreputable companies. Any outfit that values its name shouldn't need to tout for business. Likewise, be wary of companies offering free rides in from the airport, no matter how slick their patter.

**Off-road driving** Driving off-road in national parks is illegal and destructive. Plenty of companies do it, though, even some of the big ones (excluded from this book). Test a company's moral resolve by innocently asking whether it would be possible to drive off-road for that perfect shot of a lion or leopard.

**Comments book** Even the worst companies will show you guest books overflowing with wild praise, but as no company asks dissatisfied punters to pen their opinions, they're not much use. Here's a trick that works though: ask the company what kind of complaints they receive. There isn't a single safari outfit, in any price range, that doesn't receive complaints from time to time, so if they say they never receive complaints, they're lying.

0755/208423, ⓦ www.maasaiwanderings.com.
Tanzanian arm of the very ethical IntoAfrica; see p.22
for review.

**Safari Makers** Behind AICC Sports Club off the
Old Moshi Rd ℡ 027/254 4446 or 0754/300817,
ⓦ www.safarimakers.com. A US/Tanzanian outfit
with good vehicles, a solid reputation, and flexible
itineraries, from budget camping and Crater Highlands
jaunts (up to ten days) to lodge-based trips. They're
also licensed for Kilimanjaro and Mount Meru.

**Sunny Safaris** Colonel Middleton Rd ℡ 027/250
8184 or 0754/268475, ⓦ www.sunnysafaris.com.
A long-established, family-friendly and reliable budget
and mid-range outfit, whose 4WDs have roof hatches
and guaranteed window seats. They also offer trips
using walk-in tents at special campsites, Crater
Highlands treks, and Kilimanjaro climbs (for which
they're also licensed).

### Mid-range

**Dorobo Tours & Safaris** Olasiti, 6km along the
Dodoma road, then 3km south ℡ 027/250 9685,
ⓔ office@dorobo.co.tz or dorobo@habari.co.tz.
A small, very ethical and personable outfit run by
three American brothers, who were first off the
mark with cultural tours, in the early nineties.
Their exclusive tailor-made trips feature an
enjoyable and instructive blend of culture and
wildlife in mostly little-travelled locations, and excel
in rugged treks outside the national parks. If you
have enough time and money, a two- or three-week
trip is recommended to really get under the skin of
rural Tanzania.

**East African Safari & Touring Company** Sakina,
off the Nairobi Highway ℡ 0787/293727,
ⓦ www.eastafricansafari.info. A flexible and
pleasingly offbeat Australian/Tanzanian outfit with an
excellent reputation for off-the-beaten-track tours,
priced to suit all budgets. Their speciality is Tarangire
Conservation Area (where they own *Naitolia* and
*Boundary Hill* lodges), the Crater Highlands and Lake
Natron, and Tanzania's far northwest. Other offerings
include birding, mountain biking, and a bumper
21-day "Tanzania Explorer".

**Green Footprint Adventures** Sekei
℡ 027/250 2664, ⓦ www.greenfootprint.co.tz.
Dutch/South African company offering mid- to
high-end trips featuring smaller, out-of-the-way
lodges and mobile camps. They also operate various
activities (mostly 2–3hr) from their bases at the
*Serena* lodges, including mountain biking, canoeing,
hiking and microlight flights over Lake Manyara,
and run eight-day wildlife courses in April, May
and November.

**Nature Discovery** 5km west along the
Nairobi Highway, Sakina ℡ 0732/971859,

ⓦ www.naturediscovery.com. An efficient, safety-
conscious, ethical and keenly priced firm offering
4WD camping and lodge safaris, plus a number of
interesting hiking options in the Crater Highlands,
donkey trekking from Longido, birding, and walks along
the eastern side of Lake Eyasi. Mountain climbing
is another speciality – they're licensed and enjoy an
outstanding reputation for Kilimanjaro, on which they
carry oxygen and a portable altitude chamber.

**Tropical Trails** *Masai Camp*, Old Moshi Rd
℡ 027/250 0358, ⓦ www.tropicaltrails.com.
A highly respected firm offering affordable camping
safaris as well as personalized safaris, either by
vehicle or on foot outside the parks (anything up
to two weeks), with knowledgeable guides. They
also offer Crater Highlands treks, walks in the Rift
Valley with Maasai guides, and Kilimanjaro climbs
(licensed).

### Expensive

**Amazing Tanzania** Based at *Gibb's Farm* in
Karatu, 140km west of Arusha ℡ 027/253 4302,
ⓦ www.amazingtanzania.com. Attention to detail
and personal service is the hallmark here. Most
options are tailor-made and feature luxurious mobile
camps; they also have plenty of experience with
elderly clients.

**Coastal Travels** ATC House, Boma Rd ℡ 027/250
0087, ⓦ www.coastal.cc. See p.53.

**Hoopoe Adventure Tours** India St ℡ 027/250
7011, ⓦ www.hoopoe.com. Specialists in off-the-
beaten-track safaris, often staying in intimate luxury
tented camps in Tarangire Conservation Area, their
own concessions at Loliondo next to Serengeti,
Ngorongoro, and West Kilimanjaro, or in searingly
expensive mobile camps.

**Summits Africa** India St ℡ 0787/130666,
ⓦ www.summits-africa.com. A mountaineering outfit
renowned for its fair treatment of porters and staff,
offering a range of expeditions on Kilimanjaro, Meru,
and in Kenya, plus an ever-expanding selection of
mountain-biking expeditions. Their conventional game
drives are run by Hoopoe.

## Safari companies in Dar

The following are mostly mid-range and
upmarket companies, useful for both the
"**southern circuit**" (mainly Mikumi, Selous
and Ruaha), and the western parks of
Katavi, Mahale Mountains and Gombe
Stream, access to which is usually by
plane. Budget travellers should be wary
of self-proclaimed "budget" operators in
Dar, especially in Kisutu area, as few if any
of those are licensed or recommendable.

Luckily, access to each of the southern circuit parks can be arranged locally, so you don't actually need a safari company.

**Authentic Tanzania** Kawe Beach, 10km north of Dar ☎0786/019965 or 0784/825899, ⓦwww .authentictanzania.com. A responsible and reliable operator offering innovative itineraries throughout southern and western Tanzania, plus Zanzibar and Mafia. Choose from tailor-made flying safaris, extended road trips, mid-range fly-camping trips, or unusual activities for Tanzania such as horse-riding, mountain biking or ornithology. Great guides, too, and not snobbish either.

**Coastal Travels** Upanga Rd, also at the airport ☎022/211 7959, ⓦwww.coastal.cc. Pioneers of Tanzania's "flying safaris", Coastal's airline, Coastal Aviation, flies more routes than any other. As such, the company offers good-value trips all over, including tailor-made, but are best for southern and western Tanzania: they have their own camps in Selous and Ruaha, and are one of the few companies offering trips to Rubondo Island. All safaris can be combined with Mafia or Zanzibar.

**Easy Travel & Tours** Raha Tower, Bibi Titi Mohamed Rd ☎022/212 1747 or 0754/602151, ⓦwww.easytravel.co.tz. See p.51.

**Foxes African Safaris** TAZARA railway station, Nyerere Rd ☎0713/237422 or 0784/237422, ⓦwww.tanzaniasafaris.info. A long-established, highly regarded and ethically run English family affair emphasizing luxurious but keenly priced off-the-beaten-track forays, often flying using their Safari Airlink airline. Nights are usually spent in their own lodges in Mikumi, Selous, Ruaha and Katavi, and, away from the animals, at *Lazy Lagoon Island Lodge* near Bagamoyo, and *Mufindi Highlands Lodge* in the south.

**Hippotours** Nyumba ya Sanaa, Ohio St ☎022/212 8662 or 0754/267706, ⓦwww .hippotours.com. One of the most reliable mid-range operators for southern circuit trips, including the coast, all tailor-made but not necessarily pricey: they're happy offering Selous with overnights outside the reserve, for instance.

**Leopard Tours** *Mövenpick Royal Palm*, Ohio St ☎022/211 9754, ⓦwww.leopard-tours.com. Huge yet efficient mid-market operation, often dealing with package tours (towing luggage in trailers is a clever touch), and reasonably priced for the quality – though in high season you risk travelling in convoy. Has a branch in Arusha.

**Tent with a View Safaris** Zahra Tower, corner Zanaki/Makunganya St ☎022/211 0507 or 0713/323318, ⓦwww.tentwithaview.com. A reliable, enthusiastic and relatively affordable outfit with its own lodges in Selous (*Sable Mountain Lodge*) and Saadani (*A Tent With a View Safari Lodge*).

**Wild Things Safaris** Farasi St, Mbezi, 14km north of Dar ☎022/261 7166 or 0773/503502, ⓦwww.wildthingsafaris.com. Another enthusiastic and efficient British-run company very much committed to sustainable tourism, and the only one specializing in the otherwise almost wholly unknown Kilombero Valley, a birding paradise south of the Udzungwa Mountains, trips to which are run in conjunction with local communities. They also operate temporary mobile camps in Mikumi and Ruaha. The guides are second to none (including for birds), and they also offer trekking and cultural tours.

## Complaints

First off, you've only yourself to blame if a $100-a-day safari bought off the street turns sour. Also, be understanding about things outside a company's control – like bad weather, lack of animals (unless they explicitly promised sightings), and breakdowns caused by things like broken fuel-injection pumps, which even the best mechanics cannot predict. For justified complaints, operators should at least offer a partial refund or replacement trip. Should the operator not be forthcoming, there's little you can do to force redress, but you can make things difficult for them in future: alerting the tourist board may result in the company being blacklisted, and TATO (see p.50) can expel errant members. Posting your experiences online also helps, and you can write to the guidebooks (we're at ⓦwww.roughguides.com); the updates for this book are at ⓦwww.bluegecko.org /tanzania.

## Arranging your own safari

Arranging your own trip has the advantage of **flexibility** and being able to choose your companions, but isn't necessarily cheaper than going through a company if you're going to need a vehicle, unless you can fill all the seats (usually five or seven). You'll also be paying full "rack rates" on mid-range and upmarket accommodation, which might otherwise be discounted if booked through a safari company.

Parks and reserves that can be entered **without vehicles** are Gombe Stream, Kilimanjaro (requiring prepayment in Arusha), Kitulo, Mahale Mountains, Rubondo Island

and Udzungwa Mountains. At a few others, you can get close on **public transport** and arrange things there: these are Katavi (at Sitalike), Mikumi (Mikumi village), Ngorongoro (Karatu), Ruaha (Iringa or Tungamalenga), and Selous (Mloka). For all other parks you'll need a **4WD vehicle**; advice on renting is given on p.30.

The basic **daily costs** are park fees ($20–100 per person plus $40 per vehicle; details are given throughout this book), car rental ($140–200 a day excluding fuel but including the driver and his costs), meals, maps, guidebooks, tips, a guide or ranger (sometimes optional; $10–20), and accommodation. The cheapest stays inside the parks are camping or using park-run *bandas* (both $30 per person), but you'll need to be self-sufficient. To stay in a lodge or a tented camp, expect to pay anything from $150 to over $2000 a double, depending on its standard, exclusivity, and whether or not it's inside the park or reserve.

**Entry fees** are paid on arrival. Rates for tourists ("non residents") are in dollars. At most places, payment is in dollars cash, but at the more popular northern parks – Arusha, Kilimanjaro, Lake Manyara, Mkomazi, Serengeti and Tarangire – you can only pay electronically. This means buying a prepaid **TANAPA Card** at TANAPA headquarters in Arusha (p.307), as there's no guarantee that credit cards will work. Check the situation beforehand, however, as things were fluid at the time of writing.

# Activities

Tanzania boasts plenty of wholesome outdoor activities, and not just wildlife safaris: take your pick from diving or snorkelling, boating, canoeing or hiking. Alternatively, indulge in a spot of birdwatching, or sample some of the country's pioneering cultural tourism projects.

## Cultural tourism

Most tourists come to Tanzania for a beach-and-bush experience, and perhaps also to climb Kilimanjaro, but an increasing number find that mixing with the locals is the real highlight of their stay. We wholeheartedly agree, and it's simple to arrange, as well.

Tanzania's pioneering **Cultural Tourism Programme** (ⓦwww.tanzaniaculturaltourism .com) was set up in 1995 by SNV, a Dutch NGO, in response to a request from Longido's Maasai community for help establishing tourism that would benefit them directly. The programme is now coordinated by the tourist board in Arusha, and offers intimate hands-on experiences in **over thirty locations**, most of them accessible by public transport. The concept is as simple as it is effective: visitors get to know locals, their way of life, history and environment in intimate, respectful and invariably memorable ways; in turn, villagers benefit directly from receipts (for guides, food, accommodation, entrance fees), and through "development fees" funding community-managed projects such as irrigation, dispensaries and schools.

The various "modules" range from two hours to over a week, and **costs** are reasonable, especially if you book direct or via the tourist board in Arusha (p.307) – typically no more than $30 or $40 for a full day and night. You'll pay a premium if going through a safari company as part of a safari, but there are no ethical worries as the basic costs mentioned above stay with the community. A **warning**: only book at the offices or places mentioned in this book or on the project's website, as the project's success has in some places attracted scammers and dupers. A full **list** of the country's cultural tourism options is included under "Cultural tourism" in this book's index.

## Hiking

Hiking gives you unparalleled contact with nature as well as locals, and that delicious feeling of being one with the world, something you'd never get by just driving around. For a sheer challenge, it's hard to beat a six- or seven-day climb up and down Africa's highest peak, the 5891m **Mount Kilimanjaro**. It's a distinctly masochistic undertaking, for your wallet as well as you, as you won't get much change out of $1500. Cheaper and a little easier, but equally invigorating, is a two- or three-day ascent of **Mount Meru** (4566m), the beautiful hulk that looms up over Arusha. Other climbable peaks include the 3417m **Mount Hanang** near Babati (an almost perfect volcanic cone), and the carbonate-spewing **Ol Doinyo Lengai** volcano (2889m, at least before its last eruption in 2008), between Ngorongoro and the wild desert around Lake Natron. Climbs up Mount Hanang are arranged locally; the others can be organized through safari companies (also overseas) or with specialist hiking companies based in or around Moshi. None of the climbs needs special skills, but you do need to be in good shape, and both Kilimanjaro and Meru require some preparations: see pp.266 & 268.

Getting to the top of mountains is one thing. Just as rewarding can be exploring the rainforests on their flanks, for which there are few places better in Africa than the ancient **Eastern Arc mountains**, a disparate chain of isolated ranges that include North and South Pare, West and East Usambara (including the "Galapagos of Africa", Amani Nature Reserve), the Ulugurus, and Udzungwa Mountains National Park, all of which are easily explored on foot. The rewards are many: enchanting liana-draped forest scenery, hidden brooks and waterfalls in which to refresh tired limbs, and some of the most biodiverse terrain on earth, with hundreds of unique species of plants and flowers, birds and bugs (including butterflies), and primates. Further south, Tanzania's **southern highlands** beckon, a land studded with crater lakes, hot springs, and the dormant 2960m Mount Rungwe volcano, which can be climbed in a day

or, better, over three. The jewel of this area is **Kitulo National Park**: dubbed "God's Garden" by locals, the highland plateau is home to over fifty species of orchid as well as the newly discovered kipunji monkey and, for now, receives virtually no tourists whatsoever.

Equally wild for walking, but for a few hours rather than days, are wildlife parks and reserves, where a **bush walk** – in the company of an armed ranger or guide – can get you face-to-face with elephants, buffalo, antelopes and other beasts. The walks are best arranged through a safari company or lodge, as you can't just turn up at the gate and start marching. Particularly good are: Arusha National Park to explore the lower inclines of Mount Meru; Gombe Stream and Mahale on the shore of Lake Tanganyika for tracking chimpanzees; Ruaha for classic savanna wildlife; Ngorongoro for the "Crater Highlands", a trek of several days; Katavi for unimaginable quantities of hippos and crocs; and Selous, simply because it's beautiful.

## Birding

Tanzania boasts around 1200 **bird species**, including dozens of endangered "Red Book" endemics found only in particular forests or mountain ranges. The best time for birding is from November to March, when residents are joined by Eurasian and Palearctic migrants. It's impossible to recommend one area over another, as every place has something special, but highlights include: Tarangire National Park and its adjacent Conservation Area, which contain over 550 recorded species; Lake Natron for immense flocks of flamingos and rare raptors; Lake Manyara, also for flamingos and almost four hundred other species; and Rubondo Island in Lake Victoria, paradise for water birds. For endemics, the rainforest at Amani Nature Reserve in East Usambara is the place to head be, while other Eastern Arc mountain ranges – including Uluguru and Udzungwa – also contain rare endemics.

A few **safari companies** offer specialized birding trips. Especially recommended are Dar's Wild Things Safaris (reviewed on p.53), Arusha's East African Safari and Touring Company (p.52), Birding & Beyond (Ⓦ www.tanzaniabirding.com), and "Birdman" James Wolstencroft in Arusha

(Ⓦbirds.intanzania.com). A useful **website**, which includes checklists, is Ⓦwww .africanbirdclub.org.

## Diving and snorkelling

Caressed and nourished by the warm South Equatorial Current, Tanzania's fringing coral reefs offer exhilarating **scuba diving and snorkelling**, with an abundance of colourful and sometimes heart-stopping marine life to be seen within a short boat ride of most beaches. For snorkellers, the best areas – with plenty of shallow reefs and a myriad corals and creatures – are Mafia Island and the east coast of Zanzibar's Unguja Island. For scuba divers, the choice is more a matter of personal preference, though both Mafia and Pemba come in for heaps of praise.

### Scuba diving

Tanzania is as good a place as any to learn how to dive: there are dozens of locations with **dive centres**, almost all of them offering PADI-accredited courses. On any dive you can expect to see a profusion of colourful tropical fish in extensive **coral gardens**, together with larger open-water (pelagic) species such as giant groupers, Napoleon wrasse, barracuda, kingfish, tuna and wahoo – enormous, super-fast versions of mackerel. **Dolphins and turtles** are also seen, and year-round too, but you'll need luck (and the right season) for whale-sharks or **whales**, which migrate up the coast from southern Africa in the latter half of the year to nurse their offspring in East Africa's warm waters. Depending on the location, experienced divers can also enjoy drift dives, wreck dives, and **night dives** (great for colourful sea slugs, properly called nudibranchs).

Arguably Tanzania's most spectacular diving location, certainly with the clearest water, is **Pemba**, whose vertiginous drop-offs are stuffed with a stupendous variety of life; Misali Island is a particular gem. However, the strong currents that add spice to many a dive here are also potentially dangerous – hence, novices should learn the ropes around Zanzibar's **Unguja Island** instead, whose eastern shore is bounded by a sheltering barrier reef. Often forgotten, but also good, are the handful of islands – protected as a

marine reserve – off the coast **north of Dar**, though some of the reefs have been badly damaged by dynamite fishing. Also worth exploring are the coral gardens around the tidal Maziwe Island near Pangani, in the north. South of Dar, the reefs around **Mafia Island** rival Pemba's for beauty, and have more big fish, too. Further south, you can also dive off **Kilwa Masoko** (steep drops-offs), and in the barely known but pristine **Mnazi Bay–Ruvuma Estuary Marine Park**, on the border with Mozambique.

The **best months** for diving should be November and March, when the water is clearest and conditions calm, but as the seasons have gone haywire of late, you might find that October or February is better, as there's a chance of strong wind from November to January. June to September, the time of the *kusi* monsoon, is also windy, and the choppy seas and strong currents will restrict you to sites within lagoons or bays.

### Safety

Proportionally, scuba diving claims more fatalities than any other sport, so **safety**, not cost, should be your primary concern when choosing a dive centre. At the time of writing, the ones reviewed in this book were accredited by **PADI** (Professional Association of Diving Instructors), which unfortunately doesn't mean as much as it should do, as PADI neither visit nor vet dive centres, basing their certifications instead on the centre's throughput. Nonetheless, we'd strongly recommend you avoid companies not reviewed in this book, and even for those we list, try to interview them beforehand to get a feel for how serious they are about your safety. One thing to ask is whether they use **marker buoys**: life-savers where drifts or strong currents are normal, such as around Pemba. Have a look at the equipment, too: a messy storage area, or battered tanks and regulators, are not a good sign. The boats can tell a tale, too: the best are state-of-the-art inflatables equipped with oxygen, HF radio and powerful engines; others are converted dhows; whilst many are just normal boats with outboards. All should have life-jackets, and ideally two engines. Recommended dive centres and reefs are described in boxed sections throughout this book: look under "diving" in the index. You could also post a query on Ⓦ www.scubaboard.com.

## Courses, costs and equipment

In theory, a **medical certificate** is necessary for beginners, but it's rarely asked for. Novices can try things out with a one-day **Discover scuba course** ($70–100), or jump straight in with the standard 4–5 day **Open Water certification** ($400–500, including the obligatory manual), completion of which gives you the right to dive to 18m with any qualified diver worldwide. Details of these and other courses are given on Ⓦ www.padi.com.

For already qualified divers (bring your card), costs average $40–50 per dive, plus $20–40 a day if a long boat trip is required. You don't need to bring **equipment**, but pack specialist gear like dive computers or waterproof cameras as renting locally can be expensive. Only three Tanzanian dive centres have **Nitrox facilities** (for deeper and longer dives, averaging 40min at 30m): East Africa Diving and Sensation Divers at Nungwi on Zanzibar, and Sea Breeze Marine at Jangwani Beach near Dar es Salaam. Given the risk of the bends, most dive centres wisely refuse to take clients below 27m. The only **recompression chamber** is at the *Fairmont Zanzibar* hotel in Matemwe on Unguja, use of which your insurance should cover (the better dive centres should provide insurance in any case).

## Snorkelling

**Snorkelling** is a rewarding and cheap way of dipping beneath the ocean surface, and as most diving reefs have shallower ones nearby, snorkellers can often get there on diving boats, which cuts costs. The most accessible reefs are in Mafia's Chole Bay, and off the eastern side of Unguja, where a barrier reef encloses a series of shallow and sheltered tidal lagoons. One really special reef accessible to snorkellers but not to divers is **Chumbe Island**, southwest of Unguja, which has among the densest coral growth and diversity in Africa (over two hundred species), and provides shelter for ninety percent of East Africa's varieties of fish. For something completely different, go freshwater snorkelling at the north end of **Lake Nyasa** near Matema, remarkable for its extraordinary number of colourful cichlids.

Bring your own **equipment** if you plan to do much snorkelling, since the daily cost of renting a mask, flippers and snorkel (at least Tsh5000) soon adds up. Buying a set in Dar or Stone Town costs around Tsh30,000. The price of **renting a boat** varies: some fishermen will happily take you out for Tsh4000 per person or Tsh10,000–15,000 per boat, but some dive centres and beach hotels will charge fifteen times as much.

## Responsible diving and snorkelling

Despite their apparent solidity, **coral reefs** are among the most fragile ecosystems on earth, with even minor environmental changes wreaking disastrous results. In places, the 1997–98 El Niño event, which raised the water temperature by one measly degree for just a few months, killed over ninety percent of corals, and some of Tanzania's reefs have yet to recover fully. Minimize your own impact by following these rules:

**Swim carefully**. Coral polyps die if covered with silt or sand, commonly stirred up by careless swipes of fins (flippers). Be aware of where your feet are, and when you're close to something, use your hands to swim. If you haven't dived for a while, take a refresher course and practise buoyancy control in a swimming pool.

**No feeding**. Some irresponsible companies encourage their clients to feed fish, but this risks screwing up feeding and mating patterns.

**No touching**. Leave corals, shellfish and other critters alone: you might damage them, or they might damage you – many are poisonous or otherwise bad for your health. Also, resist the temptation to collect shells on the beach, or to buy them from hawkers: the export of many species is illegal, both in Tanzania and internationally.

## Boating

The classic way to mess about in East Africa's waters is on a **dhow trip**. If arranged specially for tourists, these are usually day-trips, or over even shorter periods (see p.32 for dhow-hopping along the coast), and can involve snorkelling, exploring mangroves and islands, or cruising lazily up a river in search of birds, monkeys, crocodiles and hippo.

The main places for dhow trips are Pangani and Saadani on the north coast (both with rivers, mangroves and snorkelling), Mafia Island in the south (various islands, snorkelling and mangroves), the Ruvuma River (wildlife and snorkelling in the marine park; most easily arranged in Mikindani), Kilwa Masoko (mainly for visiting Kilwa Kisiwani and other ancient ruins), Stone Town (sunset cruises and snorkelling trips), Nungwi and Pemba (boozy sunset cruises), Pemba (snorkelling, deserted islands and mangroves), and almost anywhere on Unguja's eastern seaboard (more snorkelling, and mangroves).

As Tanzania has few rivers navigable for more than a few dozen kilometres, boat trips inland – beside ferry journeys on the lakes – are limited to wildlife **cruises** on the Rufiji in Selous, and for getting to Gombe, Mahale and Rubondo Island national parks. **Dugouts** are useful for exploring Lake Babati and Lake Nyasa (from Matema), but take care as they're inherently unstable: you don't want to become someone's next meal. You can also **canoe** at two places near Arusha: the Momela Lakes in Arusha National Park, and Lake Duluti (a crater lake) nearby.

# Crime and personal safety

Despite the often paranoid "travel advisories" from certain terrorism-obsessed governments, Tanzania is a safe and peaceful country to travel around in, and if you stick to the following mostly common-sense advice, you're unlikely to run into trouble.

## Robbery and theft

Your chances of being **robbed** in Tanzania are slim but you should nonetheless be conscious of your belongings, and never leave anything unguarded. In addition, be careful where you walk, at least until you're settled in somewhere; known trouble spots are mentioned throughout the guide. Be especially alert in bus and ferry terminals, and if you can't help walking around with valuables and are in town for more than a couple of days, vary your route and schedule. For advice on keeping things safe in a hotel, see p.37.

The best way to avoid being **mugged** is not to walk around at night unless you're sure the area is safe, and not to carry unnecessary valuables, especially anything visible. It should go without saying that you shouldn't wear dangling earrings or any kind of chain or necklace, expensive-looking sunglasses or wristwatches. Not so obvious is that certain brands of sports shoes (sneakers) can also be tempting, but which brands is impossible to say, as it depends on fashion. Similarly, try to avoid carrying valuables in those handy off-the-shoulder day bags or even small rucksacks, as these provide visible temptation. Old plastic bags are a much less conspicuous way of carrying cameras. If you clearly have nothing on you, you're unlikely to feel, or be, threatened.

If you do get mugged, **don't resist**, since knives and guns are occasionally carried. It will be over in an instant and you're unlikely to be hurt. You'll have to go to the nearest police station for a statement to show your

## Carrying money safely

The safest place for banknotes, passports and credit cards is a flat **money belt**, strapped around your waist under your clothes. Avoid nylon belts as these can irritate your skin. If you sweat a lot, wrap your things in a plastic bag before putting them away. Although the belts are effectively invisible, it still makes sense to stash some emergency money and perhaps a spare credit card elsewhere, perhaps in the lining of a suitcase or rucksack. The voluminous "**bum bags**" (also called "fanny packs") should definitely be avoided, and not just for linguistic reasons, as even if worn back to front, they're one short step away from announcing your stash with flashing neon lights. Equally dumb are pouches hung around your neck, and ordinary wallets are a pickpocket's dream.

Place daily **spending money** in a pocket or somewhere else accessible: you don't want to be rooting around your groin every time you have to pay for something, and you'll feel safer with at least some money to hand, as few muggers will believe you have nothing on you whatsoever.

---

insurance company, though you may well be expected to pay a "little something" for it. You can usually forget about enlisting the police to try and get your stuff back. In fact, their lackadaisical attitude, and that of the courts, favours **mob justice**. So, as angry as you may feel about being robbed, if you shout "Mwizi!" ("Thief!" in Kiswahili) **be ready to intercede** should a crowd manage to turn up the thief, as he might otherwise be killed.

### Driving hazards

Don't leave **valuables** in an unlocked or unguarded vehicle. In towns, find an *askari* (security guard) to keep an eye on it: Tsh500 is enough for a few hours. If you can, **avoid driving at night**: armed hold-ups in remote areas are sporadically reported, and in cities, you risk grab-and-run robberies if your doors are unlocked or the windows open. Don't worry too much about car-jackers though: they tend to shun the typical (ie slightly battered) Land Rover or Land Cruiser you'll likely be driving.

### Police, bribes and politics

Though you might sometimes hear stories of extraordinary kindness and amazing bursts of efficiency, **Tanzanian police** are notoriously corrupt, and it's best to steer clear. If you need to deal with them, patience and politeness, smiles and handshakes always help, and treat even the most offensively corrupt cop with respect (greeting him with "Shikamoo, Mzee"

for starters). Having said this, in unofficial dealings the police can go out of their way to help you with food, transport or accommodation, especially in remote outposts. Try to reciprocate. Police salaries are low and aren't always paid on time, so they rely on unofficial channels to get by.

Unless you're driving a car, police are rarely out to solicit **bribes** from tourists, although on Zanzibar robberies at fake police roadblocks (possibly manned by real police) have been reported. If you *have* done something wrong, it really is best to pay the full fine (with receipt) than go for the cheaper bribe. Still, if a bribe it is (in which case there'll be no receipt), wait for it to be hinted at, then haggle as you would over a purchase; Tsh2000 or so is often enough to oil small wheels, though traffic police may expect something more substantial from tourists. Bribery is, of course, illegal – if you've done nothing wrong and are not in a rush, refusing a bribe will only cost a short delay until the cop gives up and tries someone else. Insisting on seeing his ID may help, too. If the officer persists in his pursuit, insist on going to the police station to sort things out, where you'll be able to kick up a fuss with his superior, or threaten legal action, demand legal assistance and so on – a time-consuming rigmarole that hopefully won't be worth the corrupt cop's time, or his job.

### Drugs

Tourists in Arusha, Dar and Zanzibar are occasionally offered **marijuana**. Grass (*bangi*)

## Scams

Visitors are most likely to be **ripped off** in their first day or two, when they're still a little green. Most scams are confidence tricks, and though there's no reason to be paranoid (indeed, one or two scams are a play on paranoia), a healthy sense of cynicism is helpful. Here's a quick run-down of the most popular tricks:

**Ticket scams**: A tout sells you a ticket for a non-existent ferry, or you buy a ticket at cheaper "resident" rates, only to be pulled over by the inspector to pay the full fare plus a fine. Solution: don't buy anything from touts, and if there are "non-resident" rates, well, that's what you have to pay.

**Greedy victim scams**: Should a stranger, finding a wad of cash, wish to share it with you – say, down a convenient alley – well, at least the resulting robbery would vindicate Darwin.

**Money changers**: Changing money on the street carries way too many risks, and won't get you better rates than a bank or forex either. The most popular scams are either straight swindles on the exchange rate, being given invalid banknotes, or the money changer dashing off at full clip. Admirably more subtle is a surprisingly common trick involving sleight-of-hand: the man switches the bundle of shillings he showed you for a roll of paper wrapped in a single banknote. He tells you it's dangerous to count money on the street and saunters off, cool as a cucumber. Incidentally, there are no regulations obliging visitors to buy Tanzanian shillings on arriving at land borders, so if someone feeds you that line, you'll know he's just a scammer warming up.

**Drugging on public transport**: A nasty one, this, but hardly ever reported from Tanzania: someone strikes up a friendship with you, gives you food, drink or even a cigarette. When you come to, your new friend, and all your stuff, has vanished.

**Dope scams**: Buying marijuana (*bangi*) on the street is asking for trouble, man: you risk being trailed and then either robbed or being shaken down by complicit cops.

**Fake sponsorship**: "School children" or "students" approach you with a sponsorship form. Well, it may be true, but schooling is now free, so most requests are just cons.

---

is widely smoked and remarkably cheap, but attitudes vary considerably, and it's illegal, so you should be discreet if you're going to indulge, and watch out who you get high with. It's best to buy from a real friend, not someone you met that day or the day before, and never on the street – you're guaranteed to be conned or, worse, shopped to the police. If you're caught in possession, you'll be hit with a heavy fine, and possibly imprisoned or deported, depending on the quantity. Anything harder than marijuana is rarely sold and will obviously get you in much worse trouble.

### Political unrest

Wherever you are, avoid **rallies and demonstrations**, particularly on Zanzibar where political violence (and police brutality) is a constant theme, reaching a bloody crescendo at election time: the next ones are scheduled for November 2010. Pemba Island and Ng'ambo area in Zanzibar Town are particularly incendiary flashpoints. One last thing: if you're driving and see dozens of **police motorcycles**, pull off the road and stand by your vehicle, for it is He – His Excellency, the President (no photos please). That, or the chief of police.

# Culture and etiquette

Tanzanians are known for their tactfulness and courtesy, qualities that are highly valued right across the social spectrum. The desire to maintain healthy relationships with both neighbours and strangers epitomizes the peaceful and non-tribalistic nature of Tanzanian society, and expresses itself in the warm welcome given to visitors. As such, you'll be treated as an honoured guest by many people, and if you make the effort, you'll be welcomed to a side of Tanzania that too few tourists see.

There are few hard-and-fast rules about public behaviour. In **Islamic areas** you should obviously avoid dress that might be deemed indecent or displays of sexual intimacy (although holding hands is fine), and non-Muslims shouldn't enter mosques without permission. During Ramadan, it's also polite not to be seen eating, drinking or smoking in public by day.

Elsewhere, only a few things are considered offensive: these include both verbal and material **immodesty** (so don't flaunt your wealth), and **bad temper or impatience**, though there are exceptions to this: if you're a woman being pestered by a man, an angry outburst should result in embarrassed bystanders coming to your rescue. Also, it's not cool to take **photographs of people** without their permission. Always ask first, and cough up (or refrain) if they ask money in return. You should also ask permission if you want to **smoke** in an enclosed public space such as a bar or restaurant.

**Tipping** is only really expected on safari or when climbing Mount Meru or Kilimanjaro. In bars, restaurants and taxis, tips are appreciated but not required.

## Religious beliefs

The majority of mainland Tanzanians are **Christians** – if sometimes only in name. Varieties of Catholicism and Protestantism dominate: there are several thousand flavours in all, often based around the teachings of local preachers. On the coast and Zanzibar, **Sunni Islam** dominates, and is in the ascendant throughout the country. The Aga Khan's moderate **Ismaïli** sect is also influential, with powerful business interests, the profits from which are often used in (secular)

development projects. Unless you're given permission, **mosques** should only be entered by Muslims. **Hindu** and **Sikh** temples are found in most large towns, and there are adherents of **Jainism** and **Bahai** faith, too.

An ever decreasing minority still hold **traditional beliefs**, which are not so much religions as world-views or cosmologies. These are mostly based on the idea that so long as deceased **ancestors** are remembered and honoured by the living, frequently via offerings of food or drink, they remain alive in the spirit world, where they're able to influence God in matters of weather, disease and other things beyond human control. Sadly, these beliefs, together with much collective wisdom, traditional music and modes of life, are gradually being destroyed by the expansion of Christianity, even among conservative peoples such as the Maasai and Barbaig, so traditional beliefs are now confined to remote areas.

## Appearance

Tanzanians make an effort to appear well dressed, and so should you. The simple rule is to wear comfortable and decent **clothes** (you'll feel cooler in loose cotton); they should also be clean, within reason.

Although Islamic moral strictures tend to be generously interpreted, in Muslim majority areas – mainly the coast and all of Zanzibar – visitors should **cover up** when not on a beach frequented by tourists. This means wearing long trousers and any kind of shirt for men, and a long dress, skirt, *kanga* or trousers for women. Uncovered shoulders are fine, and there's no need for headgear either, but don't show cleavage or any other part of your torso. Although people are far too polite to admonish strangers, tourists who ignore the dress code – which is posted in pretty much every hotel on Zanzibar – are viewed with considerable scorn.

The other reason for covering up, other than minimizing the risk of Caucasians turning lobster-red, is that you'll attract less **hassle** in the main tourist centres of Arusha, Moshi, Dar es Salaam, Stone Town, and the more popular Zanzibari beaches. Whilst it's impossible not to look like a tourist (expats are known by all), you can dress down and look like you've been travelling for months, so that hustlers will assume you're streetwise. Avoid wearing anything brand new, especially white, and make sure your shoes aren't too shiny. Some tourists swear by sunglasses to avoid making unwanted eye-contact; while this usually works in fending off hasslers, it also cuts you off from everyone else... the same people that make Tanzania so special.

## Greetings

**Lengthy greetings** – preferably in Kiswahili – are important, and people will value your efforts to master them. Elderly men and women are invariably treated with great deference. The word for greeting anyone older than you is *Shikamoo*, best followed by an honorific title. If you're addressed with "Shikamoo" – usually by children in rural areas – do respond with the requisite "Marahaba" (pulling a silly face goes down a storm, too). For these and other **common greetings**, see the "Language" section on p.622.

As well as the verbal greeting, younger women do a slight **curtsy** when greeting elders, while men invariably shake hands both at meeting and parting. It's especially polite to clasp your right forearm or wrist with your left hand as you do so. Younger people have a number of more elaborate and ever-changing handshakes that anyone will be happy to teach you. Incidentally, if someone's hands are wet or dirty when you meet, they'll offer their wrist instead. You should always use your right hand to shake, or to give or receive anything.

## Gifts

When invited into someone's home, bring small **presents** for the family. Elderly men often appreciate tobacco, whether "raw" (a piece of a thick, pungent coil that you can buy in markets everywhere; ask for *tumbako*) or a couple of packets of filterless Sigara Nyota or Sigara Kali cigarettes, nicknamed *sigara ya babu* – grandfather's cigarettes. Women appreciate anything that helps keep down household expenses, be it soap, sugar, tea, meat, or a few loaves of bread. Kids, of course, adore sweets – but give them to the mother to hand out or you'll end up getting mobbed.

If you're **staying longer**, slightly more elaborate presents are in order. Increase the number of practical things you bring, and perhaps buy a *kanga* or *kitenge* for the mother and grandmother (see p.65). Ballpoint pens and notepads will always find use, and kids will like books (Tanzania's literacy rate, though down from a peak of ninety percent-plus which it reached in the 1980s, is still high by African standards). Most bookshops sell gorgeously illustrated children's books in Kiswahili. For other gift ideas, ask your host before coming – and insist beyond their polite insistence that the only presents you need to bring is your own presence.

Lastly, **do not give gifts to children** if you don't know them already: it encourages begging, as proved in touristic areas by the chirpy choruses of "Mzungu give me money/pen/sweet..." If you really want to give something, hand it to an adult to share out, or make a donation to the local school. If you'll be travelling or staying for some time and really want to prepare, get a large batch of photos of you and your family with your address on the back. You'll get lots of mail.

## Sexuality

Sexual mores in Tanzania are generally quite open. The price is the prevalence of sexually transmitted diseases. At least one in ten Tanzanians carries **HIV**, so it goes without saying that casual sex without a condom is a deadly gamble and you should assume any sexual contact to be HIV-positive. **Condoms** are openly sold in pharmacies and supermarkets; a reliable brand is Salama, but check the expiry date and don't buy ones whose boxes have been bleached by sunshine.

Despite the risks, **female prostitution** flourishes openly in urban areas, particularly in bars and nightclubs frequented by better-off Tanzanians and foreigners. On Zanzibar, **male**

**gigolos** abound, with enough female tourists indulging in sexual adventures to make flirtatious pestering a fairly constant feature, but don't kid yourself: your cute dreadlocked potential lover probably romances for a living. The attention can of course be irritating as well as amusing, but fortunately really obnoxious individuals are usually on their own. A useful trick for women travelling unaccompanied by men is to wear a "wedding" ring (silver ones are less likely to attract robbery), though for this to be really credible it helps to take along a picture of a burly male friend à la Mike Tyson with a suitably husband-like message written on the back as "proof".

Male **homosexuality** is officially illegal. Although men holding hands is normal, up to a point (ie if someone's leading you by the arm), public displays of affection are guaranteed to offend, and may even get you up to 25 years in the slammer. As such, there are no overtly gay or lesbian venues in Tanzania, and few hotels will let two men share a room. Women sharing a room should be fine. *Shoga* is the word for gay man; *msagaji* is a lesbian.

## Hassle

Most Tanzanians will go well out of their way to help visitors, but in touristic areas it's possible to fall prey to misunderstandings with young men – generally known as **flycatchers** or, on Zanzibar, *papasi*, meaning "ticks" – offering anything you might conceivably want, from safaris and hotel rooms to drugs and souvenirs, and themselves as guides, helpers or even lovers. You shouldn't assume anything they do is out of simple kindness. It may well be, but if not, you're expected to pay. If you're being bugged by someone whose "help" you don't need, just let them know you can't pay for their trouble. It may not make you a friend, but it's better than a row later on.

Far less likely to harangue you are **beggars** – common in Arusha, Dar es Salaam and Dodoma, but rare elsewhere. Most are visibly destitute. Some are cripples, lepers or blind; others are homeless mothers with children. A Tsh100 coin suffices; Tsh200 will often delight. More common, especially in Arusha, are **street children**. Some may be AIDS orphans or may have escaped physical abuse; others may be begging on an adult's behalf; some are lost to the world on glue; all are persistent. Western sensibilities make them hard to ignore, especially when they trail you around murmuring pitifully until you cough up. If you want to help, it's probably best giving food, or getting in touch with an orphanage, as handing out money arguably promotes dependency.

# Shopping

There are heaps of attractive souvenirs you could bring home with you from Tanzania, from well-crafted woodwork to colourful kangas and kitenges. While many items are portable, others – like life-size statues of Maasai warriors – require the services of a shipping agent, which the seller should be able to arrange. Rooting around markets for groceries is fun too: coffee and honey make great souvenirs, as do essentials oils from Zanzibar.

For basic goods and services used by the majority of Tanzanians, which includes food, the prices are known by all, so even an ignorant foreigner isn't likely to be overcharged by much. Where, as a tourist, you *will* get ripped off – unless your haggling hat is on straight – is when buying souvenirs, where the opening "special price, my friend" can be ten times what the vendor is really prepared to accept. Once you get into bargaining, though, you'll rarely end up paying more than double the going rate, but don't

## Tips and tricks for haggling

**Know your limit** If buying souvenirs, visit a gift shop in a large hotel first to get an idea of the maximum price. For other things, ask disinterested locals about the real price beforehand. The bottom line though is that if you're happy with a price, then it's a good price, irrespective of what locals might have paid.

**Bargain only for what you want** Don't start haggling for something you'll never buy.

**Dress down** Put that camera away, brush up on your Kiswahili, and definitely don't wear swimming trunks or a bikini while shopping. The less you look like a tourist, the lower the price.

**Feign disinterest** If a seller knows you're hooked on something, the price is going to stick. Insouciance is what you need.

**Bluff** Bargaining is basically just bluffing, so don't be shy of making a big scene (it's all part of the fun). If things really aren't going your way, say it's too much, thank the seller for his time, get up and start to walk away. That's often all that's needed to elicit a better offer.

**Buy in bulk** Striking a good deal is easier if you have more items to play with.

**Show your money** Once you're close to finalizing, pull out the cash: the sight of greenbacks may encourage the seller to squeeze the price down just that little bit more. Or not, if you time it badly…

take it to extremes and start quibbling over a few hundred shillings for a few lemons. The box above should help you along.

## Woodwork

**Woodwork** souvenirs are ubiquitous, most famously from Southern Tanzania's **Makonde tribe** (see p.190), who have literally carved a global reputation for themselves. Their best-known works are the "tree of life" or "people pole" carvings in the **Ujamaa style**: intricately carved columns of interlocking human figures representing unity, continuity, and communal strength or power known as *dimoongo* in Kimakonde. In the carvings, the central figure is a mother surrounded by clinging children, supporting (both literally and symbolically) later generations, on top. Lively and full of movement, rhythm and balance, these are the works that justly brought the Makonde their fame. Less well-known is the naturalistic **Binadamu style**, which represents traditional modes of life such as old men smoking pipes, and the more abstract **Shetani style**, depicting folkloric spirits in distorted and often fantastically grotesque ways. Though the tradition's roots allude to the birth of the Makonde themselves (see p.190), the modern carvings are mostly made with an eye to the tastes of tourists and collectors. They're not always by Makonde either, prompting

some to decry their output as mere "airport art". But don't listen to the snobs: even mass-produced carvings possess a grace and elegance that easily endures repeated viewing.

**Also worth** buying are **bao boards**. Known elsewhere in Africa as *mancala* and by a host of local names, bao is the quintessential African board game, and you'll see it being played throughout Tanzania. The board, either carved or just a series of depressions scratched into the ground, typically has four rows with eight holes each. The basic idea is for two players to take turns in distributing counters (seeds, beans or stones) from one of the holes on the row closest to them into adjacent holes, clockwise or anticlockwise, one seed per hole. The objective is to clear your opponent's inner row by capturing their seeds. The permutations are mind-boggling and, as with chess, the best players ruminate over many moves in advance. Like chess, too, bao has ancient roots: wooden game boards survive from the sixth century, and there are much older "boards" etched into rocks at various Stone Age sites, possibly including Matombo near Morogoro (p.210).

Other woodwork items include walking sticks, Maasai spears (you can't take those in your hand luggage), combs, animal figures, and rather excellent "goat boards" (*kibao cha mbuzi*), which are foldable stools with an attached metal grater for gouging out the contents of coconuts. With the notable exception of motorbike-style "helmet masks" from the Makonde, called *mapiko*, **masks** are notably absent: what you can find, other than rather ugly stylized warrior heads, are reproductions of central African designs. Beware: almost all of them are fake, no matter how much congealed cow dung appears to fill the crevices.

## Tingatinga paintings

Apart from Makonde carvings, Southern Tanzania's other great "airport art" tradition is **Tingatinga paintings** – vibrantly colourful tableaux of cartoon-like people and animals daubed in bicycle paint and sold virtually everywhere. The style takes its name from Eduardo Saidi Tingatinga, born in 1937 to a rural Makua family. He moved to Tanga when he was sixteen, and when not working on building sites, made paintings and signboards for shops. In the mid-1960s, he began selling his paintings from the **Morogoro Stores** in Dar es Salaam, and quickly garnered a reputation as Tanzania's foremost artist. In particular, it was his use of *shetani* ("spirit") imagery that caught the eye – often amusingly grotesque beings gobbling their feet or those of other figures, and which apparently inspired the Makonde's Shetani style of woodcarving. Tingatinga was shot dead in 1972, when police mistook him for a criminal.

His style lives on, but the subjects of most modern versions are, as might be expected, typically touristic scenes depicting wildlife, baobabs and Kilimanjaro, but that's not to dismiss them – they make singularly cheerful

and attractive souvenirs, and are portable too. If you're more of a purist, hunt around in Dar es Salaam's galleries or at ADEA in Mtwara for some imaginative new takes on the genre. **Prices** are generally very reasonable, with a large A3-sized painting not costing more than Tsh15,000 if you're adept at bargaining.

## Kangas and kitenges

The colourful printed cotton wraps worn by many Tanzanian women are called **kangas** ("guinea fowl", alluding to early polka dot designs imported by Portuguese merchants). Two *kangas* joined together are called **doti**, and are often cut in two by the buyer, one part being worn around the body, the other around the head or shoulders. *Kanga* designs always include the words of a **proverb or riddle** (*neno* – statements): a way of making public sentiments that would be taboo in another form. So, a wife wishing to reprimand her husband for infidelity or neglect might buy a *kanga* for herself with the proverb, "The gratitude of a donkey is a kick" (*Fadhila ya punda ni mateke*), while one reading "A heart deep in love has no patience" (*Moyo wa kupenda hauna subira*) might be bought for a woman by her lover, expressing his desire to get married.

Similar to a *kanga*, but without the proverb or riddle, is a **kitenge**, made of thicker cloth and as a double-pane; their size makes them ideal for bedlinen. **Prices** for simple *kangas* range from Tsh5000 to Tsh8000 depending on the design and where you buy it, while *doti* and *kitenges* go for Tsh7000–10,000. Women will be happy to show you some ways of tying it. For more ideas,

## What not to buy

The purchase or export of most items sourced from wildlife is illegal, internationally and in Tanzania, not that you'd ever guess it looking at the products for sale in touristic areas. This includes **ivory**, **turtleshell** (often miscalled "tortoiseshell"), **seahorses**, **coral**, and many species of **seashells**. If caught you risk a heavy fine or imprisonment. Similarly off-limits are **animal skins and game trophies** lacking the requisite paperwork, and even with the right papers, possession of them may still be illegal in other countries. Finally, when buying carvings, if you must go for **ebony** (*mpingo* in Kiswahili), consider making a donation to the African Blackwood Conservation Project (⊛ www.blackwoodconservation.org), which strives to avoid the exhaustion of this fast-diminishing resource.

Tanzania's bookshops should have one of either *Kangas: 101 Uses* by Jeanette Hanby and David Bygott, or *The Krazy Book of Kangas* by Pascal Bogaert.

## Other souvenirs

The country's distinctive **toys** make good souvenirs: most worthwhile are beautifully fashioned buses, cars, lorries and even motorbikes made out of wire and cans. Also recycled are small **oil lanterns** called *kibatari*. **Batiks** are common but rarely outstanding; reams of them will shoved under your nose in Arusha by hawkers. Other frequently seen items include a huge variety of **sisal baskets**, jewellery (especially iconic is colourful Maasai **beadwork**), and **soapstone carvings** imported from Kisii in Kenya.

Imitations of **traditional crafts**, often smaller and more portable in scale than the originals, include weapons, shields, drums, musical instruments, stools and headrests.

There's also some really nice **pottery** about, especially in West Usambara, and on the north shore of Lake Nyasa, but little that's easily portable. Much more pocketable are some unusual **cures**, such as *jiwe ya punju*, a little stone for treating snake bites, and small clay cylinders (the names differ locally) stuffed with minerals that are useful during pregnancies. On Zanzibar, root around for **essential oils** (*mafuta*), which are great way of being reminded of Africa's "spice islands" long after you've returned home. Clove oil is the main one, but also worth seeking out is lemongrass. You can also find aromatherapy oils, which use coconut oil for their base.

Lastly, if you're in Dar or Bagamoyo, have a look at some **contemporary art**: paintings especially often display an eye for movement and colour (not necessary gaudy, like Tinga-tinga paintings) that has long been absent from Western art.

# Responsible tourism

Tourism is Tanzania's second-biggest foreign exchange earner. If well managed, it can boost local economies and even preserve cultural traditions that might otherwise be swept away. But unbridled tourism can wreak havoc on local communities and cause irreversible environmental damage.

Unfortunately, **Zanzibar** is case a point. Some coastal villages there have been all but bought out by all-inclusive package holiday resorts. Although land prices are now in the millions of dollars, the first resorts managed to buy up vast acreages for a pittance. Cocooned within their tall walls, often topped with shards of broken glass, razor wire or electrified wires, rarely do these newcomers contribute much to the local economy, and some of them even import the most basic foodstuffs. Others take the lion's share of already stretched water resources, and the bulk of the profits rarely get anywhere close to Tanzania, as most of the big hotels are foreign-owned. We can blame the entrepreneurs, corrupt politicians

and bureaucrats, too, but individual tourists aren't blameless, either. Circa 1995, it was unheard of for kids in Zanzibar to demand "presents" of tourists. Now, you're as likely to be greeted with a chorus of "Give me money!" as you are the traditional "Jambo!" Zanzibar's age-old tolerance is also being pushed to the brink. In Stone Town, you'll likely catch sight of female tourists wearing little more than bikinis, which is astonishingly disrespectful given that almost all locals are Muslim. It's perhaps no coincidence that the rise of mass market tourism has coincided with the increased adoption of veils, and even full-on burkas. As a tourist, then, do please take your responsibilities seriously.

## Six steps to a better kind of travel

At Rough Guides we are passionately committed to travel. We feel strongly that only through travelling do we truly come to understand the world we live in and the people we share it with – plus tourism has brought a great deal of **benefit** to developing economies around the world over the last few decades. But the extraordinary growth in tourism has also damaged some places irreparably, and of course **climate change** is exacerbated by most forms of transport, especially flying. This means that now more than ever it's important to **travel thoughtfully** and **responsibly**, with respect for the cultures you're visiting – not only to derive the most benefit from your trip but also to preserve the best bits of the planet for everyone to enjoy. At Rough Guides we feel there are six main areas in which you can make a difference:

• Consider what you're contributing to the **local economy**, and how much the services you use do the same, whether it's through employing local workers and guides or sourcing locally grown produce and local services.

• Consider the **environment** on holiday as well as at home. Water is scarce in many developing destinations, and the biodiversity of local flora and fauna can be adversely affected by tourism. Try to patronize businesses that take account of this.

• Travel with a purpose, not just to tick off experiences. Consider **spending longer** in a place, and getting to know it and its people.

• Give thought to how often you **fly**. Try to avoid short hops by air and more harmful night flights.

• Consider **alternatives to flying**, travelling instead by bus, train, boat and even by bike or on foot where possible.

• Make your trips "**climate neutral**" via a reputable carbon-offset scheme. All Rough Guide flights are offset, and every year we donate money to a variety of charities devoted to combating the effects of climate change.

## Eco-tourism: myth and reality

Most wildlife lodges and camps like to vaunt themselves as "eco-friendly", but few really are. For a start, their very existence in "unspoiled" areas takes a toll on the **environment**, no matter how many safeguards are in place. Indeed, many establishments seem to equate "ecological" with their extensive use of natural materials, when in fact the opposite is the case. Tropical hardwoods, mangrove poles, and wood for firing limewash are all exploited in wholly unsustainable and usually illegal ways. In short, don't believe the hype.

On the positive side, an encouraging trend outside national parks has been to involve local communities, not just as staff but sometimes as part-owners and managers. In **our reviews** for accommodation and safari companies, we've tried, as far as possible, to keep environmental and ethical matters in sight, and have excluded obvious offenders (with the exception of lodges around Ngorongoro Crater, all of them environmental blights but which cannot practically be excluded due to the huge number of tourists staying there). We've also excluded companies known for **other abuses**, including racism, physical violence towards staff, miserly contributions to local communities, and involvement in the corruption-riddled world of trophy hunting. Of course, it's not possible to guarantee that all companies featured in this book are ethical: if you know better, please let us know – your feedback is very welcome.

## Resources

Among the most active **organizations** concerned with responsible tourism are Tourism Concern (ⓦ www.tourismconcern .org.uk) and Transitions Abroad (ⓦ www .transitionsabroad.com), whose websites contain heaps of practical advice, lists of recommended tour operators, and much more. Tourism Concern publishes the *Ethical Travel Guide*, which reviews community-based tourism initiatives in twenty African countries, and elsewhere. Transitions Abroad offers free **downloads** of its annual *Responsible Travel Handbook*, and Rough Guides offer *The Rough Guide To A Better World* (ⓦ www.roughguide-betterworld.com), also for free.

# Travel essentials

## Costs

For tourists, Tanzania is not cheap unless you're content with cultural tourism as your main activity: safaris, Kilimanjaro climbs, scubadiving, chimp-tracking, and anything involving rented cars will all blow a hole in your budget. Having a **youth or student card** (ⓦ www.isiccard.com) may get you reductions on international flights, but nothing in Tanzania itself. With the exception of food, most costs are **negotiable**, so it's worth honing your bargaining skills; see p.64. One thing you can't bargain is your status: foreigners pay **"non-resident" rates** for touristic services, which are usually priced in dollars and always more than the "resident" rates paid by locals. It's a rip-off, definitely, albeit legally sanctioned and, if you think about it, justifiable: why should people who earn fifty times Tanzania's average salary pay the same as locals?

For **basic costs**, excluding activities but including two simple meals and a couple of drinks, solo travellers can get by comfortably on $20 a day (roughly £14, €15 or Tsh27,000, or double than on Zanzibar), but if you're unfussy and don't drink alcohol, this can drop to $10–15 on the mainland, or $30 on Zanzibar. To this add transport: bus fares average $1 an hour, and no more than $2 a journey on Zanzibar. Couples sharing a room will end up paying less per person: from $15 each on the mainland, and $25 on Zanzibar, including a couple of drinks. Factoring in **activities**, costs begin to spiral: $1200 and up for a six-day ascent of Kilimanjaro, $500–600 for a four- or five-day wildlife safari, and $400–500 for an Open Water scuba diving course. More affordable, and rarely costing more than $30 a day, is snorkelling or cultural tourism.

On **mid-range** trips, costs vary enormously, as it all depends on where you eat and sleep, and how you travel around. Minimum costs for two people sharing a decent three-star standard hotel room, eating in good but not overly-expensive restaurants with a couple of drinks each, and travelling by taxi in towns, is $100, or $65 if travelling alone, but doubling those costs would give you far greater choice of accommodation. To this add on **activities**: upwards of $1000 for a four- or five-day wildlife safari, and $1500 for a six-day ascent of Kilimanjaro. If you want to travel by rental car instead of public transport, add on $120–150 per day for the vehicle. **Upmarket**, the sky's the limit. Most travellers in that range come on package holidays, prices for which, excluding international flights but including a safari, transport and full board start at around $350 a day but can easily double or triple depending on the options.

## Gratuities

When **tipping**, keep in mind that the average Tanzanian salary is less than $100 a month. In local hotels, bars and restaurants, tipping is not customary, but if you wish to do so, the gesture is appreciated. In tourist-class establishments, on safari, and when climbing Kilimanjaro, staff generally will expect tips, not just because you're "rich", but because they may not be paid at all, tips being their only source of income.

For small services, Tsh500 is fine, with Tsh1000 reasonable for portering a lot of luggage. **On safari**, expectations vary widely, but anything less than $10 a day from each safari-goer to each member of staff would be mean, so count on $30 per day in all. If service was excellent, by all means tip more. On the other hand if the driving was dangerous or the guiding awful, tip less or not at all – but do explain why. Lack of wildlife is no reason to tip less, however – animals don't keep to schedules.

## Electricity

Tanzania uses British-style square three-pin plugs – theoretically 220V, though in practice, the range fluctuates between 160–260V. Power cuts, surges, spikes, drop-offs and rationing are very frequent, especially in Dar, and particularly at the end of dry spells, when reservoirs are too low to run hydroelectric stations. Most rural areas are not connected to the national grid: electricity in those places, if any, is provided by local oil-fired power stations. The result is that many businesses, including hotels, have their own generators.

## Entry requirements

Visitors to Tanzania need a passport valid for six months beyond the end of your stay; possibly a yellow fever **vaccination certificate** if travelling from elsewhere in Africa (see p.23); and a visa, which can be bought without fuss at airports and land borders. The standard three-month **tourist visa** costs $50 (cash only), except for US and Irish nationals, who pay $100. A **multiple-entry visa** is next to impossible to obtain, even though it appears as an option on the form you fill in. Contrary to what you might read on the internet, tourist visas are *not* valid for the rest of East Africa.

**To extend your stay** beyond three months is awkward. Officially, you need to give a letter to an immigration office in Tanzania explaining why you need to stay longer, which should get you a one-month extension. In practice, it's simpler to spend a few days in a neighbouring country and re-enter on a new visa.

**Customs** officials are unlikely to show tourists much interest unless they're carrying a mountain of specialized gear. Items that are obviously for personal use (binoculars, cameras, even laptops) pose no problem, particularly if they aren't in their original packaging: at worst you'll have to sign (and pay) a bond, redeemable when leaving the country. If you're taking expensive presents, however, you'll have to pay duty.

## Insurance

Travel insurance is big business, but not the most transparent one: most policies are masterpieces of exclusionary legalese, so **read the small print** to be sure you're getting the coverage you need. For Tanzania, expect to pay around $75/£40 per month. The good news is that **you may already be insured**, at least partly, by all-risks home insurance policies, private medical schemes and health plans, student cards, and credit card companies.

The most useful component of even the most basic travel insurance policy is **medical coverage**, which should adequately cover hospital fees, medical evacuation, medicines, and injuries. Not compensated are injuries caused by obviously dangerous activities, including riding motorbikes over 125cc. If you're going to be in the wilds for

## Tanzanian diplomatic missions

Visas for volunteering or work need to be arranged beforehand via an embassy or high commission:

**Australia & New Zealand** Will need to send passports to Japan for relevant paperwork. Tokyo ☎+81 3425-4531, ⊛www.tanzaniaembassy.or.jp

**Canada** Ottawa ☎613/232-1509, ⊛www.tzrepottawa.ca

**South Africa** Pretoria ☎012/342 4371, ⊛www.tanzania.org.za

**UK & Ireland** London ☎020/7569 1470, ⊛www.tanzania-online.gov.uk

**US** Washington ☎202/884-1080, ⊛www.tanzaniaembassy-us.org

an extended period, you might consider buying temporary membership of Tanzania's First Air Responder **air evacuation** service (Ⓦwww.knightsupport.com), or Kenya's flying doctors (Ⓦwww.amref.org). If you're **renting a vehicle**, it should come with its own third-party insurance.

Compensation for **lost or stolen money** is adequate so long as you're not carrying your entire stash as cash. Neither credit cards nor traveller's cheques are a worry as they'll be replaced or refunded by the issuing company. In policy small print, "**personal effects**" covers theft or loss of valuables, but normally excludes anything you might actually want to claim for, namely electronics, cameras and jewellery, and you may need the original receipt when making a claim. Check these exclusions, also the per-article limit, the maximum pay-out (rarely more than $400/£220), and fees deducted for each item claimed for. Another section to read carefully is the one on so-called **dangerous activities**, which often lists exclusions unless additional premiums are paid; these include scubadiving, mountaineering and safaris. The other tricky section is **personal liability**, assuming it's included at all. This should cover you if you're sued because you caused loss, injury or death to other people, but the small print tends to exclude almost all imaginable scenarios.

If you need to **make a claim**, keep receipts for things you're out of pocket on, and in almost all events you must obtain an official statement from the police (who may demand a few thousand shillings for the favour).

## Internet

Most Tanzanian towns are blessed with satellite-based broadband, and a handful of **internet cafés**. Most post offices also have access. Prices average Tsh500–1000 an hour (under a dollar). Bigger hotels may provide wi-fi or modem sockets, usually at no extra charge. Unless you're technically confident, avoid internet banking or making payments from public computers, as many are infested with malware.

## Laundry

There are no laundromats in Tanzania. When washing your own clothes (they'll dry fast),

beware of the all-dissolving New Blue Omo soap powder. Most bigger hotels have expensive laundry services; in more humble places, staff are happy supplementing their wages with a bit of washing and ironing. Tsh2000 for a modest bundle should be gladly received.

## Mail

Tanzania's **postal service** is slow but things do eventually arrive: airmail should take about five days to Europe, ten to North America or Australasia. For something more urgent, the post office's EMS service is reliable, and cheaper than an **international courier**, though the latter are best if you're sending valuables: DHL and FedEx have branches throughout Tanzania.

Couriers are also useful for **parcels** but, if you're not in a rush, surface parcel post (taking up to four months) is cheaper: for 20kg, Canada, UK and New Zealand $100; $80 to the US; Ireland $60; Australia $65; and South Africa $40.

To receive mail, **poste restante** works for major towns: ask correspondents to underline and capitalize your surname. Smaller post offices also hold mail, but your correspondent should mark the letter "To Be Collected". If you're expecting a parcel, you'll probably have to pay import duty: having the sender mark packages "Contents to be re-exported from Tanzania" can be helpful. There's no home delivery in Tanzania: **addresses** are always box numbers (PO Box or SLP, its Kiswahili equivalent) or, out in the sticks, "Private Bag" with no number.

## Maps

The best **general map of Tanzania** is Reise Know-How's waterproof *Tanzania, Rwanda, Burundi* (1:1,200,000), packed with detail, and with relief shown as both contours and colouring. Almost as detailed, and just as accurate, is harms-ic-verlag's *Tanzania, Rwanda and Burundi* (1:1,400,000). If you can't find these, Nelles Verlag's *Tanzania, Rwanda, Burundi* (1:1,500,00) is perfectly fine.

For **Zanzibar**, the best is harms-ic-verlag's *Zanzibar*, with Unguja at 1:100,000, and insets of Pemba and Stone Town. **Zanzibar's dive sites** are presented on Giovanni Tombazzi's *Zanzibar at Sea* (Maco Editions,

ⓦwww.gtmaps.com), an attractive compilation of painted plans. Giovanni Tombazzi's painted maps also beautifully cover the **northern safari circuit**, most useful being *Arusha National Park*, *Kilimanjaro*, *Lake Manyara*, *Ngorongoro*, *Serengeti* and *Tarangire*. All are double-sided: the wildlife ones come with a dry-season version on one side and wet-season on the other (showing the changes of vegetation and illustrating commonly seen plants and trees). The most accurate map of Ngorongoro is harms-ic-verlag's *Ngorongoro Conservation Area* (1:230,00).

Apart from Tombazzi's plan, good **Kilimanjaro** maps are ITMB's *Kilimanjaro Trekking Map* (1:62,500), with 100m contours and tinting; Andrew Wielochowski's *Kilimanjaro Map & Guide* (1:75,000 and 1:30,000); and harms-ic-verlag's *Kilimanjaro National Park* (1:100,000).

For completely **off-the-beaten-track hiking**, you need 1:50,000 topographical sheets available at the Government's Mapping & Surveys Division in Dar es Salaam (Kivukoni Front; Mon–Fri 8am–3.30pm; ☏022/212 4575), which cover the whole country. They've run out of popular sheets, but it may be possible to buy photocopies. A caveat: most were produced between 1959 and 1962, so whilst the topographical detail remains more or less accurate (though don't expect the forest cover to be anywhere near as extensive), things like roads and villages will have changed.

## Money

Tanzania's **currency** is the shilling ("Tsh"). It floats freely against major hard currencies, so **changing money** on the street is both pointless and risky. Plastic is the most useful way of accessing money, but it's common sense to take cash and perhaps traveller's cheques too. You can change money safely at banks and foreign exchange bureaux ("forexes"); the former have better rates but may whack you with commission (ask first), and queues can be long. **Exchange rates** in mid-2009 were US$1/Tsh1300, €1/Tsh1700, £1/Tsh1850, Can$1/Tsh1000, Aus$/Tsh850, NZ$/Tsh650, and ZAR10/Tsh1250. Rates on Zanzibar are typically ten percent less. ⓦwww.oanda.com has the latest rates.

## Cash

Never carry more **cash** than you're prepared to lose: for budget travellers, the equivalent of a few hundred dollars suffices for a couple of weeks. US dollar banknotes can also be useful, and are essential for paying national park entry fees. $100 bills attract better rates than smaller denominations, but $500 notes are rarely accepted. Also avoid dollar notes printed before 2000. If you need more dollars, Tanzanian forexes will oblige, but you'll be round-tripped via shillings. When changing money into shillings, ask for a spread of notes, not just Tsh10,000 ones, as these can be difficult to find change for in non-touristic areas.

## Cards and ATMs

**Credit cards and debit cards** are the easiest way to access money in Tanzania, via several 24hr ATM networks, all of which dole out shillings. The machines can be moody, however, so bring at least two cards – ideally Visa and/or MasterCard, as there's no guarantee of others working. A useful take on Visa is **Travel Money**, a prepaid debit card that works in most ATMs. You load up your account with funds, and can top up the card online, not that you should trust Tanzania's internet cafés for that. There are several flavours. Easiest to find is Travelex's "Cash Passport" (ⓦwww.cashpassport.com), which can be bought at various banks, high street retailers, travel agents and forex bureaux in the UK, US, Canada, Australia, New Zealand and South Africa, but not Ireland. In Ireland (and the UK), post offices sell Travel Money cards.

The most useful **ATM network** is NBC's, with sixty machines nationwide; CRDB's network is larger but sometimes temperamental. The same applies to Barclays and Exim, the latter taking MasterCard only. Most ATMs are in cubicles watched over by security guards; if you're worried about security, get a friend to cover your back. Cards with **six-digit PINs** may work using only the first four digits, but check with your issuing company first. If you'll be travelling two months or more, set up a **standing order** to cover monthly charges.

Direct **payments** with cards are rarely possible for anything other than the most expensive accommodation and services (flights, safaris and car rental), and attract premiums of five to ten percent on Visa or MasterCard, and up to twenty percent on American Express, if accepted at all.

## Traveller's cheques and wiring money

**Traveller's cheques** can only reliably be cashed in Arusha, Dar es Salaam and Stone Town, and at rates at ten to thirty percent worse than cash. Nonetheless, we'd recommend you take a few hundred dollars' worth along in case you lose your card(s). Thomas Cook and American Express cheques are the most likely to be accepted. When cashing them, you'll need to show your purchase receipt with the serial numbers: make photocopies and stash them away. As a last resort, you can **wire funds** via Western Union (Ⓦ www.westernunion.com) or MoneyGram (Ⓦ www.moneygram.com). Both have agents throughout the country.

## Opening hours and public holidays

Most **shops** are open Monday to Friday from 8.30am to 5pm, sometimes to 7pm, and sometimes with a lunch break; they're also open Saturday mornings until around noon. Supermarkets, and stores and kiosks in residential or rural areas, may be open later. **Government offices** have slightly variable times, but you'll always find them open Monday to Friday from 8am to 2.30pm. Other opening times: **post offices** Mon–Fri 8am–4.30pm, Sat 9am–noon; **banks** Mon–Fri 8.30am–4pm, Sat 8.30am–1pm (rural branches close at 12.30pm weekdays, 10.30am Sat); **forex bureaux** variable, but often Mon–Fri 9am–4.30pm, Sat 9am–noon.

Tanzania's diverse ethnic patchwork provides for many eclectic local celebrations. In additional, Islamic festivals lend some more colour to coastal regions, including Zanzibar. Particularly enjoyable events to coincide with are covered on p.45-46. Government offices, banks, post offices and other official establishments are closed on **public holidays**, including Christian and Muslim celebrations (except Ramadan). If a holiday falls on a weekend, the following Monday is the day off. Holidays with **fixed dates** are: January 1 (New Year); January 12 (Zanzibar Revolution Day); April 7 (Karume Day); April 26 (Union Day between Zanzibar and Tanganyika); May 1 (Workers' Day); July 7 (Industrial Day); August 8 (Farmers' Day); October 14 (Nyerere Day); December 9 (Independence Day); December 25 (Christmas); December 26 (Boxing Day). Holidays with **variable dates** are Easter (Good Friday and Easter Monday) and the four Muslim celebrations. Dates for the latter are approximate as they depend on moon sightings:

**Maulidi** Feb 26, 2010; Feb 15, 2011; Feb 4, 2012; Jan 24, 2013.

**Start of Ramadan** Aug 11, 2010; Aug 1, 2011; July 20, 2012; July 9, 2013.

**Idd al-Fitri** Sept 10, 2010; Aug 30, 2011; Aug 19, 2012; Aug 08, 2013.

**Idd al-Haj (Idd al-Adha)** Nov 27, 2009; Nov 16, 2010; Nov 6, 2011; Oct 26, 2012; Oct 15, 2013.

## Phones

TTCL operates Tanzania's terrestrial network; reliability is improving, but is still smitten by power cuts and the theft of copper wires. As such, Tanzanians have embraced **mobile phones** with gusto. Tanzania's networks use GSM. Local "phone mechanics" (*fundi simu*) can unlock most such handsets for no more than $15, letting you swap in a Tanzanian SIM card (from $1). Alternatively, buy a handset on arrival ($40 and up). International calls can be as cheap as $0.50 a minute; sending an SMS averages $0.15, or is free. Phones are topped up with a scratch card (a *vocha*, voucher), available everywhere. Zain has the widest network, covering most places you're likely to visit, including most of the national parks; Zantel, partnered with Vodacom on the mainland, winkles a bit more out of Zanzibar.

With no mobile, you can call from a hotel (usually extortionate), or use **public phones**. These include a cumbersome "operator-assisted" procedure inside TTCL offices; coin- or card-operated phones outside TTCL offices, at bus stations, and in some bars and hotels; and informal "assisted call" centres, often around bus stations. Costs are rarely

## Phone numbers and calling home

Most **land lines** have seven-digit subscriber numbers plus a three-digit area code (022 to 028), which can be omitted when calling locally; **cell phones** have four-digit operator codes beginning "07" which must be always be dialled. The initial "0" should be omitted when calling from outside Tanzania. Tanzania's **country code** is 255, but from Kenya or Uganda dial ☎004 instead.

**Calling from Tanzania**, dial ☎000 followed by the country code and phone number, omitting any initial "0". The exceptions are Kenya (☎005 followed by the area and subscriber number) and Uganda (☎006). Some **country codes**: Australia 61, Canada 1, Ireland 353, New Zealand 64, South Africa 27, UK 44, US 1.

less than $0.80 a minute for international calls. Cheaper are VoIP phone services such as Skype offered by a handful of Internet cafés, mostly in Arusha and Stone Town. **Collect calls** (reverse charge) cannot be made from Tanzania.

## Photography

**Digital photography** is the way to go: equatorial light can be tricky, as can dark skin on bright backgrounds, so feedback is invaluable. For quick snaps and photographing people, you'll feel most comfortable with a compact camera, but for wildlife – for which you need a proper zoom – an SLR is much better, and also lets you use UV or polarizing filters.

Whatever you take, protect it from **dust** (zip-lock freezer bags are ideal). Bring **spare batteries**, and plenty of memory cards (or film). For digital, a USB memory card reader will let you transfer or send photos online at internet cafés, or back things up to CD or DVD.

**Animal photography** is more a question of patience (and luck) than equipment. Morning and evening light is best. When **photographing people**, never take pictures without asking permission first, and pay for the right if asked: the Maasai have made quite a business of it. Blithely aiming at strangers may well get you into trouble, and remember that in Islamic areas popular belief equates the act of taking a picture with stealing a piece of someone's soul.

It's also a bad idea to snap things that could even vaguely be construed as **strategic targets**, including police stations, prisons, airports, harbours, bridges, and the president. It depends who sees you, of course – but protesting your innocence won't appease small-minded officials with big shoulder chips.

## Time

Tanzanians – and their transport timetables – begin counting the day's hours at 6am (roughly sunrise) and 6pm (roughly sunset), so that six o'clock (*saa sita*) in "Swahili time" equates to noon or midnight as you know it. In other words, just add or subtract six hours.

Tanzania is three hours ahead of GMT year-round, meaning two hours ahead of Britain in summer, three in winter. It's seven or eight hours ahead of US Eastern Standard Time; one hour ahead of South Africa; and seven hours behind Australia (Sydney).

## Toilets

Tanzania's few **public toilets** are not places you want to mess with: usually reeking long-drops covering by two slabs of concrete for positioning the feet, with no guarantee of water, and certainly no paper. Better would be to find a mid-range hotel or restaurant and ask politely. These tend to have Western-style toilets with flushes, and should have toilet paper to hand. In lowlier places, such toilets may lack seats, and be flushed with a bucket. Asian-style "squats", often in the same cubicle as showers, are mostly quite hygienic, and may also have flushing mechanisms. Locals rarely if ever use toilet paper, and there's a reason: in the tropical heat, rinsing your nether regions with water (using your *left* hand) is much cleaner than wiping with tissue, so long as you wash your hands afterwards. There's invariably a tap to hand, with a bucket for flushing and a plastic jug for rinsing. If you can't or won't adapt, you can find toilet paper in towns.

## Tourist information

The Tanzania Tourist Board (TTB) has no offices overseas, but does maintain two tourist information offices, in Arusha and Dar, and both are helpful. Apart from these, and a handful of privately-run information centres mentioned in this guide, information on the ground is difficult to find without being half-fluent in Kiswahili. The best source of information (other than guidebooks), then, is the internet. The **tourist board** is at ⓦwww.tanzaniatourist board.com. Other good general websites include:

ⓦ**www.africatravelresource.com** Detailed reviews of Tanzania's upmarket lodges.
ⓦ**www.fodors.com/community** A busy forum mainly patronized by upmarket travellers.
ⓦ**www.safarilands.org** A comprehensive tourism portal, including news and features.
ⓦ**www.tanzaniaparks.com** Official national parks site; informative and nicely illustrated.
ⓦ**www.travbuddy.com** A great collection of blogs.
ⓦ**www.tripadvisor.com** Candid client reviews of mostly upmarket lodges.
ⓦ**www.zanzibar.net** A good portal for the isles.

### Travel advisories

**Travel advisories** are where governments post advice and warnings about other countries. They always err on the side of caution, especially as regards terrorism, so read them with a pinch of salt: Australia ⓦwww.smartraveller.gov.au; Canada ⓦwww .voyage.gc.ca; Ireland ⓦwww.foreignaffairs .gov.ie; New Zealand ⓦwww.safetravel.govt .nz; UK ⓦwww.fco.gov.uk/travel; US ⓦtravel .state.gov.

## Travellers with disabilities

Tanzanian **attitudes** towards disabled people are schizophrenic. Officially, there's very little support, as you'll see from the polio- or leprosy-afflicted beggars in Arusha, Dar and Dodoma. In some areas, too, lingering superstitions mean that families prefer to keep physically and mentally handicapped people out of sight. But overall things are gradually improving, sometimes quite spectacularly: read our description of Neema Crafts Centre on p.470.

In the company of a helper, a Tanzanian holiday for physically disabled people is quite feasible, although you should expect physical knocks, just like everyone else, while **on safari**, even with a mollycoddling driver, as the roads are often awful. The most comfortable national parks to access by road are (from Arusha) Lake Manyara, Tarangire, Ngorongoro and Serengeti (also from Mwanza) and, from Dar es Salaam, Mikumi. For other parks, **flying** is recommended, though on some planes there's simply no room for movement, or a wheelchair, so ask beforehand.

Semi-accessible **accommodation** can be found virtually everywhere, if only because most hotels have ground-floor rooms. A number on the coast have ramped access to public areas, and larger hotels in Arusha and Dar, and some in Stone Town, have elevators. With help, many wildlife lodges and camps are also just about accessible. Almost any **safari companies** touting "tailor-made" tours should be able to provide suitable itineraries. Alternatively, there are two **specialist operators**: the highly recommended Go Africa Safaris in Kenya (ⓦwww .go-africa-safaris.com), and Eco-Adventure International in the US (ⓦwww.eaiadventure .com/access).

Navigating **towns** can actually be more challenging: pavements are invariably pot-holed or blocked by parked cars and hawkers, there are few if any ramps, and taxis are small, but with a little perseverance you should be able to find a minibus taxi (which are the norm on Zanzibar). With the exception of Scandinavian Express' "Royal Class" coaches (ⓦwww.scandinavia group.com), **public road transport** is not disabled-friendly (it's not exactly "abled-friendly" either). That said, catching a **train** is possible, though you'd have to be carried aboard, and possibly also to the toilets, as the corridors are narrow.

For more information, get Gordon Rattray's *Access Africa* **guidebook** (ⓦwww.bradt -travelguides.com), which includes Tanzania among the six countries covered. Rattray's own website, ⓦwww.able-travel.com, has some handy travel tips. Other useful **websites** include ⓦwww.gimponthego.com and ⓦwww.tourismforall.org.uk.

## Travelling with children

Assuming you can keep your child healthy, Tanzania is a great country for kids, especially of school age. Most Tanzanians are simply gaga about children, who should make friends easy, thereby also serving as an introduction for you to get to know Tanzanians outside of the touristic context.

You won't have any trouble finding people to look after the little 'uns should you need a break, and **breast-feeding** in public is perfectly acceptable, even in Zanzibar (with the help of a well-placed *kanga*). Tinned baby milk can be bought in supermarkets in larger towns and cities, together with nappies (rarely used locally; it's cheaper and more ecological to wash and reuse cloths).

The big worry, however, is **malaria**. This is a particular concern as none of the drugs used for adult prophylaxis are recommended for young children. Instead, you'll need to rely on bug spray, repellent and mosquito nets (buy a dinky cot-covering tent for babies). Your family doctor should be your first point of contact, who will also advise you about inoculations (see p.23). The other concern is protecting the little ones from the **sun**: keep them smothered in sunblock, insist on hats, and also T-shirts when swimming. Sunglasses are also a good idea, even for babies: you can always find little novelty ones to fit. And of course, be sure they drink plenty of water.

For a family with under-fives, **going on safari**, especially a shared one, probably isn't a great idea: young children aren't overly excited about seeing animals from a distance, and the long drives can be tedious. Hiring a car with a driver is quite feasible, however, and gives you the flexibility and privacy you need for changing nappies, toilet stops and shouting at each other. Few are the cars in Tanzania with working (or even fitted) seat belts, however, so you will be taking a risk, even if you bring a detachable baby seat. The most child-friendly parks, needing only short drives, are Arusha National Park and, if your kids can cope with a two- or three- hour drive, Ngorongoro and Tarangire (which has lots of elephants – a big favourite). Many lodges and hotels "discourage" children, often under-sixes, sometimes under-twelves, either because wildlife tends to wander through the grounds, or just to avoid having noisy brats tearing around.

Much more fun for kids are **beaches**. We'd recommend staying in Jambiani on Zanzibar, which has a really pleasant village feeling, and shallow sheltered waters that retreat at low tide exposing all sorts of interesting critters in coral pools. Larger hotels should be able to provide babysitters given a few hours' notice, and a handful – mentioned in our reviews – offer a full range of children's activities.

## Volunteering

A great way of getting to know Tanzania is **voluntary work**. In exchange for your time, you gain work experience, pleasure at being able to help out, and – just as important – meaningful interaction with locals. You can arrange things directly with the organization in Tanzania or, easier, via an agency. ⓦwww.studyabroad.com and ⓦwww.world volunteerweb.org have useful listings.

Some projects accept anyone, but most require **specialist skills**, such as teaching, biology, IT or accounting. Volunteers usually pay for their own upkeep, but if you're expected to pay a substantial amount, take care as the voluntary sector is infested with **get-rich-quick schemes**. The internet is your friend here: check whether the ideals of an NGO as espoused in their blurb has ever translated into something concrete (and whether your payment can reasonably be squared with the results). You should also check whether they're really registered as charities or non-profits, but be aware that there are few controls over who can register an NGO in Tanzania. Respectable places welcoming volunteers include Iringa's Neema Crafts (p.470), and Mikindani's *The Old Boma* (p.180). Genuine international organizations involved in Tanzania include:

**Frontier** UK ☏020/7613 2422, ⓦwww.frontier .ac.uk. A profit-making company placing paying volunteers for three to twenty weeks. Environmental surveys are the main thing: in Tanzania, either marine conservation (lots of diving), or the Eastern Arc mountains.

**Peace Corps** US only ☎1-800/424-8580, ⓦwww.peacecorps.gov. Places Americans with specialist skills in 27-month postings, mostly in education or AIDS awareness.

**Student Partnership Worldwide** UK ⓦwww.spw.org; US & Canada ⓦwww.spwusa.org. Registered charity offering placements in southern Tanzania; volunteers need to find £3600/$6500 in fund-raising.

**Volunteers for Peace** US ⓦwww.vfp.org. Mostly two-week placements run by partner organizations; around $600, no skills required.

**Voluntary Service Overseas (VSO)** UK ⓦwww.vso.org.uk, Ireland ⓦwww.vso.ie, US & Canada ⓦwww.cuso-vso.org, Australia and New Zealand ⓦwww.australianvolunteers.com. Government-funded agencies for placing skilled volunteers.

# Guide

# Guide

www.roughguides.com

# Dar es Salaam and around

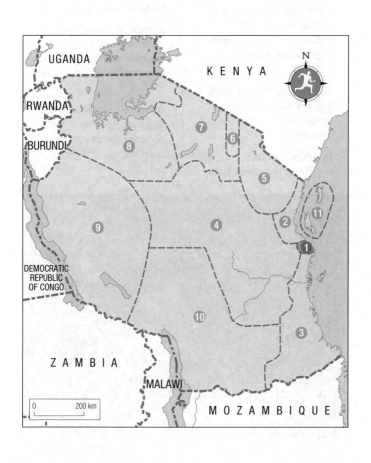

CHAPTER 1  # Highlights

✳ **Kariakoo Market** Crowded, hectic, bewildering, exhilarating… a pungent feast for the senses. See p.93

✳ **National Museum** Covers every angle on Tanzanian culture and history, from Nutcracker Man and prehistoric fish to **wooden** bicycles and xylophones. See p.95

✳ **Food** It wasn't so long ago that Dar was a gastronomic desert. Not any more: *karibu chakula!* See p.100

✳ **Nightlife** With bars, nightclubs and dance halls galore, Dar is heaven for night owls. See p.103

✳ **Traditional music** Radio Tanzania sells over a hundred recordings of "music of the ancestors", as well as guitar-rich *muziki wa dansi* – a national treasure. See p.108

✳ **Wonder Welders** Some of the weirdest and most inspirational metalwork you've ever seen, and light enough to carry home. See p.108

✳ **Beaches** Escape the city and head north for a range of watersports south for a quiet respite. See p.97 & p.112

▲ Dar es Salaam's buzzing nightlife

# 1

# Dar es Salaam and around

From a moribund settlement of three thousand people little over a century ago, **DAR ES SALAAM** ("Dar" for short) has grown into East Africa's largest metropolis, with almost four million inhabitants, over seventy percent of whom make do without electricity, running water or basic sanitation. Their nickname for the city is **Bongo**, meaning "brain" or "wits" – these being what's needed to survive.

Despite the realities of urban poverty, the city is a likeable place, friendly and easy-going, having managed to absorb immigrants from all around the country, and beyond, without ever completely alienating them, or their cultures. On the pot-holed pavements, in buzzing markets and smoke-belching daladalas, you'll see Swahili women dressed in shrouding black *buibuis*, Indian women in billowing sarees, broad-shouldered "big ladies" showing off the latest *kanga* designs, Muslims in white gowns and caps, Maasai medicine men wearing car-tyre sandals and red *shuka* gowns, red-faced expats donning shorts and briefcases, smart businessmen, seedy touts, lamentable beggars, even Catholic nuns. Dar is very much the "melting pot" of the old cliché, where wooden dhows bob alongside freighters and oil tankers in the harbour, and delicate architectural gems from colonial times huddle in the shadows of blue-glass high-rises; a place where gluttonous 4WDs share the fume-filled streets with hand-cranked tricycles ridden by polio victims. In short, a scruffy maelstrom for the senses.

For most travellers, Dar es Salaam is just a stepping-stone to Zanzibar or southern Tanzania, but it does boast a modest collection of museums, and, better yet, a **vibrant music and arts** scene. If you choose to stick around, there are several **outlying attractions** to explore, including decent beaches, a couple of islands, good scuba diving, medieval ruins at Kunduchi, plus a community tourism-based project at Gezaulole, and hikes in the Pugu Hills.

## Some history

Dar es Salaam dates from 1862, when Zanzibar's **Sultan Seyyid Majid** chose the Zaramo fishing village of **Mzizima** as the site for a new summer palace, which, he hoped, would replace Stone Town as capital of the Busaïdi dynasty. The location was ideal: its fine natural harbour was perfectly placed to exploit the flourishing trade in **ivory and slaves**; and, unlike Bagamoyo

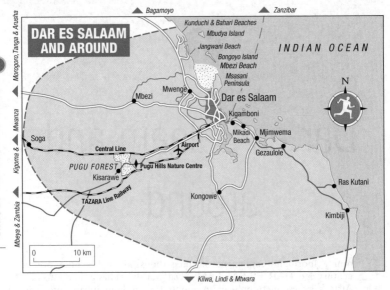

DAR ES SALAAM
AND AROUND

▲ Bagamoyo      ▲ Zanzibar

Kunduchi & Bahari Beaches
Mbudya Island
Jangwani Beach
Bongoyo Island
Mbezi Beach
Msasani
Peninsula

*INDIAN OCEAN*

Mwenge
Mbezi
Dar es Salaam

Kigamboni

Mikadi
Beach    Mjimwema

Soga
Central Line       Airport
PUGU FOREST    Pugu Hills Nature Centre
Kisarawe         Gezaulole
TAZARA Line Railway
Kongowe        Ras Kutani

Kimbiji

N

0        10 km

▼ Kilwa, Lindi & Mtwara

and Kilwa Kivinje, whose caravans were routinely pillaged and disrupted, Dar was untroubled by warlike neighbours. Sultan Majid named the place **Bandar es Salaam** – the "Peaceful Harbour".

By 1867, Majid's palace was sufficiently complete to host a lavish banquet in honour of European and American consuls, whose economic and military might the Sultan unwisely courted. Hadhramaut Arabs from Yemen were invited to develop coconut plantations in the hinterland, and, with the arrival of Indian merchants, the fledgling city seemed set to flourish. The sultan, however, died before his plans could be realized (ironically, breaking his neck in his new palace), and his successor, **Sultan Barghash**, showed no interest in the project whatsoever, particularly after the British forced him to prohibit the sea-borne slave trade in 1873, and the mainland slave trade three years later.

With little economic *raison d'être* left, the dhows and caravans returned to Kilwa and Bagamoyo, and Dar returned to being a fishing village, albeit one with a palace. So it remained until 1887, when the **Deutsch-Ostafrikanische Gesellschaft** – the commercial front for Germany's colonial effort – established a station here, and swiftly asserted their authority by torching Majid's palace. In 1891, with the German conquest in full and bloody swing, the capital of German East Africa was transferred from troublesome Bagamoyo to Dar, and the construction of the city began in earnest. Benedictine and Lutheran missionaries were among the first on the scene, their churches serving as bases for the spiritual conquest of the natives. Dar es Salaam's economic importance was sealed by the **Mittelland Bahn** – now the Central Line railway – which facilitated commerce with Central Africa via Lake Tanganyika and, after World War I, via Lake Victoria too.

Following the war, the **British** took over Tanganyika. Retaining Dar as their commercial and administrative centre, they divided it into three racially segregated zones. **Uzunguni**, in the east, was for Europeans, and benefited from tree-lined avenues, stone buildings, a hospital, a botanical garden inherited from the Germans, and other amenities. The more compact **Uhindini** area in the centre was reserved for Asian "coolies" brought in by the British to construct the new colony; the shops and businesses of their descendants still form the city's commercial heart. Lastly, **Uswahilini**, to the west, was left to Africans, who were deprived of even the most basic facilities.

As the city and its African population grew, so did social and political awareness. The **Tanganyika African Association**, an ethnically diverse welfare agency and social club, was founded in Dar in 1927 to advocate the betterment of the African lot. Spreading to rural communities, it eventually merged with the Tanganyika African National Union (TANU) to become the driving force behind the push for independence. Throughout this period, the city expanded relentlessly, and following **Independence** in 1961 became the capital of Tanganyika and, subsequently, Tanzania.

Alas, President Nyerere's well-meant but economically disastrous **Ujamaa** policy (see p.585) effectively bankrupted the city, which also lost its capital status to Dodoma in 1973. Two decades of stagnation followed before the effects of economic liberalization finally kicked in. These days, with the economy booming, Dar es Salaam is undergoing the biggest building spree in its history, with blue-glass high-rises shooting up all over the place, even in the poorest districts. But for all the construction work and shiny new motors choking the streets, **poverty** remains a daily reality for the great majority, and with more people migrating to the city each year, the challenges are enormous. It may take ten, twenty or thirty years for the economic benefits of current policies to filter through, but if history be a guide, Dar's resilient sense of community will continue to hold everything together. Especially with a generous dose of *bongo*…

# Arrival and information

Arriving in Dar can be disorienting, especially if there are hustlers or touts about. If you're at all nervous, catch a taxi to catch your breath.

### By air

Dar es Salaam's **airport** lies 11km southwest of the city along Nyerere Road, roughly half an hour by road. **International flights** use Terminal 2, which has a car-rental agency, an ATM, and a forex (bad rates). Avoid the safari operators here unless we've reviewed the companies (see pp.52–53), and be wary of touts. Most **domestic flights** use Terminal 1, whose facilities are limited to a snack bar, toilet and charter airline offices.

**Taxis** from the airport are expensive: Tsh25,000 to the city centre, Tsh35,000 to Msasani Peninsula, and Tsh50,000 to the northern beaches. You can book them at a desk outside each arrivals hall. Haggling might get you Tsh5000 off,

---

### Avoiding trouble

Although Dar es Salaam is relatively **safe**, do keep your *bongo* (wits) about you, especially if you're new to Tanzania. Basic advice on staying safe is given on p.58; it's worth repeating that you should be on your guard for **thieves** in crowded markets and transport terminals, and don't go **walking around at night** unless you're absolutely sure the area is safe (the general rule is the more people, traffic and lights there are around, the less the risk). **Walking by day**, even in crowded suburbs, poses no problem so long as you're not visibly nervous, or carrying anything that looks valuable. The exceptions are the beach running alongside **Ocean Road** and parts of **Coco Beach**, where you should take care if there aren't many people around.

but given that you'll likely be hot, tired and sweaty, you might as well resign yourself to paying full whack. If you're feeling fresh and don't have a mountain of luggage, **daladalas** (Tsh300) can be caught on Nyerere Road, 500m from either terminal. The most useful are to Posta in the city centre; avoid ones to Kariakoo unless you know the area, as you'll likely be dropped on or just off Msimbazi Street, chaotic at the best of times.

### By bus
Most buses terminate at **Ubungo Bus Station**, 8km west of the city along Morogoro Road. The fenced-in terminal is relatively calm, but there are enough hawkers and touts to keep you on your toes. **Taxis** charge around Tsh15,000 from here to the city centre; there are frequent **daladalas** (Tsh300) to Kariakoo, Posta or Mwenge. If you arrive late at night, the *Terminal Hotel* inside the bus station has decent en-suite rooms with air conditioning (☎022/245 0228, ✉rikihotel@raha .com; ❷); the bus station also contains bars and basic restaurants. Some buses – including Dar Express, Royal and Takrim – continue on to their **old terminals** in Kisutu, close to the main budget hotels. Scandinavian Express also pass through Ubungo before finishing at their terminal on Msimbazi Street, on the edge of Kariakoo. Almost opposite is the terminal for Akamba Bus.

Arriving directly **from Kilwa**, you'll probably be dropped in Temeke, a crowded suburb to the south. Taxis to the centre charge Tsh15,000; daladalas (Tsh300) run to Posta, Stesheni or Kariakoo. Coming **from Bagamoyo**, most minibuses finish at Mwenge, from where there are plenty more daladalas into the centre.

### By train
The **TAZARA Line station**, for trains from Mbeya and Zambia, is 5km west of the centre along Nyerere Road, from where there are lots of daladalas (Tsh300) into the city and taxis (around Tsh10,000). **Central Line Train Station**, for services from Kigoma and Mwanza, is just off Sokoine Drive in the city centre; Stesheni daladala stand is behind the shops facing the station.

### By sea
The **ferry terminal** for boats from Zanzibar is on Sokoine Drive in the city centre. It's ok to walk from there, but you'll likely be accompanied by flycatchers. Posta Zamani daladala stand, two blocks east, has frequent services to most of the city until around 9pm.

### By car
**Driving** into Dar is simple – Kilwa Road heads in from the south, becoming Msimbazi Street in Kariakoo. To get to the beaches south of the city, turn right at Kongowe, 20km before Dar. Coming from elsewhere except Bagamoyo, you'll arrive along Morogoro Road. Our hotel reviews mention where there's safe **parking** for guests. Parking space on the street can be difficult to find, even in Kariakoo: once you find a space, buy a parking ticket from attendants in orange bibs.

---

### Safaris from Dar

Dar es Salaam is the main base for the **Southern Safari Circuit**, which includes Mikumi and Ruaha national parks, and Selous Game Reserve. The various options, and recommended companies, are reviewed in Basics on pp.46–54. Don't get taken in by **companies touted by flycatchers**, or those focusing on the cluster of budget hotels in Kisutu, few if any of which are licensed.

## Bird walks

A different way of getting a feel for the city is on a two- to four-hour **bird walk**, organized by the Wildlife Conservation Society of Tanzania (WCST, Garden Avenue ☏022/211 2518, ⓦwww.wcstonline.org). These leave from their office on the first and last Saturday of each month at 7.30am. It doesn't cost anything except transport, but participants are encouraged to join the society ($50 annual membership), or make a donation. Andrew Majembe, who runs *Warthog Camp* in Saadani village (see p.132), offers similar trips for around Tsh20,000 per person, excluding transport: contact him on ☏0784/490399 or ⓔwildlife2001tz@yahoo.com.

# Information and tours

Dar's helpful **tourist office** (Mon–Fri 8am–4pm, Sat 8.30am–12.30pm; ☏022/213 1555, ⓦwww.tanzaniatouristboard.com) is on the ground floor of Matasalamat Mansions on Samora Avenue, four blocks southwest of the Askari Monument. They have hotel rates, a register of licensed safari operators, transport schedules and a good city map (free), and can answer pretty much any question.

For information about forthcoming events, restaurant reviews and practical listings, pick up a **monthly listings booklet**: the glossy *Dar es Salaam Guide* (the online version, ⓦwww.mhgallery.net, has articles only), the similar *What's Happening in Dar es Salaam*, or – for classifieds and day-by-day listings – the weekly *Advertising in Dar* (also at ⓦwww.advertising-dar.com). All are free and are distributed at the tourist office, major travel agents, hotels, restaurants and bookshops.

A number of travel agents (p.112) offer **city tours**, covering most of the main sights. Prices depend on group size, but average $170 per vehicle. It's cheaper to strike a deal with an English-speaking taxi driver.

# City transport

Most tourists use **taxis**. Way cheaper, but unsuitable if you're carrying luggage or physically inflexible, are **daladalas** – hectic, packed shared minibuses (invariably falling apart) that cover every corner of the city.

### Taxis

**Taxis** can be found almost everywhere, especially outside hotels, clubs, restaurants, bars, and at major road junctions. Licensed cabs are white and have white number plates; others risk being pulled up by the police, at your inconvenience. **Fares** for point-to-point trips within the city shouldn't top Tsh4000; journeys to the inner suburbs cost Tsh8000, and Tsh10,000–15,000 to Msasani Peninsula or Mwenge. These, and other fares quoted in this chapter, are the usual tourist rates; if you're an able bargainer, you might pay twenty percent less. Hourly or daily rates can be negotiated: starting prices are around Tsh60,000 per day excluding fuel.

### Daladalas

Despite periodic complaints in the press about dangerous driving, dirty uniforms and unsociably loud music (all true), Dar es Salaam's **daladalas** are surprisingly efficient and will get you almost anywhere within a

## Useful daladala terminals

Daladala terminals are called **stands**, or *stendi*. Throughout this chapter, we've noted useful daladala **routes**; if just the route is given (eg "Posta–Mwenge") with no further directions, you can assume the vehicle passes right by the entrance.

### Central terminals

**Kariakoo** Various stops along and off Msimbazi Street, between Mkunguni Street and Uhuru Street, 3km west of the city centre. Daladalas that start on Msimbazi Street itself head all over the city. Vehicles to Mwenge and Msasani congregate at the north end of Kariakoo market on Mkunguni Street. One block west are daladalas to Tegeta, close to the northern beaches.

**Kivukoni** East end of Kivukoni Front. Mainly for getting to and from Kigamboni ferry, for the southern beaches. Has services to/from Posta Zamani, Stesheni, and further west and south.

**Mnazi Mmoja** Uhuru Street as it crosses Mnazi Mmoja Grounds. Westbound services to Ilala, TAZARA and the airport, most of which pass via Kariakoo.

**Peacock** Bibi Titi Mohamed Road, facing *Peacock Hotel*. Posta–Ubungo and Posta–Mwenge daladalas pass here.

**Posta** Comprises two places: "Posta Mpya" (New Post Office) along Maktaba Street (mainly for dropping off), and, at the street's southern end along the harbour, "Posta Zamani" (Old Post Office), serving most destinations.

**Stesheni** One block east of Central Line Train Station. Mainly southbound, including Kilwa Road (Mgulani) and Temeke.

### Terminals out of town

There are plenty of daladalas from Posta, Kariakoo and Peacock to the following:

**Mwenge** 9km northwest at the junction of New Bagamoyo and Sam Nujoma roads. For services further north, including Jangwani and Kunduchi (though you'll need a taxi for the last bit). Also to the university (Chuo Kikuu) and Bagamoyo (Chapter 2).

**Ubungo** A few hundred metres west of the main bus terminal on Morogoro Road. For the western outskirts, Mwenge, and the university (Chuo Kikuu).

twenty-kilometre radius of the city for only a few hundred shillings (currently Tsh300 for most journeys). Most services operate 5am to 9pm. Routes are **colour-coded** (a thick band around the vehicle), with destinations clearly marked on the front. The only potential hassle is at major terminals, where you'll have to contend with touts competing to get you on their vehicles: the fullest ones are most likely to leave first.

# Accommodation

Dar es Salaam has a broad spread of **accommodation**, but at the budget end, finding decent digs for under Tsh20,000 a double, or Tsh30,000 with air conditioning, can be awkward – we've winkled out the best of them. If money's really tight, decent and safe is the *Salvation Army Hostel* on Kilwa Road in Mgulani, 3.5km south of the centre (℡022/285 1467, ℻022/285 0542; Tsh8000 per person), with 68 individual bungalows in a grassy garden, all with bathrooms, fans, pure nylon sheets and towels, and most with box nets. Catch any daladala from Kariakoo, Stesheni or Posta marked "via Kilwa Road".

From **October to February** rooms can be exceedingly hot: be sure yours has a good fan and ventilation, or air conditioning, or base yourself just outside the city at one of an ever-growing number of **beach hotels**: Mikadi, Mjimwema and Kawe beaches are covered below; for Jambiani and Kunduchi further north, see p.113. The nearest **campsites** are at Mikadi and Mjimwema. You can also pitch up at *Silver Sands Hotel* on Kunduchi Beach, at Gezaulole in the south (p.113), or at Pugu Hills Nature Centre (p.115).

## Kivukoni

The leafy former **European quarter** contains a trio of modest budget places, and central Dar's leading hotels, the latter all with wi-fi, swimming pools, restaurants and bars. All except *YWCA* have safe parking.

**Holiday Inn** Upanga Rd/Maktaba St ☎022/213 5888, ⓦ www.holidayinn.com. A blue-glass tower aimed at corporate types, so slick but soulless. The rooms are on the small side but have good views over the city or the ocean, as does the eleventh-floor rooftop bar and restaurant. There are more eating and drinking places on the ground floor, and an internet café and gym. BB ❼

**Kilimanjaro Kempinski** Kivukoni Front ☎022/213 1111, ⓦwww .kempinski-daressalaam.com. It took more than a lick of paint to transform this once sombre 1960s monolith into an airy five-star. With high standards throughout, it's a very dependable choice. The front rooms have great harbour views, but avoid the rear-facing ones, which are within earshot of the Bank of Tanzania's generators. Has a casino and rooftop pool. BB ❾

**Luther House Centre Hostel** Sokoine Drive ☎022/212 0734, ✉luther@simbanet.net. An adequate but pricey Christian-run backpackers' haunt, often fully booked. All rooms have a/c (not always working though), and back rooms have harbour glimpses. Poor restaurant. BB ❸

**Mövenpick Royal Palm** Ohio St ☎022/211 2416, ⓦwww.moevenpick-daressalaam.com. Along with the *Kempinski*, this is Dar's leading five-star, larger, with a little less personality but just as plush. The best rooms, at the back, overlook the golf course and ocean beyond. Also has a gym. BB ❾

**New Africa Hotel** Azikiwe St ☎022/211 7050–1, ⓦwww.newafricahotel.com. Once Dar's leading address, it's very tired these days, but the harbour-facing rooms are reasonable value. There's also a casino. BB ❼

**Southern Sun** Garden Ave ☎022/213 7575, ⓦwww.southernsuntz.com. A five-storey hotel beside the Botanical Gardens, and the only one of the biggies whose architecture – a take on British Raj – fits the area's heritage, but overall it feels a little cramped. BB ❽

**YMCA Youth Hostel** Upanga Rd ☎022/213 5457. A real dump, this, with all the charm of an army barracks (only half-finished, at that), and gloomy staff to match. The bedrooms, sharing bathrooms, are ragged but clean, and have nets and fans. On the positive side, there's a quiet courtyard garden, a cafeteria mostly dealing in beer and soda, and it's extremely cheap for its location. BB ❷

**YWCA** Ghana Ave ☎0713/622707, ✉ywca .tanzania@africaonline.co.tz. Best budget choice in the area, this also admits men and couples, and is friendly if the matriarchs take a shine to you. The rooms are a little scruffy (though for some, "en suite" just means a sink), have nets and fans, and there's a cheap restaurant. The *askari* will let you in after the curfew. Also has flats: Tsh25,000 for two beds, Tsh30,000 for three. Reservations advisable. BB ❷

## Kisutu and Mchafukoge

The **Asian district** retains much of its original character, and contains Dar's main backpacker hostels (all with signs forbidding "women of immoral turpitude", in those words exactly). The area has a handful of local boozers, the excellent *Chef's Pride* restaurant, and a small contingent of mostly harmless safari touts. In addition to the following are a handful of cheaper guesthouses (under Tsh15,000 a room): *Pop Inn* and *Tamarine*, both on Sofia Kawawa Street, and *Zanzibar Hotel* above a bar on Zanaki Street, facing Libya Street; security at them cannot be guaranteed however. Walking at night between local restaurants and hotels is generally safe (there are *askaris*), but do ask local advice, especially if venturing further afield.

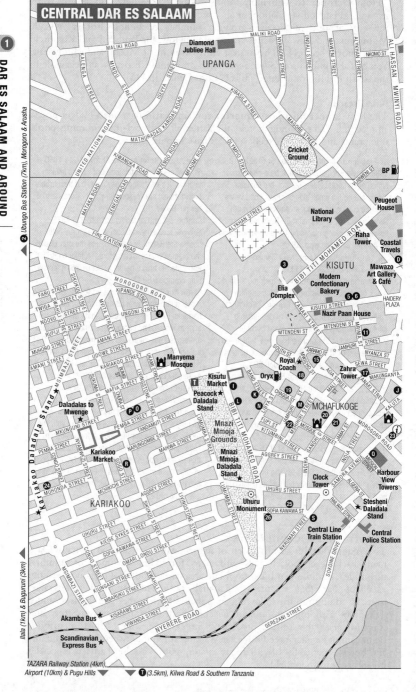

# CENTRAL DAR ES SALAAM

MALIKI ROAD

**Diamond Jubliee Hall**

UPANGA

MALIKI ROAD

NYANGORO STREET
UNGAI STREET
MAVENI STREET
ALYKHAN STREET
NKOMO ST
ALI HASSAN
MWINYI ROAD

KALENGA STREET
MINDU STREET
ISEVYA STREET
KIBASILA STREET
MAGORE STREET

MATHURADAS KARIDAS ROAD

KIWANUKA ROAD
MATENGO ROAD
OLYMPIO STREET

UNITED NATIONS ROAD

**Cricket Ground**

BP

MATAKA ROAD
SENEGAL ROAD
ALYKHAN STREET

**Peugeot House**

FIRE STATION ROAD

VUGA STREET

**National Library**

JAMHURI STREET

**Raha Tower**

**Coastal Travels**

BIBI TITI MOHAMED ROAD

KISUTU

**Mawazo Art Gallery & Café**

MOROGORO ROAD

KIPANDE STREET

UNGONI STREET

❸

**Modern Confectionary Bakery**

**Elia Complex**

ZANAKI STREET

KISUTU STREET

❺❻

HAIDERY PLAZA

**Nazir Paan House**

FARU STREET
SWAHILI STREET
TWIGA STREET
NDOVU STREET
RUFIJI STREET

MTENDENI ST
MTENDENI ST

❾

MUHORO STREET

AMANI STREET

UDOWE STREET

SOUTH ST

ZARAMO ST
KISIWANI ST

MARIMA ST
JAMHURI ST
NYANZA ST
SEWA STREET

❶❶

AMANI STREET

MSIMBAZI STREET

UKAMI STREET
KARIAKOO ROAD
BIBITI
LIVINGSTONE STREET

**Manyema Mosque**

**Royal Coach**

❶❺

MKWEPU ST

**Zahra Tower**

ASIA STREET

MAKUNGANYA

❶❼

SUKUMU STREET

MAFIA STREET

SUKUMA STREET

**Kisutu Market**

❶

**Peacock Daladala Stand**

**Oryx**

❶❽

CHAGGA ST

❶❾

MANSFIELD ST
MAIN ST

MCHAFUKOGE

JAMAL ST

❿

**J**

KALUTA

**Daladalas to Mwenge**

MKUNGUNI STREET

❼ P O

**L**

**K**

**N**

BAND STREET

FUPI ST

MOSQUE ST
GANDHI ST

MSIMBAZI STREET

**Kariakoo Market**

PEMBA STREET

TANDAMUTI STREET

**Mnazi Mmoja Grounds**

KITUMBINI STREET

❷❷

❷❶

MOROGORO ROAD

❷❸

**i**

**O**

CONGO STREET
NWANZA STREET

NARUNGOMBE STREET

MAHIWA STREET

GOGO STREET

**R**

MCHIKICHI STREET

**Mnazi Mmoja Daladala Stand**

AGGREY STREET

INDIRA GANDHI STREET

INDIA STREET

SAMORA AVENUE

ALGERIA ST

**Harbour View Towers**

❷❹

MUHONDA STREET

AGGREY STREET

LIVINGSTONE STREET

UHURU STREET

**Clock Tower**

**Stesheni Daladala Stand**

**KARIAKOO**

UHURU STREET

SIKUKU STREET

SOFIA KAWAWA ST

**Uhuru Monument**

❷❺

❷❻

**Central Line Train Station**

PALM WAY STREET

**Central Police Station**

KIESE SYKES STREET

SOFIA KAWAWA STREET

OMARI LONDU STREET

SIKUKU STREET

LIVINGSTONE STREET

NKRUMAH STREET

**S**

KUNGANI STREET

MSIMBAZI STREET
CONGO STREET

MBARUKU STREET

KIGARAWE STREET

VIWANDA STREET

NYERERE ROAD

SOKOINE DRIVE

GEREZANI STREET

**Akamba Bus**

**Scandinavian Express Bus**

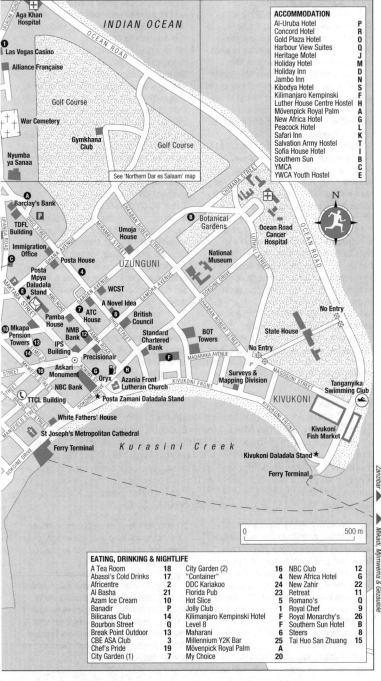

**Harbour View Suites** Harbour View Towers, Samora Ave ☎022/212 4040, ⓦ www.harbourview-suites.com. Perched way up on top of the shopping centre, this is primarily aimed at business executives, with lots of large, very well-appointed rooms (the suites have balconies and huge plasma screen TVs), most of them indeed facing the harbour (or ocean), and all with fully equipped kitchens and internet access. There's also a swimming pool, gym, and Cajun-style rooftop bar and restaurant. Safe parking. BB rooms ❼, suites ❽

**Heritage Motel** Katuta St/Bridge St ☎022/211 7471, ⓦ www.heritagemotel.co.tz. A new, six-storey hotel with lift access and bright, well-kept rooms with a/c, TV and internet. Also has a restaurant. The only downside is that the surrounding area is undergoing extensive construction work. Street parking. BB ❻

**Holiday Hotel** Jamhuri St ☎022/211 2246, ⓔ yasinmjuma@hotmail.com. A secure and perfectly decent backpackers' choice, cheaper than the *Jambo* and *Safari* nearby. Doubles are good, especially those with street-facing balconies, and some have bathrooms, but singles are tiny and stuffy. ❷–❸

**Jambo Inn** Libya St ☎022/211 4293, ⓦ www .jamboinnhotel.com. The most popular backpackers' haunt, but ask to see a selection of rooms as they vary greatly: all are en suite, some with good-sized nets and some with a/c, but others are hot and badly kept, with small beds, nylon

sheets and no nets. Rooms at the front are noisy but their balconies are a boon. Internet café and overpriced restaurant (closed Wed). Mediocre breakfast included. BB ❸

**Kibodya Hotel** Nkrumah St ☎022/211 7856. Above a branch of Barclays, this is suitably secure. The rooms, doubles or twins, are tatty but reasonably priced, and have TVs. Fans ❷, a/c ❸

**Peacock Hotel** Bibi Titi Mohamed Rd ☎022/212 0334, ⓦ www.peacock-hotel.co.tz. Two buildings wrapped in a single blue-glass shell, with lift access. Facilities include internet throughout, two bars, small swimming pool, and a windowless restaurant. Well-run, but neither the location nor the rooms are anything special at the price (and avoid rooms facing onto the dark internal courtyard). BB ❻

**Safari Inn** Off Libya St ☎022/213 8101–2, ⓦ www.darsafariinn.com. Another backpackers' haunt, with small but bright, clean and airy en-suite rooms with big double beds, fans and nets, and some with a/c. The bathrooms can be smelly, and the welcome at times perfunctory, but it's decent nonetheless. Internet café and cheap restaurant, and good breakfast included. BB ❸

**Sofia House Hotel** Bibi Titi Mohamed Rd ☎022/211 2521, ⓦ www.sophiahouse.com. Unexciting but well-priced mid-range option, all rooms with TVs, fans and a/c, but smelling of bug spray. The better rooms (twins) face Mnazi Mmoja Grounds. Safe parking. ❺

## Kariakoo

Over the last decade, the former mud-and-thatch district of **Kariakoo**, sprawling westwards from Mnazi Mmoja Grounds, has been utterly transformed by mushrooming high-rises. Many of them are hotels, most of them rather dingy and overpriced. The better ones are reviewed below, but do check the rooms first, as new buildings sprouting next door can easily turn bright and breezy rooms into hot and dark cells. If you're staying close to a mosque, listen out for the haunting ethereal *dhikri* chants early in the morning. Kariakoo is *not* safe to walk around in at night, or with valuables by day.

**Al-Uruba Hotel** Mkunguni St ☎022/218 0133–4, ⓕ 022/218 0135. The east-facing rooms in this Somali-run block have lost their views to the adjacent *Gold Plaza*, but if you get a west-facing one (overlooking Kariakoo market), it's excellent value. Staff are friendly, and the well-kept rooms have bathrooms, desk and chair, window nets, hot water, ceiling fan and TV, and some have a/c. *Banadir Restaurant* downstairs has fantastic Tanzanian food (no alcohol). Couples need proof of marriage. ❷

**Concord Hotel** Sikukuu St ☎022/218 2547. A high-rise with lift access, friendly staff, and

bright modern rooms, all with large windows, TV, a/c and good-sized beds, but no nets (rooms are sprayed). There's also a restaurant and two bars. ❸

**Gold Plaza Hotel** Mkunguni St ☎022/218 2306, ⓦ www.goldplazahotel .co.tz. The reception area in this nine-storey block is unpromising, but the rooms themselves – singles, doubles or twins – are in excellent shape and very good value, with a/c, fans and TVs. Lift access (after five steps). Couples require proof of marriage. ❸

## Msasani Peninsula and Kawe Beach

The plush suburbs on **Msasani Peninsula**, 6km north of the centre, contain mostly upmarket hotels, and similarly well-to-do restaurants, bars and clubs. It's actually illegal to build on the seaward side of the shoreline road, not that you'd ever guess. Still, what's done is done – some hotels have the advantage of ocean views, but no amount of *chai* could grant them beaches, as most of the shoreline is rocky. Taxis charge Tsh8,000–12,000 from the city centre, or Tsh35,000 from the airport. Posta–Masaki daladalas pass by *Q-Bar* and the *Golden Tulip* to finish at the *Sea Cliff*. For a proper beach, head to the *Mediterraneo* on **Kawe Beach**, 10km from the centre; catch a daladala from Posta or Kariakoo to Kawe, then walk 600m. There's safe parking at all the following, although *Q-Bar's* is on the street, watched by *askaris*.

**Coral Beach** Close to Sea Cliff Village, Msasani Peninsula ☎022/260 1928, ⓦwww .coralbeach-tz.com. Seen from the outside, this is an uninspired stab at a beach resort, hampered by rather too many buildings for the available space, and a lack of beach (it's on a low headland). That said, the rooms are very well equipped, and those in the new wing – all sea-facing – are positively regal. The fine swimming pool also has sea views, and there's a gym, restaurant and bar. BB ➐

**Golden Tulip** Touré Drive, Msasani Peninsula ☎022/260 0288, ⓦwww.goldentuliptanzania.com. Despite the Arabian styling, this huge resort-style hotel remains impersonal (better for conferences than holidays), but is amply endowed, including a massive swimming pool, and most rooms have sea-view balconies. BB ➐

**Mediterraneo** Off Kawe Rd, Kawe Beach ☎022/261 8359, ⓦwww.mediterraneotanzania .com. A cluster of low, Mediterranean-style buildings in gardens within walking distance of the beach. Amenities include a beach bar and Italian restaurant, a small pool, and a boat for island trips. BB ➏

**Peninsula Sea View Hotel** Chui Bay Rd, off Kimweri Ave, Msasani Peninsula ☎022/260 1273, ⓦwww.peninsulaseaviewhotel.com. A small four-storey hotel that packs it in: ten well-appointed rooms (spend more for a magnificent sea view), rooftop swimming pool, and the excellent

*O'Willies Irish Whiskey Tavern* (p.103), with a sea-front terrace and great food. Internet throughout. BB ➏

**Q-Bar & Guest House** Off Haile Selassie Rd, Msasani Peninsula ☎0754/282474, ⓦwww.qbardar.com. Three good reasons to stay here: a four-bed backpacker room ($12 per person); the peninsula's liveliest nightlife downstairs; and a wide selection of very good value en-suite rooms, all with satellite TV, a/c, fridge and window nets (cheaper ones share bathrooms). Internet throughout, and plenty of shops and facilities in the area. BB ➍–➎

**Sea Cliff Hotel** Touré Drive, Msasani Peninsula ☎022/260 0380–7, ⓦwww.hotelseacliff.com. With over one hundred rooms in a thatched monolith and in an adjacent shopping centre, this isn't the most graceful of constructions, but it's stylish inside, and if you get a bright sea-facing room, the views – from the cliff at peninsula's tip (no beach) – are spectacular. There's a mass of facilities, too, including internet access, several restaurants, cafés and bars, a swimming pool, health spa, gym, a casino, and even a bowling alley. BB ➐–➒

**The Souk** The Slipway, Msasani Peninsula ☎022/260 0893, ⓦwww.slipway.net. Modern creature comforts wrapped in Arabian style, on three floors, but with limited if any sea views. The spacious rooms and apartments have a/c and satellite TV, and The Slipway's restaurants and bars are at your feet. ➎

## Mikadi and Mjimwema beaches

**Mikadi Beach**, just south of the city, is a popular stop for truck tours, and staying overnight can be a lot of fun if you're happy slipping into road-trip mentality. There are fewer dazed *wazungu* at **Mjimwema**, 5km further on, which is calmer and more intimate. **Camping** is possible at all three places below, costing Tsh4000–5000 per person. *Mikadi Beach Camp* can provide tents for an additional Tsh2000; *Sunrise Beach Resort* charges Tsh15,000 if you have no tent, but that's for one or two people, and includes breakfast. South of Mjimwema are a number of privately owned **beach houses** for rent over a week or more; see *Advertising in Dar* (p.85).

To reach either place, catch the **ferry** from the eastern end of Kivukoni Front, an eight-minute hop to Magogoni on Kigamboni Peninsula (sailings every 30min 5am–1am; Tsh200, vehicles Tsh1500). Watch your bags and pockets, don't allow yourself to be harried by touts, and don't try to walk from there to the beaches – there's a risk of mugging. Instead, catch a **daladala** (6am–8pm; Tsh300). A taxi shouldn't cost more than Tsh4000 to Mikadi, Tsh7000 to Mjimwema, and a *bajaji* perhaps half that.

**Kipepeo** Mjimwema: 7.5km south of Kigamboni, then 1.3km along a dirt track ☎0732/920211, ⊕www.kipepeocamp.com. Spread out along a huge sandy beach, intimate *Kipepeo* ("butterfly") is recommended whatever your budget. It's actually two places: *Kipepeo Beach Camp*, with fourteen simple but comfortable thatched beach *bandas* with large nets, fans and lights; and the more expensive *Kipepeo Village*, a row of twenty cosy, locally styled "chalets" on stilts in the bush behind the beach, all en suite, with hot water and power. The food's good (also weekend barbecues), as is the sweetly named *Swimming Cow Pub* (their beach bar). Beach *bandas* ❸, chalets BB ❻

**Mikadi Beach Camp** Mikadi Beach, 2km from Kigamboni ☎0754/370269, ⊕www .mikadibeach.com. A long-standing favourite with overlanders, this has been thoroughly revamped, and now sports a dashing swimming pool, and an open-sided thatched beach bar and restaurant (great home-made burgers). Most people camp (plenty of shade), but there are also twelve thatched *bandas* on stilts facing the beach, each with two beds, big nets, fans and lockable door. Boat trips can be arranged. ❸

**Sunrise Beach Resort** Mjimwema, 7km from Kigamboni ☎022/218 0196, ⊕www.sunrisebeachresort.co.tz. Another quirky and friendly place, Indian-run, with good if rather tightly spaced rooms in both cottages and two-storey rondavels. The beach is a peach, and has recliners and parasols. Sea-view rooms, some with a/c, are double the price, but still worth it. All have TV, fridge, and Zanzibari four-posters. Add in a swimming pool, a restaurant specializing in flambées, two bars (one on the beach), children's activities, camel and horse rides, boat trips to Sinda Island (see p.113), and (often noisy) watersports, and you have great value for money. BB ❸–❻

# The City

Dar es Salaam is a patchwork of influences, but one with an underlying motif: the British apartheid divisions of Uzunguni ("European area"), Uhindini ("Indian area") and Uswahilini ("Swahili area"). Although the names are no longer in use, the racial stamp is still apparent in the architecture and feel of each zone, and it's those contrasting flavours that provide the city's main interest, since conventional tourist attractions are thin on the ground. For a **bird's-eye view** of the whole thing, take an elevator up to the 21st floor of Benjamin Mkapa Pension Towers on Maktaba Street (no roof access, though).

## Kisutu and Mchafukoge

Historically, the city's commercial heart – a square kilometre bounded by Bibi Titi Mohamed Road, Samora Avenue and Maktaba/Azikiwe Street – was Uhindini, the area reserved by the British for Indian "coolies" (manual labourers) shipped in to construct the city.

Nowadays split into **Kisutu and Mchafukoge**, it remains a hive of activity, with hundreds of stores selling almost anything you might need, from motor spares to gold jewellery, together with tea rooms, restaurants and sweet shops, and dozens of temples and mosques. There's no real centre to either district, nor any specific sights. The pleasure lies in details, such as seeing men selling beautifully arranged flower petals outside temples, or spying intricate wooden latticework balconies up above, so keep your eyes open as you wander around. Non-Muslims

▲ Watermelon seller, Kisutu Market

aren't allowed inside mosques, but other communities will happily to show you around their temples: start on the recently renamed Pramukh Swami Street, better known as **Kisutu Street**. This street is also a great place to sample **Indian sweets** (try Modern Confectionery Bakery, or Bhog 56 almost next door; also good is Al-Muazzin on Makunganya St, near Asia Street). For a taste of *paan*, one of India's stranger cultural exports, head to Nazir Paan House, at the west end of Kisutu Street. Essentially a mildly narcotic dessert, you choose from a range of sweet spices, chopped nuts and bits of vegetable, which are then mixed with syrup, white lime and *katu* gum, and wrapped in a betel leaf (*tambuu*) – the bit that strokes your synapses. Pop the triangular parcel in your mouth, munch, and spit out the pith when you're finished.

Unfortunately, greed (often confused with progress) is fast hammering its way through Mchafukoge's not inconsiderable architectural heritage (Art Deco, primarily, but also some very pleasant Indo-Swahili-European fusions), though the eastern end of **Uhuru Street** still has a few nice old balconied houses. And don't miss the atmospheric if insalubrious little **Kisutu Market** (daily 8am–5pm) on Bibi Titi Mohamed Road, a gentler introduction to African market life than Kariakoo further west. Among the stalls selling fruit and vegetables, honey, beans and pulses are others peddling baskets of squawking chickens, dried fish, and some gorgeously pungent herbs.

## Kariakoo

West of Kisutu and Mchafukoge, beyond the grassy Mnazi Mmoja Grounds, lies **Kariakoo**, at the heart of what the British called Uswahilini ("Swahili area"). Chaotic, potentially disorienting and definitely dangerous to walk around in at night, it's also by far the city centre's liveliest and most stimulating district.

Kariakoo got its name from the barracks of the hated British Carrier Corps, into which thousands of Tanzanians were conscripted during World War I to serve as porters. After the war, Kariakoo and Ilala, further west, were left – actually abandoned – to the African population: no amenities were provided, and some parts still lack the most basic of facilities. But things are changing, and fast. Barely a decade ago, the district's characteristic mud-walled "Swahili houses" were even touted as an attraction by the tourist board. Not any more: Kariakoo is transforming, at an ever-accelerating pace, into a jungle of high-rises.

In spite of the massive changes, and the poverty that remains evident everywhere, Kariakoo exudes a solid sense of community that manages to combine both tribal and religious identities. In many ways, the district is a microcosm of the country, so it's fitting that it plays host to **Kariakoo Market** (daily sunrise–sunset), which occupies the site of the Carrier Corps barracks, sitting under a bizarre roof resembling a forest of upturned parasols. In it, and in the maze of shops and stalls surrounding it, you'll find everything, whether from sea, land or factory: exotic fruit and vegetables, blocks of compacted tamarind paste (that might raise eyebrows at airports, given the resemblance to hashish), and all manner of meat, whether fresh and abuzz with flies, or cooked, or still bleating. There are also aromatic spices, herbs, Kilimanjaro coffee, handicrafts, textiles, local brews (*pombe*), and children's toys made from wire and recycled tin cans. You'll also see Maasai, both men and women, selling medicinal herbs, potions, and powders in little bottles salvaged from hospitals, as well as bundles of tree bark, dried lizards and seashells with curative properties. Elsewhere, great squawking bundles of trussed-up chickens clamour for freedom, whilst in other parts of the market you might be offered tart baobab seeds, snuff tobacco or dodgy imported electronics branded with deliberate misspellings such as "Soni".

Other than the maelstrom of sights, smells and sounds, what's also striking is the care with which everything is displayed, whether pieces of cloth rolled into tight cones and propped up on the ground, or little pyramids of oranges and other fruits, or fresh flowers inserted between mounds of coconuts. Take precautions against pickpockets, and sure as hell don't walk around here after dusk, at least not without a trustworthy escort.

For a breather, join the locals at the famous **DDC Kariakoo Social Hall** on Muhonda Street. Tanzania's oldest African bar, it also serves up a wide range of cheap and tasty Tanzanian dishes, before – on Tuesdays, Saturdays and especially Sundays – turning into one of Dar's best-loved live music venues.

## Kivukoni

With much of the rest of Dar es Salaam disappearing under concrete and steel, the city's best-preserved district is the former European area, Uzunguni, between the Asian area and the shore. With its broad tree-lined streets, gardens, imposing yet delicate colonial-era structures, a hint of sea breeze, and, well, not all that many people, **Kivukoni** – as the area is now known – comes as quite a change. As you might expect, it's still the administrative centre, and includes State House, home to the Tanzanian president.

Apart from some lovely wood-balconied buildings, the colonial presence is recalled by the **Askari Monument** along Samora Avenue. Designed by James Alexander Stevenson, the bronze statue depicts an African *askari* advancing, rifle ready, in honour of Carrier Corps porters who lost their lives in World War I, and replaced a statue of Hermann von Wissmann, the German explorer, soldier and governor.

Dar es Salaam's first buildings, erected during Sultan Majid's rule in the 1860s, faced the harbour. Though most have long since disappeared, a notable exception is the **White Fathers' House** (Atiman House), on Sokoine Drive near the corner with Bridge Street. This served as the Sultan's harem until being put to holier uses by the Society of Missionaries of Africa, a Roman Catholic order founded by French Algerians. The mission still occupies the building today. The nearby **St Joseph's Metropolitan Cathedral**, consecrated in 1897, is a major city landmark and a good place to experience Dar's church music (*kwaya*), best heard during Sunday Mass. The cathedral is notable for its twin confessionals, one in Baroque style, the other Gothic. The competing **Azania Front Lutheran Church**, 200m east, is unmissable thanks to its fancy Rhineland-style tower. It also has a *kwaya*, rivalling that of St Joseph's.

### Kivukoni Fish Market and Ocean Road

Heading east along the harbour, **Kivukoni Front** leads past a number of graceful German buildings, most adorned with wooden Indian-style balconies, which are nowadays occupied by government ministries and offices. At the eastern end of Kivukoni Front, in the shadow of a spanking new marine traffic control tower, is the ferry terminal for Kigamboni and, almost opposite, **Kivukoni Fish Market** – not that you need directions to get there as the smell is unmistakable. Unsurprisingly, this is the best place in Dar for seafood, with red snapper, kingfish, barracuda, squid, crab, lobster and prawns all usually available if you arrive early in the morning. Should you feel peckish, plenty of women are on hand to work magic over wide frying pans, or put their muscle into huge pots of *ugali* and cassava porridge. On the other side of the road is the fruit and veg section with yet more street food, hidden behind a row of stalls selling beautiful seashells, starfish and other marine curios. Please don't succumb to temptation: the export of many of these is illegal, even if they're openly available here.

The **beach** starts just north of the fish market, but the water can be polluted, so most people just sit around to feel the breeze, sip coconuts bought from nearby vendors, or stroll out onto the extensive flats at low tide. For clean water, the nearest stretches are Mikadi and Mjimwema a few kilometres to the south, and Coco Beach on Msasani Peninsula, to the north. Heading up Ocean Road from Kivukoni, the big, white, guarded building on your left is **State House**. Built by the Germans, it currently houses the Office of the President – which means no photos. Five hundred metres along is **Ocean Road Cancer Hospital**, built in 1886 as the German Malaria Research Laboratory. This was where **Robert Koch**, who in 1905 was awarded a Nobel Laureate for his discovery of tuberculin (wrongly believed to be the cure for TB), developed the standard laboratory method for preparing pure bacterial strains, the Koch Method. He went on to discover that flea-infested rats were responsible for the bubonic plague, and that the tsetse fly was the vector for sleeping sickness.

### National Museum and Botanical Gardens

A five-minute walk southwest from the Cancer Hospital is Tanzania's **National Museum**, on Shaaban Robert Street (daily 9.30am–6pm; Tsh6500, photography Tsh13,000; ⓦwww.museum.or.tz). Established in 1940 as the King George V Memorial Museum, it's quite a happening place these days, and well worth visiting.

Starting at the beginning, the **Hall of Man** traces human evolution (the Rift Valley being, as far as we know, the "Cradle of Mankind"). Highlights include a cast of Ngorongoro's "Laetoli footprints", which showed our ancestors were walking upright way before anyone had imagined, and fossilized skulls from Oldupai Gorge and elsewhere, including the 1,750,000-year-old partial skull of *Australopithecus boisei*, whose impressive jaw led to him being dubbed "Nutcracker Man". Don't miss the hilarious letter from an irate newspaper reader in 1958 fuming about the "hideous" suggestion that man might have evolved from apes... some things never change.

The **History Room** is a pleasant hotchpotch, covering a little bit of everything: explorers, wars and revolts, the slave trade, Independence (in photographs, and the original "Uhuru Torch" planted atop Kilimanjaro on December 9, 1961), and beyond… to the moon, with bits of rock brought back from the Apollo missions. The medieval mercantile Swahili civilization is amply represented through Indian trading beads, Chinese porcelain prised off gravestones, Mediterranean coins, and Persian friezes – all proof of the vitality of Indian Ocean trade prior to the Portuguese conquest.

The **Biology Hall** at the back contains a large collection of seashells (including a truly giant clam), corals, a couple of dull fish tanks, and – more interesting – an enormous pickled **coelacanth**, largely unchanged since its species' genesis some 350 million years ago.). The museum's real gem though is its **ethnographic collection**, with rich and informative descriptions, providing a fascinating journey through Tanzania's many and varied cultures. Even if ethnography per se leaves you indifferent, you're bound to find something to tickle your fancy, be it a fully functional wooden bicycle (still occasionally seen in central Tanzania), a gorgeously resonant Zaramo xylophone, a canoe made of sewn leather, a somewhat kinky beaded smock from Lake Eyasi, or grotesque clay figurines traditionally used in initiation ceremonies and for sexual education. Last but definitely not least is the **House of Culture**, the new building on your left as you enter, which should become a powerhouse both for traditional and contemporary arts (see p.107). It should also have a restaurant, serving traditional dishes.

The **Botanical Gardens**, adjacent to the museum (entrances on Samora and Garden avenues; daily sunrise–sunset; free), are ever more modest these days, most recently having lost a chunk for a tourism training college. Still, what's left is a shady and peaceful oasis. Established in 1893 as a testing ground for cash crops, the gardens still contain a few species of palm trees, some primeval fern-like cycads, and a raucous population of wing-clipped peacocks. The gardener's office has an explanatory leaflet.

## Msasani Peninsula and Kawe Beach

Six kilometres north of the city centre, **Msasani Peninsula** is the address of choice for diplomats, civil servants, NGOs and the otherwise rich, privileged or corrupt, and upmarket hotels, bars and restaurants are scattered all over it. The exception is **Coco Beach**, on the peninsula's eastern side, which has been a favoured weekend spot for ordinary Tanzanians for as long as anyone can remember. With a sturdy pair of legs (and a sun hat), you can walk here from central Dar in just over an hour. At weekends, you reach the first informal street-food, coconut and beer sellers opposite Oyster Bay Shopping Centre, but aim for *Coco Beach Bar* (p.104), which is also accessible by daladala (Posta–Masaki). If you're carrying valuables, be wary of the beach's quieter stretches, but walking along the road is fine. Taxis charge Tsh10,000–12,000 from the centre. Coco Beach has the advantage of being within stumbling distance of *Q-Bar* (p.104), the peninsula's alcoholic pulse for expatriates and other well-heeled revellers, and *Police Mess* (p.104), lovely by day and sometimes with live music at night.

Coco Beach's sand is mixed with coral ragstone, but the water is clean enough for swimming at high tide. For something smoother underfoot, **Kawe Beach**, stretching 4km north from the peninsula, is the place. There are several good beach bars scattered along (see p.104), and which, like Coco Beach, are popular with Tanzanians at weekends. To get here, catch a Posta–Kawe daladala, or Kariakoo–Kawe marked "via A.H. Mwinyi Rd". Taxis charge Tsh12,000–15,000. A good place to aim for is *Msasani Beach Club* (p.104), with live music on Sunday. However, things can change quite quickly as regards bars and bands, so get current recommendations before heading out. For a more private stretch of sand, the *Mediterraneo Hotel* (p.91), at the north end of Kawe, has excellent food, lovely views, and very nice rooms. **Swimming** at Kawe, as at Coco Beach, is only possible at high tide: the *Dar es Salaam Guide* (p.85) has tide tables.

## Mikadi and Mjimwema beaches

Dar's nicest beaches, and making do without the breakwaters that have scarred Jambiani and Kunduchi to the north, are **Mikadi and Mjimwema**, just a few kilometres south of the city. Somehow, so far, both of them have eluded a tidal wave of development, and – as long as not too many overtruck calls have called in – offer quite a meditative experience: perfect if you're after a bit of peace and quiet, but not so great if you want do stuff, as "activities" are largely limited to

▲ Coconut seller

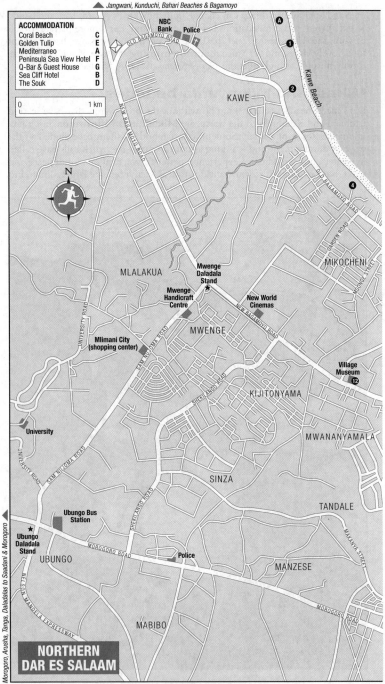

Jangwani, Kunduchi, Bahari Beaches & Bagamoyo

**ACCOMMODATION**

| | |
|---|---|
| Coral Beach | C |
| Golden Tulip | E |
| Mediterraneo | A |
| Peninsula Sea View Hotel | F |
| Q-Bar & Guest House | G |
| Sea Cliff Hotel | D |
| The Souk | B |

0 _____ 1 km

N

NBC Bank
Police

KAWE

Kawe Beach

OLD BAGAMOYO ROAD

MIKOCHENI

GARDEN ROAD

MSONGE STREET

MLALAKUA

Mwenge Daladala Stand

Mwenge Handicraft Centre

New World Cinemas

NEW BAGAMOYO ROAD

Mlimani City (shopping center)

MWENGE

Village Museum

KIJITONYAMA

SAM NUJOMA ROAD

SHEKILANGO ROAD

University

MWANANYAMALA

UNIVERSITY ROAD

SINZA

TANDALE

MAKANYA STREET

Ubungo Bus Station

Ubungo Daladala Stand

UBUNGO

MOROGORO ROAD

Police

MANZESE

MOROGORO ROAD

NELSON MANDELA EXPRESSWAY

MABIBO

## NORTHERN DAR ES SALAAM

Tazara Train Station, Airport & Mgulani

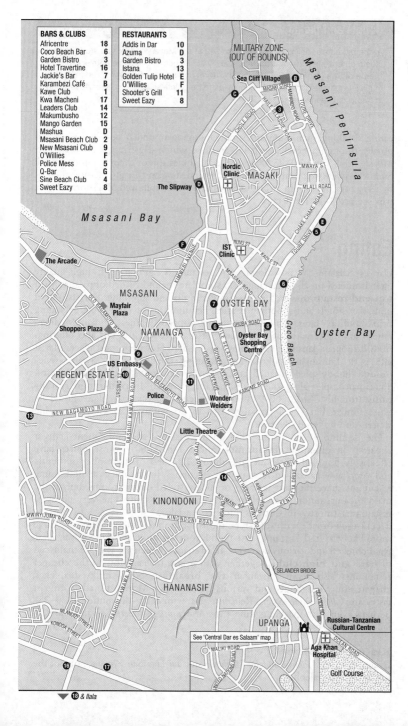

**BARS & CLUBS**

| | |
|---|---|
| Africentre | 18 |
| Coco Beach Bar | 6 |
| Garden Bistro | 3 |
| Hotel Travertine | 16 |
| Jackie's Bar | 7 |
| Karambezi Café | B |
| Kawe Club | 1 |
| Kwa Macheni | 17 |
| Leaders Club | 14 |
| Makumbusho | 12 |
| Mango Garden | 15 |
| Mashua | D |
| Msasani Beach Club | 2 |
| New Msasani Club | 9 |
| O'Willies | F |
| Police Mess | 5 |
| Q-Bar | G |
| Sine Beach Club | 4 |
| Sweet Eazy | 8 |

**RESTAURANTS**

| | |
|---|---|
| Addis in Dar | 10 |
| Azuma | D |
| Garden Bistro | 3 |
| Istana | 13 |
| Golden Tulip Hotel | E |
| O'Willies | F |
| Shooter's Grill | 11 |
| Sweet Eazy | 8 |

## Buffets and theme nights

At the big hotels, dollops of cash (up to $42 at the *Mövenpick*) let you stuff yourself stupid on **eat-all-you-want buffets**, usually at lunchtime. The same hotels also offer **theme nights** (seafood, Swahili, Indian, Italian and so on, sometimes with matching music), but these change so frequently as to be pointless detailing here; *Advertising in Dar* (p.85) has the latest.

eating, drinking, swimming, and simply lounging around. Access to the beach is usually through a hotel (see p.92), at all of which day-trippers are welcome. *Mikadi Beach Camp*'s Tsh5000 entry fee includes use of their swimming pool; *Sunrise Beach Resort*'s similar charge is refunded against meals. Getting there is by ferry over the mouth of Dar es Salaam's harbour, followed by a short daladala trip: see pp.91–92 for details.

# Eating

Dar es Salaam has no shortage of restaurants, and enough high-quality establishments (in all price ranges) to stimulate the most jaded of palates. Most **top-end restaurants** are on Msasani Peninsula and adjoining districts, and in upmarket hotels and shopping centres. For upwards of Tsh24,000, excluding drinks and taxi fares, you'll find the usual suspects (Chinese, Indian, Mediterranean and "international" – the land of prawn cocktails), but also offerings from Ethiopian, Japanese and Malaysian cuisines. However, most places play it safe with Tanzanian cooking by restricting themselves to "Swahili-style" seafood (lightly spiced, if at all, and cooked in coconut sauce), and avoid most Tanzanian staples altogether (*ugali*, cassava, plantain). In **mid-range restaurants** (roughly Tsh12,000–24,000), what ends up on your plate should be quite similar, but you'll probably have to do without sea views, hovering waiters and polished silverware.

The domino effect of the 2008 oil price shock and subsequent crisis is apparent in **cheaper restaurants** (under Tsh12,000), whose prices have effectively doubled since our last edition. The best of these offer authentic and very tasty Tanzanian fare, as well as curries, pizzas and fast food. Some restaurants have pleasant terraces or nicely styled dining rooms, but in the main the surroundings are plain, or even hot and stuffy. The very cheapest restaurants (mostly in districts such as Kariakoo) still manage to provide decent *ugali* or rice with stew-type meals for around Tsh3000, though you're more likely to find Tanzania's fast-food favourites: *mishkaki*, *chipsi mayai*, *ndizi*, fried chicken and various other pre-fried snacks, which are also the mainstays of **bars and nightclubs**, together with *nyama choma*. Most of the cheaper restaurants also serve Tanzanian-style **breakfast**, being milky tea, eggs, chapati, sour doughnuts and various fried snacks. More attuned to tourist tastes are *Chef's Pride*, *Steers*, *Romano's* and – for blow-out buffets ($20–25), perhaps even with sparkling wine – the *Mövenpick*, *Southern Sun* and *Kilimanjaro Kempinski* hotels.

## Kisutu and Mchafukoge

Except for *Break Point Outdoor*, *Maharani* and *Tai Huo San Zhuang*, none of the following serve alcohol.

**A Tea Room** Jamhuri St/Morogoro Rd. The best of several unfussy "tea rooms" around here, serving a wide range of traditional snacks (potato and meat balls, samosas, doughnuts and so on), a filling chicken *pilau* lunchtimes (Tsh4000), and chicken or mutton biriani for Sunday lunch (Tsh4000–4500).

**Abassi's Cold Drinks** Zanaki St. A friendly Indian place for breakfast, with a selection of refreshing fruit juices and snacks including samosas and rice cakes.

**Al Basha** Indira Gandhi St. Genuine Lebanese food (good for vegetarians: the *labneh* – strained yoghurt – is nicely refreshing) in a plain cafeteria. Snacks under Tsh3000, meals over Tsh7000. Closed Sun lunch.

**Azam Ice Cream** Jamhuri St/Upanga Rd. No-frills fixes for *gelato* junkies.

**Break Point Outdoor** Simu St. A large, lively and friendly outdoor bar that's also handy for food: *nyama choma*, *ndizi* and *chipsi mayai* all day long, plus Tanzanian lunches (*ugali* or rice with beans, stews or fish, all around Tsh4000).

**Chef's Pride** Chagga St. A busy and deservedly popular Tanzanian restaurant offering an embarrassment of choice, most of it freshly cooked, whether Zanzibari-style fish in coconut, birianis, or tender roast chicken. It also dishes up fast-food favourites, pizzas, snacks and great breakfast combos, with nothing much over Tsh6000.

**City Garden (2)** Mkwepu St. With a similar menu and prices to its namesake (p.102), this is better known as *Java Café*, and is the latest incarnation of an originally German bakery. As the Cosy Café, it was one of few places where races could mingle socially, and it was here that British officials met Nyerere, then still a teacher, to discuss the move to Independence. Nowadays, it's been tarted up as a swanky restaurant: dodge the awfully stuffy interior and take a table on the attractive, tree-lined veranda. Closed during Ramadan.

**Hot Slice** Kisutu St. Elegant, cool and calm little pizzeria also offering brilliant salads, lots of ice creams (well-tended, so no worries), shakes and coffee. Pizzas Tsh6500–11,000, depending on size.

**Maharani** Kisutu St. Modest Indian place that's seen better days, but with fresh and tasty food, best sampled via the lunchtime buffet: Tsh6500 vegetarian, Tsh7500 with meat.

**My Choice** Indira Gandhi St. Very cool a/c is one reason to come here; the other is genuine Tanzanian cooking, especially from the north. Try the *matoke* banana stew (Tsh4000 with meat). Closed Sun.

**New Zahir** Mosque St. A favourite with Kisutu's Muslims, this does reasonable curries and birianis for under Tsh4000, some Tanzanian dishes and real espresso, but juices aren't the real thing, and it's all a bit run-down. Has a few tables outside.

**Retreat** Mrima St. Don't let the stark dining room put you off – very popular with Tanzanian-Indians, this place serves up seriously good South Indian vegetarian fare, as well as Punjabi dishes and *paneer*, and a selection of more average Chinese dishes. The lunchtime *thalis* are good value at Tsh6000; otherwise Tsh10,000 a meal. Closed Mon.

**Romano's** Harbour View Towers, Samora Ave. An Italian bistro inside the shopping mall with seats in the atrium, great for comfort food: lasagne and pizza from Tsh11,000, plus cheaper burgers, toasted sandwiches, and good coffee.

**Royal Monarchy's** Bibi Titi Mohamed Rd/Sofia Kawawa St. One of several cheap eateries in this area. Has lunchtime chicken *pilau*, and some tables on the pavement outside.

**Tai Huo San Zhuang** Jamhuri St. The cream-themed dining room is the first impression here, something like a Victorian powder room. The cuisine is genuine Chinese (as are most of the clientele), and is well priced at around Tsh10,000 for mains with rice, less for vegetarian or noodles. The lunchtime specials are a bargain at Tsh4500, but the service is impatient. Well-stocked bar.

## Kariakoo

Apart from the following, Kariakoo has loads of cheap no-frills eateries, especially along the unsurfaced streets west of Msimbazi Street in Ilala, where you can fill up for under Tsh3000.

**Banadir Restaurant** *Al-Uruba Hotel*, Mkunguni St. Popular with locals, especially Somalis, this has a wide choice of often superb Tanzanian dishes you won't find elsewhere, including very tasty vegetable stews. Tsh6000 gets you stuffed. Also has fresh juices and fruit. No alcohol.

**DDC Kariakoo Social Hall** Muhonda St. Dar's longest-running bar and live music venue is also one of the best places for a really cheap eat, packing them in with metal platters of *pilau*, beans and stews for Tsh2000. Also has great *supu* for breakfast.

**Royal Chef** Lumumba St. Run by the same folks as *Chef's Pride*, and also highly recommended: this is one of the city's best Tanzanian restaurants. The tasty food, including

## Street food

Out on the streets, you can find some really tasty and often dirt-cheap food, especially around markets and transport terminals. **Kivukoni Fish Market** has some of the finest grilled fish on the coast. For fuller **meals**, try one of the *mama lisha* ("feeding ladies") in the Swedish-built buildings on the harbour side of Kivukoni Front, who dish out rice and *ugali* with stew or beans, fried fish or *mishkaki* (skewers of grilled goat meat), chicken kebabs wrapped in chapatis, bananas cooked in coconut milk, all delicious and costing under Tsh2500. On Kivukoni Front itself are hawkers aplenty, peddling **snacks** such as samosas, rice cakes, roasted maize cobs, mangos (which are peeled for you), and delicious roast cassava doused in light chilli sauce, a far cry from the usual mealy, mouth-drying tuber. In addition, *mama* (and some *baba*) *lisha* at the west end of Garden Avenue serve full meals, as do stalls at most road junctions in Kisutu, even by day.

To cap a meal on the move, look for **coffee vendors** (also in the morning), especially in the Asian district, Kariakoo, and at daladala stands, who dole out their brew in tiny porcelain cups. You can also find fruit, including finely peeled oranges and chunks of sugar cane, and lastly, should a strangely chirpy, fairground-ride-style rendition of *O Sole Mio* (or Presley's *It's Now or Never*) meander into your ears, you'll know that an **ice-cream vendor** (and his tricycle) are nigh.

grills, meat, seafood and vegetarian, comes quickly and in large portions, and there's an attractive streetside veranda to boot. Full meals around Tsh7000. No alcohol.

### Kivukoni

**City Garden (1)** Garden Ave/Pamba Rd. The outdoor location, under trees and awnings, is one reason to eat here. Another is its weekday lunchtime buffets (Tsh14,000), which are among the cheapest in town. A la carte (Tsh8000 a plate) can feel a little pricey in comparison, but the food is good, especially fish (try the seafood pasta) and salads. No alcohol. Closed Ramadan.

**"Container"** Ohio St. This is what a garden restaurant should be: friendly, relaxing, breezy, with plenty of well-spaced tables under trees (hopping with talkative Indian crows), scrawny cats at your feet, and proper Tanzanian meals (*ugali*, rice or *pilau* with great stews) for under Tsh4000. The name? The shipping crate housing the kitchen.

**Kilimanjaro Kempinski Hotel** Kivukoni Front. The *Oriental* is the more interesting of the two restaurants here, serving inspired blends of Japanese, Chinese and Indian cuisine. Lunchtime buffets Tsh34,000; à la carte similarly priced.

**Mövenpick Royal Palm Hotel** Ohio St. Two ground-floor restaurants, with some tables outside: *L'Oliveto* (closed Mon) for Italian, and *Serengeti* for international, including buffets (Tsh42,000) and theme nights (Tsh38,000). A la carte isn't much cheaper. If you're counting the pennies, light meals including shawarmas and baguettes, salads and pasta at the *Kibo Bar* are under Tsh15,000.

**New Africa Hotel** Azikiwe St ☎022/211 7050–1. Forget the humdrum first-floor *Bandari Grill* (buffets Tsh18,000), and get up to the *Sawasdee* (evening only; best to book ahead) on the ninth-floor rooftop for fabulous à la carte Thai (around Tsh30,000) and nocturnal harbour views.

**Southern Sun Hotel** Garden Ave. Both dining rooms here (the *Baraza* and *Kivulini*) have swish service but unexceptional surroundings; it's best to eat outside. Recommended for grills and Swahili-style seafood (around Tsh14,000), and well-priced lunchtime buffets (Tsh18,000).

**Steers** Samora Ave/Ohio St. Fast food as it should be (and *halal* too): fresh, well made, perhaps even good for you: everything from toasted sandwiches to toffee ice cream, and good coffee. There's also a pizzeria and curry house, internet café, and seats under parasols on the street corner. No alcohol.

### Msasani Peninsula and around

Msasani contains dozens of upmarket restaurants, of which the following (all serving alcohol) are just a selection – new places open and old ones close constantly, so ring ahead before going. Expect to part with upwards of

Tsh15,000 for a full meal with drinks. See also the reviews of Msasani's bars (p.104), many of which serve (decidedly cheaper) food.

**Addis in Dar** 35 Ursino St, off Bagamoyo Rd, Regent Estate ☎0713/266299. Attention to detail is everything in this north Ethiopian place, from the traditional decor to the wafting incense. The basic staple is *injera*, a huge sour dough pancake that you share with your partner, using it to mop up a variety of highly spiced sauces and stews. Good coffee. Posta–Mwenge daladalas to Rashidi Kawawa Rd, then walk 500m. Closed Sun.

**Garden Bistro** 498 Haile Selassie Rd, Msasani Peninsula ☎022/260 0800. A couple of restaurants here, the special one being *Shamiyana*, for fine Indian dining in a shady garden. Also has a *shisha* lounge, popular sports bar, and nightclub. Posta–Masaki daladalas to Sea Cliff Village, then walk 200m.

**Golden Tulip Hotel** Touré Drive, Msasani Peninsula ☎022/260 0288. Theme nights and expensive buffets at the *Sanaa* restaurant, but recommended for its children's activities on Sunday afternoon. Use of the swimming pool costs Tsh10,000. Posta–Masaki daladalas.

**Istana** Ali Hassan Mwinyi Rd, Mwananyamala ☎022/276 1348. Welcoming and friendly Malaysian restaurant, with plenty for vegetarians. Also has good buffets (Tsh10,200). Posta–Mwenge daladalas. Evenings only.

**O'Willies Irish Whiskey Tavern** *Peninsula Sea View Hotel*, off Kimweri Ave, Msasani Peninsula ☎022/260 1273. Pub grub to assuage any Gaelic or British homesick yearning: from BLTs and fish and chips to Irish stew and shepherd's pie. Main courses around Tsh8000. See our bar review on p.104.

**Shooters Grill** 86 Kimweri Ave, Namanga, Msasani Peninsula ☎0754/304733. Carnivore paradise on a hunting theme, famed for whopping 1kg T-bones. Live music Sun. Posta–Kawe daladalas to Kimweri Ave, then walk 200m.

**The Slipway** Msasani Peninsula ☎022/260 0893. Upmarket shopping centre with several restaurants and bars. The *Mashua* terrace (Italian food) distinguishes itself with a sweeping view over Msasani Bay, whilst *Azuma* has excellent Japanese and Indonesian cuisine, including *sashimi*. Masaki–Posta daladalas to IST, then walk 1.5km. *Mashua* open daily; *Azuma* closes Mon and weekend evenings.

**Sweet Eazy** Oyster Bay Shopping Centre, Touré Drive/Ghuba Rd, Msasani Peninsula ☎0755/754074. Authentic Thai (marinated raw tuna *jodari* is exquisite), plus inventive African dishes. Eat inside (a/c) or on the terrace. Posta–Masaki daladalas to Touré Drive, then walk 400m.

# Drinking and nightlife

For a quick drink or three, Dar's central **bars** are perfectly fine, but head out into the suburbs, to places like Ilala, Sinza and Kinondoni, and you'll discover not just bars but a wealth of **clubs** brimming over with people dancing to exuberant live bands, a scene that few expats or indeed well-off locals know anything about. If the local scene isn't to your liking, upmarket areas like Msasani have more than their fair share of places too, as glitzy, brash or as downright expensive as you like, though many also attract prostitutes on the prowl. The upmarket crowds are a fickle lot, so you'd do well to check a venue's popularity before heading out.

On nocturnal escapades, get around by **taxi**. Getting home is no problem as even the smallest bar or club will have cabs outside, even at the most unsociable hours. Lastly, should too much money be weighing on your conscience, absolution is available at the **casinos** inside the *Kilimanjaro Kempinski* and *New Africa* hotels in town, at *Sea Cliff Hotel* on Msasani Peninsula, and *Las Vegas Casino* on Ali Hassan Mwinyi Road.

## Bars and clubs

See also our reviews of live music venues, most of which operate as bars when not hosting bands. In addition, the big hotels all have bars, usually expensive and rather anodyne affairs, albeit fluent in the language of cocktails; the better ones are reviewed below.

## City centre

**Bilicanas Club** Simu St. Dar's most popular disco-thèque, with good lighting and sound, occasional live bands, and oodles of prostitutes.

**Bourbon Street** Harbour View Towers, Samora Ave. A terrific harbour view is the big draw at this rooftop Louisiana-themed bar and restaurant, complete with wrought-iron balustrades, and matching music. There's also a restaurant, serving buffet lunches and à la carte evenings.

**Break Point Outdoor** Simu St. A big upcountry-style *nyama choma* bar slap bang in the centre. Lots of tables in a large gravel-strewn enclosure, plenty of food (including a lunchtime buffet), and In Africa band playing Friday nights (to 1am).

**CBE ASA Club** College of Business Education, Bibi Titi Mohamed Rd. The most laid-back local bar in the centre, hidden in the college grounds. Calm by day (plenty of tables under thatch or trees), this can be lively at night if there are promotions or live bands. Also has *nyama choma* and *ndizi*.

**Florida Pub** Mansfield St. Dark and pricey a/c bar with haughty barmaids. There's Castle lager on tap, a mute TV, two pool tables, and reasonable food. Closed weekends.

**Jolly Club** Beside *Las Vegas Casino*, Ufukoni St, Upanga. A huge, partially outdoor bar, with fancy lighting, TVs all over, tables in cosy thatched nooks, and a zillion prostitutes waiting in them. Things get really steamy at weekends, when there's a band (free). Good food, including *nyama choma*.

**Level 8** *Kilimanjaro Kempinski*, Kivukoni Front. Expensive drinks, expansive harbour views from the rooftop of Dar's best hotel. 5pm–1am.

**Millennium Y2K Bar** Sofia Kawawa St. Best of the bunch in this area, a friendly local dive with tables in a courtyard at the back. There's a pool table, cheerful Congolese music, full meals until 4pm and snacks and *mishkaki* thereafter. Be careful walking back at night if you're staying in the area.

**NBC Club** Pamba Rd. This is where the nation's bankers went to drown their sorrows in the good old days of economic decline. Now, the bar's declining, but it remains popular. It has two sections, one inside with a TV, the other outside with a dartboard. Good food, including hangover-dispelling *supu*.

## North of the centre

**Coco Beach Bar** Touré Drive, Msasani Peninsula. The peninsula's most popular local joint, with a great beachfront location (swimming possible). Beers are cheap by Msasani standards, and a wide range of food is served. Pool tables, and a Sunday disco from 4pm onwards. Posta–Masaki daladalas.

**Garden Bistro** 498 Haile Selassie Rd, Msasani Peninsula. A relaxed, upmarket place with restaurants, bar and nightclub, popular for its Friday disco, and live band on Thursday. Posta–Masaki daladalas to Sea Cliff Village, then walk 200m.

**Jackie's Bar** Haile Selassie Rd, Msasani Peninsula. Popular but nonetheless calm respite from the nearby *Q-Bar*'s whores and hordes, with plenty of outdoor tables by the roadside. Posta–Masaki daladalas.

**Karambezi Café** *Sea Cliff Hotel*, Msasani Peninsula. Tasty light meals and jaw-dropping ocean views (and prices) at the tip of the peninsula. Posta–Masaki daladalas.

**Kawe Club** Old Bagamoyo Rd, Kawe Beach. A breezy old colonial beach club established in 1952 by the Tanganyika Packers (lapsed purveyors of corned beef). Currently being renovated, this is always a good place at weekends, when it often has live music. Posta–Kawe daladalas, or Kariakoo-Kawe marked "via A.H. Mwinyi Rd".

**Mashua** The Slipway, Msasani Peninsula. The location's the thing: an open terrace overlooking Msasani Bay. Also serves pasta, pizza and grills. Masaki–Posta daladalas to IST, then walk 1.5km.

**Msasani Beach Club** Kawe Beach. A cavernous, army-owned place with a scrubby beach-front garden, tables under parasols, and lovely swimming at high tide. Food is the usual *chipsi* and *nyama choma*, but you can also bring a picnic. Sunday is the big day, featuring Congolese-style Akudo Impact band from 3pm onwards (kids are welcome). Daladalas as per *Kawe Club*.

**O'Willies Irish Whiskey Tavern** *Peninsula Sea View Hotel*, off Kimweri Ave, Msasani Peninsula. It had to happen: Tanzania's first Irish pub, complete with Victorian-style trimmings, quizzes, bands, karaoke, traditional British pub grub, whisk(e)y galore, and, goodness, real Guinness (Tsh5000 a pint). There's also a sea-facing terrace. Kariakoo–Msasani Mwisho daladalas, then walk 100m, or Posta–Masaki to before Chole Rd, and walk 1km.

**Police Mess** Touré Drive, Msasani Peninsula. Astride a low ragstone headland in a lovely bayside location, this mostly open-air bar has the crowds hopping on Friday and Saturday night, when Kilimanjaro Band strum their *njenje* style into the early hours. Posta–Masaki daladalas.

**Q-Bar** Haile Selassie Rd, Msasani Peninsula. Popular with locals, expatriates, tourists, and a welter of well-dressed prostitutes. It's liveliest on Friday (Roots Rockers band) and also busy on Wednesday (live band or football) and Thursday (In Africa band). Also has good food, pool tables, and TVs screening sports. Posta–Masaki daladalas.

**Sine Beach Club** Kawe Beach. Popular with locals (and families) for its beach at weekends, this has hit-and-miss food, live bands Thursday and Saturday evenings, and a chance of live music Sunday afternoon. Daladalas as per *Kawe Club*.

**Sweet Eazy** Oyster Bay Shopping Centre, Touré Drive/Ghuba Rd, Msasani Peninsula

☎0755/754074. Apart from excellent food (p.103), this has an open-air bar (sadly, hardly any ocean view) and is currently *the* place for upmarket crowds on Saturdays. Live music Thursday. Posta–Masaki daladalas to Touré Drive, then walk 400m.

## Live music

You didn't really come to Tanzania to sit at a British-style pub or in a five-star hotel's piano bar and pay first-world prices, did you? Leave your valuables at the hotel, stuff some money in your pockets, and head out to the suburbs to explore Dar's effervescent live music scene. The mainstay is **dance music**, *muziki wa dansi*: the older bands play brassy, guitar-rich sounds popular with all ages; newer ones favour Congo's raunchier rhythms and butt-shaking style (for a run-down, see pp.613–614). A handful of **Taarab** venues are included below, but "underground" styles such as **rap**, **hip-hop** and even mainstream **Bongo Flava** are rarely performed: your best bet is the two-day **B-Connected Festival** at the end of May (🖳www.musicmayday.org). Performances of **traditional music** and dance are given at the Village Museum (Sat & Sun 4pm; $4), and at Nyumba ya Sanaa (Fri 7.30pm; Tsh2000).

**Up-to-date information** on bands and venues is hard to come by. The "what's on" section at 🖳www.dar411.com covers the bigger names. For the rest, taxi drivers may know a thing or two, and the Saturday editions of Kiswahili newspapers such as *Nipashe* or *Uhuru* may have listings on the inside back page. More upmarket events are covered in Dar's listings booklets (p.85).

Most **venues** are open-air, with a dance floor between the tables and the band; venues worth visiting by day (when they operate as normal bars) are reviewed in the preceding sections. When bands are playing, **entrance fees** shouldn't be more than Tsh5000. In the main, things heat up after 10pm, the exception being Sunday, when many bands kick off the proceedings at around 4pm. Sundays can be great fun for families, especially at beachside venues. **Other venues** worth asking about include *Amana Club* and *Max Motel*, both in Ilala, *Lions Club* and *Vatican City* (for big events), both in Sinza, and, south of town, *TCC Club* in Chang'ombe and *Equator Grill* in Mgulani.

**Africentre** Kigogo Rd, Ilala. The new base for much-loved old-timers, Msondo Ngoma (formerly OTTU Jazz Band), who draw crowds of all ages every Sunday. Take a taxi.

**DDC Kariakoo** (also called *DDC Social Hall*) Muhonda St, just off Msimbazi St, Kariakoo. Tucked under a vaulted roof, this is Dar's oldest bar, and home on Sunday (from 4pm) to the famous DDC Mlimani Park Orchestra. Taarab features on Tuesday (Jahazi Modern Taarab) and Saturday (Zanzibar Stars).

**Kwa Macheni** 2.5km along Morogoro Rd, before *New Bondeni Hotel*. An infamous yet highly enjoyable 24hr dive, with live music some evenings (free entry) and dancers nightly. It gets packed at midnight, and slowly fizzles out around 4am. Posta–Ubungo or Kariakoo–Ubungo daladalas.

**Leaders Club** Tunisia Rd, Kinondoni. Home turf for the various pro-Government "TOT" bands, this large club is run by the ruling CCM political party.

It's best on Sunday afternoon for its "Leaders Bonanza", with different bands each week (often Twanga Pepeta or Vibration Sound). Saturday afternoons may be lively too. Posta–Mwenge daladalas to before Little Theatre, then walk 200m.

**Makumbusho** Village Museum, New Bagamoyo Rd, Kijitonyama. Part of the museum's grounds serve as a live music venue; the currently hugely popular FM Academia play Saturday night, with Akudo Impact following on Sunday. Posta–Mwenge daladalas.

**Mango Garden** Mwinyijuma Rd, Kinondoni. Consistently one of the best venues for dance music, with live bands from Wednesday to Sunday (including weekend afternoons). Currently starring FM Academia (Wed), Diamond International (Fri), and Twanga Pepeta (Thurs and either Sat or Sun from 4pm). Catch a taxi.

**New Msasani Club** Old Bagamoyo Rd, Namanga. Occupying a huge and largely empty outdoor plot, this fills up on Sunday when FM Academia are at home. Posta–Kawe daladalas, or Kariakoo-Kawe marked "via A.H. Mwinyi Rd"; get off at Ubalozi. **Hotel Travertine** (also called *Lango La Jiji*) Kawawa Rd/Morogoro Rd, Magomeni. A major

Taarab venue west of town, currently home to Jahazi Modern Taarab (you'll likely hear them, or East African Melody, any night from Thurs–Sun).

# Film, theatre and the plastic arts

**Cultural events** are pretty thin on the ground, with neither film nor theatre having much prominence, and **dance** limited to the Contemporary Dance Festival in October (contact Mawazo Gallery for details), which may become an annual event. The plastic arts fare much better, with the output of contemporary Tanzanian artists presented in a number of galleries. For **information** on what's happening and where, see the monthly listings booklets (p.85), or talk with Rachel Kessi at Mawazo Gallery, Yves Goscinny at La Petite Galerie, or Aggrey Mwasha at Wasanii Art Centre; all are reviewed below.

## Film and theatre

Dar es Salaam has just two **cinemas**, both modern: for Hollywood, go to Cinemax in Mlimani City, Sam Nujoma Road (℡022/277 3053; Posta–Mwenge daladalas, then one towards Ubungo); Bollywood is the flavour at New World Cinema, New Bagamoyo Road (℡022/277 2178; Posta–Mwenge daladalas, alighting at "TV"). **Screenings** are announced in *Advertising in Dar* (p.85), and at ⓦwww.dar411.com. If you're around in October, there's the three-week **European Film Festival** where you might see otherwise very rare Tanzanian productions.

**Theatre** is limited to the Dar es Salaam Players, who put on a production roughly once a month at the Little Theatre, off Haile Selassie Road near Ali Hassan Mwinyi Road. The plays cater mainly for English-speaking expats and the Europhile Tanzanian elite; they also have Christmas pantos. Details through *Advertising in Dar* (p.85).

## Galleries and cultural centres

The acclaimed **East African Art Biennale** (December of odd-numbered years; contact Yves Goscinny at La Petite Galerie) is a major showcase, assembling works

---

### The Village Museum

Roughly 8km along New Bagamoyo Road is the open-air **Village Museum** (daily 9.30am–6pm; $4; ℡022/270 0437; Posta–Mwenge daladalas to Makumbusho), founded in 1966 to preserve some of the nation's architectural and material traditions. Spread out over the site are houses in the styles of sixteen tribes, each furnished with typical household items and utensils, and surrounded by small plots of local crops and animal pens. Although laudable, the aims of the museum became grimly ironic in the years following its establishment, when President Nyerere embarked on his economically disastrous Ujamaa policy, in which the majority of rural Tanzanians were forcibly moved into collective villages, ultimately wrecking the very traditions the museum undertook to preserve.

Traditional arts and crafts, including carving, weaving and pottery, are demonstrated by resident "villagers", and a blacksmith explains the intricacies of an art that has existed in East Africa for at least two millennia. The finished products are sold in the museum shop, which also stocks books and souvenirs. There's a small café serving drinks and Tanzanian food, performances of **traditional dance** (Tues–Sun 2–6pm), and storytelling sessions on Tuesday and Thursday, primarily for school groups.

by over a hundred painters, sculptors, photographers and cartoonists – much of it extraordinarily powerful as well as beautiful. The superb exhibition catalogue ("Art in Tanzania"), and its predecessors, are sold in Dar's better bookshops.

**Alliance Française** Off Ali Hassan Mwinyi Rd, next to *Las Vegas Casino* ☎022/213 1406, Ⓦwww.ambafrance-tz.org. The most energetic and relevant of the foreign cultural centres, with frequent exhibitions, music and arty gatherings, often combining Francophone African with Tanzanian artists or performers. Also has a first-floor terrace bar. Mon–Sat 8am–6pm, plus evenings for special events.
**House of Culture** National Museum, Shaaban Robert St Ⓦwww.houseofculture.or.tz. This Swedish-funded museum extension – dedicated to preserving Tanzania's traditional heritage and fostering contemporary genres – could well become the nerve centre of the city's arts scene, with exhibitions, a theatre, music studio, information centre, hands-on children's activities, an art gallery, and restaurant with traditional food. Daily 9.30am–6pm.

**La Petite Galerie** Oyster Bay Shopping Centre, Touré Drive/Ghuba Rd, Msasani Peninsula ☎022/260 1970, Ⓔygoscinny@hotmail.com. Serious contemporary paintings and sculptures, and great books. Posta–Masaki daladalas to Touré Drive, then walk 400m. Mon–Sat 10am–5.30pm, Sun 10am–4pm.
**Mawazo Gallery** *YMCA* compound, Upanga Rd ☎0784/782770, Ⓔmawazogallery@gmail.com. A leading contemporary arts centre with monthly exhibitions of high-quality original work, and with a great gift shop too. Mon–Fri 10am–5.30pm, Sat 10am–2pm.
**Wasanii Art Centre** The Slipway, Msasani Peninsula ☎0754/572503. Exhibitions often showcasing young (and hopefully upcoming) artists. Masaki–Posta daladalas to IST, then walk 1.5km. Mon–Fri 1–8pm, Sat 1–6pm.

# Shopping

As the nation's commercial capital, you'll find almost anything in Dar. For fresh produce, **markets** have the best prices: Kisutu (p.93), Kariakoo (pp.93–94) and Kivukoni (p.95). If you're up for a bit of adventure, the daily **Ilala Market** – probably Tanzania's largest – is a massive sprawl along Uhuru Street west of Kariakoo (most daladalas to Buguruni, leaving from Kariakoo, Posta and Kivukoni, pass by the entrance). It's particularly good for fabrics and clothes, whether new or secondhand. The main central **supermarkets** are listed on p.112.

## Shopping centres

To assuage a bout of homesickness, Dar's **shopping centres** duly oblige, most of them containing a selection of Western-style restaurants, fast-food outlets and bistros, plus a variety of stores, pharmacies, supermarkets or big groceries (at Western prices), internet cafés and ATM machines. The best are on Msasani Peninsula (reviewed below), and further north, including the enormous Mlimani City on Sam Nujoma Road, which also has a cinema. In the city centre, the main one is the modest Harbour View Towers, also called JM Mall, on Samora Avenue.

**Oyster Bay Shopping Centre** Touré Drive/Ghuba Rd, Oyster Bay. A nice little collection of speciality shops, including a deli, Italian ice-cream parlour, jewellery store, La Petite Galerie (see above), and *Sweet Eazy* restaurant and bar (p.105). Posta–Masaki daladalas to Touré Drive, then walk 400m.
**Sea Cliff Village** Next to *Sea Cliff Hotel*, Masaki. The biggest of the three, with plenty of expat-oriented restaurants and cafés, including a branch of South Africa's *Spur* steak house chain. Also a good bookshop. The adjacent hotel has a

bowling alley and stunning ocean views from its *Karambezi Café*. Posta–Masaki daladalas terminate here.
**The Slipway** Masaki. Facing Msasani Bay, this includes Wasanii Art Centre (see above), a good bookshop, a deli, supermarket, good restaurants (including *Azuma* Japanese, p.103), and the *Mashua* for drinks at sundown (p.104). It's also the departure point for trips to Bongoyo Island (p.114), and has an arts and crafts market at weekends. Posta–Masaki daladalas to IST, then walk 1.5km.

## Buying recorded music

For traditional music (*ngoma ya kiasili*), make for one of the **Radio Tanzania Dar es Salaam** (RTD) shops: the main one (daily 6am–4pm) is at the entrance to its studios on Nyerere Road, on the left just before the TAZARA train station (daladalas from Mnazi Mmoja or Kariakoo; ask for TAZARA), but often better stocked is the one inside Ubungo bus station (Mon–Fri 8am–3.30pm), on the first floor of the building facing Scandinavian Express' enclosure. Both sell cassettes (*kandas*) from around sixty Tanzanian tribes, plus over one hundred tapes of popular Tanzanian music from the heady days of "Twist" to the present day. The tapes (not CDs, unfortunately) cost Tsh1000 each, the quality is generally good, and the music itself – much of it no longer played – is a national treasure. Some recommendations: anything from the Gogo, Haya, Kuria or Luguru tribes.

If it's just dance music you're after, the dusty **Dar es Salaam Music & Sports House** (Mon–Fri 9am–5pm, Sat 9am–1pm) on Samora Avenue, opposite Harbour View Towers, has a great selection of classic *muziki wa dansi*.

## Souvenirs

The spread of souvenirs isn't as wide as in Arusha, but there's still plenty to choose from. Apart from the shops below, there are a couple in the departure lounge of the airport's international terminal. Art galleries (see p.107) are also good sources of souvenirs, as is the Village Museum (p.106). For **kitenges** and **kangas** (see p.65), rummage around the shops on Uhuru Street between the clock-tower and Bibi Titi Mohamed Road, or those on Nyamwezi Street south of Kariakoo Market. In November, there's the **Makutano Arts & Craft Fair** (ⓦwww.makutanotz.com, or ask at Mawazo Gallery).

**Karibu Art Gallery** Mbezi Beach area, 15km along the road to Bagamoyo. A great choice at reasonable prices, with an especially wide selection of wood carvings, including *mapiko* ("helmet masks") from the Makonde. Mwenge–Tegeta daladalas. Closed Tues.

**Mawazo Gallery** *YMCA* compound, Upanga Rd ☏0784/782770, ⓔmawazogallery @gmail.com. A fantastic selection of funky, unique souvenirs, including Wonder Welders' marvellous output (see below).

**Morogoro Stores** Haile Selassie Rd, Msasani Peninsula. It was here that Eduardo Tingatinga (p.65) first sold his work, and it's still the best place for paintings in his style, together with other crafts. Posta–Masaki daladalas.

**Mwenge Handicraft Centre** Sam Nujoma Rd, Mwenge, 12km north. Almost a hundred shops, representing the spectrum of Tanzanian arts and crafts. Especially strong on wood carvings (you can see carvers at work): Makonde and Zaramo figures, Zanzibari chests, masks, bao games, coconut shredders, even Ethiopian-style idols. Posta–Mwenge or Kariakoo–Mwenge daladalas, then walk 600m.

**Nyumba ya Sanaa (Nyerere Cultural Centre)** Ohio St, beside *Mövenpick Royal Palm*. A rather somnolent venue in which young artists can create and sell their work (mostly touristic stuff, given the adjacent hotel).

It's rather better for hands-on courses in painting, drawing, batik and printing. Traditional dances are performed Fridays at 7.30pm (Tsh2000), and there's a modest restaurant for lunch (Tsh6500 buffet). Shops Mon–Fri 8am–8pm, Sat & Sun 8am–4pm; workshops Mon–Fri 8am–3pm (free).

**The Slipway** Msasani Peninsula. Upmarket mall containing several crafts shops, and with a handicrafts bazaar on weekends (till around 6pm). Masaki–Posta daladalas to IST, then walk 1.5km.

**Tanzania Curio Shop** Bridge St/Mansfield St. Attractively poky store packed to the rafters with a mixture of pure junk and kitsch, modern souvenirs, tribal crafts, and antiques, including lovely Zanzibari silverwork. Closed Sat afternoon & Sun.

**Wonder Welders** 1372 Karume Rd, Namanga ☏022/266 6383 or 0754/051417, ⓦwww.wonderwelders.org. The artists behind some of the country's most inspired, and inspiring, souvenirs are a collective of polio victims and other disabled people, who started out producing figurines and masks from scrap metal. They also make recycled glass jewellery, handmade paper and soap, and baby-friendly wooden toys, but it's the metalwork that's utterly captivating, and, given the raw materials, unique. Posta–Masaki daladalas, then walk (signposted) from TTCL on Haile Selassie Rd. Mon–Fri 8.30am–5pm, Sat 9am–2pm.

### Bookshops

Dar's best **bookstore** is A Novel Idea (Ⓦwww.anovelideatanzania.com), which has four shops: two on Msasani Peninsula (at The Slipway and Sea Cliff Village; both Mon–Sat 10am–7pm, Sun noon–6pm); one in town (Ohio St, beside *Steers*; daily 10am–7pm); and, biggest, at Shoppers Plaza (Old Bagamoyo Rd; Mon–Sat 9.30am–7pm, Sun 9.30am–5pm). All offer a lavish spread of coffee-table tomes, novels, academic works, guidebooks and maps, but are weak on locally published titles. For these, try Dar es Salaam Bookshop or School Text Books (both east end of Makunganya St), General Publishing House (south end of Mkwepu St), or the University Bookshop at the university, but all are poorly stocked. **Secondhand** bookstalls cluster along Samora Avenue on both sides of the Askari Monument, and along the southern part of Pamba Road.

# Listings

**Air charters** Tanzanair, *Mövenpick Royal Palm*, Ohio St Ⓣ022/211 3151, Ⓦwww.tanzanair.com. Local airlines Coastal Aviation, Precisionair, Safari Airlink and ZanAir (see below) also do charters.
**Airlines (international)** For websites, see p.20. Air Malawi, see Walji's under "Travel agents"; Air Zimbabwe, see Easy Travel & Tours under "Travel agents"; British Airways, *Mövenpick Royal Palm*, Ohio St Ⓣ022/211 3820; Emirates, 6th floor, Haidery Plaza, India St/Kisutu St Ⓣ022/211 6100; Ethiopian Airlines, TDFL Building, Ohio St Ⓣ022/211 7063; Kenya Airways, Peugeot House, Bibi Titi Mohamed Rd/Upanga Rd Ⓣ022/216 3917; KLM, Peugeot House, Bibi Titi Mohamed Rd/Upanga Rd Ⓣ022/216 3914; LAM, see Walji's under "Travel agents"; Qatar Airways, Elia Complex, Bibi Titi Mohamed Rd Ⓣ022/219 8300; South African Airways, Raha Tower, Bibi Titi Mohamed Rd Ⓣ022/211 7044; Swiss, Luther House Centre, Sokoine Drive Ⓣ022/211 8871.
**Airlines (local)** For websites, see p.32. Air Excel, see Easy Travel under "Travel agents"; Air Tanzania, ATC House, Ohio St/Garden Ave Ⓣ022/211 7500; Coastal Aviation, Upanga Rd Ⓣ022/211 7959; Precisionair, Pamba Rd Ⓣ022/216 8000; Regional Air Ⓣ027/250 4164 (Arusha); Safari Airlink Ⓣ0784/237422; ZanAir, Airport Terminal 1 Ⓣ022/284 3297 or 024/223 3670 (Zanzibar).
**Airport information** Ⓣ022/284 4324.
**Ambulance** Private ambulances: Knight Support Ⓣ0754/777100 or 0784/555911 (both 24hr); Ultimate Security Ⓣ0713/123911 (24hr).
**Banks and exchange** 24hr ATMs can be found at banks all over town, inside upmarket hotels, in shopping centres, even in Kariakoo. If you're having connection problems, try the one at Stanbic, Ohio St/Samora Ave. Foreign exchange bureaux with reasonable rates that accept traveller's cheques include: Money Link, Samora Ave facing the tourist office; and Crown Forex, India St/Zanaki St. Bad rates but with good hours is Equity, inside *Mövenpick Royal Palm* (Mon–Sat 8am–8pm, Sun 10am–1pm). The only forex open on holidays is Karafuu, ground floor, Mkapa Pension Towers. Banks changing traveller's cheques without commission (taking time instead) include: National Bureau de Change, Samora Ave; NBC, Sokoine Drive/Azikiwe St.
**Car rental** The following companies are reliable and have TALA licences for national parks, but read p.30 first. Avis (Skylink Tours), TDFL Building, Ohio St Ⓣ022/211 5381, Ⓦwww.avistz.com, and at *Kilimanjaro Kempinski* Ⓣ022/212 1061; Green Car Rentals, Nkrumah St Ⓣ022/218 3718 or 0713/227788, Ⓦwww.greencars.co.tz; Hertz (formerly Leisure Tours), Nyerere Rd Ⓣ022/218 2612 or 0754/333133, Ⓔhertz@cats-net.com; Xpress Rent-A-Car (no self-drive), Haidery Plaza, India St/Kisutu St Ⓣ022/212 8356, Ⓦwww.xpresstours.org.
**Dentists** Three Crowns Swedish Dental Clinic, *Mövenpick Royal Palm*, Ohio St Ⓣ022/213 6801 or 0713/353 435.
**Embassies and consulates** Australia, represented by Canada; Burundi, 1007 Lugalo Rd, Upanga Ⓣ022/211 7615, Ⓔburundemb@raha.com; Canada, 38 Mirambo St Ⓣ022/216 3300, Ⓦwww.daressalaam.gc.ca; Ireland, 353 Touré Drive, Masaki Ⓣ022/260 2355, Ⓦwww.embassyofireland.or.tz; Kenya, 127 Mafinga St, Kinondoni Ⓣ022/266 8285, Ⓦwww.kenyahighcomtz.org; Malawi, NIC Life House, Ohio St/Sokoine Drive Ⓣ022/211 3240 or 0784/481740, Ⓔmhc@africaonline.co.tz; Mozambique, 25 Garden Ave Ⓣ022/212 4673, Ⓔembamoc.tanzania@minec.gov.mz; New Zealand, represented by High Commission in South Africa Ⓦwww.nzembassy.com; Rwanda, 32 Ali Hassan

## Moving on from Dar

You can reach almost anywhere from Dar in one or two hops; for **frequencies and journey times**, see "Travel details" at the end of this chapter. For **safaris**, see p.46.

### By bus

Dozens of bus companies operate out of Dar, almost all of them (the main exceptions being Scandinavian Express and Akamba; see below) starting at **Ubungo Bus Station**, 8km along Morogoro Road (reachable on daladalas from most central stands, including Posta). The tourist office has timetables. To be sure of getting a reliable company, and to choose your seat, buy your **ticket** two or three days before – at Ubungo, from the booths outside the station. If not, arrive at Ubungo no later than 5am.

Other than daladalas to **Bagamoyo** (for which you'll need to get to Mwenge, north of the city), the only major route that doesn't touch Ubungo is **Kilwa**, direct buses to which depart from Temeke and Mbagala districts to the south. Unfortunately, there's no single bus station for these or their ticket offices, and as you don't want to be wandering around those areas at 5am, safer and easier, if a little more expensive (you'll be charged the fare for Lindi), is to catch a bus for Lindi, Mtwara, Masasi or Nachingwea at Ubungo. Get off at Nangurukuru, from where there are frequent daladalas.

**Safety** should be paramount when choosing a bus. Companies with reputations for recklessness include Abood, Air Bus, Air Msae, Amit, Buffalo, Dar Express, Hood, Kilimanjaro Express, Mohamed Trans, Saibaba, Tashriff and Tawfiq. Takrim can be OK, but sometimes not. At the time of writing, the safest mainline operators from Dar were the following (for other destinations, consult the "moving on" boxes in the relevant chapters of this book, where recommended companies – if any – are mentioned):

**Akamba** Terminal: Msimbazi St, Kariakoo ☎022/218 5111; office also at Ubungo bus station. For Moshi, Arusha, Nairobi, extensive onward connections in Kenya, and Mwanza via Nairobi.

**Royal Coach** Office: Libya St/Mwisho St, Kisutu ☎022/212 4073; office also at Ubungo bus station. For Moshi and Arusha.

**Scandinavian Express** Terminal: Msimbazi St, Kariakoo ☎022/218 4833 or 0784/218484; also with a fenced enclosure at Ubungo bus station. For Morogoro, Dodoma, Iringa, Mbeya, Moshi, Arusha, Tanga, Mombasa, Nairobi and Kampala.

**Shabiby** Ubungo bus station ☎0754/753769. For Morogoro and Dodoma.

**Sumry** Ubungo bus station ☎022/218 0169. For Morogoro, Iringa, Mbeya, Sumbawanga and Songea.

Mwinyi Rd ☎022/212 0703, ⓦtanzania.embassy .gov.rw; South Africa, Mwaya Rd, Msasani ☎022/260 1800, ⓔsntombelal@foreign.gov.za; Uganda, 25 Msasani Rd, Msasani ☎022/266 7391, ⓔugadar@intafrica.com; UK, Umoja House, Garden Ave/Mirambo St ☎022/211 0101, ⓦukintanzania .fco.gov.uk; US, Old Bagamoyo Rd ☎022/266 8001, ⓦtanzania.usembassy.gov; Zambia, Ohio St ☎022/212 5529, ⓔzhcd@raha.com.

**Football** Tanzania's top teams, Simba and Young Africans (Yanga), both play at the fancy new National Stadium on Nelson Mandela Expressway, Mgulani. No problem buying tickets there on match day, but the difficulty is finding the schedule: in Dar,

the simplest approach is just to ask around; online, try ⓦwww.rsssf.com/tablest/tanz09.html. It might also be worth trying the federation (ⓦwww.tff-tz .org) or the sponsor (ⓦwww.vodacom.co.tz).

**Golf** Gymkhana Club's course covers both sides of Ghana Avenue, its "greens" made from sand and engine oil. Enquire at *Mövenpick Royal Palm* hotel.

**Hospitals and clinics** Best for emergencies is Aga Khan Hospital, Ocean Rd ☎022/211 5151. Also good is TMJ Hospital, Old Bagamoyo Rd, Mikocheni ☎022/270 0007. For non-urgent treatment, best is the Dutch-run IST Clinic, Inter national School of Tanganyika Campus, Ruvu St, Masaki ☎0754/783393 (24hr) or 022/260 1307.

### By train

Tanzania's railways both start in Dar. For route descriptions, schedules and sample fares, see pp.30–31. The **TAZARA Line**, to New Kapiri Mposhi in Zambia, departs from the TAZARA station, 5km west along Nyerere Road (ticket office Mon–Fri 7.30am–12.30pm & 2–4.30pm, Sat 9am–12.30pm; ☏022/286 0340). There are frequent daladalas from Posta and Kariakoo (get one marked U/Ndege, Vingunguti or Bugurini). Taxis charge Tsh10,000.

The **Central Line**, to Kigoma and Mwanza on lakes Tanganyika and Victoria respectively, starts at the station on the corner of Railway and Gerezani streets in the city centre (ticket office Mon–Fri 8am–1pm & 2–5pm, Sat & Sun 8am–1pm, and from two hours prior to departures; ☏022/211 0600, ⊚www.trctz.com).

### By boat

The **ferry terminal** is on Sokoine Drive. You can minimize the hassle from the pushy touts by buying your ticket the day beforehand (unencumbered by bags) from one of the offices to the left of the terminal entrance (definitely not from a tout); read about scams on p.60. To **Stone Town**, fastest are the *Sea Express*, *Sea Star*, *Sea Bus* and *Sepideh* (all $35 economy, $40 first-class, including port tax; 2hr–2hr 30min). Even in low season you should find sailings at 7–7.30am, 10.30am, 2pm and 4pm. Cheapest but slowest are *Flying Horse*, *Aziza* and *New Happy* ($20–25 economy, including port tax; 3hr 30min–5hr), one of which should head off daily at around noon.

For **Pemba** (via Stone Town), boats and schedules change constantly, usually three or five a week (there are more boats from Stone Town). The *Sepideh* takes around six hours ($60 economy, $70 first-class, including port tax). Other boats, if any (ask about the *Spice Islander*), leave Dar at noon to reach Mkoani at dawn.

### By plane

Dar es Salaam International Airport lies 11km southwest of the city – half an hour by road, but allow an hour in case you get stuck in heavy traffic. Domestic **flights** on light aircraft take off from Terminal 1; international flights, and domestic flights on bigger aircraft (Air Tanzania and some Precisionair routes) use Terminal 2. A $5 departure **tax** on domestic flights is payable if not included in the fare (taxes on international flights are always included). You can book directly with the airline or via a travel agent – see "Listings". A taxi from the city centre should be no more than Tsh20,000 (less than *from* the airport). Alternatively, catch a daladala: from Posta, Kariakoo or Mnazi Mmoja to U/Ndege, P/Kajiungeni or Vingunguti; or from Ubungo towards G/Uboto.

---

**Immigration** Ohio St/Ghana Ave ☏022/211 8637.
**Internet access** Viral infections aside, the most reliable places are Hotspot, Harbour View Towers, Samora Ave (Mon–Fri 6.30am–8pm, Sat 9am–8pm, Sun 9am–5pm), and Digital City, 1st floor, Mkpa Pension Towers (Mon–Fri 8am–8pm, Sat 8am–6pm). Try also the post office, Maktaba St; *Jambo Inn* and *Safari Inn*, both in Kisutu. The ones inside *Mövenpick Royal Palm* and *Kilimanjaro Kempinski* are very expensive (Tsh6000 per hr).
**Language courses** KIU, Salvation Army complex, Kilwa Rd, Mgulani, and at Nyumba ya Sanaa, Ohio St (☏022/285 1509, ⊚www.swahilicourses.com); Tanzania Swahili Language School, The Arcade,

72 Old Bagamoyo Rd, Mikocheni (☏022/277 2234, ⊚www.tanzaniaswahili.or.tz).
**Libraries** Maktaba Kuu ya Taifa (National Library), Bibi Titi Mohamed Rd (Mon–Fri 9am–6pm; Tsh500 per hr day). The library of the Wildlife Conservation Society of Tanzania, Garden Ave (Mon–Fri 8.30am–4.30pm), is for environmental and ecological matters.
**Maps** The Surveys & Mapping Division, Kivukoni Front (Mon–Fri 8am–3.30pm; ☏022/212 4575), has 1:50,000 plans of the country suitable for hiking.
**Optician** Eyeline, Sewa St ☏022/212 1869.
**Pharmacies** Harbour View Towers and Mkapa Pension Towers both have pharmacies (Mon–Fri plus Sat mornings). On Sundays, basic pharmacies

are open in Kariakoo, for example along Mkunguni St. Open 24/7 is the pharmacy inside Ebrahim Haji Health Centre, Asia St ☎022/211 4995.

**Police** Emergencies ☎112. To report theft and deal with insurance paperwork, Central Police Station, Sokoine Drive ☎022/211 7362.

**Post and couriers** Main post office on Maktaba St. Courier: DHL, Peugeot House, Bibi Titi Mohamed Rd/Upanga Rd ☎022/211 3171 (Mon–Fri 8am–6pm, Sat 8am–2pm).

**Supermarkets** The most central are City Supermarket (Harbour View Towers, Samora Ave; daily 9am–7.30pm); Imalaseko (Pamba House, Garden Ave/Pamba Rd; Mon–Fri 9am–7pm, Sat–Sun 10am–4pm); and PATCO (1st floor, Mkapa Pension Towers, Maktaba St; Mon–Sat 8am–8pm).

**Swimming pools** Central hotels restrict their pools to overnight guests. Day-trippers can choose from *Mikadi Beach Camp* 2km south of Kigamboni ferry (p.92; Tsh5000); *Golden Tulip Hotel* on Msasani Peninsula (p.91; Tsh10,000); and the enjoyably outrageous Wet 'n' Wild water park at Kunduchi Beach (see below; Tsh5500).

**Telephones** TTCL, Bridge St, off Samora Ave (Mon–Fri 7.45am–midnight, Sat & Sun 8.30am–midnight).

**Travel agents** Easy Travel & Tours, Raha Tower, Bibi Titi Mohamed Rd ☎022/212 1747, ⓦ www .easytravel.co.tz; Rickshaw Travels, *Mövenpick Royal Palm*, Ohio St ☎022/213 7275, ⓦ www.rickshawtz .com; Walji's Travel, Zanaki St/Makunganya St ☎022/211 0321, ⓦ www.waljistravel.com.

# Jangwani and Kunduchi beaches

Dar's main beach strips start 20km north of the city, and benefit from resort-style hotels and tons of activities, including boat trips, snorkelling, or diving around the islands of Dar es Salaam Marine Reserve. Sadly, a series of break-waters intended to hinder erosion appear to be having the opposite effect, and don't do much for the beach paradise illusion either, so if you're up for a longer beach stay, you'd be better off on Zanzibar, or at Pangani, covered in chapter 2.

The liveliest resort strip, attracting city folk in need of a little pampering, is **JANGWANI**. To its north, separated by an inlet, is **KUNDUCHI**, which comes complete with the astonishingly brash **Wet 'n' Wild** waterpark (Tsh5500; closed Mon), with over twenty water slides and tubes, seven swimming pools, and reams of other activities (at additional cost) including kite-surfing, jet-skiing, beach buggies, slot machines and even a go-kart track. In complete contrast, and just 600m north of Wet 'n' Wild, are the infrequently visited **Kunduchi ruins**, comprising a sixteenth-century mosque and various other remains set in a grove of baobabs and bushes, together with graves dating from the eighteenth and nineteenth centuries. The gravestones are of particular interest: many bear distinctive obelisk-like pillars; others are ornately carved from coral ragstone, and inset with blue-and-white Chinese porcelain bowls – one of the few sites where the bowls are still in their original setting. Their presence is a reminder of the scope of the Indian Ocean's monsoon-driven dhow trading network, now long gone. Unfortunately, the site has been known for muggers, so the safest access is by car (ask for the *magofu*, "ruins"). If you want to try walking, get a reliable local to escort you, or ask at the police station in Mtongani, 1.7km from the Bagamoyo road and 2km from the site: it's an informal arrangement for which a decent tip is in order.

## Arrival

The access roads to the beaches start on the road to Bagamoyo. With the exception of Wet 'n' Wild and *Kunduchi Beach Hotel*, which have daladalas right outside (Mwenge–Kunduchi), access is either expensive or awkward, not favouring frequent trips into Dar. **Taxis** charge Tsh25,000 from the city centre. You can slash the cost by covering most of the route by **daladala**:

Posta–Mwenge then Mwenge–Tegeta, or Kariakoo–Tegeta, getting off at the signposted turnings for the beaches, from where you'll need a taxi (Tsh4000–5000), a *bajaji* rickshaw (Tsh2000–3000), or a bicycle "taxi" (Tsh500–1000). Don't walk.

## Accommodation, eating and drinking

Given that walking unaccompanied on the access roads away from the hotels isn't too safe, **eating and drinking** – unless you hire a bicycle – is mainly limited to restaurants and bars inside hotels, and to the two water parks. The following **hotels** can arrange trips to Mbudya Island for snorkelling (p.114), and scuba diving through Sea Breeze Marine (p.114). The **campsite** at *Silver Sands Hotel* ($3 per person) has good security and clean showers.

**Beachcomber Hotel Resort** Jangwani Beach, 4.5km from the Bagamoyo road ☎022/264 7772, ⓦwww.beachcomber.co.tz. A relatively informal package-tour place, with an airy and cheerful design (side-on sea views from most rooms, though), but suffering from a ragged beach (one too many breakwaters), and rather ragged rooms too. Has plenty of amenities, including a huge pool, a good restaurant, and kids' activities. BB ❻

**Kunduchi Beach Hotel & Resort** Kunduchi Beach, 3km from the Bagamoyo road ☎022/265 0050, ⓦwww.kunduchiresort.com. Once threatened by erosion, this reopened in 2005 as a huge and, well, kitsch resort complete with spanking new beach (made from sand dredged from who knows where), and an obsession with providing as many facilities as possible, including countless watersports, several restaurants and bars, and a huge free-form swimming pool (and that's on top of the adjacent Wet 'n' Wild water park). Most of the 200 rooms and apartments are sea-facing, and there's plenty for kids, starting with a crèche. BB ❼

**Silver Sands Hotel** Kunduchi Beach, 4.2km from the Bayamoyo road ☎022/265 0567,

ⓦwww.silversandshotel.co.tz. The oldest of the north coast hotels, still ambling along after almost five decades. It's extremely good value, and its campsite makes it a popular port of call for overland tour trucks. As well as rooms (all a/c, some with TV), there are four-bed dorms with nets and shared bathrooms. Facilities include a bar and beachside restaurant, swimming pool, 400m of beach (cut by breakwaters), a snorkelling centre, and excursions, best being the trip to Kunduchi-Pwani village and the Kunduchi ruins, followed by a dhow sail to Mbudya Island for snorkelling. BB ❹

**White Sands Hotel & Resort** Jangwani Beach, 4.2km from the Bagamoyo road ☎022/264 7620, ⓦwww.hotelwhitesands.com. On the beach, this has well-equipped rooms with sea-view verandas (only complaint: some views are obscured by trees, so get one on top and away from the main building). There's a large octagonal pool, a dive centre, several bars and restaurants, theme nights, and a great Sunday lunch at the beach café with spit-roast lamb, live music and acrobats. Also has a flashy nightclub (Fri & Sat). Transfer from Dar included. BB ❼

# Gezaulole

Fourteen kilometres south of Dar es Salaam, beyond Mikadi and Mjimwema beaches, is the coastal settlement of **GEZAULOLE**, a cosmopolitan little place thanks to its having been a "collective village" during President Nyerere's Ujamaa experiment and, earlier, an entrepôt for ivory and slaves. Its inhabitants nowadays survive on agriculture, fishing, and some seaweed harvesting, but it looks like the old days are numbered: developers have already dumped an upmarket housing estate on the place, and more is likely to follow. For the time being, the reason to visit is a sadly neglected **cultural tourism programme**, whose health you should enquire about in Dar before setting out: contact Mr Kimonge Oriyo, AGRIS, 2nd floor, TANCOT House, Sokoine Drive (☎0732/323163 or 0713/323163, ⓔkonsult@cats-net.com), facing the *Luther House Centre*. Should it still be kicking, several options are possible, including – besides merely chilling out – **dhow trips** to the uninhabited islands of Sinda

## Dar es Salaam Marine Reserve

The reefs and islands of Bongoyo, Mbudya, Pangavini and Fungu Yasini north of the city are part of **Dar es Salaam Marine Reserve** (entry fees included in the cost of trips; ⓦwww.marineparktz.com). Despite heavy damage from dynamite fishing, the reefs still have plenty of underwater interest, and with lovely **beaches**, they're the perfect get-away from Dar.

### Boat trips and snorkelling

**Snorkelling** conditions are best around **Mbudya Island**, 3km off Kunduchi Beach, which has shady casuarinas, baobabs and palms, and a population of endangered coconut crabs. Underwater, you might see butterfly fish, sweet lips, giant clams, octopus and, with luck, either hawksbill or green turtles. Enterprising locals sell barbecued fish (and chips, if you like), sodas, and sometimes beer; hence the island's nickname, "Mini Bar". You can also rent *bandas* for the day. Trips by motorboat are run by the *Mediterraneo* hotel on Kawe Beach (p.91), Sea Breeze Marine on Jangwani Beach (see below), and *Silver Sands Hotel* on Kunduchi Beach (p.113), and can also be booked at hotels in the area. Count on around Tsh20,000 per person for a half-day's snorkelling in a party of four; if there are fewer of you, go at the weekend, when you won't have to wait long for other punters to turn up.

Msasani Peninsula's The Slipway shopping centre is the starting point for trips to **Bongoyo Island**, popular with picnickers at weekends. The island has some nature trails, and good snorkelling (equipment can be bought at The Slipway). Snacks, drinks and grilled fish (around Tsh7000) are available, and you can rent deck chairs and *bandas*. Motorized dhows (Tsh16,000 return) push off at 9.30am, 11.30am and 1.30pm for the 6km, thirty-minute crossing, returning at 12.30pm, 2.30pm and 5pm.

### Scuba diving

The **scuba diving reefs** are in mixed condition, having suffered from dynamite fishing in the 1990s before the reserve was created. **Fungu Yasini** is easiest to visit, and has a wide variety of corals (down to 40m), home to all sorts of smaller fish (including oddities such as crocodile fish, lionfish and pufferfish), a surprising variety of colourful nudibranchs (sea slugs), but also a lot of coral-devouring crown-of-thorns starfish. **Big T Reef** (Mbudya Patches), further out, is in better shape, so you're more likely to see large pelagic species, including kingfish and tuna, perhaps even bull sharks or white-tipped reef sharks. Whales have on occasion also been sighted, or heard. Advanced divers can relish a rarely undertaken **wreck dive** – the *Schlammerstadt*, scuttled in Oyster Bay in 1908 following a fire.

The main **dive centre**, safety conscious and with good equipment, is Sea Breeze Marine at *White Sands Hotel*, Jangwani Beach (☎0754/783241, ⓦwww.seabreeze marine.org), who have Nitrox facilities for experienced divers, and offer an array of PADI courses, including Open Water ($380) and Dive Master ($650).

---

and Latham (Tsh15,000–20,000 per boat), both with superb beaches and snorkelling (bring your own equipment). There's also a thought-provoking **historical walk**. The village's first inhabitants were Zaramo fishermen who used the site as a temporary camp. After a while they decided to settle permanently and so – according to legend – asked their soothsayer for advice. He chillingly ordered a young virgin be buried alive, and added, "then *gezaulole* (try and see) whether you can stay here". The walk includes the unfortunate girl's tomb, and some early Muslim graves nestling – as in so many other coastal sites – in the shade of a majestic old baobab tree.

## Practicalities

**Access** is by ferry from Dar to Kigamboni, then by daladala past a series of villages set amidst thick coconut, banana and mango plantations. The vehicles run roughly hourly from 7am to 6pm. On arrival, follow the signs for *Kim Beach & Kampsite*. Given the quasi-abandoned state of the project, **costs** for most things are negotiable (but reasonable): bicycle rental should be around Tsh3000 a day, camel rides about the same, and a **guide** for half a day shouldn't be more than Tsh10,000. Basic **rooms** (❶) are available, and you can **camp** at *Kim Beach & Kampsite* (Tsh3000: bring a tent). **Meals** are provided by local families: Tsh4000 a head would be just dandy.

# The Pugu Hills

Until the sixteenth century, much of the seaboard from Somalia to Mozambique was covered by forest. Watered by ten million years of metronomic Indian Ocean monsoons, the forests were incredibly rich and diverse ecosystems. Sadly, population pressure over the last few centuries has decimated them, leaving only a few isolated patches, of which Tanzania's Amani Nature Reserve (chapter 5) and Kenya's Arabuko-Sokoke Forest are the best preserved. Up to fifty years ago, the **PUGU HILLS**, 25km southwest of Dar es Salaam, might have rivalled them, its forests at that time extending to within 10km of the city, and providing a habitat for lions, cheetahs, leopards and hyenas, hippos and black-and-white colobus monkeys, all of which have since disappeared. Indeed, despite official "protection" as two forest reserves, the **destruction** of Pugu Hills' forests is a case study in how *not* to go about preserving places of exceptional biodiversity: corruption, obstinate bureaucracy, poverty, and demand for cheap charcoal having conspired to eliminate almost every last acre of Pugu's primary forests, and conservation projects have now been abandoned.

Lest all this sound depressing, cheer up: Pugu's secondary and tertiary forests still contain a good variety of trees and birds, and unusual **mammals**, too, including giant elephant shrews, monkeys, bush pigs and banded mongooses. Suni antelopes and duikers can also be seen, and bush babies at night. Entering the forest reserves (Pugu and Kazimzumbwi) *legally* is next to impossible without oodles of time to navigate the bureaucratic obstacles between you and the $30 permit, but you can visit the privately managed **Pugu Hills Nature Centre**, just outside Pugu Forest Reserve's eastern boundary (reservations essential, even for day-trips; ☎0754/565498, ⓦ www.puguhills.com). A gem of a place, the centre is involved in environmental education, and has been busy planting trees representative of Pugu's original forest, and from the rest of Tanzania. Good excuses for **hikes** include a few surviving patches of original forest just outside the reserves, a viewpoint over Dar es Salaam (on clear days), an enjoyably lively cattle market, and local villages and schools, including Pugu Secondary School, where Nyerere taught before becoming President.

## Practicalities

**Access** is via Pugu Kajiungeni village, 12km beyond the airport; Kariakoo–P/Kajiungeni **daladalas** go direct, and Kariakoo–Kisarawe ones pass by. Getting off at Pugu Kajiungeni's petrol station, continue 200m along the surfaced main road (ie towards Kisarawe), then turn left on to a small track crossing a stream. Asking for "Bwana Kiki" will get you to the football field beside the centre after some fifteen minutes. If you're **driving**, or fancy a longer walk, turn left at Pugu

Kajiungeni before its petrol station, on to the signposted asphalt road for Chanika. A dirt road on your right, 1km along (150m before the rail crossing) takes you to the nature centre (1.5km).

The centre's Tsh2000 entry fee includes use of their swimming pool, and the **restaurant** rustles up excellent meals (around $10). Staying overnight, you can **camp** ($7 per person), or splash out on an enchanting **banda**: four luxurious open-sided bamboo huts on stilts (BB ❺), one of them with a "sultan bath" for you and your partner. If these are out of your league, Pugu Kajiungeni village has basic **guesthouses** (❶).

# Travel details

See the box on pp.110–111 for more information on moving on from Dar.

## Buses

Most bus services peter out by noon or early afternoon, so "hourly" in the frequencies below refers to services up to that time. Asterisks denote routes prone to delays or closure during heavy rains (for the road south of Dar, this is a 50km stretch south of the Rufiji River, set to be asphalted by 2011/2012).

**Dar** to: Arusha (20 daily; 9hr); Bagamoyo (hourly; 1hr); Dodoma (hourly; 6–8hr); Ifakara (3 daily; 7hr); Iringa (hourly; 6–7hr); Kampala (2–3 daily; 26hr); Karatu (2 daily; 12hr); Kilwa (2–3 daily; 5–6hr); Kyela (4 daily; 13hr); Lindi (3–4 daily*; 9hr); Lushoto (3–5 daily; 5hr); Mahenge (2 daily*; 12hr); Mang'ula (2 daily; 6hr); Masasi (3–4 daily; 11–12hr); Mbeya (10 daily; 11–12hr); Mombasa (3 daily*; 9–11hr); Morogoro (1–2 hourly; 2hr 45min); Moshi (20 daily; 8–9hr); Mtwara (3–4 daily*; 10hr); Musoma via Kenya (2 daily; 21–24hr); Mwanza via Kenya (2 daily; 24–27hr); Mwanza via Singida (4 daily*; 32–34hr); Nairobi (4 daily; 12–14hr); Newala (daily*; 11–12hr); Njombe (5 daily; 9hr); Singida (2 daily*; 13–16hr); Songea (3 daily; 9–11hr); Tanga (6–8 daily; 6hr).

## Trains

Central Line trains currently leave Dar on Tuesday, Friday and Sunday (not to Mwanza) at 5pm.
**Dar (Central Line)** to Dodoma (13hr); Kigoma (36hr 30min); Morogoro (6hr); Mwanza (36hr 30min); Singida via Dodoma or Manyoni (24hr); Tabora (23hr 30min).

**Dar (TAZARA)** to: Kisaki, for Selous (Tues & Fri; 4hr); Mang'ula, for Udzungwa (Fri; 7hr); Mbeya (Tues & Fri; 20hr); New Kapiri Mposhi, Zambia (Tues; 38hr).

## Ferries

**Dar** to: Pemba (3–5 weekly but unreliable; 6hr or overnight); Stone Town (5–9 daily; 2–5hr).

## Flights

Airline codes used below are: AE (Air Excel), AT (Air Tanzania), CA (Coastal Aviation), PA (Precisionair), SA (Safari Airlink), TA (Tropical Air), and ZA (ZanAir). Where more than one airline flies to the same destination, the one with most frequent flights and/ or shortest journey times is listed first.

**Dar** to: Arusha (PA, ZA, CA, AE: 6 daily; 1hr 15min–2hr 30min); Dodoma (CA: daily; 4hr); Kigoma (PA, AT: 1–2 daily; 3hr 10min); Kilimanjaro (PA, AT: 4–5 daily; 1hr–1hr 15min); Kilwa (CA: daily; 1hr 10min); Mafia (CA, TA: 2 daily; 30min); Manyara (CA: daily; 4hr); Mikumi (SA: daily; 30min); Mtwara (AT, PA: 1–2 daily; 1hr); Musoma (PA: 4 weekly; 2hr 10min); Mwanza (AT, PA, CA: 4–5 daily; 1hr 30min–3hr); Ngorongoro (CA: daily; 4hr 15min); Pangani (SA: daily; 40min); Pemba (ZA, CA: 3–4 daily; 1hr–1hr 30min); Ruaha (CA, SA: 2 daily; 2hr 30min); Saadani (SA: daily; 20min); Selous (CA, SA, ZA: 4 daily; 45min); Serengeti (ZA, CA: 2 daily; 3hr 30min–6hr); Tabora (AT, PA: 1–2 daily; 2–3hr); Tanga (CA: daily; 1hr 35min); Zanzibar (CA, ZA, PA, AT, SA, TA, AE: hourly; 20–25min).

# The north coast

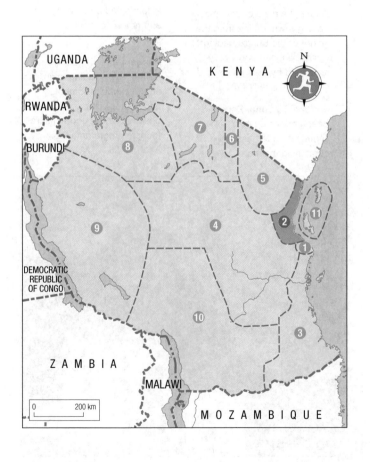

CHAPTER 2    # Highlights

✱ **Bagamoyo** A major slaving port in the nineteenth century, its name meaning "lay down my heart". Atmospheric and poignant, it's now the heart of a lively arts scene. See p.119

✱ **Kaole** The ruins of a medieval trading town, dating from the height of the Shirazi trading civilization, and now partly reclaimed by mangroves and the ocean. See p.128

✱ **Saadani National Park** Beach meets bush; a shoreline wilderness combining marine, savanna, forest and riverine environments. See p.130

✱ **Amboni Caves** Winding passageways, dripping stalactites, colonies of bats, an assortment of unlikely legends and a nearby forest and hot-water springs. See p.139

✱ **Pangani** Like Bagamoyo, a former slave-trading town, and delightfully somnolent and decrepit. It has superb beaches, and a good cultural tourism programme too. See p.142

▲ Holy Ghost Mission, Bagamoyo

# 2

# The north coast

N orth of Dar es Salaam the beach resorts give way to a string of little-visited fishing villages interspersed by mangrove forests and sweeping sandy beaches that have been largely overlooked by tourism: the Sirenic charms of Zanzibar, just offshore, have seen to that. But there is plenty to enjoy, and not just beaches. **Bagamoyo**, the first major settlement north from Dar, is a hugely atmospheric town. In the nineteenth century it was East Africa's foremost slaving port, from which time there are many picturesque reminders, and German colonial remains, too. Heading back further in time, the nearby ruins of **Kaole** hint at the luxuries of coastal life almost eight centuries ago.

North of Bagamoyo, **Saadani National Park** combines the pleasures of beaches with wildlife, whether on game drives, bush walks, or in a boat. It also has a cultural tourism programme, as does the chilled-out fishing village of **Pangani**. It's the only place on the mainland to seriously rival Zanzibar as a beach destination, with a string of attractive, small-scale hotels on near-deserted strands either side of town. Pangani also offers boat tours, snorkelling, scuba diving, and a scatter of ruins related to slavery and colonialism. Closer to Kenya, the harbour town of **Tanga** has been in gradual decline for over half a century, which may turn out to have been a blessing in disguise: the lack of building development has left its colonial centre largely intact, making it one of Tanzania's prettiest towns. It's also a handy base for visiting Amani Nature Reserve (chapter 5) and, closer in, the Amboni **cave complex**, and extensive **Shirazi ruins** at Tongoni.

There's **public transport** between Dar and Bagamoyo, and – along the highway running inland – from Dar to Tanga, from where you can catch onward transport to Pangani. Getting to and around Saadani is easiest in a private vehicle or on safari, but can be done by daladala and pick-up. Note that the road north from Bagamoyo to Saadani is blocked at the Wami River, whose rope-pulled ferry, washed away in the 1997–98 El Niño floods, was never replaced. A bridge is planned for 2010, and should be worth asking about in Dar or Bagamoyo.

## Bagamoyo and around

Set on a beautiful mangrove-fringed bay 72km north of Dar, tumbledown **BAGAMOYO** makes an attractive day-trip, and has enough of interest to reward longer stays, too. Now little more than a large village, it positively wallows in its sordid past, when, in the nineteenth century, it was East Africa's

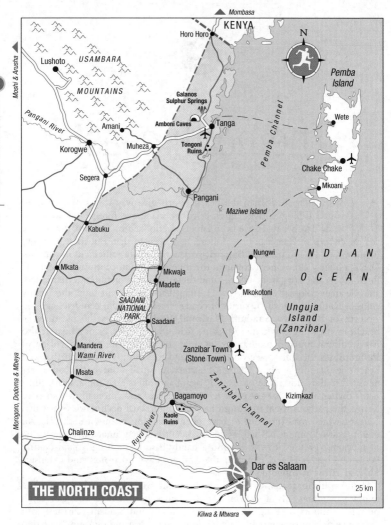

main port for the ivory and slave trade. Bagamoyo's wealth of buildings from those times are gradually, very gradually being restored (too slowly for some, alas, which have already collapsed). The town is not, incidentally, a World Heritage Site, as often claimed: corruption and bureaucracy are likely to keep it on UNESCO's "tentative" list for the foreseeable future.

Theoretically, Bagamoyo also has the ingredients for a good **beach holiday**, but there's no swimming at low tide, muggings are not unheard of, and with better stretches of sand at Pangani to the north, and on Zanzibar, it really doesn't stand a chance. As such, most beach hotels concentrate on corporate shindigs and conferences. Should you take a liking to the place (and there are some good hotels), the town's **arts scene** is vibrant, and with time you can go bird-watching or hippo-spotting on the **Ruvu River**, or explore the medieval ruins of **Kaole** nearby.

## Some history

Bagamoyo's proximity to Zanzibar, 42km away, is key to the town's historical importance. During the eighteenth and nineteenth centuries, trade in the western Indian Ocean was controlled by Zanzibar's Busaïdi Sultanate, which became one of the wealthiest dynasties Africa has ever seen. Their riches stemmed from the export of goods from the mainland, especially **slaves and ivory**, which were exchanged for cotton, beads and other manufactured goods. An estimated 769,000 slaves were transported from the East African coast during the nineteenth century, most of whom passed through Bagamoyo, which served as the major caravan terminus for routes from Lake Tanganyika and Lake Victoria, both over 1000km away. Countless more died, uncounted, along the caravan routes long before reaching the ocean.

Given its trading links, Bagamoyo was a logical starting or ending point for many a European foray into the "dark continent". Stanley, Burton, Speke and Grant all passed through, as did a number of Christian missionaries and, most famously, the body of David Livingstone. In the 1880s, following the groundwork laid by explorers and missionaries, the European **colonization** of East Africa began in earnest, and for the Germans – who had been accorded the territories

### The Abushiri War

Before the European conquest, northern Tanganyika's coastal strip was ostensibly ruled by Zanzibar. In reality, though, only in **Bagamoyo** – the most important slaving port – was Zanzibari dominion assured, thanks to a much-feared garrison of **Baluch mercenaries** from Oman. So when the British forced Zanzibar's Sultan Barghash to ban the sea-borne slave trade in 1873, it was Bagamoyo that took the hit. For Bagamoyo's more independently minded rivals, **Pangani and Saadani**, the following fifteen years proved to be immensely profitable.

Saadani's leader was **Bwana Heri**, a slave trader from the Zigua tribe whose influence stretched as far as Unyamwezi (Tabora). A missionary writing in 1877 described slave caravans passing daily into Saadani, each with a hundred children in chains. With the profits, Bwana Heri bought arms with which to tighten his grip on power. He would need them. In November 1884, **Karl Peters**, charged with securing German interests in Tanganyika (part of Germany's spoils from the "scramble for Africa"), set off from Saadani to strike a series of bogus treaties with tribal chiefs, effectively grabbing their land. Bit by bit, Bwana Heri's influence over the interior was usurped, but it was not until 1888 that he and other slaving magnates, notably **Abushiri ibn Salim al-Harthi**, a wealthy Arab trader in Pangani, began to see their political and economic might directly threatened, when Zanzibar's sultan granted Germany the right to extract customs duties on the mainland.

With local passions already inflamed by the desecration of a Pangani mosque by German soldiers and dogs, and various other instances of perceived arrogance, Saadani and Pangani erupted in **popular rebellion**, and by September 1888, the Germans had been expelled from all but two enclaves – Dar and Bagamoyo. The German response took time to arrive, but was brutal. In April 1889, **Major Hermann von Wissmann** and an army comprised mostly of Sudanese Nubians and South African Zulus began the first major assault of the **Abushiri War**. Saadani was bombarded and taken in June and Pangani followed in July. Fleeing inland, Bwana Heri built a series of forts, each destroyed by the pursuing Germans, until he surrendered in April 1890. Abushiri, for his part, lost control of the rebellion in November 1888, half a year before the German attack, and began a futile six-month siege of Germany's colonial capital, Bagamoyo. He was captured in December 1889 and hanged at Pangani. His **grave** is unknown: it's possibly in the garden of Pangani's *Pangadeco Bar*, or in the mass graves uncovered at Pangani's Boma.

now comprising Tanganyika, Burundi and Rwanda – Bagamoyo was an obvious choice for the capital of German East Africa. It was a status it enjoyed for less than a decade, as the **Abushiri War** of 1888–89 (see p.121) prompted the Germans to shift their capital to Dar es Salaam. Bagamoyo continued as provincial capital, but with the slave and ivory trades at an end, and with Bagamoyo's shallow harbour eclipsed by new facilities at Dar es Salaam, Tanga and Mombasa, the town entered a long period of economic decline from which, as any glance at the old town's crumbling buildings will tell, it has yet to escape.

## Arrival and information

Bagamoyo is an hour's drive by **daladala** from Dar's Mwenge terminal (Tsh2000; throughout the day). The town's **bus and daladala station** is southwest of the centre, on the same road as NMB Bank. Some tourists walking from there to the beach hotels, 2–4km away, have been mugged in the past, so use **taxis** (around Tsh3000) or motorized **rickshaws** (Tsh1500).

The town's unofficial **tourist office**, at the end of the road in from Dar (daily 8am–8pm; ☏0784/869652, ✉bagamoyo2007@gmail.com), is primarily a feeder for guides. Short **tours** within town or to Kaole are overpriced, but half- and full-day trips (minimum two people) are a more reasonable $25 per person, and include some cultural tourism and visits to a traditional healer. They can also arrange Kiswahili lessons. Guides are also available inside the Old Fort, but don't hire anyone on the street.

The Roman Catholic Mission Museum (p.124) is well informed about historical matters, and has several good books and booklets for sale. The best **website** is ⓦwww.bagamoyo.com, with unmatched historical coverage, and reasonably up-to-date practical information.

## Accommodation

Most **beach hotels** garner their business from conferences, which means they're either full of paunchy execs on expense accounts, or resoundingly empty – but always expensive. There are some nice exceptions, though, and plenty of basic **guesthouses** in town, especially at the west end of Uhuru Road and around. **Camping** is possible at *Travellers Lodge* ($12 per person) and, with no fixed prices, at *Bagamoyo Beach Resort* and *Moyo Mmoja Guesthouse*.

### Town centre

**Kizota Guest House** Uhuru Rd. A comfortable if basic choice, with box nets, fans, and clean shared bathrooms (hot water in buckets). ❶

 **Moyo Mmoja Guesthouse** 400m southeast of the post office (signposted)

☏023/244 0236, ✉guesthouse@moyommoja.org, ⓦwww.moyommoja.org. Ten minutes from the beach, this is the best budget choice, with a nice homely feel. There's a big garden, a fully equipped kitchen (they can provide meals), and six rooms: three in the main house and three more in a couple of cosy

---

### Bagamoyo: lay down my heart

The name "**Bagamoyo**" derives from *bwaga* (to put down) and *moyo* (heart). As exact meaning in Kiswahili depends upon the context in which it is spoken, so there are two theories behind the name. The first contends the words were uttered by slaves on reaching the coast, where the impending sea voyage to Zanzibar crushed any lingering hopes of escape. For them, Bagamoyo meant "crush your heart". More likely, however, is that the words were spoken by caravan porters on arriving from the interior. For them, *bwaga moyo* was a place to "lay down the burden of your heart" – an expression of relief.

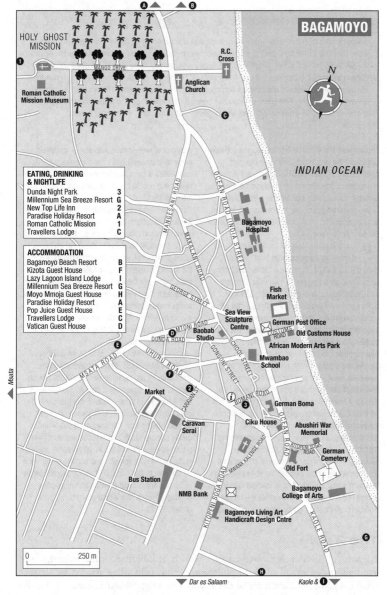

**BAGAMOYO**

HOLY GHOST MISSION

Roman Catholic Mission Museum

MANGO DRIVE

R.C. Cross

Anglican Church

*N*

INDIAN OCEAN

**EATING, DRINKING & NIGHTLIFE**
| | |
|---|---|
| Dunda Night Park | 3 |
| Millennium Sea Breeze Resort | G |
| New Top Life Inn | 2 |
| Paradise Holiday Resort | A |
| Roman Catholic Mission | 1 |
| Travellers Lodge | C |

**ACCOMMODATION**
| | |
|---|---|
| Bagamoyo Beach Resort | B |
| Kizota Guest House | F |
| Lazy Lagoon Island Lodge | I |
| Millennium Sea Breeze Resort | G |
| Moyo Mmoja Guest House | H |
| Paradise Holiday Resort | A |
| Pop Juice Guest House | E |
| Travellers Lodge | C |
| Vatican Guest House | D |

Bagamoyo Hospital

MANGESANI ROAD

MAFALANI ROAD

OCEAN ROAD (INDIA STREET)

GEORGE STREET

Fish Market

Sea View Sculpture Centre

Baobab Studio

German Post Office

Old Customs House

MTONI ROAD

DUNDA ROAD

MSATA ROAD

UHURU ROAD

CARAVAN ST.

SCHOOL STREET

GONGONI STREET

BOMANI ROAD

African Modern Arts Park

Mwambao School

Market

Caravan Serai

Ciku House

German Boma

Abushiri War Memorial

KITOPENI SOGA ROAD

German Cemetery

MWANA KALENGE ROAD

Old Fort

Bus Station

NMB Bank

Bagamoyo Living Art Handicraft Design Cntre

Bagamoyo College of Arts

KAOLE ROAD

| | |
|---|---|
| 0 | 250 m |

▲ Msata

▼ Dar es Salaam

Kaole & ▼

tribal-style garden huts. All are cheerfully decorated, have fans and box nets. Profits fund programs for orphans and vulnerable children. Book ahead. ❷

**Pop Juice Guest House** Msata Rd ☎023/244 0318. A perfectly decent cheapie, with basic clean rooms with or without bathrooms (squat toilets). Can be noisy. ❶

**Vatican Guest House** Dunda Rd. Similar to *Pop Juice*, also with some en-suite rooms. ❶

## Along the beach

**Bagamoyo Beach Resort** ☎023/244 0083 or 0754/588969, ✉bbr@baganet.com. Run by a French couple and their friendly staff, this is

## Staying safe

Bagamoyo's chronic unemployment explains the pilfering of carved doors and stones from historic buildings, and the town's sorry reputation for **muggers and touts**. Areas to be wary of (in other words, don't carry valuables, wear fancy clothes or flashy footwear) include beaches away from hotels, places near mangroves, the fish market in the afternoon when the dhows return, the road to Kaole, and, unfortunately, almost anywhere at night. The local police don't give a monkey's, so the onus is on you: catch a taxi or *bajaji* to your hotel, and when going out carry only what you'll need.

popular with families. The eighteen rooms are well back from the beach but have large box nets, comfy beds, big patios and a/c. There are also four cheap beach *bandas* lacking bathrooms but with fantastic views. Amenities include a (not always clean) swimming pool, bar and restaurant, internet, boat trips, sailing, windsurfing, and even minigolf. BB *bandas* ❸, rooms ❹

🎿 **Lazy Lagoon Island Lodge** Near Kaole, 6km from Bagamoyo by boat, 10km by road ☎0784/237422, ⓦwww.tanzaniasafaris .info. Snug as a bug on its own island replete with bushbabies, wild pigs, genets, baboons, duiker and suni antelopes, this British-run place oozes opulence – and though expensive, is excellent value, and perfect for lovers. The main building is a spectacular vaulted affair; bedrooms are in twelve wood-and-thatch sea-facing cottages with hammocks and lofts (great for kids). The wonderfully designed restaurant and bar have panoramic views, and there's a swimming pool, not that you need one with all that beach around. The price includes kayaking, sailing and snorkelling. FB ❽

**Millennium Sea Breeze Resort** 200m beyond Bagamoyo College of Arts ☎023/244 0201, ⓦwww.millennium.co.tz. The most characterful and welcoming of the conference-style places, on the town's best stretch of sand (shared with locals, except – if the guards remain vigilant – hustlers). Holiday-makers won't go far wrong – rooms are in a cluster of well-spaced, two-storey rondavels, some with (shared) sea-view balconies, all a/c, and there's a good beachside restaurant, swimming pool, a couple of bars, disco, and internet. BB ❺–❻

**Paradise Holiday Resort** 600m north of the Anglican church ☎023/244 0000, ⓦwww .paradiseresort.net. Shoehorned into a narrow plot, this is the most luxurious of the north-end resorts, albeit impersonal, with over eighty rooms. Avoid the small "standard" ones overlooking the car park; better are the well-appointed "deluxe" ones, some with ocean views. Has a big swimming pool, tennis court, fitness centre, internet, bars, and excellent cuisine. Activities include windsurfing, and dhow trips for snorkelling or poking around the Ruvu River mouth. BB ❻

🎿 **Travellers Lodge** ☎023/244 0077 or 0754/855485, ⓦwww.travellers-lodge .com. Run by an engaging German/South African couple, this is Bagamoyo's best mid-range hotel, and a bargain to boot – indeed, the friendly and easy-going atmosphere, lush gardens (with an improbable but true 131 species of palm) and gently sloping sandy beach recommends it over pricier options. Rooms are in 26 attractive en-suite cottages, all with veranda and a/c, the better ones on the beach. The bar and restaurant (great break-fasts) has some mind-blowing Makonde-style carvings; there's also a wild playground. Book ahead. BB ❺

# The Town

Bagamoyo's history is embodied in a wealth of buildings, some ruined, some achingly poignant, all of them photogenic, especially when framed by slender coconut palms and glimpses of the ocean. The town's historic centre is locally called Mji Mkongwe – "Stone Town."

## Holy Ghost Mission and Museum

At the north end of town in what used to be a slave-worked coconut plantation, the Catholic **Holy Ghost Mission** occupies a series of whitewashed buildings whose plain appearance belies their historical importance. Also called **Freedom Village**, the mission was founded in 1868 by French missionaries instructed to spend as much as they could on buying slaves their freedom. Although the immediate impact was limited to a few hundred souls, the moral boost it gave the Abolitionary movement may well have heralded the beginning of the end for the East African slave trade. In 1873, Sultan Barghash, under pressure from the British, abolished the slave trade between Zanzibar and the mainland, although the trade continued illicitly for several decades more.

The church itself, built in the midst of the 1872 cholera epidemic, is East Africa's oldest Catholic building. Its squat tower – the so-called **Livingstone Tower**, topped with a combination of arches and pinnacles resembling a mitre – is named after the explorer-cum-missionary, whose body was laid out here for a night on February 24, 1874, having been carried on an epic eleven-month journey from Chitambo, in present-day Zambia, by his extraordinarily devoted servants Abdullah Susi and James Chuma. The following morning his body was taken to Zanzibar aboard the wryly named MS *Vulture*, and thence to England, for burial in London's Westminster Abbey. For more on Livingstone, and his "discoverer" Stanley, see p.431.

The colonnaded **Fathers' House** facing the church was completed in 1873, and in 1876 a small chapel (also called the Grotto) was dedicated to Our Lady of Lourdes, who'd made her miraculous appearance in France in 1858. Over the following years, especially during a second cholera outbreak during the Abushiri War, Freedom Village's population increased as people sought refuge, and it's from them that many of Bagamoyo's present-day inhabitants descend.

The story of the mission and its fight against the slave trade is told by the **Roman Catholic Mission Museum** (daily 10am–5pm; Tsh2000), housed in the Sisters' House of 1876. There's a small collection of woodcarvings, books and booklets for sale, and plenty of material documenting not only the arrival and progress of Christianity, but also Bagamoyo's pre-history, with extensive explanations in English. Other items include Indian and Arab door frames, and shackles, chains and whips, though even these are not as disturbing as the photographs of slaves tied together with chains around their necks.

The baobab tree outside the mission office was planted in 1868. Poking out of its trunk is a short piece of metal **chain**. The story goes that sometime after 1895 a certain Madame Chevalier, who had been running a dispensary in Zanzibar, arrived as a volunteer. She fastened a chain around the tree in order to tie her donkey to it, and eventually forgot all about it. Since then, the tree's circumference has swelled by over seven metres, engulfing all but a foot or so of the chain.

### Livingstone Memorial Church

At the junction of the mission's driveway and Ocean Road are a cluster of pushy woodcarvers, and the small **Anglican church**. A sign reads, "Through this door David Livingstone passed", a fine example of linguistic sophistry: Livingstone did indeed pass through it, but at the time the door was 1200km away on the shore of Lake Tanganyika. It was donated by an Anglican parish in 1974 following the construction of the present church, which is thought to occupy the site of the tree under which Livingstone's body was laid whilst awaiting the high tide to carry him to Zanzibar. Set in a small garden by the shore is a **stone cross**, not without its own touch of spin: inscribed "First Cross of the RC Church in East Africa planted 17.6.1868", it's made of concrete.

### Ocean Road

Walking south along Ocean Road, the first major building you reach, on your left, is **Bagamoyo Hospital**. Built in 1895, it's one of several public works from **Sewa Haji**, a Pakistani trader whose condition for financing the hospital was that it would admit people of any race or religion. The Ismaïli branch of Shiite Islam to which Sewa Haji belonged has long enjoyed a tradition of trans-religious altruism, most visible these days under the patronage of the Aga Khan Foundation. Sewa Haji's own unstinting philanthropy was rewarded with a knighthood from Queen Victoria. Half a kilometre along is the old **German Post Office** (East Africa's first telegraph office) and, down by the shore, the **Old Customs House**, with its keyhole arches. On the north side is the **fish market**, busiest in the afternoon when boats return.

Just inland is another of Sewa Haji's gifts: the three-storey **Mwambao Primary School**. Built in 1896, it was donated to the colonial government on condition that it remained multi-racial. Restored in 2006 with German funding, its most famous pupil is the incumbent Tanzanian President, Jakaya Kikwete.

Continuing south along Ocean Road brings you to the **German Boma**, once Bagamoyo's most striking edifice, but now a most pitiful sight. Built in 1897 to replace Liku House (see below) as the seat of the German regional administration, it's flanked by twin crenellated towers similar to the single-towered Boma at Mikindani on Tanzania's south coast. Long neglected, its roof collapsed after the 1997 El Niño rains, and the building's guts – including a gorgeous arabesque gallery – spilled out a few years later, to be carted off by locals for building something more useful. All very sad, though not much of a concern for the resident bats.

Just south of the Boma, **Liku House** – currently housing the immigration department – was built in 1885 as the headquarters of the Deutsch-Ostafrikanische Gesellschaft (German East Africa Company). The building is linked to **Emin Pasha**, originally a German Silesian Jew called Eduard Schnitzer, who adopted a Turkish name and Muslim way of life while serving as Ottoman governor of northern Albania. In 1878 he was appointed Pasha of Sudan's Equatorial Province by **General Charles George Gordon**, whose mission was to extend Anglo-Egyptian rule over the Sudan. The resulting Mahdist Uprising cost Gordon his life (and gave him heroic status in Victorian Britain). Emin Pasha, however, felt his position was secure enough, and had to be reluctantly "rescued" from the "furious hordes" by **Henry Morton Stanley**. Evidently in need of another scoop to cap his meeting with Livingstone, Stanley subsequently published *In Darkest Africa, or The Quest, Rescue and Retreat of Emin, Governor of Equatoria*. Together with their sizeable entourage (albeit reduced to 196 from an original 708), Stanley and Emin Pasha arrived in Bagamoyo in December 1889. To celebrate their safe passage, the Germans threw a lavish party at Liku House, at which Emin Pasha, "supremely gay and happy" in the words of Stanley, but also short-sighted, tumbled fourteen feet off the balcony and fractured his skull. He did recover, but was murdered two years later by Arab slavers in the Congo.

### The Old Fort

Just south of Liku House is the **Old Fort** (or Arab Fort; Tsh2000 entrance), large, whitewashed and unadorned. The original structure dates from 1856, but was totally remodelled and fortified in the 1870s during Sultan Barghash's reign. Its serene location, set amidst coconut palms overlooking the ocean, is grimly ironic thanks to its (legendary, at least) nineteenth-century role as a holding place for slaves. Held in small, dark and overcrowded cells, it's said that the slaves were led blindfolded through the courtyard and up a treacherously steep flight of stairs to the upper level of the fort, from where they were led back down along another stairway and out to the waiting dhows – a disorienting procedure intended to foil last-minute escapes. The fort subsequently served as a German military camp, a British prison, a customs office and police headquarters.

## Arts and crafts in Bagamoyo

Bagamoyo is a major arts centre, with an arts college, sculpture school, and several artists' collectives and studios to its name. The latter crop up but also disappear frequently enough, and whilst most are aimed squarely at tourists, hunt around and you'll find some truly extraordinary stuff, such as the delightfully surreal life-sized busts sculpted by **Dula Bute** (ask for him at the top end of Mangesani Rd). The annual **Bagamoyo Arts Festival** (early Oct; ⊛www.bagamoyo.com has dates), showcases plastic arts plus theatre, music and dance, from both college students and abroad.

**Bagamoyo College of Arts** Kaole Rd ☎023/244 0032, ⊛www.sanaabagamoyo .com. Tanzania's oldest arts college, teaching drama, fine arts, handicrafts, music and dance, and even acrobatics. You're welcome to watch classes (and buy the students' work) and performances. For personal tuition, say on traditional musical instruments, you'll pay $10 an hour. Mon–Sat 8am–3pm.

**Bagamoyo Living Art Handicraft Design Centre** Facing the post office ☎0754/834430, ⊛www.jamani.nl/site/BLACC.html. An NGO training disadvantaged women in handicraft and business skills; their showroom sells pottery and ceramics, textiles, embroidery, basketry and clothes. You're welcome to visit the women at work. Mon–Sat 9am–4.30pm.

**Baobab Studio** Near Sewa Haji School ⊛www.baobabstudio.net. One of three places supported by the Zukri Foundation (the others are Sea View Sculpture Centre and African Modern Arts Park, both on Ocean Road at the junction with Customs Rd), primarily concerned with teaching skills, such as art, hip-hop and even boxing, as a means for youths to escape poverty, or at least find some pride. The studio is a colourful little place stuffed with paintings, including, amidst the touristic guff, some real gems. Mon–Sat 9am–5pm, usually also Sat.

### The German Cemetery and gallows

A short walk east of the fort are a couple of reminders of the 1888–89 Abushiri War (p.121). The **German Cemetery**, down a path beside the former BADECO Hotel (now government offices), contains the graves of about twenty soldiers killed during the uprising, and over the following years when the *Schutztruppe* was almost constantly engaged in quelling resistance. The African dead, of which there were thousands, are commemorated by a small plinth just inside the former hotel's gate, marking the **gallows** where Abushiri's supporters were executed in December 1889.

### The Caravan Serai

About 800m west of the Old Fort, and one block north of the bus station, is the **Caravan Serai**, once the assembly and arrival point for caravans, complete with temporary rooms for porters, a slave camp on its western side (possibly where the covered market is now), and pens for pack animals. The present building, from German times, is a large rectangular enclosure, symbolically rather than architecturally important, and contains a modest **museum** (daily 9.30am–6pm;Tsh2000) covering the slave and ivory trade and German colonization, mostly in photos.

## Eating, drinking and nightlife

The beach hotels offer a good range of **seafood**, including prawns, and both Italian and Indian favourites, though at touristic prices (from Tsh10,000–15,000 a meal).There's cheaper and more basic fare in town, and street food around the market in the evening.

## Moving on from Bagamoyo

The bus station has frequent daladalas to Dar. If you're **heading north**, ask about the planned Wami River bridge for accessing Saadani. For now, heading north means either backtracking to Dar to catch a bus or, if you don't mind possibly having to stand, going by daladala to **Msata** on the highway and flagging down a passing bus there. Lastly, *Bagamoyo Beach Resort* can help arrange a **dhow to Zanzibar**; for more on dhow-hopping, see p.32.

There's a reasonable selection of **bars** in the centre, and at the beach hotels: the astonishing Makonde-style woodcarvings alone make the *Travellers Lodge* worth a visit. Consistently the most popular local joint is the friendly *New Top Life Inn.* Also popular, and sometimes with **discos**, is *Dunda Night Park* on Bomani Road. If you're into **live music**, traditional or modern, ask at the arts college.

### Restaurants

**Millennium Sea Breeze Resort** The beachfront restaurant here enjoys a fine reputation, albeit for filling rather than fancy food– the waiter won't bat an eyelid if you ask for chips along with your red snapper à la coconut sauce. Also has lunchtime buffets, and a swimming pool.

**Paradise Holiday Resort** This has arguably Bagamoyo's best kitchen, which you can sample in several elegant dining areas, including on the beach edge. Excellent seafood, and themed lunchtime buffets (Mediterranean, Oriental and Africa) most days except in low season.

**New Top Life Inn** Uhuru Rd/Caravan St. Apart from drinks, this serves up very good and cheap local dishes such as *ugali* or rice with *mishkaki*, stewed goat, fish or roast chicken. A full plate shouldn't top Tsh3500. Also has a streetside patio.

**Roman Catholic Mission** The small area with thatched *bandas* at the rear of the mission buildings is good for cheap lunches (under Tsh5000) and soft drinks.

**Travellers Lodge** Open-air restaurant dishing up consistently good Swahili-styled food, especially aquatic (fresh from fishermen), including a famous seafood platter (Tsh42,000 for two).

## Listings

**Banks and exchange** NMB, same road as the bus station, changes traveller's cheques and has an ATM.

**Health** The Holy Ghost Mission's St Elizabeth's dispensary (T023/244 0253) does reliable malaria tests and is useful for minor emergencies. Bagamoyo Hospital, Ocean Rd (T023/244 0008), also does blood tests.

**Internet access** There are several internet cafés in the area around *New Top Life Inn*, at the arts college (also wi-fi), in the post office, and, more expensive, in larger beach hotels.

**Police** Kaole Rd (T023/244 0026) but rarely helpful.

**Swimming pools** Using hotel pools largely depends on who's at reception and how much you're willing to pay.

## The Kaole ruins

The atmospheric ruins of the once prosperous trading town of **KAOLE**, 5km south of Bagamoyo, include what may be the oldest mosque on the East African mainland, and are among Tanzania's most impressive remains from Shirazi times. The town went into decline following the arrival of the Portuguese in the 1500s, and by the time the Omanis gained control of Bagamoyo in the eighteenth century, Kaole's harbour had silted up and was abandoned. Kaole's original name was Pumbuji, but was renamed "Kalole" by the Zaramo after the town's desertion, meaning "go and see" what had been left behind. The attribution is similar to that of Gezaulole, south of Dar es Salaam (p.113), which means "try and see". Much of the town has now been reclaimed by sea and mangroves.

▲ Kaole ruins

As well as the thirteenth-century **mosque**, which includes a well-preserved *mihrab*, and another mosque from the fifteenth century, Kaole contains **twenty-two tombs**, which are of particular interest for the pillars rising from their headstones. Such "pillar tombs" are unique to the East African coast, and appear to have their roots in pre-Islamic fertility rites: the twelfth-century Iberian geographer Al-Idrisi reported the "worship" of fish-oil-anointed megaliths (menhirs) in Somalia. Kaole's earliest pillar tombs are from the fourteenth century, the latest – with a legible inscription – from 1854 (1270 in the Muslim calendar). That pillar's five depressions formerly held Chinese porcelain bowls: three were stolen, the other two are in Dar's National Museum. Also unusual is the double "**Love Grave**", said to house the remains of a couple drowned at sea, and "**Sharifa's grave**", a "hut tomb" of a holy woman still venerated by women today, who pray to her for help and leave modest offerings in a small metal bowl inside the tomb.

The ruins are 1km beyond Kaole village (daily 8am–5.30pm; Tsh3000 entry, plus tip for an optional but recommended guide); the admission fee includes entry to a small but interesting **museum** containing pottery shards, oil lamps and other artefacts, some of them Chinese. There's **no public transport**, and walking carries a risk of mugging, so go by bike (around Tsh5000 a day) or taxi (Tsh10,000 return is fair). Just before entering Kaole village, look for the two glaringly phallic **pillar tombs** on your right, quite different from the pillar tombs found in the archeological site, but likely stemming from the same tradition.

## The Ruvu River

The road to Msata, west of Bagamoyo on the Dar to Tanga/Arusha highway, was the last leg of the old slaving route, passing through the beautifully verdant if swampy **Ruvu River valley**, whose diminutive villages consist of tiny houses perched on stilts. The area positively pullulates with colourful **birds**, and if you're determined you'll also see monkeys and, in the river, **hippos**. For more than a fleeing glimpse from a daladala, hire a bicycle in town (it's a 30min ride), but to explore the river itself you'll need to arrange a **boat trip** in Bagamoyo, either with fishermen, or through a hotel or the tourist office ($100 for two people for a full day).

# Saadani National Park

The rarely visited 1062-square-kilometre **Saadani National Park**, 45km north of Bagamoyo, is unique in combining marine, terrestrial and riverine environments. Bush walks are the thing here, sometimes hair-raising, always fascinating, and there's fantastic birding throughout (see box below). But even though you won't likely see big game on the beach (as is sometimes touted), the plains and swamps behind the shore are home to thirty-odd species of large mammals. A history of poaching means many are both rare and shy, so don't come expecting a wealth of photo-ops. That said, their very elusiveness makes spotting them all the more thrilling. Denizens include warthog, elephants (most likely in the north), buffalo, zebra and giraffe, and a host of antelopes: Liechtenstein's hartebeest, wildebeest, waterbuck, bushbuck, dikdik, eland, kudu, oryx and the rare Roosevelt and Roan sables. The most numerous **predators** are leopards, though lions are more visible.

## Practicalities

The **best time to visit** is June to October, when animals converge on the river. January and February, after the short rains, are visually rewarding, when the park is painted green. Access roads are better than they were, so the park is now only rarely cut off during the long rains (heaviest April & May), but the internal road network, especially in the south, can get waterlogged.

### Arrival

Access is easiest on an **organized safari**; reliable companies are reviewed on p.53. **Drivers** need 4WD. It's four hours from Dar (300km), so day-trips are only possible from Pangani (2hr each way; informal car rental averages $200). Other access roads start from the Dar–Tanga/Arusha highway. The better one goes from Mandera to Saadani village (58km; 2hr); longer, and more likely to be blocked during rains, is the road from Mkata to Mkwaja. Saadani's lodges offer road transfers from Dar ($150–250 per vehicle). The direct road **from Bagamoyo** has been impassible since the rope-pulled ferry over the Wami River was washed

---

### Birdlife in Saadani

With its mix of habitats, Saadani's **birdlife** is rich and varied, whether along the Wami River, in acacia woodland, in Zaraninge Forest, or along the shore. **Waders** include the woolly-necked stork, yellow-billed stork, open-billed stork, common sandpiper and grey heron. The dense **acacia woodland** in the south also has spectacular birding: colourful lilac-breasted rollers, fork-tailed drongos, grey hornbills, bee-eaters, flocks of Meyer's parrots and red-cheeked cordonbleus can all be seen. **Birds of prey** include palmnut and white-backed vultures, yellow-billed kites, and various eagles, including the eye-catching African fish eagle, which perches in trees awaiting prey carried up on the high tide.

away, but with a new bridge in the offing, it's worth asking about. Whichever route you take, arrive before 6pm or you won't be admitted.

Access by **public transport** is possible, but if you want to see wildlife, arrange activities such as game drives and walks through a lodge beforehand (see below). Saadani village is the best target: catch a pick-up **from Mandera** on the highway no later than 3pm, or the daily 1pm bus **from Dar** (from "Ubungo Maji", 300m west of Ubungo daladala stand on Morogoro Rd; Tsh10,000, 5hr). Less useful is the approach **from Pangani** (actually from Bweni, facing it): the midday bus to Mkwaja isn't reliable, and there's no regular onward transport to Saadani village. There's currently no road transport **from Bagamoyo**, but if/when the Wami River bridge gets built, this may change. For now, *Saadani Safari Lodge* offers boat transfers from Bagamoyo at $195 per boat (3 passengers).

Expensive scheduled **flights** are operated by Safari Airlink (Ⓦwww.safariaviation.info) from Dar, Zanzibar, and various airstrips in southern Tanzania, including Mikumi, Ruaha and Selous.

### Entrance fees and information

**Entrance fees**, payable at gates on the park boundary, are $20 per person plus $40 per vehicle (both for 24hrs), dollars cash only. Although Saadani village itself is outside the park, you'll still have to pay even if you plan on spending all your time there. The park **headquarters** are 8km northwest of Mkwaja village, 6km off the road from Pangani (daily 7.30am–5.30pm; Ⓔhnguluma@yahoo.co.uk, Ⓦwww.saadanipark.org). The best **guidebook** is TANAPA's colourful *Saadani and Bagamoyo*.

### Activities

The upmarket lodges have heaps of activities for guests (included in the price), and possibly for others, too, if arranged in advance. *Saadani Safari Lodge* for one are happy to oblige so long as they're not too busy, and you give them at least 24 hours' notice (Ⓣ0713/555678, Ⓔinfo@saadanilodge.com): they charge $45 per three-hour activity. The following are the "standard" activities; others unique to specific lodges are mentioned in our accommodation reviews.

**Game drives**, in open-sided vehicles, are best up north where the park headquarters are (and where you can hire a guide; $10). Outside the park, *Kisampa Camp* offers spotlit night-time drives: lots of glowing eyes. **Bush walks** – in the company of an armed ranger (available in theory if not always in practice at the park headquarters; $20) – are an often heart-stopping way of eyeballing Saadani's denizens, and getting to see Zaraninge Forest. **Boat cruises** on the Wami River are nirvana for birders, with countless specimens in and around the flanking forest, but don't rock the boat: those floating logs are crocodiles, and there be hippos, too. **Cultural tours** are also possible (see p.132).

### Accommodation

If you're coming from Pangani and get stuck in **Mkwaja village**, there's the basic *Mwango Guest House* (❶). **Camping** is cheapest at *Warthog Camp* in Saadani village (Tsh8000 per person, Tsh10,000 if you use their tent). The park's own campsites ($30 per person) are on the beach at *Saadani Guest House*, and, requiring a vehicle, at Kinyonga on the Wami River and Tengwe, 8km northwest of Saadani village.

**Kisampa Camp** Outside the park's southwestern boundary Ⓣ0754/927694 or 0753/005442, Ⓦwww.sanctuary-tz.com. Set on a ridge in a conservation area also comprising grasslands, hills, riverine forest and ox-bow lakes, *Kisampa* is run in partnership with five villages, and is one of Tanzania's best examples of responsible tourism. On the menu, beside the usual activities,

## Cultural tourism in Saadani

Saadani's upmarket lodges all offer cultural interactions, but to really get it on down with the locals, get in touch with the **Saadani Cultural Tourism Programme**, based at *Warthog Camp* (see below). On the menu are visits to traditional healers, dance performances, story telling, tours of historic Saadani (including nineteenth-century ruins), market forays, chinwags with fishermen, and sampling the local *wanzuki* honey hooch. Wildlife is on the cards, too, especially birding (the project coordinator's big flutter): a trip to the pink salt pans to the south should be rewarded with plenty of waders, including flamingoes. Canoeing on the Wami River is also possible. **Costs** are reasonable: bush walks or birding are Tsh21,000 per person; most other activities are Tsh16,000. Bicycle rental is Tsh3500 a day.

are butterfly walks and birding, visits to a bee-keeping project and school funded by the camp's activities, village visits, and wobbling around in dugouts on the nearby Wami River. Accommodation is in seven large, open-sided thatched *bandas*; "rustic simplicity" means no electricity in the *bandas*, and bucket showers (hung from trees). To change scenery, you can camp in the bush, or on the beach – they have a patch north of Madete. Children are welcome. All-inclusive ($300 per person) ⑨

**Saadani Guest House** 1.5km north of Saadani village; book through the park headquarters. This simple park-run hostel, with ten pleasant twin-bed rooms, is worth trying to book as it's right on the beach (there's a great terrace), but it hasn't always been open to tourists. Sometimes has running water and solar-powered light. ④

**Saadani Safari Lodge** 1km north of Saadani village ☎022/277 3294 or 0713/555678, ⓦwww.saadanilodge.com. The most traditional of the lodges, with nine comfortable "tented cottages" strung along the beach – large and airy, with wooden floors, big Zanzibari four-posters, lots of draperies, and ocean-view verandas. Special activities include forest walks and snorkelling. There's also a tree house overlooking a waterhole, a swimming pool, bar and library, and a superb restaurant (especially

for seafood). No children under 6. Full-board ($260 per person including park fees) ⑨

**A Tent with a View Safari Lodge** 7km south of Mkwaja, outside the park ☎0713/323318 or 022/211 0507 (Dar), ⓦwww .saadani.com. On the beach in a former coconut plantation, this is stylish without being frilly. Special activities include birding by canoe along the mangrove-lined Mafue River, and admiring newly hatched turtles. Accommodation is in ten comfortable solar-powered tents pitched along the blissful beach, eight of them on stilts under thatched roofs, all with large ocean-view balconies (and hammocks), and making nicely inventive use of driftwood in their decor. Honeymooners have three secluded suites (FB $295 per person). The restaurant also has sea views, and there's a hide overlooking a waterhole. No children under 6. FB $195 per person, all-inclusive $295 per person. ⑨

**Warthog Camp** Saadani village ☎0784/490399, ⓔwildlife2001tz@yahoo.com. If you're fine with long-drops and bucket showers, the base for Saadani's cultural tourism programme (see above) is perfect for an extended stay in the area. Apart from camping, they have simple tented *bandas*, and cheap meals can be provided. The beach is close by, for swimming and snorkelling. ③

# The park

The **beach**, of course, is an attraction in itself. As for shoreline wildlife, baboons and sometimes waterbuck are all you'll likely see, and perhaps mongooses at night, out hunting crabs. While snorkelling or on a boat, look for bottle-nosed **dolphins**, which are common off the southern shore, as are small **sharks** – who prefer prawns to humans. Saadani's nesting sites for endangered **green turtles** can be visited through *A Tent with a View Safari Lodge*, who also maintain an egg incubation and hatching centre. Time things right (contact them beforehand) and you might catch a "hatch out" (year-round), when the hatchlings make their D-Day dash into the ocean.

The park's **northern sector** sustains some fifty **elephants**, but their memories of poaching are fresh (in Saadani's days as a Game Reserve, rangers knew the area as Kosovo), so take care as they're less predictable than elsewhere. Two **rare antelope species** are the greater kudu, well camouflaged and hard to see (they spend much of the day under bushes), and sable antelope, mainly southwest of Mkwaja. These are smaller and lighter in colour than the common sable, and have shorter horns, which for a time led zoologists to class them as a separate species. While you're in the area, pay your respects to the lugubrious hippos along the seasonal Madete River.

The **Wami River** marks the park's southern boundary: there's fabulous birdlife all along (including flamingoes in the estuary), plus **hippos and crocs**, and, in the flanking forest, black-and-white **colobus monkeys**, given away by the crashing of branches as they flee. In swampy areas, Eastern Bohor **reedbuck** can be seen in reed beds, but bushbuck, whilst common, hide out in dense riverside bush. In the southwest, low hills are covered with rare remnants of coastal woodland, of which **Zaraninge Forest** is the jewel, with several primates including black-and-white colobus and blue monkeys, and yet more birds.

# Tanga and around

Located on a large, pear-shaped bay 200km due north of Dar es Salaam (but 350km by road), **TANGA** is Tanzania's second-busiest port and the country's third largest town, with 200,000 inhabitants. Not that it feels anything like that big. Founded in the fourteenth century by Persian traders, all that remains of their presence are graves and ruins on Toten Island in the bay, and the town's seafaring name: *tanga* is a woven sail, as in "tweka tanga" – to set sail.

Omani Arabs sailed into the harbour in the eighteenth century, and under their tutelage the port become a major entrepôt for **ivory** (not so much for slaves) bound for Zanzibar. Inevitably, Tanga's trading links attracted European interest, and by the 1880s the town had become a major focus for the **German conquest** of the interior. As their regional headquarters, Tanga looked set to prosper, especially when construction began on a railway to Moshi. The real driving force was **sisal** (see box, p.134) but when the market collapsed after World War II (synthetics having edged out natural fibres), Tanga entered a period of decline from which it's still struggling to emerge. Once the country's second most powerful economic region, Tanga now bumps along in sixteenth place.

Tanga Bay is lined with mangroves so there are no proper beaches, but that's not to say you shouldn't linger: outlying attractions include the **Amboni Caves**, **Galanos Sulphur Springs**, the medieval **Tongoni ruins**, and yet more ruins, as well as mangroves, on **Toten Island** in the bay. There's also the town itself: economic decline has had the felicitous side effect, so far, of keeping blue-glass, high-rise development away. As a result, the town's **colonial heart** is remarkably well preserved, its many beautiful buildings making it one of Tanzania's most photogenic towns.

## Arrival and information

Tanga's **bus stand** is a ten-minute walk into the town centre along Pangani Road, but if you're coming on Scandinavian Express, you'll be dropped centrally by the stadium on Ring Street. Daily **flights** from Arusha, Dar and

## Sisal

Tanga Region was once the world's biggest producer of **sisal** (*katani*), the fibre extracted from aloe-like plants (*mkonge*) used for making ropes and sacks. The plants, originally from Yucatan, Mexico, were introduced to Tanganyika in 1892 by the German botanist Richard Hindorf. Despite only 62 of the thousand plants surviving the journey, sisal proved to be spectacularly well adapted – by 1908 there were over ten million sisal plants in Tanganyika, and at its height the region was producing 250,000 tonnes of fibre a year (compared to 20,000 tonnes in 2000). The plantations, which stretch westwards from Tanga along much of the plains edging the Usambara Mountains, still constitute the region's major cash crop, and the new millennium has brought some reason for hope: a greener global consciousness, and rising interest in bio-fuels, appears to be reviving the once left-for-dead market in sisal.

Zanzibar are operated by Coastal Aviation; the airport is 4km southwest of town, Tsh5000 by taxi.

**Taxi** rides within town cost Tsh3000. **Bicycles** are a popular way around, and cost a few thousand shillings a day (ask at the tourist offices). **Walking** by day is safe (though pay attention in and around the bus station), and the colonial part of town should be safe at night, too, as there are plenty of *askaris* about, but do seek local advice.

Tanga has two unofficial **tourist offices**, both of them primarily offering tours: TAYODEA, at the corner of Independence Avenue and Usambara Street (Tanga Youth Development Association; Mon–Sat 8.30am–5pm; ☎027/264 4350 or 0713/260027, Ⓦwww.tayodea.org), who also coordinate overseas volunteers, and Ilya Tours, at *Ocean Breeze Hotel* (daily 8am–8pm; ☎0713/560569 or 0784/660569, Ⓦwww.ilyatours.com).

## Accommodation

Tanga has plenty of accommodation in all ranges, and two **campsites** (both $5 per person): the best is *Kiboko*, off Bombo Road (☎0784/469292, Ⓔjda-kiboko @bluemail.ch), which has pitches under a couple of old mango trees, clean toilets and showers, a barbecue area, beers, and an expensive restaurant; they can provide tents for free if you're going to eat there. Further up, *Raskazone Hotel* also allows camping (shadeless), and has a cheap restaurant and bar.

### Town centre

**Ferns Inn** Usambara St ☎027/264 6947 or 0784/481609. Run by a sweet Goan, this has clean en-suite rooms with fans and (round) nets, and three with a/c (and double beds). All have cable TV. There's a small friendly bar, and good cheap food (see p.138). BB fans ❶, a/c ❷

**Hotel Kola Prieto** India St, close to Custom Rd ☎027/264 4206, Ⓔkolaprieto@hotmail,com. A four-storey, supposedly business-class hotel that's past its best, but reasonable if you can negotiate a good price. The rooms are attractively designed, with big double beds, satellite TV, phone, fridge and a/c (which can be loud). There's a formal restaurant (no alcohol), but no lift. BB ❸

**Malindi Hotel** Ring St ☎027/264 2791. A four-storey affair (with a pool table at the entrance) offering good value for money, and clean cotton sheets. The atmosphere is a mite tawdry, however, and it all feels rather dark. Cheaper rooms share bathrooms. BB fans ❶, a/c ❷

**Ocean Breeze Inn** Clock Tower St ☎027/264 4545. The best central budget choice, especially if you get a top floor room with north-facing balcony, for views of Tanga Bay between the trees. The rooms, all en suite with TVs (local stations), are fine, albeit with dodgy plumbing, and some of the a/c units prefer rattle to hum. There's also a bar and restaurant. BB fans ❶, a/c ❷

**TANGA**

RAS KAZONE

Toten Island ▲

Tanga Bay

Tanga Port

Tanga Bay

Canoe & Dhow Moorings

Popatlal Secondary School

Bombo Hospital

European Cemetery

Harbour Offices

St Anthony's Cathedral

Police

MISITU

NGAMIANI

Mkwakwani Stadium

Train Station

See inset map for detail

**ACCOMMODATION**
| | |
|---|---|
| Dolphin Inn | I |
| Ferns Inn | M |
| Inn by the Sea | A |
| Kiboko | D |
| Kiboma Ivory Inn | G |
| Hotel Kola Prieto | L |
| Malindi Hotel | N |
| Mkonge Hotel | C |
| New Mbuyukenda Hostel | F |
| Ngorongoro Guest House | H |
| Ocean Breeze Inn | E |
| Panori Hotel | B |
| Raskazone Hotel | K |
| Sea View (Bandari) Hotel | J |

**EATING, DRINKING & NIGHTLIFE**
| | | | |
|---|---|---|---|
| A.R.D. Coffee Tree Motel | 13 | New Mbuyukenda Hostel | F |
| Chichi Night Club | | Octopus Exotica | 9 |
| Club La Casa Chica | 8 | Panori Hotel | E |
| Dolphin Inn | | Patwas | 12 |
| Ferns Inn | M | Raskazone Swimming Club | 3 |
| Food Palace | | Splendid View Hotel | 11 |
| Harbours Club | 4 | Tanga Bathing Club | 6 |
| Kiboko | D | Tanga Hotel | 2 |
| Loilondo Gate | 7 | Tanga Yacht Club | 5 |
| Mkonge Hotel | C | | 1 |

**Inset map (TANGA town centre):**

Clock Tower

Jamhuri Gardens

Barclays Bank

EXIM Bank

CRDB Bank

Usambara Court House

Vila Esperança

Library

Uhuru Park

Market

NMB

Clock Tower Street

Mkwakwani Stadium

Scandinavian Express

Train Station

Eckernforde Avenue

INDEPENDENCE AVE

MARKET STREET

USAMBARA STREET

INDIA STREET

ARAB STREET

SWAHILI STREET

CUSTOMS ST

RING STREET

TAIFA ROAD

MKWAKWANI ST

100 m

▼ Daladala Stand, Tongoni ruins (20km) & Pangani (43km)

◀ Galanos Sulphur Springs (10km)

▲ Amboni Caves (10km),

◀ Mombasa Road

◀ Dar es Salaam & airport

◀ Muheza, Moshi,

SWAHILI STREET

INDIA STREET

USAMBARA STREET

RING STREET

ECKERNFORDE AVENUE

MKWAKWANI ST

CUSTOMS STREET

INDEPENDENCE AVENUE

MARKET STREET

6TH STREET

1ST STREET
2ND STREET
3RD STREET
4TH STREET
5TH STREET
6TH STREET
7TH STREET
8TH STREET
9TH STREET
10TH STREET

MPIRA STREET

TAIFA ROAD

PANGANI ROAD

RING STREET

CHUMBAGENI POLICE ROAD

GOVERNMENT ST

BOMA ROAD

INDEPENDENCE AVENUE

AMANI STREET

COAN STREET

ECKERNFORDE AVENUE

KILIMANJARO AVENUE

NEW KOROGWE ROAD

MOMBASA ROAD

BOMBO ROAD

ONATO ROAD

TASMA ROAD

KISAUNI ROAD

BOMBO ROAD

0    400 m

0    100 m

N

www.roughguides.com

Sea View (Bandari) Hotel Independence Ave ☎0713/254052. It took almost a decade, but this sweet old colonial hotel has finally been renovated. Good thing too, especially if you get one of the four front rooms on the first floor, whose private balconies have spectacular harbour views. All rooms are large, have a/c, and mosquito nets are available on request. The downstairs bar has a lovely streetside terrace, where you can also eat take-outs from *Octopus Exotica* next door. BB ❸

## Ras Kazone

The verdant (and humid) **Ras Kazone peninsula** has an almost rural feel. Unfortunately there's no real beach to speak of other than a handful of clearings cut from the mangroves years ago, and now occupied by swimming clubs, the yacht club and *Inn by the Sea*. There are loads of daladalas running up and down Bombo Road (Tsh400).

Inn by the Sea 1.5km along Bombo Rd ☎027/264 4614. Perched on a low cliff among lush bougainvillea hedges, this somewhat narcoleptic place sees little trade, but has the peninsula's best location (and you can swim, too). The rooms, in two rows plus a few more in the main building, are perfectly acceptable if run down. No food, but there's *Raskazone Swimming Club* next door. BB fans ❷, a/c ❸

Mkonge Hotel 1.25km along Bombo Rd ☎027/264 3440, ✉mkongehotel@kaributanga .com. Tanga's leading abode, set in a baobab-studded lawn by the bay. The fringing mangroves mean no swimming, but a swimming pool compensates. The main building, containing the bar, restaurant (see p.138) and internet café, is a sensitively restored hulk dating from the happier days of the sisal industry; less enticing is the 1970s accommodation block accessed along a long dark corridor, although its large rooms – with polished parquet – are cheerfully furnished and equipped with a/c (no nets), satellite TV, spotless bathrooms and small terraces. The better ones have fine bay views, albeit through trees and a fence; best from the top floor. ❺

New Mbuyukenda Hostel 400m along Bombo Rd ☎027/264 5564. Run by the Lutheran Church, this has a few prim and proper cottages (12 en-suite rooms) set in mature gardens with hugely impressive trees, making it an excellent choice for families (no shoreline though). Also has a sleepy restaurant (see p.138). BB fans ❷, a/c ❸

Panori Hotel 3km from the centre ☎027/264 6044, ✉panori@africaonline.co.tz. A poor location, being close to a stretch of beach owned by the military and over 1km from the bathing clubs and public transport, but the welcome is warm, and all rooms have private bathrooms and a/c, though the smell of bug spray is pervasive. The better rooms in the New Wing have parquet floors, TVs and big bathrooms. There's also a bar and a good restaurant wrapped around a tree. BB ❹

Raskazone Hotel 200m off Bombo Rd near *Tanga Bathing Club*, 2km from the centre ☎0713/670790. A quirky place complete with life-size sculptures of crocs and monsters in its garden. It functions mainly as a bar these days, with food too. The rooms (a handful with a/c) have seen better days, but are reasonable value if you can bargain the price down a bit; unusually for Tanga, it also has (significantly cheaper) single rates. BB ❷–❸

## Kana area

If you're on a tight budget, **Kana area**, just south of the railway tracks, has decent guesthouses, and as many bars and nightclubs. Seek local advice about walking around at night.

Dolphin Inn Just east of the railway tracks ☎027/264 5005. Probably the best hotel in the area, efficiently run, with thirteen rooms with nets, fans, tiled bathrooms, big beds and cotton sheets. There's also a hair salon and a lively bar. BB ❶

Kiboma Ivory Inn 8th St ☎027/264 3578. Cheap and secure, but check the mosquito nets for size. A handful of more expensive singles have bathrooms. Also has a quiet bar and very slow restaurant. ❶

Ngorongoro Guest House 8th St ☎027/264 3512. An excellent budget choice with large, clean rooms with private bathroom, fans, good showers, huge comfortable beds with cotton sheets and suitably sized nets. There's also a quiet bar, but the food is average. BB ❶

# The Town

Tanga is two places. The colourful crowded streets and haphazard structures of the dusty (or muddy) grid-like **Ngamiani district**, inland, is where the bulk of the population live and work, and is fun to explore, especially if you're looking for something (a needle, say). But in the old **colonial district**, between the railway and the harbour, there's little to dispel the gently mouldering atmosphere, with a wealth of gorgeous old buildings gradually wilting in the humidity and heat, despite the sterling efforts of the **Tanga Heritage Project** (ⓦwww .geocities.com/urithitanga) to rescue the more impressive ones. But they're a resilient bunch, Tanga's buildings: no matter how dilapidated they look, they still stand – it might have something to do with the quality of the cement (which, along with sisal, is Tanga's main export). There's no real focus to this part of town, but any walk is rewarding, as most streets contain a least a handful of photogenic old buildings, many of them colonnaded, or with beautifully carved wooden balconies. Tanga's **architecture** has a strong Indian flavour, the town having received its first immigrants from the subcontinent in the 1830s, and subsequently a Baluchi garrison, to collect taxes on the Sultan of Zanzibar's behalf.

The **British period** was Tanga's heyday, and a very cosmopolitan time, with Greek sisal planters adding to the mix. A particularly fine example of the resulting cross-cultural pollination is the 1930 **Vila Esperança** at the east end of Ring Street, gracefully combining Goan and Art Deco with a hint of Portuguese; its Portuguese name ("Hope Town") reflects the aspirations Tanga enjoyed before the collapse of the sisal market laid waste to its prospects. Walking west along Ring Street brings you to another attractive memento of British rule: the lovely green-and-white gabled **train station**. The rusty steam locos and carriages in the sidings and sheds behind are fenced off, but the stationmaster should be amenable to the pleadings of ardent train buffs.

## The "Battle of the Bees"

From the British point view, **World War I** in East Africa was a disaster from the start, when, on November 2, 1914, General Arthur Aitken ordered: "Tanga is to be taken tonight." It was not to be. The 48-hour delay in landing troops gave the Germans plenty of time to organize their defences, and when confrontation finally came, the eight thousand Allied troops, mostly Indian reserves, found themselves facing **Paul Emil von Lettow-Vorbeck**'s well-trained, thousand-strong force of mostly African *askaris*, lying in wait on the far side of the railway cutting at the neck of **Ras Kazone** peninsula. Although some Allied forces fought their way into the town centre, others were ambushed at the railway, got lost in rubber and sisal plantations, or were famously stung by **bees** enraged at having had their hives pierced by stray bullets, hence the battle's name. The inept nature of the assault was typified by the story of 25 **cattle** stolen by the British to feed their beleaguered troops. The following night, the African cattle herders snuck in behind British lines and took them back, without anyone even noticing. After three days and 795 casualties, the British retreated to Mombasa, leaving behind sixteen machine guns, 455 rifles and 600,000 rounds of ammunition – enough for a year's fighting. Lettow-Vorbeck went on to harry British forces throughout the war, and was undefeated when the 1918 Armistice forced his surrender.

The northern section of Tanga's **European cemetery**, east of the centre, includes the graves of forty-eight African and sixteen German soldiers who died in the battle. One of them contains **Tom von Prince**, commander of the German army's bitter 1894–98 campaign against Chief Mkwawa of the Hehe (see p.474), but his and many other gravestones, or their inscriptions, are sadly missing. The cemetery also contains British graves.

The **German period** is best represented by the restored neo-Gothic **Usambara Court House** on Usambara Street, formerly the German Governor's House. Other reminders of German times include the fancy **clock tower** (1901), close by on Independence Avenue, and the **obelisk** in the adjacent Jamhuri Gardens, commemorating German marines who died in the Abushiri War. The gardens overlook the bay, and benefit from sea breezes and a children's playground. Also good for a rest is **Uhuru Park**, two blocks inland, whose few surviving benches are arranged around a bizarre missile-like monument celebrating Independence.

## Eating

**Street food** in the town centre is restricted to a handful of fruit stalls, coconut-juice vendors and peanut and cashew pedlars rhythmically marking their presence with seed rattles. The area around the bus station has more choice, and the narrow beach beside the canoe and dhow moorings just east of St Anthony's Cathedral is the best place for fried fish. As for **restaurants**, there's not a huge selection, but what there is can be unusually good (the big speciality is prawns). You can also find (rather average) *nyama choma* and *chipsi mayai* in some bars, and *supu* in the morning.

**A.R.D. Coffee Tree Motel** Usambara St/India St. Local bar serving filling Tanzanian dishes like *ugali* with fish, or meat and banana stew (all around Tsh1500), with tables on a veranda outside. See also p.139.

**Ferns Inn** Usambara St. Small, friendly Goan-run place offering chips or *ugali* with meat, fish, curried squid or roast octopus (all Tsh1500), and prawns (Tsh5000). Also a well-stocked bar, and there are a couple of streetside tables.

**Food Palace** Market St. Ever popular with expats and Tanzanian Indians, the menu isn't extensive but the food reliably good, and includes pizzas, Gujarati dishes, evening barbecues (Fri–Sun), and excellent snacks (good for breakfast). Full meals under Tsh5000. The streetside veranda has a few tables. Daily 7.30am–3.30pm, plus Fri–Sun 7–10.30pm.

**Kiboko** Off Bombo Rd. One for gastronomes with wallet-opening dedication. With several thatched shelters in a jungly garden, this serves up seriously good prawn dishes (Tsh15,000), and the chicken garners good reports too (Tsh11,000), but meat, including pork, takes pride of place – and an even bigger chunk of your savings. Massive portions.

**Mkonge Hotel** 1.25km along Bombo Rd. A surprisingly affordable restaurant given the plush surroundings, with most mains under Tsh10,000 (prawns Tsh12,000). Also has cheaper Tanzanian dishes, and rather boring vegetarian options. Eat in the garden for bay views (through a wire fence).

**New Mbuyukenda Hostel** 400m along Bombo Rd. Hugely ambitious menus are not normally a good sign, but most of the stuff on this one is easy enough to make: excellent sandwiches and omelettes (both under Tsh2000), full-on breakfasts (Tsh3000), and

cheap hot meals (under Tsh3500 with meat, Tsh4500 for fish). Extra brownie points are earned for its glorious garden; eat under one of two enormous mango trees. No alcohol, and don't come if you're in a rush.

**Octopus Exotica** Beside *Sea View (Bandari) Hotel*, Independence Ave. A converted shipping crate that serves up delicious and cheap food, including octopus, prawns, kingfish and curry rice. You can eat it on the hotel's lovely streetside terrace next door.

**Patwas** Mkwakwani St. Occupying a bright and sometimes breezy former factory, this has ambled along for almost half a century, dispensing very good juices and milk shakes, snacks (be sure they're fresh, as some sit around) and full meals, including curries (around Tsh5000). Closed Sun. No alcohol.

**Raskazone Swimming Club** 1.6km along Bombo Rd. Scattered along a steep and thickly vegetated slope over the bay, and with direct access for swimming, this is the better of the two swimming clubs, serving alcohol as well as meals. *Masala*-spiced dishes are the thing, whether prawn or chicken (both Tsh5500). Tsh500 admission.

**Tanga Bathing Club** 1.9km along Bombo Rd. Similar to *Raskazone Swimming Club* but with two big differences: no alcohol, and much cheaper meals (nothing much over Tsh1500). Tsh300 admission.

**Tanga Yacht Club** 2.3km along Bombo Rd. If you're okay with the expat vibe, this comes recommended for its bayside views and excellent meals (over Tsh10,000), especially prawns. Also has a small beach (and showers). Tsh2000 admission, Tsh5000 minimum spend.

# Drinking and nightlife

Tanga is famous for nightlife: there are **drinking** holes all over town, with things getting lively after 8pm. Other than places mentioned below, the nocturnal focus is a cluster of lively bars and clubs in Kana district: try the *Loliondo Gate* or *Dolphin Inn*, both on Chuda Road. There are also more dignified but sleepy bars at the *Mkonge*, *Raskazone* and *Panori* hotels. At dusk and at night, take a taxi.

**A.R.D Coffee Tree Motel** Usambara St/India St. A nice sleepy bar for an afternoon tot, with TV inside and tables on a wide veranda outside. Also serves decent food, and has a pool table.

**Chichi Night Club** Independence Ave, beside *Sea View (Bandari) Hotel*. Partly outdoor bar and disco-thèque, sleepy by day, lively weekend nights and sometimes also on Thursdays.

**Club La Casa Chica** Top floor, Sachak House, Independence Ave. A popular Western-style disco, often with live music too, but with the appearance of a fire trap. Wed & Fri–Sun from 9pm; Tsh3500–4000.

**Harbours Club** Off Bombo Rd. A bay-side venue that's lively when they host visiting bands, whether

Taarab or *muziki wa dansi* (usually Fri; around Tsh3000 entrance).

**Splendid View Hotel** Eckernforde Ave. Live music venue, including big-name bands from Dar (most likely on Sat).

**Tanga Hotel** Eckernforde Ave/Chumbageni Police Rd. One of the most popular town-centre bars, large and not too noisy, with as many women as men thanks to the friendly atmosphere (and police station around the corner). There's also passable *nyama choma*, a restaurant, satellite TV, dartboard and pool table. Good chance of live bands on Wed, Sat & Sun (Tsh3000).

# Listings

**Airlines** Coastal Aviation, Tanga Airport ☎0713/566485 or 0784/810608.

**Banks and exchange** Best for cash and traveller's cheques (but be patient) is NBC, Bank St/Sokoine Ave. All banks have ATMs; there are several on Independence Ave.

**Hospitals and clinics** Bombo Hospital, Bombo Rd ☎027/264 2997. Private clinics: Fazal Memorial Hospital, Independence Ave ☎027/264 6895; Tanga Medicare Centre Hospital, Independence Ave ☎027/264 6920, also with a dentist.

**Internet access** Fast connections at Vircoms, Market St (daily 9am–9pm), and Ahaa, Arab St/ Customs St (Mon–Sat 9am–7pm).

**Library** Tanga Library (George V Memorial Library), in a lovely Arab-inspired building on Independence

Ave, is surprisingly well stocked (Mon–Fri 9am–6pm, Sat 9am–2pm; Tsh500 per day).

**Police** Off Independence Ave near Tanga Library ☎027/264 4519.

**Post and couriers** Main post office, Independence Ave; DHL, Market St, opposite *Food Palace* ☎027/264 6523.

**Shopping** Woodcarvers sell their work in stalls facing the north side of the small produce market, between Market St and Independence Ave. The main market area is in the streets behind the bus station. There's a lively clothes market at the junction of Pangani Rd and 8th St on Tues, Thurs & Sat.

**Telephones** TTCL, Independence Ave. Cheap international calls (Tsh100 per min) can be made over the internet at Vircoms, Market St (daily 9am–9pm).

# Around Tanga

Except for Toten Island, the following places can be reached by bicycle, taxi or daladala (followed by a short walk). If you want a guide – recommended if you're not on a strictly shoestring budget – contact either Ilya Tours or TAYODEA (see p.134), who are invaluable for arranging jaunts to Toten Island. Prices are negotiable, depending on group size and your perceived wealth, but even starting prices are not unreasonable at no more than $15–30 per attraction, depending on type of transport.

## The Amboni Caves and Galanos Sulphur Springs

With their winding passageways and galleries, dripping stalactites, suggestive stalagmites and unlikely legends, the limestone **Amboni Caves** ("Mapango ya Amboni"; daily 9am–4pm; $3) are among the region's highlights. Thought to have formed during the Bathonian Period (176–169 million years ago), the caves cover fifteen square kilometres, making them the most extensive known in East Africa. They contain at least ten networks of caverns and passageways, two of which – 3a and 3b – can be visited. There's no light, and even with your guide's torch it takes a few minutes for your eyes to adjust, so the first thing you'll notice is the soft ground, and the smell. Both are the product of **bats** (*popo*), living in colonies numbering tens of thousands. For most of the day they hang around upside down in enormous bunches, but if you hang around the entrance at sunset, you'll see clouds of them flitting out to feed – an amazing sight in itself.

Inside are various **chambers**, most with nicknames, some of which allude to their stalagmites: among them are a miniature Mount Kilimanjaro, a doppelgänger Virgin Mary, and the Statue of Liberty. Others reflect tall tales. The **Mombasa Road Cavern**, for instance, is said to go all the way to the Kenyan port. Another passage is rumoured to lead to Kilimanjaro, a story that started after World War II, when two Europeans exploring the caves apparently disappeared without trace. Their dog was found dead a few months later outside another cave 400km away, near Kilimanjaro. Sadly, the fun was scotched by a German-Turkish survey in 1994, which concluded that the longest of the caves extended no further than 900m from the entrance.

Of more genuine significance is Mzimuni, the **Chamber of the Spirits**, which locals believe is inhabited by a snake-like force, Mabavu, capable of granting fertility to childless women. They come here to pray and leave offerings; the chamber floor is littered with bottles, flags, charcoal and the remains of food. Another cavern, containing the chillingly named **Lake of No Return** (not always included in tours), is said to have been the place where the Digo tribe threw albino babies, which were believed to be bad omens. **Albinos** have a hard time of it in Tanzania: a spate of grisly murders and dismemberments since 2007 (apparently because of a belief that albino body parts have magical or at least medicinal properties) has made international headlines, and prompted a high-profile and ongoing campaign by the government and NGOs to educate people about the reality of the albino condition.

After your visit, go see the patch of **riverine forest** above and around the caves, which affords good bird- and butterfly-watching, and chance encounters with black-and-white colobus monkeys. Rounding off your trip, 3km east, are the **Galanos Sulphur Springs**. Named after a Greek sisal planter, the springs are rarely visited and the small spa beside them has been derelict for years, but it is possible to bathe in the hot, green and stinky water – particularly beneficial, it is said, for arthritis and skin ailments. Coming from Amboni, you'll have to cross the **Sigi River** by dugout (your guide will arrange this): look out for crocodiles and, needless to say, don't swim.

A guided **bicycle trip** to the caves and springs from Tanga and back takes about five hours and shouldn't cost more than $20–25 per person: visiting just the caves takes about three hours, and doesn't cost much less. Without a guide, cycle or catch a daladala 8km along the Mombasa road, then turn off 2km to Kiomoni.

## Tongoni ruins

The first European to visit **TONGONI**, a now ruined town beside a village of the same name, was **Vasco da Gama** in 1498, when, en route to opening the sea route to India, one of his ships ran aground on Mtangata shoal nearby. Likely founded in the thirteenth century, the original Tongoni was long ago reclaimed by the ocean: a ruined mosque and a jumble of graves are all that

## Moving on from Tanga

### By bus and daladala

Most **buses** depart early, with the last ones leaving shortly after noon. The bus stand, along Pangani Road, has signposted bays. Buy your ticket the day before, when, unrestrained by luggage or time, it's easier to avoid the duplicitous touts – most ticket offices are around the bus stand. The **safest** bus company for Dar and Mombasa (dry season only) is Scandinavian Express, departing from their office on Ring Street, by Mkwakwani Stadium (☎027/264 4337).

For other **long-distance destinations** (Arusha, Dodoma, Morogoro, Moshi), ask around beforehand as to the safest buses: at the time of writing, Simba Video Coach had a reasonable reputation. The wildest route from Tanga is across the Maasai Steppe to Kondoa in central Tanzania: Mwambao Bus cover this twice a week in the dry season, taking over 24 hours (there's an overnight stop along the way). For **Amani Nature Reserve**, get yourself to Muheza: any southbound bus or daladala with the exception of ones to Pangani pass by. **Lushoto** is covered by daladalas.

### By air

Coastal Aviation **fly** daily (4pm) to Pemba ($70), Zanzibar ($100) and Dar ($130). A taxi to the airport, 4km along the road to Dar, costs Tsh5000.

### By boat

The theory: Tanga port has weekly **passenger ferries** to Pemba, costing $20. The reality: companies, boats, departure days and times, even the destination (sometimes Wete, sometimes Mkoani) change on a quasi-monthly basis. And at times of political turmoil on Zanzibar (a dead-cert around elections, the next ones being due at the end of 2010, with the fall-out likely to last until mid-2011), there's nothing at all. That said, since 2006, Tuesday mornings (9am) have been a good bet for ferries to Pemba, currently Wete, arriving mid-afternoon. Given the fluidity of the situation, even the tourist offices can be misinformed, so verify things at the port. The next sailing should be chalked up at the entrance. If not, talk with the harbour master (office just inside the entrance; ☎027/264 3078).

The harbour master is the also the one to ask about **dhows** (to Zanzibar), although customs and immigration are likely to throw up insurmountable obstacles. Less painful is arranging things in Pangani. For more on dhow-hopping, see p.32.

---

remain of the evidently once-prosperous town, but the site remains evocative and atmospheric.

The **mosque** measures 12m by 13m, large for its time, though you'll need a lively imagination to picture what it might have looked like: its roof disappeared long ago, leaving only pillars, ragged walls and a finely arched *mihrab*. Surrounding the mosque on three sides is East Africa's largest collection of **Shirazi tombs**, over forty in all, with doubtless many more having succumbed to the creeping ocean. About half date from the fourteenth century, when the Shirazi–Swahili civilization was at its height. Their curious **pillars** are characteristic of Shirazi tombs in East Africa: some are square, others octagonal, but at Tongoni only one of the latter still stands erect. As with Kunduchi near Dar, and Kaole, the recesses in some of these pillars originally held Chinese or Islamic ceramic bowls, of which no trace remains. Other tombs bear traces of fine relief work, all testifying to the town's former riches; the extent of Tongoni's trading links were shown by one tomb which bore an imported glazed tile with a Persian inscription – the only such example ever found in East Africa – and which has since rather scandalously been "lost". More recent tombs, crude in comparison, date from Tongoni's brief revival in the eighteenth and nineteenth centuries, when it was occupied by **Kilwan migrants** who marvellously named the place *Sitahabu*, meaning "better than there".

## Practicalities

The ruins (9am–4pm) lie close to the beach 20km south of Tanga, ten minutes on foot from the Pangani road. A **caretaker** (who will likely be the guy dashing across the fields to meet you) collects a $3 entry fee. If it's not too hot, **access** is simplest and cheapest by bicycle from Tanga; alternatively, taxis charge Tsh25,000 for the round trip. Tanga's tourist offices ask a negotiable $20 per person if cycling with a guide, or $30–35 if travelling by car. You can also get here on any Pangani-bound bus or daladala (Tsh1000), but to be able to get back to Tanga (or carry on to Pangani), don't leave too late, as it's wise not to rely on the last bus back (for either direction), supposedly passing Tongoni around 5pm.

### Toten Island

Should Tongoni have woken the sleeping archeologist in you, the mangrove-cloaked **Toten Island**, 1km offshore in the middle of Tanga Bay, harbours another cluster of ruins, and a handful of graves, both Shirazi and (from World War I) German. Getting there is easiest via one of the tourist offices (a negotiable $35 per person by dhow or motorboat). Assuming your guide actually knows the place, once you've trudged ashore through the mangroves, finding the graves and the overgrown mosque remains (seventeenth-century, if not earlier) is simple enough, but a quest for the other mosque surveyed in the 1960s will likely end in an impassable tangle of undergrowth.

# Pangani and around

Located at the mouth of the Pangani, Tanzania's second-longest river, the small and very friendly town of **PANGANI** served in the nineteenth century as a **slaving port**, before becoming a focus for the Abushiri uprising against the German presence. There are over a dozen atmospherically decayed **buildings** from those

---

## Pangani and Rhapta

According to some, Pangani's origins – or possibly those of Bweni village on the south bank – can be traced back almost two millennia to a trading centre called **Rhapta**, mentioned in the *Periplus of the Erythraean Sea* (c.130–140 AD), an anonymous account of the considerable trade that flourished along the coast at that time. A fuller account, describing the journey of a Greek merchant named Diogenes, was given in Claudius **Ptolemy**'s *Geography*, written a century or so later, in which the metropolis of "Rhaptum" marked the end of the known world. Beyond it, according to Ptolemy, lived *anthropophagoi* – cannibals.

The identification of Pangani with Rhapta is given credence by Diogenes' claim to have "travelled for a twenty-five days journey [from Rhapta] and reached a place in the vicinity of the two great lakes and the snowy mountains from where the Nile draws its sources". Although doubted by those who consider 25 days too short a time to reach Lake Victoria (700km distant), never mind the Ruwenzori Mountains, there's nowhere else on the coast that's closer, and the mountains could be mounts Kenya and Kilimanjaro. In any case, the account proves that European knowledge of the interior was a great deal more advanced in those times than it was in the middle of the nineteenth century.

times, some with lovely carved doors. Historical interest aside, Pangani has some of the country's best **beaches** (the only niggle, for late risers, being that the sun sets inland), with a string of intimate beach hotels either side of town. Cap this with **cultural tourism**, dhow trips, snorkelling, and a couple of **dive centres** to the south, and you have a perfect place for a few days, or even weeks, of pure languor.

## Arrival and information

Apart from the road up from Saadani National Park (the ferry across the Pangani River, linking the town with Bweni village, operates between 6am and 6pm), there are two approaches, one from Tanga, the other Muheza. Neither is surfaced, and may require 4WD in the rains if they haven't recently been graded, especially the Muheza road which passes over easily waterlogged soil.

**Coming from Tanga** (43km), five buses and a few daladalas lurch along the bumpy road each day (roughly 7.30am–5pm; the first is Raha Leo). Buy tickets early to be sure of a seat. The road winds through sparsely populated marshland (look for herons and other waders) and a sisal estate, then passes farming communities surrounded by ragged coconut groves. If you're staying at one of the beach hotels north of Pangani, ask to be dropped at the appropriate turning. Taxis from Tanga charge around Tsh50,000 (Tsh30,000 to *Peponi* or *Capricorn*).

**Coming from Muheza**, there's at least one daily bus during the dry season (2–3hr), plus a few battered Land Rovers and daladalas, which leave Muheza between 10am and 3pm – get there early to be sure of a ride. The Muheza road joins the Tanga road 3km north of Pangani.

Arusha-based Regional Air (☎027/250 4164, ⓦ www.regionaltanzania.com) offers Pangani as an optional stop on their daily Arusha–Dar–Zanzibar–Arusha **flight**, arriving late afternoon ($100 from Dar); the airstrip used depends on where you're going. Safari Airlink offers the same from Dar, Zanzibar and various places in southern Tanzania, but is more expensive.

Pangani's only **bank**, NMB, has an ATM, and should in theory be able to change traveller's cheques, but as there are no fall-back options, it's best to change money before coming. Pangani is hassle-free, so there's no problem wandering around with your bags on arrival. For reliable **information** and advice, visit the cultural tourism programme (p.144).

## Pangani's cultural tourism programme

Pangani's **cultural tourism programme**, based opposite the market (Mon–Sat 8am–4pm; ☎0784/489129 or 0784/539141, ✉sekibahaculturetours@yahoo.co.uk), is well established, with most of the cultural tours offered by beach hotels being the same thing but with a mark-up. The development fees fund an educational trust.

Among the **guided walks** (roughly Tsh10,000–15,000 per person) are a two-hour historical town tour, and an extensive agricultural and nature excursion (which can be split into separate walks), combining visits to local farmers, the coconut-processing area at the mouth of the river and the German fort on the opposite bank, **sisal estates** and the 200- to 300-million-year-old fossilized remains of **dinosaurs**, concluding with dinner in a local home. Also possible are sunset **river cruises** (with a chance of spotting colobus monkeys), **dhow trips** to Maziwe Island for snorkelling (see box, p.148), and traditional dancing. The project can arrange **bicycle hire**: around Tsh5000 a day.

## Accommodation

Pangani's central hotels are quite basic; much better, and not always bankbreaking, are a string of intimate **beach hotels** either side of town. Pangani's **water supply** comes from badly maintained boreholes; purify tap water if you're going to drink it (that is, if the water supply is functioning at all).

For **camping**, *Peponi Beach Resort*, 17km north of town ($4 per person; $5 for a thatched shelter with electric socket), gets top marks for its gorgeous location, right on the beach. Other pitches are at *Tinga Tinga Lodge* ($6 per person) and, south of town, *The Beach Crab Resort* (Tsh4000) and *Tulia Beach Lodge* ($10).

### Central Pangani

*Pangadeco Bar* used to have four very cheap rooms (two with sea views over the garden), but these are currently bottle stores: worth enquiring about, though, as it's a great location. At the following, check mosquito nets for size and holes before settling in.

**River View Inn** Jamhuri St, 500m east of the ferry ☎027/263 0121. The town's cheapest is, despite a little shabbiness, acceptable. Most of the nine rooms share bathrooms. The bars has soft drinks only; meals available. ❶

**Safari Lodge** ☎027/263 0013. Very average en-suite rooms with showers and Western-style

toilets (but no seat or paper), and linoleum floors. There's also a (loud) bar and restaurant. ❷

**Stopover Guest House** 1km east of the ferry, Funguni Beach ☎0784/498458. Within staggering distance of *Pangadeco Bar* and its beach, this is the town's newest choice, with well-kept en-suite rooms. ❶

### North coast

These hotels are signposted off the Tanga road. All but *Capricorn* and *Peponi* are astride low headlands, with the beaches below disappearing at high tide. The farther north you go, the clearer the water.

**Capricorn Beach Cottages** 17km north of Pangani, beside *Peponi Beach Resort* ☎0784/632529, ⊛www.capricornbeachcottages .com. Relaxed and friendly, this has just three secluded and well-furnished self-catering cottages, with lovely ocean views, framed by baobabs, from their verandas. Each cottage has a

kitchen, bathroom, big beds with box nets and fans. The barbecue area is perfect for seafood bought from local fishermen, and the lodge stocks smoked fish, bread, cheese, wine and other treats. Snorkelling and dhow trips can be arranged. Internet access. BB ❻

▲ Sisal plantation, Pangani

**Mkoma Bay Tented Lodge** Mkoma Bay, 5km north of Pangani ☎027/263 0000 or 0786/434001, ⓦwww.mkomabay.com. This pleasingly idiosyncratic place is a stylish blend of traditional architecture and modern quirkiness. The cheaper rooms are in bungalows, and nothing to write home about; more attractive and twice the price (but also lacking views) are safari-style tents on platforms under *makuti* roofs, each with a small veranda, Zanzibari beds, box nets and bathroom. There's also a self-catering family house with four bedrooms (minimum four people; $75 each), a small swimming pool, a very good restaurant (with great sea views), and wi-fi. Rates include bicycles and kayaks; cruises and snorkelling trips are extra. BB bungalows $70, tents ❼

**Pangani Beach Resort** Mkoma Bay, 3.5km north of Pangani ☎0712/994342 or 0784/686660. A friendly place with ten clean if slightly musty and smallish en-suite rooms (no singles) in a motel-like environment, all with hot water, small twin beds (some triples also) and ripped linoleum floors, and no views. Also has a sleepy bar. BB ❸

🏃 **Peponi Beach Resort** 17km north of Pangani, 30km south of Tanga ☎0784/202962 or 0713/540139, ⓦwww.peponiresort.com. Welcoming, well-run and extremely good value, with eight comfortable two- to six-bed cottages set back from the beach in grassy gardens. Each is made from mangrove poles, coconut leaves, fibre and sisal, and has a bathroom, fans and box nets. The food is delicious and reasonably priced (à la carte or set menus), but ring ahead if you're not staying overnight. The sandy beach is a peach, there are mangroves nearby, and the hotel has its own dhow for birding and snorkelling. There's a sea-view swimming pool, too. "Peponi" means paradise – can't argue with that unless being miles from anywhere is somehow irksome. BB ❹, HB ❺ (backpackers and under 25s: BB ❸, HB ❹)

**Tinga Tinga Lodge** Mkoma Bay, 3km north of Pangani ☎027/263 0022 or 0786/364310, ⓦwww.tingatingalodge.com. Set back from the beach in rolling, spacious gardens (also home to vervet monkeys), this newly tarted up place is friendly and well run, with ten very large, circular rooms in semi-detached bungalows, each with TV, ceiling fan and plenty of furniture, but no ocean views. You can also camp using their tents. Good restaurant. If you're staying for a while, they offer package deals including cultural tourism and visits to Amani Nature Reserve. Tents BB ❸, rooms BB/HB ❻

## South coast

The south coast hotels are at **Ushongo Beach**, the turning to which is 11km south of Bweni. Unfortunately, with only very occasional exceptions, the two or three buses stick to the road 5km inland, leaving you with a 5–7km walk to the hotels. Better to arrange a transfer (usually free) or, for day-trips, a bicycle.

**The Beach Crab Resort** 18km south ☎0784/543700 or 0784/253311, ⓦwww .thebeachcrab.com. German-run, this is the cheapest place on Ushongo, with six safari tents pitched under thatched shelters (each with double bed, box net and electricity) sharing bathrooms, and some very cool, spacious en-suite bungalows made of mangrove poles and palm weave, well furnished and with verandas. Activities (not included in the price) include snorkelling, surfing, biking and scuba diving (p.148), and there's an excellent multilevel beach bar and restaurant (see p.149; great breakfasts, too). Tents BB ❸, HB ❹; bungalows HB ❻

**Emayani Beach Lodge** 16km south ☎027/264 0755, ⓦwww.emayanilodge .com. An intimate, relaxed and breezy Dutch-run place set in a coconut grove on an area of the beach with tidal pools, with plenty of activities including snorkelling, birdwatching (in nearby mangroves), river trips, windsurfing and sailing. The twelve cool and spacious thatched en-suite bungalows, nicely irregular, are decked out in castaway style, and have beach-facing verandas with jaw-dropping views. Breakfasts are lavish,

meals are reasonably priced (see p.149), and there's a well-stocked bar, too. Activities (extra cost) include snorkelling, sailing, birding, sunset cruises, and diving at Kasa Divers (see p.148) next door. HB ❼

**The Tides Lodge** 17km south ☎0784/225812, ⓦwww.thetideslodge.com. Another intimate albeit expensive British-owned place, classy yet rustic and unostentatious, in a lovely beachfront location among palm trees. There are seven individually styled thatch-roofed chalets (all very attractive), a couple of suites and a family house, plus a beachside bar, swimming pool, and one of Tanzania's best seafood restaurants, perfect for romantic candlelit dinners (see p.149). Activities include snorkelling around Maziwe Island, dhow trips, kayaking, and guided walks around Ushongo village (free). They also arrange trips to Saadani National Park. Internet access. HB ❽

**Tulia Beach Lodge** 16km south ☎027/264 0680, ⓦwww.tuliabeachlodge.com. Next to *Emayani* and with the same owners, this is more affordable, with six plain but comfy thatched sea-view cabins, good food and bar, and the same activities as *Emayani*. BB ❺, HB ❻

## The Town

Pangani is small enough to be walked around in an hour or so, but its sombre past is best explored on the cultural tourism programme's **historical walk** (see box, p.144). Whether or not you're with a guide, a walk is always a pleasure – there are picturesque tumbledown buildings all over the place, and kids are invariably ecstatic to greet visitors (as are adults, for that matter).

### The Boma and around

At the west end of town is Pangani's oldest building, the **Boma**, with particularly fine carved doors. Built in 1810 by an Omani slave trader, it's said he buried a live slave in each of its corners to ensure strong foundations (a belief that was also current in Zanzibar). The Germans made it their district office, a function it retains today. Behind it is the "**slave prison**", also from German times: despite the abolition of the slave trade, slavery itself continued well into the British period. Subsequently, the building served as the district hospital, and presently houses government offices and, once more, some cells. Two hundred metres northwest of here is the **German cemetery**. Some of its graves apparently date from the Abushiri War, others possibly contain the remains of seventeenth-century Portuguese mariners, but as all have lost their inscriptions, no one's really sure. A handful were excavated a few years ago, not by archeologists, but by locals believing the Germans had left treasure.

### The riverfront

Heading to the shore, the small **memorial garden** by the ferry slipway contains a crumbling "pillar" commemorating the handful of Germans who died in the Abushiri War (surprisingly, no memorial exists to the thousands of African victims). Walking east along the riverfront, you'll see the imposing **Customs House**, which took four years to build, opening in 1916 just before the Germans were ejected. It's used to store coconuts, most of them from plantations across the river – a legacy of the slave trade when cheap labour was plentiful. In the 1930s, **Shaaban Robert**, Tanzania's foremost poet, worked here as a customs official: his broken and rusty typewriter sits in the office. Almost next door, the **Slave Depot**, derelict and close to collapse, used to have a whipping platform where slaves were punished, and a tunnel which led to the river for ferrying blindfolded slaves to the dhows. A particularly gruesome story concerning the building tells of a slave-owner's wife's request to see an unborn child, for which a pregnant slave had her stomach sliced open while still alive.

### The market and Uhindini Street

The **market**, up the street beside the Slave Depot, makes an enjoyable detour. Look for an *mbuzi* – not a goat (though those are available too), but a coconut shredder. Properly called a *kibao cha mbuzi* ("goat board"), it resembles a small bookstand or foldable wooden chair, from one end of which – resembling a goat's tail – protrudes a serrated metal spatula. You sit on the chair part and then grate off the flesh of half a coconut on the blade. One street east of here is the road in from Tanga, whose southern continuation is **Uhindini Street** (Indian St), the place for tailors, many of

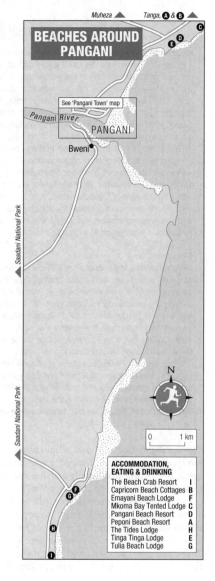

**ACCOMMODATION, EATING & DRINKING**

| | |
|---|---|
| The Beach Crab Resort | I |
| Capricorn Beach Cottages | B |
| Emayani Beach Lodge | F |
| Mkoma Bay Tented Lodge | C |
| Pangani Beach Resort | D |
| Peponi Beach Resort | A |
| The Tides Lodge | H |
| Tinga Tinga Lodge | E |
| Tulia Beach Lodge | G |

whose businesses and buildings date from the 1870s when Calcutta linen was the economic mainstay of Pangani's Indian immigrants.

### Kiwanjani and the beach

Back on the river, the area between Uhindini Street and the river mouth is called **Kiwanjani** ("fallow land"). This is where some fifty workers de-husk giant mounds of **coconuts** with sharp iron crowbars, leaving behind a surreal debris of tens of thousands of coconut husks that are carried out to sea whenever the river

## Maziwe Island Marine Reserve

**Maziwe Island Marine Reserve**, 13km southeast of Pangani, was established after the island's fringing corals were badly damaged by dynamite fishing and careless anchoring. It protects one of the north coast's best reefs for **snorkelling and diving**, with some especially beautiful coral heads ("bommies") and sea fans providing food and shelter for hundreds of tropical fish species, including moray eels, poison-barbed lionfish, butterfly fish, leaf fish, clownfish, starfish and octopus. Keep your eyes peeled on the way out, as bottlenose **dolphins** are frequently seen. Divers may also get to see green turtles and blue-spotted rays.

The island itself has a **strange history**. Nowadays merely a sandbank, until the 1960s it was wooded with casuarina trees, fringed with mangroves, and its beaches served as East Africa's most important nesting ground for three species of turtle. By 1976, the last casuarina had been felled, and the final blow came during the 1978–79 war with Idi Amin's Uganda, when, it is said (not entirely plausibly), the remaining mangroves were cleared away for security reasons. The mangroves never returned, and the ensuing erosion – coupled with rising sea levels – causes the island to be completely submerged at high tide.

### Practicalities

On **snorkelling trips**, costs are $20–50 per person including equipment, according to group size, boat used (motorboat or *ngalawa* outrigger), and where you arrange things: hotels are more expensive, cheaper is the cultural tourism programme. Outriggers take ninety minutes, motorboats about half that. A modest marine park fee ($1) and $2 donation to the Friends of Maziwe (an association of hoteliers, boat owners and fishermen, the reserve's effective custodians) should be included in the cost. Sailing out from Pangani, notice the German fort (1916) on the river's south bank, half-hidden by vegetation.

There are two PADI-accredited **scuba diving centres** on Ushongo Beach, south of town: the Belgian-run Kasa Divers (ⓦwww.kasa-divers.com) between *Emayani* and *Tulia* lodges; and the eponymous outfit at *The Beach Crab Resort* (ⓦwww .thebeachcrab.com). Both offer the usual array of courses. It's best to stay at one of the south coast hotels, as bus times don't really fit.

---

floods. Pangani District's vast coconut plantations constitute about half of Tanzania's production. Beyond the husking ground, either follow the shore itself as it curls north into **Funguni Beach** and the ocean proper, or follow the road a few hundred metres along to the *Pangadeco Bar*, which also has beach access. Although the water doesn't look too enticing (the brown colour comes from the silt gathered along the river's 400km journey), it's apparently safe to bathe here so long as you stay to the left, away from the river, but **be careful** of currents: the river pushes its waters out a good few kilometres before losing itself in the ocean. At low tide you can walk almost 1km out to sea over the sand flats, but keep an eye on the tide. It's fine to walk up the beach to Mkoma Bay (4km) if you're not carrying valuables.

## Eating and drinking

Pangani's best restaurants – many offering quite stupendous seafood, and equally delicious ocean views – are in the **beach hotels** north and south. Most of them happily receive day-trippers for lunch, but ring beforehand (see our hotel reviews for contact numbers) as they may be busy with their own guests. Eating out in Pangani itself is very limited, so unless you're content with chips/rice with fried chicken/fish, **order early**. The cheapest eats, including stewed or grilled octopus, are at the **foodstalls** along Jamhuri Street near the ferry.

Given that Pangani is mainly Muslim, the ever-growing battalion of **bars** is quite a surprise, and a source of considerable exasperation for the elderly **muezzin** of the main mosque, who is famous for his unusually blunt early morning exhortations to the not-so-faithful, starting with a strident series of loudspeakered "*Amka!*" ("Wake up!"), followed by a litany of colourful curses which invariably include the line, "If you sleep now, your bed shall be your bier and your sheets your shroud!"

## Central Pangani

**Central Bar** For good, cheap and filling portions of *nyama choma* (evenings), grilled chicken and *chipsi mayai*, this is definitely the place to be, and it stays open late. There are tables on the street corner veranda, a dartboard, cheerful music and satellite TV.

**Pangadeco Bar** Funguni Beach. Chilled-out if slightly tawdry, thanks to the prostitutes who frequent the bar, this enjoys an unbeatable beach-front location, and has plenty of tables under creaking trees in the gardens, and a wonderful beach close by (see p.148). Without at least two hours' notice you're likely to find only basics after 3pm. Pre-ordered, meat, fish, octopus or prawns cost Tsh4000–6000, depending on the season. Hosts discos Wed, Fri & Sun.

**Safari Lodge** Functions mainly as an (often loud) bar. The food is reasonably priced, with most dishes around Tsh5000, all with fresh salad.

## North coast

**Mkoma Bay Tented Lodge** Mkoma Bay, 5km north of Pangani. Great views, good seafood, a snappy menu (including light lunches), and the bonus of genuine espresso and a good wine list. Diners may also be able to use the swimming pool. Meals $10–15.

**Tinga Tinga Lodge** Mkoma Bay, 3km north of Pangani. Great seafood and fantastic ocean views. A la carte starts at around $10 a plate; seafood barbecues, including lobster, cost $20 per person, minimum four (and order a day in advance). There's also good Indian and Cajun.

## South coast

**The Beach Crab Resort** 18km south of town. The enchanting multilevel beach bar and restaurant here has a great reputation for inspired use of local ingredients, whether home-made seafood ravioli, marinated octopus, or vegetable stews. Also bakes its own bread. Light lunches Tsh5000, three-course dinners Tsh13,000.

**Emayani Beach Lodge** 16km south of town. A good target for day-trips if you can be sure of transport back, and very reasonably priced ($5 lunch, $12 dinner). They're happy catering for unusual diets, too.

**The Tides Lodge** 17km south of Pangani. Some people have been known to fly in just to have lunch at this elegant open-sided restaurant. Understated sophistication is the thing, and quite spectacular seafood – including a $20 platter you can share. Main courses, like prawns in garlic and herb butter, average $8–10.

### Moving on from Pangani

The first **buses** and **daladalas**, for Tanga and Muheza, leave between 6am and 6.30am. You should definitely catch one of these if you're heading on to Amani Nature Reserve or Dar, and buy your onward ticket as soon as you arrive. The last guaranteed vehicle to Muheza leaves at 8am. The last bus to Tanga departs at 4.30pm. If you're **driving**, there's an adventurous and infrequently travelled route south of Pangani into Saadani National Park (see p.131 for details).

Getting a passage from Pangani on a **dhow to Zanzibar** (either to Mkokotoni or, more usually, Nungwi village, both at the northern tip of Unguja Island; read the general advice on p.32) is relatively straightforward, with at least two motorized dhows each week, taking four hours if things run smoothly – ask at the cultural tourism programme, or at hotels. Costs are $20–45 per person depending on the number of passengers.

**Flying** out of Pangani is possible if there were enough passengers warranting a stop in the first place: Regional Air for Arusha (ⓦwww.regionaltanzania.com), or Safari Airlink for Dar, Zanzibar and the southern circuit (ⓦwww.safariaviation.info).

# Travel details

## Buses and daladalas

The bus companies Hood, Tashriff (Tawakal), Takrim and Tawfiq have reputations for reckless driving and should be avoided. During the long rains, usually March–May, the road to Mombasa from Tanga can be blocked.

**Bagamoyo** to: Dar (hourly; 1hr 30min); Msata (every 2hr; 2–3hr).

**Pangani** to: Muheza (2 daily; 2–3hr); Tanga (5 daily; 2–3hr).

**Tanga** to: Arusha (6 daily; 6hr); Dar (6–8 daily; 6hr); Kondoa (2 weekly, dry weather only; 26hr); Korogwe (hourly; 1hr 30min); Lushoto (5 daily; 3hr); Mombasa (4 daily; 4–7hr); Mombo (hourly; 2hr); Morogoro (4 daily; 5–6hr); Moshi (3–4 daily; 5hr); Muheza (frequent; 45min); Pangani (5 daily; 2–3hr).

## Flights

**Pangani** (Regional Air) to: Arusha (daily; 2hr).
**Pangani** (Safari Airlink) to: Dar (2 daily; 50min); Mikumi (daily; 2hr 50min); Ruaha (daily; 4hr 20min); Selous (daily; 2hr); Zanzibar (2 daily; 20min), and various southern Tanzania airstrips.
**Saadani** (Safari Airlink) to: Dar (2 daily; 1hr); Mikumi (daily; 3hr); Ruaha (daily; 4hr 30min); Selous (daily; 2hr 10min); Zanzibar (2 daily; 15min), and various southern Tanzania airstrips.
**Tanga** (Coastal Aviation) to: Dar (daily; 1hr 35min); Pemba (daily; 25min); Zanzibar (daily; 1hr 5min).

## Ferries

**Tanga** to: Pemba (weekly; 6hr), but unreliable.

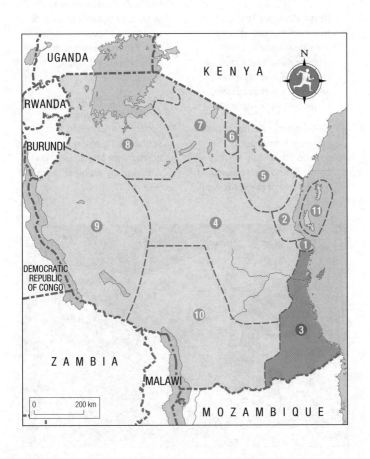

**3**

# The south coast

CHAPTER 3 # Highlights

* **Mafia archipelago** Superb scuba diving, equally good snorkelling, plenty of messing about in dhows, heaps of historical interest, and one of Tanzania's best beaches. See p.155

* **Kilwa Kisiwani** The ruins of this medieval island state, in its time the wealthiest metropolis in East Africa, are among the country's most impressive and evocative historical sites. See p.166

* **Kilwa Kivinje** An atmospheric and very tumbledown nineteenth-century slaving harbour, whose rise signalled the demise of Kilwa Kisiwani. See p.172

* **Mikindani** Another old slaving port with plenty of ruins, a pleasantly laid-back atmosphere and one of Tanzania's nicest hotels. See p.179

* **MaKuYa** It's just once a year, but Mtwara's festival of traditional Makonde, Makua and Yao music is reason enough to head south. See p.186

* **Mnazi Bay-Ruvuma Estuary Marine Park** Superb beaches, snorkelling and scuba diving along the border with Mozambique, and virtually no other visitors. See p.187

▲ Gereza Fort, Kilwa Kisiwani

# The south coast

U ntil recently, the south coast was Tanzania's forgotten quarter, cast adrift from the rest of the country during the rains when the roads in from Dar, Songea and Mozambique turned into impassable swills of mud. Whilst access has improved significantly with the construction of bridges over the Rufiji River and over the Ruvuma from Mozambique, the coast still retains a backwater feeling: tourist development is minimal, few locals speak English, and whilst there are a few nice beaches, the lack of sanely priced beach hotels in most of these restricts that pleasure to upmarket travellers. Where the south coast comes into its own is for some of best **scuba diving** in Africa, and **historical sights** – from the earliest days of the Persian landfall over a thousand years ago to the slave trade and German conquest of the nineteenth century.

Combining both these attractions is the **Mafia archipelago**, whose coral reefs are highly rated by scuba divers and snorkellers alike, and where you can also explore old Swahili ruins, or just swan around by dhow exploring mangroves. The other big pull is **Kilwa**, beyond the swampy Rufiji River delta, which is actually three towns: tumbledown Kilwa Kivinje, steeped in the history of slavery and German colonialism; Kilwa Masoko, the main base for visitors; and Kilwa Kisiwani, the impressive ruins of a medieval island-state.

Further south you'll find **Mikindani**, a fishing village with links to slaving times, but no beach. For that, excursions can be arranged to **Mnazi Bay–Ruvuma Estuary Marine Park**, along the border with Mozambique, and which, like Mafia, is positively brimming with aquatic life. Heading inland from the port towns of Mtwara or Lindi, you can explore the **Makonde Plateau**, home of the famous woodcarving tribe. Further west there's little to detain you, but those with a degree of immunity to physical discomfort could attempt the road to Lake Nyasa, indubitably one of Tanzania's most adventurous roads when travelling by public transport.

With the exception of Mafia, mainstream tourism is a novelty, so there are some **practical issues** to be aware of. For a start, a 50km stretch of road south of the Rufiji River has yet to be asphalted, so until it's completed, driving all the way from Dar may be impossible in the heaviest rains. Also, off the main roads neither public transport nor accommodation can be relied on, so if you want to see much more than the places summarized above, it's best to be driving in **your own car** (and have someone fluent in **Kiswahili** tagging along). Alternatively, you can arrange tours in Mikindani, Newala, and – informally – in Kilwa. If you're on a budget, bring a **tent**, as there are only a few guesthouses you might actually *want* to stay in. Money is also tricky: don't rely on being able to change **traveller's cheques**, so bring cash, or cards for use at ATMs (Lindi and Mtwara only). Lastly, be sure to pop those pills, as **malaria** is rife.

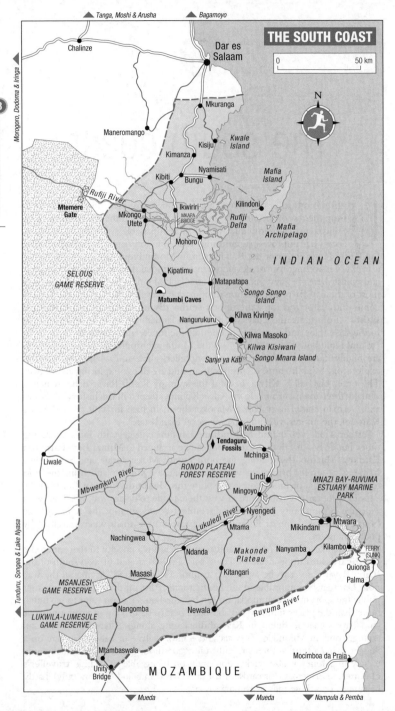

THE SOUTH COAST

0          50 km

N

Tanga, Moshi & Arusha          Bagamoyo

Chalinze

Dar es
Salaam

Morogoro, Dodoma & Iringa

Mkuranga

Maneromango

Kisiju          Kwale
Island

Kimanza

Kibiti     Nyamisati          Mafia
     Bungu          Island

Rufiji River

Mtemere
Gate

Ikwiriri          Kilindoni
          MKAPA
Mkongo     BRIDGE     Rufiji
Utete          Delta     Mafia
          Archipelago
     Mohoro

INDIAN  OCEAN

SELOUS
GAME RESERVE

Kipatimu

Matapatapa     Songo Songo
          Island

Matumbi Caves

Nangurukuru     Kilwa Kivinje

          Kilwa Masoko
          Kilwa Kisiwani
Sanje ya Kati     Songo Mnara Island

Kitumbini

Tendaguru
Fossils
          Mchinga

Liwale          RONDO PLATEAU
          FOREST RESERVE     Lindi     MNAZI BAY-RUVUMA
          ESTUARY MARINE
          Mingoyo          PARK

Mbwemkuru River          Lukuledi River     Nyengedi

          Mtama     Mikindani     Mtwara

Tunduru, Songea & Lake Nyasa

Nachingwea          Nanyamba     Kilambo
          Ndanda     Makonde          FERRY
          Plateau          (SUNK)
          Kitangari          Quionga
Masasi
          Palma
MSANJESI
GAME RESERVE

LUKWILA-LUMESULE          Nangomba     Newala     Ruvuma River
GAME RESERVE

Mtambaswala

Unity
Bridge          MOZAMBIQUE          Mocímboa da Praia

Mueda          Mueda     Nampula & Pemba

# The Mafia archipelago

Just 25km offshore from the Rufiji delta, and 130km south of Dar, is the **Mafia Archipelago**, comprising Mafia Island, the much smaller islands of Chole, Juani and Jibondo, and a host of minor atolls. Girdled by one of the world's richest marine habitats, much of it a protected **park**, Mafia's main attraction is its sea life, but that's not all it has to offer. A series of overgrown **ruins** provide picturesque reminders of medieval and colonial times, and you can also explore remnants of coastal **forest** in search of duikers, monkeys, wild pigs, bushbabies, or black and rufous elephant shrews, and there are even "dwarf" **hippos**. **Birdlife** is plentiful, too, with 130 recorded species. **Awkward access** (there are no ferries from Dar) means that Mafia receives few tourists, the bulk of them coming in July and August, and, encompassing the main diving season, between November and March.

## Some history

Recent discoveries of ancient Egyptian, Mediterranean and Indian pottery in a cave on Mafia's Juani Island show the archipelago was well embedded in the western Indian Ocean's trading network no later than 700 BC, a thousand years earlier than previously thought. Whether the first inhabitants were Africans or immigrants remains open to debate, but Iron Age forges show that an agricultural people had crossed over from the mainland no later than 200 AD. Around that time, the mainland trading port of **Rhapta** (possibly in the Rufiji delta, or at Pangani; see p.142) was, according to the *Periplus of the Erythrean Sea*, ruled by the Yemeni state of Ma'afir, whose name may have stuck to the archipelago. Alternatively, "Mafia" may derive from the Arabic *morfiya*, meaning group, and, by extension, archipelago.

The archipelago was a natural stopover for Arab and Persian dhows plying the ancient trade routes between East Africa and Arabia, and archeological finds show that Mafia, in its heyday, was trading as far afield as **Ming-dynasty China**. Following its conquest by the **Portuguese** captain Duarte Lemos in 1508, Mafia's

## The Rufiji River delta

The swampy, mosquito-infested **Rufiji River delta**, roughly 130km south of Dar, is the reason why the road to Kilwa was so often cut during the rains, and also explains the underwater marvels of the Mafia archipelago just offshore: flanking the delta's myriad streams, lakes, tidal marshes and sandbanks is East Africa's largest **mangrove forest**, covering 5300 square kilometres. This serves as a gigantic filter for Tanzania's largest river, letting through micronutrients whilst retaining sediments that would otherwise suffocate Mafia's corals.

During the long rains, the river jumps its banks by up to fifteen kilometres, fertilizing the surrounding land and feeding innumerable lakes and pools. The waters are important breeding grounds for prawns, shrimps and fish, and coupled with the largely intact riverine forest, attract incredibly rich **birdlife** (the delta is a RAMSAR conservation site). The plain-backed sunbird, longbills, lovebirds, and the majestic African fish eagle are commonly seen, while rarer species include the African pitta, found north of the river, and Livingstone's flycatcher, to the south. There are moves afoot to establish community-based tourism in the delta, but for now the only practical approach is a **boat trip** from Mafia arranged at one of the lodges, which will cost a pretty penny.

fortunes nose-dived, culminating in the destruction of Kua, the island's main town, by cannibalistic Madagascan visitors, the Sakalava, in 1829. The archipelago's fortunes revived briefly after 1840 under the control of Zanzibar's **Busaïdi dynasty**, but the days of the slave trade were numbered. In 1890, when Zanzibar was forced to become a British "protectorate", its sultan was forced to sell Mafia to Germany for four million marks. The British seized Mafia in 1915 for use as a base in their hunt for the cruiser **Königsberg**, which had taken refuge in the Rufiji delta – a cat and mouse affair that tied down British troops and resources for over eleven months. Once the cruiser was located (and sunk by the Germans, who escaped with the ship's guns), Mafia became the backwater it is today.

This eclectic history is reflected in the archipelago's **inhabitants**. Apart from the Mbwera, believed to be related to Mafia's first African inhabitants, there are Shirazis, Hadhramaut Arabs, Omanis, Indians, and Madagascan and Comoran

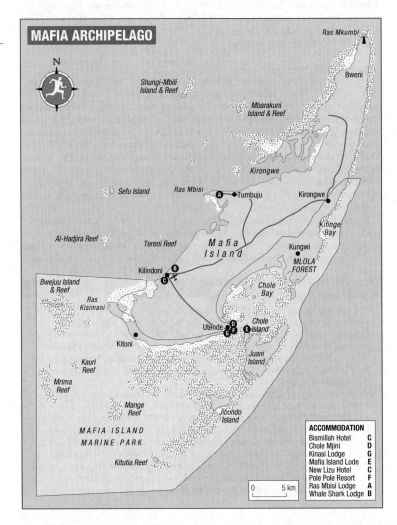

## MAFIA ARCHIPELAGO

N

Ras Mkumbi

Bweni

Shungi-Mbili
Island & Reef

Mbarakuni
Island & Reef

Kirongwe

Sefu Island    Ras Mbisi    Ⓐ ●Tumbuju    Kirongwe

Kifinge
Bay

Al-Hadjira Reef    Tereni Reef    *M a f i a
I s l a n d*    Kungwi

MLOLA
FOREST

Kilindoni    Ⓑ
Ⓒ

Bwejuu Island
& Reef    Chole
Bay

Ras
Kisimani

Chole
Island

Utende    ⒹⒺ
ⒼⒻ

Kitoni

Juani
Island

Kauri
Reef

Mrima
Reef

Mange
Reef

Jibondo
Island

MAFIA ISLAND
MARINE PARK

Kitutia Reef

| ACCOMMODATION | |
|---|---|
| Bismillah Hotel | C |
| Chole Mjini | D |
| Kinasi Lodge | G |
| Mafia Island Lode | E |
| New Lizu Hotel | C |
| Pole Pole Resort | F |
| Ras Mbisi Lodge | A |
| Whale Shark Lodge | B |

0    5 km

traders. But the majority descend from slaves, including northern Kenya's Pokomo tribe. More recent immigrants include Pakistani Baluch on the south side of Mafia Island near Kitoni, who arrived in the nineteenth century as members of an expedition sent by the Zanzibari sultan, and Makonde, who settled in Utende as recently as 1991, having fled Mozambique's civil war.

# Mafia Island

The largest by far of the archipelago's islands is **Mafia Island**, spanning 55km from northeast to southwest, much of it covered by coconut plantations. The main town and port is **KILINDONI**, a scruffy, dozy little place for most of the time (especially during the rains), but endowed with a nice beach, an attractively poky market and an animated harbour. It's also useful for mundane things, as it has a bank, post office, telephones and a pharmacy. Try to coincide with a **full moon**, when an age-old ritual procession brings the place alive. Starting in the evening, the milling crowd is headed by women singing to the rhythms of a brass band and drummers, as kids dash around in an excitable frenzy. The music resembles Swahili Taarab, not only in rhythm and melody, but because it's women who dictate the words and therefore the mood. Although the new moon is important in Islam, marking the months of the Hegira calendar, the significance of the full moon is rooted in pre-Islamic times. Respect for more orthodox Islam is evident when the procession falls silent as it moves past the Friday Mosque (only to pick up with more verve on the other side).

In the east, **Chole Bay** is where most dhow trips start. *Mafia Island Lodge*, the only hotel here with a decent beach (and with fine swimming at high tide), is a good target for day-trippers, and will happily lay on snorkelling excursions, meals and drinks. Keen **bird-watchers** may care to linger awhile: waders, falcons and fish eagles, lilac-breasted rollers, black kites and crab plovers are frequently seen in the bay and in the woodland behind.

**Ras Kisimani** – the "Headland of the Wells" – is Mafia Island's westernmost point, and was a major port until 1872, when it, and much of its headland, was washed away by a cyclone. Potsherds and other remnants still turn up on the beach, the oldest having been dated to the twelfth century (see box, p.162). Chole Bay's lodges run trips to Kisimani for around $200 per boat or $40–50 per person.

## Arrival

The archipelago is most easily reached by plane. **Mafia airport**, a grand name for a dirt runway plus shed, is a five-minute walk from Kilindoni, and has daily flights from Dar ($115) and Zanzibar ($150) on Coastal Aviation and Tropical Air.

For stricter budgets, there are passenger-carrying **cargo boats** (Tsh7000; 3hr) which leave each afternoon from **Nyamisati**, 145km south of Dar (the turning is at Bungu, 120km along). Daladalas from Dar's southern terminals of Mbagala or Rangi Tatu go all the way (Tsh4000; 3hr). More adventurous, but potentially dangerous (see p.32), is to catch a **dhow** from Kisiju (Tsh5000 for locals), 90km south of Dar, which can take anything from five to twenty hours. From Dar, catch a southbound bus or daladala and get off at Mkuranga, from where very crowded pick-ups cover the remaining 45km (count on two hours for this bit, as the road is very sandy). The boats sail at high tide, and may stop over at Kwale or Kome Islands en route. Kisiju has rudimentary guesthouses, but also a reputation for petty theft, so take care. One more piece of advice: use the toilets in Kisiju, unless you fancy testing the cantilevered contraptions slung over the vessel's side.

▲ Hawksbill turtle, Mafia Island

## Accommodation

Upmarket travellers have their pick of posh places at **Chole Bay** in the east, and one on the west coast, but budget travellers are limited to **Kilindoni**, the main town and port on Mafia. You'll have to splurge (albeit modestly) to get the most from your stay, whether you're snorkelling, or visiting Chole, Juani and Jibondo islands by dhow. Daladalas, including pick-up trucks, are hit-and-miss for **day-trips**, but if you're patient, and happy to rely on luck for the ride back, they are possible. Better, though, is to arrange a trip through your hotel, or rent a bicycle – it's just 14km to Chole Bay.

### Kilindoni and around

Apart from *Whale Shark Lodge*, the town's best **restaurant** – not that there's much competition – is *Al-Watan*. Run by a couple of friendly women, it's a basic *mgahawa* around the corner from *New Lizu*, and if you order early enough they can prepare all manner of tasty dishes. Also good are the foodstalls by the market and at the harbour. The only local **bar** is a spartan room at *New Lizu*. **Camping** is possible at *Whale Shark Lodge* (Tsh5000 per person).

**Bismillah Hotel** 50m from the *New Lizu* in an unmarked blue building. Very basic and with horrid shared long-drops and bucket showers, but it's safe, and all rooms have ceiling fans – make sure you get one with a mosquito net. *Kijuju Guest House*, 300m from *New Lizu* along the Utende road, is similar. ❶

**New Lizu Hotel** At junction of the roads from the airport, and harbour, 500m from either ☎023/240 2683. For a long time this was the only option in town, and is past its prime. Although the rooms have bathrooms, they're overpriced given that most lack mosquito nets (but they do at least have fans). Food is available but order early for octopus or prawns. ❷

**Ras Mbisi Lodge** 16km northeast of Kilindoni ☎0754/663739 or 0734/284397, ⓦwww.mafiaislandtz.com. No question about it: this British-owned lodge, an hour's drive from Chole Bay, is one of the best along any stretch of Tanzanian coastline. Situated in a remote location on an ever-so-sweet beach, complete with swaying palm trees, this sustainably built place has an intimate vibe, friendly staff and a swimming pool, so it's great for families as well as smoochy couples. The accommodation isn't half bad either: the nine beachside *bandas* are all made from coconut wood, coconut poles and thatch. The food is fabulous, and its ethics are more than just words, with biogas-powered electricity, extensive use of coconut wood, solar heated water, and good local relations. Activities (at an extra cost) include snorkelling, diving, sunset cruises, canoeing and various land excursions. Rates include transfers. Closed April and May. FB

 **Whale Shark Lodge** On the beach behind the hospital, 1.5km northeast of

Kilindoni ⊤ 0755/696067 or 023/201 0201, Ⓔ carpho2003@yahoo.co.uk. A nicely oddball (and always helpful) Italian place, with a beautiful stretch of sand and a fantastically sited bar/restaurant. Best of all, it's affordable, with five clean and comfortable two-bed *bandas*, and you're welcome to pitch a tent. Meals cost $7, and they have plenty of contacts for excursions. BB ❸

## Chole Bay

Airport transfers to Chole Bay's lodges cost $20–30 per vehicle, or are free if you're staying at *Pole Pole*. Before choosing a hotel, do read other travellers' reviews (good websites are on p.74), as standards can be surprisingly changeable. Also, be aware that there's no **swimming** at low tide, and the only hotel with a decent **beach** is *Mafia Island Lodge*; *Chole Mjini* has no beach at all, while the other two only have silty clearings amidst the mangroves. On the plus side, all offer loads of activities, including scuba diving. All lodges are closed from Easter to the end of May or mid-June.

**Chole Mjini** Chole Island ⊛ www.cholemjini.com. Run by a South African couple who are passionate about diving. Rooms are in six alluring, Robinson Crusoe-style tree houses built from wood, thatch and mangrove poles; each has two floors, a double bed, and a bucket shower and composting toilet in a straw shelter at the base. There's also one ground-level room. The lack of electricity might just be an attraction, but the lack of beach (or swimming pool) is a real drawback, even if you get some beach lounging on the snorkelling and dhow trips included in the rates. It's quite basic for the price, although $10 a head goes to the local community. FB ❾

**Kinasi Lodge** Chole Bay ⊛ www.mafiaisland.com. A slightly strange place, half-way between classic holiday resort and boutique hideaway. It has a swimming pool, dive centre, and plenty of facilities, but lacks the charm of *Pole Pole* and *Chole Mjini*. Rooms are in fourteen large and airy *makuti*-roofed bungalows set on a low hillside, six facing the sea. The open-plan lounge area is a delight, with a bar, satellite TV and an extraordinary reference library: they really know their stuff, as shown by a superb selection of excursions (at an extra cost), whether historical-, cultural- or natural-themed. Bicycles,

kayaks and windsurf boards are provided free of charge. FB ❾

**Mafia Island Lodge** Chole Bay ⊛ www .mafialodge.com. This is a welcome transformation of a once-stark government-run hotel into an attractive, unpretentious and affordable, *makuti*-thatched resort that wouldn't look out of place on Zanzibar. The forty rooms are in long coral-stone blocks, and are comfortable if nothing special; all have a/c, hot water, fans and nets, and bay-view verandas. The excellent (and natural) beach compensates for the lack of intimacy. Facilities include a seafood restaurant and terrace bar, a dive centre, and a full range of excursions (not included). Internet access. HB ❼

 **Pole Pole Resort** Chole Bay ⊛ www .polepole.com. An intimate and well-managed Italian-run lodge with a well-regarded dive centre. It's the most stylish of the lot, with attentive service and fittingly *eccellente* cuisine. There are just seven exquisitely designed and furnished ocean-facing bungalows on stilts with private verandas, including two for families. The lodge is run on sound ethical principles, with good local relations, and a hand in development projects. Rates include dhow trips and snorkelling. FB ❾

# Excursions from Chole Bay

Mafia's main **historical attractions** occupy a trio of **islands** accessed from Chole Bay, boat trips to which are offered by Chole Bay's hotels. If you're staying elsewhere, there are three possibilities: get your hotel to arrange things; arrange things through one of the Chole Bay hotels beforehand; or do it yourself. For the latter, get to Chole Bay as early as you can to strike a deal with fishermen (on the beach) for the boat.

## Mafia Island Marine Park

Established in 1995, **Mafia Island Marine Park** (ⓦwww.marineparktz.com; $10 entry fee paid on arrival at Chole Bay) protects 822 square kilometres of coastline, reefs, mangroves and remnant coastal forest, and includes the islands of Chole, Jibondo and Juani, and Mafia Island's southeastern shore from Chole Bay down. Altogether, over four hundred species of fish have been recorded in the area, together with forty-nine genera of hard corals and a dozen soft (including giant table corals, huge stands of blue-tipped staghorn, whip corals and delicate sea fans), 140 forms of sponge, seven mangrove species, 134 species of marine algae, and a seagrass area inhabited by the locally near-extinct **dugong** – a blubbery mammal that's apparently behind old seafarers' tales of mermaids. The archipelago is also an important nesting site for **hawksbill and green turtles**, some migrating from as far away as South Africa or Aldabra Atoll in the Seychelles. Turtle populations have declined dramatically over recent decades, a result of *jarife* shark nets for fishing, and habitat damage through the use of beach seine nets and dynamite fishing. However, the efforts of the WWF, and now a community-based NGO, Sea Sense (ⓦwww.seasense.org), have had positive results: now some 250 nests and over twenty thousand hatchlings are protected annually.

### Snorkelling

Snorkelling is best inside **Chole Bay**, with plenty of coral outcrops 2–8m below the surface. It's a fantastic place to see East Africa's colourful marine life, including lionfish, damselfish, angelfish, sponges, sea cucumbers and all sorts of crustaceans. Other good snorkelling areas are Okuta Reef around **Jibondo Island**, the Blue Lagoon south of **Juani Island**, and **Kifinge Bay** on the northeast side of Mafia Island, which is also a nesting site for green turtles. With more time (and money for the boat),

# Chole Island

The tiny, lushly vegetated **Chole Island**, 1.5km east of Chole Bay, is the archipelago's oldest continuously inhabited settlement, having taken over Kua's mantle as capital when the latter was sacked in 1829. Under Busaïdi rule from Zanzibar, Chole gained notoriety as one of East Africa's main **slave-trading** centres, so much so that the much larger Mafia Island was for a time known as "Chole's Farm", as its coconut plantations were owned by slavers from Chole. But the slave trade was nearing its end, and now all that remains of the once-wealthy nineteenth-century town is a picturesque collection of ruins overgrown with the twisted roots of strangling fig trees.

Access to the island is by **boat** from Chole Bay. Small outriggers, basking in the grandiose title of "ferries", shuttle between the beach in front of *Mafia Island Lodge* and the island; the ten-minute trip costs Tsh300. Alternatively, the Chole Bay hotels offer half-day trips for $10. The boats land next to a church-like building, erected in the 1990s as a fish market but now used to sell high-quality woven mats, made from the fronds of *mikindu* phoenix palms. These colourful, naturally dyed mats have been made for centuries and come in two forms: large, rectangular floor mats (*majamvi*), or oval prayer mats (*misala*).

Immediately behind the market, in the lee of a glorious stand of frangipani trees, is Chole's most impressive ruin; a coral ragstone façade and foundations that were once part of the **German governor's residence** between 1892 and 1913, when the island's capital was shifted to Kilindoni. Prior to colonization, an Omani slave trader owned the house, and it's from this period that Chole's other ruins date. The old **prison**, almost next door amidst a fantastic tangle of fig-tree roots, has weathered the years somewhat better than its neighbour, with its eight

**Kitutia Reef** to the south of Mafia Island is also recommended, and has a lovely sand bank on which, tides permitting, you could have lunch.

**Access** to the reefs is by *mashua* dhow or *ngalawa* outrigger, which can be rented informally with fishermen on the beach facing *Mafia Island Lodge* ($20 per person including equipment). It's best to arrange things the day before, and you'll need a measure of luck with tides and winds. More reliable are motorboats (minimum four or six people), as provided by the lodges: $40–60 for a full day's snorkelling, including lunch.

### Scuba diving

Mafia has some of the best scuba diving in East Africa, although visibility isn't all it's cracked up to be. Conditions are best in November (with a good chance of sharks, too), and in February, but strong winds between June and September, and sometimes December and January, may confine you to Chole Bay. But there's still plenty to see at a range of diving depths, especially at **Kinasi Wall**, a glorious drift dive whose dense coral formations are home to huge groupers, large shoals of snappers, stingrays and ribbontail rays, and occasional "heavyweights" such as white-tipped reef and tiger sharks, barracuda and turtles. Also good inside the bay is **Chole Wall**, which has fewer big fish but pristine corals, and good odds for seeing turtles close-up.

All three Chole Bay hotels, and *Chole Mjini*, have PADI-accredited **dive centres**. But the related outfits at *Mafia Island Lodge* and *Pole Pole Resort* have a better reputation for beginners, and are cheaper than the rest, both charging $390 for the Open Water course (plus $70 for the manual), or $300 including equipment for a ten-dive package if you're already qualified. Drift dives or night dives are $60 each. For general information on scuba diving in Tanzania, see p.56.

small cells – said to have held up to fifty inmates each – still intact, though missing their roofs. The inmates were (presumably) mostly slaves, as the free population of Chole would surely never have needed so large a jail. Further along the broad "Market Street", which is said to have had lanterns arrayed along its length (something that's difficult to imagine), a series of rectangular stumps within a low wall are said to have been the tethering pillars of the **slave market**, although some say the structure was merely a warehouse. The ruins of a Hindu temple further on have, like the prison, acquired an impressive encrustation of fig-tree roots, which appear to be the only things keeping the walls upright. A mosque, wells and other stone houses can also be seen.

Among Chole's other curiosities are colonies of giant **Comoros fruit bats** (also called "flying foxes") that roost by day in big mango trees and which – unlike their cave-dwelling cousins – rely on eyesight rather than sonar to navigate. The colonies are included on a **bat trail**, whose winding pathways provide an ideal way of acquainting yourself with the island's lush vegetation. Leaflets detailing the trail and other walks can be picked up at *Chole Mjini* lodge. For more information, ask at the lodge for the excellent *Chole Booklet* (Tsh5000) by Dudley Iles and Christine Walley; you might also find copies at Chole Bay's hotels.

## Jibondo and Juani islands

An hour's sail south of Chole is the most traditional of the archipelago's settlements, **Jibondo Island**. Most of its two thousand inhabitants engage in shark fishing and octopus baiting, but seaweed farming – introduced by an NGO in 1992 – also provides income. Traditionally, the islanders also caught **turtles**, but the turtles and their nesting grounds are now protected by the marine park. Until

## Kua, Kisimani and cannibals

Mafia's strategic location made it a coveted base for traders, and it created plenty of **rivalries**, too; initially between Persian and Arab immigrants, and later between the archipelago's main towns, **Kua and Kisimani**, allied to Kilwa and Zanzibar respectively.

Legend tells the dark tale of a large *jahazi* **dhow** that was to be launched at Kisimani. The people of Kua were invited over for the celebrations, but on arriving, their children were bound, laid in front of the dhow and then crushed as the dhow was launched. **Revenge** took time to come, but was impassive when it did. After a few years, the people of Kua invited their rivals for a wedding. The people of Kisimani, assuming they'd been forgiven for killing the children, arrived unsuspecting. The wedding feast was held in a beautifully decorated underground chamber, from which, one by one, the people of Kua excused themselves, until only a very old man remained to entertain the guests. The chamber entrance was sealed off, and the scores were settled.

Historians still debate the **catastrophe** that subsequently overtook Kua. According to one story, a harsh queen ruled Kua at the start of the nineteenth century and some of her opponents travelled to Madagascar to seek help from the ruling **Sakalava**. The Sakalava people agreed to help overthrow the queen on condition that they be allowed to rule Kua, but when they arrived, in 1829, with a force of eighty canoes, they proceeded to sack the entire town, regardless of allegiance, allegedly eating many of its inhabitants in the process. A good proportion of the three thousand survivors were sold into slavery, and by 1840 the last inhabitants had deserted Kua to start new lives on Kome Island, halfway between Mafia and Kisiju on the mainland. Locals say that both Kua and Kisimani were destroyed for their wickedness, Kisimani having been erased from the map by a cyclone in 1872.

recently, the islanders were also famed for their skill in **building dhows** without using iron, or even nails, a tradition going back almost two millennia. Sadly, the art is now obsolete, although ongoing repairs and small-scale construction of *mashua* dhows keep some of the craftsmen in business. A trip to Jibondo can easily be tacked on to a snorkelling trip from Chole Bay: the hotels charge $25–30 per person for a group of four.

Separated from Chole Island by a narrow waterway, **Juani Island** is the archipelago's second largest island, supporting a number of monkeys, feral pigs (introduced by the Portuguese), and diminutive blue duiker antelopes. The island is also the main nesting site for **turtles**; the best time to see hatchlings is from May to September. Amateur archeologists can visit a limestone **cave** in which recent excavations unearthed Mediterranean and Lower Egyptian sherds dating to the start of the first millennium BC, and Indian sherds from over two thousand years ago: evidence of the scope of western Indian Ocean trade.

Juani's main attraction is the ruins of **Kua**. According to legend, the town was founded early in the eleventh century by Bashat, son of the Shirazi founder of Kilwa, on the mainland. Believed by locals to be haunted, the old town languishes almost forgotten on the west side of the island amidst a dense tangle of baobab-studded undergrowth. Excavations in 1955 unearthed a grid of streets, along with Chinese and Indian coins from the thirteenth and fourteenth centuries. Kua appears to have covered about one and a half square kilometres, and its **ruins** (see box above) include a palace dating from the eighteenth century, two graveyards, fifteen houses and seven mosques, the oldest from the fourteenth century. Exactly what you see depends on the state of the vegetation. **Access** is by *mashua* dhow from Chole Bay, and trips include the pretty mangrove-lined Kua Channel at the island's southern end; Chole Bay's hotels charge around $25 per person.

# The Kilwas

South of the Rufiji River delta, the asphalt road resumes after a particularly nasty 50km of (as yet) unsurfaced road. Leaving the delta behind, the first place of note is the Kilwa peninsula. At the southern end of the peninsula is the modern town of **Kilwa Masoko**, which is probably where you'll be staying. It has a couple of nice beaches, but the main reason for coming is to visit the oldest and most fascinating of the Kilwas, **Kilwa Kisiwani**, 2km offshore. In medieval times, this was one of Africa's wealthiest towns, thanks to its monopoly over the gold trade from what is now Mozambique and Zimbabwe. Ruins are all that remain, but, as ruins go, they're very well preserved (enough to have been declared a World Heritage Site), and it requires little effort to picture what the place must have been like during its heyday. Should Kilwa Kisiwani leave you pining for more, there are similar, smaller sites on the islands of **Songo Mnara** and **Sanje ya Kati**, nearby. At the top of the peninsula you'll find **Kilwa Kivinje**, a major nineteenth-century slave-trading centre whose historical core is in a woefully dilapidated but picturesque state.

## Kilwa Masoko

For the handful of visitors who make it down here (including a disproportionate number of hunters taking breaks in between shooting stuff in Selous), the small town of **Kilwa Masoko** ("Kilwa of the Market") is the main base, with access to **Kilwa Kisiwani**, and a couple of **beaches** to flop around on: Jimbiza Beach, in the middle of town, which harbours Kilwa's modest dhow fleet, and the more tide-dependent but secluded Masoko Pwani Beach, 5km north. Locals seem somewhat reserved in their dealings with foreigners at first, and their long stares can be unsettling, but once you get used to them, and they get used to you, Kilwa is as friendly as anywhere else, especially the kids, who've taken to greeting foreigners with cheery choruses of "bye-bye!".

### Arrival

There are Coaster **minibuses from Lindi** and sometimes Masasi to Kilwa Masoko, but choose carefully as driving skills can be shocking, and the road is fast. Coming from **Dar es Salaam**, the easiest option is to catch a bus from Ubungo bus station, usually at 6am, towards Lindi, Mtwara, Nachingwea or Masasi. Akida's Coach is slowest, so theoretically less likely to crash. Get off at **Nangurukuru**, at the top of Kilwa peninsula, from where there are frequent daladalas to Kilwa Kivinje or Kilwa Masoko.

Kilwa Masoko's **airport** (a grass strip and a wooden shed) is two kilometres north of town; if there are enough passengers, Coastal Aviation flies from Zanzibar ($200) via Dar ($160) and Mafia ($110). If you can't arrange a lift on arrival, turn right out of the airport building on to a dirt road, and right again beyond the runway to reach the main road.

Kilwa has some **taxis**, and cheaper motorized **rickshaws** (*bajaji*), but the latter will struggle on the rough track to Masoko Pwani Beach. **Bicycles** can be rented informally.

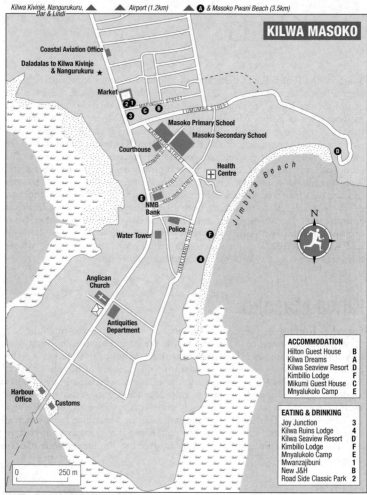

▼ Kilwa Kisiwani, Sanje ya Kati & Songo Manara

## Accommodation

Kilwa Masoko has a handful of attractive **beach hotels**, but they aren't cheap. In comparison, the **guesthouses** are a profoundly dismal bunch: uniformly run-down, poorly ventilated, and with no guarantee of running water or reliable electricity. **Camping** is possible at *Kilwa Seaview Resort* ($5 per person; Tsh5000 for breakfast), but *Kilwa Dreams* ($10 including breakfast) has the better location.

**Hilton Guest House** Mapinduzi St ☎0777/547588. If you're on a really tight budget, stay here – basic, but nowhere near as squalid as the rest. Rooms have fans, and some have bathrooms with clean long-drops – the shared ones are insalubrious. The downside is bed sheets and mosquito nets that are too small – use repellent. ❶

**Kilwa Dreams** Masoko Pwani Beach, 4–5km north of town ☎0784/585330, ✆www.kilwadreams .com. This small Tanzanian/Danish place is the most affordable beach stay, but it's quite a walk from town. Occupying a wild plot dotted with palm trees and backed by a narrow saltwater creek, it has simple but well-maintained sea-facing bungalows (one with four beds), all en suite and quite breezy, so no fans or a/c. Swimming is possible at high tide, and there's hardly anyone else around. There's also a good bar, and generous portions of excellent seafood (from Tsh12,000). Boat trips cost around $25 per person, and can be arranged for snorkelling (they have equipment), birding, or visiting Kilwa Kisiwani. BB ④

**Kilwa Seaview Resort** Jimbiza Beach ☎023/201 3064 or 0784/613335, ⓦwww.kilwa.net. A sleepy place atop a crumbling cliff at the north end of Jimbiza Beach – the nearest swimmable section is a few hundred metres west, beyond the fishing boats. The concrete-walled, *makuti*-roofed cottages are decently fitted out, if slightly tatty, and those at the front have bay views: it's best value for four people sharing. The open-sided restaurant does reasonable food, there's a separate bar, and a murky swimming pool. Unfortunately, most of the sea views are obscured by vegetation. Excursions to Kilwa Kisiwani are $30 a head; other dhow trips (say to Songo Mnara and

Sanje ya Kati, or exploring mangroves) cost $100 per boat. HB ⑥

**Kimbilio Lodge** Jimbiza Beach ☎0787/034621, ⓦwww.kimbiliolodges.com. This Italian place has five pink rondavels with thatched roofs set in a scrubby lawn, all spacious and stylishly decorated, with big beds and washed cement floors. Three have ceiling fans, one has a/c, but there's no backup generator. Also has a great bar and restaurant, both with views, and a dive centre. BB ⑥, HB ⑦

**Mikumi Guest House** Mapinduzi St. Try this one if the *Hilton* is full: basic, with shared squat toilets and bucket showers, but cheap and quite friendly. ①

**Mnyalukolo Camp** On the main road ☎0787/112055. A messy hotchpotch of buildings, shelters and container crates by the roadside, but it's the town's only decent lower mid-range choice, with three modern guest rooms at the back: tiled floors, fans, clean bathrooms, reliable water and a backup generator. There's also a bar, restaurant and billiards table. The owner is knowledgeable about the region and happy to set up tours. BB ②

## Eating and drinking

Kilwa's **restaurants** rarely have anything more than a sackful of rice in their larders or days-old oily snacks in their display cases. Better are the beach hotels, whose specialities include prawns, lobster, squid, meaty *kolekole* fish, and stewed or grilled octopus. For coconut juice and grilled dorado, try the **market**, which is bounded by mango trees; even though the produce is limited, snooping around there is always fun, and it stays open well into the night. The best-located **bars** are on Jimbiza beach at *Kilwa Ruins Lodge* and *Kimbilio Lodge*. For a more local vibe, try any of the joints on the main road either side of the market – at weekends, these can even be lively. **Walking at night** is safe until around 11pm.

**Joy Junction** On the main road. An expanded street-food place with tables, serving *chipsi mayai* and chicken and sodas. No alcohol. Popular after sunset.

**Kilwa Seaview Resort** Jimbiza Beach. Average but filling meals, taking about an hour to prepare. Lunch or dinner costs Tsh10,000 (prawns,

Tsh12,000). There's also a well-stocked bar around a baobab tree.

**Kimbilio Lodge** Jimbiza Beach. Just above the high-tide mark, this Italian-run place has Kilwa's best restaurant, good sea views, and you're welcome just for a drink. The menu consists of half a dozen dishes, chalked up on a blackboard.

---

### Diving and snorkelling off Kilwa

Kilwa's reefs – mostly steep drop-offs – are good for seeing large, open-water species such as sharks and turtles, blue marlin (best in Sept), tuna (Dec), and even calving humpback whales (most likely from Aug–Nov). Kilwa Masoko's *Kimbilio Lodge* is the only PADI-accredited **dive centre** between Mafia and Mikindani, and an Open Water course (including the manual) costs $450 as does a ten-dive package, including equipment.

Unfortunately, the dive sites are too deep for **snorkelling**: the closest reefs for this are 4km further north off Masoko Pwani Beach, for which staying at *Kilwa Dreams* makes sense. To go snorkelling with *Kimbilio* costs $30 per person, minimum four.

Seafood is the biggie, but they're also happy catering for vegetarians. Around Tsh12,000.

**Mnyalukolo Camp** On the main road. Handy for a quick drink in pleasant company – it's run by a charming Tanzanian/German couple. There are a couple of thatched shelters, and, if you order two hours in advance, good home-cooked food.

**Mwanzajibuni** Mapinduzi St. A ramshackle shed that's the best of the really cheap places, with good Tanzanian-style breakfasts including *supu*, and full

meals of *pilau* or rice with fish or meat (under Tsh2000). No alcohol.

**New J&H** Beside *Hilton Guest House*, Mapinduzi St. Very modest and often has next to nothing, but capable, with advance notice, of rustling up some prize nosh for under Tsh3000, including fresh squid and prawns. No alcohol.

**Road Side Classic Park** On the main road. Primarily a bar with lots of shaded and secluded seating, and a pool table. Food is acceptable when it's busy, but otherwise terrible.

# Kilwa Kisiwani

Just 2km across the water from Kilwa Masoko are the spectacular ruins of **Kilwa Kisiwani** ("Kilwa of the Island"), on the mangrove-rimmed island of the same name. At its height the island-state – known at the time as just Kilwa – was the most important trading centre on the East African coast, and ruins include a fourteenth-century palace that was the largest stone structure in sub-Saharan Africa. There are also several mosques, dozens of Shirazi graves set amidst gigantic baobab trees, and a well-preserved Omani fortress.

### Some history

According to the **legend** (see p.579), Kilwa was founded in 975 AD by Hassan bin Ali, son of the king of Shiraz (now Iran). After being shipwrecked on the island, Ali bought it from a local chief in return for a quantity of cloth. While archeologists dispute the date (their evidence points to the ninth century), the gist of the story may well be true. Persians were extensively involved along the East African coast at that time, both as traders and, over the following century, as refugees fleeing internecine conflict.

Kilwa reached its apogee in the fourteenth and fifteenth centuries, from which time the bulk of the surviving ruins date. Key to Kilwa's success was its control of maritime trade in the western Indian Ocean, in particular the port of **Sofala** in central Mozambique, which was the main conduit for **gold** produced by Zimbabwe's Monomotapa kingdom. At its height, Kilwa boasted sub-Saharan Africa's largest stone building, its largest mosque, and the very first mint. Its ruling class lived in stone houses with indoor plumbing, wore silk and fine cotton, and ate off Chinese porcelain. In 1332, **Ibn Battuta**, Morocco's

## Moving on from Kilwa

If you're based in Kilwa Kivinje and are moving on by road, get yourself down to Kilwa Masoko (hourly daladalas) the day before. Currently, the vehicles are all large Coaster or DCM minibuses, and run daily to **Dar and Lindi**. They leave at dawn from their "offices" (signboards beside tables) on and off Mapinduzi Street near Kilwa Masoko's market. Vehicles to **Masasi** can hang around in Lindi for hours, so get to Lindi first and change there. Some vehicles are more carefully driven than others, so ask for local advice. Wherever you're going, buy your ticket a day or two before, and forget about finding a seat on a full-size bus passing through **Nangurukuru**: you'll almost certainly have to stand. For **plane tickets**, there's an unofficial agent along the main road north of the market with a big Coastal Aviation logo painted outside. Alternatively, contact Coastal in Dar (p.109) or Zanzibar (p.529).

celebrated globetrotter, described Kilwa as "amongst the most beautiful of cities and elegantly built" and also remarked on the sultan's generosity, but, curiously, stated that the buildings were made of wood and roofed with reeds. There's not one mention of stone, which either suggests that Battuta was telling lies about having visited Kilwa, or that he was confused by the more humble dwellings of the general populace that presumably surrounded the stone buildings, and of which no trace remains.

The **Portuguese** arrived in 1498, when Vasco da Gama's flotilla pulled in en route to opening the sea passage to India. They found a flourishing and powerful city, exporting gold, silver, precious stones, ivory, myrrh, animal skins, frankincense, ambergris and a few slaves, receiving spices and metal goods in return. It was revenge that prompted **Vasco da Gama's return** in 1502, demanding payback for the "unfriendly" welcome that ruler Amir Ibrahim had accorded Pedro Álvares Cabral two years earlier. Da Gama threatened to burn the city and kill its inhabitants unless he was paid tribute. Wisely, the Amir coughed up.

In 1505 **Dom Francisco d'Almeida**, who was about to assume the post of viceroy of the newly conquered territories of India, took a liking to the town, "Kilwa, of all the places I know in the world, has the best port and the fairest land that can be." Fine words, but insufficient to sway him from ransacking the town. The Portuguese eventually left Kilwa in 1513, and with its trading links destroyed, the town limped on towards a gruesome finale when, in 1587, forty percent of its population was massacred, some of them allegedly eaten, by the marauding **Zimba tribe**, who were first recorded in 1570 by the Portuguese in northwestern Mozambique.

Only in the eighteenth century did Kilwa's fortunes revive, when – fuelled by demand from European plantation colonies – the **slave trade** supplanted gold as the coast's major commodity. But in 1842, Kilwa was easily captured by Omani Arabs from Zanzibar, a move calculated merely to stifle competition. The slave caravans were diverted to the new port of Kilwa Kivinje, 30km to the north, and Kilwa Kisiwani was once again abandoned, this time collapsing into the ruins you see today.

## The ruins

The **ruins** – complete with walkways and signboards – are scattered in and around the present-day settlement of Kilwa Kisiwani, whose simple mud houses provide a stark contrast to the wealthy city Kilwa once was. The bulk of the ruins are in the northwest, and cover little more than one square kilometre. Husuni Kubwa and Husuni Ndogo sit together 2km to the east, accessed by narrow footpaths wending between plots of irrigated farmland, cashew plantations, mango groves and acacia and baobab thickets where, with a keen eye, you may spot bee-eaters and bulbuls.

### The Gereza fortress

The crenellated **Gereza** (also known as the fort or the prison) is Kilwa Kisiwani's most prominent building, and has commanding views over the waterway to Kilwa Masoko, and of the open ocean beyond. Parts of the northern walls have crumbled into the sea, but the Gereza is otherwise in fine fettle. The first fortress on the site was erected by the **Portuguese** in, it's said, under three weeks: in the ever-florid words of Francisco d'Almeida, writing to the king of Portugal in 1505, "We built a fortress which if it were possible I would give years of my life for Your Highness to see, for it is so strong that the King of France could be awaited there".

He overestimated its strength, however: when the **Omanis** gained control, early in the nineteenth century, they had to rebuild the entire thing with the exception of the tower foundations, and this is the building you see today. In keeping with its defensive nature, there's only one entrance, through a relatively modern door. Above the entrance is a slot for muskets; there are more slits along the parapet. Inside, the courtyard has a number of benches along the walls, and spy holes from the middle level of the surrounding three-storey edifice – you'll find the best-preserved rooms in the southeast corner, on your left as you enter. The chamber set in the southern wall may have been a gunpowder magazine. Excavations in the northeast corner have unearthed cannonballs, musket shot, and thousands of trading beads.

### The Great Mosque

The **Great Mosque** (or Friday Mosque) lies on the edge of the present-day village, in an area frequented by goats. In its time the largest mosque in East Africa, it was excavated between 1958 and 1960 by Neville Chittick, who reconstructed parts of it and also somewhat carelessly left behind a short length of railway and an upturned carriage, which had been used to clear debris. The mosque is a truly beautiful building, and the play of light and shadow on the mildewed archways and walls makes it supremely photogenic. Its architecture reflects Kilwa's rising prosperity over the centuries. The roofless **northern section** is the oldest part, built no later than the **twelfth century** when the gold trade was in its infancy. Its flat, coral-concrete roof was supported by nine sixteen-sided wooden columns set in rows of three, on top of which three beams were laid running north to south. The wood of course rotted away long ago, leaving only the gaps in the masonry into which the beams and pillars fitted. As Kilwa prospered, the mosque's **southern extension** was given an elaborately vaulted roof surmounted by 22 domes, all supported by thin octagonal stone pillars. Indisputably elegant, they were unable to bear the weight of the roof, which collapsed around 1350. The pillars were replaced with coral limestone blocks, most of which stand today; the original pillars lie discarded beside the eastern wall, and the domes' interiors are occupied by bats. At the southern end of the mosque is a porch that was used as the **ablutions area**, with a bench, water trough, and a slab of round sandstone on which the faithful could wash their feet. If you peer into the well beside the mosque, you'll see two **underground passages** leading off it about halfway down. The one on the eastern side is said to lead to the Gereza and may have been used for moving slaves, while the one to the west goes to Makutani Palace.

### The Small Domed Mosque

The **Small Domed Mosque**, 150m southwest of the Great Mosque, is the best preserved and most attractive of Kilwa's medieval buildings, with more than half its original roof intact. It dates from the middle of the fifteenth century when Kilwa's prosperity was at its height. Other than the thick buttresses, the first thing that strikes you is the partly broken octagonal pillar jutting upwards from the central dome, from which you can draw comparisons with the pillar tombs found at other Shirazi sites, such as Kaole and Kunduchi, and on Pemba Island. **Inside**, the mosque is an architectural gem. As with the Great Mosque, the African influence is visible in the overall form of the building, which is based on a rectangular prayer hall with a roof supported on numerous pillars, rather than on the contemporary Arabian "pavilion" style featuring arcaded courtyards. The central dome was inlaid with circles of green-glazed ceramic bowls, some of which can still be seen, and there's an

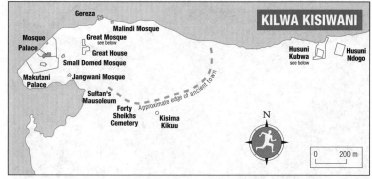

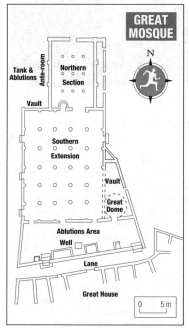

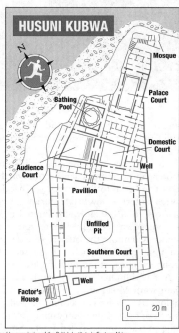

Adapted from John Sutton (1998), in Azania 33. Reproduced by permission of the British Institute in Eastern Africa.

elegant *mihrab* in the north wall that is home to easily startled bats. The **ablutions area** to the southwest is more complex than that in the Great Mosque, and contains a latrine and two water tanks. Like the Great Mosque, there are also some circular foot-scrubbing stones.

## The Makutani Palace and around

Close to the western shore is the **Makutani Palace**. Its name means "gathering place", suggesting a mode of rule that valued collective decisions, as was traditional among many Tanzanian tribes before the turmoil of the nineteenth century turned everything upside down. With the exception of the perimeter walls, most of the fifteenth-century structure was demolished at the end of the

▲ Great Mosque, Kilwa Kisiwani

eighteenth century to provide building material for the new palace, which is still largely intact, and surrounded by enormous defensive outer walls that open only to the shore.

The old palace consists of a **residential section** to the west and barracks or storerooms around a large **courtyard** to the east. The rusty cannon in the courtyard adds to the impression that defence was a prime concern, as does the water cistern – invaluable during a siege. Both wings of the palace had long, narrow rooms, their width limited by the length of the mangrove poles that supported the ceilings. The reception rooms and living quarters were on the upper two floors, the latter provided with toilets. The decor is hinted at by traces of pink plaster, which can be seen halfway up the walls of the corridor connecting the stores with the palace antechamber.

A few hundred metres southeast of the palace are the scant remains of **Jangwani Mosque**, of interest mainly to archeologists on account of the unique ablutionary water jars set into its walls just inside the main entrance. Just to the south of the mosque, you can cut across the salt-crusted sands of the inlet at low tide to reach the so-called **Forty Sheikhs Cemetery**, part of which has been eroded by the sea. Like the vast majority of known Shirazi grave sites, the tombs nestle in groves of **baobabs**, including one of the biggest you're ever likely to see. The presence of the trees is explained by the legend that when a sultan died, a pair of baobab saplings would be planted at either end of his grave; these would eventually grow together, effectively making the tomb part of the tree. The story certainly fits the atmosphere of the place, at once sacred and meditative.

### Husuni Kubwa

Built on a rocky spur high above the fringing mangroves 2km east of the Gereza, **Husuni Kubwa** ("Great Palace") was, in its time, the largest permanent building in sub-Saharan Africa, and remains one of its most enigmatic constructions. Walking along the footpath from the Gereza and the village, the undergrowth suddenly clears as your eyes meet a grey maze of courtyards, hallways, galleries, staircases and rooms up to three storeys high. Excavations suggest that the construction was never fully completed, nor lived in by more than three generations of sultans before the dynasty decamped to the Makutani Palace. No one really knows why the building was abandoned, especially as the cliff-top location was surely ideal, benefiting from continuous sea breezes as well as commanding views.

A plaque found in the palace sings the praises of Sultan "al-Malik al-Mansur" ("the Conquering Ruler") al-Hasan ibn Sulaiman, and dated the bulk of the palace's construction to the 1320s. The very size of the palace spectacularly illustrates the wealth that was accruing from the gold trade at that time – if you've seen the display on Kilwa in the National Museum in Dar, with its Chinese porcelain bowls, elaborately engraved friezes, oil lamps, pottery and coins, it's not too difficult to imagine the opulence that once existed here.

The palace complex had two main parts: the palace itself, in the north, and a rectangular commercial section to the south, which is the first area you reach. Heading down a flight of steps, you pass a well and enter the large **southern court**, enclosed by a double range of rooms. No roof was found during the excavations, and as the walls of the rooms are uncommonly thick, they may have been intended to carry another storey. Near the centre of the courtyard is a large irregular pit, which was either used as a quarry or may have been intended to form a cistern.

North of the Southern Court is the **palace** itself, occupying the north- and west-facing tip of the headland. Entering from the southern court, you pass through the **domestic court**, which is surrounded by terraces. To the west is the **pavilion** in which the sultan would have received visitors and conducted public business. A short flight of steps below the pavilion on the western edge of the complex is the **audience court**, flanked by wide terraces which may also have been used for receptions and dances, and which offer a fine view westwards over the coast and harbour. The wall niches were probably occupied by oil lamps.

After passing through the audience court, you'll reach an octagonal **bathing pool**, set in an unroofed square enclosure; some eighty thousand litres would have been needed to fill it, which – given the lack of channels – would have been hauled by hand from the well beside the Domestic Court. The sheer scale of palace fittings, like these, suggests why the site might have been abandoned prematurely: its upkeep may simply have been too expensive, even for Kilwa.

North of the Bathing Pool and through the rectangular **palace court**, steps lead down to a landing creek in the mangroves, where most dhows collect passengers before returning to Kilwa Masoko. Before leaving, you may wish to have a look at **Husuni Ndogo**, separated from Husuni Kubwa by a deep gully. This "Small Palace" is believed to have been constructed in the fifteenth century, though archeologists are at a loss to explain much about the building. With the exception of its outer walls and turrets, it contains virtually no internal structures, and dense thorny shrubs render access difficult.

## Practicalities

Visitors to Kilwa Kisiwani, Songo Mnara and Sanje ya Kati (see p.172) need a **permit** (Tsh1500) from the Antiquities Department in Kilwa Masoko, housed in the administrative block facing the post office (Mon–Fri 7.30am–3.30pm; ☏023/201 3016 or 023/201 3019). While you're there, ask to see or buy a copy of John Sutton's fascinating *Kilwa: A History of the Ancient Swahili Town*.

The romantic approach is by sail-powered *mashua* **dhow**. If there are other passengers, likely at 7am (get your permit the day before), it shouldn't cost more than Tsh500 each way, but if you want the dhow to yourself – as the captain is likely to assume you do – you'll pay anything from Tsh10,000 to Tsh20,000 (per boat) for the return trip, more if it has a motor. Less enchanting, but more reliable, is the **motorboat** owned by the Antiquities Department, which charges Tsh30,000 per boat there and back (or Tsh60,000 to Songo Mnara), including the guide. Trips arranged through Kilwa Masoko's beach hotels cost $25–30 per person. Before embarking, pay your Tsh300 **port tax** at the office inside the harbour gate.

Boats usually drop you at the Gereza where the captain will locate a **guide**. You're then shown around as many ruins as you want, and finish up (if you can face the walk) 2km east at Husuni Kubwa, where, with luck, your boatman will be waiting. The guiding fee is negotiable: Tsh10,000–15,000 per group would be fair. Should you fancy spending the night on the island, ask at the Antiquities Department before heading off: they have a basic **rest house** (beds, tattered sheets and nets, but no fixed price; likely Tsh5000 per person). An *askari* can help collect water from a nearby well. **Camping** may also be possible – again, nothing fixed.

## Songo Mnara and Sanje ya Kati

To the south of Kilwa Kisiwani are several other islands with yet more ruins, including Songo Mnara and Sanje ya Kati. Those at **Songo Mnara** (15km by boat), which are included with Kilwa as a World Heritage Site, are the most impressive. Mostly dating from the fourteenth and fifteenth centuries, they comprise an extensive palace complex, at least four mosques, and dozens of graves and houses, all surrounded by a defensive wall. Diminutive **Sanje ya Kati**, formerly known as Shanga, is 3km to the west and contains the foundations of oblong houses and a tenth-century mosque, although they're little more than rubble.

You need a **permit** (see p.171) to visit either site. If the cost of hiring a boat (see above) is prohibitive, Songo Mnara is also accessible by irregular *mashua* **dhow ferries** (2–3hr; Tsh1000 for locals) sailing between Kilwa Masoko and Pande, further south; you'll have to wade through the water to get ashore. Be sure to double-check arrangements for your pick-up on the return trip, as there are no facilities on the island. Songo Mnara has a **guide** who will expect a tip (and may put you up for a night).

# Kilwa Kivinje

Facing the ocean at the top of Kilwa peninsula, 30km north of Kilwa Masoko, is the totally dilapidated, rarely visited but strangely charming town of **KILWA KIVINJE**: "Kilwa of the Casuarina Trees". In its brief efflorescence in the mid-nineteenth century, under Omani rule from Zanzibar, it usurped Kilwa Kisiwani as the major **slaving terminus** on the route from Lake Nyasa (chapter 10). Over twenty thousand slaves were shipped out from here in the 1860s, either to the market in Zanzibar, or straight to the French colonies of Madagascar, Réunion and Mauritius. Later it became a **German garrison** town and as such played a key role in the suppression of the **Maji Maji Uprising**, but it's now little more than a large if slumberous fishing village. Many of its historic buildings have collapsed, and with no beach to entice developers or tourists, it's difficult to not feel sorry for the place. Still, if history is your thing, Kilwa Kivinje has more than one tale to tell.

# The Town

The road in from Nangurukuru finishes at the fishing harbour, separated from the commercial harbour just to the west by a clump of mangroves. The town's somnolent **market** is three blocks back from the commercial harbour. The sandy streets between these areas are perfect for a gentle wander, with some really beautiful **balconies and carved doors**, the latter invariably in better condition than the houses they guard. Kilwa Kivinje's most impressive historical building is the ruined two-storey **German courthouse**, facing the fishing harbour. The cannon mounted on a replica carriage outside dates from Omani times, and there are two more unmounted cannons a few metres away on the grimy beach, which get covered at high tide. The **beach**, silty and scattered with mangroves, isn't much good for swimming (or sun-bathing; it's in the middle of town), but at low tide the sea recedes by almost a kilometre, making for fine walks along the shore.

Heading inland back along the road to Nangurukuru you'll see a couple of historical monuments. The first, facing the daladala stand, is a small **German memorial**, with four cannons pointing downwards at its corners. It honours two Germans killed in September 1888 during the **Abushiri War** (see box, p.121), defending, according to the inscription, "the house of the German East Africa Company in heroic fashion". Locals have another version: the Germans, they say, had been hunting warthogs or wild boar, and after the hunt skinned the animals to prepare the meat. Unfortunately for them, the meat was stolen by a local, who proceeded to eat it with his family and friends. On discovering that what they had just eaten was a kind of pork and thus *haram* (forbidden), the good Muslim thief returned to lynch the hapless Germans.

Kilwa put up strong resistance during the war, and was one of the last places to be "pacified" when, in November 1895, its leader **Hassan bin Omari Makunganya** was hanged from a mango tree. The tree has disappeared, but the site – **Mwembe Kinyonga**, meaning "hangman's mango tree" – can be visited: it's on the right-hand side of the Nangurukuru road heading back from Kilwa Kivinje, 1km beyond the German memorial. Surmounting a small obelisk is a wooden figurine of an old man (missing its arms), which is either Makunganya, or **Kinjikitile Ngwale**, who was a soothsayer from a village in the Matumbi Hills northwest of Kilwa, and the spark that ignited the **Maji Maji Uprising** of 1905–06. Kinjikitile claimed to have discovered a spring of water which, when sprinkled on a person, gave protection against bullets. Within months, word of the charm had spread and the entire south of the country rose up in arms against the Germans. Kinjikitile was one of the first victims of the German reprisal, and was hanged in Kilwa Kivinje.

The British finally ejected the Germans during World War I. If you look around the beach at the top of the slipway in the commercial harbour, you can still see a thick, armour-plated **gun hatch**. Where it comes from, nobody knows for sure.

## Practicalities

**Getting there** is the same as for Kilwa Masoko (see p.163), the difference being that there's nothing direct, so jump on a daladala at Nangurukuru, or come on a day-trip from Kilwa Masoko (daladalas charge Tsh1200). Note that most **road maps** of Tanzania get the Kilwa peninsula completely wrong: the road from Nangurukuru to Kilwa Masoko *doesn't* go through Kilwa Kivinje, but passes its junction 6km inland. **Arriving** in Kilwa Kivinje, daladalas drop you on the main road 250m short of the harbour. **Security** isn't a worry by day so long as you're not dangling anything tempting, but get someone reliable to escort you at night, as muggings have been reported.

③

> ### Dhows
>
> Kilwa Kivinje is one of few places where **catching a dhow** is still a real possibility, especially between November and March (for dhow hopping, see p.32). The first place to head for is the commercial harbour, to find a boat that's able to take passengers. There are no fixed prices, and it's wise to ask locally about the seaworthiness of any vessel, and the character of the skipper. There are boats to **Songo Songo** island most days, some continuing to **Mafia**. Songo Songo Island itself occasionally has vessels going all the way to **Zanzibar**. Heading south, there are less frequent dhows to **Lindi**. An **exit stamp** is unlikely to be necessary if you're staying within Tanzania, but it'd be wise to check at Kilwa Masoko's administrative block, facing the post office, just in case.

Kilwa Kivinje has a handful of cheap but very basic **guesthouses** (all ❶), of which the more bearable, if you don't mind doing without electricity and private bathroom, is the *Savoye*, beside the commercial harbour, with cleanish rooms, mosquito nets, and friendly owners (Kiswahili only). Equally lacklustre are the town's **restaurants**, with the best eats at the ramshackle stalls on the beach in front of the ruined German courthouse, where you'll find delicious grilled fish and squid, and seasonal fruit. The ducks waddling around here don't appear to feature on anyone's menu. As for proper restaurants, the best of the bunch – not meaning an awful lot – is *Kivulini Beach Bar*, facing the mangroves west of the harbour, which also has reasonably cool beers. For breakfast, try the friendly *Boys Corner Hotel* beside the market, with *andazi* doughnuts, scalding hot sweet tea, chapatis and *ugali* with sauce. Advice on **moving on** is given on p.166.

# Lindi, Mtwara and Mikindani

The big port towns of **Lindi and Mtwara**, 450km and 560km south of Dar respectively, are not much of a draw in themselves, but if you've just arrived from Kilwa or have braved the overland route east from Lake Nyasa, they'll feel like oases of civilization. As a bonus, both have access to some very nice beaches. Without a beach, but much more attractive in itself, is the former slave-trading town of **Mikindani**, just west of Mtwara, with a palpable sense of history, one of southern Tanzania's best hotels and an NGO offering a variety of excursions. In addition, the town has an excellent **scuba diving** centre, whose speciality is the otherwise almost unknown **Mnazi Bay-Ruvuma Estuary Marine Park**, along the border with Mozambique.

## Lindi

Founded in the eighteenth century as a caravan terminus on the slave and ivory route from Lake Nyasa, the Indian Ocean port of **LINDI** ("Deep Channel") is the capital of one of Tanzania's most impoverished regions, having long suffered from poor soil, the development of Mtwara (at Lindi's expense), and, together with the rest of southeastern Tanzania, geographical isolation. But all this may well become just a bad memory: the construction of the "Unity Bridge" to Mozambique, the road to which passes through Lindi, is expected to boost both tourism and trade.

For now, the feeling of abandonment is most obviously expressed in Lindi's crumbling infrastructure. After the rains, when clouds of mosquitoes and flies descend on the town, it's hard to imagine that Lindi was once home to a thriving expatriate community. Most of them cleared out after Independence and only a handful remain, generally NGO workers and missionaries. Few people speak English, but the locals are unfailingly friendly (if initially reserved) and the town is enjoyable enough, with a number of attractive buildings dating from the first half of the twentieth century. The location is lovely, too. Nestled on Lindi Bay at the mouth of the Lukuledi River, the town is flanked by hills on both its landward and river sides, and by the ocean to the northeast, where dhows under sail are a common sight.

## Arrival and information

Lindi's **bus stand** is in the middle of town between Makongoro Road and Msonobar Street. There are at least three daily buses from Dar, with Akida's Coach having the "best" reputation; buses and minibuses to and from Mtwara,

*Mtema Beach (3km)*

**LINDI**

INDIAN OCEAN

N

*Airport (18km), Kilwa & Dar es Salaam*

Food Stalls

Commissioner's Residence

SHULE ST  School

Transmitter

Police

Market

Pentecostal Church

CRDB Bank

Air Tanzania

German Boma

SHEIKH BADI STREET

Bus Stand

NMB Bank

Regional Administration

SABA SABA STREET

Precisionair

UHURU AVENUE

Obelisk

AMANI STREET

Commercial Harbour

NZUNDA STREET

EILAT ROAD

EILAT ROAD

Omani Minaret

SWAHILI STREET

NBC Bank

Anglican Church

Motorized Canoes

Fishing Harbour

0    200 m

**EATING & DRINKING**

| | |
|---|---|
| Lindi Malaika Hotel | C |
| Lindi Paris Club | 4 |
| Magereza Social Club | 1 |
| Nankolowa Guest House | D |
| Santorini Club | 2 |
| Titanic Bar | 3 |

**ACCOMMODATION**

| | |
|---|---|
| Adela Guest House | E |
| Adela Hotel | F |
| Another Coast Guest House | A |
| Coast Guest House | B |
| Lindi Malaika Hotel | C |
| Lindi Oceanic Hotel | G |
| Nankolowa Guest House | D |

*Mtwara & Masasi* ▼   **F** *(200m),* ▼ **G** *(2.5km), Mtwara & Masasi*

Masasi, Newala and Nachingwea also pass through. There are no flights at present; though they may resume (Precisionair was the company); the **airport** is 18km towards Kilwa.

Cashing **traveller's cheques** in Lindi – at NBC, south of the harbour – is uncommonly painful and can take hours, so change money before coming or try the ATM at NBC. For internet access head to Lindi Net, on the corner of Amani St and Karume St (daily 8am–6pm). The post office is also on Karume St and telephones can be found at TTCL, next door.

## Accommodation

Lindi has lots of cheap but mostly so-so **guesthouses**, and a somewhat anodyne but far more comfortable conference-style place on the shore. Incidentally, the beaches 3–5km north of town are sitting ducks for hotel developers, and with the completion of Unity Bridge between Tanzania and Mozambique, and the road from Dar almost completely asphalted, it's probably just a matter of time before they move in: keep your eyes peeled for hotel signs on the left of the road in from the north.

**Adela Guest House** Swahili St ☎023/220 2571. A welcoming and safe budget option with dozens of cell-like rooms with clean but stained sheets, large box-nets and quiet fans, shared showers and squat toilets. ❶

**Adela Hotel** Ghana St, four blocks south of Swahili St ☎023/220 2310. Pricey but reasonable rooms, all with tiled bathrooms and hot running water (but broken toilet seats), box nets and fans. There's a quiet bar at the back (guests only), food to order and safe parking. BB ❷

**Another Coast Guest House** Jamhuri St. Fresher than *Coast Guest House* (same owner), but the ocean view is partially obscured by the buildings opposite. ❶

**Coast Guest House** Facing the beach near the top of Makongoro Rd. Basic and smells musty but who cares when it's this close to the sea, although only two rooms have sea views (through wire mesh windows). Most share bathrooms, all have box nets and fans. ❶

**Lindi Malaika Hotel** Market Ave ☎023/220 2880. Best of the "budget" guesthouses, if still a tad basic. All rooms have a shower and Western toilet, fan, large box net(s) and TV, and there's also an "executive room" containing an enormous bed (too large for its net), a desk, and a horrendous three-piece suite. BB ❷

**Lindi Oceanic Hotel** On the bay 3km south of town ☎023/220 2829, ⓦwww.lindioceanichotel .com. A large, inoffensive but comfortable conference-oriented hotel, sitting beside a silty beach along the river. All rooms have a/c, and the "executive" ones have satellite TV. There's also a swimming pool, bar and restaurant. Fifty more rooms are planned for 2010. BB ❹–❻

**Nankolowa Guest House** Rutamba St ☎023/220 2727. A safe budget choice with various rooms, most sharing bathrooms, all with ceiling fan and big box-nets. It can get a bit musty during the rains. ❶

## The Town

Despite the loss of its economic importance, Lindi retains a lively and bustling air, best experienced around the bus stand and in the **market** at the west end of Market Street. Heading east from here takes you to the Chinese-built stadium,

### Dhow hopping from Lindi

If you want to try **dhow hopping** from Lindi (see p.32), your first stop should be the Dhow Registrar (Mon–Fri 8am–4pm; ☎023/220 2162), on the right as you enter the commercial harbour. Kilwa is the most likely destination. There are no regular dhows into Mozambique; even if you find one, you'll need to have bought a Mozambican visa in Dar, as you can't get one on arrival.

from where a left turn along Makongoro Road heads up to the **beach**. The coast road back into town skirts a pleasantly green quarter that was favoured by colonial Europeans for their residences and offices, most of them now in ruins. Notable among these is the marvellously dilapidated **Commissioner's Residence**, its flags and bunting replaced by festoons of ivy, and just before the road veers inland and into Uhuru Avenue, the old **German Boma**, which is now so run-down that a veritable forest of fig trees has sprouted inside.

Heading south from the commercial harbour you'll come to the small **fishing harbour**, which also has a small market, and stalls selling freshly grilled fish. Just behind is the **Anglican Church**, a clumsy stab at the formal proportions of Neoclassicism, not helped by the battleship-grey cement. Heading back into town along Karume Street you'll find arguably Lindi's oldest construction, a battered and lopsided domed **Omani minaret** dating from the nineteenth century; it's just north of Swahili Street, beside a more recent mosque.

The town-centre **beaches** are mainly used by fishing boats, and for the most part are lined with houses, offering you neither privacy nor – if you're a woman – much chance to respect Islamic sensibilities. More suitable are the beaches north of town, which get better the further you go; the best stretch is **Mtema Beach**, which starts 3km off the top of our map, just beyond a headland that's being gnawed away by a quarry.

Even better, if you have time, would be to catch a motorized **canoe** (Tsh300) at the fish market for the five-minute crossing across the Lukuledi, from where a thirty-minute walk north between the mangroves and the shore brings you to an absolutely beautiful sheltered beach, with all the shades of turquoise you could wish for. It should also be possible to rent a whole canoe, with its owner, to explore the wide river estuary, containing a number of secluded beaches and creeks, mangroves, outlandish limestone formations, crocodiles, and the small island of **Kisiwa cha Popo** ("Bat Island"), which is a daytime roost for fruit bats.

## Eating and drinking

Lindi has a handful of half-decent **restaurants**, but what's really recommended is the row of **street vendors** inside the bus stand who every evening rustle up roast or fried chicken, eggs and chips for hungry travellers. There are chairs and tables arranged at the front, so you can sit under the stars and watch the world go by in the flickering light of *kibatari* oil lamps. Waitresses from nearby bars bring sodas and beers, and the atmosphere is very friendly, with kids dancing about to music blaring from surrounding stores. Street food, including king-size prawns, can also be sampled at the fishing harbour, and just north of *Coast Guest House* facing the beach, where you'll find especially good grilled fish.

There are plenty of **bars**, though, once again, for a different nocturnal experience, the bus stand beckons. Walking around at night is relatively safe, but being escorted by a reliable local would be wise as there are no street lights.

### Restaurants

**Lindi Malaika Hotel** Market Ave. Lindi's best restaurant, serving up great breakfasts and fresh juices, but arrive early for lunch or dinner as the food is generally gone by 8.30pm. Portions are generous and prices low: Tsh2500 for *pilau* or banana and meat stew, Tsh3000 for their special biriani.

**Lindi Paris Club** Uhuru Ave/Makonde St. A pleasantly quiet daytime haunt that gets busy on weekend nights, when people gather for its discos; it also occasionally hosts live bands. There are tables in a large covered courtyard and unspeakable toilets.

**Nankolowa Guest House** Rutamba St. Enjoys a good reputation and has an extensive menu to choose from, with most dishes under Tsh3000 (until 9pm), but order early.

### Bars

**Magereza Social Club** North end of Makongoro Rd. Operated by the prison authority, this is popular in the evenings for its coastal breezes. You can also drink in the nicely overgrown garden facing the bar – a lovely daytime refuge.

**Santorini Club** On the coast at the top of Makongoro Rd. Mtwara's main nightspot, with heaving discos weekend nights, and a gaggle of prostitutes, too.

**Titanic Bar** Market Ave. A good local place if you want to hit the beers; the tables outside by the pavement are the main reason for coming.

# Around Lindi

To reach anywhere worth visiting in Lindi Region, you need a 4WD, an experienced driver, and someone who definitely knows the way, as giving accurate directions is way too complicated. Also, the roads off the main asphalt artery are rough going even in the dry season, and are often impassable during the rains. There's no reliable public transport, either, nor accommodation, and camping probably isn't too clever given the ever-present, but unlikely, risk of lion attacks. But with a healthy dose of curiosity, there are a couple of destinations offering enough rewards for the effort expanded in getting there.

## The Rondo Plateau Reserve

The **Rondo Plateau Forest Reserve**, 77km by road from Lindi (asphalt as far as Nyengedi, 27km west of Mingoyo, then north along a dirt track) provides a soothing contrast to the coastal swelter. Largely trashed during the British period, the approximately 18 square kilometres of surviving semi-deciduous coastal forest are surprisingly **biodiverse**, including dozens of unique plants, a newly discovered species of bushbaby (galago), and some very **rare birds**, among them the East Coast akalat, spotted ground thrush and Rondo green barbet. Those without wheels needn't fret: *The Old Boma Hotel* in Mikindani (p.182) offers a two-day trip at a bargain £60 (charged in sterling; approximately $100) per person in a couple, including a night in the former plantation manager's residence with oil lamps, serenading cicadas and frogs, and as much forest hiking as you want. There are also some rock paintings.

## Tendaguru Hills

A more challenging target are the **Tendaguru Hills**, northwest of Lindi, famed among paleontologists as Africa's richest deposit of **late Jurassic fossils**. Their similarities to the Morrison Formation in the western USA illustrate the existence, some 150 million years ago, of land bridges between various continents. Unless you're an avid fossil freak, the various trenches dug by researchers (or looters) aren't much to look at, but poke around and you'll come to recognize a litter of fossil fragments. The site was discovered for science by a German mining engineer, Bernhard Sattler, in 1907, while searching for garnets. Locals were already acquainted with the fossils, saying they were the remains of a **man-eating ogre** whose toes had been slit open by warriors to release the people that he had eaten. The excavation of Tendaguru began in 1909 under the auspices of Berlin's Museum für Naturkunde, which still houses the finds, including a twelve-metre-tall **Brachiosaurus brancai**.

First stop is the Natural Resources Officer (Afisa ya Maliasili; ☎023/222 0501) at the regional headquarters near Lindi's commercial harbour, from whom you need a **permit**. He should also be able to suggest a suitable guide, and possibly transport. If not, you'll need a sturdy 4WD, and a knowledgeable driver. In dry weather, the drive takes about four hours each way.

# Mikindani

Heading south from Lindi, the asphalt road forks after 26km, one branch heading west to Masasi, the other south to Mikindani and Mtwara. **Mingoyo**, the village at the junction (also known as Mnazi Mmoja; "One Palm Tree" – in fact there are thousands), has hawkers aplenty peddling a variety of tasty snacks, including fruits, cashew nuts, bundles of freshly chopped sugar cane, and all sorts of seafood, including octopus and unspeakably succulent king prawns – well worth stopping for. Should you get stuck (or hooked on the food), several decent guesthouses oblige.

Lindi is pleasant in its way, but **MIKINDANI**, 11km before Mtwara, is beautiful. Set inside an almost circular, mangrove-lined bay, the village is home to some fifteen thousand people, for whom the ocean is their livelihood. As in so many other coastal villages, the peaceful, almost languid atmosphere belies a brutal past, when the town was one of the coast's major seaports for ivory- and slave-carrying **caravans**. Mikindani's stone buildings, many in ruins, are eloquent and picturesque reminders of more prosperous times, while sandy beaches on the far side of the bay, a wide choice of excursions, a scuba diving school, and one of southern Tanzania's most beautiful hotels make it a great place to get away from it all.

### Some history

Mikindani's sheltered location offered an ideal base for early traders sailing up and down the coast, and the town – or rather Pemba village, on the northern spur of land guarding the bay's entrance – was swiftly incorporated into the Indian Ocean trading network, as proven by some of Tanzania's earliest signs of Arab habitation. The arrival of **Arabs** stimulated trade, and by the end of the fifteenth century – when Mikindani proper replaced Pemba as the main port – the town was trading inland as far as present-day Malawi, Zambia, Angola and Congo.

Decline set in with the arrival of the **Portuguese**, but the town's fortunes picked up once more in the eighteenth century, after the Portuguese had been unseated by two rival Arab dynasties. Mikindani's real boom began during the reign of the Zanzibari sultan **Seyyid Barghash**, whose rule saw the consolidation of the town's importance and the construction of several fine buildings, notably the Friday Mosque. The legacy of the **slave trade** is reflected in the village's tribal make-up, which includes descendants of Yao, Makua and Mwera slaves, as well as Ngoni who first came as caravan porters working for the Arabs, and Makonde, some of whom had been slave traders themselves.

**German rule** was marked by the introduction of cash crops such as sisal, rubber, coconut and oil seed, but failed to reverse the decline in the town's fortunes that followed the abolition of the slave trade. Things changed little under **British rule** and by the 1950s Mikindani Bay had also outlived its usefulness as a harbour, as it was too shallow for the vessels of the day. Come Independence, most of the area's colonial plantations were abandoned, and the town's buildings began to crumble as Mikindani reverted to its original status as a humble fishing village.

## Arrival, information and accommodation

**Daladalas** run from Mtwara throughout the day (Tsh400); transport to Mtwara from Masasi, Lindi and all points further north also pass through. The bus station is in the western part of town, but you can ask to be dropped at either of the hotels, a few hundred metres to the east. **Leaving Mikindani**, it's best to go to Mtwara first (by daladala), even if you're heading north, as vehicles passing Mikindani tend to be full. Mikindani's hotels are useful sources of **information**, especially *The Old Boma Hotel*, which has dozens of useful sheets covering attractions here and in southeastern Tanzania in general. **Trade Aid**, the British NGO running the hotel (ⓦwww.tradeaiduk.org), is involved in education, and the preservation of the village's historic buildings.

If you're on a shoestring, the town can be visited as a **day-trip** from Mtwara. With six months to spare and skills in microfinance, self-help development, hospitality, accounts or teaching English, you may be able to **volunteer** at *The Old Boma Hotel*.

**The Old Boma Hotel** (☏0784/360110, ⓦwww .mikindani.com). Set inside the beautifully restored German Boma above the village, this is southern Tanzania's best hotel by miles, with bags of atmosphere, outstanding accommodation, and a wide range of activities and excursions (see p.182). There's also a sophisticated restaurant and bar, free internet access, wi-fi and a welcome swimming pool. The eight high-ceilinged rooms, some with balconies, have large timber beds and are decorated with local handicrafts. There's no a/c, but the thick walls, sea breeze and ceiling fans keep things cool. It's worth spending a little more for a view. No smoking inside the building. Credit cards accepted. BB ❻–❼

**Ten Degrees South Lodge** (☏0784/855833, ⓦwww.eco2.com) Facing the bay over the road, this small but welcoming and informal place is associated with the eco2 dive centre two doors down and has two types of room. "Guesthouse" rooms are in a cool, thick-walled old house, boasting solid Zanzibari beds, walk-in mosquito nets with fans *inside* them, clean cotton sheets and shared bathrooms; the rooms in a new wing by the roadside are less atmospheric but have private bathrooms and hot water. There's also Mikindani's best bar, good food, and free internet. BB "guesthouse" ❸, en suite ❹

## The Town

Mikindani is small enough to walk around, and the plentiful trees provide enough shade. If you want a guide, contact *The Old Boma Hotel*. As you're wandering along the narrow, winding streets, look for the attractive first-floor wooden balconies (*uzio*) and the elaborately carved wooden doorways, both typical of Swahili coastal settlements. Most of the stone buildings, many of them in ruins, date from the slaving era and are constructed of coral rock (ragstone) embedded in lime mortar. Much of the original lime stucco facing and cream or white limewash has disappeared, but where patches of limewash remain, the buildings make singularly photogenic subjects – kids are happy having their pictures taken, but most adults aren't, so ask before snapping.

### Friday Mosque

Notable among the buildings dating from the reign of Sultan Barghash is the **Friday Mosque** in the centre of town. The beautiful carved door was the work of an Ndonde slave called Gulum Dosa (the Ndonde are closely related to Makonde), who belonged to an Indian customs officer in the Zanzibari government. The three **stone graves** outside the mosque are believed to date from the fifteenth century, and face north towards Mecca. They're marked by baobab trees, which has led some to believe that they belong to sultans.

### Livingstone House and the Slave Market

At the bottom of the hill leading to the Boma, the near-derelict **Livingstone House** has long been earmarked for renovation by Trade Aid, but looks very sorry for itself. The building – a rather bland three-storey construction with little decoration – was erected by the British government in 1952 in memory of the famous missionary and explorer, and supposedly occupies the site of Livingstone's camp in 1866 at the start of his fifth and final expedition to the

Great Lakes, which became famous for his encounter with Stanley (see p.431). Although his journal isn't too clear about the matter, it's more likely that Livingstone actually stayed in Pemba village on the northern lip of the bay, first camping, and then in a house rented for four dollars a month.

When the Germans arrived, twenty years after Livingstone, slaves were still the town's most valuable asset, and it took them some time to eliminate the trade. Indeed, according to some accounts, it was the Germans themselves who built Mikindani's "**Slave Market**", at the bottom of the grand cobbled roadway leading to the German Boma. Some confusion remains about whether the building really was used as a slave market, or if it was simply built on the site of an older one. The thick walls, up to 60cm in places, seem to point to the former, which would show that slavery was at least tolerated during the early years of German occupation. Sadly, renovation has completely destroyed the charm of the previously ruined building – its wonderful pastel-shaded arches and vaults now hidden by internal walls enclosing various offices, a modest restaurant and a bar. Art lovers can indulge at Mr Kuchele & Son, the yellow shack next door, where father and son produce all manner of **paintings**. Prices are reasonable and it's not just tourist guff. More arts and **crafts** are sold at the *The Old Boma Hotel*, with profits funding various projects.

### The German Boma and Bismarck Hill

A more sensitive example of restoration than the slave market is the **German Boma**, which has been beautifully spruced up and converted into the luxurious *Old Boma Hotel*. Built in 1895 as the seat of the German colonial administration, the limewashed building is the town's most distinctive and attractive landmark, combining German, Arab and Swahili architectural elements. The gardens surrounding the Boma are attractive too, with frangipani and flame trees providing splashes of colour and shade, and shelter for blue monkeys. Visitors are welcome to look around. On entering, have a look at the stunning door carvings, the work of Gulum Dosa, who also carved the mosque's doorway. Inside is a cool courtyard, with rooms arranged around it on two floors. One corner of the building has a three-storey tower with crenellated battlements, resembling an Andalucian minaret: scale two steep flights of steps for a sweeping view over the town and its bay.

Just behind the Boma above the coconut groves stands **Bismarck Hill**, named after the first chancellor of unified Germany – it's worth the thirty-minute climb to the top, not only for the views but also for a curious piece of history. The hill is popularly known as Baobab Hill, because of the lone baobab (*mbuyu*) on its summit. These trees are traditionally thought to be inhabited by benevolent spirits, and so were considered safe places to bury things, like money, which gave rise to the common belief that the Germans buried treasure near baobabs when they left. In this case, the great big hole on top was made by a batty treasure-seeking *maganga* (traditional healer), who, sadly for him or her, failed to find anything.

## Around the bay

Mikindani's big drawback, from a tourist's point of view, is its lack of beach, at least one within easy reach. In case you're tempted by the silty shore facing either hotel, resist: this part of the bay functions as the town's latrine. Much cleaner, and largely out of sight, is a narrow stretch of sand by the **Yacht Club**, 1.5km towards Mtwara from the hotels. The club itself is almost defunct, with no facilities other than a few tables and, for now, free use of its toilet and shower.

More private, and definitely more romantic, is a small patch of sand on the bay's southern lip, to which eco2 can help arrange dhow trips. On the bay's western lip is another good stretch of sand, **Naumbu Beach**, about 7km from Mikindani. To walk or cycle there, head up the road towards Lindi and bear right before the bridge and past the boatyard. The track follows an old railway embankment between the bay and the electric fence of Mikindani Estate (watch out for snakes). If you stay on the track closest to the bay you'll eventually come to **Pemba**, which has the remains of an old Arab mosque (possibly from the ninth century), and some graves. The beach is on the ocean side of the village – ask for directions.

## Excursions from Mikindani

Mikindani's hotels are happy acting as intermediaries if you want to rent **bicycles, dugouts or ngalawa outriggers**. The latter (up to Tsh30,000 a day for the boat) are a wonderful way to explore Mikindani Bay, and get you to some nicely secluded beaches.

For landlubbers, *The Old Boma Hotel* has a wide choice of trips. Prices are in sterling (£1 being $1.65 at the time of writing), and are per person for a couple. These include leisurely guided **rambles** in and around town (£5–15); **classes** in Tingatinga painting, cooking and Kiswahili; nocturnal **fishing trips** by canoe (£10); day-trips to **Mnazi Bay** (p.187) or the **Ruvuma River** for a spot of hippo watching (each trip £40); and overnight trips to the **Rondo Plateau** (£60; see p.178). If you're enthusiastic enough, you might also be able to convince them to arrange a trip to Tendaguru (p.178) or a safari to Lukwika-Lumesule (p.194).

Southern Tanzania's marine experts are **eco2**, two doors along from *Ten Degrees South Lodge* (Ⓣ0784/855833, Ⓦwww.eco2.com). As the only PADI-accredited **dive school** between Kilwa and Mozambique, they're the ones to contact for the enchanting underside of **Mnazi Bay-Ruvuma Estuary Marine Park** (p.187). Headed by a British marine biologist, eco2 offers the full range of PADI dive courses, and a few marine biology courses of their own. **Snorkellers** are welcome to tag along ($30 per person). A particular wow not needing any immersion is **humpback whale-watching;** key months for seeing them are September and October, when cetacean mothers-to-be return to East Africa's warm waters to calve, often in the company of a "midwife" ($40 per person, minimum four people; no guarantees).

## Eating and drinking

Mikindani is just a village; the following **restaurants** and **bars** are virtually all there is.

**CCM building** Behind the bus stand. This is basically an empty courtyard where discos are held, supposedly every Wednesday, Friday and Saturday from 7pm–2am. Tsh1000 admission. No alcohol: the dancing kings and queens tank up at *Muku's*, opposite.

**Ismaili's Bar** In the Slave Market. Given that almost all the locals are Muslim, it's a bit of a surprise to see this bar, but there you go – good for a dissolute dabble. Open daily to 10pm, closed Ramadan.

**The Old Boma Hotel** Consistently delicious and inventive cooking, courtesy of Mama Joyce and her mates. The menu features great vegetable soups

(Tsh4000) and unbeatably fresh salads and herbs from their own garden. The menu is extensive, but we'd recommend you just ask what looks good that day: upwards of Tsh12,000 for a main course. Eat under parasols or trees, and cool off in the pool (Tsh6000 if you're not staying the night). There's also a quiet bar in the reconstructed tribal court-house, which was first built by the Germans.

**Samaki Restaurant** In the Slave Market. A simple but effective *mgahawa* for tea, snacks and very cheap meals (fish with rice for under Tsh1000), and handy for breakfasts too. Closes around 3pm.

**Ten Degrees South Lodge** Big portions are the style here. The mashed potato deserves a mention, and the seafood is always good, especially the Thai prawn curry (Tsh10,000), all going down a storm with expats and aid workers alike. Mind you, the real attraction might just be the bar – good music, cold drinks, some of Tanzania's cheapest wine (Tsh15,000 a bottle), satellite TV, and often lively conversation. Open until the last punter falls down.

# Mtwara and around

The south coast's largest town, **Mtwara** is 82km south of Mingoyo, close to the border with Mozambique. Once dubbed "Siberia" by civil servants thanks to its isolation from the rest of Tanzania, this modern town is something of an anomaly, and testimony to the failure of the **Groundnut Scheme** – a grand plan for regional development put into action by the British colonial powers after World War II, and which saw the establishment of Mtwara itself in 1947. Unfortunately, the British never once considered whether the soil was suitable for growing groundnuts (peanuts) – it was not – and the project collapsed amidst colossal losses and bitter recriminations. The 211-kilometre railway from Mtwara to Nachingwea that had been built as part of the scheme was ripped up, leaving only the empty spaces that intersperse Mtwara's broad street layout to bear witness to the grandiose and short-sighted dreams of the past.

The cashew-nut economy that replaced the Groundnut Scheme has been the victim of fickle market prices, and the Mtwara Region has suffered. The area is now a favoured base for NGOs and aid organizations. Still, things are looking up: several million dollars have been spent modernizing Mtwara's harbour, Tanzania's third busiest, and with the asphalt road from Dar es Salaam almost a reality, it looks like Mtwara is finally emerging from its long Siberian winter... even if locals are now worried that the new **Unity Bridge** over the Ruvuma River, the road to which doesn't come close to Mtwara, might condemn it once more into the cold.

For visitors, Mtwara's modern origins mean that it lacks even a single building or sight of note. It does, however, sit on one of Tanzania's most beautiful stretches of coastline, while the **Mnazi Bay-Ruvuma Estuary Marine Park** to the south offers superlative swimming and snorkelling, some of Tanzania's best scuba diving reefs, and miles of palm-fringed sandy beaches. The town is also a handy springboard for **Mikindani** (see p.179).

## Arrival and accommodation

The **bus station** is in the southeast of town, beside the market and the **airport** is 6km to the south; Precisionair fly in daily from Dar. Mtwara's expansive street layout isn't overly conducive to walking: the best way around is in a motorized *bajaji* **rickshaw**, which can be found at the bus stand, at Uhuru Torch round about, and at the corner of TANU and Uhuru roads. Taxis charge Tsh3000–4000 for most journeys, *bajajis* half that.

Mtwara has a good selection of **accommodation**, including one place on the beach, but nothing overly posh. **Camping** is possible at *Msemo Hotel* (Tsh10,000 per tent) and in the lush grounds of *Drivein Garden & Cliff Bar* (Tsh5000 per person), both just a few metres from the sea. Electricity is quite reliable by Tanzanian standards (it's fed by a gas-to-electricity project in Mnazi Bay), but Mtwara's **tap water** may contain sediment, so is unsafe to drink.

**Bambo Guest House** Sinani Rd/Makonde Rd ☎023/233 4056. Basic and a bit tatty but acceptable. All rooms, twins or singles, can be shared, and come with en suites, big beds, box nets and fans, but water is supplied in buckets. ❶

**Bondeni Lodge** West of TANU Rd, near the police station ☎023/233 3769. En-suite rooms with

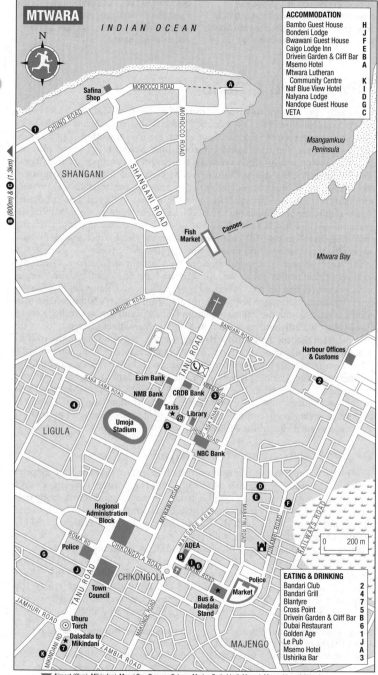

# MTWARA

*INDIAN OCEAN*

N

**ACCOMMODATION**

| | |
|---|---|
| Bambo Guest House | H |
| Bondeni Lodge | J |
| Bwawani Guest House | F |
| Caigo Lodge Inn | E |
| Drivein Garden & Cliff Bar | B |
| Msemo Hotel | A |
| Mtwara Lutheran Community Centre | K |
| Naf Blue View Hotel | I |
| Nalyana Lodge | D |
| Nandope Guest House | G |
| VETA | C |

MOROCCO ROAD

Safina Shop

CHUNO ROAD

SHANGANI

SHANGANI ROAD

MOROCCO ROAD

**①**

**Ⓑ** (800m) & **Ⓒ** (1.3km) ◀

*Msangamkuu Peninsula*

Fish Market

Canoes

*Mtwara Bay*

TAMHURI ROAD

BANDARI ROAD

TANU ROAD

SABA SABA ROAD

Exim Bank

NMB Bank

CRDB Bank

Taxis

@ Library

**③**

MINISTRY

AGA KHAN ROAD

UHURU ROAD

**⑤**

**④**

LIGULA

Umoja Stadium

NBC Bank

**Harbour Offices & Customs**

**②**

Regional Administration Block

MTWARA ROAD

MAKONDE ROAD

MABATINI ROAD

KINANGI ROAD

RAILWAYS ROAD

**Ⓓ**

**Ⓔ**

**Ⓕ**

0        200 m

BOMA RD

Police

**Ⓖ**

CHIKONGOLA ROAD

ADEA

**Ⓗ** **Ⓘ** **⑥**

SINANI ROAD

**Ⓙ**

Town Council

TANU ROAD

CHIKONGOLA

Bus & Daladala Stand

**★**

Police Market

JAMHURI ROAD

Uhuru Torch

MIKINDANI RD

Daladala to Mikindani

**⑦**

ZAMBIA ROAD

MAKONDE ROAD

**Ⓚ**

MAJENGO

**EATING & DRINKING**

| | |
|---|---|
| Bandari Club | 2 |
| Bandari Grill | 4 |
| Blantyre | 7 |
| Cross Point | 5 |
| Drivein Garden & Cliff Bar | B |
| Dubai Restaurant | 6 |
| Golden Age | 1 |
| Le Pub | J |
| Msemo Hotel | A |
| Ushirika Bar | 3 |

▼ *Airport (6km), Mikindani, Mnazi Bay-Ruvuma Estuary Marine Park, Lindi, Masasi, Mozambique & Newala*

cleanish squat toilets, fan, one bed, which can be shared, and round nets. The rooms behind the bar are small and quite basic; the ones at the side are better – a little larger with sofas and local TV. The bar has food to order. ❶

**Bwawani Guest House** Kunambi Rd, 600m north of the bus stand. A small, friendly, family-run place, with basic but well-kept rooms, shared bathrooms, big beds and box nets, and quite breezy, too. Very cheap, especially singles. ❶

**Caigo Lodge Inn** Off Mabatini Rd ☎0784/766580 or 0784/538647. A modern but slightly solemn place with large, well-kept en-suite rooms, all with large double beds, a/c, fan, satellite TV, cotton sheets and box nets. Secure parking. BB fans ❶, a/c ❷

**Drivein Garden & Cliff Bar** 1.5km west of Safina Shop, Shangani ☎0713/503007 or 0784/503007. On the land side of the road next to the shore (which comes right up to the road), this occupies a lushly vegetated former ragstone quarry. Starting as a garden bar and campsite, it now also has a restaurant and a proper house for long-term stays ($500/month), and some rooms should be ready by the time you read this. BB ❹

🏃 **Msemo Hotel** Shangani ☎023/233 3206 or 0786/678283. Currently the town's only beachside hotel, hence the recommendation. The sea-facing rooms are pretty good, too – large with high ceilings, and some of them in individual rondavels. All have big *semadari* beds and box nets, a proper chair and table, local TV, fan, and a terrace. The beach is mainly wild and strewn with jagged blocks of blackened coral, but there's a sandier section at one end. Has a restaurant and bar (both with views), souvenir shop and even mini golf. Good value. BB ❹

**Mtwara Lutheran Community Centre** 100m south of Uhuru Torch roundabout ☎023/233 3294. The quiet and gentle atmosphere of this place makes it Mtwara's best budget choice, but don't plan on crawling back late, as the gate closes at 10pm. All rooms have box nets and standing fans, and some also have bathrooms, ceiling fan and local TV. For an extra Tsh10,000, you get a/c. Has soft drinks, but rarely any food. BB ❶, en suite ❷–❸

**Naf Blue View Hotel** Sinani Rd ☎023/233 4465, ✉nafblueview@yahoo.com. Unfortunate naming aside, this has the novelty of two rooms with desktop computers and internet for Tsh10,000 more. All rooms have big double beds, not leaving much space for anything other than a/c and flat-screen satellite TV. Also has a gym and a small restaurant serving mainly Indian and Chinese dishes (under Tsh10,000). No alcohol. BB ❹

**Nalyana Lodge** Off Mabatini Rd ☎0755/777715. Very similar to the *Caigo*, opposite, but with only six rooms. Also has a bar at the back with tables under a tree. Safe parking. BB ❷

**Nandope Guest House** 200m beyond *Bondeni Lodge* ☎023/233 4060. Two very different standards of room here: very basic singles with just a bed and box net, sharing bathrooms; and very small but new en-suite rooms with icy a/c, fan and local TV. Safe parking. ❶, en suite BB ❷

**VETA** 2km west of Safina Shop, Shangani ☎023/233 3453, ✉vetasoutheast@yahoo.com. Attached to a training institute, this walled-in hotel has eager-to-please staff and well-tended rooms equipped with TVs. Singles can be shared by couples; if you need more space, go for a suite. Decent restaurant. It's 200m back from the beach, which is shallow and rocky, so not much good for swimming, but it's in a beautiful location. BB ❷, suites ❸

## The Town

Mtwara's liveliest area is around the **market** (Soko Kuu) near the bus station, but its most interesting "sight" is the whole area north of here, where the wide spaces between the roads – intended to have been populated by a city that never was – are now filled with almost village-like life, complete with small farms and plots and pecking chickens: really quite endearing for a city centre.

Probably the most interesting architectural sight – and that's stretching it – are the two terraces of two-storey concrete stores facing one another on **Aga Khan Road**, the town's main commercial drag, where pirated Nigerian videos sell well. Dating from the 1950s to the 1970s, the pillared shop fronts are the modern equivalent of the traditional balconied Swahili town houses you can still see in Mikindani, Kilwa Kivinje and elsewhere.

The town's main beaches are in the NGO-colonized suburb of **Shangani**, a couple of kilometres north of town. There's no public transport so *bajajis* are best unless you're happy walking. The beach on the north side is quite rocky and has little sand, but the views (variegated blues and greens) are blissful, as is

## ADEA and the MaKuYa Festival

Mtwara's **African Development through Economics and the Arts** (ADEA) is a great one. Founded in 2003, the NGO prioritizes **art** as a means of development, but took a gamble in 2008 with the inaugural **MaKuYa Festival** of traditional music. They were rewarded with a smash success. The festival's name is a contraction of three major southern Tanzanian tribes: the Makonde, Makua and Yao, all of them endowed with vivid **musical traditions**, including the Makonde's quite wonderful *sindimba* stilt dance; various masquerades, capable of scattering children, and women's groups with powerful displays of drumming.

Mid-August looks set to be the date for subsequent editions, but at any time of year you're welcome at ADEA's base on Sinani Road (Mon–Fri, sometimes also at weekends; ☏0784/503076 or 0784/491471, ⟲www.adeaafrica.org) to have a chat, see the artists at work, or buy some rather excellent **handicrafts**, including high-quality work in the Tingatinga style, clothes, carvings and some very cool paintings that defy categorization.

– for most of the year – the breeze. Swimming is only possible at high tide; at low tide, kids will like rummaging around the exposed coral pools in search of crabs and other critters. The water is quite clean, although the beaches can get covered in seaweed. Access to the shoreline is possible all the way along, so there are plenty of fine **picnic** sites to choose from. You can buy basic supplies and a few treats, including brown bread and cheese, at Safina Shop, a container crate run by a very charming Polish lady.

With more time, you could head across the bay to more attractive beaches at **Msangamkuu** – the "Big Sand" – a giant sand spit across the harbour entrance. Regular canoe ferries (around Tsh500) cross throughout the day from the jetty behind the Catholic church. Don't bring valuables, but if you must, don't leave them unattended, even if the beach appears deserted.

## Eating and drinking

For **eating out**, all bars or local *hotelis* will serve up perfectly acceptable *nyama choma*. For real restaurants, you're pretty much limited to the following. Mtwara has plenty of enjoyable **bars** to choose from, and a modest night scene, too.

### Restaurants

**Bandari Grill** *Mtwara Peninsula Hotel.* Dine on decent continental and Indian grub in arctic a/c. They don't always have meat, but can rustle up lasagne whenever they have mince. Mains around Tsh6000–8000.

**Drivein Garden & Cliff Bar** 1.5km west of Safina Shop, Shangani. A great excuse for a wander along Shangani's shoreline, the lovely garden here covers what was once an eyesore quarry, and comes complete with a tidal pond. A walkway over it leads to one of several gazebos scattered around. Great for a drink, or the "speciality" chicken and chips; order in advance for anything else at Safina Shop, which is owned by the same couple.

**Dubai Restaurant** Sinani Rd. One of several good cheap restaurants in this area, serving both snacks and full meals (under Tsh2000) in efficient cafeteria style.

**Golden Age** 500m west of Safina Shop, Shangani. A couple of converted container crates nicely dumped under a bunch of shady trees, and which dish up some famously good squid.

**Msemo Hotel** Shangani. The restaurant here has seen better days, and is pricey by local standards (grilled seafood Tsh12,000, meat a little cheaper), but who cares with views like this. The menu is mainly continental fare, including steaks, pasta and seafood with chips. It also has a well-stocked bar.

### Bars

**Bandari Club** Port Rd. A lively and friendly weekend nightspot (from 7.30pm; Tsh1000 entry), with the Boka Ngoma band on Friday and Saturday, and a disco on Sunday. It's a somnolent bar the rest of the time.

**Blantyre** Uhuru Torch roundabout. A major venue for one-off events, especially Taarab music. Also

has a pool table and bar food (very slow service). **Cross Point** TANU Rd. Busy central boozer that stays open all night; also has good cheap food. **Le Pub** *Bondeni Lodge*, west of TANU Rd. Unremarkable but nonetheless popular outdoor bar.
**Ushirika Bar** Mindu Rd. The outdoor disco here on Fri & Sat is popular; Tsh1000 entry.

## Listings

**Banks** NBC on Uhuru Rd, and CRDB and Exim, both TANU Rd, all have ATMs. CRDB should be able to change traveller's cheques. Also try NBC, but both are excruciatingly slow.
**Internet access** Info Solution at the CCM building on Uhuru Rd is reliable with good opening times (daily 8am–9pm). Also try the post office (Mon–Fri 8am–4.30pm, Sat 9am–noon).

**Library** "Mtwara Intellectual Service Station" is on Uhuru Rd (Mon–Fri 9.30am–6pm, Sat 9am–2pm; Tsh500 per day).
**Pharmacy** Bus Stand Pharmacy, at the bus stand ☏023/233 3359.
**Post** TANU Rd/Uhuru Rd.
**Telephones** TTCL, beside the post office (Mon–Fri 7.45am–4.30pm, Sat 9am–12.30pm).

## Mnazi Bay-Ruvuma Estuary Marine Park

Established in 2000, **Mnazi Bay-Ruvuma Estuary Marine Park** covers a large part of the land and ocean southeast of Mtwara between Msangamkuu Peninsula and the mouth of the Ruvuma River on the Mozambique border, encompassing a network of estuarine, mangrove, tidal, peninsular, island and

## Moving on from Mtwara

Several buses leave each day for **Dar** at around 6am. **Safety** is a perennial headache, especially now that the road is, except for 50km south of the Rufiji, perilously fast: Akida's Coach and White Star are generally considered safest, but that's no guarantee. There are also hourly departures for **Lindi** on large minibuses, and a handful going to **Newala** or **Masasi**. If you can't find anything direct to **Kilwa**, go to Lindi, from where there are two or three a day. For **Mikindani**, catch a pale-blue-banded daladala (Tsh400) at the Uhuru Torch roundabout, running every half-hour or so throughout the day.

**Flights** to Dar es Salaam are operated by Precisionair; its office is beside CRDB Bank on TANU Road (call centre ☏0787/888417 or 0787/888408–9). For information on crossing into **Mozambique**, see p.194.

coral reef environments. The reefs offer superb snorkelling and diving, especially on **Ruvula Reef**, off the north end of Msimbati Peninsula, which slopes steeply right up to the shore, whilst the **beaches** – with all the white sand, fringing palm trees and warm turquoise water you've dreamed of – are among Tanzania's most enthralling.

The easiest beach to access is just beyond **Msimbati** village and the park gate, though it's used by fishermen for peeling prawns and cleaning fish. Much nicer is the one after **Ruvula**, 6km northwest of Msimbati village on the tip of the peninsula, and backed by thick vegetation. It's possible to arrange **dhow trips** with local fishermen at Ruvula to Namponda Island, 3km offshore; with more time, you could also explore Mongo Island and the diminutive Kisima Ndogo Island nearby. A word of caution when swimming: there's a **dangerous undertow** at Msimbati beach and possibly elsewhere at spring tide (new moon and full moon), and people do get swept away from time to time, so seek local advice.

## Practicalities

The heart of the park, Msimbati Peninsula, is a couple of hours from Mtwara by **daladala**, which go as far as Msimbati village, 2km short of Msimbati beach. To get to Ruvula, at the tip of the peninsula, either walk the remaining 8km along a sandy track, or wait for a lift – you stand a better chance at weekends. If you're **driving** from Mtwara (count on an hour), head south from Uhuru Torch round about for 900m and turn left. After 3.7km, turn left again, off the tarmac, on to the wide *murram* road for Kilambo. The turning for Msimbati is at Madimba, 17.5km along the *murram* road. The rest of the drive is deep sand. **Day-trips** are offered by *The Old Boma Hotel* in Mikindani, costing $56 per person (charged in sterling). To really get to know the area, **snorkelling and scuba diving** trips in and around the marine park are organized by **eco2**, also based in Mikindani (p.182), which is also thinking about extended "dive safaris" with nights spent under canvas.

If you're coming by boat (from Mikindani), **park fees** ($10 for 24hr, also payable in shillings) are collected by the company you're with. Otherwise, pay at the gate just beyond Msimbati village. The park **website** is Ⓦwww .marineparktz.com/mnazi_bay.htm; for more **information** contact eco2.

The park's only regular **accommodation** is the Belgian/Congolese-run *Ruvula Sea Safari*, wonderfully located at Ruvula beach (☏0784/367439, Ⓦwww.ruvula.net; FB ❻), which charges monopoly rates for simple but nonetheless attractive thatched stone *bandas* (sharing bathrooms). The food's good, and you can arrange to be picked up from Mtwara. It also has a **campsite** ($12 per person). Otherwise, **fly camping** is the only option, on the beach at Msimbati or beyond Ruvula village. There are no facilities other than the restaurant at *Ruvula Sea Safari*, but fishermen will happily sell you part of their catch, including oysters, prawns or even barracuda, whilst villagers may be persuaded to rustle up some chickens for a barbecue. There are no **security** problems at present but there have been in the past: asking permission from village elders minimizes the risk, and is also polite.

# The Makonde Plateau and westwards

**Heading inland** from Lindi or Mtwara, tourists are virtually unheard of, and outside major centres there's little in the way of accommodation. It's not because there's nothing to see en route to Mozambique or the region around Lake Nyasa, there's plenty, but the practicalities are a mite awkward unless you're fluent in Kiswahili and have your own wheels.

Rising just north of the Ruvuma River is the **Makonde Plateau**, a river-gouged massif peaking at 900m and the region's main geographical feature. The plateau's abrupt southern edge is quite spectacular, but the plateau itself is pretty rather than beautiful, the main attraction being its deeply rural nature. The main town is **Newala**, on the plateau's southwestern edge and within walking distance of jaw-dropping views over the Ruvuma River and Mozambique. Dusty **Masasi**, in the lowlands to the west, is Tanzania's cashew-nut capital, with several climbable granite inselbergs (outcrops, usually devoid of vegetation) nearby, two of which have **Neolithic rock paintings**. Beyond, the only town of note is **Tunduru**, a rough and ready gemstone mining town.

The region's big news – and big hope – is the **Unity Bridge** between Tanzania and Mozambique, which promises major changes once its access roads are asphalted (the road is already open albeit rough). Coming from the coast, the road from Mingoyo to Masasi is fast tarmac. The next section to Tunduru has funding for asphalt, but we won't hazard a guess as to exactly when this might actually happen. The last leg of the journey to Songea, for access to Lake Nyasa and the southern Highlands, is still a very tough, bone-rattling experience, and likely to be impassable (or, at best, a gear-grinding mudfest) in the rains. Needless to say, it shouldn't be attempted by drivers not completely confident on loose sand or mud, or suitably equipped with a reliable high-clearance 4WD, shovel, tow rope, spare oil, water and brake fluid.

## Newala

A fine base for exploring the Makonde Plateau is the town of **NEWALA**, perched right over the plateau's southwestern rim, and a pleasant stopover if you're taking the direct but unsurfaced road from Mtwara (much prettier

## The Makonde and their carvings

The Makonde Plateau, as you might guess, is home to the **Makonde**, one of Tanzania's largest and most heterogeneous tribes, who have achieved worldwide fame for their woodcarvings (see p.64). They're also one of Tanzania's more traditional societies, having historically preferred to keep themselves isolated from their neighbours, and wisely so: for much of the eighteenth and nineteenth centuries, southern Tanzania was lacerated by slave raids, but the steep-sided plateau was left largely untouched.

The birth of the woodcarving tradition is entwined with the **mythical origin** of the Makonde themselves, similar to the story of Adam and Eve. Instead of a rib, the lonely male forebear carved a female figure from a piece of wood, and placed it beside his dwelling. Presto, the following morning the figure had transformed into a beautiful woman. They conceived a child, but it died three days later, so they moved upriver, but their second child died as well. So, they moved up in to the highlands, where their third child was born and survived.

The myth alludes to the Makonde's **migration** away from the frequently flooded lowlands of northern Mozambique. Up on the plateau, their isolation from other tribes meant that they kept some traditions that were lost elsewhere, including matrilineal descent. Motherhood is also a quasi-sacred state of being, and such is the female domination of Makonde society that older men travelling alone may take a carved female figurine with them for protection.

Another traditional form of Makonde carving is **masks**, representing spirits or ancestors and commonly used in dances for initiation ceremonies and harvest celebrations. There are three main kinds: face masks, body masks (which cover the dancer's torso) and helmet masks (*mapiko*), worn over the head like helmets, and which represent a terrifying force: whether traditional spirits, turbaned slave traders, or even Europeans. The masks are made and kept in a secret bush location known as *mpolo*, which women are forbidden to approach. *Mapiko* dances and *sindimba* dances (in which the dancers perform on stilts called *machopila*) still take place every year when a new generation is initiated into adulthood. If you can time your visit with Mtwara's annual MaKuYa festival in August (p.186), you're almost guaranteed to see this. For more on the Makonde, pictures and sound clips, visit ⓦ www.bluegecko.org /kenya/tribes/makonde.

than the paved road via Mingoyo). The views from the edge of town, where the plateau gives way to the valley of the Ruvuma River half a kilometre below, are utterly spectacular. Equally refreshing is the town's relatively cool climate: considered glacial by locals, it should be just right for visitors after the swelter of the coast, even if you'll still have to contend with mosquitoes.

The town centre is at the junction of the roads from Mtwara and Masasi. The **market** (and post office) is 200m southwest of here at the start of the town's main street, a broad, tree-lined avenue of vibrant orange sand that heads 1.3km southwest to Newala's oldest building, the squat **German Boma**, unusual for its sloping black walls. The Boma is occupied by the police, who are quite happy having tourists poke around; indeed, they have a guest book, and will likely give you a guided tour, too. Behind the Boma, which is built on a spur of land jutting out from the plateau rim, the land plunges away on three sides, giving fantastic **views** over a distance of nearly 100km, including the Ruvuma River (the beige band of sand), Mozambique, and the isolated peaks around Masasi in the far west. If this grabs you, you'll love **Shimo la Mungu** ("God's Hole"), a particularly vertiginous drop just to the north. The easiest way there is to backtrack 400m along the avenue from the Boma, then turn left (north) along another tree-lined road. After 700m you cross the west end of the airstrip and the escarpment is just beyond it on your left.

## Practicalities

If you're **driving** from Mtwara during heavy rains, take the longer route via Mtama (on the paved Mingoyo–Masasi road), as the direct road via Nanyamba is prone to flooding and sections of it can be very muddy. Newala's **bus stand** is on the road in from Mtwara, 800m northeast of the town centre. There's roughly hourly **transport** to and from Masasi until 4pm. If you're leaving Newala to travel to Mtwara, Lindi or Dar, it's best to start early: the first buses head off at 5am. You can rent **bicycles** at a stand facing the side of the post office at the edge of the market (just remember that what goes down has to be ridden or pushed back up). For longer or lazier excursions, including down to the Ruvuma River, *Country Lodge* offers Land Cruisers complete with driver for Tsh1500 per km.

There's a scatter of decent **guesthouses** (❶–❷) on the road leading into town from the bus stand, and several more around the market and off the road to the German Boma, but the latter now receive little trade since the bus station shifted to its present location, and standards are slipping. The most comfortable of the lot is *Country Lodge* (☏023/241 0355 or 0755/387799, ⓦwww.countrylodgetz.com; BB ❸), a proper **hotel** 900m along the Masasi road (1.8km from the bus stand), with fine en-suite rooms, twin or double beds with matching nets, plus a sofa, chair and table, and local TV. Newala has **water** problems, so don't drink the tap water, and don't expect hotel showers to work. Also, don't count on electricity: if they receive more than a few hours' supply a day, the locals feel blessed.

The best **restaurant** is a large thatched affair at *Country Lodge*, with uncommonly good seafood (Tsh6500, a little more for prawns). It also functions as a

▲ A Makonde woodcarver

bar, and has cold beers. Earthier venues for drinks and bar food, filled with young women and older men, lie between *Country Lodge* and the town centre, and around the corner from the post office facing the market.

# Masasi

The scruffy crossroads town of **MASASI** is west of the Makonde Plateau, at the start of a weird and wonderful landscape characterized by isolated inselbergs. It's also the place you're most likely to pass through if heading into Mozambique (see p.194). The town is mainly of interest to **cashew-nut** (*korosho*) traders; for most other travellers it's likely to be an overnight stop if you're heading on to Tunduru. The Makua tribe who populate the region these days were not its first inhabitants, as shown by prehistoric **rock paintings** tucked away in natural shelters on some of the inselbergs beside the town. Unlike Kondoa-Irangi's rock art (see p.235), Masasi's paintings – mostly in red ochre – are abstract, geometric, and include what are arguably "sun symbols" (circles with radiating lines) and stylized axes. The easiest site to visit is on **Mtandi Hill**, behind the Anglican cathedral 4km back towards Lindi; ask there for a guide. Before visiting any of the Masasi's sites, read the section on rock art etiquette on p.236.

## Practicalities

Masasi sprawls along almost 5km of road, but, other than the inselbergs on its northern side, it lacks an obvious focus. Most **buses and daladalas** terminate at the west end of the paved road, at the junction to Nachingwea,

### The Makua

The **Makua**, like their neighbours the Makonde and Yao, were originally from what's now northern Mozambique, and settled in the region around Masasi most likely in the sixteenth century. They called their new home *Machashi*, describing the head of the wild millet plant, which was large and heavy with grain here. In the eighteenth and nineteenth centuries, Masasi – as the first properly productive land encountered by caravans arriving from the west – became an important stopping point for **slavers**, who picked up not just victuals but many of the inhabitants, who were scattered far and wide: some of their descendants include a community of over 200,000 Makua in Madagascar.

The caravan road also attracted **missionaries**, including Masasi's first Anglican bishop, **William Vincent Lucas**, who made his mark by pioneering (in 1925) a Christian version of the traditional *Jando* **initiation ceremony** for boys. The combination of circumcision and Christian confirmation flew in the face of more orthodox Christian beliefs, and the new rite was even accused of being "little better than an orgy". But Lucas's show of respect for local traditions – which he rather unfortunately once described as "a wonderful opportunity ... for the Christian priest of getting into real personal touch with his boys" – won over the Makua. Another winsome Bishop that graced Masasi (1960–68) was **Trevor Huddlestone**, a long-standing opponent of southern Africa's apartheid regimes.

For a good **overview of Makua traditions**, which in many ways mirror those of other Tanzanian tribes, there's the excellent *Excerpts of Makua Traditions* by Father Kubat and Brother Mpokasaye, at Ⓦ www.sds-ch.ch/centre/artyk/articel/makua.htm.

Newala and Tunduru. Vehicles coming from the east stop first at another stand 1.4km short of the junction, near the market and post office. **Leaving Masasi**, you'll find buses and daladalas to Mtwara and Newala, and sometimes to Lindi, until around 4pm. The road to Tunduru and Songea is covered later in this chapter.

### Accommodation

Masasi has dozens of ever-changing **guesthouses**, the bulk of them on the main road between the two bus stands. Tracking down a decent one used to involve quite a foot slog, but no more: the town's cheap *bajaji* rickshaws are a handy way of checking out several options without wearing out your soles. The *Holiday Motel* (☎0784/727911 or 0786/105487; BB **❶**), diagonally opposite the main (western) bus stand, has seven small but perfectly acceptable en-suite rooms, some with local TV, and some swanky new rooms are being built at the side. At the east end of town, past the Mkuti petrol station, try *Sayari Guest House* (☎023/251 0095; **❶**), which, while past its best, is still popular, and has a good bar.

### Eating and drinking

Most of Masasi's **restaurants**, like its hotels, can be found between the two bus stands, and are primarily bars that also happen to serve food, mainly the ubiquitous *ugali*, *nyama choma* and sometimes fried fish. You won't find much to write home about, but the local **relish** sold in the markets is worth searching out: ask for *kiungo cha embe* if you like mangoes, or *kiungo cha ndimo* for the one made with lime.

You're spoilt for choice when it comes to **drinking**. The *Mahenge Transit Cassino & Bravo Bar* has a great atmosphere, helped along by a generator that ensures a non-stop supply of eminently danceable Congolese music and Bongo Flava. The *Masasi Club* opposite is a friendly and more intimate venue, with the bonus of video shows in the back room: the quality is eye-meltingly bad and the sound is terrible, but it's great fun all the same. Next door to the *Holiday Motel*, there's a large street-side bar that also serves food, has pool tables and shows football on the telly. The *Sayari Guest House's* bar is another good place, with a decent restaurant and upbeat music. If you're feeling brave, seek out the local brew made from the distilled fermented juice of "cashew-apples" (*mabibo* or *makanju*) – the pulpy fruit that grows just above the nut.

# Masasi to Songea

The road from Masasi to Songea is usually covered over two days, though with the road as far as Tunduru in as fine condition as it has ever been, you could just about manage it in a day in bone-dry conditions if you're self-driving and set off before sunrise. The first leg – the 196km **road to Tunduru** – is covered by two or three buses a day in either direction, including buses that pass through Masasi in mid-afternoon. These take no more than five hours in good weather, but up to ten if it's been raining. If you miss these, try to pay for a lift in the back of a lorry. It's an attractive route, ducking and swooping between huge eroded inselbergs before entering a forested area south of Selous Game Reserve, a vital wildlife corridor between Selous and Mozambique's Niassa Reserve, and the reason why the region is infamous for lion attacks (see p.195).

## Crossing into Mozambique

The south coast is the obvious overland approach to Mozambique (the other is by ferry via Malawi on Lake Nyasa). Things should be simple enough with the imminent opening of the Unity Bridge, but be aware that, for now at least, you cannot buy a **Mozambican visa** at a land border or port; instead, visit their High Commission in Dar before heading south.

### Unity Bridge crossing

The 720-metre **Unity Bridge** is almost complete, with border posts and access roads in place, although the access roads aren't all sealed. When ready, this will be the main crossing. Access on the Tanzanian side is via Nangomba, 40km west of Masasi. The bridge starts 66km south of there.

### Kilambo crossing

The old landing craft over the Ruvuma River, at Kilambo, 40km south of Mtwara, currently sits on the riverbed. There are plans to salvage it (for the latest, see ⊛www .eco2.com/ferry), but this may take years, if at all. Travellers without vehicles can cross on large canoes, but vehicles need rafts made of two or more canoes lashed together: precarious, and expensive, at upwards of $200. Mtwara to Kilambo is covered by pick-ups and daladalas, but the remaining 5km across the floodplain will be impassible during rains should the causeway be washed away and, as is sadly likely, not repaired. Once in Mozambique, *chapas* (daladalas) cover the 8km to the immigration post at Namoto.

### By boat

The only **ferries** to Mozambique are on Lake Nyasa via Malawi. On the coast, you might find a **commercial dhow or motorboat** from Mtwara to either Mocímboa da Praia (at least 48hr; $15 or so) or Pemba (not the Zanzibar one!): enquire at Mtwara's harbour office in the main port complex (Mon–Fri 8am–5pm; ☏023/233 3243). You'll need to clear customs in the port complex, and immigration at the Regional Administration Block on TANU Road. Be prepared to grovel, as service with a smile is not the style.

# Lukwika-Lumesule Game Reserve and around

There are next to no settlements on the way to Tunduru, so the only even vaguely touristy attractions are a couple of obscure game reserves, which occupy part of the migratory corridor between the Selous Game Reserve and Niassa Game Reserve in Mozambique. They're rarely visited, and not just on account of their remote locations: from July to December, they're closed to all but trigger-happy hunters, and the rains mean that June is the only certain month for mere camera-toting mortals, with January and February plausible if it hasn't been chucking it down.

The closer of the two is **Msanjesi Game Reserve**, 45km west of Masasi, but more interesting – both scenically and for wildlife – is **Lukwika-Lumesule Game Reserve**, 110km southwest of Masasi along the Ruvuma River, whose perennial waters attract lions, leopards, hippo, crocodile, antelope and numerous bird species, as well as elephants, who routinely trek across the river from Mozambique. There's no accommodation, but **camping** is possible. To get to (and around) either reserve you'll need a 4WD, and a permit from the Office of Natural Resources in Masasi: it's at the west end of town, a short distance beyond the bus stand near the District Commission buildings (☏023/251 0364). The permit will likely cost $30 per person, but the Wildlife Department being the shambles it is, you never know. You'll probably also need to shell out for an obligatory armed ranger. Without your own wheels, Mikindani's *The Old Boma Hotel* (p.182) is the only place in southern Tanzania offering **safaris** to Lukwika-Lumesule, usually over two days.

## Tunduru and on to Songea

The reward for braving the road is a night at the rough gemstone mining town of **TUNDURU** (alexandrite is what makes local eyes shine). The town's **guesthouses** (all ❶) are a sorry lot, with particularly rank squat toilets-cum-showers, though most do at least have some en-suite rooms with large mosquito nets. The most acceptable is *Annex Hunters Guest House* (no phone), 100m west of the bus stand and just off the right side of the road to Songea, which is friendly and secure, but lacks running water. Similarly uninspired are Tunduru's **restaurants**: the best is *The Mainland Hotel*, 300m from the bus stand towards Songea, whose printed menu is wishful thinking but at least their stock dish of rice with meat or beans is a welcome respite from the bombardment of carbonized chicken and chips that assails the region.

The 273km road from **Tunduru to SONGEA** (see p.503), mostly through thick, tsetse fly-infested *miombo* woodland, is one of the worst in the country, and buses only cover this route in the dry season. More "reliable" (a distinctly relative concept around here) are changed "110" Land Rovers, departing either town at 6am (usually Tsh20,000, but fares vary according to the state of the road), and whose drivers are capable of astonishing dexterity behind the wheel. They can take as little as eight hours, but from November to February (after which the road becomes impassable), and also after the long rains, fifteen to twenty hours is considered good going. If you're **self-driving** outside the dry season (during which loose sand is the main problem), getting stuck in mud is a certainty, so it's best to fill up with as many passengers as possible to provide the necessary muscle power for when horse power fails. Alternatively, travel in a convoy. Food and drink, at inflated prices, can be bought at a handful of isolated villages along the way. The only **accommodation** between the two towns is *Malinyi Hotel and Guest House* (❶) at **Namtumbo**, 72km east of Songea.

---

### Tunduru's man-eaters

Apart from terrible roads, Tunduru district's other claim to ignominy is its **man-eating lions**, for which reason you should avoid camping wild, and, if you've broken down, stay close to your vehicle.

The gruesome attacks have been occurring on and off for over three decades, even on the edges of Tunduru town – in 1986, a single lion claimed the lives of 42 inhabitants. The problem has been given a surreal slant by superstitious locals, who have long feared the unusually powerful reputation of Mozambique's **witch doctors**. The tale goes that a man had a quarrel with a neighbour, so crossed over the border to consult a witch, who gave him a rope that could be turned into a lion to attack his neighbour if he followed strict instructions. The man returned home and created the lion, but forgot the instructions and was promptly gobbled up by it, which is how the lions acquired their taste for humans. The more prosaic explanation is that Mozambique's brutal sixteen-year civil war turned the country's wildlife habitats inside out, with the result that the big cats started looking elsewhere for their meals.

# Travel details

## Buses and daladalas

The usual time for long-distance buses is 5am or 6am. The asterisks below denote routes that can be blocked during very heavy rain (frequently March–May, occasionally Nov–Dec): the tricky sections are a 50km stretch south of the Rufiji River, the direct Mtwara to Newala road, and the road west of Tunduru.

**Kilwa Kivinje** to: Kilwa Masoko (frequent daladalas; 30min); Nangurukuru (hourly; 20min).
**Kilwa Masoko** to: Dar (2–3 daily*; 5–6hr); Lindi (2 daily; 3–4hr); Nangurukuru (hourly; 30min).
**Lindi** to: Dar (3–4 daily*; 9hr); Kilwa Masoko (2 daily; 3–4hr); Masasi (4–6 daily; 2hr 30min); Mikindani (hourly; 1hr 30min); Mingoyo (hourly; 30min); Mtwara (hourly; 1hr 30min).
**Masasi** to: Dar (3–4 daily*; 11hr); Lindi (4–6 daily; 2hr 30min); Mikindani (3–4 daily; 3hr 30min); Mtwara (4–5 daily; 4hr); Newala (hourly; 2hr 30min); Tunduru (2–3 daily; 4–5hr).

**Mikindani** to: Lindi (hourly but you'll have to stand; 1hr 30min); Mtwara (frequent daladalas; 20min).
**Mtwara** to: Dar (3–4 daily*; 10hr); Lindi (hourly; 1hr 30min); Masasi (4–5 daily; 4hr); Mikindani (frequent daladalas; 20min); Newala (1–2 daily; 5–6hr).
**Nangurukuru** to: Kilwa Kivinje (hourly; 20min); Kilwa Masoko (frequent daladalas; 30min).
**Newala** to: Dar (daily*; 11–12hr); Masasi (hourly; 2hr 30min); Mtwara (1–2 daily; 5–6hr).
**Tunduru** to: Masasi (2–3 daily; 4–5hr); Songea (2 Land Rovers daily*; 8–24hr).

## Flights

All flights are daily. Mafia is served by Coastal Aviation (also Kilwa) and Tropical Air; Mtwara by Precisionair.

**Kilwa** to: Dar (1hr 10min); Mafia (30min); Zanzibar (1hr 45min).
**Mafia** to: Dar (30min); Kilwa (30min); Zanzibar (1hr 5min).
**Mtwara** to: Dar (1hr 20min).

# Central Tanzania

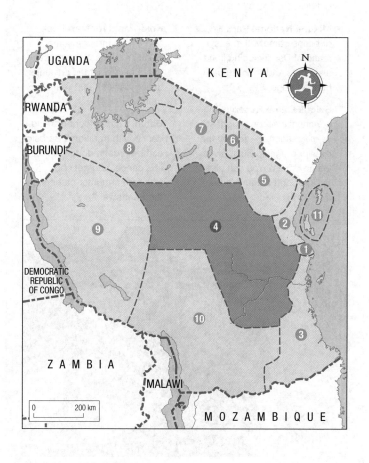

**4**

CHAPTER 4 # Highlights

* **Uluguru Mountains**
  Waterfalls galore, forests, and enjoyable encounters with the Luguru are some of the attractions when hiking (or biking) around these rugged old hills. **See p.207**

* **Mikumi National Park** Heaps of plains game within easy reach of Dar, including lions, elephants and even African hunting dogs. **See p.211**

* **Selous Game Reserve** The continent's second-biggest wildlife sanctuary, fed by the ever-photogenic Rufiji River. Game drives? You can also walk, or drift along in a boat. **See p.215**

* **Udzungwa Mountains**
  Stretch your legs for an hour, or over five days, in Tanzania's most immaculate rainforest, which dozens of unique animal species call home. **See p.222**

* **Kolo-Irangi rock art** Peek at the past through some of Africa's oldest and most beautiful prehistoric paintings, dating back 19,000 years, or more. **See p.235**

* **Babati** Climb Mount Hanang, dance with traditional Barbaig cattle-herders, dodge hippos in a canoe, and get chatty with former hunter-gatherers, the Sandawe. **See p.239**

▲ Barbaig women dressed in goatskin

# Central Tanzania

anzania's heartland is an amorphous region but has something for everyone: forest-cloaked mountains, unspoiled wildlife, swamps and meandering rivers, fascinating cultures, and art created back in the mists of time. First stop from Dar is the lively town of Morogoro, sitting snug in the lee of the rain-soaked **Uluguru Mountains**, whose rich ecology and the equally vibrant Luguru culture provide an excellent reason to linger, especially as Morogoro's cultural tourism programme is one of Tanzania's best. The **Udzungwa Mountains** are great for hikers, and, like Uluguru, are also part of the ancient Eastern Arc mountain chain. The pristine rainforest in the mountains is an extraordinarily species-rich sanctuary, especially for primates, butterflies and birds, in which you can walk for a few hours or for up to a week. For most visitors, though, central Tanzania boils down to a couple of wildlife areas that are included in the so-called Southern Safari Circuit. The usual starting point is **Mikumi National Park**, for a chance to quickly spot most of the species you might want to see in Tanzania, including otherwise rare African hunting dogs; but for something really special, head to **Selous Game Reserve**, Africa's second-largest protected wildlife area, which you can explore on foot or by boat as well as on a game drive. The reserve's blissfully beautiful northern sector, watered by the **Rufiji River**, is a haven for animals (including birds, crocodiles and hippos), and heaven for safari-goers, though you'll need to be patient, as Selous' luxuriant vegetation can make animals difficult to spot.

Heading west from the parks and reserves, the very centre of Tanzania comes as quite a shock: unremittingly dry and dusty, and only sparsely vegetated, it's home to the hardy **Gogo tribe**, owners of one of Africa's most bewitching musical traditions. In the middle of their traditional terrain is **Dodoma**, the planned (if never quite completed) city that has served, in name at least, as Tanzania's capital since 1973. North of here the land rises sharply into the Irangi Hills, which contain some of the oldest and most beautiful **paleolithic rock paintings** on earth. The paintings can be visited via **cultural tourism** programmes, one in Kondoa, the other in Babati further north (also accessible from Arusha), which also organize climbs up the perfectly conical **Mount Hanang** volcano, and intimate get-togethers with the traditionalist **Barbaig** cattle-herders, or with former **hunter-gatherers**, the Sandawe.

**Getting around** by bus is usually quick and easy enough, even for the parks and reserves. The main roads, from Dar to Dodoma and from Morogoro southward, are asphalted. Other roads are unsurfaced, but only the

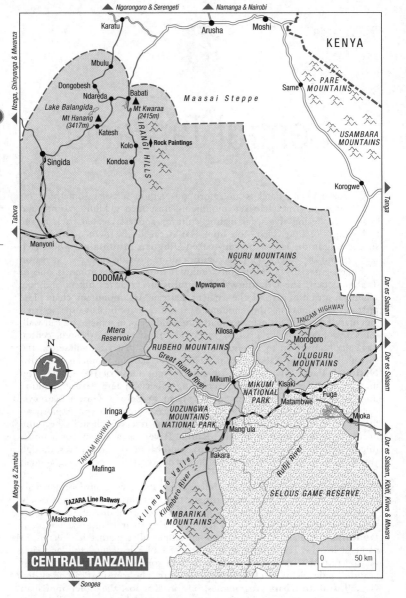

**CENTRAL TANZANIA**

0        50 km

Dodoma–Babati stretch is likely to be blocked during the rains. The Central Line railway passes through Morogoro and Dodoma, but is slow so mainly useful for getting to or from western Tanzania. The TAZARA Line, heading south, is quite erratic and tends to pass through at night.

# Morogoro and the Uluguru Mountains

The bustling crossroads town of **Morogoro**, 190km west of Dar es Salaam, owes its prosperity to an immensely fertile hinterland. The town is also the base for exploring the **Uluguru Mountains**, one of Tanzania's best hiking destinations. Part of the ecologically rich Eastern Arc range, the mountains and their forests are blessed with bountiful natural wonders, and a heap of **cultural interest**, too, all accessible via a cultural tourism programme.

## Morogoro

The first thing that strikes you as you approach **MOROGORO** is its beautiful location at the foot of the rugged **Uluguru Mountains**. On clear mornings, as the sun rises above the mist to bathe the town in warm tones of orange and gold, even the bus station gets momentarily imbued with a certain charm. Although seemingly nothing remains of Simbamwenni, the town's nineteenth-century precursor, the legacy of that century's Muslim-dominated **caravan trade** lives on. In the town centre, the passage of time is marked by calls to prayer from the mosques, and Morogoro is one of few places outside Zanzibar where you'll see women wearing black *burkas*. The cultural compote is enhanced by a thriving Indian community, Maasai warriors in full tribal drag, and a dishevelled army of expats, be they NGO workers, tobacco plant employees, dodgy gemstone prospectors, or missionaries by the bushel.

### Simbamwenni: the vanished town

In the nineteenth century, central and southern Tanganyika was in a state of considerable **turmoil**: slavers and then German soldiers were drilling in from the east, Ngoni immigrants were battling their way up from the south, and the equally militaristic Maasai were pushing down from the north, ever-avid for grazing land and cattle.

A disastrous time for most tribes, the chaos allowed wilier leaders to carve out short-lived empires, including Chief Mirambo of the Nyamwezi, the Hehe's Chief Mkwawa, and, in Morogoro, **Kisabengo**. Unusually, Kisabengo wasn't a tribal chief, but the leader of a group of fugitive slaves, who acquired power and eventually land through force of arms, and the kidnapping of neighbouring tribespeople. Kisabengo's domain, although small, included part of the major caravan route from the coast to the Great Lakes, and thus his capital, modestly named **Simbamwenni** (the "Lion King"), became an important base for traders. When **Stanley** passed by in 1871, en route to his famous encounter with Livingstone, he estimated the population at up to five thousand, and was most impressed by the town's stone fortifications and towers.

Given the extensive use of building stone – most unusual except on the coast – it's a mystery why no trace of Simbamwenni appears to have survived. If you want to try your hand at finding it, Stanley's account – published in his *How I Found Livingstone* – suggests it should be somewhere along the Ngerengere River west or north of town.

The town's population is growing fast, having doubled in the last decade to almost 300,000, but it retains a likeably small-town feel, and is a prosperous place by Tanzanian standards. Its region is the country's second-largest producer of rice, and source of much sugar, cotton, sunflower oil, millet, maize, coffee and sisal. Morogoro is also home to one of East Africa's largest munitions factories, a legacy of the town's role as a major base-in-exile for South Africa's ANC, whose cadres were trained in the mountains.

## Arrival and information

The **bus station** is 4km north of town at Msamvu roundabout on the Tanzam highway, at the turning for Dodoma, and is used by all except Scandinavian Express, whose hassle-free terminal is over the roundabout, diagonally opposite. Arriving at the main bus station, however, you're greeted by a welter of pushy touts, hustlers and taxi drivers frantically trying to grab your attention, or your bags. To escape the chaos, just walk towards the main road – few hustlers will follow, as they'll miss other potential pickings. Daladalas into town charge Tsh300, taxis Tsh4000, but be sure they're licensed (white number plates). The **train station** is 1.5km northeast of the centre; you'll arrive at night, but there are plenty of taxis, and several hotels nearby.

For **tourist information**, visit the excellent Chilunga Cultural Tourism Programme on Rwagasore Street (daily 8am–5.30pm; ☎0754/477582, 0713/663993 or 023/261 3323, ⊛www.chilunga.or.tz), whose main purpose is organizing trips into the mountains (see p.207). You can rent **bicycles** at their entrance (Tsh1000 per day). **Taxis** around town cost Tsh3000.

## Accommodation

Morogoro's mid-range **hotels** are a decent bunch, but cheap *and* decent **guest-houses** are a rare breed: many subsist on "short time" clients, but exceptions are reviewed below. At these, single rooms can usually be shared by couples if the beds are big enough. **Camping** is possible in the grounds of the *New Acropol*: free, including toilets and showers, if you buy a few meals or drinks. Lastly, don't drink **tap water**, rumoured to be contaminated with heavy metals, and, in the past, typhoid.

**"B" One Lodge** Shamba St ☎023/261 3080 or 0784/930151. This is actually four, virtually identical tarted-up guesthouses whose owners missed an obvious naming trick ("B" One, "B" Two…). Two of them are on this road. The rooms are all clean en-suite doubles with satellite TV, fans, box nets and hot showers, some also with a/c and fridge. Safe parking. BB ❷

**Hilux Hotel** Old Dar es Salaam Rd ☎023/261 3946, ⊛hiluxhotel@gmail.com. A good-value but sterile conference-friendly place with 58 rooms crammed into two three-storey blocks, all with a/c, satellite TV, big box nets, table and chair, and spotless bathrooms. The better rooms are on the left side. Also has a restaurant, two bars, and computer for internet access. Safe parking. No single rates. BB ❹

**Masinga Hotel** One block east of Lumumba St ☎0782/823035, ⊛masingahotel@yahoo.co.uk.

Quiet, reasonable and well-kept if darkish rooms (some en suite), all with cotton sheets, box nets, fans and satellite TV. The brighter rooms, sharing bathrooms, are upstairs. Internet café and snack-bar are next door. BB ❶–❷

**Morogoro Hotel** Rwagasore St ☎023/261 3270, ⊛morogorohotel@morogoro.net. The town's largest hotel, with a cluster of 1970s buildings designed to look like traditional Luguru homesteads but which bear an uncanny resemblance to flying saucers. The bedrooms – smallish but with high ceilings and therefore cool – are in saucer segments, all with excellent bathrooms (and bathtubs in the suites), huge beds, box nets, a/c, fridge and satellite TV. Facilities include tennis courts, access to the golf course across the road, a large tree-studded garden with great views of the Uluguru, internet access, a (hit-and-miss) restaurant and bar. Safe parking. BB ❹

# MOROGORO

▲ *Tanzania Highway, Msamvu Bus Station (3km),* ❶ ❷ *Dar es Salaam & Dodoma*

▲ ❺ *(2km) & Selous Game Reserve*

## EATING

| | |
|---|---|
| Blue Room | 12 |
| "Chacha" | 9 |
| Dragonaires | 5 |
| Hearts Snack Bar | 11 |
| High Classic Hotel | 7 |
| Lucky Star Café | 8 |
| Mama Pierina's | 6 |
| Morogoro Hotel | J |
| New Acropol Hotel | F |
| Hotel Oasis | D |

## DRINKING & NIGHTLIFE

| | |
|---|---|
| Chipukizi Club | 10 |
| Glonency 88 Hotel | 1 |
| King Tom Club | 3 |
| Makuti | 2 |
| New Acropol Hotel | F |
| New DDC Club | 4 |
| New Savoy Hotel | A |
| Ze Club | 13 |

## ACCOMMODATION

| | |
|---|---|
| "B" One Lodge | B & C |
| Hilux Hotel | E |
| Masinga Hotel | G |
| Morogoro Hotel | J |
| Mount Uluguru Hotel | I |
| New Acropol Hotel | F |
| New Savoy Hotel | A |
| Hotel Oasis | D |
| Sofia Hotel | H |

▶ *Morningside, German Boma &* ❸

▶ *(250m) & Rocky Garden (2.5km)*

▼ *SUA*

**Mount Uluguru Hotel** Mlapakolo Rd ☎ 023/260 3489, ℻ 023/261 4079. This five-storey hulk is the best value for money in the town centre, the nicest rooms at the top facing the mountains. All come with twin beds (which can be joined), big nets, fan, wall-to-wall carpet, fridge and bathroom, and an either/or choice of local TV or a/c (same price). There's a large, caged-in bar at the front, and a restaurant inside. BB ❷

🏃 **New Acropol Hotel** Old Dar es Salaam Rd ☎ 023/261 3403 or 0754/309410, ⓦ www .newacropolhotel.biz. Morogoro's most stylish abode, Canadian-run, with seven spacious en-suite rooms and two suites (one with two bedrooms, ideal for families), all tastefully decorated and with big four-posters (twin or double), a/c and fan, cable TV and fridge. There's also an excellent restaurant and bar, wi-fi, an adjoining massage room (women only), and use of *Hotel Oasis'* swimming pool. Safe parking. BB ❹

**New Savoy Hotel** Station Rd. Formerly the *Bahnhof*, this is slightly dilapidated, has saggy beds and lacks running water, but compensates with a warm welcome and positive vibe. The fifteen rooms, all en suite, are a pot-pourri, though all have clean cotton sheets, box nets, and some have

TV. The best are the twins on the second floor of the building closest to the train station, which have fans. Also acceptable are the big-bedded "suites" below (with a/c), but single rooms in the building beside the reception are grim. Also has a restaurant and big bar, with live music most weekends (Fri–Sun from 8.30pm). BB ❷–❸

**Hotel Oasis** Station Rd ☎ 023/261 4178 or 0754/377602, ⓦ www.hoteloasistz.com. Set around a swimming pool, this large and bland but well-run place attracts conferences and civil servants. The rooms are big and comfortable, some better than others, all with box nets, fridge, cable TV, fans, a/c, and tiled bathrooms. There's a bar and an excellent restaurant (especially for Indian), plus internet access. Safe parking. BB ❹

**Sofia Hotel** John Mahenge St ☎ 023/261 4848 or 0786/535555, ℮ sofiahotel@yahoo.com. On two storeys, this is getting shabby but remains a good budget choice if you don't mind sharing (rather grubby) bathrooms. The en-suite rooms are overpriced unless you absolutely need a/c, fridge or TV. All have two beds, cotton sheets, round nets and mosquito screens. There's a tiny bar at the front with streetside tables, and a bland but cheap restaurant at the back. BB ❶–❷

## The Town

Central Morogoro is pleasant but largely devoid of things to do other than visiting the main **market**, off Madaraka Road, where villagers from the mountains sell whatever they have that day: tomatoes, snow peas, delicious sweet tangerines, bananas, papayas and coconuts, as well as delicately woven baskets, woodcarvings and coconut-wood chairs. Historical sights are limited to the German-era train station, the *New Savoy Hotel* facing it (see box opposite), and the pink German Boma, still housing the local administration, a few kilometres along Boma Road.

Also south of town, and ideal for a lazy afternoon, is **"Rocky Garden"** (Tsh2000), 3km along Rwagasore Street. It's a beautiful patch of natural, boulder-strewn forest flanking a wild stream that's deep enough in parts for a dip. Romantic locals like it, and a small shop at the entrance sells sodas and beers. For something equally different, ask at Chilunga Cultural Tourism Programme about the school for disabled children, which offers **drum and dance lessons**.

## Eating

Morogoro's **street food** is very good: the stalls at the corner of Madaraka Road and John Mahenge Street get going towards dusk, when the air fills with aromatic plumes of smoke spiralling from dozens of charcoal stoves: grilled goat meat, roast bananas and maize cobs, chips and eggs are the staples. For chicken, no one beats "Chacha", the guy 100m east of the clock tower, along Station Road on the left. For dessert, seek out someone with a mangle for sugar cane juice, one of Azam's ice-cream vendors (on tricycles), or a *dafu* coconut vendor. **Bar food** is also decent, with *supu* broth, *nyama choma*, *mishkaki* and pork (*kiti moto*) among the favourites.

## Schmutz for Smuts

World War I in Tanganyika was a cat-and-mouse affair, with the mouse very effectively played by a small but mobile force led by the German commander, **Paul von Lettow-Vorbeck**. His tactic was simple: tie down Allied forces and resources by avoiding full-on confrontations. Having taken control of a string of towns south of Moshi, his pursuer, **General Jan Smuts**, believed that the Germans would make their last stand at the railway in Morogoro. He was mistaken. Before beating a hasty retreat in August 1916 (Lettow-Vorbeck was still running around in 1918 when the armistice forced his surrender), his troops left a coin-operated mechanical piano playing Deutschland über Alles in the *Bahnhof Hotel*, now the *New Savoy*, together with rather more earthy "presents" deposited on chairs and tables…

**4**

**Blue Room** Makongoro St. Cheap snacks and full meals (Tsh2500; ignore the menu, just ask what they have) in a clean but dull interior, or at streetside tables, where there's also a grill.

**Dragonaires** 2.5km along Old Dar es Salaam Rd. An expat hangout, especially on Fridays and Sundays, when American-style spare ribs and pizzas are the thing (but really, *hot dog* pizza?). The tables, outside, have great mountain views, but let bug spray be your companion. There's also a pool table, and a bar – sometimes with live music, other times country & western.

**Hearts Snack Bar** South end of the road from *Masinga Hotel*. A big outdoor *nyama choma* bar, also with *mishkaki*, chicken-and-chips and proper meals. It's a nice place to watch the world – and the hawkers – go by.

**High Classic Hotel** Lumumba St. A popular local joint, with no-fuss meals (under Tsh3000), including stews. Handy for breakfast. No alcohol.

**Lucky Star Café** Behind Pira's Cash and Carry. Has a full range of fresh Tanzanian snacks, including egg chops, *katlesi* (balls of mashed potato and minced meat), *kababu* and *sambusa*, plus packaged ice cream and good juices. No alcohol.

**Mama Pierina's** Station Rd. The menu here (mostly Tsh5000–7000) pays respect to the family's Greek-Italian roots, occasionally including (ask nicely the day before) lasagne, moussaka, home-made pesto (with cashew nuts replacing pine kernels), great pancakes, salads, and *mezedes* – salami, cheese, olives and tomato. Eat inside or on the porch. You're welcome just for drinks, too.

**Morogoro Hotel** Rwagasore St. Great on a sunny day, when you can eat in the garden in view of the mountains. The menu covers authentic Indian and Chinese as well as Tanzanian favourites like *pilau*, *uji* porridge (for breakfast; ask the day before), *matoke* banana stew and coconut-sauced fish or meat. No more than Tsh10,000 a meal.

**New Acropol Hotel** Old Dar es Salaam Rd. Splitting the honours with *Hotel Oasis* as Morogoro's best restaurant, this has a sophisticated if quirky ambience and is excellent value (nothing much over Tsh7000). It caters to all tastes and diets, including vegetarian (home-made tofu and cheese, and plenty of pulses), and has a nut-free guarantee, too. The pork selection is particularly impressive: try the *piccata* (sautéed in butter and white wine, with capers). Also does sandwiches, burgers, nachos, and good stir fries, and their arabica from Utengule, near Mbeya, is excellent.

**Hotel Oasis** Station Rd. Some of the best Indian food in Tanzania (amazingly succulent chicken masala, and superb vegetarian options too), but cover yourself in insect repellent if you're eating in the garden. A curry with naan and a drink or two shouldn't top Tsh8000. There's also a swimming pool.

## Drinking and nightlife

Morogoro is an excellent place for a tipple or five, but the **dance bands** for which it was famous – Morogoro Jazz and Super Volcano – are long gone. Still, Levent Music Band (Fri–Sun at the *New Savoy*) goes some way to fill the void, and it's worth enquiring about **visiting bands**, whether dance, hip-hop or (if you're not yet sick of it) Bongo Flava. The "in" venues change constantly, but are likely to be on the Tanzam highway north of town: currently favoured is *Makuti* by the bus station, and *Glonency 88 Hotel*, towards Dar. The clubs get busy around 10pm, and stay so until 2am or later. Don't walk north of the railway **after dusk**, and elsewhere take a taxi after 8pm.

## Moving on from Morogoro

Eastbound **trains** to Dar es Salaam are very slow. More useful are those to Kigoma or Mwanza via Tabora, currently leaving around 2am on Wednesday and Saturday; there's also a faster train to Kigoma around 11pm on Sunday. Buy your ticket in advance if you want a bed, and to check the schedule.

**Buses** leave from Msamvu 4km north of town on the highway; get there on a Kihonda daladala, or by taxi (Tsh4000). The parking bays have destinations marked on the far side, away from the road. Scandinavian Express have their own terminal (☏023/260 1279) on the other side of the roundabout. Try to buy your ticket a day or two before to be sure of a good seat, and to avoid reputedly **dangerous companies**, which include Abood, Hood, Mohamed Transport (to Mwanza and Bukoba) and Saibaba. The **safest** operators are Sumry and Shabiby, between them covering Dar, Iringa, Mbeya, Kyela, Songea and Dodoma. Scandinavian Express (Dar, Mbeya and Dodoma) are also safe enough but charge considerably more.

**Chipukizi Club** Makongoro St. One of the largest and busiest local places, open all day and often far into the night, with a wide range of beers, good cheap food, and a TV alternating between global channels and pirated videos with Arabic subtitles (afternoons).

**King Tom Club** Station Rd. A sprawling outdoor bar with plenty of seats under thatched shelters or trees, plus good *nyama choma*, duck (with luck) and pork.

**New Acropol Hotel** Old Dar es Salaam Rd. With a spray of colonial antiques, walls adorned with fake game trophies, prints and paintings, and cats and dogs at your feet, what's not to like about this upmarket bar? Also has a billiards, low tables facing the front garden, and great food.

**New DDC Club** Nkomo Rd. One of several big, *nyama choma*-garden-style bars along and off this road. Weekend nights are big, sometimes with live music. Be careful walking around.

**New Savoy Hotel** Station Rd. Nights can be busy here from Friday to Sunday, when Levent Music Band pump out a mix of jazz oldies and newer Congolese-flavoured tunes (Tsh2000). By day it's nicely quiet (unless a conference rolls in), and there's basic food.

**Ze Club** 2.5km south along Boma Rd. Two discos in one enjoyably schizophrenic package: a posh disco (Tsh5000 entry keeps hookers at bay) favouring Euro trash and other packaged pap, and another (free) for more African sounds and, sometimes, Bruce Lee films. Take a taxi.

## Listings

**Banks and exchange** Traveller's cheques are getting awkward to cash: try NBC or CRDB, both on Old Dar es Salaam Rd, but check the commission first. All banks have ATMs; beware of Exim's card-gobbling reputation.

**Car rental** Nothing official: ask at *Hotel Oasis* or the *New Acropol*.

**Football** Jamhuri Stadium hosts Premier League side Polisi Morogoro; struggling Moro United are now based in Dar.

**Health** For blood tests and minor ailments, go to Aga Khan Clinic, Boma Rd ☏025/250 2043 or 025/250 2265. Best in emergencies, open 24hr, is Shalom Mazimbu Clinic (ask a taxi driver). The government-run Regional Hospital is on Rwagasore St ☏023/232 3045.

**Internet access** Connections are generally slow. Try the post office on Old Dar es Salaam Rd, Valentine's by the stadium, Daus beside *Masinga Hotel*, or Matunda facing *Sofia Hotel*.

**Post and couriers** Post office: Old Dar es Salaam Rd. DHL: Boma Rd ☏023/260 4528.

**Supermarkets** Best, also stocking wine, is Pira's Cash & Carry, Lumumba St (daily until late). Try also Murad's at the MT petrol station, Dar es Salaam Rd.

**Swimming pool** *Hotel Oasis* (Tsh3000).

**Telephones** TTCL, Kitope St beside the post office (Mon–Sat 7.30am–10pm, Sun 8am–8pm).

# The Uluguru Mountains

South and east of Morogoro and rising to over 2600m, the spectacular **Uluguru Mountains** contain some of the most luxuriant – but sadly threatened – indigenous rainforest in the country. Spanning 100km north to south and 20km east to west, the range is one of several in the 25-million-year-old **Eastern Arc mountain chain** (see box, p.279). Their great age, coupled with a wide altitudinal range, high rainfall, and stable climate over the ages, have favoured the development of some of the world's richest and most species-diverse **rainforests**. The Ulugurus contain eleven endemic reptilian and amphibian species and over a hundred endemic plants, including African violets, busy lizzies and begonias. **Mammals** include yellow baboons, blue monkeys, black-and-white colobus monkeys, wild pigs and duiker antelopes. But where Uluguru really comes into its own is its **birdlife**, which includes fifteen rare or unique species. Notable among these are the Usambara eagle owl, which was found here in 1993 – only its third known habitat – and the endemic Uluguru bush-shrike, critically endangered thanks to ongoing deforestation on the lower slopes.

In the early 1960s, most of the mountains were still covered with forest, but a glance from Morogoro today tells a sorry tale of destruction, either deliberate – by timber extraction or clearance for cultivation – or accidental, by fire (whose depressing plumes are a daily feature of the skyline). Whilst the ambitious **Uluguru Biodiversity Conservation Project** appears to have run out of steam (or into a wall of intransigent bureaucracy), a fortunate spin-off has been the establishment of a **cultural tourism programme** aiming to provide alternative sources of income for local communities via low-impact tourism, thereby lessening some of the pressure on the forests. For the visitor, this means an exciting range of walks and hikes, combining natural attractions (forests, streams, waterfalls and beautiful views) with equally fascinating encounters with the Luguru tribe (see box, p.208), all at very affordable prices.

## Practicalities

Hiking (or biking) is best arranged through ⚐ **Chilunga Cultural Tourism Programme** in Morogoro (p.202), whose youthful guides are both conscientious and knowledgeable. **Costs** are Tsh40,000 a day per guide for up to four tourists plus Tsh10,000 a day per person in fees. To this, add food, accommodation and transport (if any), and – if you'll be entering **forest reserves** – $30 for an official permit (Tsh3000 for Tanzanians) from the Regional Catchment Forest Project Office, 1km along the road to Msamvu, on the left just after the railway (Mon–Fri 7.30am–3.30pm). Two great **websites** are ⓦ www.easternarc.or.tz/uluguru and www.africanconservation.com/uluguru.

The **best time to visit** is the dry season from July to September. The main rains fall between February and June, with the patchier – and these days most unpredictable – short rains coming sometime between October and January. All routes are steep in places, so bring good **walking boots** or at least worn-in shoes with good tread, especially if it's raining (when you'll also need a raincoat). You should also take water, some food, suncream, and – from June to September – a light fleece. Regular accommodation is limited to non-existent, so expand your options by **camping**. The cultural tourism programme rents tents for $5 day.

## The Luguru

The Uluguru Mountains are the traditional home of the 1.5-million-strong **Luguru tribe**, whose name means "people of the mountain" (*guru* being "mountain" or "high"). Although most now live in the lowlands, a hundred thousand or so live on the mountains' lower slopes, using self-composting ladder terraces and other tricks to eke the most out of the already very fertile soil and abundant rains.

Despite growing Christian and Islamic influence, Luguru society remains strongly **matrilineal**, and land is often the property of women. It passes from mother to daughter, either in their own name or in that of one of fifty clans to which all Luguru belong, which in turn are subdivided into around eight hundred **lineages** (essentially extended families). Although a man may inherit land from his mother, it reverts to his sister's children on his death, even if he has children of his own. This system gave Luguru women uncommon independence from their husbands, and those who displeased them were sent packing with nothing more than the clothes on their backs. Things are changing, however: the traditional system, coupled with the location along the road to Zambia (dubbed the "AIDS Highway") has brought with it the devastating spectre of HIV. Population pressure has also trashed the forests on the mountains' lower slopes, and with land now scarce, inheritance patterns are shifting.

Still, some things don't change, not least the so-called "**joking relationships**" (*utani*) between rival villages, and also between the Luguru and other tribes, which historically circumvented conflicts via an institutionalized form of friendship, neighbourly assistance and good humour. Villages in an *utani* relationship were (and still are) expected to share food with each other at times of hardship, in return for which donors were allowed to jibe at their neighbours' expense. But if you hear kids laughing their heads off on seeing you, well, there's probably another explanation...

## Exploring the mountains

A great thing about the cultural tourism programme is its **flexibility**: you can walk for up to six days, camping or staying with local families, without ever retracing your steps. The main options are covered below. In addition, if you're around on a Saturday, ask for the fortnightly **Maasai market** (*mnada*), 30km along the Dodoma road.

### Morningside

The views from the half-abandoned colonial settlement of **MORNINGSIDE**, a two- to three-hour walk south of Morogoro, are well worth braving the steep path for, and the cool mountain air makes for a bracing and welcome change from Morogoro's habitual swelter. Other than this, though, Morningside doesn't have much more to offer, and the old German building, which functioned as a hotel until the 1970s, is crumbling away. Energetic folk can continue an hour up a steep track or along the winding road to the forest boundary, marked by an enormous eucalyptus tree planted in the 1960s. The transmitter-topped **Bondwe Peak**, in the forest reserve beyond, can be climbed if you have a forest permit.

Start early for Morningside, as the lower part of the walk – through open farmland – gets hot. There's a shop halfway up with sodas, a waterfall nearby, and, further up, **Ruvuma village**, whose female potter welcomes visitors. Although you could walk this route without a guide, there have been reports of unaccompanied tourists being mugged (especially on the way down), and Morningside itself can be hard to find when it's misty or cloudy.

## Choma

The village of **CHOMA**, a three-hour walk east of Morogoro (8km), is the main place for cultural encounters, and has a number of activities for tourists, including seeing mats and baskets being made from the fronds of the *mkindu* phoenix palm. A mat takes about two months to finish, as the weavers only have evenings in which to work on them – daylight is for fields. The local women are also talented musicians, and for a small fee will introduce you to the delights of traditional Luguru **music and dance** (if you're in Dar, do drop by one of Radio Tanzania's stores, see p.108, to buy their two tapes of "Kiluguru" music, where you'll hear flutes blended with voices to mesmerizing effect). You can also see the production of "soil cake", a calcium-rich supplement used by pregnant women. Finish your visit with a **traditional lunch**, but take it easy with the various *pombe* home-brews unless you're staying over: some families offer **homestays**, and the cultural tourism programme is planning a **campsite** along the route.

## Madola

Huddled up against a bare rock face, the tiny hamlet of **MADOLA**, two to three hours on foot from Morogoro (6km) is known locally for its woodwork (including dolls and figurines), but is more famous for Bibi Maria, a remarkable **traditional healer**. Her supernatural powers were revealed to her in a series of dreams when she was six. She now uses dreams, and premonitions, to diagnose illness and determine the appropriate remedy – invariably a coupling of physical (medicinal plants) and spiritual (ritual). The track is steep and difficult to follow in places, but you're rewarded with beautiful views, patches of forest between fruit orchards and vegetable plots, and a small waterfall. Bibi Maria charges foreign visitors Tsh10,000, whether for an interview or consultation.

## Lupanga and Kimhandu peaks

For that top-of-the-world feeling, set your sights on the 2150-metre **Lupanga Peak**, the closest to Morogoro, which can be scaled and descended in about six hours. It's tough going, though, and inside the forest it gets dangerously slippery in the rains, but you may be rewarded by glimpses of the rare Loveridge's sunbird or Fulleborn's black boubou, or by the more easily seen (or heard) Livingstone's turaco and silvery-cheeked hornbill. Longer hikes include a challenging four-day trek to the range's highest point, the 2638-metre **Kimhandu Peak** in South Uluguru. Both climbs require $30 per day forest permits once you reach the tree-line (see p.207).

## Bunduki and around

The area east of **BUNDUKI** village, a challenging three-hour drive south of Morogoro (turn left at Kipera and left again at Mgeta, where the Luguru first settled), offers some great hiking possibilities, including along the **Lukwangule Plateau** separating the mountains' northern and southern ranges. Just over an hour's walk east of the village are the impressive **Hululu Falls**, where water spills out of the forest over a rocky forty-metre drop: go with a local or a guide as the site is sacred. If you want to hike higher up, through Bunduki Forest Reserve, you'll need a forest permit ($30); the extra cost is surely worth it for the superb east-facing views from the ridge, and, for keen birders, a chance of sighting the otherwise very rare **Mrs Moreau's warbler**. Bunduki's inhabitants are happy to rustle up food, swimming is possible in the river, and you're welcome to **camp**.

**Matombo**

On the eastern flank of the Ulugurus is **MATOMBO** village, straddling the unsurfaced road that goes to Selous Game Reserve's Matambwe Gate (route description on p.218). You can get here by 4WD, or, for a bit of exercise, by bicycle (65km from Morogoro) or on foot from Bunduki (30km of very rough terrain). The village is worth visiting for two very unusual attractions. The first is a **sacred cave** that contains a natural stone formation resembling a naked woman, and from which Matombo draws its name (it means "breasts"). The other attraction is in the river itself, at a place called **Usolo**: it's a curious rock (visible unless there's heavy rain) bearing rows of evidently man-made, circular depressions. Although archeologists are at a loss to explain the significance of such "cup marks" (which are also found in Europe and Asia), locals know better. They say that a long time ago, two Luguru chiefs finally made peace after having quarrelled for many years. One of them, a certain Chief Hega, tapped his heel on the rock to magically create the depressions, then invited his erstwhile adversary to join him in a game of *usolo* – the local word for the traditional African board game of *bao* (see p.64).

# Mikumi, Selous and Udzungwa

The southern foothills of the Uluguru Mountains mark the start of an incredible ecosystem that covers a vast swath of central and southern Tanzania, and includes the easily visited **Mikumi National Park**, and the untrammelled wilderness of **Selous Game Reserve**, visiting which requires a bit of planning if you've yet to win the lottery. The ecosystem's wealth in wildlife stems both from the perennial **Rufiji River**, and from the dry **miombo woodland** that covers almost three-quarters of it. Unlike the scrubby savanna vegetation prevalent in northern Tanzania, *miombo* is dominated by deciduous *Brachystegia* trees. The leaves that are shed each year form the basis of a complex food chain, ultimately creating an ideal habitat for dozens if not hundreds of **large mammal species**. That humans haven't trashed the area is due to *miombo* woodlands being the perfect habitat for **tsetse flies**, pernicious vectors of sleeping sickness. Wild mammals have acquired resistance, but domestic livestock and humans have not (but don't worry, your chances of contracting it are minute). The *miombo* woodlands are at their most beautiful in October and November, before and during the short rains, when they put out new leaves in all shades of red, copper, gold and orange, as well as green. For real forest, though, get yourself down to **Udzungwa Mountains National Park** south of Mikumi, a biological wonderland that offers possibly the most exhilarating walking in Tanzania, whether you're up for an adventurous hike over several days, or a quick saunter in search of monkeys, birds, butterflies and waterfalls.

# Mikumi National Park

An hour's drive southwest of Morogoro, the 3230-square-kilometre **Mikumi National Park** is the first stop on most "Southern Circuit" safaris, and famed among photographers for its spine-tinglingly rich light. Framed by the Uluguru, Rubeho and Udzungwa mountains, and bounded by Selous Game Reserve to the south, Mikumi's grassy plains and thick *miombo* woodland are an oasis for wildlife. For those on really tight budgets, buses along the **Tanzam highway** pass

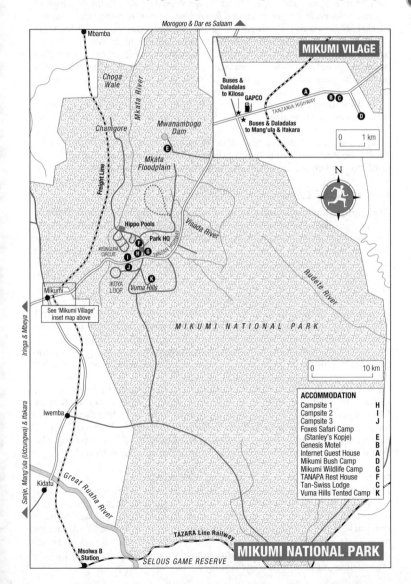

ACCOMMODATION

| | |
|---|---|
| Campsite 1 | H |
| Campsite 2 | I |
| Campsite 3 | J |
| Foxes Safari Camp (Stanley's Kopje) | E |
| Genesis Motel | B |
| Internet Guest House | A |
| Mikumi Bush Camp | D |
| Mikumi Wildlife Camp | G |
| TANAPA Rest House | F |
| Tan-Swiss Lodge | C |
| Vuma Hills Tented Camp | K |

straight through the park, giving you a good chance – best in the dry season – of seeing elephants, giraffes and antelopes. Mikumi actually owes its protection to the road, whose construction caused a massive increase in poaching, leading to the park's hasty creation in 1964. In spite of an 80kph speed limit and dozens of speed bumps, most drivers treat the highway as a race track. Smaller creatures like mongooses and, lamentably, African hunting dogs, obviously aren't worth wearing out brake pads for, as the assortment of flattened roadkill bears witness.

Heading off the highway into the park itself, **plains game** is easily seen, including elephants and impala. Most guides should be able to locate a **lion** or three, but leopards are more elusive (your best chance is along watercourses). Black-backed jackals can sometimes be seen in the evenings, but the highlight is the **African hunting dog**, one of Africa's rarest mammals, which (a matter of luck) are sometimes seen in packs. **Birdlife** is profuse, with over four hundred recorded species, including red-billed oxpeckers, marabou storks, pretty lilac-breasted rollers and malachite kingfishers, black-bellied bustards, and, between October and April, Eurasian migrants.

The **best times to go** are December to March, when wildlife numbers are their highest (and resident elephant herds are joined by their cousins from Selous and the Rubeho Mountains), or the dry season from mid-August to October, when animals are concentrated around water sources. Bad times are during the long rains, when most of the park's internal roads are impassable, and just before, when the landscape can be scarred by controlled fires.

## Practicalities

**Arranging your own safari** is easy: it's cheapest to sort things out in **Mikumi village**, a roadstead at the junction to Udzungwa just outside the park. Reliable companies are reviewed on p.53. Forget about one-day safaris from Dar (286km; 4hr each way), and you might also feel short-changed on "two-day" trips, which are actually one night with two game drives. **Flying safaris**, from Dar or Zanzibar, are operated by Foxes African Safaris (p.53), who operate *Foxes Safari Camp*, *Vuma Hills Tented Camp*, and other camps in Ruaha, Selous and elsewhere.

If you're planning to make your own way here note that only 4WD vehicles are admitted to the park, and there's no fuel available, so fill up beforehand. There are no passenger trains, so by **public transport**, catch a bus to Mikumi village, where you can arrange car rental (with driver) at *Genesis Motel* or *Tan-Swiss Lodge* for $130–150 per day, excluding park fees. Hiring an **official guide** ($10 plus tip for a few hours) at the park headquarters is recommended: they can spot leopards' tails from half a kilometre away.

The **park headquarters** are in the middle at Kikoboga, just off the highway (☎023/262 0487, ⓦwww.tanzaniaparks.com/mikumi.html). **Entrance fees** are $20 per person ($50 if staying overnight), plus $40 per vehicle; tickets are valid for 24 hours. There's no charge if you're just passing along the highway. The park headquarters sell a map and an excellent **guidebook** ($10), which you can also find in the lodges, and at bookstores in Arusha, Dar and Stone Town.

### Accommodation, eating and drinking

**Inside the park** is a rest house and a trio of upmarket places – none of which are fenced, so close encounters with animals are possible, be it elephants or, at night, civets, bushbabies and perhaps a honey badger. Mikumi village, **outside the park**, is basically an overgrown truckers' night stop, but has some decent motel-style options as well as a dirty dozen tawdry guesthouses "serving" commercial drivers in more ways than one. None of these have any kind of bush feeling: for that, try the enchanting *Mikumi Bush Camp*.

**Camping** outside the park is possible at *Chella Lodge, Genesis Motel, Tan-Swiss Lodge* (all $5 per person) and *Mikumi Bush Camp* ($15). Campsites inside the park ($30 per person on top of entry fees; pay at the gate) are: *Campsite 1*, near the park gate, with running water, pit latrines, shower, fireplace and firewood; *Campsite 2*, along the Kisingura Circuit, under an old baobab with a toilet but no water; and *Campsite 3*, just south of the highway under a large fig tree, with just a toilet. Be wary of baboons while camping: don't eat in their presence, and keep food in sealed containers.

## Outside the park: Mikumi village and around

**Genesis Motel** 4km east of Udzungwa junction ☎023/262 0461 or 0713/470262, ⓦwww .genesismotel.com. Pricey but often included in budget safaris, this has thirty good en-suite rooms, each with two beds and satellite TV, but the claimed hot water is erratic. Also has an expensive restaurant and bar, and a motley collection of snakes and tortoises in boxes and pens next door ($5 entry for non-guests). BB ❹

**Internet Guest House** 500m east of Udzungwa junction ☎023/262 0419. Very basic digs, acceptable if you're used to that kind of thing (no guarantee of electricity or running water), but there's a good bar, and decent food: try anything with cassava leaves. ❶

🏃 **Mikumi Bush Camp** 6km east of Udzungwa junction, then 2km south ☎022/550 0200, ⓦwww.mikumibushcamp.com. Run by Tanzanians and close to the park boundary, this is the only bush-style option outside the park, and if you don't mind basic food and accommodation, actually trumps the lodges and camps inside the park for its in-the-wild atmosphere. There are six smallish tents under thatched shelters (no platforms, so muddy when it rains) with shared bathrooms and toilets. The restaurant is in the open, and there's a campfire most nights. No electricity: hurricane lanterns provide lighting. FB ❺

🏃 **Tan-Swiss Lodge** 4.2km east of Udzungwa junction ☎0755/191827, ⓦwww.tan-swiss.com. Run by a charming Swiss/Tanzanian couple, this is a cheerful take on the classic US motel, complete with colourful murals. Rooms are comfortable and come with satellite TV and box nets, and the restaurant is well priced, its menu veering all over the place. Also has Mikumi's best bar (cocktails and South African wines), and a children's playground. BB ❹–❺

## Inside the park

**Foxes Safari Camp (Stanley's Kopje)** Mkata floodplain, 25km north of the park ⓦwww .tanzaniasafaris.info. This is Mikumi's classiest option, and the only one that doesn't have distant views of buses on the highway. Set on a rocky kopje in prime game-viewing terrain (elephants are occasional visitors, attracted by Mwanambogo Dam nearby), it boasts 360° views from its hilltop restaurant and bar. Accommodation is in twelve large and quirkily elegant en-suite tents on wooden platforms, their verandas giving sweeping views. There's also a small swimming pool. FB $450; game package $610 ❾

**Mikumi Wildlife Camp** Kikoboga ☎022/260 0352, ⓔmwc@bol.co.tz. The best place for spotting wildlife from the comfort of an armchair, as two waterholes nearby attract elephant, buffalo, wildebeest and impala. Accommodation is in twelve spacious African-style *bandas* with drapes for windows and big verandas. There's a swimming pool with sundeck and hot-tub, a look-out tower with 360° views over the plain, and a bar. Meals are taken around a campfire in a dining area overlooking a floodlit waterhole. FB ❽

**TANAPA Rest House** Kikoboga (book through the park headquarters, or TANAPA in Arusha; see p.307). The park's cheapest accommodation at $30 per person, with two double rooms, shared toilets, a kitchen and sitting room. The park's social hall is in the same complex should you fancy a bite or a drink. Book ahead. ❹

**Vuma Hills Tented Camp** 7km southeast of the park gate ⓦwww.tanzaniasafaris.info. Welcoming, relaxed and luxurious, with good food and smart service, this is also suitable for families. There are sixteen spacious if rather closely spaced en-suite tents on raised wooden decks, with grassland vistas from their verandas, plus a small swimming pool and sundeck overlooked by the bar and restaurant, and a commendable library. FB $450; game package $610 ❾

# The park

The park's main focus is a network of tracks in the Mkata River floodplain, north of the highway, especially the "Kisingura Circuit" (accessible year-round) in **Kikoboga** near the park headquarters. It's an area characterized by baobabs,

▲ Giraffe running, Mikumi National Park

amarula trees, and tall borassus palms (*mikumi*), which have strangely graceful swellings halfway up their trunks. Kikoboga is most famous for **elephants**, especially after the short rains (Dec & Jan), when they're drawn in by the gastronomic delights of swamp grass and the plum-like amarula fruit. Elephants gobble them by the thousand, even shaking the trees to get them to fall. Proof of the fruit's impressive laxative qualities lie scattered all over. **Other mammals** commonly seen around the floodplain are herds of eland and buffalo, Liechtenstein's hartebeest (often close to the river where it crosses the highway), and good odds on lions (sometimes in trees), leopards (also up in trees), and, occasionally, small packs of African hunting dogs. In the dry season, you'll find plenty of hippo and waterbirds around **waterholes**, especially 5km northwest of the park headquarters, and further north at Chamgore (also good for Bohor reedbuck), and at Mwanambogo Dam, which has the additional attraction of **pythons**, either at the water's edge or coiled up in trees. Take care: it may be non-venomous, but a body blow from this constrictor can topple an impala. You'll need a park ranger ($10) to venture further north to the picnic site at **Choga Wale**, a pretty glade of *Hyphaene* palms, acacias, strangling fig trees and pink jacarandas, the bark of which finds use against witchcraft.

Although the bulk of the park lies **south of the highway**, it's seldom visited, and only the "**Ikoya Loop**" is easy enough to follow without a guide (the park may insist you hire one in any case). In the dry season, hippos and other animals can be seen at Ikoya waterhole, but the best time is June to November, when the cassia thickets are covered in fragrant yellow flowers. The area beyond Ikoya, including the ridges close to Selous Game Reserve, is mostly *miombo* woodland, home to sable antelope, greater kudu, Liechtenstein's hartebeest, black-and-white colobus monkey… and clouds of tsetse flies. There are also hot water springs.

# Selous Game Reserve

Checking in at 54,600 square kilometres, **Selous Game Reserve** – a World Heritage Site – is Africa's second-largest wildlife sanctuary (after southern Africa's Great Limpopo Transfrontier Park), and the Southern Safari Circuit's undisputed highlight. Taken in combination with Mikumi and a number of adjoining reserves, Selous' rich and diverse ecosystem is home to an estimated 750,000 large mammals, including the world's largest populations of elephants, African hunting dogs, leopards, crocodiles, buffaloes and hippopotamuses.

Most of the reserve is set aside for hunting, but the small northern sector for "photographic tourism" is not just the reserve's but arguably one of the country's most beautiful places, its habitats ranging from grassy plains and rolling *miombo* woodland to dense patches of groundwater forest and the magnificent **Rufiji River**, best experienced from a boat. It's in Selous that the river – Tanzania's longest – is at its finest, its labyrinthine network of lagoons, channels, islets and swamps stuffed with hippos and crocs, and dressed in riverine forest a-chatter with **birds**: over 450 species have been recorded inside the reserve.

Terrestrial wildlife isn't lacking, either, and can be seen either on a game drive or, more thrillingly, on a **bush walk**. Elephants are abundant, as are zebra, giraffe, and all manner of antelopes, including wildebeest and impala, waterbuck, reedbuck, Roosevelt's sable, and Liechtenstein's hartebeest. Smaller **nocturnal mammals** such as lesser bushbabies and small spotted genets are often seen or heard around camps at night, and mongooses are often seen scampering across tracks. The forests backing the waterways are good places for **primates**, including vervets, large troops of olive and yellow baboons, black-and-white colobus monkeys, and, just as shy, blue monkeys. Rarer animals include Sharpe's grysbok, a tiny population of red colobus monkeys in the far northwest near the railway, and approximately 150 **black rhino**, the locations of which are closely guarded secrets.

Of the **predators**, lions – often in large prides – are the most visible; leopards, despite their considerable population, are more elusive. Cheetah and spotted hyena are also occasionally seen, but the real highlight is the **African hunting dog**, amongst the rarest of Africa's predators, which has found in Selous one of its last refuges: their population peaks in September and October.

For all these riches, don't count on being able to tick off species as you would in northern Tanzania, which is one of the reasons why tour operators recommend longer stays in the "hidden" Selous. The other reason is profit: factoring in entrance fees and activities, you won't find a double room inside the reserve for less than $680 a night. Should the prices scare you off, or the all-white, neo-colonial atmosphere prick your conscience, don't despair: with a tent, or simply staying just outside the reserve, the overall cost can actually be less than in northern Tanzania's more emblematic national parks.

The **best months** for large mammals are July to September/October, when the vegetation is lower and animals are clustered around the river and its lakes. The short dry spell in January and February is perfect for birds (including migrants), but terrestrial wildlife is more dispersed at that time, and the temperature can feel intense thanks to the gathering humidity. This culminates in the long rains (mid-March to late May), when most roads are cut off and the majority of lodges and camps inside the reserve are closed.

## Arrival

Most visitors to Selous arrive by plane, but a handful of **safari companies** offer cheaper road safaris, but you'll waste a full day getting here from Dar, and another back, so it works best if you're on an extended trip. The cheapest approach is by **public transport** to one of several camps and lodges just outside the reserve's eastern gate, all of which can arrange safaris (see pp.220–221).

### Organized safaris

Reliable **safari operators** are reviewed on p.53. On a **driving safari**, lodges and campsites outside the reserve's eastern gate are the usual base. Access roads

---

### Hunting, shooting and conservation

One superlative that few brochures will tell you about is that Selous Game Reserve is the only place in Tanzania where the gentlemanly sport of **elephant hunting** is permitted, even if only a few dozen kills are made each year. In fact, all but three of the reserve's forty-five "management blocks" are for hunting, the rationale being that plugging lead into animals provides eighty percent of the reserve's income.

It's an uneasy state of affairs, whose roots stretch back to 1896, when the German administration formed several hunting reserves after an epidemic of sleeping sickness gave them a handy excuse to shift the locals elsewhere. The reserve's present name comes from **Captain Frederick Courteney Selous**, a British explorer killed at Beho Beho in January 1917 while scouting for the 25th Royal Fusiliers. Selous, a professional hunter, had spent much of his life shooting his way through a colossal amount of central and southern African wildlife ("not for mere sport," he explained, "but also to gain the goodwill of the natives"). There must have been heaps of goodwill for sale, as the reserve's elephants were being hunted at the rate of several tens of thousands a year. Come the British, the various German reserves were combined and expanded, a process that continues to the present day, with each enlargement having seen villagers evicted, sometimes by force. So it was that by the 1970s, resentful villagers relocated outside the reserve were only too willing to engage in commercial poaching. Between 1981 and 1989, they obliterated over 75,000 of Selous' elephants (two-thirds of the original population) and all but a hundred of the reserve's three thousand black rhino.

The ecological catastrophe was only stemmed at the end of the decade when a global ban on ivory and rhino horn trading came into force. The elephant population has since doubled to around 60,000, but the rhinos, still numbering barely 150, remain critically endangered. Still, things are looking up, as the reserve's management finally appear to be paying more than lip-service to the idea that the best way to conserve Selous is not by excluding but including local communities. As such, fifty-odd villages bordering the reserve now benefit from limited hunting quotas (which they can use or sell), in return for patrolling **Wildlife Management Areas**, effectively buffer zones. For the first time in decades, relations between those villages and the authorities can now be described as constructive, a far cry from the days when a farmer trapping animals destroying his crops was persecuted as a poacher.

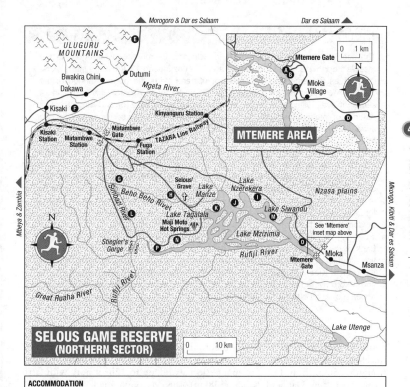

**MTEMERE AREA**

*Mkongo, Kibiti & Dar es Salaam*

Nzasa plains

See 'Mtemere'
inset map above

Msanza

**SELOUS GAME RESERVE**
**(NORTHERN SECTOR)**

0    10 km

*Mbeya & Zambia*

**CENTRAL TANZANIA** | Selous Game Reserve

**4**

**ACCOMMODATION**

| | | | | | |
|---|---|---|---|---|---|
| Beho Beho Camp | **H** | Mivumo River Lodge | **P** | Selous River Camp | **A** |
| Beho Beho Bridge campsite | **G** | Rufiji River Camp | **O** | Selous Riverside Safari Camp | **D** |
| Jimbiza Lodge | **C** | Sable Mountain Lodge | **F** | Selous Safari Camp | **I** |
| Jukumu Scout Station | **E** | Sand Rivers Selous | **N** | Selous Wildlife Lodge | **L** |
| Lake Manze Camp | **J** | Selous Impala Camp | **M** | | |
| Lake Tagalala campsite | **K** | Selous Mbega Camp | **B** | | |

and roads within the reserve are rough, so don't pinch pennies when choosing an operator: you'll need a reliable vehicle, competent driver, and HF radio should things go pear-shaped.

If you're staying inside the reserve, the usual approach is by **plane**. Flying safaris are offered by the lodges themselves, safari companies and travel agents. You'll be picked up at one of several airstrips, not always for free. Coastal Aviation, via Coastal Travels (p.53), offer alluring out-of-season deals for *Lake Manze Camp* and *Selous Impala Camp*, whilst Safari Airlink (part of Foxes African Safaris, p.53) do the same for *Rufiji River Camp*. ZanAir also offer packages.

If you buy a **game package** (ie full board with game drives and other activities included), get a guarantee about the kind of vehicle to be used (open-sided jeeps are best); whether – if it's not open-sided – you'll get a window seat; and what's not included (transfers, entrance fees, drinks, and all kinds of sneaky supplements).

### Arranging your own safari: self-drive

High-clearance **4WD** in excellent condition is essential, but even if you have one forget about driving during the long rains. Few rental companies will trust you self-driving in Selous (nerve-racking even for experienced drivers), so

## Getting to Selous via Matambwe

The scenic if finger-biting approach to Selous is by road from Morogoro to the reserve's northwestern **Matambwe Gate**. The unsurfaced 155km route starts along Old Dar es Salaam Road (see map, p.203) and skirts the northern fringe of the Uluguru Mountains before turning south along the rugged eastern flank, passing a series of lively villages (see the Matombo account on p.210) and almost jungly patches of forest interspersed with cracking views. The rocky and sometimes steep surface makes the first 80km slow going if passable, taking two-and-a-half to five hours depending on the road's state of repair. If the mountain scenery grabs your attention and you have a tent, the gorgeously sited *Jukumu Scout Station* **campsite** ($5 per person) at Kilengezi, near Mvuha village at Mambarawe Ridge, 55km before Kisaki, has friendly locals and sweeping views over northern Selous. There are two creeks with waterfalls nearby where you can swim, and plenty of dense forest to explore. Water is available from a pump, and there are toilets, showers and firewood for sale. The site is run by community game scouts who are, unsurprisingly, excellent guides, though there's nothing formally arranged for tourists.

Leaving the Uluguru foothills, the road descends 45km towards the swampy north bank of the Mgeta River. If recently graded, this stretch is passable in most conditions, but if not it can get blocked after even moderate showers. The stretch beyond the river to **Kisaki village** and its train station, where the road crosses the Rudete and Msoro rivers before following the railway to Matambwe Gate, is fine. The only accommodation outside the park in this area is *Sable Mountain Lodge*.

you'll be provided with a driver. There are two main routes: the **Matambwe route** in the northwest, from Morogoro, is utterly spectacular but potentially treacherous; see the box above. Easier and quicker is the **Mtemere route** (roughly 250km from Dar; 6hr in a perfect world, up to 12hr if not), with fast tarmac between Dar and Kibiti (138km), then a rough road southwest to Mkongo (32km), right towards Mloka (77km) and on to Mtemere Gate (3.5km). The nearest petrol stations are at Morogoro, Kibiti and Ikwiriri. The reserve's gates close at 6pm, and you can't drive after 6.30pm.

### Arranging your own safari: public transport

The only public road transport goes via the Mtemere route, getting you to **Mloka village**, 3.5km shy of Mtemere Gate, and within walking distance (at your own risk; there are animals around) of several lodges and camps just outside the reserve. A direct but excruciatingly uncomfortable daily bus should leave from Dar's southern suburb of Temeke at 5am, arriving around 3pm, but at the time of writing road works meant it was leaving from Mbagala. Either way, get there the day before to be sure of the location and your ticket, and on the morning of departure catch a taxi. Alternatively, catch a 6am bus from Dar's Ubungo bus station or later daladala from Tegeta or Mbagala to **Kibiti** (any bus or daladala going further south passes by), where you'll likely have to spend the night (try *Victoria Guest House*; ❷) before catching an onward pick-up or bus the next day. Returning to Dar, the bus leaves Mloka when full, being any time between 4.30am and 7am.

## Information and entrance fees

It seems as if the reserve's management take the "hidden Selous" moniker a little too seriously: there's no website, no official publication, no information centre, and any queries sink straight into the bureaucratic mire that is the Ministry of

Natural Resources and Tourism (if you want to try: Ivory Room, Nyerere Rd, PO Box 1994 Dar es Salaam; ☎022/286 6064, ✉sgrmp@raha.com). On arriving at the reserve gate, however, you should be able to buy a copy of Rolf Baldus and Ludwig Siege's excellent *Selous Travel Guide* **guidebook** (Gallery Publications), and, with luck, the 1:500,000 *Visitor's Map of the Selous Game Reserve North of the Rufiji* **map** published by GTZ, showing relief, vegetation, accommodation, some walking trails, and good places for spotting given species. The map is hard to find elsewhere, but the book can be bought in Arusha, Dar and Stone Town. The best **website** is ⓦwww.wildlife-baldus.com.

**Entrance fees**, valid 24 hours, are $65 per person ($75 if staying inside the reserve, or $80 if flying in), and are paid in dollars cash. The services of an **armed ranger**, doubling as a guide (obligatory if self-driving), costs $20 a day.

## Accommodation

**Camping** is the cheapest way of staying in or around Selous; see box on p.220. Otherwise, the most affordable options lie just **east of the reserve** along the Rufiji's north bank. Although terrestrial wildlife isn't as profuse here as inside the reserve, the river is much the same, and all places offer walks, drives and boat trips. **Inside the reserve** is an ever-expanding collection of luxury tented camps and lodges, all of which are soul-crushingly expensive.

### Inside the reserve

Excepting the two public campsites (see p.220), Selous' cheapest digs start at $330 **full board** for two people sharing (excluding reserve entry fees and only for clients arriving in their own vehicles), and upwards of $530 a day for a **game package** (see p.217). If you're up for these, read recent reviews from other clients on the internet (see p.74 for websites) for way more personal – and occasionally damning – reports than we could ever legally publish. Prices quoted below are 2009 rack rates for two people sharing, and exclude reserve entry fees; substantial **discounts** may be available if booking via travel agents or safari companies. The five choices reviewed below offer the best cost-to-value ratio; if money's no object, there's also *Beho Beho Camp* ($2050; ⓦwww.behobeho.com), *Mivumo River Lodge* and *Selous Wildlife Lodge* ($1720 and $1220 respectively; both ⓦwww.malalaluxurylodges.com).

**Lake Manze Camp** ⓦwww.adventurecamps.co .tz. Twelve secluded tents amidst doum palms and terminalia trees, all with lake views. Quite plain but does the trick, and cheap by Selous' shocking standards. Children under 6 discouraged. FB $330; game package $530. ⓭

**Rufiji River Camp** ⓦwww.rufijirivercamp .com. Overlooking the river, this is unfussy, unpretentious and relaxed, with excellent guides for extended wildlife walks. The fourteen rustic tents are tucked away in the forest, each with a veranda for river and sunset views. There's also a shaded

## Selous by train

The **TAZARA railway**, linking Dar to Zambia, dips tantalizingly into Selous Game Reserve's northwestern corner. Alas, for budget travellers at least, cadging a free safari en route isn't on the cards for now, as the trains (two a week in either direction) pass through at night – useful only if you're staying at *Sable Mountain Lodge*, outside the reserve, who can pick you up. That said, it's worth keeping an eye on the schedule, just in case. The good news, for upmarket travellers, is that the private **Selous Safari Train**, operated by Foxes African Safaris (p.53), is due to resume in June 2010, providing a suitably swanky introduction to the neo-colonial chic of Selous' lodges.

## Camping in and around the Selous

The most exciting, often hair-raising, and potentially cheapest way of experiencing Selous – and the nocturnal concerts given by bush babies, bull frogs, lions, hippos and hyenas – is to camp. **Inside the reserve** are two public campsites: *Beho Beho Bridge*, and *Lake Tagalala* ($20 per person, plus park fees and $20 for the obligatory armed guard). Both have long-drop toilets and water (which needs purifying). Campfires are permitted if dead wood is used. **Outside the reserve**, you can pitch a tent at *Selous River Camp* ($10 per person) or *Jimbiza Lodge* ($15). Wherever you camp, don't do it without an **armed guard** – there be man-eating lions about.

### Luxury fly-camping

It may be camping, Captain, but not as we know it: some of Selous' upmarket camps and lodges offer optional **fly-camping excursions**, involving walks through bush and forest guided by white-hunter-type chaps, accompanied by armed rangers, and, for a gratuitous dab of colour, Maasai warriors. The camps are set up ahead of your arrival in the afternoon, and come with hot bucket showers hung from trees, long-drop or chemical toilets, evening banquets around campfires and champagne breakfasts. Prices start at a wallet-melting $450 per person per day (minimum two nights) – rather rich given that you'll probably be sleeping on a camp bed in a small dome tent. More comfortable are the tents used by companies operating upmarket **seasonal tented camps** (also called "mobile camps" or "private camps"): Authentic Tanzania (@www.authentictanzania.com) have a good reputation for Selous.

swimming pool, library, and superb Tuscan-style cuisine. Children welcome. FB $400; game package $590. ⑨

**Sand Rivers Selous** @www.nomad-tanzania .com. Stylish "rustic chic" perfect for a preposterous pampering, with eight cottages on a hippo-filled river bend, and great wildlife guides. No children under 8. Game package $1420. ⑨

**Selous Impala Camp** @www.adventurecamps .co.tz. The location is the thing here, amidst borassus palms and tamarinds on the Rufiji's north bank, but even with the accent on wildlife, it's too plain for the price. All tents have river-view verandas, and there's a swimming pool. Children welcome. FB $760; game package $890. ⑨

**Selous Safari Camp** @www.selous.com. Set in *miombo* woodland behind Lake Nzerekera, understated elegance is the hallmark: thirteen luxurious tents, personal butlers, some of Tanzania's best food, expert guides, and great wildlife viewing even within the camp. Also has two swimming pools. No children under 8. Game package $1250. ⑨

### Outside the reserve

Accommodation **outside the reserve** is much cheaper, and offers the chance of village walks ($10–25 per person), in addition to boat trips, bush walks and game drives ($35–50 per person, $70–100 for a full day, plus $65 per person if entering the reserve). For cruises or drives with fewer than four tourists, you may have to pay more.

**Jimbiza Lodge** On the river, 3km from Mtemere Gate ⓣ022/261 8057 (Dar) or 0784/629409, @www.jimbizalodges.com. An nicely unfussy Tanzanian-run place with a spread of decent accommodation and a laid-back vibe. The *bandas* are nothing special at the price (they resemble guesthouse rooms); the tented rooms fare better, but the best deal is camping, either in your own tent or using theirs ($25 per person), to which add $10 a meal, and $5 to use the pool. Tents (no meals) $50, *bandas* (FB) ⑧

**Sable Mountain Lodge** 10km from Kisaki village outside Matambwe Gate @www .selouslodge.com. Occupying three peaks of the Beho Beho Mountains above thick forest, with eight simple but stylish stone cottages and five luxury tented *bandas* facing the Uluguru Mountains, all secluded and with verandas and solar-powered light. The best – two "honeymoon *bandas*" – have private plunge pools and beautiful views down a valley towards a waterhole. A tree house nearby provides good game viewing; there's also a "snug" for star-gazing, two restaurants and bars, swimming pool, evening campfire, and warm relations with local villages (who are paid a percentage of profits; good village tours). No children under six. FB $290–390; game package, including reserve fees $550–650 ❽–❾

**Selous Mbega Camp** On the river, 1.4km from Mtemere Gate ☏ 022/265 0250 (Dar) or 0784/624664, ⓦ www.selous-mbega-camp.com. Nestled amidst lush riverine woodland (colobus monkeys – *mbega* – are sometimes seen), this has a dozen large, en-suite tents pitched on attractive wooden platforms, ten with river-facing verandas, and various more permanent buildings in a mixture of European and African styles. Also has a restaurant enveloping a mahogany tree, and is planning a swimming pool. Discounts for backpackers arriving by bus, if booked direct. FB ❼

🏕 **Selous River Camp** On the river, 1.2km from Mtemere Gate ☏ 0784/237525, ⓦ www.selousrivercamp.com. An affordable self-catering place on the forested riverbank, run by a charming Tanzanian/British couple. You can camp, or – booking ahead – stay in their delightful en-suite mud hut, which has a raised wooden veranda with wonderful views. The bar has similar vistas, but bring your own food (or stock up on the very basics in Mloka village): a cooking fire is provided, or you can hire a cook. ❺

**Selous Riverside Safari Camp** 6km outside Mtemere Gate, 2.5km southeast of Mloka ☏ 022/212 8161 (Dar), ⓦ www.selousriversidecamp .com. Several kilometres downstream from the other east-side options, this is, for now, nicely isolated and unpretentious, but pricey. It has ten very large and attractively furnished tents (with mosquito screens) raised on wooden platforms under *makuti* shelters, with dense forest behind, all with river-view verandas. Meals are taken on a wooden deck beside a swimming pool, also with views. Tasty, mostly Tanzanian food, efficient staff, and good guides. FB $400; game package $550 ❾

# The reserve

The magnificent **Rufiji River** is the heart and soul of Selous, and ineffably beautiful it is, too – its labyrinthine channels, lagoons, islets and their abundant wildlife making it easy to forget the ugly fibreglass-and-canvas boats used for cruises. **Birdlife** is plentiful throughout the wetlands: on the lagoons, look out for African skimmers, pink-backed and great white pelicans, ducks and Egyptian geese, giant kingfishers and white-fronted plovers, while the shallows and sandbanks are ideal for waders like herons and storks as well as kingfishers, African skimmers (again) and white-fronted bee-eaters. The groves of *mikumi* palms lining the shore in many parts are also rich twitching territory, including morning warblers, palmnut vultures, red-necked falcons, nesting African fish eagles, yellow-billed storks, ibises and palm swifts. **Lake Tagalala**, actually a lagoon, is the main destination for boat safaris. The lake apparently contains the densest population of crocodiles on earth, presumably fed by the profusion of wildlife that comes here to drink, and there are also plenty of hippos, though you shouldn't get too close as they will charge a boat if feeling threatened. Another good destination is **Stiegler's Gorge**, where the Great Ruaha River flows into the Rufiji. The gorge takes its name from a hunter who was killed here by an elephant in 1907, and offers a fair chance of spotting leopard.

The **riverine forest** is best visited on a **bush walk**, during which you might catch glimpses of black-and-white colobus monkeys, or hear the crashing of branches as they flee your approach. The walks are generally two- to three-hour affairs in the company of an armed ranger: necessary, as heart-stopping encounters with elephants, lions or buffalo are frequent enough. Bush walks are also good for spotting details you would otherwise miss, like the sticky secretions dikdiks deposit on top of grass stems to mark their territorial latrines, or the tracks and spoors left by animals whose bellowings kept you up the night before.

On a traditional **game drive**, your itinerary really depends on the state of the reserve's tracks, and what your guide reckons is best at the time, but there are a couple of places you could aim to include among all the bumping and sliding:

the sulphurous **Maji Moto hot springs** on the eastern slope of Kipala Hill, near Lake Tagalala, which are cool enough in places for swimming (also visitable by boat); and **Captain Selous' grave**, at Beho Beho.

# Udzungwa Mountains National Park

Even with a thesaurus to hand, it's difficult to do justice to the wonder that is **Udzungwa Mountains National Park**, an immaculate forest-cloaked wilderness whose 1900 square kilometres are among the most biodiverse on earth. Protected as a national park in 1992, the driving rationale was to conserve the **catchments** of the Kilombero and Great Ruaha rivers, lifeblood of the Selous and of human populations elsewhere. The authorities of course also knew that the area they were protecting was rich in species, but just how rich continues to amaze. Forget about rare bugs and plants, new discoveries of which are two to a penny: Udzungwa still has the habit of turning up *mammals* hitherto unknown to science, the latest being the world's largest shrew (60cm from tip to toe), and not just a new species but an entirely new genus of monkey, which turned up at the same time it was also found at Kitulo National Park.

Like the Uluguru and Usambara mountains, the Udzungwas are part of the **Eastern Arc** (see box, p.279), a disjointed chain of ancient mountains whose great age and isolation, and a steady rain-soaked climate, has allowed its forests to evolve independently from each other, and quite spectacularly. But whereas most of the Eastern Arc's ranges have suffered major environmental damage over the last 150 years, Udzungwa is pristine, thanks both to its unusually steep terrain (limiting human intervention to the lowlands), and **taboos**. Locals around Udzungwa believe the mountain's forests are the abode of ancestral spirits (a belief that crops up elsewhere in Tanzania in places with long-established primate populations), and as such they restricted access to ceremonial purposes, and for burials. To disturb the spirits or the graves, people say, will bring great calamity, and should anyone dare cut down a *mitogo* tree, they're sure to become a lion's next meal… The result is the only place in East Africa with an unbroken virgin forest canopy from a low-point of 250m above sea-level to over 2km high, covering *miombo* woodland, bamboo and lowland forest containing trees 50m tall, to montane rainforest up in the clouds.

Udzungwa's wildlife can be seen all year round, but as you'll be hiking the **best times to visit** are the dry months from June to October and December to February.

### Biodiversity

Given its exceptionally well-preserved forest cover, Udzungwa's wildlife is rich, if not always easy to see. The park contains Tanzania's widest selection of **primates**, its twelve species including the recently discovered **kipunji** monkey, and four **endemics**: the Sanje crested mangabey, the Iringa (or Uhehe) red colobus, and two species of dwarf galago or bushbaby. Other primates include the thick-tailed galago, blue monkey and black-and-white colobus. The primates are concentrated in the east of the park, which is great news for hikers as this is where the main walking trails are located. Also frequently seen are **buffalo** (keep your distance), but the most you're likely to see of **elephants** is their droppings, or patches of vegetation flattened by portly backsides. **Rarer animals** include the red-legged sun squirrel, the recently rediscovered Lowe's servaline genet (previously seen seventy years ago), the red duiker, Abbot's

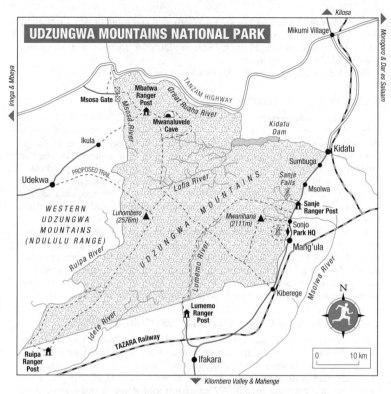

UDZUNGWA MOUNTAINS NATIONAL PARK

Kilosa

Mikumi Village

Morogoro & Dar es Salaam

Iringa & Mbeya

TANZAM HIGHWAY

Great Ruaha River

Msosa River

Mbatwa Ranger Post

Msosa Gate

Mwanaluvele Cave

Ikula

PROPOSED TRAIL

Udekwa

Lofia River

WESTERN UDZUNGWA MOUNTAINS (NDULULU RANGE)

Luhombero (2576m)

Ruipa River

UDZUNGWA MOUNTAINS

Lumemo River

Kidatu Dam

Kidatu

Sumbuga

Sanje Falls

Msolwa

Sanje Ranger Post

Mwanihana (2111m)

Sonjo Park HQ

Mang'ula

Msolwa River

Kiberege

N

Idete River

Lumemo Ranger Post

TAZARA Railway

Ruipa Ranger Post

Ifakara

0    10 km

Kilombero Valley & Mahenge

duiker (also called blue duiker), Livingstone's suni, bush pig, bushbuck, spiny mice, the comical chequered elephant shrew (named after its trunk-like snout), and, also recently discovered, Philips' Congo shrew and the grey-faced sengi – a truly **giant elephant shrew** (whose wispy 700g somehow fill a 60cm-long frame). **Birders** are in for a treat, too, with possible sightings of rufous-winged sunbirds or Udzungwa partridges, both of them rare endemics. Other endemics include millipedes, a tree frog, over seventy species of spider, a gecko, a skink, and the nattily named pygmy bearded chameleon.

Whether it's nature that turns you on, or you're just up for a yomp, you'd be insane to give this place a miss.

## Arrival

Turning south off the Tanzam highway at Mikumi village, you leave safari land behind and, after 40km or so, you leave the sealed road, too. The dirt road continues south, wending its bumpy and dusty way between the lime-green expanse of sugar cane plantations and rice paddies in the Msolwa Valley to the east, and the increasingly green and heavily forested Udzungwa Mountains to the west. The park headquarters, where you pay your entry fees, are 200m west of the road at **Mang'ula**, 60km from Mikumi village. Trains are not useful (only one a week, arriving at night), so you'll need to catch a **bus** or a large "Coaster" daladala from Morogoro (the 10am Islam's Bus is safest), or from Dar, or – more likely – from Mikumi village. The first vehicles leave Mikumi around 10am (roughly hourly thereafter), but are usually packed and badly driven, so it might be better waiting for Islam's Bus, around 11am. **Leaving Mang'ula**, buses for Dar pass through around 11am; Coaster minibuses to Mikumi and Morogoro are roughly hourly until 4pm.

For information on accessing the park's western slopes, see p.473.

## Information and costs

The **park headquarters** (☎023/262 0224 or 0784/370536, ✉udzungwa @gmail.com) sell a map and a colourful **guidebook**. The park's **website** is ⓦwww.udzungwa.org. Strictly speaking, the $20 **entrance fee** (valid 24hr) is for single entry only, but for now the wardens don't mind visitors spending the night outside the park and returning the next morning. All but the Prince Bernhard trail require an official guide or **armed ranger** ($20 per day). Suggested daily fees for (optional) **porters**, hired through the park, are Tsh8000 for a 16–20kg load on the Sanje Falls Circuit, Tsh12,000 for Mwanihana Peak, and Tsh15,000 for Luhombero Peak.

There's only one (short) trail starting from the park headquarters; for the others, pay your fees then either drive, catch a Coaster or rent a Land Rover from the park to reach the starting point. Prices for the vehicle are approximately $20 per group for a lift to Sanje Ranger Post 9km north, where several trails start, or, for longer journeys, $100 for 100km. If you're coming in your own vehicle, leave it at the park headquarters; they'll look after bags too.

## Accommodation, eating and drinking

Lying outside the park, but within ten minutes' walk of the headquarters, are several **hotels** geared to hikers, and (in planning) an upmarket lodge. There are more basic **guesthouses** in Mang'ula village, 2km southeast: to get there from the main road, walk south past *Udzungwa Mountain View Hotel*, turn left at the post office and continue straight. All have **food and drink**, and there also basic bars and restaurants in the village, albeit none venturing far beyond the land of *kuku na chipsi*. **Camping** is possible at *Hondo Hondo* (see below; $5), and – much more expensive – inside the park ($30 per person plus entrance fees). Best of the park's three permanent sites (with pit latrines but nothing else) is "number 2", in a beautiful patch of forest 2km inside the gate near a bubbling brook with swimmable rock pools.

**Hondo Hondo** 100m north of the park headquarters ☎022/261 7166 (Dar) or 0773/503502, ⓦwww .udzungwaforestcampsite.com and ⓦwww .udzungwaforestlodge.com. Run in collaboration with villagers by Wild Things Safaris (p.53), unrivalled experts on Udzungwa and Kilombero, further south, this has something for all budgets. At the lower end, *Udzungwa Forest Campsite* has well-kept Western-style toilets and showers, a shop for snacks and essentials, tent hire ($10 per person), and four simple but comfortable mud-and-thatch *bandas* with double beds and nets, all with views over the valley. For upmarket travellers, *Udzungwa Forest Lodge*, under construction at the time of writing, promises to be a fine retreat. Lodge (FB) ❽, *bandas* ❸
**Mountain Peak Lodge** Mang'ula village, 876m from the main road (so sayeth the sign)

☎0784/650392. Best of the local guesthouses, clean and with safe parking. Some of its rooms have bathrooms (squat toilets), all have fans and box nets, and there's a bar and restaurant (chicken or beef with chips or rice). ❶
**Twiga Hotel** 1km east from the park headquarters (signposted), same contacts as the park headquarters. Set in shady gardens, this pleasantly rambling old place is now run by the park authority, and with a renovation in the offing, the price may rise (currently $20 per person). For now, it has plenty of simple but perfectly good twin-bed rooms, some with bathrooms, all with large nets, balconies and TV. Tasty food available (around Tsh5000), and drinks. ❹
**Udzungwa Mountain View Hotel** 600m south of the park headquarters ☎023/262 0218 or

▲ Blue monkey, Udzungwa National Park

0784/454481, ⓦ www.genesismotel.com. Owned by Mikumi's *Genesis Motel*, this is similarly costly and also in need of renovation, but enjoys a nice location under a thick canopy of trees. It has twenty en-suite, twin-bed rooms, with a choice of fan or a/c. The restaurant charges upwards of Tsh10,000 a plate, but does have prawns and, somewhat worryingly, impala. There's also a bar with TV. BB ❹

## Hiking in the park

The park's established **hiking trails** range from an easy hour's dawdle to a full-on five-day affair, or six days if you can convince a ranger to rise to the challenge. **Equipment** should include good walking shoes (all routes have steep and/or slippery sections), light waterproofs in the rains, a water bottle, something for purifying water (there's plenty of water along the trails), and camping equipment for overnight trails. A gas or kerosene stove is also useful. All overnight trails, with the exception of the eastern approach to Luhombero Peak, have **campsites** equipped with toilets and shelters.

### The trails

The only walk from the park headquarters is the **Prince Bernhard Trail** (1km; 40min; no guide needed), going to two waterfalls: the small Prince Bernhard Falls, named after the then Dutch president of the WWF who cut the park's ribbon in 1992, and the Njokamoni Falls en route. Red duikers are frequently seen, as are habituated baboons and mangabeys (hide food and take care). Another short trail, the **Sonjo Trail** (2.5km; 2hr; guide needed), starts 5km north of Mang'ula at Sonjo, passing through *miombo* woodland to two other waterfalls. Primates and birds are the main animal attractions here. The most popular route is the **Sanje Falls Circuit** (5km; 4hr; guide needed), from Sanje Ranger Post 9km north of Mang'ula. The trail heads through various forest zones to the Sanje Falls, a sequence of three cascades dropping over 170m. The first two provide a refreshingly misty experience, and you can swim in their splash pools. The third and longest fall is difficult to see as you emerge from the dense forest right on top of it, though the hollows and undulating channels gouged into the rock by water are interesting. You can see the falls clearly on the way down to Sanje village, or on the bus from Mikumi for that matter. Primates are frequently seen, as are birds and butterflies. The **Campsite 3 Circuit** (13km; 10hr; ranger or guide needed) is best for wildlife (or at least their dung), and also gives good odds on seeing bushbuck and duiker as well as primates, birds and butterflies. The trail starts at Campsite 3, 100m north of *Udzungwa Mountain View Hotel*, and ends 3km north of Mang'ula.

The **Mwanihana Trail** (38km; three days, two nights; armed ranger needed) starts at Sonjo, 5km north of Mang'ula, and is the highlight of many a visit to Tanzania, taking you to Udzungwa's second-highest peak, Mwanihana (2111m). Be warned however: the walk is exhausting (19km uphill, returning the same way) and you need to be sure-footed. The trail follows the Sonjo River for the most part, its steep and narrow valley necessitating at least fifteen crossings; in the dry season this just means wading across, but in the rains you'll be struggling through torrents while hanging on grimly to a guide rope, so unless you're covered by ample life insurance avoid this one from March to May. At other times you have the pleasure of passing through every one of the park's forest zones, before emerging onto the grassy plateau by the peak. The park blurb promises duiker, elephant and a herd of buffalo, but you'd be lucky to see any of them. More likely are glimpses of various monkeys. There are also lots of butterflies and birds.

The park's newest walk is the **Lumemo Trail** (65km; at least four nights; ranger needed), a clockwise circuit up the Lumemo River and down along the northern side of Mwanihana Peak. Access to the start of the trail is through Lumemo Ranger Post near Ifakara, around 50km south of Mang'ula. The cheapest way there is to arrange for the rangers to pick you from Ifakara train station, which you can reach by Coaster. If you're driving, turn right at the train station, and it's 12km along. A hike up to the park's highest point, **Luhombero Peak** (2576m; six days; armed ranger needed), is a serious and rarely attempted undertaking, as the trail is difficult to follow.

# Dodoma and northwards

Tanzania's geographical centre – an arid plateau gouged by sand-filled gullies and studded with weathered granite outcrops – is inching ever closer to fully-blown desert. At its heart lies the planned city of **Dodoma**, Tanzania's political capital, and a reminder of a time when ideology and ideals carried more weight than common sense. The city has little of interest to tourists, but it's a pleasant stop nonetheless. More gratifying are a number of places to the north, including the Irangi Hills, which contain some of Africa's oldest **prehistoric rock paintings**, and some of the most recent, left barely a century ago by the Sandawe, who at the time were hunter-gatherers. You can visit them, and the resolutely traditional cattle-herding Barbaig, via a cultural tourism programme in **Babati**, which also offers hikes up Tanzania's fourth-highest peak, **Mount Hanang**. Cultural tourism is also possible in **Kondoa**, closer to the rock paintings.

## Dodoma's fragile environment

Passing through in the 1870s, Henry Morton **Stanley** was enchanted by Ugogo – the land of the Gogo. "In the whole of Africa", he wrote, "there is not another place whose environment has attracted me as much as this". Mr Stanley, one presumes, would have been somewhat surprised to see the changes that have occurred since. A large part of the region is savanna plateau whose little rain falls in heavy bursts in December, and in March or April, leaving the rest of the year unremittingly dry, windy and dusty. As a result, the region has long been prone to **drought**, a natural cycle whose challenges the Gogo traditionally mastered via a cyclical system of communal grazing that ensured no one piece of land was ever exhausted.

The **Europeans**, however, made every effort to discourage the Gogo's nomadic lifestyle, which they considered backward (not unlike the present government's attitude to the Barbaig and Maasai). Land was confiscated, increasing pressure on what grazing land remained, and the Gogo were "encouraged" to settle. But without irrigation (the region's dams are more recent) or agricultural techniques attuned to semi-arid conditions, the results were disastrous: two famines after World War I killed thirty thousand people, and the **slash-and-burn** farming technique adopted (a very bad move in such a fragile environment) caused erosion on a whopping scale. Nyerere's idealistic **Ujamaa** policy (see p.585) had an equally catastrophic impact. Human and animal population densities in critical areas increased by fifty percent as a result of the establishment of centralized "Ujamaa villages". Pastures were trampled to dust, water points exhausted, and groundwater tables sank ever deeper. The region's present-day lunar landscape is the visible legacy.

With a population of over 1.3 million, the Gogo today can hardly turn back the clock, even if many still dress as their ancestors did. One **solution** being developed by the forestry department is to introduce sustainable modes of agriculture and plant varieties that won't leave the soil uncovered. But this will take time – and time, unfortunately, has all but run out.

# Dodoma

As Tanzania's political capital since 1973, **DODOMA** is testimony to President Nyerere's idealistic plans for nation-building. Although he got it right most of the time, his choice of Dodoma was less felicitous. Straddling the Central Line railway, the site was chosen primarily on account of its location at the country's geographical heart, which, unfortunately, happens to be a disconsolately arid nowhere. Inspired by the artificial cities of Brasília (Brazil) and Abuja (Nigeria), Dodoma was supposed to be the centrepiece of Tanzania's multitribal identity, a kind of giant Ujamaa village. But the remote location, the billowing dust storms and the 40°C-plus temperatures were never going to facilitate things. The country's parliament has been there since 1996, but the government itself – well, every time it half-heartedly tries to shift itself from Dar es Salaam, twelve months later you'll find that the ministries and departments have snuck back to the coast.

Inevitably, this means that Dodoma is never really going to appeal much to visitors, but it's a pleasant enough place, and there's a appealingly gentle anarchy about it, too, and not just in the broken street-numbering system. The city is gradually outgrowing the rigidity of its original blueprint, and large sections originally earmarked for ministries or parks are now occupied by a maze of dusty roads packed not only with businesses but homes, even in the city centre, and with children all over the place, even at night, Dodoma has a distinctly village-like feeling. Perhaps Nyerere's dream wasn't so far-fetched after all.

## Dodoma: that sinking feeling

Dodoma's name is a corruption of the Kigogo word *idodomia* or *yadodomela*, meaning "sinking" or "sunk". The prosaic explanation is that it was a metaphor for the fate of invaders unable to escape the spears and arrows of the brave Gogo defenders, but a taller tale refers to an elephant that came to drink in the Kikuyu River, got stuck and began to sink – to the delight of newspaper critics ever-fond of the old "white elephant" jibe. Another tale tells of Gogo warriors secretly lifting a herd of cattle from the Hehe, their southern neighbours. The Gogo feasted on the cattle, leaving only the tails, which they then stuck into the ground. When the Hehe came looking for their herd, the Gogo pointed to the tails and exclaimed, "Look, your cattle have sunk into the mud!"

## Arrival and city transport

Dodoma is a six- to eight-hour drive from Dar (469km; good asphalt); it's also a major stop on the Central Line railway to Kigoma and Mwanza. The unsurfaced roads from Tabora and Arusha are rough, and become impassable for days at a time during and after heavy rains. The direct road from Iringa fares better, but most drivers find it quicker to take the longer route via Morogoro. A walk or taxi ride from town, the **bus stand** is on Dar es Salaam Avenue on the southeast side of town, next to a big roundabout; Scandinavian Express' terminal is on the other side of the roundabout. The **train station** is ten minutes' walk southeast of the centre. The **airport** is 4km north: Coastal Aviation come here "on inducement", meaning if there are enough passengers to turn a profit.

**Daladalas**, locally nicknamed "Express", leave from Jamatini Stand on Dar es Salaam Avenue, and cover the whole city (Tsh300 for most journeys). **Taxis** congregate at transport terminals and outside the market; trips within the city cost Tsh3000–4000. Dodoma has plenty of (rarely pushy) **beggars**, often living with polio: you'll feel better with some coins to hand. The sun is more wearying; you could invest in a colourful parasol, as many locals have done.

## Accommodation

Dodoma has an ever-growing selection of **accommodation**. A good thing too, as at times you'll have to visit three or four places before finding a free room. Government expense accounts have pushed prices higher than elsewhere, with the cheapest (decent) double starting at Tsh15,000; single rooms can usually be shared by couples. Standards are generally good. The main concentration of hotels is in the fan-like grid of numbered streets west of Kuu Street, while there are more mid-range choices east off Dar es Salaam Avenue, and up in Area "C", a shadeless thirty-minute walk from the centre (or daladala trip from Jamatini stand towards Mnadani). Dodoma's **water** supply is unreliable and may be tainted by pesticides.

**Cana Lodge** 9th St ☎0754/919996, ⓕ026/232 1716. Not the warmest of welcomes, and with similar but cheaper options nearby, this is now a stand-by, albeit still reasonable, with well-kept rooms all with cable TV, fans and nets. The better rooms are upstairs. There's also a modest restaurant and bar, and safe parking. ❷
**CCT Centre** Zuzu roundabout ☎0713/475741, ⓔcct_ctc@yahoo.com. Run by the Anglican

Church, this has lots of bare rooms in polygonal clusters connected by open-sided corridors, mostly with shared bathrooms. Maintenance isn't divine – there are holey mosquito nets and window screens, and water problems – but the beds are clean, and there are also two- and three-bedroom units sharing sitting rooms, useful for families. Singles are cheap by local standards (Tsh8000). Internet café and basic restaurant. BB ❷

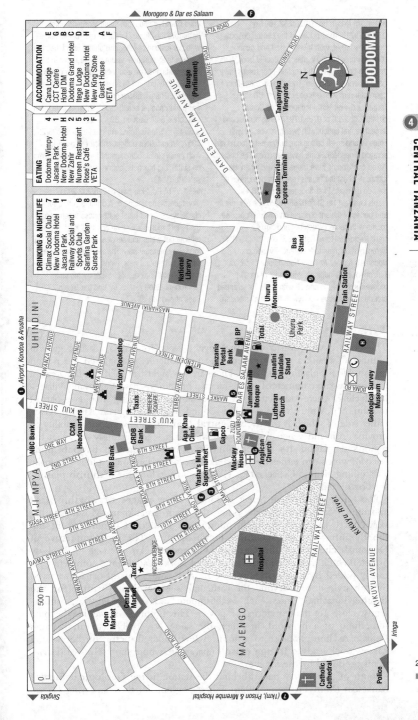

▲ Morogoro & Dar es Salaam    ▲ **⒡**

**DODOMA**

N

## ACCOMMODATION
| | |
|---|---|
| Cana Lodge | E |
| CCT Centre | G |
| Hotel DM | B |
| Dodoma Grand Hotel | D |
| Itege Lodge | C |
| New Dodoma Hotel | H |
| New King Stone | A |
| Guest House | |
| VETA | F |

## EATING
| | |
|---|---|
| Dodoma Wimpy | 4 |
| Jacana Park | 1 |
| New Dodoma Hotel | 2 |
| New Zahir | 5 |
| Nureen Restaurant | 3 |
| Rose's Café | 8 |
| VETA | F |

## DRINKING & NIGHTLIFE
| | |
|---|---|
| Climax Social Club | 7 |
| New Dodoma Hotel | H |
| Jacana Park | 1 |
| Railway Social and | 6 |
| Sports Club | |
| Sarafina Garden | 8 |
| Sunset Park | 9 |

Bunge (Parliament)

Tanganyika Vineyards

Scandinavian Express Terminal

Bus Stand

National Library

Uhuru Monument

Uhuru Park

Train Station

VETA ROAD

BUNGE ROAD

DAR ES SALAAM AVENUE

MASHARIKI AVENUE

RAILWAY STREET

BOMA RD

UHINDINI

MWANZA AVENUE
ABORA AVENUE
MBEYA AVENUE
LINDI AVENUE
TEMBO AVENUE

Victory Bookshop

Taxis

MTENDERE SQUARE

MTENDENI STREET

MARKET STREET

Tanzania Postal Bank

BP

Total

Jamatini Daladala Stand

Jamatkhana Mosque

Lutheran Church

KUU STREET

NBC Bank

CCM HEADQUARTERS

ONE WAY

2ND STREET

MMB Bank

CRDB Bank

Aga Khan Clinic

Gapco

ZUZU ROUNDABOUT

6TH STREET
7TH STREET
8TH STREET
9TH STREET
10TH STREET
11TH STREET
12TH STREET

MADARAKA AVENUE

Yasha's Mini Supermarket

Mackay House

Anglican Church

SIASA STREET
4TH STREET
9TH STREET
10TH STREET
DAIMA STREET

MWANZA AVENUE

Taxis

INDEPENDENCE SQUARE

Central Market

Open Market

NDOVU ROAD

MAJENGO

Hospital

KIKUYU RIVER

RAILWAY STREET

Geological Survey Museum

Catholic Cathedral

Police

KIKUYU AVENUE

▼ Singida

▼ **⒧** (1km), Prison & Mirembe Hospital

▲ **⒤** Airport, Kondoa & Arusha

▼ Iringa

0    500 m

4

**CENTRAL TANZANIA**

**Hotel DM** Ndovu Rd ☎026/232 1001 or 0752/229718. Best-priced of the central options, near the market, with friendly staff and good rooms: a/c, satellite TV, massive double beds, fans, and nice bathrooms. The second-floor rooms have nets; others are sprayed. There's also a top-floor bar/restaurant with a breezy terrace. BB ❷

**Dodoma Grand Hotel** Independence Square ☎026/232 3280 or 0785/079777. The newest and largest central option, with twenty rooms, all with cable TV and small ceiling fan, but no nets (rooms are sprayed if needed). Some have balconies. The pricier "executive" rooms have fridges but are otherwise identical, whilst the "suites" are overpriced, even if they do have a/c. First-floor restaurant. BB ❸

**Itege Lodge** 11th St ☎0755/763574. A friendly and perfectly decent cheapie on several floors. All rooms with cable TV, box net and fan. ❷

**New Dodoma Hotel** Railway St ☎026/232 1641, ✉reservation_newdodomahotel@yahoo.com. Dodoma's former *Railway Hotel* is one of central Tanzania's best lodgings, with most of its 91 rooms, mostly twins and all with cable TV, wrapped around an attractive courtyard. The small standard ones have big beds (but small mosquito nets); better are the slightly larger deluxe rooms, some with a/c instead of fans, and others with balconies. Service is as polished as the marble floors in the restaurants and bar, and there are plenty of tables in the courtyard next to an amusing pool and fake waterfall. There's also a proper if slightly murky swimming pool, a health "spa", internet café, wi-fi and forex. Safe parking. BB ❹–❺

**New King Stone Guest House** 9th St ☎026/232 3057. An excellent budget choice but often full, with small clean rooms, squat toilets (some rooms en suite), big box nets, cotton sheets, fan, even satellite TV. ❶

**VETA** VETA Rd, 2km east ☎026/232 2931, ✉vetadom@do.ucc.co.tz. A training centre for chefs, waiters and hotel staff whose teachers know their stuff: rooms are clean and well kept, there's reliable hot water and service is excellent, making for a very pleasant stay. The 39 rooms have TVs, singles with round nets, twins (can be pushed together) with box nets; cheaper rooms share bathrooms. Good restaurant and bar (see p.232). Book ahead. BB ❷–❸

## The City

The city's busiest district is **Mji Mpya** ("New Town"), a fan-like grid of numbered streets: a simple system that has nonetheless confused the person responsible for placing road signs. There are no "sights" as such, but the area – a mix of low-rise commercial and residential buildings – has an enjoyably village-like feeling, where kids getting all excited about the passing stranger is part of the fun. Mji Mpya's western edge is bounded by the stagnant Kikuyu River, either side of which is the lively **Central Market**, renowned for its ability to provide fruit and vegetables even out of season – mysteriously so, given the region's desolation. It's a good place to sample bittersweet **baobab pods** (*ubuyu*), which can either be sucked like sweets or laboriously pulped to make a refreshing vitamin C-packed juice. You could also look for a "**thumb piano**"; see box on p.231.

The south end of Kuu Street is dominated by **places of worship**, each apparently vying to outdo the other: the brick Jamatikhana Mosque with a very church-like clock tower, the minimalistic Lutheran Church adjacent, and the Byzantine-domed Anglican Church opposite. The most impressive of Dodoma's churches is the **Catholic Cathedral**, 2km west along Railway Street. Rebuilt in 2001, the fantastical brickwork facade comes complete with overly gilded Byzantine-style mosaic frescoes, and a pair of ornately carved Swahili-style doors. Beyond the cathedral is **Mirembe Hospital for the Insane**, Tanzania's largest such establishment, and some might say, conveniently close to the corridors of power. The hospital's name has become something of a by-word, in much the same way that Victorian Britain's Bedlam Asylum gave rise to a noun. A few hundred metres further west, a narrow track leads to **Isanga prison** (*magereza*), whose shop sells sisal (*katani*) items produced by the inmates.

South of the railway tracks, behind the station, is the **Geological Survey Museum** (Mon–Fri 8am–3.30pm; Tsh500) – look for the sign saying *Wizara*

## The music of the Gogo

The Gogo are famous throughout Tanzania for their musical prowess, and one of their number, the late Hukwe Ubi Zawose, even made inroads on the World Music circuit. The ensemble of traditional Gogo music is called **sawosi** (in Kiswahili, *ngoma ya kigogo*), and is some of the most beautiful, haunting and subtle music you're ever likely to hear.

In common with the musical traditions of other "Nilotic-speaking" groups such as the Maasai, **multipart polyphony** is the thing: a subtle interweave of different rhythms, in which each musician plays or sings just a small part of one rhythm, which they're free to embellish within the greater scheme of things. This allows for a quasi-mathematical complexity.

Whilst for the Maasai this is a purely vocal trick, for the Gogo the technique reaches its hypnotic apogee in an intricate interplay of voices with instruments: single-stringed **zeze** fiddles, and **marimba ya mkono** hand xylophones (or "thumb pianos"), also known by their Shona name, *mbira*. The marimbas are the Gogo's calling card: hand-held wooden sound boxes, either rectangular or rhomboidal, fitted with an array of metal forks which, nowadays, more often than not are metal shafts taken from screwdrivers.

Highly **recommended listening** are two tapes of Gogo recordings sold at Radio Tanzania in Dar es Salaam (see p.108). For CDs (rarely available in Tanzania), see p.617. If you're a dedicated music fanatic, the best time for *sawosi* (in Dodoma Region's villages, not in town) is the harvest and circumcision season from June to August, especially July, which features the *cidwanga* dance conducted by healers, in which ancestors are remembered and praised.

*ya Nishati na Madini*. This is a hall filled with display cases containing gemstones and minerals, the more valuable of which (gold, platinum, ruby) are notably absent but for their labels and the patches of glue that once held them in place. Still, there's enough remaining to keep you interested for half an hour or so, including some enormous fossilized ammonites, flaky sheets of mica resembling plastic, and a large wall map of Tanzania's minerals with blinking lights linked to a massive control panel.

Heading east along Dar es Salaam Avenue takes you past a heap of informal stalls between the daladala stand and bus station, at which traditional Maasai doctors and hairdressers take pride of place. Behind them is the dusty **Uhuru Park**, whose monument to independence has seen better days: the spear-brandishing hand is still here, but the shield and machine gun have disappeared, as has the replica Uhuru Torch topping the abstract representation of Mount Kilimanjaro. In finer fettle is Tanzania's parliament, the **Bunge**, 1.5km further east, being a inspired futuristic take on traditional styles. No photography, alas, and access to debates is restricted.

## Eating

Dodoma has **restaurants** for all tastes and pockets, including a number of decent if unexciting places in mid-range hotels. You'll find **street food** and coffee vendors around the market, and along Dar es Salaam Avenue.

**Dodoma Wimpy** Zuzu roundabout. No relation to the multinational, this popular outdoor meeting place serves fast-food snacks like samosas, fried chicken, chips and *kababu*; excellent *mishkaki*; plus coffee, tea and sodas; and – for breakfast – *supu*. Also has full lunches (under Tsh3000), but get there early for the full choice. No alcohol.

**Jacana Park** Arusha Rd, Area "C". A great outdoor bar under a lovely stand of trees, serving up an excellent range of food, including *supu ya mbuzi* (a stew of various bits of goat in hot chilli broth), beef, chicken and *chipsi mayai*. Daladalas from Jamatini to Chang'ombe or Mnadani pass by.

**New Dodoma Hotel** Railway St. Contains two restaurants, the more interesting being *China Garden* (closed Tues lunch) for genuine Cantonese cuisine, including *mapo* (tofu), sizzlers and fresh salads. Vegetarian meals from Tsh5500 including rice, otherwise upwards of Tsh8000 or so. You can eat in the courtyard outside, which has a great children's play area and *nyama choma* bar.

**New Zahir** Mtendeni St. So long as the squillion dead flies on the floor don't put you off, this is a great place for cheap and proper meals, serving big portions of *pilau*, stews and birianis, and real juices, too, including tamarind. No alcohol.

**Nureen Restaurant** Dar es Salaam Ave. A down-at-heel Indian place, but their curries can be very good (unlike their snacks). Good *mishkaki* is sold on the street outside. No alcohol. Lunchtimes only, closed Sun.

**Rose's Café** 9th St, close to *Cana Lodge*. Cheap Tanzanian-Indian place, handy for snacks as well as full meals: curries and masalas with rice or chapati cost Tsh3500–5000. Good lunchtime vegetarian *thali*, too (Tsh5000). Closed Sun.

**VETA** VETA Rd, 2km east. Part of the training school, the chef being the instructor, the staff his students: they're doing good work, as both food and service are excellent. There's a wide choice of tasty dishes (but nothing vegetarian) as well as pastries and, if you order a day early, a selection of set menus. Main courses cost Tsh5000 and up. The bar outside has *nyama choma* from 7–11pm.

# Drinking and nightlife

Dodoma has a good number of attractive outdoor **beer gardens** (see also *Jacana Park* on p.231), all dishing up excellent *nyama choma*, grilled bananas, chicken and other snacks. The city's nocturnal scene is ever-changing, especially as regards venues for **live bands.** These tend to be in well-to-do outskirts, especially Area "D" district northeast of the airport: *Royal Village* was the main place here at the time of writing. Posters announcing upcoming gigs are displayed throughout the city, and there are also banners strung over Independence Square near the market.

**Climax Social Club** 3km west of the centre beyond the prison. Until Independence, this was Dodoma's main colonial hangout, and is still favoured by expats. As well as its bar and restaurant, there's a swimming pool. Daily membership Tsh2000.

**New Dodoma Hotel** Railway St. Expensive drinks in the hotel's wonderful courtyard, or indeed at a rondavel perched over its fanciful "swimming" pool. There's also a full-sized pool at the back (Tsh5000).

**Railway Social and Sports Club** East side of Uhuru Park, off Dar es Salaam Ave. A pleasant

bar-cum-restaurant, somewhat in the shadow of the much busier (and shadier) *Sunset Park* next door, with a TV and good traditional Tanzanian food.

**Sarafina Garden** Kuu St. Friendly outdoor place, but watch you don't come a cropper on the foot-snagging woodwork beside the bar, intended to stop people stealing the stools.

**Sunset Park** East side of Uhuru Park. An oasis of shady trees and shrubs with plenty of secluded seating, this is very popular with workers at the end of their shifts (and yes, there *is* a sunset, over the bus stand). Good music, *nyama choma* and snacks.

## Dodoma wine

For something completely different (really, *completely* different), do sample the region's **wine**, either at *New Dodoma Hotel*, or courtesy of a supermarket. The art was introduced by Italian missionaries a century ago, but evidently lost something in translation, as the output from Dodoma's Tanganyika Vineyards company is so bad it's probably best left for those with a solid sense of humour (and stomach); faring much better is Bihawana Red, made at Bihawana Mission along the Iringa road.

## Moving on from Dodoma

### By bus

None of the bus companies operating from Dodoma have completely unblemished reputations as regards safety; ones with particularly reckless reputations include Abood, Amit, Hood, Mohamed Trans, Tawfiq, and possibly Tashrif/Takrim. For **Dar**, safest companies are Shabiby (T0755/683976), with its own enclosure adjoining the bus station, and Scandinavian Express (T026/232 2170), on the other side of the roundabout. Shabiby also go to **Mwanza** and **Arusha**, both of them potentially taking fifteen hours plus. Six buses a week make the journey to **Tabora**, along a dirt road flanking the railway; there are no buses to Kigoma. For **Tanga**, clamber aboard Simba Video Coach (7.30am Wed, Fri & Sun). Most buses to **Iringa** go via Morogoro; the direct (but unsurfaced and slow) route via Mtera Dam is covered by two or three daily buses (Urafiki, Upendo and King Cross), which tend to be uncomfortably packed. For **Kondoa**, there's a steady stream of buses and daladalas until around noon unless it's raining heavily.

### By train

Train schedules are likely to change, so check in advance. Currently, services are as follows: **Mwanza, Kigoma and Tabora** (7am Wed & Sat, plus – not Mwanza – Mon); **Dar es Salaam** (7.30pm Mon, Wed & Fri); **Singida** (10am Wed, Fri & Sun; 3rd-class only). If you need a bunk, buy your ticket in advance. The office is at the station (Mon–Fri 8am–noon & 2–4pm, Sat 8–10.30am, and 2hr before departures).

### By air

Coastal Aviation fly from Dodoma if they have enough passengers: destinations are Arusha ($220), Tarangire ($250), Ruaha ($250) and Selous ($350).

## Listings

**Banks and exchange** Quickest for changing cash is Massive Bureau de Change at *New Dodoma Hotel*, Railway St (daily 8am–9pm). The main banks are on Kuu St, all with ATMs; NBC should be able to change traveller's cheques.

**Health** Best are the private Aga Khan Clinic, 6th St (T026/232 2455), and Mackay House, west end of Dar es Salaam Ave (T026/232 4299), also with a good dental clinic. The main government-run place is Dodoma General Hospital, off Railway St T026/232 1851. A reasonable pharmacy is Central Tanganyika Chemist, Dar es Salaam Ave, west of Zuzu roundabout (T026/232 4506).

**Internet access** The most reliable places are *New*

*Dodoma Hotel* (daily 7.30am–10pm), and the post office.

**Police** Kikuyu Ave, on the way to Iringa T026/232 4266.

**Post** Railway St.

**Supermarket** Yashna's Mini Supermarket, 6th St, behind GAPCO near Zuzu roundabout (Mon–Sat 8.30am–6.30pm, Sun 9am–2pm), stocks expensive imported treats guaranteed to please, plus a full range of Dodoma's wine.

**Swimming pool** *New Dodoma Hotel* charges non-guests Tsh5000.

**Telephones** TTCL, Railway St beside the post office (daily 7.30am–8pm).

# Kondoa and around

Some 158km north of Dodoma along an infamously bad road is the small and dusty/muddy town of **KONDOA**, a handy base for visiting the ancient **rock paintings** of the Irangi Hills. The town's inhabitants are mostly Rangi, but there are also Gogo and Sandawe, the latter having been hunter-gatherers until a few decades ago. Islam is the dominant religion: if you're awake at 5.30am, listen for hauntingly ethereal recitations of the ninety-nine names of

## The Rangi

The main tribe in Kondoa and the Iringi Hills are the **Rangi** (also called Langi), an extraordinarily friendly and welcoming people. Wherever you go you'll be greeted with broad smiles, effusive greetings and handshakes, and gleeful kids going berserk as you pass by. Nowadays primarily agricultural, the Rangi's cattle-herding past is reflected in the saying "it is better to hit a person than his cattle", so if you're driving, take extra care. Originally plains-dwelling, the Rangi moved up into the hills a couple of centuries ago to avoid the inexorable advance of the warlike **Maasai**, and built their villages into wide natural hollows, rendering them almost invisible from the surrounding steppe. Nowadays, with no reason to hide, Rangi villages are notable for their use of **brickwork**, sometimes decorated with geometrical relief patterns similar to styles used in parts of Ethiopia and the Sahara. The Rangi's expertise in earthenware is even more artfully shown by their beautiful **black cooking pots**, which can be bought for a few hundred shillings at any of the region's markets (there's one every day somewhere in the hills – ask around). You'll see the pots perched on people's houses along with pumpkins – roofs are the only place where pots can be dried after washing without being smashed by the above-mentioned hyperactive children...

Allah. Perhaps because of its shared religion, the town has a strong if easy-going sense of identity, doubtlessly strengthened by the feeling that the government has ignored the region for too long – in spite of years of promises, all roads leading to Kondoa remain unsurfaced, and are liable to be blocked in the rains. Unsurprisingly, the region is a stronghold of the opposition Civic United Front (CUF).

Apart from its **cultural tourism** programme, Kondoa itself has no real attractions, although the weird sight of gigantic baobabs growing in the town centre is memorable enough, and the town's **markets** are always fun; the main one adjoins the bus stand, and there's a tiny produce market a few blocks to the east beside a church, whose aged vendors are well worth the extra few shillings they'll winkle out of you. Few speak English, but no matter – people are eager to help out, and even the touts at the bus stand are uncommonly apologetic in their advances.

## Practicalities

Kondoa lies 3km west of the Arusha–Dodoma road, slow-going on either side of Kondoa, and potentially **treacherous** in the rains, with the road from Dodoma, especially, likely to be blocked for days at a time between March and May. The **bus stand** is at the west end of town, one block south of the main road in. NMB **bank** at the east end of town changes cash, but don't bank on traveller's cheques, and there's no ATM (yet).

Best of the **hotels** is the friendly and welcoming *New Planet Guest House* (☎0784/669322; BB ❷), 200m west of the bus stand along the continuation of the road in, whose spotless rooms, some en suite, have large and comfortable beds, fans and TVs, and a wide choice of tasty Tanzanian and continental dishes for under Tsh4000. There are more hotels along Usandawe Road (the road to Singida) which runs west from the south side of the bus stand: closest, 200m along, is the cheap but very basic *Kijengi Guest House and Tea House* (❶). Just beyond is *New Geneva Africa Hotel* (❷), with big beds and private bathrooms. Further down, 800m from the bus stand, is *Sunset Beach Guest House* (❷), which has a TV in its reception, some cheaper rooms sharing bathrooms, and food to order, but no alcohol. Or beach.

The bus stand is the focus for **street food** and coffee vendors. A popular local **bar**, also with bar food, is the cheerfully noisy 24-hour bar attached to the *New Splendid Guest House*, signposted 300m north off the main road from the bus stand, which plays good African music and has satellite TV.

## Cultural tourism around Kondoa

The **Kondoa Irangi Cultural Tourism programme** is coordinated by a young man named Moshi Changai, based both in Kondoa and Arusha, so it's best to contact him in advance in case he's out of town (☎0784/948858 or 0777/948858, Ⓦwww.tanzaniaculturaltours.com). If you're already in Kondoa, ask for him at *New Geneva Africa Hotel*. **Prices** are higher than other cultural programmes on account of vehicle costs from Kondoa: for standard tours, a full day and night for two costs around $80 each. You should get a discount for cycling tours, or if you have your own vehicle.

A welter of **activities** include rock-painting tours, birding (and bird-trapping) with locals, honey-harvesting (best immediately after rains), traditional dances, consultations with a medicine woman, school visits, and a marvellous hike in the Sambwa Hills to Ntomoko Falls where, myth has it, you might catch sight of Satu the snake, protector of the water source. Coming from **Arusha**, you might consider a seven-day round trip, which includes the Barbaig tribe, Lake Eyasi, and nights spent in traditional flat-topped *tembe* houses (or camping). A women's co-operative provides meals.

## The Kondoa-Irangi rock paintings

The area between Singida and the Maasai Steppe to the east harbours one of the world's finest and most beautiful collections of rock art, collectively known as the **Kondoa-Irangi rock paintings** (or "Kolo rock paintings"), which give a vivid and fascinating insight into not just Tanzania's but humankind's earliest recorded history, and way of thinking. A World Heritage Site since 2006, the bulk of the paintings – an estimated 1600 spread around almost two hundred different locations – are in the **Irangi Hills** east of the Babati–Kondoa road. The most recent date from just a century or two ago, but the oldest may have been daubed an astonishing 28,000 years ago, placing them among the world's most ancient known examples of human artistic expression. There are fourteen major sites, each with an average of three painted shelters within a hundred metres or so of each other. The paintings are either on vertical rock faces with overhangs above, or on angled surfaces resembling cave entrances, both offering

### Moving on from Kondoa

Most departures are at 6am, so buy your ticket in advance to be sure of a seat. There are several daily buses and daladalas to **Arusha**, none of whose companies have unblemished safety records: Mtei Express is probably the "best" of this bad bunch. Heading south, there are buses all the way to **Dar**, but to increase your chances of a safe ride beyond Dodoma (on devilishly fast tarmac), it's best to change in **Dodoma**, meaning an overnight stop. Similarly, heading to **Singida**, go to Babati or Dodoma and change there, as although the direct route from Kondoa (via Kwa Mtoro) is served by pick-ups, you risk being stranded if the vehicle doesn't go all the way. For a wild run across the Maasai Steppe to **Tanga** via Korogwe, catch Mwambao Bus (Tsh20,000) on Tuesday or Friday. It leaves at noon, stops overnight at a guesthouse along the way, and arrives at 2pm the following afternoon.

protection from millennia of rain, wind and sun. Most are located on the eastern edge of the Irangi Hills, giving striking views over the Maasai Steppe (and, more significantly, of the rising moon or sun).

Many of Tanzania's rock paintings have deteriorated at an alarming rate over the last few decades thanks to **vandalism**. Most obvious is the graffiti left by both Tanzanians and foreigners, which at two of Kondoa-Irangi's sites at least has defaced almost fifty percent of paintings that had hitherto survived thousands of years. Other panels have been disfigured by misguided "cleaning" efforts, while others have been damaged by attempts to enhance colours and contrast for photography by wetting the paintings with water, Coca-Cola or even urine. Wherever you see rock art please don't touch the paintings or the surrounding rock, as direct contact of any kind can dislodge pigments, and the traces of oil and acid in your sweat will destroy them over time. Don't wet them either: wet paintings may look better on camera, but each soaking fades and dissolves pigments, eventually washing them away.

### Practicalities

The gateway to the Irangi Hills is **Kolo** village, 27km north of Kondoa and 82km south of Babati. **Getting there** is easiest in the dry season, as in the rains the road from Babati can be extremely muddy, and the one from Kondoa is likely to be blocked. Assuming the road is open, 6am buses from Arusha to Kondoa or Dodoma pass through Kolo in the afternoon. There are also several buses and daladalas from Babati, the last leaving around 10am. From Kondoa,

---

## Kondoa-Irangi rock paintings: history, style and meaning

Kondoa-Irangi's rock paintings are remarkable not just for their quantity and quality, but for their astonishing timespan, the oldest possibly 28,000 years old (definitely 19,000), the youngest mere centenarians left by ancestors of the present-day **Sandawe and Hadzabe**, both of them traditionally **hunter-gatherers**. The Sandawe, nowadays living west of the Irangi Hills, were forced to abandon their ancient way of life a few decades ago, but the Hadzabe, around Lake Eyasi further north, still persist, albeit against increasingly unfavourable odds. In the broader context the paintings are part of a stylistically similar chain of sites looping down from the Ethiopian Highlands to southern Africa, so it's no coincidence to find that the Hadzabe and Sandawe are the only Tanzanian tribes with languages characterized by clicks, similar to the languages of the Kalahari's "San" or "Bushmen", who were also prolific rock painters.

### Style

The Kondoa-Irangi paintings vary greatly in terms of style, subject, size and colour: the most common are depictions of animals and humans done in red or orange ochre (iron oxide bound with animal fat). Particularly remarkable are the fine **elongated human figures**, often with large heads or hairstyles, whose hands generally only have three fingers, the middle one being much longer than the other two. The large heads are intriguingly similar to a "round-head" style found in the Sahara's Tassili n'Ajjer Plateau, which has provoked all sorts of crackpot theories – including proof of helmet-wearing aliens.

At Kondoa-Irangi, the figures are depicted in a variety of **postures** and activities, some standing, others dancing, playing flutes, hunting and – in an exceptional painting at Kolo B1 dubbed "The Abduction" – showing a central female figure flanked by two pairs of males. The men on the right are wearing masks (the head of one clearly resembles a giraffe's) and are attempting to drag her off, while two unmasked men on the left attempt to hold her back. Animals are generally portrayed realistically, often with an amazing **sense of movement**, and include elephant,

catch any vehicle for Babati or Arusha, or wait for the midday "Rombo Bus" which goes to Pahi, deep in the Irangi Hills, returning the next day at 4am.

With the exception of the "Kolo B" paintings, which can be visited on foot from there (6km each way), **access** to the rock art sites is really only feasible by bike, using Kolo as your base (where you should be able to rent bicycles) or by 4WD, as the paintings are spread out over a 35km radius, and both public transport and accommodation are extremely limited in the hills. Alternatively, you can arrange visits through the cultural tourism programmes in Kondoa or Babati (p.239), or as part of a safari from Arusha.

Visitors to the rock art sites are legally obliged to obtain a **permit and a guide** from the Antiquities Department on the main road in Kolo. The permit costs Tsh3000 and covers as many sites as you wish. The congenial guide-cum-curator is not paid a fortune, so a decent tip is in order. Depending on their orientation, the sites are best viewed in the **morning or late evening**, when the low sunlight enhances the paintings and lends a rich orange cast to the rock, making for wonderfully vivid photographs.

The only formal **accommodation** is *Silence Guest House* at Kolo village (❶), which lacks electricity but can arrange tasty meals. In the hills themselves, you're limited to whatever you arrange with locals, or camping, although the only vaguely official pitch is on the riverside just 4km from Kolo, close to "Kolo B" rock art site. There are no facilities, however, nor water in the dry season, and locals advise you only use the site if you're in a large group (three or four tents at least), as there have been robberies in the past.

kudu, impala, zebra and giraffe, which occur in around seventy percent of central Tanzania's sites and which give their name to the so-called **giraffe phase**, tentatively dated to 28,000–7000 BC. The later **bubalus phase** (roughly 7000–4000 BC), generally in black (charcoal, ground bones, smoke or burnt fat), depicts buffalo, elephant and rhinoceros. Of these, the highly stylized herds of elephants at Pahi are uncannily similar to engravings found in Ethiopia. The more recent paintings of the **dirty-white phase**, from 2000 to 100 years ago, were made from kaolin, animal droppings or zinc oxide and generally feature more abstract and geometric forms such as concentric circles and symbols that in places resemble letters, eyes or anthropomorphs (stylized human figures).

### Meaning

As to the meaning of the paintings, the once favoured "art for art's sake" explanation has been completely debunked, leaving us with plenty of theories but no certainties. Some hold that the paintings had a **magical-religious purpose**, whether shamanistic or as a form of sympathetic magic, the idea being to bring an animal's spirit to life by painting it, often from memory. This may have been to enable a successful hunt, or part of a more complex belief system which summoned the spirits of certain sacred animals to bring rain or fertility. The latter is evidenced by the practice of Kalahari shamans "becoming" elands when in a state of **hallucinogenic trance**. Another theory has it that rock shelters – as well as baobab trees – are **metaphors** for the "aboriginal womb" of creation. Indeed, the Sandawe *iyari* ritual surrounding the birth of twins once included rock painting, and intriguingly, the Hadzabe were also in the habit, even in the last two decades, of retouching certain paintings for ritual purposes. For **further information**, the expensive but extraordinarily beautiful *African Rock Art: Paintings and Engravings on Stone*, by David Coulson and Alec Campbell (Harry N. Abrams Publishers, New York, 2001; ⊛www.abramsbooks.com), features Kondoa-Irangi in its East Africa chapter.

▲ Kondoa-Irangi rock paintings

The weekly cycle of **produce markets** is good for roasted maize cobs, freshly grilled beef and goat meat, as well as dried fish, sugar cane, live chickens and ducks, sandals made from car tyres, all manner of clothing and, of course, the beautiful Rangi cooking pots. **Eating out** is limited to a handful of basic *mgahawa* joints in each village, which are tiny restaurants dishing up tea, coffee and simple dishes like rice with beans.

# Babati and around

The fast-growing town of **BABATI**, 105km north of Kondoa and also easily reached from Arusha, is a great place to hunker down in for a few days, as it enjoys not just a pretty location on the north shore of Lake Babati, but an excellent **cultural tourism programme**. As well as boat trips and jaunts up the nearby Mount Kwaraa (2415m), this offers encounters with local **Barbaig** and **Sandawe** communities, and challenging hikes to the top of Tanzania's fourth-highest mountain, the solitary 3417-metre volcano, **Mount Hanang**.

Babati's *raison d'être* is its position at the crossroads between Arusha, Dodoma and the Great Lakes. Given the roads' historically atrocious states of repair, Babati was an unavoidable stop, so much so that it became a thriving market centre. The land around Babati is also fertile, quite unlike the semi-desert tracts to the north, and is a major producer of maize. Now with a population of over forty thousand, Babati is the capital of newly formed Manyara Region.

The town's major cultural event is the grand **monthly market** (*mnada*), held on the seventeenth of each month, 4km south of town on a hillside along the

Kondoa road. The event attracts thousands of people, many from outlying districts, and for some town-dwellers the market provides a perfect excuse to bunk off work and indulge in grilled beef, fresh sugar-cane juice and local brews at inflated prices (many are the tall stories of hung-over revellers waking up in the early hours to see packs of hyenas scavenging over the remains). The cattle auction is perhaps the day's highlight, and draws Maasai and Barbaig from all around. All in all, a great day out.

## Practicalities

Babati lies 68km beyond the end of the sealed road from Arusha (68km that were meant to have been surfaced years ago). There are several daily buses from Arusha, Kondoa and Singida, one or two from Tanzania's northwest, and – weather permitting – Dodoma. The **bus stand** is just off the main road in the town centre. It has a chaotic reputation, not helped by the cultural tourism programme employing **touts**. As there's no guarantee they're not just thieves, decline their services as politely as you can and make your own way to a hotel or the programme; directions are given in the box below.

### Accommodation

Try to arrive early as Babati's new status as regional capital means decent **guesthouses** fill up quickly. Enquire at *Kahembe's Guest House* for **camping** ($5): you can pitch a tent at Mr Kahembe's house 2km east of town, or on his farm at the foot of Bambaay Hill, 10km away.

Classic Guest House 200m beyond the cultural tourism programme office on the same road ☎0784/390940. An excellent budget choice, with well-kept rooms (some en suite) with large box nets, and safe parking. BB ❶
Dodoma Transport Motel On the highway ☎027/253 1089. Very cheap and clean en-suite rooms, plus a decent restaurant. ❶
Kahembe's Guest House Behind the cultural tourism programme office ☎0784/397477, ⓦwww.kahembeculturalsafaris.com. Eight small en-suite rooms set around a courtyard, with

mosquito nets, hot showers, TV and full English breakfast, but pricey if not included as part of a trip with the cultural tourism programme. BB ❸
Paa Paa Motel By the bus stand ☎027/253 1111. Another good cheapie (and often full), with clean en-suite singles (no hot water) and doubles sharing bathrooms. Also has a small restaurant, lively bar, and safe parking. ❶
Paris Guest House Turn right beyond *Classic Guest House* ☎0784/721958. Another good choice, similar to the *Classic*, all en-suite rooms, also with safe parking. ❶

### Babati-Hanang cultural tourism programme

The reason for the steady trickle of tourists to Babati is its long-established **cultural tourism programme**, whose office is at *Kahembe's Guest House*. To get here from the bus stand, walk back along the main road towards Arusha for 200m until you reach *Ango Bar & Garden* on your right. Turn left, and the office is 200m along on the right. **Costs** average $60 per person for 24 hours, excluding transport ($5 for a bicycle, $5 per canoe), drinks and tips. A portion of the fees is used to improve primary school facilities.

The programme offers a wide variety of flexible itineraries, including half-day dugout outings on **Lake Babati**, climbs up **Mount Hanang** (see p.241), various **cycling** expeditions, walks over several days in the Mang'ati Plains to meet the traditional **Barbaig** (who may put on a mock fight to illustrate how they got their name; see p.242), **rock art** tours in the Irangi Hills (see preceding section), encounters with former hunter-gatherers the **Sandawe**, and various options for short-term **volunteers** combining hands-on help with wildlife safaris.

## Eating, drinking and entertainment

Lamentably, Babati's **fish** – for which it has long been famous – is currently trucked in dry from Lake Victoria, as overfishing in Lake Babati collapsed stocks and prompted a ban. Still, there's good **food** to be had. The thatched *Ango Bar & Garden* on the highway, with a nicely atmospheric wood-and-thatch interior and some tables outside, is best at lunchtime for its regal buffet. Breakfasts are also good (tasty snacks), but evening fare is very limited. Also good for lunch, especially Indian-style, is *Abida Best Bites Café*, 100m south of the cultural tourism programme office. For dinner, you can't go wrong with the goat meat *trupa* (a particularly tasty stew of pretty much everything) at *Dolphin Bar*, between the cultural tourism programme office and *Classic Guest House*. It also does good *nyama choma*, as does *Paa Paa Motel*.

There are a multitude of **bars** to choose from. Ever popular both day and night (when satellite TV is the big draw) is the one at *Paa Paa Motel*, which has tables facing the bus stand. *Ango Bar & Garden* is also good, whilst the large *makuti*-thatched *Dolphin Bar* is the town's main nightspot, with **live music** some nights, and tapes of dance music otherwise.

## Around Babati

A pleasant way to spend a day is to visit **Lake Babati**, a 2km stroll south of the cultural tourism programme office: walk down the Kondoa road, and take the track to your right that starts at an old mango tree facing the District Court. The lake – one of few freshwater bodies of water in the Rift Valley – is a paradise for **birds**: over three hundred species have been recorded so far, including flamingos.

Given the lack of a known outlet, the lake's level varies wildly according to the rains: during the 1997–98 El Niño rains, it rose so high that it flooded the Kondoa road in two places – a boon for fishermen who made a tidy profit ferrying people across. Parts of the town itself were also flooded, and locals joke that all they had to do for their dinner was reach out of a window to grab a fish. The event prompted an NGO to build an overflow pipeline from the lake to a river at lower altitude, which should prevent such flooding in future. The lake is said to be free of bilharzia, and kids are happy swimming in it, but not adults – the resident **hippos** are unpredictable and definitely dangerous, so swim or canoe at your own risk.

Although you don't really need a guide – you can follow the water's edge for most of the way, though a couple of swampy areas force you briefly back to the road – taking one from the cultural tourism programme is a good way to meet locals, and also gets you on a wobbly dugout in search of hippo (at your own risk) and, if or when the ban on fishing is lifted, chinwags with local fishermen.

### Mount Kwaraa

The flat-topped mountain rising 3km east of Babati is **Mount Kwaraa**. Its 2415-metre peak is swathed in heavy forest and usually also in mist, so don't expect panoramic views if you climb it. What you will see is some fascinating and virtually untouched forest. The mountain is used by migratory herds of elephant and buffalo: you almost certainly won't see them, but the presence of fresh dung and crushed undergrowth is enough to give most spines a tingle. The lower slopes, up to around 1750m, are mainly scrub, with dry montane forest and stunted woodland dominating the higher sections, which is part of the protected **Ufiome Forest Reserve**. The mountain can be climbed in a day, but two days (with a tent) is preferable as you'd have much more time to explore.

The first bus to **Arusha** leaves at 4am, the last around 2pm. Heading south towards **Kondoa or Dodoma** is no problem in the dry season, with at least two buses a day, but the stretch beyond Kondoa can be impassable during and after heavy rain (usually March to May, sometimes also November or December). Most buses leave around 6–7am, although late risers can buy a ticket a day or two before for a seat on a through bus from Arusha to **Singida or Mwanza**; they pass by between 10.30am and 1pm. The best company for all routes is Mtei Express: their buses may be old and not overly reliable, but the company has a safer reputation than the others, not that that's saying all that much.

If you're **driving**, ensure your vehicle is in good condition before proceeding west or south, as the roads are a trial. Also, be sure not to get caught out after dark: the road to Singida is known for nocturnal **car-jackings** and hold-ups.

To go above the forest line you need a guide, and a $30 permit from the Forestry Office in Babati, along the Kondoa road. The cultural tourism programme can arrange this. If you have the energy, **Bambaay Hill** – part of Mount Kwaraa – can also be climbed, though this is better over two days, giving you time to visit the Gorowa village of Maisaka, whose elders are happy regaling guests with traditional tales and fables.

# The road to Singida

The road between Babati and Singida is one of Tanzania's most beautiful, running for much of its 178km along the southern flank of the Rift Valley's Malbadow Escarpment and past the lone volcanic peak of **Mount Hanang**. Starting from Babati, the road crosses the floodplain of Lake Babati, then twists up into the hills amidst beautiful and ever-changing scenery before levelling out in a broad valley, with Mount Hanang to the south and the long barrier of the Malbadow Escarpment to the west. The road forks at **Ndareda**, 26km from Babati. A right turn takes you along a minor road (difficult or impassable in the rains) to the lively market town of **Dongobesh** and on to **Mbulu**, from where there's an even less-travelled but stunningly beautiful route north to **Karatu**, near the eastern entrance of Ngorongoro Conservation Area (upwards of 4hr from Ndareda). The route makes a fascinating diversion from the Northern Safari circus, but you'll need your own 4WD and ideally an experienced driver. This is the land of the **Iraqw**, a Cushitic tribe which is culturally more akin to Ethiopians and northern Kenyans than to the Bantu-speakers who dominate Tanzania; for more about them, see p.365.

## Mount Hanang

Taking the left fork at Ndareda, the Babati–Singida road veers south towards Tanzania's fourth-highest mountain, **Mount Hanang**. An almost perfect volcanic cone, it rises up from the Mang'ati Plains to three summits, the highest at 3417m. Hanang is sacred to the Barbaig and Gorowa (or Fiome) tribes: it's tall enough to condense water vapour from clouds, making **Lake Balangida** one of the Rift Valley's most important watering points. The high water table also supports a surprisingly rich groundwater forest on the mountain's lower slopes. Higher up, this gives way to montane and upper montane forest, with

## The Barbaig

The **Mang'ati Plains**, an unremittingly dry expanse of savanna extending south from Mount Hanang, are at first sight a deeply inhospitable place. Yet they're home to some 200,000 **Barbaig** (or Barabaig), a semi-nomadic, cattle-herding people distantly related to the Maasai. The key to their existence is the freshwater **Lake Balangida**, on the far side of Mount Hanang. The lake is fed by the mountain, which ensures that even when it's dry (an increasingly common occurrence), the deep wells that have been dug around its periphery still contain enough water for the Barbaig's cherished herds.

Tall, handsome and proud, the Barbaig are at first glance very similar to the Maasai. They dress alike, and cattle occupy a pivotal place in their culture. Like the Maasai, too, their society is organized into clans (*doshinga*) and age-sets (formalized generations of people of similar age, who undergo the various life stage ceremonies at the same time) that govern pasture and water rights. But for all their similarities, there's no love lost between the two. The Maasai have two names for the Barbaig. One is **Mbulu**, which means "unintelligent people". The other, reserved for the Barbaig alone, is **Il-Mang'ati**, meaning "the enemy", a simple tag which, coming from East Africa's most feared and warlike people, is almost a compliment. The name Barbaig itself comes from *bar* (to beat) and *baig* (sticks), alluding to a unique dance that is still performed today, in which fights are mimicked using sticks for weapons – all good training.

The Barbaig are one of nineteen tribes that originally made up a broader cluster of people called **Datooga** (or Tatoga). Like the Maasai and Kenya's Kalenjin, the Datooga are linguistically classed as Nilotic, meaning that they share a common origin, presumed to be in Sudan's Nile Valley. A fascinating relic from this time, which could also explain the extreme ritual importance of cattle in all Nilotic societies, is the Barbaig word for God, *Aseeta*, which is related to the Kalenjin word *Asiis*, which also means sun. Both words have their root in the name of the ancient Egyptian goddess **Isis**, who wore a solar disc and the horns of a cow and was the focus of a cattle and

trees up to 20m tall on the wetter southern, eastern and northern slopes, and dry montane forest on the western slopes. Above 2100m the forest gives way to grassland, thicket and bushland, while above 2700m moorland predominates.

Despite recurring problems with illegal logging, much of Hanang's forest has survived intact, apparently thanks to the Gorowa belief in **underground earth spirits** called Netlangw. The Netlangw are said to live under large trees where springs emerge, which makes Mount Hanang's girdling groundwater forest of prime importance. They are guardians of the water; if offended, say by forest clearance, they move away, taking the water with them. The logic is clear and unassailable: destroy trees and you destroy your water supply.

### Katesh

Whichever route you take to climb Hanang, first stop is **KATESH**, 76km southwest of Babati, where you should visit the Forestry Department to pay $30 for every day you plan to spend on the mountain. The **bus stand** is halfway along the road through town, and is nothing more than a tree with the Mtei Express timetable nailed to its trunk. The ride from Babati takes about ninety minutes, and there are at least three buses a day from Arusha – basically, any service that goes to Singida.

The town is liveliest on the tenth and eleventh of each month during the *mnada* **market**, held 2km south of town along the Singida road. The market's popularity explains Katesh's profusion of pretty decent **guesthouses** (all ❶) from east to west along the Babati–Singida road, these include the *Colt* (the best,

fertility cult throughout much of antiquity. According to Roman mythology – which adopted many Egyptian cults – the beautiful Isis, whom the Romans called Io, was kidnapped by an amorous Jupiter, but her mother, Juno, gave chase. Rather than give her back, Jupiter rather unfairly turned Io into a cow, and compounded the injustice by calling down a bumble bee from the heavens, which he commanded to sting the cow. Not terribly enchanted with this treatment, the miserable Io fled to Egypt, where she cried so much that her tears formed the Nile.

The Datooga's southward **migration** is believed to have started around 3000 years ago, possibly prompted by massive climate changes that coincided with the expansion of the Sahara. Around 1500 AD, the Datooga arrived at Mount Elgon on the Kenya–Uganda border, where they stayed until the eighteenth century, when they migrated south once more into Tanzania. The Datooga first settled at Ngorongoro before being pushed on by the Maasai, after which they separated into various tribes, many of which have now been assimilated by others. Lamentably, the Barbaig's southward migration continues even today. Loss of their ranges to commercial ranches, flower farms and seed-bean plantations, and encroachment by Maasai (who have themselves been pushed south by the creation of the Serengeti and Tarangire national parks) mean that the Barbaig are among Tanzania's poorest people. Child mortality rates are high, as is the incidence of cattle disease. The fact that none of this used to be the case supports the Barbaig claim that nothing other than the loss of their traditional land has caused these problems, but unfortunately the scattered nature of Barbaig society means that they have largely been absent from politics, and have consequently been marginalized. Their latest efforts to regain access to their land via a series of legal actions in the courts have stalled on the absurd grounds that they lack legally recognized title to the land.

For more information on the problems Barbaig culture faces, see *Passions Lost* by Charles Lane (Initiatives Publishers, Nairobi, 1996).

with en-suite rooms), *Matunda*, *Tip-Top* (by the bus stand, also with en-suite rooms), and *Hanang View*. *Kabwogi's Hotel* has good **food**. There's a small **daily market** on the east side of the road beyond *Hanang View Guest House*. The NMB **bank**, past the police station on the left on the way out south, may change money, but you shouldn't bank on it, as it were.

### Climbing Mount Hanang

The easiest way to arrange a **climb** is through Babati's cultural tourism programme (see box, p.239), which also offers an excellent four-day trip combining an ascent with a visit to a Barbaig community. They charge $155–170 for a two-day ascent, including transport from Babati. For general advice on mountaineering, read the Kilimanjaro section in Chapter 5. **Camping** is possible on all routes, but you need to be fully self-sufficient; take enough water as there's none near the summit and no guarantee of any further down. Don't underestimate the mountain: it gets pretty cold at 3417m so come suitably equipped. Altitude sickness isn't a major worry – you might get a headache, but nothing more serious.

The shortest and most popular ascent is the **Katesh route**, from Katesh up the southwestern ridge: five to six hours to the summit, camping at 3000m, and a three-to four-hour descent the following day. You can go up and down in one day if the physical challenge is more important than enjoyment, but do start early. Allow time to arrange transport from Babati to Katesh, and to pay the forest fee, so count on a minimum of two or three days in total.

To vary the scenery, descending via the **Ngendabi route** is recommended, or alternatively ascending along it and descending to Katesh. The route starts 16km (3hr) northwest from Katesh at Ngendabi village, which levies a $2.50 fee on visitors. Accommodation in Ngendabi may be offered informally by teachers from the primary school, but shouldn't be counted on. The main alternative to the Katesh and Ngendabi routes is the **Giting route**, from Giting village on the northeast side of the mountain. You might need your own 4WD, as public transport is currently suspended on account of the bad road. You'll also need to visit Katesh first to pay the forest fee. Accommodation along this route has been planned for years to take advantage of the beautiful view of Lake Balangida; enquire whether this has finally happened in Babati.

# Singida

The town of **SINGIDA**, 178km southwest of Babati, lies at the northern end of a Central Line railway branch from Dodoma, and is also an overnight stop for trucks plying between Lake Victoria and Arusha or Dodoma. Improvements in the roads (and new regulations letting buses roll on until midnight) mean that only a few buses now spend the night here, but if you do need a stop somewhere between Babati and Mwanza, Singida is the most attractive place for it, surrounded by a boulder-strewn, kopje-studded landscape and flanked by two **freshwater lakes**, Singida to the north, Kindai to the south. The town itself is built around several more outcrops, and, coming from Babati, the road threads through a narrow "gate" made from two boulders, one painted with a big advert for Salama condoms. Singida's main tribe is **Nyaturu**, whose last chief, Senge Mghenyi, achieved fame during the military mutiny of 1964. To pledge his support to President Nyerere, he walked all the way from Singida to State House in Dar es Salaam, accompanied by a hyena – the traditional guardian of Nyaturu chiefs.

On the west side of town, 100m from Lake Singida, **Singida Regional Museum** could be worth a visit (ask for Makumbusho ya Mkoa; ☎026/250 2449; Mon–Fri 9am–6pm; free, but tips appreciated). It's in the unmarked building on your right, 200m beyond *J-Four Singida Motel*. If no one's around, ask at the District Council nearby. Singida is known for **chickens**, which are sold as far away as Dar (hence the sorry spectacle of fowl stuffed into wicker baskets at the bus stand). The town's other speciality is especially fine **honey** (*asali*), sold in the market.

## Practicalities

The **train station** is 2km southwest of town along Karume Road; the **bus station** is just off Karume Road in the centre. NBC **bank**, between the post office and phone office at the start of Mwanza (Shinyanga) road, has an ATM.

There are dozens of cheap and currently quite decent **hotels** (something that may change given fewer overnight stops), but be sure of a good mosquito net – there may be zillions of the whiny vampires about. There are two good options on the Babati–Mwanza road, three blocks north of the bus station (walk up Karume Road until you get to the TRA building on your right). Cheapest is the *Lutheran Centre*, 200m west of the junction (no phone; ❶), with good twin-bed rooms opening onto a courtyard, some with Western-style toilets and showers. Seven hundred metres further west, past the hospital,

## Moving on from Singida

The roads around Singida are much improved but asphalt has still not arrived (one day, *mungu akipenda* – God willing). Most buses leave at 6am. Mtei Express is best for **Arusha** and **Mwanza**. NBS Coach also runs to Arusha (Wed, Thurs & Sat), and is the main company for **Tabora** (currently Wed & Sat). **Trains** to Dodoma leave at 7am on Monday, Thursday and Saturday.

is *J-Four Singida Motel* (☎026/250 2193; ❷). Often empty and slightly run-down, it does boast a lovely garden (and bar), complete with tables under parasols, children's swings and mongooses. Heading east from the TRA building towards Babati, turn right after 100m for Sokoine Road and two more choices: the ever-popular if slightly pricey *Stanley Hotel* (☎026/250 2351; ❶–❷), which has TVs in its en-suite rooms; and *Cheyo Guest House*, beside it but accessed from the back (☎026/250 2258; ❶), whose good-value doubles share bathrooms and powerful showers.

Only *Cheyo* of the places to stay doesn't have a **restaurant**, though it does have a bar. The bus stand, and Soko Street on its northeast side, have plenty more **bars and cheap eateries**, but don't expect much of the town's other restaurants: trade is slack.

# Travel details

## Buses and daladalas

Asterisks denote routes liable to be blocked during the rains (usually Nov & Dec and most of March–May).

**Babati** to: Arusha (5 daily; 4–5hr); Dodoma (1–2 daily*; 7–10hr); Katesh (1 daily; 1hr 30min); Kondoa (2–3 daily*; 3–5hr); Mwanza (2 daily; 11–14hr); Singida (2–3 daily; 4–5hr); Tabora (2 weekly*; 24hr).

**Dodoma** to: Arusha (1–2 daily*; 12–14hr); Dar (hourly until noon; 6–8hr); Iringa (4–6 daily; 9hr); Kondoa (5 daily*; 4–5hr); Morogoro (1–2 hourly until noon; 3–4hr); Mwanza (2–3 daily*; 12–15hr); Singida (3–4 daily*; 6–7hr); Tabora (6 weekly; 9–12hr); Tanga (3 weekly; 9–10hr).

**Kondoa** to: Arusha (3–4 daily*; 8–9hr); Babati (3–4 daily*; 3–5hr); Dar (3 daily*; 11hr); Dodoma (5 daily*; 4–5hr); Kolo (5–6 daily*; 1hr); Morogoro (3 daily*; 8–9hr); Pahi (1 daily*; 2–3hr); Tanga (2 weekly; 24hr).

**Mang'ula** to: Dar (2 daily; 5–6hr); Mikumi (2 daily plus hourly Coasters; 1hr 30min–2hr 30min); Morogoro (2 daily plus occasional Coasters; 4hr 30min).

**Mikumi** to: Dar (hourly to 4pm; 5hr); Iringa (hourly; 3hr); Mang'ula (2 daily plus hourly Coasters; 1hr 30min–2hr 30min); Mbeya (hourly; 8–9hr); Morogoro (hourly; 2–3hr).

**Morogoro** to: Arusha (daily; 8–10hr); Dar (1–2 hourly until 4pm; 2hr 45min); Dodoma (1–2 hourly until noon; 3–4hr); Iringa (hourly; 6hr); Mang'ula (2 daily plus occasional Coasters; 4hr 30min); Mbeya (hourly; 11–12hr); Mikumi (hourly; 2–3hr).

**Singida** to: Arusha (4–5 daily; 8–9hr); Babati (3–4 daily; 4–5hr); Biharamulo (5 weekly; 10–12hr); Bukoba (5 weekly*; 14hr); Dar (2 daily*; 13–16hr); Dodoma (3–4 daily*; 6–7hr); Morogoro (1–2 daily*; 9–10hr); Mwanza (2 daily; 6–8hr); Tabora (2 weekly*; 6hr).

## Flights

Airline codes used below are: CA (Coastal Aviation), SA (Safari Airlink) and ZA (ZanAir). Where more than one flies to the same destination, the airline with most frequent flights or shortest journey times is listed first.

**Dodoma** to: Arusha (CA: daily; 55min); Ruaha (CA: 45min); Selous (CA: 3hr 5min); Tarangire (CA: 1hr 25min) – all these "on inducement", meaning with enough passengers.

**Selous** to: Arusha (CA: daily; 5hr); Dar (CA, SA, ZA: 5 daily 35min–1hr 15min); Manyara (CA: daily; 5hr 30min); Ruaha (SA, CA: 2 daily; 1hr 30min); Tarangire (CA: if enough passengers; 5hr); Zanzibar (CA, ZA: 4 daily; 1hr 5min–1hr 40min).

## Trains

**Dodoma** to: Dar (3 weekly; 13hr); Kigoma (3 weekly; 22hr 30min); Morogoro (3 weekly; 6hr); Mwanza (2 weekly; 22hr 30min); Singida (3 weekly; 8hr); Tabora (3 weekly; 9hr 30min).
**Mang'ula** to: Dar (2 weekly; 7hr).

**Morogoro** to: Dar (3 weekly; 5hr 30min); Dodoma (3 weekly; 7hr); Kigoma (3 weekly; 30hr 30min); Mwanza (2 weekly; 30hr 30min); Tabora (3 weekly; 17hr 30min).
**Selous** (various stations) to: Dar (2 weekly; 4hr–5hr 30min); Mbeya (2 weekly; 14–18hr).
**Singida** to: Dodoma (3 weekly; 9hr 30min).

# The northern
# highlands

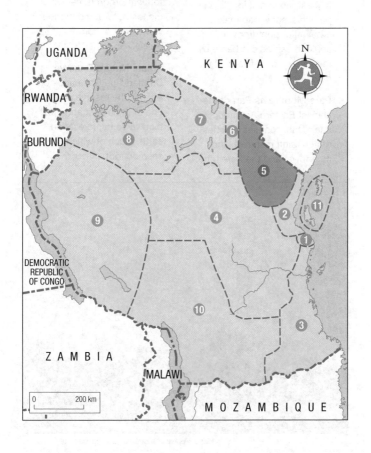

CHAPTER 5    # Highlights

✳ **Coffee** A brew of Kilimanjaro's heavenly *arabica* at Moshi's *The Coffee Shop* might just convince you to never go instant again. See p.255

✳ **Mount Kilimanjaro** Africa's highest mountain, its perennial snow cap makes a beautiful sight from any angle. It can be climbed – by the hardy – over five to eight days. See p.262

✳ **Pare Mountains** Part of the ancient Eastern Arc mountain chain, this contains patches of rich rainforest, highland meadows, and the Pare tribe, renowned for their healers and witches. See p.277

✳ **West Usambara** Also part of the Eastern Arc, and home to the welcoming Sambaa tribe. Best visited through Lushoto's excellent cultural tourism programme, which blends nature and glorious views with culture. See p.283

✳ **Amani Nature Reserve** Dubbed "the Galapagos of Africa", the reserve contains one of the oldest and most biodiverse rainforests on earth, much of which can be seen on foot. See p.295

▲ Herd of elephants and the snow-capped Mount Kilimanjaro

# The northern highlands

T he lush and fertile **northern highlands** are one of the most scenically dramatic areas in Tanzania, running inland from the coast through a series of mountain chains and culminating in the towering massif of **Mount Kilimanjaro**, Africa's highest peak. The region's attractions are manifold, ranging from the arduous trek to the summit of Kilimanjaro itself to less strenuous but hugely enjoyable hikes in the **Usambara** and **Pare mountains**, whose great age and climatic stability has resulted in the development of a unique and extraordinarily rich plant and animal life. The jewel is **Amani Nature Reserve** in the Eastern Usambaras, which protects some superb montane rainforest.

The region's main centre is **Moshi**, best known to visitors as the base for climbing Kilimanjaro, of which – clear skies permitting – it has fantastic views. The nicest town in the highlands, however, is **Lushoto**, capital of the Western Usambaras, whose friendly inhabitants, cool climate, spectacular vistas and well-established **cultural tourism programme** entice many visitors to stay longer than planned. Indeed the same could be said of the entire northern highlands – take your time; it's a vividly beautiful and hugely rewarding region to explore.

# Kilimanjaro Region

At almost 6000m, the massive volcanic hulk of **Mount Kilimanjaro** is Africa's highest mountain, and dominates much of the region named after it, spiritually as well as physically and economically. Although some forty thousand tourists are drawn to "Kili" every year by the challenge of trekking to the summit, only a few spend more than a couple of days in the towns at its base, of which the bustling and friendly **Moshi** is by far the biggest.

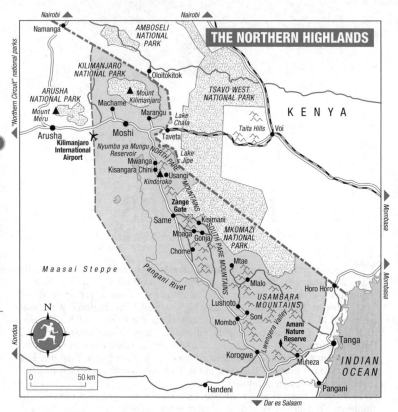

Efforts have recently been made, however, to spread the economic benefits of tourism, resulting in community-based cultural tourism programmes being set up in **Marangu** and **Machame**, the villages at the start of Kilimanjaro's most popular hiking routes, and close to the band of tropical rainforest that skirts much of its base. The programmes include a variety of half- and full-day hikes into the forests to see waterfalls, hot springs, and places with spiritual or historical significance. Similar trips can be made from Moshi itself, although little is properly organized.

# Moshi

An hour's drive east of Arusha, the busy commercial town of **MOSHI** is the capital of Kilimanjaro Region and beautifully located beneath the summit of the mountain. The views are unforgettable, especially when the blanket of cloud that clings to Kili by day dissipates – with luck – just before sunset, to reveal glimpses of Kibo and Mawenzi peaks: accompanied by the tweeting of thousands of wheeling swallows. The mountain's influence is pervasive. Meltwater streams permit year-round agriculture, especially of **coffee**, while the mountain is alluded to in the town's name: *moshi* in Kiswahili means "smoke", either from Kilimanjaro's last, minor eruption in the 1700s, or because of the smoke-like cloud that often covers the mountain. The town itself is refreshingly open and spacious, with broad, tree-lined avenues and leafy suburbs, and – despite a population of over 200,000 – it's decidedly more laid-back than Arusha. There's a wealth of good hotels to suit all pockets, and a few excellent restaurants, too, making the town an ideal base for the climb up Kilimanjaro.

## Arrival, town transport and information

International **flights** land at Kilimanjaro International Airport (KIA), 34km west of Moshi off the road to Arusha. See p.303 for details about arriving there and travelling to Moshi. Most public transport stops at the combined **bus and daladala stand**, south of the clock tower between Market Street and Mawenzi Road, though some bus companies have their own terminals: Dar Express is on Boma Road, Kilimanjaro Express on Rengua Street, and Akamba by the *Buffalo Hotel*.

Passengers arriving on one of the **Nairobi shuttle buses** can be dropped at any central hotel: Impala finish at their office on Kibo Road, next to *Chrisburger*; Bobby Shuttle next to the Duma Internet Café, just down from *The Coffee Shop* on Hill St, and Riverside at the THB Building, on Boma Road. **Flycatchers** touting for hotels and hiking companies are quick to spot new arrivals and, though harmless, can be persistent and intimidating to new arrivals.

### Town transport

Moshi's compact centre is easy to negotiate on foot and, unless you're carrying visibly tempting valuables, **safety** isn't much of an issue either. The exceptions

## The Chagga

Numbering over a million, the **Chagga** occupy the southern and eastern slopes of Kilimanjaro and are among East Africa's wealthiest and most highly educated people. Their wealth stems from the fortunate conjunction of favourable climatic conditions and their own agricultural ingenuity. Watered by year-round snow and ice melt, the volcanic soils of Kilimanjaro's lower slopes are extremely fertile and are exploited by the Chagga using a sophisticated system of intensive irrigation and continuous fertilization with animal manure, permitting year-round cultivation that can support one of Tanzania's highest human population densities. *Arabica* coffee has been the Chagga's primary cash crop since colonial times, although maize and bananas remain staple foods. The cultivation of bananas is traditionally a man's work, as is that of eleusine seed (*ulezi*), which is boiled and mixed with mashed plantain to brew a local beer (*mbege*), still used as a form of payment to elders in their role as conflict arbiters.

In the past, the potential for such conflicts was great: even today there are some four hundred different Chagga clans – indeed it's barely a century since the Chagga finally coalesced into a distinct and unified tribe. Most are related to the Kamba of Kenya, who migrated northwards from Kilimanjaro a few centuries ago during a great drought. Other clans descend from the Taita, another Kenyan tribe, and others from the pastoral Maasai, whose influence is visible in the importance attached to cattle as bridewealth payments and in the grouping of men into age-sets analogous to the Maasai system. Today, the Chagga wield considerable political and financial clout, because of both their long contact with European models of education and Christianity (both of which dominate modern-day political and economic life) and their involvement in the coffee business, which remains the region's economic mainstay in spite of volatile world prices. Indeed, the Chagga are the one tribe you're almost guaranteed to meet in even the most obscure corners of Tanzania, working as traders, merchants, officials, teachers and doctors.

are the Kuheshimo area, about a kilometre south of the central market, and the bus and daladala stand, which has pickpockets and bag snatchers. The cheapest way to the suburbs is by **daladala**, nicknamed *vifordi* – alluding to the town's first-ever vehicle, a Model-T Ford. Most leave from the north side of the bus and daladala stand; journeys cost Tsh300. Daladalas heading along the Dar–Arusha highway can also be caught on Kibo Road.

**Taxis** park outside larger hotels, at major road junctions, around the bus and daladala stand, and on the west side of the Central Market on Market Street. A journey within town costs Tsh1500; rides to the outskirts shouldn't cost over Tsh3000 though expect to be asked for much more.

### Information

Moshi lacks a **tourist office**, so don't be misled by hiking companies displaying "tourist information" signboards; it's just a ruse to get you inside. The best source of information is the annual *Moshi Guide* (Tsh4000), containing listings of pretty much everything you'll need, which is available at *The Coffee Shop* on Hill Street. There's also the informative **website**, Ⓦ www.kiliweb.com and you'll find **notice boards** at *The Coffee Shop* and a smaller one outside the *Indoitaliano Restaurant* but be warned that not all the safari and hiking companies featured on it are reputable or licensed.

## Accommodation

**Town centre hotels** are plentiful and generally good value, though all but the very cheapest have hiked-up "non-resident" (tourist) rates. A handful have rooftop "summit bars" for views of Kili; one or two also have some rooms with views. Given Moshi's low altitude (810m), **mosquitoes** and malaria are prevalent: good-sized mosquito nets are preferable to window screens and/or bug spray.

The cheapest and most cheerful **campsite** is the *Golden Shower*, 2km east of town (Ⓣ027/275 1990; $3 per person), which also has a restaurant and bar, weekend discos, and plays host to occasional overland trucks, when it can get a bit noisy. *Green Hostels* also allows camping ($3 per person). To reach the out-of-town accommodation, you'll need to take a daladala or taxi, unless you're in training for a Kili climb.

### Town Centre

**Budget**

**Backpackers' Hotel** Mawenzi Rd Ⓣ027/275 5159, Ⓔ hoteldacosta@yahoo.com. An attractive cheapie with creaky floorboards and a good restaurant-bar on the second floor with a street-view terrace, but no Kili views. Rooms (sharing bathrooms) have fans, nets, and a table and chair. The twin-bed rooms are fine, but the cell-like singles are hot and stuffy. Breakfast included. Dorm $5. ❷

**Buffalo Hotel** New St Ⓣ027/275 0270, Ⓔ buffalocompany2000@yahoo.com. An affordable, clean and well-run three-storey hotel. The mostly en-suite rooms have fans, box nets and phones; the better ones are larger, or have balconies facing Kilimanjaro. There's also a restaurant, free luggage store, and good adjacent internet café. Breakfast included. ❷

**Green Hostels** Nkomo Rd Ⓣ027/275 3198, Ⓔ greenhostels2@yahoo.co.uk. A friendly, family-run place, with ten rooms situated in peaceful grounds. The three en-suite rooms with bathtubs are reasonably good value, even though there's not always hot water; the ones with shared bathrooms are less enticing. Food and drinks are available. Breakfast included. ❷

**New Coffee Tree Hotel** Off Old Moshi Rd Ⓣ027/275 1382. Popular with budget travellers, this charmless four-storey block (with lift) is central Moshi's largest hotel, and OK if you don't mind linoleum floors, saggy beds and the occasional cold shower. Rooms, with or without bathroom (those without have washbasins) are large and breezy, though most lack fans and the nets can be too small. The hotel has one towering advantage: matchless Kilimanjaro views from almost half its rooms, and

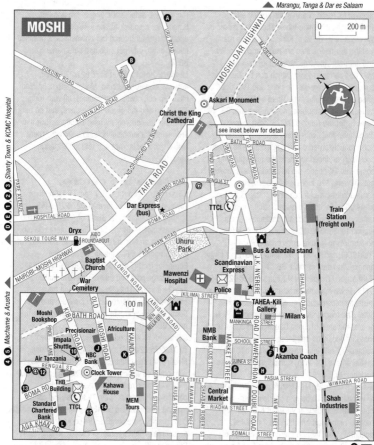

▲ Marangu, Tanga & Dar es Salaam

# MOSHI

0    200 m

URU ROAD

SOKOINE ROAD

IKWORO RD

MOSHI-DAR HIGHWAY

KILIMANJARO ROAD

Shanty Town & KCMC Hospital

**A** Askari Monument

Christ the King Cathedral

see inset below for detail

BATH ROAD

OLD MOSHI ROAD

GHALLA ROAD

KIBO ROAD

KAUNDA ROAD

RINDI LANE

Rengua St

NGORONGORO AVENUE

TAIFA ROAD

HOROMBO ROAD

@

PARE AVENUE

HOSPITAL ROAD

SEKOU TOURÉ WAY

Dar Express (bus)

BOMA ROAD

**TTCL** ✆

Train Station (freight only)

Oryx

KIBO ROUNDABOUT

AGA KHAN ROAD

Uhuru Park

★ Bus & daladala stand

NAIROBI-MOSHI HIGHWAY

Baptist Church

RENGUA ST

FLORIDA ROAD

Mawenzi Hospital

Scandinavian Express

J.K. NYERERE

War Cemetery

(KILIMA) STREET

Police ★

KILIMA STREET

Machame & Arusha

0    100 m

OLD (ARUSHA ROAD)

BATH ROAD

Moshi Bookshop

Precisionair

Africulture

**J**

MOSHI ROAD

KAUNDA ROAD

BEN BELLA ST

MANKINGA

**6** TAHEA-Kili Gallery

Milan's

MANKINGA ROAD / STREET

Impala Shuttle

**10**

Air Tanzania

RINDI RD

KIBO ROAD

**J** NBC Bank

**K**

NMB Bank

SCHOOL STREET

MAWENZI ROAD / STREET

**7** Akamba Coach

RENGUA ST

**11** @ **12**

THB Building

BOMA RD

✆ Clock Tower

**8**

SEUSS STREET

GUINEA ST

**G**

PASUA STREET

**H**

WIWANDA ROAD

**13**

Kahawa House

CHAGGA STREET

KENYATTA STREET

KUSA STREET

SHARON ROBERT STREET

Central Market

DOUBLE ROAD

NEW STREET

Shah Industries

KARAAMA STREET

Standard Chartered Bank

**TTCL**

MEM Tours

**14**

RIADHA STREET

AGA KHAN RD

**15**

**L**

SOMALI STREET

GHALLA ROAD

MARKET STREET

**9** ▼

| ACCOMMODATION | | EATING | | DRINKING & NIGHTLIFE | |
|---|---|---|---|---|---|
| Backpackers' Hotel | I | Abbas Ally Hot Bread Shop | 13 | Glacier Bar | 1 |
| Bristol Cottages Kilimanjaro | L | Central Garden | 15 | La Liga | 9 |
| Buffalo Hotel | F | Chrisburger | 10 | Malindi Club | 12 |
| Green Hostels | B | The Coffee Shop | 6 | Pub Alberto | 10 |
| Keys Hotel | A | Corner Café | 11 | Sal Salinero | D |
| Kilimanjaro Crane Hotel | K | El Rancho | 3 | The Watering Hole | 5 |
| Kilimanjaro Impala Hotel | E | Friendship Restaurant | 14 | | |
| Kindoroko Hotel | H | Indoitaliano Restaurant | 7 | | |
| Leopard Hotel | G | Mama Clementina's | 4 | | |
| New Coffee Tree Hotel | J | Leopard Hotel | G | | |
| Sal Salinero | D | Panda Chinese | 2 | | |
| YMCA Youth Hostel | C | Salzburger Café | 8 | | |
| | | The Watering Hole | 5 | | |

from the top-floor bar and restaurant. Especially good value for singles (Tsh8000). Breakfast included. **2**

**YMCA Youth Hostel** Junction of Taifa and Kilimanjaro rds ✆027/275 1754. Large institution-type place where clean, bright rooms with nets, fans and good beds share bathrooms. The main draw is the superb swimming pool (with views of Kilimanjaro).

There's also a poolside snack bar, good restaurant and curio shop. BB. **2**

## Mid-range

**Bristol Cottages Kilimanjaro** Rindi Lane/Aga Khan Rd ✆027/275 5083, ℗www.bristolcottages.com. Clean and efficient, though this has lost some of its rustic charm since adding a three-storey accommodation block. The better rooms in the block have views of Kili (and a phone mast), and the top-floor suites are huge, and have TVs and bathtubs; they're cheaper too, than the twin-bed cottage rooms, which don't have views but do have clunky old a/c units and TVs. One gripe – no mosquito nets. There's also a coffee house, cheap restaurant and safe parking. BB. ❹

**Keys Hotel** Uru Rd ☎027/275 2250, ⓦwww .keys-hotel-tours.com. Long-established, friendly hotel vaguely styled on an English inn. The fifteen cool, high-ceilinged rooms in the main building come with TV, phone, fan and (not always reliable) hot showers; $20 more gets you a/c. There are also some unattractive African-style cottages for the same price. Facilities include a sauna, a small and rather grotty pool, a bar and restaurant (mains around Tsh3800–6000, and one of only a few restaurants to feature *mtori* banana stew (Tsh1700), and a hiking company. Also has a larger annexe 3km east of town. BB ❹

**Kilimanjaro Crane Hotel** Kaunda Rd ☎027/275 1114, ⓦwww.kilimanjarocranehotels.com. A large, perfectly decent and unexciting business-class hotel. The rooms, all en suite, have phone, TV, fan or a/c, and smallish nets. Doubles and suites have massive beds (and bathtubs), and some have balconies. Facilities include a rooftop bar, two restaurants, a gift shop, swimming pool and safe parking. BB. ❹

**Kindoroko Hotel** Mawenzi Rd ☎027/275 4054, ⓦwww.kindoroko.com. A spotless four-storey hotel with spectacular views of Kili from the rooftop restaurant and bar. Most doubles are decently sized, though there are a couple of small and cheap twins with shared bathroom; all

rooms have satellite TV, phone, fan and net. Singles vary, so ask to see a selection. There's another restaurant and bar downstairs, a licensed hiking outfit, internet café and safe parking. BB ❸

**Leopard Hotel** Market St ☎027/275 0884, ⓦwww.leopardhotel.com. Modern and calm, with clean en-suite twins and doubles, all with fridge, TV, phone and fan or a/c (same price), but no nets – rooms are sprayed. All have balconies, but they are mainly facing neighbouring buildings. There's also a good restaurant, bar and small parking area. BB. ❹

## Outside the centre

**Kilimanjaro Impala Hotel** Lema Rd, Shanty Town, 4.5km north of town ☎027/275 3443, ⓔimpala@kilinet.co.tz. Sister of Arusha's main business hotel, but this place is far more relaxed. The stylish architecture, international standards of accommodation, fine Indian, Chinese and European food (Tsh6500–7000) in the restaurant, plus a large pool and an internet café make it excellent value. The eleven bedrooms have parquet flooring, reproduction furniture and TVs. Some also have a/c, others have huge double beds. BB. ❺

**Sal Salinero** West off Lema Rd, Shanty Town ☎027/275 2240, ⓔsalinerohotel@yahoo.com. Moshi's smartest address, a huge Italianate villa with polished wooden floors and seven enormous, ornate en-suite rooms (with more being built); packed with facilities, from TV to tea- and coffee-making facilities. Also boasts a gorgeous swimming pool, manicured grounds and a popular restaurant that screens English Premier League football every Saturday. BB. ❻

# The Town

If you can cope with the persistent – if generally friendly – attentions of the flycatchers, especially around the clock tower and along Mawenzi Road, Moshi is a relaxing place to wander around, although there are few actual sights, since most of the town dates from the 1930s onwards. The liveliest place is the bustling **central market**, south of Chagga Street (Mon–Sat 8am–4.30pm, Sun 8am–noon), which sells a garish cornucopia of imported plastic and aluminium goods, as well as locally produced coffee, cardamom, spices, fruits and vegetables. Keep an eye out for traditional **herbalists** in and around the market (usually old men sitting beside vast quantities of glass jars containing multicoloured powders). One block north, Guinea Street has some **jua kali** (literally "sharp sun") craftsmen, who specialize in turning old tin cans into superb oil lamps, coffee pots, kettles and pans. Two more markets worth exploring include **Mbuyuni market**, four blocks south of the central market (daily by daylight; don't take any valuables with you), and **Kiboriloni market** (Tues, Wed, Fri & Sat; best in the morning), 5km along the highway

## Coffee

The Kilimanjaro Region produces high-quality **Arabica coffee**, characterized by its mild flavour and delicate aroma. Most of the coffee farms are smallholdings whose production is collected and marketed by the Kilimanjaro Native Coffee Union (KNCU), providing a guaranteed minimum income to farmers at times when world coffee prices slump, something that these days happens with alarming frequency.

Coffee bushes flower during the short rains (Oct–Nov), when they become covered in white blossom and give off a pervasive, jasmine-like scent. The best time to visit if you're interested in seeing how coffee is processed is between July and September, when the berries are harvested. Following harvesting, the beans' sweet pulpy outer layer is mechanically removed, after which they're fermented in water and then dried in sunlight on long tables. After a few days, the outer casing (the "parchment") becomes brittle, and is easily removed at the coffee mill, after which the beans are graded for sale according to size and weight.

Moshi's *The Coffee Shop* is the best place to sample a brew, and may also be able to point you in the right direction should you want to visit a working coffee farm. The process can also be seen as part of the cultural tourism programme at Tengeru near Arusha (see p.329).

to Dar, known as far as Arusha for its cheap second-hand clothes, as well as hardware and food. There are frequent daladalas from the main daladala stand and from along Kibo Road.

Moshi's only monuments of note are the structures dominating a trio of roundabouts, including the central **clock tower**. A few hundred metres north, the **Askari Monument** rises from the roundabout at the junction with the highway. The statue of the soldier, rifle at the ready, commemorates African members of the British Carrier Corps who lost their lives in the two world wars. On the south side of the roundabout is the Catholic **Christ the King Cathedral**, famed for its colourful Sunday Masses (6.25am, 8.30am, 10.30am & 4.30pm); the best is the 10.30am service, which attracts many families and features plenty of traditional Chagga singing – worth catching even if you're not religious.

**Kibo roundabout**, 1km west along the highway (Taifa Road), is marked by a stylized **Uhuru Torch**. The original was placed atop Kilimanjaro on the day of Tanzania's Independence in December 1961 to – in the words of President Nyerere – "shine beyond our borders, giving hope where there is despair, love where there is hate, and dignity where before there was only humiliation." At the time, Kenya – whose border skirts the north and east side of the mountain – was still under colonial rule, having only recently emerged from the bloody Mau Mau Rebellion. The short walk from here to **Arusha Road Cemetery** is worth the effort, as part of it contains the graves of British and Tanzanian soldiers who fought in World War I; it can be reached along a path at the north end of Florida Road.

## Eating

Moshi has lots of **restaurants**, one or two of which are quite outstanding. Many of the better restaurants can be found in the salubrious Shanty Town, an expat haven 2km north of the centre. Look out for regional speciality *mtori*, a thick mash of bananas usually served with meat. More ubiquitous, especially in bars, are *nyama choma*, *ndizi* and *chipsi mayai*: the busier the bar, the better the food. **Street food**, mainly roasted maize cobs, is found throughout town. For your own **provisions**, fresh fruit and vegetables are best at the market. Also try the local **supermarkets** (see p.259).

## Town centre

**Abbas Ally Hot Bread Shop** Boma Rd. Popular for snacks and light lunches, with good samosas, sandwiches, cakes, cappuccino, ice cream and waffles. Closed Sun.

**Central Garden** Facing the clock tower. Serves drinks, snacks or full meals in a lovely shady garden. The menu ranges from steaks and fast-food favourites to Indian dishes. Also has good juices and coffee. Daytime only.

**Chrisburger** Kibo Rd. Handy for breakfast and cheap fast-food style lunches (under Tsh2500), plus burgers and hot dogs. Closes 4.30pm weekdays, 2pm weekends.

**The Coffee Shop** Hill St. A superb place with a warmly decorated dining room, a garden at the back with tables and a few more on the shady street-front terrace. Serves a wide range of delicious meals and snacks, including soups, pies, mouthwatering cakes, samosas and ice cream. Best of all is the heavenly Kilimanjaro arabica coffee – probably the best brew in East Africa. It's also a travellers' meeting place, has a notice board with ads for local artists and art centres, and has the Our Heritage crafts shop. Mon 8am–5pm, Tues–Fri 8am–8pm, Sat 8am–6pm.

**Corner Café** Rengua St, up the hill from Dot Internet Café. Serves sandwiches (Tsh2100), toasties (Tsh2300) and salads (Tsh1800), all made by the older girls from the charity Kilimanjaro Young Girls in Need (@www.kygn.org), with all profits going to the charity.

**Friendship Restaurant** Mawenzi Rd. Popular with locals throughout the day, dishing up good cheap food and drinks, including *nyama choma.*

**Indoitaliano Restaurant** New St, opposite *Buffalo Hotel.* One of the nicest places in the evening, with a cool street-side veranda, friendly service and – oddly – Indian and Italian food, including delicious pizzas and a wide range of curries (Tsh5000 upwards). Turn up before 8pm, however, or you could well end up queuing on the street.

**Leopard Hotel** Market St. Probably has the cleanest and most modern kitchen in town (it's open plan), and is good value too, with most mains – including delicious chilli chicken – costing around Tsh7000. They also boast a decent wine list

(Tsh18,000–25,000 per bottle) and a wide range of pizzas.

**Salzburger Café** Kenyatta St. Pleasingly bizarre spot, decorated like an Austrian bar and with lots of memorabilia from the local Volkswagen Members Club. The menu has been much reduced recently, but the food is good and it remains cheap – everything, including steaks, is under Tsh6000.

## Outside the centre

**El Rancho** 200m off Lema Rd, Shanty Town, 5km from town – take the second right after the *Kilimanjaro Impala Hotel.* Tasty North Indian cuisine and a wide selection of European dishes in an affluent suburb popular with expats at weekends. A full à la carte stuffing with a drink or two costs around Tsh15,000 and its famous Sunday lunch buffet costs Tsh7500. There are also evening barbecues (no beef or pork), an excellent cocktail and wine list, plus a pool table, minigolf and table football. Closed Mon.

**Mama Clementina's** 2.5km west of Kibo round about, then 500m south just after Karanga Bridge ☏027/275 1746. This women's vocational training centre makes some great food, with à la carte dishes daily (full meals around Tsh5000), plus a range of three-course set menus including – if you're in a group and order in advance – Mexican. Eat inside or on the terrace. Order all food at least 1hr prior to arrival.

**Panda Chinese** Off Lema Rd, Shanty Town, 500m before *Kilimanjaro Impala Hotel*; 4km from town. Excellent and authentic Chinese cuisine, with a wide selection of generous dishes. The soups and seafood are particularly good, especially the prawns (Tsh8500, or Tsh16,000 for jumbo prawns). Open all day at weekends; also does takeaway (☏0754/838193 or 0784/875725).

**The Watering Hole** 2.5km west of Kibo round about, then 500m south just after Karanga Bridge ☏0784/876427. Situated next to *Mama Clementina's* west of the town centre, this place has two lovely decks on the riverbank, and offers different cuisines for each night, including excellent Tex-Mex on Thurs. Food must be ordered in advance. Closed Mon–Wed.

### By bus

The **bus and daladala stand**, between Market Street and Mawenzi Road, has ticket offices in its central building, and clearly marked bays on either side: those on the north are for local daladalas, those on the south are for longer-distance minibuses and buses. The following **safer bus companies** (all running between Arusha and Dar) have their own terminals or offices: Akamba, on the corner of School and New streets (℡027/275 3908; also goes to Nairobi); Dar Express, on Boma Road (℡0786/811070; also goes to Karatu); Royal Coach, on Kaunda Street (℡0754/298274); and Kilimanjaro Express (℡0787/478125) on Rengua Street.

The **Moshi–Arusha Highway** is perilous, and the antics of the average driver are enough to induce visions of your life in flashback; the Coaster minibuses, especially, crash with alarming – and fatal – frequency. Note that a popular Coaster scam involves having a sane and respectable-looking gentleman occupying the driver's seat whilst the vehicle is at the bus stand, only for him to be replaced by a red-eyed teenage lunatic at the exit…

Whilst the Moshi–Arusha Highway is Tanzania's most dangerous, you should also be on your guard on the run to Dar. Your safest bet is to travel only with one of the companies mentioned above. **Companies to avoid completely**, even if this means having to do a journey in two legs rather than one, include Abood, Air Bus, Air Msae, Buffalo, Hood, Tashriff and Tawfiq.

Getting to Nairobi is easy, with three companies operating daily shuttle buses ($30) via Arusha. The safest is Impala Shuttle (℡027/275 1786, office on Kibo Rd beside *Chrisburger*; daily 6.30am & 11.30am). All shuttles can pick you up at your hotel if you pre-book. Kenyan visas, currently $50, are easily bought at the Namanga border.

### By air

The easiest way to **Kilimanjaro International Airport** if you're flying with Air Tanzania or Precisionair, is on their shuttle buses; contact their offices (see p.258) for more information. A taxi to the airport costs $35–50 depending on your bargaining skills.

# Drinking and nightlife

Whilst Moshi at night is not as lively as Arusha, there's plenty to keep you busy, and a couple of places host **live bands**. There are lots of friendly local **bars** throughout the town, few of which see many tourists. Walking around the centre at night is generally safe, but if you're going more than a few blocks, it's wiser to catch a cab. Several **hotels** have "summit bars" with views of Kili.

**Glacier Bar** Shanty Town, bottom of Lema Rd. Spacious, reggae-heavy place with tired pool table and table football, dancefloor and well-stocked bar. Open Fri–Sun only. Live music on Sat nights.

**La Liga** Bondeni City, past Shah Industries. The "Number 1 Nightclub in Tanzania" boast may be stretching the truth a little, but nevertheless this place has been making a big noise since its arrival on the scene. The endless rules can be a bit trying, but otherwise this is a fun place with a large dance floor surrounded by viewing balcony, impressive lighting system, and even a free taxi to and from the centre of town. Tsh5000 entry.

**Malindi Club** Rengua St. Entrance to Moshi's friendliest bar is through a set of giant concrete elephant legs. Once inside, you'll find a spacious, unpretentious place with televisions posted around the walls.

**Pub Alberto** Kibo Rd. Moshi's brashest nightclub, with all the loud music, lasers and spinning mirrored globes you might want, and plenty of spangled prostitutes too. The music's pretty run-of-the-mill but there's a pool table, and food is served throughout the night. Closed Mon.

**Sal Salinero** West of Lema Rd, Shanty Town. Mentioned here partly because of its gorgeous grounds, partly because of its outdoor pool table, and partly because of its popular Saturday afternoon screening of English football.

**The Watering Hole** Just up from *Mama Clementina's* (☏0784/876427, ⊛ www.twhmoshi .com) Tucked behind the scruffy jeep park of a local safari company, this Swedish-run riverside restaurant-cum-bar is gaining popularity amongst Moshi's *wazungu* population thanks to its Saturday-night theme parties and Sunday-night movie screenings. Also has wireless internet and offers a free taxi ride from town.

## Shopping

Moshi has far fewer **souvenir shops** than Arusha, but this is no bad thing – it's easier to choose, and a number of places stock stuff you simply won't find elsewhere.

Local **bookshops** major on stodgy Christian texts, with little of interest for visitors except for some illustrated children's books which make great presents: try Moshi Bookshop, on the corner of Kibo Road and Rindi Lane, and the Lutheran Centre bookstore on Market Street. *Kilimanjaro Crane Hotel*'s gift shop stocks coffee-table books. For Western novels, try the second-hand bookstall at the corner of Mawenzi Road and Mankinga Street. The Twiga internet café on Old Moshi Road operates a book rental system (Tsh1500 per week).

### Crafts and souvenirs

**Africulture** Old Moshi Rd. One of the biggest crafts shop in town, and also happy to tailor clothes.

**I Curio** Round the side of the *Kindoroko Hotel*. The best choice for souvenirs in Moshi, with a good selection of T-shirts, carvings and Tinga Tinga paintings.

**Shah Industries** Karakana St. A crafts workshop occupying an old flour mill, some of whose forty employees are disabled. They're happy to give free guided tours around the workshops and gardens, and also have a shop. Great for unusual curios fashioned out of cow horn, leather and pressed flowers, plus woodcarvings and batiks. Mon–Fri 8am–5pm, Sat 8am–1pm.

**TAHEA-Kili Gallery** Hill St, facing *The Coffee Shop*. Great batiks, carvings, fabrics and jewellery from a vocational training programme for young people and women.

## Listings

**Airlines** Air Tanzania, Rengua St, near the clock tower ☏027/275 5205; Precisionair, Old Moshi Rd ☏027/275 3498. Also see "Travel agent".

**Banks and exchange** Reliable foreign exchanges include Trast, Mawenzi Rd/Chagga St (Mon-Sat 8am–4.30pm); and Chase, Subzali Building, Rindi Lane (Mon–Fri 8am–5pm, Sat 8am–2pm; Visa cards accepted). Most banks levy hefty commissions; NBC, by the clock tower, is the exception, but takes forever.

**Car repairs** Workshops along Bath Rd between Kaunda and Old Moshi roads. The *Golden Shower* campsite (see p.252) also has competent mechanics.

**Health** KCMC (Kilimanjaro Christian Medical Centre), 6km north of town past Shanty Town (☏027/275 0748), is the best hospital in northern Tanzania but that's not saying much and you need to be referred by a doctor unless it's an emergency. Blood tests can be done at Sima Hospital, Kenyatta St (☏027/275 1272; 24hr) and the dispensary there is also open 24hr. Other well-stocked pharmacies include Hapa Majengo Dispensary, near Majengo Block Supply (Mon–Fri 9am–4.30pm, Sat 9am–12.30pm; ☏027/275 0280); and Shanty Town Dispensary (Mon, Wed, Thurs & Fri 9am–1pm & 3–5pm, Tues 1.30–4pm, Sat 9am–1pm; ☏027/275 1418).

**Immigration** The Immigration Office is in Kibo House, Boma Rd, by the clock tower (Mon–Fri 7.30am–3pm; ☏027/275 1557).

**Internet access** Internet cafés usually charge Tsh1500/hr. Easy.com, Kahawa House, by the clock tower (daily 8am–8.30pm); Duma, Hill St (daily 9am–7pm); and the café at the *Buffalo Hotel* (daily 7.30am–9pm; Tsh1000; see p.252).

**Library** Moshi Regional Library, Kibo Rd (Mon–Fri 9am–6pm; daily membership Tsh500).

**Police** Market St ☏027/275 5055.

**Post and couriers** The main office faces the clock tower. There's also a branch in a converted shipping crate on Market St, facing the police station. DHL, Kahawa House, by the clock tower (☏027/275 4030; Mon–Fri 8am–6pm, Sat 8am–12.30pm).

Sport The Kilimanjaro Marathon (and half
marathon) is held every February: register through
ⓦ www.kilimanjaromarathon.com
Supermarkets Carina, Kibo Rd near *Pub Alberto*
(Mon–Sat 8am–6.30pm); MDC, Kawawa St/Florida
Rd (Mon–Sat 7.30am–9pm); Highway Supermarket,
Karanga Bridge (daily 7.30am–10pm); Mr Price,
Kilimanjaro Rd by the turning to *Green Hostels*
(Mon–Sat 8am–9.30pm).

Swimming pools *YMCA Youth Hostel* (25m),
*Kilimanjaro Impala Hotel* and *Sal Salinero*; all cost
Tsh3000.
Telephones TTCL, next to the main post office
on Market St (Mon–Fri 7.45am–4.30pm, Sat
9am–noon).
Travel agent Emslies, Old Moshi Rd ⓣ027/275
2701, ⓔ emslies.sales@eoltz.com.

# Around Moshi

A number of flycatchers and hiking companies offer **day-trips** to various nearby
sights, but there's nothing really organized. Costs average $25–50 per person per
day depending on group size, mode of transport and bargaining skills. **Bicycles**
can be rented informally at most hotels; the cost should be Tsh10,000 a day.
Possible destinations include hikes in **Kilimanjaro Forest Reserve** at Kibosho
(15km north of town) and **Rau Forest** (10km northeast), and trips to see hot
springs, waterfalls – and crocodiles, so take care.

For something more established, consider the **cultural tourism programmes**
in Marangu and Machame (see p.260) and east of Arusha (p.261), most of which
can also be accessed from Moshi.

## Marangu

The base for most climbs up Kili is **MARANGU** village, an hour's drive
northeast of Moshi. Marangu actually consists of two villages, both situated on
the sealed road leading to the park gate: **Marangu-Arisi** is the section closest
to the park, whilst **Marangu-Mtoni** is at the crossroads to Mamba and Rombo,
5.6km short of the park.

There's more to Marangu than just a base for climbing the mountain,
however. Marangu's hotels can arrange a number of **guided walks** in the area
– the scenery is superb, especially close to the park, where you get unobstructed
views of the Pare Mountains, Nyumba ya Mungu reservoir and Kibo (weather
permitting), plus Kenya's Taita-Taveta plains and Lake Jipe.

### Practicalities

Frequent **daladalas** from Moshi (roughly 8am–6pm) cover the 30km to
Marangu-Mtoni. From there to the park gate, take a shared taxi for Tsh500.
**Camping** is possible at *Bismark Hut Lodge*, *Kibo Hotel*, *Kilimanjaro Mountain*

---

### The Kenyan border at Taveta

It's possible to cross into Kenya at **Taveta**, 34km east of Moshi. Daladalas run hourly
from Moshi to the border. The drawback is an hour's walk on the Kenyan side, if you
can't find one of the enterprising locals running bicycle taxis from the border into
town. Taveta has a bank, plenty of decent accommodation, and provides access to
**Lake Chala**, set in a stunningly picturesque volcanic crater on the eastern flank of
Kilimanjaro – there's a hotel by the lake, but swimming isn't recommended, because
of the crocodiles in the lake. Onward travel in Kenya is by bus or *matatu* (daladala) to
Voi or Mombasa.

*Resort* and at *Coffee Tree Campsite.* **Hotels** are lacking in the budget range, but the price to quality ratio improves as you move upscale. Ensure your bed has adequate mosquito nets – Marangu's zillion banana plants favour the critters. All hotels have luggage stores for climbers.

**Babylon Lodge** 1km east of Marangu-Mtoni off the Rombo road ☎027/275 6355, ⓦwww .babylonlodge.com. Thirty recently renovated, good if rather pricey en-suite twins and doubles in modern buildings scattered across a slope; functional rather than memorable. There's also a restaurant, bar and safe parking. BB. ❹

**Hotel Capricorn** 2.7km from the park gate ☎027/275 1309, ⓦwww.capricornhotel.com. A large, attractive option surrounded by lush gardens and dominated by a vast conical roof. Rooms in the old cottages have bathtubs; new wing rooms, for $25 more, have showers, balconies, digital TV, fridge, phone and safe. Try to get a room facing south, as the others are very dark. Good restaurant (meals $10–12), atmospheric bar, and gift shop, but no pool. BB. Cottages ❸, new wing ❹

**Coffee Tree Campsite** 2km from the park gate ☎027/275 6604, ⓦwww.alpinesafari.com. The spartan but clean dorm-like accommodation here ($12 a mattress) is handy for a cheapish night before a climb, and paradise when you return, thanks to its sauna. It also has internet access and camping ($8 per person or $10 including tent hire).

🏃 **Kibo Hotel** 1.4km west of Marangu-Mtoni ☎027/275 1308, ⓦwww.kibohotel.com. A rambling old hotel from German times with tons of charm; set in slightly wild gardens where camping is

available ($5 per person including the use of the kitchen and pool). The entire place is adorned with old prints, maps and antiques, including expedition flags and T-shirts in the dining room. Facilities include a small pool, cosy bar, a huge central fireplace in the lounge, and good meals (three-course lunch $10, dinner $14; à la carte mains around $6). BB ❹

**Kilimanjaro Mountain Resort** 1.5km west of *Kibo Hotel* ☎027/275 8950, ⓦwww .kilimanjaromtresort.com. A mountain of money was used to build this vaguely Neoclassical place, more like a private mansion than hotel. The rooms are well appointed, with shiny bathrooms (which have large bathtubs), phone, digital TV and fridge. There's also a restaurant (mains $10–12), internet access, a duck pond and kids' playground. You can also camp here ($12 or $20 with tent hire). BB ❻

**Marangu Hotel** 2km south of Marangu-Mtoni ☎027/275 6594, ⓦwww.maranguhotel.com. Originally a coffee farm started by Czech immigrants in 1907, this became a guesthouse in the 1930s. The rooms are darkish and very basic for the price, but facilities include a good swimming pool, croquet lawn, bar, filling and tasty meals (light lunches, including lasagne, mostly Tsh2000–2500, or a five-course set dinner for $12 – pre-order) and safe parking. Their hiking operation has an excellent reputation. HB ❻

## Walks around Marangu

You can get hassled a lot walking around Marangu: the persistent attention from young men wanting to take you to one of Marangu's waterfalls quickly becomes tedious. Marangu's **cultural tourism programme** circumvents some of the hassle, and of course opens the door to a side of local life you might not otherwise see. The tours are all easy half-day walks that can be combined into one- or two-day trips and include: excursions inside the park to **Mandara Hut** (including Maundi Crater and a waterfall); **Mamba village**, 3km east towards Rombo, for traditional blacksmiths and underground caves, where villagers would hide their cattle and family during times of war; a 120-year-old Catholic mission church at **Kilema village**, its relics include what is purported to be a piece of Christ's cross, and in whose grounds Kilimanjaro's first coffee tree was planted; and a nature hike up **Ngangu Hill** on the west side of Marangu, for a great view and a cave containing the remains of a former chief. Seven **waterfalls** around Marangu can also be visited: the closest are Kinukamori Falls, 1km north of Marangu-Mtoni; Ndoro Waterfalls, where you can swim in the splashpool, are 2km west of Marangu-Mtoni past *Kibo Hotel*; and Kilasiya ("Endless") Waterfall, near the *Mountain Resort Hotel*. You can visit the waterfalls on your own, as they're signposted (admission fees average Tsh3000), but you'll probably be followed by a gaggle of wannabe guides.

Unfortunately, the tourism programme lacks a central office, so trips are arranged through the hotels reviewed above. The most reliable place to book tours is *Kibo Hotel* (see p.260), which charges $20 per person for a half-day tour including entrance fees and lunch.

Lastly, there's the modest **Chagga Life Museum**, just outside *Kilimanjaro Mountain Lodge* (daily 10am–5pm; Tsh3000), which traces the history of the Chagga, especially the Marangu's Marealle clan, back over seventeen generations, and also displays all sorts of tools, implements and drums, all labelled in English. The **Cultural Temple** by Kinukamori Falls is less interesting and informative, but is included in the entrance fee to the falls.

## Machame

On the southwestern side of the mountain, **MACHAME** – the village at the start of Kilimanjaro's second most popular climbing route – is set in a beautiful area of steep valleys, thick forests, streams and fertile farmland, and has good views of the summit to boot. Most visitors only pass through en route to climbing the mountain (the Machame route is for ascent only), so there are no tourist facilities other than an infrequently visited **cultural tourism programme**, which offers a variety of guided walks and the chance to meet the locals.

### Practicalities

**Daladalas** run hourly (7am–6pm) from Moshi's main bus stand, taking about an hour. Alternatively, catch a daladala or bus towards Arusha and get off at the signposted junction 12km west, where other daladalas connect with Machame – 14km to the north – every ten minutes or so from 8am to around 6pm. The park gate lies 4km beyond the village.

Apart from **homestays** arranged through the cultural tourism programme (around Tsh3000 per person), and *Makoa Farm* for horse riders (see Ⓦwww .makoa-farm.com), **accommodation** is limited to the much-recommended *Protea Hotel Aishi Machame* (Ⓣ027/275 6948, Ⓦwww.proteahotels.com; BB ❻), 6km from the Moshi–Arusha Highway. The hotel boasts thirty well-equipped rooms with TVs in a stylish three-storey block with tree bark roof tiles, or in bungalows, all set in lush gardens with ponds, boardwalks and hundreds of banana plants. Facilities include a good restaurant (meals $13–15), solar-heated swimming pool (Tsh5000 for day visitors), sauna and steam room.

### Walks around Machame

The **cultural tourism programme**, run by Foo Development Association or FODA (Ⓣ027/275 7033, Ⓔfodamachame@yahoo.com) is based at Kyalia near Foo village, about 1km beyond Machame. Costs should be no more than $25 a day, all included. Make sure you arrange things through the office itself and not through someone on the street. There are several hikes, including the fascinating **Sienye-Ngira tour** (4–6hr) through Sienye rainforest to Masama village, southwest of Machame. The trip can be extended over two days to include **Ng'uni**, upstream from Masama, with great views over the plains, where you can learn about constructing traditional *mbii* houses.

# Mount Kilimanjaro

**As wide as all the world, great, high, and unbelievably white in the sun, was the square top of Kilimanjaro.**

Ernest Hemingway, *The Snows of Kilimanjaro*

The ice-capped, dormant volcano that is **Mount Kilimanjaro** has exerted an irresistible fascination since it was "discovered" by Europeans in the mid-nineteenth century. Rising over 5km from the surrounding plains to a peak of 5892m, Kilimanjaro – a national park, and a World Heritage Site since 1989 – is Africa's highest mountain, the world's tallest free-standing massif and one of the world's largest volcanoes, covering some 3885 square kilometres. It is also an exceptionally beautiful mountain, both from afar and close up, and fills up brochures as easily as it does the horizon.

The mountain was formed during the most recent faulting of the Great Rift Valley two to three million years ago, an event that also produced Mount Meru and Mount Kenya. Kilimanjaro has three main peaks, together with parasitic volcanic cones and craters dotted around its sides. The youngest and highest peak is the distinctive snow-capped dome of **Kibo**, actually a large crater that was formed around 460,000 years ago during the last period of major volcanic activity. The pinnacle, Uhuru Peak, is 5892m high, but most maps mark it as 5895m – from the days before satellite surveys. The jagged, pimple-like **Mawenzi**, 11km to the east of Kibo (and is connected to it by a broad lava saddle), is all that remains of a volcanic cone that lost its eastern rim in a gigantic explosion; its highest point is Hans Meyer Peak (5149m). The oldest peak is the **Shira Ridge**, on the west side of the mountain.

For many visitors, the prospect of scaling the mountain, which can take anything from five to eight days, is as exciting as it is daunting. The fact that no technical climbing skills are required to reach the summit (it's said to be the world's highest non-technical climb) means that Kilimanjaro has acquired something of an easy reputation – a dangerous misconception, and one which you should ignore. The

▲ Hikers tackle a steep path on Kilimanjaro

## Meltdown: the end of Kilimanjaro's ice cap?

Incredible though it might seem, Kibo's emblematic white cap may soon be no more. Kilimanjaro is heating up, and its ice cap and glaciers are retreating at an alarming rate. In 1912, the ice cap covered just over twelve square kilometres. By 2005, it had shrunk to under two square kilometres, having diminished by a full third over the previous fifteen years.

The primary cause is **global warming**, as worryingly proven by research using core samples of the ice cap as a weather archive. Hapless park and forest management has also done little to stop the ongoing **destruction of forest cover** on the mountain's lower slopes, through illegal logging and uncontrolled fires courtesy of honey-gatherers, poachers and careless farmers. Forests trap solar heat, so less forest means warmer ambient air, in turn hastening the big thaw.

Some researchers believe that the ice cap will have disappeared completely sometime between 2014 and 2021 – whereas others proffer a more hopeful 2040 as the year in which we'll see the final demise of the glaciers – eleven thousand years after the peak last lost its snowy crown.

high altitude and the possibility of a quick ascent mean that an average of a dozen people lose their lives every year, usually as victims of **acute mountain sickness** (see box, p.268). In addition, almost everyone suffers with screaming headaches and utter exhaustion on summit day, meaning that of the forty thousand people who attempt the climb every year, only about two thirds make it all the way to Uhuru Peak. Having said this, if you take your time and stay attentive to your body's needs, there's no reason why you shouldn't be able to make it to the top. The mountain also offers plenty of less strenuous alternatives for those for whom the prospect of summiting smacks of a mite too much masochism: a walk on the lower slopes, through rainforest and on to the edge of sub-alpine moorland, makes no extreme fitness demands, and can be done in a day.

### Some history

Non-Africans have known Kilimanjaro since at least the thirteenth century, when Chinese mariners reported a "great mountain" inland. Europe, however, remained ignorant of Kilimanjaro until 1848, when the German missionary **Johannes Rebmann**, having given up trying to convert coastal tribes to Christianity, headed inland to try his luck elsewhere. His report of a snow-capped mountain three degrees south of the Equator was met with scorn and ridicule back home, and it wasn't until 1861, when Kilimanjaro was scaled to a height of around 4300m by Dr Otto Kersten and Baron Karl Klaus von der Decken, that his report was accepted by the likes of the Royal Geographical Society. The first Europeans to reach the summit were the German geographer **Hans Meyer** and Austrian mountaineer **Ludwig Purtscheller**, who reached Kibo on October 6, 1889. Mawenzi was climbed in 1912.

The origin of the **mountain's name** is confusing. To some explorers, it meant "that which cannot be conquered", to others it was the "mountain of greatness", or the "mountain of caravans". In both Kiswahili and Kichagga (the Chagga language), *mlima* means mountain, while *kilima* is a hill. The use of the diminutive could be affectionate, though Chagga place names are often preceded with *ki*, as are names around Mount Kenya. The second half of the name remains vague: *njaro* may be related to a Kichagga word for caravan, a throw-back to the slave and ivory trade, or to an old word for God, *kyaro*. An alternative meaning stems from the Maasai word *ngare*, meaning river – Kilimanjaro, of course, being the source of life for several of these.

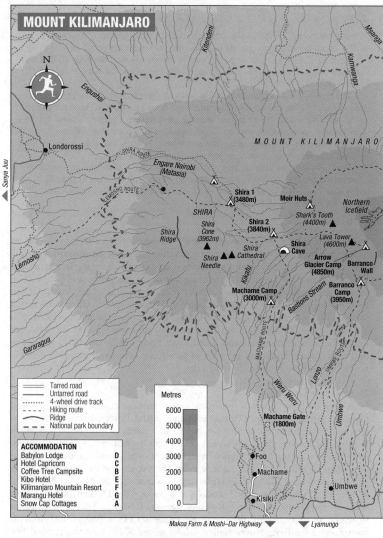

**MOUNT KILIMANJARO**

N

MOUNT KILIMANJARO

Londorossi

*Sanya Juu*

*Engushai*

SHIRA ROUTE

Engare Nairobi
(Matasia)

Shira 1
(3480m)

Moir Huts

Northern
Icefield

SHIRA

Shark's Tooth
(4400m)

Shira 2
(3840m)

*Kitendeni*

*Kamwanga*

*Msanga*

LEMOSHO ROUTE

Shira
Cone
(3962m)

Shira
Ridge

Shira
Cathedral

Lava Tower
(4600m)

Barranco
Wall

*Lemosho*

Shira
Needle

*Kikelu*

Shira
Cave

Arrow
Glacier Camp
(4850m)

Barranco
Camp
(3950m)

Machame Camp
(3000m)

*Bastions Stream*

MACHAME ROUTE

*Gararagua*

*Weru Weru*

UMBWE ROUTE

*Lonzo*

*Umbwe*

**Metres**

| | |
|---|---|
| 6000 | |
| 5000 | |
| 4000 | |
| 3000 | |
| 2000 | |
| 1000 | |
| 0 | |

Machame Gate
(1800m)

Tarred road
Untarred road
4-wheel drive track
Hiking route
Ridge
National park boundary

**ACCOMMODATION**

| | |
|---|---|
| Babylon Lodge | D |
| Hotel Capricorn | C |
| Coffee Tree Campsite | B |
| Kibo Hotel | E |
| Kilimanjaro Mountain Resort | F |
| Marangu Hotel | G |
| Snow Cap Cottages | A |

Foo

Machame

Umbwe

Kisiki

*Makoa Farm & Moshi–Dar Highway*   *Lyamungo*

The Chagga have a wonderful tale about the origin of Kilimanjaro's main peaks, **Kibo and Mawenzi**, who, they say, were sisters. Kibo was the wiser of the two, and was careful to store away food for times of hardship. Her sister, Mawenzi, however, had no such cares for the future, and fell into the habit of asking Kibo for help whenever times were bad. Eventually, Kibo became angry with her sister's begging, and hit her on the head with a spoon; hence Mawenzi's ragged and broken appearance. Another Chagga legend speaks of a great treasure on the mountain, one protected by powerful spirits who punished those foolhardy enough to dare climb it – extreme cold, exhaustion and altitude sickness are the very real modern forms of those spirits.

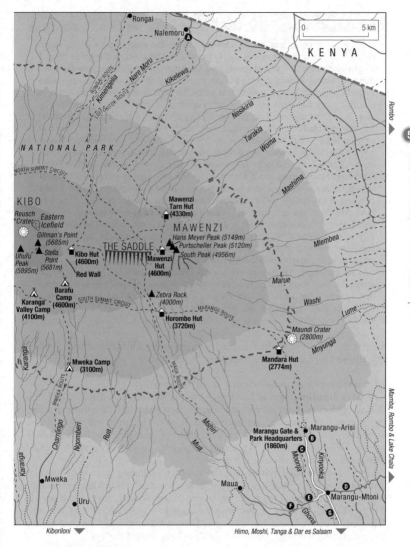

Map labels:
Rongai
Nalemoru
A
KENYA
0      5 km
Rombo ▶
Mamba, Rombo & Lake Chala ▶
NATIONAL PARK
RONGAI ROUTE
Kimengelia
Nare Moru
LOITOKITOK ROUTE
Kikelewa
Nesikina
Tarakia
Woma
Mashima
NORTH SUMMIT CIRCUIT
KIBO
Reusch Crater
Eastern Icefield
Gillman's Point (5685m)
Uhuru Peak (5895m)
Stella Point (5681m)
Kibo Hut (4600m)
Red Wall
THE SADDLE
MAWENZI
Mawenzi Tarn Hut (4330m)
Hans Meyer Peak (5149m)
Purtscheller Peak (5120m)
South Peak (4956m)
Mawenzi Hut (4600m)
Miembea
Marue
Washi
Lume
Barafu Camp (4600m)
Karanga Valley Camp (4100m)
SOUTH SUMMIT CIRCUIT
Zebra Rock (4000m)
MARANGU ROUTE
Horombo Hut (3720m)
Karanga
Mweka Camp (3100m)
MWEKA ROUTE
MAIN ROUTE
Maundi Crater (2800m)
Mnyunga
Mandara Hut (2774m)
Charongo
Ngomberi
Rua
Mshini
Mua
Marangu Gate & Park Headquarters (1860m)
Marangu-Arisi
B
C
Moonja
Kinyooka
Mweka
Uru
Maua
Marangu-Mtoni
D
E
F
G
Ghona
Kiboriloni ▼
Himo, Moshi, Tanga & Dar es Salaam ▼

## Practicalities

**Kilimanjaro National Park** covers the entire mountain above the tree line (approximately 2750m), together with six forest corridors running down to around 2000m. The most popular **routes up the mountain** start at the villages of Marangu, Machame and Lemosho respectively. Increasingly popular, too, is the Rongai route, the only one to start on the northern side of the mountain.

Anyone wanting to climb Kilimanjaro must be accompanied by an officially accredited guide and a trekking company with a TALA licence. Reliable companies in Moshi and Marangu are reviewed on p.271; see also the Arusha

## What to take

A good pair of boots and lots of warm clothes are the essentials for a Kilimanjaro climb. Your trekking agency will supply tents etc, though you will need to bring a warm (rated down to −10ºC) **sleeping bag**. Check to see if they will supply a **ground mat** or whether you need to bring this too. You don't need cooking equipment, as the porters bring this. There's a kiosk just inside the gate at the park headquarters at Marangu Gate that rents out some pretty good gear, from balaclavas to sleeping bags: as an idea of costs, hiring a sleeping bag with foam mat costs $70 per climb.

Regarding **clothing**, the important thing is to wear layers – several levels of clothing worn on top of one another provide better insulation than fewer but bulkier items. **Thermal underwear** and **fleeces** are essential, and as you won't have much chance to dry things out (open fires are no longer permitted), **waterproofs** are vital. Don't forget **sunglasses** and a **sunhat**, as well as a **woolly hat** and **gloves** (prefereably a thinner inner layer and a thicker, waterproof outer glove) for the colder climates. A **headtorch**, **toilet paper**, **walking poles** and **water bottles** (enough to carry three litres) are all pretty much essential. **Plastic bags** for keeping things dry, **towel**, **sweets** and **money** (for tips, and to buy drinks at the huts) are all useful too. High-altitude medication (see p.268), plasters, bandages and gauze, lip salve, and suncream (minimum factor 25) and rehydration powders/solutions should all be added to your standard **medical kit** (see p.24).

As for carrying it, the porters will take your main backpack but tend to dash off ahead, so you'll need to bring a **small daypack** to carry stuff you'll need during the day, such as water bottles, snacks, camera, waterproofs, suncream and sunglasses. Don't pack too much weight, and ensure your pack is comfortable.

safari company reviews in Chapter 6. Incidentally, **children under 10** are not allowed further than the tree line.

### Information, guidebooks and maps

The **park headquarters** at Marangu Gate (daily 8am–6pm; ☏027/275 3195, ✉kinapa@habari.co.tz) are useless for specialized queries, but the shop opposite the registration counter sells maps and books. The most up-to-date and comprehensive **guidebook** is Henry Stedman's *Kilimanjaro: The Trekking Guide to Africa's Highest Mountain* (Trailblazer) or pick up Jacquetta Megarry's *Explore Mount Kilimanjaro* (Rucksack Readers).

There's lots of **information** on the internet, including dozens of journey accounts. The most comprehensive site is ⓦwww.climbmountkilimanjaro.com, with a regular "Kilimanjaro news" section and plenty of information and advice. The park's official page is ⓦwww.tanzaniaparks.com/kili.html. See also the Kilimanjaro Porters' Assistance Project at ⓦwww.kiliporters.org, a site dedicated to ameliorating working conditions for Kili's long-abused porters.

Given that you'll be accompanied by a guide, **maps** aren't essential, but taking one is recommended for plotting your route, putting names to geological features and gauging distances and elevations – a guide's conception of "not far" can differ radically from your own. The easiest to find is Giovanni Tombazzi's hand-painted *New Map of Kilimanjaro*, with good inserts on flora. The best and newest, however, is by Swiss company Climbing Maps (ⓦwww.climbing-map.com/en/maps/kilimanjaro.html), though it's currently not that widely available in Tanzania.

### Costs

Climbing Kilimanjaro is an **expensive** business, even if you brave the hassle of arranging things yourself. Going with a hiking company, you won't get much change from $1100 for a budget trip, or $1600–1800 for a mid-range one. Incidentally, some companies' quoted rates exclude park fees; so don't get too excited if you're offered a hike for $500. Prices don't just depend on the quality of the company you climb with but the route you choose too, with the Shira/Lemosho and Rongai routes tending to cost a little more, as they are the furthest away from Moshi/Arusha so transport costs are higher.

The lion's share of the costs is taken up by **park fees**: $60 per person for 24hr, plus $50 for a night's camping or $50 for hut space on the Marangu route. There's also a one-off $20 rescue fee. Then you need to pay for your crew: the obligatory **guide** as well as **porters** and a cook. **Additional costs** include food, equipment rental, and transport to and from the park gates.

Don't forget to factor in **gratuities**. One tenth of the total cost of the trip would be about right, though exactly how much to tip is a perennial headache (leaving unneeded equipment with the guide and porters after the climb is welcome, but no substitute for a cash tip), not helped by the sour mood of some climbers who fail to reach the top or by the constant and not-so-subtle hints from the guide and porters that can plague some trips. The best way to deal with it is to say you'll pay when you get down, but don't tie the promise of tips with a successful summit attempt: you'll be encouraging the guide to take risks, and success depends more on your body and attitude than on the guide and porters. On the other hand, if the guide or porters were terrible, don't tip at all – but do explain to them why.

## When to go
The most popular climbing **season** is December to February, when the weather is generally clear. June to September is also good, though there's a chance of rain in June, and September can be devilishly cold. Kilimanjaro can be climbed during the intervening **rainy seasons**, but the lower slopes will be exceedingly muddy and there's no guarantee of clear skies higher up. The southeastern slopes receive most rain, meaning that the Machame and Shira/Lemosho routes are generally drier than the Marangu route. It can snow on or near the summit all year round, though chances are highest during and shortly after the rainy seasons. Try to coincide with a **full moon** on summit day – it avoids the need for flashlights, and lends an eerie beauty to the scene.

## Guides and porters
These days all trekkers have to sign up with a TALA-registered agency. They in turn will provide you with guides and porters who will help you up the mountain. KINAPA (Kilimanjaro National Park) insist that all groups must be accompanied by a licensed **guide**, at the ratio of one licensed guide to every two trekkers. Most of the guides are superb: many have climbed the mountain innumerable times, and they're usually fluent in English. That said, if you have a chance you should ask your agency if you can meet your guide in advance, to see how you get on – after all, he's going to be your companion for the next week, and you are putting your life in his hands.

Your agency will also provide you with **porters** – usually about two or three per trekker. Porters are limited to carrying no more than 20kg each, plus 5kg of their own gear. Incidentally, porters don't scale the summit – though some of them will climb with you to the Crater Campsite (see p.273) if you have booked a night there – but instead stay at the last hut or campsite and meet up with you again on the way down. Though the amount they carry is now regulated, the porters still face one of the hardest jobs on the mountain, and many still perish in the course of doing their job. A good place to start

## Altitude sickness

Air gets thinner the higher you go; on the summit of Kilimanjaro, a lungful contains only half the oxygen you would inhale at sea level. Given enough time, the human body can adapt to an oxygen-scarce environment by producing more red blood cells. But, without weeks to acclimatize, almost everyone climbing Kili will experience the effects of high altitude, known as **altitude (or mountain)** sickness: these include shortness of breath, light-headedness, headaches, nausea, insomnia and, naturally enough, exhaustion. The symptoms appear towards the end of the second or third day. Staying hydrated is absolutely essential at high altitude and normal altitude sickness isn't much to worry about, although vomiting should be treated seriously.

Much more serious is **acute mountain sickness (AMS)**, the chronic form of altitude sickness. Symptoms of AMS include most of the above, plus one or more of the following: severe headache; shortness of breath at rest; flu-like symptoms; persistent dry cough; blood-tinged saliva or urine; unsteadiness or drowsiness; lack of mental clarity or hallucinations; and chest congestion. In these cases, **descend immediately** to a lower altitude. Be aware that mental fuzziness may convince the victim that he or she is fit to continue – they're not. A porter will usually accompany the victim, so the whole party won't have to turn back. Ignoring the symptoms of AMS can be fatal: complications like pulmonary oedema and cerebral oedema claim the lives of about a dozen climbers each year. Predicting who will get sick is impossible: AMS affects young and old alike, the fit and the not so fit, so don't deny the signs if you start feeling them, and heed your guide's advice.

Some **drugs** are claimed to eliminate such problems. **Diamox** (the trade name for acetazolamide) seems to be the most reliable and achieves the best results, however, opinion is sharply divided over their pros and cons, so consult a doctor before taking anything. The drug has two well-known short-term side effects: your fingers tingle, and it's an extremely efficient diuretic, so you'll be urinating every few hours day and night – drink lots of water to compensate. Some (unconfirmed) reports suggest that in rare cases the tingling or numbness in fingers may persist for several years. Nonetheless, most climbers do tend to have an easier time of things when on Diamox. As an alternative, some climbers swear by ginkgo biloba (120mg taken twice a day, starting a few days before the climb). Don't take it if you bleed easily.

Given the confusion over medication, **prevention** is a better approach: let your body acclimatize naturally by taking an extra day or two when climbing the mountain (at least six days, whichever route you're taking, ideally seven or eight – or else climb Mount Meru the preceding week to help you acclimatize); stay hydrated; climb slowly; and if you ascend a lot in one day, camp at a lower altitude, if possible. Lastly, don't go higher than the tree line (2700m) if you're suffering from fever, nosebleed, cold or influenza, sore throat or a respiratory infection.

looking for reputable companies is the website of **KPAP (Kilimanjaro Porters Assistance Project)** at Ⓦwww.kiliporters.org, where they list all their "partner" companies – those trekking agencies that have a good record of treating their porters well and paying them a fair salary. You should also have one **cook** in your crew – and you'll be amazed at how good they are at rustling up some surprisingly delicious nosh.

### Preparation and pacing

It cannot be said enough that the more days you have on the mountain, the higher are your chances of success – and the more time you'll have to enjoy the scenery. Small group sizes are also better, as the guide can be more attentive to your needs. A positive **mental attitude** is the key to success: climbing Kilimanjaro is difficult and usually painful, so brace yourself for a big effort and don't be overly confident – the bigger they come, the harder they fall. Being adequately equipped and in good **physical condition** also helps your attitude. You don't have to be an athlete, but cut down on alcohol a few weeks before the climb, go cycling and walk or jog to tune up your lungs and get your legs in shape. If you have the time and money, a climb up Mount Meru is recommended to help your body acclimatize. On the mountain itself, take care of your body's needs. Your appetite may vanish at high altitude, so make the effort to eat properly. You should also drink enough to keep your urine clear (generally 3–4 litres of water a day), taken in sips throughout the hike. Also, try to sleep properly, though this can be difficult at high altitude. For the night of the summit attempt, bring lots of energy foods and water.

The other key to success is to **take your time** – start early at a deliberately slow pace and take frequent rests and you'll find the ascent much less painful than if you charge up. On summit day, go very slowly (not that you'll feel like running), take five-minute rests every half-hour and drink plenty of fluids. When short of breath, inhale and exhale deeply and rapidly four or five times. Near the top, stay focused: don't be put off by grumbling climbers descending after failed attempts, and remember that the pleasure lies in the journey, not necessarily in reaching the destination. Also, be aware of your limitations, and listen to your guide – if he suggests you go no further, don't – as he knows what he's talking about. Lastly, when **descending**, take it slowly – the greatest risk of injury is on the way down, so use a walking stick or ski pole, and resist the temptation to slide down the scree.

## The routes

There are three main routes up Kilimanjaro. Descent is usually along the Mweka or Marangu routes in the south. **Overnights** on the Marangu route are in a chain of relatively comfortable cabins; all other routes require camping, usually at recognized campsites equipped with long-drops and nothing much else. The "uniport" huts along these routes are for rangers only.

The **Marangu route**, approaching from the southeast, is the quickest, steepest and most popular way up (and down). Though usually offered as a five-day trek, an extra day considerably increases your chances of reaching the top.

The **Machame route**, from the southwest, is the next most popular, requiring at least six days, seven being recommended. It's slower and more sedate than the Marangu (but with the occasional very steep section), has campsites instead of huts, and enjoys more varied scenery.

The third main route is the distinctly less-travelled **Lemosho Route**, the longest route on the mountain, with eight days being the normal completion time.

Other routes include the short, scenic but steep **Umbwe route** from the south, and the increasingly popular **Rongai route** from the northeast. A good base for the latter is the Swiss chalet-style *Snow Cap Cottages* in Nalemoru (☎027/275 4826, ⓦwww.snowcap.co.tz/cottages.html; HB ❻), they also arrange hikes.

### The Marangu route

The **Marangu route** is the choice of seventy percent of climbers who ascend Kili. It's a short, beautiful but steep trail that's anything but easy, especially if done over only five days – which probably explains why fewer than one in three climbers on this route reaches Uhuru Peak. Extending the trek over six days, as described below, or even seven days, is preferable and greatly increases your chances of success. Depending on the season (see p.267), the Marangu route can be cloudy and muddy, and is often busy. The route's popularity means that the path is badly eroded in many places, and the lower slopes turn into a mudfest in the rains. At times, there's also a lot of litter left by dumb climbers (hence the trail's nickname, the "Coca-Cola Route"), and graffiti adorns the three large **accommodation huts**: Mandara, Horombo and Kibo. These are equipped with mattresses, solar lighting, kitchens, toilets and a rescue team. Snacks and drinks, including beer, are available at all the huts – but wait until you descend to indulge in the booze. Bunks must be reserved through the park headquarters at Marangu Gate (your hiking company can do this for you). Camping isn't allowed except for those who took the Rongai Route to ascend but who use this route for their descent.

### Day 1: Marangu Gate to Mandara Hut

The Marangu route starts 5.6km north of Marangu village at **Marangu Gate** (1860m), where you pay the park fees and hire a guide and porters if you're not on an organized climb. You can also buy last-minute supplies like energy food here. Start as early as possible to give yourself plenty of time to enjoy the tangle of rainforest and to increase the odds of avoiding showers, which tend to fall in the afternoon. The entire day's walk (8km; count on around 3hr) becomes very slippery and muddy in the rains, so take care. You may get soaked along this section, even if it's not raining, as the cloying mist drenches everything.

Immediately after the gate, the broad track plunges into dense forest. While the porters take the wide track to the right, you should be led along the narrower signposted track to the left, a slightly longer alternative that follows a small stream and gives a better view of the forest. Both tracks merge after some 5km at Kisambioni. **Mandara Hut** (2705m) is 3km further on. If you arrive early and feel up to it, there's a pleasant walk from Mandara Hut to the rim of **Maundi Crater** (2800m) 1.5km northeast, the remnant of a volcanic vent from where there are glorious views. The crater can also be worked into the next day's walk.

Mandara Hut, just inside the upper boundary of the forest, comprises a complex of comfortable wooden cabins, most containing two rooms with four bunks apiece. The exception is a large two-storey house that has a large dormitory on top and the communal dining area downstairs. Eat well, as you might lose your appetite higher up.

### Day 2: Mandara Hut to Horombo Hut

After an early breakfast (try for 6.30am), the trail emerges from the rainforest and veers northwest. If the sky is clear, there's a great view of the craggy Mawenzi Peak to the north and of the plains to the south from here. The trail heads up through alpine meadows and crosses a stream to emerge onto grassland, eventually thinning into surreal moorland scattered with bushes and short trees. If it's cloudy, don't fret – the vision of the plants emerging from the mist in a cocoon of silence can be magical, and you stand a reasonable chance of clear skies in the afternoon. As you approach Horombo Hut, 12km from Mandara, across a series of moorland ravines, ragged stands of giant groundsels and giant lobelia take over (see box, p.273), lending an equally strange and unearthly quality to the scene, often complemented by Horombo's magnificent sunsets. **Horombo Hut** (3714m), in a rocky valley, comprises a collection of huts similar to Mandara. There are some old-fashioned long-drops down the slope, and newer toilets flushed with piped water from a stream behind the huts. It gets cold very quickly after sunset, so wrap up well. Count on five to seven hours for the day's walk.

### Day 3: Horombo Hut

Most people begin to feel the effects of altitude on the walk up to Horombo Hut, so a **rest day** at Horombo is advisable even if you're in good physical shape: no great hardship given the stunning location. You can help yourself acclimatize more easily if you spend at least a couple of hours walking to a higher altitude: most people head for **Zebra Rock** (4000m), named after its

## Kilimanjaro hiking companies

Any company directly organizing Kilimanjaro climbs needs a current **TALA Mountaineering Licence**: the national park offices at Marangu and Machame gates have lists of licensed companies, as do the tourist offices in Arusha and Dar es Salaam.

Those reviewed below are among the more reputable, licensed outfits in Moshi and Marangu. For recommended Arusha-based companies, read the safari company reviews on pp.51–52. One company not reviewed here as it only deals with tour companies, but with an excellent reputation, is African Environments (🕸www .africanenvironments.co.tz). Be wary of other companies not reviewed in this book – appearances are not everything. In addition, don't necessarily believe recommendations on the internet: several companies are adept at plugging themselves. And if a flycatcher claims to work for one of the following, ensure that you end up at the correct address – there have been cases of disreputable outfits "borrowing" the names of other companies to snare clients. Lastly, given that the cost of climbing is so much already, **don't scrimp** by going with a dodgy company: it's not worth the saving if you're going to end up with inexperienced guides, dud equipment, or the blot on your conscience if you use a company that exploits its porters.

### Companies in Moshi

Unfortunately, Moshi's trekking agencies have a bad reputation for mistreating their porters – a town-wide malaise with only a couple of exceptions, noted here.

**Ahsante Tours & Safaris** Arusha Road ☎027/275 1971, 🕸www.ahsantetours.com. Helpful, friendly company, which has long been the budget trekkers' agency of choice, Ahsante aren't as cheap as they used to be and their new offices out on the way to Arusha are hardy convenient. That said, they still offer one of the most reliable and best-value services on Kilimanjaro: six-day climbs start around $1100. Also licensed for wildlife safaris and a member of TATO (Tanzania Association of Tourist Operators).

**Summit Expeditions and Nomadic Experience (SENE)** ☎027/275 3233, 🕸www .nomadicexperience.com. Run by the irrepressible Simon Mtuy – holder of the record for the fastest combined ascent and descent of Kilimanjaro, and the only Chagga guide to own his own expedition company – SENE offers climbs on the Lemosho and Machame Routes, with each trek preceded by a couple of days relaxing on Simon's farm at Mbahe, in the foothills of the mountain. Not cheap, at $2500–3000 per expedition, but highly recommended by those who've sampled Simon's hospitality and a partner of KPAP (see p.268).

### Companies in Marangu

**Kibo Hotel** ☎027/275 1308, 🕸www.kibohotel.com. One of the best mid-range companies for the Marangu route as long as you're adequately equipped (hiring stuff here is expensive), offering a six-day Marangu trip for $1185–1340, a seven-day Machame trip for $1590–1680 plus $230/group for vehicle transfer, and seven days on the Rongai route for $1463–1560 plus $170/group vehicle transfer.

**Marangu Hotel** ☎027/275 6594, 🕸www.maranguhotel.com. Long-established company with excellent guides and a reputation for thorough preparation. Offers a choice of "fully equipped" climbs, for which all you need to bring is warm clothes and a good pair of boots, and "hard-way" climbs, where you supply everything and the hotel arranges guides, porters and accommodation for a $50 fee. A fully equipped six-day Marangu hike costs around $1300; a seven-day Machame hike costs $1600. TATO member and KPAP partner.

peculiar weathering pattern. If you're feeling particularly fit, you could try a day-trip to **Mawenzi Hut** (4538m), at the foot of Mawenzi Peak.

## Day 4: Horombo Hut to Kibo Hut

The next stage, 9.5km up to Kibo Hut, can be tough if your body hasn't fully acclimatized, so keep an eye out for symptoms of acute mountain sickness beyond simple headaches, and leave Horombo early, as you'll have little time to sleep in the evening before the wake-up call for the summit attempt. The whole stage takes five to seven hours.

Just beyond Horombo, two trails diverge, both heading up to the **Saddle** – the broad lava-stone ridge between Mawenzi and Kibo peaks. The right-hand trail, which is very rocky and eroded, veers north, and is the quicker, albeit the more difficult, of the two (2–3hr compared to 3–4hr). From the Saddle, a track heading east takes you to the 4538-metre mark on **Mawenzi** – as far up that peak as you can get without technical gear. Ignore this track and carry straight on instead – Kibo Hut is three to four hours away, across an otherworldly alpine desert of reddish gravel and boulders. The alternative route from Horombo to the Saddle takes upwards of four hours, but leaves you a little under 2km from Kibo Hut. Both routes have a number of steep uphill and downhill sections.

**Kibo Hut** (4713m) is a stone construction with a dining room and accommodation in bunks. There are long-drops outside the huts – take care at night. There's no water, so fill up near Horombo, either at one of the tarns on the eastern route, or at "Last Water" stream on the western route. Assuming you're up for the ascent the same night, try to catch some sleep in the afternoon and evening as the next stage, starting around midnight, is by far the hardest.

## Days 5 and 6: Horombo to the summit and back down

The summit push on **day 5** is the steepest and most strenuous part of the hike, taking five to six hours up to Gillman's Point (and an extra ninety minutes to Uhuru Peak if you're still standing), followed by a nine- or ten-hour descent. After a generally fitful night's sleep due to the cold and the altitude, hikers set off between 11pm and 1am for the final ascent. Temperatures are well below zero, and visibility is difficult, especially if there's no moon or if flashlights conk out. The trail leads past **Hans Meyer Cave** – handy for a sheltered rest – before turning into a painful series of single-file zigzags up loose scree, for which a Zen-like mindset helps. At the top of the zigzags, a short rocky scramble gets you to within staggering distance of Gillman's Point. The thin air forces frequent stops, and most climbers get lightheaded and nauseous along this stretch, and suffer from headaches.

**Gillman's Point** (5685m), on the crater rim, is where many people call an end to their attempt, to be consoled with the stupendous view and the sun rising from behind Mawenzi Peak. If you're up to it, an even more exhausting ninety-minute clockwise walk around the crater rim past **Stella Point** – where the Machame route joins up – and Hans Meyer Point brings you to the roof of Africa, **Uhuru Peak** (5892m). Those ninety minutes (or two hours if you're really whacked) may not sound like much, but are likely to be the hardest, most painful and – with luck – most rewarding ninety minutes of your life. Sunrise here above a sea of clouds is unforgettable (though the majority of climbers arrive about an hour after sunrise), as is the feeling of elation, even if, right then, your only desire is to get down as quickly as possible. There's a summit log you can sign, and remember to take a photograph with that famously battered yellow sign – the pounding headache that you will more than likely be feeling means that many people forget.

## Kilimanjaro's high-altitude flora and fauna

Kilimanjaro is covered by a series of distinctive habitat zones, determined by altitude. Above about 1800m, farmland ceases and forests take over. Up to around 2000m, much of the forest is secondary growth, but beyond here is dense primary **cloudforest**, containing over 1800 species of flowering plants. In its lower reaches, the forest is dominated by ferns, podocarpus and camphor trees, and is home to three primate species: blue monkey, western black-and-white colobus, and bushbaby (galago). Leopards also live here (though you're most unlikely to see one), preying on mountain reedbuck and members of the world's largest population of Abbot's duiker.

Rainfall is less heavy at higher altitudes, so from around 2400m the forest becomes less dense. The tree line (2800–3000m) marks the start of the peculiar **afro-alpine moorland** (also called upland grassland) and the land of the giants – giant heather, giant groundsel (or tree senecio) and giant lobelia. The cabbages on stumps and the larger candelabra-like "trees" are two forms of the giant groundsel, which can have a sheaf of yellow flowers. The giant groundsel favours damp and sheltered locations such as stream beds; they're slow growers but, for such weedy-looking vegetables, they may be extraordinarily old – up to two hundred years. Higher up, in the alpine bogs, you'll see groundsel together with another strange plant, the tall and fluffy giant lobelia – the animal-like furriness insulates the delicate flowers. A number of mammals habitually pass into the moorland zone from the forests: grey duiker and eland are most commonly seen; bushbuck, red duiker and buffalo are more rare. There are few birds: the most common is the white-necked raven, often seen at campsites.

Above 4600m is the barren alpine desert zone. The sub-zero conditions here mean that few plants other than mosses and lichens are able to survive, although the daisy-like *Helichrysum newii* has been seen on Kibo's summit caldera at 5760m close to a fumarole. Even stranger was the mysterious leopard whose frozen body was found close to the summit in 1926 and which featured in Hemingway's *The Snows of Kilimanjaro*. No one knows what it was doing so far up the mountain.

It's possible to **hike into the crater** if this is arranged in advance with your guide (at extra cost). Measuring 2km in diameter and 300m deep, the crater contains another, smaller crater named after Dr Richard Reusch, who in 1926 discovered the frozen leopard later made famous by Hemingway (see box above). In the centre of this is an ash pit, and there are some small but active steam fumaroles on its northern and eastern rim. Incidentally, it's not a good idea to spend a night on the summit (**Furtwangler Camp**, 5600m) unless you're taking at least nine days for the hike, as you'll need to be totally acclimatized to avoid coming down with AMS.

Most folks only spend a few minutes at the bitterly cold summit before **heading back down**. Try to avoid the temptation of "skiing" down the scree – it makes things even more difficult for climbers after you, and, of course, you risk a painful and potentially limb-breaking tumble. Most climbers get back to Kibo Hut around 10am, take a rest, and then retrace their steps to Horombo, for their last night on the mountain.

The **final day** (day 6) should be bliss, but by now your knees may be complaining – take it easy, and use a walking stick. Mandara Hut is usually reached by lunch time, and the park gate in the afternoon. Don't forget your certificate at the gate.

### The Machame route

Nicknamed the "Whiskey Route" because of the more upmarket trash left by the wayside up until a few years ago, the long, winding and dramatic **Machame**

**route** is the second most popular way up after the Marangu route. Encounters with eland and other wildlife are no longer so common, and you'll see dozens of other climbers along the way – the official daily limit of sixty climbers a day is apparently not enforced. Six days is usual for the ascent along this route, but seven or even eight is recommended. The walk is more difficult than the Marangu, but the advantage is that, being longer, acclimatization is easier and so the success rate is higher. There are a couple of routes to the summit from the **Shira Plateau**, with the Mweka Route (a mudfest in the rains) the normal descent route, so all in all you get to see a lot of the mountain. Nights are spent camping: the campsites are usually called "huts" on maps, but the metal "uniports" there are for guides and porters only.

### Day 1: Machame Gate to Machame Camp

Count on an hour for the drive from Moshi and at least an hour to complete formalities at the **gate** (1800m). Aim to leave the gate no later than 11am because the day's walk takes five to seven hours.

From the gate, the trail heads up to the west of Makoa stream into dense, steamy and ever-changing **rainforest** alive with birdsong (look out for wild orchids). The trail narrows after thirty minutes to follow parts of a rocky ridge, where the vegetation becomes thicker, characterized by giant heather, and beard-like Spanish mosses hanging from the trees. The trail is steep, muddy and very slippery in places, especially beyond the two- to three-hour mark. As you approach **Machame Camp** (3032m), the vegetation thins out and the path emerges onto alpine moorland. The camp, occupying a clearing on the ridge, has long-drop toilets, water from a nearby stream and great views of the Western Breach.

### Day 2: Machame Camp to Shira Camp

So long as you're in good shape, this is a very pleasant and easy day's hike (around 5hr) that brings you out of the forest (usually above the clouds, though it can still be misty) and onto the drier and rockier **Shira Plateau**. From Machame Camp, the trail continues northeast along a steep and rocky ridge (some scrambling required) scattered with giant heather, and passes several clearings with great views of Mount Meru in the west. The top of the ridge – after three hours or so – ends in a small cliff, up which a rudimentary staircase has been built. Lunch is taken on the top. From here, the incline lessens and the trail veers northwards across several ravines, through land studded with giant lobelia and giant groundsels. This leads on past Shira Cave (actually more of a rock shelter), before reaching the exposed **Shira Camp** (3847m) on the edge of the Shira Plateau, an immense, gently sloping expanse of desolate moorland marked by **Shira Cone** – the remnants of Kilimanjaro's oldest peak. There's a good view of the Western Breach from the camp, and awe-inspiring sunsets over Mount Meru. Night-time temperatures usually stay a few degrees above freezing, but the wind chill makes it feel much colder. The first symptoms of altitude sickness can appear here.

### Day 3: Shira Plateau

The Shira Plateau is a great place to spend an extra **rest day** acclimatizing. The main attraction is **Shira Cone** at the west end of the plateau, rising some 200m above the plateau. South of here are two impressive pinnacles – volcanic plugs named Shira Needle and Shira Cathedral – while behind is the Shira Ridge, the so-called "third summit" of Kilimanjaro, formed by the first big eruption that formed the Kilimanjaro massif. Eland are sometimes seen on the lower reaches of the plateau.

If you're feeling OK, however, you may prefer to acclimatize later on; the next day's hike to Barranco Camp is particularly good for this – rising to around 4530m before dropping back down to 3985m.

## Day 4: Shira Camp to Barranco Camp
There are **two routes** to the summit from Shira Camp: either via Barranco Camp and Barafu Camp to Stella Point, or straight up the Western Breach. The former, described below, is by far the easier. For a description of the Western Breach route, see p.277.

The boulder-strewn trail to Barranco Camp (Umbwe Hut on some maps) takes five to seven hours and is extremely beautiful in a lunar kind of way. The walk starts with a gentle incline east towards Kibo. At the top of a ridge marked by a rock called the **Shark's Tooth** (4400m), the trail veers south to cross a series of shallow valleys at the base of the Western Breach and the 4600-metre **Lava Tower**, gradually descending to **Barranco Camp** (3985m). Set in alpine tundra, the camp has a great view of the icy Western Breach as well as the Barranco Wall – which you'll be climbing the next day; it appears intimidatingly vertical from here. If you're going to suffer badly from altitude sickness, it really kicks in at Barranco, so be reasonable with your expectations.

## Day 5: Barranco Camp to Barafu Camp
Although the following is a one-day route description from Barranco to Barafu Camp, this section is often done in two four-hour segments, with an overnight halfway in the Karanga Valley camp. This is especially recommended if you didn't spend a day acclimatizing at Shira.

Although steep, only a few stretches of **Barranco Wall** require hands-and-feet climbing. The path is narrow, so "experienced" climbers can get huffy about the slow pace – ignore them, and take your time. The wall normally takes ninety minutes to scale and your reward at the top is a great view of the Heim, Kersten and Decken glaciers. The path then follows a spectacular traverse east along the base of Kibo. The top of the icy **Karanga Valley** (4130m) is usually reached by noon, giving you a lazy afternoon to rest and sleep before heading off the next day to Barafu.

Continuing on from Karanga Valley, the track continues its eastward traverse, after about two hours reaching the crossroad with the Mweka route. Turn left for Barafu Camp – an exhausting ninety-minute climb up a steep and rocky lava ridge. It often snows, and in the rainy seasons this area can be blanketed. **Barafu Camp** (4681m) is on the ridge close to the southern edge of the Saddle, and has a great view of Mawenzi Peak. The downside is the often filthy state of the campsite – take your rubbish down with you. The long-drops are close to the ridge edge – take care at night, as several climbers have fallen to their deaths from here. Go to sleep no later than sunset.

## Days 6 and 7: Barafu to the summit and back down
**Day 6 – summit day** – is the most exhausting, and involves at least seventeen hours of hiking, from Barafu Camp to the summit (6–8hr) and down to Horombo Hut on the Marangu route, or to Mweka Camp on the Mweka route. The "day" starts before midnight, when you're woken for breakfast, and most climbers set off between midnight and 1am. The trail follows an increasingly steep valley on the edge of scree fields, before passing between the Rebmann and Ratzel glaciers to emerge at **Stella Point** (5672m) on the southern rim of Kibo; the last few hundred metres are the hardest section on the climb. **Uhuru Peak** (5895m) is about an hour further along an ice-covered trail; see day 5 of

the Marangu route (p.272) for a description. The trail for the most part is steep with extremely loose scree, making for painfully slow progress.

Heading **back down**, most people reach Barafu Camp around 9–11am, where an hour's rest is followed by a long hike down, either along the Mweka or Marangu routes, for your last night on the mountain. **Day 7** is generally just a few hours of relatively easy – if sometimes very muddy – downhill walking. Take it slowly.

## The Lemosho Route

The Lemosho route replaces the original route across the Shira Plateau, known as the Shira route, which is now a driveable road used by emergency vehicles to take suffering trekkers off the mountain. Though that trail is still very occasionally used by trekkers, more often than not the Lemosho route is the trail taken by those looking to cross the Shira Plateau on their way to the summit – even though, confusingly, it is sometimes referred to as the Shira Route.

Extremely photogenic, the Lemosho route approaches the mountain from the west, through forest used as a migration route by elephants (hence the more open canopy than in the south), and joins the Machame route on the fourth day at the foot of Kibo near the Lava Tower. Seven days is the minimum trekking time, with eight being ideal.

Once patronized only by upmarket companies, the Shira or Lemosho routes now feature on most hiking company brochures, though they're still nowhere near as busy as the Machame and Marangu routes.

### Day 1: Londorossi Gate to Mti Mkubwa

From either Arusha or Moshi the drive to the Londorossi Gate is a long one: about three hours from Moshi, slightly longer from Arusha. Having registered and had all your luggage and equipment weighed, you then rejoin your transport to take you up the lower slopes of Kilimanjaro. The path itself begins at the lower reaches of the forest at about 2000m, where a troop of colobus monkeys seem to have taken up almost permanent residence. The walk on this first day is only a couple of hours long (around 6km), and meanders through one of the best stretches of forest on the whole mountain – an extensive stretch of untamed wilderness where elephants still stroll through and leopards stalk at night. The destination on this first day is **Mti Mkubwa** ("Big Tree") Campsite (2650m), attractively located in the shade of a spreading podocarpus tree.

### Day 2: Mti Mkubwa to Shira 1 Campsite

This second day, covering a distance of around 7km, takes you out of the forest on a relentlessly uphill march towards the **Shira Ridge**. This ridge was the southwestern rim of the original Shira Crater, formed by the first volcanic explosion. Crossing heath and moorland, you reach the top of the ridge (3610m) after around 5–6 hours, from where there are great views of the Kibo summit. Just twenty minutes or so after dropping off the ridge onto the Shira Plateau, you'll reach your campsite for the night, **Shira 1** (3480m), close to one of the many streams that cross the plateau.

### Day 3: Shira 1 Campsite to Shira Huts Campsite

The third day on this trek is a short and, relatively speaking, not too strenuous trudge across the Shira Plateau, though nowadays many trekking agencies are varying the route by taking an excursion south to **Shira Cathedral**. This large ridge (3720m) on the southwestern lip of the plateau affords great views down

## The Western Breach route

For experienced climbers taking the Machame, Umbwe or Shira/Lemosho routes, a challenging alternative to the ascent from Barafu Camp is the approach over the **Western Breach**, a steep slope that was created when the western rim of Kibo exploded. Nicknamed "the Torture Route", the Western Breach ascent is very steep and potentially dangerous – landslides and rock falls are not uncommon. The path was closed in 2006 following the deaths of three trekkers in a rockfall, and since its reopening many agencies refuse to use the path. Those that do, usually insist that their climbers wear helmets (which the agencies supply) and many also ask their clients to sign a waiver form before agreeing to take them up. Another danger is that turning back on the last part is impossible without proper climbing equipment, so if you feel anything more than just a headache, turn back well before.

The route separates from the main trail at Lava Tower (4660m), four hours from Shira Camp, or higher up the slopes of Kibo at the equally dramatic **Arrow Glacier Camp** (4871m), next to an area of boulders and snow fields. It takes at least six hours to the crater rim from Arrow Glacier, and around nine hours from the Lava Tower.

towards the Machame Route on the southern side of the mountain. Whatever route you take, your destination at the end of the day is **Shira Huts** (aka Shira 2; 3840m), a large and smart campsite in the heart of the plateau, surrounded by crisp white flowers.

### Day 4: Shira Huts Campsite to Barranco Huts

The path for today is around 9km and heads almost due east across the plateau to the Kibo summit and a union with the Machame route (see p.275) near the Lava Tower. If the skies are clear this is a wonderful day for photos – the light at this altitude is particularly special and the Kibo summit is particularly impressive (and imposing) from this angle. The walking itself is relentlessly uphill – but never steep – to **Lava Tower** (4610m), where most groups take lunch. Assuming you're not taking the Western Breach route (see above), your path from here contours around the southwestern face of Kibo before plummeting to **Barranco Huts Campsite** (3895m).

For a description of the trail from Barranco to the summit, see p.275.

# The Pare Mountains

To the southeast of Kilimanjaro rise the much older but equally beautiful **Pare Mountains**, a green, fertile and infrequently visited region divided into two distinct ranges – north and south. The practical business of getting around is not as difficult as it was, thanks to the establishment of three **cultural tourism programmes** (see p.54), two in the north at Usangi and Kisangara Chini, another at Mbaga in the south. Each programme offers a range of affordable activities based around guided walks in the mountains and their forests, and encounters with the rural culture of the **Pare** tribe, who have been living in the mountains for the last six hundred years.

The Pare is northeastern Tanzania's most traditional tribe. In the same way that the geologically separate Eastern Arc forests have developed an especially rich flora and fauna (see box opposite), so the isolation of the Pare from other tribes has resulted in their strong and distinctive culture and sense of identity. Whereas traditional knowledge of plants and their uses is fast disappearing elsewhere, the Pare have kept much of their knowledge intact, and are famed throughout northern Tanzania for the power of their healers, and sometimes feared for witch-craft – witches, called *ndewa* in Kipare, are invariably associated with botanical knowledge garnered over many centuries. It's thanks to the continuity of Pare culture that many of the mountains' indigenous forests have been preserved, despite high human population densities, since the Pare consider the forests sacred places, guarded by the spirits of their ancestors. Add to all this the fact that the Pare, like their Sambaa cousins to the south (see box, p.290), are an unfailingly welcoming bunch, and you have an immensely rewarding place to visit.

In the plains between the mountains and the Kenyan border lies the **Mkomazi National Park** (see p.282), which became the scene of controversy following the forced expulsion of Maasai cattle herders in 1988. It contains a rhino sanctuary, but otherwise probably isn't worth the effort if the Northern Safari Circuit figures in your plans.

# North Pare

The **North Pare Mountains** are best visited through the cultural tourism programme at **Usangi**. Another programme, at **Kisangara Chini** on the Dar–Arusha highway, also offers walks into the mountains, but is better for trips to Nyumba ya Mungu reservoir in the plains to the west.

## Usangi

The base for the North Pare Mountains' cultural tourism programme is **USANGI** village, 25km east of the highway in a beautiful location surrounded by no fewer than eleven peaks. Try to visit on a Monday or Thursday, when the village's **market** is held. The cultural tourism programme offers a range of trips; profits are currently used to help a local clinic.

**Transport** from Arusha or Moshi is on the daily Sahara Coach (10am from Arusha, passing Moshi around 11.30am; and leaving Usangi at 6am). Coming from Dar es Salaam, catch a bus for Moshi or Arusha and get off in the district capital, **Mwanga**, 50km southeast of Moshi, from where a handful of daily buses grind uphill along a good sandy road to Usangi (60min). At Usangi, get off at Lomwe Secondary School and ask for the project co-ordinator and school headmaster, Mr Nelson Kangero (℡0784/813787). If you get stranded in Mwanga, the school for deaf children has a good little guesthouse (℡027/275 7727; ❷).

In Usangi, several families – most of them connected to the secondary school – offer **accommodation** (❶) through the cultural tourism programme, and camping is possible (Tsh2000). The school itself also has a guesthouse, sleeping eight, and there's a guesthouse in the village near the mosque. **Meals** are provided by the Usangi Women's Group with dinner or lunch both Tsh4000.

### Guided walks and tours

A guided half-day walk takes in farms on the lower slopes of the Pare Mountains before climbing to **Mangatu moorland** (1600m), near the sacred forest of the Mbale clan, with superb views of Kilimanjaro and Lake Jipe on

## The Eastern Arc Mountains

The Pare Mountains are part of the Eastern Arc Mountains, an isolated range of ancient massifs that stretch from the Taita Hills in southeastern Kenya into Tanzania, where the range includes the Pare Mountains, East and West Usambara, the Ulugurus near Morogoro and the Udzungwa Mountains. Despite the proximity of the northern part of the Eastern Arc to the volcanic massifs of Mount Meru and Kilimanjaro, the steep crystalline ridges and peaks of the Eastern Arc are a much older and geologically separate formation. The current ranges began to take shape some 100 million years ago, and attained their present form at the start of the Miocene epoch, 25 million years ago.

The great age of the Eastern Arc Mountains, along with the physical isolation of the various ranges from one another, is one reason for their exceptional **biodiversity**. Another is the region's remarkable climatological stability over the last forty million years, thanks to the proximity of the Indian Ocean, whose monsoon system dictates weather patterns over much of the Eastern Arc, producing ample mist and rainfall from moisture-laden clouds coming in from the ocean. Together, these factors have fostered the evolution of the mountains' tremendously rich ecological systems, notably their forests, which contain literally thousands of plant and animal species found nowhere else on earth – not for nothing is the Eastern Arc often referred to as the "Galapagos of Africa".

the Kenyan border. A full-day trek can be arranged up North Pare's highest peak, **Mount Kindoroko** (2113m), 9km south of Usangi, for grand views of Kilimanjaro, Mount Meru, Lake Jipe and Nyumba ya Mungu reservoir. The walk goes through the surrounding rainforest, home to blue monkeys and birds, and you can also visit a women's pottery co-operative, a traditional healer and listen to a storyteller. Another day-trip goes up **Mount Kamwala**, whose forests are sacred. Walks over several days can also be arranged; Ugweno village, near **Lake Jipe** on the Kenyan border, is a handy base both for walks and canoeing on Lake Jipe (watch out for the hippos and crocodiles), and has accommodation at the local school. You can also camp in the mountains, but will need to bring your own gear.

If you're not up for long hikes, there are several things to do in and around Usangi, including visits to a brick-making co-operative and to other artisans producing pottery, clothes and traditional sugar-cane beer (*denge*). **Costs** include a guide fee of Tsh10,000 (for a group of up to five people) per day (plus Tsh6000 if you wish to camp overnight), and a Tsh2000 Village Development Fee.

## Kisangara Chini

The easiest of Pare's cultural tourism programmes to visit is at **KISANGARA CHINI**, 12km south of Mwanga on the highway, sandwiched between vast sisal plantations in the shadow of Mount Kindoroko, North Pare's highest peak. **Buses** running between Dar and Arusha (or Moshi) pass through.

The **cultural tourism programme** (Mrs Grace Msafiri Mngara ☎027/275 7789, ✉msafirigrace@yahoo.com) is thirty minutes' walk east of the village. It's not signposted, so keep asking for "Mama Grace". The turning on the highway is at the sign for Shule ya Msingi Chanjale, 100m north of the Total filling station. You pass over a small stream after 70m. Go on, then turn right at the T-junction into a square with a big tree. Keep left and exit the square. The compound is 1.5km further on, on the right as the road veers left (east) towards the mountain.

Mama Grace and her family are exceptionally welcoming, and run the project as part of a boarding school. The project offers **rooms** in cottages with cold showers (❸), and a **campsite** (Tsh10,000 per person). There are a couple of simple guesthouses in the village (both ❶), plus the smarter *Kindoroko Mountain Lodge* (☎027/275 7786; BB ❹), behind the Total petrol station, which boasts its own internet café. Food and drinks are also available. Kisangara Chini's **market days** are Thursday and Sunday.

### Guided walks and tours

The "must-do" is a hike up **Mount Kindoroko** (also offered by Usangi's cultural tourism programme), combined with visits to sites of ritual importance. The programme also arranges day-trips to **Nyumba ya Mungu** ("House of God") reservoir in the plains to the west, for bird-spotting, fishing excursions by canoe and encounters with local fishermen, some of whom emigrated here from Lake Victoria. Closer to Kisangara Chini, various **half-day walks** combine visits to carpentry workshops, brick and sisal factories, a traditional brewery producing beer from sugar cane or Lembeni Herbal Hospital, with traditional dancing performed by a women's group, and crash courses in Pare cookery, storytelling and Kiswahili. **Costs** include a Village Development Fee of Tsh5000, a guide fee of Tsh10,000 for groups of up to five people (plus Tsh5000 for overnight excursions), and, should you wish to see it, a traditional dancing fee of Tsh3000.

# South Pare

The district capital of the Pare region, **Same**, sits 52km south of Mwanga, at the western end of a lowland corridor separating North from South Pare. The mountains of **South Pare** are similar in many respects to their northern twin – just as beautiful, and with a superb cultural tourism programme at **Mbaga**, which may well entice you to stay longer than planned. If you're just passing along the highway, a recommended **overnight stop** is *Pangani River Campsite* ($6), between the railroad and river in the shadow of the Pare's southernmost peak. Despite the river reeds, there aren't as many mosquitoes as you might fear. It's a welcoming and laid-back place, with lots of shady doum (*mikweche*) palm trees, a bar and thatched restaurant, an electricity generator, tents for hire ($3–4) and a two-bed *banda* (❷). They can also guide you up and down the forested peak (7hr). There's another campsite, the *Tembo*, further south at Mkumbara and amply signposted, but it has little to recommend it other than its swimming pool.

## Same

Straddling the highway at the foot of the South Pare Mountains lies **SAME** (pronounced *sah-mê*). The main attraction is its **Sunday market**, drawing farmers from all over the mountains. A local speciality is honey (*asali*); the normal variety, called *msiku*, is from tended hives hung from trees; the sweeter and superior variety (the bee stings are also said to be more painful) is called *mpako*, and comes from wild beehives in the ground. Another item worth seeking out is the local **scorpion and snakebite cure**, called *nkulo*. Sold in powdered or stick form, it literally sucks venom out of wounds.

### Practicalities

Same is 116km southeast of Moshi and can be reached on any **bus** travelling between Dar or Tanga and Moshi or Arusha. **Leaving Same**, most buses pass through between 7am and 3pm; see p.257 for recommended bus companies, and ones to avoid. *PADECO Safari Grill*, facing the bus stand, has **information** about Mbaga's cultural tourism programme. **Change money** at NMB, near the bus stand.

There's lots of **accommodation**, most of it in rather tawdry guesthouses doubling as brothels. In the rains, mosquitoes infest Same and malaria is present, so check bed nets carefully. The most comfortable place is *Elephant Motel*, 1.4km south of the bus stand on the highway (℡027/275 8193, ✉sgeneralsame@elct.org; BB ❸; camping $5), which has large, clean en-suite rooms with box nets and satellite TVs, safe parking, and a bar and restaurant. The best of the cheapies, with safe parking, is the pious *Amani Lutheran Centre* (℡027/275 8107, ✉pd@elct .org; ❷), 250m uphill from the bus stand, with en-suite rooms and round nets (but no fans) overlooking an enclosed garden.

Same's **restaurants** are pretty basic, tending to function as "groceries" (bars) for truckers and other travellers. An exception is *Elephant Motel*, with good, filling meals such as grilled elephant poussing (actually not an elephant at all, but chicken cooked with garlic and herbs). For **drinks**, the nicest place is *Honey Port Bar*, whose pleasant shaded outdoor terrace facing the bus stand is a perfect place to watch the world go by. They also do *nyama choma*.

## Mbaga and around

South Pare's **cultural tourism programme** – one of Tanzania's best – is at **MBAGA**, a former missionary station set in a lush area of terraced cultivation up in the mountains. It offers a wide variety of walks to various attractions and small villages that are little-changed from centuries ago, and gives you a chance to experience local life and culture. Profits from the project have already paid for the construction of a pre-school building and dispensary, and now subsidize energy-efficient stoves, vocational scholarships and road maintenance. A good time to come is Wednesday, coinciding with the weekly **market**.

### Practicalities

Mbaga is also known as Manka. There are two roads from Same: via the eastern flank of the Pare Mountains past Mkomazi National Park, then uphill from Kisimani village (treacherous even in dry weather; 4WD essential); or, much easier, up the western flank of the mountains via Mwembe village. The latter route is advisable if you're **self-driving**, taking just ninety minutes: the road starts 2km south of Same's *Elephant Motel* along the highway; there's no sign, so ask for *njia panda kwenda Mwembe* (Mwembe crossroads). At Mwembe, turn left (east) and up towards Mbaga. By **public transport**, Mangare Bus leaves Same every day sometime after 2pm, taking two and a half to three hours; it leaves Mbaga at 5.30am. There's also an occasional daladala or pick-up, but no more than one a day.

Transport stops outside *Hill-Top Tona Lodge*, the base for Mbaga's **cultural tourism programme** (Mr Elly Kimbwereza ℡0754/8520, ⓦtonalodge .org). The lodge's main building was the residence of a German missionary named **Jakob Dannholz**, who wrote what are still the best works on Pare culture, including *Lute: The Curse and the Blessing*, available at the lodge (Tsh2500) – it's a rare, insightful read, and is highly recommended.

**Accommodation** at the lodge (BB ❶) consists of four modest rooms in the main building, and several more in brick cottages a few minutes away, each with electricity and bathroom with running water. **Camping** is also possible (Tsh3000); bring your own tent. Extraordinarily delicious traditional **meals** (Tsh2500) are available if ordered early; try *makande*, a light stew of maize and beans cooked with milk and vegetables, or anything with bananas. There's more basic accommodation (and food) at *Sunrise Lodge*, 5km beyond Mbaga along the road to Gonja, and *Adela Guest House* in Gonja itself.

## Guided walks and tours

The cultural tourism programme offers a range of walks from easy half-day hikes to treks of three days or more; they can also arrange a day's safari in Mkomazi National Park (see below), though if you don't have wheels you'll need to wait a day or two for them to rent a vehicle in Same. One fascinating (and rather disturbing) half-day walk goes to the **Mghimbi Caves** and **Malameni Rock**. The caves provided shelter from slave raiders in the 1860s, whilst the rock, further up, was the site of child sacrifices until the practice was ended in the 1930s. The rock can be climbed, but you need to be instructed on the appropriate behaviour by an elder first – your guide can arrange this.

Other good half-day destinations include **Mpepera Viewpoint**, giving views – on clear days – of Kilimanjaro and Mkomazi; and the hilltop **Red Reservoir** near the Tona Moorlands, frequently covered with water plants and good for bird-watching. A recommended full-day trip is to the tiny and beautiful agricultural village of **Ikongwe**, said to have been a gift from God, or to the 136-metre **Thornton Falls**, a ninety-minute walk from Gonja. Overnight stays in Ikongwe can be arranged with local families, and the trip can be combined with Mpepera Viewpoint.

**Costs** are very reasonable: Tsh10,000 per person for the guide, Tsh2000 per person for the village, meals (Tsh2500), porter (Tsh2000) and Tsh1000 for a consultation with a traditional healer. Camping away from Mbaga costs Tsh2500, though you'll need your own tent. The Tona Traditional Dancing Troupe can be hired for Tsh5000 plus tips.

## Chome village

**Chome village**, hidden in a lush green valley at the western base of Shengena Peak, is one of Pare's gems: a small, traditional and immensely friendly place, despite having suffered the mysterious abduction of dozens of villagers in 1929 – no one knows where they ended up. The village can be visited as part of Mbaga's cultural tourism programme (it's a day's walk along narrow footpaths), or through *Kisaka Villa Inn* in Chome itself (☎0754/288858, ✉kisakas@yahoo.co.uk; BB, en suite ❸), a large and modern two-storey alpine-style building with a rather religious atmosphere (no alcohol or smoking). Public transport from Same, 41km away, is limited to irregular Land Rovers and pick-ups, usually leaving Same in the afternoon. If you're driving, instead of turning left at

---

### Mkomazi National Park

Tanzania's newest national park, Mkomazi was only gazetted in 2008 and still sees few visitors. At the moment the wildlife is rather sparse, thanks at least in part to Mkomazi's former incarnation as a hunting reserve, but TANAPA has high hopes for this scenic stretch of baobab-studded savanna adjoining Kenya's giant Tsavo National Park.

Entrance to the park costs $20, and the main attractions are the 400-plus species of birds and some rare creatures including the gerenuk, an agile antelope that gets up on its hind legs to reach food higher up. In addition, there's a rhino sanctuary – which also plays host to a pack of African hunting dogs – though visits here must be arranged in advance. For more information, visit ⓦwww.tanzaniaparks.com /mkomazi.html.

Mwembe for Mbaga, just keep going until you reach a signposted turning, leaving you with 26km to Chome. You might have to push your vehicle at the end, as the last part is very steep.

Apart from the hike up **Shengena Peak**, local attractions – most of which can be walked to in a few hours – include the Namoche Valley (scene of a victorious battle against the Maasai), warriors' graves, German ruins, local farms, waterfalls and viewpoints, and the **Kings' Stone**, once used for human sacrifices: victims were thrown off the top. It's a very steep and slippery climb through thick bush.

# The Usambara Mountains

Southeast of the Pare Mountains, and also belonging to the ancient Eastern Arc chain (see p.279) are the craggy and often mist-shrouded **Usambaras**, which rise with startling abruptness over a kilometre above the dusty plains below, forming two rocky, forest-cloaked ranges. The larger and more densely populated is **West Usambara**, home to the ever-friendly Sambaa people. It contains some of Tanzania's most spectacular hiking terrain, and plenty of swivel-eyed chameleons, too. The area is easily and most enjoyably explored via a cultural tourism programme. **East Usambara**, separated from the western range by the Lwengera valley, is equally alluring: the monsoon-fed rainforests of the Amani Nature Reserve, clinging to its vertiginous slopes, are the second-most biodiverse place in Africa.

## West Usambara Mountains

The only road up into West Usambara, from Mombo on the highway, follows the twisted, boulder-strewn gorge of the **Bangala River**. If you can stop worrying about the unfenced chasm to your left, it's a dramatic ride that takes you from the flat and dry expanse of the Maasai Steppe into a lushly forested and quite spectacular land, where you'll glimpse mountain peaks towering over waterfalls, and some precariously balanced ridge-top villages and farms. The district capital of **Lushoto** is the main base for one of Tanzania's best cultural tourism programmes, with plenty of guided tours around West Usambara from half-day trips to week-long hikes.

### Lushoto

The base for most visitors to the Usambaras is **LUSHOTO**, 34km from Mombo and the highway. Despite being Usambara's biggest town, it's an intimate, friendly and instantly likeable sort of place, and enjoys an especially beautiful setting among high-forested peaks. Lushoto's altitude (almost 1400m) ensures a cool and temperate climate all year round, and made it a favoured mountain retreat for German officials, who named it **Wilhelmstal**, in honour of their Kaiser. For a time, it even served as the unofficial "summer

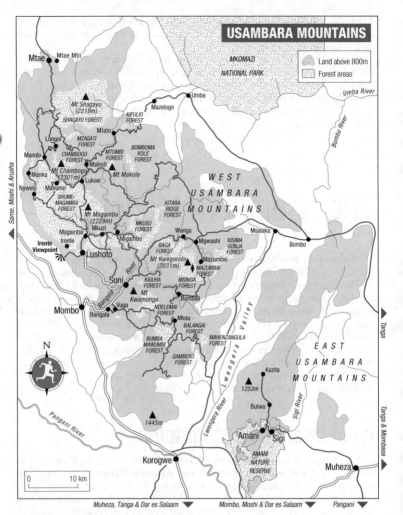

capital" for German East Africa – a welcome change from the sweltering heat and humidity of Dar es Salaam. The first European to visit was the missionary **Johann Ludwig Krapf**, who in 1849 was given a warm welcome by the local chief, Kimweri I. European interest remained marginal until 1886, when arch-colonist **Karl Peters** – "a model colonial administrator" in the words of Adolf Hitler – "persuaded" the ruler to sign away his domain for a pittance. The subsequent German advance was made easier because at the same time Usambara was racked by chaos: the **slave trade** had turned its sights to the mountains, and at the same time the Sambaa's Kilindi dynasty was caught up in a civil war against East Usambara's Bondei, who wanted independence. Many buildings survive from the period of German rule, including a bizarre construction at the top end of town whose belfry is topped by an onion-shaped steeple made from iron sheeting.

Apart from the history, the scenery and cultural tourism, Lushoto's other attraction is its colourful **market**, which is liveliest on Thursday and Sunday when farmers descend from all around. Sunday is especially good for traditional pottery – either plain, or incised with geometric motifs inspired by plants. **Fruit** is another speciality, especially apples and pears (Easter), peaches and plums (Dec–Feb), jackfruit (Mar–Jun), tamarind (Nov–Jan), loquats (Jun & Jul), and berries all year round. Look out also for traditional medicinal herbs and bark (*madawa asili*, "ancestor medicine"), honey (*asali*) and *viungo vya chai* – powdered ginger (*tangawizi*) mixed with other spices for adding to tea. The best deals are made late, when vendors want to go home.

### Practicalities

Lushoto is served by early morning **buses** from Arusha, Dar, Moshi and Tanga, and by daladalas from Tanga until mid-afternoon. If you miss these, get to **Mombo** on the highway (take any Arusha–Moshi or Dar–Tanga bus), from where there are frequent daladalas to Soni (1hr) and Lushoto (1hr 30min): catch them at the start of the road 100m off the highway. Should you want to explore the surrounding area under your own steam, mountain bikes can be rented through the cultural tourism programmes or from the *Lawns Hotel* (Tsh6000–10,000 a day).

Change traveller's cheques before you arrive, as it may be awkward to change them once you're here. NMB (near the tourist office) will change cash without fuss, but there's no ATM as yet. The District Hospital can be found 1.5km back along the road to Soni (☎027/264 0098), and internet access is available at ELCT, beside *Tumaini Hostel* (Mon–Sat 8am–6pm).

### Accommodation

The town itself has a good spread of budget and mid-range **accommodation**; the cheaper ones are southwest of the centre – haunt of an uncommonly tuneless muezzin who wakes all and sundry at 5am. **Camping** is possible at *Lawns Hotel* (Tsh6000 per person).

There are a handful of great **places to stay** at in the hills around Lushoto and in addition to these, the cultural tourism programmes can organize **homestays** for no more than Tsh10,000 per person per night; for Soni's

▲ Market, Usambara Mountains

## Staying safe

Given Lushoto's popularity with backpackers, there are sometimes **aggressive touts** in Lushoto or Mombo, and robberies are occasionally reported. So, take care of your bags on arrival (Lushoto's bus stand, though small, can be chaotic), and don't hire a guide on the street or on public transport, no matter how slick their patter or genuine their ID card appears to be; instead, arrange things at one of the cultural tourism programmes (see p.290), or at *Maweni Farm* in Soni.

*Maweni Farm*, one of northern Tanzania's best (and most affordable) hotels. **Camping** is possible at *Irente Farm* (Tsh5000 per person); unfortunately, Irente viewpoint's cliff-top campsite (the aptly named "Bellavista" with its dizzying views) had been abandoned at the time of writing, but it's worth asking about in case it reopens.

### In town

**Karibuni Lodge** 1km along the road to Soni ☎027/264 0104 or 0784/474026. The luxuriant forest location, complete with vervet monkeys and birds, is what recommends this simple, charming and cosy colonial-era place. Apart from a four-bed dorm (Tsh6500 per person), there are four en-suite rooms, all with wooden floors, box nets and hot water. Dinner can be arranged (Tsh5000), and there's a book swap. BB ❷
**Kialilo Green Garden Motel** ☎027/264 3464. One of the best options, this tiny place has clean and bright but narrow rooms with tiled bathrooms, hot water, TV, crisp linen and box nets. Friendly staff, and safe parking. BB ❷
**Kilimani Guest House** ☎027/264 0014. Past its prime: twelve cell-like rooms (two with badly kept bathrooms and squat toilets) flanking a courtyard and somnolent bar. There's a livelier beer garden, which can be noisy weekends. Food is available and there's safe parking at the side. ❶
**Kimunyu Guest House** ☎0717/640930. A good budget option, with a friendly welcome and simple but clean rooms and shared bathrooms; the better ones have big box-nets. ❶
**Lawns Hotel** ☎027/264 0005, ⓦwww .lawnshotel.com. Over a century old, this Cypriot-run place is both quirky and charming – that is so long as you heed the belligerent "complaints won't be tolerated" sign in the reception… You have a choice of rooms with or without bathrooms (those without are less than half price) but all vary considerably in style and quality: the better ones have creaky floorboards, old fireplaces, heavy Art Deco beds and cast-iron baths. There's a good restaurant and bar, friendly dogs, a small putting green, internet access, and safe parking. BB ❷; en suite ❸
**Lushoto Executive Lodge** 1.5km along the road to Magamba ☎0784/360624 or 027/260 0076,

ⓦwww.lushotoexecutivelodge.co.tz. Set in a hilly, lawned garden, the lodge is aimed at tourists as well as conferences. The main building is from German times, now with a modern extension; there are also a few new cottages. The rooms are smart and comfortable, with four-posters, box nets and satellite TV. It also has a restaurant, gym, health "spa" and golf putting course, all in all making it very good value. BB ❹
**Lushoto Sun Hotel** ☎027/264 0082. For a long time this was the main backpackers' haunt, but is now well overpriced and flagging pretty badly, some of its rooms even touching on dingy. Recommended only if it (or at least its bathrooms) has been renovated. The restaurant's average (no alcohol). Safe parking. ❸
**Mandarin Grand Hotel** ☎0784/533816. A half-complete hotel on which construction stalled years ago, so it resembles a building site in parts, but the view over Lushoto – and the warm welcome – are its saving graces. The twenty rooms are well kept and spacious: single rooms share bathrooms, but there are better-value en-suite doubles (with box nets), twins (round nets), triples and suites, some with bathtubs *and* enough hot water to fill them. There's also a sleepy bar and restaurant. BB ❷
**Sarafina Teachers' Club** ☎027/264 0087. Basic, cheap, calm and friendly, with clean rooms and shared bathrooms. Good value despite the erratic water supply. ❶
**Tumaini Hostel** ☎027/264 0094 or 0784/563214, ⓦwww.elct-ned.org. This Lutheran Church place is a calm and decent choice, but is often full. The bright, simple rooms all come with box nets, some with good bathrooms; there are three dorms (Tsh5000 a head), and a suite with two beds that can be pushed together. Also has a good restaurant, foreign exchange, and safe parking. BB ❷–❸

**View Point Guest House** ☏ 027/264 0031. Despite the name, there's no view. This is a quiet and very basic family-run place with seven sometimes musty rooms, all with nets, table and chair, most sharing squat toilets and bucket showers. ❶

**White House Annex** ☏ 0784/427471. One of the better cheapish options, with ten rooms, two sharing bathrooms (squat toilets), plus some overpriced suites with TVs, but all have mosquito nets. There's also a popular bar with outside tables, a TV in the reception, and a restaurant (order early). Safe parking. ❶

## Out of Town

🏃 **Irente Farm (Mkuyu Lodge)** 4.5km west of town, before Irente viewpoint ☏ 0784/502935 or 0788/503002, ⊛ www.elct-ned .org. A bucolic place recommended primarily for its food, a true Epicurean delight. It has just five rooms, so book ahead: two three-bed ones in a long green-roofed building with a kitchen; two small doubles; and a flat sleeping three. Meals cost Tsh5000–6000, including possibly the best breakfast in Tanzania (see p.291 for the basic ingredients). Walk there, or catch a taxi for under Tsh10,000. ❸

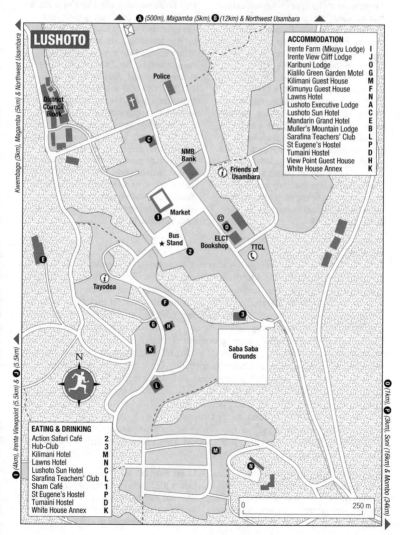

**LUSHOTO**

Ⓐ (500m), Magamba (5km), Ⓑ (12km) & Northwest Usambara

Kwembago (3km), Magamba (5km) & Northwest Usambara

Ⓘ (4km), Irente Viewpoint (5.5km) & Ⓙ (5.5km)

Police

District Council Block

**ACCOMMODATION**

| | |
|---|---|
| Irente Farm (Mkuyu Lodge) | I |
| Irente View Cliff Lodge | J |
| Karibuni Lodge | O |
| Kialilo Green Garden Motel | G |
| Kilimani Guest House | M |
| Kimunyu Guest House | F |
| Lawns Hotel | N |
| Lushoto Executive Lodge | A |
| Lushoto Sun Hotel | C |
| Mandarin Grand Hotel | E |
| Muller's Mountain Lodge | B |
| Sarafina Teachers' Club | L |
| St Eugene's Hostel | P |
| Tumaini Hostel | D |
| View Point Guest House | H |
| White House Annex | K |

NMB Bank

ⓘ Friends of Usambara

Ⓒ

Ⓔ

Market

ⓘ Tayodea

@ Ⓓ

★ Bus Stand

ELCT Bookshop

TTCL ☎

Ⓕ

Ⓖ Ⓗ

Ⓚ

Ⓔ₃

Saba Saba Grounds

N

Ⓛ

Ⓜ

Ⓝ

**EATING & DRINKING**

| | |
|---|---|
| Action Safari Café | 2 |
| Hub-Club | 3 |
| Kilimani Hotel | M |
| Lawns Hotel | N |
| Lushoto Sun Hotel | C |
| Sarafina Teachers' Club | L |
| Sham Café | 1 |
| St Eugene's Hostel | P |
| Tumaini Hostel | D |
| White House Annex | K |

0          250 m

Ⓞ (1km), Ⓟ (3km), Soni (16km) & Mombo (34km)

**Irente View Cliff Lodge** 6km west of town, at Irente viewpoint ☎027/264 0026, ⓦwww.irenteview.com. Something of an eyesore right on the cliff edge, this ostentatious complex – a conference venue, really – boasts vertiginous views from the balconies of its sixteen rooms, albeit through loosely spaced iron grilles (the management evidently wishing to avoid free-falling guests). The best views are from the standard rooms in the main building, all with satellite TV. The "superior" rooms, larger and with bathtubs, are in two rows; those at the front have good views, the ones further back overlook a canyon and cliffs. The restaurant and bar in the main conical *makuti*-thatched building lack views. Hikes can be arranged, and there's internet access. Free pick-up from Lushoto if you book ahead. BB ❺

**Maweni Farm** 2.5km east of Soni, 18km from Lushoto ☎027/264 0427 or 0784/307841, ⓦwww.maweni.com. A great base for cultural tourism (see p.290) is this 1920s farmhouse, in the lee of a imposing cliff. There are thirteen well-kept rooms with box nets, most with bathrooms, plus four en-suite, walk-in tents pitched on a concrete platform overlooking an ornamental pond. Accommodation aside, the food is superb, much of it raised or grown organically on the farm. There's also fast Internet, a telescope, a wood-panelled lounge and dining room, a playgroup for kids, holistic treats (including yoga and reiki), and stacks of locally produced documentaries. BB ❹

**Muller's Mountain Lodge** 12km northeast of town, at Mkuzi ☎027/264 0204 or 0715/315661, ⓦwww.mullersmountainlodge.co.tz. Set in orchards and farmland close to Mkuzi Forest, this is a grand, two-storey 1935 farmhouse in the style of an English country manor (brick walls and steep, thatched gable roof), and blessed with a fittingly old-fashioned interior, including a cosy living room with a big fireplace and board games. There are seven bedrooms, some en suite (including a two-bedroom cottage; $100), all with big beds and fluffy pillows and duvets. Amenities include a bar and restaurant, great walking guides, and trips by car. To drive here, turn right at Magamba and right again after 5.3km at the signpost. Free lift from Lushoto if you stay two nights; taxis charge upwards of Tsh20,000. BB ❹

**St Eugene's Hostel** 3km towards Soni, at Ubiri ☎027/264 0055 or 0784/523710, ⓔsteugenes_hostel@yahoo.com. A source of funding for projects run by the Catholic Mission of the Montessori Sisters, this is perfect so long as you're okay with the cocoon-like atmosphere. The two-storey guesthouse – a starkly modern building whose green roof touches the ground – contains fourteen spotless and very comfortable guest rooms, all en suite, some with balconies. There's also a kitchen, great breakfasts, and equally good lunches and dinners ($7). Walk, or catch a daladala. BB ❹

## Eating

Lushoto is a delight if you're **self-catering**. Your first stop should be the market, for fruit and vegetables – amazingly cheap, even by Tanzanian standards. Also well worth stopping at is *Tumaini Hostel*, which sells some of the exceedingly fine output of **Irente Farm** (see p.291 for a mouthwatering list). Giving Irente Farm a run for its money is the Catholic Mission at Ubiri, 3km south of Lushoto, which also makes good cheese and rye bread, but is famed both for its "gooseberry" jam (actually cape gooseberry), and banana wine. If you'll be staying overnight with locals as part of a cultural tour, see whether you can get someone to cook up **bada**, a Sambaa speciality consisting of a thick, greenish-brown porridge of pounded maize flour and dried fermented cassava, mixed with hot water and oil and served in aromatic banana leaves. It's exceedingly tasty, and is eaten, like *ugali*, dipped in sauces. *Bada* is usually served with chicken or meat, fried bananas or potatoes.

The following are the pick of the town's better **restaurants**; try also the bars near the bus station, where you'll find good *nyama choma* (roughly Tsh2500 for half a kilo of beef).

**Action Safari Café** Friendly and welcoming place near the bus stand that's accustomed to tourists, so offers spaghetti as well as local dishes (from Tsh1200). Also has snacks, and brews a wicked spiced tea.

**Lawns Hotel** Delicious three-course lunches or dinners (Tsh10,000) in a quirky dining room decorated with commemorative plates from around the globe, plus snacks and light meals for under Tsh4000. You can also eat on a veranda.

## Moving on from Lushoto

Lushoto has daily **buses** to Arusha, Dar and Tanga, as well as to Mtae. As usual, most departures are early in the morning, though you can still find transport to Arusha as "late" as 10am, but it's best to check things out the day before. There are several daily buses to Dar, the better ones being Umba River Tours and Shambalai (both 8am). For Tanga and Muheza (for Amani Nature Reserve in East Usambara), the last bus leaves around 10am; Tashriff also covers the route but has a mixed safety record. Alternatively, catch a daladala down to Mombo (every 30min), and change there for another one to Tanga (the last one leaves around 3pm). If you want to catch one of the better buses to Dar, Moshi or Arusha, phone their offices in Arusha or Dar es Salaam (see the "Moving on" sections in those chapters) to book a seat, and tell them you'll board at New Liverpool Hill Breeze, a bar/restaurant/bus stop 1km north of Mombo along the highway where most long-distance buses take a short break.

**Lushoto Sun Hotel** Average but cheap food (under Tsh3000) that you can eat at the street-side terrace. No alcohol, but you're welcome to bring your own.
**Sham Café** A great little place for cheap and unfussy meals, and they're happy to rustle up something special if you contact them beforehand. They also provide hot milk – a favourite with locals and just right on a cold day.
**St Eugene's Hostel** 3km towards Soni. The convent's nuns dish up great breakfasts: virtually everything is home-made, including the bread, butter, jam and an array of cheeses. Other meals cost $7.

**Tumaini Hostel** There are two restaurants here: a bland-looking one indoors for touristic fare such as burgers, vegetarian moussaka, pizza, and a good range of meat and fish; and a more attractive one in the garden for Tanzanian fare. It's pricey for snacks, but good value for more substantial dishes (Tsh3500 and up). Also has ice cream, juices and shakes. No alcohol.
**White House Annex** Not a patch on what it once was, but it still serves up half-decent meals, including spaghetti and pepper steak, mostly under Tsh3000.

### Drinking and nightlife

The following are the best of the town's numerous **bars**. Many sell the local **sugar cane hooch**, *boha*, popular with both men and women – especially the latter during festivities such as "Kibwebwe", an all-night, women-only drumming celebration held after the birth of a mother's first child. At posher places, ask for the Montessori Sisters' surprisingly palatable "Dochi" **banana wine**. If you're still thirsty, the Benedictine Fathers in Sakharani, near Soni (⊕027/264 0452), make Tanzania's best **grape wine**, a Chenin Blanc under the "Sakharani" label.

**Hub-Club** A normal bar by day, this hosts lively discos on Saturday nights.
**Kilimani Hotel** There are two bars here; the one worth mentioning is the beer garden, sometimes with discos on Friday or Saturday. There's also a wide choice of food, including hangover-quashing *supu*.
**Lawns Hotel** Contains Lushoto's nicest bar, very cosy and pub-like, and equipped with satellite TV.

The Cypriot owner offers a free drink in exchange for unusual foreign coins to add to the zillions glued to the counter. There's also a veranda.
**Sarafina Teachers' Club** A pleasant and laid-back place open past midnight; also does good *nyama choma*.
**White House Annex** Near the *Sarafina* and equally friendly and relaxed, with plenty of tables outside.

# Around Lushoto

The practical nitty-gritty of getting around West Usambara is a breeze thanks to an affordable **cultural tourism programme**. Originally developed in the 1990s by villagers with the assistance of NGOs, the result is over a dozen different and well-established **guided tours** around the mountains, ranging from three-hour strolls to challenging week-long hikes or cycling trips through some of Tanzania's most inspiring terrain. The most popular trips, or "modules", are described in the following pages, and can often be combined.

The original cultural tourism programme is run by the **Friends of Usambara**, whose office – also functioning as a tourist information centre – is behind Lushoto's NMB bank and is signposted from the bus stand (open daily 7.30am–6pm; ☏0784/689848 or 0784/423917, ✉usambaras2005@yahoo.com). Best of the copycats, and often happily enthusiastic, is **TAYODEA** (Tanga Youth Development Association), a self-help group established by formerly unemployed youths. Their office, also in Lushoto, is beside *Green Valley Annex*, 200m southwest of the bus stand (☏0787/246169, ✉youthall2000@yahoo.com). Alternatively, base yourself at **Maweni Farm** in Soni (p.288); the manager, Juma Kahema, has been involved with the Friends of Usambara since day one, and knows the mountains better than anyone else.

Although you're not obliged to take a **guide**, you'll need one for anything but the walk to Irente viewpoint, unless you fancy rambling around in circles. Most guides know the trails backwards, speak reasonable to excellent English, and provide a great introduction for getting to know the locals more intimately. By taking a guide, part of your fee also benefits local communities. **Costs** vary according to the tour and, in part, on your perceived ability to pay (it's always worth bargaining). Starting prices shouldn't be more than Tsh30,000–45,000 per person per day including meals, more if you're staying overnight, using a vehicle, or entering gazetted forest reserves (an additional $30).

## The Lion King of Usambara

Unlike many East African tribes, for whom contact with the modern world came abruptly, traditional Sambaa culture had time to adapt to modern times rather than simply being swept away, thanks to the inaccessibility of its mountain terrain.

The Sambaa's agricultural way of life, and settled communities, favoured systems of leadership based around individuals rather than councils of elders. Their first great chief, a founding father of sorts, was **Mbega** (also spelled Mbegha), born in the late 1600s to a Zigua chief in Ngulu, down on the plains. Oral histories recount that Mbega was cheated of his inheritance and forced into exile. He wandered for many years, gaining a reputation as a skilled and generous hunter. At the time, the Sambaa were experiencing problems with an infestation of bush pigs, which were uprooting their crops, so they asked the famous hunter for assistance in ridding them of their problematic swine. Mbega set about his work, all the while distributing gifts of meat to the local people. Word of his skill, wisdom and fairness spread swiftly, and soon Mbega became sought after for his skills in settling disputes, too. So much so that the people of Vuga, near Soni in West Usambara, asked him to become their leader.

During his reign, which was characterized by intelligence and consideration, Mbega united the Sambaa clans into the **kingdom of Kilindi**, named after the place where Mbega had settled before coming to Usambara. Mbega himself became known as Simbawene, **the Lion King**. The Kilindi dynasty reached its height at the start of the nineteenth century, when the Sambaa ruled not only over Usambara, but also over the Pare Mountains and much of the plains south and east. By the 1840s, however, the Zigua tribe from the plains were becoming dominant thanks to their involvement in the **slave trade**, which gave them access to firearms, and by the time the Germans arrived in the 1880s, the Sambaa's military weakness was such that they capitulated without a fight.

The Kilindi dynasty was granted limited power by the Germans, and by the British who followed, but their rule ended in 1962 when the Tanzanian government abolished tribal chiefdoms. Nonetheless, the lineal descendants of Mbega are still known by his title, the Lion King.

## Soni and around

The busy little town of **SONI**, between Mombo and Lushoto, is famed for its twice-weekly **market** (Tuesdays and Fridays), where the entire array of West Usambara produce can be found. Fruits are especially good, including plums, passion fruit, mountain papaya (sweeter and more delicate than the lowland variety), coconuts and pineapples. Soni is easily reached by daladala from Mombo or Lushoto, or on long-distance buses to Lushoto.

There are a number of good half- or full-day excursions in the area, which can be arranged through Soni's *Maweni Farm* (see p.288), or via Lushoto's cultural tourism programmes. Apart from a quick visit to (and possibly a swim in) **Soni Falls**, where the Mkuzi River becomes the Bangala, seek out the **"Growing Rock"** near Magila village, which seems to grow taller each year. In fact, it's the soil around the base that's disappearing, thanks to erosion. Then head to Mount Kwamongo, to take in good views and see lots of butterflies. The best trip is a five-day hike (three if you drive back) to the **Mazumbai Rainforest**, West Usambara's best-preserved primary forest. It's a challenging trip, covering a variety of up-and-down terrain, and is particularly recommended for **birdwatchers**. Two of the birds will be on any birders'"must-see" list: the Usambara alakat (*Sheppardia montana*), and the endangered Usambara weaver (*Ploceus nicolli*). *Maweni Farm* charges $180 per person for the three-day version.

## Irente and around

The walk to and from **Irente Viewpoint**, 6km west of Lushoto, is the most popular short trip offered by the cultural tourism programmes (expensive at Tsh20,000–30,000 per person), and although you don't actually need a guide to be able to follow the road, a spate of muggings a few years ago (and a few irritating wannabe guides along the way) means it's best to take one along to be on the safe side. If you decide to go it alone, the only tricky point is 800m off to the left of our Lushoto map, where you reach a small hamlet with two wide dirt roads turning off on your right. Take the second one (it should be signposted), and just follow it all the way.

The viewpoint, perched on the southwestern edge of the Usambaras, offers a truly breathtaking panorama over the Maasai Steppe almost exactly one kilometre below. The isolated range facing you, with the knuckle-shaped outline, is Mount Mafi, and the settlement below is Mazinde. You can **stay overnight** at the over-the-top (in both senses) *Irente View Cliff Lodge* (p.288), or have lunch there, although its restaurant has no views.

On your return, stop by the Lutheran-run **Irente Farm**, 1.7km back along the road, an ideal picnic break with plenty of seating in colourful shaded gardens. The farm shop sells quite delicious **organic food**: heavy German-style rye bread, jams, pickles and other preserves, macadamia nuts, arabica coffee, flavoured teas picked by the patients of Lutindi Mental Hospital near Korogwe at the base of the mountains, and – best of all – superb cheeses, including German-style Quark curd cheese, and one just like Tilziter. Contact the farm in advance (p.287) if you'd like them to prepare lunch, an extravagant picnic for just Tsh3000.

Adjacent to the farm is **Irente Children's Home**, also run by the church, around which the matron will be happy to escort you. Poverty and AIDS are the main problems, the latter having in some cases wiped out entire generations. The home houses over twenty orphans, disabled children and children of parents with psychiatric disorders, and also trains older girls – who look after the little ones – in pre-nursing care and basic schooling. Nearby are two special-needs schools, also run by the church: **Irente Rainbow School** for autistic children, and **Irente School for the Blind**; you're welcome to visit either of them.

## Magamba Rainforest

The physically demanding but rewarding walk through **Magamba Rainforest**, north of Lushoto, gives you a shot at spotting black-and-white colobus monkeys, horned chameleons, exotic birds, such as the paradise flycatcher, plenty of butterflies, and weirdly extravagant fungi. It's done as a round trip from Lushoto (5–6hr), and can be extended to a full day by visiting the wild **Mkuzi Falls**, a narrow cascade in the thick of the forest off the road east of Magamba, and where you can swim. Arranged through the cultural tourism programmes, the walk, including Mkuzi, **costs** around Tsh40,000 per person.

The standard tour begins with a stiff uphill hike along tracks to the east of the Lushoto–Magamba road, passing through the former colonial settlement of Jaegerstal and a camphorwood forest. Just north of Magamba village at the junction to Mkuzi, a track delves into the forest on your left. Emerging onto a forestry road, you continue uphill to a ridge giving expansive views over Lushoto and the Maasai Steppe. From the ridge, the track continues south to a rest house atop **Kiguu Hakwewa Hill**, whose name translates as "unclimbed by short leg", a delightful way of saying steep. There are 360-degree views and a toilet. If you (literally) stomp around here, you'll notice that the hill appears to be hollow, as indeed it is: it was excavated by German residents during World War I for use as a **bunker**. The bunker is said to contain almost one hundred rooms; it definitely contains bats. You're free to explore, but you'll need a torch, and watch out for snakes; the entrance is 100m downhill on the southeastern flank. From the hill, a steep and rocky path heads down through farmland to the royal village of **Kwembago**, one of the seats of the Kilindi dynasty, and which has good views over Lushoto.

## Mlalo

The walk to **MLALO**, north of Lushoto, takes three or four days there and back, including travelling some sections by bus, but is best combined with a visit to Mtae (see below) for an excellent six- or seven-day trip; expect to spend Tsh25,000–35,000 per day, including a guide. The walk includes Magamba Rainforest, followed by a bus ride direct to Mlalo, or to Malindi, from where you walk. There are several good markets in the area. **Kileti village's** (also called Kwemieeti) is the main one, and is also one of the best places for meeting female **potters**. The Sambaa liken the art of pottery to the creation of life in a mother's womb, so it's no surprise that pottery is traditionally a woman's occupation, with knowledge and rituals connected with the craft being passed from mother to daughter. Although men are allowed to collect clay, they are excluded from the pot-making process itself – it's believed that their presence may anger spirits, who might crack the pots during firing or, worse still, cause sterility. There's simple and generally perfectly decent **accommodation** in several villages along the way. Recommended in Mlalo itself is the *Silver Dollar Guest House* (❶), with clean rooms, shared bathrooms and a good restaurant.

## Mtae and around

The journey to **MTAE**, a village perched on the northwestern edge of the mountains, is the most popular long excursion from Lushoto, taking three to five days depending on how much you cheat by catching the bus. Although the trip can be done without a guide, you'll miss much of the context and contacts

## The goat and the leopard

Mtae's motto is *Kesi ya mbuzi hakimu ni chui haki hakuna*, which means, if the leopard is the judge when a goat brings a court case against a lion, there will be no justice. The saying is illustrated by paintings hung up in some of the village's bars, and depicts a courtroom presided over by a leopard. The plaintiff is a lion, the defendant a goat. The saying alludes to colonial times, when there was little chance of justice for an African from a German judge when the plaintiff was a German farmer.

that make this walk so special. The views are simply gobsmacking, especially as you approach Mtae, and the villages between are as fascinating and pretty as they are friendly, offering plenty of opportunities to meet the locals.

Passing by Shume-Magamba rainforest (where you might glimpse black-and-white colobus monkeys, even from the bus), **Lukosi** is the first stop, an attractive village set in a high valley, which has a couple of basic guest-houses (❶). North or west of here, look for the unusual two-storey houses with intricately carved wooden balconies, accessed via external staircases, which are also found in the Pare Mountains. Also distinctive are whitewashed houses whose facades and interiors are decorated with geometric designs reminiscent of Ndebele house paintings in South Africa, or Ethiopian religious art – perhaps no coincidence, as some oral histories place the origins of the Sambaa in Ethiopia.

The village of **Mtae** itself is utterly enchanting, and delights the eye with views you'll remember for the rest of your life. The location is everything, isolated on a spur that juts out from the northwestern edge of the mountains – in some places you have a plunging 270-degree view over the plains almost a kilometre below, giving the impression you're flying. With clear skies, especially in the evenings, you can see the Taita Hills in Kenya to the north, and the Pare Mountains and sometimes even Kilimanjaro to the northwest – before the sun disappears in a kaleidoscope of colours and smoke from kitchens drifts into the air. In warm weather, night-time can be just as humbling, with the twinkling of fireflies seemingly reflecting that of the stars above. Don't sleep in, mind: during and just after the rains you might wake to the extraordinary sight of being above a blanket of clouds.

At any time of year, your alarm clock will be the drifting sound of crowing cocks and lowing cattle, followed by goats and children, while on Sundays the bells ring out from the **Lutheran church**, complete with its boisterous (if not always tuneful) brass band. The church was founded at the end of the nineteenth century on land that locals knew was haunted by spirits. The idea, at least if you believe the church's version of the story, had been to scare off the newcomers; but the church prospered, prompting many a local to convert to Christianity. Others remained true to their beliefs: the area around Mtae is renowned for the power of its traditional healers.

### Practicalities

Mtae is best visited as part of the cultural tourism programme (see p.290), with which you can walk all or part of the way. **Public transport** is limited to two daily buses. The ride up from Lushoto, along a narrow dirt road, often with sheer drops on one side, is one of the bumpiest (if most scenic) in Tanzania, and isn't advisable in the rains. The buses leave Lushoto between 2pm and 3pm, to arrive in Mtae three or four hours later. Heading back from **Mtae**, the first bus leaves at the unearthly time of 3am or 4am, the other no later than 6am.

The best **restaurant** is attached to *Mwivano Guest House 1*, and for **drinking**, try *Mtitu wa Ndei* next to the *Pendo Guest House*. If you need medical attention, visit the dispensary at the Lutheran mission. Mtae's high altitude, exposed location and strong winds make it chilly at night, so bring a sweater, and be aware that the sun burns more quickly at this altitude.

## Accommodation

**Accommodation** is limited to the following small places, all on the main (and only) road, within a few hundred metres of each other. **Camping** is available at the *Lutheran Mission* (no more than Tsh5000 per person).

**Kuna Maneno Guest House** ☎027/264 0200. The only establishment in the village with electricity, albeit powered by a none-too-reliable generator. There are eight doubles and one twin (shared bathrooms only) and reliable piped water, plus a large but usually empty bar. **①**

**Lutheran Mission** c/o ELCT in Lushoto ☎027/264 0102. This place has atmospheric and spacious rooms, all with high ceilings and creaking floorboards, in a wing adjacent to the church. Food is available if ordered in the morning for the evening. **①**

**Mount Usambara Guest House** (no phone). Eight rooms with shared facilities (and hot water in buckets). Two rooms have fantastic views over Lake Kalimawe and the Pare Mountains beyond. **①**

**Mwivano Guest House** ☎027/264 0198. This is actually two hotels on the main road. *Number 1* sits next to a restaurant and has cell-like singles with clean, shared showers and toilets. *Number 2*, 200m back on the left, is more attractive, and has double rooms with shared bathrooms and stunning views through chicken wire-covered windows over Mkomazi Game Reserve. **①**

### Mtae Mtii

A leisurely and recommended four-hour walk goes from Mtae to the small village of **MTAE MTII**, the last seat of the Kilindi dynasty in northwestern Usambara before chiefdoms were abolished in 1962 (the main seat was at Vuga near Soni), and you can do the return journey in a day. Mtae Mtii was also the site of a semi-mythical nineteenth-century battle between the Sambaa and the Maasai, who lived in the plains below. The story goes that the Maasai believed that the king of Usambara had the power to bring rain to the plains, so one day they went to ask him for rain. He refused, and the Maasai resolved to fight. Although the Maasai were better equipped, the Sambaa vanquished their attackers by rolling boulders down the steep inclines, killing most of them. As spoils, the Sambaa seized the Maasai's cattle. Locals say they are the ancestors of all the cows you see grazing contentedly in the mountains today.

The last king of Mtae Mtii died in the late 1990s. His **compound** can be visited as part of the cultural tourism programme and has a fantastic location on a crag overlooking the Mkomazi plains. Next to the surprisingly humble (and now abandoned) hut where the king lived is an enclosure made from branches, bushes and young trees.

# East Usambara

Rising abruptly from the coastal lowlands a mere 40km from the ocean, the steep and lushly forested escarpments of the **East Usambara Mountains** level off about a kilometre above sea level onto a deeply furrowed plateau. The range is separated physically and biologically from West Usambara by the 4km-wide Lwengera Valley. With the exception of dry lowlands to the north, the climate is warm and humid, influenced by the proximity of the Indian Ocean. Rainfall averages 2000mm a year, which, together with the deeply weathered red loam soils, has created ideal conditions for the evolution of an astonishingly rich and complex **tropical rainforest ecosystem**.

The figures speak for themselves: of East Usambara's 230 tree species, sixteen are unique, whilst of the well over two thousand vascular plant species recorded so far, over a quarter are found nowhere else on earth. Most species of **African violet** originated in East Usambara, and are now the pride and joy of gardeners all over the world. Their genus, *Saintpaulia*, is named after Baron Walter von Saint Paul Illaire, the Tanga district commissioner of German East Africa. In 1892, he shipped a consignment of the small blue flowers to Berlin, starting a horticultural craze that continues to this day. The African violet's hidden genetic make-up tells of the forests' immense age: blue or violet in the wild, gardeners and botanists have managed to tease all sorts of colours from the plant's genes, from red and pink to white and even green – genetic diversity in evolution increases as time goes on.

The proportion of endemic **animal** species is just as astounding, ranging from ten to sixty percent depending on family and genera. Denizens include over thirty kinds of snakes and chameleons, amongst them the terrestrial pygmy leaf chameleon, the larger arboreal three-horned chameleon and a remarkable species of toad, *Nectophrynoides tornieri*, which gives birth to live offspring instead of eggs. There are also over two hundred species of butterfly and close to 350 types of bird.

## Amani Nature Reserve

The most accessible part of East Usambara is the **Amani Nature Reserve**, its name aptly meaning "peace". Established in 1997, this mountainous and heavily forested reserve is one of Tanzania's most attractive and least-visited destinations, offering beautiful scenery, weird and wonderful flora and fauna, a constant chorus of cicadas and tree frogs (joined by the screeching of bushbabies at night), one of Africa's largest botanical gardens, and enough hiking trails through primeval rainforest to keep you in raptures (or blister packs) for weeks. Even if your interest in things botanical is limited to the greens on your plate, the sight of the towering camphor trees festooned with vines, lianas or strangling fig trees that flank much of the drive up to the reserve is the stuff of dreams.

**Bird-watchers** will also be in heaven; despite difficult viewing conditions (the forest canopy conceals well), over 335 species have been seen, including the endangered Amani sunbird, the long-billed apalis, and the banded green sunbird, which, although rare outside East Usambara, can sometimes be seen at Amani in

▲ Chameleon, Amani Nature Reserve

flocks of up to sixty. Other rare species include the Usambara red-headed bluebill, long-billed tailorbird, Sokoke scops owl (named after Arabuko-Sokoke forest in Kenya), Usambara eagle owl, Tanzanian weaver and the green-headed oriole.

There are few large **mammals** in the forest, which makes sighting them all the more rewarding, though all you're likely to see of the shy black-and-white colobus monkey is a flash of a tail in the canopy as it retreats deeper into the forest. Other primates include yellow baboons and blue monkeys, both pests for farmers – it's said that if you throw stones at blue monkeys to chase them off, they just pick them up and hurl them back, often with a surer eye. The Tanganyika mountain squirrel is the most common of the three squirrel species; and if you're really lucky, the rufous elephant shrew may put in a fleeting appearance on the forest paths.

## Access

Amani is accessed via **MUHEZA**, a messy little town on the highway 45km southwest of Tanga, and served by daladalas from Lushoto, Mombo and Tanga, and buses connecting Tanga to Dar or Arusha. Get to Muheza in the morning if you can, as public transport into the reserve can be erratic. With a few hours to kill, Muheza's busy **market** is worth a rummage: you'll find lots of herbalists here, and delectable honey, too. If you get stranded, there are a few basic guest-houses near the market and along the highway.

Some **vehicles to Amani** start at Muheza's bus stand, but most hang around at the start of the road to Amani itself: walk 200m into town from the bus stand (with the stand on your left), bear right where the road forks, then turn right again. The unmarked stand is 50m along on the left before the railway, facing the interestingly named Death Row Electronics. Two buses to Amani leave Muheza between 1 and 2pm, and carry on past Amani to Kwamkoro or Bulwa. There's also usually a pick-up or two, or a lorry or occasional daladala a little later, but rarely after 4pm. The reserve's **Sigi Gate** is 26km west of Muheza along an all-weather *murram* road. The following 9km to **Amani village**, much of it hairpin bends, is treacherously slippery in the rains, when a 4WD is

### Conserving Amani

Up until the end of the nineteenth century, East Usambara was way more extensively covered by forest than it is now, and had only a small human population. The advent of colonialism, however, had catastrophic consequences, even if the initial impact was indirect. The expulsion of farmers outside the Usambaras, to make way for commercial ranches and plantations, pushed people up into the hills, where they set about clearing forests to make farmland. But it didn't take long for the colonists to turn their gaze upwards. For both the Germans and the British, forestry meant commercial exploitation, not conservation, and extensive forest clearance for commercial **tea plantations** was a major blow, as was large-scale **logging**. The figures are sobering – from an estimated thousand square kilometres of prime forest cover in 1900, East Usambara now contains only 330, of which only a tenth remains relatively intact and undisturbed.

From the 1970s, the timber industry was actively supported by the Finnish government's development agency. Only in 1986 did the Finns realize just how grossly they had underestimated the ensuing ecological damage. Performing a perfect volte-face, commercial logging was terminated, and the Finns turned to conservation, spearheading the creation of **Amani Nature Reserve**. Although the forest's destruction has now been stemmed, many challenges remain, notably the provision of sustainable alternative sources of livelihood for communities living around the forests.

## The Sigi–Tengeni Railway

Amani's information centre occupies the delicately restored wooden German Stationmaster's House, at the terminus of the short-lived **Sigi–Tengeni Railway**. Built between 1904 and 1910, the narrow-gauge line opened up 120 square kilometres of forest to timber exploitation, but fell into disuse after World War I, and was dismantled in the 1930s when the road from Muheza was opened. Apart from the Stationmaster's House, all that remains is a diminutive freight carriage and a square block in front of the house, which housed the station bell. There's also a giant cogwheel from a demolished sawmill.

recommended. If you're feeling energetic, you could catch a vehicle to **Kisiwani village**, 3km short of Sigi Gate, for a very pleasant uphill walk through forest (watch out for snakes at night, though).

### Entry fees, information and accommodation

Unusually for Tanzania, Amani's **entrance fees**, paid at Sigi Gate or at the reserve headquarters, have no time limit: $30 per person, plus $30 per vehicle, and you can pay in shillings. Sigi Gate's **information centre** provides leaflets detailing the various trails, which are also downloadable at ⓦ www.easternarc.or.tz/eusam, together with a heap of academic papers. The **reserve headquarters** are in Amani village (ⓣ 027/264 0313, ⓔ amaninaturereservefbd@yahoo.com), where you can rent **bicycles** ($5/day), a vehicle (expensive at $300 per day for under 80km), and access the internet.

### Accomodation

There's **accommodation** at Sigi Gate and in Amani village, both of which are bases for walks. **Camping** along the various hiking trails costs $30 per person (or $40 including tent hire), but none of the sites, with the exception of Kiganga on the Kwamkoro trail, have any facilities at all.

**Amani Conservation Centre Rest House** Amani village, 9km from Sigi Gate (reservations through the reserve headquarters). Modern and comfortable, with nine large, triple-bed rooms with electricity, mosquito nets, hot showers and use of a kitchen. The rooms are treated as dorms ($10 per person), so if there are many visitors, you'll have to share. A small bar and restaurant sells cold sodas and beers, and rustles up great meals (Tsh4000). ❸

**Amani Malaria Research Centre Rest House** Amani village, 9km from Sigi Gate ⓣ 027/264 0311. In a medical research complex established by the Germans in 1893, this place has several spacious and funky bedrooms, a cosy lounge with a huge fireplace, and decent food. For drinks, try the *Welfare Club* nearby. FB ❹

**Sigi Rest House** Sigi Gate (reservations through the reserve headquarters). This place is identical in every respect to *Amani Conservation Centre Rest House*. ❸

### Exploring the reserve

There are eight **walking trails**, none longer than a day, some starting at Sigi Gate, others at Amani village, and others from elsewhere. In addition there are three "driving routes", actually better by **bicycle** (rental costs $5 a day). The reserve headquarters can advise you about combining campsites with trails, giving you two or more days in the wild without having to return to Sigi or Amani village. **Guided walks** cost $25 per person per day: expensive, but recommended for the guides' extensive botanical knowledge, and for not getting lost (easy enough, even with a map, as none of the trails are well marked). The guides can be hired at both Sigi Gate and at the reserve headquarters.

## Moving on from Amani

Most transport to Muheza, including a bus from Kwamkoro and another from Bulwa, passes through Amani village between 6am and 6.30am, reaching Sigi Gate half an hour later, and arriving in Muheza in time to catch onward transport to Pangani, Tanga, Dar or Mombo (for Lushoto). If you miss the buses, you'll have to hitch – payment will be expected. Tickets for Scandinavian Express buses from Muheza to Dar or Mombasa (Kenya) can be booked at their office on the highway (℡027/264 1214).

The rainforest is best seen along the **Amani–Sigi Mountain Trail** (3–5hr from Sigi Gate), a fairly tough and steep round trip that climbs 450m through primary and secondary lowland and submontane forest to the top of a ridge. The area has particularly tall trees (many over 60m); on the lower stretches, you may see bright orange land crabs hiding under fallen leaves. Another good trail, especially for getting between Sigi Gate and Amani village, goes through **Amani Botanical Garden**. Founded in 1902, the garden contains around three hundred tree species (indigenous and exotic), a large expanse of original forest, a spice garden, and a palmetum, whose indigenous cycads – an ancient and primitive species of palm – hint at the great age of the forests. The plants are not labelled, so take a guide if you want names.

Other trails detailed in the reserve's leaflets include visits to tea plantations (and a tea factory), waterfalls, villages and farms, viewpoints overlooking West Usambara, and cultural sites including sacred caves and the remains of a fortified Iron Age settlement. There's also a **butterfly-breeding project** with walk-in cages at Shebomeza, 2km from Amani village (Tsh2500; ℡0784/802899, Ⓦwww.amanibutterflyproject.org).

For the more adventurous (a guide is essential), try scaling **Lutindi Peak** (1360m; one day with transport, three days entirely on foot) for jaw-dropping views over the Lwengera Valley, or a **five-day hike to West Usambara**, for which you'll need a tent, and a couple of days beforehand to arrange guides, food and other practicalities. The route can also be done in reverse (ask at *Maweni Farm* in Soni, see p.288). Lastly, short **night walks** are also possible, and particularly recommended should tree frogs or chameleons turn you on.

# Travel details

There are no scheduled flights from Moshi. For flights from Kilimanjaro International Airport, see p.334.

## Buses

**Lushoto to:** Arusha (2 daily; 5–6hr); Dar (3–5 daily; 6hr); Mombo (daladalas every 30min until 5pm; 1hr); Moshi (2 daily; 4–5hr); Mtae (2 daily; 3–4hr); Muheza (3 daily plus daladalas until mid-afternoon; 2hr); Tanga (3 daily plus daladalas until mid-afternoon; 3hr).

**Moshi to:** Arusha (3 hourly; 1hr 45min); Dar (hourly until 2pm; 8–9hr); Iringa (1–3 daily; 9–10hr); Karatu (3 daily; 5hr); Kisangara Chini (2 hourly; 1hr); Lushoto (3–4 daily; 4–5hr); Machame (hourly; 1hr); Marangu

(hourly; 45min); Mbeya (1–3 daily; 15hr); Morogoro (3–4 daily; 6–7hr); Muheza (3–4 in the morning; 4hr); Mwanga (1–2 hourly; 1hr); Nairobi (6 daily; 8hr); Same (1–2 hourly; 2hr); Shinyanga (1 weekly; over 24hr); Tanga (3–4 in the morning; 5–6hr); Taveta (hourly; 45min); Usangi (1 daily; 4–5hr).

**Muheza to:** Amani (2 daily 1–2pm, plus irregular transport until 4pm; 1hr); Arusha (3–4 each morning; 5hr 30min); Dar (3 daily; 4–5hr); Lushoto (every 2hr until mid-afternoon; 2hr); Mombo (hourly; 1hr); Morogoro (every 2hr until 1pm; 4–5hr); Moshi (3–4 in the morning; 4hr); Pangani (2 daily except in the rains; 2–3hr); Tanga (every 30min; 45min).

**Same to:** Arusha (2 daily; 3hr 30min); Mbaga (1 daily; 2hr 30min).

# 6

# Arusha and around

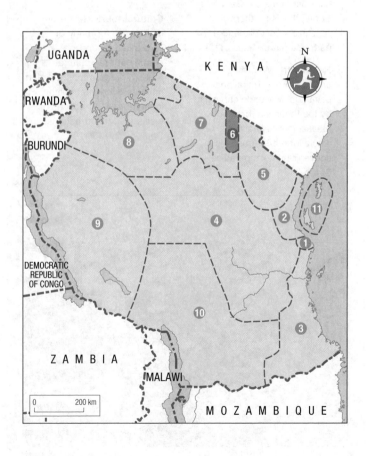

CHAPTER 6 # Highlights

✳ **Safaris** As the capital of Tanzania's "Northern Safari Circuit", most trips to Serengeti and Ngorongoro start here. See p.46

✳ **Via Via** A lively restaurant-cum-bar in the old German Boma, this is northern Tanzania's best place for the performing arts. See p.313

✳ **Handicrafts** With vivid and humorous Tingatinga paintings, Makonde carvings by the thousand, beaded Maasai jewellery and a whole lot more, Arusha is a souvenir-hunter's paradise. See p.316

✳ **Mount Meru** Tanzania's second-highest peak can be climbed in three days, ideally four, and offers stunning scenery all the way, along with views of Kilimanjaro. See p.325

✳ **Cultural tourism** Arusha is the base for many of Tanzania's ground-breaking, community-run cultural tourism programmes, offering intimate encounters with local tribes, and dozens of walks to local attractions. See pp.327–334

▲ Mount Meru, seen from Arusha

# 6

# Arusha and around

H eading west from Moshi, the last major town before the rolling savanna of the Rift Valley kicks in is **Arusha**, Tanzania's safari capital and third-largest city. The town receives around 400,000 visitors each year. Most only use Arusha as a base from which to explore the nearby wildlife parks, but the town's lively shops and markets, vibrant nightlife, cultural tourism and some excellent restaurants provide plenty to justify a longer stay.

Overlooking Arusha is the magnificent **Mount Meru**, a dormant volcanic cone that, at 4566m, is Tanzania's second-highest mountain; the three- or four-day hike to the top passes through some exceptionally beautiful (and bizarre) scenery. Another climbable mountain close by is the mist-shrouded **Mount Longido**, which can be climbed as part of a Maasai-run **cultural tourism programme**. There are more such programmes in other rural locations, giving visitors the opportunity of combining meeting local people with hikes to unspoilt forests, rivers and waterfalls, and even camel-back safaris.

# Arusha

Nestled among the lush foothills of Mount Meru, the booming town – officially now a city – of **ARUSHA** is northern Tanzania's major commercial centre and the country's undisputed safari capital. In clear weather, the sight of Mount Meru's near-perfect cone rising majestically to the north provides the town's abiding memory, while the exceptionally rich volcanic soils on and around Meru's slopes account for Arusha's prosperity – every inch of the area seems to be taken up by *shambas* and settlements, producing half of the country's wheat and substantial amounts of coffee, flowers, seed-beans and pyrethrum for export, along with bananas, maize, millet and vegetables. The rainforests on higher ground are the traditional land of the **Meru and Il Larusa (Arusha) tribes**.

Despite a burgeoning population of around 400,000 people, Arusha has a remarkably laid-back, small-town atmosphere, an impression accentuated by the unexpected sight of small fields of maize and vegetables running straight through the centre of town, along the banks of the Naura, Goliondoi and Themi rivers. Even so, Arusha is a cosmopolitan and diverse place. The presence

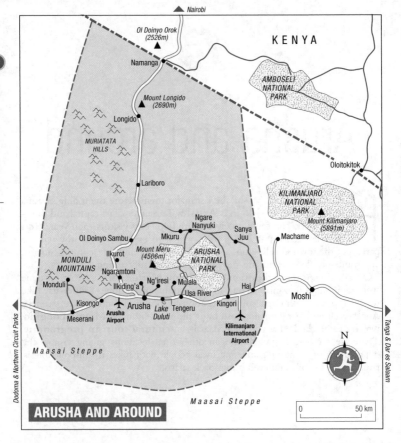

ARUSHA AND AROUND

of tourists and expatriates keeps Western culture prominent, while around the market Asian and Muslim businessmen dressed in loose white or pale blue cotton garments mingle with Nike-capped youths and streetboys, and on the balconies above you might see African women in brightly patterned kangas talking to Asian neighbours dressed in lurid sarees.

And, of course, there are the **Maasai**: the men in red or purple tartan *shukas* (cloth replaced leather towards the end of the nineteenth century), the women with shorn heads and huge disc-like necklaces (*esos*) sewn with hundreds of tiny beads. Some look bewildered in the metropolitan setting, but most are as nonchalant and at ease with themselves as they are in the savanna. And then there's you, the tourist, being followed by trains of young men brandishing reams of batiks, stacks of newspapers or crumpled brochures from safari companies. If you can weather the attentions of the flycatchers, Arusha is one of the most vibrant and ultimately enjoyable towns in Tanzania.

Arusha's altitude, at around 1500m, ensures a temperate **climate** for most of the year, and also – apparently – prevents malaria; the cold season (mid-April to mid-Aug) requires nothing thicker than a sweater, though nights can be truly chilly in July. It gets fiercely hot in November before the short rains start.

## Some history

Arusha is, unsurprisingly, home to the Arusha (properly called Il Larusa) people and the related Meru. The **Meru** seem to be the original inhabitants of the foothills of the mountain that bears their name and are related to disappeared hunter-gatherer communities, whereas the **Il Larusa**, the agricultural cousins of the Maasai, are said to have migrated here about two centuries ago from south of Moshi. The reason for the migration is unclear: one theory holds that they were taken or captured by Maasai to dig wells and build irrigation furrows, and later intermarried. Their Maasai heritage is evidenced by their language, a dialect of Maa, and by the fact that Il Larusa practise horticulture rather than agriculture, dispensing with ploughs – a remnant of the Maasai taboo against breaking soil: cattle are sacred, and so too is the soil that nurtures the grass that feeds them.

The town of Arusha came into existence in the 1880s during **German colonial rule**. In 1886, a military garrison was established, and the settlement that grew up around it became the main market centre for the surrounding European-owned plantations. Later, it became a stopover for vehicles travelling down from Nairobi in Kenya on what became known as the **Great North Road**, which continued south into Zambia. Arusha's increasing importance was confirmed when it was made capital of Tanganyika's Northern Province. While under British rule, a 1929 brochure for the province, published to coincide with the opening of the railway from Moshi, enticed prospective settlers with the offer to recreate a little piece of England.

In some respects, the dream remained half-complete. The planned extension of the railway to Mwanza never happened, but Arusha's importance as a commercial and agricultural centre continued. Even so, the population remained surprisingly small, with the 1952 census putting it at just under eight thousand, of which less than half were Africans. After **Independence**, the pace of development increased dramatically, and by 1980, the population had rocketed to 100,000. The present population numbers well over 400,000, the majority of them migrants seeking waged employment.

# Arrival and information

Arusha is well connected to the rest of Tanzania (and with Nairobi in Kenya) by both road and air.

### By air

International flights touch down at **Kilimanjaro International Airport (KIA)**, 46km east of Arusha, 6km south of the Moshi Highway. Passport formalities are efficient, and you can buy your visa at immigration if you haven't already got one (usually $50; see p.69). There are **foreign exchange bureaux** at passport control and in the arrivals hall, offering reasonable rates for traveller's cheques, though rates for cash are about twenty percent lower than at the forexes in town. There's also a Barclays ATM just by the front entrance. The airport has a couple of gift shops, a restaurant and bar, a post office and pharmacy, though all but the post office are inaccessible to everyone except those taking a flight out.

For passengers arriving on Air Tanzania, there's a free **shuttle bus** to Arusha or Moshi; KLM passengers pay $15 for a similar service (run by Impala Shuttle, to Arusha only), and Precisionair passengers pay Tsh10,000. Arriving on another

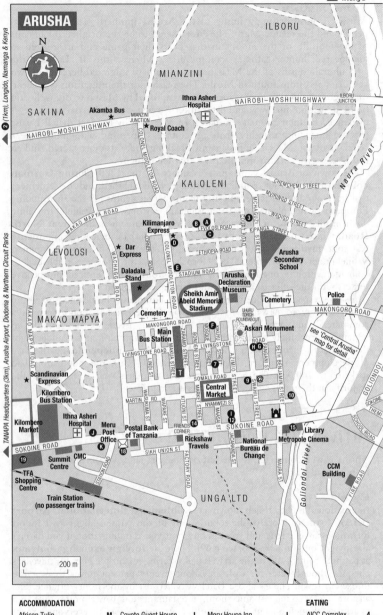

| ACCOMMODATION | | | | | EATING | |
|---|---|---|---|---|---|---|
| African Tulip | **M** | Coyote Guest House | **I** | Meru House Inn | **J** | AICC Complex | **4** |
| Annex Hotel Arusha by Night | **E** | Hotel Fort des Moines | **G** | Monje's Guest House | **A & C** | Big Bite | **9** |
| Arusha Backpackers | **K** | Giraffe Motel | **B** | The Outpost | **O** | Blue Heron | **11** |
| Arusha Centre Tourist Inn | **H** | Golden Rose Hotel | **D** | | | Bollate | **8** |
| Arusha Crown Hotel | **F** | The Impala Hotel | **N** | | | Dolly's Patisserie | **12** |
| Arusha Tourist Inn Hotel | **J** | Le Jacaranda | **L** | | | Everest Chinese | **20** |

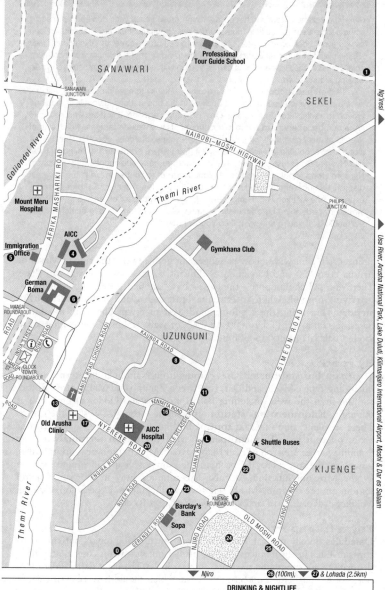

Ng'Iresi ▼

▶ Usa River, Arusha National Park, Lake Duluti, Kilimanjaro International Airport, Moshi & Dar es Salaam

SANAWARI

Professional Tour Guide School

SANAWARI JUNCTION

SEKEI

Goliondoi River

AFRIKA MASHARIKI ROAD

NAIROBI–MOSHI HIGHWAY

Themi River

PHILIPS JUNCTION

Mount Meru Hospital

AICC

Immigration Office **5**

German Boma **6**

MAASAI ROUNDABOUT

Gymkhana Club

MICHUY ROAD

INDIA STREET
BOMA ROAD

MAKAO ST
MAEDA ST
ROAD
CLOCK TOWER ROUNDABOUT

KAUNDA ROAD

UZUNGUNI

**8**

SIMEON ROAD

KALUSA ROAD (CHURCH ROAD)

**11**

**13**

Old Arusha Clinic

**17**

NYERERE ROAD

KENYATTA ROAD
**16**

HAILE SELASSIE ROAD

AICC Hospital
**20**

VIJANA ROAD

**L**

★ Shuttle Buses

La Bella Luna **21**

**22**

KIJENGE

ENGIRA ROAD

RIVER ROAD

**M** **23**

Barclay's Bank

Sopa

SERENGETI ROAD

Themi River

**0**

NJIRO ROAD

KIJENGE ROUNDABOUT
**N**

**24**

**25**

KIJENGE JUU ROAD

OLD MOSHI ROAD

▼ Njiro

**26** (100m), ▼ **27** & Lohada (2.5km)

| | | | | | | |
|---|---|---|---|---|---|---|
| Flame Tree | 16 | Masai Café | 5 | Stiggys | 25 | |
| Greek Club | 23 | McMoody's | 14 | Via Via | 6 | |
| Green Hut | 15 | Pizzarusha | 3 | | | |
| Khan's | 7 | Sazan | 17 | | | |
| L'Oasis Lodge & Restaurant | 1 | Shanghai Chinese | 18 | | | |
| Le Jacaranda | L | Spices & Herbs | 22 | | | |

**DRINKING & NIGHTLIFE**

| | | | |
|---|---|---|---|
| AICC Sports Club | 24 | Matongee Arusha | |
| Colobus Club | 26 | Club | 13 |
| Empire Sports Bar | 19 | Silk Club | 10 |
| La Bella Luna | 21 | Triple-A | 2 |
| Le Jacaranda | L | Via Via | 6 |
| Masai Camp | 27 | | |

## Security

Given the volume of tourists that pass through Arusha each year, don't be surprised if some people treat you as little more than an easy source of income. That said, as long as you avoid booking with safari companies touted on the street by "flycatchers" (see "Safaris" and "Trouble" in Basics), there's little to worry about. If you're still uncomfortable, *Via Via* in the German Boma can fix you up with a guide to accompany you when walking around town.

As to **theft and robbery**, you'd be extremely unlucky to have problems by day, but keep a close eye on your bags and pockets in the bus stations, daladala stands and around markets. After dusk, taking a taxi is strongly advised. If you are walking, there are a number of **areas to avoid after sunset**. These include bridges, which attract thieves as they give the victim little room to escape; the ones over the Themi River along the Nairobi–Moshi Highway, Sokoine Road where it crosses the Goliondoi River and Nyerere Road just east of the clock tower are notorious. Indeed, the entirety of **Nyerere Road** should be avoided at night. North of town, **Sanawari** is the roughest district, though serious incidents are rare. In the town centre, **Sokoine Road** – especially the junction with Factory Road known as Friend's Corner, and the western stretch towards Kilombero Market – is known for opportunistic bag-snatchers and pickpockets. If you're driving, roll up your windows.

airline, catch a lift with fellow passengers, or grab a **taxi** – the ride to Moshi or Arusha costs $50, and bargaining is difficult, so it's cheaper if you can share. There's no public transport – the closest buses are 6km away on the highway.

Arriving from elsewhere in Tanzania, most flights land at the small **Arusha airport**, 7km along the Dodoma road west of town. There are no shuttle buses, so rent a taxi (Tsh10,000–15,000), or walk 1.5km to the main road to catch a daladala (every 15–30min; Tsh300).

### By road

The **main bus station**, for buses coming from Nairobi and eastern Tanzania (including Tanga, Moshi and Dar) is between Zaramo and Makua streets; buses coming from the west (including Babati, Kondoa and Dodoma) drop you at the messy **Kilombero bus station** off Sokoine Road, just west of the centre. There are plenty of pushy **taxi touts** at both places, so stay cool and keep your hands on your bags. **Bus companies with their own terminals** include Scandinavian Express, on Makao Mapya Road; Mtei Express next door; Jordan, just across the street; Royal Coach, in the Bamprass Star Gapco petrol station by the Mianzini Junction; Akamba, five minutes away in the Sango petrol station on the Nairobi–Moshi Highway; Kilimanjaro Express, on Colonel Middleton Road; and Dar Express, on Wachagga Road.

### Town transport

**Daladalas** (locally nicknamed *vifordi*) cover much of the town's outskirts; most trips are Tsh300, but if you're heading further out of town it costs a little more; destinations are painted on the front of the vehicles. The main **daladala stand** is north of the bus station off Stadium Road, which should have labelled bays. At present, some vehicles **heading northwest** along the Nairobi–Moshi Highway leave from Wachagga Road one block west, whilst services **heading east** to Usa River and Tengeru (for Lake Duluti) are best caught at Sanawari junction, between Afrika Mashariki Road and the Nairobi–Moshi Highway. Daladalas to the **eastern suburbs** of Kijenge and Njiro (including *Masai Camp*) can be boarded on Sokoine Road between Swahili and Seth Benjamin streets.

Taxis – invariably white Toyota saloons – are found throughout town, and at night outside most bars, restaurants and clubs. A ride within town as far as the Nairobi–Moshi Highway costs Tsh2000. Although **taxis** are usually safe (ignoring their parlous and often comical state of disrepair), avoid taking a cab if there's already a passenger inside – although most are just friends of the driver, cases of robbery have been known. Make sure your taxi has a white number plate too, an indication that the cab is licensed.

### Information and tours

The helpful **Tanzania Tourist Board office** is on Boma Road (Mon–Fri 8am–4pm, Sat 8.30am–1pm; ☎027/250 3842, ✉ttb-info@habari.co.tz). They have hotel price lists covering most of Tanzania, a free town map, an invaluable bus timetable and a list of licensed safari operators, and a sporadically updated blacklist of really bad ones. They also stock information about the various **cultural tourism programmes** in the Arusha Region and nationwide (see pp.327–334 & p.54). **National parks information** can be obtained at the Ngorongoro Conservation Area Office (Mon–Fri 8am–5pm, Sat 8am–1pm; PO Box 776 ☎027/254 4625 ⓦwww.ngorongorocrater.org) a few doors down, and at the **TANAPA headquarters**, unhelpfully located 5km along the Dodoma road (Mon–Fri 8am–4pm; PO Box 3134 ☎027/250 3471, ⓦwww .tanzaniaparks.com). A taxi from town costs around Tsh4000, but it's cheaper to catch a daladala towards Monduli (Tsh300) and get dropped off a few hundred metres beyond African Heritage.

Additional local information can be found in the often humorous *Arusha Times* (every Saturday; ⓦwww.arushatimes.co.tz). The main travellers' **notice boards** are outside *The Patisserie* on Sokoine Road and in the corridor leading to *Jambo's Makuti Garden* on Boma Road.

Several safari companies offer guided minibus **city tours**, averaging $20–30 per person. Cheaper and just as good are the **guided walks** offered by *Via Via* (see p.313). These take in most of the central sights, plus a range of more intimate experiences in the suburbs, including weekly markets, coffee farms and villages. Access is usually by daladala.

# Accommodation

Arusha has lots of **accommodation**, ranging from dirt-cheap, town-centre guesthouses, with shared squat toilets and bucket showers, to mid-priced hotels and top-dollar neo-colonial places in the town's leafy suburbs and coffee plantations further out. Central Arusha only has a couple of **campsites**. *Arusha Vision Campsite* (Boma Rd ☎0754/040810) sits above the Themi River (more like a stream) and is a surprisingly central oasis. The location leaves niggling worries about safety, although there hasn't been an incident for years, but you'll get hassled by flycatchers from the resident safari companies. There's a bar and basic restaurant, a laundry and (sometimes) hot water (Tsh3000 per person).

*Masai Camp* (Old Moshi Rd, 2.5km east of Kijenge ☎0754/507131, ⓦwww .masaicamp.com) has an excellent restaurant, bar and children's play area, and is also the base for Tropical Trails safaris. Camping ($5 per person) is not recommended on Fri and Sat when it hosts Wild & Whacky nights and the noise can go on until at least 4.30am. There are a handful of basic rooms (singles ❷), and a four-bed dorm (❶). Don't come here if dogs bristle your hair – there are plenty. *Meserani Snake Park*, 30km west of town (see p.332) is recommended, too. See also the accommodation reviews for Arusha National Park, pp.324–325.

## Safaris from Arusha

Thanks to its location close to the northern circuit of national parks, Arusha is a great place to arrange a safari, if you haven't already done so. A safari of **three days** (one full day and two half-days) gives you time to enjoy game drives in the nearby parks of Tarangire, Manyara and Ngorongoro. Over **four days**, the Serengeti is a possibility, though five or six days are recommended. Most of the larger and more expensive safari companies are now based in the suburbs and are best contacted by email via their websites. Some of the budget companies still maintain city-centre offices that are good places to find out more about what safaris are on offer, what's included and to get an idea of prices. For more information on organising a safari, see p.46.

## Town centre

The main concentration of **budget accommodation** is in Kaloleni district, north of the stadium; it's pretty safe, in spite of its dilapidated appearance, unsurfaced roads and numerous local boozers. The streets around the main bus station and central market are also lively and have some decent **mid-range** options. Other areas are distinctly quieter.

**Power cuts** are frequent (the better hotels have generators), so water supplies are also erratic: part of the town's supply depends on electric pump-powered boreholes, and many hotels use pumps to fill their tanks.

The "mid-range and expensive" options listed all include breakfast in their rates; the more expensive choices accept Visa and MasterCard.

### Budget

**Annex Hotel Arusha by Night** Colonel Middleton Rd, entrance on Stadium Rd (☎0713/485237). Adequate and good value for couples, with large, clean, en-suite twin-bed rooms off a dark corridor. All have nets and hot showers, and there's also safe parking and an average restaurant and bar. Can be a little noisy. BB ❷

**Arusha Backpackers** Sokoine Rd ☎027/250 4474, ⓦwww.arushabackpackers.co.tz. As the name suggests, this is the number one place for backpackers in Arusha. There's nothing special about the rooms; none are en suite but they're clean and comfy enough and this is one of the very few places with a (four-bed) dorm (Tsh7000). It's safe, friendly, and the restaurant on the roof is a lovely place to lounge around and gawp at Meru. Book in advance, as it's often filled with groups of American students. BB ❷

**Arusha Centre Tourist Inn** Off Swahili St ☎027/250 0421, 0782/749962 ⓔicerestaurant @yahoo.co.uk. Nineteen recently renovated but small en-suite rooms on three floors (no lift), with nets and TV. There's a cheap restaurant downstairs. BB ❸

**Coyote Guest House** Azimio St ☎027/250 5452. On the first floor, this is a friendly and safe place to stay. Some rooms have cold showers and squat toilets (only shared bathrooms have hot water), and beds have nets. There are also some large twin-bed doubles. ❷

**Giraffe Motel** Levolosi Rd ☎027/250 4618, 0754 /817912. One of the smartest options in Kaloleni following its renovation; thirteen squeaky-clean tiled rooms, all en suite and with box nets. It's only let down by the service. ❷

**Meru House Inn** Sokoine Rd ☎027/250 7803, ⓦmeruhouseinn@hotmail.com. Popular with backpackers, this place has small but comfortable rooms on three floors (including triples) with nets and hot showers. Some rooms have street-side balconies, others are en suite and there's a pleasant café-bar squeezed onto the first-floor walkway with satellite TV and OK food. Safe parking. ❶

**Monje's Guest House** Levolosi Rd, Kaloleni (☎0754/462308, ⓔjanemonjes@yahoo.com). Actually three guesthouses in Kaloleni, with another one being built nearby. "B" is quiet, has no flycatchers, massive rooms, good mosquito nets, and piping hot showers whenever there's electricity. "A" is smaller and less welcoming and does not offer breakfast in the price. Best of all is "C", with bright rooms, free coffee and TV in the en-suite rooms. ❷

**YMCA** India St ☎027/254 4032. Seedy rather than pious, but friendly. There's a local bar and drinks in a courtyard at the back. The seven rooms are old and basic but very tidy and have nets and washbasins (all share bathrooms with erratic water supply). Basic cheap meals are available. BB ❷

## Mid-range and Expensive

**African Tulip** Serengeti Rd ☏ 027/254 3004, ⓦ www.theafricantulip.com. This safari-agency-owned establishment offers supremely comfortable accommodation in its 29 huge, individually designed en-suite rooms, with each boasting inter-active TV, a/c, mini-bar and safe. Also has a pool and wi-fi access. **❼–❽**

**Arusha Crown Hotel** Makongoro Rd ☏ 027/250 8523, ⓦ www.arushacrownhotel.com. Efficiently run and oddly upmarket for the area, the better rooms have views of Mount Meru and the football stadium. Also has a sophisticated restaurant. Good value. **❻**

**Arusha Naaz** Sokoine Rd ☏ 027/250 2087, ⓦ www.arushanaaz.net. Long-established place in the heart of the action; the surly receptionist and rather scruffy entrance disguise a hotel that has some surprisingly smart and clean en-suite rooms with TV and a/c. Try to get one at the back to avoid the hubbub from the road. **❹**

**Arusha Tourist Inn Hotel** Sokoine Rd ☏ 027/254 7803, ⓔ atihotel@habari.co.tz. Situated behind the Meru House Inn, and sharing the same management and entranceway, this shiny hotel gleams in the Arusha sun, putting its budget neighbour to shame. The 29 en-suite rooms come with all the facilities you'd expect (including satellite TV) but being hemmed in by high-rises means they don't have views. Still a safe and decent choice. No singles. **❹**

**Hotel Fort Des Moines** Pangani St ☏ 027/254 8523, ⓦ www.bimel.co.tz/. Arranged over four floors (no lift) and getting tatty but still reasonable value. Carpeted en-suite rooms (double or twin) have ceiling fans, phone, nets and hot water; and some have views of Mount Meru. **❸**

**Golden Rose Hotel** Colonel Middleton Rd ☏ 027/250 7959, ⓦ www.goldenrosehoteltz.com. Friendly and decent, if overpriced. The en-suite twins and doubles all have big beds with nets, though they do get musty in the rains. Facilities include an internet café next door and safe parking. **❹**

**Le Jacaranda** Vijana Rd, Kijenge ☏ 027/254 4945, ⓦ www.chez.com/jacaranda. It's still one of the most atmospheric places in Arusha but this colonial-era house with mostly en-suite rooms is in need of attention. The best room is on the first floor with a large balcony; the worst – by some distance – are the minuscule singles in a separate block. There's also a good but expensive restaurant, plus a bar and mini-golf. **❹**

**The Arusha Hotel** By the clock tower ☏ 027/250 7777, ⓦ www.thearushahotel.com. Established in the 1920s, this rambling hotel – the best in town – is one of Arusha's oldest and most attractive. Extensively renovated, its 86 rooms (some with a/c) come with electronic safes, satellite TV, large box nets, and bathtubs. An extra $10 gets you a balcony and slightly larger bed(s). Amenities include lift access, a swimming pool set in pleasant gardens, two bars, a terrace restaurant, slot machines, gift shops, gym and safe parking. **❼–❾**

**The Impala Hotel** Kijenge roundabout ☏ 027/250 8448, ⓦ www.impalahotel.com. Still popular and good value despite the lack of attentive service, most of the 160 rooms at *The Impala* are in a nine-storey block fitted with panoramic lifts running up the outside. Some have TV, others offer great views of Mount Meru; all have nets and phone. Amenities include three restaurants, two bars, small swimming pool, foreign exchange and an internet café. **❻**

🏃 **The Outpost** Serengeti Rd, off Nyerere Rd ☏ 027/254 8405, ⓦ www.outposttanzania .com. Great for families – this place is good value and likeable. There's a family room, bar and restaurant in the attractive colonial-era house, plus en-suite rooms (including triples) in fourteen bungalows and cottages around the gardens. Also has a gift shop, internet café, pool and mini golf. **❹**

## Out of town

The advantage of staying outside town is the peaceful and rural – if often somewhat neo-colonial – atmosphere. On clear days, most places also have views of Mount Meru, but take the "Kilimanjaro view" claims with a pinch of salt – it's in cloud for much of the year. For a description of the Nairobi–Moshi Highway and several of Arusha's cultural tourism programmes, which also offer accommodation, see pp.327–334; see also the reviews for Arusha National Park (pp.324–325). The following include breakfast in their rates.

**Arumeru River Lodge** 15km east of town at Tengeru: 1km south of the Nairobi–Moshi Highway ☏ 027/255 3573, ⓦ www.arumerulodge.com. On a coffee estate, this has twenty large, comfortable rooms in chalets with touches of African style. There's a small reedy swamp alive with birds, and a nearby forest for walks. Also has a swimming pool and superb restaurant (buffet lunch and three-course à la carte are both Tsh23,000). **❼**

**Arusha Coffee Lodge** 6.5km west of town at Burka, along the Dodoma road near Arusha airport (book through Elewana Afrika, Sopa Plaza,

99 Serengeti Rd, Arusha ☎027/250 0630–9, ⓦwww.elewana.com). Stylish but expensive; the luxurious, rustic-style cottages sit on wooden platforms at the edge of a coffee plantation, all have four-posters, lounge and fireplace. Also has a good restaurant, bar and swimming pool, plus guided walks around the estate. $900 ❾

**KIA Lodge** 48km east of town at Kilimanjaro International Airport ☎027/255 4194, ⓦ www .kialodge.com. Handy for late-night arrivals, this is more than just a stopover. There's comfortable accommodation in thatched cottages, with a bar, good Afro-European restaurant and hilltop swimming pool with glorious views, including Kilimanjaro. Airport transfer included. ❼

🏃 **Kigongoni Lodge** 10km east of town at Tengeru ☎027/255 3087, ⓦwww .kigongoni.net. On a beautiful, partially forested coffee estate with views of Mount Meru, the lodge funds the adjacent Sibusiso Foundation for mentally disabled children. The nineteen attractive en-suite cottages are rustic in style, with fireplaces, four-posters, and wooden verandas overlooking the forest and some jittery vervet monkeys. There's a pool with great views, free wi-fi and guided walks through nearby forest, and also to coffee, rose and trout farms, waterfalls and Lake Duluti. ❺

🏃 **L'Oasis Lodge & Restaurant** 800m north of the Nairobi–Moshi Highway at Sekei ☎027/250 7089, ⓦwww.loasislodge.com. Set in lush gardens surrounded by small farms and mud houses, and within walking distance of town, this place has cosy en-suite doubles and triples. Rooms are mostly in traditionally built rondavels, though the best are in the large wooden houses on stilts. The cheaper "Backpackers' Lodge" annexe (BB ❸) on the opposite side of the road is flanked by banana plants, and has twelve twin-bed rooms in a long house on stilts, each with a washbasin (shared bathrooms). The open-air restaurant is superb; there's also a bar, internet café, and swimming pool. Be warned, the guard dog often keeps guests awake all night. ❺

**Moivaro Coffee Plantation Lodge** 7km east of town at Moivaro: 1.8km south of the Nairobi–Moshi Highway ☎027/255 3242, ⓦwww.moivaro.com. A recommended coffee-estate getaway, with 40 rustic en-suite cottages, all with box nets, small verandas and fireplace. Amenities include a pool

with views of Mount Meru, bar and restaurant, jogging circuit and playground, and there's room service, too. ❼

**Mount Meru Game Lodge & Sanctuary** 22km east of town at Usa River: along the Nairobi–Moshi Highway ☎027/255 3885, ⓦwww.intimate-places .com. Founded in 1959 and recently refurbished, this welcoming choice has aged well. Styled on a colonial hunting lodge, it has seventeen large, en-suite rooms in wooden bungalows with verandas giving eyeball-to-eyeball views with denizens of the adjacent wildlife sanctuary. There's also a bar and good restaurant, and walks are possible through the estate, or to villages and farms. ❼

🏃 **Onsea House (Guest House)** 8km east of town at Moivaro: 2km south of the Nairobi–Moshi Highway ☎0784/833207, ⓦwww .onseahouse.com. This cosy, intimate and exclusive Afro-colonial place offers Arusha's finest out-of-town accommodation; a secluded hideaway with five first-rate rooms, gorgeous grounds and excellent food to match. Also has a swimming pool and a hot tub with a view of Mount Meru and the Maasai steppe. ❼

🏃 **Rivertrees Country Inn** 22km east of town at Usa River: 300m south of the Nairobi–Moshi Highway ☎027/255 3894, ⓦwww .rivertrees.com. A stylishly rustic house that is part of a flower and vegetable farm. There are ten en-suite rooms (can be musty in the rains), two cottages and a riverside house all with classic colonial furnishings and agricultural memorabilia, and the gorgeous garden flanking Usa River is good for birdlife. Amenities include internet access, swimming pool, bar and excellent food (around $20 for lunch, $25 for dinner). Day-trips and transfers are included in the price. Trips on foot or horseback can also be arranged. ❼

**Serena Mountain Village Lodge** 13km east of town at Lake Duluti: 2km south of the Nairobi–Moshi Highway from Tengeru (book through Serena Hotels, Diamond Trust Bank Building, 2nd Floor Along Moshi-Arusha Road ☎027-250 4158, ⓦwww.serenahotels.com). A homely retreat of thatched bungalows set in tropical gardens 300m from the lake. The better rooms have pleasant lake views, and some have sunken baths; all have cable TV. It's a good place for lunch ($15 for the buffet), and there's a bar. Plus, guided walks and canoeing are available. ❼

# The Town

Arusha has two distinct centres: the old **colonial quarter** between Goliondoi and Boma roads in the east, which contains most of the shops and offices you might need plus a wealth of gemstone dealers; and the larger, earthier grid of streets around the **central market** to the west. In the east, beyond the Themi River, is **Uzunguni** ("the place of Europeans"), a spread-out area of trees and guarded houses where the local elite live, along with a good many expats. To the north and south of these three areas are the populous **residential suburbs** – areas such as Sanawari, Sekei and Sakina to the north, Unga Limited in the south, and Kijenge to the east. These suburbs are busy, bustling places, home to innumerable little stores and cottage industries, from batik designers to coffin makers, as well as the majority of the city's population.

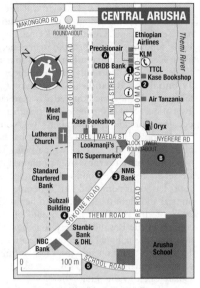

| ACCOMMODATION | EATING & DRINKING | | |
|---|---|---|---|
| The Arusha Hotel **B** | The Arusha Hotel **B** | Mawingu City | |
| Arusha Naaz **C** | Arusha Naaz Hotel **C** | Centre Club | **4** |
| YMCA **A** | Café Bamboo **2** | The Patisserie | **3** |
| | Jambo's **1** | Police Mess | **5** |

## The clock tower and the German Boma

The **clock tower**, at the bottom of Boma Road by *The Arusha Hotel*, is Arusha's best-known landmark, and also where most of the town's flycatchers, second-hand newspaper vendors and "batik boys" hang out. A small plaque at the base of the tower states that Arusha is the halfway point between Cape Town and Cairo – but it's actually somewhere in the swamps of the Congo River basin. The story seems to have come from the megalomaniacal ambitions of the British arch-colonialist Cecil Rhodes, who dreamt of seeing the entirety of eastern Africa painted red on the map. Had his vision of a projected "Cape to Cairo" railway ever come to fruition, Arusha may well have been the mid-point.

Heading up Boma Road past the tourist office brings you to a squat, white wall enclosing a number of defensive-looking whitewashed buildings. This is the **German Boma**, built in 1886 as a military and administrative headquarters during the German colonization of Tanganyika. It now houses the neglected **National Natural History Museum** (Mon–Fri 9am–5.30pm, Sat & Sun 9.30am–5.30pm; $4, $2 students), with displays on the evolution of mankind, an examination of the world of insects, while in the building on the right is a small selection of stuffed animals, together with half a dozen pictures of Tanzanian fauna by photographer Dick Persson. On the grassy slope east of the fortified quadrangle, the *Via Via* bar and restaurant (closed Sun; see p.313) hosts frequent **cultural events** such as art exhibitions and music.

## The AICC and the Maasai roundabout

Immediately behind the German Boma are the three office blocks of the **Arusha International Conference Centre (AICC)**, built in the 1960s to serve as the headquarters of the original, ill-fated East African Community (resurrected in 2001, and which will also be based in Arusha). The triangular design of the three wings – named Kilimanjaro, Serengeti and Ngorongoro – represent Tanzania, Uganda and Kenya. The original community collapsed in the 1970s following ideological differences between Nyerere's socialist Tanzania and Jomo Kenyatta's capitalist Kenya, and sour relations with Idi Amin's Uganda.

The complex currently houses offices and the **International Criminal Tribunal for Rwanda** (ICTR; ⓦwww.ictr.org), set up by the UN in 1994 following the horrific hundred-day genocide that same year which claimed the lives of over 800,000 people. The tribunal delivered the world's first condemnation for genocide in September 1998, when former Rwandan Prime Minister Jean Kambanda was found guilty, but has been dogged by controversy for much of its life – not the least of which being the UN's characteristically lavish and ineffectual **bureaucracy**: over a billion dollars to the end of 2007 (the last trials are set to conclude around 2012). Indeed, fifteen years after the genocide, the court has so far convicted just 34 people and acquitted six. Twenty-three remain on trial and eight trials have yet to begin. However, the successful conviction in 2008 of the so-called 'mastermind' of the genocide, Theoneste Bagosora, a colonel in the Rwandan army, together with two of his cohorts, was seen as a sign that the tribunal is producing results. All three were given life sentences. The notice board outside the Press & Public Affairs Unit on the ground floor of the Kilimanjaro Wing has a weekly timetable of **court hearings**; they're usually open to the public (free).

Just southwest of the AICC, the so-called **Maasai Roundabout** at the junction of Afrika Mashariki and Makongoro roads is actually graced by a statue of an elephant and a rhino, commissioned by the municipal council following attempts at expropriation by a local bar. Heading west, Makongoro Road crosses the Goliondoi and Naura rivers before reaching, after 1km, a far more imposing roundabout monument – the concrete-arched **Uhuru Torch** – symbolizing the torch that was set atop Kilimanjaro on the eve of Tanganyika's Independence (*uhuru* means freedom). Sadly, the "eternal" flame flickered out ages ago, but the relief panels in the sides of the monument have been repainted in colourful detail, and show mainly agricultural scenes.

On the northwest side of the roundabout, the **Arusha Declaration Museum** (daily 7.30am–6pm; $4) mostly contains rare documentary photographs, and tells Tanzania's history from just before colonial times to **Ujamaa** – President Nyerere's economically disastrous experiment in self-reliant rural socialism. Nyerere's policy stressed the importance of hard work and longer working hours as the key to Tanzania's future economic success, rather than dependence on foreign aid, loans and industrialization.

## The Central Market

The city's enjoyable **central market** (Mon–Sat 7am–6pm, Sun 7am–2pm) is five minutes' walk southwest from the Arusha Declaration Museum, in the thick of the Muslim district. Don't be intimidated by the swarming mass of people (but do beware of pickpockets) – the market and the streets to the west of it offer a dazzling variety of produce, from fruit and vegetables, meat and fish (fresh or sun-dried) to herbs, spices, traditional medicine, cooking implements, colourful kangas, clothing and sandals made from truck tyres and traditional grass baskets, all displayed with geometric precision. A couple of other unusual things worth seeking out are pale pink baobab seeds that are used to make juice, or sucked like sweets; and fresh tamarind (at the end of the year), which is good for juices and sucking, and great for cooking with.

# Eating

Visitors have a wide selection of top-notch restaurants to choose from, as well as the cheaper (but still good) local eateries. Those functioning also as bars, or marked as "licensed", also sell alcohol. The town is famed for **beef** (*ng'ombe*), whether grilled or dished up in a variety of stews, notably *trupa* (or *trooper*), which is a mix of bananas, beef or chicken, seasonal vegetables and potatoes – it sounds weird but is rather tasty, and comes in portions sufficient for four or five people. Another speciality is a thick banana mash called *mashalali*. For your **own supplies**, check out the central market or the various supermarkets and groceries (see p.319).

There's also plenty of **street food**. Roasted maize cobs, *mishkaki* meat skewers, fried cassava and sometimes even stir-fries can be bought from vendors along Swahili Street one block south of *Big Bite*, as well as in Kaloleni, and at various other street corners in the western part of town. For more upmarket fare, the TFA complex at the western end of Sokoine Road has several very good restaurants, including *Sapporo*, serving Japanese food; and *Chocolate Temptation*, the best place for cakes in the city.

In addition to the restaurants below, don't forget the **bars** (see p.315), all of which rustle up cheap and filling meals, mainly based on meat, eggs and chips, and often accompanied by *supu* broth in the morning.

## In the centre

**The Arusha Hotel** Facing the clock tower. The Tsh15,000 lunchtime buffet is popular with safari groups. There's also light à la carte, including nachos and vegetarian pie, for Tsh6000. And chocolate mousse…

**Arusha Naaz Hotel** Sokoine Rd. Long-standing establishment renowned for its lunchtime buffet (Tsh7000) with a good selection of grilled meats, vegetables and staples from chips to *ugali*.

**Café Bamboo** Boma Rd. A bright, cheerful and friendly place, especially popular for breakfast. Serves up home-made cakes, ice cream, fresh juices, milk shakes, Kilimanjaro coffee and great *chai tangawizi* (ginger tea). Also has light lunches and dinners (Tsh4000–6500) especially good fish and salads. Daily 7am–9pm.

**AICC Complex** Off Afrika Mashariki Rd. The cafeteria in the Serengeti Wing has simple but good lunch buffets, including vegetarian, for Tsh11,000. There are also three snack bars, including the excellent AHTI bakery for bread, pies, cakes and brownies.

**Jambo's** Boma Rd. Two interconnected places either side of the tourist office: the unfussy *Coffee Shop* at the front (7.30am–6pm) and the beautifully decorated but dark, thatch-roofed *Makuti Garden* at the back for meals and drinks (9am–10pm). When it's busy, lunches tend to be light, such as stuffed chapatis (Tsh5500–6500), with more substantial evening meals (Tsh6000–8000 for two courses).

**Masai Café** Simon Boulevard ☎0755/765640. Part Italian-owned pizza and pasta joint that's chock-a-block with expats and well-heeled locals during the day – thanks largely to its location opposite the AICC building – but which can be deathly quiet in the evenings. A bit of a shame, as the food is fine and the service satisfactory. Also does takeaway.

**The Patisserie** Sokoine Rd. Bakery-cum-internet café popular with overlanders. The light meals and snacks are reasonably priced, and they also do coffee, fresh juices, ice cream, cakes, and fresh bread. Mon–Sat 7am–6.30pm, Sun 7am–2pm.

**Via Via** German Boma, Boma Rd. Popular with travellers and locals alike, this is a bar, restaurant and lively cultural venue rolled into one. Sitting on the grassy bank of the Themi River, there's plenty of shaded seating, and excellent food (mains around Tsh7500): a cosmopolitan mix of European and African (the tilapia in white wine is especially tasty). They also do toasted sandwiches, soups and salads, fresh juices, milk shakes and coffee. Food until around 10pm. Closed Sun.

## West of the centre

**Big Bite** Swahili St/Somali Rd. One of the best Indian restaurants in East Africa, and reasonably priced at that (curries from Tsh7000). The naff name and grimy street outside belie the exquisite Mughlai and tandoori cooking. Both the chicken and mutton in spinach purée are unbelievably succulent, and even simple dishes, such as buttered naan, are full of subtle flavours. There's also a wide vegetarian choice and, as the name suggests, the portions are big. Ask for the day's specials. Closed Tues.

**Dolly's Patisserie** Sokoine Rd. Excellent cakes, buns and freshly baked bread.

**Green Hut** Sokoine Rd. Good fast food, with hamburgers, great samosas, *kabalu*, juices and cheap full meals (around Tsh2500). Good for breakfast.

**Khan's** Mosque St, just north of central market. Star of magazine articles and TV features the world over, Khan's is a garage by day and a pavement restaurant at night, serving delicious, gourmet street food. So successful that they now print their own T-shirts, *Khan's* is a bit of a tourist trap but you can't knock the quality of the kebabs or chicken, nor some of the deliciously fiery sauces that accompany them. There's a second branch at Njiro.

**McMoody's** Sokoine Rd. Likeable East African version of Western junk-food chain but with table service. Fast food from burgers (from Tsh3120) to pizzas, fish fingers to fired chicken. Delicious shakes (Tsh3000) too. Daily 7.30am–10pm. Also has a branch at Njiro. No alcohol.

**Shanghai Chinese** Behind Meru Post Office, Sokoine Rd, ☏027/250 3224. Genuine Chinese cuisine with good sizzling platters, ginger crab with spring onion (Tsh7500), and soya lemon prawns (Tsh7800). Does takeaway too.

### East of the centre

**Blue Heron** Haile Selassie Rd. Incredibly swish, German-run expat hangout has gorgeous grounds dotted with capacious, comfy chairs – the ideal place to drink coffee and try one of their home-made pies (lemon meringue is particularly delicious). Gift shop attached. Closed Sun.

**Bollate** Kaunda Rd (☏0732/975263). Tasty and authentic Mexican dishes (fajitas from Tsh6500, enchiladas from Tsh8000) as well as a fine Italian selection, served in the peaceful, shaded grounds of a old colonial house. Open daily to 10pm.

**Everest Chinese** Nyerere Rd. Yet another good Chinese, with seating indoors, on the terrace or in a shaded corner of the garden. The business lunches are good value at Tsh7500; otherwise it's around Tsh10,000 for a main course with drinks – the sizzlers are especially tasty.

**Flame Tree** Kenyatta Rd (☏0754/377359). Arusha's most inventive and classiest restaurant, with dishes such as smoked venison slices in lemon and olive oil for starters (Tsh7000) and main courses that include jumbo T-bone steaks (Tsh25,000), fondues (Tsh30,000 per person), and Swiss cheese. Best of all, however, is the heavenly

dessert selection (Tsh5000) that majors in chocolate. Closed Sun eves.

**Greek Club** Nyerere Rd. Established in the 1930s by Greek planters (behold the Corinthian facade), this remains popular with expats and well-to-do-locals, especially at weekends, when it becomes a sports bar. But the main reason for coming is the superb Greek food, particularly its salads, famed moussaka, and souvlaki in pitta bread. Also does a selection of jacket potatoes (Tsh7000–7500). Mon 11am–4pm, Tues, Wed, Fri–Sun 11am–midnight.

**Le Jacaranda** Vijana Rd. Set on the breezy first-floor terrace of the guesthouse, this is a pleasant venue with Italian, Chinese and Swahili menus. Main courses average Tsh7000–10,000, and a three-course splurge could relieve you of Tsh20,000. Game such as wildebeest and gazelle can also be seen migrating across the menu on occasion (around Tsh15,000 per person depending on how you want it cooked). There's also a bar, seating in the garden, and mini-golf.

**Sazan** Nyerere Rd. Arusha's first Japanese restaurant and surprisingly reasonable value. As you'd expect sushi and sashimi feature heavily, though the wisdom of eating raw fish this far from the coast in Africa is debatable. Nevertheless, it's popular and the tuna and marlin mixed sashimi (Tsh5400) is delicious.

**Spices & Herbs** Simeon Rd. Excellent Ethiopian cuisine, also suitable for vegetarians, with a quiet and dignified atmosphere, and some seats on the lawn. Try their *siga beyayinetu*, a mix of spicy stews and pickles placed on the traditional Ethiopian bread-cum-plate of *injera* – a huge soft pancake. There's also Western food if you don't like spices – Ethiopian food is *hot*.

**Stiggy's** Old Moshi Rd, Kijenge. A well-regarded place which is popular with expats and specializes in Thai and South Seas seafood. There's also a pool table and bar. Closed Mon.

### North of the centre

**L'Oasis Lodge & Restaurant** Sekei: 800m north of the Nairobi–Moshi Highway. Whether you eat by the bar, in the garden with its crowned cranes, or up in the tree house, this is one of Arusha's tastiest gastronomic experiences, with everything from pizzas (around Tsh9000) and lamb kebabs (Tsh5000) to seasonal dishes such as squid and prawn (both around Tsh12,000) gaining plaudits from even the most jaded of palates. Also does a variety of huge salad bowls (Tsh6000–9000).

**Pizzarusha** Court Rd. Now occupying new premises but still in Kaloleni and still, in their own words, making the best damn pizza in Africa. Friendly, cheap, with a small menu of curries, sandwiches, and yes, delicous pizzas (Tsh4000–5000), with basil, oregano and garlic rolled into the dough.

### Out of town

Most of the out-of-town hotels also have perfectly good tourist-standard restaurants, but only two of them are really worth a special trip:

**Mount Meru Game Lodge & Sanctuary** 22km east of town at Usa River: along the Nairobi–Moshi Highway ☎027/255 3885. Especially popular with weekenders, the main draw here is the game sanctuary (daily 7am–5pm; Tsh1000), which started off as a zoo for ill or orphaned animals, and also has a pond with flamingos, pelicans and herons and gardens grazed by eland and a lone zebra – perfect for a lazy Sunday afternoon with the kids. Lunch $20; Sunday roast $18. Catch a daladala towards Usa River or Kikatiti.

**Onsea House** 6km east of town. Possibly the finest dining in East Africa, with food cooked by a Belgian chef with plenty of experience in Michelin-star restaurants in Europe. Lunch ($25) is à la carte while dinner ($50) is a six-course set-menu extravaganza, from *amuse-bouche* at the start to coffee and cake.

# Drinking and nightlife

Arusha's main **nightlife** happens along the Nairobi–Moshi Highway, which has a slew of bars from Sakina in the west, to Sekei in the east. Places go in and out of fashion frequently, so if one of the following has fallen out of favour, you shouldn't have problems finding somewhere better nearby. The ever-changing scene makes tracking down what's really hot an enjoyable challenge. The owners of *Via Via* in the grounds of the German Boma keep up with the latest, and also offer an innovative guided **nightlife tour** in the populous outskirts (Tsh10,000 excluding drinks and taxis, though you may have to carry your guide home). Tune into Triple-A FM (88.5Mhz) for lots of Bongo Flava.

For **live music**, *Triple-A* is the most likely venue for rap and hip-hop. *Via Via* is renowned for its Thursday live music nights (Tsh3000 including free drink), while the *Empire Sports Bar* round behind *Stiggbucks* at the TFA Complex hosts live music most Saturdays. The *Empire* also hosts an annual three- to four-day music festival in June.

Worth trying at least once is Meru banana wine, which comes in two varieties – sweet and dry. You'll find it in some of the local bars, and in supermarkets, or you can find locally brewed versions in villages closer to Mount Meru, which can be visited as part of the cultural tourism programmes; see p.327. Don't walk at night but catch a taxi; you'll find them outside virtually every bar and club that's still open. Make sure you get one with a white number plate; this proves it is licensed.

### Bars

**AICC Sports Club** Old Moshi Rd, 150m east of Kijenge roundabout. Remains a favourite among local drinkers attracted by good *nyama choma*, grilled bananas, and roast gizzards (*filigisi*); especially popular with families on Sunday afternoons.

**Empire Sports Bar** TFA complex, Sokoine Rd. Expat-heavy club that's heaving most weekends, particularly their Friday reggae nights. Also has pool table and screens fooball and other sports.

**La Bella Luna** Simeon Rd. Large but fairly humdrum open-sided restaurant and bar under a thatched roof, enlivened by the presence of acrobats and live music most Saturdays.

**Le Jacaranda** Vijana Rd. Whether you drink in the garden or on the first-floor terrace, this is a lovely afternoon hideaway. There's also mini-golf (Tsh500), and live music at weekends.

**Masai Camp** Old Moshi Rd, 2.5km east of Kijenge. One of the best, especially lively whenever the overland tour trucks are in town. Also has pool tables, darts, satellite TV and internet café.

**Matongee Arusha Club** Nyerere Rd. Next to the Themi River, this is a good local bar with plenty of outdoor seating, and great *nyama choma* too (Tsh3500 for 0.5kg).

**Police Mess** School Rd, off Sokoine Rd. Forget the indoor bar (unless you fancy a game of pool) and head to the beer garden beside it, a lovely relaxing place that, yes, also has superb *nyama choma*.

**Via Via** In the grounds of the German Boma, top end of Boma Rd. One of the nicest and friendliest bars in town, with great music (including a stack of traditional *ngoma*), good food, a pool table, and a grassy lawn to chill out on. There's also live music on Thursdays. Closed Sun.

### Clubs

**Colobus Club** Old Moshi Rd, 500m east of Kijenge roundabout. Now owned by the manager of *Via Via*, this place remains a favourite with expats, despite being open only two nights per week (Fri & Sat, 10pm until late; Tsh5000). This brash, lively and extremely loud place plays a mix of music and also has pool tables and internet access.

**Masai Camp** Old Moshi Rd, 2.5km east of Kijenge. The tourists' and overland truckers' favourite also has "Wild & Whacky" club nights every Fri and Sat. A mixed local/tourist clientele enjoy eclectic, DJ-spun tunes and the occasional live band. Entrance is free to residents and campers, Tsh3000 otherwise.

**Mawingu City Centre Club** Sokoine Rd /Goliondoi Rd. This club is yet to find its feet but the guys behind it are the same ones behind the old Hotel Saba Saba's legendary discos, so it's worth keeping an eye on, and the city-centre location is hard to fault.

**Silk Club** Seth Benjamin St. Once the Crystal Club (Arusha's oldest nightspot), this place still pulls 'em in with lots of dancing and a young, easy-going crowd. The covered outside bar is for those who prefer a more sedate pace, and shows English Premier League football on Saturdays. Entrance to the club is Tsh3000.

**Triple-A** Nairobi–Moshi Highway, Sakina; opposite Nairobi Rd. Arusha's favourite disco, more mellow than *Colobus Club*, and with a more African feel too. Particularly popular on a Wednesday when it's Ladies' Night, though there is a disco every night of the week. Also hosts live bands (usually Fri & Sat), including rap and Bongo Flava, and music contests.

# Shopping

Arusha has a vast range of **souvenirs** to choose from, bringing together arts and crafts from all over the country, as well as from Kenya (luridly coloured soapstone carvings) and reproduction tribal masks from Central and Western Africa. Typical items include Makonde woodcarvings, bright Tingatinga paintings, batiks, musical instruments (the metal-tongued "thumb pianos" of the Gogo, from around Dodoma, are great fun, as are the slender *zeze* fiddles) and Maasai bead jewellery.

The **souvenir shops** are concentrated in the eastern part of the centre between Goliondoi and Boma roads. Most of the salesmen have mastered the "but how am I going to feed my family" line of patter, so you might like to pay a first visit with no money to get a feel for it. **Prices** are rarely, if ever, fixed, and depend entirely on your bargaining skills. Luckily, getting a decent final price isn't too difficult thanks to the wealth of competing stalls (you can play them off against each other). For advice on bargaining techniques, see p.64.

For more upmarket souvenirs head to the TFA at the western end of Sokoine Road where several shops offer superior souvenirs, from handmade cards to beautiful trunks and tables fashioned (so they say) from the wood of dhows. You'll also find Zoom here, a photo gallery with some lovely pictures of the Serengeti and Kilimanjaro, and Msumbi Coffees, selling beans and freshly ground arabica from Kilimanjaro. Prices tend to be fixed at these establishments.

▲ Earrings made from bottle tops, Arusha

**Afrihope** Engira Rd. Owned and run by a 56-member cooperative of craftsmen. Plenty of wooden statues as well as some nice soapstone boxes and toy trucks made from recycled cans. A good place to visit first, just to get an idea of what's on offer in town. Open daily.

**Blue Heron** Haile Selassie Rd. Part of the café and stuffed with tasteful souvenirs and gifts. Good fabrics (cushion covers embellished with Maasai bead designs and embroidered bedspreads), glassware and wooden furniture. Closed Sun.

**The Craft Shop** Goliondoi Rd. A good place to get an idea of prices, with loads of Makonde carvings, some Tingatinga paintings. Closed Sat pm and Sun.

**Lookmanji Curio Shop** Joel Maeda St. One of the best selections in town, especially for carvings, and keenly priced, too. They also stock carvings from Kenya's Kamba tribe, who make good figurines. Other stuff includes Congolese and Malian masks, and – occasionally – a circumcision mask from Tanzania's Luguru. Closed Sun pm.

**"Maasai market"** Joel Maeda St/Boma Rd by the clock tower. An impromptu pavement market where Maasai women make and sell beadwork necklaces and bracelets, and men hawk scary-looking daggers and spears. Most days except Sun.

**The Travel Market** TFA Complex, Sokoine Rd. Superior handicrafts and a fine book selection; this is the best place for present shopping in Arusha. Prices are fixed.

# Arts and culture

After lying dormant for decades, Arusha's **arts scene** has woken up with a satisfying jolt. The main venue for performances and art exhibitions is *Via Via* in the grounds of the German Boma, which has an outdoor stage beside the Themi River (seating is in a grassy amphitheatre). There's at least one event each week, usually a local band although film screenings are also popular. Hands-on activities at *Via Via* include: drumming lessons (Tsh9000); a three-day **drum-making workshop** (Tsh50,000); courses in batiks (Tsh10,000 plus Tsh10,000 for materials); and Tanzanian cooking (Tsh10,000

## Buying tanzanite

Northern Tanzania – specifically the Mererani Hills between Arusha and Moshi, and an as-yet undeclared location in the Pare Mountains – is the only place on earth known to contain **tanzanite**, a precious transparent gemstone discovered in 1967. In its natural form, the stone is an irregular brownish lump, but when heated to 400–500°C it acquires a characteristic colour and brilliance, predominantly blue, with other shades ranging from violet to a dullish olive green. Determining the real colour isn't too easy however, as the stone is trichroic, meaning it shows three different colours when viewed from different angles: blue, purple or red. The facets are made by gemologists.

The whole business of mining tanzanite is beset by controversy. Local miners have gradually been pushed out by multinational enterprises whose heavy-handed tactics in dealing with "scavengers" – as they refer to artisanal miners – are frequently reported in the press. The mines themselves have a lamentable safety record, and in 2008 65 miners drowned following heavy rainfall – the third large-scale disaster at the mines in ten years.

Arusha is the main marketing (and smuggling) centre for tanzanite and other gemstones – ruby, green garnet (locally called tsavorite), green tourmaline, emerald and sapphire – some of them spirited in from Congo and Mozambique. There's no official **grading system** for tanzanite, although unofficially stones are classified into five main grades from AAA (the finest) to C. The price depends on colour (deep and radiant is most expensive), size and grade, with A-grade stones, for example, costing $250–500 per carat. Do your research before buying tanzanite; its many shades make **scamming** easy; a common trick is to pass off iolite (which costs $10 per carat) as tanzanite.

plus ingredients which you shop for at the local market at the start of the day). If you're around at the end of August or early September, ask about the annual **Arusha Street Festival**, which is held along Boma Road and combines music with a carnival atmosphere. June is the time for the *Via Via*-organised music festival, and a film festival in October is also planned.

The Century **Cinema**, at Njiro shopping mall east of the centre, screens Hollywood and Bollywood blockbusters (Tsh5000–7000).

# Listings

**Airlines** Air Excel, Subzali Building (over Exim Bank), Goliondoi Rd ☎027/254 8429, @reservations@airexcelonline.com; Air Tanzania, ATC House, Boma Rd ☎027/250 3201, @www.airtanzania.com; Air Uganda, Swahili St ☎027/254 6385, @www.air-uganda.com; Coastal Aviation, ATC House, Boma Rd ☎027/250 0087, @www.coastal.cc; Ethiopian Airlines, *New Safari Hotel*, Boma Rd ☎027/250 4231, @www.flyethiopian.com; Kenya Airways, see Precisionair; KLM, *New Safari Hotel*, Boma Rd ☎027/250 8062, @www.klm.com; Northwest Airlines, see KLM; Precisionair, *New Safari Hotel*, Boma Rd ☎027/250 8589, @www.precisionairtz.com; Regional Air, Nairobi Rd – turn north after Kilombero Market ☎027/250 4164, @www.regionaltanzania.com; Rwanda Air, Sokoine Rd (☎0732/978558, @www.rwandair.com); ZanAir, Summit Centre, Sokoine Rd

☎027/254 8877, 0784 320818, @www.zanair.com. Tickets for other airlines can be booked through travel agents.

**Airport information** Kilimanjaro International Airport ☎027/275 4252; Arusha Airport ☎027/250 5980.

**Ambulances** AAR ☎027/270 1121.

**Banks and exchange** There are banks and foreign exchange bureaux throughout town. Bank rates are around ten percent better than forexes, particularly for traveller's cheques, but check the commission first. There are also ATMs dotted throughout town. Forexes are quicker than banks but many only change cash rather than traveller's cheques.

**Books and maps** The best bookshop for locally published works is Bookpoint on Swahili St, which also has a good selection of coffee-table books, maps and some Tanzanian novels in English. Also worth a rummage are either of Kase Bookshop's branches (Boma Rd and Joel Maeda St).

**Camping equipment** Safari Care (Mon–Sat 9.30am–5pm) at the TFA on Sokoine is, by some distance, the best-equipped camping shop in Arusha, though it's not cheap. Don't rely on it to have just what you want in your size – its boot selection is particularly poor – but it's good for GPS systems, knives, water purifiers, batteries, hats and head torches.

**Car Rental** Avis Skylink Travel & Tours, Goliondoi Rd ☎027/250 9108, ⑩www.skylinktanzania.com. Suzuki Vitara self-drive $130 per day, including 110km ($500 excess liability); Land Cruiser $180 per day ($1000 excess). With driver, add $20 to each figure, excluding fuel. Arusha Naaz Rent A Car, *Arusha Naaz Hotel*, Sokoine Rd ☎027/250 2087 or 0754282799; ⑩www.arushanaaz.net. Land Cruiser from $120 a day with driver, includes 120km free per day.

**Football** Matches are held at Sheikh Amri Abeid Memorial Stadium; the local team is Arusha FC. Tickets (Tsh500) at the gate on Makongoro Rd.

**Health** AICC Hospital, Nyerere Rd ☎027/254 4113 is the best, and also has a good paediatrician. For minor ailments and tests, visit the Old Arusha Clinic, Nyerere Rd ☎0754/888444. Pharmacy: Moona's, Sokoine Rd, just west of NBC Bank (Mon–Fri 8.45am–5.30pm, Sat 8.45am–2pm; ☎027/250 9800).

**Immigration office** Afrika Mashariki Rd (Mon–Fri 7.30am–3pm; ☎027/250 3569).

**Internet access** Arusha has loads of Internet cafés, one on virtually every street in the centre. Prices average Tsh1500 an hour.

**Language courses** Via Via, at the north end of Boma Rd, offers lessons at Tsh7000 for around 45 minutes.

**Library** Arusha Regional Library, Sokoine Rd (Mon–Fri 9am–6pm, Sat 9am–2pm; Tsh500 daily membership).

**Police** Emergency ☎112. Report thefts for insurance paperwork at the station on the north side of Makongoro Rd ☎027/250 3641. Facing it is the regional police headquarters.

**Post and couriers** The main post office is on Boma Rd (Mon–Fri 8am–4.30pm, Sat 9am–noon), and has a stationery shop and philatelic bureau. To send international parcels, you need to arrive before 10am (Mon–Fri), when the customs officer is on duty. There are two branches on Sokoine Rd, and another in the AICC complex. For courier services: DHL, Sokoine Rd beside Stanbic Bank ☎027/250 6749; EMS, at the clock tower and AICC post offices.

**Sports and health clubs** AICC Sports Club, Old Moshi Rd, has squash, tennis, darts and volleyball; there's mini, golf at *Le Jacaranda* (Tsh500), and *The Arusha Hotel* has a gym (Tsh7000, or Tsh10,000 if using the pool too). *Stiggy's* on Old Moshi Rd is the venue for the Hash House Harriers' weekly runs (Fri 5.30pm; usually 5km, with or without beers to start with).

**Supermarkets and groceries** Largest is Shoprite in the TFA Shopping Centre, Sokoine Rd (Mon–Fri 8am–7pm, Sat 8am–5pm, Sun 8am–1pm). Smaller but more central is the anonymous supermarket by the clock tower (Mon–Fri 9am–5pm, Sat 9am–noon, and Rushda (same hours, also open Sun), under *Coyote Guest House* on Azimio St. Meat King (Mon–Fri 9am–5pm, Sat 9am–noon), Goliondoi Rd, is favoured by expats for imported beef, cheese, smoked hams, sausages and salami.

**Swimming pools** Nicest is the outdoor pool at *The Arusha Hotel* (Tsh5000); the one at the *Impala Hotel* (Tsh5000) is quite small. There are also pleasant and not too busy public baths at Njiro (Tsh4000). All are open daytime only.

**Telephones** TTCL is on Boma Rd (Mon–Fri 8am–4.30pm, Sat 9am–noon). Be very careful with phone services offered by some foreign exchange bureaux, which can charge exorbitant fees. The cheapest way of ringing abroad is via internet call: try *The Patisserie* on Sokoine, which offers little privacy but is cheap (Tsh300 per minute to the UK).

**Travel agents** Reliable agents for arranging rail, bus and plane tickets, car rental, safaris and trekking include Easy Travel & Tours at *New Safari Hotel*, Boma Rd ☎027/250 3929, ⑩www.easytravel-tanzania.com.

# Around Arusha

For all the hundreds of thousands of tourists passing through Arusha each year en route to the Northern Circuit, only a tiny proportion see much more of **Arusha Region** than the highway. Yet there are lots of things to keep you occupied.

## Moving on from Arusha

Arusha is northern Tanzania's transport hub, with several daily **bus connections** to all major towns in the north and east, and to Nairobi and Kampala. There are frequent **flights** to most national parks, northwestern towns, Dar and Zanzibar. For approximate journey times and frequencies, see p.334.

### By road

**Road conditions** to Dar, Ngorongoro, Tanga and Nairobi are surfaced, but the stretch up to Namanga on the Kenyan border is prone to flooding during heavy rains. Conditions on routes heading west vary with the season, as the sealed road only goes as far as Tarangire National Park before the road splits: northwest towards the Northern Circuit parks (sealed until Ngorongoro), and southwest towards Dodoma via Babati and Kondoa. The section south of Babati is extremely tricky, if not totally impassable, during the rains (heaviest March–May), as is most of the road network west of Singida.

The main hazard on sealed roads is **reckless driving**, especially between Arusha and Moshi. If you're driving yourself, be on your guard when the road swoops down towards bridges, as fatal high-speed crashes and collisions are depressingly common. The route is safest in the morning when drivers are less tired. **Safer bus companies** mentioned below include Akamba on the Nairobi–Moshi Highway (☏027/250 9491); Kilimanjaro Express, on Colonel Middleton Road; Royal Coach, in the petrol station at Mianzini Junction; and Scandinavian Express, at the Kilombero Bus Station on Makao Mapya Road. Companies with particularly **dangerous reputations** include Air Bus, Air Msae, Buffalo, Hood and Tawfiq.

**Bus tickets** for most companies can be bought at the main bus station, and some of the larger bus companies, including Scandinavian, also have offices/lots at Kilombero Bus Station. Buy tickets the day before, or leave very early: most buses are gone by mid-morning.

### Buses eastwards

To **Dar es Salaam**, some twenty buses head off between 6 and 8.30am: safest are Dar Express (6am, 7.30am, 8am, 8.30am and 9.15am, plus their bus from Nairobi which calls in at Arusha at about 10.45am before continuing to Dar; Tsh23,000); Scandinavian Express (8.30am and 11.30am; Tsh20,000–24,000); Royal Coach (9am; Tsh23,000) and Kilimanjaro Express (6.30am, 7am and 8am; Tsh23,000). These buses are also useful for getting to the **Usambaras** (change at Mombo) or the **Pare Mountains** (change at Mwanga or Same), though there are also direct buses to Lushoto (daily at 6am with Fasaha and Chakito) and Usangi (10am with Sahara Coach). For Moshi, 'Coaster' buses (Tsh2500) run every half an hour or so from the main station, but the only company with a good reputation on this route is Ibra Line. For **Tanga**, buses leave between 8am and 10.30am; Simba Video Coach is the safest company.

For **Morogoro**, safest is probably Islam Bus (7am), but as none of the companies have particularly safe reputations, it's best to go to Dar and move on the next day. The only company covering **Iringa and Mbeya** is the perilous Hood (daily 5am).

---

The fertile lands either side of the highway, east of Arusha, were among the first in northern Tanzania to be colonized by Europeans, who grew tobacco to barter with Maasai for livestock. **Coffee** took over later, and remains the area's major crop – you can stay on a coffee estate, or see the coffee-making process as part of a cultural tourism programme based at Tengeru, close to the bird-filled **Lake Duluti**. There are several more **cultural tourism programmes** in the vicinity of Arusha, providing intimate glimpses into rural life among the Maasai, Meru and Il Larusa (Arusha) tribes. A good destination for hikers is **Mount Meru**, part of **Arusha National Park**. The mountain is Tanzania's

### Buses westwards

Heading west, things are getting better as the road network gradually improves, with the road to **Mwanza** now completely sealed. Mtei is probably the safest company serving **Babati** (5.30am) **Kondoa** (5.30am) and **Singida** (6.30am, 7.30am). **Dodoma** is most easily covered in two legs, changing at Babati or Kondoa; of the direct buses, Shabiby (daily; 5.45am) is safe. **Tabora** is covered Wednesday to Saturday at 6am by NBS; the journey can take as little as twelve hours. For towns around the **national parks**, there are three buses a day to Mto wa Mbu and Karatu (most leaving in the afternoon) as well as daladalas. There are three approaches to the **Lake Victoria region**: via Singida, via Ngorongoro and Serengeti, and via Kenya. Via Singida, buses to Mwanza (the safest are Air Jordan, Bedui or Mohamed Trans; Tsh31,000) all leave at around 6am and can cover the route in a day, assuming there are no breakdowns.

### Buses to Kenya

**Mombasa** is served by three buses a day: Tashif via Tanga at 8.30am and Perfect and Rakibu via Moshi at 7am. **Nairobi** is covered by mainline operators: Scandinavian (daily 4pm; Tsh25,000) and Dar Express (3pm; Tsh22,000) are the safest. More convenient, if slightly more expensive, are the **shuttle minibuses**. The latter leave at 8am and 2pm, with all but one departing from the *La Bella Luna Guest House* (the exception being the Impala Shuttle, which leaves from the car park of its namesake hotel). That said, all of them can pick you up at your hotel if you buy the ticket in advance, and on occasion they'll drop you at your hotel in Nairobi too. Shuttle companies include: Impala, at *Impala Hotel* (☏0754/550010; $30); Bobby Shuttle (☏027/250 3490), at Bobby Tours on Goliondoi, and Riverside (☏027/250 3916 or 0754270089; $25) on Sokoine near the river. **Kenyan visas** are issued without fuss at Namanga ($50 for most nationalities, or $20 for a transit visa; bring dollars in cash).

### By air

Airline offices are listed on p.318. A $6 **departure tax** is levied on internal flights; the $35 tax on international flights is included in the fare. Most domestic flights take off from **Arusha Airport**, 7km along the Dodoma road: catch a Monduli daladala (6am–3pm; Tsh300) and get off at the airport sliproad, a 1.5km walk away, or catch a taxi, which should be no more than Tsh8000. **Kilimanjaro International Airport (KIA)** lies 48km east of Arusha, 6km off the Moshi Highway. Air Tanzania operates free **shuttle buses** for their passengers; KLM charges $15 (enquire at the offices on Boma Road) while Precisionair charges their passengers Tsh10,000. For other airlines, a taxi is the only way: you'll do well if you bargain it down to Tsh30,000. Buses to Moshi can also drop you at the airport turning, leaving you 6km to walk or hitch. KIA closes after the last flight, reopening at 6am, so you can't spend the night there – the upmarket *KIA Lodge* is nearby (see p.310).

second-highest peak, and achingly attractive, whether you want to scale it or nose around its lower slopes, either on foot or on a game drive.

# Arusha National Park

In spite of its proximity to Arusha town, **Arusha National Park** is little-visited – which is good news for visitors who do make it here, as they can enjoy the park's stunning volcanic scenery, expansive views (especially of its

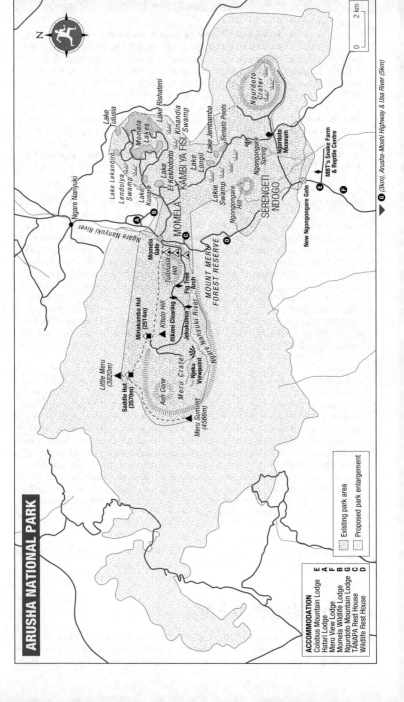

# ARUSHA NATIONAL PARK

ACCOMMODATION
Colobus Mountain Lodge    E
Hatari Lodge    F
Meru View Lodge    B
Momela Wildlife Lodge    G
Ngurdoto Mountain Lodge    C
TANAPA Rest House    D
Wildlife Rest House

Existing park area
Proposed park enlargement

0    2 km

N

giant neighbour, Kilimanjaro), hauntingly beautiful rainforest and plentiful wildlife in relative solitude.

Dominating the park is the volcanic **Mount Meru** (4566m), Tanzania's second-highest mountain. While Meru appears as an almost perfect cone when viewed from Arusha, from the east it shows the effects of the cataclysmic volcanic event which a quarter of a million years ago blew away the entire eastern side and top of the mountain – which was once taller than Kilimanjaro – in a series of gigantic explosions which hurled boulders over 70km to the east and unleashed a devastating flood of water, rocks, mud, ash and lava. Although the volcano is now classed as dormant, earth tremors still occur, and a series of minor eruptions were recorded in colonial times, the most recent in 1910.

The national park and its fringing forest reserve encloses much of the mountain, including the 3.5km-wide **Meru Crater** on the summit and the entire shattered eastern slope, as well as the mountain's eastern foothills. Here you'll find **Ngurdoto Crater**, an unbroken three-kilometre-wide caldera whose wildlife has earned it the nickname "Little Ngorongoro", and the shallow, alkaline **Momela Lakes**, known for their birdlife, especially flamingos. **Wildlife** you're likely to see includes buffaloes (especially in forest glades), elephants, hippos, giraffes, warthogs, antelopes, zebras, black-and-white colobus and blue monkeys. Leopards and hyenas are present but rarely seen (there are no resident lions), and while there are also some extremely rare black rhinos, the park authorities are understandably loath to make too much noise about them, given the ever-present risk from poachers. There are also 575 bird species, and butterfly fanatics are in for a treat, too.

## Arrival and information

Access to the park is easiest through **Ngongongare Gate**, 7.5km north of Usa River and the Arusha–Moshi Highway. **Momela Gate**, 17km further north, is the starting point for hikes up Mount Meru, and also houses the park headquarters.

Most visitors come on organized safaris, but visiting the park **independently** is feasible, given that hiking is possible in the western sector as long as you're accompanied by a ranger – they can be hired at Momela Gate. To reach the park by **public transport**, catch the daily Urio Bus from Arusha towards Ngare Nanyuki; it leaves Arusha at 1pm, and returns back through Momela Gate at around 7am. Alternatively, catch a daladala to Usa River, from where Land Rovers and trucks run every hour or two up to Ngare Nanyuki. If you're **hiring a car**, 2WD is sufficient for most roads in the east of the park during the dry season, but 4WD is nonetheless advisable, and essential during or shortly after the rains.

The **best time to visit** depends on what you want to do. Mount Meru can be climbed throughout the year, but is best avoided during the long rains (March–May), when you can get very wet, cold and muddy. Skies are clearest in September (when the mountain is bitterly cold), and again from December to February (when the temperature is marginally more clement). Bird-watching is best between May and October, when migrants visit.

### Information and fees

The **park headquarters** are at Momela Gate, 24km north of Usa River (daily 6.30am–6.30pm; ☎027/255 3995, ⓦwww.tanzaniaparks.com/arusha.html); this is where rangers, guides and porters can be hired. **Entry fees** are paid here or at Ngongongare Gate: $35 per person for 24 hours.

If you're **driving**, the services of an official guide ($15) are optional. If you're **hiking** (only possible west of Momela Gate), an armed park ranger is obligatory ($20 per group per day; tips expected), whilst climbers also pay a one-off $20 rescue fee if going beyond Miriakamba Hut. The total cost for a self-arranged four-day ascent and descent of the mountain works out at $300 including hut fees but excluding transport, food, porters and additional guides. **Porters** come from nearby villages: the set daily rate is around Tsh6000 for carrying a maximum of 20kg. A four-day hike arranged through a safari company in Arusha averages $450–500 per person.

The only decent **map** is Giovanni Tombazzi's painted version – ensure you get the "New" one – available at the park gates, Arusha's bookshops and the Ngorongoro Conservation Authority office on Boma Road.

## Accommodation

The two **mountain huts** ($20 per person) along the Mount Meru climbing route are clean and have bunk beds and toilets. Water is also available, but at Saddle Hut you may have to collect it from the lower gorges during the dry season. Although the huts are rarely full, the park advises climbers to book ahead, either at the gate or at TANAPA's headquarters in Arusha (see p.307). **Camping** is possible outside the huts and at three park-run campsites a kilometre or two southwest of Momela Gate (all $30 per person), and at three special campsites ($50) with no facilities. You can also camp at *Colobus Mountain Lodge*, outside Ngongongare Gate ($5 per person).

### In the park

*Hatari Lodge* and *Momela Wildlife Lodge* are just outside the park, but access is usually through the park so park fees are payable.

**Hatari Lodge** 1km north of Momela Gate ℡0754/510195, ⊛www.hatarilodge.com. Welcoming and nicely idiosyncratic place decked out in 1960s and 1970s style – a refreshingly funky change from the neo-colonial mood of most lodges. There are just nine en-suite rooms (spacious and peaceful and with fireplaces), a good "John Wayne" bar, delicious food, library and a veranda with views of Meru and Kili. Immediate wildlife interest is good, too: giraffes frequently come right up, bushbabies and genets are seen at night, a boardwalk accesses a clearing with buffalo, waterbuck, eland and giraffe. Walks, game drives ($125 each) and canoeing can be arranged. FB ❽

**Momela Wildlife Lodge** 2km north of Momela Gate ℡0787/005062, ⊛www.lions-safari-intl.com. Large and far from intimate but cheap, with 57 faded rooms in a series of mundane wooden thatch-roofed *bandas* supposedly styled after an African village. Still, there's hot water and good views of Mount Meru, while for film buffs, this is where the cheesy John Wayne movie *Hatari* was shot. There's a bar and lounge with a fireplace, a big swimming pool (guests only) and free early-morning bird walks. Game drives are $150 each. BB ❼

**TANAPA Rest House** 1.3km south of Momela Gate; turn east at the signpost for "Halali" (book through TANAPA in Arusha; see p.307). Perfectly decent bunks and bathrooms. ❸

**Wildlife Rest House** 6km south of Momela Gate (book through Mweka College of African Wildlife Management ℡027/275 6451, ⊛www .mwekawildlife.org). In a grassy forest clearing beside the roadside, this has just two beds, solar electricity, a toilet and bucket shower. ❶

### Outside the park

The following all include breakfast.

🧗 **Colobus Mountain Lodge** 300m west of Ngongongare Gate, 7.3km north of Usa River ℡027/250 2813, ⊛www.colobusmountain .lodge.com. Next to an unsightly sawmill, this good-value 18-room establishment centres on a large *makuti*-thatched bar and restaurant, and also has occasional internet access. Rooms – including triples and others accessible to wheelchairs – are in two-room thatch-roofed stone *bandas* with fireplaces and verandas. ❻

**Meru View Lodge** 6.5km north of Usa River on the right ℡0784419232, ⊛www.meru-view-lodge.de. A quiet, charming and well-priced option run by a Tanzanian–German couple. Surrounded by colourful gardens containing aviaries and wild birds, the bright, comfortable cottages are divided into two en-suite rooms with big double beds. There's also a swimming pool, and hiking can be arranged. Great food and drinks. ❺

**Ngurdoto Mountain Lodge** 2.5km north of Usa River, then 1km east ☎027/255 5217, 🌐www .thengurdotomountainlodge.com. The area's best-appointed and biggest hotel (it's more like a resort), with rooms decked out in classic Africana, most with hot tubs. Its size, overly landscaped gardens and Disneylandish architec-ture detract from the experience, but it's good value, and has a pool, golf course and rooms for disabled guests. ❼

# Ngurdoto Crater and Momela Lakes

The highlights of the **eastern section** of the park, covering the forested foothills of Mount Meru, are the Momela Lakes and Ngurdoto Crater. Both can be visited on an organized day-trip from Arusha. **Walking** may be possible in the area if accompanied by a park ranger.

The **Momela Lakes** in the northeast of the park comprise seven shallow, alkaline lakes formed from the volcanic debris created when Mount Meru blew its top 250,000 years ago. The alkalinity is ideal for various forms of algae, which account for the lakes' opaque shades of emerald and turquoise and provide an ideal habitat for filter feeders such as flamingos. Other birds include pelicans, ducks, and a host of migrants, especially between May and October. Glimpses of black-and-white colobus monkeys are virtually guaranteed in the forests around the lakes, and you may also catch sight of blue monkeys, bushbucks, buffaloes, hippos, giraffes and zebras. **Canoeing** is possible on Little Momela Lake; contact Green Footprint Adventures at *Serena Mountain Village Lodge*, Lake Duluti (☎027/253 9267; see p.310). It costs $50 per person, and there's also a $20 canoeing fee payable to the national park, in addition to standard park fees and transport.

Three more lakes and Lokie Swamp flank the drivable road south from Momela Lakes to **Ngurdoto Crater**, an unbroken, 3km-wide, 400m-deep volcanic caldera (inevitably dubbed "Little Ngorongoro") produced when two volcanic cones merged and finally collapsed – you can walk along the crater's western and southern rims. Like Ngorongoro, Ngurdoto plays host to a rich variety of wildlife, including buffaloes, elephants, baboons and occasionally rhinos. To protect this little Eden, especially the highly endangered rhinos (which were hunted to the brink of extinction in the 1980s), visitors aren't allowed to descend to the crater floor. Instead, you can view the crater's denizens from a series of viewpoints on the south side of the rim, which also gives good views of Kilimanjaro, weather permitting.

The **Ngurdoto Museum** (daily 6am–5pm; free), 2km west of the crater, has modest displays of butterflies, moths, insects, birds and – more worryingly – snares used by poachers. The most startling exhibit is a rhinoceros skull with a wire snare embedded several centimetres into it; the rhino survived several years before the wire finally killed it. Back on the main Usa River–Momela road, 1km south of Ngongongare Gate, **MBT's Snake Farm & Reptile Centre** (daily 8am–5pm; Tsh3000) breeds snakes, turtles and reptiles for export. There's an extensive collection of scaly critters on display, including chameleons and crocodiles.

Heading back towards Momela, keep an eye out for wildlife in the diminutive patch of grassland to the right; dubbed **Serengeti Ndogo** ("Little Serengeti") it contains a variety of plains game, including a population of zebra introduced following the collapse of an export scheme.

# Mount Meru

**Mount Meru** is sometimes treated as an acclimatization trip before an attempt on Kilimanjaro, and although the summit is over a kilometre lower, the climb

www.roughguides.com

325

can be just as rewarding, with spectacular scenery and dense forest. The mountain's **vegetational zones** are similar to Kilimanjaro's, though the high-altitude glaciers and ice fields are absent. Evergreen forest begins at around 1800m, which is moist, cool and thick at first, then thins as you rise. The higher forest, including giant bamboo thickets (up to 12m tall), offers an ideal habitat for small duiker antelopes and primates, notably blue monkeys and black-and-white colobus monkeys, which are often seen by climbers. The forest disappears at around 2900m, giving way to floral meadows where you might spot buffalo, giraffe or warthog. The meadows are followed by a zone of giant lobelia and groundsel (see p.273), and finally – above the last of the trees at 3400m – bleak alpine desert where the only sounds, apart from your breathing, are the wind and the cries of white-necked ravens.

### The ascent

Climbs of Mount Meru are usually done through a safari company, though if you're suitably equipped (see p.266), you can save a modest amount of money by arranging things yourself. The ascent starts at Momela Gate (1500m), where rangers, guides and porters can be hired. The trek is usually done over three days (two up, one down); those on a four-day climb will find that the extra day is spent on the descent (stopping for a second time at Miriakamba Hut) rather than on the ascent, so there is no advantage, acclimatization-wise, of taking the extra day. Although **altitude sickness** isn't as much of a problem on Mount Meru as on Kilimanjaro, symptoms should nonetheless be treated seriously. If you come down with the mild form of altitude sickness, Little Meru Peak, also on the crater rim but 750m lower than Meru Summit, is an easier target than Meru summit itself.

**Day one** (4–5hr) goes from Momela Gate to **Miriakamba Hut** (2514m). There are two routes; the steeper and more direct one heads up due west (and is mainly used by walkers when descending), and the longer and more pictur-esque route follows a drivable trail to the south which begins by hugging the boulder-strewn **Ngare Nanyuki** (Red River); look for tawny eagles in the yellow-bark acacia trees here. The trail curves around **Tululusia Hill** (Sentinel Hill), in the lee of which stands an enormous strangling fig tree whose aerial roots have formed a natural arch; there's a waterfall on the Tululusia River near the tree. A kilometre beyond the tree is **Itikoni Clearing**, a popular grazing area for buffaloes (there is also a "special campsite" here), and 1km further on is Jekukumia, where a small diversion takes you to the confluence of Ngare Nanyuki and **Jekukumia** rivers. At around 2000m both routes enter the rainforest, characterized by the African olive tree (rare elsewhere thanks to its useful timber), and bushbuck may be seen here. Buffalo and elephant droppings mean you should be careful when walking around Miriakamba Hut at night.

**Day two** heads on up to **Saddle Hut** (3570m) below the northern rim of the summit's horseshoe crater (2–3hr). If you have time and energy, a short detour to **Little Meru Peak** (3820m) is possible (5–6hr from Miriakamba Hut), though the symptoms of altitude sickness kick in on this day. **Day three** starts no later than 2am for the 4–5hr ascent to **Meru Summit** (4562.13m according to the sign at the top), following a very narrow ridge along the western rim of the crater, to arrive in time for sunrise over Kilimanjaro. Lunch is taken on the way down at Saddle Hut, and Momela Gate is reached by late afternoon. Alternatively, you could take it easy and spend an extra night at Miriakamba Hut, some four to five hours' walk from the summit.

# Cultural tourism programmes around Mount Meru

Although Arusha National Park covers only the eastern flank and summit of Mount Meru, the southern and northern slopes can also be visited through a number of **cultural tourism programmes**, which combine beautiful views, intimate encounters with the local Maasai, Il Larusa (Arusha) and Meru tribes and dozens of walks to local attractions. Access to some can be a little awkward, given their rural locations off main roads, though the tourist office in Arusha is helpful at arranging transport. **Costs** for the programmes depend on group size, but you can estimate about Tsh15,000–25,000 per person for half a day, Tsh25,000–45,000 for a full day, or Tsh45,000–60,000 for a day and night trip, though longer trips of a few days are available too. The money you pay is put to good use by the villages involved, with some of it funding local primary and nursery schools and healthcare programmes, while elsewhere is subsidizes other worthwhile causes, such as the purchase of energy-efficient stoves.

## Ilkiding'a

On the southern slopes of Mount Meru, 7km northwest of Arusha, is the Il Larusa village of **ILKIDING'A**. Its **cultural tourism programme**, most of whose members perform in the Masarie Cultural Dance Group, offers half- to three-day guided tours, including walks through farms, visits to a healer and local craftsmen, and hikes along Njeche Canyon (which has caves to explore) and up Leleto Hill. The three-day hike (or one day by mountain bike) also features forest reserves and local markets, with nights spent camping or in family homes.

There's no public **transport**, but as it's only 7km from Arusha, walking is the best way there: turn north at the signpost for *Ilboru Safari Lodge* on the Nairobi–Moshi Highway and follow the signs. The road is bad, so taxi drivers charge up to Tsh30,000 for the return trip. Arrange **bookings** through Eliakimu Ole Njeche ☏0713/520264, ✉enmasarie@yahoo.com.

## Mkuru

On the north side of Mount Meru, some 70km from Arusha, the Maasai settlement of **MKURU** is famed for its camels, which were introduced in the early 1990s, as they fare better in semi-arid conditions than cattle. Mkuru's **cultural tourism programme** offers **camel rides** (from a few hours to a week-long expedition to Ol Doinyo Lengai and Lake Natron), bird-watching, encounters with Maasai, and a short but stiff climb up the pyramidal Mount Ol Doinyo Landaree (3hr 30min return trip).

At least one overnight in Mkuru is needed, preferably several; **accommodation** is in three two-bed cottages at the camp (bring your own bedding, food and drink). **Access** is expensive unless you're coming as part of a regular safari to Arusha National Park. Catch the daily Urio Bus service from Arusha (1pm) to Ngare Nanyuki: it goes through the park, so you'll have to pay the $35 entrance fee. From Ngare Nanyuki, walk the remaining 5km (signposted) west to Mkuru or rent a pick-up (Tsh20,000). **Bookings** can be made through Mr Isaya Ishalavel ☏0784/756162, or with *Momela Wildlife Lodge* (p.324).

▲ Camel safari, on a cultural tourism trip near Mount Meru

## Mulala

On the southeastern slopes of Mount Meru, 34km from Arusha, is the beautifully located Meru village of **MULALA**. The cultural tourism programme is
run by a women's group, who will show you their cheese dairy (which supplies
a good many tourist hotels), bakery, stores, farms, and perhaps a few nifty dance
moves. You can also visit a school, explore **Mount Meru Forest Reserve**
(birds and monkeys), and hike through coffee and banana farms to Lemeka Hill
(views and a traditional healer), along the Marisha River (thick tropical vegetation, birds and monkeys), or to **Ziwa la Mzungu** – White Man's Lake – where
legend says that a European disappeared while fishing, after frightening
demonic sounds came from the lake. The various walks can be combined into
a full day, or spread over two days if you have a tent – a better option.

To get to Mulala by **public transport**, catch a daladala towards Usa River
and get off 1km before at the signboard for "Dik Dik Hotel". From here,
catch a pick-up or Land Rover for the 9km to the Ngani (pronounced *njani*)

Cooperative Society; alternatively, the society can arrange transport for Tsh25,000 each way. Ask for Mama Anna Pallangyo (☎0784/378951, ✉agapetourism@yahoo.com), whose house is nearby.

## Ng'iresi

On the verdant southern slopes of Mount Meru, 6km north of Arusha, lies **NG'IRESI** village where the Il Larusa tribe is currently in transition from cattle-herding and life in Maasai-style *bomas* to agriculture and permanent stone buildings. Several easy tours are offered as part of the cultural tourism programme, from half-day walks to three-day camping trips (bring your own equipment), and include an encounter with a traditional healer (an additional fee of Tsh10,000), hikes through Olgilai Forest Reserve, Songota and Navaru waterfalls, viewpoints on the Lekimana Hills, a climb up Kivesi Hill to the crowning forest, and visits to development projects. The local women's group provides meals.

**To get here**, walk 5km up the road that goes past the *Summit Club* from the Nairobi–Moshi Highway, just east of *Mount Meru Hotel*, or arrange transport via the tourist office in Arusha (Tsh20,000 there and back). **Bookings** can be made through Mr Loti Sareyo of Kilimo Youth Group: ☎0754/320966, ⓦwww .ngiresischool.org.

## Tengeru and Lake Duluti

**TENGERU** lies 12km east of Arusha with its bustling, recently modernized market – busiest on Wednesday and Sunday (all day). Tengeru's cultural tourism programme is five minutes' walk north of the highway: head down the road facing the Natoil petrol station where daladalas from Arusha drop you (ones to Usa River and Kikatiti also pass by), turn right after 350m, then left at the signpost for "Tengeru Campsite". The **campsite** has hot water (BB Tsh10,000), it also has a tent for hire (an extra Tsh5000), and a self-catering apartment (❸). Mountain bikes and good food are also available. For **bookings**, contact Mr Brightson Pallangyo ☎0754/960176, ✉tengeru_cultural_tourism@yahoo.com.

Other experiences on offer include the chance to visit a traditional healer, stone grinding finger millet (*ulezi*) to make *uji* porridge, coffee roasting (you can take some home), and tree planting. They also offer a hike along the **Malala River**, whilst the three-day tour includes a visit to the gruesome spot where hundreds of Maasai drowned in a war with the Meru in the nineteenth century

The main reason for coming to Tengeru is **Lake Duluti**, a small crater lake 2km to the south, visits to which can be made through the cultural tourism programme, *Via Via* in Arusha, or independently. Formed at the same time as Mount Meru, it's partially flanked by a thin slice of forest through which wends a nature trail. It's a pretty place, probably best savoured at the end of your trip – if you have the money, at *Serena Mountain Village Lodge* near the east shore (see p.310). Sunsets are a particular joy, both for the sky-show and the many birds. Unfortunately, **swimming** is out of the question: the floating papyrus beds suggest bilharzia, whilst volcanically induced currents may be dangerous.

The lake and its forest are a reserve managed by Arusha Catchment Forestry (☎027/250 9522, ✉tourismduluti@yahoo.com), which charges $8 **entry**, plus $2 per person for a guide and $12 for an inflatable canoe or fishing gear. Their office is next to the (signposted) Duluti Club on the lake's western shore, a lovely 1.5km walk from the Natoil junction on the highway through a coffee plantation and patches of woodland. The office also has a **campsite**.

# The road to Kenya

The bus ride from **Arusha to Kenya** is a delight, especially early in the morning when the mist shrouding Mount Meru begins to dissipate. The rolling hills and acacia-studded plains beyond can be fantastically green after the rains, but the lush appearance is illusory: like the area to the west of Arusha, the plains north of Mount Meru suffer from massive erosion as a result of overgrazing by Maasai cattle herds, itself a consequence of their expulsion from traditional pastures following the establishment of the region's wildlife parks and commercial ranches.

Several settlements between Arusha and the border with Kenya run cultural tourism programmes, enabling you to get to know the area's tribes and wildlife spot while exploring the plains and mountains.

## Ngaramtoni

Rounding the southwestern flank of Mount Meru, the first major settlement you come to is **NGARAMTONI**, 12km from Arusha (daladalas from Arusha's daladala stand or the main bus station). Signposted from Ngaramtoni is the **Osotwa cultural tourism programme**, a two-kilometre walk east of the highway. You may be met by guides – ensure they're carrying an ID card. The best time to come is Thursday or Sunday, to coincide with **Ngaramtoni market**, where you'll find fantastic spherical pots at throwaway prices.

Rather than being a place, *osotwa* means "good relations between people", and the project covers nine neighbouring villages. On offer are various walks accompanied by Il Larusa guides and visits to traditional healers, crafters, and a sacred fig tree ("strangling fig" vines have long been venerated by East Africa's peoples). You can also walk along the Ngarenaro River, or clamber up the 2000m Sambasha Hill to its crater and forest for great views, and to spot birds, butterflies, and both colobus and blue monkeys.

At present, the longest trip is just a day and night – there are various **campsites** (Tsh4000), or you can stay in one of several **homestays** (Tsh5000) in the village or on the edge of a forest plantation. **Costs** vary according to group size: Tsh10,000–20,000 per person for half a day, plus a forest fee (Tsh6000) and community development fee (Tsh8000). Taxis from Arusha are Tsh15,000 one way, or it's Tsh500 in a daladala. Profits subsidize energy-efficient stoves. For **bookings**, contact the Chairman on ☎0754/960905, ⓦwww.osotwa.com.

## Ilkurot

Whereas Ngaramtoni is largely inhabited by settled Maasai, the drier terrain further north is the domain of their cattle-herding cousins. One of the best places to get to know them is through the **Ilkurot cultural tourism programme** (contact Jeremia Laizer ☎0784/459296, ⓔmaasaitourism @yahoo.com, ⓦmaasaiwanderings.com), 8km towards Nairobi from Ngaramtoni, or 20km from Arusha.

Thoroughly recommended are visits to (or overnights in) Maasai *bomas*, and three- to five-day walking or **riding trips** (by camel or donkey) for a unique insight into semi-nomadic life, as well as glimpses of plains game and sweeping views of mounts Meru, Kilimanjaro, Longido and Kilimamoto. Shorter trips include a half-day hike up **Ngorora Hill**, followed by a visit to a blacksmith, women's handicrafts groups and a *boma*; for a full day, there's also time to climb **Kilimamoto mountain** to its crater, or to visit beekeepers. Saturday is market day at nearby **Ol Doinyo Sambu** (no photos). Should you wish to witness a Maasai-style goat slaughter (and subsequent transformation into succulent *nyama choma*), just ask.

**Access** by daladala is easy: take one to Ngaramtoni, then change to another for Ol Doinyo Sambu and get off at Sitau: the project is based at the campsite 400m west of the road from here. A taxi from Arusha is about Tsh35,000. If you're not staying under canvas (you'll need to bring your own tent; there's a Tsh5000 charge for camping), **accommodation** is available on traditional skin-and-grass beds in a Maasai *boma* (Tsh5000), or in a guesthouse (❶). **Costs** are reasonable: Tsh11,500–19,000 per person for half a day depending on group size; Tsh16,000–23,500 for a full day; longer stays are also available. Part of the fees benefit widows and orphans, and also pay for primary schools and health care.

## Longido

Located 80km north of Arusha along the Nairobi Highway in the heart of Maasai land, **LONGIDO** is the most distant but probably the most popular of the cultural tourism programmes around Arusha.

Rising abruptly in the east, **Mount Longido**'s 2690-metre elevation makes for a dramatic change of vegetation, winding up through dense cloudforest before following a series of buffalo trails across drier montane forest and scrub. The climb is possible in a day (8–9hr return trip), but two days, with overnight camping at Kimokouwa (bring your own tent), is recommended. With clear skies, the views from the summit are stunning; good weather is most likely from May to October. **Other walks** are possible in the plains around the mountain, including a half-day hike to Maasai *bomas* at Ol Tepesi, and a day-trip to Kimokouwa's "Valley of Wells" (the wells lead to an underground river used by Maasai herders); both of the hikes offer the chance of sighting gerenuk (common in southern Kenya but rare in Tanzania), lesser kudu and klipspringer, giraffe, zebra, gazelle and buffalo. The guides are all young Maasai warriors, and most speak reasonable English.

The best **day to visit** is Wednesday, to coincide with the weekly cattle market, where you can also buy *kiloriti*: a root taken as an infusion for its stimulating properties – which may explain the astonishing ability of the Maasai and other pastoral tribes to cover enormous distances on foot, seemingly without fatigue. **Buses** and Peugeot shared taxis leave from Arusha's main bus station every hour or so, and take ninety minutes. The **cultural tourism programme** office is signposted a short distance from the highway in Longido. There's a basic and clean **guesthouse** (❶) in the village, and three **campsites** connected to the tourism programme. **Food** is available from local *hotelis* (restaurants) and the FARAJA Women's Group. **Costs** depend on group size, from Tsh10,000–30,000 for a half day. The cost for climbs up Mount Longido varies but shouldn't be much more than Tsh50,000, half that if you're in a group of twelve or more. Profits fund the construction and maintenance of cattle dips. **Bookings** can be made via Mr Ally Mwaiko of Longido Village Committee on ☏027/253 9209 or 0787/855185.

## Namanga

Passing Mount Longido, the road veers northeast towards **Ol Doinyo Orok** mountain (2526m), sacred to the Maasai. At its base, 110km north of Arusha, is the bustling settlement of **NAMANGA**, which straddles the Kenyan border. **Buses, daladalas and Peugeot pick-ups** to Namanga run once or twice an hour throughout the day from both Nairobi and Arusha; the trip from Arusha takes ninety minutes to two hours. Locals pass between Kenya and Tanzania with impunity, but tourists wishing to **cross the border** have to complete formalities, which can take up to half an hour on each side. **Visas** ($50 for either country) are usually paid in dollars cash; you may be able to pay in sterling, but don't rely on it. There's a KCB **bank** on the Kenyan side, and an NBC in Tanzania within the customs area. Don't be suckered into changing money on the street, and if someone says you need to have Tanzanian/Kenyan shillings to enter Tanzania /Kenya, ignore them – it's just a ruse leading to a money-changing scam.

The Kenyan side of the border is famed for its admirably tenacious Maasai women, who sell trinkets and pose for photos. The Tanzanian side is marginally calmer if you can avoid the red-eyed daladala touts, but watch your luggage on both sides – there are a lot of drugged-up young men hanging about. If you want or need to spend the night at Namanga, there's a slew of cheap **guest-houses** (all ❶) on either side, the better ones are in Tanzania.

# West of Arusha

Heading **west from Arusha** along the Dodoma road, towards the wildlife parks and central Tanzania, the landscape changes with startling abruptness from Mount Meru's lushly forested foothills, into a broad and largely featureless expanse of savanna. Although it turns green in the rains, for much of the year it's an unremittingly dry and unforgiving area, where the disastrous effects of **overgrazing** are depressingly apparent. With little plant cover left, the soil no longer absorbs rainwater as it should, and the resulting floods have gouged deep, lunar gullies across the land, which in the dry season are the playground of spinning dust devils. Often seen as an indictment of the Maasai obsession with cattle, the massive erosion is actually more the result of the eviction of Maasai herders from their traditional ranges further west, which has created unnaturally high population densities elsewhere.

## Kisongo and Meserani

**KISONGO** village, 16km from Arusha, is the first settlement of any size along the highway west, and hosts a lively cattle market on Wednesdays (all day) attended by herders from all over the area. To catch the best of it, you'll have to stay over the night before: there are cheap and basic **rooms** (❶) at *Sinya Bar* and *Millennium 2000 Bar*, on the left of the main road at the west end of the village; both places also have food and drink. The Kisongo Maasai Gallery and Cultural Centre, 800m east of the village, is one of several **souvenir emporiums** along the road to the parks: you'll have to bargain hard, and bear in mind that if you're on safari, your driver will be paid a twenty to thirty percent kickback on anything you buy. Credit cards are accepted, but whether you can trust them with your card details is another matter. **Daladalas** from Arusha's main bus stand to Monduli (6am–3pm, to 6pm on Sun) also pass through.

Past Kisongo, the landscape becomes increasingly bleak, especially in October before the onset of the short rains, when the flat brown plains and distant inselbergs (rocky outcrops) are danced over by spiralling dust devils. The next major settle-ment is **MESERANI**, 30km from Arusha, which holds livestock auctions on Tuesdays (all day; mornings are best). There are several cheap and basic **guest-houses** with bars and restaurants: try the *Perselian* (❶). Much better, if you have a tent, is **Meserani Snake Park** beside the highway at the west end of the village (☎0754/440800 or 0754/445911, Ⓦwww.meseranisnakepark.com). Started by a South African family in 1993, the park was almost wholly desert when they arrived, but the judicious planting of drought-resistant indigenous trees has created an oasis. Most of the snakes are collected from local farms and villages; in return for not killing them, locals benefit from free antivenom. Highlights include black and red spitting cobras, several green mambas and two black-mouthed mambas – not that you'd have much time to savour the sight. There are also lizards and a crocodile pool, the fence serving mainly to keep out drunken overlanders.

Adjacent to the snake park and run by the same people is an excellent **Maasai Cultural Museum**, containing dozens of dioramas of figures in various situations (daily life, dance, an *orpul* meat feast, circumcision, and "milking" blood from a cow, amongst others). The guide will explain anything that catches your eye. Entrance to the museum and snake park costs $10, and **camping** is free. There's good, touristy grub and one of East Africa's funkiest bars (cold beers, cool cocktails, good atmosphere and zillions of flags), which becomes something of a riot whenever overland truck groups are in residence.

Behind the museum are some thickly thatched houses built by Maasai, who sell **handicrafts**; there's little hassle, so take your time. If you don't find something to your liking, there's more choice at Tingatinga Art Gallery in the centre of Meserani, and Oldoinyo Orok Arts and Gallery (both open daily; free admission) at the north end of the settlement. The Maasai outside the snake park can also arrange **camel rides** (Tsh12,000 for two hours), and guided walks through the village. To get to Meserani from Arusha, catch a **daladala** (Tsh1000) from the main bus station towards Monduli.

## Monduli

The **Monduli Mountains**, north of Meserani, act as condensers for rainfall, and so are of obvious importance to the Maasai, providing year-round water and pasture. The area's main town is **MONDULU CHINI** (Lower Monduli; usually just called Monduli), 12km north of Meserani and the highway, at the foot of the mountains. **MONDULI JUU** (Upper Monduli), 10km further into the mountains, is actually a cluster of four Maasai villages: Emairete, Enguiki, Eluwai and Mfereji. Emairete is the main one, and occupies a crater that was once considered sacred. If you can, it's worth coinciding with Emairete's weekly market on Saturday. **Maasai** are of course the main reason to visit.

**Access** to both Monduli Chini and Monduli Juu is difficult, with buses to the former stopping at least a ninety-minute walk away, and up to four hours from Monduli Juu. For this reason, by far the best way to visit is to sign up with Oreteti Cultural Discovery, an organization that grew out of NGO Aang Serian and that still helps to build schools and various projects with and for the Maasai. While the founders of Oreteti continue to adopt many of the ethical tenets that made Aang Serian stand out (paying fair wages and putting back much of what they earn into the villages they work with), they are no longer an NGO or not-for-profit operation.

Nevertheless, Oreteti do run some interesting tours and are your best bet if you wish to visit Monduli and get a real handle on the day-to-day life of the inhabitants. Three main programmes are offered: a two-day Beadwork Tour in Monduli Chini, where you learn from the ladies who make the often fantastic beadwork you see for sale on the streets of Arusha; a two-day Indigenous and Modern Masai Education, also in Monduli Chini, where you get to visit a local school; and, most popular of all, the three-day Medicine tour in Monduli Juu, where you meet with such local characters as a herbalist, medicine man and even a fortune teller, and where you may also get to watch a local goat being slaughtered for medicinal reasons.

Prices for the two-day "experiences" start at $135 per person if there are ten or more of you, though can be as much as $310 if you are on your own, but this does include all food, transport and accommodation, either in a Maasai home or camping. The three-day "Medicine" tour starts at $150 per person for a large group, or $365 for solo travellers.

To find out more, visit Oreteti Cultural Discovery's website at ⓦ www.oreteti .com, or visit its offices below the *Sinka Court Hotel* in the centre of Arusha (☏0784 193591).

# Travel details

Full details on moving on from Arusha are given on pp.320–321.

## Buses

Routes marked with an asterisk are liable to delays or cancellations during the rains.
**Arusha** to: Babati (5 daily; 4–5hr); Bukoba via Kenya and Uganda (2 weekly*; 26–30hr); Bukoba via Tanzania (3 weekly*; 16–18hr); Dar (20 daily; 9–11hr); Dodoma (1–2 daily*; 12–15hr); Iringa (1 daily; 12hr); Karatu (3 daily plus hourly daladalas; 3hr); Kondoa (1–3 daily*; 8–9hr); Lushoto (2 daily; 6–7hr); Mbeya (1 daily; 15hr); Mombasa (4 daily; 6hr); Mombo (20 daily; 5hr); Morogoro (4 daily; 8–10hr); Moshi (20 daily plus Coasters; 1hr 20min); Musoma via Nairobi (2 daily; 16–18hr); Musoma via Serengeti (3 weekly; 10hr); Mwanza via Nairobi (6 daily; 18–20hr); Mwanza via Serengeti (4 weekly; 10hr); Mwanza via Singida (1–2 daily; 12–14hr); Nairobi (12 daily; 4–6hr); Namanga (14 daily plus daladalas; 2hr); Ngorongoro (1–2 daily; 4hr); Same (21 daily; 3hr); Singida (4–5 daily; 8–9hr); Tabora (2 weekly*; 12–13hr); Tanga (6 daily; 6hr); Usangi (1 daily; 4hr).

## Flights

Airline codes used below are: AE (Air Excel), AT (Air Tanzania), CA (Coastal Aviation), PA (Precisionair), RA (Regional Air) and ZA (ZanAir). Where more than one airline flies to the same destination, the one with most frequent flights and/or shortest journey times is listed first.
**Arusha Airport** to: Dar (PA, CA, AE, ZA: 5 daily; 2hr–3hr 30min); Dodoma (CA: 3 weekly; 2hr); Kilimanjaro (RA: daily; 10min); Kilwa (CA: daily; 4hr); Mafia (CA: daily; 3hr 15min); Manyara (AE, RA, CA: 5 daily; 20–30min); Mwanza (CA: daily; 3hr 30min); Ngorongoro (CA: daily; 1hr); Pemba (ZA, CA: 2 daily; 2hr 15min–2hr 50min); Ruaha (CA: daily; 3hr 30min); Rubondo (CA: 2 weekly; 4hr 30min); Selous (CA: 1–2 daily; 3–5hr); Serengeti (AE, RA, ZA, CA: 6 daily; 1hr–2hr 40min); Tanga (CA: daily; 3hr 20min); Zanzibar (PA, CA, ZA, AE: 5 daily; 1hr 10min–1hr 35min).
**Kilimanjaro International Airport** to: Arusha (RA: daily; 10min); Dar (AT, PA: 3–4 daily; 1hr–3hr); Manyara (RA: daily; 55min); Mwanza (PA: 6 weekly; 1hr 20min–2hr 5min); Serengeti (RA: daily; 2hr–2hr 35min); Shinyanga (PA: 3 weekly; 1hr 10min); Zanzibar (PA: 1–2 daily; 2hr–2hr 30min).

# The Northern Safari Circuit

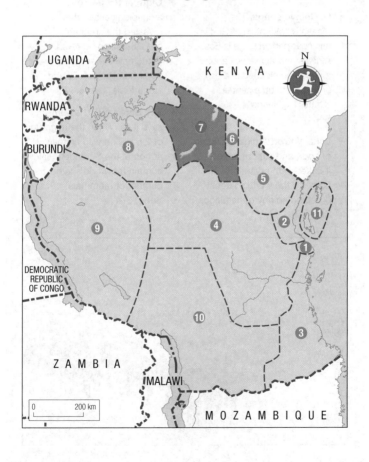

# CHAPTER 7

# Highlights

* **The Maasai** East Africa's emblematic tribe, and one of the most traditional. Aside from their imposing appearance, their singing is among the continent's most beautiful. See pp.356–357

* **Ol Doinyo Lengai** The Maasai's "Mountain of God", this near-perfect cone is East Africa's only active volcano, and can be climbed in a day, or as part of an extended "Crater Highlands" hike. See p.360

* **Lake Natron** A gigantic sump of soda and salt, much of it caked with crystals, and home to the world's largest breeding colony of flamingos. See p.361

* **Ngorongoro Crater** When a volcano collapsed 2.5 million years ago, it left a huge crater, which now contains the world's biggest concentration of predators. See p.371

* **Oldupai Gorge** The archeological site that revealed the cranium of 1.75-million-year-old "Nutcracker Man", and many other hominid fossils and stone tools. See p.373

* **The Serengeti** The name says it all. When the migration of 2.5 million wild animals is at home, the Serengeti Plains contain the world's largest number of mammals. See p.374

▲ Wildebeest migration, Ngorongoro Crater

# The Northern Safari Circuit

H ead west out of Arusha and the land quickly turns to dry and dusty savanna, marking the start of traditional Maasai pastureland, and the journey to paradise for hundreds of thousands of safari-goers each year – eighty percent of Tanzania's visitors. The pride of the country's blossoming tourist industry is a quartet of wildlife areas between Arusha and Lake Victoria, collectively known as the **Northern Safari Circuit**.

The most famous of its destinations, known worldwide through countless wildlife documentaries, is **Serengeti National Park**. Its eastern half comprises the Serengeti Plains, which in the popular imagination are the archetypal African grassland. If you time your visit right, they offer one of the most spectacular wildlife spectacles on earth: a massive annual **migration** of over 2.5 million wilde-beest, zebra and other animals, from the Serengeti Plains north into Kenya's Maasai Mara Game Reserve and back down, following the life-giving rains. Even if you can't coincide with the migration, there's abundant wildlife, and the plains are as good a place as any for seeing lions, often in large prides, and packs of hyenas.

The Northern Safari Circuit's other undeniable jewel is the **Ngorongoro Conservation Area**, the centrepiece of which is an enormous caldera (volcanic crater) – one of the world's largest – whose base, comprising grassland, swamp, forest and a shallow alkaline lake, contains an incredible density of plains game, and a full complement of predators. Ngorongoro is also one of few Tanzanian wildlife areas to tolerate human presence beyond tourism: the undulating grasslands around the crater belong to the cattle-herding **Maasai**, whose red-robed, spear-carrying warriors are likely to leave an indelible impression. To cynics, Ngorongoro's popularity makes it resemble little more than a zoo, with the presence of dozens of other safari vehicles all looking for that perfect photo opportunity. Nonetheless, Ngorongoro is the highlight of many a trip, and its popularity is a small price to pay for the virtually guaranteed sight of lion, buffalo, leopard, cheetah, and highly endangered black rhino.

East of the Serengeti and Ngorongoro, in the **Great Rift Valley**, are two more national parks, less well known, but each with its own appeal. **Lake Manyara**, at the foot of the valley's western escarpment, is one of Tanzania's smallest national parks but, despite that, its wide variety of habitats attracts disproportionately dense wildlife populations. The bushy terrain, while not as immediately gratifying as the dramatic wide-open spaces of Serengeti and Ngorongoro, can still make for

sudden, heart-stopping encounters with animals. The lake itself is a popular feeding ground for large flocks of flamingos, and has a series of picturesque hot springs on its shore. Southeast of the lake, only two hours by road from Arusha, is **Tarangire National Park**, a likeably scruffy place, where millenarian baobab trees dwarf even the park's substantial elephant population; in the dry season, this is probably the best place in all of Africa to see pachyderms. Adjoining the park's northeastern boundary is **Tarangire Conservation Area**, a vast conjunction of community-managed wildlife areas, where the main attractions are guided bush walks, night game-drives illuminated by spotlights and some wonderfully romantic accommodation.

But it's not all about wildlife. Three **cultural tourism programmes**, at Mto wa Mbu near Lake Manyara, Karatu near Ngorongoro, and at Engaruka, a remote Maasai settlement, offer intimate and enlightening encounters with local communities, and there are also a number of **archeological sites** worth visiting. Engaruka contains the ruins of seven villages and their irrigation network, while the Serengeti's weathered granite outcrops have rock paintings of shields and animals daubed by Maasai warriors, and an enigmatic **rock gong**, part of a huge boulder that was once used as a musical instrument. Ngorongoro, for its part, was where the **origin of mankind** first began to make sense, in the paleontological paradise of **Oldupai Gorge**.

Fans of really wild places also have a couple of destinations to head to. **Lake Natron**, in the desolate north, is an enormous soda sump, much of its surface covered by a thick crust of pinkish-white soda crystals. At its southern end rises the perfectly conical and supremely photogenic **Ol Doinyo Lengai**, the Maasai's "Mountain of God", which is East Africa's only active volcano. It can be climbed in a day, or as part of a longer hike from Ngorongoro's **Crater Highlands**.

Almost everyone comes on an **organized safari** from Arusha (p.51), though companies in Mwanza (p.402), and Dar (p.52) also offer trips, albeit at a slight mark-up – ensure they have the requisite TALA licence for safaris or tour operators. It is possible to visit the parks under your own steam, the easiest way being to **rent a vehicle** (preferably with an experienced driver worked into the bargain) – the price is competitive if you fill all the seats. There are car rental companies in Arusha, Dar and Mwanza, and vehicles can also be rented in Karatu, close to Ngorongoro.

Access to the parks by **public transport** is limited, but you'll need a car to enter Tarangire or Lake Manyara, and to see more of the Serengeti than the highway between Arusha and Lake Victoria, which is covered by a few buses each week. Ngorongoro is more viable – take the bus from Arusha to the conservation area headquarters, from where you can arrange guided walks from a few hours to several days, as long as you have a tent.

**Guidebooks** and **maps** are sold at the park gates and lodges, but are not always in stock: buy them beforehand in Arusha, Dar es Salaam or in Stone Town (Zanzibar). For practical advice on arranging safaris and avoiding dodgy companies, and for information on what to expect, see pp.46–54.

# The Great Rift Valley

The **Great Rift Valley**, which furrows its way clean through Tanzania from north to south, is part of an enormous tectonic fault that began to tear apart the earth's crust twenty to thirty million years ago. This geological wonderland runs from Lebanon's Bekaa Valley to the mouth of the Zambezi River in Mozambique, passing through a network of cracks across Kenya and Tanzania – a distance of 6600km.

The gigantic fracture is at its most dramatic in East Africa, where the valley reaches up to 70km in width, and whose floor has sunk more than a kilometre beneath the surrounding plains in places. There are actually two distinct rift valleys in Tanzania: the western branch, which includes depressions occupied by Lake Tanganyika and Lake Nyasa; and the eastern Great Rift Valley, which is at its most spectacular west of Arusha, where it's marked by a long and almost unbroken ridge. In places, however, the exact limits of the fault are blurred by associated volcanic activity: mounts Kilimanjaro, Meru and Hanang are products of these cataclysms, as is the still-active Ol Doinyo Lengai.

Three major lakes fill depressions within the Great Rift Valley: Natron, Manyara and Eyasi. The southernmost is **Lake Eyasi**, at the base of the Ngorongoro Highlands. The surrounding woodland is home to one of Africa's last hunter-gatherer tribes, the **Hadzabe**, whose future looks as bleak as the lake itself. Increasing encroachment on their territory, the conversion of scrubland around their habitat into farmland and ranches, and insensitive tourism hyped around "Stone Age" images, may soon consign their way of life to oblivion, so it's best to stay away.

**Lake Manyara** is situated at the foot of the highest and most spectacular section of the escarpment, and its northern extent is protected as a national park. The lake's water, though alkaline, is fresh enough for animals, including dense populations of plains game and large flocks of flamingos. **Mto wa Mbu**, the village serving as the base for visits here, has a popular cultural tourism programme that provides a good way of getting to know some of the dozens of tribes that have settled here, attracted – as with the wildlife – by the year-round water supply. There's another cultural tourism programme at **Engaruka** to the north, an excellent place for getting to know Maasai. The village lies within walking distance of one of Africa's most enigmatic archeological sites: the ruins of a city about which little is known other than that it was founded around six hundred years ago and abandoned in the eighteenth century.

North of Engaruka is the bleak and windswept terrain around **Lake Natron**, a vast and largely lifeless soda lake that will appeal to desert aficionados. At the lake's southern end rises **Ol Doinyo Lengai** ("The Mountain of God"), one of the few volcanoes in the world to spew out sodium carbonate (soda), with the result that the lake's water is exceedingly alkaline – a thick, pinkish-white crust forms on its surface in the dry season. The unremittingly dry and desolate nature of the lake and its shore excludes most forms of life, the major exception being **flamingos**, which thrive on the soda-loving diatom algae; the lake is their most important breeding ground in the world. At times, literally millions of birds paint the horizon with a shimmering line of pink; Lake Natron is protected as an Important Wetland Area under the international RAMSAR Convention.

Safari operators usually offer trips to Lake Manyara as an either/or choice with **Tarangire National Park**, southeast of the lake. But the two parks actually complement each other, both for wildlife and visually. Tarangire is the more open of the two, with lots of (partly seasonal) plains game and an immense variety of birds – over 550 species at the last count. It is also one of the best places in Africa to see elephants, especially in the dry season when animal densities in the park are second only to those of the Serengeti–Ngorongoro ecosystem.

# Tarangire

Occupying almost four thousand square kilometres of pure Rift Valley wilderness southeast of Lake Manyara, **Tarangire** comprises **Tarangire National Park** and the adjacent **Tarangire Conservation Area**. Uncrowded and unspoiled, they possess a wild and unkempt beauty, and contain pretty much every animal species you're likely to see on safari with the exception of rhino, which were wiped out here by poachers in the 1980s. Tarangire's signature attractions are **elephants** (head counts of several hundred a day are not unusual), and **baobabs**, weird, ungainly and hugely impressive trees that can live for several thousand years, providing wonderful silhouettes for sunset photographs.

The area's ecological importance stems from the **Tarangire River**, which loops through the park in an anticlockwise direction, emptying into the shallow and alkaline **Lake Burunge** just outside the park's western boundary. A bare string of isolated waterholes in the dry season, the river is in spate during the rains, and is the catalyst for an annual **wildlife migration** (see box, p.344). Many

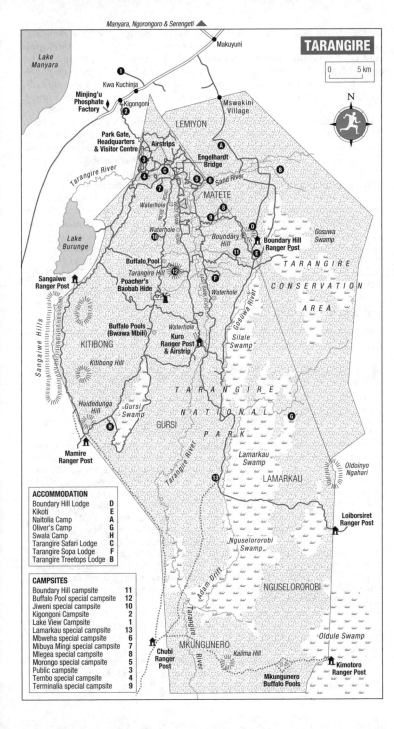

**TARANGIRE**

0      5 km

N

*Manyara, Ngorongoro & Serengeti* ▲
Makuyuni

Lake
Manyara

Kwa Kuchinja ❶

Minjing'u
Phosphate
Factory ▼
Kigongoni ❷

Mswakini
Village

LEMIYON

Park Gate,
Headquarters
& Visitor Centre
Airstrips

Ⓐ

Engelhardt
Bridge

Ⓑ

*Tarangire River*

❸
❹ Ⓒ
❼
❺ ❻ *Sand River*

MATETE

Waterhole

Ⓓ

❽

❾

Waterhole
⑩

*Boundary
Hill*

Boundary Hill
Ranger Post

*Gosuwa
Swamp*

Lake
Burunge

Ⓔ

⑪

T A R A N G I R E

Buffalo Pool
*Tarangire Hill* ⑫
Poacher's
Baobab Hide

Ⓕ

C O N S E R V A T I O N

Sangaiwe
Ranger Post

Waterhole

A R E A

*Sangaiwe Hills*

Buffalo Pools
(Bwawa Mbili)

Waterhole
Kuro
Ranger Post
& Airstrip

*Silale
Swamp*

KITIBONG

*Kitibong Hill*

T A R A N G I R E

*Haidedunga
Hill*

*Gursi
Swamp*

N A T I O N A L

Ⓗ

GURSI

P A R K

Ⓖ

Mamire
Ranger Post

*Lamarkau
Swamp*

*Oldoinyo
Ngahari*

⑬

LAMARKAU

Loiborsiret
Ranger Post

*Nguselororobi
Swamp*

NGUSELOROROBI

www.roughguides.com

*Oldule Swamp*

*Tarangire River*

*Adam Drift*

Chubi
Ranger
Post

MKUNGUNERO

*Kalima Hill*

Kimotoro
Ranger Post

Mkungunero
Buffalo Pools

341

**ACCOMMODATION**

| Boundary Hill Lodge | D |
| Kikoti | E |
| Naitolia Camp | A |
| Oliver's Camp | G |
| Swala Camp | H |
| Tarangire Safari Lodge | C |
| Tarangire Sopa Lodge | F |
| Tarangire Treetops Lodge | B |

**CAMPSITES**

| Boundary Hill campsite | 11 |
| Buffalo Pool special campsite | 12 |
| Jiweni special campsite | 10 |
| Kigongoni Campsite | 2 |
| Lake View Campsite | 1 |
| Lamarkau special campsite | 13 |
| Mbweha special campsite | 6 |
| Mibuya Mingi special campsite | 7 |
| Mlegea special campsite | 8 |
| Morongo special campsite | 5 |
| Public campsite | 3 |
| Tembo special campsite | 4 |
| Terminalia special campsite | 9 |

animals stay all year round however, including significant numbers of elephants, buffaloes, giraffes, zebras, ostriches and warthogs, and a full range of **antelopes**. Also present are **predators** – lions can usually be viewed lazing around by the river and, with luck, you might also catch sight of a leopard (best seen in the adjacent conservation area, where night game-drives by spotlight are allowed). Cheetahs exist but are rare, as the long grass doesn't favour their hunting technique, and you'd also be lucky to see hyenas, whether spotted or striped.

The **best time to visit** is July to October or November for the national park, when wildlife concentrations are second only to the Serengeti–Ngorongoro ecosystem. The conservation area is also good at this time, but even better when the migration is passing through, during December–March and May and June, though long grass immediately after the rains may hinder visibility.

Strangely, there seems to be some prejudice against Tarangire, particularly on the web, with some reviews even going as far as to say that a trip to Tarangire isn't worth the effort expended to reach it. While we can't be certain, we can be fairly sure that some of these opinions come from the safari companies themselves, who are reluctant to visit the park because of the extra fuel involved in reaching here (as opposed to the other parks that all conveniently lie on the same axis). The extra petrol costs eat directly into their profits, and so they like to run the place down. Suffice to say that amongst the tourists who have managed to visit it, Tarangire sits alongside Ngorongoro as one of the most popular and beautiful parks in Tanzania.

## Practicalities

The main **national park** entrance gate is 7km south of the highway from Arusha. The first 104km to the junction at Kigongoni village are on a fast

---

### Birdwatching in Tarangire

With its wide variety of habitats and food sources, **birdwatching** in and around Tarangire is a major draw, with over 550 species recorded to date, the highest count of any Tanzanian park, and about a third of all Tanzania's species. In the swampy floodplains in the south and east, Tarangire also contains some of earth's most important breeding grounds for **Eurasian migrants**. Wherever you are, you'll rarely be left without song: birdsong starts well before dawn, and continues deep into the night.

It's impossible to give a full list of what's around, but to give an idea, the **woodlands** are particularly good for hoopoes and hornbills, brown parrots and the white-bellied go-away-bird (named after its curious call), and for game birds such as helmeted guinea fowl, yellow-necked spurfowl and crested francolin. Other commonly sighted birds include yellow-collared lovebirds and lilac-breasted rollers, barbets and mouse-birds, swifts, striped swallows and starlings, bee-eaters, hammerkops, owls, plovers and cordon bleus. There are also four **bustard species**, including the kori, the world's heaviest flying bird, albeit usually seen on the ground. High above, especially close to hills, soar bateleur eagles, their name – "tumbler" in French – aptly describing their aerobatic skills. Over fifty other species of **raptors** (birds of prey) have been recorded, from steppe eagles (migrants from Russia) and giants such as lappet-faced vultures, to the tiny pygmy falcon.

The **best months** for birdwatching are from September or October to April or May, when the winter migrants are present, though access – especially to the swamp areas – can become impossible at the height of the long rains from March to May. A recommended safari company offering **specialist birding safaris** is The East African Safari & Touring Company in Arusha (p.52), whose trips are based at *Naitolia Camp* or *Boundary Hill Lodge* in the conservation area, and cost a very reasonable $140–200 per person per day.

sealed road; the remaining 7km are all-weather gravel. The gate is open 6.30am–6.30pm and driving is not allowed after 7pm. **Entrance fees**, valid for 24 hours, are $35 per person, plus Tsh10,000 for a vehicle. An optional **wildlife guide**, handy if you're self-driving, can be hired at the gate for $20 per drive.

Special permission is required to enter or leave through other gates (marked on our map as ranger posts); the most useful of these is Boundary Hill in the northeast, for access to **Tarangire Conservation Area** (no entrance fees at present). To access the conservation area otherwise, turn south off the Arusha highway 3km west of Makuyuni, the village at the junction to Lake Manyara, Ngorongoro and Serengeti. The start of the dirt track is marked by a sign for Naitolia School. Self-drive is difficult as there are few other signposts along the way. The track is passable by 2WD as far as *Naitolia Camp* (18km), but you'll need 4WD to get in deeper, or in the rains. It's possible to enter the national park at Boundary Hill, but you'll need to have paid the entrance fee at the main gate first.

All of Arusha's **safari operators** cover Tarangire, usually tacked on to a trip to Ngorongoro and/or Serengeti. Day-trips are possible, but bear in mind that you'll be spending at least two hours on the road in either direction. Particularly good value is an overnight trip offered by the East African Safari & Touring Company (see p.52) for $180 per person, which includes a night at *Naitolia Camp* in the conservation area, a five-hour guided walk and night game drive; the minor catch is that you have to make your own way from Arusha to Makuyuni (several daladalas and buses cover the route daily, including Mtei Coach), where they'll pick you up. A similar trip over two nights costs $330, and can be extended.

The national park headquarters are 1km inside the gate; nearby is the **Tarangire Visitor Centre**, which has loads of information, a viewing platform built around a baobab tree, and an artificial waterhole for wildlife. The official **website** is ⓦ www.tanzaniaparks.com/tarangire.html; for the conservation area, see ⓦ www.tarangireconservation.com. For more detail on the park, get one of TANAPA's **guidebooks**, which can bought in bookshops in Arusha, Dar and Stone Town, or at the park gate. The old black-and-white version ($5) is comprehensive but out of date for roads; the new full-colour version costs $10. The best map is Giovanni Tombazzi's beautiful hand-painted version, with two plans, one each for the dry and rainy seasons; ensure you get the "New" version, as the road network on the old one is wrong.

## Accommodation, eating and drinking

Apart from some very basic guesthouses along the highway at Makuyuni and Kigongoni, the cheapest **accommodation** is camping, either outside the park in some very average campsites, or – much better – inside the park. There are lodges and tented camps in both the park and adjacent conservation area; the latter has the edge in being able to offer night game-drives and bush walks, though walks should eventually also be possible inside the park (currently only from *Oliver's Camp*), but probably only for overnight visitors.

The park's **public campsite** ($30 per person) is 4km south of the main gate. There's plenty of shade, few tsetse flies, flush toilets and cold showers. Deeper in the park are several **special campsites** ($50 per person), which should be booked and paid for in advance at TANAPA headquarters in Arusha (see p.307), though you may strike lucky if you just turn up. None has facilities of any kind, and they are often unnervingly close to wildlife; hiring an armed ranger ($20)

## Tarangire's wildlife migration

Albeit nowhere near as grand as Serengeti's world-famous migration, Tarangire is the centre of an annual **migration** that includes up to 3000 elephants, 25,000 wildebeest and 30,000 zebras, as well as such rare creatures as the fringe-eared oryx. In the dry season, from July to late October or early November, animals concentrate along the Tarangire River and its waterholes, before the onset of the short rains prompts wilde-beest and zebra to head off north towards Lake Manyara, and east into the Simanjiro Plains of the Maasai Steppe. By April or May, when the long rains are at their height, the migration is also at its peak, with animals scattered over an area ten times larger than Tarangire, some even reaching Kenya's Amboseli National Park, 250km northeast on the northern side of Kilimanjaro.

When the rains come to an end, usually between mid-May and early June, the plains dry up and eland and oryx turn back towards Tarangire, followed by elephants, and then, by July, zebra and wildebeest. In August, with the weather now hot and dry, the bulk of the migrants are back in Tarangire, where they will stay a few months before the whole cycle begins anew.

at the park headquarters may be necessary for staying at some of them. Firewood collection is forbidden, so bring gas cans, or buy charcoal at Kigongoni or Kwa Kuchinja before entering the park.

There are also a few **privately run campsites** outside the park, none of them anything special but handy for a cheap night ($5 per person), the best two being *Kigongoni Campsite*, 1km south of Kigongoni towards the park gate with hot showers available mornings and evenings and a kitchen (but no food); and *Lake View Campsite,* 2km east of Kigongoni along the sealed road, then 1km northwest, with toilets, showers and soft drinks but no kitchen.

For **food**, most safari-goers pack a picnic or a lunchbox – available at all the lodges and tented camps. There are some basic *hotelis* and bars in the villages along the highway, and you're welcome for drinks or lunch ($20–25) at *Tarangire Sopa Lodge* and *Tarangire Safari Lodge*, both of which also have swimming pools.

### Accommodation in the National Park

**Oliver's Camp** East of Silale Swamp, 70km inside the park (book through Asilia Lodges & Camps, Arusha ☏ 027/250 2799, Ⓦ www.asilialodges .com). Painfully expensive but with fine views of nearby swamps and good wildlife guides – especially if birds are your thing, as the location is a twitcher's paradise. It's also the only place inside the park to offer bush walks. Accommodation is in comfortable en-suite tents. Closed mid-March to mid-June. All-inclusive $400 per person. **⑨**

**Swala Camp** Close to Gursi Swamp, 67km inside the park (book through Sanctuary Lodges, Njiro Hill, Arusha ☏ 027/250 9816–7, Ⓦ www .sanctuarylodges.com). Sheltered in an acacia grove, the nine luxurious en-suite tents are stuffed with period furniture and each has a terrace overlooking a waterhole frequented by waterbuck, the said *swala* (impala), lion, elephant and leopard. Closed April & May. All-inclusive $650 per person. **⑨**

**Tarangire Safari Lodge** High above the Tarangire River, 10km inside the park Ⓦ www .tarangiresafarilodge.com (book at 50 Serengeti Rd, Arusha ☏ 027/254 4752). Cheapest lodge in the park, and none too quiet given its 86 rooms and popularity with package tours, but the location is superb overlooking the river below. The rooms and permanent tents are fine (but lack nets). There's also a large swimming pool. Half price April & May. HB **⑥**

**Tarangire Sopa Lodge** South of Matete, 32km inside the park (book through Sopa Lodges, 4th floor, Sopa Plaza, 99 Serengeti Rd, Arusha ☏ 027/250 0630–9, Ⓦ www.sopalodges.com). Large and functional rather than beautiful, built on a wooded hillside east of the Tarangire River. Views are good and the bedrooms (four with disabled access) are spacious. There's also a small pool. Half price April & May. HB **⑧**

## Accommodation in the Conservation Area

**Boundary Hill Lodge** 47km from the highway ⓦ www.tarangireconservation.com (book through The East African Safari & Touring Company in Arusha; see p.52). Perched high on the rocky hillside, this is a truly eco-friendly lodge – relying on rainwater, solar panels and wind turbines – and the local Maasai owns fifty percent. The eight spacious rooms each have spectacular views over Silale and Gosuwa swamps, as does the large swimming pool built into the rock. Included in the cost are game drives (also at night with spotlights) and sundowners on Sunset Hill. All-inclusive ❼

**Kikoti** 6km from the park, 61km from the main gate (book through Safari Legacy ☎ 027/250 8790). Eighteen thatched, en-suite, twin or double *bandas*, each one raised on a platform and boasting a lovely large veranda. Pleasant, without being spectacular; it does at least have 24hr power and hot water – but at this price, you would expect a bit more. ❽

**Naitolia Camp** 18km from the highway ⓦ www .tarangireconservation.com (bookings as for *Boundary Hill Lodge*). Located in baobab- and acacia-studded woodland, this is an informal place with friendly staff. Accommodation is in four secluded stone-and-canvas rooms, or in a romantic tree house with spectacular views of the savanna. All have flush toilets and bucket showers but no electricity. The same activities as at *Boundary Hill Lodge* are available, plus fly-camping ($285 per person). All-inclusive ❼

**Tarangire Treetops Lodge** 37km from the highway (book through Elewana Afrika, 4th floor, Sopa Plaza, 99 Serengeti Rd, Arusha ☎ 027/250 0630–9, ⓦ www.elewana.com). The ultimate in bush chic, though with prices that leave you seeing stars. Twenty quirkily romantic tree-house tents with two beds, stone bathrooms, electricity and sweeping 270-degree views from their balconies. The dining room is built close to a small swimming pool and waterhole used by elephants. Optional extras include night game-drives and bush dinners. Closed April & May. FB $550–630 per person. ❾

# Tarangire National Park

Tarangire contains a range of different habitats, from grassland and woods in the north, to low hills, scrub and swampland further south. Cutting through these habitats is an evergreen corridor, the **Tarangire River**, which empties into Lake Burunge in the west. The river is the key to life here, and its northern extent – close to the park gate and *Tarangire Safari Lodge* – is the most popular area for game drives. In the dry season, when the bulk of the migration congregates around the river and its water pools, the area is phenomenal for game viewing. Fauna on the gently inclined grassland and woodland either side of the river is thinner, but the chance of spotting rarer animals like klipspringers and Bohor reedbuck, and rich birdlife, makes up for this, and the **baobab forests** in both areas are a big attraction.

With an extra day or two, you can venture farther afield. The shallow and saline **Lake Burunge** is an attractive destination, and usually has flocks of pink flamingos. South of here is **Gursi Swamp**, one of many marshes dominating the park's southern half and a paradise for birds. The **far south** is extremely remote, with access only guaranteed in dry weather. **Walking in the park** is theoretically possible, but currently only allowed for guests of *Oliver's Camp* – enquire at the park headquarters or with a safari company. You'll almost certainly need a vehicle to reach the walking zone, as it's likely to be in the south.

## Lemiyon and Matete

The park's northern sector consists of **Lemiyon** and **Matete areas**. Their proximity to the park gate makes them easy to visit, and there's an extensive network of roads and tracks throughout the area. Together, they encompass a broad range of habitats, from grassland plains (where fringe-eared oryx can be seen), umbrella and flat-topped acacia woodland (great for birds) and more open woodland to the east, dominated by **baobab trees**. The acacia

## Baobab trees

The one thing that never fails to amaze Tarangire's visitors is its giant **baobab** trees. Known in Kiswahili as *mbuyu* (plural *mibuyu*) and popularly as the calabash tree, the baobab is one of Africa's most striking natural features. With its massive, smooth silver-grey trunk and thick, crooked branches, it's the grotesque and otherworldly appearance of the trees that impresses more than anything. The **trunk's circumference** grows to ten metres after only a century, and by the time the tree reaches old age, it may be several times more. Most live to at least six hundred years, but exact dating is difficult, as the tree leaves no rings in its often hollow trunks. Radiocarbon dating, however, suggests that the **oldest** can reach three thousand years or even more.

Needless to say, the baobab is supremely adapted to its semi-arid **habitat**, its range stretching right across Africa and eastwards to Australia, where it's known as the bottle tree. One of the secrets to its longevity is its fibrous wood, which is extremely porous and rots easily, often leaving a huge cavity in the trunk that fills with water during the rains. The immense water-carrying capacity of the trunks – anything from three hundred to a thousand litres – enables the tree to survive long spells of drought. For this reason the baobab has long been useful to humans, and the legends of Kenya's Kamba tribe (who migrated north from Kilimanjaro five centuries ago) say that they moved in search of the life-giving baobabs: the Ukambani Hills, where they settled, are full of them.

The tree's shape has given rise to several **legends**. Some say that baobabs used to walk around the countryside on their roots, until one day God got tired of their endless peregrinations and resolved to keep them forever rooted to the soil, replanting them upside down. On the Tanzanian coast, a pair of baobab saplings were traditionally planted at either end of the grave of an important person; in time they grew together to form one tree, enclosing the tomb within their roots. Baobabs were also, therefore, considered a propitious place to bury treasure, as the spirits of the ancestors would ensure their safekeeping.

The baobab has myriad other more **practical** uses. The gourd-like seed pods or calabashes, which grow up to 25cm long, form handy water containers and bailers for boats, and the seeds and fruit pulp ("monkey bread") are rich in protein and vitamin C, and effective against dysentery and circulatory disease. They're also a source of "cream of tartar" (found in baking powder). When soaked in water, the seeds make an invigorating drink (you can buy baobab seeds, *ubuyu*, at Arusha's market); and when roasted and ground, they taste similar to coffee. Young leaves are edible when boiled, and also have medicinal uses, and the bark, when pounded, yields a fibre suitable for making rope, paper and cloth, while glue can be made from the pollen. It's not just humans who benefit from the baobab though. Bees use the hollow trunks for hives, hornbills nest in their boughs, and elephants like to sharpen their tusks by rubbing them against the trees. In exceptionally dry seasons, they gouge deeper into the trunk to get at the water stored in the fibrous interior: the scars left by these activities are clear wherever you go in Tarangire.

woodland is always good for wildlife viewing, providing year-round shelter and food, and there's abundant birdlife. Vervet monkeys and olive baboons are common in both areas, especially around picnic sites where they scavenge for food – be wary of **baboons**, which can be dangerous, especially if you have food in view.

### The Tarangire River

The park's peerless attraction is the **Tarangire River**, which forms Lemiyon's southern and Matete's western boundary. Although good for wildlife all year round, the river is at its best in the dry season, when the migration is at home around the river's water pools. The section where the river flows from east to west has sandy cliffs along much of its northern bank, where there are several **viewpoints** and a picnic site – bring binoculars.

This east–west section of the river can be crossed at two points: across a concrete **causeway** in the west (dry season only) towards Lake Burunge, and over **Engelhardt Bridge** close to *Tarangire Safari Lodge*, which offers access to two south-running routes: Ridge Road down to Gursi Swamp, and West Bank Road which hugs the river. Following the east bank is another road, accessed from Matete, which heads down to Silale Swamp. Any of these riverside drives is ideal for getting close to wildlife. In the dry season, a number of **water pools** attract large numbers of thirsty zebra, wildebeest, elephant (who are responsible for creating a good many pools themselves by digging up the dry riverbed with their tusks), giraffe, eland, gazelle, impala, warthogs and buffalo. Olive baboons are resident, and lions too are often found nearby. The bush on either side is ideal for hartebeest, lesser kudu and leopard, which usually rest up in the branches by day, their presence given away by little more than the flick of a tail. This part of the river, before it veers west, can be crossed along various dry-season causeways and small bridges.

There's a pleasant **picnic site** by the river south of Matete, about 6km north of the turning for *Tarangire Sopa Lodge*. The site, by a huge mango tree, gives a good view of the river, at a point where there's a popular mud wallow for elephants.

## Lake Burunge

The Tarangire River empties into **Lake Burunge**, a shallow soda lake just outside the park's western boundary, which is home to flocks of flamingos from July to November. The lake is surprisingly large, and makes a pretty picture with the Great Rift Valley's western escarpment in the background. There's no outlet, so salts and other minerals washed in by the river have turned the lake inhospitably saline, although during the rains the water is fresh enough to serve as a watering point for animals, including elephants and lions (look for their tracks in the mud). The lake's shallowness (barely 2m) means that its extent fluctuates widely. It tends to dry up completely at the end of the dry season, leaving only a shimmer of encrusted salt on its surface.

The road from the north – the last 3km of which are impassable in the rains – crosses the Tarangire River south of the park gate. It's not the most spectacular game-viewing area, but you may catch glimpses of lesser kudu or eland, steinbok in undergrowth, and small herds of shy and rare fringe-eared oryx. Closer to the lake are plains of tussock grass and clumps of fan palms, hemmed in by acacia woodland and scattered baobabs, and weirdly imposing cactus-like "trees" – **candelabra euphorbia**. Their sap is extremely corrosive, so the trees are usually left well alone by wildlife: the exceptions were the rhinos, which sadly were poached to extinction in the park in the 1980s.

The plains are best for wildlife at either end of the migration, when they fill up with large herds of wildebeest and zebra. But the main species to leave a mark, literally, are **tsetse flies**, clouds of them, especially in the vicinity of wildebeest.

## Ridge Road

A right fork just south of Engelhardt Bridge marks the start of **Ridge Road**, a superb 40km drive south through acacia woodland to Gursi Swamp, which in places offers beautiful vistas over much of the park and further afield. While wildlife is not as dense as around the river, there's still a decent selection, with mostly solitary elephants, giraffe, eland, warthog and buffalo. They're best seen at two sets of signposted **buffalo pools** along the way.

The other main attraction here is **Poacher's Hide**, its name possibly explaining the unusual jumpiness of the area's elephants. The hide is an enormous old baobab tree out of whose hollow trunk a small door has been carved, to resemble the dwellings of elves and sprites in children's books. The artificial doorway has led to lots of speculation about the original use of the hide: it seems likely that hunter-gatherers, possibly ancestors of Lake Eyasi's Hadzabe tribe (see box, p.364), used it as a shelter or for keeping honey beehives. The hide was certainly used by poachers in the 1970s and 1980s, hence its name – thick grass around the site, and a boulder that could be rolled across the entrance, completed the disguise. The hide is now used by animals: hyena cubs, bats and bat-eared foxes have all been seen inside – so take care.

### The swamps

In the dry season, access to the **swamps** of central and southern Tarangire is possible. The swamps, which feed the Tarangire River, are among the richest areas in Tanzania for **birdlife**, especially water birds from November to May. During the dry season as the swamps begin to dry, the receding waterholes and remaining patches of marshland also offer superb game viewing, including large buffalo herds up to a thousand strong, and elephants longing for mud baths. The easiest to visit are Gursi Swamp, at the end of Ridge Road close to *Swala Camp*, and Silale Swamp at the end of the East Bank Road on the park's eastern border.

A game track runs all the way around **Gursi Swamp** and much of the grassland on its periphery is studded with tall termite mounds. Bushy-tailed ground squirrels are common, as are giraffes in the woodland. **Silale Swamp**, which should be accessible all year round, is perhaps better for birdlife; and lions, preying on herds of zebra and wildebeest, are often seen on the western side in October. The fringing woods are said to contain huge tree-climbing pythons.

At its southern end, Silale merges into the enormous **Lamarkau Swamp** (whose name comes from *il armarkau*, Maasai for "hippo"), which itself merges into **Nguselororobi Swamp** (Maasai for "cold plains"). Both areas, together with Ngahari Swamp and Oldule Swamp in the park's southeastern extremity, are exceedingly remote and virtually unvisited.

## Tarangire Conservation Area

Contiguous to the national park's northeastern boundary is Tanzania's first community-controlled wildlife area, **Tarangire Conservation Area**. Trophy-hunting safari misfits used (and abused) the area until the turn of the millennium when local villages were finally given official title to the land, and turned it over to photographic tourism. The communities derive income from various lodges and camps, one of which (*Boundary Hill*) is half-owned by villagers – another admirable first.

Although the conservation area lacks the perennial flow of the Tarangire River, a number of seasonal "sand rivers" turn into a series of water pools during the dry season, at which time wildlife viewing can be better than in the park. Likely sightings include impala, Thomson's gazelle, oryx and dikdik, ostrich, giraffe and wildebeest, and of course **elephants**, which inhabit the area all year round. But the area's real magic lies both in some wonderfully romantic accommodation, and in not being tied by park regulations: **guided bush walks** are offered by all the camps and lodges, and provide the perfect way to get a feel for the wild. Just as unusual are **night game-drives**, giving you the chance of seeing otherwise elusive animals such as leopards and fringe-eared oryx. Strangely, they seem unfazed by the spotlights. To visit the area, you'll either need to come on an organized safari, or stay overnight at one of the lodges or camps.

# Lake Manyara and Mto wa Mbu

One of Tanzania's most dramatically located wildlife areas is **Lake Manyara**, a shallow soda lake at the foot of the Great Rift Valley's western escarpment. The lake's northwestern section may be one of Tanzania's smallest national parks, but its varied shoreline habitats shelter a wide variety of animals, including elephants, great flocks of pink flamingo, large hippo pods, and much-hyped "tree-climbing lions". The park has been a UNESCO World Biosphere Reserve since 1981.

Although the park is usually tacked onto the end of a safari, after Ngorongoro or Serengeti, the grandiose nature of those places means that Manyara is best visited at the start of a trip, before you become too jaded with wildlife – unless birds are your thing, in which case Manyara can be a grand finale. A day is sufficient to see most of the park's sights.

The park is accessed through the bustling town of **Mto wa Mbu**, which has a wide range of accommodation and a good **cultural tourism programme** – perfect for getting up close to the town's many tribes, including the Maasai. For spectacular views, take the road up from Mto wa Mbu to the top of the escarpment en route to Ngorongoro and the Serengeti, which gives increasingly breathtaking views of Lake Manyara and the green expanse of vegetation around its shore with every hairpin bend. There's a **viewpoint** on top, as well as a number of lodges and a recommended campsite.

## Mto wa Mbu

The verdant, oasis-like area around **MTO WA MBU**, whose name means "River of Mosquitoes", was a thinly populated patch of scrubland until the 1950s, when the colonial government began an ambitious irrigation project aimed at controlling Lake Manyara's cyclical floods, and to turn "unproductive" swampland into farmland. The project was a big success, attracting farmers from all around. In the 1960s, Mto wa Mbu was declared a collective **Ujamaa village** as part of Tanzania's ultimately disastrous experiment in "African socialism", into which thousands of people were sometimes forcibly resettled from outlying rural areas. In Mto wa Mbu, the main effect of the Ujamaa period is the town's extraordinary **ethnic diversity**: the population represents almost fifty tribes, including Hehe from Iringa; Gogo, Gorowa, Mbugwe, Nyamwezi and Rangi from central Tanzania; Barbaig, Hadzabe and Maasai from close by; Ha from Kigoma on the shore of Lake Tanganyika (who introduced oil palms); and the Il Larusa, Chagga, Iraqw and Meru from the north and northeast. Some of these tribes can be visited as part of a **cultural tourism programme**.

### Arrival

The 113km from Arusha is all sealed road. Three **buses** leave Mto wa Mbu in the morning (the last around 10am), and turn back from Arusha in the afternoon; they take around two and a half hours. The bus stop is outside *Red Banana Café* on the highway, the base for the cultural tourism programme.

## Accommodation

Mto wa Mbu has a wide range of **accommodation**, from cheap (and not-so-cheap) campsites and guesthouses in town, to mid-range places in woodland and expensive safari lodges atop the escarpment overlooking the town and the lake. None of the escarpment places has much in the way of wildlife except for birds but the views can be great. Nonetheless, at the price, there are much better pampered retreats elsewhere. See also the accommodation reviews for the national park on p.354.

**Camping** (around $7 per person) is possible at *Migunga* (quietest, and in the shade of a pretty acacia forest); *Panorama Safari Camp* (matchless views); *Twiga Campsite & Lodge* (popular with overlanders); *Njake Lake Manyara View* and at *Jambo Lodge*.

### Budget and mid-range

**Jambo Lodge** On the main road towards the eastern end of town by the petrol station ☏027/250 1329, ⓦwww.njake.com. Now rivalling Twiga as the largest and busiest tourist place in town, Jambo is a welcoming campsite bordered by half a dozen two-storey 'houses' split into smart, en-suite rooms; those on the upper floors are brighter. Camping is available ($7, or $20 if hiring a tent), and there's a pool too. ⑤

**Kiboko Tented Lodge** 2.5km east of town along the highway, then 2km south ☏027/250 2617, ⓦwww.equatorialsafaris.com. Dominated by a huge *makuti*-thatched dining room and bar, this place boasts six big walk-in tents raised on platforms, each with two beds, big box nets, bathroom, and amusing decor (an animal painted on the door, and sculpture of said animal's head on the veranda railing). Now looking a little tired and losing ground to its neighbour *Migunga* but OK nevertheless. BB ④

**New Sunlight Guest House** On the main road in the centre of town ☏0784312553. Best of the cheapies, without any frills whatsoever save for a good internet café (Tsh3000 per hour). ②

**Panorama Safari Camp** On the escarpment, 500m north of the highway beside the mobile-phone mast ☏0784/418514, ⓦwww.panoramasafari.com. Kudos to this gorgeously sited campsite; some of the pitches have great views and they provide tents with bedding for those without – free of charge. There's electricity, piped water and hot showers, and guided walks can be arranged through Mto wa Mbu's cultural tourism programme. Bookings advisable. $7 per person.

**Twiga Campsite & Lodge** 1.5km east of town ☏027/253 9101, ⓔtwigacampsite@yahoo.com, ⓦwww.twigacampsite.com. The best of the moderately priced places, *Twiga* has 18 good en-suite twins and triples with hot water in the mornings and evenings (and more rooms are nearing completion). There's a bar, restaurant and satellite TV. Camping $10. BB ⑤

### Expensive

**E Unoto Retreat** 10km north of Mto wa Mbu, accessed off the road to Lake Natron starting 4km east of town ☏027/254 8542, ⓦwww.maasaivillage.com. On a ridge overlooking small Lake Miwaleni – and its resident hippos – the 25 bungalows (some with disabled access) are styled after Maasai homesteads. There's a swimming pool and activities including cycling to Maasai villages. However, there have been some complaints about how much the staff demand tips. FB ⑧

**Kirurumu Tented Lodge** On the escarpment, 6km northeast of the highway (book through Kirurumu Tented Camps & Lodges, India St, Arusha ☏027/250 7011, ⓦwww.kirurumu.net). Twenty-two large, mostly twin-bed, en-suite tents on the ridge, some with lake views from their shady verandas. The excellent restaurant serves produce from their organic garden, and ethno-botanical walks accompanied by Maasai warriors are offered. Good value compared to the other luxury options. FB from $560. ⑨

**Lake Manyara Hotel** On the escarpment, 3km southeast of the highway (book through Hotels & Lodges Ltd, 2nd floor (Block B), Summit Centre, Sokoine Rd, Arusha ☏027/254 4595, ⓦwww.hotelsandlodges-tanzania.com). A 1970s concrete hulk with magnificent views over the lake from most of the one hundred bedrooms, but it's all rather bland for the price. There's also a swimming pool. FB $440–460. ⑨

**Lake Manyara Serena Safari Lodge** On the escarpment, 2km northeast of the highway past the airstrip (book through Serena Hotels, 2nd floor, Diamond Trust House, Arusha ☏027/253 9160, ⓦwww.serenahotels.com). Poshest hotel of the lot – the overly formal service makes it hard to remember you're on safari. Only a few of the 67 two-storey rondavels have lake views but the pool has good views. FB $550. **❾**

**Migunga Forest Camp** 2.5km east of town along the highway, then 2km south, 200m before *Kiboko Bushcamp* (book through Moivaro Lodges & Tented Camps, *Moivaro Coffee Plantation Lodge*, Arusha ☎027/250 6315, ⓦwww .moivaro.com). Sitting in a forest of yellow-bark acacia trees, this Dutch-run place has 19 en-suite tents and three bungalows, all with balconies facing a central lawn. There's a pleasant open-sided bar and dining room, and activities (at an extra cost) include cycling safaris and nature walks. The campsite has fixed tents ($15 per person), or you can bring your own and camp for $8. FB $187. **❼**

**Njake Lake Manyara View Lodge** On the escarpment, just off the highway ☎027/250 1329, ⓦwww.lakemanyaraview.com. A massive, thatched dining-cum-reception area sits in overgrown grounds surrounded by 33 rooms, while tucked away in a corner are a couple of concrete baobabs containing comfy en-suite rooms. Overpriced, but how often do you get to spend the night in a concrete tree? Camping $7. **❻**

## The Town

Given Mto wa Mbu's ethnic diversity, it's no surprise that the town's **markets** are among the liveliest and most colourful in the country. The central market on the south side of the highway is a mishmash of shops and stalls where you'll find pretty much anything that's produced locally, including many of the town's estimated eighty varieties of **bananas**. One corner of the market, the so-called "Maasai Central Market", is a tourist trap flogging the usual trinkets such as Maasai beadwork jewellery and tartan *shuka* cloth, but an enjoyable one at that. Much more authentic is the Thursday **animal auction** held at the roadside 5km east of Mto wa Mbu (1km beyond the junction for Engaruka), and a **monthly market** (*mnada*) on the same site on the 22nd of each month, which attracts buyers and herders from as far away as the Zanaki tribe of the Mara Region. Some of these herders continue to Arusha and a handful even make it to Dar es Salaam – an epic journey of over 900km.

Mto wa Mbu's ethnic diversity is best experienced through the town's **cultural tourism programme** (☎027/253 9303 or 0784/606654, Ⓔmtoculturalprogramme@hotmail.com), based at *Red Banana Café* on the highway. The **guides** are former pupils of Manyara Secondary School and speak good English (some speak Spanish and French too). To avoid hustlers and conmen, do not hire guides on the street or elsewhere, and ensure you get a receipt. Incidentally, the cultural tours offered by some upmarket tour operators and lodges are not necessarily the same thing, and can't guarantee that locals will profit from your visit.

While the various **guided tours**, each lasting a reasonably long day, are not as immediately exciting as those of similar projects elsewhere, they are good for getting to know a wide variety of **tribes**, as all include visits to farms, local artisans and small-scale development projects. There are four main tours. Starting at the market, the **farming tour** covers a number of *shambas* north of town, where you'll meet farmers and see banana beer being brewed by some of the local Chagga people who have settled here, and taste the result. A visit to the papyrus-fringed **Lake Miwaleni**, 5km north of town at the foot of escarpment, together with a waterfall, is accessed by trails along small streams. There are trips to **Lake Manyara** by bike (without entering the National Park), to view the game as well as some enormous baobabs, and a visit to a local school is a popular option. The final option includes a visit to a Maasai *boma*.

**Costs** start at Tsh33,500 per tour if you're on your own, though drop significantly if there is more than one of you (to less than Tsh15,000 per person if there are four of you). Traditional meals, provided by a women's group, cost

**7**

**THE NORTHERN SAFARI CIRCUIT** | Lake Manyara and Mto wa Mbu

www.roughguides.com

351

Tsh7500, though again the price drops the more people there are on the tour. **Bicycle rental** is Tsh6000 a day (or a mean $25 for a mountain bike).

### Eating and drinking

Mto wa Mbu has lots of basic **restaurants**, especially south of the market and highway, most doubling as bars. One of the best, despite appearances, is the *Rembo* (one block south of the market; turn south at Oryx petrol station and then left), which rustles up tasty and filling meals for under Tsh1500. The more touristy hotels also have restaurants: try *Twiga Campsite & Lodge* (meals around Tsh10,000, but sometimes limited to the chickens running around its grounds). Meals at the upmarket lodges average $15–30.

The main cluster of **bars** is one block south of the Oryx petrol station, and east from there along the road to *Mashanga Guest House*; the *Rembo* and *Fiesta Complex* are both lively. Also good, and popular with tourists and locals alike, is the cavernous *Red Banana Café* on the highway.

## Lake Manyara National Park

Set against the impressive 600m-high backdrop of the Great Rift Valley's western escarpment, **Lake Manyara National Park**, which covers the lake's northwestern corner, is a rare flash of green in an otherwise unremittingly dry land. Much of the park's land area is covered by groundwater forest or thick bush, which – though it makes spotting wildlife harder – allows an intimate and heart-stopping sense of being in the wild when an animal suddenly appears as you turn a corner.

For its small size, the park contains a wide range of **habitats**: evergreen groundwater forest in the north fed by springs; a swampy fan delta crowning the top of the lake; acacia woodland at the foot of the scarp scattered with baobab trees; a small grassy plain; and, of course, the lake itself. Together, they provide an oasis for wildlife, and the presence of year-round water also makes the lake part of the same migratory system at the heart of which is Tarangire (see box, p.344).

▲ Pelicans at Lake Manyara

## Lake Manyara's ailing ecosystem

For all Lake Manyara's riches, all is not well. Migratory **wildlife routes** have been blocked by Mto wa Mbu in the north and by commercial ranches and farms (the same problem that afflicts the Hadzabe hunter-gatherers to the south), whilst **lake levels** have dropped drastically over recent years due to recurring droughts and unsustainable water use by Mto wa Mbu's burgeoning population (now around 25,000, compared to 3500 in the early 1970s). Combined with clearance of swamps, woodlands and forest for arable land, continued **poaching**, and the insidious **pollution** of lake waters from both commercial and subsistence farms in its catchment area, the balance of the entire ecosystem has never been more precarious.

Human interference has exacted a terrible toll with the **local extinction** of at least nine mammalian species: lesser kudu (1957), wild hunting dogs (1963), cheetah (1980), mountain reedbuck and hartebeest (1982), eland and oribi (1983), black rhino (1985) and the common reedbuck (1991). And if that was not enough, in 2004 ten thousand of the lake's emblematic flamingos perished – victims of **toxins** accumulated in algae that had reached deadly levels following several years of drought. Short of wholesale changes in the entire region's farming methods, there's little real hope that the lake's gradual degradation can be halted, never mind reversed.

Manyara is perhaps most memorable for its **elephants**, which number around three hundred – down from 640 in the 1960s but recovering well from the disastrous poaching of the 1980s. Other impressive denizens include **buffalo**, sometimes in large herds, which feed on sedge by the lakeshore, and two hundred **hippos**, seen in water pools in the northern fan delta. **Antelope** include impala, bushbuck and waterbuck, and agile klipspringers on the rocky escarpment wall. Other plains game include zebra, giraffe, mongoose and warthog, together with their predators: leopards and, famously, **tree-climbing lions**, which are sometimes seen resting up in the boughs of acacia trees south of the groundwater forest – your best bet for spotting them is between June and August. The reason for their arboreal prowess is a mystery, though there's no shortage of possible explanations, the most plausible of which is their attempt to avoid the unwelcome attention of tsetse flies. The phenomenon isn't unique to Manyara – lions have also been seen up in trees at Tarangire, Serengeti, Ngorongoro and Selous.

The shallow lakeshore is especially favoured by **water birds**, including pelicans, storks, herons, ibis, jacanas, egrets, plovers and lots of ducks and geese. But the undoubted avian stars are the vast flocks of pink **flamingos**, attracted by the profusion of algae in the lake's shallow, alkaline waters.

**Primates** are represented by blue monkeys and vervet monkeys in the forest, and numerous baboon troops. The vervets are preyed on by crested hawk eagles, one of Manyara's over 380 **bird species** – for many visitors, the park's great highlight. Birdlife is at its most spectacular in the form of large flocks of flamingos feeding on the lake's algae. The algae are supported, in turn, by a series of picturesque **hot springs** along the shoreline, heated by geothermal activity associated with the Rift Valley's ongoing expansion.

### Arrival, information and entrance fees

The park gate is 2km west of Mto wa Mbu, 115km west of Arusha. If you've come on public transport you'll still need a vehicle for visiting the park unless you're taking one of the walking safaris: the main tourist hotels can help out, or contact the cultural tourism programme (see p.351). A 4WD is recommended, although 2WD will get you to most places in dry weather.

The national park is open year round, but is best avoided during the heavy rains (most likely March–May), when road access can be limited to the far north. The **best time to visit** for big mammals is June or July to September or October, and again in January and February. For birds, November to May is best. The best source of information is the TANAPA **guidebook** to Manyara, available in Arusha ($10). The park's **internet** site is Ⓦ www.tanzaniaparks.com /manyara.html. There's an accurate **map** published by Harms-Ic-Verlag in association with TANAPA, not that you really need one for getting around, and a more attractive hand-painted one by Giovanni Tombazzi.

Park **entry fees**, valid for 24 hours, are $35 per person and Tsh10,000 for a vehicle. As most accommodation is outside the park, it's possible to exit and re-enter on the same ticket.

## Accommodation

Accommodation inside the park is limited to park-run campsites and *bandas*, and an obscenely overpriced tented camp that has not been reviewed.

TANAPA Bandas Just inside the park gate (bookings – not always required – through TANAPA in Arusha; see p.307). A complex of ten brick cottages which, although basic, are comfortable, and have hot showers, proper toilets and electricity but no nets. There's no food, but firewood is supplied free of charge, and there's a kitchen and dining room. $20 per person.

TANAPA Public Campsites Just inside the park gate (bookings not required; pay at the park gate). Three sites close to the *bandas*, each occupying a lovely forest clearing, all with toilets and cold showers. Although camping in Mto wa Mbu is much cheaper, the beauty and intimacy of these sites can't be matched. Don't bother with the three "special" campsites further into the park ($50), which are nothing special at all. $30 per person.

## The park

From the gate, a small network of tracks covers most of the vegetational zones in the northern section, and a single-track (with some short game-viewing loops) heads south along the narrow strip of land between the lake and the escarpment.

### The groundwater forest

Heading west out of Mto wa Mbu and over its eponymous river, the abruptness with which thick green forest appears to your left is quite startling. This is part of Manyara's evergreen **groundwater forest**, a soothingly cool, refreshing and very special habitat that dominates the northern section of the park next to the escarpment. Although it looks and feels like rainforest, Manyara's average annual rainfall of 760mm would be nowhere near sufficient to sustain trees of this size on its own. Instead, groundwater forest is fed by water from mineral springs, which seep through the ground's porous volcanic soil.

The tall mahogany, croton and sausage trees, tamarind, wild date palms and strangling fig trees are home to a variety of wildlife, including blue monkeys, vervet monkeys and baboons (all of whom are fond of crashing around in the branches, especially at the park gate's picnic site), and there's plenty of **birdlife** too, though seeing anything more than a flitting form disappearing into the foliage is a challenge. More easily seen are ground birds, including two species of guinea fowl, and the large silvery-cheeked hornbill, which lives in the canopy but is often seen on the ground. Also look out for forest plants benefiting from the shade of the trees such as orchids. **Elephants** are occasional visitors, and partial to using larger trees as back-scrubbers, much

## Activities at Lake Manyara

Walking safaris are an option in Manyara, a refreshing change from being stuck in a car all day, though do bear in mind that you won't be able to venture as far into the park on foot as you would by vehicle. Walks tend to last about three or four hours on average and it costs $20 to hire a ranger in addition to the park fees of $35. Contact the chief park warden (☎027/253 9112, ✉manyara@tanapa.org) to arrange a walk.

In addition, a number of "**soft adventures**" inside Manyara National Park are offered by Green Footprint Adventures, based at *Lake Manyara Serena Safari Lodge* (ⓦwww.greenfootprint.co.tz). Apart from canoeing excursions ($45 for two hours or so plus a canoeing fee of $20 and park fees) and mountain biking (outside the park), worth doing at least once is a **night game-drive** (3hr; $130–170 including park fees), and it can be combined with a romantic bush dinner.

to the anguish of the park authorities that have tried to deter them by dressing some trees in prickly corsets of chicken wire.

### The fan delta and hippo pools

About 4km southwest of the park gate along the main track is a signposted left turn towards a loop road around **Mahali pa Nyati** – the Place of Buffaloes – which, as you might expect, is a good place for spotting those rather cantankerous and temperamental beasts, which are invariably accompanied by ox-peckers and buff-backed herons feeding on insects disturbed by the passing of their hosts. South of the buffalo circuit is another loop leading to the mouth of the Mto wa Mbu River, and a series of **hippo pools**.

### The acacia woodland, Msasa and Ndala rivers

To the south and east of the groundwater forest is more open **woodland**, dominated by umbrella acacias and dotted here and there by ancient baobab trees. It's a good habitat for all sorts of big game, especially elephant, giraffe and buffalo, and is good for spotting **birdlife** too, including various species of plover and kingfishers, larks and wagtails.

South of the groundwater forest, the park's main track crosses a series of small rivers, sometimes by bridge, other times by causeways that can become impassable if the rains hit hard. The main watercourse in the park's northern section is the **Msasa River**. This area is good for seeing solitary old male buffaloes, and if you're going to see **lions in trees**, it'll be here. There's a signposted picnic site under a big tree with benches, tables, a lake view and often uncomfortably close sightings of buffalo. There are two more picnic sites near the **Ndala River**, 9km south of the Msasa River, one of which has good lake views. The presence of buffalo, often in large herds, means tsetse flies start to be a nuisance south of the Msasa River.

### The hot springs

Flamingos can also be seen on the western shore, close to a series of pungently sulphurous **hot springs**, of which there are two main groups. The smaller but most accessible are **Maji Moto Ndogo**, 22km south of the park gate, which keep to a very pleasant 33°C and get covered whenever the lake level is high. Just over 17km further south, past the patch of grassland formed by the modest delta of the Endabash River, are the bigger and more scalding **Maji Moto Kubwa** springs, whose temperature averages 76°C – hot enough to give you a nasty burn and melt the soles of your shoes if you wander too close. They're at

## The Maasai

Exotic, noble, aristocratic, freedom-loving, independent, savage, impressive, arrogant and aloof … you'll find these adjectives scattered all over travel brochures whenever they talk of the **Maasai**, one of East Africa's most emblematic tribes.

Meeting a Maasai warrior, with his red robe, spear and braided ochre-smeared hair, is one of the high points of many a safari holiday. Depending on the tour company or your ability to haggle, **visits** to spend half an hour in a "genuine" Maasai village (*boma*) in Ngorongoro, or along the road coming from Arusha, cost anything from a few dollars to $50. The money buys the right to take photographs and perhaps witness a dance or two, though you may also be mercilessly pestered by old ladies selling beaded jewellery and other trinkets. Depending on your sensibilities, the experience can either be an enlightening and exciting glimpse into the "real" Africa, or a rather disturbing and even depressing encounter with a people seemingly obliged to sell their culture in order to survive.

### Some history

In the popular imagination, the Maasai – along with South Africa's Zulu – are *the* archetypal Africans, and as a result a disproportionate amount of attention has been lavished on them, ever since the explorer Joseph Thomson published his best seller *Through Maasailand* in 1885. In those days, the Maasai were seen as perfect "**noble savages**", but their story is much more complex.

What we know of their distant history is little more than conjecture proposed by romantically minded Western scholars. Some say that they are one of the lost tribes of Israel and others that they came from North Africa. Still others believe that they are the living remnants of Egyptian civilization, primarily, it seems, on account of their warriors' braided hairstyles. Linguistically, the Maasai are among the southernmost of the Nilotic-speaking peoples, a loosely related group that came from the north, presumably from the Nile Valley in Sudan. It's thought that they left this area sometime between the fourteenth and sixteenth centuries, migrating southwards with their cattle herds along the fertile grasslands of the Rift Valley. The Maasai eventually entered what is now Kenya to the west of Lake Turkana, and quickly spread south into northern Tanzania, whose seasonal grasslands were ideal for their cattle. They reached their present extent around the eighteenth century, at which time they were the most powerful and feared tribe in East Africa. Their tight social organization, offensive warfare, deadly cattle raids, and mobility as semi-nomadic cattle herders ensured that they could go where they pleased, and could take what they wanted. Their **military prowess** and regimentation meant that they were rarely defeated and as a result, their history before the arrival of the British was one of ceaseless expansion at the expense of other people.

Their combined Kenyan and Tanzanian territory in the seventeenth century has been estimated at 200,000 square kilometres. But all this is just one side of the story. The other is told by their territory today, which is less than a quarter of what it was before the Europeans arrived. The Maasai have been progressively confined to smaller and smaller areas of land. The British took much of it away to serve as farms and ranches for settlers, and in recent decades the land expropriations have continued, this time to form the wildlife preserves of Serengeti, Tarangire, Mkomazi, and part of Ngorongoro, to which the Serengeti Maasai were relocated when they were evicted.

their most impressive when the lake level is low, and then especially in the rains when the water erupts in a series of highly pressurized flumes, due to the higher water pressure. Even when the lake level is high, however, there are some small springs closer to the road, which have remarkably beautiful colours and patterns formed by the heat- and sulphur-loving algal blooms, lichens and assorted moulds growing in and around the shallow pools.

### The Maasai today, and in the future

Politically and economically, the Maasai remain marginalized from the Tanzanian mainstream, having stubbornly refused to abandon their pastoralist way of life, or their traditions, despite repeated attempts by both colonial and post-Independence governments, and missionaries, to cajole or force them to settle. Many men persevere with the status of **warriorhood**, though modern Tanzania makes few concessions to it. Arrested for hunting lions, and prevented from building *manyattas* (cattle enclosures) for the *eunoto* transition in which they pass into elderhood, the warriors (*morani*) have kept most of the superficial marks of the warrior without being able to live the life. The ensemble of a red or purple cloth *shuka* tied over one shoulder, together with spear, sword, club and braided hair is still widely seen, and after circumcision, in their early days as warriors, you can meet young men out in the bush, hunting for birds to add to their elaborate, taxidermic headdresses.

But the Maasai **lifestyle** is changing: education, MPs and elections, new laws and new projects, jobs and cash are all having mixed results. The traditional Maasai staple of curdled milk and cow's blood is rapidly being replaced by cornmeal *ugali*. Many Maasai have taken work in the lodges and tented camps while others end up as security guards in Arusha and Dar es Salaam. A main source of income for those who remain is provided by the **tourist industry**. Maasai dancing is *the* entertainment, while necklaces, gourds, spears, shields, *rungus* (clubs, also known as knobkerries), busts and even life-sized wooden warriors (to be shipped home in a packing case) are the stock-in-trade of the curio and souvenir shops.

For the Maasai themselves, the rewards are fairly scant. **Cattle** are still at the heart of their society but they are assailed on all sides by a climate of opposition to the old lifestyle. Sporadically urged to grow crops, go to school, build permanent houses and generally settle down, they face an additional dilemma in squaring these edicts with the fickle demands of the tourist industry for traditional authenticity. Few make much of a living selling souvenirs, but enterprising *morani* can do well by just posing for photos, and even better if they hawk themselves on the coast; one or two can even be seen in Zanzibar.

For the majority, who still live semi-nomadic lives among a growing tangle of constraints, **the future** would seem to hold little promise. However, the creation of community-run conservation areas outside the parks and reserves looks promising; generating income from annual land rents paid by tourist lodges and tented camps, and often a percentage of profits or overnight receipts. That stubborn cultural independence may yet insulate the Maasai against the social upheavals that have changed the cultures of their neighbours beyond recognition.

Unless you're really short on time, a much more satisfying and less voyeuristic way of meeting Maasai than in the touristic "cultural *bomas*" is via Tanzania's community-run cultural tourism programmes, several of which are run by Maasai (see below for Engaruka, and pp.327–334 for projects around Arusha). In addition, the cheaper Crater Highlands treks (see p.371) from Ngorongoro to Lake Natron are usually guided in part by Maasai, and may include overnights in genuine, non-tourist-oriented *bomas*. For **more information**, see Ⓦ www.bluegecko.org/kenya/tribes/maasai, a comprehensive resource about Maasai culture, including their marvellously hypnotic singing.

# Engaruka

The most enigmatic of northern Tanzania's attractions is a complex of stone ruins at **ENGARUKA**, at the foot of the Great Rift Valley's western escarpment north of Mto wa Mbu. The ruins comprise at least seven villages and a complex irrigation system of stone-walled canals, furrows and dams. The question of who

▲ Maasai tribespeople

was responsible for creating a settlement that would originally have supported a population of over five thousand people in this inhospitably dry location continues to leave archeologists baffled.

First recorded in 1883 by the German naturalist, **Dr Gustav Fischer**, the ruins extend over 9km of the escarpment base. The site was founded early in the fifteenth century, but was mysteriously abandoned between 1700 and 1750. Most of Engaruka's present-day occupants are Maasai, but the absence of any tradition mentioning Engaruka indicates that the settlement had already been abandoned when they arrived, almost two centuries ago, and consequently little is known of Engaruka's original inhabitants.

Research shows that Engaruka's residents were most likely to have been the ancestors of the **Iraqw** tribe (see box, p.365), who have a similar system of self-contained agriculture and now live south of Karatu. Iraqw history recounts their last major migration, some two hundred to three hundred years ago, following a battle with Barbaig cattle herders (who, until the arrival of the Maasai, occupied the "Crater Highlands" above Engaruka). This fits with the presumed date of Engaruka's desertion. Another present-day tribe that has been linked to Engaruka is **Sonjo**, who live 100km north of Engaruka west of Lake Natron (see p.387). Their last migration also coincides with Engaruka's dates, and their traditional method of building houses on raised stone platforms is identical to remains found at Engaruka.

Apart from the Iraqw's story of the Barbaig war, a likely factor contributing to Engaruka's desertion was environmental. Engaruka's very success at irrigation in such a dry land may have proved counter-productive, when the demands of a vastly increased human population became too much for the area's limited water supplies.

Engaruka not only provides a fascinating and thought-provoking glimpse into the history of pre-colonial Tanzania, it serves as a reminder that we still have much to discover about the continent's history.

## Arrival

Getting to Engaruka has become easier over the past few years, though it can still be tricky particularly during the rains, when the road may well be impassable. Unless you're coming from the Serengeti's Klein's Gate across Loliondo, the only access is from the road junction 1km east of Mto wa Mbu where the road to **Selela village** and beyond is well graded. Bear in mind that the road to Engaruka initially veers away from the escarpment to avoid gullies and hills. The ride from Mto wa Mbu takes ninety minutes depending on the state of the road.

**Public transport** is limited to Land Rover pick-ups every day or two from Mto wa Mbu and the daily "Kiazi Kitamu" bus (its name means sweet potato) from Arusha. Both leave for Engaruka in the afternoon, and head back the following morning before 7.30am. There is a $5 'development fee' to enter the village.

## Accommodation and eating

There are two Engarukas in addition to the ruins – a dusty spread of huts at Engaruka Chini along the road from Mto wa Mbu to Lake Natron, and the bustling Maasai market centre of Engaruka Juu, spreading 2–4km west of here along the way to the ruins.

The only **accommodation** is at the basic *Mlezi Guest House* (**❶**) in Engaruka Juu (2km west of Engaruka Chini and the main road), or camping at either *Engaruka Ruins Campsite* (about 2km from the main road), which boasts solar-powered electricity, or *Jerusalem Campsite* (6km west of Engaruka Chini and close to the escarpment, in the grounds of Engaruka Primary School). *Jerusalem Campsite* has no electricity but better views, and despite being signposted is awkward to find: turn left just beyond *Mlezi Guest House*, cross the river immediately, and take the right fork on the opposite bank; the campsite is 4km on along a rough track. You're best bringing your own food. Both sites charge Tsh10,000.

## The site

Old Engaruka can only be visited on foot. A guide from the village (compulsory) costs $5 per group, plus there's the $10 entrance fee and the $5 village development fee.

Two curious features characteristic of Engaruka are cairns and stone circles. The **cairns**, up to 5m long and 2m high, appear to be little other than places where rocks and stones cleared from fields were gathered, although their carefully arranged square or angular faces suggest something rather more useful, or spiritual, than just a heap of stones. A human skeleton was found under one cairn but, other than that, excavations have yielded few clues as to their real purpose. More readily explained are the large **stone circles**, especially south of the river, which measure up to 10m in diameter and functioned as cattle pens. The clusters of **raised stone platforms** on ground unsuitable for irrigation mark the sites of Engaruka's seven villages. The platforms served as bases for houses; the Sonjo tribe still build their homes this way.

For **more information**, John Sutton's exhaustive and scholarly work about Engaruka is available at *Jerusalem Campsite*, Kase bookshop in Arusha, and A Novel Idea bookshop in Dar.

# Ol Doinyo Lengai

Rising up at the south end of Lake Natron is East Africa's only active volcano, **Ol Doinyo Lengai**, whose Maasai name means "The Mountain of God". Despite its active status, very little is known about the mountain other than that it tends to erupt explosively every twenty to forty years, and manages smaller **eruptions** every decade or so. The last significant eruption was in 2007, continuing into 2008, so you should be safe for the next few years.

For **geologists**, the special thing about Ol Doinyo Lengai is that it is one of few volcanoes worldwide to emit sodium carbonate and potassium, whose run-off accounts for the extremely alkaline and corrosive swill of neighbouring Lake Natron. For **photographers**, Ol Doinyo Lengai's perfectly conical shape is a delight, whilst the lava flows on the summit can be every bit as terrifying and awe-inspiring as you might imagine. **Climbers** are also in for a treat, despite the volcano's summit (2889m) being but a pimple compared to the majesty of its giant but dormant brothers to the east – Meru and Kilimanjaro. Admittedly, any pleasure gained by climbing the mountain (which can be done without any special equipment) is distinctly masochistic: the searing sun, the notoriously prickly vegetation and rough surface, reported sightings of spitting cobras near the summit (and leopard tracks), and the almost 45-degree slope. But as a reward for your travails, there's the weird, wonderful, eggily pungent and quite positively perilous sight and sound of **lava flows** bubbling at 510°C on top. There are two summit craters: the southern one is dormant or extinct and almost filled to the brim with ash, but the northern one, over 200m deep, remains active (occasionally lobbing lava bombs into the sky) and should be treated with **extreme caution**, particularly so given the highly fluid and hence potentially quick moving (or explosive) nature of natrocarbonatite lava. Ⓦ frank.mtsu .edu/~fbelton/lengai.html is a great **internet site** dedicated to the mountain, with lots of up-to-date practical info, photos and links.

## Practicalities

**Climbing** must be done with a guide who knows the mountain and its caprices. There are two ways of going about it: the easiest is simply to tackle the mountain as part of an extended "Crater Highlands" trek (see box, p.371) from Ngorongoro to Lake Natron. Many of Arusha's safari operators offer this as a regular trip, but do check that they have both their own experienced guides, and that – if you need it – there's adequate back-up (vehicles rather than donkeys, and HF radio for emergencies). For more modest budgets, it's perfectly feasible to arrange things at the campsites in Engaresero (see p.361).

The climb starts about 10km south of Engaresero village, and takes at least seven hours: four hours up and three back down. If you don't have a vehicle and don't fancy walking from Engaresero to the start of the trail, you'll have to wait until a vehicle is available. The ride shouldn't cost more than a few thousand shillings. The ascent is steep and mostly on loose and uncompacted soil, and there's no shade, so set off before dawn to arrive at the summit by mid-morning. It's possible to camp on the summit – the inactive southern crater makes a distinctly safer campsite than the active northern one.

With your own vehicle, you also could try searching out one of several **volcanic cones** and craters on the eastern side of the mountain, the biggest of which is called Shimo la Mungu ("God's Hole").

# Lake Natron

To desert rats, the land around **Lake Natron** – a vast, shallow soda lake bordering Kenya in Tanzania's far north – is something of a dream: hellishly hot, dry, desolate and bizarrely beautiful, especially with the grandiose peak of Ol Doinyo Lengai rising at its southern end. This volcano is the cause of the lake's extreme alkalinity, which forms a pinkish-white crust of soda crystals across much of its surface in the dry season, cracked into a polygonal patchwork.

Covering over 1300 square kilometres, the lake, like the smaller Lake Magadi just over the border in Kenya, lacks any outlet, and receives only 400mm of rain a year, part of it falling as "phantom rain", meaning that the raindrops evaporate before hitting the surface. The amount lost by **evaporation** is eight times that; the shortfall is made up by volcanic springs and temporary streams, whose waters leach through Ol Doinyo Lengai's caustic lava flows before reaching the lake. The concentration of salt, sodium carbonate (soda, or natron) and magnesite in the lake water is highly corrosive and the surrounding land isn't much more hospitable.

Not surprisingly, the lake isn't the most conducive to life, the big exception being a flourishing population of sometimes several hundred thousand **lesser flamingos**, who feed on the lake's microscopic diatom algae, and who have made the lake the most important flamingo breeding ground in the world.

## Practicalities

The only settlement of any size is **ENGARESERO** (also called Ngara Sero or Natron Village), near the lake's southwestern shore, 56km north of Engaruka and 124km from Mto wa Mbu. Engaresero contains a handful of poorly stocked **stores**, a couple of **bars** (the *Magogo* being the best) – and that's about it. There's no petrol or diesel, and the place has all the charm of a frontier outpost, which of course it is.

The easiest way to get to Lake Natron is on an **organized safari**. Companies running trips through this area include The East African Safari & Touring Company (p.52), and the cultural tourism programme in Karatu (p.366). The lake also features on a growing number of **Crater Highlands treks** from Ngorongoro (see p.371).

The next easiest way to Lake Natron is to rent a vehicle with a driver in Arusha or through the cultural tourism programme in Mto wa Mbu (p.351), as there's **no public transport** north of Engaruka. Theoretically, the drive from Mto wa Mbu should only take four or five hours, but the road is often impassable in the rains. Locals either walk or wait around, sometimes for a day or three, for a lift on one of the very few private vehicles that make it up here, usually carrying supplies for Engaresero's shops. Alternatively, if you're staying at *Lake Natron Camp*, they can arrange a ride from Mto wa Mbu.

Ngorongoro District Council has a **toll gate** 6km south of Engaresero, which charges tourists $15 for entering the area; this covers Engaresero, the lake and Nguruman Escarpment, and Ol Doinyo Lengai.

In between visiting the lake and climbing the volcano there isn't much to do in Engaresero, though you can always laze by the small **pool** at *Lake Natron Tented Camp* ($5 for those not staying at the campsite) or visit the **waterfalls** ($25 per guide); a 25-minute walk upstream from the Waterfalls Campsite.

For information about the rough route to Lake Natron **from Loliondo**, see pp.386–387.

## Accommodation

In addition to the following, there are a number of 'unofficial' campsites that spring up from time to time, often owned by one of the major safari companies in Arusha.

**Lake Natron Camp** Turn right at the tollgate and continue for 2km towards the lake (☎027/255 3638, 0787/560555, ⊛www .ecoTZ.com). Set in a bone-meltingly hot location not far from the lakeshore, this place resembles an army camp. Nevertheless, it's still one of the best choices; seven eco-friendly tents (self-composting toilets and solar-generated electricity) stylishly done out. They also run a full range of activities. Camping $10. ❺

**Lake Natron Tented Camp & Campsite** Around 1km west of Engaresero (book through Moivaro Lodges & Tented Camps, *Moivaro Coffee Plantation Lodge*, Arusha ☎027/255 3242, ⊛www.moivaro.com). It comes as something of a surprise to find such luxury in dusty Engaresero. The nine permanent, en-suite tents are stylish and comfortable and come with electricity. There's also a public campsite ($10 per person), a bar and good simple food, internet access and a swimming pool. FB ❼

**Riverside Kamakia Campsite** In a ravine beside the Engaresero River; turn right as you approach the escarpment (no phone). Despite being less shady than *Lake Natron Camp*, this has a much nicer and marginally cooler location, and there are rock pools in the adjacent river where you can take a dip. Drinks and meals are available, and there's a full range of guided walks but you will need to bring your own tent. $15 per person.

# Around Engaresero

Engaresero itself has little to detain you, but is the only base for visiting a number of attractions. The most obvious, of course, is Natron's **lakeshore**, 4km away across scorching grey sand (the level of the lake varies). As you approach the edge, soda and salt crystals appear, concealing a foul-smelling slurry of mud, which can burn your skin. To reach the **hot springs** on the eastern shore calls for a 4WD and a driver experienced on loose sand. Take care not to drive too close to the shore, where you're likely to get bogged down. The soda flats in the southeastern corner are used by **flamingos** to mate and nest between August and October; the nests, which you can see from a distance, are made from mud and resemble miniature volcanoes – rather fittingly, given the location. Flamingos can usually also be seen in Moniki area, roughly 10km north of Engaresero village. Other birds you might see include pelicans, ibis, ducks and geese, together with eagles and plovers. **Terrestrial wildlife** is also present, especially close to the springs, albeit in small numbers, and includes zebra, wildebeest, gazelle, ostrich, golden jackal, and – more rarely – fringe-eared oryx, lesser kudu and gerenuk.

The **Nguruman Escarpment**, within walking distance of Engaresero, contains a number of attractions, including a volcanic implosion crater, ravines containing nesting sites for Ruppell's griffon vultures, and several waterfalls along **Engaresero Gorge**. Swimming is possible, though women are expected to cover up while bathing – shorts and a T-shirt. Walks further up the escarpment can be arranged at the campsites, they can also fix up visits to a Maasai *boma*.

# Ngorongoro and around

One of Tanzania's best-known wildlife refuges is **Ngorongoro Conservation Area**, which together with the adjoining Serengeti National Park forms an immensely rich ecosystem. Ngorongoro's highlight is an enormous volcanic crater, providing one of Africa's most stunning backdrops for viewing a glut of wildlife, especially lion, elephant and highly endangered black rhino. There's plenty of upmarket **accommodation** inside the conservation area and more affordable campsites, plus a good range of hotels in **Karatu town**, outside Ngorongoro's eastern gate.

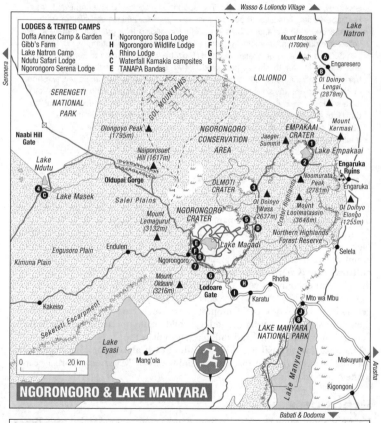

**LODGES & TENTED CAMPS**

| | | | |
|---|---|---|---|
| Doffa Annex Camp & Garden | I | Ngorongoro Sopa Lodge | D |
| Gibb's Farm | H | Ngorongoro Wildlife Lodge | F |
| Lake Natron Camp | A | Rhino Lodge | G |
| Ndutu Safari Lodge | C | Waterfall Kamakia campsites | B |
| Ngorongoro Serena Lodge | E | TANAPA Bandas | J |

**NGORONGORO & LAKE MANYARA**

**CAMPSITES**

| | | | | | |
|---|---|---|---|---|---|
| Empakaai special campsite 1 | 1 | Ndutu campsite | 4 | TANAPA (Manyara) | |
| Empakaai special campsite 2 | 2 | Nyati special campsite | 7 | public campsites | 8 |
| Lemala special campsite | 5 | Simba A public campsite | 6 | Tembo Aspecial campsite | 5 |
| Nanokanoka special campsite | 3 | Simba B special campsite | 6 | Tembo B special campsite | 5 |

## Lake Eyasi and the Hadzabe

Occupying a shallow trough in the shadow of Ngorongoro's Mount Oldeani is **Lake Eyasi**, another of the Rift Valley's soda lakes. In the dry woodland around its edges live the **Hadzabe** tribe. Numbering between five hundred and 2500, depending on how "purely" you count, the Hadzabe are Tanzania's last hunter-gatherers, a status they shared with the Sandawe further south until the latter were forced to settle forty years ago. Sadly, the Hadzabe appear to be heading the same way: much of their land has been taken by commercial plantations and ranches, which also form effective barriers to the seasonal wildlife migrations on which the hunting part of the Hadzabe lifestyle depends, whilst the unwelcome attentions of outsiders – notably tourists – is rapidly destroying their culture.

Being absolutely destitute in monetary terms, the Hadzabe are in no position to resist the more pernicious elements of modernity, with its trade, enforced schooling, cash economy, AIDS and indeed tourists. The supposedly backward and primeval form of Hadzabe society has also attracted researchers, whose dubious activities range from the "discovery" that grandmothers are useful for feeding their grandchildren, to thinly veiled attempts by multinational pharmaceutical companies to patent their DNA.

In 2000, a news report stated that the Hadzabe were preparing to leave their land and way of life for the brave new world of Arusha. Though at that time the story turned out to be a hoax, within five to ten years it may sadly become a reality. Short of convincing the Tanzanian government to protect Hadzabe land and its wildlife routes (most unlikely given the government's previous attempts to forcibly "civilize" the Hadzabe), the best thing you can do is to help preserve their culture. In the absence of any kind of tourism that directly benefits and is controlled by them, this means leaving them well alone.

# Karatu

The dusty town of **KARATU** – periodically swept by red twisters in spite of the new sealed road – is the main supply base for Ngorongoro Conservation Area, 18km to the northwest, and an obvious base if you can't afford Ngorongoro's lodges and don't want to camp there. Capital of a densely populated district, the town has little of interest in itself other than a new **cultural tourism programme**, which offers a range of walks and drives in the area and encounters with Barbaig, Iraqw and Maasai.

Given the steady stream of safari vehicles passing through, tourists are generally seen as a source of money: most hotels have shamelessly hiked-up their rates for non-Tanzanians, and local children are unusually insistent in their demands not just for pens and shillings, but dollars too.

The **best day to visit** is on the seventh of each month, for a big market and livestock auction (*mnada*) that attracts thousands of Maasai and Barbaig cattle herders, and Iraqw farmers.

## Practicalities

Karatu is about three hours' drive from Arusha along a good sealed road. **Buses** leave Arusha around 3–4pm, arriving in Karatu before sunset; Dar Express, which starts in Dar, is probably the safest. All buses leave Karatu at daybreak. You can change money at NBC **bank**, which also has a Visa/MasterCard ATM. To **rent a 4WD**, ask at Karatu's hotels, petrol stations or the cultural tourism programme; prices average $160 for a day's rental including driver and fuel, but excluding food and park entry fees.

## Accommodation

A rare beast is a Karatu hotel that doesn't charge **outrageous rates** to tourists, putting it on a par with Zanzibar. As such, **camping** is the way to stay flush, though there are still some basic local guesthouses charging standard rates. Karatu has **mosquitoes** but not malaria, so get a room with a net.

**Bougainvillea Safari Lodge** About 1.5km west of the town centre ☎027/253 4083, ⓦwww.bougainvillealodge.net. Pricey but definitely worth the money, *Bougainvillea* has 24 supremely cosy bungalows with fireplace, fridge, phone and box nets. The complex also boasts a pool and internet service (Tsh5000 for thirty minutes). ❼

**Bushman (BM) Camp** 700m south of the highway, signposted at the west end of town ☎0755/814579, ⓔfaidabushmancamp@yahoo .com. One of few sanely priced places, with pleasant flowering gardens for camping and hot showers. Meals are $5. ❶

**Crater Rim View Inn** 500m south of the highway opposite *Bytes* (no phone). Friendly,

clean and well run, with eight beautifully appointed double rooms, and a good restaurant. BB ❸

**Doffa Annex Camp & Garden** Just off the highway beside *Paradise Garden Restaurant* ☎027/253 4305. A pleasantly grassy campsite with hot showers and a basic restaurant: meals cost around Tsh2000 (no alcohol), and they have *supu* for breakfast. Their main site is 8km west of town – a lovely breezy place under jacaranda trees and with a bar. ❶

🏃 **Gibb's Farm** (*Ngorongoro Safari Lodge*) 5km off the highway northeast of town ☎027/253 4397, ⓦwww.gibbsfarm.net. This working farm – surrounded by dry forest and coffee plantations – is by far the nicest place to

## The Iraqw

Karatu's main tribes are the cattle-herding Barbaig (see p.242) and the agricultural Iraqw. The history of the 200,000-strong **Iraqw**, who occupy much of the area between Karatu and Mbulu town in the south, is fascinating, though the theory that they originally came from Mesopotamia (Iraq, no less) is too simplistic, given their name, to be likely. Nonetheless, the Iraqw language is related to the "southern Cushitic" tongues spoken in Ethiopia and northern Kenya, meaning that at some point in their history they migrated southwards along the Rift Valley, something you can also tell by their facial features, which are finer than those of their neighbours and similar to those of Ethiopians.

Exactly when the Iraqw arrived in Tanzania is not known, but a number of clues are offered by their agricultural practices – the use of sophisticated terracing to limit soil erosion, complex irrigation techniques, crop rotation and the use of manure from stall-fed cattle – and provide uncanny parallels to the ruined irrigation channels, terraces and cattle pens of Engaruka (see p.357), at the foot of the Great Rift Valley's escarpment.

Iraqw **legend** makes no mention of Engaruka but does talk of a place called **Ma'angwatay**, which may have been their name for it. At the time, the Iraqw lived under a chief called **Haymu Tipe**, whose only son, Gemakw, was kidnapped by a group of young Iraqw warriors and hidden in the forest. Finally locating him, Haymu Tipe was given a curious ultimatum: unless he brought the warriors an enemy to fight, his son would be killed. So Haymu Tipe asked the cattle-herding Barbaig, who occupied the Ngorongoro highlands, to come to fight, which they did. It seems that the Iraqw lost the battle, as Haymu Tipe, his family and his remaining men fled to a place called Guser-Twalay, where Gemakw – who had been released as agreed – became ill and died. Haymu Tipe and his men continued on to a place called Qawirang in a forest west of Lake Manyara, where they settled. Subsequently, population pressure in Irqwar Da'aw led to further migrations; the first Iraqw to settle in Karatu arrived in the 1930s.

For more information, see Bjørn-Erik Hanssen's *Three stories from the mythology of the Iraqw people* at ⓦwww.leopardmannen.no/hanssen/english/afrika.html.

## Karatu cultural tourism programme

The best place to learn more about the **Iraqw** is through the Karatu cultural tourism programme, which is next to *Paradise Garden Restaurant* on the highway (T027/253 4451 or 0784/326274, Ejparess@yahoo.com). The project has its roots in the independent **Sandemu Iraqw Art & Culture Promoters Centre**, roughly one and a half hours' walk west of Karatu. The centre (entry Tsh15,000 per group) is built in the form of a traditionally painted and fortified house, nestling so snugly into the hillside that it only needs a front wall (similar to the former fortified houses of the Rangi; see p.234). Historically, fortification and camouflage was essential to avoid the warlike attention of the Maasai and Barbaig. The centre contains displays of weapons, tools, grinding stones and furniture, and sells mats, baskets, traditional clothes and jewellery, gourds and calabashes. Given enough time, they can also arrange performances of traditional music and theatre, and lay on traditional meals. Camping costs $5.

**Other tours**, most of which need a vehicle unless you're used to walking longer distances, include a 5km (2–3hr) hike up and down Gyekurum Hill for views over Karatu (no car needed); a 25–30km circuit to Baray Gorge south of Sandemu centre for forest, birds and hides excavated in baobab trunks; and a half-day excursion to the western escarpment of the Great Rift Valley for views and the Kambi ya Simbi caves, whose nine chambers are home to bats, porcupines and insects. This trip can be extended to a full day to include waterfalls, Mto wa Mbu town and Lake Miwaleni. Two-day trips include one to the Iraqw heartland of Mbulu to see rock paintings and climb Mount Guwangw, and another covering Engaruka, Ol Doinyo Lengai and Lake Natron in the Rift Valley.

**Costs** average $20–30 per person per day plus transport, which usually means a car as buses and pick-ups rarely have useful timings; vehicle rental for a half-day for a 60km round trip shouldn't be more than $70. Part of the profits fund a kindergarten and soil conservation measures.

---

stay around Ngorongoro, despite (or perhaps because of) the slightly formal colonial atmosphere. The best rooms are in the 1920s farmhouse, while other rooms occupy garden bungalows, and the food is top-notch. Guided walks are included and safaris can be arranged. Open all year round. BB ❽

**Kudu Lodge & Campsite** 500m south of the highway, signposted at the west end of town T027/253 4055, Wwww.kuducamp.com. Set in attractive gardens, this has 25 nicely decorated but wilfully overpriced rooms. Campers fare better at $10 per person, with clean bathrooms and cooking huts. There's a bar and decent restaurant (meals $19, snacks around $6), and internet access (Tsh8000 per hr). Bike tours around the local area ($15 for 2 hours) are available. ❻

**Tanzanite Guest House** Opposite *Bytes*, T027/253 4446. Ten self-contained rooms arranged round a courtyard. Clean, quiet, conveniently located opposite the town's best restaurant – and yet to inflate its prices, which makes it rather special indeed. ❷

**The Octagon Lodge** 1.2km south of the highway, off the same road as the *Kudu Campsite* T027/253 4525, Wwww.octagonlodge.com. Run by an Irish–Tanzanian couple, this place has twelve bright rooms in individual raised wooden chalets vaguely resembling garden sheds, all with verandas facing the garden and its resident crowned cranes and guinea fowl. There are also cottage suites for four people, a nice Irish-themed bar and good, fresh food. FB ❻

## Eating and drinking

Karatu has lots of cheap and basic restaurants and bars, and most hotels also provide sustenance.

**Bytes** Crater Highlands Service Station on the highway, 300m east of *Karatu Lutheran Hostel*. Karatu's best restaurant, with great food in a

polished, pub-like interior. Its several menus wander all over, including paninis and lasagne to an extensive selection of snacks but it's strongest on English and American cooking, with sterling favourites such as cottage pie, fried breakfasts and T-bone steak (Tsh12,500). Prices are reasonable, with most mains around Tsh6000–8000. There's also a sophisticated bar (and great coffee), gift shop and dairy produce store. Closed Mondays. **Gibb's Farm** 5km northeast of town. Something of a time warp back to the days of the British Empire – and pleasingly so. With nouvelle cuisine presentation, natural farm-grown ingredients and some game meat, such as eland. Meals here are always an experience, served with flair; for example sorbet served in a croquant cup as a starter (lunch $21; dinner $28). Digest it all with a guided walk around the coffee farm, or to some waterfalls. Book ahead (☏027/253 4040).

# Ngorongoro Conservation Area

"The eighth wonder of the world" is the clarion call of the brochures, and for once they're not far wrong. The spectacular 8288-square-kilometre **Ngorongoro Conservation Area** occupies the volcanic highlands between the Great Rift Valley and the Serengeti Plains. It's the product of the volcanic upheavals that accompanied the formation of the Rift Valley, and its varied habitats virtually guarantee sightings of "the big five" – elephant, lion, leopard, rhino and buffalo. For animals, this place is a haven; for tourists, it's something close to heaven.

Coming from the east, the magic begins the instant you pass through Lodoare Gate. The road begins to climb up through the tall and liana-festooned Oldeani Forest, giving way to an unforgettable view of **Ngorongoro Crater**, an ever-changing patchwork of green and yellow hues streaked with shadows and mist. At its centre Lake Magadi reflects the silvery sky, while on the western horizon, there's the seemingly endless shimmer of the Serengeti Plains. The 19km-wide crater is Ngorongoro's incomparable highlight, a vast, unbroken caldera left behind when an enormous volcano collapsed. Its grasslands, swamps, glades, lakes and forests contain vast numbers of herbivores, together with Africa's highest density of predators. **Game viewing**, needless to say, is phenomenal, as is the abundance of photo opportunities, the crater's deep, bluish-purple sides providing a spectacular backdrop to any shot. The crater also contains a few highly endangered **black rhino**, which despite their disastrously reduced population (now about twenty), are easily seen. **Birdlife** is pretty decent, too, and includes ostriches, Verreaux's eagles, Egyptian vultures, kori bustards and lesser flamingos, the latter feeding on soda lakes occupying Ngorongoro and Empakaai craters, and at Lake Ndutu on the border with Serengeti.

Although the crater is often all that tourists see of Ngorongoro, there's much more besides. In the west, the rolling hills give way to the expansive grassland of the **Salei Plains**, which receive a good part of the Serengeti's annual wildlife migration between December and April. Both hyena and cheetah are frequently seen here, though in the dry season the plains resemble a desert. Right on the edge of the plains is a remarkable geological fissure, **Oldupai Gorge**, famous among paleontologists as the site of important hominid finds dating back millions of years. To the northeast, close to the edge of the Great Rift Valley's escarpment, are two smaller craters, **Olmoti and Empakaai**, which are also rich in wildlife yet see very few visitors. The craters form part of the so-called **Crater Highlands**, which can be visited on foot if accompanied by an armed ranger – an exciting if hair-raising prospect. For those with more time, and a sturdy pair of legs, it's also possible to walk across the highlands from Ngorongoro to Lake Natron via

Ngorongoro is a wilderness, but one that has also long been inhabited by humans, originally by hunter-gatherers collectively known as **Dorobo**, and later by cattle herders, including the ancestors of the Barbaig (see p.242) and then the Maasai (see p.356). As with the Serengeti, humans were and are very much part of Ngorongoro's delicate ecological balance, a balance that has become increasingly precarious since the end of the nineteenth century, when Europe began to colonize East Africa.

The first *mzungu* to set eyes on Ngorongoro and its famous crater was the German explorer **Dr Oscar Baumann**, who in March 1892 reported a magnificent abundance of game, and promptly went on to bag three rhinos. So began a long history of European involvement, first for hunting, then for conservation, and which, for all their efforts and theories, has witnessed a massive decline in animal numbers.

Originally heavily exploiting the area for hunting, the British administration soon realized that their activities were having a detrimental effect on Ngorongoro's wildlife, and in 1921 Ngorongoro became a **Game Reserve**. Seven years later, locals were prohibited from hunting and cultivating in the crater, although – hypocritically – Europeans continued to do as they wished until the end of the 1930s, when trophy hunting was finally banned. In 1951, Ngorongoro became part of Serengeti National Park, and in 1958 the Maasai – under formidable pressure – formally renounced their claim to Serengeti. The following year, they were evicted and moved into Ngorongoro, which was declared a multiple land use area. This special status still allows Maasai to settle and graze their cattle in coexistence with wildlife, but this admirable idea conceals a more disturbing reality.

Although the **law** states that in cases of human-wildlife conflict in Ngorongoro, Maasai rights are to take precedence, this has rarely been the case, and relations between the authorities and the Maasai have at times been extremely bitter. Settlement in the crater itself was banned in 1974, and cultivation, which the Maasai increasingly had to adopt, was prohibited throughout Ngorongoro in 1975, and only periodically allowed since. Livestock too has been excluded from the crater since the early 1990s, denying the Maasai a critical dry-season pasture for their cattle, and the last decade has been peppered with deeply troubling allegations. For more details see ⓦwww2.warwick.ac.uk/fac/soc/law/elj/lgd/2000_1/lissu.

The underlying problem is that the Maasai presence is barely tolerated by Ngorongoro's authorities, which have progressively made it harder for them to scrape a living from their diminishing resources. Having lost water and pasture rights to the crater (and eighty percent of the land they controlled until a century ago), the Maasai have also been forbidden from hunting or cultivating. An estimated forty percent of Ngorongoro's Maasai are considered destitute, owning less than two livestock units per household. Some conservationists see **tourism** as the solution, but to date the Maasai have seen little of Ngorongoro's gate receipts beyond the construction of a few wells, dams and dispensaries.

Ngorongoro's problems aren't just with the Maasai, however. The changing ecological balance caused by the ban on subsistence hunting and the exclusion of cattle from large areas has favoured increased wildebeest and buffalo populations, with the unfortunate knock-on effect of an increased incidence of **malignant catarrh fever**, which is fatal to cattle. Diseases affecting wildlife have also become more common, disastrously so in 2000 and 2001, when an outbreak of tick-borne Babesiosis claimed the lives of over six hundred animals, including three rhino. The changing ecological balance may also have been responsible for swarms of aggressive blood-sucking flies, *Stomoxys calcitrans*, which killed at least six lions and injured 62 more in 2001.

It can only be hoped that Ngorongoro's authorities can find the wisdom to settle their differences with the Maasai once and for all. As has been shown in several other protected areas in Tanzania, the key to successful wildlife conservation lies in fully involving local communities, in both the running and the profits of wildlife areas.

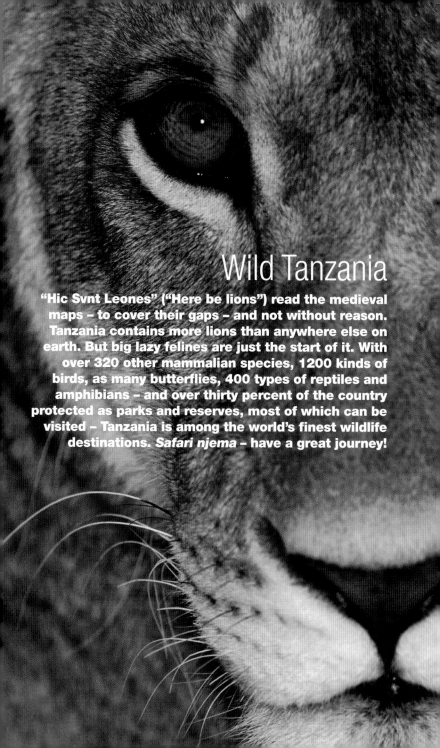

# Wild Tanzania

"Hic Svnt Leones" ("Here be lions") read the medieval maps – to cover their gaps – and not without reason. Tanzania contains more lions than anywhere else on earth. But big lazy felines are just the start of it. With over 320 other mammalian species, 1200 kinds of birds, as many butterflies, 400 types of reptiles and amphibians – and over thirty percent of the country protected as parks and reserves, most of which can be visited – Tanzania is among the world's finest wildlife destinations. *Safari njema* – have a great journey!

# In the land of giants

**Tanzania has long been a land of giants, starting with the 150-million-year-old twelve-metre-tall fossilized Brachiosaurus found at Tendaguru in southern Tanzania. The giants these days are black rhino, hippo, elephant and buffalo.**

## Hippo ▲

Weighing in at 1.5 tonnes, the hippopotamus (Latin for "water horse") is Africa's second most dangerous animal, after malaria-carrying mosquitoes. What looks like an idle yawn is actually a warning. Hippo jaws are capable of applying over a ton of pressure per inch, and they will charge anyone who unwittingly finds themselves between them and the water because their delicate skin cracks with alarming speed when not swaddled in mud or water.

## Rhino ▼

Looking like they've stepped out of the Jurassic period for a breather are Africa's rarest giants, black rhinos, which were poached to the brink of extinction in the 1980s for their horns – used to make dagger handles in the Arabian peninsula and pep-potions in China. Tanzania's population is now under two hundred, compared to ten thousand in the 1960s, and authorities like to keep rhino locations a secret, apart from at Ngorongoro Crater.

## Buffalo ▲

The big, bad boy of the cattle world, the African buffalo weighs close to a tonne and has an unpredictable temper. Try to be understanding: their eyesight is bad, and as their calves make easy prey, adults will charge anything that looks or even smells vaguely like a threat. Oxpeckers are the exception and help to keep buffaloes parasite-free.

## Elephant ▼

Standing 3.5m tall and tipping the scales at as many tonnes, African elephants are the world's heftiest land animals. They are socially complex, emotional and blessed with excellent memories: they periodically return to the remains of deceased family members to place the bones back together. Elephants communicate by touch and sound: trumpeting, and low-pitched, almost sub-sonic rumbles that can travel 50km underground, to be detected not by ears but feet. The elephant's trunk, a blend of lip and nose, can uproot a tree, yet is dexterous enough to pick up a single blade of grass.

# Perfect predators

**Watching predators go in for the kill is a guilty pleasure, the yarns of which fill the evening air at many a safari lodge.**

## Cheetah ◀

The cheetah is the most elegant hunter – a streamlined take on the leopard. When it comes to continuously powered movement they're the world's fastest land animals, topping 110kph (70mph) in their headlong dashes. Speed is one cheetah trick, eyesight is the other, helped by distinctive dark streaks under their eyes which keep down the glare.

## African hunting dog and jackal

The continent's rarest predators are African hunting dogs, also called wild dogs or painted wolves. Like hyenas, they favour teamwork, and are known for tearing their prey apart while it's still alive. Also related to wolves are jackals: they're known as scavengers, but are primarily hunters, settling for birds, small mammals and even insects.

## Lion ▼

Africa's top cat is the lion, packing the power to snap a zebra's back in a single lunge. There are only two things they defer to: elephants (no arguing with those feet), and red-robed Maasai warriors (no arguing with those spears). Females do most of the hunting, while males, distinguished by shaggy manes, patrol the pride's territory, which can as big as 260 square kilometres.

## Leopard ◀

Where lions use power, leopards use stealth. Primarily night-time hunters, by day you might see them up in trees, a tactic born of necessity: by stashing their prey off the ground, they avoid lunchtime bullies (lions) and the irksome attentions of tsetse flies. Their forested habitat has served leopards well: out of sight of poachers, they're Tanzania's most numerous big cats.

## Hyena ▶

Laughing, limping and mean… history hasn't had a good word to say about the hyena, but it's a fascinating creature. Bigger and stronger than their mates, females get first dibs on food, and to assert their dominance have evolved fake penises. Hyenas are also efficient: pack hunting doubles the odds of success compared to lions, and they eat everything, even bones.

## Crocodile ◀

Africa's most terrible predator is the Nile crocodile, scourge of any sentient being needing to cross a river or lake, or drink from its banks. Lurching out of the water, their victims are snatched, dragged under and spun around until the creature either drowns or falls apart. Simple, brutal and time-tested: other than an evolutionary downgrade in size (today's crocs are a measly 6m from tail to snout), they're virtually identical to their Jurassic forebears. Their teeth are continuously replaced – around two hundred a year.

# Surviving the savanna

For most predators, dinner is a four-legged vegetarian: antelopes, zebras, even young buffalo and giraffe. Under constant threat of attack, survival strategies vary.

## Zebra ▶

Naturalists still argue about zebra stripes. Some say they confuse tsetse flies, others that they camouflage them from lions (which are colour blind), while others posit that they simply disorient: picking out individuals from a rippling mass of stripes is difficult even for a keen-eyed cat. Predators treat them with caution; a kick from the hind legs of an adult can be fatal.

## Gazelle ▶

Gazelles are every predator's favourite repast, but catching them takes work. Their top speed isn't far off a cheetah's and, to confound chasers, herds will explode in all directions when startled. They are extremely agile leapers, turning 180 degrees in little more than a stride.

## Dikdik ◀

Named after its alarm cry, the dikdik is Africa's Bambi: an adorable little thing no larger than a hare, whose lack of defensive tricks makes it prefer bushes, in which it hides. Dikdiks are highly territorial, and mark their territory with sticky secretions produced by dark glands beside their eyes. They mate for life, and are usually seen in pairs.

## Wildebeest ▲

Also called gnus, wildebeest are fast food for predators. Half a million calves are born in the Serengeti at the start of the year, coinciding with the lush grazing afforded by the long rains, before they begin an epic migration to Kenya's Maasai Mara. There's security in numbers: the larger the herd, the better the chances of newborns surviving.

## Giraffe ◀

Gliding along the savanna, heads 5m up, are giraffes. Evolution stretched their necks to let them browse the upper branches of acacias without having to compete with other species; but surprisingly their necks are supported by seven vertebrae, just like ours. Giraffes also have record-breaking tails (over 2m long), and rather dandy tongues: half a metre of branch-stripping muscle painted blue, apparently to avoid sunburn.

### The Great Migration

The Serengeti owes its hallowed place in our imagination to the annual eight-hundred-kilometre migration of over 2.5 million animals, the largest mammalian migration on earth. A continuous, milling and unsettled mass, over half of which are wildebeest, the migration offers visitors one of nature's most staggering displays, one in which the predators play vital roles. River crossings are the biggest obstacles, namely the Grumeti in Serengeti, and the Mara along the Kenyan border. Both can be the scene of true carnage as panicked herds struggle across the raging flows in a writhing mass of bodies, while the weak, injured or careless are picked off by crocodiles and lions. The hazards of the migration are such that only one in three newborns survive.

# Apes, great and small

Closest to us on the evolutionary ladder, primates are easy animals to relate to. They are found all over Tanzania; to spoil yourself, have a gander through the forests of the Udzungwa Mountains.

## Bushbaby ▶

The bushbaby's blood-curdling screams are what gives them their name. This unbelievably cute, tree-dwelling creature has enormous saucer eyes that give it bionic eyesight at night. Equally impressive, especially given its small size, is its jump: bushbabies store energy in their tendons on landing, which, on release, can catapult them upwards by 2m.

## Chimpanzee ◀

Chimpanzees share between 94 and 99 percent of our genes, and chimp tracking – either in the Mahale Mountains or at Gombe Stream, both on the shores of Lake Tanganyika – will provide memories for a lifetime. Their intelligence and tool use has long been acknowledged: "fishing" for termites by poking long sticks into termite hills is a trick that Tanzanian chimps have adopted. Not as well known is their ingestion of certain plants for specific medical purposes, and their propensity for violence, which in one infamous case – at Gombe – resulted in the extermination of an entire clan.

## Colobus monkey ◀

Gentle in their manners, the most common colobus monkey is the black-and-white, which lives in forest canopies but is very shy. Easier to see, and photograph, is Zanzibar's unique red colobus monkey, a large troop of which resides by the entrance of Jozani Forest. Locals calls them poison monkeys, as they can safely gobble normally toxic foods, courtesy of their fondness for eating charcoal. Their name derives from the Greek for "incomplete" as they lack thumbs.

## Baboon ▶

Living in large and rigidly hierarchical communities, baboons are intelligent and highly adaptable, making them champion survivors. They'll eat anything from scorpions to baby antelopes, and will quite happily steal your lunch, too. Mutual grooming keeps parasites at bay and reinforces social bonds. During ovulation, a female's backside swells and turns bright pink – subtlety isn't a baboon thing.

## Vervet monkey ▶

Brazen in their approach to humans (and partial to snatching cameras as well as sandwiches), the vervet monkey is small, agile and unruly, and frequently seen around wildlife lodges scavenging for scraps. They have a sophisticated predator warning-system, with three distinct alarm calls: for snakes, eagles and leopards. Male vervets have blue scrota; the deeper the colour, the higher the rank.

# Life beneath the waves

Tanzania's beaches are spectacular, but there's more to the coast than blissful sands: a short dip or boat trip away are some of Africa's richest coral reefs, explorable with a mask and snorkel, or scuba gear. At the heart of the ecosystems are microscopic animals called polyps, whose exoskeletons grow at the pace of fingernails, to eventually form reefs: perfect habitats for a bewildering array of marine life.

## Moray eel ◀

Even though the moray measures 1.5m, the most you're likely to see of it is its fearsome head gawping out from a crevice in the coral. They're ambush predators, snatching anything that swims within striking distance – including overly inquisitive fingers. To swallow prey, morays have a second set of mobile jaws that drag the fish into their guts.

## Nudibranch ◀

Sea slugs to you and me, nudibranchs are the (toxic) Christmas Tree baubles of the deep: vividly coloured, bizarrely patterned and weirdly shaped. In fact, everything about them is weird, including sex: nudibranchs are hermaphrodites. A favourite with scuba divers, the Spanish dancer is named after its fetching red "skirt".

## Turtle ▶

Green turtles are believed to migrate from Australia just to lay eggs on Africa's shores. The exercise serves them well: they tend to live longer than humans, and turtles have changed little over the last 250 million years. All five turtle species in Tanzania are endangered, but efforts are underway to protect them and their nesting beaches.

# Dugong

Among the rarest of mammals, on the brink of extinction, the dugong or manatee (*nguva*) is a seal-like mammal related to dolphins and whales, and an unlikely inspiration for sailors' tales of mermaids. The legends may have had something to do with the dugong's habit of floating around on its back, letting a pair of bobbing, ample breasts work their magic on the mariners of yore.

# Octopus

The master of the art of camouflage, the octopus cannot only instantly change its colour to match its surroundings, but its texture, too, making it difficult to spot unless on the move. Octopuses are also clever, capable, for instance, of unscrewing discarded jars in order to use them as homes.

# Dolphin

Tanzania's most common marine mammal is the gregarious dolphin, especially the bottlenose and humpback. Dolphins communicate using sound, including squeaks, whistles and body language noises such as slapping their tails on the water. They're most easily seen off southern Unguja, Zanzibar.

# Manta ray

With a "wing" span topping 7m, a gliding manta ray (from the Spanish for "cloak") is an awe-inspiring sight, and may be seen by scuba divers off Pemba Island. Mantas rid themselves of parasites by scrubbing themselves against coral reefs, and are often accompanied by remora – hitch-hiking fish that hold on using sucker-shaped fins.

# Between heaven and earth

Tanzania's birdlife is astonishingly diverse, with around 1200 species, from the thumb-sized cordon bleu to the ostrich. Independent birdwatchers can expect to encounter over three hundred species in a ten-day trip, while on a specialist tour, you can reasonably hope for a hundred more. Over forty unique species are to be seen, and there are many more near-endemics, too.

## Flamingo ◀

The pretty pink so characteristic of lesser flamingos comes from their diet: a rich soup of soda-loving algal blooms. Flocks of tens or even hundreds of thousands can be seen on Lake Manyara, where they feed, and on the caustic sump of Lake Natron, where they breed – far away from the attentions of predators.

## Weaver ▶

Africa's weavers, including (right) the vitelline masked weaver, are extraordinarily skilled nest-builders, and it's the shape of the nests – anything from socks and cloche hats to doughnuts – that tells the various species apart.

## Hornbill

Hornbills are commonly seen, given away by their erratic flap-glide flying technique and raucous calls. Also unusual is the breeding habit of the red-billed hornbill: the male incarcerates its mate inside a hollow tree, leaving a hole through which he feeds her while she incubates the eggs and rears the young.

## African fish eagle ◄

The elegant African fish eagle is, as the name suggests, an expert catcher of fish. They spend much of their time perched in trees beside lakes, rivers and shores, on the look-out for signs of a quick snack, then swoop low over the water to grab the meal in their talons.

## Ostrich ▼

The pink-legged ostrich is the world's largest and heaviest bird. Fly it can't, but run it sure can, cruising at 50kph, and sprinting up to 70kph. If surprised by a lion, a well-aimed kick can kill its attacker. Ostriches don't hide their heads in the sand, incidentally, but they do sleep with their heads tucked under their wings.

## Marabou stork ◄

The marabou is hard to miss: 1.5m tall, it's a macabre character with a long funnel-like beak, and plumage resembling that of a disgruntled butler. Like vultures, they're primarily carrion eaters, but will also hunt – including young flamingos. Their 3.2-metre wingspan matches that of the Andean condor.

# Habitats

Tanzania's natural habitats range from classic African savanna and acacia bushland to deciduous woods, monsoon-fed rainforests, high-altitude tundra, lakes, rivers, swamps and marshes, mangroves and coral reefs. Almost a third of the country is under some form of official protection, much of which can be visited.

## Savanna ▶

Africa's archetypal savanna is the Serengeti, whose plains are centre stage for an epic migration of over 2.5 million wildebeest, zebra and gazelle. Included in the migration is Ngorongoro, whose blown-out volcanic caldera contains the world's densest concentration of wild mammals, including a glut of predators. Tarangire, framed by forests of gigantic baobab trees, is the place to see elephants.

## Forests ▶

The most intimate wildlife experiences are on foot, with forests especially enchanting: the Udzungwa Mountains (right) are paradise for primates and birds, and Amani Nature Reserve is one of the world's top four biodiversity "hot spots". Also memorable are Gombe Stream and Mahale Mountains on Lake Tanganyika, both famed for chimpanzees. On Zanzibar, Jozani Forest has unique red colobus monkeys, and Pemba's incredibly lush Ngezi Forest has great birding.

## Coral reefs

Snorkellers and divers are in for a treat. The pick of the best: Pemba Island for exhilarating drift dives; Pangani to combine with a mainland beach holiday; Zanzibar's Unguja island for a bit of everything; Mafia Island for big open-water species; and Mnazi Bay–Ruvuma Estuary in the south, to go where few have gone before.

## The Riddles of Kilimanjaro

Life on the icy tundra surrounding Kilimanjaro's 5892-metre summit – Africa's highest – is untenable for all but a handful of birds. But in *The Snows of Kilimanjaro*, Ernest Hemingway mentioned a frozen leopard, one that really was found up here, over 5km high, in 1926. Just what it was doing, no one knows, but it wasn't alone: elephant bones were found in the same area, and in 1964 a buffalo skeleton was found on Mawenzi Peak, two years after the explorer Wilfred Thesiger was trailed to the very top by a pack of African hunting dogs. With Kili's last glaciers melting away at a depressing rate, who knows what else might be found...

# Rivers and swamps ▼

Water is life, an equation nowhere more evident than in Selous, where the Rufiji River spills into an enormous inland delta, attracting a riot of wildlife. Saadani National Park is also good for boat safaris along the shore or up a mangrove-lined creek filled with hippos and crocs. Visit Katavi in the dry season, when zillions of hippos congregate in a few muddy wallows on the receding floodplain.

# Lakes ▼

The caustic waters of lakes Natron and Manyara, along the Rift Valley, are inimical to life, except soda-loving algae, which attract flocks of flamingos. Lake Victoria, the world's second-largest freshwater lake, has superb birdlife, and the other Rift Valley lakes, Tanganyika and Nyasa, have hundreds of unique fish species.

# The little five

**Much is made of the Big Five – lions, elephants, leopards (or cheetahs), rhinos and buffaloes – but it can be just as rewarding glimpsing a shy antelope or a rare bird, as it can be watching a pride of fly-infested lions gorging on a kill. For a little structure to your quest, might we suggest...**

## Ant lion

The ravenous larval stage of a kind of lacewing that makes funnel traps in loose sand to catch prey.

## Rhino beetle ▶

With a huge horn protruding from its head, the Hercules of the insect world can lift several hundred times its own weight. It's often given away by hissing squeaks, intended to ward off rivals.

## Leopard tortoise ◀

The blotched carapace (shell) accounts for its name. You'll often spot it on roads, and the female outweighs the male threefold.

## Buffalo weaver

An enterprising bird that hitches rides on the backs of buffaloes and other beasts, eating bugs disturbed by their passing.

## Elephant shrew ▶

Note the resemblance? This beauty resembles a hobbling big-footed mouse with a trunk-like snout. The name was coined long before DNA tests showed that it isn't a shrew at all, and is, in fact, most closely related to ... you guessed it, elephants!

Ol Doinyo Lengai volcano, a journey that can take anything from two to seven days (see p.371).

Another attraction is the chance to meet the red-robed **Maasai** for whom the conservation area provides year-round pasture. Package tours are catered for by **cultural bomas** – "traditional" Maasai villages set up expressly for tourists. The experience can feel uncomfortably staged and voyeuristic at times, but for many it's the only time they'll be able to meet one of Africa's traditional tribes. With more time, much better would be a Crater Highlands walk, which passes clean through Maasai territory, or a visit to one of Tanzania's cultural tourism programmes; see p.357.

Given these manifold attractions, Ngorongoro is Tanzania's most visited wildlife area, attracting over 300,000 tourists annually, and this, in fact, is the main drawback. To some, large numbers of visitors make Ngorongoro resemble a zoo, and spoil the experience of being in a true wilderness – something the authorities are now attempting to tackle with massive increases in entrance fees. Nonetheless, for all the tourists, the hype and the expense, Ngorongoro – designated a World Heritage Site in 1979 – is still a place that enchants, and few people leave disappointed.

## Arrival

Pretty much every tour operator in Tanzania offers **safaris** to Ngorongoro, and the sealed road, running all the way from Arusha to Ngorongoro's Lodoare Gate, means most safari vehicles cover the 160km in less than three hours. If you're adept at bargaining and have access to enough backsides to fill seats, it's cheaper to arrange **car rental in Karatu** (see p.364). Self-drive is possible as everything is signposted, but you won't be allowed into the crater without an officially licensed **guide** or driver-guide; they can be hired at the park gate for $20 a day. Open-topped vehicles are not admitted.

It's not possible to get around the conservation area by **public transport**, but there is a bus run by the Ngorongoro Conservation Area Authority (NCAA) from Arusha (10am Mon–Fri; returning in the afternoon) to its headquarters close to the crater (and a few buses each week between Arusha and Musoma or Mwanza), where you should be able to hire a ranger for walks, and possibly a vehicle. There's no guarantee of either however, so enquire at the conservation area's office on Boma Road in Arusha before heading out.

## Entrance fees and information

**Entry fees**, paid at Lodoare Gate if you're coming from the east or at Naabi Hill Gate coming from Serengeti, are currently $50 per person for 24 hours, plus $5 for a vehicle permit, and $200 per vehicle for a morning or afternoon spent inside Ngorongoro Crater (the "crater fee"). Cash is currently acceptable. **Armed rangers** are obligatory for Crater Highlands treks and cost $20 a day.

There is a **tourist information centre** at Lodoare Gate where you can pick up a **guidebook** published by Ngorongoro Conservation Unit ($10), which contains a wealth of information about the region, its history, geology and inhabitants (animal and people), and is accompanied by a number of other booklets covering geology, birdlife, wildlife, trees and plants, and prehistory. The most detailed and accurate **map** is Harms-Ic-Verlag's. Not as detailed but more visually attractive is the painted dry-season/wet-season map by Giovanni Tombazzi.

**7**

# Accommodation

The only regular **accommodation** inside Ngorongoro is at a number of expensive **lodges**; all but one on the crater rim – and that one is often fully booked months in advance. Environmentally and ethically, however, none of the crater-rim lodges enjoys an unblemished reputation. Camping is in many ways better – for the feeling of being in the wild and because it's much cheaper – it costs $30 or $50 per person depending on the site. There are more campsites, and also much cheaper hotels, outside the conservation area in Karatu (see p.365). All of the following are marked on the map on p.363.

## Camping

**Campers** can choose between one public campsite, which doesn't require reservations, and several "special campsites" which are often block-booked by safari companies months if not years in advance. In Arusha, you can ask about availability – and book – at Ngorongoro's tourist office in Arusha; see p.307.

The **public campsite** ($30 per person, paid at the gate) is *Simba A* on the southwestern rim of Ngorongoro Crater, which has toilets and showers, but gets packed, noisy and often filthy in high season. Nonetheless, the crater views are jaw-dropping, there's electricity (good for charging your camera) and the Woodstock/Glastonbury feel appeals to many, despite the discomforts.

The **special campsites** ($50 per person) are usually in very scenic locations but have no facilities at all. The only one to be avoided is *Nyati*, near Ngorongoro Crater, which lacks any kind of views. The rest, all recommended if you can find them free for a night, are: *Simba B*, which has similarly good views to *Simba A* 1km away; *Nanokanoka*, close to Olmoti Crater and Nanokanoka village, which means you can wander in for a chat with local Maasai; two sites next to Empakaai Crater, perfect for descending into it the next day; and three sites on the wooded northeastern rim of Ngorongoro Crater, *Tembo A*, *Tembo B* and *Lemala*, all of which occasionally see elephants. There are also seven special campsites around Lake Ndutu in the west, often very crowded.

## Lodges

Day-visitors can take **lunch** at the lodges: prices range from $25 (*Rhino*) upwards. Room **rates** drop considerably April–June.

**Ndutu Safari Lodge** Next to Lake Ndutu on the border with Serengeti ℡ 027/250 2829, ⓦ www.ndutu.com. A welcoming and friendly place well off the beaten track, with 32 comfortable bungalows – the best at the front facing the lake. There's an open-sided bar, a lounge and dining room with superb food. FB ❽

**Ngorongoro Serena Lodge** On the crater rim (book through Serena Hotels, 2nd floor, Diamond Trust House Building, Arusha ℡ 027/253 9160, ⓦ www.serenahotels.com). The usual high standards of creature comforts from this chain make this a stylish yet impersonal place. Most of its 75 rooms have verandas overlooking the crater, and the restaurant and a terrace have views. FB $550. ❾

**Ngorongoro Sopa Lodge** On the crater rim (book through Sopa Lodges, 4th floor, Sopa Plaza,

99 Serengeti Rd, Arusha ℡ 027/250 0630–9, ⓦ www.sopalodges.com). The only hotel on the eastern rim, this is perfect for sunsets, but also the largest and least personal of the lodges, with 90 mostly twin-bed rooms. The external architecture is an eyesore, but the views are fantastic, whether from public areas, the balconies of most of the rooms or the swimming pool. HB $530. ❾

**Ngorongoro Wildlife Lodge** On the crater rim (book through Hotels & Lodges Ltd, 2nd floor (Block B), Summit Centre, Sokoine Rd, Arusha ℡ 027/254 4595, ⓦ www.hotelsandlodges-tanzania.com). Another architectural mess, this place – nicknamed the "ski lodge" – was government-owned for years, but has raised its rates rather more than its standards. On the positive side, the views are superb, whether from the 78 bedrooms (just four with balconies), or from the lounge. FB $460. ❾

## The Crater Highlands

The Crater Highlands is the informal term for the mountainous eastern part of Ngorongoro that forms the lush forested ridge of the Great Rift Valley's western escarpment, and which the Maasai call Ol Doinyo Ildatwa. The area includes Ngorongoro Crater, the 3216m Mount Oldeani to its south, the isolated Gol Mountains in the north, Olmoti and Empakaai craters in the northeast, Mount Loolmalassin (the range's highest point at 3648m) and Ol Doinyo Lengai, East Africa's only active volcano (see p.360), which rises in a perfect cone just outside the conservation area's northeastern corner.

One of Ngorongoro's major attractions is a **Crater Highlands trek**, which can be as short as half a day, or as long as a week, giving you ample time to get to Lake Natron, perhaps including a climb up Ol Doinyo Lengai along the way. The exact distance, and number of days required, depends on where you start and whether you're being driven part of the way. For example, a two-day (44km) trek to Lake Natron starts at Empakaai Crater, while a seven-day trip allows you to amble at your leisure from the rim of Ngorongoro Crater to the desolately beautiful Lake Natron, overnighting at Maasai *bomas* or camping wild. Most safari companies offer five-day trips as standard.

**Costs** vary according to the level of service and back-up: count on between $250–400 a day. Upmarket operators offer something close to bush luxury, where a full camp attended by plenty of staff is set up ahead of your arrival, including mess tents, furniture, chemical toilets and ingenious bucket showers. Much cheaper, more adventurous and definitely more "authentic" are humbler trips where the gear (dome tents, usually) is carried by donkey, which will also carry you if you're tired. These trips are often guided by Maasai warriors, who make up for their sometimes limited knowledge of English with tremendous practical botanical know-how and an astounding ability to spot all sorts of wildlife.

For **one-day trips**, contact the conservation area headquarters (see p.307), which can fix you up with an armed ranger, or Green Footprint Adventures (Ⓦwww .greenfootprint.co.tz) at *Ngorongoro Serena Lodge*. For longer forays, see the safari company reviews for Arusha (pp.51–52); some of Moshi's hiking companies (p.271) also offer Crater Highlands treks.

---

**Rhino Lodge** Just a few metres south of the crater rim, 15km from Lodoare Gate ℡0762/359055, Ⓔrhino@ngorongoro.cc. Cheapest of the hotels on the crater rim, the *Rhino* resembles an army barracks from the outside but the 24 rooms are thankfully much more appealing. ❼

# Ngorongoro Crater

Some 2.5 million years ago, the reservoir of magma under an enormous volcano towering over the western flank of the Great Rift Valley emptied itself in an enormous explosion, leaving a vacuum that caused the mountain to implode under its own weight. In its wake, it left an enormous 600-metre deep crater (caldera), its 19-kilometre diameter now making it the world's largest unbroken and unflooded caldera. This is **Ngorongoro Crater**, one of Tanzania's wonders, covering approximately three hundred square kilometres and providing a natural amphitheatre for the wildlife spectacle on its floor. The crater contains 25,000 to 30,000 large mammals, which when viewed from the rim are a blur of pulsating specks arranged in fluid formations, while above the crater, eagles, buzzards, hawks and vultures circle.

The main feature on the crater floor is the shallow and alkaline **Lake Magadi**, whose extent varies according to the rains – flocks of flamingos feed here in the dry season. On the western shore is an enigmatic scattering of stone **burial**

www.roughguides.com

**mounds**, believed to have been left by the Datooga (Tatoga), ancestors of Barbaig cattle herders who occupied the crater until the Maasai pushed them out. At the lake's southern edge is **Lerai Forest**, a large patch of acacia woodland that takes its Maasai name from the dominant yellow-barked acacia, and is a good place for seeing waterbuck and flitting sunbirds. Swamp, thorn scrub and grassland fill the rest of the crater, and provide the bulk of the game viewing.

The majority of the animals are **herbivores**, supported by year-round supplies of water and fodder, and include vast herds of wildebeest (up to fourteen thousand), zebra, buffalo, Grant's and Thomson's gazelle, eland, hartebeest and mountain reedbuck, warthog and hippo, and two of Africa's giants: elephants, of which a handful of bulls are always present, and a small population of **black rhino**. Once rhinos where common across all of eastern and southern Africa, but poaching in the 1970s and 1980s took a terrible toll on this magnificent creature, decimating the population from 108 in the 1960s to only fourteen in 1995. Although poaching is now under control (if not completely eradicated), Ngorongoro's rhino suffered a major blow in 2000–2001, when tick-borne Babesiosis killed three of them. There are now around twenty.

Apart from rhino, the big draw is the transfixing sight of Africa's densest population of **predators** in action. Lions are very common and easily seen (best in the dry season), as are hyenas and jackals. Cheetahs are also sometimes present, as are leopards, which require some patience to spot, as they rest up in trees or thick bush by day.

There are three **access roads**. The eastern Lemala route, from *Lemala* and *Tembo* campsites, can be driven in either direction. In the south, the steeper Lerai route from Lerai Forest on the crater floor is for ascent only, while the Seneto route in the west is only for descent. A **fee** of $200 per vehicle for six hours applies (in practice, a morning or afternoon's game drive), in addition to entry fees, and you'll need to hire an official guide if you're driving yourself (this doesn't apply if your driver is licensed by the authorities, or if you're on an organized safari). Only 4WD vehicles are allowed in the crater, and in theory they need to carry a heavy-duty jack, chains or a towrope, a shovel or hoe, and an axe or *panga*. The speed limit is 25kph, and you must be out by 6pm, so start ascending no later than 5.30pm. Visitors must stay in their vehicle except at two **picnic sites**: one next to Lerai Forest at the foot of the Lerai ascent route, the other at Ngoitokitok Springs in the east next to a small lake.

## Olmoti and Empakaai craters

North of Ngorongoro Crater are two smaller craters, Olmoti and Empakaai. The rims of either can be reached by vehicle, but are best seen on foot, ideally prearranged as part of a Crater Highlands trek. Though ranger posts are close to both craters, if you're intending to walk it's best to organize in advance with the conservation area headquarters (see p.307) for a ranger to accompany you.

The shallow and grassy **Olmoti Crater**, accessed from Nanokanoka village (there's a special campsite there), contains several antelope species, and there are waterfalls nearby on the Munge River. Accompanied by an armed ranger (the post is in the village), the crater rim and its fringing forest can be explored on foot, taking anything from two to seven hours.

Northeast of here is the stunningly beautiful, 6km-wide **Empakaai Crater**, much of which is filled with a forest-fringed soda lake. This is better for wildlife than Olmoti, and resident species include bushbuck, reedbuck and waterbuck, buffalo, monkeys and an abundance of birds, including flamingos. You can walk along the rim (again, if accompanied by an armed ranger – the post is about 5km southeast) and into the crater itself (at least 7hr). There are two special campsites on the rim: enquire with a safari operator, or Green Footprint Adventures (@www.greenfootprint.co.tz).

## Oldupai Gorge

Gouged from the edge of the Salei Plains, **Oldupai (or Olduvai) Gorge** is a steep-sided, 48km-long ravine with depths reaching 150m in places. Furrowed out of the volcanic land by the capricious Oldupai River, the eroded rock strata on either side of the gorge have exposed the fossilized remains of animals and over fifty hominids dating back almost two million years – an archeological trove of inestimable importance for understanding the origins of humankind.

The fossils were first noted in 1911 by **Professor Kattwinkel**, a German butterfly collector, who found them by chance and took the fossilized remains of a three-toed horse back to Berlin's Museum für Naturkunde. Two decades later, Kattwinkel's findings aroused the curiosity of Kenyan-born British anthropologist, **Louis Leakey**, and in 1931 he began excavating at Oldupai.

For almost thirty years, Leakey and his wife Mary found only stone tools, the oldest belonging to the so-called **Oldowan industry** (1.2 to 1.8 million years ago). Spurred on by the belief that the remains of the hominids that had created the tools could not be far behind, they persevered, and their patience was finally rewarded in 1959 by the discovery of two large human-like teeth and a piece of skull. Four hundred additional fragments were eventually found, which were painstakingly reassembled to form the 1.75 million-year-old skull of *Australopithecus boisei* ("southern ape"), nicknamed **Nutcracker Man** on account of his powerful jaws. The tool-maker had been found, and the discovery – at the time, the oldest known – provoked a sea change in paleontological circles, especially as the skull's size and dentition displayed uncanny similarities with modern man. The unavoidable conclusion was that the Leakeys had unearthed a direct ancestor of modern man, and that the much vaunted "missing link" had been found.

### Laetoli

For all Oldupai's paleontological wonders, perhaps Tanzania's most astonishing prehistoric find occurred at **Laetoli** (or Garusi), 40km south of Oldupai, which offered up its first fossils in 1938. The most spectacular discoveries came in the 1970s, the first of which were thirteen jaw fragments dating back 3.6 million years. They belonged to a species called *Australopithecus afarensis*, taking its Latin name from the first finds of the species in Ethiopia's Afar desert, which in 1974 introduced the world to "Lucy" – a half-complete female skeleton which evidence suggested had been bipedal, and was dubbed Dinquenesh ("you are amazing") by Ethiopians.

In 1979, Laetoli offered up something equally amazing: a trail of **fossilized footprints** that had been left in wet volcanic ash by two adults and a child. The discovery was dated to around 3.75 million years ago, and attracted worldwide attention as it provided incontestable proof that hominids were walking (and running) upright way before anyone had imagined. Further research suggested that *Australopithecus afarensis* stood fully erect, was about 100–150cm tall, and weighed up to 50kg. The skull, although only fractionally larger than that of modern chimpanzees, had dentition similar to modern humans.

**Access** to Laetoli is not possible, and the footsteps have been covered up again, but plaster casts are on display at Oldupai Museum, both museums in Arusha, the National Museum in Dar and Nairobi's National Museum.

The theory was accepted until disproved by much older finds from Ethiopia, and from Laetoli, south of Oldupai (see box, p.373), and since then poor old Nutcracker Man has been consigned to history as an evolutionary dead end. His importance remains, however, in showing that hominid evolution was not a simple linear progression. The find sparked a flurry of **further excavations** at Oldupai, which showed conclusively that two other hominid species, almost certainly our ancestors, lived contemporaneously with Nutcracker Man – *Homo habilis* ("handy man") and *Homo erectus* ("upright man").

Over the years, various claims have been made for one place or another being the "cradle of mankind", but it's way too early to say this with any certainty. What is certain, however, is that the incredible journey into our prehistory first began to make sense at Oldupai, and it's a journey that, if it can be traced at all, should happily continue to baffle humankind for many years to come.

### Practicalities

Oldupai Gorge can be seen on foot or by vehicle, and even if old bones and stones don't appeal, the gorge itself is a pleasant diversion off the road to Serengeti, and there's also a range of fast-moving black sand dunes to explore. The entrance to the gorge, next to a small but fascinating museum documenting the finds, lies about 30km west of Ngorongoro Crater, and 7km north of the road to Serengeti. The Tsh3000 **entrance fee** also gives access to the museum; in theory, this includes the services of an **official guide** for the gorge, but in practice they won't join you unless you pay a fairly hefty tip; $15 per group would be reasonable. That said, the guides do know their stuff – they reel off entertaining lectures and can put a context to even the most mundane-looking of rocks or fossil fragments. The average tour lasts thirty minutes to two hours if you're in a car.

Despite its modest size, **Oldupai Museum** (daily 8am–4.30pm; ☎027/253 7037) packs in a bewildering amount of information. There are three rooms that are full of well-documented bones, tools and skilful reproductions of skulls (the original Nutcracker Man is at Dar es Salaam's National Museum; see p.95).

### The Shifting Sands

Providing an appropriate metaphor for Oldupai's immense sweep though time are the **Shifting Sands**, roughly 15km northwest of the museum and beyond the northern edge of the gorge, which are a range of elegant black sand dunes forever being pushed eastward by the wind (an estimated 17m a year). Taking a guide is obligatory as you have to pass through the gorge to get there, and the authorities also discourage folk from clambering over the dunes, which destroys their fragile plant cover and hastens their onward advance.

# The Serengeti and around

As one of the world's most famous wildlife areas, the **Serengeti** needs little introduction. Bordering Ngorongoro in the east, Kenya's Maasai Mara Game Reserve in the north, and reaching to within 8km of Lake Victoria in the west, the Serengeti is also Tanzania's largest national park, and any safari here promises wildlife galore, especially when the **annual migration** of plains game – mainly wildebeest and zebra and their natural predators – is in residence. The migration, which swings up to Maasai Mara, also passes through **Loliondo**, a remote and little-visited wilderness sandwiched between Serengeti, Ngorongoro, Lake Natron and the Kenyan border. Loliondo contains a number of upmarket tented camps offering much of Serengeti's wildlife in exclusive wilderness concessions, and if you're coming by rented car, a rough road through the area from Serengeti gives an alternative – and highly adventurous – way of getting to and from Lake Natron.

# Serengeti National Park

As Tanzania's oldest and largest national park, and one of the world's best-known wildlife sanctuaries, the 14,763-square-kilometre **Serengeti National Park** is one of the jewels in Tanzania's wildlife crown. Protected

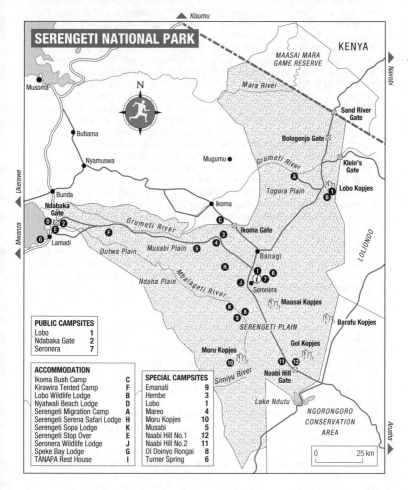

**SERENGETI NATIONAL PARK**

Kisumu

KENYA

MAASAI MARA GAME RESERVE

Musoma

N

Mara River

Nairobi

Sand River Gate

Butiama

Bologonja Gate

Nyamuswa

Mugumu

Grumeti River

Klein's Gate

Lobo Kopjes

Togora Plain

Ukerewe

Bunda

Ndabaka Gate

Ikoma

Grumeti River

Ikoma Gate

Mwanza

Lamadi

Outwa Plain

Musabi Plain

Banagi

LOLIONDO

Ndoha Plain

Mbalageti River

Seronera

Maasai Kopjes

Barafu Kopjes

**PUBLIC CAMPSITES**

| Lobo | 1 |
| Ndabaka Gate | 2 |
| Seronera | 7 |

SERENGETI PLAIN

Gol Kopjes

**ACCOMMODATION**

| | |
|---|---|
| Ikoma Bush Camp | C |
| Kirawira Tented Camp | F |
| Lobo Wildlife Lodge | B |
| Nyatwali Beach Lodge | D |
| Serengeti Migration Camp | A |
| Serengeti Serena Safari Lodge | H |
| Serengeti Sopa Lodge | K |
| Serengeti Stop Over | E |
| Seronera Wildlife Lodge | J |
| Speke Bay Lodge | G |
| TANAPA Rest House | I |

**SPECIAL CAMPSITES**

| | |
|---|---|
| Emanati | 9 |
| Hembe | 3 |
| Lobo | 1 |
| Mareo | 4 |
| Moru Kopjes | 10 |
| Musabi | 5 |
| Naabi Hill No.1 | 12 |
| Naabi Hill No.2 | 11 |
| Ol Doinyo Rongai | 8 |
| Turner Spring | 6 |

Moru Kopjes

Simiyu River

Naabi Hill Gate

Lake Ndutu

NGORONGORO CONSERVATION AREA

Arusha

0    25 km

## The Great Migration

The Serengeti owes its hallowed place in our imagination to the annual 800km **migration** of over 2.5 million animals, the largest mammalian migration on earth. A continuous, milling and unsettled mass, including almost two million wildebeest and close to a million other animals, the migration offers visitors one of nature's most staggering displays, one in which the ever-vigilant predators – lions, cheetahs, African hunting dogs and spotted hyenas – play a vital part. The river crossings are the biggest obstacle, namely the Grumeti in Serengeti, and the Mara along the border with Kenya in the north, and both can be the scene of true carnage as the panicked herds struggle across the raging flows in a writhing mass of bodies while the weak, injured or careless are picked off by crocodiles and lions.

The migration's ceaseless movement is prompted by a seasonal search for fresh water and pasture dictated by the rains. It moves in a roughly clockwise direction, concentrating in the national park from **April to June**, towards the end of the long rains, before leaving behind the withering plains of the Serengeti and journeying northward towards the fresh moisture and grass of Kenya's Maasai Mara Game Reserve, which the migration reaches in August. By **September** and **October**, the bulk of the migration is concentrated in Maasai Mara. By **late October** and **early November**, the Mara's grasslands are approaching exhaustion, so the migration turns back towards northern and eastern Serengeti, following the fresh grass brought by the short rains. In this period, the migration is widely spread out, and a large part of it circles through Loliondo and into Ngorongoro, beyond the Serengeti's eastern border. From **December to March**, the migration settles in the Serengeti Plains and western Ngorongoro, where it remains until the onset of the long rains. The wildebeest take advantage of this temporary pause to give birth (especially from late Jan to mid-March), accounting for half a million calves annually. The timing of this mass birthing provides security in numbers: predators will eat their fill, but within a few months, the surviving calves are much stronger and able to outrun their pursuers; nonetheless, the hazards of the migration are such that only one in three calves makes it back the following year. By April, the migration is once more concentrated inside Serengeti, and the whole cycle starts again.

The exact time and location of the migration varies annually, depending on the rains and other factors, so coinciding with it cannot be guaranteed. Nonetheless, as a general rule, the **best months** for seeing the migration in the Serengeti are from December to July, especially February and March in the plains when the wildebeest herds are dotted with new-born, and April to June when animal concentrations are at their highest. June is also the best time for catching the migration's perilous crossing of the Grumeti River, while the spectacular Mara River crossing, best seen from Kenya but also in northern Serengeti, is at its most awesome (and gruesome) in July and August.

since 1929, at a time when trophy hunters were wreaking havoc on wildlife populations, and declared a national park in 1951, the Serengeti is also – together with Ngorongoro – a UNESCO World Heritage Site and International Biosphere Reserve. And with good reason – the Serengeti lies at the heart of the world's largest and most impressive **wildlife migration** (see box above), at the peak of which it contains the highest concentration of mammals on earth.

Serengeti takes its name from the flat **grassland plains** that cover the eastern section of the park next to Ngorongoro, which the Maasai called *siringet*, meaning "endless plain". Along with the Kalahari, these plains are the Western imagination's archetypal African landscape, and the highlight of many a visit, certainly when the migration is in full swing. Even outside the migration, there's plenty to see, including large clans of hyenas and thriving lion prides, and a series of weathered granite outcrops called **kopjes** (pronounced kop-yees; from the Afrikaans for "little head"), one of which contains rock paintings, and another a mysterious "rock gong".

There's more to Serengeti than the plains though, which cover only one third of the park. In the hilly centre, around **Seronera** – where a good deal of the park's accommodation is located, along with an excellent visitors' centre – a series of lightly wooded valleys provide excellent year-round game viewing, while in the **north**, along a 40km-wide corridor connecting with Kenya's Maasai Mara Game Reserve, rolling hills and thorny acacia woodland dominate. To the west, another corridor of land runs along the **Grumeti River** to within 8km of Lake Victoria. The river's flanking evergreen forests are another special habitat, providing a home for primates as well as lurking leopards, whilst the river itself and its swamps are as perfect for water birds as they are for crocodiles preying on thirsty wildlife, a sight as enthralling as it is gruesome when the migration is passing through.

**Wildlife**, of course, is why people come to Serengeti, and the figures are flabbergasting. Of the five million animals to be found during the migration (double the resident population) there are wildebeest, who numbered almost two million at the last count, gazelle, both Grant's and Thomson's, who are estimated at around half a million, and some three hundred thousand zebra. But even when the migration is up in Maasai Mara, or spread out across Ngorongoro and Loliondo, the park contains substantial populations of **plains game**, including buffalo, giraffe and warthog, and a wide range of antelopes, including dikdik, bushbuck, waterbuck and mountain reedbuck, eland and impala, and the rarer oryx and topi. Some two thousand elephants, too, are present, though they are largely migratory and can easily be missed.

But all this is to forget perhaps the most memorable of Serengeti's animals, its **predators**, who thrive off the regal banquet on offer. Indeed, apart from

▲ Lions lounging on a Serengeti *kopje*

Ngorongoro, Serengeti is probably the best place in Tanzania to see predators in action. Foremost are nearly eight thousand much-maligned spotted hyenas, which live in clans of up to eighty individuals. Also very visible are the park's three thousand or so lions, whose males have characteristic black manes. Other predators include cheetahs, which have been the subject of ongoing research since 1975, leopards and bat-eared foxes. Scavengers, apart from hyenas (which also hunt) include both golden and side-striped jackals and vultures. There are six species of vulture, representing a fraction of Serengeti's 520 **bird species** (including Eurasian winter migrants) – the country's second-highest count after Tarangire National Park. Keen birders can expect to see several hundred species in a two- or three-day safari, including many of the park's 34 raptors.

The **best time to visit** depends on a combination of weather and the extent of the migration. All things considered, June to July is probably the optimum time to visit. The Serengeti is at its busiest from December to February and, to a lesser extent, in July and August. Still, it's a big park, so you won't get anything like the congestion that beleaguers Ngorongoro. The driest months are June to October and mid-December to January or early February. The scattered **short rains** fall between November and December, while the **long rains** are from February or March to the end of May. The wildlife migration passes through Serengeti between December and July (see box, p.376).

## Arrival

Serengeti's eastern entrance, shared with Ngorongoro Conservation Area, is **Naabi Hill Gate**, 17km inside Serengeti, 45km southeast of Seronera Visitor Centre and approximately 300km from Arusha. The western entrance, 145km from Seronera, is **Ndabaka Gate**, next to the Mwanza–Musoma Highway. Two other, less used, gates are **Ikoma Gate** north of Seronera, and **Klein's Gate** in the northeast, which gives access to Loliondo and the wild road to Lake Natron (see p.386). You can't visit Serengeti in any meaningful way using public transport, though you can get a feel for the place on one of the roughly daily **buses** between Arusha and Musoma or Mwanza; you'll still have to stump up the entrance fee, though (and another $50 for Ngorongoro), so it's an expensive glimpse.

All this means that most visitors come on an organized safari from Arusha (pp.51–52) or Mwanza (p.402), whether by road or, for upmarket packages, by light aircraft, or in a rented 4WD.

**Renting a 4WD**, in Arusha, Karatu or Mwanza, gives you more flexibility than a standard safari, and works out pretty cheaply if you can fill all the seats. **Self-drive** is possible, although in theory this restricts your movements to the main roads through the park, so it's better to rent a vehicle with a driver (who usually doubles as a wildlife guide), or to hire an official guide at the park gate ($20 per day), pretty essential in any case given that Serengeti's roads aren't particularly well signposted. Fill up on **fuel** wherever you can, as supplies are limited and expensive. The cheapest fuel is at Seronera village in the centre. Much costlier, and sometimes reluctant to sell it except in emergencies, are the garages at *Lobo Wildlife Lodge*, *Serengeti Migration Camp*, *Serengeti Serena Safari Lodge* and *Serengeti Sopa Lodge*.

## Entry fees and information

**Park entry fees**, valid for 24 hours, are $50 per person and Tsh10,000 for a vehicle. Curiously, at Naabi Hill Gate they only accept MasterCard, while at

## Crossing the Kenyan border

The **Sand River border** crossing between the Serengeti and Kenya's Maasai Mara Game Reserve is only open to private vehicles, and – being unofficial – may leave you open to having to pay bribes on the other side: anything up to $50 in *chai* in addition to visa and nature reserve fees. Tanzanian immigration is at Seronera Visitor Centre; in Kenya, the nearest is in Narok. The closest **official border crossing** is at Sirari along the Mwanza–Kisumu road in the west; there's a rough road on the Kenyan side into Maasai Mara.

Ndabaka Gate it's Visa. For those on an organized safari this won't matter – your safari company will sort out the payment – but for those travelling by bus or independently it's important to have the correct card for the correct gate, so check before you get there. The park's **administrative headquarters** are just outside Ikoma Gate and of little use to tourists, but the park also maintains more useful offices behind the excellent **Seronera Visitor Centre** (see p.384). There's also tourist information at **Naabi Hill Gate**, which has a viewpoint over the plains, and an informative park office at *Lobo Wildlife Lodge*.

Maps and guidebooks can be bought at the park gates (if they're not out of stock), in Arusha, Dar and Stone Town (Zanzibar), or at the park's lodges. The best **guidebook** is the full-colour, pocketsize edition published in 2000 by TANAPA. Given that driving off the main routes is only allowed with a professional guide or driver-guide, finding a decent **map** isn't that important. As ever, a good bet is Giovanni Tombazzi's hand-painted version. For Seronera, the park publishes an A4 leaflet (available at the gates) containing a detailed map showing all the routes and road junction markers. There are lots of **internet sites** dedicated to Serengeti; the official one is ⓦ www.serengeti.org.

## Accommodation

There's plenty of accommodation both inside and outside the park, but the **luxury tented camps** and **lodges** inside the park are often fully booked months ahead, even for low season, despite their prohibitive prices. For most visitors, the choice just depends on how close you want to be to the wildlife migration (see box, p.376). When choosing, don't forget *Ndutu Safari Lodge* (p.370), in Ngorongoro right on the Serengeti border.

If you have at least three days to spare, it's best to stay in two **different places** to give you a better chance of getting close. But the most atmospheric (and nerve-jangling) way of spending a night is to camp.

### Camping

Apart from TANAPA's rest house, **camping** is the only cheap way to stay in Serengeti – $30 a person for a pitch in a public campsite, and $50 in a "special campsite". Outside the park, camping is possible off the Mwanza–Musoma Highway at *Serengeti Stop Over* and *Speke Bay Lodge*, neither charging more than $10.

The park's **public campsites** – one at Ndabaka Gate, another at Lobo in the north and the others in a tight cluster a few kilometres northeast of Seronera Visitor Centre – have water, toilets and showers (which don't always work). The **special campsites** are spread all over the park, have no facilities whatsoever, and need to be booked months if not years ahead through TANAPA in Arusha (see p.307), which can give details on locations. However, you may strike lucky if you enquire at the park gate on arrival.

## Luxury camping around the Serengeti

A handful of safari companies operate blindingly expensive **luxury tented camps** in and around the Serengeti, mainly on private concessions in neighbouring Loliondo. All offer walking safaris, game drives in open-topped vehicles, and optional fly-camping in small dome tents. The following companies are recommended if you have the money ($450–800 per person per day) and want a neo-colonial feel:

**Asilia Lodges & Camps** Ⓦwww.asilialodges.com for *Sayari Camp*.

**Kirurumu Tented Camps & Lodges** Ⓦwww.kirurumu.net for the mobile *Kirumuru Serengeti Camp*.

**Sanctuary Lodges and Camps** Ⓦwww.sanctuarylodges.com operates *Kusini Camp*.

Neither style of campsite is fenced, so wildlife comes and goes. As a result, Seronera's public campsites have become notorious for nocturnal visits by **lions**. Though the last attack on humans was in 1965, needless to say, take extreme care. The lions are generally just curious, so the rule is to stay calm and remain inside your tent. Similarly, take care with **baboons**, which are well used to people and quite capable of mauling you: don't tempt or tease them, and keep food in airtight containers.

Collecting **firewood** in the park is prohibited, so bring your own fuel for cooking. If you're staying at Seronera, you're permitted to drive along the shortest route to *Seronera Wildlife Lodge* in the evening for dinner, so long as you're back by 10pm (driving elsewhere is forbidden after 7pm).

### Inside the park

Wildlife and scenery vary greatly from one lodge and tented camp to the other, but don't believe the hype about the **migration** passing right under your nose. A rough indication of the best months for each of the following places is included, but as you'll have a vehicle, you can always catch up with the herds elsewhere. Room rates can drop by half in low season; the rates vary according to the lodge's location on the migratory route.

**Kirawira Tented Camp** Kirawira Hills, 100km west of Seronera (book through Serena Hotels, Diamond Trust Building, Arusha ☏027/253 9160, Ⓦwww.serenahotels.com). On a hilltop overlooking the savanna in the western corridor, this place will pamper you silly with its valets, luxurious double tents, plunge pool and refined cuisine. Massively overpriced, but ideally placed for catching the migration May–July. FB $1450. ❾

**Lobo Wildlife Lodge** Lobo Kopjes, 76km north of Seronera (book through Hotels & Lodges Ltd, 2nd floor (Block B), Summit Centre, Sokoine Rd, Arusha ☏027/254 4595, Ⓦwww.hotelsandlodges-tanzania .com). Built around the crest of a high kopje, this enjoys awesome views of a vast game-filled plain that receives a small part of the migration; there are also large resident lion prides nearby. Each of the 75 rooms has views, as does the swimming pool and its terrace. FB $460. ❾

**Serengeti Migration Camp** Ndassiata Hills, 80km north of Seronera (book through Elewana Afrika, 4th floor, Sopa Plaza, 99 Serengeti Rd, Arusha ☏027/250 0630–9, Ⓦwww.elewana .com). Built into a kopje overlooking the Grumeti River, this is a good location for wildlife. There are 21 super-luxurious tents, an open-sided bar, and small pool. A floodlit waterhole attracts wildlife including hippos. Like *Lobo* nearby, the rocky location doesn't favour disabled visitors. Closed April & May. FB $980. ❾

**Serengeti Serena Safari Lodge** Mbingwe Hill, 24km northwest of Seronera (book through Serena Hotels, AICC Ngorongoro, Room 605, Arusha ☏027/262 1507, Ⓦwww.serenahotels.com). Hidden behind acacia trees are the lodge's 23 two-storey, thatch-roofed rondavels. There's a pool, two rooms for disabled guests, and bush dinners for an extra $30. The migration passes April & May. FB $550. ❾

Serengeti Sopa Lodge Nyarboro Hills, 46km southwest of Seronera (book through Sopa Lodges, 4th floor, Sopa Plaza, 99 Serengeti Rd, Arusha ☎027/250 0630–9, ⓦwww.sopalodges.com). Occupying a ridge, this is an architectural blot, but things perk up considerably inside where warm ochre tones and chunky armchairs with big cushions dominate public areas. The 79 rooms are large and have balconies with sweeping views, and there's a pool on a panoramic terrace. Feb–June is the main migration time, especially April. HB $530. ❾

Seronera Wildlife Lodge Seronera (book through Hotels & Lodges Ltd, 2nd floor (Block B), Summit Centre, Sokoine Rd, Arusha ☎027/254 4595,

ⓦwww.hotelsandlodges-tanzania.com). This breezy place has aged well and still looks good, though the 75 rooms are a little basic. The best, and with better views, are at the back. The migration is in Seronera April–July. FB $460. ❾

TANAPA Rest House 1km from Seronera village and the Visitor Centre (bookings advisable: contact TANAPA in Arusha, p.307; pay at the park gate). This park-run place has three en-suite twin rooms, but lacks any "in the wild" feeling. Still, it benefits from the proximity of Seronera village, which has three *hotelis* dishing up cheap meals, bars and shops selling everything from chocolate to champagne. ❹

## Outside the park

Ikoma Bush Camp 3km outside Ikoma Gate (book through Moivaro Lodges & Tented Camps, north of AICC, Arusha ☎027/255 3243, ⓦwww.moivaro.com). In a great location on the edge of the western migratory routes (May–July & Nov–Jan), this place has sixteen large and comfortable en-suite tents in a relaxed and friendly atmosphere. The camp offers reasonably priced excursions on foot (outside the park) or by vehicle, and night game-drives ($20 per person). FB $450 ❾

Nyatwali Beach Lodge 4.5km north of the gate, then 4km west towards the lake ☎028/262 0534, ⓦwww.afrilux.net. Pleasant, quiet lodge and adjacent campsite ($7 per person) on the lakeshore, with an open-air bar and simple brick-and-thatch *bandas* lining a sandy beach. ❺

Serengeti Stop Over On the highway 2km south of Ndabaka Gate ☎028/262 2273 or 0784/422359,

ⓦwww.serengetistopover.com. A pleasant if largely shadeless place within walking distance of Lake Victoria (no swimming due to bilharzia). Ten small, clean *bandas* with two beds, big nets and bathrooms (good showers). Meals available ($4–10), but the main reason for staying is for its cultural tours including visits to a traditional healer ($20–100 per group) and fishing trips ($10). Camping $7. BB ❻

Speke Bay Lodge 13km south of Ndabaka Gate; the turning is 6km south of Lamadi ☎028/262 1236, ⓦwww.spekebay.com. On the lakeshore (no swimming due to bilharzia) on a lightly wooded plot with lots of birdlife, and great sunsets over the lake. Accommodation is either in tents without bathrooms and views, or in eight attractive bungalows on the shore. BB ❹–❻

# Eating and drinking

**Picnic lunches** are the norm. Lodges provide guests with "lunch boxes", either as part of a full-board package, or for an extra $10–20. For little more, it might

## Balloon safaris

From the ground, the wildebeest migration is a compelling phenomenon, bewildering and strangely disturbing, as you witness individual struggles and events. From the air, in a **hot-air balloon**, it resembles an ant's nest. At $499 for the sixty- to ninety-minute flight (including a champagne breakfast), **balloon safaris** are the ultimate in bush chic. The inflation and lift-off at dawn from the launch site either near *Seronera Wildlife Lodge* or in the Western Corridor is a spectacular sight, and the landing is often interesting, to say the least, as the basket may be dragged along before finally coming to rest.

You don't need to stay at the lodge to fly; they'll pick you up from any of the central lodges or campsites before dawn. There are only two balloons, one for twelve people the other for sixteen, so book in advance, whether through a lodge or safari company, or directly with Serengeti Balloon Safaris (ⓦwww.balloonsafaris.com).

▲ Hot-air ballooning, Serengeti National Park.

be better splashing out on an all-you-can-eat **buffet** at one of the lodges. With the best views, and use of their swimming pools included in the price, are *Lobo Wildlife Lodge* ($20) and *Serengeti Sopa Lodge* ($25). Cheap **local meals** (no more than Tsh2500) are cooked up at three *hotelis* in Seronera village.

## The park

Serengeti National Park has four main sectors: the Serengeti Plains and their kopjes; Seronera in the centre; the Western Corridor; and the north. Each warrants at least half a day, meaning that two or three days overall is recommended to see a bit of everything. Coming from the east, the road from

Ngorongoro Crater to central Serengeti is one long game drive in itself, passing through the heart of the **Serengeti Plains**. Scattered around the plains are a number of weathered granite outcrops called kopjes, which are miniature ecosystems, providing some shade, and limited water supplies in pools left in the rock after the rains.

Before starting a game drive, check the latest rules regarding **off-road driving** with the park authorities, because it is only allowed in certain areas (mainly the western edge of the plains). The rule when off the main roads is never to follow tracks left by other vehicles, as this hastens soil erosion. However, at the time of writing all off-road driving had been banned for environmental reasons following recurring droughts. **Restricted areas**, which require special permission to visit ($10), include Gol Kopjes in the east, which is a vital habitat for cheetah (whose hunting patterns are easily disturbed by safari vehicles), and sometimes Moru Kopjes.

### The Serengeti Plains

The undulating, semi-arid **Serengeti Plains** are the cornerstone of Serengeti's ecosystem. For a bird's-eye view, walk up the kopje behind **Naabi Hill Gate**; this viewpoint and picnic site is ideal for observing the **migration** (see box, p.376) between January and April, especially February and March, when literally hundreds of thousands of wildebeest, zebra and gazelle munch their way across the grasslands below. The popularity of the plains with wildlife appears to owe something to the alkaline nature of the soil, whose volcanic ash was laid down during the eruptions of Ngorongoro's Crater Highlands, and is therefore rich in **minerals** – something accentuated by the annual cycle of rain and evaporation, which sucks minerals to the surface. The main ones are calcium, potassium carbonate and sodium carbonate, which recent studies have shown are an essential component of many animals' diets, especially when lactating, and which explains why eighty percent of Serengeti's wildebeest give birth on these plains.

Even when the migration moves out of the area, and the plains turn into a dry and dusty shimmer of straw, there's still plenty of resident **wildlife** around, including lion prides, unusually large clans of hyenas (up to eighty strong), plus hartebeest, topi, warthog and ostrich. **Birdlife** is richest during the rains; through you'll see secretary birds and kori bustards throughout the year. Another bird worth looking for is the **black-throated honey guide**, which has a remarkable symbiotic relationship with the ratel (honey badger). The honey guide, as its name suggests, leads the ratel to wild beehives in trees, which the ratel – seemingly immune to the stings – pulls down and breaks open. The ratel eats the honey, and the honey guide treats itself to beeswax.

### Moru Kopjes

The flat plains are broken in several places by isolated and much-eroded granite "islands" called **kopjes**. Also known as inselbergs ("island hills"), the kopjes were created millions of years ago when volcanic bubbles broached the surface and solidified, and were subsequently eroded by rains and floods, carving out the singularly beautiful and sensuous forms you see today. Rainwater run-off from the kopjes and permanent water pools caught in rocky clefts make them particularly good for spotting wildlife in the dry season, when **lions** like to lie in wait for other animals coming to feed or drink – for this reason, take care when walking around kopjes.

Humans, too, have long been attracted to kopjes, both hunter-gatherers such as the Dorobo, who were evicted in 1955, and seasonal "migrants" such as

Maasai cattle herders. The Maasai, evicted in 1959, left their mark – literally – in a rock shelter on one of the **Moru Kopjes** 32km south of Seronera. Here, a natural rock shelter is daubed with **rock paintings** (in red, white and black) of Maasai shields identical to ceremonial shields still used today. The paintings, accompanied by drawings of elephants and less distinct animal and human forms, were left by young Maasai warriors (*morani*) for whom the site was the location of an *orpul* meat-feasting – as you can tell from soot lining the shelter's ceiling. According to Maasai custom, junior warriors were prohibited from eating meat, at least in public, so they'd steal a cow and bring it here. As with all rock art, the paintings are perishable (see p.236).

Another thoroughly enigmatic kopje, 1km away, contains **rock gongs**, which are an ensemble of three loose boulders. One in particular – a large lemon-shaped wedge – bears dozens of circular depressions, created by people repeatedly striking the rock with stones to produce weirdly reverbative and metallic sounds (the sound differs depending where you strike the rock). Although rock gongs are nowadays played only by tourists, the wedge-shaped one was certainly used as a instrument way before the Maasai arrived a couple of centuries ago (they lack any musical tradition involving percussive instruments) and similar gong rocks have been found as far south as Zimbabwe. However, as little is known of the now vanished hunter-gatherers who presumably made and used the gongs, their exact age and purpose remain a mystery. Incidentally, time spent poking around the boulders may turn up a surprise – in 1992, a species of **tree frog** hitherto unknown to science was discovered in one of the rock gong's depressions.

### Seronera

The central part of Serengeti is **Seronera**, which comprises the wooded valleys and savanna of the Grumeti River's main tributaries. There are a large number of drivable circuits in the area, which your driver or guide should know well, and the wildlife is representative of most of Serengeti's species. For many, the highlight is Seronera's famous **black-maned lions** – the cause of many sleepless nights at the campsites. **Leopards** also abound, though you'll need a dash of luck, as they chill out by day in the leafy branches of yellow-barked acacias close to the rivers. The migration usually moves up to Seronera from the plains in April, before continuing on north and west.

A great place to head for after an early-morning game drive is **Seronera Visitor Centre** (daily 8am–4.30pm; ☎028/262 1515), close to Seronera village, the public campsites and *Seronera Wildlife Lodge*. This brilliantly designed centre is a real pleasure, combining permanent exhibits, displays and wildlife video screenings at lunchtime (if the generator's working), with a humorous **information trail** around a nearby kopje. There's also a shop with drinks and snacks and a picnic site where semi-tame rock hyraxes and birds, including hoopoes and adorable Fischer's lovebirds, eye up your lunch. The centre's gift shop should have a booklet containing the information presented on the trail, and also a leaflet with a map and detailed descriptions of the various game drives around Seronera. The staff can usually fill you in on recent predator sightings and road conditions, and a number of park wardens are also based here for more detailed queries.

A quick rundown of the **main trails** follows. Most have numbered road junctions corresponding to those on the leaflet. The **Seronera River Circuit** (junctions 1–26) starts at Seronera Hippo Pool and follows the river, and offers sightings of lions, leopards, crocodiles and waterbuck, as well as hippos, giraffes, vervet monkeys, baboons and many birds. The circuit can be combined with the **Kopjes Circuit** (junctions 52–62; enter at junction 18 on the east bank of the Seronera River), which goes anti-clockwise around Maasai, Loliondo and Boma Kopjes. Climbing on the rocks is forbidden. **The Hills Circuit** (junctions 27–29) cuts through grassland to the wooded foothills of the Makori and Makoma Hills west of the Seronera Valley, and is good for hyena, zebra, ostrich, warthog, gazelle, topi and hartebeest. A drive along this circuit is best combined with the **Songore River Circuit** (junctions 30–34), which loops into the plains south of the Seronera River. Thomson and Grant's gazelle, topi, hartebeest and ostrich are frequent, as are cheetah during the dry season. Lastly, the **Wandamu River Circuit** (junctions 40–49) covers similar habitats to the Seronera River Circuit, and hugs the banks of the Wandamu River, especially popular with buffaloes.

### The Western Corridor

The **Western Corridor** is the unlovely name given to the forty-kilometre-wide strip that reaches out from Seronera to within 8km of Lake Victoria. The forests and swamps of the **Grumeti River** mark the northern boundary, while to the south is an area of grassland flanked by low wooded hills. The area receives the annual migration between May and July, after which time the bulk of the herds head on north over the Grumeti River towards Maasai Mara. This is the best time to visit the area, especially if the river is in flood, when the crossing is extremely perilous. At first hesitant, the herds surge headlong with a lemming-like instinct into the raging waters, while crocodiles and lions lie in wait for those injured in the effort, too weak for the strong currents or who get stuck in the muddy quagmire at the river's edges. You can find the crossings just by looking for vultures circling overhead.

A small part of the migration forgoes the pleasures of the river crossing to stay behind in the grasslands in the western part of the corridor, which also contains substantial populations of **non-migratory animals**, including some wildebeest and zebra, and smaller populations of giraffe and buffalo, hartebeest, waterbuck, eland, topi, impala and Thomson's gazelle. Hippo are present in large numbers, and in the dry season can always be seen at **Retima Hippo Pool**, 20km north of Seronera. Given the abundance of food, predators flourish, too, **leopards** in the lush tangled forests and thickets beside the river, and **crocodiles** – especially around Kirawira in the west – for whom the migration's river crossing provides a Bacchanalian feast. A speciality of the forest is a population of **black–and–white colobus monkeys**, though you'll need time and patience to track them down. The forests are also rich in **birdlife**, especially during the European winter. With luck, you might see the rare olive-green bulbul.

### Northern Serengeti

The patches of acacia woodland at Seronera begin to dominate the rolling hills of northern Serengeti. The area contains at least 28 acacia species, each adapted to a particular ecological niche, and the change in species is often startlingly abrupt, with one completely replacing another within a distance of sometimes only a few dozen metres. The undulating nature of the landscape makes it easy to spot animals from a distance and, further north, especially around **Lobo Kopjes**, higher ground provides fantastic views of the migration in the grasslands to the east (the best months are July–September when it heads north, and November and December when it turns back). Elephant, buffalo, zebra, gazelle and warthog can be seen all year.

There's a game-drive circuit to the east of *Lobo Wildlife Lodge*, whose waterholes attract a variety of wildlife, although the natural spring mentioned on older maps has now been capped by a pump.

# Loliondo

Located outside the Serengeti's northeastern boundary, and hemmed in by Ngorongoro, Lake Natron and the Kenyan border, is **Loliondo**, a wild and little-visited region. Nowadays the area is offered by a handful of mainly upmarket safari companies (see box, p.380) as a venue for off-the-beaten-track wildlife trips. Loliondo will also appeal to lovers of wild and desolate landscapes – the drive across Loliondo, from Serengeti's Klein's Gate to Lake Natron (see p.361), is spectacular and, in places, hair-raising (especially the hairpins down Nguruman Escarpment in the east). It's also potentially dangerous, thanks to past incidents involving **armed bandits**.

Yet for all its aridity and wild frontier feeling, Loliondo is also a subtly beautiful land, even in the dry season, when – if you look carefully – even the leafless trees and bushes are full of colour, from the blue or yellow bark of some acacias, through violet and rusty orange bushes, and the mauve and green of thorn trees.

The area is especially good for **wildlife** in November and December when a good part of the annual migration heads back down from Maasai Mara – as a consequence, trophy hunters have long favoured Loliondo.

### Klein's Gate to Wasso

There's no reliable public transport to or within Loliondo, so other than buying a safari, you'll need your own 4WD, an experienced local driver and plenty of petrol and water. A decent map would be helpful, too. Note that the western section of the route, between Klein's Gate and Wasso, goes across patches of **black cotton soil**, which can make it impassable in the rains, while the zigzagging road down the Nguruman Escarpment in the east sometimes loses entire sections of road.

Leaving Klein's Gate, the road heads southeast towards Wasso, 70km away, passing through impressively craggy hills, heavily wooded save for clearings made by Maasai for their cattle and limited agriculture. The road is easy to follow for the most part, although there are some confusing forks: just keep asking for Wasso. Along the way you pass many Maasai who, unlike their cousins in Ngorongoro, are not accustomed to tourists, so make a point of always obtaining (or paying for) permission before taking photos.

**Wasso**, about two hours from Klein's Gate, is the first major settlement. A government building on the left with a flag, and a transmitter on the right, marks the entrance. There's a small river crossing beyond here, then a junction. Bear left for Loliondo village, or turn right into Wasso itself and the road to Lake Natron and Ngorongoro Conservation Area. Wasso Hospital has three **guest rooms** (BB ❸), and there's a campsite in the village.

### Loliondo village

Before the sealed road from Kenya to Tanzania via Namanga was built, Loliondo was a major stop on the Great North Road from Nairobi to Arusha, which ultimately went on to Cape Town in South Africa. The sight of **Loliondo village**, about 6km northeast of Wasso, is probably the biggest surprise you'll have in the region. Amidst such desolate terrain, the village is an oasis of lush vegetation, and its high altitude gives it a pleasantly breezy and cool climate, which can be quite nippy at night. A handful of Europeans settled here early on, and the village still has an old colonial feeling to it, both in the style of its buildings, and the wide main road which some thoughtful soul long ago planted with beautiful purple-flowered jacaranda trees. There's a post office, a branch of NMB bank, fuel and a **campsite**: ask for *Simon Kamakia's Oloolera Maasai Campsite* (☎0786562617; $15, or $30 if you borrow a tent – which needs to be booked in advance).

### Wasso to Sonjo

Entering Wasso from the west (Serengeti), turn right after the river crossing, where a decently graded road heads south. If you're on the right road, you'll pass the entrance to Wasso airfield on your right after 2km. Bear left at any road fork, and continue for another 13km (15km from Wasso), where the road forks again. The right fork heads on down to Ngorongoro Conservation Area, while the left one continues south/southeast for 8km before turning east into a valley. Follow this until the road turns south again (there's a beautiful viewpoint near the top).

    **Sonjo village**, a large cluster of round thatched huts in the lee of an escarpment, is 5km south of the viewpoint, and the main settlement of the agricultural **Sonjo tribe**. The Sonjo, who supplement their subsistence agriculture by hunting, may be one of the peoples responsible for having constructed the now-ruined villages and intricate irrigation complex at Engaruka, 100km to the south (see p.357), and have similar stone bases for building houses on. They settled in their present location at least three hundred years ago, but their more distant origins remain unknown, and academics can't agree on whether their language – quite distinct from Maasai – is Bantu or Cushitic, though it's probably a bit of both. There's no accommodation, and you'll need to obtain permission before taking pictures.

### Sonjo to Lake Natron

From the north side of Sonjo village, the road veers east once more, starting a long, straight and very dusty drive due east to the edge of the Nguruman Escarpment. The low craggy mountain that gradually appears to the southeast is **Mount Mosonik**, rising on the southwestern side of Lake Natron. Beyond its peaks is the distinctive pyramidal mass of Ol Doinyo Lengai. The road is extremely sandy in places, and a 4WD is helpful even in dry weather. Along the way, there are fantastic candelabra euphorbia trees to admire, as well as bizarre giant aloe, which resemble palm trees with upturned fronds. With luck, you'll also see ostrich.

    At the edge of the escarpment, the road – now a narrow rocky trail barely wider than a 4WD – twists down a frightening stretch known as **Seventeen Corners**. Some sections get washed away in the rains, so check on the road's condition at the army post before Sonjo (or at Engaresero if you're coming from the lake). Once down, the road heads south across a weird and extremely beautiful moonscape pitted with craters and gullies, before skirting the lake to arrive at Engaresero, an hour's drive from Seventeen Corners. Engaresero, and the route from Mto wa Mbu to Lake Natron, are covered on pp.357–362.

# Travel details

## Buses

**Engaruka** to: Arusha (1 daily; 4–5hr); Mto wa Mbu (1 daily; 2hr).

**Mto wa Mbu** to: Arusha (3–4 daily plus daladalas; 2hr 30min–3hr); Engaruka (1 daily; 2hr).

**Karatu** to: Arusha (3 daily; 4hr); Dar (2 daily; 13hr); Moshi (3 daily; 5hr 30min).

**Kigongoni** to: Arusha (4 daily; 2hr); Babati (4 daily; 2–3hr); Singida (3–4 daily; 6–7hr).

## Flights

Airline codes used below are: AE (Air Excel), CA (Coastal Aviation), RA (Regional Air) and ZA (ZanAir). Where more than one airline flies to the same destination, the one with most frequent flights and/ or shortest journey times is listed first. Most flights to Serengeti land at both Seronera in the centre and Grumeti in the west; some also go to Klein's Gate in the north, or to Serengeti South.

**Manyara** to: Arusha (AE, RA, CA: 5 daily; 20–25min); Dar (AE: daily; 2hr 45min); Kilimanjaro (RA: daily; 45min); Mwanza (CA: daily; 2hr 45min); Ruaha (CA: 3 weekly; 3hr); Selous (CA: 3 weekly; 4hr 35min); Serengeti (AE, RA, CA: 5 daily; 30min–1hr 30min); Zanzibar (AE: daily; 2hr 10min).

**Ngorongoro** to: Arusha (CA: daily; 1hr); Mwanza (CA: daily; 2hr 15min); Serengeti (CA: daily; 1hr).

**Serengeti** to: Arusha (AE, RA, ZA, CA: 6 daily; 1hr 5min–2hr 20min); Dar (AE, ZA: 2 daily; 3hr 30min–5hr 20min); Kilimanjaro (RA: daily; 1hr 35min–2hr 15min); Manyara (AE, RA, CA: 5 daily; 30min–2hr); Mwanza (CA: daily; 1–2hr); Pemba (ZA: daily; 4hr); Rubondo (CA: 2 weekly; 2–3hr); Selous (CA: daily; 5hr); Zanzibar (ZA, AE, CA: 3 daily; 3–4hr).

# 8

# Lake Victoria and northwestern Tanzania

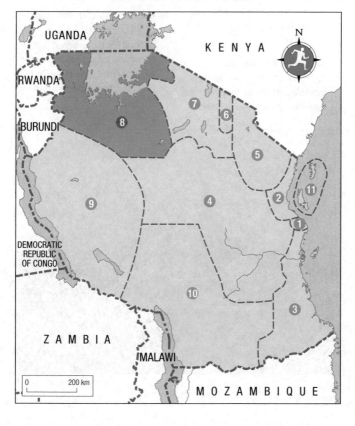

UGANDA

KENYA

N

RWANDA

BURUNDI

7

6

8

5

9

4

2

11

1

DEMOCRATIC
REPUBLIC
OF CONGO

10

3

ZAMBIA

MALAWI

0    200 km

MOZAMBIQUE

# CHAPTER 8

# Highlights

* **Lake Victoria** The world's second-largest freshwater lake is also the fabled source of the Nile, an enigma that baffled Europeans until Speke stumbled upon it in 1858. See p.398

* **Sukuma Village Museum** At Bujora near Mwanza, a great place for getting to know the Sukuma, Tanzania's largest tribe, and seeing their annual dance competitions. See p.403

* **Ukerewe and Ukara** Long-inhabited and heavily agricultural, these lake islands are way off the beaten track, and ideal for getting a feel for an existence largely untouched by the twenty-first century. See p.404

* **Bukoba** A pleasant port town connected to Mwanza by ferry and by road to Uganda and Rwanda. A lovely beach, laid-back feel and lots of cultural activities are the reasons to linger. See p.412

* **Rubondo Island** Sitting in the lake's southwestern corner, its difficult (or expensive) access is compensated for by a host of endangered animals and breeding bird colonies. See p.419

▲ Bismarck Rock, Lake Victoria

# Lake Victoria and northwestern Tanzania

D
ominating Tanzania's northwest is **Lake Victoria** (Lake Nyanza), which fills a shallow depression between the Western and Eastern Rift Valleys. Covering an area of 69,484 square kilometres, and with a shoreline of 3220km, the lake is Africa's largest, and the world's second-largest freshwater lake. It's also the river Nile's primary source, providing it with a steady, year-round flow.

The lake region is densely inhabited by farmers and cattle herders, and also by people living in the major cities on its shores, including Kampala and Jinja in Uganda, Kisumu in Kenya, and **Mwanza**, **Bukoba** and **Musoma** on the Tanzanian side. Bukoba is a great base for exploring the previously virtually inaccessible northern reaches of Kagera Region bordering Uganda and Rwanda. Several islands also warrant exploration, notably **Ukerewe** and **Ukara** between Mwanza and Musoma, and **Rubondo Island** in the lake's southwest corner – its diverse birdlife includes elephants, chimpanzees and sitatunga antelopes and it is protected as a national park.

The most enjoyable way of getting to, and around the region is on one of Lake Victoria's **ferries** (from Mwanza to Bukoba or Ukerewe Island), or by train from Dar and Tabora. But whilst the region's trunk roads have improved massively, cutting driving times from Arusha to under a day, unsurfaced roads can still become impassable during heavy rains, and getting off the beaten track by public transport can be an interesting experience to say the least, one that's definitely not recommended for those with old bones or claustrophobia: daladalas and buses really pack 'em in. Renting a car is of course another option; see p.29 for more information.

Whichever way you travel, you will need plenty of **time**, as connections aren't guaranteed. But then, getting stranded in the back of beyond is all part of the fun.

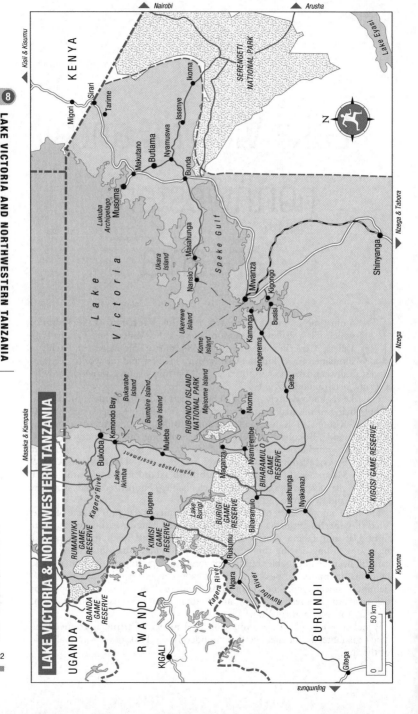

## LAKE VICTORIA & NORTHWESTERN TANZANIA

▲ *Nairobi*

▲ *Arusha*

◄ *Kisii & Kisumu*

◄ *Masaka & Kampala*

► *Nzega & Tabora*

► *Nzega*

► *Kigoma*

► *Buvumbura*

*Lake Eyasi*

N

**KENYA**

**UGANDA**

**RWANDA**

**BURUNDI**

KIGALI

GITEGA

*SERENGETI
NATIONAL PARK*

Nairobi

Arusha

Migori

Sirari

Tarime

Ikoma

Issenye

Nyamuswa

Makutano

Butiama

Bunda

Musoma

*Lukuba
Archipelago*

Masahunga

*Ukara
Island*

Nansio

*Speke Gulf*

Mwanza

Kigongo

Busisi

*L a k e

V i c t o r i a*

*Ukerewe
Island*

Kamanga

Sengerema

Shinyanga

*Kome
Island*

Geita

Nkome

*Maisome Island*

*RUBONDO ISLAND
NATIONAL PARK*

*Bukarabe
Island*

*Bumbire Island*

*Iroba Island*

Mueba

Kemondo Bay

Bukoba

*Lake
Ikimba*

*Kagera River*

*Nyamilyango Escarpment*

Maganza

Nyamirembe

*BIHARAMULO
GAME
RESERVE*

Lusahunga

Nyakanazi

Biharamulo

Kibondo

*KIGOSI GAME RESERVE*

Bugene

*Lake
Burigi*

*BURIGI
GAME
RESERVE*

Rusumo

*RUMANYIKA
GAME
RESERVE*

*KIMISI
GAME
RESERVE*

*IBANDA
GAME
RESERVE*

Ngara

*Kagera River*

*Ruvubu River*

50 km

0

Just over a century ago, Lake Victoria contained one of the richest freshwater ecosystems on earth, with an estimated five hundred species of fish, including many brilliantly coloured cichlids. Today, only two hundred remain, the rest having vanished in the biggest mass extinction of vertebrates since the demise of the dinosaurs, while the lake itself is being systematically polluted, starved of oxygen and invaded by water hyacinth – all of which offers a bleak prospect for the thirty million people who depend on it for survival.

The alarming collapse of Lake Victoria's ecosystem can be traced back to the arrival of the railways in colonial times and the subsequent development of lakeside cities, such as Mwanza (Tanzania), Kisumu (Kenya) and Kampala (Uganda), which began to place unsustainable pressure on the lake's resources. The Europeans also started commercial fishing, which rapidly depleted traditional fish stocks; by the 1950s, catches of the two main edible species of tilapia fish had fallen to uneconomic levels. In a bid to find an alternative, moves were made to introduce non-native **Nile perch** (*mbuta*) into the lake. It was hoped that its size (up to 250kg) and carnivorous habits would convert smaller and commercially worthless cichlid species into profitable dinner-table protein. Scientists, who correctly predicted ecological disaster, fiercely opposed the proposal. Nonetheless, Nile perch found their way into the lake, having either been surreptitiously introduced, or having swum in along the Victoria Nile from Lake Kyoga in central Uganda. From a commercial point of view, the arrival of Nile perch in the lake was an enormous success, and catches spiralled, fuelling a lucrative export trade to Europe and Asia. Ecologically, however, the Nile perch was an unmitigated disaster: by the 1970s, Lake Victoria's cichlid populations, which had previously constituted eighty percent of the lake's fish, had fallen to under five percent (they're now estimated at just one percent). The Nile perch were quite literally eating their way through the lake's native species.

Sadly, the Nile perch are only part of the problem: **pollution** on a massive scale is the major cause of the lake's oxygen depletion. The British and Germans were keen to use the lake's fertile hinterland for commercial plantations, and set about clearing vast areas of forests and other natural vegetation. With no permanent cover, soil erosion became an acute problem, as shown today in the sludge-brown colour of many of the region's rivers. In addition, the drainage of lakeside swamps (which are natural filters of silt and sediment) removed the barrier between the lake and the rain-carried chemical residues from farms (especially pesticides and fertilizers) and gold mines, whose slurry is poisoned by mercury and other heavy metals. Add to this vast quantities of untreated effluent from the lakeside cities (Mwanza alone discharges an estimated 65 million litres of sewage into the lake every day) and you have some idea of the scale of the problem.

The resulting unnaturally high levels of nutrients in the lake water, especially nitrates, has caused the proliferation of algae near the lake's surface and the acidification of the water, which in turn has provided an ideal habitat for another unwanted species, **water hyacinth**. This pernicious (albeit beautiful) floating weed is native to South America, and was introduced to Africa as an ornamental pond species. Apart from hindering shipping, the blanket of weed cuts off sunlight to the water beneath, creating stagnant areas and leading directly to an increased incidence of diseases such as cholera, malaria and bilharzia. The weeds also deplete oxygen levels, which has much the same effect on cichlid populations as the jaws of the Nile perch.

Now, the vicious cycle of destruction appears to have turned full circle: Nile perch stocks are dwindling for want of food – unbelievable for a lake that, at its height, produced half a million tons of fish a year. The whole sorry mess features as the subject of the documentary *Darwin's Nightmare* (ⓦwww.coop99.at/darwins-nightmare), by Austrian director Hubert Sauper, which parallels the lake's ecological catastrophe with the dire social consequences of globalisation in Mwanza.

# Mwanza Region

**Mwanza Region**, on the south side of Lake Victoria, is dominated by the port city of **Mwanza**. The region, much of it undulating plains scattered with large granite outcrops called kopjes, is home to the **Sukuma**, cattle herders by tradition, though many are now subsistence farmers. Mwanza is a handy base for a number of nearby attractions, including the **Sukuma Museum** and the islands of **Ukerewe** and **Ukara**, and also serves as a potential base for visiting Serengeti National Park, whose western border is barely 5km from the lakeshore.

# Mwanza

Located on Mwanza Gulf on the southeast shore of Lake Victoria, the scruffy and weather-beaten but lively and friendly city of **MWANZA** is Tanzania's second-largest metropolis, one of Africa's fastest-growing cities (twelve percent a year), and the country's busiest inland port, handling most of Tanzania's trade with Uganda.

The city was founded in 1892 as a cotton-trading centre, but cotton has declined in importance as a result of low world prices, erratic rains and mismanagement. Now fishing, trade, some light industry, and particularly receipts, legitimate or otherwise, from the region's **gold and diamond mines** have stepped in to fill some of the economic gap. Mwanza's inhabitants, many of them economic migrants, now number around one and a half million, seventy to eighty percent of whom live in insalubrious slums on and around the hills on the city's outskirts. The pace of population growth has now far outstripped the development of the city's infrastructure, much of which is in a pitiful state, where it exists at all. For many, the main source of protein is "punky" – fishbone waste sold off by fish-processing factories. Still, things are looking up: the city's streets, notorious for having more holes than asphalt, have finally been patched up and even expanded, and the location – sitting among rolling lakeside hills with great views – is handsome indeed.

## Arrival and information

Mwanza has good **transport connections** by road, plane and ferry to Bukoba and by train to Tabora and Dar, and, indirectly, to Kigoma. Most buses terminate at the **Buzuruga bus stand** 5km east of the centre. There are plenty of daladalas from here to the daladala stand in the centre (Tsh300). Some of the better companies have their offices nearer to the centre, such as Akamba, under *Majukano Hotel* at the west end of Liberty Street.

If you're **driving from the west**, you'll have to catch a ferry across Mwanza Gulf. The quickest route is the northern crossing from Kamanga to the city centre (Mon–Sat from 8am until 6pm, Sun until 5pm; every hour or so; Tsh3500 for a car with driver, plus Tsh800 for each passenger; 30 min). There's another roll-on roll-off ferry from Busisi to Kigongo further to the south (daily from 8am until 9pm; every hour or two; same prices), although this leaves you with a 30km drive into the city once you're across. Arriving at night, vehicles are supposed to travel in convoy, with armed policemen at the front and rear, to deter bandits.

Most **ferries** dock at the ferry port in the city centre. The exceptions are the Kamanga ferry, which arrives just to the south, and the MV *Airbus* from Ukerewe, which ties up at Kirumba Mwaloni 3km north along Makongoro Road. Despite the welter of people and hawkers that greet ferry passengers, there's not much hassle, but keep an eye on your bags.

**Mwanza Airport** lies 8km northeast of the centre. Daladalas into town cost a few hundred shillings. The normal taxi fare is Tsh7000–10,000, but drivers will try it on for more.

Mwanza is the terminus of the **Central Railway Line**'s northern branch, served by three trains a week from Dar (a fascinating if exhausting 37hr ride) via Dodoma, Tabora and Shinyanga. The station is 500m south of the centre on Station Road, and within walking distance of most hotels, although you could always catch a taxi.

The city centre is small enough to walk around. **Taxis** can be found everywhere: a short ride costs Tsh1500–2000, though tourists may be overcharged. A comprehensive source of **tourist information** is ⓦwww.mwanza-guide.com. Tap water needs purifying for drinking.

## Accommodation

There's lots of central accommodation in all price ranges, and most hotels will let couples share a single room.

### Budget

**Deluxe Hotel** Uhuru St/Kishamapanda St ☏028/254 0543. A welcoming four-storey place with bright and breezy rooms, especially higher up. The mattresses are sagging, but otherwise the rooms – all en suite with large box nets and writing tables – are pretty good value. There's also a bar and restaurant. ❶

**Kishamapanda Guest House** Uhuru St/Kishamapanda St ☏0755/083218. The entrance – shared with the *New Geita* – is through a bar. There are eight clean rooms, all with fans; the cheaper ones share bathrooms. It's best to skip the food, since the kitchen is none too salubrious. ❶

**Lake Hotel** Station Rd ☏028/250 0658. A funny old place near the train station where rooms are accessed through a dark and sprawling bar that is popular with elderly gents. There are 48 en-suite rooms (singles, twins and triples), and they're

pretty simple but good value if you don't mind the noise (upstairs rooms are quieter). Food is available in the bar. ❷

**New Binza C Guest House** Uhuru St (no phone). Good, cheap and basic with clean rooms (shared bathrooms only). Located in the thick of a busy local area with plenty of cheap restaurants and food stalls nearby. ❶

**New Geita Lodging** Uhuru St/Kishamapanda St ☏028/254 0033. Sharing its dissolute entrance and kitchen with the *Kishamapanda*, the twenty rooms here (some of which are en suite) are quite decent – all tiled, and with large double beds, TV, ceiling fan, net, and fine squat toilets. Breezier rooms are upstairs. ❶

### Mid-range

All of the following include breakfast in their rates.

**Aspen Hotel** Uhuru St ☏028/250 0988. A large, modern place with well-appointed en-suite rooms

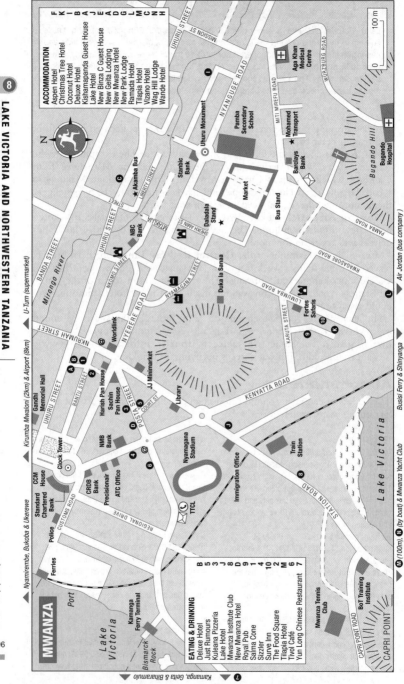

# MWANZA

**LAKE VICTORIA AND NORTHWESTERN TANZANIA**

8

www.roughguides.com

396

*Lake Victoria*

*Port*

Kamanga Ferry Terminal

Bismarck Rock

Ferries

Police

Standard Chartered Bank

CCM House

Clock Tower

Customs Road

Regional Drive

TTCL

Immigration Office

Nyamagana Stadium

Precisionair

ATO Office

CRDB Bank

NMB Bank

Library

Nyerere Road

JJ Minimarket

Harish Pan House

Sachin Pan House

POSTA STREET

COURT ST

Bantu Street

Uhuru Street

Nkrumah Street

Worldlink

Nyamagana Street

Duka la Sanaa

NBC Bank

Mtakuja Street

Liberty Street

Momo Street

Banda Street

Mirongo River

Gandhi Memorial Hall

Uhuru Street

Akamba Bus

Uhuru Monument

Uhuru Street

Pamba Secondary School

NYANGUGE ROAD

MISSION 1ST

UHURU STREET

UHURU STREET

SHEIKH AMIN ROAD

Daladala Stand

Market

Bus Stand

Stanbic Bank

Barclays Bank

Mohamed Transport

Aga Khan Medical Centre

MITI MIREFU ROAD

WURZBURG ROAD

*Bugando Hill*

Bugando Hospital

PAMBA ROAD

RWAGASORE ROAD

LUMUMBA ROAD

KARUTA STREET

Fortes Safaris

KENYATTA ROAD

*Lake Victoria*

Train Station

STATION ROAD

CAPRI POINT ROAD

BoT Training Institute

Mwanza Tennis Club

CAPRI POINT

Kapri Point

Train Station

### ACCOMMODATION
| | |
|---|---|
| Aspen Hotel | F |
| Christmas Tree Hotel | K |
| Coconut Hotel | I |
| Deluxe Hotel | B |
| Kishamapanda Guest House | A |
| Lake Hotel | J |
| New Binza C Guest House | E |
| New Geita Lodging | A |
| New Mwanza Hotel | D |
| New Park Lodge | G |
| Ramada Hotel | L |
| Tilapia Hotel | M |
| Vizano Hotel | C |
| Wag Hill Lodge | N |
| Wande Hotel | H |

### EATING & DRINKING
| | |
|---|---|
| Deluxe Hotel | B |
| Just Rumours | 5 |
| Kuleana Pizzeria | 3 |
| Lake Hotel | J |
| Mwanza Institute Club | 8 |
| New Mwanza Hotel | D |
| Royal Pub | 9 |
| Salma Cone | 1 |
| Sizzler | 4 |
| Surve Inn | 2 |
| The Food Square | M |
| Tilapia Hotel | 6 |
| Tivol Café | — |
| Yun Long Chinese Restaurant | 7 |

▲ *Nyamirembe, Bukoba & Ukerewe*

▲ *Kirumba Mwaloni (2km) & Airport (8km)*

▲ *U-Turn (supermarket)*

▲ *Buzuruga bus stand (5km), Bujora & Musoma*

▲ **E, F, G & H**

▲ *Buzuruga bus stand*

▲ *Kamanga, Geita & Biharamulo*

▲ *Air Jordan (bus company)*

▲ *Busisi Ferry & Shinyanga*

▲ *(100m), (by boat) & Mwanza Yacht Club*

N 0 100 m

(doubles or twins), all with cable TV, phones, fans, nets and cotton sheets, most with balconies. Safe parking. ❸

**Christmas Tree Hotel** Off Karuta St ☎&🖷 028/250 2001. All 27 rooms have cable TV, phone, fan, double bed and well-kept bathroom. A handful of rooms (the best are on the third floor) have great views of the inlet and Saa Nane Island. There's also a bar. Good value and often full. ❸

**Coconut Hotel** Liberty St ☎ 028/254 2373, 🌐 www.coconuthotel-tz.com. A clean-ish, modern-ish choice overlooking the filthy Mirongo River. All rooms are en suite with TV, fan, carpet and reliable hot water. There's a stuffy restaurant downstairs, and a nicely breezy bar (also with food) on the first- and second-floor terraces. No single rates. ❸

**New Park Lodge** Uhuru St ☎ 028/250 0265. Spotless en-suite "singles" (that can be shared by couples) with huge double beds, box nets, fan and cable TV, and some have bathtubs as well as showers. The best rooms – with views over town – are on top. There's also a bar and restaurant. ❷

**Ramada Hotel** Rwagasore St ☎ 028/254 0223. Good and secure, despite the noisy location, this place has bright and breezy rooms, some with views over the bay, others with balconies. All the rooms have TVs, phones, big beds and fans but no nets (rooms are sprayed). There's a nice restaurant and bar, too. ❷

**Vizano Hotel** Uhuru St ☎ 028/254 1790, 📧 vizanohotel@yahoo.com. Smart hotel, in a bustling part of town, with facility-packed rooms including hot water, telephone, a/c and satellite TV, while the suites also boast internet access. Friendly and good value. ❹

**Wande Hotel** Off Uhuru St ☎ 028/250 3373. This friendly place has en-suite rooms with TV, fridge and fan; singles have huge beds, doubles have two beds and are a bit dark. Food and drink are available. Safe parking. ❷–❸

## Expensive

The following include breakfast in their rates.

**New Mwanza Hotel** Posta Rd ☎ 028/250 1070, 🌐 www.newmwanzahotel.com. A rather soulless, but perfectly adequate, "international" class hotel with 54 en-suite rooms (double or twin), all with minibar, phone, a/c and satellite TV. Facilities include a swimming pool, room service, 24hr coffee shop, bar and restaurant, internet, health club and a casino. ❻

**Tilapia Hotel** Capri Point ☎ 028/250 0517, 🌐 www.hoteltilapia.com. A posh bayside place that's been popular with expats and package tourists for years (hence the upmarket hookers in the bar). Rooms have cable TV, phone, big bed(s), fan, a/c, minibar, safe, and internet access; the better ones have lake views. The more atmospheric rooms are on a houseboat called the *African Queen* and suites have fully equipped kitchens. Yacht cruises are also available. ❺–❻

🏃 **Wag Hill Lodge** On the west side of Mwanza Gulf; accessed by boat from Mwanza Yacht Club ☎ 028/250 2445 or 0754/917974, 🌐 www.waghill.com. Up above the western shore of Mwanza Gulf in a protected patch of indigenous forest, this romantic, eco-friendly lodge enjoys a gloriously lush location teeming with birds. There are just three secluded, cosy bungalows, all built from natural materials, with balcony views of both forest and lake. There's also a swimming pool, fine food, and an open fire in the evenings with views across the lake. Rates include guided forest walks, fishing trips, and boat transfers. All-inclusive $550. ❾

# The city and around

Most of Mwanza's burgeoning population lives on the outskirts, in unplanned slums spread all over various boulder-strewn hills and outcrops, the most famous of which is **Bugando Hill**, crowned by the Government hospital. The area at the hill's base, stretching westwards towards the city centre, is a hive of activity, reaching a crescendo in the **market area** around the bus and daladala stands. Nearby, just north of the Uhuru Monument on both sides of a footbridge straddling the foul Mirongo River, are several **Maasai herbalists**, who apart from providing locally esteemed medicinal concoctions also sell cowrie-shell necklaces and other trinkets you won't easily find elsewhere.

Close to the ferry ports, a plaque next to the **clock-tower roundabout** at the west end of Nyerere Road commemorates the "discovery" of Lake Victoria and hence the source of the Nile in 1858 by the English explorer

Speke, who first saw the lake "from Isamilo Hill one mile from this point" (see box below). The traffic island also contains a small **memorial** to the men who died in the two world wars; the British as soldiers and the Africans as conscripted porters.

Mwanza's neglected lakeside **Botanical Gardens** are four hundred metres north of here off Makongoro Road and are a pleasant target for a short walk. The **lakeshore** is, of course, Mwanza's main attraction, best savoured on either side of the hilly **Capri Point peninsula** south of the centre – the city's most affluent district, home to millionaires who have grown fat off diamonds and gold, and the fishing, processing and export of the lake's remaining tilapia and Nile perch. None of these industries have done any favours for the environment, or for locals dispossessed of their land by mining conglomerates, or pushed out of their fishing grounds by trawlers.

Heading south from the clock tower or ferry port you'll see the city's most photographed landmark, **Bismarck Rock**, a weathered granite kopje just offshore. Although kids are fond of swimming around it, it's not recommended due to the city's lamentable lack of sewage treatment, and sadly the same applies to all the beaches close by. Continuing beyond Bismarck Rock, the road veers away from the western shore and across Capri Point to the eastern shore. On this side there's a small jetty used by ferries going to the **Saa Nane Island Game Reserve**, sitting in the inlet between Capri Point and Bugando Hill. The island is attractive, and the big rocks that stud it make popular picnic spots, but the "game reserve" itself – established in 1964 as a quarantine station during the creation of Rubondo Island National Park – encapsulates all that's most

## The riddle of the Nile

Africa's Great Lakes – Victoria (Nyanza), Tanganyika and Nyasa – remained virtually unknown outside Africa until the second half of the nineteenth century, when they suddenly became the centre of attention amidst the scramble to pinpoint the **source of the Nile**. This was no mere academic exercise, for whoever controlled the Nile, controlled Egypt.

Yet it was a riddle that had bamboozled geographers and travellers alike since ancient times, when **Herodotus**, the "Father of History", had wrongly stated that West Africa's Niger was a branch of the Nile. Pliny the Elder compounded the confusion with his belief that the Nile had its head in a "mountain of lower Mauritania, not far from the [Atlantic] Ocean", whilst early Arab geographers didn't help matters by calling the Niger *al-Nil al-Kebir*, meaning the Great Nile.

In February 1858, the English explorers **John Hanning Speke** and **Richard Francis Burton** became the first white men to set eyes on Lake Tanganyika. The impetuous Burton instinctively believed Lake Tanganyika to be the Nile's source, but Speke argued – correctly, it turned out – that the lake lay too low. Leaving behind a grumbling and poorly Burton, Speke headed north, having been told of Lake Victoria by an Arab slave trader. As soon as he reached the shore, where Mwanza is now, in August 1858, Speke was convinced that the quest was finally over.

To verify his theory, Speke returned to the lake in October 1861, accompanied by the Scottish explorer **James Augustus Grant** and, after circling half the lake, sailed down the Nile in 1863 all the way to Cairo. "The Nile is settled," he wrote in a telegram from Khartoum to the Royal Geographic Society. Many people remained sceptical of Speke's claim, however, while Burton himself continued to insist that Lake Tanganyika was the true source of the Nile. In the end, it took a circumnavigation of Lake Victoria by Stanley in 1875 to prove Speke right. Sadly, Speke didn't live to enjoy his triumph, having died in a hunting accident in 1864.

▲ Igogo slum, Mwanza

dismal and depressing about zoos, as exemplified by a thoroughly depressed caged chimpanzee, which has endured decades of taunts from visitors. The **ferries** sail daily at 11am, 1pm, 3pm and 5pm (returning half an hour later); the Tsh800 return fare includes entry to the reserve.

To get to **the top of Capri Point**, walk past the Saa Nane museum and turn right before *Tilapia Hotel*. Take the first left, then right – ascending all the time. You should pass an enormous yellow mansion on your left (the road here is surfaced). Keep going straight up until the drivable road stops. From here, a footpath wends along the edge of the summit, giving fantastic views of Mwanza Creek, Lake Victoria and dozens of islands.

## Eating

At night, Uhuru Street is a good place for **street food**, with numerous stalls dishing up grilled meat (goat is best), fish and bananas cooked on smoky charcoal *jikos* (barbecues). For a taste of *paan* (see p.93), try *Harish Pan House* or *Sachin Pan House*, both at the junction of Nyerere Road and Posta Street.

**Deluxe Hotel** Kishamapanda St. Popular at lunchtimes, this has the usual range of Tanzanian favourites plus excellent *matoke* (a stew made from bananas). Food costs around Tsh1000 a dish.
**The Food Square** Bantu St. A reliably good cheap place in the centre, on two floors, with great *pilau* and other full meals (from Tsh1300 to Tsh2500 for chicken and chips), plus *supu*, various snacks, fresh juices, and grills in the evening. No alcohol.
**Kuleana Pizzeria** Posta St. Semi-outdoors, this cheerfully decorated place is as popular with locals as travellers, so get there early to be

sure of a table. The food – strictly vegetarian – is invariably delicious, once the sullen waitresses finally get round to you: large pizzas for around Tsh6000, sandwiches, and a good range of cakes, biscuits and fresh bread.
**New Mwanza Hotel** Posta Rd. Here's a rarity, a smart city hotel offering what it calls "street food" from South India. It's delicious, too, with a particularly tasty *saag paneer*.
**Salma Cone** Bantu St. Snacks such as samosas, cakes and buns, ice creams and good juices, including sugar cane. Opposite, *City Fries* does a

### By road

**Mwanza's bus stand** has moved from Pamba Road in the centre to **Buzuruga**. Unfortunately, the move did nothing to improve the chaos that so distinguished the old station. If you can travel out to the station to buy tickets a day or two before – unencumbered by bags – so much the better. You should also enquire about the correct fare with your hotel, as you'll almost certainly get ripped off otherwise. Incidentally, the bus companies that still have offices at the old town-centre location tend to be those operating at the cheaper end of the market, so are unreliable – if not downright dangerous – and best avoided.

Also worth avoiding are the touts, though evasion is no easy matter. Tell them you're just after information: "Naomba maelezo tu" is the phrase to use. Incidentally, if a tout offers a "discount", you'll still be charged over the odds.

If you're heading north into Kenya (or back into Tanzania via Namanga in Kenya to Arusha and Dar), you can avoid all this as the best companies have their own offices and terminals: Akamba are safest (*Majukano Hotel*, west end of Liberty St, ☎028/250 0272). Add $100 in visa fees ($70 if you can wangle a Kenyan transit visa) to the fare if you're re-entering Tanzania and lack a multiple-entry visa. There are two other ways of reaching **Arusha**: the main one (dry season, but should soon be all-weather) passes through Shinyanga, Nzega and Singida, and takes a full day (around Tsh38,000). The other is **through Serengeti and Ngorongoro**, which will add $100 to the fare in park entrance fees; the companies are Kimotco on Wednesday, and Coast Line on Monday, Tuesday and Thursday.

The road to **Biharamulo** via the gold-mining town of Geita starts at Kamanga on the west side of Mwanza Gulf, accessed by vehicle ferry from the end of Posta Street (approximately every hour; Tsh3500 per vehicle and Tsh800 per person). Two buses cover the route daily; board the bus at the ferry terminal but buy your ticket at the bus stand the day before. The road all the way to Geita is sealed – after that, things get a little difficult.

There are no buses to **Bukoba** – go to Biharamulo and change there (next day), or catch the ferry. Services to **Kigoma** are sketchy and prone to change, and to delays and cancellations in the rains. Two buses – Adventure Connection and Saratoga Line

---

mean trade in kebabs: Tsh200 per skewer, with juicy salad, tamarind sauce and chilli accompaniment. No alcohol.

**Sizzler** Kenyatta St. Unpretentious and pleasant restaurant in the centre of town serving good, cheap, no-nonsense grub such as pepper steak (Tsh4000) or a mixed grill (Tsh5000), as well as Indian dishes, while CNN broadcasts in the background. Takeaway available.

**Surve Inn** Lumumba Rd. A good, calm and clean *hoteli* that is especially good for breakfast, with decent *supu*, tea, samosas and even espresso. Open daytime only; closed Sun. No alcohol.

**Tilapia Hotel** Capri Point. The hotel houses various restaurants serving up Italian, Chinese, Indian Japanese and (especially good) Thai cuisine, with tables by the lakeside, others on breezy terraces or by the pool. Starters Tsh6000 and main courses Tsh10,000–12,000.

**Yun Long Chinese Restaurant** Nasser Drive, beyond Bismarck Rock. The only completed part of an abandoned project to build a posh resort-style hotel on the lakeshore. Despite this, it's Mwanza's most attractive eating venue – its delightful lakeside terrace offering unmatched views. The menu is Chinese and Tanzanian (chips, rice or *ugali* with chicken, fish or stews). For Chinese, most dishes cost Tsh8500 including rice. Open daily until midnight.

## Drinking and nightlife

The most popular **discos**, for the latest Bongo Flava or whatever style is making waves, are in the northern suburbs. Try the *Hotel La Kairo*, 2km north off Makongoro Road (taxi Tsh3000), which also has a swimming pool and access

– operate on alternate days, both leaving at 5am to arrive late the same day. **Tabora** has two or three buses daily, including Mohamed Transport (☏0784/566501), whose office is off Miti Mirefu Road.

### By ferry

A more comfortable and sedate approach to **Bukoba** is on the MV *Victoria*, sailing at 9pm Tuesday, Thursday and Sunday, stopping en route at **Kemondo**, 21km south of Bukoba. There are also daily ferries to **Ukerewe Island** (see p.404).

The **tourist fare** to Bukoba is Tsh30,600 first-class (two bunks per cabin), Tsh20,600 second-class (six bunks), Tsh17,100 second-class seated. Cabins are recommended if you want to arrive refreshed, so buy your ticket several days before. For **information**, contact Marine Services Ltd: ☏028/250 0880, ©marine @africaonline.co.tz.

### By train

A leisurely if tiring way to **Dar es Salaam** (almost forty hours) is by train (6pm on Thursday and Sunday). Change in **Tabora** for **Mpanda** or **Kigoma**: the trains from Mwanza will give you a full day in Tabora (you arrive before dawn and leave after dusk).

The **station** is on Station Road (☏028/250 2781, ⓦwww.trctz.com). **Fares** from Mwanza to Dar range from Tsh16,200 (third class) to Tsh53,600 (for first-class sleeper). For Tabora they range from Tsh7300 to Tsh21,200. For sleepers, buy your ticket a few days – indeed weeks – before to be sure of a compartment.

### By plane

The **airport** is 8km north of town. Daladalas cost Tsh300, or taxis charge Tsh7000–10,000. There are daily **flights** to Arusha, Bukoba, Dar, Lake Manyara, Ngorongoro and the Serengeti, and less frequent flights to Entebbe, Kilimanjaro and Rubondo Island. See p.422 for more route details, and "Airlines" (p.402) or "Travel agents" (p.402) for booking information. For an idea of **fares**: Mwanza–Arusha one-way on Coastal Aviation costs $230.

to a grubby beach, and *Casanova Disco* in Kiroreri area east of the airport (taxi at least Tsh5000).

**Just Rumours** Posta St/Court St. Something like a wine bar (lots of mirrors, glass and polished wood), and with Castle lager on tap. There are discos on Friday and Saturday from around 10pm (Tsh3000), when the dancing continues until daybreak. Open from 3pm; closed Mon.

**Lake Hotel** Station Rd. A large, friendly and popular old-timers' bar with satellite TV. There's also a reasonable restaurant (meals around Tsh2500), but eat in the bar rather than the glum dining room.

**Mwanza Institute Club** Station Rd. A pleasant and peaceful place for a drink, with seats in a shady garden at the back.

**New Mwanza Hotel** Posta St. The first-floor *Kipepeo Bar* terrace is the city's most reliable venue for live music, with Jambo Stars playing every Saturday (9pm–3am; Tsh5000). There's also a casino upstairs.

**Royal Pub** Off Karuta St. This Tanzanian beer garden is popular throughout the day and well into the night, and has mellow music to boot. It also does good nourishing breakfasts of chapati and *supu*, and sells cakes and sweets.

**Tilapia Hotel** Capri Point. The well-stocked bar here has great views over the inlet to Bugando Hill and Saa Nane Island, and is the main weekend hangout for the well-to-do. There's also a big TV screen for sports.

**Tivol Café** Posta St. The first-floor street-side balcony attracts the after-work crowd. Also has food.

**Yun Long Chinese Restaurant** Nasser Drive. A lovely place for a lakeside drink, and good service, too.

# Listings

**Air charters** Auric Air, Mwanza Airport ℡028/256
1286, ⓦwww.auricair.com; Precisionair, Kenyatta Rd
℡028/250 0819, ⓦwww.precisionairtz.com; Coastal
Aviation, Mwanza Airport ℡028/256 0441, ⓦwww
.coastal.cc.

**Airlines** Air Tanzania, Kenyatta Rd ℡028/256
1846, ⓦwww.airtanzania.com; Coastal Aviation,
Mwanza Airport ℡028/256 0441, ⓦwww.coastal
.cc; Precisionair, Kenyatta Rd ℡028/250 0819,
ⓦwww.precisionairtz.com.

**Banks and exchange** Quickest for cash or
traveller's cheques are the forexes at the *New
Mwanza Hotel* (also Sun) and Serengeti Services &
Tours, Posta St. NBC bank on Nkomo St gives
better rates but is slow.

**Car rental** See "Safari companies", below.

**Health** Bugando Hospital, Bugando Hill, top of
Würzburg Rd (℡028/250 0513), is government-
run. Better for non-emergencies is the Aga Khan
Hospital Medical Centre, Würzburg Rd/Miti Mirefu
Rd ℡028/250 2474. The FDS Pharmacy, *New
Mwanza Hotel* building, Posta St (℡028/250 3284),
is reasonably well stocked.

**Immigration** Station Rd, before the train station
℡028/250 0585.

**Internet access** Most reliable are Karibu Corner
Internet Café, Kenyatta St/Posta St (Mon–Fri
8am–8.30pm, Sat 8am–6pm, Sun 9am–5pm),
and the post office. Both charge Tsh1500 per hr.
Access also at the *Tilapia Hotel* and dozens of
places around town.

**Library** Mwanza Regional Library, Station Rd
(Mon–Fri 9am–6pm, Sat 9am–2pm; Tsh500 daily
membership).

**Mechanics** There are lots of car workshops
along Pamba Rd, and spares at the Land Rover
garage to the south of Fourways roundabout on
Station Rd.

**Police** Customs Rd outside the ferry port.

**Post and couriers** The post office is on Posta
St; there's also a branch at Pamba Rd near the
former bus stand. DHL can be found on
Kenyatta Rd (℡028/250 0890) and Skynet
couriers at the *New Mwanza Hotel*, Posta St
(℡028/250 2405).

**Supermarkets** Mwanza's supermarkets are
expensive. U Turn, north of the centre at the
junction of Nkrumah St and Hospital Rd, has the
best selection. Imalaseko, CCM Building by the
clock tower, is more convenient for the centre.

**Swimming pools** *New Mwanza Hotel* charges
day-guests Tsh3000 to use its pool; *Tilapia Hotel*
Tsh5000.

**Telephones** TTCL, Posta St beside the post office
(Mon–Fri 8am–4.30pm, Sat 9am–noon). Karibu
Corner offers internet calls of Tsh140/min to the
UK, US or Canada.

**Travel agents** Fourways Travel Service, Station
Rd/Kenyatta Rd ℡028/250 1853, ⓦwww
.fourwaystravel.net and Serengeti Services &
Tours, Posta St ℡028/250 0061, ⓦwww
.serengetiservices.com.

## Safari companies

Mwanza can provide an alternative base to Arusha for **Northern Circuit
safaris**, since it's better placed for Serengeti and has good connections to the
little-visited bird haven of Rubondo Island National Park. Prices depend on
the cost of car rental and the style of accommodation: a "budget" camping trip
starts at $220 per person per day. **Car rental** averages $200–250 per day,
depending on the distance covered, and includes a 4WD with driver, fuel, and
the driver's expenses (park fees, food and accommodation) – self-drive outside
Mwanza is generally not possible. The following companies are licensed for
safaris and it's worth shopping around, as none have fixed prices.

**Dolphin Tours & Safaris** Mwanza Airport,
℡028/256 1286, ⓦwww.auricair.com. Reliable
and keenly priced Northern Circuit safaris by road
or light aircraft (the company is owned by a
charter airline). Straight 4WD rental costs $100
per day including 150km, driver and driver's
allowance, but excludes fuel; the same but with a
camping vehicle (a tent folds out of the
bodywork) costs $120 per day.

**Fortes Car Hire** Lumumba Rd, near Karuta St
℡028/250 1804, ⓦwww.fortessafaris.com.
Primarily a car rental firm but offers safaris too;
rates are cheaper if you book online.

**Fourways Travel Service** ℡028/250 1853,
ⓦwww.fourwaystravel.net. Useful for air charters;
also arranges car hire and safaris.

## The Sukuma

The lake's southern and eastern hinterland, strewn with impressively eroded granite boulders, is the land of the six-million-strong **Sukuma**, Tanzania's largest tribe. Their long-horned Ankole cattle – startlingly different from the short-horned Maasai race – provide the first inkling that central Africa is near. But the region is far from being a rural Nirvana: the area is notorious for its modern **witch-slaying** tradition – usually poor old ladies with red eyes caused by one too many years of hunkering over smoky kitchen fires. In Shinyanga Region alone, one old woman has been murdered every day, on average, since the mid-1990s. Fear of witchcraft is part of the problem, but so is greed for land: an old lady's soil, once inherited, may yield more than just crops: **diamonds** have been mined in the region since the 1920s, and the region's **gold reserves** – currently exploited by foreign mining corporations – are also staggering.

Whilst the slayings are the most notorious facet of Sukuma superstition, the age-old Sukuma belief in magic is also more cheerfully expressed through **dance competitions**. Held in June and July, and sometimes also in August after the harvest that follows the long rains, they're particularly exuberant examples of a successful synthesis between old and new. The two oldest **dance societies** (*wigashe*), both of which perform annually at Bujora, are the Bagika and Bagalu, which were founded in the mid-nineteenth century by **rival healers** (good witches, if you like), Ngika and Gumha. As the two could not agree which of them had the most powerful medicine (*dawa*), a dance contest was organized to decide the issue.

The format, which remains unchanged, is for two competing dance societies to perform at the same time, with the crowd being free to move between the two – the better the medicine, the bigger the crowd. Obviously, good preparation is the key to success, and nothing is more important than **good luck medicine** (*samba*). This is dispensed by each dance society's healer (*nfumu*), and is intended to make the dancers, especially the dance leader (*mlingi*), appealing to the crowd. Given that crowd size is the key to success, each passing year sees new and innovative dance routines, tricks and costumes – in 1995, one group won by using a plastic toy monkey given to them by a Japanese traveller. Others used articulated wooden puppets as props, stilts or fire breathing, while all dancers possess the most outrageous gymnastic agility. Although dance moves and lyrics change annually, there are some enduring favourites, notably the *Bugobugobo* **snake dance**, a hugely theatrical affair starring live pythons, which is a speciality of the Ngika Society.

The dance contests are best experienced at Bujora's two-week **Bulabo festival** following the Christian festival of Corpus Christi (usually early or mid-June). Alternatively, the Sukuma Museum at Bujora can arrange dances at any time of year.

# Around Mwanza: the Sukuma Museum

The **Sukuma Museum** (Bujora Cultural Centre, Mon–Sat 8.30am–6pm, Sun 1–6pm; ☎0754/772439; entry Tsh8000) at Bujora makes an excellent day-trip from Mwanza. Just 18km east of the city, 2km off the Musoma highway, it covers in great detail the culture and traditions of Tanzania's largest tribe, the Sukuma. The museum is in the compound of the **Bujora Catholic Mission**, founded in 1952 by a Canadian missionary, Father David Clement. Clement's open-minded approach saw Sukuma music, dance and history introduced into the mission's religious services, and is also reflected in the mission's **church**. Modelled along Sukuma lines, the church has a round peaked roof resembling a traditional Sukuma house, and is decorated inside with symbols of chiefly power: the altar is in the shape of a royal throne, and the tabernacle resembles a chief's house (*ikulu*), complete with a shield and crossed spears on the door.

The entrance to the **museum** is marked by a monument depicting a painted royal drum placed on a bas-relief map of Tanzania. The exhibits, covering every aspect of Sukuma life from the humdrum to the ritual, sacred and chiefly, are contained in a number of startlingly designed and colourfully painted pavilions. The Dance Society Pavilion has a wealth of information on the competing Bagika and Bagalu dance societies, whilst Sukuma history is presented in the Royal Pavilion, designed in the form of a royal throne and containing a mass of genealogy, as well as royal drums, fly whisks, headdresses and other objects donated by the descendants of former chiefs.

### Practicalities

**Buses and daladalas** run approximately every half-hour from Mwanza to Kisesa, 16km along the Musoma road. The museum is a 2km walk north of Kisesa – turn in at the sign for "Shule ya Msingi Bujora". A taxi from Mwanza won't cost more than Tsh20,000, though the driver may need convincing to cover the last 2km from Kisesa. **Accommodation** is available at the centre, either in small rooms with nets (❶) or at a large campsite (Tsh3000 per person).

Performances of **traditional drumming and dancing** can be arranged with a day's notice (Tsh80,000), and you can take lessons in traditional arts. For more about the museum and its activities, visit ⓦwww.mwanza-guide.com/bujora .html or ⓦphilip.greenspun.com/sukuma: the former has practical information; the latter features hundreds of jaw-droppingly gorgeous photographs and reams of text.

# Ukerewe and Ukara Islands

Lake Victoria's largest island is **UKEREWE ISLAND**, due north of Mwanza and separated from it by Speke Gulf. Nicknamed "UK" by locals, this densely populated island of low wooded hills, craggy outcrops, granite boulders and subsistence farms is the district capital of an archipelago comprising 26 other islands and islets, including **Ukara Island** where you can discover the legend of the Dancing Stone (see p.407). Despite its proximity to Mwanza, Musoma and the tourist traffic in the Serengeti, these islands are among the least-known areas in Tanzania. Don't come expecting anything exceptional – there are few sights apart from the views – but do expect to encounter a kind of rural Arcadia that has remained virtually unchanged from before colonial times. The isolation, in fact, is a good part of the attraction, though it makes travelling here – and around the islands – something of an adventure.

## Arrival

There are two ways of **reaching Ukerewe**, either by road from Bunda via Masahunga, with a short ferry crossing over the narrow Rugezi Channel, or by ferry from Mwanza.

### By ferry from Mwanza

Daily **ferries** connect Mwanza with Ukerewe's main town, Nansio, taking two and a half to three hours (seats Tsh4600–6600). The MV *Claris* and the MV *Butiama* leave daily from the ferry port at the end of Customs Road (Sun–Fri at 9am, Sat 8am; returning from Nansio Mon–Fri 2pm, Sat 4pm). The smaller MV *Airbus* departs daily from Kirumba Mwaloni, 3km north of Mwanza, at 2.30pm, having set out from Nansio at 8am.

**8**

### By road from Bunda

The 83km from Bunda, on the Mwanza–Kenya highway, to the ferry at **Masahunga** (or Kisoria), passes through attractive countryside scattered with the small homesteads of the Luo tribe, between which marshy areas attract a wealth of **birdlife**, including grey herons, egrets, marabou storks, vultures, fish eagles and weavers. The trip is a two-hour drive in good weather if you have your own vehicle, or three to four hours by **bus**. The **bus stand** is about 1km west of the highway. Two companies – Bunda Bus and Trans Africa – cover the route daily, continuing on to Nansio after the ferry crossing; Bunda Bus is the more reliable, leaving Bunda every day at 10.30am to arrive in Nansio around 3.30pm. Its office in Bunda is 150m from the highway at the start of the road to Masahunga.

Should you get stuck, there's no shortage of good, cheap **accommodation in Bunda**. These include the friendly *Bhukenye Bar & Guest House* (☎028/262 1232; ❶): from the bus stand, head north and then first right back towards the highway, and it's on the second road left (signposted). Or for something more salubrious, there's the terrific-value *Spice Rite Hotel* (☎028/262 2288, 0756/375857; ❷) that has large en-suite rooms with TV, hot water, fan and box nets. To find it, head 200m up the hill across the main road from the turn-off to the post office. There are plenty of other choices lining the Mwanza–Musoma highway. For food, you're pretty much limited to your hotel, a helping of *nyama choma* at one of the bars in town, or one of the street stalls.

The **ferry** from Masahunga on the mainland to **Rugezi** on Ukerewe takes twenty to thirty minutes and can carry up to six cars (Tsh5000 for a car with driver, Tsh200 for each passenger or pedestrian). The ferry leaves Masahunga daily at 9.30am, 11.30am, 1.30pm, 3.30pm and 6pm, and Rugezi at 8.30am (Tuesday 8am), 10.30am, 12.30pm, 2.30pm and 5pm. The ferry is met in Rugezi by daladalas going to Nansio. Should you get stranded in Masahunga, there are a couple of hotels (both ❶): the *Bwanza* is very basic, the *Deo Guest House*, on the left before the jetty, is much better.

## Information and accommodation

The island's capital, **Nansio**, is one of Tanzania's doziest towns – even the market is a low-key affair. Travellers are rare, and people are visibly startled to see tourists. You can **change money** at NMB between the bus stand and the market. The one internet café, Delka computers, is just 100m from the port on the tarmac road.

Unless you're planning to decamp to the even sleepier "town" of Bwisya on Ukara, Nansio will be your base for the duration as it contains Ukerewe's only guest **rooms**.

**La Bima** Behind the post office ☎028/251 5146. Surprisingly smart hotel with 26 presentable rooms (no singles), each with mosquito net, TV and, on occasions, hot water. There's also a bar and restaurant. ❸

**Kazoba Lodging & Boarding** Posta St, opposite the NMB ☎028/251 5146. A quiet, peaceful place to stay with basic rooms (some en suite) with nets. Avoid the stuffy singles, which lack windows. ❶

Monarch Gallu Beach Hotel 600m west of the ferry jetty on a headland facing Nansio Bay ☎028/251 5303, ⊛www.monarchhotelmwanza .com. Not to be confused with the *Gallu Beach Hotel* restaurant that organizes tours, this is

Nansio's best lodging – a breezy place on the lakeshore with wide lawns, an attractive view and a bar and restaurant. The rooms are spacious, but overpriced. Electricity (from a generator) runs from 7–10pm, but there's no running water. BB ❸

# Eating and drinking

Apart from a couple of *mishkaki* (snack) stalls along the main road between the ferry jetty and *Monarch Gallu Beach Hotel*, and a couple of basic cafés at the west end of town, the following are virtually the only places on the island where you can buy **cooked food**. Another good place for a **drink** is *Picnic Villa* (or *Sunset Beach*), 50m from the ferry jetty, which has some tables in a small lakeside garden.

Bima Hotel Behind the post office. Unexceptional restaurant serving standard fare, improved by its sometimes lively bar and slightly upmarket feel.
Gallu Beach Hotel On the main street, off on the right when walking towards the *Monarch*. Ukerewe's best cuisine (and breakfasts); sit at the tables outside under thatched parasols. But the main

reason for chewing the cud here is to organize tours, and chat with the management, who are knowledgeable about all things concerning the island.
Monarch Gallu Beach Hotel A nice location, and good meals for around Tsh9000. It's also a civilized place for a drink, with tables under parasols in a garden by the lake.

# Exploring the islands

Public transport on the islands is scant, so **hiring a bicycle** is the best way to get around: ask at Nansio's market, or arrange things through *Gallu Beach Hotel* restaurant (see above; ☎028/251 5094, ✉gallubeachhotel@yahoo.com), the base for a number of enticing **day-trips** around Ukerewe and Ukara. Costs vary but count on about $25–40 per day including lunch and a guide, which should cover the main sites.

The islands are not blessed with much in the way of tourist attractions, though a pleasant day can be spent travelling around them, calling in at the following sights as you go. The closest attraction to Nansio is the semi-ruined **Bukindo Palace** (8km north of Nansio and 2km north of Bukindo village). The palace is a few hundred metres to the right of the road in a stand of trees, but isn't signposted so you'll have to ask for directions: ask for Kasale Victor Mazura Rukumbuzya, who owns the place and is the grandson of the last king of Ukerewe. Built in 1928, apparently by an Italian architect named Tonerro, the palace is a grand, colonial-style two-storey construction, surrounded on both levels by a wide balcony. It served as the palace of **Chief Gabriel Ruhumbika** (who died in 1938) and then of his son, **Chief Rukumbuzya**, who was the last king of Ukerewe; after his death in 1981, the palace was abandoned by the family. To get there, catch a **pick-up** from Nansio to Bugolora, which run at irregular intervals throughout the day.

Returning to Nansio then heading northwest for 10km you come to Mahande, from where it's not far to **Handebezyo Museum** – not so much a museum as a glorified picnic site. The site is perched on top of one of several low granite hills in the centre of the island, all named after 1960s African leaders. The small **cave** at the base of the highest hill was placed under guard by the kings (*watemi*) of Ukerewe, so that their subjects could deposit valuables in cooking pots for safekeeping – a kind of bank. Concrete steps have been built all the way to the top (at 172m above the lake surface, Ukerewe's highest point), giving sweeping views over much of the island and lake. If you're driving, head 2km along the road towards Bukindo then turn left at the school and ask for directions from

> ### The Dancing Stone
>
> Even further off the beaten track is **Ukara Island**, an hour's boat ride north of Ukerewe, and home to the Kara tribe. Like Ukerewe, it's heavily populated and has few attractions you can pin down, other than the isolated rural ambience and a clutch of distant legends.
>
> The most vivid of these concerns the **Dancing Stone of Butimba**, on the western shore, which is a boulder balanced on top of another boulder. The best way to see Ukara and the Dancing Stone is to take the thirteen-hour **day-trip** offered by *Gallu Beach Hotel* in Nansio, but give them two days' notice. If you want to try getting there under your own steam, Ukara Island is accessed by boat from **Bugolora**, on the north side of Ukerewe Island. One DCM minibus and two daladalas run daily from Nansio, the first leaving around 7am, the last heading back to Nansio at 4pm.

there. By **public transport**, catch the first daladala from Nansio to Rubya and get off at Mahande, leaving you with a pleasant three-kilometre walk.

Aside from these 'official' tourist sites, the other main attractions on the islands are the beaches. The only beach that is definitely free of bilharzia is beyond **Rubya Forest** in the far west. Two daladalas cover this route: if you're not planning on camping overnight at the beach, the 11.30am run is your only option, giving you around three hours by the lake before the last daladala returns from Rubya (around 4pm). The most accessible beaches, such as the one beside the *Monarch Gallu Beach Hotel*, may or may not be infected.

# Mara Region

The eastern shore of the Tanzanian portion of Lake Victoria is part of **Mara Region**, named after the **Mara River**, which rises to the north of Kenya's Maasai Mara Game Reserve. The river is famed as the scene of the carnage that results every year when massive herds of wildebeest and zebra attempt to cross the raging river on their great migration (see p.376), providing a feast for countless crocodiles, lions and other carnivores. By the time the river approaches the lake, however, it has become one of the most sedate and beautiful of East Africa's rivers, creating a labyrinthine network of lazy waterways bounded by papyrus and reeds. While there's not an awful lot to do in the region, the area's natural beauty makes any journey a pleasure in itself.

## Musoma

Mwanza's expansion has been at the expense of **MUSOMA**, a small port town located on a peninsula in Mara Bay, 120km south of Kenya. Laid-back and charming, it has a refreshingly different climate from the strength-sapping humidity of Mwanza. Other than informally arranged **boat trips** to various isles for fishing and bird-watching there aren't any sights as such, though a walk

## The Lukuba Archipelago

Roughly 15km offshore, and visible from the west side of Musoma Peninsula, the **Lukuba Archipelago** consists of three large islands and several smaller ones, and is traditionally used as a base by fishermen. Being too rocky for extensive agriculture, the islands are rich in wildlife, especially **birds**, and the rare **spotted-necked otters**.

Other than informally arranging things with fishermen at Musoma town's eastern beach, there are two ways of **visiting** the archipelago. Either rent a large motorboat for a few hours via *Tembo Beach Hotel* (a bargainable $80–90 depending on where you go; space for up to thirty people), or contact *Lukuba Island Lodge* (🖳www .lukubaisland.com), which offers day-trips from Musoma for $60 per person including lunch, for a minimum of four people. The cost of **staying overnight** in one of the lodge's five stone-walled, lake-facing bungalows is $280 per person, to which you should add the cost of guided hikes and (expensive) watersports, including Nile perch fishing. There's also a swimming pool and sundeck.

to the end of the peninsula is always fun, both for the views and for the local **birdlife**, especially waders and raptors (which can be found around the papyrus beds that fringe the beaches), kingfishers, and all sorts of wonderful, garishly coloured birds. There are also a couple of small **markets**: one by the lakeshore to the east of town close to where fishing boats are repaired, the other a more generic affair next to the bus stand in the centre.

Unfortunately, **swimming** – although popular with local children – doesn't appear to be terribly safe, despite local assurances. The papyrus and reed beds at the waterline offer an ideal habitat for bilharzia-infected blood flukes.

## Practicalities

The **bus stand**, just off Kusaga Street in the centre, is an orderly affair, and there are taxis on hand. The Mohamed Trans bus company has its office and stop on Kivukoni Street; Coast Line is several blocks south near the corner of Mukendo Road and Uhuru Street. If you're coming on a long-distance bus bound for Mwanza or Nairobi, chances are it'll drop you at **Makutano junction** 10km from town, from where you can catch a shared taxi for a modest Tsh1500. The only scheduled **flight** is with Precisionair (see p.410).

### Accommodation

Musoma has dozens of **guesthouses**, most to the east of Mukendo Road, some grotty, most perfectly sound. The *Tembo Beach Hotel* is on the **beach** and has **camping** ($7) on the sand. The following include breakfast unless otherwise noted, and couples can share most single rooms.

**Afrilux Hotel** Afrilux Rd ☎028/262 0031, 🖳www .afriluxhotel.net. At four storeys, this is Musoma's highest building, and also the town's largest and most established hotel. Rooms are en suite, most with cable TV, and those on the upper floors have good views of Mara Bay. There's also a bar and restaurant, room service and safe parking. ❸
**Hotel Matvilla** Gandhi St ☎028/262 2445, ✉matvilla_hotel@yahoo.com. Friendly staff and smart accommodation (built above a strip of shops in the centre of town) make this a good choice. All

rooms are en suite and come with cable TV, hot water and box nets. ❹
**Mujungu Annex Inn** Diamond Rd ☎028/262 0017, ✉mujunguinn@yahoo.com. Cheap, clean, calm and obliging family-run guesthouse. All rooms are en suite, the better ones have satellite TV, and all have big beds and box nets. As with all the cheaper hotels, it has water problems. Secure parking. ❷
**Pyramid Inn** Aman St ☎028/262 2201, ✉rafikien@yahoo.com. Lurid green high-rise in

the centre of town containing some surprisingly tasteful, gleaming rooms with TV, internet access, fridge, bath and a/c. Quiet, clean and friendly. ❸

**Tembo Beach Hotel** 1km north of town by the beach off Lakeside Drive ☎028/262/2887, Ⓔ tembobeach@yahoo.com. Sitting right on the

(grey sandy) beach, this hotel has seven en-suite rooms in a graceless two-storey block (more rooms are being added nearby), all with views of the beach and bay. Also has a bar on the beach and meals in the *kuku na chipsi* tradition (Tsh2500). No single rates. ❸

## Eating

There's not a big choice of food, but what is available is good.

**Afrilux Hotel** Afrilux Rd. Relatively upmarket and expensive with a huge menu (including Indian dishes), and shady outdoor seating.

**Mara Dishes Frys** Kivukoni St. Escape from *chipsi*-land: this self-service place cooks up big vats of inexpensive traditional food including a tasty brown *ugali* made from corn flour and cassava, *matoke*, and good bean, liver and tripe

stews. Tsh2500 will get you fed handsomely, and a soda or juice. No alcohol.

**Salamander Hotel** Market St/Afrilux Rd. A great local place for snacks, including Musoma's take on a *kababu* (a meatball wrapped in a pancake), and combo-plates of tasty African food including fresh fish, meat, chicken or liver, all for Tsh1000–1500. No alcohol.

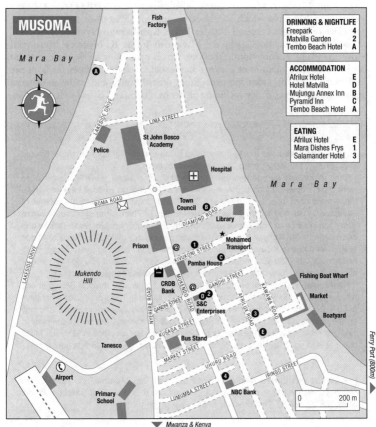

**MUSOMA**

*Mara Bay*

N

Fish Factory

LAKESIDE DRIVE

LIMA STREET

St John Bosco Academy

Police

BOMA ROAD

Hospital

*Mara Bay*

Town Council

DIAMOND ROAD

Library

Prison

KIVUKONI STREET

Mohamed Transport

Pamba House

Mukendo Hill

LAKESIDE DRIVE

NYEREFRE ROAD

CRDB Bank

GANDHI STREET

MKENDO ROAD

GANDHI STREET

S&C Enterprises

AFRILUX ROAD

KAWAWA ROAD

Fishing Boat Wharf

Market

Boatyard

Tanesco

KUSAGA STREET

Bus Stand

MARKET STREET

UHURU ROAD

IRINGO STREET

Airport

Primary School

LUMUMBA STREET

NBC Bank

0      200 m

| DRINKING & NIGHTLIFE | |
|---|---|
| Freepark | 4 |
| Matvilla Garden | 2 |
| Tembo Beach Hotel | A |

| ACCOMMODATION | |
|---|---|
| Afrilux Hotel | E |
| Hotel Matvilla | D |
| Mujungu Annex Inn | B |
| Pyramid Inn | C |
| Tembo Beach Hotel | A |

| EATING | |
|---|---|
| Afrilux Hotel | E |
| Mara Dishes Frys | 1 |
| Salamander Hotel | 3 |

Ferry Port (800m) ▶

▼ Mwanza & Kenya

## Drinking and nightlife

Most **bars** also serve limited food and are often good for *nyama choma*.

**Freepark** Down a little cul-de-sac off Mukendo Rd. This has tables under shady trees and is lovely by day, and atmospheric at night – a great place to meet people. There's a wide range of drinks and bar food, too.

**Matvilla Garden** Gandhi St. Pleasant, shaded garden in the heart of town, serving cold, cold beers. The best place in the centre to escape the heat of the day. Also serves food.

**Tembo Beach Hotel** Off Lakeside Drive, 1km north of town. If it's beach you're after, this is the place. Apart from cold beers and sodas, served up at tables on the beach, they can also rustle up some basic but good food including *nyama choma* and sandwiches.

## Listings

**Airlines** The agent for Precisionair and Air Tanzania is Global Travel, Gandhi St ☏028/262 2707.
**Banks** CRDB and NBC, both Mukendo Rd; NBC charges lower commission and has a 24hr Visa/MasterCard ATM.

**Internet** Musoma Communications Centre, Gandhi St (8am–7pm); Tsh1500 per hr.
**Telephones** TTCL is behind Mukendo Hill near the airport. There are card phones at the *Afrilux* and *Orange Tree* hotels.

# Around Musoma

Apart from Musoma, Mara Region's other major town is **BUTIAMA**, 45km southeast of Musoma, which would be an unremarkable place were it not the birthplace of Tanzania's revered founder, **Julius Kambarage Nyerere** (see p.583), whose life is commemorated by the **Mwalimu Julius K. Nyerere Memorial Museum** (daily 9.30am–6pm; Tsh6000), which opened in 1999, just before his death. There are a mixture of personal items such as clothing, shoes, his favourite (and very battered) radio, presents from official tours and archival material documenting his presidency, including plenty of photos, an *Ujamaa*-style Makonde

---

### Moving on from Musoma

There are no scheduled ferries (formerly to Kisumu in Kenya) from Musoma. Should they resume, the **ferry port** is 2km southeast of town.

Most minor **bus companies** have offices at the bus stand, while the larger ones have their offices on Uhuru Street either side of Mukendo Road. Mohamed Trans (ⓦwww.mtl.com) has its on Kivukoni Street and Coast Line's is by the corner of Mukendo Road and Uhuru Street (☏0754/598863). There's transport to **Mwanza** every half-hour or so from 6am to around 3pm and frequent daladalas to **Tarime** and on to Sirari on the **Kenyan border**, where you can catch a *matatu* (daladala) to Migori or Kisii, or a bus to Kisumu. The border formalities don't take too long, though you'll need to pay the $50 visa fee ($20 if you're in transit) in cash if you don't have one already. Akamba runs daily to Nairobi (you can buy these tickets in advance).

For **Arusha**, you have three options: the quickest is straight through Serengeti and Ngorongoro (add $100 in entry fees to the Tsh32,000 fare). There are buses most days at 5am: the better companies are Coast Line and Kimotco. Just as expensive is to stay on the sealed road and go through Kenya (add $70 in visas). The safest company is Akamba, which leaves in the afternoon, though it only has an office in Mwanza. Much cheaper is to go to Mwanza and catch a bus via **Shinyanga** and **Singida** from there.

#### Flights
Precisionair operates a triangular route between Dar, Musoma and Mwanza on Mondays, Wednesdays, Fridays and Sundays; book through Global Travel on Gandhi St (☏028/262 2707). The airport is 500m west of the town centre.

## The Kuria

Heading north from Musoma, the landscape becomes hillier and beautiful as the road drops down into the valley of the Mara River, which begins life north of Kenya's famous Maasai Mara Game Reserve. Much of the valley here is occupied by the **Masura Swamp**, consisting of extensive papyrus beds through which the river meanders. It is here that you'll find Tarime, the main market town for the Kuria tribe. Straddling the border with Kenya, the ancestors of the **Kuria tribe** were among the first Bantu-speaking peoples to have settled in East Africa, possibly over two thousand years ago. Although traditionally cattle herders, larger and more powerful groups – such as the Luo on the lakeshore, and the Maasai in the plains – have restricted the Kuria to the hill country just east of **Lake Victoria** and forced them to adopt a settled, agricultural way of life. Nonetheless, cattle remain ritually important, especially in marriage negotiations, where hefty dowries – paid for in cattle – remain the norm. Rainfall is generally favourable, allowing the cultivation of cash crops such as coffee, sugar cane, tobacco and maize. Another cash crop is **marijuana** (*bangi*), which serves the same purpose as locally brewed beer elsewhere, being taken communally by elders when discussing tribal affairs. Disputes over marijuana-producing areas, however, have been the main cause of bloody clashes between rival clans, which have claimed dozens of lives.

**Music and dance** accompany almost every traditional ceremony and rite of passage for the Kuria, especially weddings and circumcisions, and also serve as entertainment in their own right. The music itself is characterized by one of Africa's largest lyres, the *iritungu*, which gives a distinctly metallic timbre, the strings' deep and resonant buzzing providing a hypnotic impetus. For more information about Kuria music and culture, see ⓦwww.bluegecko.org/kenya/tribes/kuria, which includes music from the Kuria, as well as the Luo and Maasai, and has full-length sound clips. You can also buy tapes locally, and at Musoma's bus stand.

carving (see p.64) depicting the founding members of TANU who had spearheaded the drive for Independence, and an oddly beautiful set of carved plaques commemorating the 1978–79 Kagera War with Idi Amin's Uganda. You should also be able to visit his **grave**, close to the museum, which has been enclosed in a mausoleum, contrary to his wish to be buried in a simple manner.

The visit can be done as a half-day trip; access by **public transport** is easiest from Musoma, where daladalas run every hour or two. If you're driving from Musoma, the museum is signposted at several places along the highway, but these disappear in Butiama itself, so you'll have to ask: it's at Mwitongo, about 1km west of the centre along a tree-lined avenue that passes a transmitter mast. Hang around, or ask at the army base just before the museum, and the curator will come to let you in. Butiama also has a few simple places to stay and eat.

# Kagera Region

The thickly forested hills, rain cloud-filled skies and vibrant red laterite soil of **Kagera Region** in Tanzania's far northwest provide a welcome, beautiful and truly tropical contrast to the unremitting scrub of central Tanzania. Connected to Mwanza by passenger steamer, Bukoba is an attractive and

Properly called Bahaya, the **Haya** of Tanzania's northwestern Kagera Region number around two million people. Their history is complex, mirroring that of Rwanda and Burundi, thankfully without the tragedy of their neighbours. The Haya have two distinct ethnic elements: the Iru and the Hima.

The region's original inhabitants, whose descendants constitute the Haya's present-day **Iru clan**, were Bantu-speaking farmers and fishermen who excelled in steel production. Excavations have revealed 1500-year-old forges that were capable of producing a higher grade of steel than that produced in eighteenth-century Europe, and using a fraction of the fuel. But the **kingdoms** for which Haya later became famous were founded by aristocratic cattle-herding northern immigrants in the fifteenth or sixteenth century, **the Hima**. Imposing a rigidly hierarchical social structure upon the Iru, the Hima feudal kingdoms effectively oppressed the Iru in much the same manner as the Tutsi had dominated the Hutu in neighbouring Burundi and Rwanda.

Although the German and British colonial powers tacitly favoured the Hima, rising tensions between the two groups were thankfully defused after Tanzanian Independence. President Nyerere's emphasis on equality and togetherness across all tribes, and his **abolition of traditional chiefdoms** and kingdoms, brought an abrupt but peaceful end to the social divisions that had threatened to go the same way as Burundi and Rwanda. For more on Haya culture, especially music and epic poetry, see the excellent and wide-ranging *The Last of the Bards: The Story of Habibu Selemani of Tanzania (c.1929–93)* by M.M. Mulokozi, available to view at ⓦwww.questia.com.

lively base for the region, with some delightful beaches and an innovative tour company offering dozens of trips in northern Kagera, including prehistoric rock paintings, and ruined palaces that were part of eight traditional kingdoms. With more time, there's also the little-visited **Rubondo Island National Park** in the lake's southwest corner to explore – a wonderland if birds are your thing. The park's isolation, and hence inaccessibility to poachers, has also made it a preferred place for relocating species endangered elsewhere, including chimpanzees, black rhinos and even elephants.

# Bukoba

Tanzania's only major town on Lake Victoria's western shore is **BUKOBA**, a bustling, upbeat and friendly place. Most tourists who come here are generally passing to or from Uganda, but it really is worth hunkering down for a while: the surrounding region contains a feast of attractions, whilst the gorgeous lakeshore location backed by boulder-strewn and thickly vegetated hills, and plentiful birdlife in the surrounding swamps, make it a pleasant destination in its own right.

## Arrival and information

The **bus stand** is at the west end of town off Kawawa Street and there are plenty of taxis. The **airport** is near the lakeshore at the end of Aerodrome Road; there are rarely any taxis there, but the walk into town is very pleasant. The **ferry port** lies 2.5km southeast of town. There's a bar and canteen at the port, but beware of pickpockets and thieves. A taxi into town from here costs Tsh3000, or you can catch a daladala for a few hundred shillings.

Bukoba's unofficial **tourist office** is Kiroyera Tours on Sokoni Street (Mon–Sat 8am–6pm; ☎028/222 0203, ⊛www.kiroyeratours.com), which can recommend hotels, and offer a huge range of trips around Bukoba and Kagera Region (see p.417).

## Accommodation

The main concentration of budget **guesthouses** is on Miembeni Street, about 600m east of the bus stand. Mid-range places are situated closer to the lake, with one right on the shore. **Camping** is best at *Kiroyera Beach Campsite* (☎0787/222 0203), where you can choose from camping in your own tent (Tsh4000), borrowing one (Tsh5000), or sleeping in a small but sweet *banda* (❶).

**Balamaga B&B** 2km south of town ☎0787/757289, ⊛www.balamagabb.com. Run by a Dutchman who married a local, this B&B is a lovely place to stay. Two of the four rooms are en suite and all have box nets and cable TV, but it's the gorgeous gardens that set this place apart – they are filled with tropical plants and have views over the lake. Wonderful. ❸

**ELCT Bukoba Hotel** Airport Rd ☎028/222 3121, ⊛www.elctbukobahotel.com. Run by the Lutheran

Church, the hotel enjoys large and beautiful grounds with lawns, mature trees and many birds. The 22 rooms range from doubles with shared bathrooms to en-suite twins (better ones with TVs and box nets) and suites. All the rooms are clean and have phones. There's also internet and safe parking. ❸

**Lake Hotel** Shore Rd ☎028/222 1024. A colonial survivor going to seed in gardens near the lakeshore, and apparently where Humphrey Bogart

▲ Bukoba's market

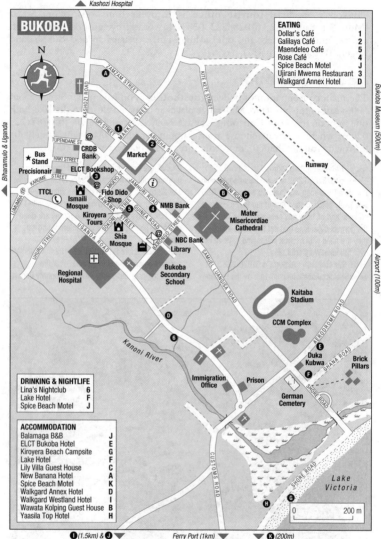

## BUKOBA

▲ Kashozi Hospital

**EATING**

| | |
|---|---|
| Dollar's Café | 1 |
| Galilaya Café | 2 |
| Maendeleo Café | 5 |
| Rose Café | 4 |
| Spice Beach Motel | J |
| Ujirani Mwema Restaurant | 3 |
| Walkgard Annex Hotel | D |

**DRINKING & NIGHTLIFE**

| | |
|---|---|
| Lina's Nightclub | 6 |
| Lake Hotel | F |
| Spice Beach Motel | J |

**ACCOMMODATION**

| | |
|---|---|
| Balamaga B&B | J |
| ELCT Bukoba Hotel | E |
| Kiroyera Beach Campsite | G |
| Lake Hotel | F |
| Lily Villa Guest House | C |
| New Banana Hotel | A |
| Spice Beach Motel | K |
| Walkgard Annex Hotel | D |
| Walkgard Westland Hotel | I |
| Wawata Kolping Guest House | B |
| Yaasila Top Hotel | H |

Bukoba Museum (500m) ▶
Airport (100m) ▶

Biharamulo & Uganda ◀

▲ Ⓛ (1.5km) & Ⓙ ▼     Ferry Port (1km) ▼     ▼ Ⓚ (200m)

and Katherine Hepburn stayed for the film *The African Queen*. The rooms are huge, contain two beds, box nets, phone and washbasin; the better ones have lake views or bathrooms. There's also a basic restaurant and bar. Tatty but still charming. BB en suite ❷; shared bathroom ❶

**Lily Villa Guest House** Miembeni Rd (no phone). Cheap and welcoming place with twin rooms and shared clean bathrooms with surprisingly powerful showers. Check the mosquito nets – some are too small. ❶

**New Banana Hotel** Zamzam St ☎028/222 0892. Good-value rooms with decent beds and nets, cable TV and phone, and well-kept Western-style toilets. There's also a quiet bar and restaurant, and secure parking. ❷

**Spice Beach Motel** On the beach 2km south of the centre ☎0713/451904. The breezy lakeside location's the thing here; the motel occupies a neat cluster of old German buildings near a patch of kopjes and boulders facing Musila Island. The six en-suite rooms (double or twin) are big and bright, with box nets, cable TV, clean showers and Western-style toilets. There's also a beachside bar and restaurant. ❷

**Walkgard Annex Hotel** Uganda Rd ☏028/222 0626, ⓦwww.walkgard.com. A two-storey business-style option with good-value, en-suite rooms, all of which have TV, hot water and phone (some also have balconies). The suite-like doubles come with large beds, box nets and a sofa. BB ❸

**Walkgard Westland Hotel** 3km south of town ☏028/222 0935, ⓦwww.walkgard.com. Occupying a high bluff overlooking the lake, this architectural mishmash has Bukoba's best accommodation – all thirty rooms have cable TV, phone and minibar. There's also a good restaurant, a couple of bars and a swimming pool. The hotel arranges similar tours to those offered by Kiroyera Tours. HB ❹

**Wawata Kolping Guest House** Miembeni Rd ☏028/222 1289. Run by the Catholic Church, this has a fittingly calm and meditative atmosphere. There's one en-suite double room (❶), and a single-sex dorm with six beds and a shared bathroom, which you can either rent in its entirety (Tsh12,000) or by the bed (Tsh2000). Breakfast and lunch available.

**Yaasila Top Hotel** On the beach, 2km south of the centre ☏028/222 1251, ⓦwww.yaasila.com. Occupying a great spot overlooking the beach with a bar on the sand, this hotel has the smartest rooms of all the lakefront properties. Each room is en suite and comes with TV, telephone, hot water and fridge; try to nab one of the ten rooms in the main building, which boast balconies with views over the lake. ❹

## The Town

One of the things you'll notice in Bukoba – aside from zillions of harmless lake flies – is the presence of lots of earnest-looking *wazungu* working for aid agencies and Christian NGOs, many of which deal with AIDS. The aid workers are merely the latest in a long line of *wazungu* – the influence of their predecessors, the European missionaries, is visible throughout town in the form of several large churches. The biggest is the half-built yet grandiose Catholic **Mater Misericordiae Cathedral** (Africa's first Cardinal, Laurian Rugambwa, was from Bukoba), at the corner of Barongo Street and Samuel Luangisa Road, which now serves as a roost for a raucous colony of hadada ibis.

Daily life centres on the bus stand and the lively, colourful **market** to its east, in the middle of town. The market's a good place to buy *robusta* coffee, the region's major cash crop, and bananas, which form local inhabitants' staple food.

About twenty minutes' walk southeast of the market area is the **lakeshore**, backed by pretty freshwater swamps full of papyrus and reed beds which are a good place to see water birds. There's also a narrow but attractive stretch of beach between the swamp and the lake – *Spice Beach Motel*, at its south end, is a wonderful base, and has a bar and food. According to locals, **swimming** is safe, though the swamps behind the beach could be a possible breeding ground for the parasite-carrying flukes. There are no reports of crocodiles round here (but best to check with locals on the latest situation) but there are hippos in the waters around the rocky **Musila Island**, facing the beach. The island can be visited by boat, most easily through Kiroyera Tours ($50 per boat carrying up to five people plus $2 community fee on arrival at Musila; lifejackets provided).

There's a reminder of colonial rule at the corner of Shore and Aerodrome roads in the form of **Duka Kubwa** ("Big Shop"). Now mostly abandoned and covered by truly spectacular mosses and dust-encrusted spider webs (as are most of the trees around here – quite surreal), it served as the town's first general store in German times. Also ruined are the three **brick pillars** (access from a footpath off Shore Rd), often said to have been built during the 1978–79 Kagera War with Uganda for use as look-out posts but which were actually part of a German wirless transmissions tower, shelled by the British in World War I.

Lastly, to the north of the airport is the small but reasonably absorbing **Kagera Museum** (daily 9.30am–6pm; $2). It contains a collection of traditional tools, Haya artefacts, and an extensive photographic display of the region's wildlife by Dick Persson. The easiest way to reach it is from the beach; walk along the sand past the end of the airport then take a sharp turn left, following the road running alongside the airport's fence; the museum is 300m along the road.

## Eating

Restaurants in Bukoba close when their supply of food for the evening is finished, meaning that whatever's on offer is cooked in a great big pot, and when it's empty, that's your lot. This means you should either find a place early, or risk encountering locked doors and an empty stomach. The local speciality is **ebitoke** (or *matoke*), a thick banana stew which, when well made, is similar to a sticky potato stew.

**Dollar's Café** Market St. This has a limited menu of Tanzanian dishes, even fewer of which are actually available, but what there is is good. Full meals, such as *pilau* or meat with *ugali*, cost Tsh1000–1800. Closed Sat evenings and Sun. No alcohol.

**Galilaya Café** Arusha St. A small and unassuming place that serves some of the best food in town – it's also pretty much the only cheap place guaranteed to be open at night or on Sunday. Stuff yourself silly with a gorgeously aromatic *pilau* and steamed or broiled fish, for under Tsh1500. They also have fresh milk (hot or cold) and real juices. No alcohol.

**Maendeleo Café** Sokoni St. Next to and run by Kiroyera Tours, this place does simple snacks and hot drinks as well as basic meals served with *ugali* or *kashuri* (yam).

**Rose Café** Jamhuri Rd. A longstanding favourite, this place has good breakfasts and snacks, and

simple but filling meals, including *matoke* and hamburgers. Open daytime only, closed Sun. No alcohol.

**Spice Beach Motel** On the beach 2km south of the centre. A brilliant location and very good food, served under parasols facing the beach (there's no dining room as such). *Nyama choma* is available all day, but there's a wait for anything ordered off the menu: mains cost from Tsh3000.

**Ujirani Mwema Restaurant** Market St. The large dining room here is popular for quick bites or a cup of tea or coffee, though arriving at a time when they have full meals is pot luck. Erratic hours; closed Sat evenings. No alcohol.

**Walkgard Annex Hotel** Uganda Rd. Serves up the usual – roast chicken, fried tilapia and chips – plus burgers. Most dishes are around Tsh5000.

## Drinking and nightlife

The local **banana beer** is *olubisi*; when distilled it becomes *nkonyagi* ("Cognac").

**Lina's Nightclub** Uganda Rd. You can take the 'Open 24hr' sign with a pinch of salt, but nevertheless this is Bukoba's best nightspot, with live bands, well-stocked bars and a disco that's packed till the wee small hours most weekends.

**Lake Hotel** Shore Rd. The lake view from the terrace

or the tables on the lawn is the main draw in this calm, dignified but increasingly dilapidated place.

**Spice Beach Motel** On the beach 2km south of the centre. A stunning lake view, brisk breezes, sandy shoreline, lots of booze, good food, and it's open until midnight too – languorous bliss.

## Listings

**Banks and exchange** NBC, Barongo St/Jamhuri Rd, is helpful and efficient.

**Bookshop** ELCT Bookshop, Kawawa St/Market St, has a good book on Haya proverbs, and also sells beads, necklaces, basketry and carvings.

**Car repairs** ELCT Garage and the adjacent Naushad Auto Works, both on Kawawa St.

**Health** Hospitali ya Mkoa, Uganda Rd

☎028/222 0927, is reasonably well equipped. MK Pharmacy, opposite *Rosé Café*, Samuel Luangisa Rd ☎028/222 0582; also open Sun.

**Immigration** Immigration office on Uganda Rd, ☎028/222 0067.

**Internet** Best at the post office, Barongo St (Mon–Fri 8am–8pm, Sat 8am–6pm, Sun 10.30am–4pm; Tsh1000 per hr). There's also New

Heading to Mwanza, it makes sense to catch the overnight MV *Victoria* **ferry**, which sails from Bukoba at 9.30pm on Monday, Wednesday and Friday. The ticket office is at the port 3km south of town. For a $3 mark-up, Kiroyera Tours on Sokoni Street will buy the ticket for you – get it a few days in advance to be sure of a berth rather than just a seat. Tickets cost Tsh30,600 first-class (two bunks per cabin), Tsh20,600 second-class (six bunks per cabin), and Tsh16,300 for a second-class seat.

**Bus services** from Bukoba are sketchy and usually deeply uncomfortable experiences, and bus frequencies and schedules change frequently; the following is just a rough guide. For **Biharamulo**, there's a daily bus except Sunday; do catch a bus rather than a daladala, which really *is* uncomfortable. For Arusha via **Nzega** and **Singida**, Kimotco is the company, heading off on Tuesday, Thursday and Saturday and taking one day, with no overnight stop. For **Kigoma**, Visram Bus leaves on Monday and Wednesday, and Saratoga Line on Tuesday and Saturday; all buses leave at 6am and arrive before midnight on the same day. There are no direct buses to **Mwanza**: change in Biharamulo (next day) or catch the ferry.

Tanzania's only overland crossing into **Uganda** is at Mutukala (Mutukula), 80km northwest of Bukoba. There's the daily Dolphin Bus at 7am for Kampala (roughly four hours), and several uncomfortably packed daladalas and pick-ups every hour or so to the border. **Immigration** can be awkward if the official decides to be, well, officious – be patient and polite. There are moneychangers at the border.

The only **flights** out of Bukoba are a twice-daily service (around 7am and 2.15pm) to Mwanza operated by Precisionair, whose office is on Karume Street (☏ 0713/316806). A taxi to the airport from the town centre should be no more than Tsh1500.

---

Bukoba Cyber Centre, Kashozi Rd/Tupendane St (Mon–Sat 8.30am–9pm; Tsh1000 per hr), and a couple of terminals at the *ELCT Bukoba Hotel* on Airport Road (Tsh1500 per hr).
**Library** Barongo St (Mon–Fri 9am–6pm, Sat 9am–2pm; Tsh500 daily membership).

**Post office** Kawawa St/Barongo St.
**Supermarket** Fido Dido Store, Jamhuri Rd.
**Swimming pool** *Walkgard Westland Hotel* charges Tsh3000 for day guests.
**Telephones** TTCL, Uganda Rd near the bus station.

## Around Bukoba

Kagera Region is both a political boundary, sharing its borders with Uganda, Burundi and Rwanda, and a natural one, marking the transition from East African flora and fauna to vegetation more typically Central and West African. It's also a wildly beautiful region, with scattered lakes, hills cloaked in deep forests, impressive escarpments (and caves), and villages built in traditional style with artfully designed beehive-shaped grass houses (*mushonge*) thatched down to the ground. Add in a cornucopia of attractions, from game reserves to prehistoric rock paintings and ruined palaces, and there's more than enough to keep you busy for weeks.

The region sees very few tourists, though this has not deterred **Kiroyera Tours** in Bukoba (Sokoni St; ☏ 028/222 0203, ⓦ www.kiroyeratours.com) – owned and ably managed by five local women – from offering quite possibly the largest number of trips and activities of any Tanzanian tour operator: a pleasingly bewildering assortment with something for all interests, from history and archeology to wildlife, culture and cooking. Itineraries can be customized, and trips extended over several days. **Costs** largely depend on transport: half-day bicycle trips around Bukoba are upwards of $10 per person, while a two-day tour of Kagera's far northwest could easily relieve you of $200 per person. On average, though, expect to pay $40–60 per person per day, plus $35 per group for transport: not especially cheap, but reasonable given the cost of car rental otherwise.

Some sample tours (see Kiroyera's excellent website for more) include **Lake Ikimba**, 40km southwest of Bukoba, which shares a curious Sodom and Gomorrah-style myth with several other lakes around Lake Victoria, in which the disobedience of a newly wed bride caused the lake to emerge from a cooking pot. The trip includes **hippo watching** at Engono River. South of here is the steep but climbable **Nyamilyango escarpment**, which has caves, freshwater springs and waterfalls. The trip can be extended over two days to include Muleba Palace, Kishaka Island and tea farms.

# Biharamulo

The small, lively and friendly town of **BIHARAMULO** is set on a high ridge crowned by an unusually well-fortified **boma** founded by the Germans in 1902 (now a hotel). The town, which was only endowed with electricity and direct-dial phones in recent years, is a handy overnight stop if you're heading to Bukoba by car or bus. It's also a possible jumping-off point for visits to Rubondo Island National Park, via the fishing village of Nyamirembe (see p.420).

## Practicalities

The **bus stand** is at the bottom of town on the road in. There are buses to Bukoba on Tuesday, Thursday and Saturday afternoons, and Monday morning, as well as hugely uncomfortable daladalas every morning (get there for 7am to be sure of a seat), though these may only go as far as Muleba, where you'll have to change (plenty of daladalas from there). There's also at least one daily bus (except Sat) between Biharamulo and Mwanza, at 6am. Buses to Kigoma start in Bukoba, and whilst the companies – Visram Bus on Monday and Wednesday, and Saratoga Line on Tuesday and Saturday – have agents at Biharamulo's bus stand, there's no guarantee of a seat until you reach Kibondo.

If you're **driving north**, there is no longer any need to pick up an armed guard at the police post just north of town, though this rule may be reinstated depending on the stability of the region. **Heading south**, there's a good unsurfaced road as far as Lusahunga (31km) at the junction of the sealed road into Rwanda. The road south of here towards Kigoma is in a bad shape until you reach the first of the refugee camps near Kibondo. Again, depending on the security situation in these, you may have to pick up an armed escort at **Nyakanazi**, at the junction with the sealed road that goes most of the way to Shinyanga. If you get delayed, there are several guesthouses in both Kibondo and Kasulu.

Change money at NMB **bank**, 800m uphill from the bus stand. TTCL is nearby; turn left along Makongoro Road just before reaching the bank. The post office is at the northwest corner of the bus stand. There's **internet access** beside *Robert Hotel*.

### Accommodation, eating and drinking

The town has a good spread of cheap **hotels**, where hot water is provided on request in buckets. There's not much in the way of **restaurants**: the best place for food or drinks is *Robert Hotel* (opposite the bus stand); the *Sunset Inn* next door is fine too. Both also do breakfast – try the *supu* broth. **Street food** is limited to roast maize cobs sold at the bus station until around 10pm.

**Boma Guest House** 1.5km uphill (west) from the bus stand, at the end of the District administration offices ☎028/222 3486. Occupying the fortified German boma, this is Biharamulo's classiest option, if still far from luxurious. Rooms come in pairs: two en-suite rondavels in the courtyard, two singles and two doubles sharing bathrooms, and a couple of "VIP" suites. Meals, other than breakfast, need to be pre-arranged. ❸

**Victoria Guest House** ☎028/222 3418. Ntare Rd: walk down Mwinyi St, on the west side of the bus stand, and take the second right. This friendly place has clean and extremely cheap rooms with good-sized beds, nets and shared bathrooms (water in buckets). ❶

# Rubondo Island National Park

Tucked in to the lake's southwestern corner, **Rubondo Island National Park** is one of Tanzania's least-visited and best-preserved wildlife areas. It covers 457 square kilometres, little more than half of which is land, and includes eleven minor islets in addition to Rubondo Island itself. Most of the main island is scattered with the granite outcrops so characteristic of the lake region, and covered by moist evergreen forest – butterfly paradise. The rest is grassland, open *miombo* woodland, sandy beaches and papyrus swamps. The variety of habitats favours a diversity of plant and animal species, something that is especially

▲ Egyptian goose and chicks, Rubondo Island

419

evident in **birdlife** – close to four hundred species have been recorded so far. Among the more easily identifiable birds are hammerkops, cormorants, Goliath herons, saddle-billed storks, egrets and sacred ibises, kingfishers, geese, darters, bee-eaters, flycatchers, parrots, cuckoos, sunbirds and birds of prey, including martial eagles and the world's highest density of African fish eagles. A particular highlight is an unnamed islet to the east, which serves as a breeding ground for tens of thousands of birds.

In addition to the park's birdlife, a number of **endangered mammals** have been introduced, since the island's isolation makes it inherently safer from poachers. While attempts to introduce black rhinos and roan antelopes haven't met with much success, the introduced populations of elephants, chimpanzees, black-and-white colobus monkeys, suni antelopes and African grey parrots are flourishing and – with the exception of the elephants – can be seen with relative ease. The forest-dwelling **chimpanzees** descend from a population of seventeen individuals rescued from smugglers and introduced in the late 1960s – most had been kept in cramped cages, some for as long as nine years. It speaks for the adaptability of chimps (like humans) that these ragged survivors apparently had few problems in establishing themselves on Rubondo, and their population now numbers around 35. The chimps are still being habituated by researchers, so are out of bounds to tourists.

Of the native species, the undoubted stars (together with the birds) are the amphibious **sitatunga antelopes**, an unusual species with splayed and elongated hooves, though unless you catch a glimpse of one straying into the forest, you probably won't see them in all their glory, as they spend much of their lives partly submerged in the marshes and reed beds along the shore. Other frequently seen animals include vervet monkeys, bushbucks, large numbers of hippos and crocodiles and a number of small predators including genets, spotted-necked otters and marsh mongooses.

The **best time to visit** depends on how important clear skies are to you: the best weather is in the dry season from June to the end of September or October, but butterflies and flowers – most spectacularly forest orchids, fireball lilies and red coral trees – are at their showiest during the rains (Oct–Nov & March–May), at which time migratory birds also arrive in abundance.

## Arrival

The easiest access is by light aircraft, but as there are currently no scheduled flights to Rubondo, you'll have to charter a plane: around $500 one way for a five-seat Cessna from Mwanza.

The alternative approach, by **boat**, can be awkward. The place to aim for is **Maganza**, 68km northeast of Biharamulo, leaving you with a roughly ten-kilometre boat crossing to the park headquarters at Kageye. If you're booked at the upmarket *Rubondo Island Camp* they'll organize the crossing ($120 return); otherwise either arrange things locally with fishermen in Maganza, or well in advance through TANAPA in Arusha (see p.307). There are two or three daladalas most days from **Biharamulo to Maganza** via Nyamirembe. There's no accommodation in Maganza, so catch the first daladala (11am), which – should you be unsuccessful in arranging a boat ride that day – gives you the chance to catch the last daladala back to **Nyamirembe** where there's the basic *Maendeleo Guest House* (❶), 1km from the lake. Nyamirembe also has a small dairy that makes delicious cheese; it's the last building on your left before the lake.

Alternatively, you can book a tour. Kiroyera Tours in Bukoba (see p.417) run three-day/two-night tours including transport to the island, accommodation, park fees and walking tours. The price varies depending on the number of people and the kind of accommodation on Rubondo but starts at $335 per person full-board if there are five or more of you and you opt to stay in the TANAPA-run *bandas*.

## Information and accommodation

The **park headquarters** are at Kageye, halfway up the island. **Entry fees** are $20 for 24 hours. The park's **internet** site is Ⓦwww.tanzaniaparks.com /rubondo.html and TANAPA's **guidebook**, available in Arusha, Dar and Stone Town (Zanzibar) covers Lake Victoria.

You have three choices for **accommodation**: a campsite, simple park-run *bandas*, and a luxury tented camp. The campsite ($30 per person) is close to the park headquarters, and offers unnervingly close contact with grazing hippos at night (never position yourself between them and water, which panics them and usually prompts an attack). The *bandas* ($20–30 per person) only have six beds, so you're advised to book ahead at TANAPA in Arusha (see p.307). Bring enough food and drink for the duration whether you're camping or staying in the *bandas*. The upmarket option is *Rubondo Island Camp*, overlooking the lake (book through Safari Legacy in Arusha ☎027/250 3090, Ⓦwww.safarilegacy .com FB Ⓕ which has ten large, twin-bed tents under thatched roofs between the forest and the shore, each with attached bathroom, electricity and lake views from a terrace. There's a bar and swimming pool, and bathing in the lake is also possible.

There are no vehicles, so **getting around** the park is either on foot or by boat. **Guides** are obligatory ($20 per walk per group). There are several walking trails from the park headquarters, including crocodile and sitatunga habitats. **Boats** for excursions (no more than $60 for a few hours) can be rented at *Rubondo Island Camp* or the park headquarters.

# Travel details

### Buses, daladalas and pick-ups

The following journey times are minimums; breakdowns, washed-out roads and bridges and prolonged stops play havoc with timetables. Routes that are especially prone to delays and cancellations during the rains are marked with asterisks.

**Biharamulo** to: Bukoba (4 weekly plus daladalas*; 3–5hr); Kigoma (4 weekly; 12–14hr); Maganza (3 daily; 3hr); Nyamirembe (3 daily; 1hr 30min).
**Bukoba** to: Arusha via Tanzania (3 weekly*; 16–18hr); Arusha via Uganda and Kenya (2 weekly*; 26–30hr); Biharamulo (1–2 daily plus daladalas*; 3–5hr); Dar via Uganda and Kenya (2 weekly; 34–40hr); Kigoma (4 weekly; 15–18hr); Nzega (3 weekly*; 8–10hr); Singida (3 weekly*; 10–12hr); Uganda border (hourly; 2hr).
**Musoma** to: Arusha via Kenya (2 daily; 16–18hr); Arusha via Serengeti (4–6 weekly; 9–11hr); Dar via Kenya (2 daily; 25–27hr); Butiama (every 2hr; 1hr 30min); Mwanza (hourly; 3–4hr); Shinyanga (daily; 10–11hr); Sirari (hourly; 2hr); Tarime (hourly; 2hr).
**Mwanza** to: Arusha via Kenya (6 daily; 18–20hr); Arusha via Serengeti (4 weekly; 10–12hr); Arusha via Singida (1–2 daily; 12–14hr); Biharamulo (2 daily*; 9–11hr); Bunda (hourly; 2hr); Dar via Kenya (3–4 daily; 27–29hr); Dodoma (1 daily*; 22–25hr); Kigoma (1 daily*; 14–18hr); Morogoro (4–5 daily*; 22–27hr); Moshi via Kenya (2–3 daily; 20–22hr); Musoma (hourly; 3–4hr); Nairobi (6 daily; 14–15hr); Nzega (3–4 daily; 10–12hr); Shinyanga (5 daily; 5hr); Singida (2 daily*; 20–22hr); Sirari (hourly; 5–6hr); Tabora (2–3 daily*; 8hr).

### Ferries (Lake Victoria)

**Bukoba** to: Mwanza (3 weekly; 11hr).
**Mwanza** to: Bukoba (3 weekly; 11hr); Nansio (2–3 daily; 2hr 30min–3hr).

**Nansio (Ukerewe Island)** to: Mwanza (2–3 daily; 2hr 30min–3hr).

## Flights

Airline codes used below are: AA (Auric Air), AT (Air Tanzania), CA (Coastal Aviation) and PA (Precisionair). Where more than one airline flies to the same destination, the one with most frequent flights and/or shortest journey times is listed first.

**Bukoba** to: Mwanza (PA: 2 daily; 45min).
**Mwanza** to: Arusha (CA: daily; 3hr 15min); Bukoba (PA: 2 daily; 45min); Dar (AT, PA: 3–4 daily; 1hr 30min–2hr 15min); Entebbe (AA: 2 weekly; 1hr); Kigali (CA: daily; 1hr); Kilimanjaro (PA: 6 weekly; 1hr 20min); Manyara (CA: daily; 2hr 45min); Ngorongoro (CA: daily; 2hr 40min); Rubondo (CA: 2 weekly; 30min); Serengeti (CA: daily; 1hr 55min).
**Rubondo Island** to: Arusha (CA: 2 weekly; 4hr 5min); Mwanza (CA: 2 weekly; 30min); Serengeti (CA: 2 weekly; 1hr 30min–2hr 35min).

## Trains

**Mwanza** to: Dar (3 weekly; 37hr); Dodoma (3 weekly; 24hr 10min); Morogoro (3 weekly; 31hr 35min); Tabora (3 weekly; 10hr).

# Lake Tanganyika and western Tanzania

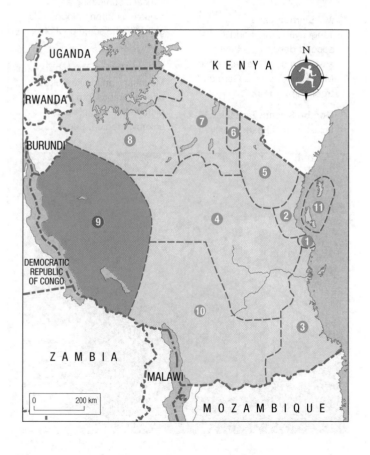

CHAPTER 9 Highlights

* **Ujiji** Now a fishing village, Ujiji was at the start of a 1200-kilometre slave route to Bagamoyo, and where Stanley gave the world those immortal words, "Dr Livingstone, I presume?" See p.430

* **MV Liemba** Lake Tanganyika, the world's second deepest, is best savoured from the venerable MV *Liemba*, an old German troopship. See p.435

* **Gombe Stream** Tanzania's tiniest national park is only accessible by boat; Gombe's chimpanzees have been studied since 1960. See p.437

* **Katavi National Park** A remote wilderness where biomass really looks like it means something as thousands-strong hippo pods gather in the same pool of mud. See p.455

* **Rukwa Region** The Mbizi Mountains and Lake Rukwa offer a glimpse into this picturesque and almost unknown region. See p.460

▲ Hippos in the Katuma River, Katavi National Park

# 9

# Lake Tanganyika and western Tanzania

W estern Tanzania is as fascinating and rewarding to explore as it can be frustrating to get around, especially during the rains, when most roads become impassable. The region is dominated by **Lake Tanganyika**, which separates the semi-arid *miombo* woodland of Tanzania's Central Plateau from the lush forests of Central Africa. The lake also marks the border with Burundi, Zambia and the Democratic Republic of Congo (formerly Zaïre), and as such is a veritable cultural crossroads. This mixture is best seen in the region's largest town, **Kigoma**, on the northeast shore of the lake, though for tourists Kigoma's main attraction is **Ujiji**, the former slave-trading centre nearby where Stanley and Dr Livingstone famously met. Kigoma is also the starting point for the weekly ferry to Zambia, calling at a string of fascinating places along the way, and the most convenient base for visiting **Gombe** and **Mahale national parks**, both of which contain **chimpanzees**.

Heading away from the lake to the east, the Central Line Railway follows the line of the old caravan routes across the Central Plateau, bringing you to the large and bustling town of **Tabora**. Occupying the historically strategic junction of routes from Lake Tanganyika and Lake Victoria, Tabora controlled much of the **slave trade** in the latter half of the nineteenth century, though like Kigoma it owes its modern importance to the railway. The region **south of Kigoma and Tabora** is seldom visited, mainly because of the difficulty of getting around, although a branch line of the Central Line Railway runs to Mpanda, just beyond which is **Katavi National Park**, dominated by tsetse-fly-infested *miombo* woodland and rich wildlife, especially hippo, buffalo, crocodiles and birds. Further south, **Lake Rukwa** and the **Mbizi Mountains** are completely off-the-beaten-track destinations for adventurous travellers, both reached from the area's only significant town, **Sumbawanga**.

Travel in western Tanzania is for the most part a wild, adventurous and hugely time-consuming affair. **Language** is limited to Kiswahili and local tongues, though if you really get stuck some bus drivers and hotel managers can usually muster a few words in English. **Road conditions** throughout the region are dreadful. In the **dry season** you can get through to anywhere if you don't mind a slow, dusty, bumpy – and, on public transport, a remarkably body-crunching – ride. During the **short rains** (Oct–Dec) you can still get to most places but may be delayed waiting for the road to dry out; in the **long rains** (March–May),

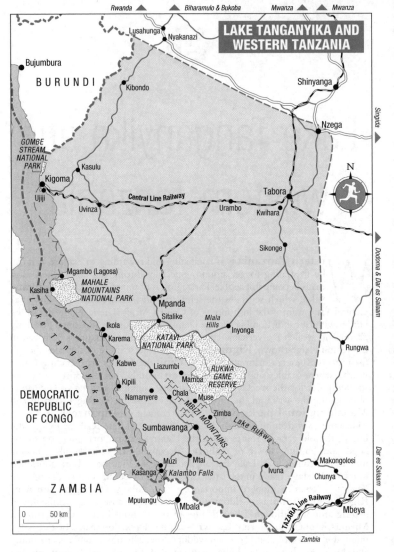

LAKE TANGANYIKA AND
WESTERN TANZANIA

however, you can forget about roads, as most routes are closed for weeks on end. The only half-decent stretches are between Tabora and Mwanza, and south from Mpanda to Sumbawanga, but these are likely to become impassable if not properly maintained. Wherever you're driving, always seek local advice about the state of the road before heading off, as well as **security**: there's a slight but ever-present risk of attack from armed bandits, especially around Kigoma and northwards. If things are considered risky, you'll be offered armed escorts at roadblocks when leaving towns. The one all-weather route is the **Central Line Railway**, from Dar es Salaam to Tabora and Kigoma, with a southward branch to Mpanda (timetables on Ⓦwww.trctz.com).

# Lake Tanganyika

Occupying the southern end of the Western Rift Valley, and bordered by Tanzania, Burundi, Congo and Zambia, **Lake Tanganyika** is the **world's longest freshwater lake**, measuring 677km from north to south, fed by the Malagarasi and Kalambo rivers on the Tanzanian side, and the turbulent Ruzizi River from Lake Kivu on the border of Burundi and the Democratic Republic of Congo. The lake's maximum recorded depth of 1436m (the deepest part of the lake lies 358m below sea level) also makes Tanganyika the **world's second-deepest lake** after Siberia's Lake Baikal, though lake life only inhabits the top two hundred metres, as there's little or no oxygen further down. Covering some 32,900 square kilometres, Lake Tanganyika is also **Africa's second-largest permanent lake** (Lake Victoria is the biggest) and, last but not least, is also one of the **world's oldest lakes**, having been formed around twenty million years ago during the tectonic upheavals that created the Rift Valley. Its great age, size, freshness, ecological isolation and geological and climatological stability have fostered the evolution of a remarkably diverse local flora and fauna. Animals which can be spotted here include various species of crabs, molluscs and crustaceans, hippos and crocodiles, and over 250 species of fish, most of which are small and often brightly coloured cichlids.

The main settlement on the Tanzanian shore is the lively harbour town of **Kigoma**, at the end of the Central Line Railway from Dar es Salaam, which has a weekly ferry south to Zambia via a string of Tanzanian fishing villages, some of which have road access inland towards Mpanda and Sumbawanga. The old Arab slave-trading town of **Ujiji**, 10km south of Kigoma, is the place where the immortal words "Dr Livingstone, I presume?" were uttered by Henry Morton Stanley. Accessible by boat from Kigoma are two expensive but very special national parks – **Gombe Stream**, and **Mahale Mountains**, both famous for their chimpanzees.

# Kigoma

Tucked into the southeastern corner of Kigoma Bay at the end of the Central Railway line, the bustling harbour town of **KIGOMA** is Lake Tanganyika's busiest port, handling most of Burundi's foreign trade and serving as the main arrival point for refugees fleeing Central Africa's interminable conflicts. Head out of town and you're bound to come across a long-term UN refugee camp. In town you'll hear plenty of French, the lingua franca of Burundi, Rwanda and Congo, and many business signs include French translations in addition to Kiswahili and English. The refugee presence also means that people are well used to seeing foreigners, the majority of whom work for one of the plethora of international aid organizations based here.

The town itself is very attractive, its lush tropical vegetation providing a welcome contrast to the monotonous *miombo* woodland that covers much of central Tanzania. For tourists, the town serves as the base for the **Gombe Stream** and **Mahale Mountains** national parks, and for day-trips to **Ujiji**, scene of Stanley's famous meeting with Livingstone. There are also a few beautiful beaches if you want to escape the strength-sapping heat and humidity.

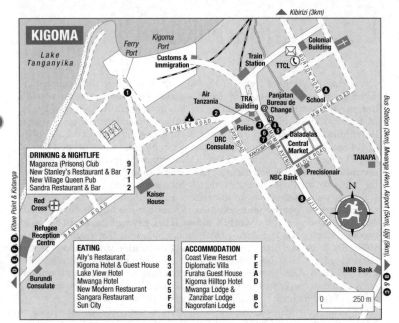

**KIGOMA**

Lake Tanganyika

Kibirizi (3km)

Ferry Port · Kigoma Port · Customs & Immigration · Train Station · Colonial Building · TTCL · BURTON ROAD

Air Tanzania · TRA Building · Panjatan Bureau de Change · School · MWANGA ROAD

Police · DRC Consulate · Daladalas · Central Market · TANAPA

STANLEY ROAD · KAYA ROAD · KAKOLWA ROAD · MLOLE ROAD

NBC Bank · Precisionair

Kaiser House

Red Cross

BANGWE ROAD

Refugee Reception Centre

Burundi Consulate

UJIJI ROAD

NMB Bank

Bus Station (3km), Mwanga (4km), Airport (5km), Ujiji (9km)

Kilwe Point & Katanga

N

0      250 m

**DRINKING & NIGHTLIFE**
Magareza (Prisons) Club ... 9
New Stanley's Restaurant & Bar ... 7
New Village Queen Pub ... 1
Sandra Restaurant & Bar ... 2

**EATING**
Ally's Restaurant ... 8
Kigoma Hotel & Guest House ... 3
Lake View Hotel ... 4
Mwanga Hotel ... C
New Modern Restaurant ... 5
Sangara Restaurant ... F
Sun City ... 6

**ACCOMMODATION**
Coast View Resort ... F
Diplomatic Villa ... E
Furaha Guest House ... A
Kigoma Hilltop Hotel ... D
Mwanga Lodge & Zanzibar Lodge ... B
Nagorofani Lodge ... C

## Some history

In the nineteenth century, Lake Tanganyika was the major source of the Zanzibari-controlled **slave trade**. Slaves were captured as far west as the Congo Basin, from where they were transported across the lake to a number of transit centres on the Tanganyikan shore, of which **Ujiji** was the most infamous. For much of this time, Kigoma was a small fishing village, and it wasn't until towards the end of the nineteenth century that its importance grew, just as Ujiji's began to wane. The slave trade was at an end, and Germany controlled much of what is now Tanzania, Rwanda and Burundi. Kigoma's sheltered location inside Kigoma Bay gave it the edge over Ujiji, and the site was consequently developed into the regional headquarters. The town really took off in February 1914, when the 1254-kilometre **Central Line Railway** from Dar es Salaam finally reached the lake nine years after construction had begun, establishing a reliable and rapid connection between the Indian Ocean and Lake Tanganyika which has ensured the town's livelihood to this day. The Germans had little time to enjoy the fruits of their labour however: World War I erupted, and in 1916 they were ejected by troops from the Belgian Congo.

The indigenous population of Kigoma (and of Kasulu and Kibondo districts to the north) is the **Ha tribe**, who number nearly a million. They call their country Buha, which before the arrival of the Germans contained six independent chiefdoms organized into elaborate hierarchies of sub-chiefs and headmen similar to that of the Haya (see p.412) and Nyamwezi (p.447). Over the last three centuries the Ha have developed close ties with Burundi's **Tutsi**. Through intermarriage and commerce, the two tribes have come to share a good part of their language, and the Ha have adopted the Tutsi cattle-herding culture in the grasslands south of Kigoma. The Ha's longhorn Ankole cattle play a vital social role as tokens of inter-family bonds and friendship, especially in marriage, when cattle are exchanged as bridewealth paid to the bride's family.

## Arrival

The easiest way to reach Kigoma is by **train** from Dar es Salaam or Tabora. The **bus station** – for services from Bukoba and Mwanza – is 4km uphill at Mwanga, from where there are taxis (you'll probably arrive too late to catch a daladala). Kigoma **airport** lies 3km beyond Mwanga and Precisionair fly in daily from Dar es Salaam via Tabora.

**Daladalas** start at the Central Market off Lumumba Avenue. **Taxis** can be rented at the airport, at the bus and daladala stands, and along Lumumba Avenue. Short journeys cost Tsh1500.

## Accommodation

The better guesthouses are those up in Mwanga district, 3km up Ujiji Road from the centre. But as you're on Lake Tanganyika, much nicer – unless you're on a really tight budget – is to stay at one of the three **lakeshore hotels**. In the cheaper places, "single" rooms can be shared by couples, as "double" means two beds. **Water supplies** are erratic, so shower when you get the chance.

**Coast View Resort** 2.5km southwest of town, signposted from Bangwe Rd ☎028/280 3434, ✉coastviewresort@yahoo.com. This shiny, tiled affair fails to make use of its hilltop location, with only the outside bar offering any view of the lake, but the fourteen en-suite rooms are smart. There's also an internet café and restaurant. ❸

**Diplomatic Villa** 2.5km southwest of town, signposted from Lumumba Ave and Bangwe Rd ☎028/280 4597. Up on a dusty hillside, this vaguely colonial-style place has a nice garden and *banda* for drinks. The nine reasonable en-suite rooms in the main house have big beds and box nets, local TV, fan and window screen. Good food is available to order. ❸

**Furaha Guest House** Burton Rd ☎028/280 3665. Another acceptable and calm central cheapie; all rooms have fans and nets, saggy beds, and clean squat toilets (either sharing or en suite), plus one "special" en-suite room with Western-style toilet. ❶

**Kigoma Hilltop Hotel** 4km southwest of town on a headland high above the shore ☎028/280 4437, ✉kht@raha.com. Kigoma's poshest place by miles, but the electric fence, armed guards and wildlife trophies gracing the lobby hardly make for a happy first impression, and the service isn't all it could be. There are thirty rooms in chalets strung out across the headland, giving spectacular views over the lake from their balconies. Facilities include two restaurants, swimming pool (with lake views), sandy beach, tennis court and gym. The hotel also runs trips to Mahale and Gombe. FB ❺–❻

**Mwanga Lodge** and **Zanzibar Lodge** Ujiji Rd, Mwanga (no phone). Kigoma's best budget guest-houses, under the same management and within 100m of each other. The beds have big nets, and the bathrooms (shared and en suite) with their showers and squat toilets are relatively clean. *Zanzibar Lodge* also has a restaurant, and some of its upper-floor rooms give glimpses of the lake. ❶

**Nagorofani Lodge** Lumumba Ave ☎028/280 4626, 028/280 5371. This is a quiet, safe choice with 10 en-suite rooms, each fitted with TV and a/c. An internet café and gym are also planned; though expect prices to rise if/when these are installed. ❸

## The lakeshore

Lake Tanganyika's surface water is a very pleasant 23°C, and according to locals, **swimming** near Kigoma is safe as long as there's no reedy vegetation nearby; if there is there might be a risk of bilharzia. **Crocodiles** are sometimes sighted in the area, although there have been no reports of attacks, but **water snakes** may dwell near rocks. If you want to take the risk (and plenty do, including tourists), then the area around the closed *Lake Tanganyika Beach Hotel* is a lovely place for a dip, or just to spend a blissfully lazy afternoon doing nothing more energetic than watching crows and distant dhows. If you don't want to chance it, *Kigoma Hilltop Hotel* charges Tsh2000 for the use of its pool. **Women should cover up** when bathing to avoid offending Islamic sensibilities – indeed, this applies to the whole lake. There are two private beaches 7km south of town near Kitwe Point. The best is **Jacobsen's Beach** (Tsh2000), which has coarse red sand and a few parasols in a small secluded cove, but no facilities. Just to the south, less sheltered and with pebbles instead of sand, **Zungu Beach** (Tsh1000) has three parasols, a couple of shelters and some warm sodas and cans of Castle lager for sale, but no food. Tsetse flies can be a pain but don't carry sleeping sickness. To get to either beach, take a taxi (Tsh5000) or catch a daladala to Katonga village from outside the TRA Building at the start of Bangwe Road – these will leave you at the junction for the track leading to the shore (there's a green sign to Zungu Beach); it's a sweltering three-kilometre walk over the hills to either beach. The intermittent signposts aren't much help – for Zungu, turn left at the first fork after about 2km and bear right at the next junction; for Jacobsen's, just keep right at every fork.

**Kibirizi**, 3km north of town (follow the rail tracks, catch a daladala, or take a taxi), is the best place to see how **dagaa** – the lake's main commercial catch – is dried. These diminutive fish, which measure between 2cm and 10cm, live in immense shoals near the surface, and are caught at night using pressure lamps mounted on wooden boats. At a given moment, the fishermen beat on the sides of the boat to panic the fish into tight shoals, which are then scooped up in nets. The flotilla leaves Kibirizi late in the afternoon in pairs, the lead boat towing the other to conserve fuel, and you can see their lights bobbing up and down from the coast at night; the season peaks in the second half of September. The fish are spread out the following morning to dry, either on gravel or over a suspended wire mesh.

## Ujiji

The pleasantly relaxed atmosphere of **Ujiji**, 10km southeast of Kigoma, belies a terrible past when, as the main Arab trading post on Lake Tanganyika, it was the place from where tens of thousands of shackled slaves began their gruelling 1200-kilometre march towards the Indian Ocean. The journey from Ujiji to Bagamoyo, Saadani or Pangani took anything from three to six months, and many died along the way, perishing either from exhaustion or being shot when they became too ill to move or tried to escape – it's thought that during the fifty years when Zanzibar controlled the route, over a million Africans (mostly from eastern Congo) were enslaved. Now little more than a suburb of Kigoma, Ujiji has few visible reminders of its infamous past other than its distinctive Swahili-styled houses (more typical of the Indian Ocean coast) and a profusion of mango trees, said to have grown from stones discarded by slaves.

From the 1850s onwards, **European explorers** venturing into the interior also used the slave routes, and – so long as they were armed with letters of recommendation from the sultan in Zanzibar – generally had little to fear. The first to visit Ujiji and set eyes on Lake Tanganyika were Richard Burton and John Hanning Speke, who arrived in February 1858 during their search for the source of the Nile (see p.398). Ujiji was also the scene of Henry Morton Stanley's legendary meeting with David Livingstone. The alleged site of the famous encounter is marked by the **Livingstone Memorial**, halfway along Livingstone Street some 500m before the harbour; coming into town along Kigoma Road, the junction for Livingstone Street is on the right before the *Matunda Guest House*. A plaque beside two mango trees – said to have been grafted from the tree under which the duo allegedly met – marks the spot. The small **museum** (daily 8am–5.30pm; Tsh5000) contains local paintings depicting the famous encounter, and some offbeat, larger-than-life sculptures of Livingstone and Stanley raising their hats to each other in greeting, and not much else.

Missionary-turned-explorer David Livingstone made his name with a bestseller, *Missionary Travels and Researches in South Africa*, but lasting fame came from his serialized *Journals* – graphic and impassioned tirades against the horrors of the slave trade, particularly the massacre of hundreds of market women at Nyangwe in Congo by Arab slavers:

"Shot after shot continued to be fired on the helpless and perishing. Some of the long line of heads disappeared quietly; while other poor creatures threw their arms high, as if appealing to the great Father above, and sank."

Livingstone's words obliged the British Government to blockade Zanzibar, forcing a reluctant Sultan Barghash to close Stone Town's slave market, thus hastening the end of the slave trade, and ultimately of slavery, in East Africa.

Born on March 19, 1813, near Glasgow in Scotland, the introspective **Livingstone** travelled to Cape Town in 1841 (under the auspices of the London Missionary Society), where he married a missionary's daughter and set to work as a preacher and doctor. On his early expeditions he crossed the Kalahari Desert and "discovered" Lake Nyasa, but his most famous discovery, in November 1855, was that of Mosi oa Tunya (the "Smoke that Thunders") which he dutifully renamed **Victoria Falls**. His fourth major expedition (1858–64) covered the area between the Lower Zambezi River and Lake Nyasa.

After a brief sojourn in Britain, he returned to Africa in 1866, having been commissioned by the Royal Geographical Society to explore the area between Lake Nyasa and Lake Tanganyika and to solve the riddle of the Nile's source. So began the five-year odyssey that was to end with the famous **encounter with Stanley**. At the time of the meeting, Livingstone was suffering from dysentery, fever and foot ulcers, but within two weeks had recovered sufficiently to explore the northern shores of Lake Tanganyika with Stanley, before returning to Kazeh near Tabora, where Stanley headed to the coast.

Livingstone stayed behind awaiting supplies, and then set off on his fifth and final expedition in August 1872, during which he again fell ill with dysentery and died at **Chitambo** village close to Lake Bangweulu (in present-day Zambia) in May 1873. He was buried as a national hero at Westminster Abbey on April 18, 1874.

### ...and Stanley

Among Livingstone's pallbearers was **Henry Morton Stanley**. Twenty-eight years Livingstone's junior, Stanley was born at Denbigh, Wales, on January 29, 1841. During his childhood he spent nine years in the workhouse before taking work on a ship from Liverpool to New Orleans at the age of 17. Just eleven years later he was working as the *New York Herald*'s scoop journalist and was commissioned to cover the inauguration of the Suez Canal and then find Livingstone, who had been "missing" for five years.

The expedition set off from Zanzibar and exactly 236 days later, on November 10, 1871, having buried eighteen porters and guards, his two European companions, both his horses, all 27 donkeys and his watchdog, Stanley arrived in Ujiji. "I would have run to him," wrote Stanley, "only I was a coward in the presence of such a mob – would have embraced him, but that I did not know how he would receive me; so I did what moral cowardice and false pride suggested was the best thing – walked deliberately to him, took off my hat, and said: 'Dr Livingstone, I presume?'"

After the meeting, Stanley abandoned journalism and dedicated himself to exploring Africa. He was knighted in 1899, and died in London on May 10, 1904. His summation of Livingstone: "He is not an angel, but he approaches to that being as near as the nature of a living man will allow."

Frequent **daladalas** run to Ujiji from the east side of the market in Kigoma, dropping you along Kigoma Road, from where it's a ten-minute walk to the Livingstone Monument. A taxi there and back from Kigoma costs Tsh6000–7000.

## Eating

The local delicacies are **migebuka**, which looks like a thin mackerel and tastes similar, and of course **dagaa**, which is best roasted in palm oil (*mawese*, which gives it a nutty taste) and served with dark *ugali* made from cassava. **Street food**, especially fried cassava, roasted maize cobs and seasonal fruit, is best along Lumumba Avenue between the daladala stand and the train station. There are also plenty of dirt-cheap grilled meat and *chipsi mayai* places around the daladala stand and market. Mwanga, a few kilometres uphill along Ujiji Road, is especially good in the evenings, with dozens of stands serving up fried *dagaa* and tasty *mishkaki* (goat-meat skewers). There are also cheap *hotelis* facing the railway station.

**Ally's Restaurant** Lumumba Ave. A friendly place busy with locals at lunchtime. Some of the pre-cooked snacks are a bit grim but the aromatic cinnamon-laced tea is wonderful, the chicken *supu* a delight, and full meals (Tsh1500–3000), including biryanis if ordered in advance, are also good. No alcohol.

**Kigoma Hotel & Guest House** Lumumba Ave. Food is limited to rice or *ugali* with fish or chicken (Tsh1800), but there's a breezy if loud (blaring music) street-side terrace.

**Lake View Hotel** Lumumba Ave. Snacks, beers and a TV, with *supu* for breakfast, good mashed potato *chops*, and a nice shady terrace. No lake view, incidentally.

**Mwanga Hotel** 3km up Ujiji Rd, Mwanga. The *migebuka* fish here is usually good, as is the *dagaa*, and it's very cheap, costing under Tsh1500 for a meal. No alcohol.

**New Modern Restaurant** Lumumba Ave. Unspectacular menu of standard African fare (chicken and chips etc) or, if ordered in advance, more 'specialist'

### Moving on from Kigoma

**By train**

**Trains** to Dar via Tabora, Dodoma and Morogoro (change in Tabora for Mwanza or Mpanda) depart at 5pm (Tues, Thurs & Sun). The ticket office is open 8am–noon and 2–6pm on these days, and 8am–noon and 2–4.30pm on others; buy your ticket in advance to be sure of a first- or second-class bunk. **Fares** to Dar es Salaam are Tsh54,300 in first-class sleepers, Tsh39,700 in second sleeping, and from Tsh17,160 for a seat. The **timetable** is posted at ⑩www.trctz.com.

**By plane**

**Scheduled flights** are limited to the Precisionair service to Dar es Salaam every evening (Tsh250,000 one-way), and the Air Tanzania service direct to Dar on Sundays and Wednesdays at 10.30am, and to Tabora and then on to Dar at 10.15am.

**By road**

The only practical **road** out of Kigoma is north via Kasulu and Kibondo to Biharamulo and Bukoba (Visram Bus Wed & Fri, Saratoga Line Thurs & Sun), or to Shinyanga and Mwanza (six weekly: served by Saratoga Line, whose office is in the *New Centre Guest House* on Lumumba Ave in Mwanga, or Adventure Connection, whose office is just 100m or so further up the hill), either of which takes a full day, or two days with breakdowns or rain. During the rains the stretch between Kibondo and Nyakanazi can be impassable. Buy tickets – from the offices at the bus stand in Mwanga – at least two days in advance to avoid having to stand, though even seated, it can be uncomfortable. There is no public transport to **Mpanda** and the rough road is impassable during the rains.

meals such as beef curry. That said, the place is spotlessly clean, the food good value (large portions and nothing over Tsh4000) and the service from the uniformed staff is both attentive and polite. No alcohol.

**Sangara Restaurant** *Kigoma Hilltop Hotel*, 4km southwest of town on a headland high above the shore. Expensive Continental and Indian-style

meals in an anodyne atmosphere, compensated for by superb lake views and a swimming pool (Tsh3000). There's also an ice-cream parlour. No alcohol, but they don't mind if you bring your own.

**Sun City** Lumumba Ave. Jauntily painted place that's good for simple breakfasts (samosas, juices etc) though it remains open throughout the day to serve simple local staples.

## Drinking and nightlife

Unsurprisingly, considering Kigoma's location, **Congolese music** rather than Bongo Flava reigns supreme, with the sound of long-established stars Koffi Olomide, Le General Defao et al pouring from radios and tape players in the streets and in a number of bars, which sometimes double as discos. Incidentally, **don't walk** around Kigoma at night, but catch a taxi.

**Magereza (Prisons) Club** 2km along Bangwe Rd, just before the prison on the right. A popular place on the beach – its Sunday afternoon discos give the prisoners next door something to dance to.

**New Stanley's Restaurant & Bar** Kakolwa St. The restaurant serves food and drinks all day, but most people come for the disco, sometimes featuring live bands (Wed & Fri from 9pm, Sun from 3pm).

**New Village Queen Pub** 50m up from the ferry port. Advertising itself as "the home of fine beer"

as well as inviting you to "experience indifference (sic) services", this place is ideal if you're waiting for the ferry. Music pumps out both day and night – regardless of whether there are any punters – but the service is warm and the grounds not unattractive.

**Sandra Restaurant & Bar** Stanley Rd. Handy place if awaiting a train or ferry, with a pleasant beer garden at the back, and good *nyama choma* and fried bananas (Ts3500).

### By boat

Open-topped **lake taxis** (nicknamed *kigoma-kigoma*) leave from Ujiji for ports to the south, and from Kibirizi, 3km north of Kigoma, for ports to the north. Their unpleasant reputation is due not so much to the risk of sinking, nor because they can be massively uncomfortable and offer no shade, water or toilets, but because they sometimes carry "dangerous passengers" – usually drunks but occasionally armed bandits.

Much safer and more comfortable if you're heading south is the historic **MV Liemba ferry** (Marine Services Company ☏028/280 3950, ✉marine@africaonline .co.tz), sailing from the ferry port southwest of the commercial harbour every Wednesday at 4pm for Mpulungu in Zambia, if all goes well arriving around 10am on Friday, turning around at 2.30pm the same day to arrive back in Kigoma on Sunday. It stops more or less everywhere, offering a number of feasible if rough-going overland connections in the dry season to Mpanda, Katavi National Park and Sumbawanga – see p.434 for details of port hopping on Lake Tanganyika. The MV *Liemba* is also helpful for getting to Mahale Mountains National Park (see p.442) and has also resumed services to Bujumbura in Burundi. However, every few weeks the ferry interrupts its passenger service to ferry refugees back to Congo or Burundi; it's worth asking in advance to find out if it is still doing this, and how services will be interrupted. **Tickets** for non-Tanzanians must be paid in dollars cash. **Fares** range from $16–28 to either Bujmbura or Mgambo, and $41–66 to Mpulungu in Zambia.

## Listings

**Airlines** Air Tanzania, 1st floor, New Nation Housing Building, Lumumba Rd (☎028/280 3286); Precisionair, Mlole Rd, facing the Central Market ☎028/280 4436, ✇www.precisionairtz.com. Zantas Air is a charter company running occasional services to Arusha from Kigoma. Though most of the passengers are on a pre-booked package, it might be worth enquiring if there are seats free; visit Mbali Mbali at *Kigoma Hilltop Hotel* for further details.

**Consulates** Burundi, Bangwe Rd ☎028/280 2865, ✉consbdi@africaonline.co.tz; Congo, Bangwe Rd /Kaya Rd ☎028/280 2401. Travelling to either country is currently not recommended, and there's no regular public transport into either.

**Health** Kigoma's hospitals are in Mwanga. The best is the mission-run Baptist Hospital (☎028/280 2241) about 1km from Kasulu junction: turn left at the junction then first right. A check-up costs $15. The government-run Maweni Hospital (☎028/280 2671) on Ujiji Rd beyond Kasulu junction and

Mwanga Market lacks resources. Kigoma Pharmacy is on Lumumba Ave, facing the market.

**Immigration** Exit formalities for Zambia are done on the ferry. The main immigration office is on Ujiji Rd in Mwanga, 100m beyond Maweni Hospital on the left.

**Internet access** Aifola and Baby Come & Call are on Lumumba Ave (both daily 8am–6pm; Tsh2000 per hr).

**Money** NBC Bank, Lumumba Ave/Mlole Rd, changes cash and traveller's cheques and has a 24hr Visa/MasterCard ATM. The only forex, handy for changing cash quickly, is Panjatan Bureau de Change, Lumumba Ave (erratic hours, usually Mon–Sat 10am–1pm & 3–4pm).

**Police** Bangwe Rd, near the TRA building, and in the train station.

**Post office** Kiezya Rd (Mon–Fri 8am–1pm, 2–4.30pm, Sat 9am–noon).

**Telephone** TTCL, round behind the post office on Burton Rd (Mon–Fri 8am–4.30pm, Sat 9am–noon).

# Port hopping along Lake Tanganyika

For the truly adventurous, **port hopping** along Lake Tanganyika south of Kigoma is a time-consuming yet strangely rewarding exercise. Given that the **ferry** (usually the MV *Liemba*; see opposite for fares and departure times) sails only once a week, to "hop" more than one port means either hunkering down in a lakeside village for a week to await the ferry's return, or risking local **lake taxis** – a potentially dangerous form of transport. Most of the villages that the

▲ Boarding the MV *Liemba*, Lake Tanganyika

## The MV Liemba

A much-loved feature of Lake Tanganyika is the **MV Liemba**, which has been ferrying passengers and cargo up and down the lake once a week for over eighty years. Originally christened the **Graf von Götzen** (after a former governor of German East Africa), the 1300-tonne steamship was constructed in Germany in 1913, then cut apart and transported by train from Dar es Salaam to Kigoma in the early stages of World War I, where she was reassembled for use as an armed troop transport. In June 1916 the ship was bombed by Belgian aircraft but escaped with light damage. However, when the British took control of the Central Line Railway the following month, the Germans **scuttled** the ship at the mouth of the Malagarasi River south of Kigoma rather than have her fall into enemy hands. The *Graf von Götzen* remained submerged for eight years until, following an unsuccessful effort by the Belgians in 1921, the British finally salvaged the vessel in 1924 and renamed her the MV *Liemba*, after the lake's original name.

Any journey on the MV *Liemba* (or the MV *Mwongozo* for that matter) is a memorable one – gorgeous sunsets over Congo's eastern highlands, and the frenetic activity that erupts in the port villages along the way whenever the ferry arrives: the ferry drops anchor offshore, with passengers, luggage and cargo carried to and from land in small lighters, invariably eliciting chaotic scrambles as people jostle to get on or off. The ship is engaged for approximately one week per month in ferrying Congolese and Burundi refugees back to their respective countries. This operation should have finished by the time you read this though do check on the latest situation before planning any itinerary.

ferry calls at also have road access to Mpanda or Sumbawanga (both covered later in this chapter), so bailing out is also an option, at least in the dry season – in the rains, none of these roads is even passable.

## Ikola and Karema

Sailing south from Kigoma, Thursday morning sees the ferry drop anchor off **IKOLA**, famed among tropical aquarium fanatics for giving its name to a highly prized family of cichlid fish. There's connecting road transport to Mpanda (at least 5hr), a **guesthouse** (Tsh9000) owned by local taxman Mr Mollo, and a basic restaurant – buy the ingredients at the market and let the chef work his magic.

If the lake – or its history – appeals, rent a bike from Ikola's guesthouse or stay on the ferry until **KAREMA** (or Kalema), 15km to the south. During the nineteenth-century **slave trade**, the lake region was convulsed by war and slave hunting, and as a regular staging post for the slave trade, the Europeans were inevitably attracted to Karema. The first to occupy Karema was the Belgian Comité d'Études du Haut Congo in 1879, which named the place **Fort Leopold** in honour of King Leopold II, whose notoriously tyrannical rule over Central Africa only recently made it onto Belgium's school curriculum. Belgium went on to claim the sardonically named Congo Free State as its African domain, but was obliged to relinquish Karema in 1885 following the European partition of Africa, when Germany took over Tanganyika. With the slave trade effectively at an end, it was the **Missionaries of Africa** ("White Fathers") who inherited Fort Leopold, and who ransomed four or five hundred slaves to found the village proper. Their church was erected in 1890, and the fortified mission house – which still stands – was completed in 1893.

The Catholic Mission in Karema has a **rest house** (❶), and there are regular **Land Rovers to Mpanda** (upwards of six hours) most days around noon, and certainly when the ferry calls.

## Kasanga and Muzi

**KASANGA** is the last Tanzanian port before Zambia, and is where **Tanzanian border formalities** are dealt with. The immigration officer is unusually helpful, and boards the ship on arrival. In German times, Kasanga was known as **Bismarckburg** – the ruins of its fort are outside the village but on military land, so there's no access. With time, the **Kalambo Falls** (see below) are an attractive target from here. The ferry usually arrives at Kasanga between midnight and dawn on Friday. For **accommodation**, there's the *Mwenya Guest House* (❶) on a hill behind the harbour, with a bar and – novelty of novelties – a TV.

The tranquil fishing village of **MUZI**, 5km north of Kasanga (90min on foot, or squeeze into a local boat for Tsh2000), also has a hotel – *Muzi Guest House* (no nets but plenty of mosquitoes; ❶), a small *mgahawa* restaurant, nice views and plenty of friendly people.

Daily Land Rovers and pick-ups to Sumbawanga leave Kasanga 6–7am, the badly rutted road taking four to five hours in the dry season and nine hours in the rains. Returning from Sumbawanga, they head off around 9am.

## Kalambo Falls

Sitting right on the border with Zambia a few kilometres east of Lake Tanganyika, the breathtaking 215-metre **Kalambo Falls** are Africa's second-highest

---

### Gombe's chimpanzees

**Chimpanzees** are our closest living relatives: they share 98.5 percent of our genome, and of course – unless you're a Creationist – we share common ancestors. Like us too, chimpanzees are intelligent social creatures that feel and share emotions, and are able to adapt to different environments and foods, pass on knowledge, and make and use simple tools. They also hunt in a human way, use plants medicinally, raid each other's communities and sometimes descend into a state of war. We owe much of our knowledge of chimpanzees to two ongoing research projects in Tanzania, one at Gombe, the other at Mahale (p.444); both of which started in the early 1960s. **Dr Jane Goodall** began a fifteen-year study of Gombe's chimpanzees in June 1960, having been encouraged by the Kenyan palaeontologist Louis Leakey, who believed that by observing the behaviour of great apes we could reconstruct something of the early life of mankind. The studies continue under the patronage of the Jane Goodall Institute (ⓦ www.janegoodall.org).

The study's first surprising discovery was that chimpanzees were capable of making and using simple **tools**. This is best seen in November at the start of the rains, when they go "fishing" for termites by inserting sticks into termite mounds, and then withdraw the probe to lick it clean of insects. The study has also demonstrated chimpanzees' knowledge and use of **medicinal plants**, in their use of *Aspilia mossambicensis* to clean their intestines of worms. The leaves contain an antibiotic and worm-killer, and are eaten in the morning before moving on to other foods. The method of eating the leaves is as important as their chemical content: using their lips, the chimps carefully remove one of the rough and hairy leaves from the plant and pull it into their mouths using their tongue. This causes the leaves to fold up like an accordion, which are then swallowed without chewing, thereby not only killing but physically removing worms.

Studies revealed that chimpanzees are omnivorous rather than vegetarian. Indeed, their success rate at **hunting** – primarily of red colobus monkeys, young bush pigs and bushbuck – is far higher than that of some specialized predators such as lions. The

uninterrupted falls, their waters plunging into the canyon of the river that forms the border with Zambia. Aside from the falls' natural beauty, they're also a breeding ground for the giant marabou stork, and several sites in the vicinity have great archeological importance: 300,000-year-old Stone Age tools have been uncovered, as well as some of the oldest evidence for the use of wood in construction, dating back sixty thousand years. Excavations of early Iron Age villages and campsites have also revealed a wealth of earthenware pottery – mainly globular pots and shallow bowls – the earliest of which have been dated to around 350 AD.

**Access** to the falls, which lie 130km southwest of Sumbawanga, is easiest from Kasanga: catch a pick-up at around 6am to Kalambo village, 5km north of the falls, from where you'll have to walk. Seek local advice about crocodiles.

# Gombe Stream National Park

Just 16km north of Kigoma, **Gombe Stream** is the smallest but one of the most inspiring of Tanzania's national parks – and also the most expensive. Its 52 square kilometres cover a narrow strip of hilly country rising from Lake Tanganyika to the eastern ridge of the Western Rift Valley escarpment, cut by thirteen steep-sided river valleys running east to west. The variations in altitude and the variety of habitats make the park one of the country's most rewarding

secret of their success is co-operative hunting, as several chimps can block any possible escape routes; it has been estimated that chimps may be responsible for killing fifteen percent of the red colobus population every year. Goodall's study also found that most of the dominant **"alpha" males** in the studied community were not necessarily big or physically strong, but gained their status through persistent or inventive macho displays of power. In one case, the alpha male used empty fuel-cans to terrify his peers; in another, two brothers – one of whom had lost an arm through polio – worked as a team to intimidate their competitors; others use family connections to gain influence. All in all, uncomfortably human. The parallels became even more unsettling when the study revealed that chimps also engaged in **warfare**, which had all the depressing hallmarks of our own conflicts. On occasion different groups of chimps invade neighbouring territories, attacking and sometimes killing any strangers encountered, with the exception of young females without young who are taken into the community. In a series of raids between 1974 and 1977, the males of the Kasakela community exterminated those of the Kahama community, with whom they had formerly been allied. The males also attacked strange females, and in three cases the stranger's child was killed and later eaten in a savage act of cannibalism. And in one infamous alleged incident in 2002, a male snatched and killed the baby of the wife of a park ranger. It would appear that these behavioural extremes may be related to **environmental pressures**, certainly in Gombe: hemmed in by humans on three sides and the lake on the fourth, forest habitat suitable for chimpanzees is limited – and shrinking. Indeed, all is far from well: human viruses have killed several chimps since 2000, and the feeding station has been abandoned due to the increasingly aggressive behaviour of the chimpanzees.

Good books include the lavishly illustrated *40 Years at Gombe* (1999) by Stewart, Chabori and Chang, and numerous works by Jane Goodall, including: *In the Shadow of Man* (1971); *The Chimpanzees of Gombe: Patterns of Behaviour* (1986); *Through a Window: My Thirty Years with the Chimpanzees of Gombe* (1991); and *Reason for Hope* (2002).

places for observing wildlife and flora, but you can forget about the "Big Five" – the Gombe ecosystem is a far subtler affair. Lake Tanganyika and the unremitting *miombo* woodland that stretches to the east have acted as a natural barrier for the last twenty million years, and as a result Gombe contains several plant and animal species common in West Africa but unknown further east. The evergreen riverine forests are especially diverse, and are the abode of the park's famous **chimpanzees** which have, since 1960, been the subject of what is now the world's longest-running study of a wild animal species; one troop has been habituated to humans and can be visited. Other **primates** include the olive baboon, along with less common red colobus, redtail and blue monkeys. The redtail and blue monkeys are unusual in that, despite their striking physical differences, they have only recently diverged as separate species, and hybrids occur, usually with the redtail's white nose and the blue monkey's dark tail and larger size. Other **mammals** include grey duiker antelope, bushbuck and marsh mongoose, as well as the chequered elephant shrew, which eats insects and can be seen patrolling the forest floor – it's named on account of its comical trunk-like snout and long legs. Over 230 **bird species** have been recorded, along with 250 species of butterfly.

Gombe's diminutive size, and dense human population surrounding it on three sides, make it highly vulnerable to **environmental degradation**, something that sadly appears to be coming to a head, thanks in part to the unsustainable needs of **refugees** from Burundi, barely 20km to the north. Despite efforts by various authorities both inside and outside the national park to keep deforestation in check, it seems destined to be a losing battle. That said, the recent cessation of fighting in Burundi and the ongoing return of refugees should help to alleviate the pressure on Gombe.

## Arrival and information

Gombe can only be reached by **boat** (half an hour to three hours), and visitors get to see the place on foot accompanied by an official guide – nothing too strenuous, but you need to be reasonably fit.

**Organized safaris** are the easiest way in, offered by a handful of safari operators based in Arusha (p.51), Mwanza (p.402) and Dar (p.52), which generally fly their guests into Kigoma on upmarket packages, and by one in Kigoma: Mbali Mbali (formerly Chimpanzee Safaris) at *Kigoma Hilltop Hotel* (p.429), which runs Gombe's tented camp and charges $550 per person all-inclusive. If your budget doesn't stretch to these prices the companies may still be useful for information or for organising transport to the park.

**Arranging your own safari** is possible but fiddly and not necessarily cheaper. You may need to book a chimp-trekking slot, and a *banda* if staying over, through TANAPA in Kibirizi (see p.439). As a rough guide, a boat holding ten to twelve passengers costs $250 return through Sunset Tours, based at the now defunct *Acqua Lodge*, or $550 for one of Mbali Mbali's speedboats (capacity 20 people). **Lake taxis** are overcrowded, potentially dangerous and offer limited if any shelter from the sun, but are cheap. They leave for Gombe from Kibirizi, 3km north of Kigoma, at around 1pm (Mon–Sat; 2–3hr; $4). As well as boat costs there are park fees, food and accommodation to pay for. Returning to Kibirizi, park staff can help you find a boat; 5–6pm appears to be the best time.

### Entrance fees and information

**Entrance fees** cost a whopping $100 per person per 24 hours, plus $10 per group for the obligatory guide.

## Monkey trouble

Wherever you are in Gombe, **beware of baboons**, which can be extremely dangerous if teased or tempted as they're completely unfazed by humans. The golden rules for avoiding hassle are to keep all food (and valuables) out of sight, keep tents and rooms closed, never eat outdoors, and never stare at a baboon (if threatened, look away, turn your back, and move away slowly). Should a baboon snatch something from you, don't resist but alert the park staff instead, who'll try to get it back. The same might be said of Gombe's **chimpanzees**, which have become increasingly violent towards humans.

The **park headquarters** are on the shore at Kasakela where the boats tie up; The brand new TANAPA Visitor Information Centre in Kigoma (PO Box 185 Kigoma, ℡0713/158320) is also nearing completion. **Chimp tracking** is limited to four groups a day (maximum six people each including the guide), so if you're arranging things yourself, enquire at the office in Kibirizi beforehand to be sure of a free slot. They'll also be able to tell you whether camping on the beach is still allowed (meaning safe from baboons), and if there's room in the overnight *bandas*. The best source of **information** is the excellent guidebook published by TANAPA, available in Arusha, Dar and Stone Town. It contains masses of information on the park's wildlife and the chimpanzees, and also covers Mahale Mountains National Park. The park's official **website** is ⊛www.tanzaniaparks.com/gombe.html.

The **best time to visit** depends on your interest. Photography is best in the dry season (July to mid-Oct and mid-Dec to Jan), but the chimps are easier to see in the rains (roughly Feb–June and mid-Oct to mid-Dec), when the vegetation on the higher slopes is at its greenest and most beautiful. There are occasional windy thunderstorms during April and May and from August to September.

Special **equipment** to bring includes dull-coloured clothes, a pair of shoes which have a good grip in wet conditions, rain gear, a torch for walks along the beach at night and bottled water if you're planning long hikes. Binoculars are pretty much *de rigueur*, and flash photography is not permitted. For swimming, a face mask and snorkel are an advantage. Fish can be bought from fishermen on the beach, but bring all other food, and conceal it in sealed containers to avoid unpleasantness with baboons.

## Accommodation

Despite the white sandy beach and glorious lake views, neither of Gombe's **accommodation** options is perfect, mainly thanks to increasingly threatening behaviour from both chimps and baboons, which has led to communal eating areas being screened with wire mesh. Whilst **camping** – either in the campsite near the *bandas*, or on the beach – is still allowed ($20 per person), it appears to be a mite dangerous these days, and you'll need permission first from the park warden in any case – enquire at the TANAPA office in Kibirizi.

**Gombe Forest Lodge** book through Mbali Mbali, ℡027/254 7007, 022/213 0553, ⊛www.mbalimbali .com. On a wide sandy beach at the mouth of the Mitumba streams in the north, is a rather simple tented camp consisting of seven spacious en-suite twin-bed tents set on wooden platforms in the shade of mango trees. Rather detracting from the romantic setting is the wire mesh covering the dining banda, installed to prevent attacks by aggressive baboons. That said, evening sundowners and dinner can be taken around a campfire. Other features include a small library, shop, bar and lounge. Rates include park fees but *not* transport. $500 per person. FB ❾

**TANAPA Bandas** Kasakela. Very basic and uninspiring breeze-block *bandas* near the beach, which – like the tented camp – have their verandas fitted with wire mesh to keep out chimps and baboons. There should be bed sheets and mosquito nets, but you'll need to be self-sufficient food-wise. ❸

# The park

Whilst **chimp trekking** is the main reason for visiting Gombe, there are a number of other possible **hikes** in the park, both along the shore and up through the forest to the crest of the mountain ridge – attractions in their own right, and handy for filling in the time whilst waiting for a slot with the chimps. **Night walks** are an exciting novelty, especially around full moon when you can dispense with a torch, giving glimpses of nocturnal animals such as genet, white-tailed mongoose, the slow-moving giant rat (up to 90cm long, including the tail), porcupine and bushbuck. You might also hear the loud cracking of palm nuts, a favourite with the hairy bush pig and also popular with palm civets.

## The shore

You can walk along the **beach** without a guide. The temporary camps along the sand are occupied by *dagaa* fishermen, who spend about ten days a month here in the dry seasons around the full moon, when the catches are best. The mango trees and oil palms in the bays are human introductions, the latter a familiar sight in West Africa, but largely unknown in Tanzania. In parts, the forest reaches down to the beach, but there's little other permanent vegetation along the shore. As a result, hippos and crocodiles are rare if not completely absent; seek advice from park staff before **swimming**. Bilharzia is also believed to be absent. If you're given the all-clear, head to the river mouths or the rocky shore just north of Mitumba beach, where a mask and snorkel will reveal many beautifully coloured cichlid fish. In deeper water

---

## Chimpanzee etiquette

Despite living in a national park, Gombe's chimpanzee population has dwindled from 150 in the 1960s to around a hundred today, due to poaching and outbreaks of human-transmitted diseases. The following rules are designed to protect both you and the chimps.

**Do not visit chimpanzees if you are ill** Chimpanzees are susceptible to many of our diseases without necessarily possessing our immunity: an epidemic of infectious pneumonia killed almost a third of Gombe's main study community in the 1980s.

**Always wear a face mask when visiting the chimps** You will be given a surgical mask by your guide before visiting the chimps. Wear it at all times when in the presence of the chimps, and make sure it covers both your mouth *and* your nose.

**Keep your distance** Never approach closer than 10m. If approached by a chimp, move away quietly or, if you can't, ignore it.

**No food** Visitors are not allowed to eat or display food in front of chimpanzees, nor to feed them.

**Sit while observing chimps** Standing upright can intimidate.

**Stay with your group** Do not spread out, as surrounding chimpanzees disturbs them.

**Respect chimp feelings** Don't follow chimps who appear to be shy or are avoiding you, and talk quietly.

**Photography** Be patient and don't try to attract the chimps' attention. Flash photography is not allowed.

**Safety** Chimpanzees are much stronger than us and can attack humans. Never come between a mother and her child. Should a chimp charge you, stand up, move quickly to a tree and hold on tightly to signal that you're not a threat. Do not scream or run away.

you may see the harmless Lake Tanganyika jellyfish, a tiny (2cm diameter) semi-transparent pulsating disc. Many beach strollers here are spooked by the sight of harmless **Nile monitor lizards**, which look like little crocodiles, but these skittish fellows are just as easily spooked as you and dash off into the water when approached. Gombe's most common primate, the stocky and thick-furred **olive baboon**, is generally the only mammal seen by day on the shore, where they scavenge for fish and occasionally swim and play in the water – keep your distance.

The lack of mud flats, weeds or perches means there's little **birdlife**, though the reeds at the mouths of streams are good habitats. Pied kingfishers, African pied wagtails and common sandpipers are most frequently seen, the giant kingfisher less so, while fish eagles are comparatively rare. Palm-nut vultures can sometimes be seen over the lake angling for fish. Winter migrants include white-winged black terns, hobbies and the lesser black-backed gull.

### Evergreen riverine forest

Of Gombe's various habitats, the narrow **evergreen riverine forests** are the undoubted highlight, especially in the north. These originally formed part of the great forests of Central and West Africa, but became isolated by climatic change during the last eight thousand years, and more recently from each other by human activity. The nearest forest is straight up the Kakombe Valley from Kasakela: a high, tangled canopy of trees and vines. As you walk along, crushed undergrowth marks the hasty retreats beaten by chimpanzees, red colobus, redtail or blue monkeys. Your guide should know where chimpanzees were last seen. The walk ends at the beautiful twenty-metre **Kakombe waterfall**.

**Forest birdlife** is melodious but difficult to see, usually no more than a brief flash of colour disappearing into the undergrowth or up into the canopy. The more easily seen birds are crimson-winged turacos: the mainly green Livingstone's; and Ross's with its blue body, yellow face and red crest – both have raucous calls. Of the four species of fruit-eating barbets, the only one you're likely to see is the tiny yellow-rumped tinkerbird, which has black-and-white facial stripes, a yellow rump and a monotonous "tink, tink, tink" call. More pleasant to the ear are the flute-like calls of the tropical boubou, a black-and-white shrike that duets in dense foliage. The African broadbill gives itself away by periodically flying up from its perch to do a somersault, emitting a small screech. The ground-feeding Peter's twinspot is an attractive finch with a red face and a white-spotted black belly. Winter migrants include various species of cuckoo, Eurasian swifts, bee-eaters and rollers, and four species of flycatcher. With a good deal of luck, you might also spot the pennant-winged nightjar, or one of two species of warbler (icterine and willow).

### Dry woodland and upper ridges

The drier valleys and higher slopes, especially in the south of the park, are neither as rich nor as interesting as the forest, and the semi-deciduous woodland and thorn scrub that covers them can look rather bleak in the dry season – the result of fires which formerly devastated large areas. Firebreaks have now been made by the park authorities by lighting controlled fires at the start of the dry season. In the wet season it's a different world, with the vivid green grass being scattered with pink gladioli and giant heather. The poor soil and lack of year-round food supports few mammals however, the exceptions being olive baboons, vervet monkeys and bushbuck. Even so, a hike to the top of the escarpment (over 700m above the lake) is rewarded with sweeping views over the park, a luxuriant contrast to the dry and crowded farmland to the east. On ridges, you might also see **crowned eagles** circling over the forests in search of imprudent monkeys. There are several routes to the top, all of them steep; leave early in the morning, and don't expect to be back until around nightfall.

# Mahale Mountains National Park

Located 120km south of Kigoma on a wide peninsula jutting out into Lake Tanganyika, **Mahale Mountains National Park** is one of the country's least-visited (and indeed least accessible) parks. Covering 1613 square kilometres, it's dominated by the heavily forested **Mahale Mountains**, which rise up from the pristine sandy beaches on the lakeshore to the 2462-metre peak of Mount Nkungwe.

Like Gombe, the park's ecology is characterized by a curious **mixture of habitats and species** typical of both the East and West African bio-geographical zones, and includes forest, mountain, savanna, *miombo* woodland and lake environments. As might be expected, Mahale is exceptionally rich in **birdlife**, and also has lots of **butterflies**, including over thirty species of fast-flying charaxes that feed on animal dung. **Mammals** include elephant, buffalo, lion and leopard, giraffe, kudu and eland, as well as rarer species such as roan and sable antelope and the brush-tailed porcupine, but it's for the eight species of primates that Mahale has gained international renown – especially its **chimpanzees**, of which one group has been habituated to humans and can be visited.

## Arrival and information

Given its remote location, visiting Mahale is either **expensive**, or just **plain awkward**. And as with Gombe, there are no roads into or within the park, so **walking** is the only way around – a sometimes heart-stopping but always memorable experience.

The easiest way of seeing Mahale is on an **organized safari**, either flying in from Arusha or Mwanza, or by boat from Kigoma. Mbali Mbali at *Kigoma Hilltop Hotel* (p.429) has a number of trips to Mahale, with a five-day excursion costing $2000–2500 per person depending on group size and where you stay.

---

### Mahale's first conservationists: the Batongwe and Holoholo

The Mahale Mountains are the traditional home of the **Batongwe** and **Holoholo** (the latter also known as Horohoro or Kalanga) tribes. Following the establishment of the Mahale Mountains Wildlife Research Centre in 1979, however, all human habitation was demolished to make way for the national park (created 1985), despite the fact that the Batongwe and Holoholo's lifestyles were highly adapted to the local environment. The Batongwe lived in compact communities of around forty people and practised sustainable shifting cultivation over a cycle of thirty to fifty years, giving ample time for forest regeneration. They practised little or no commercial hunting, and fished with nets whose mesh size was no smaller than 12cm, while some parts of the land, considered the sacred abodes of guardian spirits, were left untouched. So whilst proponents of "high-cost, low-impact tourism" stretch moral boundaries to justify $500 a night, the real conservators of the Mahale Mountains, the Batongwe and Holoholo, who lived in near-perfect symbiosis with their environment, have been excluded from their ancestral land, and their traditional livelihoods.

Alternatively, you can arrange things yourself. **Flights** are currently limited to charters from Arusha, Mwanza, Katavi and Ruaha. The park headquarters at Bilenge are around 3.5km from the airstrip, accessible by boat. If you're booked in at one of the private camps in the park, the transfer from the airstrip to the camp will be included in the package. If you're staying at one of the TANAPA *bandas*, however, make sure you let them know when you're arriving and they'll send someone to meet you. On the way you'll call in at the headquarters first in order to pay all your park fees, before continuing by boat south for a further 30 minutes to Kasiha, where the *bandas* are situated. The exact price of the trip from the airstrip to the *bandas* seems to depend on the whim of the person in charge on the day; expect to pay at least $25 (though they are trying to introduce an official price of a jaw-dropping $65 one-way, $130 return).

Otherwise, the only access is by **boat from Kigoma**, 130km to the north, which takes up to ten hours. Given spiralling fuel costs, hiring a motorboat is bitterly expensive unless you can muster a large enough group, with costs starting at $900 for a vessel seating eight or ten people. You could also check with the TANAPA office in Kigoma (see p.439) whether they have a trip heading down to Mahale, as they may have spare seats.

Considerably cheaper is to catch the **MV Liemba** ferry on Wednesday at 4pm (see p.433), which drops anchor off **Mgambo** (also called Lagosa), 35km north of the park headquarters, before midnight the same day (first class $28; second $26 and third – just a chair rather than a bed – $16). You'll need onward boat transport from there to the park headquarters, which should ideally be arranged in Kigoma: contact TANAPA's office in Kibirizi, which should be able to **radio call** the park to let them know you're coming. If you arrive in Mgambo without having contacted the authorities, you'll need to rent a local boat for the trip to the park headquarters at Bilenge, and on to the *bandas* (a further 45 minutes to an hour). You might strike lucky at night, but it's far safer to wait till sunrise before setting off. Getting back to Kigoma is just as awkward, with the MV *Liemba* – if it's running – passing Mgambo in the wee hours of Sunday morning.

Lastly, whilst it's possible to catch a **lake taxi** (Tsh10,000) all the way from Ujiji to Kalilani, a walkable 1.5km from the park headquarters, the lengthy (16–24hr) trip is anything but comfortable, and is also potentially dangerous. Taxis depart from Ujiji on Sat, Mon and Fri at around 6pm, returning to Ujiji on Mon, Wed, Thurs and Sat around 11am.

### Entrance fees and information

**Park fees** are $80 per person for 24 hours. The obligatory guide/armed ranger costs $20 per walk, more if you're fly-camping and he stays overnight. **Children** under ten are not allowed on chimp treks, and may not be admitted inside the park.

The park is **best visited** during the dry season (May to mid-Oct). TANAPA's *Gombe* **guidebook** has a good section on Mahale, and is available in Arusha, Dar and Stone Town; alternatively, a good **coffee-table book** is *Mahale: a photographic encounter with chimpanzees* by Angelika Hofer et al (Sterling, 2000).

## Accommodation

Accommodation in Mahale is either basic and comparatively cheap ($30 per person in *bandas* or camping, plus park fees), or scaldingly expensive but beautifully pampered. Most of the accommodation is at Kasiha, around thirty minutes by boat from the park headquarters at Bilenge. Solar power is the norm.

**Flycatcher** At Kasiha, around an hour by boat from the airstrip. Scruffy yet charming and refreshingly unpretentious series of eight single and double tents on the beach, with a small but smart new dining room-cum-library and bar. Open June–Oct only. ❼–❽

**Mango Tree Park Bandas** At Kasiha, just south of *Flycatcher*. Run by TANAPA (bookings rarely if ever required), this former guesthouse 50m from the shore provides Mahale's cheapest rooms and perfectly reasonable ones at that, with eight en-suite twin rooms and a kitchen. They have some cooking equipment (though no tin opener!) but you'll need to bring food and drinks. ❹

**Kungwe Luxury Tented Camp** On the beach between the Kasiha and Sinsiba streams, 40 minutes south by motorboat from the park headquarters Ⓦ www.chimpanzeesafaris.com (book through Mbali Mbali at *Kigoma Hilltop Hotel* in Kigoma, see p.429, or in Arusha, ☎ 027/254/ 7007). Ten en-suite, twin-bed tents on wooden platforms spread across two beaches. There's an attractive reception area on the beach with seats fashioned from wooden canoes split into two, beach loungers, and evening campfires. Canoes and snorkelling gear are available. Chimp trekking and forest walks included, boat trips and park fees extra. Closed March to mid-May. FB $465 ❾

**Nomad Mahale Camp** (aka *Greystoke Mahale* and *Zoe's Camp*) Two hours by dhow from the airstrip Ⓦ www.nomad-tanzania.com This French-run set-up inspires travel hacks to pen purple prose, some of it justified, as well it should be given the shocking cost: the main reason being the idyllic location on a small sandy bay backed by palm trees and forested slopes. The guides are good, as are the meals and the six two-storey thatched *bandas* decorated with furniture fashioned from driftwood and old dhows are exquisite. All in all, satisfyingly pretentious glamour in the wild. Rates include chimp tracking, forest walks, dhow trips (in search of hippo or to the nearby village), snorkelling, fishing and even alcohol. Closed March–May. No children under six. $850–970. ❾

**TANAPA Campsites** The main site is close to the park headquarters, though you'll probably need to catch a boat to see the chimps as it's quite far from their usual territory. Facilities here are limited to long-drops and water. Alternatively you can camp by the *Mango Tree Bandas*. Camping in the bush is possible elsewhere, but has to be arranged with the park headquarters. Bring enough food for the duration. ❹

## Mahale's chimpanzees

The Mahale Mountains are one of the world's last strongholds for **wild chimpanzees**, with a population estimated at seven hundred to a thousand individuals in fifteen to twenty communities; several more of which are believed to exist outside the park. Despite their number, the chimps can be difficult to see, so be patient. Visits are limited to an hour, and group sizes of no more that six (including a guide), with no more than twenty tourists allowed every day. Read the box on "Chimpanzee etiquette" on p.440.

Wildlife research in the Mahale Mountains has been dominated by Japan's **Kyoto University** since 1961, when primate expert Junichiro Itani and his colleagues began exploring the shoreline south of Kigoma. The primatologists' work has focused on two communities in the northwest of the park in the Kasoge area, close to the tourist accommodation. Areas of research include their use of medicinal plants, predatory behaviour, infanticide and cannibalism, temporary adoption of infants and "dialects" in their gestural language (there's an excellent essay on chimpanzee communication at Ⓦ www.mnsu.edu/emuseum/cultural /language/chimpanzee.html).

Mahale's chimps have been separated from Gombe's for quite some time, as their social behaviour, use of tools and diet differ markedly – Gombe's chimps eat termites by probing the mounds with sticks, for example, but do not eat tree ants, whereas Mahale's chimps catch tree ants in the same way but leave the termites alone. Mahale's chimps also have a unique "handshake". For more **information** about chimp research at Mahale, see Ⓦ http://jinrui.zool.kyoto-u.ac.jp/ChimpHome /mahaleE.html (keep the mixed case or it won't work).

▲ Chimpanzee mother and baby, Mahale National Park

## The Park

Mahale offers a wide range of **walks**. An armed guard should accompany you, who will be able to advise you about recent sightings of chimps and leopards. The **lakeshore**, with its reeds, swamps and grassland is good for birds, including nesting speckled mouse-birds in the stands of oil palms around Kasiha. Large game is rare on the shore, although antelopes come here to drink and African hunting dogs are also seen from time to time. Mahale's richest habitat, however, is the lowland **gallery forests** in the northwest of the park, where the mountains rise from close to the shoreline, ascending to around 1300m. Apart from the famous chimpanzees and the leopards, the forest – like Gombe's – contains several animal and plant species more typical of western than eastern Africa, including the brush-tailed porcupine, the red-legged sun squirrel, the giant forest squirrel and the bushy-tailed mongoose. Forest birds to look out for are the crested guinea fowl and Ross's turaco – the latter is evasive, despite its vivid colour, as it spends all its time in the forest canopy.

The misty **mountains** themselves are also home to a small population of black-and-white colobus monkeys. Their range is restricted to the belt of bamboo and montane forest above 2000m on Mount Nkungwe. Above 2300m the forests give way to grassland. One- or two-night camping hikes up and down **Mount Nkungwe** are possible, but must be arranged in advance with the park authorities or the tented camps; longer trips can be arranged to explore the drier **eastern slopes** of the mountains, which are covered by *miombo* woodland, acacia and "terminalia" savanna (characterized by termite mounds). Plains game is abundant, and includes elephant, giraffe, zebra, buffalo and warthog, together with rare roan antelopes and their predators – lion, spotted hyena and the endangered African hunting dog.

# Unyamwezi

Occupying much of the tsetse-fly-infested *miombo* woodland of the Central Plateau, the Tabora region is more popularly known as **Unyamwezi** after the dominant tribe. The region used to straddle two of East Africa's most lucrative nineteenth-century ivory and slave caravan routes to the Indian Ocean: from Ujiji on Lake Tanganyika, which was the main transit point for slaves from the Congo Basin, and from Lake Victoria in the north. The routes converged on **Kazeh** ("Kingdom"), 15km southwest of Tabora, which at its height in the 1860s saw an estimated half a million porters and uncounted slaves pass through each year. Later, the focus of trade shifted to Arab-controlled **Tabora**, now a bustling town of two hundred thousand people and the regional capital. Tabora's importance as a trading centre has remained, thanks to the **Central Line Railway**, which follows the routes of the old caravan trails almost exactly, and provides easy access westwards to Kigoma on Lake Tanganyika and north to Mwanza on Lake Victoria. The legacy of the slave and ivory caravans lingers on in the form of Islam, which is becoming the region's dominant religion, and in the name of the region's major tribe, the million-strong **Nyamwezi**, which means "of the moon" in Kiswahili – an appellation used by the coastal Swahili and Arabs to describe a number of tribes to the west, where the moon sets.

# Tabora

Whereas Kazeh has all but disappeared, its hot and dusty neighbour **TABORA** has continued to prosper as a major trading centre thanks to its position on the Central Railway line. Like the old slaving routes, the railway branches at Tabora; the northern line heading to Mwanza on Lake Victoria, the western one going on to Kigoma on Lake Tanganyika, and to Mpanda. Except for a handful of German buildings, there's not all that much to see in town, but it's a friendly place, and the shady, tree-lined streets provide an attractive and soothing break

It was only in the nineteenth century that the Nyamwezi tribe coalesced into a unified state, **Unyanyembe**; largely built on the wealth they accrued from the ivory trade. The appearance of wealthy Nyamwezi traders in the coastal ports aroused the avarice of the Zanzibari sultanate, which from the 1850s onwards launched increasingly confident incursions along Nyamwezi caravan routes, dealing not only in ivory but also increasingly in slaves. As a result, the balance of power between hundreds of central Tanzanian clans and tribes broke down, and a new generation of leaders with little respect for the established way of things rose to prominence.

One of these was **Chief Mirambo-ya-Banhu**, who by 1871 had managed, mainly through conquest, to establish a rival state to Unyanyembe called **Unyamwezi**, which at its zenith between 1876 and 1881 extended into northwest Tanzania and Congo. Mirambo controlled the western caravan route from Tabora to Ujiji, as well as another caravan route heading up the western shore of Lake Victoria towards Uganda's Buganda empire. Not without reason did Stanley dub him "this black Bonaparte"; like Napoleon, Mirambo's rule was very much a product of his character. "He is tall, large chested and a fine specimen of a well-made man. As quiet as a lamb in conversation, he's rather harmless looking than otherwise, but in war the skulls which line the road to his gates reveal too terribly the ardour which animates him," effused Stanley in 1876.

Mirambo's success was manifold. Geographically, his empire blocked the Arab trade routes to Lake Tanganyika. Militarily, the vast wealth that the Nyamwezi had gained from the ivory and slave trades enabled the purchase of firearms and the hiring of *Ruga-Ruga* mercenaries from the Ngoni tribe (originally from southern Africa), all of which means that Mirambo's empire was engaged in **incessant warfare**, be it against Arabs or neighbouring chiefs. To consolidate his power, Mirambo reappointed governors of captured territories as agents and consuls, and even made an alliance with Sultan Barghash of Zanzibar.

The fact that the empire was held together largely by war, and the force of Mirambo's personality, meant that it quickly disintegrated following his death in 1884, paving the way for the arrival of the Germans a few years later. Nowadays, Mirambo is considered something of a national hero, not so much for his empire-building skills as for the fact that he managed to trump the Arabs over so many years.

---

from the blistering *miombo* woodland that stretches for hundreds of kilometres around, making it a good place to break the exhausting (37–39hr) train journey from Dar es Salaam to Kigoma or Mwanza. There's also a pleasant side trip to the **Livingstone Museum**, 15km southwest of town at Kwihara, the modern incarnation of Kazeh.

Tabora's **climate** is hot all year round, with temperatures peaking at an average of 32°C in September and October before the arrival of the short rains. Still, it's perfectly bearable if you've arrived from the sweltering humidity of Kigoma or the coast. The long rains – scattered heavy showers rather than continuous downpours – generally fall from February to May.

### Some history

The history of Tabora and its forerunner Kazeh is very much the history of the **Nyamwezi people**, who by the mid-1700s had come to dominate the ivory trade of central Tanzania. A century later, with the Omani-dominated slave trade eclipsing ivory, Nyamwezi traders and porters were commonly seen on the coast, having followed the trading routes that they had developed, while the Nyamwezi themselves also organized slave hunts. By the 1850s, under the rule of chiefs Swetu I and Saidi Fundikira I, both Tabora and Kazeh were well established, and over the following decade an estimated half a million porters passed through the twin towns every year. The towns – and the Nyamwezi – grew rich on taxes levied on caravans, as well as from the profits of caravans operated by the Nyamwezi themselves, whilst their increasing power was typified by the establishment of a short-lived but extremely powerful new state established by Chief Mirambo (see box, p.447), which successfully challenged Arab hegemony over the slaving routes in the 1870s.

During the **German conquest** of Tanganyika, an outpost and then a fort (the still-existing Boma) were raised in Tabora, surviving an armed rebellion in 1891 led by Chief Isike "Mwana Kiyungi" of Unyanyembe. The German victory made a considerable impression on lesser chiefs, some of whom took to sending envoys to Tabora for help in local conflicts. In signing treaties with the Germans, they effectively handed over their land to the colonists, and with the Nyamwezi "pacified", the Germans set about developing Tabora itself. The **Central Line Railway** (*Mittelland Bahn*) from Dar es Salaam reached Tabora in 1912. German efforts to open up the territory were in vain, however: in September 1916 they were ejected from Tabora after a fierce ten-day battle with Belgian troops from Congo, under the command of Colonel Tombeur. The British took control of Tabora after the war, and in 1928 gave the go-ahead for the extension of the railway from Tabora to Mwanza, thereby assuring the continued prosperity of both towns.

## Arrival

The **train station** is at the east end of Station Road, 1.5km from the bus stand; motorcycle taxis and bicycle taxis – as well as regular taxis – all converge on the station whenever a train is due. Trains from Dar and Dodoma should arrive at 6.30pm; coming from Mwanza or Kigoma, they should pull in around sunrise. The train from Mpanda rolls in at 2.45am, at least in theory; the *Orion Tabora Hotel*, 400m from the station, will let you in at this time. If you're looking for somewhere cheaper, hang around for a few hours until sunrise – the 24-hour *Police Mess* on Boma Road sells food and drinks.

**Buses** use the central bus stand beside the open-air market. There are daily buses from Mwanza and Nzega, and less frequent services from Arusha, Dodoma, Singida and Mbeya. Tabora **airport** lies a few kilometres south of town; the only flight is the daily Precisionair service from Dar. **Taxis** can be found at the junction of Market and Lumumba streets, outside the market, and at the bus stand.

## Accommodation

Reviewed below is Tabora's only mid-range **hotel**, plus the best of the budget ones – there are many other cheap **guesthouses** (all ❶) spread out around the junction of Boma Road and Manyema Street. "Single" rooms (those with one bed) can be shared by couples, except at the *Moravian Church Hostel* and *Orion Tabora Hotel*. Tabora's **tap water** is, on the rare occasions it flows, highly discoloured but drinkable if properly purified.

**Fama Hotel** North off Lumumba St ☎026/260 4657. A lovely little place tucked away in a quiet corner with a few shady Indian almond (*mkungu*) trees. The 13 rooms are tatty but clean, the restaurant is good, and there's also safe parking. BB ❷

**Golden Eagle Hotel** Market St/Jamhuri St, entrance through the car park ☎026/260 4623, ✆www.goldeneaglefies.com.

Under new management, this excellent-value place is set to become the travellers' favourite. All rooms have TV and box nets, and whether sharing a bathroom or in an en suite, there should be hot water available. The restaurant is good and the bar well stocked. ❶

**Moravian Church Hostel** Kapembe St/Mwanza St ☎026/260 4822, ✉mcwt@taboraonline.com. The

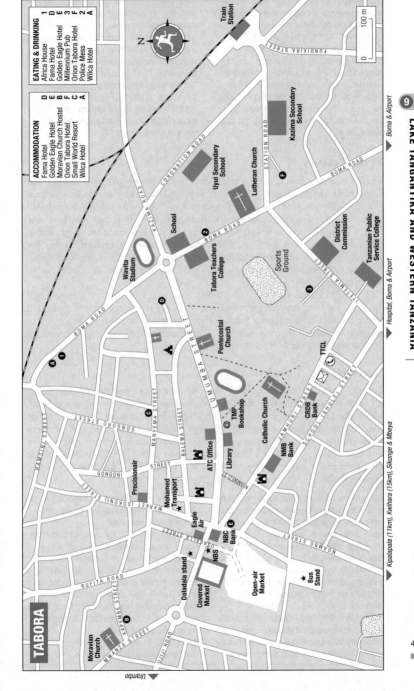

TABORA

▲ Nzega, Singida, Shinyanga & Mwanza

**ACCOMMODATION**

| | |
|---|---|
| Fama Hotel | D |
| Golden Eagle Hotel | E |
| Moravian Church Hostel | B |
| Orion Tabora Hotel | F |
| Small World Resort | C |
| Wilca Hotel | A |

**EATING & DRINKING**

| | |
|---|---|
| Africa House | 1 |
| Fama Hotel | D |
| Golden Eagle Hotel | E |
| Millennium Pub | 3 |
| Orion Tabora Hotel | F |
| Police Mess | 2 |
| Wilca Hotel | A |

Train Station

Kazima Secondary School

▼ Boma & Airport

Uyui Secondary School

Lutheran Church

KAZIMA ROAD

CORONATION ROAD

STATION ROAD

BOMA ROAD

FUNDIKIRA STREET

Wavita Stadium

School

Tabora Teachers College

Sports Ground

District Commission

Tanzanian Public Service College

TETEMIA STREET

BOMA ROAD

▼ Hospital, Boma & Airport

Pentecostal Church

Catholic Church

TMP Bookshop

Library

ATC Office

Precisionair

Mohamed Transport

Eagle Air

TTCL

NMB Bank

CRDB Bank

JAMHURI STREET

SCHOOL (ISHULI) STREET

NBC Bank

NBS

Daladala stand

Covered Market

Open-air Market

Bus Stand

Moravian Church

▼ Urambo

LUMUMBA STREET

MANYEMA STREET

BALEWA STREET

GONGONI STREET

MARKET (SOKONI) STREET

HAMSINI STREET

SONGORO STREET

RUFITA ROAD

KAPEMBE STREET

MWANZA STREET

JIJI ROAD

USAGARIA STREET

MJIMWEMA STREET

NJOMBO STREET

▼ Kipalapala (11km), Kwihara (15km), Sikonge & Mbeya

0    100 m

N

best-value budget option in town. The clean, cool rooms have mosquito nets and washbasins. Food is available if ordered well in advance. ❶

🏃 **Orion Tabora Hotel** Station Rd, 400m from the station ☎026/260 4369, ©orion@spidersat.net. This charming German railway hotel has been completely renovated and expanded, but still retains its allure. Rooms have big beds, net, fan, digital TV, and balconies facing the gardens. There's also a restaurant and two bars (live music Fri, discos Wed & Sat), and safe parking. BB ❺

**Small World Resort** Manyema St ☎026/260 5992. One of the better budget places, this has a choice of clean rooms that have large beds with nets, squat toilets and bucket showers, or cheaper ones with shared bathrooms. Food is limited to the usual *chipsi mayai* and *mishkaki*. ❶

**Wilca Hotel** Top of Boma Rd ☎026/260 4106. This has ten en-suite rooms in a calm and peaceful atmosphere, all with large double beds, nets on request (rooms are usually sprayed), ceiling fans and hot running water. There's also a bar, restaurant, and safe parking. BB ❷

## The Town

There's nothing much to see in Tabora itself, but the plentiful mango and flame trees shading many of its streets provide a pretty spectacle when in bloom – the mango trees are believed to have been unwittingly introduced by slaves who discarded the stones during their painful trek to the coast. Relics from German times include the **train station**, with its steep central gable and lime-green roof, and the imposingly robust **German Boma** (or fort) at the south end of Boma Road, overlooking a small valley to the east. It's now occupied by the military, so a visit (and photography) is sadly out of the question.

The lively **central market** is also worth a wander, with distinct areas set aside for anything from bicycle parts and tyre recyclers to a huge section dedicated to the diminutive dried *dagaa* fish which is brought in by rail from Kigoma. For *kangas* (the colourful wraps worn by Tanzanian women), try any of the shops on Balewa Street off Market Street.

## Eating and drinking

Tabora's perked up considerably in the food department, and isn't too bad either for nightlife, especially **live music**: Nyamyembe Stars are worth seeking out, whilst the famous and eminently danceable **Tabora Sound Band** (formerly Tabora Jazz; also known for their *Sensema Malunde* dance style) still perform several times a week. Apart from *Africa House*, reviewed below, two other places that host visiting big-name bands (and edifying events like beauty contests) are the Secretarial College on Boma Road and UHAZILI – the Tanzania Public Service College – on Itetemia Street.

**Africa House** Boma Rd. A dozy bar for most of the week (it sometimes closes mid-afternoon), things gets busy on Wednesday and Saturday when Tabora Sound Band are in residence. Food consists of the usual grills and chip omelettes.

**Fama Hotel** Signposted off Lumumba St. The pleasantly calm bar here (even the TV volume is kept down) also serves up some superb food for under Tsh3500 – the *maini* (ox liver) in particular is delicious.

**Golden Eagle Hotel** Great for Indian food, especially thalis, but also boasts a well-stocked bar and occasionally hosts a game meat evening (shot legally from the nearby hunting reserve). Friendly service.

**Millennium Pub** Off Itetemia St. Currently the most popular of several local beer-garden-style bars, also with cheap food.

**Orion Tabora Hotel** Off Station Rd, 400m from the station. This renovated old hotel is good for food and has an extremely well-stocked bar. The food is accomplished, with local dishes (around Tsh7200) featuring cassava leaves (*kisamvu*) and pumpkin leaves (*msusa*). There's also a selection of Indian and Chinese dishes (Tsh6000–7000). Tabora Sound Band plays on Fri from 8pm (Tsh2500) and there are free discos (Wed & Sat).

**Police Mess** Boma Rd. This 24-hour outdoor bar also dishes up good food (oxtail soup, *mtori* banana stew and *nyama choma*), and hosts live bands every so often, usually Saturdays, including the danceable Nyanyembe Stars:

**Wilca Hotel** Boma Rd. A calm place with a wide choice of well-prepared food, all for around Tsh4000 – the roast chicken is especially good, and there are also a few cheap vegetarian dishes.

## Listings

**Airlines** Precisionair, Old Bhakhresa Building, Market St ☎026/260 4818.

**Bookshops** TMP Bookshop, Lumumba St, has one or two interesting books on proverbs, some nicely illustrated children's books, and a ton of Christian texts.

**Football** Local matches are played at the small Wavita Stadium at the corner of Boma and Kazima roads most Saturdays. Entrance is a few hundred shillings.

**Health** The government-run district hospital is on Kitete St, west of the Boma ☎026/260 3269.

**Internet access** Tabora ComSec in the TTCl

building is reliable and fairly fast (Tsh1500 per hr). The post office next door charges similar rates.

**Library** The municipal library, Lumumba St (Mon–Fri 9am–6pm, Sat 9am–2pm; daily membership Tsh500) is well stocked with English-language works on Tanzania and Africa.

**Money** NBC Bank, Market St/Lumumba St, is the most efficient, taking around forty minutes to process traveller's cheques, less for cash, and also has a Visa/MasterCard ATM.

**Police** Jamhuri St, near the junction with School St.

**Telephones** TTCL by the post office, Jamhuri St.

# Kwihara

Known to nineteenth-century explorers as Kazeh, **KWIHARA** is 15 kilometres southwest of Tabora. Until the German development of Tabora, Kazeh was by far the more important of the two towns, serving as a major caravanserai (a stop for caravans) along the slave route from Ujiji to the coast. Speke and Burton passed through in 1857, and visited the town again in June 1858, having "discovered" Lake Tanganyika. But the most famous of Kazeh's visitors were undoubtedly Stanley and Livingstone, who arrived here in 1872 following their legendary meeting in Ujiji (see p.431). Stanley was most impressed by Kazeh: "On my honour, it was a most comfortable place, this, in Central Africa."

It seems incredible that all that remains of this famous town is a handful of crumbling earth houses, a few mango trees and coconut palms introduced by the Arabs, and a quirky **museum** dedicated to Livingstone. Despite all this, the place's historical importance, as well as the rural scenery scattered with flat granite outcrops, repays the hassle of reaching it.

## Practicalities

Kwihara is a day-trip from Tabora; taxis charge around Tsh10,000 return. Alternatively, catch a bus bound for Sikonge and alight at **Kipalapala village**, 11km south of Tabora, from where Kwihara is a four-kilometre hike though villages and farmland. At Kipalapala, turn right at the sign for Kwihara School (there's also a small, easily missed sign for Tembe la Livingstone). Heading back to Tabora, there's no guarantee of public transport from Kipalapala, so you might have to hitch. The museum is the large red building on the left just after Kwihara village – the children will alert the curator for you.

## The Livingstone Museum

The **Livingstone Museum** (Tembe la Livingstone; no set times; donations), which boasts a beautiful Swahili-style carved doorframe, is a 1957 reconstruction

### By road

Improvements on the roads between Tabora and Dodoma or Mwanza mean that **buses** are slightly more predictable these days, if only in the dry season; in the rains, huge delays (overnights stuck in tiny villages) or cancellations are still the norm, so factor in plenty of time for travelling. The new bus stand is beside the open-air market: tickets can be bought here or at a few offices elsewhere. Most buses get fully booked days in advance, so buy your ticket as early as possible. Buses are invariably overcrowded, making for intensely uncomfortable journeys, even if you're seated. Avoid seats at the back – the bumpy roads will toss you all over the place.

For **Mwanza**, daily 6am services are operated by Mohamed Trans (office on Market St; ☏0732/566505; buses depart at 6am, 8am & 10am) and NBS (Ujiji Rd, behind NBC bank; ☏026/260 5132). **Dodoma** buses leave at 5.30–6am; the companies are Anam, Mabruck Aleyck, Sabena and Supersonic. For **Dar es Salaam**, buy a ticket to Dodoma and move on from there the following day (with Shabiby the choice of those operating on this line); direct tickets are available from Mohamed Trans (daily 6am) and NBS (also 6am). For **Singida** and **Arusha**, the only direct bus is NBS (Wed & Sat 6am).

**Heading west**, there are daily buses to Urambo (around noon), but for Kigoma catch a train or plane. Heading south to **Mbeya** via **Mpanda** is a dry-season-only adventure, taking a minimum of eighteen hours: Sabena's buses run from Tabora on Wednesday and Sunday at 5.30am.

### By train

The ticket office at the train station is open daily 8am–noon & 2–4.30pm, and for two hours before departures. **Eastbound trains** for Dodoma and Dar leave at 7.25am (Mon, Wed & Fri). **Westbound** services (Mon, Wed & Sat) leave at 8.10pm for Kigoma and 9.30pm for Mwanza. Trains to **Mpanda** head off at 9pm (Mon, Wed & Fri). Fares: Dar: Tsh12,700–39,900; Kigoma: Tsh7800–22,700; Mpanda: Tsh6800–19,700. The **timetable** is at ⊛www.trctz.com.

### By plane

The only **scheduled flights** from Tabora are the daily Precisionair service to Kigoma and on to Dar es Salaam.

---

of the fortified house (*tembe*) where the good doctor stayed following his meeting with Stanley at Ujiji. The pair arrived in Kazeh on February 18, 1872, and while Stanley went back to the coast, Livingstone stayed on awaiting supplies. He left Kazeh on August 25 for what proved to be his final journey, dying eight months later at Chitambo, near Lake Bangweulu in present-day Zambia.

The house is largely empty now save for one room which has a mildly diverting display of Livingstone-associated items, including a lock of hair from the famous missionary, and a piece of the Ujiji mango tree under which Stanley allegedly met Livingstone. There's a room containing photocopies of pages from Livingstone's journals, reproductions of hand-drawn and later maps, and copies of contemporary US newspapers. The other, empty rooms bear labels: Donkeys, Kitchen, *Askaris*, Bombay. The latter refers to Saidi Mbarak Mombay, the leader of Stanley's "exceedingly fine-looking body of men" during his quest for Livingstone; he'd previously worked for Burton, Speke and Grant. During the expedition, Stanley was also accompanied by **John William Shaw**, who fell ill repeatedly and finally died in Kazeh in 1871. During their journey, Stanley and Shaw had travelled for a time with an Arab army, thinking it would offer safe passage further west; unfortunately for them it was routed by Chief Mirambo at Wilyankuru. Stanley blamed Shaw for the defeat, calling him "base and mean" in his memoirs, though the phrase is surely more applicable to the heartless Stanley himself, as amply evidenced by his own writings (*How I Found Livingstone* – Epaulet in the US; also free at Ⓦwww.gutenberg.org/etext/5157). Shaw's grave lies 100m from the museum under a coconut tree, though the iron headstone is now housed in the museum for safekeeping.

# Rukwa Region

South of the Central Railway Line between Lake Tanganyika and the western arm of the Great Rift Valley, **Rukwa Region** offers a refreshing change of scenery from the dusty *miombo* woodland to the north. The *miombo* continues to **Katavi National Park** but gives way to open rolling hills as you approach the fresh and relaxing town of **Sumbawanga**, only a few hours from the Zambian border. To the east of Sumbawanga, the **Mbizi Mountains**, still virtually unknown to the outside world, provide a picturesque backdrop. Further east, a shallow depression holds **Lake Rukwa**, a desolate, hot, humid but enchanting destination for those who really want to get away from it all – assuming you can get there at all. For details of boat travel around the southern part of **Lake Tanganyika**, see p.434.

## Mpanda

Sprawling over several kilometres at the end of the Central Railway's southern branch, the dusty town of **MPANDA** serves as a transit point for travellers heading between Sumbawanga and Mbeya in the south and Tabora in the north. For the trickle of tourists who make it here by train, the town also acts as a springboard for visits to **Katavi National Park**, 35km south.

As might be expected from its strategic location, Mpanda served as a collective village during the failed **Ujamaa** experiment of 1967–77 (see p.585). Numerous small agricultural tribes such as the Konongo, Bende, Pimbwe and Rwira were forcibly relocated here, followed in 1979 and 1998 by people evicted from Katavi National Park. Given the vastly increased population and the district's low rainfall and poor soil, the environmental outcome has been predictably destructive. The continued use of unsustainable **slash-and-burn agriculture** has removed all tree and shrub cover in many areas, causing flooding and massive soil erosion during the rains. This in turn has led to the silting up and disappearance of Lake Chada in Katavi National Park, and billowing clouds of dust in the dry season, which account for the unusually high rate of eye disease among Mpanda's inhabitants. Things haven't been helped by an influx of Sukuma **cattle herders** from the north, who have placed even greater pressure on the region's meagre natural resources. For all their woes, the people are exceptionally friendly and welcoming.

## Practicalities

Most people arrive on the **train from Tabora**; this theoretically pulls in at 10.30am, but is often delayed by an hour or two. The train station is at the west end of town; to get to the centre, follow the stream of passengers back along the rail tracks and turn left onto the first road. *Super City Hotel* is 100m ahead, and the roundabout referred to in our reviews is 50m further on.

Arriving **by road**, buses, trucks and pick-ups arrive at the **bus stand** outside *Super City Hotel*, apart from some pick-ups coming from the south, which stop at the Tawaqal petrol station on the west side of town. To get to the main guesthouses from the petrol station, turn right and walk 200m up the avenue, then take the second left. Continue straight for 800m and you'll arrive at the roundabout beside the *Super City Hotel*. For details on getting to Mpanda from the **Lake Tanganyika port** of Karema, see p.435.

NMB **bank** takes forever but does eventually change traveller's cheques; it's about 1.5km from the market on the northeastern fringes of town. The **post office** is close to the main market in the centre of Mpanda, and the **TTCL** phone office is close to the police station at the northwestern edge of town – alternatively, there's a card phone at *Super City Hotel*.

### Accommodation

There are plenty of perfectly decent cheap **hotels** scattered around town. Running water is erratic, so you'll probably have the pleasure of bucket showers (again).

**Super City Family Guest House** Mjimwema area, 400m northeast of the *Vatican Guest House* (no phone). Fifteen spotless rooms with ceiling fans, nets, showers and Western-style toilets; there's also a small bar, and food available. ❶
**Super City Hotel** By the transport stand ☏ 025/282 0160. This long-standing favourite has rooms with fans, nets and either private or shared bathrooms – the toilets lack seats, but there's

running water most of the time. There's also a good but sleepy bar in front. ❶
**Vatican Guest House** Immediately behind *Super City Hotel* ☏ 025/282 0065. A friendly, family-run budget option with large clean rooms, some with private bath, and all with ceiling fans and nets. Go down the alley on the right side of *Super City Hotel*, or walk around the parking lot by the roundabout. ❶

### Moving on from Mpanda

Moving on from Mpanda, the **train** heads back to Tabora at 1pm (Tues, Thurs & Sat), arriving just before 3am. Heading to Kigoma by train, get off at Tabora rather than Kalilua, where the lines meet, as you'll arrive at Kalilua at midnight and the onward connection leaves at 11pm the next night (or two nights later if you take the Saturday train); much better to kick around in Tabora.

**Buses**, **trucks and pick-ups** leave from the stand outside *Super City Hotel*. Buses also meet arriving trains at the station. For **Sumbawanga**, the most reliable transport is Sumry Bus (☏ 025/282 0464), which runs daily, and continues on to **Mbeya**. A handful of **pick-ups** also go to Sumbawanga, the first around 7–8am. The drive south to Sumbawanga goes via Katavi National Park and takes five hours in a private car or pick-up, or six or seven hours by bus. The road is all-weather *murram*, though be warned that if it's not properly maintained it will give way to a quagmire of black cotton soil.

Except one or two lorries a month, there's no road transport to **Uvinza** or **Kigoma**; catch the train via Tabora instead. If you're self-driving, leave before sunrise to have any hope of reaching Uvinza by nightfall (forget about Kigoma in one day), and count on an average speed of 15–20kph.

## Eating, drinking and nightlife

Mpanda's most atmospheric **restaurant** is the *Garden Club*, close to the *Paradise Discotheque*. The nameless restaurant next to *Super City Hotel* serves up tasty if somewhat dentally challenging grilled chicken with *ugali*, beans and rice (under Tsh4000), and the little brick café facing it is handy for breakfast. For **bars and nightlife**, you can break into a sweat at the *Paradise Discotheque*, southwest of the large market (open Fri & Sat nights, and Sun from mid-afternoon); it also has a shady garden and does food. Walking back isn't advisable after midnight and there are next to no taxis, so take a reliable local with you if you want to stay out late. The *Super City Hotel*'s bar is the most dignified place for a drink, and also has a TV, but the barmaids have a propensity to overcharge.

# Katavi National Park

**Katavi National Park**, 35km south of Mpanda and 143km north of Sumbawanga, covers 4471 square kilometres, making it Tanzania's fourth-largest protected wildlife area. Whilst the national park doesn't have especially spectacular scenery, its extraordinarily rich **dry-season wildlife viewing**, when vast quantities of game concentrate around rapidly receding water sources, easily makes it one of the gems of Tanzania's wildlife crown. Three species in particular offer stunning photo opportunities: one of Africa's most extensive **buffalo** herds, estimated at the last count to number around sixty thousand; and **crocodiles and hippo** packed into a handful of muddy lake-swamps, whose populations can reach several thousand in each. Other **wildlife** you're likely to see includes elephant (there are well over four thousand), giraffe, zebra, lion, gazelle, large herds of roan and sable antelopes, topi, eland and – in reed beds near the swamps – the southern reedbuck. **Birders** are in for a treat too, with over four hundred species recorded, including eagles, hawks, marabou storks and palm-nut vultures. But the main attraction for many is simply the park's remoteness, and the fact that you're pretty much guaranteed to have the place to yourself – Katavi attracts a mere 1200 visitors each year

## Arrival and information

Most visitors **fly in** to Katavi either direct from Arusha on light aircraft chartered by the upmarket tented camps or safari companies, or – usually as clients of Foxes African Safaris (p.53) – by five-seat Cessna from Ruaha National Park. As walking inside the park is allowed, arriving by **public transport** is a perfectly feasible alternative: **from Tabora**, catch the train to **Mpanda**, from where there are daily road connections to Sitalike, just 1km north of the park headquarters; You might also get a lift from one of the vehicles used by the tented camp or park staff; they usually park next to the *Super City Hotel* in Mpanda. The ride takes under an hour, and passes through desolate terrain where the villages are notable for some beautifully decorated houses painted with geometric and floral motifs. Coming from Mbeya, catch a bus to **Sumbawanga**, and from there (if there's no direct service) towards Mpanda, getting off at Sitalike. The road is decently graded and should be open year-round. Incidentally, the fifty-kilometre stretch of road that bisects the park is open 24 hours and doesn't require the payment of park fees if you're just passing through. Sitalike village, on the north side of the park, has a few sparsely stocked shops, lots of little bars and soda joints, a couple of basic restaurants and a mid-range hotel.

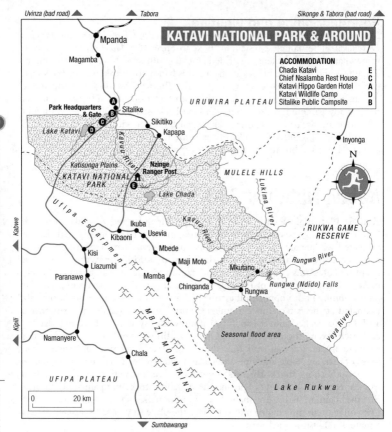

### Entrance fees and information

**Entry fees**, valid for 24 hours, are $25 per person, and Tsh10,000 for a vehicle. Although hiring a **guide** when driving is not compulsory, it's advisable given the lack of proper roads, signs or maps – the cost is $15–20 for a few hours.

The **park headquarters** are 1km south of Sitalike; after crossing the bridge into the park turn right after 100m, the headquarters are in a cluster of brick buildings. The official **website** is Ⓦ www.tanzaniaparks.com/katavi.html. The **best time to visit** is during the dry season (May–Oct, especially from July, and less so from mid-Dec to Feb). At other times the park is liable to be inaccessible due to the rains, and much of the plains game migrates beyond the park boundaries or into hillier and less accessible terrain. **Tsetse flies** are present all year round, but are especially bad in the rains.

## Accommodation

For those with obese bank accounts, there are a couple of **luxury tented camps**; guests fly in, and rates include game drives, bush walks and park fees. There's more sensibly priced accommodation at **Sitalike** on the park's northern boundary. A recommended alternative is **camping**, which enables you to do walks over several days, though you'll need to be entirely self-sufficient. Pitches are limited to *Sitalike Public Campsite* near the park headquarters ($30 per person plus park fees) and informal sites elsewhere which rangers can recommend ($50 per person if considered "special"). Basic supplies can be bought in Sitalike.

**Chada Katavi** (aka *Katavi Luxury Tented Camp* or *Roland's Camp*) On a wooded rise northwest of the Chada flood plain ⓦ www.nomad-tanzania .com. Travel hacks tie themselves in knots talking this one up, but one fact remains: it's just a bunch of tents (six, to be precise). Park fees, walks and game drives included. There's a three-night minimum stay and no kids under ten are allowed. Closed March–May. All-inclusive $850–1080. ⑨

**Chief Nsalamba Rest House** Under 1km south from the park headquarters, off the main road. Basic park-run rooms; book ahead as there are just three (most easily done at TANAPA headquarters in Arusha, see p.307). You'll have to say whether you're bringing your own food or want park staff to arrange meals or cooking equipment. There's no

problem walking along the road from the rest house to the village. ④

**Katavi Hippo Garden Hotel** Outside the park at Sitalike (ⓣ 025/282 0393). Several dozen rooms in en-suite *bandas* overlooking the Katama River. They should be able to arrange transport around the park for around $150 a day including driver but excluding park fees. ④

**Katavi Wildlife Camp** Katisunga Plains, at the mouth of the Katama River ⓦ www.tanzaniasafaris. info (book through Foxes African Safaris in Dar; see p.53). Similar to *Chada Katavi*, with its six tents set under trees and fronted by green gauze mosquito screens. Most guests fly in by Cessna from Ruaha National Park, where Foxes have another camp. Closed Dec–May. All-inclusive "fly-in" rate $700. ⑨

## The Park

**Walking** in Katavi is possible as long as you're accompanied by an armed ranger ($20 per walk, more if you camp overnight; they also double as guides). You should plan for at least two days, camping overnight, to really get anywhere. A good place to head to is the viewpoint over Lake Katavi and its flood plain, a forty-kilometre round trip from Sitalike. If you're strapped for time, it's possible to do a day's walk from the gate along the Katavi River and back through *miombo* woodland. If you've come by public transport and don't want to walk, the authorities might oblige with a lift or a spare vehicle, though there's nothing formal about this, so you certainly shouldn't count on it, and payment will of course be expected.

The park's main attraction is the **seasonally flooded grassland** occupying the area around Lake Katavi (20km southwest of Sitalike), the Katisunga Plains in the centre flanking the Kavuu River, and much of the eastern extension. In the dry season, the grasslands support vast herds of buffalo and plains game, and when they're flooded attract waterbirds in their thousands (though driving around the grasslands in the rains is treacherous if not impossible). If you're exceptionally lucky, you may see the shy and rare puku antelope (*Kobus vardoni*), about which very little is known – it's also found in

### Katabi the hunter

Katavi National Park takes its name from a semi-legendary ancestor of the Pimbwe, Fipa and Bende tribes, **Katabi**. A famed hunter in his time, his spirit is said to reside near Lake Katavi, in a small clearing around two tamarind trees. The site remains sacred, and locals still come here from outside the park to leave offerings, seeking Katabi's intercession with God in worldly matters like asking for rain. The vast hippo pods at either of the park's lakes are said to be Katabi's herds, and if you look really carefully, you might even catch a glimpse of him driving them along the shore...

Mahale, the Kilombero Valley and in isolated pockets across southern Africa. The **thickets and short grasses** around the edges of the flood plains are inhabited by leopard, lion and elephant, and various antelope species: roan and sable, southern reedbuck, eland and topi. The leopards are, as ever, difficult to spot, but your guide or ranger should be able to point out most of the antelopes.

The park's **lakes** – the palm-fringed Lake Katavi, and Lake Chada at the confluence of the Kavuu and Nsaginia rivers in the centre of the park – are nowadays little more than seasonal flood plains. Their gradual disappearance is due to river-borne silt deposits from the arid badlands between Mpanda and the park – a vivid example of the environmentally damaging consequences of concentrating human settlement in marginally productive areas, the result both of Nyerere's failed *Ujamaa* programme and of evicting people from the park. Nonetheless, both lakes retain some extraordinary wildlife viewing, most famously in the form of enormous herds of buffalo, birds in flocks of biblical proportions, and – most amazing in the dry season – literally thousands of hippos squashed together in the park's few remaining **mud pools**. At the edges of these glorious mud baths, and along riverbanks, large crocodiles also seek shelter from the dry-season sun by burrowing out nests, often stacked one atop the other. The hippos are best seen at Lake Chada, particularly at the pool close to Nzinge Ranger Post, whilst buffaloes, pelicans and marabou storks yanking out catfish from the mud are best seen from the observation hut overlooking Lake Katavi.

With your own transport, you could visit the permanent streams, small cascades and year-round springs of the cooler and wetter escarpment in the forested **Mulele Hills** (also spelled Mlala or Mlele), at the eastern boundary of the park beside Rukwa Game Reserve, while in the far southeast you might head to the **Rungwa (Ndido) Falls** on the Rungwa River, a thundering hundred-metre drop into a hippo- and croc-filled pool. If you get this far down, instead of retracing your steps you could follow the dirt road outside the park west from Rungwa village to Kibaoni, where a right turn takes you back into the park. Roughly 40km west of Rungwa you'll pass through the village of **Maji Moto** ("hot water"), just before which there are – no surprise – hot springs.

# Sumbawanga

The capital of Rukwa region is **SUMBAWANGA**, a pleasantly unimposing sort of place set in the lee of the Mbizi Mountains, whose breezes lend the town a refreshing climate – chilly at night, and just right by day. As a bonus for travellers emerging battered and bruised from a bumpy journey, there's no hassle either. The town's main attraction is the cosy **market** off Mpanda Road – just the place for cheap seasonal fruit and vegetables, *dagaa* fish from Lake Tanganyika and the traditional assortment of imported plastic and aluminium household goods from China and Taiwan. There's really nothing else to see in town, so unless you've got the patience and the stamina to arrange a hike in the **Mbizi Mountains** or down to **Lake Rukwa**, most people just stay a night before heading on towards Mpanda, Katavi National Park, Mbeya or – in the dry season – Kasanga on the shore of Lake Tanganyika.

9

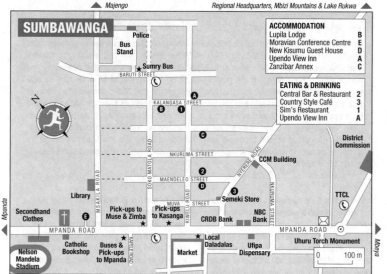

**SUMBAWANGA**

Police

Bus Stand

★ Sumry Bus

BARUTI STREET

**Ⓐ**

KALANGASA STREET

**Ⓑ** **❶**

**Ⓒ**

NKURUMA STREET

CCM Building

MAENDELEO STREET **❷**

**❸**

MUVA STREET

Semeki Store

Library

Pick-ups to Muse & Zimba ★ Pick-ups to Kasanga ★

CRDB Bank

NBC Bank

MPANDA ROAD

Uhuru Torch Monument

Secondhand Clothes **Ⓔ**

Catholic Bookshop

Buses & Pick-ups to Mpanda ★

★ Local Daladalas

Ufipa Dispensary

Market

Nelson Mandela Stadium

District Commission

TTCL

0    100 m

**ACCOMMODATION**
| Lupila Lodge | B |
| Moravian Conference Centre | E |
| New Kisumu Guest House | D |
| Upendo View Inn | A |
| Zanzibar Annex | C |

**EATING & DRINKING**
| Central Bar & Restaurant | 2 |
| Country Style Café | 3 |
| Sim's Restaurant | 1 |
| Upendo View Inn | A |

N

Mpanda

Mbeya

**LAKE TANGANYIKA AND WESTERN TANZANIA** | Sumbawanga

www.roughguides.com

## Practicalities

NBC **bank** on Mpanda Road changes traveller's cheques and has a 24-hour Visa/MasterCard ATM.

### Accommodation

The **guesthouses** immediately adjacent to the bus stand are pretty grim; the ones a few minutes' walk away in the grid of streets to the south are much better.

**Lupila Lodge** Kalangasa St ☏025/280 2418. Simple but well-kept rooms, some with private bath, all with nets. **❶**

**Moravian Conference Centre** Mpanda Rd ☏025/280 2853. Large, clean and calm if not overly welcoming Christian guesthouse; some of its 75 rooms have bathrooms (and hot water). There's also a restaurant with chapatis as flat as the overall atmosphere. BB **❸**

**New Kisumu Guest House** Maendeleo St ☏025/280 2927. A decent budget option similar to the *Lupila* – it's well kept, and some rooms have private bathrooms. **❶**

**Upendo View Inn** Kiwelu Rd/Kalangasa St ☏025/280 2242, ⒻF025/280 2502. The town's best hotel: the large clean twins (no single rates) have private bathrooms with reliable running water, Western-style toilets and even toilet paper. There's also a restaurant and bar, but the adjacent nightclub is exceedingly noisy. **❷**

**Zanzibar Annex** Off Kiwelu Rd ☏025/280 0010. An excellent choice should the *Upendo* be full, with a choice of rooms with or without private bathroom (the latter are much cheaper). Beds have nets and bathrooms have running water and clean squat toilets. **❶**

### Eating and drinking

The main concentration of **restaurants** is on Maendeleo Street, where the competition keeps standards fairly high. For your own supplies, Semeki Store, at the corner of Nyerere Road and Muva Street, has a reasonable selection of imported produce including tasty South African Ceres juices.

**Central Bar & Restaurant** Maendeleo St. Friendly local restaurant which is good for cheap breakfasts (great savoury *supus*) and lunches (under Tsh1000),

while the attached bar is great for an afternoon drink, its TV tuned to Discovery Channel and CNN during the day to keep locals glued to the screen.

## Moving on from Sumbawanga

Only two companies operate from Sumbawanga: Air Bus has a perilous reputation; much safer is Sumry (☏ 025/280 2747) on Baruti Street, which goes daily to **Mbeya and Dar es Salaam** (6.30am), and to **Mpanda** (1pm). There are also daily pick-ups and trucks to Mpanda from the petrol station on the corner of Mpanda and Kapele roads. Pick-ups to **Muse**, on the eastern flank of the Mbizi Mountains north of Sumbawanga, and **Zimba**, near the shore of Lake Rukwa, leave from Mpanda Road (see below). In the dry season, there's at least one vehicle heading to **Kasanga** on Lake Tanganyika at 9am, sometimes later. There's no regular transport to Mbala in **Zambia** (the usual border crossing is via Tunduma along the road to Mbeya), so it's a matter of asking around at the petrol station at the corner of Mpanda and Kapele roads for a truck.

**Country Style Café** Nyerere Rd. A neat little café and restaurant with a wide range of snacks and affordable meals.

**Sim's Restaurant** Kiwelu Rd/Kalangasa St. Long-established place serving up delicious and filling meals for under Tsh1000, with a choice of meat stew, roast chicken, fish or liver with *ugali* or rice, plus beans and greens. No alcohol.

**Upendo View Inn** Kalangasa St/Kiwelu Rd. This is the most kicking nightspot in town, especially on Wed, Fri and Sat. There's live music from the Rukwa International Band, plus a "*wazee* disco" (*wazee* are old men) playing Tanzanian golden oldies (possibly Fri), some *ngoma ya kiasili* (traditional music) and a children's disco (Sun 2–7pm) followed by one for adults. There's good and reasonably priced food, too.

# The Mbizi Mountains

Sumbawanga is the base for hikes in the **MBIZI MOUNTAINS**, which are almost completely unknown outside Sumbawanga – and indeed to a good many people in Sumbawanga as well. You'll need to be completely self-sufficient and have a tent, as the only **guesthouses** are at **Zimba**, a former German camp (now run by the Catholic Mission) an hour's drive from Sumbawanga on the eastern slopes of the range overlooking Lake Rukwa, and 100km to the north at Mamba, which lies 10km south of the hot springs at Maji Moto (see p.458). When camping, make sure you get permission from locals before you pitch your tent. A good source of **information** before leaving is the District Commissioner's Office in Sumbawanga (100m beyond TTCL), or the Regional HQ, 1km along Nyerere Road.

The easiest way to reach the mountains is to take one of the **pick-ups** to Zimba, which leave daily from the petrol station at the corner of Mpanda and Kapele roads between 10am and noon, returning to Sumbawanga around 4pm. From Zimba, you could explore the western shore of Lake Rukwa before heading northwest along a little-used road to Muse (40km). Pick-ups back to Sumbawanga from Muse leave around 4pm. If you want to go directly to Muse, pick-ups depart from Sumbawanga at the same place and time as those for Zimba. For something even more adventurous, the sixty- to seventy-kilometre trek northwest towards **Mamba** takes you along the eastern ridge of the mountains via the villages of Nkwilo, Mfinga, Finga and Kilida. The Amour Video Coach **bus** runs from Mamba to Mpanda, 120km north, on Monday, Wednesday and Friday, arriving in time to catch the train to Tabora the following day. **Coming from Mpanda**, they leave around noon on Tuesday, Thursday and Saturday, arriving in Mamba before nightfall.

# Lake Rukwa

Occupying the lowest part of the Rukwa Rift Valley (also called the Rukwa Trough), **Lake Rukwa** follows the same northwest–southeast fault line as Lake Nyasa to the south. The water is extremely alkaline, and there are saltpans at **Ivuna**, 15km from the lake's southern shore, fed by hot brine springs. Excavations have established that Iron Age people lived on the lakeshore from as early as the thirteenth century, working the salt, cultivating cereals, keeping cattle, goats, chickens and dogs, and hunting zebra and warthog for food. The trade in Ivuna's salt was sufficiently important to have made the southern shores of Rukwa figure as a stopover on a slaving caravan route to Bagamoyo during the nineteenth century.

Crocodiles, hippos and fish abound, of which tilapia provide the basis for a flourishing fishing industry that exports its dried catch as far away as Congo and Zambia – Rukwa's alkaline water makes for tasty and tender fish. Despite the fishery, the lake could hardly be more different from its western neighbour, Lake Tanganyika: the latter's enormous depth contrasting with Rukwa's average of a mere 3m, while the lake's size is prone to wild variations due to the lack of an outlet and the unreliability of the streams feeding it – at times it actually splits into two lakes separated by a narrow belt of swamp. During the 1820s and 1830s the lake almost dried up, and when the explorer John Hanning Speke passed by in 1859 he saw only an impassable swamp. The lake's chronic silting-up over recent decades, hastened by deforestation in its catchment area, results in it permanently flooding large expanses of formerly seasonal flood plain. The **Uwanda Game Reserve**, established in 1971 and still marked on maps, has for all practical purposes ceased to exist, as over half of it now lies permanently under water.

Rukwa's main natural attraction is its **birdlife**, with over four hundred species recorded, many of them waterfowl. The disappearance of much of the flood plain and grassland ecosystem has greatly reduced the numbers of **plains game** that once frequented the area, especially after the short rains from November onwards. Still, you might still see zebra and buffalo, rarer animals such as topi and puku antelopes, and – at least according to rumour – an albino giraffe or spotted zebra.

## Practicalities

Lake Rukwa can be accessed either from the northwest or the southeast, but whichever route you choose, take everything you'll need with you, and be prepared for the lake's unpleasantly hot and muggy atmosphere. The easier of the two routes is from **Sumbawanga** in the northwest, which has daily pick-ups to Zimba (see facing), about 5km from the lakeshore. Access along the **southeast route** from Mbeya via Chunya is much more difficult and really only feasible in your own 4WD, and even then only in the dry season. There are no restrictions on **camping** at the lakeshore (or as near as you can get without becoming stuck in a swamp), but you should seek permission from any locals you can find and keep an eye out for crocodiles and hippos. Swimming is not advisable for this reason, especially on the southeast shore, where the crocodiles are known to be particularly dangerous.

# Travel details

## Buses and pick-ups

Full details are given in the "moving on" sections throughout this chapter. An asterisk denotes that transport may not run in the rains, or may be hugely delayed.

**Kigoma** to: Biharamulo (4 weekly*; 7–9hr); Bukoba (4 weekly*; 15–18hr); Kibondo (1–3 daily*; 4–6hr); Mwanza (daily*; 14–18hr); Shinyanga (weekly*; 10–12hr).

**Mpanda** to: Karema (pick-ups*; 6hr); Mamba (3 weekly; 3–5hr); Sumbawanga (daily; 5hr).

**Tabora** to: Arusha (2 weekly; 12–13hr); Dodoma (6 weekly*; 9–12hr); Kahama (6 weekly; 4–5hr); Mbeya (2 weekly*; 18hr); Mwanza (2–3 daily; 8hr); Nzega (3–4 daily; 3hr); Singida (2 weekly; 6hr).

## Ferries (Lake Tanganyika)

Full details of ferries and lake taxis are given in "Moving on from Kigoma" on p.433.

## Flights

PA is Precisionair. Upmarket tented camps at Katavi and Mahale Mountains national parks organize charter flights from Arusha, Mwanza or Kigoma, which you can book a seat on.

**Kigoma** to: Dar (PA: daily; 2hr 40min).

**Tabora** to: Arusha (charters); Dar (PA: daily; 4hr); Kigoma (PA: daily; 55min).

**Katavi** to: Arusha (charters).

**Mahale** to: Arusha (charters).

## Trains

See p.30 for general information on Tanzania's train network. Times and days are given in the relevant arrival and moving on sections.

**Kigoma** to: Dar (3 weekly; 39hr); Dodoma (3 weekly; 24hr 10min); Morogoro (3 weekly; 31hr 35min); Tabora (3 weekly; 10hr 30min).

**Mpanda** to: Tabora (3 weekly; 13hr 45min).

**Tabora** to: Dar (3 weekly; 25hr 35min); Dodoma (3 weekly; 10hr 45min); Kigoma (3 weekly; 11hr 15min); Morogoro (3 weekly; 18hr 10min); Mpanda (3 weekly; 13hr 30min); Mwanza (3 weekly; 10hr 5min).

# Southern Tanzania

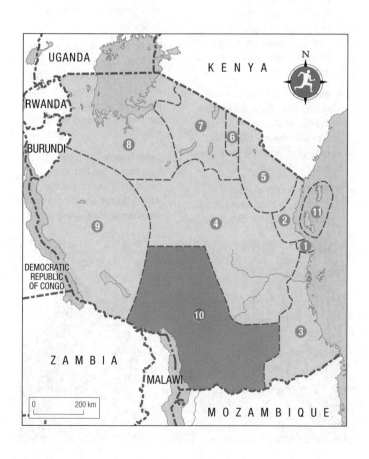

CHAPTER 10    # Highlights

* **Neema Crafts Centre, Iringa**
An uplifting arts and crafts
project for disabled people, at
which you're most welcome
to muck in, too. See p.470

* **Kalenga** The historic seat of
the Hehe tribe who, under
Chief Mkwawa, famously
resisted the Germans in the
1890s. A museum tended by
his descendants contains his
skull. See p.472

* **Isimila** spectacular series of
gullies near Iringa, resembling
the Grand Canyon in miniature,
and site of numerous finds
of prehistoric stone tools and
fossils. See p.473

* **Ruaha National Park**
"Tanzania's best-kept secret",
Ruaha contains most of the
Northern Safari Circuit's
wildlife but few of the crowds.
See p.475

* **The southern highlands**
Hike or bike from Mbeya and
Tukuyu to waterfalls, crater
lakes, a lava-stone bridge, or
up the forested peaks. See
p.486 & p.493

* **Kitulo National Park** Known
as "God's Garden", this
highland plateau contains an
immense diversity of flowers,
especially orchids. It's best
experienced during the rains.
See p.489

* **Lake Nyasa** The most
beautiful of the Rift Valley
lakes, best seen from the
weekly ferry from Itungi Port
to Mbamba Bay. See p.495

▲ Gullies, Isimila

# Southern Tanzania

L
ittle visited but often wildly beautiful, southern Tanzania is an enchanting and surprisingly easy place to explore, whether it's mountains you hanker for, or ancient forests, wildlife and birds, culture, or merely magnificent scenery. Coming from central Tanzania, first stop is **Iringa** town, a very pleasant base from which to explore the bird-filled forests of the **western Udzungwa Mountains**, a number of historical sites related to the struggle against German conquest, and the huge if fragile wilderness of **Ruaha National Park** – equal to the northern circuit for wildlife, but with only a fraction of the crowds. In the dry season, the park's waterholes attract a surprisingly rich array of wildlife; in the rains, when everything turns green, it becomes a paradise for bird-watchers.

Further south, the evergreen **southern highlands** – product of the tectonic upheavals that also wrenched apart the Rift Valley – are a giant's playground of forested peaks, crater lakes, hot springs, flower-strewn plateaux, and even a dormant volcano, Mount Rungwe. All in all quite perfect hiking terrain, access to which is simple thanks to **cultural tourism** programmes in Mbeya, the region's capital, and in the agricultural town of Tukuyu – Tanzania's wettest place. To the east, the land levels off on to the **Kitulo Plateau**, declared a national park to protect over fifty species of rare orchids, which put on delirious displays during the rains. But flowers aren't the park's only rarity: say hello to **kipunji**, an entirely new species and genera of monkey that was only discovered in 2003.

Beyond the southern highlands, the land drops down to **Lake Nyasa**, which fills a deep trough at the junction of the eastern and western branches of the Rift Valley. Flanked by the soaring Livingstone Mountains, it's a stunningly picturesque stretch of water, and provides – via a ferry ride – a short but most memorable journey. In contrast to the lake's Malawian shoreline, however, tourism on the Tanzanian side is virtually non-existent: the main beach, at Matema in the north, has just three modest hotels, whilst the southern town (and sands) of Mbamba Bay is about as far as you can get from mainstream Tanzania without tripping over the border into Mozambique.

**English** is not widely spoken, so try to get a few words of "Jambo" in advance. Virtually everywhere you'll want to go is served by some form of **public transport**, though the only comfortable rides (guaranteed seats and smooth tarmac) are along the Tanzam highway from Dar and Morogoro to Iringa and Mbeya, and, also paved, south of the highway to Songea. The only place where you'll need your **own vehicle** (or a seat on an organized safari) is Ruaha National Park, trips to which can be arranged locally, as well as in Dar. The TAZARA **railway** follows much the same trajectory as the highway, but is unreliable and not much use unless you're going straight to Zambia.

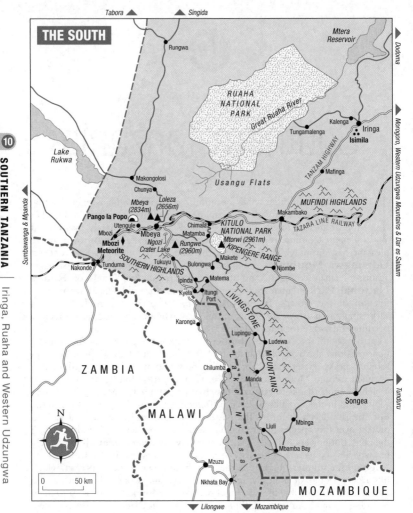

# Iringa, Ruaha and Western Udzungwa

Five hundred kilometres southwest of Dar, and just over three hundred from Morogoro, is the town of **Iringa**, a very attractive base for exploring its equally attractive region – a mix of forested hills, boulder-strewn wildernesses, fertile farmland, and dusty red lowlands that are home to most of the big game species you can also see in northern Tanzania. The main draw is **Ruaha National Park**, the country's southernmost savanna habitat and which, together with Selous and Mikumi (both in chapter 4) completes the so-called Southern Safari Circuit. Ruaha, together with the **western Udzungwa Mountains**, is also prime bird-viewing territory, with over seven hundred species recorded between them. With the exception of Udzungwa, getting around the region is simple enough, especially if you base yourself in Iringa.

# Iringa and around

Perched on an escarpment amidst jagged hills and cracked granite boulders, the town of **IRINGA** – just off the Tanzam Highway – has a very appealing location, nicely matched by its welcoming and laid-back mood. It's the main base for visiting Ruaha National Park, and travellers will also appreciate the fresh climate (1600m above sea level), which can get positively chilly in June and July. In the nineteenth century, the region was controlled by the Hehe tribe, most famously led by **Chief Mkwawa** (see p.474) who, for several years, successfully resisted German conquest. There's a museum dedicated to him at **Kalenga**, an easy half-day trip from Iringa. Similarly accessible is the Stone Age site of **Isimila**, which wouldn't be all that interesting were it not for its setting amidst a natural "forest" of bizarrely shaped sandstone pillars.

## Arrival and information

Iringa lies 3km of the Tanzam highway; the **bus stand** is in the centre of town, but coaches en route to other destinations may only stop at **Ipogoro** on the highway, from where a taxi into town costs Tsh4000, and a daladala Tsh300. As ever, keep an eye on your bags, and use **taxis** at night unless you're in a group.

Iringa's unofficial **tourist office**, operated by *Riverside Campsite*, is **Iringa Info** on Uhuru Avenue (Mon–Sat 9am–5pm, Sun 9am–2pm; ☎026/270 1988, ℮riversidecampsitetz@hotmail.com). Also helpful and well informed is Shaffin Haji, the owner of *Hasty Tasty Too* restaurant, opposite (☎026/270 2061, ℮shaffinhaji@hotmail.com).

## Accommodation

Iringa's cheapest **guesthouses** are mostly quite squalid, with anything half-decent charging over the odds. Lower-mid-range **hotels** fare better, and there are a couple of very attractive rural places out of town, both of which also have **campsites**. Lastly, Iringa's **tap water** needs sterilizing if you're going to drink it.

### Town centre

**Annex Staff Inn Lodge** Uhuru Ave ☎026/270 1344. Dreary and a little pricey by any but Iringa's standards, for which it's actually something of a bargain: secure, and with cool if cramped en-suite rooms, good beds, nets and TVs, hot water, and a nice restaurant (see p.471). No smoking. ❷

**Central Lodge Hotel** Uhuru Ave ☎0786/126888 or 0785/704988, ℮centrallodge@gmail.com. A very pleasant, almost rural alternative to the gloomy central guesthouses, with seven large en-suite rooms, some twins, with big beds and box nets, and functional plumbing (warm if not hot

water). The best thing though is the lovely garden-bar at the back. Safe parking. BB ❷

**Dr A.J. Nsekela Executive Lodge** Uhuru Ave ☎026/270 2407, ℱ026/270 2563. Run by a business school, in a large and usually very somnolent 1970s block. Has good en-suite rooms (no twins) with sporadic hot water, plus suites with bigger beds and fridges. Check nets for size. Food to order. Safe parking. BB ❷–❸

**Iringa Lutheran Center** Kawawa Rd ☎026/270 0722, ℮thelutherancenter@gmail.com. Quiet, prim, proper, and dull, just as a church hostel should be, but also expensive, and suffering from the classic hostel syndrome of too-small sheets (the nets are okay though). Rooms to the left of the reception (singles or doubles) are fine, but ones to the right haven't been properly renovated and the singles are, well, dingy. All have (local) TV and bathrooms. Food to order. Safe parking. BB ❸

**Isimila Hotel** Uhuru Ave ☎026/270 1194, ✉isimilahotel@yahoo.com. Friendly and calm with 48 en-suite rooms including suites, in several big and actually quite likeable 1970s blocks surrounded by cypress and bottlebrush trees. Despite being a bit damp and forlorn, it's comfortable and well priced. There's also a restaurant, bar and safe parking. Loud on Friday and Saturday nights (to 4am), thanks to *Twisters* in the street behind. BB ❷

**M.R. Hotel** Mkwawa Rd ☎026/270 2006, ⊛www .mrhotels.co.tz. Overlooking the bus stand, this is aimed at businessmen and is rather pricey, but has bright and mostly spotless rooms on three floors; the ones higher up being less noisy. All have (local) TV, a balcony and hot water, but no mosquito nets as rooms are sprayed instead. There's also a restaurant (no alcohol), internet café and safe parking. BB ❹

**Neema Crafts Centre** Hakimu St (see p.470). Ten en-suite rooms are being built above the workshops here, which should be up and running by the time you read this. They'll more likely than not offer Iringa's best-value accommodation... and with the guarantee that profits go straight back into the project. ❸

**New Ruaha International Lodge** Kawawa Rd/ Churchill Rd ☎026/270 0641, ✉newruaha@gmail .com. A series of red-walled green-roofed buildings occupying a gravel-strewn plot, this motel-like place has gone to town on mirrored glass and assorted renovations, but the rooms remain tiny, not all have bathrooms, and even by Iringa's standards they're overpriced. Still, you get cable TV,

and there's a quiet bar and restaurant. Safe parking. BB ❹

### Out of town

**Kisolanza Farm (The Old Farm House)** 54km southwest of Iringa along the highway (51km from Ipogoro) ☎0754/306144, ⊛www.kisolanza.com. This delightful colonial-era farm is a stopover for overland tourist trucks, who have their own campsite. There's another campsite, and a wide selection of attractive rooms, including rustic chalets sharing bathrooms, en-suite cottages with log fires, and, top of the line, a couple of luxurious "farm cottages" with their own gardens. There's also a bar (in a surprisingly authentic-looking tribal house) whose many treats include hot chocolate Amarula and cakes, and a restaurant ably showing off the farm's produce, which you can also buy from their shop. BB ❷–❻

**Riverside Campsite** 14km east of town: 12.5km towards Morogoro then 1.5km south ☎026/270 1988 or 0787/111663, ⊛www.riversidecampsite-tanzania.com. Set beside the Little Ruaha River, this lovely British-run hideaway has a campsite, six enticingly priced chalets in Hansel and Gretel style (two with kitchens), nine tented *bandas* sharing toilets, and eight "tents with beds". Good food available, often as evening buffets if there are enough people around, but the main attraction is a welter of activities, including several kilometres of walking trails, swimming in the river, village tours, mountain biking, horseriding, visits to Lugalo, Isimila and Kalenga, safaris to Ruaha National Park, and hikes in and around the western Udzungwa Mountains. A taxi from town costs Tsh17,000. Book the chalets well in advance. BB ❸–❹

## The Town

Iringa's rural essence is best sampled by rummaging around the **market**, a colourful, vibrant and hustler-free shambles built in 1940. Among the many specialities on offer are beautifully woven (and sometimes aromatic) baskets made from reeds or sisal, pumice stones and honey, bath sponges and loofahs imported from the coast, and even cow bells. There's also a riotous selection of *kanga* wraps, *kibatari* oil lamps, pungent dried fish from Mtera Reservoir (along the road to Dodoma), and pottery from various places, including – if you're lucky – the gorgeous cream-and-red ware from Lake Nyasa's Kisi tribe. For medicinal herbs and tree bark, have a mooch down the alleyway on the west side of Uhuru Park, where several Maasai sit behind their wares, together with others making and selling beaded jewellery, or plaiting people's hair. The compact **colonial quarter** occupies the streets west of the market: its most

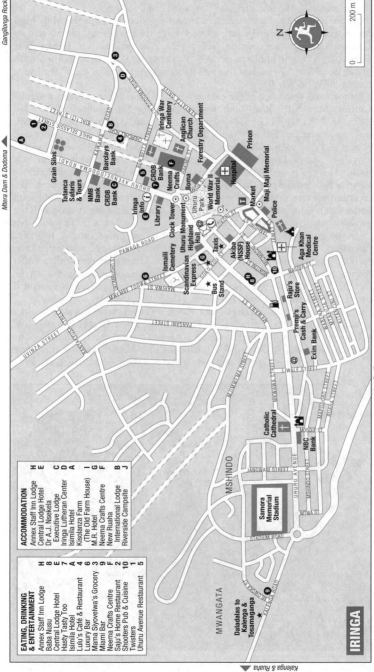

IRINGA

**SOUTHERN TANZANIA**

10

Gangilonga Rock

Mtera Dam & Dodoma

Kalenga & Ruaha

▶ **i**, **j** Ipogoro Bus Stand, Isimila, Tosamaganga, Mbeya & Morogoro

**EATING, DRINKING & ENTERTAINMENT**

| | |
|---|---|
| Annex Staff Inn Lodge | H |
| Baba Nusu | 8 |
| Central Lodge Hotel | C |
| Hasty Tasty Too | 7 |
| Isimila Hotel | I |
| Lulu's Café & Restaurant | 4 |
| Luxury Bar | 6 |
| Mama Siyovelwa's Grocery | 3 |
| Miami Bar | 9 |
| Neema Crafts Centre | F |
| Saju's Home Restaurant | 2 |
| Shooters Pub & Cuisine | 10 |
| Twisters | 1 |
| Uhuru Avenue Restaurant | 5 |

**ACCOMMODATION**

| | |
|---|---|
| Annex Staff Inn Lodge | H |
| Central Lodge Hotel | E |
| Dr A.J. Nsekela | C |
| Executive Lodge | D |
| Iringa Lutheran Center | A |
| Isimila Hotel | |
| Kisolanza Farm (The Old Farm House) | I |
| M.R. Hotel | G |
| Neema Crafts Centre | F |
| New Ruaha | B |
| International Lodge | |
| Riverside Campsite | J |

Daladalas to Kalenga & Tosamaganga

impressive building is a tall, Bavarian-style structure with a clock tower on Jamat Street; originally the town hall, it's now the Ismaïli mosque.

On the south side of the market, next to the police station, is the **Maji Maji Memorial**, honouring African soldiers who died while in the service of Germany during the uprising (see p.173). Also poignant is **Iringa War Cemetery** a couple of blocks north, which contains German as well as British graves from World War I, and those of locals (expats as well as Tanzanians) who fought in World War II.

A short walk southwest of the cemetery, on Hakimu Street, is **Neema Crafts Centre** (Mon–Sat 8.30am–5pm, workshops closed Sat afternoon; ☎026/270 2499 or 0783/0405111, ⓦwww.neemacrafts.com), a vocational handicrafts training project for disabled youths. Established in 2003 with three young deaf people and one volunteer, it now employs eighty, and is still growing – with a startlingly positive impact not just on their lives, but on local attitudes towards disabled people as well. You're welcome to tour the **workshops** (an industrious hive), or have a dabble yourself: weaving on wooden looms, printing using batiks, recycling glass to make jewellery, preparing solar panels, poking around in pottery, or making paper… from a murky vat of elephant dung. A **shop** sells the project's output, ranging from the said dung paper to cards and lamps made from maize or pineapple leaves, paintings, collages, screen prints, candles, jewellery, patchworks and wall-hangings. The first floor has a restaurant and coffee shop (p.471), a gallery, and events space: cinema on Saturday nights with a buffet dinner, pizza and games nights on Fridays, and regular live music events, including *ngoma*. There's also a book exchange, and a properly trained physiotherapist for hour-long **massages** (Tsh25,000; weekday afternoons).

One more attraction is **Gangilonga Rock** – a large, orange-streaked boulder nestling in a vale between two peaks east of town, where Chief Mkwawa – the celebrated leader of the Hehe tribe – is said to have come to meditate. The rock's name means "talking stone", alluding to a legend that the rock gave advice when asked – perhaps inspired by the whistling sound which cracks in

▲ Playing *bao* at Iringa market

the boulder emit when the wind blows in the right direction. Either way, it's a nice walk (45min each way) which rewards you with a panoramic view of Iringa (and great sunsets), though a few isolated muggings means you should get a local to accompany you – ask at your hotel, or at *Hasty Tasty Too*. You can see the rock to your right as you walk past the grain silos on Uhuru Avenue.

# Eating

Fresh milk and yoghurt is sold at the petrol station at the junction of Uhuru Avenue and Miomboni Street. The main **minimarkets**, Premji's and Raju's, are on Jamat Street.

**Annex Staff Inn Lodge** Uhuru Ave. Busy local eatery with a nice streetside terrace behind a shady vine. The liver stew is excellent. No smoking or alcohol.

**Baba Nusu** Uhuru Ave. Popular with locals, with good cheap food (*ugali*, rice, beans and meat), plenty of snacks too, even avocado milkshake. Open late. No alcohol.

**Hasty Tasty Too** Uhuru Ave. Long established, well attuned to tourists, and happy to improvise for peculiar tastes or particular diets. The cooked breakfasts (from Tsh3000) are uncommonly good, and full meals (around Tsh7000, or Tsh5000 for light lunches) are tasty, too: try the quesadillas (chapati rolls filled with beans, cheese, onion and avocado, fried and sliced). The freshly brewed arabica is good (especially with cardamom). Also sells juices, chocolates, jam and cakes. Closed Saturday afternoon and Sundays after 2pm.

**Isimila Hotel** Uhuru Ave. The second-floor restaurant here is usually empty and has a limited choice (Tanzanian staples, meaning rice or chips with everything), but the food – especially stews – can be excellent. Around Tsh4000.

**Lulu's Café & Restaurant** Churchill Rd. Like *Hasty Tasty Too*, a favourite with travellers and expats, and affordable. Quality wobbled a bit in the past, but at the last sampling was excellent, including a fantastic Greek salad (with salty, tangy home-made feta; Tsh2000), meat balls with mashed potato (Tsh3500), other Greek dishes, some Chinese, also snacks, real juices and coffee,

ice cream, and toasts. Good cheap breakfasts too. No alcohol. Mon–Sat 9am–3pm & 6.30–9pm.

**Neema Crafts Centre** Hakimu St. Above the workshops, this is a gallery and coffee shop rolled into one, and which, even if it wasn't reasonably priced (it is) would be worth it, as profits are ploughed back into the project. The foodie limelight shines brightest on its snacks, including a fabulous carrot cake; the chocolate cake isn't half bad either, especially when served hot with home-made ice cream. And where else can you slurp a baobab shake? Top marks also for the coffee: a special arabica roast from Utengule (Mbeya) which almost matches the heavenly brew from Moshi's *The Coffee Shop*. Mon–Sat 8.30am–5pm plus Friday evenings (set menu with live music). No alcohol.

**Saju's Home Restaurant** Haile Selassie St. An attractive and peaceful split-level place with a good selection of Tanzanian, Indian and Chinese options (main courses from Tsh4000; allow an hour), plus good pizzas. The chicken soup is a meal in itself, and the naan bread freshly baked, but avoid the seafood. Also does snacks. Best for lunch, as the street is unlit at night.

**Shooters Pub & Cuisine** Miomboni St. Meaty dishes and a touch of Indian and Chinese dished up in a bright dining room beside the bar. Main courses around Tsh5000.

**Uhuru Avenue Restaurant** Ben Bella St. Basic cheap snacks, and full meals for under Tsh2000. Has a few tables outside, too.

# Drinking and nightlife

The main venue for visiting **bands** from Dar is Highland Hall on Uhuru Avenue, facing the post office. There are loads of **bars** and "groceries" throughout town, especially along Mahiwa Street north of the bus stand, but few are particularly salubrious, or enticing. More attractive, even genteel, are the following.

**Central Lodge Hotel** Uhuru Ave. A calm and indeed dignified bar set in an enchanting *Alice in Wonderland*-style garden behind Iringa Info, where the shady magnolia trees, yellow-bark fever trees

and bougainvillea bushes make for a blissful setting. Currently has only typical bar food (*mishkaki*, *chipsi mayai*, *nyama choma*), but may do proper meals in future.

Luxury Bar Mwembe Togwa St. The most
appetizing of the many local bars in this area, and
worth asking about live bands, too.
Mama Siyovelwa's Grocery Kawawa Rd/Old
Dodoma Rd. Another nicely chilled-out garden bar,
with seating under thatched shelters and big trees.
Food is available, including renowned pork roasts.
Miami Bar Kalenga Rd. A lively, friendly and often
packed local bar, with – weirdly – an excellent
selection of Scotch whiskies.

Shooters Pub & Cuisine Miomboni St. Iringa's
only upmarket bar is also the nocturnal hub for
expats, with a TV (mostly international football), a
pool table, and a restaurant. You can also sit out on
a very narrow balcony overlooking the street.
Twisters Haile Selassie St, next to *Saju's*. This dark
and normally sleepy bar hosts loud discos on
Friday and Saturday (9pm–4am): a good place to
meet new friends, but keep an eye on your stuff,
and use a taxi.

## Listings

Banks and exchange You can't change traveller's
cheques in Iringa. Most banks, all with ATMs, are
on Uhuru Ave; Exim is at the west end of Jamat St.
Quickest for changing cash (at decent rates) is
Iringa Bureau de Change, 2nd floor, Akiba (NSSF)
House, Soko Kuu St (Mon–Fri 8am–6pm, Sat
9am–3pm).
Hospital Better than the regional hospital is Aga
Khan Medical Centre on Jamat St, near the market
⏀027/270 2277 or 027/270 2617.
Internet access *M.R. Hotel*, Mwembe Togwa St
(daily 8.30am–10pm), and several on Uhuru Ave:
Iringa.NET (Mon–Sat 8am–5.30pm, Sun 8am–
noon), Skynet (same building as Iringa Info; daily
8am–8pm), and the post office (Mon–Fri
8am–8.30pm, Sat 9am–6pm, Sun 11am–6pm).

Neema Crafts Centre, Hakimu St, is planning
access, and may have wi-fi.
Language courses *Riverside Campsite* (see p.468)
offers two- to sixteen-week courses: $130 per
week (plus $200/week full board). For something
less intensive, enquire at *Hasty Tasty Too*.
Library Iringa Regional Library, Uhuru Ave by the
clock tower (Mon–Fri 9.30am–6pm, Sat 8.30am–
2pm; Tsh500 per day).
Pharmacy Acacia Pharmacy, Uhuru Ave (Mon–Sat
8am–8pm, Sun 8am–2pm).
Post and couriers Post office: Uhuru Ave. Courier:
DHL, near Samora Memorial Stadium, Mshindo
area ⏀026/270 0110.
Telephones TTCL, beside the post office (Mon–Sat
7.30am–10pm, Sun 8am–8pm).

## Kalenga

An easy half-day trip from Iringa is the historic village of **KALENGA**, 15km
along the unsurfaced road to Ruaha National Park, which was the headquarters
of Chief Mkwawa (see box, p.474) until he was driven out by the Germans in
1894. The history of Mkwawa's struggle is recorded in the **Mkwawa Memorial
Museum** (no set hours – someone will open it up for you; Tsh3000), signposted
1.5km from the village. The museum, tended by the great warrior's descendants,
contains an assortment of clubs, spears and shields, as well as the shotgun with

### Moving on from Iringa

The Tanzam highway is terrifyingly fast in places, so be careful which bus company
you choose. For **Mbeya**, Chaula Bus, from the central bus stand, is recommended.
The other decent companies are Sumry (office at the central bus stand) and Scandinavian Express (around the corner on Soko Kuu Street ⏀026/270 2308): both start
in Dar, however, so you can't buy tickets before 9.30am or so on the day of departure,
and you need to board them at Ipogoro, 3km down on the highway.

Going to **Dar or Morogoro**, most through buses call in at the central bus station
(including Sumry and Scandinavian), and you should be able to buy your ticket in
advance. The only daily bus to **Arusha** (and Moshi) is run by the notoriously reckless
Hood; better to catch a bus to Dar and head on the next day. **Dodoma** is covered by
at least two daily buses, via the unsurfaced road that passes Mtera Dam; the road is
slow, so safety isn't a worry, but the buses are uncomfortably stuffed.

which Mkwawa committed suicide. The chief exhibit is **Mkwawa's skull**, which was returned to the Hehe in 1954 after a 56-year exile in Germany. Outside the museum are tombs of Mkwawa's descendants, including his son, Chief Sapi Mkwawa, and his grandson, Chief Adam Sapi Mkwawa. Five hundred metres away is another tomb, containing the body of **Erich Maas**, a German commando who attempted to infiltrate the fort and capture Mkwawa; the unfortunate Maas was discovered by Mkwawa, at whose hands he met his fate.

**Pick-ups to Kalenga**, at least hourly throughout the day, leave from Kalenga Road on the west side of Iringa. **Taxis** charge up to Tsh20,000 for the return journey. A trip to Kalenga can be combined with a visit to the Catholic mission at **Tosamaganga**, a pleasant six-kilometre (2hr) walk southwest. It's another 5km from there to the Tanzam highway, where there are frequent daladalas back to Iringa.

## Isimila

Just over 20km southwest of Iringa, 1km off the Tanzam highway, is **ISIMILA**, one of Africa's richest Stone Age sites. Since 1958 excavations have uncovered thousands of stone tools dating from the **Acheulian period**, some sixty thousand years ago. Even if archeology isn't your thing, the scenery – small but spectacular canyons studded with bizarrely eroded pink and orange **sandstone needles** – makes the trip worthwhile, as do the rock hyrax, swifts and sand martins.

The sandstone sculptures were created by the Isimila River, which was also responsible for uncovering the **stone tools**. Pear-shaped hand-axes and cleavers are most common; there are also cutters, hammers, picks and scrapers, and spherical balls whose use has never been fully explained. At the time the tools were made part of the site was occupied by a shallow lake, attracting both wildlife and hunters. The **fossil remains** of various animals hint at an environment not too different from today: elephants and antelopes, and various extinct mammals, including a giant hog, a short-necked giraffe and a weird species of hippo, which appears to have been even more boggle-eyed than its modern form.

There's a small **museum**, which also sells a short but informative guidebook. **Admission** to the site and museum costs Tsh3000 (tip expected; Tsh6000 per group is usual), which gets you an entertaining two-hour tour of the gully. The tools, which are lying in situ, cover much of the area – you're allowed to handle but not remove them. A **taxi** from Iringa costs Tsh30,000 return, including waiting time.

# The western Udzungwa Mountains

Rising about a hundred kilometres east of Iringa are the first peaks of the **Udzungwa Mountains**, whose forests are among Africa's most biodiverse. The thick, primate-rich forest on the east side is accessed from Mang'ula (in chapter 4), but for **birds**, the **Western Udzungwa Mountains** are best: over three hundred species have been recorded so far, including the Udzungwa partridge, rufous-winged and Moreau's sunbirds, dappled mountain robins, spot-throats, Nduk eagle owls, and Iringa akalats, all of them endemic and braggably rare. For the time being, exploring the western Udzungwas without a local guide is probably more trouble than it's worth, as both the national park and the various reserves abutting are wrapped in **red tape**, and access isn't too easy either. As such, we'd recommend you come either on a dedicated birding safari, or arrange things through *Riverside Campsite* near Iringa (p.468), which also runs

Iringa's tourist office, and is perfectly cuckoo about birds. The **best months** for birding are September to early December. With the exception of the riverside walk at Msosa (see below), hikes are strenuous up–down affairs, and it can also be very cold at night, so bring warm clothes as well as rain gear.

## Chief Mkwawa of the Hehe

In the latter half of the nineteenth century, the Tanzanian interior was in a state of chaotic flux. Incursions by **Arab slave traders** from the coast had disrupted the balance of power between clans and tribes, while the militaristic **Ngoni tribe's invasion** in the south had triggered mass migrations. This uncertain climate provided ideal soil on which opportunistic leaders such as Chief Mirambo of the Nyamwezi (see p.447) could plant their own personal kingdoms.

Another who emerged triumphantly was a Hehe chief named Mtwa Mkwawa Mwamnyika ("Conqueror of Many Lands"), better known as **Chief Mkwawa**. Born near Kalenga in 1855, Mkwawa's ambitious character was well suited to his time. By 1889, he had become undisputed leader of the Hehe, whom he made the region's dominant tribe by uniting – though force or diplomacy – more than one hundred clans and smaller tribes. It was not just numbers, but regimented **military organization** that formed the basis of Hehe power, and which gave Mkwawa the ability to stem the hitherto inexorable southward advance of the Maasai. Mkwawa also began to threaten Arab control over the lucrative slave- and ivory-carrying caravan routes that passed through his territory, though declining Arab power meant that it was not against the sultans of Zanzibar that the showdown eventually came, but against the **German colonial war machine**.

At first, Mkwawa tried to secure treaties with the Germans, but when they refused (on fair terms, that is), the Hehe turned their arms against the newcomers. On August 17, 1891, a year after the Germans had placed a garrison in Iringa, Mkwawa's troops ambushed a German expeditionary force led by Lieutenant Emil von Zelewski in the **Lugalo Hills** east of Iringa, killing nearly five hundred soldiers and capturing a vast quantity of firearms and munitions. Only two German officers and fifteen men escaped.

Mkwawa was no fool, and anticipated German revenge by building a thirteen-kilometre, four-metre high wall around his palace and military base at **Kalenga**. The Germans took time to reorganize, and it wasn't until October 1894 that they made their move, establishing themselves on a hill overlooking Kalenga, now the site of **Tosamaganga**, from where they began a two-day bombardment (the name *tosamaganga* means to "throw stones"). On October 30, the Germans under **Tom von Prince** stormed and took Kalenga with relative ease. The extent of Mkwawa's wealth can be gauged by the fact that it took four hundred porters to cart his ivory away. The Germans also found 30,000 pounds of gunpowder, which they used to level the town. For Mkwawa, the loss of Kalenga was a double tragedy, since his mother – who had been told that her son had been captured – committed suicide.

In fact, Mkwawa had escaped into the forests west of Kalenga, from where he waged a four-year **guerrilla war** against the Germans. He was finally cornered in 1898, having been betrayed by informers attracted by a five-thousand-rupee reward. Rather than surrender, he shot his bodyguard, and then himself. The Germans, arriving on the scene shortly after, placed another shot into Mkwawa's head just to be sure, then severed it. The chief's headless body was buried at Mlambalasi, 12km south of the road to Ruaha National Park, while his **skull** was sent to Berlin and then to the Bremen Anthropological Museum. There it remained until 1954, when it was finally returned – it's now the star exhibit of Kalenga's museum.

Mkwawa's death marked the end of a decade of armed resistance to German rule across Tanganyika, but the ensuing peace was short-lived: the Maji Maji Uprising was only seven years away. For more on Chief Mkwawa and the Hehe, see ⓦwww.mkwawa.com.

## Practicalities

If you want to arrange things yourself, the "easiest" option is to enter **the national park**, whose western gate is at Msosa, 10km east of Mtandika on the Tanzam highway (itself exactly 100km northeast of Iringa). Unfortunately, you can't just turn up, pay and enter, as entry fees ($40 for 24 hours including an obligatory ranger) are processed by the park headquarters in Mang'ula (chapter 4), meaning you may have to wait overnight before being let in. Luckily, *Riverside Campsite* have a **campsite** just outside the gate ($6 per person), where they have bird guide, too. They've also cleared 10km of trails along the Msosa River, along which you might see bush pigs, duikers and monkeys, as well as a waterfall. Inside the park are various possible hikes (up to three days in length), including a 20km round trip to Mdene Peak, and a day-trip to Mwanaluvele salt cave, which was used as a refuge during famine and conflict.

The alternative approach to western Udzungwa is to explore the northeastern sector of the newly formed **Kilombero Nature Reserve**, adjacent to the national park, for which you'll need a $30 permit from the Forestry Department at the corner of Mkoa Street and Old Dodoma Road in Iringa (Mon–Fri 8am–5pm; ☎026/270 2246). Once papered up, the approach is via **Udekwa**, a village whose Kihehe name means "vomiting", happily just alluding to its historically overflowing granaries. The turning is just north of Ilula village, 45km northeast of Iringa along the highway. From Ilula, it takes at least two and a half hours along the rough and often rocky 70km road to Udekwa; if you're driving, ask directions, as it's not signposted. There should be pick-ups at the junction in Ilula. Once in Udekwa, introduce yourself (and your permit) to the administrator in the building by the school, and enlist his help to locate a **guide**: no fixed price, but rarely more than $30 a day, including porter. There are no guesthouses, but there are several **campsites** in the area. The closest is *Chui Campsite*, 7km away on the edge of the reserve. A great walk from here takes you to *Mufu Camp* in the heart of the forest, giving you plenty of bird-watching opportunities, and good odds on seeing the famous Udzungwa partridge once there. Count on at least two days for the round trip.

# Ruaha National Park

Straddling the Eastern Rift Valley west of Iringa, and covering over 20,000 square kilometres, **Ruaha** is Tanzania's largest national park, and one of the least visited, too, with barely a hundred tourists on any one day. The park's rich biodiversity stems from the life-giving Great Ruaha River (see box, p.477), and the transitional location between eastern and southern Africa. The park contains over 1650 plant species, and a wealth of **wildlife**, including pretty much all the species you're likely to see in the northern parks except for **black rhinos**, whose whereabouts are now kept secret given the predations wrought by poachers in the 1980s. Also targeted by poachers were Ruaha's **elephants**, who have recovered much better: their present population of around twenty thousand is the largest and densest of any Tanzanian park. Ruaha is also noted for **antelopes**, being one of only a few areas where you can see both greater and lesser kudu, and the elusive sable and roan antelopes. Other denizens include zebra, the shy bushbuck, Grant's gazelle, eland, giraffe, impala, reedbuck, Defassa waterbuck, Liechtenstein's hartebeest, klipspringer, Kirk's dikdik, mongooses (slender, banded and dwarf) and, near water, large herds of buffalo. With so much food walking around, it's no surprise to find **predators** out in

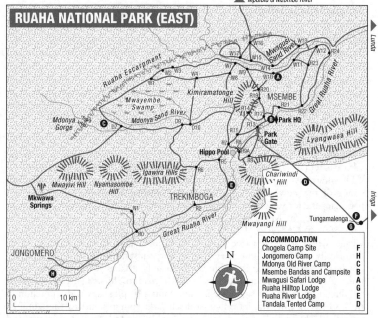

RUAHA NATIONAL PARK (EAST)

| ACCOMMODATION | |
|---|---|
| Chogela Camp Site | F |
| Jongomero Camp | H |
| Mdonya Old River Camp | C |
| Msembe Bandas and Campsite | B |
| Mwagusi Safari Lodge | A |
| Ruaha Hilltop Lodge | G |
| Ruaha River Lodge | E |
| Tandala Tented Camp | D |

force, including lions, leopards, cheetahs, jackals, crocodiles and several packs of highly endangered African hunting dogs. The park is also the southernmost range of the striped hyena. **Nocturnal animals**, which may be glimpsed in the early morning or late evening, include the aardwolf, ratel, lesser galago (bushbaby), porcupine and bats.

Ruaha's **birdlife** is equally rich and colourful, with 529 species recorded to date, many of them migrants (especially mid-Nov to March). Two special species to look out for are the rare sooty falcon, which breeds in the Sahara and the Middle East, and Eleonora's falcon, which breeds further north in the Mediterranean. Other **raptors** include the African hawk, Pel's fishing owl and eagles: bateleur, martial, long-crested and snake.

Most safari-goers are confined to the park's lower southeastern section around the Great Ruaha River, separated from the rest of the park by the Ruaha Escarpment. The area is nonetheless representative of most of Ruaha's habitats, including *miombo* woodland plateau and isolated hills in the west; undulating plains; acacia and baobab bushland; palm-fringed swamps; grassland; evergreen forest around the main rivers; seasonal "sand rivers", whose water pools draw wildlife in the dry season; and, of course, the Great Ruaha River itself.

## Arrival, information and park fees

The **park entrance** is 125km west of Iringa along all-weather *murram* (roughly 3hr). Self-drive is possible in a 4WD if you're experienced on rough roads, but the usual approach is an organized safari: by road from Dar, Iringa or Tunga-malenga (20km from the park, accessible by public transport), or by plane from Dar or Arusha, usually in combination with Mikumi National Park, Selous Game Reserve or Katavi National Park. **Park fees** (valid 24hr), paid at the gate

9km inside the park boundary if you're driving, are $50 per person, including a conservation fee, plus $40 per vehicle.

The **park headquarters** are in Msembe area, 6km beyond the entrance gate (Ⓦ www.tanzaniaparks.com/ruaha.html). The best sources of **information** are either of TANAPA's guidebooks, which can be bought at the gate, at the lodges, or in bookshops in Arusha, Dar and Stone Town. The older monochrome booklet describes game drives in scientific detail, while the full-colour edition makes a more attractive souvenir.

The **best time to visit** is the dry season (June–Oct, sometimes to mid-Nov), especially the end of that period when animals concentrate around the receding waterholes in the park's seasonal sand rivers (which unfortunately now includes the once perennial Great Ruaha). The rains start in earnest in December: the resurgent vegetation makes this a beautiful time to visit, and it's great for birds, but game is harder to see. The **rains** are heaviest in January when many tracks are likely to be cut, and continue until end-April or mid-May.

### Organized safaris

Recommended safari companies are reviewed on pp.51–53. Most visitors come on all-inclusive **flying safaris**, which can also be arranged by the park's camps and lodges. Special deals are sometimes offered by Coastal Travels (p.52), who have their own airline and also run *Mdonya Old River Camp*; and Foxes African Safaris (p.53), who operate Safari Airlink and *Ruaha River Lodge*. For just flights, it's $330 one-way from Arusha, Dar or Zanzibar, or $270 from Selous. If there are enough passengers, Coastal can also fly from Dodoma, Manyara or Tarangire.

On a **driving safari** from Dar es Salaam, your first and last day will be spent on the Tanzam highway (or a good half-day from Mikumi or Udzungwa). You can cut times, and costs, by arranging things in Iringa or through the lodges and camps located outside the park near Tungamalenga, whose costs are essentially 4WD rental (currently $200–250 a day including driver-guide) plus park fees, meals and accommodation. At the time of writing, the following **companies based in Iringa and Tungamalenga** were properly licensed: *Riverside Campsite* (p.468), also bookable via Iringa Info; *Ruaha Hilltop Lodge* and *Tandala Tented Camp*, both near Tungamalenga (p.479); and *Tatanca Safaris & Tours*, Uhuru Avenue in Iringa, just up from NMB Bank (Ⓣ 0784/881088, Ⓦ www .tatancasafaris.com).

### The Great Ruaha River – not so great?

Most tour brochures paint Ruaha in an almost Edenic palette, a picture of unspoilt wilderness abounding in wildlife. But behind the gloss, trouble stirs. Since 1993, the **Great Ruaha River**, the park's lifeblood, has dried up entirely during the dry season, each time for longer periods, thanks to unsustainable water use for rice paddies in its main catchment area north of Mbeya, and overgrazing of the swampy Usangu flats by an estimated 1.5 million cattle belonging to migrant Sukuma cattle herders, originally from Lake Victoria. A softly softly NGO-led attempt to reduce water wastage in Usangu came to nought, so with the situation critical, in 2008 the government forcibly expelled the herders, evicted villagers (who are to be compensated, unlike the herders), and enlarged the national park to include a large part of Usangu, including the sponge-like **Ihefu wetland**. The big rice farms are still there, however (possibly too many big toes to step on), so it's impossible to tell whether these measures will significantly improve the situation.

# Accommodation

The luxury **tented camps and lodges** inside the park are mostly neo-colonial in feel and searingly expensive, though their "game packages" do at least include game drives and sometimes bush walks. If you're coming by road, you should be able to get cheaper "drive in" rates – this being full board without game drives, as you won't need their vehicles. None of them are fenced, so there's always a chance of seeing (or at least hearing) wildlife pass through at night. TANAPA maintains more sanely priced accommodation in the form of **bandas** near the park headquarters, and there's also relatively cheap accommodation outside the park. All accommodation is best reserved in advance.

**Camping** inside the park is on a shadeless pitch along the Great Ruaha River, near the park headquarters at Msembe ($30 per person, paid at the gate). The site has pit latrines but nothing else, though you can use the showers at the nearby *bandas*. There are also **special campsites** ($50 per person), whose locations change every few years; those at Mbagi and Mdonya are recommended, but tend to be block-booked by safari companies. **Outside the park**, you can pitch up at the excellent *Chogela Camp Site* ($5). At a different level is the luxury **fly-camping** offered by *Mwagusi Safari Lodge* and *Ruaha River Lodge*: for a patently absurd $2000 (the lowest rate – being for two people and two nights – including park fees), you get everything laid on, from champagne breakfasts and personal butlers to game walks and drives, yet still get to enjoy the delights of bucket showers and dome tents.

## In the park

In addition to the following, a 100-bed lodge is currently under construction and should offer slightly more affordable rates (Ⓦ www.serenahotels.com); two other 100-bed places are apparently in planning. Prices below exclude park fees.

**Jongomero Camp** 63km southwest of Msembe Ⓦ www.ruaha.com. Gloriously isolated but ingloriously expensive, this swanky safari luxury occupies a grove of acacias on the north bank of the (usually dry) Jongomero River. The eight spacious tents are on raised platforms under thatched roofs, each with a veranda for wildlife viewing. There's also a swimming pool with uninterrupted views of yonder river and beyond. No children under 8. Closed mid-March to end-May. Game package $1240 ❾

**Mdonya Old River Camp** 40km west of Msembe Ⓦ www.adventurecamps.co.tz. You're paying for the isolation, intimacy and wildlife at this place, set amidst large sycamore figs and acacias beside Mdonya Sand River, rather than creature comforts, as the camp is decidedly plain. The eleven green tents have private verandas and al fresco showers, and a resident genet entertains guests at night. Children under 12 discouraged. Closed April & May. FB $360, game package $530 ❾

**Msembe Bandas** Msembe (book through TANAPA in Arusha; see p.307). Several revamped park-run chalets sleeping two to five people each. Sheets, blankets and firewood are provided,

as are hot showers all day, and there's a kitchen and dining area: bring your own food and drink. ❹

**Mwagusi Safari Lodge** 9km north of Msembe Ⓦ www.ruaha.org. In prime game-viewing territory on the banks of the Mwagusi Sand River, especially popular with buffalo. The ten large and comfortable en-suite tents (twin or double) are pitched inside thatched *bandas* with shady verandas overlooking the river, solar-powered lights and hurricane lamps. Meals are taken in a stylish *banda* decorated with branches and skulls, or on the sandy river bed. Children under 6 discouraged. Game package $860 ❾

🏃 **Ruaha River Lodge** 18km southwest of Msembe Ⓦ www.tanzaniasafaris.info. Built on and around a granite outcrop overlooking rapids with hippos and crocodiles, this is another fine place for wildlife (seen from armchairs on your private veranda, no less). The rooms are in twenty large riverside cottages (clumped into two areas) built of stone and thatch, and facilities include bars with glorious views, a split-level restaurant (ditto), lounges, evening campfires, and a library. FB $380, game package $610 ❾

## Bush walks at Ruaha

A great way of getting to experience Ruaha between June and November is on a **bush walk**, accompanied by an armed ranger. Clients at the park's lodges have priority, but it may also be possible to arrange a walk through lodges and camps outside the park – you'll need a vehicle to pick up the ranger and reach the walking zone, though. The nominal cost is $20 per ranger, plus park entry fees.

### Outside the park

The following places lie between the park boundary and Tungamalenga village (20km shy), and roughly 100km from Iringa. **Buses** from Iringa to Tungamalenga tend to leave just after midday, but timings are prone to change so ask at Iringa Info for the latest. If you don't fancy the often bone-crushing ride, lodges charge up to $200 per vehicle for the transfer.

**Chogela Camp Site** 1km west of Tunga-malenga, before the bridge ☏0782/032025 or 0717/436840. The (only) address of choice for travellers on a budget, this neat and friendly Tanzanian-run place is snuggled up to the Tungamalenga River under shady trees. Camping in your own tent costs $5, or you can use theirs (with a bed, too) for $10. Self-caterers have a kitchen and a small store, but meals can also be cooked for you (including excellent cardamom-laced pancakes). Also recommended for various culturally themed activities ($10–20 per group), including village walks, a visit to a Maasai boma, and to a waterfall. In time, *Riverside Campsite* may place vehicles here for safaris. Cyclists are also welcome: the affable young owner is a keen pedaller, and has bikes to rent. ❸

**Ruaha Hilltop Lodge** 5km west of Tungamalenga ☏0784/726709 or 026/270 1806, ⊛www.ruahahilltoplodge.com. On a scrubby hill with unforgettable views over the bush, this is an exceptionally welcoming, affordable and indeed romantic Tanzanian-run place, with fifteen beautifully decorated en-suite cottages complete with solar-heated water, electricity, verandas with 180° views, and a brick-and-thatch building lower down containing the bar and a consistently excellent restaurant. They also have a great reputation for their driver-guides, and offer walks to a Maasai village ($10 a group). FB ❼

**Tandala Tented Camp** 15km northwest of Tungamalenga ⊛www.tandalatentedcamp .com. A simple and attractive place just off the road on either side of the Mdekwa Sand River, frequently visited by elephants (the swimming pool is a handy thirst quencher, as are the river's waterholes), and occasionally by African hunting dogs. There are eleven comfortable en-suite tents on raised wooden platforms, each with a large veranda, plus a thatched bar and restaurant featuring Mediterranean cuisine, and candlelit dinners around a campfire. Activities include safaris (they're licensed), bush walks, visits to a Maasai village and hot-water springs, and nocturnal game drives. Part of the profits benefit Mbomipa village, which can also be visited. FB $470, FB including activities $630 ❾

### The park

The park's 400km of tracks mainly cover the southeastern sector around the Great Ruaha River, near the park entrance and lodges. If they haven't been trashed by elephants looking for back scrubbers, road junctions are marked by **numbered signposts**, corresponding to the park's guidebooks: unless you're with a guide, the guidebooks are essential for exploring the area beyond Msembe. **Driving** is only allowed between 6am and 7pm, and remember that off-roading is illegal and environmentally destructive. In the rains, always enquire beforehand as to which roads are open. Lastly, **be wary of elephants**: the inaccessibility of huge areas of the park, especially in the rains, makes it ideal territory for ivory poachers, an ongoing problem, albeit nowhere near as bad as it was in the 1980s. The massacres of that decade have made older elephants nervous and sometimes aggressive towards humans, particularly if they're with

▲ Baobab tree, Ruaha National Park

calves. So, treat all elephants with uncommon caution, and back off if they show signs of irritation.

The park's pristine condition owes a lot to the humble **tsetse fly**, which transmits sleeping sickness. The disease doesn't affect wildlife but does bring down domestic animals and humans, so herders have traditionally avoided the area. Don't worry about contracting the disease yourself – infections are extremely rare, and the main tsetse-infested area is in the infrequently visited *miombo* woodland. If you do go there, the usual precaution is to keep car windows closed.

### Game drives

If you're short on time, the tracks along the **Great Ruaha River** downstream from Msembe are always good for a broad range of wildlife, including elephants, lions, leopards, and most of the park's ungulates. Hippos and crocodiles also put in appearances, but you'll need luck to see sable antelopes, cheetahs or hunting dogs. There's a **picnic site** in a grove of acacia trees by junction R24, where you can leave your car. Once done, head back to Msembe along the south bank of the **Mwagusi Sand River**: elephants and plains game are frequent visitors to its dry-season waterholes, as are predators – easily camouflaged in the flanking vegetation.

**Msembe area** itself has a web of tracks, the highlights including a **hippo pool** close to junction R8, which also has crocodiles, and Kimiramatonge Hill to the north, where you might see klipspringers. Msembe's dominant tree species here is the tall *Acacia albida*, ecologically important for its role in preventing soil erosion. Unfortunately, most of the tree cover disappeared in the wake of the catastrophic poaching in the 1980s: the presence of the park headquarters led elephants to associate Msembe with safety, but their resulting high numbers ending up trashing the acacias. Things haven't been helped since by the drying of the Great Ruaha River, which has increased pressure on areas surrounding the remaining waterholes.

In dry weather, you can extend your exploration westwards. From junction W8, a trail hugs the base of the **Ruaha Escarpment**. After some 10km you

## The Mufindi Highlands

South of Iringa, the **Mufindi Highlands** are exceptionally scenic, with bright green tea estates, scattered lakes and forests, and dramatic views from peaks and ridges over the Kilombero Valley to the east. The forests are especially rich in **birdlife**, with rare species including blue swallows, the Uhehe fiscal, short-tailed pipit, mountain marsh whydah, and Iringa akalat.

Access is via one of two settlements on the Tanzam highway: Mafinga itself (also called "John's Corner"), 90km southwest of Iringa, and Nyororo ("James' Corner"), 40km further on. Other than local guesthouses, **accommodation** is at *Mufindi Highland Lodge* (Foxes African Safaris, p.53; FB ❸), 40km southeast of Mafinga. Located in an eight-square-kilometre estate, the main building is a rustic two-storey granite-and-timber affair containing a bar, dining room, TV lounge, snooker room and a large veranda with great views of the surrounding forests. The bedrooms are in twelve en-suite log cabins; room rates include guided forest walks, birding, mountain biking, horse-riding, a cultural tour to local villages and fishing for rainbow trout, and as such represent excellent value for money. Two nights at least are recommended. The easiest way to get here is for the lodge to pick you up at Mafinga ($50 per person); if you're driving, turn off the highway at Mafinga and head south into the hills until Sawala, then turn left along the road to Lupeme Tea Estate and follow the signs for 15km.

reach Mwayembe Spring, whose salty residue makes it a popular salt lick for elephant and buffalo. In the surrounding swamp, you might spot the rare Bohor reedbuck. The road continues along the escarpment base to the **Mdonya Sand River**, just below Mdonya Gorge. Returning to Msembe along the river's south bank, keep an eye out for eland, black-backed jackals, and – in the evergreen riverine forest – birds. Another good long drive follows the north bank of the Great Ruaha River from Msembe to its confluence with the (usually dry) **Jongomero River**, whose flanking trees are likely haunts for **leopards**.

With more time, but in dry weather only, you can tackle the 95km drive northwest to the **Mzombe River**. Up the escarpment, the road passes through undulating woodland where you should see small groups of elephants, and perhaps also sable antelope or Liechtenstein's hartebeest. There are some **walking trails** at Mpululu by the Mzombe River, on the border with Rungwa Game Reserve. The river is dry from July to September, when hippos congregate in pools. Walkers need to be accompanied by a park ranger or guide.

# The southern highlands

Geologically, the **Southern Highlands** are a fascinating area, having been formed by the violent plate-tectonic activity that also created the Rift Valley and its lakes, including Nyasa just to the south. The volcanic soil and heavy rainfall lends itself perfectly to agriculture, including coffee, bananas, rice, and – uniquely for Tanzania – cocoa. Despite the high human population density, a few isolated patches of **primary forest** have survived, providing one of the highlights for visitors, along with impressive waterfalls, crater lakes and hot springs. Needless to

> ## Safety
>
> Mbeya's population is a burgeoning 400,000, including a sizeable contingent of (mostly unemployed) migrants from Zambia, Malawi and Congo, who have given the town a somewhat unsavoury reputation. That said, the old colonial part – where you'll likely be staying – is a very laid-back sort of place, that is once you've extricated yourself from the hustlers and con-artists at the **bus and train stations**. Although some of the characters are genuine, unwary travellers do get tripped up, so stay cool, and keep a close eye on your bags while you get your bearings. If you're being followed, it's best to jump in a cab rather than walk the short stretch into town: there are taxis in the bus stand itself by the roadside, but be sure the vehicle really is a taxi – it should have white number plates.
>
> By day, **walking around** is quite safe so long as you're not dangling juicy carrots, but you should take taxis at night, and in the morning until around 7.30am, after sunrise, when *askaris* go home but the streets have yet to fill. This applies especially to Jacaranda Road, for the *Moravian Youth Centre Hostel*, and Jamatikhana Road.

say, the highlands are ideal for **hiking** – at its most spectacular in **Kitulo National Park**, over two and a half kilometres above sea level, and famed for orchids as well as a recently discovered species of monkey. A good place at which to base yourself, at least initially, is the town of **Mbeya**, which is also the gateway to Malawi and Zambia. Another good base, indeed quite charming in itself, is the agricultural town of **Tukuyu**, in the lee of the currently sleepy Mount Rungwe volcano. Both towns have **cultural tourism** programmes which can arrange everything for you: Tukuyu's is the cheaper of the two. For a good introduction to the region's ecology, see ⓦ www.southernhighlandstz.org.

# Mbeya and around

The regional capital of **MBEYA** is tucked into a fold between the Mbeya Range and Panda Hills, 140km north of Lake Nyasa. Founded in 1927 as a supply town during a gold rush at Lupa, in the north, Mbeya's importance was assured by its position on the **Great North Road** (now the Tanzam highway), which runs for over five thousand kilometres from Nairobi to Cape Town. The town's importance increased further in the 1960s, with the construction of the TAZARA railway into Zambia. Although there's nothing much to see in town, it has a refreshing climate, and its **cultural tourism programme** offers a wide range of equally refreshing activities in the vicinity, including hikes up nearby Loleza and Mbeya peaks, trips to hot-water springs, waterfalls, and even a giant meteorite.

## Arrival

Buses coming from the east stop first at Mwanjelwa on the Tanzam highway: get off there for *Karibuni Center Hotel*; otherwise stay on until the **bus stand** on Mbalizi Road. The **train station** is 5km southwest of the centre on the Tanzam highway; a taxi into town from here costs Tsh5000, daladalas Tsh300. The new Songwe **airport** is 22km west off the Tunduma road, and may (or may not) have flights from Dar by the time you read this. For **tourist information**, pay a visit to the town's ever-helpful cultural tourism programme, **Sisi kwa Sisi**, at the corner of Mbalizi Road and School Street (daily 8am–6pm; ☎ 0754/463471, ⓔ sisikwasisitours@hotmail.com).

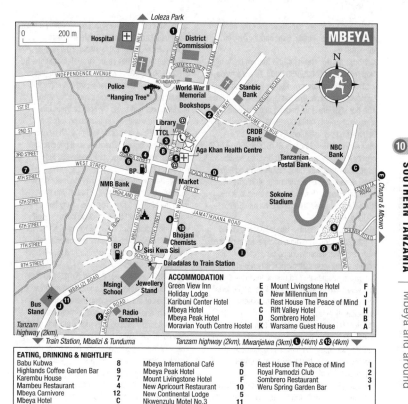

**ACCOMMODATION**

| | | | |
|---|---|---|---|
| Green View Inn | E | Mount Livingstone Hotel | F |
| Holiday Lodge | G | New Millennium Inn | J |
| Karibuni Center Hotel | L | Rest House The Peace of Mind | I |
| Mbeya Hotel | C | Rift Valley Hotel | H |
| Mbeya Peak Hotel | D | Sombrero Hotel | B |
| Moravian Youth Centre Hostel | K | Warsame Guest House | A |

**EATING, DRINKING & NIGHTLIFE**

| | | | | | |
|---|---|---|---|---|---|
| Babu Kubwa | 8 | Mbeya International Café | 6 | Rest House The Peace of Mind | I |
| Highlands Coffee Garden Bar | 9 | Mbeya Peak Hotel | D | Royal Pamodzi Club | 2 |
| Karembu House | 7 | Mount Livingstone Hotel | F | Sombrero Restaurant | 3 |
| Mambeu Restaurant | 4 | New Apricourt Restaurant | 10 | Weru Spring Garden Bar | 1 |
| Mbeya Carnivore | 12 | New Continental Lodge | 5 | | |
| Mbeya Hotel | C | Nkwenzulu Motel No.3 | 11 | | |

## Accommodation

Mbeya's cheapest **guesthouses** are a sorry lot, often with unwashed sheets, and thefts from locked rooms are occasionally reported, too. So, if you get a bad vibe, heed your instinct and look elsewhere. Ditto if door keys look like they'd open every second door in town. Sisi kwa Sisi (see p.482) can point you to reliable places. **Camping** is possible at *Green View Inn*, which has a kitchen, and at *Karibuni Center Hotel*; both charge $3 per person.

In spite of the altitude, **mosquitoes** abound, so check nets or window screens before signing in. Mbeya's **tap water** should be sterilized for drinking. **Power cuts** are frequent, and rumoured to be a punishment for voting the wrong way, and for having stoned the presidential motorcade in 2008.

**Green View Inn** Chunya Rd, 1km east of town ☎025/250 0175, ⊛ www.mbeyagreen.com. Beside a big mosque, this is in vaguely Scandinavian style, with plenty of pine furniture. There's a range of fine if rather expensive rooms, including little cottages, a trio of bright rooms on top of the main house with bathtubs and enough hot water to fill them, and much cheaper rooms sharing bathrooms. Some rooms have TVs. Drinks are

available (there's a rooftop terrace, too), but meals must be ordered four hours before. Also has a campsite. Safe parking. BB ②–③

**Holiday Lodge** Jamatikhana Rd ☎025/250 2821. A calm and friendly place with over thirty big and bright en-suite rooms in a three-storey block, all with cable TV and round but adequately sized mosquito nets. There are also some very cheap rooms sharing bathrooms behind the (average) restaurant, which are slightly shabby but clean and have excellent beds. Safe parking. ❶, en suite (BB) ❷

**Karibuni Center Hotel** Off the Tanzam highway, 4km from town ☏ 025/250 3035, ⊛ www.twiga .ch/tz/karibunicenter.htm. Run by the Swiss Mbalizi Evangelistic Church, this has good en-suite rooms with hot showers, safe parking and a decent restaurant (meals Tsh3000–6000). Safe parking. Catch a taxi the first time. ❶

**Mbeya Peak Hotel** Acacia St ☏ 025/250 3473. A breezy if slightly worn mid-range affair whose large and very good-value rooms have equally large beds, only some with nets. All rooms have TV (local channels), and the best ones look over the hotel's pleasant *nyama choma* bar. Safe parking. BB ❷

**Moravian Youth Centre Hostel** Jacaranda Rd ☏ 025/250 3263. The main backpackers' choice, with small but decent rooms, clean communal showers and squat toilets, plus an en-suite double (for which couples need a marriage certificate), all in a very calm location amidst pleasant gardens. The downside is too-small mosquito nets. Food occasionally available. BB ❶

**Mount Livingstone Hotel** Off Jamatikhana Rd ☏ 025/250 3332, ⊛ www.twiga.ch/tz /mtlivingstone.htm. A modern but somewhat gloomy fifty-room hotel aimed at tourists and conferences, but unmissable for lovers of kitsch: not just fake satin bed covers adorned with pink appliqué hearts and flowers, but, real genius this, matching flip-flops! All rooms have parquet floors, cable TV and fridge, but you'll need to ask for mosquito nets. There's also a bar, internet access, and safe parking. BB ❹–❺

**New Millennium Inn** Mbalizi Rd ☏ 025/250 0599. A secure but utterly soulless "budget" option facing the bus stand, with good clean rooms (singles only;

can be shared) with or without bathrooms. All have the unusual luxury of radio, while the more expensive ones have cable TV. Safe parking. ❷

**Rest House The Peace of Mind** Jamatikhana Rd ☏ 025/250 0498 or 0754/277410, ⓔ salu_kessy @yahoo.com. An altogether *weird* but enjoyable set-up, with just five en-suite rooms, all with marble floors and cable TV. Four of them are in a bungalow with a sun terrace on top; the other, much cheaper, is by the gate. All have a/c and internet sockets. There's also a good restaurant, bar, and, bizarrely, step machines. Safe parking. BB ❸–❹

**Rift Valley Hotel** Jamatikhana Rd/Lumumba Rd ☏ 025/250 2004 or 0784/355141. If you don't mind the slightly forlorn feel and saggy beds, this breezy four-storey business-class hotel is good value for its standard en-suite rooms – all clean, some with balconies – but the rooms with cable TV are too expensive. Also has a bar and a restaurant. Safe parking. BB ❷–❸

🏃 **Sombrero Hotel** Post St ☏ 025/250 2979 or 0762/696853, ⓔ sombrerohotel@yahoo .com. Best of the lot, efficient, friendly and accommodating, and with twenty spotless rooms on several floors, including two suites, all with good bathrooms (hot water), wall-to-wall carpet and cable TV. The upper front rooms have great views of Loleza Peak. There's also a small internet café for guests, and free pick-ups from the train or bus station. Suites are BB, others bed only. ❸

**Warsame Guest House** Sisimba St ☏ 0755/771337. Basic but acceptable, with twelve rooms in adjacent buildings, five of which are en suite, and three are twins. None of them have any furniture other than beds and nets. Security was once a concern (it was known for "short time" clients), but it appears safer these days, and has decent padlocks on the doors. ❶

# The Town

The abiding memory of Mbeya is of its views, especially the 2656-metre **Loleza Peak** looming over town from the north. From some places, the sharper outline of **Mbeya Peak** (2834m) can be seen protruding from behind it. Both can be climbed; see p.486 for details. As most Mbeyans live in crowded, slum-like suburbs south of town, the old colonial centre is eerily quiet at times. The main focus is the **market** which – although modest – is always interesting. The northwest corner has vendors selling medicinal herbs, beans, bark and assorted powders, and there are usually also some beautiful cream-and-ochre Kisi pots from Ikombe near Matema on Lake Nyasa. North of here, at the top end of Mbalizi Road by Uhuru roundabout, is the "**hanging tree**" over the river, which it's believed was used by the Germans during the Maji Maji Uprising to execute opponents of their oppressive rule. The tree in question has a metal winch with a hook attached to its largest branch, but the wire that ties it to the tree seems too slender to have supported the weight of any condemned. More certain is the sacrifice made by locals during World War II while fighting for the British; their names are inscribed on a small **memorial plaque** by the roadside just along Karume Avenue.

# Eating

Mbeya's subtly aromatic **rice** is prized throughout the country, though its large-scale cultivation is partly to blame for the drying up of the Great Ruaha River. Mbeya's arabica **coffee** isn't half bad either: if you had a good cup in Zanzibar, it was probably grown here.

**Babu Kubwa** Lupa Way. Overpriced former backpackers' favourite, recommended only for an unfussy breakfast, ideally on its streetside terrace.
**Mambeu Restaurant** Mbalizi Rd/Sisimba St. This characterful and very basic place does good snacks (especially *sambusas*), an excellent tripe *supu* for breakfast if you like that kind of thing, *mtori* banana soup, as well as very cheap lunches and dinners (under Tsh2000) – the liver stew is particularly good.
**Mbeya Hotel** Karume Ave. A wide selection of mostly Indian cuisine, including prawns, and well priced, with most mains costing Tsh6000–7000 and soups no more than Tsh2500. The place is falling apart a bit, but remains charming in the way that only 1970s hotels in Tanzania seem to manage. It also has a well-stocked bar, popular whenever there's English football on the telly. If the weather's fine, eat outside in one of several extremely battered brick rondavels.
**Mount Livingstone Hotel** Off Jamatikhana Rd. The massive à la carte menu here (main courses upwards of Tsh10,000) has almost a hundred dishes from all over the world, from Chinese and Italian to bourguignonne fondues, kedgeree chicken and seafood paellas. Amazingly, most of it is usually available, and tasty too. They cater for vegetarians with dishes like stuffed aubergine, and the desserts can be inspired, including apricot or banana fritters. The downside is the extremely gloomy dining room.

**New Apricourt Restaurant** Lupa Way. You can tell which clientele this one aims at from the menu: not just burgers but greasy delights such as chicken lollipops and even fish fingers. Unfortunately, the traditional "bites" (*kababu*, *sambusa* and so on) are equally greasy. A *pilau* or curry costs around Tsh5000, and a half chicken with chips Tsh7000. No alcohol.
**New Continental Lodge** North St. For cheap, traditional Tanzanian food, this is unrivalled, with especially good breakfasts (great *supu*, nicely crispy snacks, also juice), and, in the smoky courtyard at the back, the best *nyama choma* in town, succulent, and best enjoyed with grilled bananas. Full meals under Tsh2000.
**Rest House The Peace of Mind** Jamatikhana Rd. The spanking new restaurant and bar here somehow give the illusion of being spacious despite being tiny. The menu is a good mix, all freshly cooked, ranging from Italian (including pizza) to Indian and barbecue. At around Tsh7000 a plate, it's worth a try.
**Sombrero Restaurant** Post St. One of the town's better lunch spots (under Tsh5000), with good pasta and curries – the kidney stew is an especial wow – plus fresh juices and milkshakes. If you give them enough time, they're also happy making stuff not on the menu, including vegetarian. Evenings, when the atmosphere is stultifying, are usually limited to chicken and soup.

# Drinking and nightlife

Mbeya is considered Tanzania's second city on the **rap** scene, but unfortunately anyone who makes it big promptly absconds to Dar. It might be worth asking around though. Wherever you're going, use taxis at night.

**Highlands Coffee Garden Bar** South end of Karume Ave, facing the stadium. A nice outdoor place for a drink or food (*nyama choma* and filling Tanzanian dishes), with plenty of tables along its long grassy plot, plus slides, seesaws and swings for kids.

**Karembu House** 4th St. A great local bar, always busy, with a popular dartboard and TV for European football.
**Mbeya Carnivore** Tanzam highway, junction with Karume Rd. A popular disco and bar, open 24hr, and lively at weekends. Plays all kinds of music,

from Congolese and Tanzanian dance to Bongo Flava, pure hip-hop and reggae. Also has food and, occasionally, live bands.

**Mbeya International Café** Sisimba St. A big local bar that had a brief dalliance with tourists as "Eddy's". Despite flagging standards it remains a nice central place for a basic meal or a drink, and has some tables on a leafy veranda. Closed Sun.

**Mbeya Peak Hotel** Acacia St. A nicely relaxing garden bar with shaded *bandas* for a daytime drink or meal, including delicious *nyama choma* with grilled bananas.

**Nkwenzulu Motel No.3** Mbalizi Rd, opposite the bus stand. A large bar, busiest at night, with grim toilets and pushy barmaids. Things are much better outside, where there are plenty of seats (food also available), and a pool table.

**Royal Pamodzi Club** Lupa Way. The main uptown disco, playing a wide range of music. Fri–Sun.

**Weru Spring Garden Bar** Umoja Rd, 250m north of the roundabout. A pleasantly relaxing if run-down outdoor bar like *Highlands Coffee Garden*, but in a nicer location, next to a small stream overgrown with datura trees and bamboo. Also has a pool table, kids' playground and cheap food.

## Listings

**Banks and exchange** Quickest for changing cash or cheques (under 10min) is Stanbic on Karume Ave ($20 commission). You'll pay less at NBC down the road, but will need patience. All banks have ATMs.

**Bookshops** Mbeya's paltry bookshops, with a handful of reads in English, are Volile Investment and Golden Educational Investors, beside each other on Lupa Way. There are second-hand bookstalls outside.

**Football** Local boys Prisons FC, in the Tanzanian first division, play at Sokoine Stadium.

**Hospitals** The Aga Khan Health Centre, North St/Post St, is the first port of call ☏025/250 2896. Mbeya Regional Hospital is on Hospital Hill north of town ☏025/250 2985.

**Immigration** Behind the District Commissioner's Office off Karume Ave ☏025/250 3664.

**Internet access** Mnasi, beside *New Continental Lodge* (daily 8am–6pm). Try also Bic (TCCIA), behind the library off Maktaba St.

**Library** Maktaba St (Mon–Fri 9am–6pm, Sat 9am–1pm; Tsh500 daily membership).

**Pharmacy** Bhojani Chemists, south end of Lupa Way (Mon–Sat 8am–8pm, Sun 10am–2pm; ☏025/250 4084).

**Police** Independence Ave ☏025/250 2037.

**Post** Lupa Way/Post St.

**Supermarkets** Babu Kubwa, Lupa Way, has some imported foods.

**Telephones** TTCL, Maktaba St/Post St, beside the post office (daily 7.45am–8pm).

## Around Mbeya

Attractions in the vicinity of Mbeya are most easily visited via the Sisi kwa Sisi **cultural tourism programme** (see p.482). If you're short on time, contact them beforehand as there's not always someone around. In addition to organizing tours, they also rent bicycles and tents ($5 for a two-man). Be wary of other operators and guides; some merely lack experience, but others are out for a quick buck no matter how, so if someone tells you that they're with Sisi kwa Sisi, believe them only when you get to the office.

On offer are a wide range of day-trips and hikes, although many will be cheaper if arranged in Tukuyu via Rungwe Tea & Tours (p.492; those trips are covered on pp.493–495). Some trips include a modest "village development fee", which has so far paid for a small dispensary and books for a primary school. Sisi kwa Sisi are also the most reliable place to fix up **off-the-beaten track tours** not normally covered, for instance a ten-day hike around the highlands and down to Lake Nyasa.

### Loleza and Mbeya peaks

Dominating the skyline north of Mbeya are the two highest points in the Mbeya Range, both of which are climbable. The closest is the 2656-metre **Loleza Peak** (also called Kaluwe), which is covered in beautiful flowers during the rains (mostly Nov/Dec–May). A guide from Sisi kwa Sisi costs

$15 per person. The walk starts from Hospital Hill, off Independence Avenue, and follows a forested ridge to the top, a steep three- to four-hour climb, plus two hours back down. The summit itself is topped by an array of transmitters.

## Moving on from Mbeya

Mbeya is a road and rail hub, but other than the weekly train to Zambia, there's currently no direct transport into either Zambia or Malawi (there *are* very rough buses from Dar es Salaam to Lilongwe, but it's standing room only by the time they pass through). Mbeya's **international airport**, 22km west at Songwe, is due to open any time now.

### By bus

Most **buses** head off between 5 and 7am; buy your ticket at the bus stand on Mbalizi Road a day or two before. Long-distance **daladalas** are overcrowded and often dangerously driven; larger "Coaster" minibuses fare better, but you should always enquire about the safest companies beforehand. Of the big buses, best reputations are currently with Scandinavian Express (for Dar; ☏025/250 4305) and Sumry (Dar and Kyela; ☏025/250 0112). For Iringa, Chaula Bus is fine. **Companies to avoid** include Abood, Air Bus, Hood, Kilimanjaro Express, Super Feo, Takrim, Tashriff and Tawfiq.

The rough and wild road to **Tabora** via Chunya, Rungwa and Sikonge is travelled by Sabena (5am) on Wednesday and Sunday during the dry season, taking at least eighteen hours. The bus stand also has Coaster minibuses and daladalas going to **Tukuyu**, **Kyela** and the **Malawian border** (all hourly throughout the day), but they tend to hang around for ages on the Tanzam highway to pick up more passengers, so it's quicker catching a normal daladala to Mwanjelwa and changing there. Be careful though: Mwanjelwa is a chaotic place. Lastly, Mbeya is notorious for fake ticket salesmen: **don't buy tickets from touts** unless you want to amuse locals with yet another tale about gullible tourists shelling out wads of cash for non-existent rides (apocryphally, at least, even to South Africa).

### By train

Mbeya is the last Tanzanian stop on the TAZARA line before it enters Zambia. The **train station** is 5km southwest on the Tanzam highway (tickets Mon–Fri 8am–12.30pm & 2–4pm, Sat 8am–12.30pm, Sun 8–11am). Daladalas to the station leave from School Street at the top end of Jacaranda Road. **Timetables** change with dogged frequency; Sisi kwa Sisi can save you a needless trip out.

### Overland into Zambia or Malawi

Crossing over to Tanzania's neighbours can be quite a hassle thanks to clouds of hustlers and hucksters, and sometimes corrupt officials on the other side: be patient and polite and you'll eventually get through. **Pickpockets and bag snatchers** abound, so keep a close eye on your belongings, and avoid money-changers, too, many of whom are just con-artists. If you must change money on the street, keep it small. **Visas** can be bought on arrival, not that you'll need one: EU, US, Canadian and most other Commonwealth nationals are currently exempt. There's plenty of onward transport beyond. But get an early start as immigration calls it a day at 6pm.

For **Zambia**, the crossing is at Tunduma, 114km along the Tanzam highway. Both it, and its Zambian counterpart, Nakonde, are especially infamous for thieves. Zambian **visas**, should you need one, can be bought on arrival. For **Malawi**, the gentle approach is by ferry (see p.496); otherwise, catch a daladala or Coaster from Mbeya or Mwanjelwa to the border at Songwe River Bridge. If, as occasionally happens, the vehicle doesn't actually go to the border as promised, you'll be dumped at a junction 5km away; it's easy enough to get a lift from there, possibly even a bicycle taxi.

Slightly higher (2834m) is **Mbeya Peak** to the west; Sisi kwa Sisi charge $30 per person for their guide, excluding (optional) transport. There are at least seven routes to the summit. Easiest is from a path northwest of Mbeya, within walking distance of town. The shorter approach is from the north, starting at the end of a drivable track from **Mbowo** village, 13km along the Chunya road; a taxi to the top of the track costs Tsh30,000. From there, the path to the summit takes two hours, passing through eucalyptus forest. An alternative route, best tackled over two days, starts 9km beyond *Utengule Coffee Lodge* to the west of the mountain (see below), but is quite strenuous as parts are steep scree. The **traverse** along the 7km ridge joining Loleza and Mbeya peaks is possible but rarely attempted.

### Utengule and Pango la Popo

Located on a ridge overlooking the Rift Valley 20km northwest of Mbeya is **UTENGULE**, meaning "the place of peace". It was named in the 1870s by the Sangu tribe after having been forced out of the plains by the militaristic Hehe. The remains of a defensive structure known as **Merere's Wall** can still be seen, and it was from Utengule that the Sangu launched attacks against the Germans during the Maji Maji Uprising. If you're willing to splurge, there's an extremely pleasant **hotel** in the form of the elegant ⚑ *Utengule Coffee Lodge & Estate*, 8km north of the Mbeya–Tunduma road; the turning is at Mbalizi, 12km from Mbeya (☎0753/020901 or 0786/481902, 🖰www.riftvalley-zanzibar.com; ❻, including lift from Mbeya). Set in lovely gardens, there are sixteen large and colourfully decorated rooms and bungalows, some with views over the valley. It also has a restaurant with superb farmhouse-style cooking, a swimming pool, excursions to Pango la Popo and other local attractions, an elucidating tour of the coffee production process, and, naturally, some of the best arabica in East Africa.

Further west, 39km from Mbeya, is **Panga la Popo** ("cave of bats"), and some **hot-water springs** nearby. They're best visited in your own 4WD or in a group, as there's no public transport for the last 14km, and taxis won't take you as the road is too rocky. Head along the road to Tunduma for about 25km until Songwe, where there's a dust-belching cement factory, and turn north. Sisi kwa Sisi in Mbeya can arrange a trip by 4WD for around $60 per person; alternatively, you can come by bicycle for $25. The prices include a $5 entrance fee, which covers both sites.

### Mbozi Meteorite

Weighing in at a cool sixteen tons (it had previously been reckoned to weigh a mere twelve), **Mbozi Meteorite** – which lies on the southwestern slope of Marengi Hill, 70km west of Mbeya off the road to Tunduma – is the seventh largest known in the world. The meteorite is a fragment of interplanetary matter that was large enough to avoid being completely burned up when entering earth's atmosphere, and small enough to avoid exploding; of the estimated five hundred

---

### Throwing away the dead

In the Kisangu language, the polite way of referring to a **burial** is *kitaga umunu* – which means "to throw away a person", a curious turn of phrase that comes from ritual sites next to ravines from where the Sangu threw their dead (and, sometimes, the living, if they'd been found guilty of certain crimes, including philandery). The exceptions were chiefs, who were treated to lavish burials which reportedly included the interment of retainers or slaves. The sites are considered with apprehension by locals, so be tactful when asking about them. The closest to Utengule is known as Pitago or Kwitago, and literally means "the place for throwing away".

meteorites that fall to earth each year, only thirty percent strike land, and less than ten are reported and recorded. Mbozi has been known for centuries by locals, who call it **Kimwondo**, but the absence of legends recounting its sudden and undoubtedly fiery arrival indicate that it fell to earth long before the present inhabitants arrived, a thousand years ago. The meteorite was officially discovered in 1930. At the time only the top was visible. It was excavated, leaving a pillar of soil underneath, which was reinforced with concrete to serve as a plinth. The irregular notches on the pointed end were caused by souvenir hunters hacking out chunks – no easy task given the strength of the nickel-iron from which it's made. Most meteorites consist of silicates or stony-irons, so Mbozi is uncommon in that it's composed mainly of iron (90.45 percent) and nickel (8.69 percent), with negligible amounts of copper, sulphur and phosphorus.

**Getting there** is simple enough: catch any minibus going towards Tunduma and get off at the signposted junction (on your left) 4km before the town of Mbozi. Bicycles can be rented there (Tsh5000 is a fair price) to cover the remaining 13km due south from the highway. If you don't fancy the legwork, expect to pay $70 per person for a trip by private vehicle arranged through Sisi kwa Sisi, or $100 per group plus $30 per person if you also include Pango la Popo.

### Ngozi Crater Lake

Some 35km southeast of Mbeya in the Poroto Mountains, the two-kilometre-wide **Ngozi Crater Lake** (marked as Poroto Crater Lake on some maps) is the most popular destination for day-trippers from both Mbeya and Tukuyu. In the local Kisafwa language, Ngozi (or Ngosi) means "very big", referring to the lake rather than the 2620-metre Mount Ngozi in whose crater it resides. The lakeshore is tricky to reach (it's 200m below the crater rim along a steep and potentially dangerous footpath); the walk there is really the attraction, winding uphill through tropical rainforest, stands of giant bamboo and wild banana plants. Among the forest denizens are black-and-white colobus monkeys, many colourful birds, and vocal tree frogs. Local legend speaks of the lake's magical powers, and of a **lake monster** that has the ability to change the colour of the water. Though quaint, the tale should urge caution, as such stories are usually grounded in real-life perils, probably, in this case, volcanically induced currents. Note also that locals don't swim in the lake.

A **guided tour** from Mbeya costs $15 per person via public transport, or $35 by private vehicle. From Tukuyu, you'll pay around $10 per person. It's feasible to **make your own way there**, too. From Mbeya or Tukuyu, catch a bus or daladala to Mchangani (also called "Mbeya Moja"), where there's a signposted turn-off. It's a rough 6km west to the base of the mountain, then an hour's strenuous walk up the forested slope to the crater rim; count on two to three hours each way. A **ticket office** at the start of the road in Mchangani collects Tsh3000 per visitor and Tsh5000 per vehicle; you can hire guides there too, recommended as the last bit up the crater isn't marked.

# Kitulo National Park

The **Kipengere Mountain Range**, comprising much of the region between Mbeya and Njombe, contains areas of immense ecological importance, notably the remote grasslands of a highland plateau now protected as **Kitulo National Park**. Comprising 135 square kilometres of the plateau's northern sector, and twice as much montane forest on its western and southwestern flanks (412 square kilometres in all), the park promises more than just a taste of paradise for botanists, bird-watchers and hikers alike.

Known locally as *Bustani ya Mungu* ("God's Garden"), the plateau – which lies around 2600m above sea level – contains great numbers of endemic wild flowers, including over fifty species of **orchids** (and counting). Their protection was the primary impetus behind the park's creation, as a growing illegal trade with Zambia – where orchids were traditionally a famine food but had become more of a staple – was threatening their extinction: at the start of the millennium, an estimated four million orchids were being smuggled out of southern Tanzania each year.

Unusually for a national park, the **best time to visit** is during the rains (more or less continuous from November to May), when the plateau erupts in a glorious show of colour, contrasting beautifully with the lingering morning mists, ominous storm clouds and deep, enveloping silence. The flowers attract insects aplenty – notably moths and butterflies – in turn providing food for frogs, chameleons and lizards. The park is also home to breeding colonies of rare **birds**, including the pallid harrier, Njombe cisticola, Denham's bustard, blue swallow, and Kipengere seed-eater. There are few large **mammals**, although some may be reintroduced: the plateau's grasslands owe their existence to the grazing habits of large herbivores, whether indigenous eland, impala and montane reedbuck, or the cattle that replaced them in the 1980s – though a small population of reedbuck remain, together with a unique subspecies of black-and-white colobus monkey, and the threatened Abbot's duiker. Although heavily degraded by illegal logging, in December 2003 the fringing forest gave rise to a startling discovery: the hitherto unknown **Kipunji monkey** (*Rungwecebus kipunji*), not just a new species but an entirely new genera, genetically more closely related to baboons than to the slender mangabeys which it physically resembles. In 2004, Kipunji also turned up in the western Udzungwa Mountains, 400km away: quite an impressive entrance into the annals of zoological history. Hopefully it'll stick around: the total population is less than five hundred, ranking it as critically endangered on the IUCN's Red List. See Ⓦwww.wcs.org for the full story: tap Kipunji into its search box.

At the time of writing there was still little infrastructure in the park. Campsites, *bandas*, an interpretation centre, hiking trails and possibly driving routes are still all in planning, but so long as you have a tent and are self-sufficient, you can go anywhere you please. Recommended is a twenty-kilometre hike from Matamba village up to **Matamba Ridge** overlooking the plateau. The hike is for the fit only, as it's a strenuous up-and-down affair. Once at the ridge, you can either follow it eastwards, or descend beyond the 2750-metre Matamba Pass into the flower-bedecked **Numbe Valley**, which slopes down along the ridge towards **Numbe Juniper Forest**, many of whose trees reach a ripe old height of over 50m, making them amongst the world's tallest of their kind. Further east is **Mount Mtorwi**, at 2961m pipping Mount Rungwe by a mere metre for the accolade of southern Tanzania's highest.

## Practicalities

Accessing the park independently requires 4WD ($100–140 for a one-way trip from Mbeya), or a combination of public transport and hiking. Not entirely **organized trips** are offered by Sisi kwa Sisi in Mbeya (p.482; they're also happy renting out tents) and Rungwe Tea & Tours in Tukuyu (p.492), and by some Dar-based safari companies, although few of those have ever been to Kitulo. *Utengule Coffee Lodge* (above) and Iringa's *Riverside Campsite* could also be useful.

The **main access route** is from the Tanzam highway, by a big signpost 3km west of **Chimala** village, 70km east of Mbeya. Coming by bus or daladala (Tsh3000 from Mbeya), ask to be dropped at *njia panda ya Matamba* ("the junction for Matamba"). From here, Land Rovers (Tsh3000–4000) head off mid-afternoon to grind up a spectacular dirt road to **Matamba**, passing an eye-popping fifty-seven hairpins in the first nine kilometres. The road is extremely muddy in the rains, for which 4WD – and a driver who knows how to use it – is essential. A **western access route**, via Isongole along the road to Tukuyu, is still in the works, and at present virtually undrivable during the rains.

The **park headquarters**, where you pay your park fees, are in Matamba (Chief Park Warden, Mr Mwakilema ☎0754/362683, ⓦwww.tanzaniaparks.com/kitulo .html). There are plans to shift the HQ 20km along to the edge of the park, but things appear to have stalled. **Entry fees** are $20 for 24 hours, plus $30 for camping. Optional guides cost $20 a day. For more **information**, contact the Southern Highlands Conservation Programme in Mbeya, 100m off Karume Avenue facing CRDB Bank (☎025/250 3541, ⓦwww.southernhighlandstz.org), who also sell the highly recommended *A Guide to the Southern Highlands of Tanzania* by Liz de Leyser. The book is also available at Iringa's *Hasty Tasty Too* restaurant.

Matamba itself has lots of cheap restaurants, and four surprisingly good **guesthouses** (no phones: there's neither wire nor wireless), the best of which is the *Zebra Park* (➊), which also has en-suite rooms. More expensive but still very good value is the Lutheran Church-run *Fema* (➌). If you're passing through Iringa first, ask at Iringa Info or *Riverside Campsite* about their **campsite** 11km east of Chimala. At present it has showers, toilets and a watchman, but two tented *bandas* are planned, and guides may be stationed here too. It's nicely positioned beside a tumbling stream, safe for swimming in, or for sliding down natural rock chutes.

# Tukuyu and around

The ride south from Mbeya to Lake Nyasa is one of Tanzania's most scenic, wending up through the lush foothills of Rungwe volcano before sinking into the swampy tropical forests hugging Lake Nyasa's northern shoreline. Close to the highest point of the road, 71km southeast of Mbeya, is the rural town of **TUKUYU**. Founded just over a century ago by the Germans as a replacement for the mosquito-ridden lakeshore town of Matema (Langenburg), Neu Langenburg – as they called Tukuyu – became an administrative headquarters. The **German Boma**, whose ramparts have been incorporated into today's municipal buildings, date from this time. Tukuyu could scarcely be more different from prosperous Mbeya. There's none of the latter's cosmopolitan feeling, and the atmosphere is decidedly small town (or big village). Yet Tukuyu is certainly an attractive and refreshing place to spend some time, with wonderful views over the lushly vegetated hillocks and valleys far below, many of them extensively cultivated with tea, banana groves and sweet potatoes.

The main reason for staying is to visit various natural attractions in the surrounding area, which are accessible both under your own steam and, better, through one of two cultural tourism outfits, one in Tukuyu itself, the other at a campsite a few kilometres to the north. Foremost among the local sights are the dormant volcanic mass of **Mount Rungwe** (which can be climbed in a day, just); associated **crater lakes** in the Poroto Mountains to the west; waterfalls;

and a natural lava-stone bridge over a river. The **best months** to visit, also coinciding with the traditional drumming season following the year's main harvest, are September and October, as for much of the rest of the year it rains …and rains. With annual precipitation sloshing around the 3m mark, Tukuyu is Tanzania's wettest town.

## Practicalities

There are frequent **daladalas** between Mbeya and Tukuyu, but safer are Coasters or normal buses bound for Kyela, all of which pass through. The **bus stand** is on the west side of the road. Leaving Tukuyu, the last vehicles to Mbeya and Kyela depart around 7pm. A word on **safety**: there have been instances of tourists being robbed by newly made "friends", so insist on carrying your own bags from the bus stand.

For information and **cultural tourism**, you have two choices, both of which are unreservedly excellent. In town, **Rungwe Tea & Tours** are near the post office, signposted from the bus stand (℡025/255 2489 or 0784/293042, Ⓦwww.rungweteatours.com). Established by the local tea growers' association, they're professionally and ethically run, and have very knowledgeable guides. The other option is **Bongo Camping**, 5km back along the Mbeya road, for which see the review below. Both of them offer affordable trips to all the attractions around Tukuyu, including tea plantations, and their profits fund a variety of good causes, including schools. They both charge Tsh15,000–20,000 for a full day, a little more if you're cycling or camping.

### Accommodation

Tukuyu has few mosquitoes and no malaria. Except for *Bongo Camping*, the places below are east of the highway: walk north 100m from the bus stand and turn right. You can **camp** in the garden of the *Landmark Hotel* (no fixed price), or at *Bongo Camping* (Tsh4000).

**Bongo Camping** Kibisi village, 5km towards Mbeya ℡0784/829989 or 0784/823610, Ⓦwww.bongocamping.com. A really great place in all respects, where you'll be as much an attraction for locals as they will be to you. Firstly, you don't need a tent, as they can provide one for you (with mattress; pitches under avocado trees). Secondly, the food is excellent as well as cheap (no more than Tsh3000). Thirdly, even forgetting the various tours on offer, there's often plenty happening on site, too, whether impromptu rap sessions, Kiswahili lessons or even theatre. And last but not least, as a non-profit operation, your filthy lucre goes straight to the local community. Tent hire for two $12. ❷

**Landmark Hotel** 500m east from the highway ℡025/255 2400 or 0713/611188. A surprisingly fancy modern construction containing the town's best rooms; the most expensive ones have grand views over Mount Rungwe, the Livingstone Mountains, and – on clear days – Lake Nyasa. Also has good food, a bar, and an internet café across the street. BB ❸–❻

**Langboss Lodge** 1.5km east from the highway ℡025/255 2080. Best of the budget places, a little scruffy but quite acceptable. The best rooms are large en-suite doubles; singles share grim toilets and showers. There's also a bar and restaurant. To get here, go past the *Landmark* and turn right after a school playing field. ❶

**Laxmi Guest House** Just off the roundabout near the *Landmark* ℡025/255 2226. Humble, but clean and usually calm, with a choice of singles and doubles with or without bathroom, plus a bar and restaurant. ❶

### Eating and drinking

Tukuyu's **restaurants** mostly double as bars and are mostly pretty tawdry affairs in which some knowledge of Kiswahili is helpful to overcome small-town reticence. There are two **local brews**: *kimpuno* (made from millet), and *kyindi* (millet with maize).

**Landmark Hotel** The best restaurant, with a good choice of local and international dishes (including cheese to go with pasta), and even wine. The upstairs bar has great views.

**Langboss Lodge** Perfectly decent meals under Tsh2500, though you'll have to wait at least an hour. The bar is pretty boring, but dispenses with the *Laxmi*'s prostitutes, and also has a TV – making it a popular venue for watching European football matches.

**Laxmi Garden Centre Bar & Restaurant** Just past the post office; turn left opposite the petrol station 250m east of the highway. Downmarket but pleasant and cheerful, this is good for roast meat in the garden at the back, breakfast *supu*, and even fresh pork (*kiti moto*, meaning "hot chair"). Its bar is the town's liveliest, and gets packed at weekends and whenever it hosts live music promotions.

**Topcut Garden & Bar** Behind the football ground opposite the bus stand. An exceedingly somnolent outdoor joint with a few open-sided *bandas*, serving the usual grills, rubbery chicken, fish, chips and somewhat better liver, though you'll have to wait for ages. Good *supu* for breakfast.

# Mount Rungwe

With a full day, preferably more, a climb to the 2960-metre summit of **Mount Rungwe** is an enticing prospect, passing through wild and varied scenery. Formed 2.5 million years ago, the volcano – which comprises at least ten craters and domes – dominates the skyline for miles around. Its last eruption was two centuries ago, but **earthquakes** still occur, frequently rendering thousands homeless. Part of the mountain's forested eastern flanks have been incorporated into Kitulo National Park (see p.489). The **best time to visit** is September or October, when there's ever so slightly less chance of rain. You'll need a **guide**, available either from *Bongo Camping* or Rungwe Tea & Tours in Tukuyu, or Sisi kwa Sisi in Mbeya. Count on $20–30 per person per day.

There are two approaches to **the summit**, both passing from montane forest (around 1500m) to high-altitude bushland and heath. It's fine to take one route up and the other down. The summit itself gives breathtaking views of the Nyasa Trough to the south and the Kitulo Plateau to the east. The **northeastern route** via Shiwaga Crater is the easier of the two to climb, and arguably more scenic, but a little tricky to access initially. Catch a vehicle along the highway between Mbeya and Tukuyu as far as Isongole (also called "Number One": the first big settlement south of the Tanzam highway), and wait for a truck heading east. Get off at **Unyamwanga**, 10km along, and head up from there.

The longer **western route**, more heavily forested and thus better for wildlife, starts at **Rungwe village**, 7km off the Mbeya highway. From Tukuyu, catch the 7am daladala to Kikota, from where it's a ninety-minute walk east to Rungwe Secondary School. The base of the climb is another hour's walk east. A taxi from Tukuyu to the school costs at least Tsh20,000. The climb itself takes upwards of four to five hours to the southern rim of the summit crater, and two and a half hours back down. The last daladala to Tukuyu leaves Kikota no later than 7.30pm – if you get stranded, Rungwe Secondary School has a **hostel** (Tsh3000 per person), and as does the Lutengano Moravian Centre (Tsh4000 per person), where you can also camp. They also have a small shop.

# The Kiwira River

The **Kiwira River**, west of Tukuyu, has three distinct attractions, each of them around 20km from town: God's Bridge and the Kijungu Falls, which can be visited together as a day-trip, and the Marasusa Falls, which have to be visited separately. **God's Bridge** (**Daraja la Mungu**) is a natural lava-stone archway over the river that was formed a few hundred years ago during one of Mount Rungwe's eruptions, when river water cooled a lip of lava before it could collapse. Three kilometres northwest along the river are the **Kijungu Falls**, whose name, meaning "cooking pot", alludes to the impressive pothole in which the river disappears before reappearing downstream.

To reach either site by **public transport**, catch a daladala between Tukuyu and Mbeya and get off at Kyimo, 11km northwest of Tukuyu. There's no transport along the remaining distance, so it's best to hire a bicycle from a villager: the usual price is Tsh500 an hour. Be warned though that the bikes are past their prime, and the road is rough, and hilly. Bring your passport: the sites are on military prison land, so you need to register at the gate by the prison near God's Bridge, where you'll be assigned a guard to escort you (a tip is appreciated). Sisi kwa Sisi in Mbeya charge $25 per person for a day-trip, including a tea and coffee tour; Rungwe Tea & Tours charge Tsh15,000. There's a basic guesthouse in Kyimo should you miss the last daladala back.

Further upstream are the impressively thunderous **Marasusa Falls**. From Tukuyu or Mbeya, catch a daladala to Kiwira village, 17km northwest of Tukuyu, from where it's a 3.5km walk. Mbeya's Sisi kwa Sisi are particularly good for this trip, as they can arrange a **homestay** at Ikowe village ($20 per person for the trip). The last daladala back to Tukuyu passes Kiwira at 7pm. If you miss it or want to stay, *Mapembero Guest House* is the best of several here (all ❶).

## Kaporogwe Falls

Twenty-five kilometres south of Tukuyu, the 25-metre **Kaporogwe Falls** (also called Kala Falls) on the Kala River, a tributary of the Kiwira, are a good target for a day-trip. As well as swimming, you can walk between the tumbling torrent and enter the cave behind it, home to a concrete wall behind which Germans are said to have hidden during World War I. The discovery of **stone tools** above the waterfall – knives, scrapers, picks and core axes from the "Kiwira Industry" – indicate that the place was intensively occupied during the Stone Age. It was later abandoned, possibly when it became covered by pumice and volcanic debris from one of Mount Rungwe's eruptions.

Other than by private vehicle, **access** is via a combination of public transport and bicycle: catch one of the frequent daladalas or Coasters from Tukuyu towards Kyela and get off at **Ushirika**, 10km south. The falls are 12–15km west of the highway. You should be able to rent a bicycle in Ushirika (no more than Tsh5000) for that bit. A Tsh3000 entrance fee is collected in the car park near the falls on behalf of the local village. From Mbeya, Sisi kwa Sisi offer basically the same thing, plus guide, for $30 per person. From Tukuyu, you'll pay Tsh15,000 for the round trip by bicycle. Count on five hours in all.

## Masoko Crater Lake

An attractive by-product of Mount Rungwe's volcanic rumblings is **Masoko Crater Lake** (also called Kisiba Crater Lake), 15km southeast of Tukuyu along the unsurfaced road to Ipinda and Matema. It's easy to find, being right next to the road (on the right coming from Tukuyu). Like Ngozi Crater Lake near Mbeya, Masoko also has a legend, this one more explicable: the stone building on the crater rim housed the German Fifth Field Garrison before and during World War I, and was afterwards occupied by British troops, who later turned it into a courthouse (*mahakama*). In common with similar legends all over Tanganyika, locals believe that before the Germans were routed by the British, they buried treasure here – or, more precisely, dumped it in the lake – a theory borne out by the old German and Austro-Hungarian coins periodically washed up on the shore, encouraging intrepid locals to dive in for more (the coins are

## Age villages of the Nyakyusa

The **Nyakyusa** are the dominant ethnic group between Tukuyu and Lake Nyasa, numbering well over a million in Tanzania, and around 400,000 in Malawi, where they're called Ngonde (or Nkonde). A unique but now extinct feature of traditional Nyakyusa society was their **age villages**, brand-new villages established by boys between the ages of 11 and 13, to which they would later bring wives and start families of their own. The villages died upon the death of their last founding member, after which the land was reallocated by the district chief. Age villages served both to preserve the privileges and land of the older generation, and also to spread population pressure on the land more evenly, thereby avoiding unsustainable agricultural use. However, with each generation the available land was repeatedly divided amongst the sons of each chief, until the system finally collapsed when the land plots became too small to subdivide (a problem that also afflicts the Chagga around Kilimanjaro).

sold to tourists for under Tsh1000, though these days you're more likely to be offered coins from the British colonial period).

**Access to the lake** is relatively easy: catch the first of the two crowded daily pick-ups (8–9am) which head from Tukuyu to Ipinda and get off when you see the lake on your right. There's no entrance fee or facilities of any kind. There should be a pick-up or two in the opposite direction in the afternoon, but check in Tukuyu before leaving – there's more transport on Friday and Saturday, the market days in Ipinda and Ntaba respectively. With Rungwe Tea & Tours in Tukuyu, the trip costs Tsh15,000, or Tsh18,000 if camping overnight.

# Lake Nyasa and eastwards

Straddling the border between Tanzania, Malawi and Mozambique is the 31,000-square-kilometre **Lake Nyasa**. Also called Lake Malawi, it's East Africa's third largest lake, and probably its most beautiful. The first European to record it was a Portuguese, Gaspar Bocarro, in 1616, whose account only came to light after David Livingstone's "discovery" of the same lake in 1859. By that time, **Arab slavers** following caravan routes developed by the Yao tribe had been exploiting the region's human resources for over a century, making Nyasa a major source of slaves for Zanzibar.

Geologically, the lake is similar to Lake Tanganyika, having been formed in the same period of Rift Valley faulting some twenty million years ago. Like Lake Tanganyika, too, Nyasa is long and narrow, measuring 584km from north to south, but only 80km at its widest. It reaches a maximum depth of almost 700m at its north end, where the jagged and largely unexplored **Livingstone Mountains** rise precipitously to over two kilometres above the lake's level, providing an unforgettable backdrop to a **ferry ride**, either along the Tanzanian shore, or across to Malawi. Snorkellers are also in for a treat, as most of the lake's four hundred colourful **cichlid species** – piscine marvels of evolution – favour the rocky northeastern shoreline, accessible by boat, or dugout, from the village of **Matema**, which also has an alluring beach. Equally relaxing, and with a wonderful stretch of sand, too, is the diminutive and exceptionally friendly town of **Mbamba Bay**, near the Mozambique border, although facilities here are extremely limited. Unfortunately the price of paradise at either place is having to put up with plagues of mosquitoes: cerebral **malaria** is a problem, so be sure

## Lake Nyasa ferries

A ride on Lake Nyasa is one of Tanzania's great journeys, as much for the views and remote villages as for the unorthodox docking technique, which involves ramming the ship's prow into the beach and dropping a couple of ladders: a trick occasioned by the collapse, long ago, of every pier and jetty along the way (some of them have finally been rebuilt). There are two weekly ferries on the Tanzanian side, both starting at Itungi Port in the north. **Departure times** and days are infamously erratic, however, so ask around when you get to Mbeya, Tukuyu, Kyela or Songea: daladala or bus drivers should know the latest. In theory, though, the **MV Songea** sails from Itungi Port on Thursday at 1pm, calling at a string of minor harbours before reaching Mbamba Bay on Friday morning. All going well, it heads on the same day or Saturday to Malawi's Nkhata Bay, turning back any time between Saturday and Monday. The smaller **MV Iringa** leaves Itungi Port on Tuesday, and stops at all places down to Manda, where it stays at least 24 hours before heading back.

If you have the choice, go **first class** in a two-bunk cabin on the MV *Songea*, as **third class** (there's no second, and no first on the MV *Iringa*) is massively overcrowded, with many more passengers than seats or benches. If you do travel third class, get your ticket as soon as the office opens (three hours before departure) or you might be stuck in a steamy windowless dungeon below deck. Given that neither ferry is well maintained, it would be safer, in case of capsize, to remain on the upper deck in any case. First class to Mbamba Bay currently costs Tsh24,000; third-class is Tsh8400. There's also a Tsh500 port charge. Cheap meals and drinking water are available on both vessels.

### Principal ports

**Itungi Port** The port itself is silted up, so motorboats shuttle passengers to the ferry waiting offshore. There are no hotels, so you'll spend the night before in Kyela, 14km west. The road is generally dreadful (the oft promised tarmac never quite arrives), so count on an hour, more if it's very muddy, and leave Kyela as early as you can.

**Matema** (p.498) Three hours from Itungi Port, the MV *Iringa* stops here, but not the MV *Songea*.

**Lupingu** Five to seven hours from Itungi Port, and also accessible by buses and pick-ups from Njombe via Ludewa (or Rudewa), where there are a couple of guest-houses. The settlement's name means "protected by a charm". It's certainly charming: arriving ferries are greeted by swimming or wading women and children who have perfected the art of selling meals (fish and cassava) to passengers high up on deck via plastic jugs strapped to long poles: take the food from the jug, and put money in its place.

**Manda** The end stop for the MV *Iringa*. There are plenty of guesthouses, and a very rough road via Ludewa to the highway between Njombe and Songea.

**Liuli** With luck, you'll arrive here after dawn, to see some impressive boulders protruding from the lake. The profile of the one furthest from the shore as seen from Liuli inspired the Germans to call the place Sphinxhafen. There should be buses from here to Mbamba Bay, continuing on to Mbinga.

**Mbamba Bay** (p.501) The MV *Songea*'s last stop before Nkhata Bay in Malawi, five hours on. The Tanzanian immigration official boards the boat to stamp passports. You can change money unofficially on the boat in Mbamba Bay, or at Easy Money Ltd in Nkhata Bay, but neither of them offer great deals.

you're adequately protected. The **best time to visit** is from September to November, when the weather is hot and dry, or June to August, which is cooler and sometimes windy but has fewer bugs.

East of the lake, beyond the Livingstone Mountains, are the rolling hills of the **Kipengere Range**, a beautiful area with sweeping views over a huge expanse of land. At its heart is the highland town of **Njombe**, but as there's precisely nothing organized for tourists, you'll have to make your own tracks from here to explore the region, ideally in the company of a knowledgeable local, and with a reasonable command of Kiswahili on your part. Otherwise, just sit back and enjoy the views from the bus down to **Songea**, a scruffy tobacco-producing town at the junction of two very rough roads: one to Mbamba Bay on the lakeshore, the other east towards the Indian Ocean, a route that's covered in chapter 3.

# Kyela

The hot, mosquito-infested town of **KYELA** is no one's favourite, but a necessary overnight stop if you're catching the ferry at Itungi Port, 14km east. There's a bank, loads of accommodation, and even more bars. The safest **bus** operator from Dar is Sumry. There are also daladalas, pick-ups and Coasters throughout the day from Tukuyu, and from Mbeya, although touts at the latter aren't averse to fibbing about the vehicle's real destination, which frequently enough is Tukuyu, 55km short. The town itself is a small grid of streets 3km beyond the turning for Matema. The **bus stand** is off Posta Road by the market, three blocks left (northeast) of the highway.

The town's best **hotel** is *Kyela Resort* (☏025/254 0152 or 0753/324259, ⓦwww.kyelaresort.com; BB ❸), 1.5km back towards Tukuyu, with very comfortable rooms in a motel-like wing set in grassy gardens pocked with palm trees. The town itself has plenty of reasonable **guesthouses**, but be sure that nets fit beds and are intact. The following are all on Itungi Road: leave the bus stand with the market on your right, and turn right on to Posta Road; Itungi Road is the second one you come to. The best choice, and known locally for its boxing promotions, is *Sativa Midland Hotel* (☏025/254 0287; ❷), with just three, spotless rooms, en suite and with hot water, TV and even a/c. Much cheaper are two very basic but clean places at the corner of CCM Road, both with ceiling fans and squat toilets: the *Gwakisa* (☏025/254 0078; ❶), sharing bathrooms, and, diagonally opposite, *Makete Half London* (☏025/254 0459; ❶), with en-suite singles that can be shared by couples.

Kyela's best eats are courtesy of the ladies "manning" the **street food** stalls on Posta Road, between the bus stand and Itungi Road. Their creations are as simple as they are delicious, featuring fresh fish, fried cassava with chilli sauce, grilled goat meat and bananas, and boiled cakes, all for a pittance. The stalls are also good for breakfast, including *supu*, eggs and *uji* millet porridge. Of the proper **restaurants**, the best (so long as you avoid its toilets) is the otherwise posh-looking *Steak Inn Hotel & Bar*, which does very good fish: walk southeast down CCM Road from Itungi Road and take the second left. As might be expected from what's essentially a transit town, Kyela has scores of **bars**, mostly pretty tawdry dives where manhood – and occasionally womanhood – is apparently measured by quantities imbibed. An ability to humour dipsomaniacs is a definite asset. Of the more salubrious bars, try *Pattaya Centre* or *Mummy Classic*, both on Itungi Road, and with satellite TV.

# Matema

Tucked into Lake Nyasa's northeastern corner, between the Lufilyo River, the almost sheer Livingstone Mountains and a magnificent beach, is the fishing village of **MATEMA**. There's superb snorkelling on the rocky shoreline just to the east, while the energetic can clamber up to a waterfall, or explore the thick forest and *shambas* inland. But don't expect many mod-cons: Matema lacks mains electricity or land line telephones, and has neither restaurants nor a bank. It does however have a good hospital, run by the Lutheran Church, whose mission house resembles a Bavarian barn. Under colonial rule, Matema was briefly the regional headquarters, before mosquitoes pushed the Germans up to Tukuyu. The bay on which Matema sits is named after the imperial commissioner and former explorer **Hermann von Wissmann**, whose two side-to-side crossings of Africa spurred his country's colonizing drive. Matema is now inhabited mainly by the Nyakyusa tribe.

## Arrival

Given the cramped conditions on local road transport, **getting to Matema** can be deeply uncomfortable. The two roads, from Kyela and Tukuyu respectively, tend to alternate in terms of which one is in better condition. At present, it's the one **from Kyela**. With luck, you'll find a pick-up all the way to Matema. The plunging approach **from Tukuyu** is more scenic, and passes right by Masoko Crater Lake: vehicles leave from the roundabout facing the *Landmark Hotel*, the first between 8am and 9am. If there's nothing going, ask at the petrol station beside the bank or at the Lutheran Church offices next door, as they may have a vehicle heading down.

Chances are you'll have to change in **Ipinda**, under three hours from Tukuyu in dry weather, and as little as an hour from Kyela. From Ipinda, a handful of battered vehicles cover the remaining 20km on most days, usually in the afternoon. There are a couple of guesthouses in Ipinda should you get stuck, though they'll probably

▲ Fishing canoes on Matema Beach, Lake Nyasa

all be full on Friday, Ipinda's market day. **Leaving Matema**, get to the junction by the hospital before 6am for the first pick-ups. Alternatively, catch the weekly **ferry**, currently Tuesday afternoon to Manda (from where there's a bus to Mbamba Bay), and Wednesday or Thursday to Kyela.

## Accommodation, eating and drinking

Matema has a couple of perfectly nice church-run **hotels**, and a great backpacker-style **campsite** with *bandas*. All three are a fair distance west of the village, and share the same inspirational beach. You can camp at all three (Tsh3000 per person), and food is available at all of them, and at a basic *mgahawa* in the village itself.

**Crazy Crocodile Camp** 2.5km west of Ipinda junction ℡0783/575451, ⓦwww .crazy-crocodile.com. This funky sun- and wind-powered place backed by a heap of exotic fruit trees was founded in 2008, and looks set to stay. It's nicely chilled out, with a great bar as well as organic food. Camping is the main thing (plenty of shade), but you can also rent a tent, or stay in one of six local-style bamboo *bandas*. Also has a motorized dugout and sailing boats. Tents ❶, *bandas* ❷

**Lutheran Beach Resort** 600m west of Ipinda junction (c/o Tukuyu Lutheran Mission ℡025/255 2130, ⓔmatema.mailbox@elct.org). Idyllically located in the grounds of the historic mission and its school, the rooms and *bandas* (some en suite)

are getting run-down, but remain comfortable, and some are right on the beach. There's a small shop, excellent meals to order (including pizza, if you're nice enough), soft drinks, and a generator until 10pm. BB ❷

**Matema Lake-Shore Resort** 2km west of Ipinda junction ℡025/250 4178 or 025/256 0010, ⓦwww.twiga.ch/tz/matemaresort.htm. Run by a Swiss Evangelistic Church, this modern place has spotless rooms in four two-storey beach-front buildings (top-floor rooms have balconies), each with large box nets, and most with Western toilets. The area has been cleared of trees, so there's no shade. There's also a communal kitchen, barbecue area, cheap meals to order, snorkelling equipment, and various day-trips. ❷–❸

## The village and the beach

The diminutive **market** is at the east end of the village, beyond a river ford. If you're feeling especially lazy, a dugout ride from the hotels costs Tsh3000–6000; if walking, you'll see men hollowing out trunks en route. The market itself has only the barest necessities, though the clearing at the end by the beach usually has towers of Kisi pots made in Ikombe village (p.500) awaiting transport, which you should be able to buy. There are also a couple of people selling skewers of grilled goat meat, fish and bananas, but other than that there's little else to the village other than the fun of either amusing or inadvertently terrifying the kids.

The coarse grey sand of **Matema Beach** starts at Ipinda junction beside the hospital, a little over 2km west of the market. The water is apparently free of bilharzia, and crocodiles – which elsewhere have a habit of lunching on locals – are thankfully absent, but take any advice to the contrary seriously. The walk to the mouth of the **Lufilyo River**, 4km west of the hotels along the beach via a small lagoon, is recommended, but take care along the river itself, which is definitely home to crocodiles as well as hippo, and may also carry bilharzia.

## Excursions from Matema

A number of day-long excursions are possible, should you feel the need to rouse yourself from your Arcadian reverie. For a start, the walk back along **the Ipinda road** passes through satisfyingly thick tropical vegetation

## Precious, precocious, precarious... Lake Nyasa's cichlids

Although eclipsed in absolute size and depth by Lake Tanganyika, Nyasa (simply meaning "lake" in Kiyao) trumps its big brother in terms of **biological diversity**. Whilst Tanganyika boasts a hugely impressive two hundred **cichlid** species (fish belonging to the order of *Perciformes*, ranging in length from 2.5cm to almost a metre), Lake Nyasa contains over four hundred, representing no less than one-third of the world's known species, most of which exist only here – and in hobbyists' aquariums. Cichlids, both male and female, are devoted parents, and a good number are **mouthbrooders**, incubating eggs in their mouths and sometimes, once they hatch, keeping the fry safe, too, until they get big enough to fend for themselves. Other species, perhaps even all, can **change sex** if needed (and without the help of steroids), but the really remarkable thing is that the cichlids of Lake Nyasa and Lake Tanganyika, out of touch for millions of years, have **evolved in parallel**, with genetically different species sharing similar colour patterns, mouth adaptations or feeding techniques. For more about Nyasa's evolutionary marvels, see ⓦmalawicichlids.com.

positively awash with birdlife, and all sorts of strange fruit, including cocoa. Some of the vegetation is wild (look for vervet monkeys in the tall and bushy palms), but much is planted with banana and papaya plants, mango trees, stands of giant bamboo and sugar cane. Many of the houses in the clearings are built in traditional Nyakyusa fashion, using straight bamboo stalks lashed together for walls, and reeds for their pointed roofs. Look out too for the curious toadstool-like granaries made from woven reeds and topped by broad straw-thatch roofs. Matema also lies tantalizingly close to the northernmost spur of the **Livingstone Mountains**, which run most of the way along the Tanzanian side of the lake. The mountains' thick forests and steep slopes are sparsely inhabited, and the entire range is little explored. For a taste, there's a **waterfall** a couple of hours' walk from Matema, for which you'll need a guide: any of the hotels can arrange this.

To mess about on the water, **dugouts** can be rented from locals, but for motorboats go through a hotel. **Snorkelling** (equipment at *Matema Lake-Shore Resort* and *Crazy Crocodile*) is best off the rocky eastern shore, where you'll see many of the lake's cichlids in the crystalline water. There are shoreline **caves** nearby but access depends on the lake level, the best time being towards the end of the dry season (Oct and Nov), when the water is lower.

A trip you can do by boat or on foot is to **Ikombe village**, a few kilometres southeast of Matema on a small peninsula backed by almost vertical mountains. Its inhabitants are from the Kisi tribe, famed in Tanzania for their prowess as fishermen, and for the women's skills as **potters**. Unlike other Tanzanian potters, the Kisi women use wheels – actually thick, ash-sprinkled plates – which help create the pots' characteristically rounded forms. When the pot is ready, it's smoothed with pebbles or maize cobs and rubbed with a greyish clay to give a creamy colour after firing. After a few days of drying, the pots are decorated with red ochre and sometimes incised with motifs. The final firing is done in a shallow depression in the ground lined with dry banana leaves. The resulting pottery is ideal for cooking or storing cool liquids. The **best time to visit** is on Friday to coincide with the weekly market. Access to Ikombe is either on foot on a narrow path along the lakeshore, or by dugout from Matema, which takes just over an hour and costs Tsh2000–4000.

# Mbamba Bay

**MBAMBA BAY**, the last Tanzanian port of call for the MV *Songea*, is the nation's southernmost town, "town" being a somewhat generous term for such a dusty little place, where the streets are lined with racks for drying *dagaa* sardines, goats browse under baobabs, and locals sit pondering in the shade of mango trees. There's no running water, nor electricity, nor a bank, and the town can still, despite periodic upgrades, find its road to the rest of the world cut off during the rains. It could have been a major international border from Malawi and Mozambique (and indeed, there are plans for that, not that you should hold your breath), but the bad road and the equally treacherous stretch beyond Songea means that few travellers, or cargo, ever get off here. Good for you: the isolation is all part of Mbamba Bay's considerable charm, that and its laid-back feeling, and its **beaches**: a nice one in the bay immediately north of the ferry landing, and an immense 10km-long affair that begins 4km south of the centre, and continues, beyond a small headland, for another six. But there's one thing that really makes Mbamba Bay special: the people. Instead of running away in terror like some do in Kyela and Matema, the children here are delighted whenever they elicit a "*Marahaba*" from visitors in reply to their chirpy "*Shikamoo*".

## Practicalities

In theory, the **MV Songea** docks here twenty hours after leaving Itungi Port. It's met by two or three Land Rover **pick-ups** headed to Mbinga and Songea: you'll need to rush to get a seat, but there's really no reason to dash away from Mbamba Bay so quickly, and the daily 6am **bus** is in any case more comfortable (as ever, buy your ticket the day before). Getting to Mbamba Bay **by land** means coming from Songea. The road has been widened but is still dirt and thus liable to be impassable during and after heavy rains. There's a daily bus from Songea, or board a minibus to Mbinga, a wealthy coffee-growing centre 66km short of Mbamba Bay, where you might have to spend the night before heading on down the spectacularly steep and partly forested Matengo highlands.

### Accommodation, eating and drinking

The existence or otherwise of Mbamba Bay's **hotels** depends on the ferry to Malawi. The service was interrupted between 2006 and 2008, so at the time of writing lodgings were limited to just one, the basic and not very clean *Nyasa View Lodge* (**❶**), just under 1km north of the ferry landing overlooking the lake. Assuming the ferry doesn't get spiked once again, cheaper guesthouses should again pop up around and be signposted from the roundabout. It should also be worth asking about *Neema Guest House*, 2km south of town and beautifully located at the top of a boulder-strewn headland next to the beach.

   **Restaurants** are currently limited to *Nyasa View Lodge*, and a couple of *mgahawa* (tea rooms) in the centre, selling basic if filling meals for under Tsh1000 (usually fish with *ugali* or rice). Early in the year, more intrepid travellers might care to ask for **lake fly** (*inzi*): enormous smoke-like clouds of them float in on the wind and settle on trees, from where they're shaken into baskets, and subsequently fried.

# Njombe

Perched atop a ridge at the eastern end of the Kipengere Range, midway between Mbeya and Songea, is the agricultural centre of **NJOMBE** – one of Tanzania's highest, coolest and breeziest towns. The fresh climate and expansive views are the main attractions, making Njombe a likeable sort of place to break a journey, something you'll have to do if you arrive late from Mbeya. If you've a few hours to spare, there are two easily accessible patches of **rainforest** just outside town, one on a small hill less than a kilometre east of the cathedral, the other occupying several vales and low hills, starting 1km northwest of *Chani Hotel*, from where there's a footpath. There are also a couple of **waterfalls** next to the highway: one 800m north of NBC bank; the other 2km south of town. The **market**, one street west of the highway at the end of both Mlowezi and UWT streets, is a good place to buy naturally dyed **woven baskets** made from a reed-like grass called *milulu*; the baskets are at their freshest and most aromatic after the long rains. On Sundays, the imposing **Catholic Cathedral of St Joseph** next to the bus stand celebrates Mass (7am, 9am, 10.45am & 3pm) in effervescent musical style.

## Practicalities

The Mbeya–Songea highway runs north–south through town. The **bus stand** is on the west side of the highway at the south end of town. There are frequent Coasters and (potentially dangerous) daladalas from Makambako on the Tanzam Highway and from Songea, and fewer in number from Mbeya; **moving on**, they can be caught in Njombe until mid-afternoon, but proper buses rarely have spare seats as they're usually just passing through. Note that the roads around Njombe can get dangerously foggy in the morning – good reason to leave later if you can, as few drivers reduce their speed to compensate. The **post office** and **TTCL** office are behind the cathedral. There's **internet access** at Ngewe.com (daily 8am–8pm), beside *Wasia Hotel* one block east of the highway opposite the bus stand. The most efficient **bank** is NBC, 1km north along the highway, which has an ATM.

### Accommodation, eating and drinking

Njombe has some great-value **accommodation**, including the excellent ⌖ *Impoma Garden Lodge* off Kinyozi Street (☎026/278 2570, ✉impoma lodge@yahoo.com; BB ❶), a modern place with sixteen clean and fresh en-suite rooms (including three enormous doubles), all with cotton sheets, good nets, satellite TV and phone, and hot running water; there's also safe parking. To get here, turn left at the Total petrol station 600m north of the bus stand and it's 300m along. More upmarket but just as much a bargain is the ⌖ *Chani Hotel* (☎026/278 2357; BB ❷) off Usunguni Road: turn left at *Edina Hotel* 700m north of the bus stand, then right after *Mpoki Hotel* – 1.5km in all. It sits on the edge of the lower, partially forested part of town, its twelve comfortable rooms with wall-to-wall carpet, big comfortable beds, spotless bathrooms with hot water, and stacks of DVDs. There's also a TV lounge and safe parking. Of the really cheap places, the best is *New Magazeti Highland Green Inn* (☎026/278 2913; ❶), 100m along Usunguni Street heading towards *Chani Hotel*, whose somnolent atmosphere conceals some cheerful rooms decorated with woodcarvings and Tingatinga paintings; some are en suite (so-so squat toilets and showers). All three hotels have very reasonably priced **restaurants and bars**, the *Chani Hotel* benefiting from a lovely garden and, amazingly, silver service.

# Songea

If you can ignore the often reckless driving, the long, swooping descent from Njombe to **SONGEA** is gloriously exhilarating, passing through majestic granite scenery reminiscent of the Scottish Highlands, complete with rushing rivulets, misty moorlands and incredibly long views over the hills. Songea itself, 237km southeast of Njombe, is – despite its remoteness – a large and dirty market town you probably won't want to settle into. The only reason to come here is if you're either travelling on to Mbamba Bay, or attempting the adventurous overland route eastwards to the Indian Ocean.

## Arrival and accommodation

Songea's **bus stand** is at the west end of town on Sokoine Road, where there are taxis. There are dozens of cheap **guesthouses** scattered about, most of them very basic and uninviting, and Songea's low altitude compared to Njombe also marks the unwelcome return of **mosquitoes** – ensure your bed has a good net. Songea also experiences frequent and prolonged **power cuts**, which affect the pumped water supply of many hotels – **tap water** is unsafe to drink.

**Anglican Church Hostel** Just off the Njombe Road by the church ☏025/260 0693. The most acceptable shoestring option, with clean cell-like rooms around a courtyard, including some with bathrooms. Food can be arranged. ❶

**Annex Yapender Lodge** Deluxe St ☏025/260 2855 or 0787/126414. Getting tatty, the ten en-suite doubles at this almost catatonically calm place are nonetheless the best budget rooms in town, so arrive early. The related *Yapender Lodge* on the same street is far less enticing, but has the enjoyable *Yapender Mtini Pub* in front. Safe parking. BB ❶

**Don Bosco Hostel** ☏025/260 2004. Behind the Catholic cathedral, a five-minute walk from the bus stand, this has clean en-suite rooms with big beds (hot water in buckets), all within earshot of Sunday mass. Food can be arranged. ❶

**Golani Bar & Guest House** At the bus stand ☏025/260 2023. The most secure of a grotty (and noisy) set of hotels by the bus stand, with cheap but gloomy rooms sharing smelly bathrooms. There's a good bar and restaurant up-front with outdoor tables. ❶

**Heritage Cottage Hotel** 2km towards Njombe ☏025/260 0894. A friendly place with six motel-style

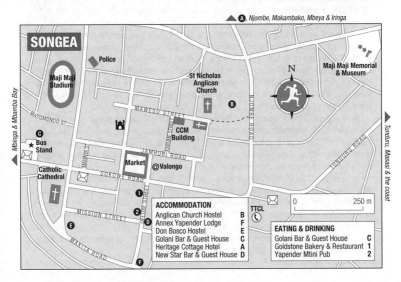

▲, Njombe, Makambako, Mbeya & Iringa

**SONGEA**

Police

Maji Maji Stadium

St Nicholas Anglican Church

Maji Maji Memorial & Museum

N

Mbinga & Mbamba Bay

MATOMONDO ST

Bus Stand

MAWESO STREET

NJOMBE ROAD

CCM Building

Catholic Cathedral

JAMHURI ROAD

Market @Valongo

SOKOWE ROAD

TUNDURU ROAD

Tunduru, Masasi & the coast

MISSION STREET

TTCL

0        250 m

MAKITA ROAD

| ACCOMMODATION | |
| --- | --- |
| Anglican Church Hostel | B |
| Annex Yapender Lodge | F |
| Don Bosco Hostel | E |
| Golani Bar & Guest House | C |
| Heritage Cottage Hotel | A |
| New Star Bar & Guest House | D |

| EATING & DRINKING | |
| --- | --- |
| Golani Bar & Guest House | C |
| Goldstone Bakery & Restaurant | 1 |
| Yapender Mtini Pub | 2 |

rooms, all with satellite TV and even hot baths – the best of the lot by a long shot. There's a good bar and restaurant with great food (especially curries), but you'll have to wait at least an hour. Internet access. BB ❸

**New Star Bar & Guest House** Deluxe St (no phone). Clean and friendly, with slightly shabby rooms sharing bathrooms, all with nets, some with fans. There's a small veranda at the front with a couple of tables for drinks, and a restaurant inside. ❶

# The Town

Songea's main attraction is the **Maji Maji Memorial and Museum** (daily 8am–7pm; donation expected), dominating the memorial ground northeast of the centre. The ground is a large square lawn flanked on three sides by the cement busts of twelve Ngoni chiefs who were captured and executed by the Germans during the Maji Maji Uprising. At its centre stands the bulky statue of a soldier with a machine-gun in his hand, while facing the ground in a pagoda is a large cement statue of Nyerere looking uncharacteristically solemn. Though crudely fashioned, the busts are rendered poignant by garlands hung around their necks. Three of the chiefs are depicted with turbans, an unwitting reminder of the Arab-dominated slave trade in which the Ngoni also participated, both as traders and captives. One of the busts represents **Chief Songea Luwafu Mbano**, from whom the town takes its

## The Ngoni invasions

Songea is the main town of the **Ngoni** tribe, who occupy much of southwestern Tanzania (they're also found in Malawi, and in scattered groups as far north as Lake Victoria). The Ngoni are relatively recent immigrants, having arrived only in the 1840s, at the end of a remarkable twenty-year, 3500-kilometre migration from KwaZulu-Natal in southern Africa.

At the beginning of the nineteenth century, the militaristic **Zulu empire** under King Shaka (or Chaka) began to make its presence felt, until by the 1830s many of southern Africa's people were on the move, either fleeing the Zulu armies or the famine and drought that accompanied the conflict. Twelve major migrations out of South Africa occurred during this period, half of which resulted in the creation of new kingdoms elsewhere: the Basotho in Lesotho; Ndebele in Zimbabwe; Gaza in Mozambique; Kololo in Zambia; and the Ngoni in Malawi and Tanzania.

The Ngoni were led by **Zwangendaba**, a former Zulu commander who had fallen out of favour. Copying the regimented military organization and strategies of the Zulu, in 1822 Zwangendaba and the Ngoni crossed into southern Mozambique, and subsequently followed the course of the Zambezi into Zimbabwe, where in 1834 they destroyed the 300-year-old Changamire empire of the Shona people. The following year, the Ngoni crossed the Zambezi and headed into Malawi, and by 1840 they had reached the Ufipa Plateau in southwestern Tanzania.

On Zwangendaba's death in 1845, the Ngoni split into several groups and continued their odyssey of conquest and migration. One group, known as the **Tuta**, headed north and settled between Lake Tanganyika and Unyamwezi, where they were welcomed by Chief Mirambo (see p.447), who took advantage of their military skills by hiring them as mercenaries for his own expansionist aims. Other groups went southwest to Malawi and eastern Zambia, while others headed east to set up independent states at Songea and Njombe in Tanzania, displacing the indigenous Ndendeule and Matengo tribes respectively, and all the while waging war against other tribes, and amongst themselves. The ensuing chaos that enveloped southern Tanzania greatly eased the German conquest of the country fifty years later – although the Germans themselves would later meet with serious opposition from the Ngoni during the 1905–07 Maji Maji Uprising.

All **buses** leave between 6am and 7am; Sumry are safest. Thereafter it's Coasters and potentially more dangerous Hiace minibuses (to Njombe, Makambako, Iringa and Mbeya). **Mbamba Bay** is served by one daily bus (variable times – ask the day before). If you miss it, plenty more buses and minibuses go roughly hourly to Mbinga, where you can spend the night before heading on: Mbinga's best hotel is *Mbicu Lodge* (☎025/264 0168; ❷), 1.5km back towards Songea. For information on the route east to **Tunduru** and the coast, see chapter 3.

name. As the most famous of the Ngoni resistance leaders, he was honoured by the Germans with decapitation rather than hanging – his cranium presumably lies in a German museum's storeroom, awaiting DNA identification and eventual repatriation – as is the case with over fifty other skulls of executed Tanzanian tribal leaders.

The curator speaks no English, but is happy to take you around. Inside are photographs and full-length paintings of the twelve chiefs, some of them pictured in the style of Ethiopian Christian icons. The upper floor contains three drums (two still playable), a couple of grinding stones, bellows used in iron-working, a beautiful tobacco horn (which might also have been used for storing marijuana, traditionally smoked by Ngoni elders), weapons and some surprisingly light hide shields. A mass grave from the uprising lies behind the building, marked by an obelisk and a low rectangular wall. Chief Songea's grave is 50m away.

Other than the museum, there's really only the **market** to keep you busy. It's a good place for sampling or smelling the dried fish from Lake Nyasa, but for *kangas* and *kitenges*, rummage through the shops and stalls at the west end of Jamhuri Road.

## Eating and drinking

Songea's eateries are almost unique in Tanzania in that they don't serve up the dentally challenging fried chicken offered in most places. The problem is actually finding a restaurant in the first place. Best of the lot is *Goldstone Bakery & Restaurant* on Deluxe Street (no sign), which, apart from full meals, does good snacks such as samosas, and very decent bread and cakes. Other than that, there's little other than the town's drinking holes for the usual chip omelettes and grilled meat. The most enjoyable **bar** is the large, *makuti*-thatched *Yapender Mtini Pub* on Deluxe Street, which plays good music and has the town's best *nyama choma*. Best of the places around the bus station is *Golani Bar & Guest House*, which screens CNN and European football.

## Listings

**Banks** NBC, Jamhuri Rd/Karume Rd, is helpful and averagely efficient, but has an ATM.

**Health** China Medical Clinic, Deluxe St (Mon–Sat 8.30am–5.30pm, Sun 8.30am–4pm) in same building as Valongo Internet Café.

**Internet access** Valongo Internet Café, Deluxe St (daily to 8pm).

**Post office** Main one at bottom of Tunduru Rd; branches in the bus stand and along Sokoine Rd.

**Telephones** TTCL is beside the main post office; attended-call offices in the bus stand and throughout town.

# Travel details

## Buses, daladalas and pick-ups

Although Iringa, Njombe and Tukuyu lie on main routes, most buses passing through are already full, so only frequencies for buses starting their journeys in those towns are mentioned. Routes liable to long delays or cancellation in the rains are marked with asterisks.

**Iringa** to: Arusha (1–2 daily; 12hr); Dar (7 daily; 6–7hr); Dodoma (3 daily; 5–6hr); Kalenga (hourly daladalas; 20min); Mbeya (hourly; 5–6hr); Morogoro (2 hourly; 3–4hr); Moshi (1–2 daily: 11hr); Songea (hourly Coasters; 8hr); Tungamalenga (1 daily; 2–3hr).

**Kyela** to: Dar (4 daily; 13hr); Ipinda (2–3 pick-ups daily*; 1hr–1hr 30min); Iringa (4 daily; 6hr); Itungi Port (pick-ups on ferry days; 1hr); Malawi border (hourly pick-ups and daladalas; 30min); Matema (2–3 pick-ups daily*; 2–3hr); Mbeya (4 daily plus hourly daladalas; 2hr 30min–3hr); Morogoro (4 daily; 10hr); Tukuyu (4 daily plus hourly daladalas; 1hr 30min).

**Mbamba Bay** to: Mbinga (1 daily plus occasional pick-ups*; 3hr 30min); Songea (1 daily plus occasional pick-ups*; 6hr).

**Mbeya** to: Arusha (1–2 daily; 15–17hr); Chunya (half-hourly Coasters; 2hr); Dar (15–20 daily; 11–13hr); Dodoma (3 weekly; 11hr); Iringa (11 daily; 5–6hr); Kyela (hourly pick-ups and daladalas; 2hr 30min–3hr); Lilongwe, Malawi (1 weekly; 18hr); Lusaka, Zambia (6 weekly; 20–22hr); Mikumi (hourly; 8–9hr); Morogoro (11 daily; 11–12hr); Njombe (hourly minibuses; 4hr); Rungwa (2 weekly*; 8–10hr); Songea (2 daily; 8–9hr); Songwe River Bridge (hourly pick-ups and daladalas; 2hr–2hr 30min); Sumbawanga (2–3 daily; 6–7hr); Tabora (2 weekly*; 18hr); Tukuyu (hourly minibuses and daladalas; 1hr 30min); Tunduma (hourly pick-ups and daladalas; 1hr 30min–2hr).

**Njombe** to: Dar (1 daily; 9hr); Iringa (1 daily plus hourly minibuses; 4hr); Mbeya (hourly minibuses; 4hr); Morogoro (1 daily; 7–8hr); Songea (hourly Coasters; 4hr).

**Songea** to: Dar (3–4 daily; 13hr); Iringa (3–4 daily plus hourly daladalas; 8hr); Mbamba Bay (1 daily plus occasional pick-ups*; 6hr); Mbeya (2 daily; 8–9hr); Mbinga (3 daily plus hourly daladalas and pick-ups*; 4hr 30min); Morogoro (3–4 daily; 10hr); Njombe (3–4 daily plus hourly minibuses; 4–5hr); Tunduru (2 Land Rovers daily*; 8–18hr).

**Tukuyu** to: Mbeya (hourly minibuses; 1hr–1hr 30min); Kyela (hourly daladalas; 1hr 30min); Ipinda (1–3 daily pick-ups*; 1hr 30min–2hr 30min); Matema (1 daily pick-up*; 4–8hr).

## Ferries

For details, see p.496.
**Itungi Port** to: Manda (1 weekly; 12hr); Mbamba Bay (weekly; 20hr).
**Mbamba Bay** to: Itungi Port (weekly; 20hr).

## Flights

Codes used below are CA (Coastal Aviation); SA (Safari Airlink).
**Mbeya (Songwe):** to commence operations in 2010.
**Ruaha** to: Arusha (SA, CA: 2 daily; 2hr 15min–2hr 40min); Dar (CA, SA: 2 daily; 2hr 5min–2hr 50min); Katavi (SA: 2 weekly; 2hr 10min); Kilwa (CA: if enough passengers; 4hr 25min); Mafia (SA, CA: daily; 3hr 30min–3hr 45min); Mahale (SA: 2 weekly; 3hr); Manyara (CA: daily; 2hr 45min); Mikumi (SA: daily; 1hr); Pemba (CA: daily; 3hr 20min); Saadani (SA: daily; 3hr 30min); Selous (CA, SA: 2 daily; 1hr 20min–2hr); Tarangire (CA: if enough passengers; 2hr 20min); Zanzibar (CA, SA: 2 daily; 2hr 35min–3hr 15min). None of these flights operate during the long rains, roughly mid-March to end-May.

## Trains

**Mbeya** to: Dar (2 weekly; 19hr 15min–22hr 30min); Ifakara (2 weekly; 11hr 40min–14hr 10min); Mang'ula (2 weekly; 12hr 20min–15hr); New Kapiri Mposhi, Zambia (1 weekly; 19hr 10min); Selous Game Reserve, various stations (2 weekly; 15hr–18hr 10min).

# Zanzibar

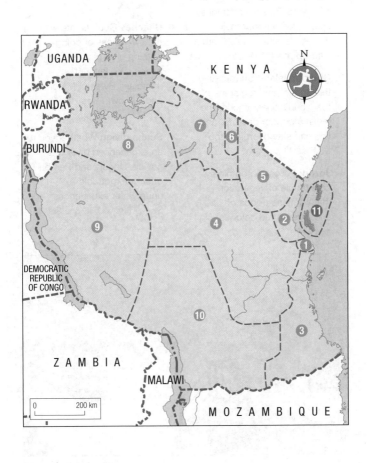

CHAPTER 11 # Highlights

* **Stone Town** Africa meets the Orient – a place where the line between reality and imagination can easily fade away. See p.509

* **Spice tours** See, touch, smell and taste Zanzibar's famous spices, learn about their myriad uses, and finish with a slap-up meal. See p.531

* **Chumbe Island** Surrounding this coral island are some of the world's finest snorkelling reefs: a perfect day-trip, and you can stay overnight too. See p.533

* **Jozani Forest** A soothingly cool tangle of vegetation that contains troops of endangered red colobus monkeys. See p.536

* **Safari Blue** A great day out from Fumba in the south-west, this excursion combines a dhow cruise, sailing in outriggers, snorkelling, and lunch on an uninhabited isle. See p.538

* **Beaches** Get intimate with the sweetness of doing nothing on a picture-perfect beach. Our favourites: Jambiani, Bwejuu, Matemwe and Kendwa. See p.542, p.547, p.553 & p.560

* **Scuba diving** Whether you're an experienced diver or a novice, Unguja and Pemba offer unforgettable underwater experiences. See p.538, p.568 & p.569

▲ Scuba diving centre, Nungwi

# Zanzibar

The **Zanzibar archipelago** is one of Africa's most bewitching destinations, the name itself evoking palm-backed beaches, languid tropical waters and colourful coral reefs. But the islands are more than just the backdrop for dedicated beach bumming. Their history is a visitors' book of peoples from around the Indian Ocean and even the Mediterranean, each of whom left their mark, whether in the form of ruined palaces, fortresses or citadels, or Zanzibar's famous cuisine, or some very strange but enjoyable cultural events, including Pemba's Portuguese-style bullfights, and Makunduchi's raucous celebration of the Persian New Year.

**Unguja** is the archipelago's main island, and the one with the best beaches. The historical **Stone Town**, part of the capital Zanzibar Town, is an alluring Arabian-style labyrinth densely packed with mansions, palaces and bazaars, most of them constructed on the back of the nineteenth-century **slave trade**, which Zanzibar controlled. Unguja's sister island of **Pemba**, 48km to the north, is quite a contrast. With few beaches to write home about, tourist facilities are extremely limited, so the main reason for coming is for **scuba diving**. History buffs can poke around a host of medieval ruins dating from the height of the Swahili trading civilization, whilst nature lovers have **Ngezi Forest**, an incredibly dense tangle that's home to unique birds, and the giant Pemba fruit bat.

# Stone Town and around

The greedy spider at the heart of East Africa's slave trade was **STONE TOWN**, the historical part of Zanzibar's capital, Zanzibar Town. Known locally as Mji Mkongwe ("Old Town"), it resembles the medinas of North Africa and Arabia, with its maze of narrow twisting streets, bustling bazaars and grand Arabian and Indian mansions. In spite of its quasi-medieval appearance (ably helped along by a most inimical climate as far as wood, masonry and roofs are concerned), the town is relatively sprightly, mostly dating from the last 150 years. Wandering about aimlessly here is a pleasure in itself, but there are also specific places to aim for, including the harrowing cells of Africa's last slave market, two cathedrals

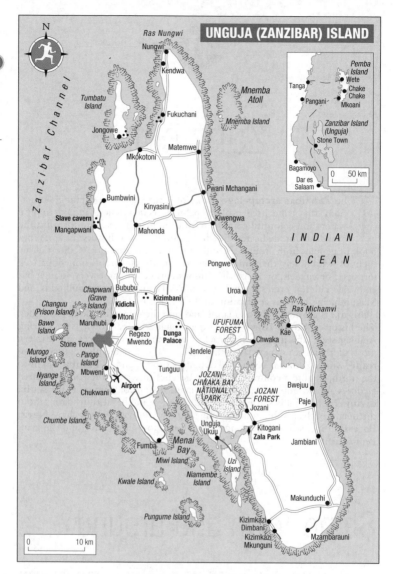

linked to the slave trade's abolition, and – along the waterfront – two majestic palaces (now museums) and a brooding Omani fortress.

Equally beguiling are several attractions within day-tripping distance, including Zanzibar's famous **spice tours**, a handful of reef-fringed **islands** for often magical snorkelling, **ruined palaces** and baths, and a former Anglican mission whose **botanical garden** is a superb spot for birding.

# Arrival

Stone Town is accessed by ferry from Dar es Salaam or Pemba, and by plane from a dozen Tanzanian airports, including Dar, Tanga and Arusha. **Zanzibar International Airport** is 7km south of town. The foreign exchange bureaux in the arrivals hall have decent rates and can also change traveller's cheques. Until around 8pm, you can catch **daladalas** from the traffic island just beyond the airport car park, which go to Darajani on Creek Road (Tsh350). The airport's **taxi** drivers are shameless in overcharging: the "normal" tourist fare should be Tsh12,000 (around $10), with locals paying half that. If you've made a booking with a tour operator or an upmarket hotel, they should be able to pick you up: usually $25 per vehicle.

The **ferry port** is at the north end of Stone Town. Tourists are expected to clear immigration inside the port, a farcical procedure given that Zanzibar is part of Tanzania. After filling in a form, your passport will be stamped, for which there's no fee. Taxis from the harbour entrance shouldn't charge more than Tsh5000 for a ride around town. If walking, stick to one of the main roads flanking Stone Town for as long as possible before diving into the maze.

# Information, city transport and tours

There's no official **tourist information** centre, but there is an unofficial help desk in the gatehouse of the Old Fort (daily 9am–5pm), who also have a few brochures. Printed **practical information** is limited to the *Swahili Coast* (ⓦ www.swahilicoast.com), a free glossy listings booklet with good articles and tide tables; pick it up at hotels, restaurants, or tour operators.

The best way of exploring Stone Town is **on foot**. Distances are short, and in any case most of the streets are too narrow for cars. A good way to get your bearings is on a **city tour** (3hr, $20–30 per person, see p.532).

# Accommodation

There's plenty of **accommodation** in and around Stone Town, but, as throughout Zanzibar, it's almost impossible to find a double room for much under $40. **Haggling** is only possible in sub-$80 places, and is easiest in April and May (long rains), and in October or November (short rains). At all times hotels can be extremely **damp**, so go for rooms as high as possible to catch a breeze.

## Hurumzi, Kiponda, Kokoni and Mchambawima

The northern part of the old town is the most picturesque, and the easiest to get lost in. Most of the following are at least five minutes from the nearest drivable road.

🏃 **236 Hurumzi** Hurumzi St ☎024/223 2784 or 0777/423266, ⓦ www.236hurumzi.com. Set in Tharia Topan's magnificent Hurumzi House (see p.523), this is East Africa's most atmospheric hotel. Effectively a reinterpretation of classic Zanzibari themes, it's a self-indulgent foray into the world of *The Arabian Nights*. Each of the sixteen rooms (accessed by steep staircases) has its own quirks, from the "Ballroom", dominated by a giant chandelier, and the "North" and "South" rooms with

Nourished by the warm South Equatorial Current, Zanzibar's fringing **reefs** abound with colourful and often heart-stopping marine life, much of it within a short boat ride of a beach. For a general introduction to diving and snorkelling, see p.56.

### Snorkelling

**Snorkelling** is the cheap way of getting face to face with the marvels dwelling beneath the surface, and can be arranged at most beaches, either through hotels, dive centres, or informally with fishermen. In most places you need a boat to get out to the best reefs, although much of Unguja's east coast – which is tidal – has reefs within walking or wading distance; you'll need to take care with incoming tides, however. Among East Africa's best snorkelling reefs – out of bounds to scuba divers, too – are those around **Chumbe Island** near Stone Town (see p.533). Other great reefs include **Mnemba Atoll** off Matemwe, and off **Misali Island** (see p.567) in Pemba. If you arrange things through a fisherman, you'll pay upwards of $15 for him and his *ngalawa* outrigger. He may also have snorkelling equipment; if not, the cost of renting a mask, snorkel and flippers averages $5–10 a day (or you can buy equipment in shops near Stone Town's Central Market; around $30). Going through a scuba diving company, you'll pay $30–50 per trip if hitching a ride with divers, for which you should get at least an hour on each of two reefs, and possibly lunch too.

### Dive sites

There are good diving reefs almost everywhere around Zanzibar. The reefs **off Stone Town** are cheapest to access, and even though visibility averages a modest ten metres, there's a good range of corals and critters, and plenty of safe locations for first-timers. Experts have a couple of wrecks, including the *Great Northern*, a cable layer that foundered on the last day of 1902.

The barrier reef off Unguja's **southeast coast**, between Ras Michamvi and Jambiani, is dominated by supremely photogenic soft corals. The shallow and sheltered coral gardens inside the lagoon offer ideal conditions for beginners (and night divers). In the very south diving is a relatively new thing: best are the sea mounts inside Menai Bay, which attract all sorts of large pelagics including sailfish and dolphins.

Off Unguja's **northeast coast** is one of Zanzibar's big diving attractions: the heart-shaped **Mnemba Atoll**, which has a huge range of reefs with something for all tastes (and abilities), a wide variety of corals and fish life, plus reasonable odds on biggies, including turtles. If you're going to be diving exclusively at Mnemba, consider basing yourself at Matemwe, as trips from elsewhere attract surcharges of up to $50 a day.

**Pemba**'s spectacular underwater realm – comprising almost half of Tanzania's reefs – is among the world's best diving destinations, particularly if you're experienced (the currents that make drift dives so exhilarating are also why novices might be better off

---

open-air bathtubs shielded from the street by wooden latticework screens, to the "Keep", "Pavilion" and "Tour" suites, which have open-sided, turret-top gazebos fitted with day beds. Most rooms have unobtrusive a/c and fans. Restaurant on top. Closed mid-April to end-May. BB ⑥ (the "Kipembe" room), otherwise BB ⑦

**240 Hurumzi** Hurumzi St, same entrance and contacts as *236 Hurumzi*. Intended for self-caterers, this has a fully equipped kitchen and dining room, and six bedrooms in similar style to *236 Hurumzi*, less extravagant but nonetheless

oozing opulence, although none have any views worth speaking of. BB ⑥–⑦

🏃 **Clove Hotel** Hurumzi St, Hurumzi
☎0777/484567, ⊛www.zanzibarhotel.nl. A modernized Dutch-run hotel with eight unfussy but comfortable rooms, the front-facing ones with balconies. What's special is the roof terrace, with fantastic views, comfy loungers, and drinks – including wine. Hearty breakfasts, free wi-fi. Closed May. BB ④

🏃 **Hotel Kiponda** Nyumba ya Moto St, Kiponda ☎024/223 3052 or 0777/431665,

learning the ropes on Unguja). The caverns, drop-offs, swim-throughs and immense coral gardens shelter a cornucopia of marine life, including an abundance of large open-water species. Other than drift dives, another highlight is **Misali Island** (see p.567), whose reefs have exceptional visibility, pristine corals, and the chance of spotting sharks, manta rays and turtles.

### Dive centres

Scuba diving can only be done through a **dive centre**. The ones below are PADI-accredited and have solid safety reputations. **Costs** average $450–520 for a four- or five-day Open Water diving course (excluding accommodation); already qualified divers pay $80–100 a day for two dives, including lunch. The only centre with **Nitrox** facilities (for those with suitable experience) is Nungwi's East Africa Diving.

**Fumba** *Fumba Beach Lodge*, Fumba Peninsula ☎0777/860504, ⓦwww.fumba beachlodge.com.

**Kendwa** Scuba Do, *Sunset Bungalows* ☎0777/417157, ⓦwww.scuba-do-zanzibar .com; Zanzibar Watersports, *Kendwa Rocks* ☎024/223 3615, ⓦwww.zanzibarwater sports.com.

**Kiwengwa** One Ocean, *Bluebay Beach Resort* ☎0777/414332, ⓦwww.zanzibarone ocean.com.

**Kizimkazi** One Ocean, *Unguja Resort* ☎0773/573411, ⓦwww.zanzibaroneocean .com.

**Matemwe** One Ocean, *Matemwe Beach Village* ☎0777/473128, ⓦwww.zanzibarone ocean.com.

**Michamvi Peninsula** Rising Sun Dive Centre, *Breezes Beach Club* ☎0774/440883–5, ⓦwww.risingsun-zanzibar.com.

**Nungwi** East Africa Diving, *Jambo Bungalows* ☎0777/420588, ⓦwww.diving-zanzibar .com; Zanzibar Watersports, *Ras Nungwi Beach Hotel* and *Paradise Beach Hotel* ☎024/223 3615, ⓦwww.zanzibarwatersports.com.

**Paje** Buccaneer Diving, *Arabian Nights Hotel* ☎0777/853403, ⓦwww.buccaneerdiving .com.

**Pwani Mchangani** One Ocean, *Ocean Paradise Resort* ☎0777/453892, ⓦwww .zanzibaroneocean.com.

**Pemba** Oxygène Pemba, *The Manta Resort*, Ras Kigomasha ⓦwww.oxygenediving .com; Swahili Divers, *Kervan Saray Beach*, Ras Kigomasha ☎0772/659805, ⓦwww .swahilidivers.com.

**Stone Town** Bahari Divers, Forodhani St, just south of the tunnel ☎0777/415011 or 0784/254786, ⓦwww.zanzibar-diving.com; One Ocean, Kenyatta Rd, just before *The Livingstone* ☎024/223 8374 or 0784/750161, ⓦwww.zanzibaroneocean.com.

ⓦwww.kiponda.com. Quiet and comfortable, with fifteen rooms, including singles and triples. The walls are thick, so the interior stays cool. Rooms vary in size and price; most have box nets, all have ceiling fans. On top is a rooftop café and bar. BB ❸–❹
**Kokoni's Hotel** Kokoni ☎024/223 0239 or 0777/451590, ⓔkokonishotel@hotmail.com. This lovely four-storey mansion towers over one side of a sweet little square. Its rooms have high ceilings; most contain nothing more than beds and box nets, but a handful have TVs, and two have bathrooms. BB ❸

**Riverman Hotel** East of Tharia St, Mchambawima ☎024/223 3188, ⓔrivermanhotel@yahoo.com. Very good value if you don't mind sharing bathrooms. All rooms have fans and box nets, and there's a pleasant courtyard for meals. BB ❸
**St Monica's Guest House** Off New Mkunazini Rd by the Anglican Cathedral, Mkunazini ☎024/223 0773, ⓔmonicaszanzibar@hotmail.com. Run by the Anglican Church, this basic hostel smells bad in the rains, but is still good value, and can't be matched for chilling atmosphere: one of the two buildings sits astride the former slave market's

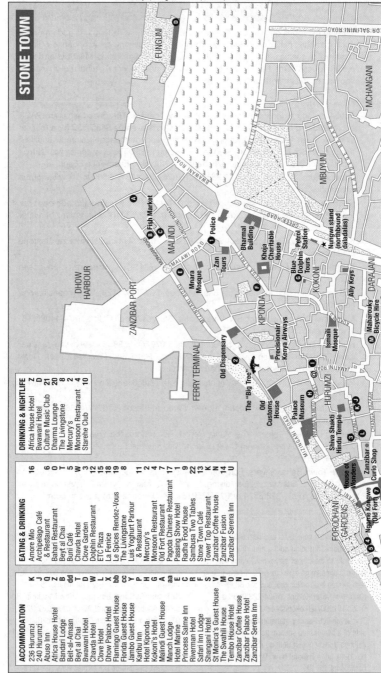

Blue Mosque, Livingstone House, Bububu, Mtoni & north ▲

**STONE TOWN**

FUNGUNI

DHOW HARBOUR

ZANZIBAR PORT

FERRY TERMINAL

**Ⓐ** Africa House Hotel
**Ⓑ** Fish Market
**Ⓒ**
**Ⓓ**
**Ⓔ** Mnara Mosque
**Ⓕ**
**Ⓖ** Blue Dolphin Tours
**Ⓗ**
**Ⓘ**
Police
Zan Tours
Bharmal Building
Khoja Charitable House
Petrol Station
Nungwi stand (northbound daladalas)
Ismaili Mosque
Maharouky Bicycle Hire
Ally Keys
Precisionair/ Kenya Airways
Old Dispensary
The "Big Tree"
Old Customs House
Palace Museum
Shiva Shakti Hindu Temple
House of Wonders
Ngome Kongwe (Old Fort)
Zanzibar Curio Shop
FORODHANI GARDENS

MALINDI

MBUYUNI

MCHANGANI

KIPONDA

KOKONI

DARAJANI

HURUMZI

| ACCOMMODATION | |
|---|---|
| 236 Hurumzi | K |
| 240 Hurumzi | J |
| Abuso Inn | Q |
| Africa House Hotel | Z |
| Bandari Lodge | B |
| Beit-al-Amaan | dd |
| Beyt al Chai | T |
| Bwawani Hotel | D |
| Chavda Hotel | W |
| Clove Hotel | L |
| Dhow Palace Hotel | X |
| Flamingo Guest House | bb |
| Florida Guest House | cc |
| Jambo Guest House | Y |
| Karibu Inn | P |
| Hotel Kiponda | H |
| Kokoni's Hotel | G |
| Malindi Guest House | A |
| Manch Lodge | aa |
| Hotel Marine | E |
| Princess Salme Inn | C |
| Riverman Hotel | R |
| Safari Inn Lodge | F |
| Shangani Hotel | S |
| St Monica's Guest House | V |
| The Swahili House | M |
| Tembo House Hotel | O |
| Zanzibar Coffee House | N |
| Zanzibar Palace Hotel | I |
| Zanzibar Serena Inn | U |

| EATING & DRINKING | |
|---|---|
| Amore Mio | 16 |
| Archipelago Café & Restaurant | 6 |
| Bahari Restaurant | 0 |
| Beyt al Chai | T |
| Buni Café | 5 |
| Chavda Hotel | W |
| Clove Garden | 3 |
| Dolphin Restaurant | 12 |
| ETC Plaza | 15 |
| La Fenice | 18 |
| Le Spices Rendez-Vous | 19 |
| The Livingstone | 8 |
| Luis Yoghurt Parlour & Restaurant | 11 |
| Mercury's | 2 |
| Monsoon Restaurant | 4 |
| Old Fort Restaurant | 7 |
| Pagoda Chinese Restaurant | 17 |
| Passing Show Hotel | 1 |
| Radha Food House | 9 |
| Sambusa Two Tables | 22 |
| Stone Town Café | 13 |
| Tower Top Restaurant | K |
| Zanzibar Fusion | 14 |
| Zanzibar Serena Inn | U |

| DRINKING & NIGHTLIFE | |
|---|---|
| Africa House Hotel | Z |
| Bwawani Hotel | D |
| Culture Music Club | 21 |
| Dharma Lounge | 20 |
| The Livingstone | 8 |
| Mercury's | 2 |
| Monsoon Restaurant | 4 |
| Starehe Club | 10 |

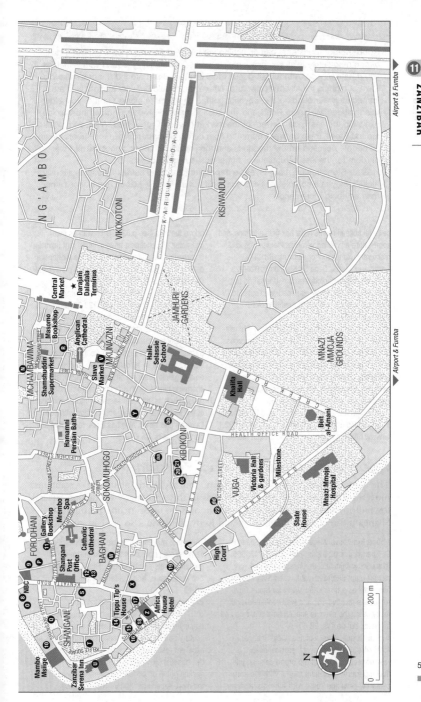

▶ Airport & Fumba

▶ Airport & Fumba

N'GAMBO

VIKOKOTONI

KISIWANDUI

K·A·R·U·M·E R·O·A·D

★ Central Market
Darajani Daladala Terminus

JAMHURI GARDENS

MNAZI MMOJA GROUNDS

MCHAMBAWIMA

Masomo Bookshop

Anglican Cathedral

Shamshuddin Supermarket

Slave Market

MKUNAZINI

Haile Selassie School

Khalifa Hall

Beit al-Amani

Hamamni Persian Baths

SOKOMUHOGO

KIBOKONI

HEALTH OFFICE ROAD

FORODHANI

Gallery Bookshop

Mrembo Spa

Catholic Cathedral

BAGHANI

Shangani Post Office

Victoria Hall & gardens

Milestone

VUGA

Mnazi Mmoja Hospital

SHANGANI

Mambo Msiige

Zanzibar Serena Inn

NBC

Tippu Tip's House

Africa House Hotel

State House

High Court

200 m

N

0

www.roughguides.com

515

**Robberies** of tourists by bag snatching are reported frequently enough, but a dash of common sense is all you need: mainly, don't go wandering around with valuables you'd hate to lose. Although it doesn't feel like it, walking around the maze-like old town at night is usually perfectly safe. Where you should be wary at night is in areas immediately surrounding the labyrinth, especially if you're alone. On the west side, this includes Mizingani Road and the section between Kelele Square and Suicide Alley. On the east side, beware of the market area on Creek Road. Also, don't walk around Stone Town between 6pm and 8pm during **Ramadan**, when the streets clear as people descend on the mosques and then return home for dinner, leaving plenty of room for the less scrupulous to target unsuspecting tourists.

As for Stone Town's many loveable **papasi** (the Zanzibari name for hustlers, literally 'ticks'), they're a complete pain to shake off but are usually just an annoyance rather than anything more serious.

cells. All sixteen rooms have box nets and fans, and some share a wooden veranda. Plain but good restaurant. No alcohol or smoking. BB ❸–❹

**Safari Inn Lodge** Dega St, Kiponda ☎024/223 6523, ⓦwww.safarilodgetz.com. Unexciting but clean, friendly, and well-equipped, with satellite TV. Also has a roof terrace with freshly cooked seafood. BB ❹

**The Swahili House** South of Kiponda St, Mchambawima ☎0777/510209, ⓦwww.theswahilihouse .com. A five-storey building with 22 swanky rooms around an internal courtyard; some have exterior balconies, others fancy stand-alone bathtubs, but the main attraction is the rooftop restaurant and bar, complete with jacuzzi. BB ❼–❽

🏃 **Zanzibar Coffee House** Tharia St, Mchambawima ☎024/223 9319 or 0773/061532, ⓦwww.riftvalley-zanzibar.com. Just eight rooms

above the café (see p.525), each with its own character. The cheapest have external (but private) bathrooms. The staff are great, and the rooftop's a delight: a cosy lounge with a wrap-around balcony. Closed May. BB ❺–❼

🏃 **Zanzibar Palace Hotel** Off Nyumba ya Moto St, Kiponda ☎024/223 2230 or 0773/079222, ⓦwww.zanzibarpalacehotel.com. A superbly renovated four-storey townhouse heavy on spangly fabrics, gilded furniture, fancy mirror frames and Persian rugs. To make the most of your stay, splash out on a "deluxe" room or, even better, on a (gigantic) suite, all different, all plush, all charming (and all with a/c, fans, and TVs). Some have balconies, others massive bathtubs, and one of the suites has a private roof terrace with sun loungers and views. Also has a fine restaurant and bar downstairs. BB ❼–❽

## Shangani, Baghani and Forodhani

The west end of Stone Town is more touristy, with plenty of restaurants, souvenir shops and internet cafés. Hotels in this area, many occupying palatial town houses, are either on or just off one of three main thoroughfares – Shangani Street, Forodhani Street and Kenyatta Road – so are easy to find.

**Abuso Inn** Above *Wings* restaurant off Shangani St, Shangani ☎024/223 5886 or 0777/425565, ⓔabusoinn@gmail.com. Unassuming and very calm (except Saturday night, when *Starehe* opposite has a disco). Unusually for Stone Town, rooms are mostly large and well-ventilated, and many catch the evening sun. All have a/c, fans and box nets, but no TVs. BB ❺

**Africa House Hotel** Suicide Alley, Shangani ☎0774/432340, ⓦwww.theafricahouse -zanzibar.com. A grand old grand colonial pile housing fourteen elegant rooms with a/c and cable TV, including some with full-on sea views.

The decor makes ample use of antiques, Persian carpets, old photographs, gilded mirrors, and golden tassels and brocades. Facilities include two restaurants, and the famous *Sunset Bar*. BB ❼–❽

**Beyt al Chai** Kelele Square, Shangani ☎0774/444111, ⓦwww.bluebayzanzibar.com. Occupying a gorgeous three-storey nineteenth-century building, on the ground floor of which is an excellent restaurant of the same name (see p.526), this has just six wooden-floored rooms, stylishly decked out in draperies and comfy antiques, with the more expensive "Sultan" rooms having bathtubs in their bedrooms. All have a/c, and the two on top have sea views over Kelele Square. Closed May. BB **7**–**8**

**Chavda Hotel** Baghani St, Baghani ☏024/223 2115, ⓦwww.chavdahotel.co.tz. Several conjoined former mansions enclosing an airy courtyard, all adorned with imported Indian fittings, reproduction furniture, and China vases. The sixteen rooms, on three floors, come with all mod cons. The more expensive twin-bed rooms have balconies, and there's a good rooftop restaurant. BB **6**

**Dhow Palace Hotel** Kenyatta Rd, Shangani ☏024/223 3012, ⓦwww.dhowpalace-hotel.com. A beautiful and tranquil 1870s mansion, preserving much of its Arabian flair. Service is smart and efficient, and the 28 spacious rooms are good value, featuring a/c, cable TV, box nets, a smattering of antiques, and blue-tiled sunken baths. Some have balconies; on the inside, these open on the swimming pool. There's also an attractive rooftop restaurant. Closed April & May. BB **6**

**Karibu Inn** Off Forodhani St, Forodhani ☏024/223 3058, ⓔkaribuinnhotel@zanzinet.com. Partly renovated but a little shabby, this is still a decent choice, its en-suite rooms scattered over four half-storeys, some on the ground floor. There are also three dorms (BB $15 per person), each with a/c and bathroom. BB **4**

**Shangani Hotel** Kenyatta Rd, Shangani ☏024/223 3688 or 0777/411703,

ⓦwww.shanganihotel.com. Hidden behind a reception resembling a gentlemen's club, complete with billiard table, is a rather charmless modern hotel, although it's decent enough for the price, especially for a room higher up. All have bathrooms, fans, a/c and cable TV, and those at the back have sea views. BB **5**

**Tembo House Hotel** Shangani St, Shangani ☏024/223 3005 or 0777/220216, ⓦwww.tembohotel.com. Built as the American Embassy in the 1830s, this is now a busy package-tour hotel, thankfully not overshadowed by its uninspiring modern wing. Whilst not as stylish as other sea-front options, and with variable standards, the beachfront location and its swimming pool are undeniable draws. Get a room with an ocean view or, better yet, an ocean-facing balcony. The hotel's *Bahari Restaurant* is right by the beach. Sunbathers have a rooftop terrace. No alcohol, but *The Livingstone* is next door. BB **6**–**7**

**Zanzibar Serena Inn** Kelele Square, Shangani ☏024/223 3587 or 0786/999020, ⓦwww.serenahotels.com. In tune with other properties in the Aga Khan's *Serena* chain, service here is faultless, standards solidly five-star, and the rooms – all sea-facing – come with all mod-cons. There are several bars and restaurants, and a large shoreline swimming pool. BB **9**

# Southern Stone Town and Vuga

The southern part of the old town contains a number of budget hotels easily reached from Vuga Road. Vuga is the broad, leafy district just south of here, whose handful of hotels should benefit from better ventilation.

**Beit-al-Amaan** Victoria St, Vuga ☏0777/414364, ⓔmonsoon@zanzinet.com. This "House of Peace" occupies a two-storey town house, and is the business for comfort and (authentic) Zanzibari style. The six large rooms and its common areas are decorated with colourful Swahili artwork, seashells, Persian carpets and all sorts of antiques. All but the huge downstairs room have private bathrooms, and there's a kitchen on top. BB **5**

**Flamingo Guest House** Mkunazini St, Kibokoni ☏024/223 2850 or 0777/491252. Cheapest of the lot ($10 a head), and not at all bad so long as the drains aren't blocked. All six rooms have box nets and fans; $2 more (per person) gets you a private bathroom. BB **3**

**Florida Guest House** Vuga Rd, Kibokoni ☏024/223 3136, ⓔfloridaznz@yahoo.com.

A reliable budget option, whose eight rooms, all with spotless bathrooms (and hot showers) come with cable TV, box nets and a/c. BB **4**

**Jambo Guest House** Off Mkunazini St, Sokomuhogo ☏024/223 3779 or 0777/496571, ⓔinfo@jamboguest.com. Popular with backpackers, with friendly staff. The eight rooms, six with a/c, share bathrooms, and are large and clean if bare. BB **3**

**Manch Lodge** Between Vuga Rd and Sokomuhogo St, Kibokoni ☏024/223 1918 or 0777/438842. Large and basic but quite acceptable, and with a small garden, too. There are twenty rooms, three with bathrooms, a handful with TVs, and all with (round) nets and fans. BB **3**

# Malindi and Funguni

Malindi district is just outside the old town, and not the most atmospheric area, but well placed if you're arriving by ferry. Bounding it is Malawi Road, good for cheap eats.

**Bandari Lodge** Mizingani St ☎024/223 7969 or 0777/423638. Especially cheap for singles, the nine high-ceilinged rooms here, all but one en suite, are relatively fresh and clean, with big beds and box nets. There's also a kitchen, and a cable TV on the top floor. BB ❸

**Bwawani Hotel** Bwawani Rd, Funguni ☎024/223 5006, ⓦwww.bwawani.com. A 1972 hulk on the edge of mudflats, this – assuming the lift is still working – is the cheapest option for physically disabled travellers. The common areas are gloomy, but the staff are friendly, and the 108 huge bedrooms are really quite decent, the best one with glimpses of the ocean. There's a basic restaurant and bar inside, also an outdoor bar, a nearby disco, and a (usually dry) swimming pool. BB ❹

**Malindi Guest House** Off Mizingani St ☎024/223 0165, ⓔmalindi@zanzinet.com. Wonderful decor throughout, and well-kept rooms with nets and fans, and most with bathrooms. Two niggles: some beds are a bit short, and it's definitely not safe to walk here at night. Good harbour views from the rooftop. BB ❸

**Hotel Marine** Mizingani Rd/Malawi Rd ☎0777/411102, ⓔhotelmarine@zanlink.com. With over twenty rooms arranged around an airy atrium, this is perfectly placed for ferries, and – so long as the price doesn't shoot up after renovation and the installation of a/c – should still be very good value. BB ❹

**Princess Salme Inn** Just off Mizingani St ☎0777/435303, ⓦwww.princesssalmeinn.com. Friendliest of the lot in this area, with twelve clean rooms, not all with bathrooms (but good showers though). The second-floor rooms, arranged around a sunny courtyard, are the best, if a little cramped. In really hot weather you'll appreciate one of the rooms with a/c. BB ❸–❹

# Out of town

Staying out of town means breezier locations, a beach, and – if you stay on an island – unbeatable romance.

**Changuu Island Private Paradise** 5km northwest of Stone Town (see p.532) ☎0786/301662 or 027/254 4595 (Arusha), ⓦwww.privateislands-zanzibar.com. This comprises a number of buildings and facilities scattered around the diminutive island, notable not only for their location, but attractive interior decor. The original "prison", enclosing a courtyard, is now a restaurant and bar. There's also a swimming pool, and floodlit tennis court. No children under 12. HB ❾

**Chumbe Island Eco-Lodge** 13km south of Stone Town (see p.533) ☎024/223 1040 or 0777/413232, ⓦwww.chumbeisland.com. A haven for snorkellers or romancers, this has just seven split-level *bandas* overlooking the ocean, with casuarina poles for walls and palm fronds for roofs. All have a large living room, handmade furniture and hammock. The ecotourism tag is genuine: rainwater is filtered and stored under the floors, hot water and electricity are solar powered (no TVs), ventilation is via cleverly designed roofs, toilets create no waste, and profits fund environmental activities. Great food (including vegetarian). There's no real beach, but with so much other beauty around you'll hardly miss it. The price includes everything except alcohol. Closed mid-April to mid-June. FB ❾

**Imani Beach Villa** Bububu, 10km north of Stone Town ☎024/225 0050 or 0773/903983, ⓦwww.imani-zanzibar.com. An intimate and sweetly run "boutique" hotel with just seven rooms in a garden beside the beach. All have good showers and a/c, and the decor is a stylish blend of Swahili and Moroccan. The outdoor restaurant, under a colourful awning, has great seafood. Good range of excursions too. Closed April–May. HB ❻

**Mtoni Marine** Mtoni, 4km north of Stone Town ☎024/225 0140, ⓦwww.mtoni.com. An elegant and well-priced beach resort nestled in palm tree-studded gardens. The beach is in two parts, one between mangroves and a jetty, the other, more open, fronted by "The Restaurant". The water is okay for swimming but the sand can feel a little slimy, so there's also a swimming pool. Very good rooms; for a private veranda and sea views, you'll need a "Palm Court" room. Amenities include three restaurants, a sports bar, a branch of the Mrembo spa (see p.523), a kids' playground, and various activities (at extra cost), including dhow cruises. BB ❻–❼

# The Town

Stone Town's showpiece is its grandiose **waterfront**, a series of monumental buildings between the port and Shangani in the southwest. This is the Stone Town that the sultans wanted you to see, and admire. Yet barely a hundred metres behind the palaces and their facades is another world entirely: the souk-like labyrinth of **central Stone Town**. Positively dripping in atmosphere, it's a bewildering warren of narrow alleyways and dead-ends, decaying mansions and colourful shops – an architectural trove, hugely photogenic, and very much lived in, which just adds to its charm. The eastern side of the old town is bounded by Creek Road – a real creek until the British drained it – beyond which lies Ng'ambo, literally "the other side" where the majority of Zanzibar Town's inhabitants live.

## Along the waterfront

Lining the **waterfront** is a wonderful strip of monumental yet delicate buildings through which the Busaïdi sultanate expressed its ever-burgeoning wealth and power. The approach by ferry, or any trip to the islands off Stone Town, gives you the best view. The main sights can easily be browsed in an hour, but to spend any time inside either of the museums, or bargain-hunting in the Old Fort, plan on half a day. Lastly, although you'll see kids happily leaping into the sea, the water here is polluted, dangerously so during the rains.

### The Old Dispensary and Palace Museum

Facing the ferry terminal is the **Old Dispensary**, a grand four-storey building which, in spite of the port robbing it of its waterfront location, is one of East Africa's finest and most beautiful landmarks. Opened as a charitable health centre, the sumptuousness of its design and decor is reminiscent of British colonial architecture in India – no coincidence, given that it was constructed by

▲ The Old Dispensary, Stone Town

craftsmen brought in from India by the dispensary's patron, **Sir Tharia Topan**. An Ismaïli businessman, Topan's wealth accrued from multiple functions as head of customs, financial adviser to the sultan, and banker to the most infamous of slave traders, Tippu Tip. Left to fall into ruin after the 1964 Revolution, the building was restored by the Aga Khan Trust for Culture in the 1990s, and you're welcome to look around – though these days it's mostly occupied by offices (daily 9am–5pm; free entry).

Walking south, the next major building is the **Palace Museum** (daily 9am–6pm; Ramadan daily 8am–2.30pm; Tsh3500 or $3), which was the residence of Zanzibar's last sultan, exiled in 1964. Unfortunately, the museum doesn't have much pulling power unless you're an incurable furniture fetishist.

### Beit al-Ajaib: The House of Wonders

With its colonnaded facade and imposing clock-tower, the Beit al-Ajaib – better known as the **House of Wonders** – is Zanzibar's most distinctive landmark. The present building, now housing the Zanzibar National Museum (daily 9am–6pm; Tsh3500 or $3), was completed as a palace in 1883. The culmination of Sultan Barghash's extravagant building spree, it was for a long time East Africa's tallest structure, and was also the first to have running water, electric light, and an electric lift (long since broken), all very good reasons for its name.

The building's entrance is guarded by two **Portuguese cannons** captured by the Persians at the siege of Hormuz in 1622. One of them bears an embossed Portuguese coat of arms, and both have Persian inscriptions. The cannons didn't help the Portuguese, but may have worked magic in protecting the House of Wonders during the **British bombardment** of August 27, 1896, when two adjoining palaces were reduced to rubble.

Walking inside, the roofed atrium is dominated by a **sewn dhow**: a *jahazi la mtepe*. Last built for real in the 1930s, this replica was constructed in Zanzibar over 2003–4. The accompanying display chronicles its construction, other forms of boat-building, traditional navigation, and the evolution of the monsoon-driven dhow trade. In a side room is a smashed-up 1950s **Ford Zephyr** automobile, once driven by President Karume – Tanzanian driving skills obviously being much the same back then.

The museum's **other displays** – all worth taking time to see properly – occupy two more floors, in rooms guarded by heavy ornamental doors whose gilded Qur'anic inscriptions were ostentatious statements of the sultanate's vast wealth. The various exhibits are exceptionally well presented, with good photographs and detailed information in both Kiswahili and English, and cover most aspects of Zanzibari life, culture and history. Highlights include a whole room dedicated to *kangas*; Dr David Livingstone's medicine chest; a thoughtful display on traditional Swahili music; several rooms on food and cooking; and a fascinating section about **traditional healing**, which includes a *pini* (charm) containing herbs and, so it is said, a dog's nose.

### Ngome Kongwe: the Old Fort

Just southwest of the House of Wonders, **Ngome Kongwe**, also called the Old Fort or Omani Fort (daily 9am–10pm or later; free entry except on evenings when performances are held), comprises four heavy coral ragstone walls with squat cylindrical towers and castellated defences, and makes for a calm and surprisingly hustler-free place to sit for an hour or two. The fort dates back to the expulsion of the Portuguese in 1698. The victorious Omanis were quick to consolidate their gains, completing the fort just three years later. It now houses craft shops, an open-air amphitheatre (concerts are announced on a sign outside), the Old Fort Restaurant (see p.525), and – in the gate house – a tourist information desk, where you might ask about the historically-themed **sound and light show** planned for the grassy enclosure in the fort's southern precinct.

### Forodhani Gardens

The formal **Forodhani Gardens** were the original site of the two cannons outside the House of Wonders, part of a battery of guns which gave their name ("mizingani" meaning cannons) to the shore-front road. The name "forodhani" – meaning a ship's cargo or a reloading place – alludes to the **slave trade**, when slaves would be landed here before being taken to the market further south in what's now Kelele Square. Despite the *papasi*, the gardens are a pleasant place to relax, but are best after sunset for the magical **street-food market** (see p.525).

## Shangani and Vuga

A footbridge from the Forodhani Gardens leads to the Zanzibar Orphanage, under which the road tunnels to emerge in **Shangani** district. This, the westernmost point of Stone Town, was where, in the mid-nineteenth century, Seyyid Saïd gave Europeans land for building their embassies, consulates and missions. Nowadays, Shangani is where you'll find most of the **upmarket hotels**, **restaurants** and **bars**, and – of course – a good many *papasi*. Further south, beyond the edge of the old town's labyrinth, is grassy **Vuga**, which was the administrative district.

### Kelele Square and Tippu Tip's House

Nowadays perfectly peaceful, **Kelele Square** – its name means "shouting", "noisy" or "tumultuous" – hints at a terrible past, when it was used as Zanzibar's main **slave market** until the 1860s. The first building on your right is **Mambo Msiige** (not open to visitors), which means "Inimitable Thing". The name apparently derives from the extravagance of its construction, for which thousands of eggs were used to strengthen the mortar, together with – according to legend – live slaves, who were entombed in the walls. The room at the very top, visibly not part of the original structure, is said to have been built for the explorer Henry Morton Stanley. The **Zanzibar Serena Inn** next door, which you can enter as long as you don't look too scruffy, occupies the perhaps overly restored telegraph office, once linked directly to Aden (Yemen) by underwater cable. A room on the first floor, beside the *Terrace Restaurant*, contains old phones and relays.

South of Kelele Square along the bizarrely named Suicide Alley (a mystery in itself) is **Tippu Tip's House**, whose door is one of Stone Town's most elaborate – look for the dandy set of black and white steps. In the middle of the nineteenth century, mainland Tanzania was in considerable turmoil, with the warlike Maasai and Ngoni pushing in from the north and south respectively, and slave traders pushing from the east. Of the latter, the most successful, and infamous, was Hamed bin Muhammed al-Murjebi, better known – on account of a facial twitch – as Tippu Tip (a bird with characteristic blinking eyes). By the late 1860s, Tippu Tip was leading **slave caravans** of more than four thousand men, and over the years became king-maker among many of the chiefdoms the caravan routes passed through, including Upper Congo, of which he was the de facto ruler. The house is currently occupied by various families, evidently undaunted by the popular belief that the house is haunted by the spirits of slaves. They're used to showing tourists around: a tip (no pun intended) is expected.

## Beit al-Amani

Walking down to the end of Kenyatta Road you reach a Doric archway, which marks the start of Vuga district: home to several "saracenic" buildings designed by J.H. Sinclair, all of them characterized by a blend of Arabian-style Orientalism and classical (European) proportions. The sweetest of these, at the south end of Kaunda Road and Creek Road, is the **Beit al-Amani** ("House of Peace"). Originally a museum, it's currently shuttered, but even seeing it from the outside is worth the walk: a squat but elegant hexagonal construction topped by a Byzantine-style dome. It's the most Islamic of Sinclair's works, dubbed "Sinclair's mosque" by his detractors, and the "House of Ghosts" by locals, for whom the concept of a museum was a strange novelty.

# Central Stone Town

Away from the waterfront, Stone Town is a spaghetti-like tangle of twisted alleyways dotted with mildew-cloaked mansions and mosques, and getting lost is unavoidable – and a pleasure. If you really get stuck, any local will help you out, or just keep walking along the busiest street – you should eventually emerge onto one of the roads bounding the old town. The **main commercial areas**, containing a clutter of shops and stalls in the manner of Arabian souks, are along and off Hurumzi and Gizenga streets, and Changa Bazaar, where you'll find dozens of antique dealers, craft shops, fabric and jewellery stores. The main streets running north to south – Sokomuhogo and Tharia/Mkunazini – are less hectic and have fewer souvenir shops, so provide a more leisurely introduction to life in the old town.

### The slave market and Anglican Cathedral

The Anglican Cathedral occupies the site of Africa's last **slave market**, closed in 1873 by a reluctant Sultan Barghash under pressure from the British. Stone Town's original slave market had been at Kelele Square in Shangani, but it's here in Mkunazini, where the market shifted in the 1860s, that the appalling cruelty of the trade hits home. Next to the cathedral, in the basement of the former mission hospital (now part of *St Monica's Guest House*), are the **slave chambers**: tiny, dingy cells that each housed up to 75 people each. The only furnishings were a pit in the centre serving as a toilet, and a low platform around the sides. There were no windows. One of the cells is now lit by artificial light; the other has been left unlit save for two slits at one end that hardly make a dent in the gloom. The cells are visitable on a **guided tour** (daily 9am–6pm; Tsh3500 or $3), which includes the cathedral. You can lunch in the guesthouse's restaurant (daily 1–3pm).

The juxtaposition of the cells with the imposing **Anglican Cathedral Church of Christ** might appear grimly ironic but, in the spirit of Christian evangelism, replacing the inhumanity of the slave trade with the salvation of God made perfect sense. The foundation stone was laid on Christmas Day, 1873, the year the market closed, on land donated by a wealthy Indian merchant. The project was funded by the Oxford-based Universities' Mission in Central Africa, and construction proceeded under the supervision of **Bishop Edward Steere**, third Anglican bishop of Zanzibar. The cathedral's design follows a basilican plan, blending Victorian neo-Gothic with Arabesque details. The unusual barrel-vaulted roof was completed in 1879, and the spire was added in 1890. A devastatingly poignant **sculpture** by Clara Sornas in the cathedral courtyard shows five bleak figures placed in a rectangular pit, shackled by a chain brought from Bagamoyo.

## Mrembo spa

**Health spas** have made a big splash at Zanzibar's beach hotels, but it's in Stone Town – sweaty and potentially heavy on the feet – where they're most useful. Particularly recommended is the German/Zanzibari family-run **Mrembo Spa** on Cathedral Street, just west of Jaws Corner (daily 9.30am–6pm; ☎0777/430117, ⊛www.mtoni.com /mrembo). The spa's design, essentially a traditional home, is a delight, and they use only natural ingredients in their scrubs and lotions. They're particularly knowledgeable, too, about the history of beauty treatments on Zanzibar, and have a shop selling fair trade handicrafts as well as Taarab CDs. Men are welcome, but should you want to preserve an aura of machismo, you can always talk football at the barbershop opposite while your better half gets revived.

The cathedral's **interior** also abounds with reminders of slavery. A red circle in the floor beside the altar marks the position of a post to which slaves were tied and whipped to show their strength and resilience before being sold, while behind the altar is the grave of Bishop Steere. The small crucifix on a pillar beside the chancel is said to have been fashioned from a branch of the tree under which David Livingstone's heart was buried. Livingstone is also remembered in a stained-glass window, as are British sailors who died on anti-slaving patrols. The cathedral organ, imported from Ipswich in England, can be heard on Sundays.

### Hamamni Persian Baths

The contrast between the slave market's misery and the slave-financed luxuries of the Persian-style **Hamamni Persian Baths** (daily 10am–4pm, ask for the caretaker across the road to let you in; $3, negotiable, including guided tour), 250m to the west, can come as something of a shock. Commissioned in the early 1870s by Sultan Barghash, the Hamamni baths (from the Arabic word for baths, *hammam*) were open to the public, with the proceeds benefiting a charitable trust (*wakf*). The baths, which are surprisingly plain, ceased functioning in the 1920s, and despite partial restoration in 1978, remain bone dry. The guided **tour** isn't up to much, but the thick walls and stone floors provide a welcome respite from the midday heat.

### The Catholic Cathedral of Saint Joseph

The towers of the **Catholic Cathedral of Saint Joseph** can be seen from pretty much every rooftop in Stone Town, but the cathedral isn't all that easy to locate on foot. The easiest approach is down Gizenga Street from Kenyatta Road, turning right immediately after the Gallery Bookshop. The cathedral lacks the historical significance of the Anglican Cathedral, but the Catholic Church was also committed to the anti-slavery movement, its main memorial being Bagamoyo's Freedom Village on the mainland. The cathedral's foundation stone was laid in July 1896, and the first Mass was celebrated on Christmas Day, 1898, two years before completion. The design is loosely based on the Romano–Byzantine style of Notre Dame de la Garde in Marseilles, while the interior is painted with deteriorated frescoes depicting scenes from the Old Testament. Sunday Mass is the best time to visit, when an organist accompanies the choir.

### Hurumzi House

Running a short distance west–east from behind the House of Wonders is **Hurumzi Street**, a great place for rummaging around souvenir and antique shops. Near the end on the right, an unassuming sign marks the entrance to the beautifully restored and opulent **Hurumzi House**, now the *236 Hurumzi* hotel (see p.511). The house was constructed by Tharia Topan, the wealthy Indian businessman who was also responsible for the Old Dispensary, and served as both the sultanate's customs house and Topan's private residence. Topan's good relations with Sultan Barghash allowed him to make it the second-highest building in Stone Town, after the House of Wonders. Its name comes from its use by the British after 1883 to buy the freedom of slaves, to ease the pain of Arab slave-owners after the abolition of slavery; "hurumzi" means "free men" (literally "those shown mercy"). The conversion into the present hotel has been gloriously done, and it's well worth looking around even if you've no intention of staying here; the rooftop restaurant (see p.527) is also the best place to see the colourful tower of the **Shiva Shakti Hindu Temple** across the road.

### Khoja Charitable House

Heading northeast from Hurumzi towards Malawi Road, fans of architecture should definitely seek out **Khoja Charitable House**, dominating a square just off Dega Street. The huge carved door and door frame is a mind-bogglingly intricate and beautiful work of art, and easily Zanzibar's fanciest. The door's inscription explains that it was founded in 1892 for use as a *musafarkhana* (a temporary rest house) for Khoja immigrants from India, most of whom arrived in the 1870s. Nowadays it serves as low-income housing, so ask if you want to take a photo, or be shown around.

# Eating

Stone Town is Tanzania's culinary apotheosis, offering an embarrassment of choice when it comes to **eating out**, from the famous nightly food market in the Forodhani Gardens to dozens of sophisticated or romantic establishments, including several right by the shore, and others on rooftops within the old town. Most menus feature **Zanzibari cuisine**, a subtle combination of the island's spices and coconuts with all manner of seafood. More conservative palates have pasta, pizza, Indian and Chinese, even burgers and chips to choose from.

Apart from the Forodhani Gardens, the market on Creek Road and the daladala stand opposite are also handy for **street food**, especially in the morning for cups of scalding uji (eleusine) porridge, and savoury supu broth. In the evenings, the stalls at the west end of Malawi Road cater to passengers catching night ferries. For something more traditional, seek out a **coffee baraza** inside the old town, where the beans are roasted, ground and brewed on the stone benches (barazas) that line the streets: a tiny cup of piping arabica costs a negligible Tsh50, and you might also find spiced tea called zamzam, named after a sacred well in Mecca. Throw in another coin and you'll also get a diamond-shaped chunk of kashata: sugared cashews, peanuts or coconut. One of the liveliest barazas is "**Jaws Corner**", at the corner of Sokomuhogo and Baghani streets. Its name derives from the film once shown on its TV.

Unfortunately, eating out during **Ramadan** can be quite expensive, as the government bans restaurants not attached to hotels from opening during the day. There are some exceptions, though the cloth screens with which the proceedings are often covered lend a furtive aspect to dining at that time.

## The Forodhani Gardens

For all its refined restaurants, the best place for eating out in Stone Town is at the open-air street food market held in the waterfront **Forodhani Gardens** after sunset, which combines a magical twilight atmosphere with a variety and quality of food to put many a five-star hotel to shame, though check seafood carefully before ordering in low season, when it's not always fresh. Tsh5000 should leave you well and truly stuffed. That said, don't necessarily believe starting prices: it's that ever-endearing Zanzibari habit of asking a "special price, my friend" of tourists.

# Budget

A full meal with soft drinks at the following shouldn't cost more than Tsh12,000. For cheaper eats, try one of the basic eateries along New Mkunazini Road, coming from Creek Road.

**Buni Café** Under the orphanage, Forodhani. A good place for breaking an afternoon's wander, in a high-ceilinged room with rattling fans, or on the veranda outside. It has an ambitious menu, but it's best for light meals and snacks, including vegetarian burgers and fajitas, fresh juices, real coffee (also iced or spiced), smoothies and ice cream. No alcohol. Closed Ramadan daytimes.

**Clove Garden** Facing *Clove Hotel*, Hurumzi St. Lots of plastic chairs and tables under parasols and palm trees, good for typical mainland meals. You're also welcome for snacks or soft drinks. Closed Ramadan daytimes.

**Dolphin Restaurant** Kenyatta Rd, Shangani. An attractive place with a chatty African grey parrot, and good value by local standards, even if portions aren't huge. Try the daily special: things like crab claws, *biriani* or *pilau*, octopus, or green lentils with fish. A la carte is mostly Swahili or Thai-style seafood. Finish your meal with a *shisha* pipe. No alcohol. Closed Ramadan daytimes.

**Luis Yoghurt Parlour & Restaurant** Gizenga St, beside Gallery Bookshop, Baghani. A quiet little place run by a friendly Goan woman with the kitchen equivalent of green fingers (try the octopus). Good for vegetarians, too, with the *thali* featuring several types of lentils, and curried beans. Closed Sun and during Ramadan.

**Old Fort Restaurant** Ngome Kongwe (Old Fort), Forodhani St. A relaxed if somewhat ignored place for lunch, with outdoor tables beside the amphitheatre. It tends to change tenants – and menus – every couple of years, but for now, it offers a good if slightly pricey selection of Asian-Swahili fusion cuisine. Try the barracuda "coco poa" in coconut masala, or red snapper in green curry. Also has snacks, milkshakes, coffee, booze, and a pool table. Closed Ramadan daytimes.

**Pagoda Chinese Restaurant** Suicide Alley, facing *Africa House Hotel*, Shangani. Offers the usual head-scratching selection. Cheap by local standards, and with a good lunchtime special for Tsh6000. No pork.

**Passing Show Hotel** Malawi Rd, Malindi. This looks like a typical Tanzanian restaurant, with linoleum-topped tables, metal-legged furniture and TVs in the corner, and so it is, but the ruckus of diners which make it difficult to find a table at lunchtime is a clue about the food: excellent, cheap and generously portioned. The *pilau*, *biriani* and stews are particularly good, including fish or cashew nuts in coconut sauce. Best for lunch when there's more choice, and for breakfast. Nothing much over Tsh3500. No alcohol. Closed during Ramadan.

**Radha Food House** Off Forodhani St beside *Karibu Inn*, Forodhani. A vegetarian Indian restaurant famed for its *thali*, and snacks, including samosas, spring rolls, lentil or chickpea cakes, refreshing lassi, and perfumed sweets.

**Stone Town Café** Kenyatta Rd. A great place for a light meal or snack, or indeed an all-day breakfast, with plenty of the healthy variety. Except for salads, it's well priced, and the menu includes quite divine cakes, real coffee (cappuccino, espresso, or cardamom-laced), falafel, grilled kingfish with olive tapenade or fillet steak with anchovy garlic, both of these costing a very reasonable Tsh7500. To finish, how about sticky date pudding? Closed Ramadan daytimes.

**Zanzibar Coffee House** Tharia St, Mchambawima. Relaxed and relaxing, sophisticated without being suffocating, and owned by Utengule Coffee Estate near Mbeya, this guarantees excellent arabica, some of which is roasted round the back. Accompanying the coffee are all manner of treats, savoury or sweet, all very reasonably priced at around Tsh3000. You can also decamp to the rooftop, for views over town. Daytime only, closed May.

## Moderate

With Tsh20,000 to spend on a main course with a starter and a drink, most of Stone Town's culinary delights are within reach.

**Amore Mio** Shangani St, Shangani. Right by the ocean under a billowing awning, the owner immodestly but accurately describes his *gelato* as the best on the island, and that – together with the sea view – is the reason for coming. There's also real coffee, milk shakes, fresh juices and salads, and full meals, including pasta, pizza, and a wicked aubergine lasagne (*Malanzane alla Parmigiana*). Usually closed May.

**Archipelago Café & Restaurant** Off Forodhani St, south end of Forodhani Gardens. On an open-sided first-floor terrace with expansive ocean views, it's not just the location that's fresh but what they conjure up in the kitchen, even if the printed menu dwells on touristic tattle such as burgers and steaks. Instead, ask for their daily specials: things like kingfish with chilli and mango sauce, or red snapper simmered in ginger and orange. Finish with sticky date pudding, or a cardamom-spiked coffee. Also has juices and shakes. No alcohol. Closed April–May, and Ramadan daytimes.

**Bahari Restaurant** *Tembo House Hotel*, Shangani St. The menu flirts briefly with most styles, and is one of few to feature a proper Tanzanian breakfast ($10 buffet, complete with cassava leaf porridge), but most delicious is the beach, popular with local kids – there's a lovely row of tables right beside it under Indian almond trees, and if you're lucky you might be able to use the swimming pool. No alcohol. Closed Ramadan daytimes.

**Beyt al Chai** Kelele Square ☎0774/444111. Occupying what may have been a teahouse for well-to-do nineteenth-century ladies, the menu here is pleasingly modest, with no more than half a dozen dishes in each category (meat, fish), providing a French spin on Swahili and mainland Tanzanian favourites (eg plantain soup). Good wine list, and dreamy cakes (think sticky toffee or chocolate).

**Chavda Hotel** Baghani St, Baghani. One of the better rooftop restaurants, open-sided, with marble-topped tables, antique chairs, wooden latticework, and good sunsets. The tempting menu covers the lot, from Zanzibari seafood, Chinese and Indian (they have a *tandoor* oven) to not so exciting European fare. No alcohol. Closed Ramadan daytimes.

**ETC Plaza** Corner of Suicide Alley and Shangani St, Shangani. A congenial and comfortable bar and restaurant with tables on the rooftop, and sea views. Very good food, be it moussaka, big sandwiches or fish: the bouillabaisse is recommended as a starter, followed by a seafood casserole simmered in creamy coconut sauce, or crab *pilipili* with ginger, fresh basil and pepper. They also do milkshakes, tea brewed in brass samovars, and fresh coffee. Closed April–May.

🏃 **The Livingstone** North end of Kenyatta Rd. Right on the beach, this occupies the former British Consulate, where David Livingstone's body was laid out in 1874 before being transported to London. Whilst primarily an upmarket bar, it also serves very good food, although the menu doesn't push the culinary boat out too far from safe touristic shores. Particularly good are its prawns. Also has proper coffee, and tables right on the beach (lit by candles at night).

🏃 **Mercury's** North end of Mizingani Rd near the Big Tree. Named after Zanzibar's most famous son, the rock star Freddie Mercury, this stylish yet informal bar and restaurant has a beautiful oceanside setting, especially striking at sunset (there are plenty of tables on wooden decking over the beach). The fun menu covers both classic Zanzibari dishes and international favourites, and includes plenty of fresh salads and pasta, excellent pizzas, and subtly seasoned seafood. Desserts are hearty: chocolate cake, mango crumble or sticky almond *halua* goo, or you could finish with a *shisha* pipe. There's live music Fri–Sun (see p.528). Closed during Ramadan.

🏃 **Monsoon Restaurant** Forodhani Gardens ☎0777/411362. Top of the range in everything but price, this is one of Zanzibar's most romantic restaurants, whether you eat outside (not during Ramadan) under a canopy of palm trees and bougainvillea, or inside, where you kick off your shoes and sit on cushions or woven rugs in a pillared dining room. The Oriental charm is especially pervasive on Wednesday and Saturday (7–10pm), when the delightful Matona Group explore the rhythmic and melodic synergies of Africa, Asia and Arabia. The menu is similarly inspired, making good use of fruits as well as spices (passion fruit with shellfish), and there are good vegetarian options such as stuffed aubergine. All main courses are accompanied by side dishes you won't find elsewhere, such as pumpkin cooked in creamy coconut. To finish, ice cream, anything with dates, or sticky *halua* should do the trick. Good wine list. Reservations advisable.

**Sambusa Two Tables** Victoria St, just off Kaunda Rd, Vuga ☎ 024/223 1979. An unusual one, situated on the first-floor veranda of a private home, complete with pillows and rugs to lounge on. The food just keeps on coming (samosas, fishcakes, marinated aubergine and superb octopus), and costs $15 for the lot. No alcohol. Reservations advisable. Closed Ramadan daytimes.

## Expensive

Over $20 (Tsh25,000) for a fishy main course is not uncommon at Stone Town's posher places, where full three- or four-course meals with a few drinks may lighten your pocket by anything up to $60.

**La Fenice** Shangani St, one block north of *Africa House Hotel*, Shangani. Italian restaurants can be relied on for style, and this one's no exception. The menu is thoroughly refined, with the full raft of Italian and French Riviera aperitifs (pastis, martinis), pizzas, and some inspired main courses such as dorado cooked with saffron, courgettes and balsamic vinegar. It's not hard to succumb to their ice creams, either, molten chocolate optional.

**Le Spices Rendez-Vous** Kenyatta Rd, Vuga ☎ 0777/410707. With an attractive terracotta-tiled interior, this is justly famed for superb (and generously apportioned) north Indian cuisine, making it impossible to recommend one dish over another. Good for vegetarians too. Closed Mon, and for a month after Easter.

**Tower Top Restaurant** Above *236 Hurumzi*, Hurumzi St ☎ 024/223 2784 or 0777/423266. Stone Town's original rooftop restaurant, and still one of the more enticing, with giant pillows, Persian rugs and inspirational views. Its popularity isn't always a good thing, however: meals can be a bit rushed, and the food isn't always up to scratch. Still, it's hard to beat for atmosphere, especially at weekends, when live music (*ngoma*, *kidumbak* and Taarab respectively) completes the mood. If current plans proceed, you should also be able enjoy light lunches here (à la carte, mostly Mediterranean). Reservations required for dinner. Closed mid-April to end-May.

**Zanzibar Fusion** *Al Johari Hotel*, Shangani. Perched on top of the hotel but below the roof, this is probably the only place in East Africa offering a St Emilion Grand Cru (Tsh165,000), or Cuban cigars. In keeping with the European pretence, most dishes are Italian-inspired, with olives, olive oil and basil featuring strongly, plus a couple of unusual but welcome Thai dishes (Zanzibar has all the ingredients), including the classic *tom yum goong* soup (prawns in a spicy lemongrass broth).

**Zanzibar Serena Inn** Kelele Square, Shangani. This five-star hotel contains two elegant restaurants, the *Baharia* for à la carte, and *The Terrace* on top, though you can also eat by the swimming pool. The various menus feature French *haute cuisine* blended with Swahili flavours and clever use of spices; for example, deep-fried crab claws coated with mustard seeds and served on a tomato and saffron *coulis*, or dark chocolate mousse with lemongrass custard. If you really want to splash out, Tsh60,000 gets you a four-course dinner. In addition to the restaurants, there's also a coffee shop.

# Drinking and nightlife

Tourism has brought with it a small but growing number of **bars and nightclubs**, which sit somewhat uncomfortably in this Muslim town – part of the reason why police have the whimsical habit of bringing an abrupt end to proceedings after midnight (if that should happen, be polite and just go home).

**Africa House Hotel** Suicide Alley, Shangani. Ever since colonial times, this has been the favoured haunt of expats, tourists and mainlanders, drawn to the first-floor *Sunset Bar* terrace, now under a voluptuous draped awning, to watch the orb slip behind the ocean. Just as inspiring is the Persian-style interior, where you lounge around on embroidered cushions and rugs amidst a scatter of samovars and low carved tables. There's also a good snack menu and all-day breakfast, whilst darts, a pool table and *shisha* pipes are available. Friday evenings feature a cheesy but cheery band playing tourist favourites (including the execrable "Jambo Bwana"… you've been warned). Daily until 10pm.

Bwawani Hotel Funguni. This has three drinking holes: *Pemba Bar* inside (daily 11am–11pm), the more pleasant *Rock Café* outdoors (whose adjacent swimming pool may, *inshallah*, one day contain more than just murky rainwater), and, open nightly until 3am or later, the ever popular *Komba Discotheque*, with nary a *mzungu* in sight. No smoking. All are closed during Ramadan.

Dharma Lounge Vuga Rd, next to *Culture Music* Club, Vuga. A small, unpretentious bar favoured by expats, remarkable only for its opening hours: daily from 7.30pm until the last punter drops, usually around 4am.

The Livingstone North end of Kenyatta Rd. A nicely laid-back and very well-stocked bar and restaurant (see p.526) popular with tourists and expats. It's an especially lovely afternoon refuge, whose indubitable draw is its decked seafront terrace (great sunsets, but you can't eat or drink there during Ramadan), partly shaded by Indian almond trees and palms. Also has tables on the beach itself. Good musical tastes except on Friday, when the touristy *Hakuna Matata* band take to the stage. Free wi-fi. Daily until midnight or later.

Mercury's Mizingani Rd. Along with *Africa House Hotel* and *The Livingstone*, this beachside venue is the place for sunsets, and can

be packed whenever there's live music (see below). The bar is very well stocked, with a ton of unique cocktails (try the "Zanzibarbarian" for a scent of cloves, or "Obama's Dawa", a take on Brazilian *caipirinha*). Good coffee, and *shisha* pipes. Daily until at least 10pm; closed during Ramadan.

Monsoon Restaurant Forodhani Gardens. Not just a great restaurant but a lovely place for an afternoon drink, especially on the leafy veranda (not during Ramadan). There's a huge selection of drinks (including one or two bottles of Tanzanian plonk, at Tsh26,000), cocktails, fresh juices, yoghurt or ice-cream smoothies, and a nice selection of teas (spiced, if you like), herbal infusions and – probably the world's best coffee (seriously) – Kilimanjaro Arabica. Daily until midnight.

Starehe Club Shangani St, Shangani. Formerly the European Yacht Club, this is a real dive accessed through a curio shop, with a terrace overlooking the beach and harbour through a chicken-wire fence. Drinks and food are cheap, but the blackboard menu is hopelessly out of touch with the kitchen's actual contents; you're usually limited to chicken with chips or *ugali* (Tsh3000), or *nyama choma* (grilled meat). It gets busy on Saturday night for its reggae disco. Daily until at least midnight.

# Live music

Ignoring tourist-oriented bands performing medleys of old pop, love songs and reggae, Stone Town's **live-music** scene is a modest affair, the big exceptions being its annual festivals (see p.529). At other times, the following venues are the most likely haunts without having to gatecrash a wedding.

Culture Music Club Vuga Rd, Vuga. Headquarters of Zanzibar's best-loved Taarab orchestra, who practice here most afternoons (visitors are welcome). They also perform weekly at *Mercury's*, currently on Friday night.

Dhow Countries Music Academy Old Customs House, Mizingani Rd (Mon–Fri 9am–7pm, Sat 9am–5pm; ☏024/223 4050 or 0777/416529, ⓦ www.zanzibarmusic.org). If anyone knows about upcoming events, venues and the latest vibes, it'll be this lot. They also host concerts on the third Wednesday of each month (8pm; Tsh2000), themed around a certain style or instrument. If you like what you hear, you can also take a course.

Mercury's Mizingani Rd. Especially recommended on Fridays (from 7pm) for Culture Music Club, and on Sundays (also from 7pm), for *kidumbak* performed by Makame Faki. Saturday's musical menu is a sop to tourists.

Monsoon Restaurant Forodhani Gardens. ☏0777/411362. Professor Matona from the Dhow Countries Music Academy plays violin here each Tuesday and Saturday night, accompanied by *tablah* and *udi*. The intimate venue (see p.526) is perfectly suited to this most meditative of performances. Free entry, but you'll be expected to dine. There's also a (gentle) display of drumming on Friday. Reservations advisable.

Ngome Kongwe (Old Fort) Forodhani St. In the dry seasons (June–Sept & Dec–Feb), the fort's open-air amphitheatre hosts evening concerts and performances. Exactly what's on, and entrance fees (if any) change from season to season; a sign outside the fort announces the next one.

Zanzibar Serena Inn Kelele Square, Shangani. Live music nightly at either the restaurants or bar, but only Culture Music Club are worth making tracks for: currently Thursday and Sunday evenings.

"The greatest cultural festival in East Africa" trumpets the brochure, and that's no exaggeration. Established in 1997, the **Zanzibar International Film Festival** (ⓦwww .ziff.or.tz) is a firm fixture on the African cultural calendar, and provides as good a reason as any to try to get to Zanzibar in July, even if you're not into celluloid: the festival also features musicians and acrobats from around the western Indian Ocean. The other big date is the four-day **Sauti za Busara festival** (ⓦ www.busaramusic.org) in February, covering everything from Taarab, Bongo Flava and mainland jazz bands to West Africa's biggest stars, and even Sufi dervishes.

# Shopping

Stone Town is shopaholic paradise, with hundreds of stores selling a huge variety of souvenirs, and prices can be reasonable, too, if you're into bargaining. Locally made items to look out for include all manner of **jewellery**, modern and antique **silverwork**, and wooden **Zanzibari chests** with brass hasps, staples and straps, and secret compartments. More portable are henna, incense, soaps and even spicy bubble bath. Also typically Zanzibari are woven **palm-weave** *mkeka* (mats) and *mkoba* (baskets). Unfortunately, the **spices** for which Zanzibar is famous usually come powdered and pre-packaged, and are nothing you can't buy back home. Rather better are **aromatic oils**, which use coconut oil as a neutral base. Clothing and **fabrics** are another speciality, especially colourful cotton *kangas* (see p.65) and *kitenges*.

The biggest concentration of souvenir and craft shops is along **Gizenga Street** and its continuation, **Changa Bazaar**. **Hurumzi Street**, which runs parallel to Changa Bazaar, is also good and has several henna "tattoo" parlours and chest-makers. The shops below open from Monday to Saturday between 9am and noon and 2pm to 6pm, and on Sunday from 9am to 1pm. The busier ones, especially on and off Kenyatta Road, stay open all day, and may also be open Sunday afternoon.

**Abeid Curio Shop** Cathedral St, facing the cathedral. The best of several antique shops along this street – anything from Zanzibari chests, silverwork and clocks to gramophones, furniture, beds, coins and British colonial kitsch.

**Lookmanji Arts & Antiques** Off Forodhani St, under *Archipelago Café & Restaurant*. A large selection covering most bases, especially good for woodcarvings, masks and batiks.

**Memories of Zanzibar** Kenyatta Rd, opposite Shangani Post Office. Tons of stuff here: reproduction maps, banana-leaf collages, batiks, rugs, some very luxurious Indian fabrics, masks, and loads of jewellery. Also stocks books and CDs. Closed weekends March–May.

**Zanzibar Curio Shop** Changa Bazaar. A glorified junk shop, packed to the rafters with fascinating stuff from old marine compasses and Omani astrolabes to gramophones and novelty tin models from British times.

**Zanzibar Gallery** Kenyatta Rd/Gizenga St. A wide selection, from clothes to pickles, reproductions of ancient maps, Indian fabrics, masks, studded wooden chests, *bao* games and scented toiletries.

**ZAYAA Gallery** Hurumzi St. Outlet for an artists' association, and the Zanzibar Henna Art project, being traditional (and somewhat psychedelic) henna designs adapted for canvas and paper.

# Listings

**Airlines** For websites, see p.32. Air Excel, no office (they're in Arusha) ⓣ024/254 8429, ⓔreservations@airexcelonline.com; Air Tanzania,

under *Abuso Hotel*, Shangani Rd, Shangani ⓣ024/223 0297; Coastal Aviation, airport ⓣ024/223 3112 or 0713/670815,

ⓔreservations@coastal.cc; Emirates, Dr Salimini Rd, just off Gulioni Rd ☏024/223 4950, ⓔemirates@zanzinet.com; Kenya Airways, behind the Big Tree off Mizingani Rd ☏024/223 2042, ⓔkenyaair@zanlink.com; Precisionair, behind the Big Tree off Mizingani Rd ☏024/223 5126 or (call centre) 0787/888417 or 0787/888408–9, ⓔfrisheid @precisionairtz.com; Regional Air, no office (they're in Arusha) ☏027/250 4164, ⓔinfo@regional.co.tz; Safari AirLink Aviation, no office (they're in Dar) ☏0784/237422 or 0713/237422, ⓔflights @safariaviation.info; Tropical Air, Creek Rd, next to Bharmal Building ☏024/223 2511 or 0777/431431, ⓔinfo@tropicalair.co.tz; ZanAir, above ZanTours, behind *Passing Show Hotel* off Malawi Rd ☏024/223 3670, ⓔreservations@zanair.com.

**Banks and exchange** NBC bank, Forodhani St (Mon–Fri 8.30am–4pm, Sat 8.30am–1pm), is slow, but has the best rates, minimal commission and an ATM. There are more banks and machines along Kenyatta Rd. Barclays Bank, ZSTC Building, Gulioni Rd, also has a machine (and one beside *Mazson's Hotel*), but won't change traveller's, cheques. Rates at foreign exchange bureaux are bad but service is much quicker: try New Malindi Bureau de Change, Malawi Rd (Mon–Sat 8am–4pm, Sun 8am–3pm), one of the few to accept traveller's cheques.

**Bookshop** Best is Gallery Bookshop, Gizenga St, facing Cathedral St (daily 9am–6pm, closes at 2pm on Sun in low season).

**Car and motorbike rental** Handled by tour operators; reliable companies include Fisherman Tours and ZanTours (p.532).

**Hospitals and clinics** The government-run Mnazi Mmoja Hospital, Kaunda Rd ☏024/223 1071, isn't brilliantly equipped but has good (Cuban) paediatricians. They also do blood tests, as do a number of clinics, whose reputations vary according to the doctor in charge: any expat will be able to recommend a reliable one. For a dentist, go to Dar es Salaam.

**Internet access** Easiest to find are various internet cafés on Kenyatta Rd, including Shangani Internet Café (daily 8.30am–9pm) and Hasinasoft, beside the post office (daily 8am–9pm). The best one, though, with huge screens and great coffee is *Palace Restaurant & Inter Café*, between *Zanzibar Palace Hotel* and *Hotel Kiponda* (daily 9am–9pm).

**Language courses** The Institute of Kiswahili and Foreign Languages, Vuga Rd (☏024/223 0724, ⓦwww.suza.ac.tz) is the place for tuition, charging $4 per hr. The shortest course is a one-week, 20hr affair. Try also KIU, based in Dar but with some courses here (ⓦwww.swahilicourses.com).

**Newspapers** There's a stall opposite *Passing Show Hotel*, a couple around Darajani daladala terminal, and a selection at Masomo Bookshop, behind the Central Market (Mon–Sat 9am–4pm, Sun 9am–3pm), which also has imported magazines.

## Moving on from Stone Town

### Daladalas and minibuses

Useful **daladala routes** are noted throughout this chapter, with most rides costing Tsh2000. The main place to catch them in Stone Town is **Darajani terminal**, being two places on Creek Road: opposite the Central Market for vehicles heading south and east, and just north of the market for vehicles heading north. The other terminals, out of town but accessible by daladala from Darajani, are **Mwembe Ladu**, 2km east along Gulioni Road, and **Mwana Kwerekwe**, 5km southeast.

The easy way to reach Paje, Jambiani, Bwejuu, Nungwi or Kendwa is on a **beach transfer minibus** for tourists, which will deposit you directly outside your chosen hotel. Most tour operators and all budget hotels in Stone Town can fix you up with a seat. Fares are negotiable, but shouldn't be more than $10. Transfers arranged through upmarket hotels and travel agents cost $75 to $120 per vehicle.

### Flights

To reach the **airport**, catch daladala #350 or #505 (both marked "U/Ndege"; Tsh350) from Darajani, or grab a cab: the normal tourist fare is Tsh12,000, but, unlike rides in from the airport, the ride out from Stone Town can quite easily be bargained down. The only flights within Zanzibar are to Pemba (ZanAir, Coastal Aviation and Tropical Air), costing $80–90. For mainland Tanzania, there are over a dozen daily flights to Dar es Salaam, and others to Tanga, Arusha, and many of the safari parks. Departure **taxes** should be included in the fare. If not, be sure you have Tsh6000 for domestic flights, or $38 (including safety levy) for international ones. Airlines are listed on p.32.

**Pharmacies** The main pharmacies are in the streets around the market, including Fahud Pharmacy, Creek Rd, just north of the market (daily 8am–midnight; ☎024/223 5669 or 0777/428888).
**Police** Malawi Rd/Creek Rd, Malindi ☎024/223 0771 or 024/223 0772.
**Post and couriers** Shangani Post Office, Kenyatta Rd. DHL, Kelele Square ☎024/223 8281.
**Supermarkets and groceries** The main outlet is Shamshuddin, off Creek Rd behind Central Market (Mon–Sat 9am–8pm, Sun 9am–2pm; closed Fri noon–2.30pm). Malkia Minimarket, with less choice, is at the south end of the tunnel in Forodhani (Mon–Sat 10am–10pm; closed 3–7pm during Ramadan). There's an unnamed supermarket on Gizenga St, one block from the post office.

**Swimming pools** *Bwawani Hotel*'s pool is the only one definitely open to day-visitors, but it's usually dry. You might get lucky at *Tembo House Hotel*, but it depends on the mood of whoever's at reception.
**Telephones** You can make international calls at several places on Kenyatta Rd, the cheapest being Shangani Internet Café (daily 8.30am–9pm; Tsh1000 per min).
**Travel agents** Coastal Travels, Kelele Square ☎024/223 9664, ⓦwww.coastal.cc; Tabasam Tours & Travel, Kenyatta Rd facing *Dolphin Restaurant* ☎024/223 0322, ⓦwww.tabasamzanzibar .com; ZanTours, behind *Passing Show Hotel* off Malawi Rd 024/223 3042 or 024/223 3116, ⓦwww.zantours.com.

# Around Stone Town

Most of the attractions around Stone Town can easily (and quite cheaply) be visited on day-trips run by local tour companies. **Spice tours** are virtually obligatory, and centre on guided walks around a farm where you're shown herbs, spices and other crops, to finish with a slap-up meal. Spice tours also include a visit to the ruined nineteenth-century **Kidichi Persian Baths**, and may also include the **Maruhubi Ruins** (see p.534) or Mangapwani's **slave chamber** (p.535). **Costs** are around $15 per person on a shared tour, or upwards of $25–35 per person on a private trip. The spice tour we'd recommend though is the "Princess Salme Tour" (see p.535), costing $55–70 per person.

### Ferries

Tickets for most **ferries** (to Dar es Salaam or Pemba) can be bought inside the port; buy in advance to be sure of a seat, and to minimize hassle from *papasi*. The offices are open until 6pm, but tickets for night ferries can be bought until departure time. If you're being trailed by a *papasi*, ensure it's you and not him who does the talking when buying. Alternatively, buy your ticket from one of the ever-changing offices outside the port: Mizingani Road or Malawi Road. **Tourist fares** ("non-residents") are priced in dollars and include $5 port tax; you can pay the shilling equivalent, but exchange rates are bad. Don't try to get the cheaper "resident" fares, or you'll run into trouble with the ticket inspector.

To **Dar es Salaam**, fastest are the *Sea Express*, *Sea Star*, *Sea Bus* and *Sepideh* (all $35 economy, $40 first-class; 2hr–2hr 30min). Cheaper but slower are *Flying Horse*, *Aziza* and *New Happy* ($20–25 economy; 3hr 30min–5hr).

For **Pemba**, boats and schedules change constantly; the following just gives a rough idea. Currently, the fastest boat, and the only one to sail by day, is the twice-weekly *Sepideh* (3hr; $40 economy, $50 first-class; ⓦwww.megaspeedliners-zanzibar.com). At the time of writing, all other sailings ($25) were overnight, leaving Stone Town around 9pm to arrive in Mkoani just before dawn. The most reliable was the large *Serengeti*, three times a week (Tues, Thurs, Sat) from the port's main section, accessed from the west end of Malawi Road. Other boats worth asking about are the *Maendeleo*, the *Seagull*, and the *Spice Islander*.

Also popular are **boat trips** to islands and reefs just offshore, most costing $30–40 per person for half a day. Other than beach lounging, **snorkelling** is the main activity: very good off Changuu Island (which also has giant tortoises), and almost miraculous off Chumbe Island. For information on **scuba diving**, see pp.512–513.

## Changuu Island

A trip to **CHANGUU (PRISON ISLAND)**, a 700m-long strip 5km northwest of Stone Town, makes a great excursion. Once a transit camp for slaves, the imposing building on the island's northeastern side was erected by the British in the 1890s to serve as a prison, but was only ever used as a **yellow-fever quarantine camp**. As even that use was limited, the island became a popular weekend retreat for the well-to-do. Snorkelling on the surrounding reefs is always fun, and the island's **coral rag forest** is home to duiker antelopes, bats, butterflies and weavers, but Changuu's long-lasting attraction is its fenced-in colony of over a hundred **Aldabra giant tortoises** (*changuu*), descended from four individuals imported from the Seychelles in 1919.

---

### Tour operators in Stone Town

Stone Town's **tour operators** are two-a-penny. Among the better ones are:

**Eco+Culture Tours** Hurumzi St, facing *240 Hurumzi* ☎024/223 3731 or 0777/410873, ⓦwww.ecoculture-zanzibar.org. A good range of options, often with a cultural spin. Their spice tour is particularly good, as is their unique tour of Unguja Ukuu and Menai Bay in the south ($45–70 per person).

**Fisherman Tours & Travel** Vuga St ☎024/223 8791, ⓦwww.fishermantours.com. Long established and efficient, offering full-day cultural tours of Nungwi or Mangapwani in addition to the usual excursions.

**Jojoba Tours** Shangani St just south of Kelele Square; also facing *Tembo House Hotel* ☎024/223 8183 or 0777/410346, ⓔjojobatours@yahoo.co.uk. The most inventive outfit, adding a cultural spin to most of their trips. Particularly recommended is their day-long "North Tour", packing in fishermen at Mkokotoni, swimming in a cave, Zanzibar's only maker of dhow nails, a women's group that makes scented soaps, and time on the beach, all for a mere $35 per person (minimum four) but excluding lunch.

**Mitu's Spice Tour** Funguni Rd, Malindi ☎024/223 4636 or 0777/418098. Self-proclaimed inventor of spice tours, Mitu's is also the cheapest: $13 per person on a shared tour.

**The Original Dhow Safaris** Mbweni, but bookable at the *Zanzibar Serena Inn* ☎024/223 2088 or 0773/723495, ⓦwww.dhowsafaris.net. Dhow cruises on one of three specially designed *jahazis*. Sailing off daily is a six-hour sandbank picnic ($80 per person), which includes Changuu Island, snorkelling, and lunch on a sandbank; and a two-hour sunset cruise ($40 per person), with drinks taken to the sound of live Taarab.

**Sama Tours** Gizenga St, also at *Hotel Kiponda* ☎024/223 3543 or 0777/430385, ⓦwww.samatours.com. Knowledgeable, unhurried, and one of few whose quoted prices include meals and entrance fees. Their unique offering is a six-hour cultural tour of Vijijini suburb south of Stone Town ($30–45 per person).

**Tabasam Tours & Travel** Kenyatta Rd, facing *Dolphin Restaurant* ☎024/223 0322, ⓦwww.tabasamzanzibar.com. Calm and professional if a little pricier than the others.

**ZanTours** Behind *Passing Show Hotel*, Malindi ☎024/223 3042 or 024/223 3116, ⓦwww.zantours.com. Thoroughly reliable; it's part of the ZanAir group.

Weighing over 200kg, the biggest – which can live to one hundred years – are second in size only to Galapagos tortoises, and like their cousins were contemporaries of dinosaurs. Tsh1000 buys you a bowl of spinach and quality bonding time, but watch out for sharp beaks.

The island's **hotel**, *Changuu Island Private Paradise*, is reviewed on p.518. Tour operators and hotels can arrange **excursions** here ($30–40 per person for half a day, including snorkelling). Boats take half an hour each way, giving you two or three hours to explore. Trips can be extended to a full day, perhaps in combination with snorkelling off Bawe Island. Arranging things yourself isn't necessarily cheaper: if you want to try, talk with the boatmen hanging around the "Big Tree" on Mizingani Road. A fair price for the ride there and back would be $35 for the boat, plus $6 per person for entrance fees. **Meals and drinks** (seafood upwards of $12) are available at the "prison" building, and at *Mathews Restaurant* on the island's eastern tip: a beautifully restored nineteenth-century holiday home built over an arcade, and with a broad patio up front overlooking the sea.

## Chumbe Island

The shallow reefs around **CHUMBE ISLAND**, south of Stone Town, enclose some of the finest coral gardens on earth, as aptly described by the island's name, which means a creature, or a being. Coral growth and diversity are among East Africa's highest, with more than two hundred species of stone corals (around ninety percent of all East African species), plus over four hundred kinds of fish, including blue-spotted stingrays, moray eels, dolphins, and – if you're lucky – turtles or batfish. Needless to say, **snorkelling** is superb, but it's not just marine life that makes Chumbe special. The island's pristine **coral rag forest** contains a surprisingly rich variety of flora and fauna, whose survival is largely due to human settlement having been limited to temporary fishermen's camps and the keeper of the lighthouse (built in 1904; its 132 steps can be climbed). The forest, which can be explored along **nature trails**, is one of the last natural habitats for two rare species: the arboreal **coconut crab**, and **Ader's duiker**. At low tide, you can explore mangroves, or poke around rock pools for starfish, crabs and other shellfish. On the bleak and rocky eastern side of the island, look out for 15,000-year-old **fossilized giant clams**.

Chumbe is visitable as a day-trip, or by staying at its intimate and justifiably expensive lodge (see p.518). The daily **boat** leaves *Mbweni Ruins Hotel*, 7km south of Stone Town, at 10am, taking half an hour for the 8km crossing. The return trip costs $80 per person, which includes snorkelling (and snorkelling guide), and lunch on a beautiful sea-view terrace. Visitor numbers are strictly limited, so day-trips must be booked exactly two days before: ☎024/223 1040 or 0777/413232, ⓦwww.chumbeisland.com.

## Mbweni

7km south of Stone Town, **MBWENI** tells part of the story of the fight against the slave trade. At its heart is a seven-acre Anglican mission established by the Oxford-based **Universities' Mission to Central Africa** in 1871. Four years later it became a colony for freed slaves. The chapel and school are in ruins, but its church – St John's – still stands, and services are held every Sunday at 9am. In its graveyard are the remains of Caroline Thackeray, the school's first headmistress and cousin of novelist William Makepeace Thackeray. Mbweni's highlight though is its cascaded **botanical garden**, founded by the Scottish physician **Sir John Kirk** during his lengthy stint as Britain's first Consul

▲ Snorkelling trip, Chumbe Island

General (1866–87). A botanist by profession (in which capacity he had accompanied Livingstone up the Zambezi), Kirk was a major authority on East African flora, and introduced many of the 650 species found in the garden, including sausage trees, Madagascan periwinkle, devil's backbone and over 150 palms. This variety has in turn attracted a wide range of birds: sixty at the last count. Many of the plants are labelled, and there's a **nature trail** which you can walk in the company of a guide from the nearby *Mbweni Ruins Hotel*, or in the company of a check-list (also at Ⓦ www.mbweni.com).

**Getting to Mbweni** is easiest by taxi: Tsh10,000 is good going. Alternatively, catch a #505 daladala from Darajani and get off at Mazizini police station beside the signposted junction for Mbweni. Follow that road and turn right after 800m. The ruins and the hotel are 900m along. The hotel has a restaurant and bar.

## The Maruhubi and Mtoni ruins

The shoreline north of Stone Town was favoured by Zanzibar's sultans for palaces, all but one of which (used by the government and therefore inaccessible) burned down many moons ago. The most easily visited **ruins**, both of them on the #502 daladala route from Darajani on Creek Road, are Maruhubi and Mtoni. The ruins of **MARUHUBI PALACE**, built by Sultan Barghash in 1882 to house his harem of 99 concubines and one wife, nestle in a grove of mango trees and coconut palms 3km north of Stone Town. Dark legend tells of concubines being killed if they did not satisfy the sultan's wishes, and of others being put to death after fulfilling the carnal desires of visiting dignitaries. The palace was gutted in 1899 and the marble from its Persian-style baths stolen, leaving only the bath-house foundations, an overgrown collection of massive coral stone pillars, and a small aqueduct that carried water from a nearby spring to cisterns. Access costs $2.

One kilometre north of Maruhubi, just beyond *Mtoni Marine* hotel (see p.518; it also has restaurants and a bar), are the older and more atmospheric ruins of **MTONI PALACE**, built by Sultan Seyyid Saïd between 1828 and 1832, and levelled by fire in 1914. At one time, the palace housed the sultan's three wives, 42 children and hundreds of concubines. The gardens contained a menagerie of wildlife, including ostriches, flamingos and gazelles. The ruins are quite substantial, and include an impressive colonnaded courtyard, but it's from love that the palace draws its fame, as it was home to **Princess Salme**, a daughter of Seyyid Saïd, whose elopement with a German merchant in 1866 caused a colossal scandal. In her autobiography, *Memoirs of an Arabian Princess*, she beautifully evokes the opulence of palace life in the 1850s and 1860s, when she was a child. The ruins can be seen off the path that goes beside the oil depot to the beach just beyond *Mtoni Marine*, but are best experienced on the **Princess Salme Tour** (☎0777/430117, ⓦwww.mtoni.com; $55–70 per person). This starts with the ruins, and continues with a boat ride to Bububu for a fanciful "coffee ceremony" in a beautiful Omani house (with an enchanting Alice in Wonderland-style garden) at which Salme is said to have spent her last night before eloping. Following this is a Salme-themed spice tour, finishing with lunch prepared by a local family. If you just want to visit the ruins, a guided tour – ask on arrival – costs $3.

## Mangapwani

Just under 25km north of Stone Town is **MANGAPWANI**, a fishing village with a lovely stretch of beach and a couple of caves in the coral ragstone facing the sea. The name means "Arabian Shore", possibly alluding to one of the caves, a man-made chamber used for hiding slaves after the trade with Oman was outlawed in 1845. The cave saw even more use after the slave trade with the African mainland was banned in 1873, when black-market prices took off. The dank and claustrophobic **slave chamber** is one of the most shocking of Zanzibar's sights and, like the cells beneath the former slave market in Stone Town, conveys the full horror of the slave trade. It consists of two rectangular cells hewn out of the soft coral rock, accessed along a deep and narrow passage and sealed by a heavy door, which was originally covered with coral ragstone, all of which served to hide slaves from the prying eyes of British Navy cruisers on anti-slavery patrols. Two kilometres south is a **coral cavern**, this one natural, and of interest for its spiritual importance to locals. The cavern, which contains a small pool of fresh water, was discovered in the early 1800s by a plantation slave-boy when one of the goats he was herding fell into the void. Like other caves in Zanzibar and on the mainland, it contains offerings to ancestors left by locals seeking their intercession in mortal affairs – a good example of the syncretic nature of rural Zanzibari Islam, which blends orthodox teachings with popular beliefs – much to the anguish of urbane imams.

Mangapwani can be visited on a spice tour if the entire group agrees. To reach Mangapwani by **public transport**, catch a #102 ("Bumbwini") daladala from Stone Town's Darajani terminal. Some daladalas turn left off the main road into the village and continue towards the coast, which is preferable if you don't fancy walking. If you're dropped on the main road, which is more likely, walk northwest through Mangapwani village. The turning for the **coral cavern** is 600m along on the left – it lies 1km south of there along a narrow track. For the **slave chamber** (Tsh1000 entry), ignore the turning and continue on to the coast. Just before the shore (roughly 1.5km from the main road, or 1km beyond the coral cavern turning), the road veers north – the slave chamber is 500m further on.

If all you want is an easy day-trip, consider taking lunch at the stunningly situated **Mangapwani Serena Beach Club**, halfway between the coral cavern and slave chamber, and right on the shore over a private beach. For $50, paid at the *Zanzibar Serena Inn* (see p.517), you get transport, a slap-up seafood buffet, and a good half-day on the beach, plus – at extra cost – snorkelling, canoeing and dhow trips. With luck, they'll have a dhow heading there from Stone Town, which will cost $60 for the package.

# Southern Unguja

Stunning beaches, romantic hotels, superb restaurants, snorkelling, scuba diving, an ancient mosque, a ruined palace, a **national park** comprising primeval forest, mangroves, monkeys, dhow trips, dolphins – **southern Unguja** has it all. And despite the proliferation of hotels, most of the area retains a local and untrammelled kind of feeling, where you're as likely to share the sand with fishermen and women harvesting seaweed as you are with fellow tourists.

The best **beaches** hug most of the southeastern shore, from **Kae** in the north to **Jambiani** in the south. In general, the hotels in this area are small-scale bungalow "resorts", and pretty good value considering their location, on some of Africa's most beautiful shores. In keeping with Zanzibar's proud culinary tradition, restaurants can be truly excellent, whether inside hotels, or run independently. As with the northeast coast, the ocean recedes by a kilometre or more at low tide, so **swimming** straight from the shore is only possible in two six-hour windows each day. Most hotels can fix you up with a dhow or outrigger for snorkelling, and there are also a handful of reliable **dive centres** (see p.513). On Unguja's southern tip, **Kizimkazi** is the other main place for tourists, not on account of its beaches (most of which disappear at high tide), but for its **dolphin tours**, and for snorkelling or scuba diving in the Menai Bay Conservation Area. Also part of the conservation area is **Fumba Peninsula** to the west, which has just one very fine hotel, a dive centre, and is the base for Zanzibar's best day-trip, the so-called "**Safari Blue**" dhow excursion. Lastly, a note on money: there are no money-changing facilities anywhere covered in this section, so change all the cash you'll need before setting off from Stone Town.

## Jozani forest and around

Driving to or from southeast Unguja, it's hard to miss the magnificent **Jozani Forest**, home to rare (but here easily seen) red colobus monkeys. Two places nearby offer a closer look at the forest's other denizens: **Zala Park**, for reptiles and dikdik antelopes, and the **Zanzibar Butterfly Centre**, a local breeding project.

### Jozani–Chwaka Bay National Park

Thirty eight kilometres southeast of Stone Town is the entrance to the fifty-square-kilometre **JOZANI–CHWAKA BAY NATIONAL PARK.** At its heart is **Jozani Forest**, a thick, tangled jungle famous for its red colobus monkeys (sightings of which are almost guaranteed), and also blue or Sykes' monkeys, bush pigs, diminutive Ader's duiker and suni antelopes, elephant shrews, chameleons, and a fluttering multitude of birds and butterflies. Several **nature trails**, from easy hour-long strolls to half-day hikes, allow you to explore all the forest has to offer at your own pace. The national park also encompasses other ecologically connected areas, including the mangroves and intertidal zones of Chwaka Bay to the north. Similar environments can be seen along the short **Pete–Jozani mangrove boardwalk**, which starts and finishes in a car park 1km south of the park entrance. Mangrove **birdlife** is rich if characteristically elusive: lucky twitchers might spot purple-banded or olive sunbirds, kingfishers or blue-cheeked bee-eaters.

The park (daily 7.30am–5pm) levies an $8 **entrance fee**, which covers the forest itself, the mangrove boardwalk and the services of a **guide**, although a tip is (rightly) expected. Taking a guide along is obligatory if you want to see colobus monkeys inside the forest, but the troop by the gate can be seen on your own. Unfortunately, some **guides** and rangers have been known to try to charge for each thing separately; feel free to refuse. The best **time to visit** is early morning when there are fewer people, wildlife is more active and the light, filtered through the lush vegetation, is deliciously soothing. It quietens down again in the evening, when conditions are superb for photography.

## Practicalities

Most people visit Jozani when returning from a dolphin tour at Kizimkazi, but it can also be reached by **public transport**: daladalas (Tsh1400) from Stone Town's Darajani terminal to Bwejuu (#3240), Jambiani (#309) and – most frequently – Makunduchi (#310), pass the gate throughout the day. The last daladala back to Stone Town passes around sunset, but it's wise to get to the road by 5pm. The various nature trails are described in leaflets available at the **information centre** at the gate, which also has a gift shop and snack bar.

### Zanzibar Butterfly Centre and Zala Park

Neatly complementing a visit to Jozani is the **Zanzibar Butterfly Centre** (ZBC), 1km west of the park entrance (daily 9am–5pm; $5 or Tsh6000; ⓦ www.zanzibarbutterflies.com), which offers visitors the chance of seeing over a dozen of the fifty-odd species of butterfly native to Jozani. They live in some five hundred square metres of tropical garden enclosed by netting, which you're free to walk around in. The centre's primary purpose is to reduce pressure on the forest's natural resources by providing an alternative source of income for villagers living on the fringes, in this case through the farming and selling of pupae to collectors internationally. Profits from the project are reinvested locally. Another local scheme worth visiting is **Zala Park** (the Zanzibar Land Animals Park), 5.5km south of Jozani along the road to Kizimkazi (daily 8.30am–5.30pm; $5 or Tsh6000, including guided tour). Founded by a schoolteacher in 1994 to educate his charges on environmental matters, it's basically a small zoo for reptiles and amphibians, but also contains dikdik antelopes as part of a breeding experiment.

# Menai Bay

Most of south Unguja's shoreline, with its innumerable mangrove-lined inlets, hidden beaches, coral atolls and sandbanks, is part of the **Menai Bay Conservation Area**, created in 1997 as a "Gift to the Earth", as a result of which hotel development is limited to just one lodge on Fumba Peninsula, and a fledgling hotel strip at **Kizimkazi**. Unless you want somewhere facing west for ocean sunsets, or wish to dive off what are still largely unexplored reefs (see p.512), the south coast isn't a patch on the powdery pleasures gracing Unguja's southeastern coast, covered later on. Kizimkazi comes into its own, however, for **dolphin tours** (see p.538), although their popularity

Menai Bay is home to resident pods of bottlenose and Indo-Pacific humpback **dolphins**, swimming with which is, for many visitors, a dream come true. However, the effects of often hundreds of suncream-smothered tourists leaping into the water each day to "play and swim with the dolphins" (as the brochures like to put it) are still subject to on-going research, so think twice before taking part in the melee. If you do decide to go, try and adhere to the following **guidelines**: encourage your skipper not to chase the pods; if you enter the water, do so away from the dolphins and with as little disturbance as possible; when in the water, stay close to the boat; avoid sudden movements; allow the dolphins to come to you and do not under any pretext attempt to touch them. Obviously, guaranteeing sightings of dolphins is not possible, but in general the **best months**, when you'd be most unlucky not to see any grinning cetaceans, are August to December.

### Dolphin tours

Zanzibar's classic **dolphin tour** lasts just two or three hours, and starts at Kizimkazi, whose former fishermen have turned the experience into a veritable industry. Buying a place on a **prearranged trip** through a tour operator (p.532) or via most hotels in Stone Town or southeastern Unguja is the easiest way to go about things. Prices start at $30–35 per person from Stone Town excluding lunch, but for that you'll be sharing with up a dozen other people. Lunch can add $3–15 depending on what and where you eat. If you combine the tour with a visit to Jozani Forest, add $8 to cover the park entry fee. Note that most of the trips are shared affairs no matter what you're paying; the only real difference with more expensive excursions is that group sizes are smaller, road transport is by Land Cruiser rather than minibus, and the boats are fibreglass rather than wood.

**Arranging things yourself**, assuming you spend the night before or after in Kizimkazi, has the advantage of being able to push off early morning or late afternoon, avoiding rush hour. It also lets you extend the trip to a full day, including, for instance, snorkelling around **Pungume Island**, 13km offshore. To avoid Kizimkazi's often offensively pushy touts, arrange things through a hotel as early as possible: *Karamba Resort* is reasonably priced, and can also arrange other trips in Menai Bay, too. The main cost is boat rental, generally $30–40 for a few hours, to which add various per-person costs: entry fee ($3), snorkelling equipment ($3–10) and, optionally, lunch. Whatever you arrange, be sure the boat has adequate shade.

### "Safari Blue" excursions

A highly recommended alternative to the standard dolphin tour is a full-day **"Safari Blue" excursion**. Starting in Fumba on the west side of Menai Bay, it kicks off with a dhow trip to a sandbank for guided snorkelling, beach lounging and snacks, before cruising on to Kwale Island for a spot of (non-harassing) dolphin-watching, a sumptuous seafood lunch and tropical-fruit tasting in the shade of some tamarind trees. The day includes a nosy around a mangrove-lined lagoon, the chance to climb an ancient baobab tree, and *ngalawa* (outrigger) sailing. The trip's success has spawned a number of imitators, but as there's not much difference in cost between those and the real thing, to guarantee quality, safety and ethics (the project employs seventy local villagers and supports a bunch of worthy projects, too), we'd recommend you settle for the original – for more information, see Ⓦwww.safariblue.net. The trips leave daily except Fridays. **Bookings** can be made through most of the Stone Town tour operators reviewed on p.532. The basic cost is $55 from Fumba, so expect to pay $80–100 per person including transport from Stone Town.

bring some ecological headaches, too: a less intrusive way of seeing dolphins is a "**Safari Blue**" dhow excursion from **Fumba Peninsula**, on the bay's western side (see p.538).

## Fumba Peninsula

The northwest side of Menai Bay is bounded by **Fumba Peninsula**, the tip of which is barely 18km south of Stone Town. There's currently only one hotel: the upmarket ⚑ **Fumba Beach Lodge** (☏ 0777/860504, ⊛ www.fumbabeachlodge .com; HB ❾), a welcoming Dutch-run place that boasts an impressive 2km of coastline containing three sandy coves accessed via steps. The twenty rooms, most with sea views, are spacious, breezy and very nicely decked out in a fresh and colourful blend of Scandinavian and Swahili styles. For something really special, spend a little more for a suite, complete with outdoor shower, rooftop terrace, or even – in the case of a "Baobab Suite" built around a tree – a double bath with a view. Amenities include a cliff-top infinity pool, a bar built into an old dhow, excellent food, therapeutic massages and other beautifications, windsurfing, kayaking, and a PADI-accredited dive centre, the latter also quite happy to arrange snorkelling or picnic trips.

## Kizimkazi

Almost at the southern tip of Unguja, 53km from Stone Town, **KIZIMKAZI** is known to tourists for its **dolphin tours**, and to historians for being one of the oldest continuously inhabited settlements on Zanzibar, one that served for a time as capital of the island's traditional rulers, the Wawinyi Wakuu, before the Omani conquest in the eighteenth century. It also contains East Africa's oldest standing **mosque** (1107 AD), which – exceptionally – can be visited by non-Muslims. Kizimkazi is actually two places. **Kizimkazi Dimbani** is the village itself, set behind a lovely sheltered bay in which dozens of outrigger canoes bob up and down at their moorings. Three kilometres to the south is **Kizimkazi Mkunguni** (also called Kizimkazi Mtendeni), which has a modest hotel strip, and a couple of ancient **baobab trees**, the older and larger of which is thought to be over six hundred years old, and was used as a transmissions mast during World War II.

Kizimkazi's **beaches**, especially Kizimkazi Mkunguni's, are strongly tidal, and disappear completely when the water is in. The shoreline behind is also rocky, so you can forget about barefooting from dawn to dusk. The prettiest beach is the bay in Kizimkazi Dimbani, although it's in full view of the village, and fishermen mending nets or making rope. Locals are used to seeing tourists in swimsuits, though, and indeed local kids messing about tend to wear nothing at all, so don't feel awkward. To get to know the place better, any hotel can arrange a guided **village walk**; the $5 fee benefits the local school.

### Arrival and accommodation

To reach Kizimkazi independently, catch a #326 **daladala** from Stone Town's Darajani terminal; they run throughout the day. Dolphin tours aside, tourism has never quite taken off here, so although there are several hotels and resorts scattered around, the cheaper ones tend to open, close or otherwise change frequently enough. If you're on a budget, arrive early and have a sniff around before settling in. Kizimkazi's location and the proximity of bushy vegetation means you can expect mosquitoes, so cover up in the evenings or use repellent.

**Coral Reef Bungalows** Kizimkazi Mkunguni, 400m south of the baobabs ☎0757/781558 or 0777/470753, ⍟www.coralreefzanzibar.com. Six cramped but clean rooms in three *bandas* at the back of a large beachside plot adjacent to *Swahili Beach Resort* (no views from the rooms), all with double beds, a/c, fan, box nets, and bathrooms with hot water. There's a good restaurant overlooking the ocean, and a warm welcome. BB ❹

🏃 **Karamba Resort** Kizimkazi Dimbani ☎0773/166406, ⍟www.karambaresort .com. This Spanish-run hotel (not really a resort) on the northern headland flanking the bay and backed by gardens is the best mid-range option, thanks in part to glorious views from each of the twenty large and bright rooms (two per bungalow), their verandas, and – in the more expensive rooms – from large open-air baths. The beach below the headland, accessed by steps, disappears at high tide, but there's a swimming pool. The large bar and restaurant is popular with day-trippers, but gets somnolent at night. Other facilities include a children's playground and aromatic massages combinable with yoga, Reiki or reflexology for a spiritual pep. Closed April & May. BB ❻

**Promised Land Beach Resort** Kizimkazi Mkunguni, 1.5km south of the baobabs ☎0773/895950, ✉shaaban1976@hotmail.com. A nice one for backpackers, albeit very spartan at present. Arranged along one side of a long, sloping rocky plot are nine tents under thatch shelters, providing Zanzibar's all-round cheapest accommodation, at just $20 a tent including breakfast. For

something more comfortable, the main house at the back has a double room, plus two dorms ($25 per person) accessed up very steep staircases (watch out if you've been boozing), plus hammocks. The beds are saggy but they have box nets, and it's all perfectly fine for the price, especially with use of the kitchen included. Food can also be cooked to order, and there's a shoreline bar. BB ❸–❹

**Unguja Resort** Kizimkazi Mkunguni, 500m north of the baobabs ☎0773/573411, ⍟www .ungujaresort.com. Set in lush gardens behind a narrow beach, this is small, personable and very stylish in a rustic way, with just twelve large, two-storey villas cleverly designed with soft, rounded forms, all with terraces, sea views and plenty of privacy. Some also have a/c, but really cool are the ones with private plunge pools! Other facilities include a swimming pool, wi-fi, fine dining, various trips, and a branch of the One Ocean scuba diving company. BB ❾

**Zanzibar Dolphin View Paradise** Kizimkazi Mkunguni, 2.5km south of the baobabs ☎024/550 1166, ⍟www.zdvp.com. Kizimkazi's biggest resort, with a proper beach in a sheltered cove, a lovely infinity pool, and thirty very large and almost pyramidal two-storey villas, all sea-facing and well-equipped, including 42-inch flat-screen satellite TVs, and – in 21 of them – private plunge pools. The resort comes complete with heaps of activities, including a health spa, and if you can fill an entire villa (six people), it's an utter bargain, costing just $45–70 per person in high season. BB ❽–❾

## Eating and drinking

Kizimkazi's popularity with day-trippers means there's plenty of choice for **eating out**. With the exception of *Jichane Restaurant*, the following remain open during Ramadan.

**Cabs Restaurant** Kizimkazi Dimbani. An enticing menu here, particularly good on seafood (straight from the fishermen). Try the seashell meat with potatoes, spices and ginger. Evening barbecues are held whenever there are enough hungry

mouths to make it worthwhile. Around Tsh10,000 a plate.

**Coral Reef Bungalows** Kizimkazi Mkunguni. A wide-ranging menu, and a lovely beachfront location on a low coral rise. It's hard to go wrong

### Kizimkazi Cultural Music Festival

A newcomer to Zanzibar's festival programme is the **Kizimkazi Cultural Music Festival**. The first event, held at the end of December 2008 at the Rasta-run *Promised Land Beach Resort* (contact them for information), pulled together an impressive line-up of Tanzanian musicians covering all styles from Bongo Flava and reggae to *ngoma* and ever popular rumba-powered *muziki wa dansi*. Whether or not it survives remains to be seen, but it's certainly worth asking about.

with grilled or marinated fish, especially when accompanied by home-made tamarind sauce. Around Tsh10,000 a plate.

**Jichane Restaurant** Kizimkazi Mkunguni, near the big baobab. This, Kizimkazi's cheapest restaurant, is where the bargain-basement dolphin tours stop by for lunch. Basic meals cost upwards of Tsh3000 (at least that's what locals pay), but if you want something other than rice with fish or chicken –

prawns, for instance – ask what's available in the morning. They also sell beer.

**Karamba Resort** Kizimkazi Dimbani. Large but still sophisticated, this gets packed for lunch and has a great reputation for seafood, featuring sushi and sashimi. The pasta is unusually good, as are as might be expected from a Spanish-run place – tapas and paella. They also cater well for vegetarians. Seafood costs upwards of $15; other mains are around $10.

---

## The Mwaka Kogwa Festival

The nebulous town of **Makunduchi**, in Unguja's southeastern corner, is a strange place indeed, not least for its faceless blocks of Soviet-style flats built in the early 1970s by East German "Friendship Brigades". Despite the visibly crumbling "veneer" of socialist modernity, it's a very traditional sort of place, something best experienced during the exuberant **Mwaka Kogwa Festival**. Held in the third or fourth week of July, the four-day shindig was introduced by Zoroastrian immigrants from Shiraz (now Iran) over a millennium ago to celebrate the Persian New Year (Nairuzi). Although the dates no longer coincide, they do align with the end of the harvest after the long rains and the traditional resumption of dhow traffic, and so as a celebration of new beginnings the festival has survived.

The proceedings begin with houses being swept clean, and a **ritual bath** in the sea (*mwaka kogwa* means "washing the year"). By mid-morning, most of Makunduchi's inhabitants descend on the centre of town, where a medicine man (*mganga*) erects a **thatched hut** accompanied by the singing of women. A group of elders enter the hut, upon which the *mganga* sets it alight. The men's subsequent "escape" gives a fine opportunity to the more theatrically inclined; the smoke that issues at this moment indicates the direction in which the fortunes of the following year will blow, and it's perhaps no coincidence that the Kiswahili word for the year's end, *kibunzi*, also means a divining board.

The burning of the hut is followed by the settling of old grievances in the form of not entirely **mock fights** between two groups of men, one from the north of Makunduchi, the other from the south, who, after taunting each other in the best football hooligan style (and chanting pleas to spirits), indulge in a fine display of unbridled machismo by flailing each other with banana stems, a dusty chaotic brawl spurred on by raucous insults from the ever-vocal women. Tourists of a masochistic bent are welcome to join in: when you've had enough flagellation, just hold your hand up to surrender.

With the new year thus cleansed of past squabbles, the following three days consist of much merrymaking, dancing and even drinking (albeit behind cloth screens). During this time, women dress in their finest *kangas*, and young girls in the frilly Edwardian-style frocks so typical of Africa. All wear lots of kohl around their eyes, vibrant lipstick and garishly painted cheeks, and have their hands and feet painted with henna arabesques. The undercurrent is desire: children born of illicit Mwaka Kogwa couplings, far from being scorned, are highly regarded socially.

The celebrations over, the bottles are stashed away, the veils rise once more and life resumes its normal course.

### Practicalities

Outsiders are welcome to join the celebrations; in fact, it's considered bad luck to be without at least one guest over this period, so you might also be invited to **stay with locals**. A good thing too, as Makunduchi has just one hotel, and that's reserved for all-inclusive Italian package tours. Any Stone Town tour operator should be able to arrange a **trip** to coincide with Mwaka Kogwa, but book well in advance, as the dates tend to overlap with the equally popular Zanzibar International Film Festival (see p.529).

# Jambiani

The long beach at **JAMBIANI**, starting around 2km south of Paje and continuing unbroken for 7km, possesses a wild and windy beauty, and is quite the best place in Zanzibar to enjoy the pleasures of both **beach and village life** without feeling hampered about where you can swim, or how you dress (on the beach, that is; obviously, cover up when in the village). The beach's name derives from the Arabic word *jambiya*, meaning a dagger with a broad curved blade, an example of which was reputedly found on the beach by early settlers. The **barrier reef** lies several kilometres out, so the lagoon in between is a mix of sandbanks, coral reefs and shallow water, great for **snorkelling**, and for poking around pools at low tide. The beach, as along much of the east coast, is very tidal, so swimming is only possible at high tide unless you fancy a long walk.

The beach is one thing that makes Jambiani special; the other is its strong **sense of community**. Unlike Nungwi and Kiwengwa in northern Unguja, Jambiani's villagers have full access to the shore, so you'll be sharing the sands with fishermen and their butterfly-like *ngalawa* outriggers, women collecting seaweed, and lots of children: sailing toy dhows made from sandals, plastic bottles or bits of wood with plastic bags for sails is a particular favourite.

## Arrival, information and accommodation

The "beach transfer" tourist **minibuses** (see p.530) take an hour to cover the 56km from Stone Town, and will drop you at your chosen hotel. **Daladalas** – #309 from Stone Town (Tsh2000) – take twice as long. There are at least two a day (the last leaving no later than 3pm), but timings are unpredictable, so enquire the day before on Creek Road, and be prepared to head out to Mwana Kwerekwe, 5km southeast of town, to catch it. **Returning** to Stone Town, the tourist minibuses leave around 10am. Daladalas leave when full: the first around 6am, the last no later than 3.30pm.

Jambiani's former main road, a sandy strip half way between the shore and the new tarmac, has a number of modest shops, including a combined post office and minimarket (daily 6am–10pm). It and a handful of other places on the same street also rent bicycles. For **internet access**, there's Beedrake & Hasu Secretarial Centre beside Casa del Mar Hotel; the Zanzibar Action Project just south of *Blue Oyster Hotel*; and the *Visitor's Inn*.

---

### Jambiani Cultural Village Tour

To get to know the villagers better, the **Jambiani Cultural Village Tour**, a modest community-run project, offers tourists short diversions to explore various aspects of **local life and culture**, the profits funding healthcare, a nursery and various educational projects. On a typical **walk** you'll be briefed on Jambiani's **history** before touring a farm, visiting a traditional herbalist (*mganga*), and seeing a seaweed farm. There's also the option of visiting a sacred limestone cave (*kumbi*), which may have been used to hide slaves after the abolition of the slave trade; it's a four-hour walk there and back, so cycling is best. The exact itinerary will be determined by your interests.

The project **office** is at Jambiani School (open most days, no fixed times; ℡0777/469118, ⓔkassimmande@hotmail.com). Expect to pay around Tsh15,000 per person for about three hours. For a day-trip from Stone Town, contact Eco+Culture Tours (see p.532), who charge $35–50 per person.

Jambiani's **hotels** are marked on the map on p.545; distances below are from Jambiani School.

**Blue Oyster Hotel** 800m north ☎024/224 0163, ⓦwww.zanzibar.de. German-run, this is an architecturally inelegant two-storey affair, but very good value, with friendly and efficient staff, and clean well-maintained rooms, the cheapest of which share bathrooms. There's also a very good beachside restaurant and bar, and excursions can be arranged. BB ❹–❺

**Casa del Mar Hotel** 500m north ☎0777/455446, ⓦwww.casa-delmar-zanzibar .com. A tasteful mid-range choice on the beach, with twelve rooms in two buildings, all with sea views, and nicely decked out in rustic style. The rooms on top, reached via steep ladders, are actually suites, each with a living room complete with king-size futon. The restaurant has a great reputation, but doesn't sell alcohol (you can bring your own). BB ❺–❻

🏃 **Dhow Beach Village** 1.1km south ☎0777/417763, ⓦwww.dhowbeachvillage .com. One for backpackers: a clean and friendly place famous for its parties (don't come here if you need to sleep on a Saturday or at full moon), with just six rooms behind the beach, quite basic but all with hot water and ceiling fans, and prettily decorated with coconut-wood furniture and colourful fabrics. Great restaurant and bar also (see p.544). BB ❹

**Jambiani Guesthouse** 600m south, beside *Pingo Restaurant* ☎0773/147812, ⓦwww .zanzibar-guesthouse.com. Danish-owned but locally-run, this pushes itself as a kind of youth hostel, but is really just a small basic holiday house right on the beach. There are just five rooms, one with its own bathroom, and a shared lounge. BB ❹

**Kimte Beach Inn** 1.8km south ☎0777/430992, ⓔkimte@lycos.com. A friendly and affordable Rasta-run place: on the land side are several rooms plus two six-bunk dorms ($15 per person with breakfast); on the ocean side is one of Zanzibar's best beach bars, and a good restaurant. Dhow trips and snorkelling can be arranged. BB ❸–❹

🏃 **Mount Zion Long Beach Bungalows** 3.2km north ☎0713/061900, ⓦwww .mountzion-zanzibar.com. Imbued with a very relaxing vibe, this friendly Rastafarian place has some of the most inspired architecture on the island: imaginative takes on traditional designs, all unique and made only from natural materials, including an outlandish three-storey affair towering over a coral-rag ground floor. It's also intimate, with just eight rooms, all with stupendous sea views, including four very affordable beach *bandas*. The honeymoon suite, however, is right next to the wall of an adjoining resort, so it feels hemmed in. There's also a large oceanside bar, a separate restaurant (same views), and a very soft beach. BB ❹

**Pakachi Beach Hotel** 3.4km north ☎0777/423331, ⓦwww.pakachi.net. Snug on a low headland a few steps above the beach but beside a dismal German-owned resort, this Tanzanian/Norwegian place has a chilled-out Rastafarian vibe. There are just three rooms, plus a bungalow ($120) and a family house ($140), all en suite and with *semadari* beds. The bar and very mellow restaurant have good views. Facilities include fishing equipment, canoes, and a motorboat for snorkelling. BB ❹

**Red Monkey Bungalows** 2.2km south ☎024/224 0207 or 0777/497736, ⓦwww.zanzibarholidays .info. German-run, on a small breezy plot at the forgotten south end of the beach, this has nine individual bungalows, each with two beds, fan, private bathroom and good water supply, plus a cheap restaurant. Free internet access. BB ❺

**Shehe Bungalows** 1.4km south ☎0777/843622, ⓦwww.shehebungalows.co.uk. Despite the sometimes surly staff, this is a decent budget choice thanks to its great location right on the beach. There are three sets of rooms (25 in all), all with box nets, fans and bathrooms. The best ones, large but a little faded, are in a row of bungalows on the north side, behind a narrow garden – all have sea views. There's also a first-floor restaurant and bar. BB ❹

**Visitor's Inn** 400m south ☎024/224 0150, ⓦwww.visitorsinn-zanzibar.com. A functional if unexpected set-up with fifteen en-suite bungalows (most with sea views) around a parking area, and ten en-suite rooms in a guesthouse set back from the beach. The rooms are well-kept and there's a large open-sided restaurant and bar. Has internet access and various activities. BB ❺

# Eating and drinking

There are lots of **restaurants** to choose from, and not just in the hotels, so prices are keen, with seafood main courses averaging Tsh8000 a plate. The locally-run restaurants right on the beach, often built with little more than palm fronds, are an ever-changing lot. At their prime they can be truly excellent, but give them at least an hour or two to prepare your meal – or, for something special, drop by the day before to discuss the options. The places below are marked on the map opposite.

**Dhow Beach Village** 1.1km south. One of Jambiani's best bars, by day or by night, plus a decent toes-in-the-sand beach restaurant (try the home-made ice cream; the pizza is good, too), famous full-moon parties, and all-night discos on Saturday nights.

**Kim's Restaurant** 900m north, near *Blue Oyster Hotel* ☎0777/457733. Among the best of the locally-run places, this one is decorated with shells and serves up tasty – and cheap – traditional meals, little of which you'll find elsewhere. For starters, you could try fish cakes, succulent fried octopus or spicy fish soup. Main courses include the classic coconut-crusted fish with mango chutney, or baby octopus grilled with ginger and chilli, and for dessert, try *kaimati* (flour, sugar and coconut), or pumpkin stewed in sweet coconut milk.

**Kimte Beach Inn** 1.8km south. Zanzibar's most chilled-out beach bar (Rastafarians know a thing or two about this), well stocked and with excellent music– from reggae and The Doors to danceable club sounds – plus evening campfires. Meals are well priced, and they also do pizzas.

**Mount Zion Long Beach Bungalows** 3.2km north. Rastafarian vibes by day, romantic candlelit dinners at night, nice music, the sound of the waves… and the food's not half bad either, particularly anything fishy. There are vegetarian options, too, and they'll jump through hoops to please.

**Pingo Restaurant** 600m south, just off the beach by *Jambiani Guesthouse*. A very cheap, simple and locally-popular bar and restaurant with a decent choice of snacks, and tasty seafood. Leisurely service but generous portions.

**Shehe Bungalows** 1.4km south. The first-floor open-front bar enjoys a fantastic view over the beach and lagoon. The limited choice of dishes should be ordered well in advance, and range from average to excellent depending on who's cooking.

**Visitor's Inn** 400m south. Reasonable value if you choose carefully, with some mouthwatering dishes such as banana fritters, marinated prawns in coconut sauce, and a large number of crab and jumbo prawn dishes. They also do milkshakes.

# Paje

The beach at **PAJE**, 51km east of Stone Town, is easy to reach by public transport, and beautiful it is, too, its white sands backed by swaying palms, and the sea more often than not imbued with heart-lifting shades of turquoise. Behind the beach is **Paje village**, whose inhabitants you'll likely be sharing the beach with, including several hundred women seaweed farmers. You needn't feel awkward about donning swimming costumes on the beach, but please cover up in the village. A word about **safety**: Paje has experienced a number of muggings of tourists over the last couple of years, and even though they appear to have been related to specific hotels known for sour community relations (and not reviewed here), do heed local advice regarding safety, especially if unaccompanied at night

## Arrival and accommodation

Coming from Stone Town, buy a seat on a "beach transfer" **minibus** (see p.530; no more than $10), or catch a #209 **daladala** from Darajani terminal on Creek Road (Tsh2000). There are four or five a day, from dawn to around 4pm, taking no more than ninety minutes. **Leaving** Paje, the last daladala heads off no later than 4.30pm.

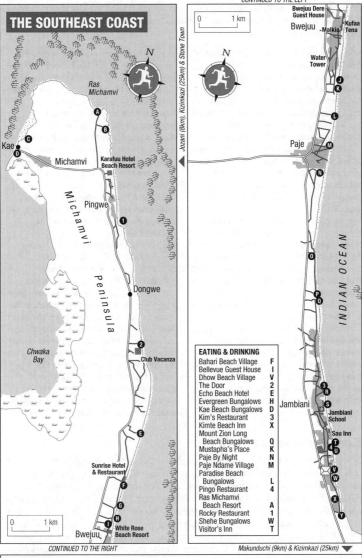

## THE SOUTHEAST COAST

CONTINUED TO THE LEFT

Bwejuu Dere
Guest House

Bwejuu · Malkia · Kufaa
Tena

Water
Tower

Paje

INDIAN OCEAN

Jambiani

Jambiani
School

Sau Inn

Ras
Michamvi

Kae · Michamvi

Karafuu Hotel
Beach Resort

Jozani (8km), Kizimkazi (25km) & Stone Town

Pingwe

Michamvi

Peninsula

Dongwe

Chwaka
Bay

Club Vacanza

Sunrise Hotel
& Restaurant

White Rose
Beach Resort

Bwejuu

0    1 km

CONTINUED TO THE RIGHT

Makunduchi (9km) & Kizimkazi (25km) ▼

### EATING & DRINKING

| | |
|---|---|
| Bahari Beach Village | F |
| Bellevue Guest House | I |
| Dhow Beach Village | V |
| The Door | 2 |
| Echo Beach Hotel | E |
| Evergreen Bungalows | H |
| Kae Beach Bungalows | D |
| Kim's Restaurant | 3 |
| Kimte Beach Inn | X |
| Mount Zion Long Beach Bungalows | Q |
| Mustapha's Place | K |
| Paje By Night | N |
| Paje Ndame Village | M |
| Paradise Beach Bungalows | L |
| Pingo Restaurant | 4 |
| Ras Michamvi Beach Resort | A |
| Rocky Restaurant | 1 |
| Shehe Bungalows | W |
| Visitor's Inn | T |

### ACCOMMODATION

| | | | | | |
|---|---|---|---|---|---|
| Bahari Beach Village | F | Michamvi Water Sports Resort | C | Sun and Sea View Resort | J |
| Bellevue Guest House | I | Mount Zion Long Beach Bungalows | Q | Visitor's Inn | T |
| Blue Oyster Hotel | R | Mustapha's Place | K | | |
| Casa del Mar Hotel | S | Paje By Night | N | | |
| Dhow Beach Village | V | Paje Ndame Village | M | | |
| Echo Beach Hotel | E | Pakachi Beach Hotel | P | | |
| Evergreen Bungalows | H | Paradise Beach Bungalows | L | | |
| Jambiani Guesthouse | U | Ras Michamvi Beach Resort | A | | |
| Kae Beach Bungalows | D | Red Monkey Bungalows | Y | | |
| Kichanga Lodge | B | Robinson's Place | G | | |
| Kimte Beach Inn | X | Shehe Bungalows | W | | |
| Mbuyuni Beach Village | O | | | | |

Some of Paje's **hotels** (marked on the map on p.545) are decidedly average; the following are the better ones. Distances below are from the junction of the road in from Stone Town.

**Mbuyuni Beach Village** 2.6km south of the junction ☎0777/843622, ⓦwww.mbuyuni.com. Halfway to Jambiani in an area known as Mwanawanu, this has the (dis)advantage of being far from central Paje, walking from which is unsafe at night, but if you're looking to strand yourself in a secluded yet affordable beachside hideaway, this could be it. Set in tropical gardens are ten large, attractively designed and stylishly equipped thatch-roofed bungalows, all with big beds and decent bathrooms. There's a reasonably priced restaurant facing the beach (mainly seafood), and frequent bonfires on the beach itself, where there are also hammocks and sunloungers. Very good value. BB ❸

🏃 **Paje By Night** 500m southeast of the junction ☎0777/460710 or 024/224 0062, ⓦwww.pajebynight.net. First off, the bad news: this is not on the beach, but 100m behind it (and *Kitete Beach Bungalows*), so no sea views. The rest is all good news, starting with its excellent bar and sublime restaurant (see below), together with a friendly, funky and laid-back atmosphere, and, rare for Italian-run places on Zanzibar, healthy community relations. Rooms are in 24 simple but well-kept rooms in colourfully painted rows, some with a/c; rates depend on how big they are and whether there's hot water. There's also a couple of quirky two-floor "jungle bungalows" likely to pit parents against their kids about who's going to sleep upstairs; these also have rooftop terraces. A range of personalized tours can be arranged with locals, including village walks, birding, time with fishermen, even Uzi Island on the south coast. Also has a nice craft shop, and hammocks slung all over the place. Rates include wi-fi (or use of a laptop). Closed mid-April to end-May. BB ❻

**Paje Ndame Village** 700m northeast of the junction ☎0777/276621, ⓦwww.ndame.info. A well-priced sixty-bed Swedish-run resort set in a grove of coconut palms behind a lovely stretch of beach. The rooms, in one or two-storey chalets (only a few have sea views), are small and not terribly inspiring, but they're comfortable enough, and cheap for families. There's also a bar, gift shop, coconut-rope loungers and parasols on the beach, and a good seafood restaurant (see below). BB ❹–❺

🏃 **Paradise Beach Bungalows** 1km north of the junction ☎024/223 1387 or 0777/414129, ⓦwww.zanzibar-paradise-bungalows.com. Run by a Japanese/Zanzibari team, this is a peaceful and likeable no-frills place snuggled in a grove of coconut palms right on the beach, and famed for its exquisite and affordable food. Its ten Swahili-styled bedrooms, all en suite – and seven with sea views – are large and comfortable even if hot water comes in buckets, and there are three stand-alone cottages at the back with covered roof terraces. Facilities include a bar, a good library, cultural tours and dhow trips, and Swahili cooking courses (see below). Bicycles and snorkelling equipment available. BB ❹

## Eating and drinking

Most of Paje's bars and **restaurants** are in its hotels, but in high season at least, you'll often find impromptu chill-out parties on the beach: just look for a campfire (but heed local advice about safety). For something deliciously different, *Paradise Beach Bungalows* can arrange a four-hour Swahili 🏃 **cooking course** with local women. It's actually more of a demonstration, including the mystical art of making coconut milk (and getting to grips with a "goat", *mbuzi* also being the word for a coconut grater). All great fun, and at just Tsh5000 per person including the resulting meal, it's a bargain. At the following restaurants, marked on p.545, you'll pay around Tsh10,000 for a meaty or fishy main course.

🏃 **Paje By Night** 500m southeast of the junction. Zanzibar's best bar, with good music and a laid-back vibe. The food (daily 10am–10.30pm), with vegetarian options is well up there too, and many ingredients are home-grown: the wood-fired pizzas please even the pickiest Italians and where else could you sample home-made ravioli stuffed with fish and almonds?

The wines (mainly South African and Spanish) are cheap for Zanzibar, starting at Tsh15,000 a bottle. Discos on Friday. Bar closes around 2am.

**Paje Ndame Village** 700m northeast of the junction. Reasonably priced Italian and Swahili dishes, including octopus and potato salad with basil and garlic, pasta with crab sauce, mixed fish grills and grilled prawns with spinach.

🏃 **Paradise Beach Bungalows** 1km north of the junction. An unusual and successful blend of Swahili and Japanese cuisine, and excellent value at Tsh7000–12,000 for a three-course lunch or dinner (the menu changes daily). The Japanese dishes are especially recommended, whether classic sushi and sashimi (kingfish, squid and tuna), or chicken teriyaki seasoned with Coca-Cola. There's also a small bar, and – for that extra thrill – a table in a tree house. Book ahead if you're not staying overnight.

# Bwejuu

The village of **BWEJUU** is 3km north of Paje, and shares the same beach, which continues northwards for another 4km until veers into Dongwe. For most of the year, the beach is a peach, backed by slender coconut palms and dozens of modest bungalow hotels, but be aware that around Christmas it can be covered in seaweed. There are some excellent **snorkelling** spots within walking or wading distance at low tide, and *Bellevue Guest House* can arrange kite surfing.

Bwejuu village is home to two women's **self-help groups**, both of which are worth supporting. Kufaa Tena & Women's Voice Project on the north side of the village, just before the collapsing *Bwejuu Dere Guest House*, make and sell woven baskets and colourful bags, and offer henna painting and massages. Livelier, and at which you're welcome to see the women at work, is Malkia, opposite *Palm Beach Inn* down the same road, who are purveyors of fine handmade clothes, and also offer internet access.

## Arrival and accommodation

Bwejuu is covered by roughly hourly #324 or #340 **daladalas** from Creek Road in Stone Town, the first leaving at around 9am, the last at 2pm. The ride takes just over an hour and costs Tsh2000, but to reach the hotels at the north end of Bwejuu, the only daladala at present is a single daily run from Stone Town to Kae (ask for Michamvi) in the afternoon, although the new tarmac road may see more vehicles joining the route soon. "Beach transfer" **minibuses** should cost no more than $10. **Leaving** Bwejuu, the first daladala (coming from Kae) passes through around 6am, and the last leaves Bwejuu at 4pm. Most hotels have **bicycles** for their guests, either free or for a nominal sum.

Bwejuu's **accommodation** (see map, p.545) is mostly in small bungalow "resorts", and is generally reasonably priced. Distances below are from the water tower at the junction of the asphalt road and the unsurfaced road into the village itself.

**Bellevue Guest House** 2.4km north ☏0777/209576, 🌐www.bellevuezanzibar.com. A friendly, Dutch-run place on a low ridge 100m back from the shore, with good views, but not being on the beach (there's a private villa in front) is a drawback. It has six rooms (four standard, plus two with hot water and other minor treats), all with huge beds, box nets, fans and good bathrooms, and the restaurant and bar has an excellent reputation. The management also run a kite surfing centre. BB ❺

**Evergreen Bungalows** 2.6km north ☏024/224 0273, 🌐www.evergreen-bungalows.com.

German-run, the beach-front plot is the thing here, though the seven rustic beach bungalows are also impressive, using plenty of driftwood, wonky beams, bamboo and mangrove poles. All have vaulted lofts (accessed by steep staircases) that serve as separate guest rooms, so there are fourteen rooms, all with box nets over their big beds. There's a well-priced restaurant (see p.547), and various excursions on offer. BB ❺

**Mustapha's Place** 800m south ☏0776/718999, 🌐www.mustaphasplace.com. Long-established and recently treated to a much-needed overhaul (and change of management), this nicely chilled-out place has seven coral-walled bungalows set in beautiful gardens a couple of minutes from the beach, each with its own style, some sharing bathrooms, others on two levels, and all decorated with colourful wildlife murals and fabrics. Also has Bwejuu's best bar, a health spa, and a new Thai-Swahili restaurant that may well be excellent. They also offer a range of locally-run trips, whether cultural or ecological. BB ❸–❺

**Robinson's Place** 3km north ☎0777/413479, ⊛www.robinsonsplace .net. Set in an almost jungly beach garden, this is a small, whimsical, unpretentious and highly recommended place run by a charming Zanzibari/ British family, who gain bonus points for having resisted the temptation to move into "boutique hotel" territory. It's also properly eco-friendly: electricity is limited to wind-powered battery chargers; lighting is by kerosene lamps; and all produce is sourced locally. There are only six rooms, including one very affordable single ($20), so book well ahead. All are eclectic in design,

though the best is at the top of a two-storey Robinson Crusoe-style house by the beach. Meals, drinks and siestas are taken in a cool beach *banda*, a circular architectural take on the traditional Swahili coffee *barazas* in soft and colourful adobe-like forms. Meals are limited to a sumptuous breakfast and dinner (guests only; around Tsh10,000). BB ❹

**Sun and Sea View Resort** 600m south ☎0773/168839, ⊛www.sunandseaviewresort .com. A cheery and affordable locally-run place with over 100m of beachfront, along the way to *Mustapha's Place*. It has ten basic but pleasant en-suite rooms, some with huge bathtubs (and hot water), plus a restaurant and bar. BB ❹

**Upepo Boutique Beach Bungalows** 3.5km north ☎0784/619579, ⊛www.zanzibarhotelbeach.com. A very small, sleepy and welcoming place on a sandy plot studded with coconut palms and backed by tropical gardens. There are just three bungalows at present, one with a full-on sea view. Also has a fine seaside restaurant and a bar. BB ❹

## Eating and drinking

Most of Bwejuu's **restaurants** are attached to its hotels. For your own supplies, there are a handful of basic shops (*dukas*) in the village. The places reviewed below are marked on the map on p.545.

**Bellevue Guest House** 2.4km north. Another great reputation here, with the basics costing Tsh12,000–15,000, but it's worth spending a little more for something fancy, such as crab in its shell. Proper coffee, either straight or laced with ginger or spice. Also functions as a pleasantly shady bar. No beach.

**Evergreen Bungalows** 2.6km north. Eat by the beach, or take a drink on a swing. Choose from a modest selection of dishes announced on a black-board: nothing fancy, but all tasty, and, at around Tsh8000 for seafood, very reasonably priced.

**Mustapha's Place** 800m south. At the time of writing, this was undergoing a sea change,

including the menu, which was about to be graced by Thai as well as Zanzibari dishes (Thai lending itself perfectly to Zanzibar's ingredients). The bar has always been popular among backpackers, and is as good a place as any in which to learn African drumming, or the finer points of playing *bao*.

**Upepo Boutique Beach Bungalows** 3.5km north. The beachside restaurant here has a fine reputation, with, as you might guess, seafood being the speciality (Tsh8000–12,000), but there's also pasta, sandwiches and various vegetarian options, including coconut milk-based curries. Finish with a chocolate pancake (Tsh4500). Good bar, complete with sangria.

# Michamvi Peninsula

North of Bwejuu is the **MICHAMVI PENINSULA**, sparsely inhabited and with three distinct areas for tourists. First up from Bwejuu is **Dongwe**. Dusty and rather dull when seen from land, the beautiful sandy beaches hidden behind the walls and thickets (gradually disappearing as more and more plots are sold to hoteliers) have attracted a number of wilfully expensive beach hotels, most of them dealing with pre-booked package tours. Lighter on the pocket, and more personal too, are a couple of hotels at **Ras Michamvi** at the peninsula's northern end, which, although on a tall headland, have lovely sandy coves down below, and great views. To the west of there is **Michamvi village**. One kilometre further west, along a sandy track, is **Kae**, which, until the developers discovered the place around 2007, had quite the perfect beach. Alas, two spanking new beach hotels, and several more in the offing, are set to turn Kae into Zanzibar's latest boutique resort, and the new walls rising along the once pristine shore are not promising.

## Arrival and accommodation

The only **daladala** currently venturing as far as Kae leaves Stone Town's Darajani terminal no later than 3.30pm, and takes about two hours (Tsh2000). Confusingly, the vehicle is marked "Bwejuu" (#324), so be sure to ask whether it goes to Kae (or, if that should draw a blank stare, Michamvi). In the opposite direction, the vehicle leaves Kae at around 5am. Tourist "beach transfer" minibuses don't cover this area.

The following **hotels** are marked on the map on p.545.

**Echo Beach Hotel** Dongwe ℡0773/593260, Ⓦwww.echobeachhotel.com. A calm, intimate and unfailingly friendly British-run hideaway, with nine spacious rooms in bungalows sweetly decorated in Afro-Arabian style, all with a/c, and sea-view terraces. Whilst there's not a mass of things to do (there is a small pool though, and a jacuzzi), you can always wander up the beach and arrange something at *Breezes Beach Club* next door. The restaurant is excellent (see p.550), and there's also wi-fi, and the (optional) attentions of an over-friendly dog. HB ❾

**Kae Beach Bungalows** Kae ℡0777/765696. Kae's oldest and cheapest lodgings, and now Italian-owned, with just three en-suite bungalows (six guest rooms) at the very end of the sandy road. Whilst basic, and lacking direct sea views, the rooms are airy and comfortable enough, have day-beds and are very good value given that it's full board. The restaurant (see p.550), which does have views, takes a couple of hours to deliver. With a bit of patience, boat trips can be arranged, including mangrove cruises, but there's no snorkelling equipment. FB ❺

**Kichanga Lodge** Ras Michamvi (turning is 2km east of Pingwe) ℡0773/175124, Ⓦwww.kichanga .com. Set on a high grassy bluff, this has a scatter of well-spaced bungalows and villas containing three kinds of room. The best are the stylish "Villa" bungalows at the front, with astounding sea views. All make nice use of fabrics, and have terraces with rope beds. The "Garden" rooms are cheaper but lack views. HB ❼–❽

**Michamvi Water Sports Resort** Kae ℡0777/878136 or 0784/758633, Ⓦwww .michamvi.com. A modest South African-run resort with a good staff vibe, a swimming pool, and twenty large, nicely decorated rooms in two-storey houses, all with a/c, furniture made from *mitumbwi* canoes, and hammocks on their verandas (partial sea views). There's also a good if pricey restaurant. As the name suggests, a heap of activities are offered, including wakeboarding, parasailing and waterskiing. Windsurfing is free, and tuition is available for all sports. Snorkelling trips cost $25–35 per person plus equipment ($10), and they can also arrange mangrove tours around Chwaka Bay (minimum $75 per group). HB ❼

🏃 **Ras Michamvi Beach Resort** Ras Michamvi ℡0774/319319, Ⓦwww .rasmichamvi.com. The awkward gate security – similar to *Kichanga*'s – comes as a surprise for a locally owned place (same people as Stone Town's *Jambo Guest House*), but once in, you get to enjoy one of the most beautiful hotel locations on the island. Like *Kichanga*, it's set on a high bluff at the peninsula's very tip, giving 180-degree sea views. There are fifteen rooms in bungalows connected by shaded wooden walkways. All are large, and come with a/c, box nets, fans and tiled bathrooms. The swimming pool is a beauty if not quite "infinity" (there's a little wall around it that stops it merging visually with the ocean). Three rooms are suitable for guests with physical disabilities, but unfortunately the two secluded beaches are accessed via long flights of stairs. Other facilities include a restaurant, well-equipped open-air gym, internet access and snorkelling trips ($30 per person). BB ❻

## Eating and drinking

For upmarket dining, any of Dongwe's hotels will oblige. Cheaper, more atmospheric **restaurants** are below and are marked on the map on p.545.

**The Door** Just north of *Club Vacanza*, Dongwe ☏0777/414962 or 0777/416932. Named after the channel in the barrier reef opposite, this is a classy but informal clifftop restaurant run by a Swahili/Italian couple. The menu – which changes daily (there's always a vegetarian option) – is a blend of Italian classics and seafood, punctuated by inventive Swahili-inspired touches such as spiced sauces or lemon-grass tea. Most dishes cost under Tsh10,000. Apart from food, there's also a beach down a long and particularly steep flight of steps, and good snorkelling within swimming distance (Tsh4000 for the equipment), and they can also fix you up with an *ngalawa* outrigger for around Tsh20,000 per boat for two or three hours. Open lunchtimes until 4pm; dinner by reservation only.

**Echo Beach Hotel** Dongwe. It didn't take long for this hotel to forge a reputation, having combined a five-star dining experience (beautifully laid-out tables) with toes-in-the-sand beach chic and knock-out views. The food itself comes in for heaps of praise: seafood, obviously, and plenty of it, but also British favourites such as lamb with mint sauce. Fine wines.

**Kae Beach Bungalows** Kae. At the end of the road, overlooking Chwaka Bay, this is a simple place on silky beach, and a perfect spot at which to sample octopus – Kae's speciality. They also have a short menu of Zanzibari and Italian favourites, but don't come if you're in a hurry.

**Ras Michamvi Beach Resort** Ras Michamvi. Don't mind the Maasai guards at the gate – the restaurant here is open to all, and whilst the menu is modest, that means everything on it should be available. The real reason for taking lunch here though is the fantastic view. Meals or snacks cost $10–14; three-course dinners go for $20–25. Sells alcohol.

**Rocky Restaurant** Kijiweni Beach, 900m south of *Karafuu Hotel Beach Resort*, Pingwe ☏0777/490681. You won't believe this place unless you see it: perched atop a tiny coral outcrop just off the beach, which at high tide becomes an island that you have to wade out to before clambering up a wonky ladder. It hasn't (yet) been grabbed by a politician or "developer", but that's probably just a matter of time. For now, it's very basic indeed, even run-down. The menu is almost entirely seafood, with most dishes costing Tsh10,000–15,000. For prawns or lobster, it's best to order the day before, but they may be willing to swim out to the fishermen on the reef to collect your order, which will be cooked in the village behind you. They don't usually have alcoholic drinks (and their sodas are warm); you're welcome to bring your own though. Order at least two hours in advance. Closed Ramadan lunchtimes.

# Northern Unguja

The beaches of **northern Unguja** were the first to be discovered by foreign beach bums, when – back in the bell-bottomed Seventies – a handful of hippy escapees started calling at Zanzibar on their cosmic journey to Kathmandu. Even today, with the bulk of the island's visitors sunning themselves in the north, hotel development has been surprisingly unobtrusive (the big bad exception being Kiwengwa in the northeast), and by and large the place still lives up to the old mantra of "peace and love", a refrain you'll hear a fair amount from dreadlocked Rasta-lookalike beach boys.

The northernmost beaches of **Nungwi** and **Kendwa** (the only ones covered by beach transfer minibuses from Stone Town) are the ones to head for if you're looking for nightlife; more sedate are **Matemwe** and **Pongwe** in the east. At all four places you can arrange **snorkelling** (for which you don't necessarily need a boat; there are shallow intertidal reefs within wading distance), as well as **scuba -diving** (see p.512) and dhow cruises. The bigger resort-style hotels have other watersports, too.

As with southern Unguja, at **low tide** the ocean recedes considerably: the exceptions, allowing swimming at all times of day, are Kendwa and Pongwe. Note that all of these beaches can be adorned by pungent **seaweed** (sometimes laced with sea urchins) between December and February, though most hotels clear their beaches. For something different, the recently opened **Kiwengwa–Pongwe Forest Reserve** promises to become a major tourist attraction.

# Pongwe

Following the abolition of the slave trade by a reluctant Sultan Barghash in 1873, a number of places along the then extremely remote northeastern coastline, especially Chwaka Bay and Pongwe, saw use as illegal **slaving ports**, continuing the trade with the Seychelles and other French Indian Ocean possessions until the beginning of the twentieth century. Still retaining a somewhat isolated feel is the tiny fishing village of **PONGWE**, 46km from Stone Town. There's nothing much to it, but the **beach** – with unbelievably clear water and lots of swaying palm trees – is the stuff of dreams, and is also the only beach on Unguja's east coast where you can swim throughout the day, irrespective of the tide. There are just three small hotels: two of them quite basic, the third swish but still intimate; all are great places to unwind in, far from the madd(en) ing crowds of *papasi*.

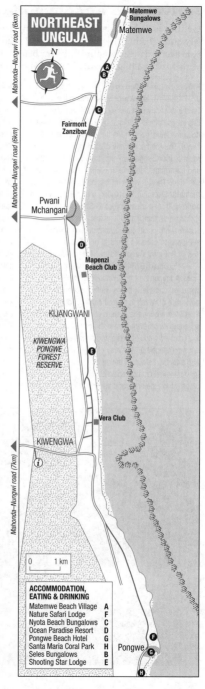

NORTHEAST UNGUJA

N

Mahonda–Nungwi road (6km)

Mahonda–Nungwi road (6km)

Mahonda–Nungwi road (7km)

Matemwe Bungalows

Matemwe

A
B

C

Fairmont Zanzibar

Pwani Mchangani

D

Mapenzi Beach Club

KIJANGWANI

KIWENGWA PONGWE FOREST RESERVE

E

Vera Club

KIWENGWA

i

0    1 km

**ACCOMMODATION, EATING & DRINKING**

| Matemwe Beach Village | A |
| Nature Safari Lodge | F |
| Nyota Beach Bungalows | C |
| Ocean Paradise Resort | D |
| Pongwe Beach Hotel | G |
| Santa Maria Coral Park | H |
| Seles Bungalows | B |
| Shooting Star Lodge | E |

Pongwe

F

G

H

## Arrival and accommodation

Getting here by **daladala** (#209 from Darajani, usually 7am; and #233 from Mwembe Ladu, variable times; both Tsh2000) can be awkward, as they don't run every day, so enquire the day before. Incidentally, don't confuse Pongwe with Mwera Pongwe (daladala #225), which is another place entirely.

**Nature Safari Lodge** ☎0777/414704 or 0777/223816, ⊛www.pongwesafarilodge.com. On a low shady cliff beside a small sandy cove, this sleepy place – owned by a retired Zanzibari doctor – lacks palm trees but the beach is still a beaut. The rooms, slightly dilapidated, are in two rows of four bungalows and have fans, box nets and bathrooms: get one at the front for a full-on sea view. There's a cheap bar and a not-so-cheap restaurant (around Tsh10,000 a plate) but with an entirely African menu (order 2–3hr before), including vegetarian options such as beans cooked with chilli, cumin, tomato and spinach, served with coconut basmati rice. BB ➍

🏃 **Pongwe Beach Hotel** Next to *Nature Safari Lodge* ☎0784/336181, ⊛www.pongwe .com. A favourite of honeymooners, this is a quiet *wazungu* enclave within a walled cocoon, the downside of which is limited contact with locals. Scattered around the mature gardens are sixteen spacious if somewhat basic thatched bungalows, with carved wooden doors and *semadari* beds. No a/c at present, but that may change. There's also a bar, a fancy restaurant doling out generous portions (and candlelit dining on the beach if you wish), a pleasant lounge area, and various pricey tours and activities. But the place really racks up the points for its utterly swoonsome beach. BB ➐

🏃 **Santa Maria Coral Park** ☎0777/432655, ⊛www.santamaria-zanzibar.com. Also enjoying a great beach, this is what *Pongwe Beach Hotel* was like before it became wazungi-fied, and at $30 a head it's one of the best-value hotels on the island for solo travellers. The grounds are also a delight, all soft white sand with lots of weird, wonderful and wild indigenous plants including tall, swaying coconut palms and bizarre screw palms. There are just five rooms, relatively basic but attractive in a rustic way, all with verandas: two single-room wooden *bandas* with attached bathrooms, a brilliant two-storey cottage (perfect for families) with a sea view from its top balcony (the only room with a view), and a stone cottage with two guest rooms. All have fans and blue box nets, and manage to keep coolish despite lacking a/c. Snorkelling can be arranged. There's also a breezy beach bar complete with a rocking rope swing, and a restaurant; meals, with seafood starting at Tsh10,000, need ordering a few hours before. Day-trippers are welcome for meals or drinks. BB ➍

▲ Traditional Swahili house, Pongwe

# Kiwengwa and Pwani Mchangani

As Zanzibar's main package-holiday destination, **KIWENGWA** is dominated by enormous all-inclusive resorts catering almost entirely to Italians, and as the beach is similar to that in far more intimate Matemwe, further north, there's frankly little to recommend Kiwengwa, although there are a couple of hotels worth considering, and those are reviewed below.

Kiwengwa is actually rather difficult to pin down, seeing as it sprawls along almost 10km of coastline. The middle bit is called **Kijangwani** (not that many people know the name), and the package-hotel strip fizzles out a couple of kilometres before **PWANI MCHANGANI** (also called Kwa Pangaa). The northern part of this is a fishing village that has so far managed to avoid selling its shoreline – and soul – to the developers, surviving instead on fishing, coconut cultivation and the farming of seaweed, which you'll see hung out to dry everywhere.

## Arrival and accommodation

Kiwengwa is covered by frequent #117 **daladalas** from Stone Town (Tsh2000), finishing at Kiwengwa village south of the main hotel strip; daladala drivers should be happy to divert for a tip (Tsh2000 might work, Tsh5000 almost certainly should). Daladalas to Pwani Mchangani, 8km north of Kiwengwa, are far less frequent: enquire about them the day before. Both routes start on Creek Road in Stone Town, just north of the Central Market. The following hotels are marked on the map on p.551.

**Ocean Paradise Resort** Kijangwani ☎0774/440990–5, ⓦwww.oceanparadisezanzibar.com. Best of the big five-star resorts on this stretch of coast, very stylish and making good use of local materials in both its rooms and common areas. Facilities include Zanzibar's largest swimming pool, tons of watersports including scuba diving (run by One Ocean; see p.513), a fitness centre and tennis courts, ocean-view restaurant, various bars and a disco. HB ❾

**Shooting Star Lodge** Kijangwani ☎0777/414166, ⓦwww.shootingstarlodge .com. Perched on a clifftop halfway between Kiwengwa and Pwani Mchangani, this intimate lodge boasts wonderful sea views (the beach is down a steep flight of steps), and is one of the

northeast coast's most romantic options. The fifteen rooms are attractively furnished, but even better are two turret-like suites, each with two floors, private swimming pool, and a bath on top. All guests have use of a small but lovely infinity pool (the horizon just goes on and on). So long as the lodge isn't jam-packed, day-trippers can also use the pool if they buy lunch. The food is exquisite and very reasonably priced, with main courses costing just $12 ($15 at night). Overnight guests can enjoy a seafood dinner on the beach in the light of candles and torches ($55 more per person). There's also a beauty spa, and other activities are arrangeable through the nearby *Bluebay Beach Resort*. HB ❼–❽, suites ❾

# Matemwe

The beautiful palm-fringed beach south of the fishing village of **MATEMWE**, 6km north of Pwani Mchangani, is the last of the main northeast-coast destinations, and one of the more intimate. The village retains a tangible sense of community, and is one of few places where you'll share the dusty roads with cows, chickens and goats, and gaggles of irrepressible kids. The beach itself is an utter delight, broad and white, and – south of the village – with few houses nearby. The near-bucolic charm might not last all that much longer though: already, the walled enclosures of larger resorts are beginning to intrude.

## Kiwengwa-Pongwe Forest

A welcome development in the Kiwengwa area was the opening, in 2009, of the 33-square-kilometre **Kiwengwa-Pongwe Forest Reserve** (daily; 7.30am to 5pm; $10), the work of the Kiwengwa Ecotourism Project (Ⓦtms.utu.fi/kiwa), which aims to get locals – especially women – to benefit from tourism, even if only modestly. The reserve, much of which is **coral rag forest** (which takes longer than most forests to recover from logging and land clearance), encloses some of the most biodiverse terrestrial habitat on the islands. **Animals** you might see include red colobus monkeys, Sykes' and blue monkeys, Ader's duikers and – among 47 bird species – the delightfully gaudy Fischer's turaco.

In the interests of preservation, visitors are restricted to three **nature trails** (200m, 400m and 2km), a small farm, and the bat-filled **Mchekeni caves**, Zanzibar's largest coral caverns: basically big gaps in what used to be coral reefs when sea levels were higher. Historically, the caves were regarded by locals with considerable dread, as they were home to all manner of malevolent spirits, as well as wild pigs and leopards (now extinct on Zanzibar), which were kept as symbols of spiritual power by witchdoctors.

To **get here**, you can walk west from Kiwengwa along the tarmac 1.7km beyond the junction for Pwani Mchangani, and turn south just after Mwanza village on to a rough track. The visitor centre is 750m along. Alternatively, catch a daladala – #117 runs along the main road – and ask to be dropped at Mchekeni. At the **entrance** you'll also find a souvenir shop, and a restaurant is under construction. For **more information**, talk with your hotel or a tour company, or contact the project: ☏024/223 8628, Ⓔmwinjuma@hotmail.com.

As with most other east-coast beaches, **swimming** at low tide is impossible unless you fancy a long walk over the coral flats (with sandals). Most hotels have kayaks and can organize sailing trips, which can also be arranged, usually for less, directly with locals. Other than just chilling out, the main reason for coming is superb **diving and snorkelling**.

## Arrival and accommodation

Matemwe is 50km northeast of Stone Town. #118 **daladalas** run throughout the day from the west side of Creek Road. **Accommodation** is quite a fluid entity at present: for a long time the beach was home to just a trio of relaxed mid-market bungalow "resorts", but these have recently been joined by a number of cheaper (and mostly cheerful) backpacker-style places and, at the opposite end of the spectrum, some swanky "boutique" hotels as well as package-tour sprawls, at either of which price is not a reliable indicator of quality. The smaller places fill up quickly, so book ahead – but given the see-sawing standards at the posher hotels, check those out beforehand online (see p.74).

The asphalt road ends at the shore; most of Matemwe's hotels are spread out over two kilometres north from there, finishing just before the village itself. The "junction" referred to below is from the asphalt road. All hotels are marked on the map on p.551.

**Matemwe Beach Village** 1km north of the junction Ⓦwww.matemwebeach.com. Located amid palm trees on a large beachside plot, this long-time recommendation needs an overhaul, but at the price is still quite reasonable. The best rooms are five suites, especially #1 and #5 which have sea views. There's a cosy bar and a decent restaurant, a swimming pool, and a branch of One Ocean (see p.513) for diving and watersports.

In brief, a lovely place to chill out in, but don't come expecting resort-style standards or facilities. HB ❼–❽

**Nyota Beach Bungalows** 800m east of the junction ☎0777/484303, ⓦwww .nyotabeachbungalows.com. A dreamy and affordable Italian-run place on a flabbergastingly beautiful stretch of sand. The ten rooms, all en suite, are darkish but comfy; some are in bungalows, others in two-storey houses; all have small fans and box nets, but only one has a proper sea view. On the edge of the beach is a charming Robinson Crusoe-esque bar-cum-restaurant on two floors, all wood and palm weave, complete with a swing. The menu offers a wide choice of mostly Swahili dishes, plus a few Italian faves; the basics are $7–10. Other facilities, at extra cost, are internet access ($5 per 30min), snorkelling off Mnemba, and bicycle and boat rental. BB ⑤

**Seles Bungalows** 900m north of the junction ☎0777/413449, ⓦwww .selesbungalows.com. If only more hotels were like this. Small, charming, laid-back, unpretentious, homely, tasteful and bursting with character: the two-storey bar/restaurant/lounge is a lopsidedly lovely creature made from mangrove poles, palm leaves, driftwood, thatch and an old dhow. The rooms, two apiece per cottage, whilst simple, are great value (and have big draped nets). Good food too (catch of the day), and they're happy to serve you breakfast in bed. BB ④

# Nungwi

From humble beginnings as a fishing village and dhow-making centre known only to a handful of hippies, **NUNGWI** – being the village and beaches either side of Unguja's northernmost point, Ras Nungwi, has become, in little more than a decade, Zanzibar's second most popular beach resort after Kiwengwa. There's plenty on offer, not least the island's liveliest nightlife, including dozens of mostly excellent seafood restaurants, as well as snorkelling, scuba diving, a turtle pool, village tours and sunset dhow cruises.

There are actually three, very different Nungwis: the village itself, which sits a short distance inland and is practically invisible from the shore, and the two main stretches of beach, where almost all the hotels, bars and restaurants are located. The **eastern shore** is very calm, with no facilities whatsoever outside of its few hotels, which makes it a nice retreat for smoochy couples. The **western shore** is a different story, having been overrun by a flurry of development, and is positively infested with tourists and associated hangers-on, including an army of often very pushy touts, as well as a surprising number of wannabe gigolos (there's evidently a market). For a long time, locals managed to shrug off the invasion, but these days there's a quite palpable sense of bitterness in the air, which you might feel when walking around the village: one too many years of idiotic tourists sauntering around the village in swimwear, and the ever-increasing number of walls around resorts that are blocking access to the coast.

## Arrival and information

Nungwi is 59km from Stone Town. #116 **daladalas** run here throughout the day (roughly 2hr; Tsh2000) from the west side of Creek Road, north of the Central Market, and drop you at the end of the tarmac, just short of the village centre. Most tourists, however, come on **shared minibuses** ($10;see p.530), bookable at Stone Town's hotels. Most leave at 8am; in high season, they may also leave at 3pm. They should drop you at your chosen hotel, but some drivers are keen to punt their passengers in the direction of *Amaan Bungalows*, or somewhere else that pays them commission.

**Bicycles** can be rented from locals and hotels; around $10 a day. An increasing number of hotels offer **internet access**, including wi-fi. Otherwise try Nungwi School (Mon–Fri daytimes); *Amaan Bungalows* (daily 7am–11pm); or *Langi Langi Beach Bungalows* (daily 8am–8pm).

# Accommodation

Nungwi has over two dozen **hotels**, mostly clusters of whitewashed bungalows with standard-issue makuti-thatched roofs. Many are quite bland, overpriced even by Zanzibar's standards, and not especially welcoming. The good news is that there are still a handful of decent places to choose from. The presence or absence of watersports shouldn't be a factor when choosing a hotel, as activities can be arranged anywhere.

The **western shore**, particularly the headland from *Z Hotel* to *Paradise Beach Hotel*, is in the thick of the tourist action, and can be busy as well as loud. South of *Z Hotel*, the beach is a little calmer as far as *Baobab Beach Resort*, currently an Italian all-inclusive. The beach north of *Paradise Beach Hotel* is also calmer but is spoiled by concrete sea walls and barricades. The shoreline east of *Smiles Beach Hotel*, including the entire eastern cape, can be covered in **seaweed** between November and January.

The beach on the **eastern shore**, which for the most part lies below a raised headland, has been left alone, and is consequently rather nicer. However, there's nothing much happening on the east side: the restaurants and bars are inside the hotels. Incidentally, **walking** along the beach east of the lighthouse can be unsafe at night.

**Amaan Bungalows** ☏024/224 0026, ⓦwww
.amaanbungalows.com. There are over fifty rooms here, but unless you're on a budget and go for one at the back, only the five sea-view ones (not sixteen as they claim) are worth staying in: small but brilliantly located in a wooden terrace built partly *over* the sea (the front of the rooms and their balconies are on stilts, which get wet feet at high tide). Those rooms are a/c, but are nonetheless quite basic for the price – easy to forgive given the views. The hotel's restaurant (*Fat Fish*) is average at best. BB ④–⑥, sea view ⑥

**Flame Tree Cottages** ☏024/224 0100, ⓦwww
.flametreecottages.com. A short distance beyond the busiest part of northwest Nungwi, this is a very calm, walled-in collection of bungalows run by a Zanzibari/Scottish couple, with a homely kind of feel. The beach wall, whilst not helping the beach paradise illusion, does at least keep out Nungwi's ever-burgeoning army of touts, though of course this means you're also less likely to meet locals. The twelve one-storey cottages, and the two-storey honeymoon suite, are simple and comfortable, with a/c, fans, fridge, a kitchen, and a breakfast terrace. The beachside restaurant varies from average to good. Village tours can be arranged with the staff. ⑥

**Jambo Bungalows** ☏0773/109343,
ⓔjambobungalows@yahoo.com. One of Nungwi's oldest and more affordable hotels, with a nice stretch of beach nearby, this has finally been tarted up a bit and whilst still a little basic (linoleum floors, hmm) it's clean and acceptable, and has partial sea views from most of its rooms (two per bungalow). Helpful staff and a good restaurant. BB ④

**Langi Langi Beach Bungalows**
☏024/224 0470, ⓦwww.langilangizanzibar
.com. Whilst not in keeping with Nungwi's traditional low-rise style, the Arabian design, both architectural and interior, isn't completely out of place, and overall this is a calm, elegant, friendly and effectively run hotel. Rooms at the back, hidden amidst lush gardens, are in semi-detached bungalows and are very well-equipped (including a/c); those at the front – with arched doorways, exposed roof pillars, and a smattering of antiques – are more expensive suites, some with spectacular sea views (and balconies too), others overlooking the swimming pool. The open-sided restaurant (see p.560) also has great views, and a solid reputation. BB ⑥–⑦

**Mnarani Beach Cottages** ☏024/224 0494 or
0777/415551, ⓦwww.lighthousezanzibar.com.
There's always a warm welcome at this small, intimate and efficiently run mini-resort on the quieter eastern flank of the peninsula, set beside a wonderful cove (accessed via steps) in lush gardens full of labelled plants and trees. The standard rooms are twelve smallish, bright orange *makuti*-thatched cottages with a/c, eight of which have sea views – and are good value. Larger rooms and family apartments also available. There are sun loungers and hammocks on the beach, a bar nestled among coconut palms, a curvaceous swimming pool, and an average-to-good seafood restaurant – dine on a terrace or, at night, on the beach. Snorkelling equipment is available, and they have a dhow for cruises and fishing. Free internet access. HB ⑥–⑧

**Ras Nungwi Beach Hotel** ☏024/223 3767,
ⓦwww.rasnungwi.com. Along with *Z Hotel*, this is

Nungwi's most expensive option, an unusually pretty 32-room resort set on a palm-dotted outcrop beside a lovely stretch of sand on the east coast, and which has resisted the temptation to add on more rooms. Prices depend on room size and proximity to the beach – in this bracket, you might as well cough up the extra for a sea-view chalet. All rooms have a/c, fans and balconies, and are attractively decorated. The hotel also boasts a swimming pool, several bars and restaurants (occasional live music, and seafood buffets twice a week), a spa (massages), internet access, and a branch of Zanzibar Watersports (see p.513) for diving as well as windsurfing and motorized sports. Closed April to mid-June. HB ❾

**Sazani Beach Hotel** ☎024/224 0014, ⓦwww .sazanibeach.com. A small, relaxed place on a lovely east-coast beach, miles from the western tourist hub. It has just ten well-equipped, en-suite rooms (they call them "snuggeries") in the colourful gardens, most with sea views from their verandas. There's also a good beachside bar and restaurant. HB ❻

**Smiles Beach Hotel** ☎024/224 0472 or 0777/417676, ⓦwww.smilesbeachhotel.com. An amusing foray into kitsch, with four two-storey Toytown houses with red tin roofs and external spiral staircases facing the sea (the beach lies beyond an unsightly seawall, as with other hotels in the area). The sixteen rooms, including triples, have a/c, sea-view balconies, satellite TV and spotless bathrooms. There's a restaurant by the ocean, a boat for snorkelling or sunset cruises, and the staff are helpful. Closed April & May. BB ❻

**Union Beach Bungalows** ☎0777/870345. Next to *Jambo Bungalows*, this is Nungwi's cheapest option and although a little run-down is a welcoming place. The rooms, all twin-bed, are in five semi-detached cottages beside the shore, fringed by an ugly scatter of rocks. There's also a small restaurant (no alcohol). BB ❹

**Z Hotel** ☎0732/940303, ⓦwww.thezhotel.com. Nungwi's first "boutique" hotel, a sadly graceless four-storey block dumped on the edge of a once beautiful coral rise – all in the best tradition of contemporary designs, meaning a complete eyesore. The love-it-or-loathe-it theme continues inside, where you can look forward to designer accoutrements in the manner of Philippe Starck, together with the latest mod-cons, including cable TV delivered via wall-mounted plasma screens, and to be fair the hotel certainly hits the mark for its intended market. Has a swimming pool on a deck in front, a nicely positioned restaurant (see p.560) with sea views, and a tapas and cocktail bar. Closed mid-April to end-May. HB ❽–❾

## Along the western shore

In spite of the tourist trade, Nungwi itself remains a traditional fishing village, whose history of seafaring and dhow building is a source of pride. The **dhow builders** use the stretch of beach beyond *Nungwi Village Beach Resort* (soon to become a *Holiday Inn*); the craftsmen are used to inquisitive tourists, but ask before taking photos. Nearby, at the back of the beach, is a cluster of wooden structures that become the daily **fish market** whenever the fishermen return (depends on the tides). Moored just offshore here are dozens of *ngalawa* outriggers.

At the northernmost tip of Unguja, Ras Nungwi, stands a lighthouse built in 1886, which is out of bounds. Just before the lighthouse is **Mnarani Aquarium** (daily 9am–6pm; $2 or Tsh2500), a natural sixty by twenty-metre pond of usually murky water that's surrounded by porous coral ragstone into which seawater seeps at high tide (the water is clearest two hours before). Housing a number of hawksbill and green turtles (ng'amba and kasakasa respectively), this started out in 1993 as little more than a money-making scheme for locals, but over time has accrued more noble aims, these days tagging and releasing excess turtles: the pool rarely contains more than twenty, and the average sojourn of an individual before being released is about three years. The turtles, both species of which are endangered, are brought in by fishermen who occasionally catch them in their nets. There's a walkway over the pond from where you can feed seaweed to the denizens; the water, whose level varies according to the tide, also contains grey mullet and trevally.

All these attractions are included in the locally run **Nungwi Cultural Village Tour**, which you can book at a hut outside the aquarium ($15 per person). The two-and-a-half-hour walk includes visits to old mosques, medicinal trees and

▲ Sunset dhow cruise, Nungwi

plants, markets, basket-weavers and a curious haunted saltwater well, much used for washing in the morning – the spirits evidently being late risers.

## Watersports and cruises

All of Nungwi's hotels can arrange **snorkelling trips** or find you equipment to rent ($5 a day is fair, but $10 is the norm), though for longer trips where safety is a concern, it would be safer to go through one of the **dive centres** reviewed on p.513. As for other watersports, it's really just a question of asking around, as outfits start up and disappear on an almost seasonal basis. For an idea of maximum prices, Zanzibar Watersports at *Ras Nungwi Beach Hotel* charges $10 an hour for **kayaking**, $30 a hour for **windsurfing** and $65 for a snorkelling trip to **Mnemba Atoll**. You should be able to get the same things for about sixty percent of those prices elsewhere. Zanzibar Watersports is the only outfit to offer **waterskiing**, however: $70 for fifteen minutes. A place on a **sunset dhow cruise** can be booked through any hotel; the cost is generally $25–30 with drinks or snacks, $15–20 without.

## Eating and drinking

The string of **restaurants** along the western side of the cape is one of Nungwi's main attractions, where competition has succeeded, in most cases, to keep standards high. Overall, they're quite similar, both in price (around Tsh12,000 for a main course) and menus (pizzas, pasta, and lots of seafood), though ones right on the shore can be lackadaisical about service and quality, given that they're guaranteed clients on account of the location. Better than menu items, in many cases, are daily specials chalked up on boards by the beach. If you're on a tight budget, there are a few **local eat houses** (*mgahawa*) in the village behind the shore, particularly around and to the east of the school. Ask for *Mama Africa*, where for Tsh2000 you'll get a perfectly good filling meal, say beef stew with rice, or *ugali* with chicken. Nungwi's **nightlife**

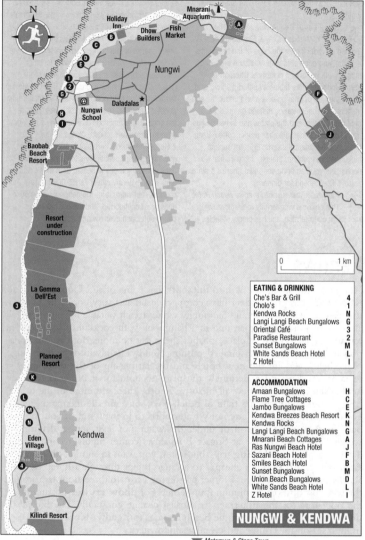

www.roughguides.com

559

is Zanzibar's liveliest, with plenty of bars to choose from along the western cape, impromptu moonlit drumming sessions on the beach, and **full-moon beach parties** at *Cholo's*.

**Cholo's** Unlike most other bars, this *Mad Max*-style Rasta refuge is right on the beach, and easily Nungwi's weirdest and funkiest joint, constructed almost entirely from flotsam. The seats are canoes, the bar is a dhow's prow, there's a motorbike up in a tree (don't ask), hammocks slung all over the place, and a cool chill-out zone perched on stilts above the bar. Drinks, including beers, fresh juices and cocktails are reasonably priced, and the limited seafood menu is good, whether for lunch or, better, for dinner (book this by lunchtime), when you can eat on the beach by a campfire, or in the chill-out zone. The music goes on till late.

🔥 **Langi Langi Beach Bungalows** The elegant *Marhaba Café & Restaurant* here is perched on a deck over the edge of the beach (it's on stilts), and decorated with Arabian reproduction antiques, old prints and octagonal Ottoman-style marble-topped coffee tables. Wonderful views, and avoids the trap of offering everything under the sun on its menu, concentrating instead on quality (seafood is great), and the pizzas and Indian dishes aren't half bad either; also has proper coffee, fresh juices, and decadent desserts. Efficient service (language is a problem, though), big portions. No alcohol, but you can bring your own (there's a store nearby). Book ahead for dinner.

🔥 **Paradise Restaurant** *Paradise Beach Hotel.* This enjoys a wonderfully romantic view from its wooden terrace, and has plenty of tables with unobstructed sea views. Both the service and the food are generally excellent, whether full meals (a wide variety of barbecued fish, also lemongrass-laced seafood), lighter bites such as pizzas (wood-fired), snacks or real coffee. Particularly good is the grilled seafood platter, which includes lobster, crayfish, crab, calamari, octopus and fish (Tsh30,000; enough for two people). The sea-view terrace, looking both north and west, is smaller than at other places, so come early for a table right at the edge. It also functions as a bar, with a preference for Tanzanian sounds. Closed in May.

**Z Hotel** Pretentious, certainly, but the restaurant and bar here are beautifully sited on a wooden deck extending over the beach. Both meals and drinks are expensive (over Tsh15,000 for main courses), but worth it for the delicious views. Also does great cappuccino, and the bar has huge comfy sofas and even swings.

# Kendwa

Nungwi's little sister, just 3km to the south, has come of age. Until 2007 or so, **KENDWA** was pure budget bliss: cheap, cheerful and very cool. The beach is still exceptional – a wide and blindingly white stretch suitable for swimming at all tides, or just lounging around in a hammock with cocktail to hand. And it remains a cheerful sort of place, too, but cheap it is no more. Both accommodation and food prices have spiralled, pushing Kendwa firmly into the mid-range. Nonetheless, despite the new hotels and the tarting-up of the older ones, it remains low-key, and is definitely the place to head for if Nungwi feels too brash, even if Kendwa's new all-inclusive resorts (there are more in the offing) have brought with them a train of beach boys, souvenir salesmen and gigolos. For now, there are few if any noisy watersports to jolt you out of your reverie, but there's plenty to do on or under the water, not least **scuba diving**, for which Scuba Do (p.513) at Sunset Bungalows comes highly recommended. They also offer **snorkelling** trips, but unless you want to snorkel off Mnemba Atoll (see p.512; $45), it's cheaper to arrange things through a hotel; Kendwa Rocks, for example, charges $15 per person for a two-to-three-hour trip around the reefs just offshore, minimum four people. For **dhow cruises**, ask around, as the operators (or the fishermen's contacts) change constantly. The big *jahazi* dhow that you might see on the beach belongs to Kendwa Rocks, and is used in high season for cruises and evening sundowners.

## Arrival and information

Kendwa lies west of the asphalt road to Nungwi. To get here **from Stone Town**, seats on daily tourist minibuses (Tsh10,000) can be booked at any hotel; they leave Stone Town at 8am, turning back around 10.30am. Cheaper is to catch a #116 Nungwi daladala from the west side of Creek Road (every half hour or so from 6am to 6pm; Tsh2000; around 2hr); get off at the signposted junction for Kendwa and walk the remaining 1.5km. To get here **from Nungwi**, 2–3km to the north, catch a daladala back down to the junction. Alternatively, ask around for a boat: there's nothing formal, but you shouldn't pay more than Tsh4000 if sharing with others, or Tsh20,000 per boat. Unfortunately, **walking from Nungwi** along the beach is not recommended: on a rising or high tide you risk getting stuck between the coral cliffs and the sea, and muggers have been known to prey on tourists.

**Internet access** is available at *Kendwa Rocks* (Tsh2000 per 30min), and there are a couple of **minimarkets** at the south end of the beach.

## Accommodation

In high season, you'll be hard-pressed to find a double room for less than $80 a night, and, given the pace of change, this may be considerably more by the time you read this. Still, despite the lurch upmarket, Kendwa's **hotels** have a more intimate feeling than the majority of those in Nungwi. The exceptions, inevitably, are a couple of all-inclusive resorts whose Italian designers evidently took a break from their otherwise irreproachable sense of style, including the stinging eyesore that is *La Gemma Dell'Est* at the north end of the beach.

The following hotels all have beach fronts, but the bulk of their rooms are on the coral bluff just behind. The only hotel whose beach is directly accessible to wheelchairs is *La Gemma Dell'Est* (ⓦ www.planhotel.com; ❾), which – architectural crimes aside – is one of Zanzibar's best-run all-inclusives. Independent establishments are reviewed below.

**Kendwa Breezes Beach Resort** ☎0774/687336, ⓦ www.kendwabreezes.com. On Kendwa's north side, this is a newcomer to the fray, and – for now at least – good value, given that the rooms have sea-view balconies. All are in spacious individual concrete bungalows cascading down the slope, their design supposedly based on Stone Town's Old Fort, but actually resembling any off-the-shelf holiday chalet but with mock crenellations on top and big glass doors. Inside, you'll find large four-posters, a/c, ceiling fans, box nets and a safe. Also has a couple of restaurants, a beachfront bar and internet café. BB ❻
**Kendwa Rocks** ☎0774/415475 or 0777/415475, ⓦ www.kendwarocks.com. This used to run neck and neck with the superficially similar *Sunset Bungalows*, but sloppy service has proved something of a theme of late. That said, it does have some of Kendwa's cheapest rooms, being very basic palm-thatch *bandas* right at the back. Costing twice as much are eight large coconut-wood cabins on stilts in a sandy clearing behind the beach, most of them containing two guest rooms; all have lots of varnished wood, rattan furniture, woven mats and partial sea views. At the back of the beach are three two-storey houses containing twelve rooms: the "Stone" ground-floor rooms are dark but have a/c, and framed masks for decoration; brighter and breezier are the upstairs rooms. Behind, on the ragged coral scarp, are several more two-storey

houses filled with fake antiques. Bar and restaurant on the beach. BB *bandas* ❸, rooms ❺–❻
🏃 **Sunset Bungalows** ☎0777/414647, ⓦ www.sunsetkendwa.com. Assuming its pricing remains sane, this is a bargain, especially the eighteen large, modern apartments right at the back, which are in excellent shape. Occupying a series of two-storey buildings, these are very well kitted out, including a/c, and have distant sea views from their verandas. The beach comes right up to the edge of the coral bluff, forming a kind of (dry) sandy inlet scattered with trees. Lining this are six small and relatively basic beach *bandas* decorated with colourful *kangas*; each has two guest rooms, but no sea views as they're side-on, and the beach bar and restaurant sit between them and the ocean. BB ❺
**White Sands Beach Hotel** ☎0773/924170, ⓦ www.whitesandhotelznz.com. A series of bungalows on top of the coral bluff behind the beach, built in generic Mediterranean style: inoffensive but nothing special. The rooms are somewhat bare but nicely decorated. There are three kinds: small and cosy ones in thatched cottages at the back with cold water and fans; slightly bigger cottages with hot water and a/c; and – better – four rooms in two cottages at the front with good views. There are hammocks slung between tamarisk trees on the beach, and a beautifully designed restaurant and bar. BB ❺–❻

## Eating and drinking

All of Kendwa's hotels have their own beach bars, **restaurants** and musical tastes; you're welcome at any of them, even the all-inclusives. At most of them, menus and prices are virtually identical, with fishy main courses going for Tsh12,000 and up. Much cheaper is an unnamed local restaurant on the rocky road leading to the hotels, at which you can eat your fill for Tsh3000; it's just south of the small shops.

If you're around on the Saturday closest to a full moon, *Kendwa Rocks* hosts a by-now very famous **full-moon beach party** (free entry, but Tsh5000 minimum spend), which kicks off a few hours after sunset with acrobats, and continues well into the night. *Kendwa Rocks* also offers a distinctly provocative evening "booze cruise" in a converted jahazi dhow, for $20.

**Che's Bar & Grill** *Duniani Lodge*. Named after the revolutionary poster boy, this is one of few restaurants to strike out with its own menu, quite different to the rest, and has an excellent reputation for seafood, including fish cakes and seafood salad. It also has plenty of vegetarian choice, for example, spinach lasagne. The bar serves great cocktails and juices. By day, relax with one of the books from the library.

**Kendwa Rocks** This *makuti*-thatched bar and restaurant, the bar itself constructed from *mitumbwi* dugouts, is plush in appearance, but the quality of the cooking is rather variable – ask other tourists for their opinion before splashing out. BBQ buffets are held on the beach whenever it's busy.

**Oriental Café** *La Gemma Dell'Est*. This massive all-inclusive resort is a grisly architectural blight, but the theatrical Ottoman-style restaurant, bar and lounge propped up at the end of its wooden jetty – right over the water – are perfectly placed, so long as your table faces out to sea. Particularly nice at sunset, whether in the company of a shisha pipe, a cup of tea or a beer. For a full meal, expect to pay at least $30.

**Sunset Bungalows** *Kendwa Rocks'* main competitor, also on the beach, and with a similarly youthful

vibe. The menu – à la carte, plus specials chalked up on a blackboard – is impressively well-rounded, with delights such as grilled calamari in ginger sauce, and no less than seven takes on lobster, including on kebab skewers. Carnivores have a good choice, too, but don't expect the steak – something of a novelty on Zanzibar – to be anything like tender. The vegetarian selection is poor other than some surprisingly decent pizzas (Tsh8000). Shoots itself in the foot with instant coffee, and (sometimes) juice from a bottle rather than freshly pressed.

**White Sands Beach Hotel** A very stylish place with upbeat music split into three areas: the bar, which also has swings; dining tables on the circular building's perimeter; and a wonderful lounge around a sand pit in the centre, with big rustic-style cushions, comfy loungers and draped lampshades, all creating a magical nocturnal mood. *Tingatinga* painters ply their art in an adjacent building. The menu is short but well thought out and enticing: say, marinated sailfish for starters, followed by crab claws with chilli, and cake and whipped cream to finish. There's always a decent vegetarian option, too.

# Pemba

The island of **Pemba**, 48km northeast of Unguja, is Zanzibar's forgotten half, traditionally conservative, religious and superstitious, and far removed from the Zanzibari mainstream. Measuring 67km from north to south and 22km from east to west, Pemba's highest point is no more than 100m above sea level, yet with its low hills gouged by gullies and entered by snaking mangrove-lined creeks, the island presents a lush and fertile profile compared to Unguja, and aptly fits the name given it by the Arab geographer Yakut ibn Abdallah al-Rumi (1179–1229), who called it *Jazirat al-Khadhra*, the Green Island – which holiday brochures have since changed to "Emerald Island".

Not that you'll find that many holiday brochures for Pemba: the island – and its tourism potential – has long been ignored by Zanzibar's Unguja-based

government, and Pemba is, if anything, sinking ever deeper into **poverty**. Few people own land (most are tenants of the government), per capita income is Tanzania's lowest, and child mortality among the country's highest. Meanwhile, the island's lamentable infrastructure continues to crumble away: roads are pitted with potholes, there's not a single working street light on the island, power cuts are a daily reality, and the water supply is more likely to be trucked in than arrive through pipes. Not surprisingly, Pemba is a

## Getting to and from Pemba

Most tourists fly to Pemba: there are daily **flights** from Stone Town ($100; 30min), Dar es Salaam ($130; 1hr) and Tanga ($80; 20min), operated by Coastal Aviation, Tropical Air and ZanAir. Flights land at **Karume airport**, 6km east of Chake Chake. The taxis outside charge $10–15 to Chake Chake, $35–40 to Mkoani or Wete, and up to $80 to the two beach hotels on Ras Kigomasha in the north. Negotiating a deal is easier if you arrange for the same driver to pick you up when you leave, or if you use him for a day-trip. If you've arranged to be picked up by a hotel, be sure it's their car you clamber into, not that of someone trying their luck. There are occasionally daladalas from the airport to Chake Chake, but their main purpose is to carry airport staff back home – likely a few hours after you touch down.

**Arriving by ferry** is cheaper, but sailings are regularly cancelled (and boats even impounded), so things up in Dar, Stone Town or Tanga. Pemba's ferry port is at **Mkoani** in the south, to which there are sailings most days from **Stone Town**, most of them overnight, and costing $25; the much faster *Sepideh* (which starts in Dar and sails by day) charges $40–50 for the two hour trip. For more details, and information on buying tickets, see p.531. Leaving Pemba, you'll find ticket offices in sheds by the port entrance in Mkoani, and an ever-changing handful of "agents" along the main roads in Chake Chake and Wete, often little more than a desk, chair and someone with a mobile. Be aware that these agents are often ill-informed about departure days and times other than for the boats they usually deal with, so if it's just information you're after, ask as many people as possible.

Sailing from **Tanga**, most boats head for the dhow harbour of **Wete**, which – since 2004 – has enjoyed a more or less weekly connection on passenger-carrying cargo boats, usually leaving Tanga on Tuesday morning, heading back Sunday morning, and taking six hours each way. If history be a guide, however, this is liable to be suspended at any time.

---

stronghold of Zanzibar's opposition party, the **Civic United Front (CUF)** (see p.586), support for which has only deepened Pemba's marginalization. Since 1995, the outcome of all this has been a recurring cycle of political unrest and brutal **repression**, especially around election time – the next ones are due at the end of 2010.

Pemba has three main towns: the capital **Chake Chake** in the centre, **Mkoani**, the main port, in the south, and the livelier dhow harbour of **Wete** in the north. There's not an awful lot to do in any of them, but they do contain most of Pemba's accommodation and are good bases for exploring further afield. Rewarding stops include the primeval **Ngezi Forest** in the north; a scatter of tumbledown **ruins** that tell the story of much of the Swahili coast; a handful of deserted, if difficult to access, beaches (part of their charm); beautiful offshore islets; and great **scuba diving** – which is really the main reason to come. Despite these attractions, there are rarely more than a few dozen tourists on the island at any one time, and facilities are extremely limited, so you should **book ahead** for beachside accommodation and diving.

Pemba's **climate** is wetter than Unguja's. The **long rains** (masika), during which it can pour constantly for weeks, fall between April and June, with May often completely washed out, as well as windy. The **short rains** (vuli), generally brief bursts early in the morning and again in the afternoon, supposedly fall between mid-October and end-November, but September can be very wet, too, as can December. Unless you're diving, the rains aren't an ideal time to be around. Nor is **Ramadan** (dates on p.72), when eating out by day is quite impossible.

# Chake Chake and around

Pemba's capital, **CHAKE CHAKE** ("Chake" for short), is the most interesting of the island's towns, and even has a modest museum in an Omani fortress. Unless you're diving, in which case it's best to base yourself at Ras Kigomasha (see p.573), Chake Chake is the most useful base for exploring the island, as there are daladalas from here to most destinations, and a couple of affordable tour companies. A special treat, especially for snorkellers, is **Misali Island** – an unspoilt gem of a place said to be the spot where Captain Kidd buried his loot. Another good excursion is to **Pujini**, for its medieval tyrant's ruined citadel.

## Arrival and accommodation

For information on getting into town from the airport, see p.564. Arriving by **daladala** from Wete (#606; Tsh1000) or Mkoani (#603; Tsh1000), you'll be dropped either at the junction by the Esso petrol station, or at the stand behind the market. Be wary of anyone offering their services as guides: reports of theft have circulated in the past, and seeing as Chake's tour companies (p.567) are reasonably priced, there's little sense in taking a risk. Bucket showers are the norm in Chake Chake's **hotels**, as the water supply, pumped from bore holes, depends on the sorry antics of Zanzibar's electricity company.

**Evergreen Hotel** Facing the People's Bank of Zanzibar ☏024/245 2633. A new, three-storey block with eight en-suite rooms (including one twin), with big nets and fans, but a very musty smell during the rains, and unsavoury bathrooms. You can minimize this unpleasantness by getting one of the three rooms with a balcony. Restaurant on top. BB ❸

**Le-Tavern Hotel** Just west of *Evergreen Hotel* ☏024/245 2660. This modern two-storey place is a reasonable option, friendly if you can surmount the language barrier and with small but clean rooms, either en suite or with shared bathrooms. The better rooms have views over town. During Ramadan, the restaurant on top (see p.567) is closed, so no breakfast. BB ❸

**Pemba Clove Inn** 550m west of the People's Bank of Zanzibar ☏024/245 2795 or 0777/420702, ✉pembacloveinn@zanzinet.com. Easily the town's best lodging, a new blue-glass business-class affair down by the mangrove swamp. There are two types of room, both a/c: most of the "Standard" ones are at the back and are loud if the generator kicks in; quieter are the "Deluxe" rooms at the front overlooking the mangroves, which have four-poster beds and box nets, fans as well as a/c, furniture made from stripy coconut wood, and satellite TV. Good restaurant (see p.567), internet access, and tours can be arranged. BB ❺

**Pemba Island Hotel** 50m west of the People's Bank of Zanzibar ☏0777/428303, ✇www.pemba-islandhotel.co.tz. A clean, modern four-storey building with en-suite rooms (smallish mosquito nets); those with two beds are $10 more and have better bathrooms. All have a/c, fan and fridge and satellite TV. There's also a restaurant (see p.567); no alcohol. BB ❹

## The Town

Chake Chake has a nicely relaxed atmosphere, and people are genuinely pleased – and curious – to see tourists looking around. The town's liveliest point is its **market** (daily from 7am; busiest Mon and Fri) where, aside from herbs and spices, you can buy aromatic essential oils, and tasty, if expensive, clove honey. Also on offer are colourfully painted straw plate-covers that look like hats, and aromatic **halua** – a sticky boiled goo (think Turkish Delight) inherited from the Omanis. Following the narrow road south of the market brings you to the **Chief Minister's Office**, a bizarre, pale blue building dominated by a round tower studded with protruding hollow cylinders, that perhaps aptly resemble the suckers on octopus tentacles. Opposite is the glorious colonial-era **Omani Court House**, with an impressive carved door and a clock tower that only tells the time twice a day.

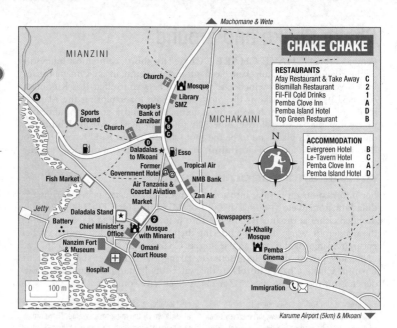

Machomane & Wete

**CHAKE CHAKE**

MIANZINI

Church

Mosque
Library
SMZ

People's
Bank of
Zanzibar

Sports
Ground

Church

MICHAKAINI

Daladalas
to Mkoani

Esso

Former
Government Hotel

Tropical Air

Fish Market

Air Tanzania &
Coastal Aviation

NMB Bank

Market

Zan Air

Jetty

Daladala Stand

Battery

Chief Minister's
Office

Mosque
with Minaret

Nanzim Fort
& Museum

Omani
Court House

Newspapers

Al-Khalily
Mosque

Pemba
Cinema

Hospital

0   100 m

Immigration

N

**RESTAURANTS**
| | |
|---|---|
| Afay Restaurant & Take Away | C |
| Bismillah Restaurant | 2 |
| Fil-Fil Cold Drinks | 1 |
| Pemba Clove Inn | A |
| Pemba Island Hotel | D |
| Top Green Restaurant | B |

**ACCOMMODATION**
| | |
|---|---|
| Evergreen Hotel | B |
| Le-Tavern Hotel | C |
| Pemba Clove Inn | A |
| Pemba Island Hotel | D |

Karume Airport (5km) & Mkoani

Continuing along the same street and turning right at the junction brings you to the diminutive **Nanzim Fort**, built in the eighteenth century by the Omanis but incorporating the foundations of a Portuguese fortress built in 1594 (the square towers are the clue, as Omanis preferred round ones). Much of the fort was demolished in the early 1900s; part of what's left is a charming **museum** (Mon–Fri 8.30am–4.30pm, Sat & Sun 9am–4pm; Tsh2000). There are just three small rooms, but the displays – in English and Kiswahili – are very well done, and cover archaeology, seafaring, and the role of Zanzibar's rulers in relation to Pemba.

For something completely different, try an evening out at **Pemba Cinema** on the main road south. Mind-bogglingly dilapidated in appearance, this is not just Zanzibar's but Tanzania's very last small cinema, and still manages to get hold of real celluloid: Bollywood weekday evenings (6pm), American B-movies on weekends. Be patient while the projectionist changes reels, as he needs to manually rewind the first before popping on the second. All in all, a great night out for a mere Tsh500.

## Eating and drinking

All but one of Chake Chake's **restaurants** are part of hotels, and charge tourist prices (around Tsh10,000 a plate for the basics). For cheaper eats, explore the area around the market, or try the street-food stalls on the main road just north of Evergreen Hotel. Busiest at night, this is where you can find everything from *chipsi mayai* and grilled goat meat to superb seafood, including succulent octopus stew, bite-sized fish cakes, grilled squid and fish, and various juices: try tamarind (*ukwaju*) or the rather wonderful *bungo*, halfway between a mango and a peach. To finish off, track down a **coffee vendor**, where for Tsh100 or less you'll be handed a tiny porcelain cup filled with scaldingly hot and bitter coffee. None of the restaurants serve **alcohol**, and there are no bars in town.

**Afay Restaurant & Take Away** Top floor of *Le-Tavern hotel*. Basic but decent, with views over town.

**Bismillah Restaurant** Facing the market. The only real cheapie, a simple *mgahawa* that dishes up meals in the "rice with fish, chicken with chips" tradition, at Tsh4000 a plate. Order early for a little more choice.

**Fil-Fil Cold Drinks** On the main road near *Le-Tavern Hotel*. Does what it says on the tin, and nothing more.

**Pemba Clove Inn** 550m west of the People's Bank of Zanzibar. Chake Chake's plushest place, with a large and a/c, if rather soulless, dining room. The menu is short and includes good vegetarian options, such as vegetable *pilau* with pickles. Officially, in Ramadan it's only open to overnight guests, but they'll likely make an exception for tourists.

**Pemba Island Hotel** 50m west of the People's Bank of Zanzibar. The third-floor restaurant has good views and a typical Swahili menu, including octopus with coconut sauce and chicken *pilau*.

**Top Green Restaurant** Above *Evergreen Hotel*. Good views but otherwise nothing special, and it's best to order half a day before.

## Listings

**Airline tickets** Coastal Aviation, at the airport ☎0777/418343, ✆aviation@coastal.cc; ZanAir, beside NMB bank ☎024/245 2990, ✆reservations@zanair.com; Tropical Air, just down from the Esso station ☎0777/859996, ✆info@tropicalair.co.tz.

**Banks and exchange** Chake's banks – NMB and the Zanzibar People's Bank on the main road, and Barclays in the former *Government Hotel* – will change cash without much fuss, but traveller's cheques will likely be impossible. They all have ATMs for Visa and MasterCard, but no guarantee that they'll be filled with money, or have electricity for them to function.

**Ferry tickets** Chake's tour operators (see below) sell ferry tickets.

**Hospital** The government-run Chake Chake Hospital beside Nanzim Fort (☎024/245 2311) is very run-down; the one in Mkoani is better. There's a good pharmacy nearby. For diagnostic tests, the Public Health Laboratory in Machomane (☎024/245 2473) is reliable.

**Internet access** Adult Training Centre, on the main road just north of Air Tanzania (daily 7.30am–4pm; Tsh1000 per hr); ZCE Internet Café, inside the former *Government Hotel* (erratic hours; Tsh1000 per hr).

**Telephones** TTCL is on the main road near the Esso station (Tsh2500 per min for international calls).

**Tour operators** The following offer affordable half- and full-day trips all over the island: Pemba Island Reasonable Tours & Safaris, under *Evergreen Hotel* ☎0777/435266, ✆www.pembareasonabletours .com; Treasure Island Tours, beside *Le-Tavern Hotel* ☎024/245 2045 or 0777/470328, ✆reasurecom pany2005@yahoo.com. More reliable than those two, but a little more expensive, is *Pemba Clove Inn* (see p.565). Tour operators also rent motorbikes: a 125cc bike (a *pikipiki*) costs around $30 a day excluding fuel.

## Misali Island

The island of **MISALI**, 17km west of Chake Chake, is a reef that emerged from the ocean some fifteen thousand years ago. It's one of Pemba's highlights, offering idyllic beaches, nature trails for spotting flying foxes (fruit bats), good snorkelling and superb diving. It also has a touch of historical romance, as the legendary pirate **Captain Kidd** is said to have used the island as a hideaway, and to have buried booty here.

A more evident treasure is Misali's rich **ecosystem**, which boasts 42 types of coral, over 300 species of fish, a rare subspecies of vervet monkey, endangered colonies of flying foxes, nesting sites for green and hawksbill turtles, and a large, if rarely seen, population of nocturnal **coconut crabs**. The island, part of a conservation area, is uninhabited except for rangers and passing fishermen. The sanctity of the island, and its name, are explained by the legend of a **prophet** named Hadhara (meaning "knowledge" or "culture"), who appeared before Misali's fishermen and asked them for a prayer mat (msala). There was none, so Hadhara declared that since the island pointed towards Mecca, it would be his prayer mat.

A $5 **entrance fee**, generally not included in quotes for tours ($50–65 per person with Chake Chake's tour operators, $35 from Mkoani), is payable on arrival. The island's **visitor centre** is on Baobab Beach where the boats pull up, and has good displays on ecology and wildlife plus information sheets that you can take with you while snorkelling or walking the trails. There's no accommodation and camping is prohibited, as is alcohol.

### Snorkelling

The shallow reef around Misali is good for snorkelling, though the current can be trying for weaker swimmers and you should stay close to the shore as currents further out can be dangerously strong; ask the folks at the visitor centre for advice. For confident swimmers, a **submerged coral mountain** off the western shore is an extraordinary place; the mountain, one of four in the area, peaks at 3–5m below sea level: you'll need a boat to get there. More accessible is the shallow reef flanking Baobab Beach, which starts a mere 10–40m from the shore. The shallower part features **conical sponges**, traditionally collected by fishermen for use as hats; further out, the reef is cut by sandy gullies and teems with life.

### Nature trails

A series of nature trails has been established around the island; pick up one of the information sheets from the visitor centre. The **Mangrove Trail** can be done on foot at low tide or in combination with snorkelling. The **Intertidal Trail** (low tide only) starts at Turtle Beach on the west side of the island, and includes a small isle connected by causeway that is popular with nesting sea birds. Mangroves and low-tide pools also feature. Another trail takes you past one of Misali's three **sacred caves**, believed by locals to be the abode of benevolent spirits. Each cave has a specially appointed traditional guardian (healer), and people leave offerings to the spirits, or to Allah, to seek intercession in worldly matters. The caves' sacred nature means that tourists should not enter if scantily dressed.

There's also a trail from Baobab Beach to Turtle Beach and to Mpapaini, whose caves contain roosts of **Pemban flying foxes**, an endangered species of bat. Go with a guide to avoid disturbing them. If you can get to Misali very early in the morning (leave before sunrise), you stand a slim chance of spotting a rare and shy subspecies of **Pemba vervet monkey**; your best bet is on the western beaches where they hunt for ghost crabs.

## The Pujini ruins

Some 10km southeast of Chake Chake, the **PUJINI RUINS** are the remains of a citadel dating from the heyday of the **Diba tribe** – possibly Persian descendants – who ruled eastern Pemba from the fifteenth to seventeenth centuries. The citadel was built by the tyrant Muhammad bin Abdulrahman, a merchant and pirate whose nickname, **Mkama Ndume**, means "grasper of men". The ruins (also known by his name) are defensively located on a hilltop and are now mostly rubble, but the presence of old tamarind and baobab trees makes them singularly photogenic. A **mosque** is the best-preserved building, but also noteworthy is a **well** half-filled with rubble, in the enclosure's northeastern corner. Legend has it that Mkama Ndume had two jealous wives; to prevent them meeting at the well, he had a dividing wall built inside it. One of the wives would use a bucket and rope whilst the other descended by a staircase – still visible – to reach the water. More likely though is that the small chamber at the foot of the staircase was a shrine to spirits (*majini*). Carved out of the soft limestone, it contains a lamp niche and a small plaster relief of a **siwa horn**. Long, heavy and frequently ornate, they were made from ivory, brass or wood and were symbols of sovereignty and authority all along the Swahili coast and on the Arabian Peninsula – the House of Wonders in Stone Town has a few examples. Another **staircase** leads up to the battlements, beyond which what looks like a dried moat was actually a canal that enabled dhows to be pulled inland for loading and offloading.

The ruins aren't signposted, so be sure that whoever accompanies you actually knows the place. **Renting a taxi** is the simplest approach; a half-day's rental costs $30–35 from Chake Chake. Alternatively, ask around about renting a **bicycle**. The site is 4km along a dirt road south of the airport, with the junction 1km before it.

# Mkoani

Pemba's main port, **MKOANI**, is where ferries from Stone Town and Dar dock, in spite of which the town is complete wasteland when it comes to facilities: it has just one combined guesthouse and restaurant, and virtually nothing else of use to travellers other than the island's best equipped hospital. Still, the market on the beach south of the ferry jetty is worth a peek before you move on, the locals are an unfailingly friendly bunch, and the guesthouse offers several very enjoyable day-trips by dhow. A pleasant way to while away a few hours is to walk up the coast to a lovely sandspit at **Ras Mkoasha**, 4km from town: just follow the road past *Jondeni Guest House*.

## Practicalities

The ferry port is 1km downhill from the town centre, where you can catch frequent **daladalas** to Chake Chake (#603, Tsh1000). The only **hotel** is the ⚓ *Jondeni Guest House* (☎024/245 6042 or 0777/460680, ⓔjondeniguest @hotmail.com; BB ❸). From the port, walk north along the broad dirt road for 800m; the guesthouse is on your left. Set on a high grassy bluff overlooking the sea, this is in fact the island's best budget hotel, and well used to backpackers, offering a wide range of affordable boat and snorkelling excursions. Accommodation ranges from dorms ($10 per person) to en-suite rooms, all with big semadari beds. There's a pleasant garden at the back with inspiring sea views, and the guesthouse doubles as Mkoani's only proper **restaurant** (no alcohol). The spiced octopus in coconut with mashed potatoes is particularly good (Tsh7000), and they're happy conjuring up something fancier, like prawns, if you order a few hours before.

Otherwise, eating out is limited to a couple of **food stalls** by the market and a couple more in front of the former *Government Hotel*, on the main road 600m east from the port, for mishkaki, grilled or fried fish, and octopus. Weirdly, the *Government Hotel*, whilst no longer offering rooms or meals, still functions as a **bar** – excepting Pemba's three beach hotels and an army barracks near Chake Chake, this is in fact the island's only bar, though its days are likely numbered.

## Boat tours and snorkelling from Mkoani

Mkoani's *Jondeni Guest House*, which owns a *mashua* dhow with twin outboards and a sun canopy, is the island's only affordable base for day-trips by boat. There are several good destinations within an hour's sail, including **Makoongwe Island**, 3km offshore, with a roost of rare Pemba flying foxes; and minuscule **Kwata Islet**, 7km west of Mkoani, which is practically all beach and has decent snorkelling and a patch of mangroves nearby.

## Bullfighting, Pemba-style

The village of **Kengeja** in Pemba's deep south would be unremarkable were it not for the curious spectacle of **bullfighting** (*Mchezo wa ngombe*), which takes place in the dry months of December to February, especially February. The fights are a hangover from the Portuguese presence, and, like the Portuguese *touradas*, don't result in the death of the animals.

The evening before a fight, villagers hold a dance called *umund* and visit graves to receive help from their ancestors and request the arrival of the rains. In the fights themselves, the bulls – initially tethered – are provoked by jostling crowds and pipe music until, sufficiently enraged, they are released, the crowd scatters and the "matador" takes over. Completely unarmed, he goads the bull with a white cloth. His skill lying in artfully dodging the bull's charges, while the pleasure for the crowd lies in observing the deft movements of the fighter (or seeing him scamper up the nearest tree whenever things get hairy).

**Tickets** for seats in the gender–segregated grandstands cost a few hundred shillings; it's free to join the crowds around the arena. **To get there**, catch a #215 daladala from Mkoani marked "Mwambe". From Chake Chake, take a #603 daladala towards Mkoani but get off at Mtambile junction and change there for a #215. There's no accommodation.

---

The isles can be visited individually, or combined as one trip for $25 per person (minimum two). Snorkelling at Misali Island (see p.567) costs $35 per person including entrance fee, and snorkelling over a shallow wreck at Panza Point in the south is $50. Jondeni also offers high-tide **mangrove tours** by dugout canoe ($10 per person) for birding and swimming, and **sailing** in ngalawa outriggers ($15 per person). All these trips require a day or two to arrange.

# Wete and around

North of Chake Chake, the land is flatter but just as lush, with extensive patches of forest surviving between cultivated areas. Rice is the staple crop here, although cloves are also grown – as your nostrils will tell you. The main town is the likeable dhow port of **WETE**, which has several good guesthouses and serves as a base for a series of attractions in the area, including **Ngezi Forest**; beautiful beaches at **Ras Kigomasha** in the far north, on which sit two of Pemba's three **beach hotels** (both with **scuba diving** centres); and several scatters of medieval **ruins**.

## Arrival and information

There are **two roads** from Chake Chake to Wete: the old and more direct one (30km; daladala #606 with the number painted in red) to the west, whose surface has all but vanished, and the fast Pemba North Feeder Road (35km; daladala #606, with the number painted in blue), which starts 7km north of Chake Chake at Melitano junction. **Daladalas** charge Tsh1000 from Chake, and finish at the side of the market in the centre of town. The best source of **tourist information** is the owner of Sharook Guest House, who also runs a variety of excursions in the area. For **souvenirs**, try the nameless but sweetly scented shop beside Pemba Crown Hotel, which is filled with herbs and spices, aromatic oils, honey, and pottery incense burners.

Internet access is available at Pemba Crown Hotel and at Benjamin Mkapa Teacher Training College nearby, both charging Tsh2000 per hr. As with Mkoani, change **money** before coming as there's no bank. **Plane** and **ferry tickets** can be bought at a number of ever-changing agents along the main road. Wete Hospital (℡024/245 4001) between the centre and the port is in reasonable shape, and Clove Island Pharmacy opposite Garden Restaurant is well stocked. **Excursions** in northern Pemba, including spice tours, can be arranged at Wete's hotels, the most experienced being Sharook Guest House: the standard cost for visiting Ngezi Forest is $30 per vehicle plus entrance fees. Wete's speciality, though, is a trip to **Fundo Island** by mashua dhow; you can either camp for the night or stay with a family for around $60–70 per person.

## Accommodation

Wete's **hotels** have improved markedly of late, even if electricity and water supplies are still at the mercy of the ZECO electric company.

**Bomani Guest House** Between the market and *Sharook Guest House* ℡024/245 4384. A sleepy, friendly and pleasingly prim-and-proper place with eight rooms (singles and doubles), all but one sharing bathrooms and with good box nets and ceiling fans. ❸

**Hill View Inn** On the way in from Chake Chake, behind the Soviet-style apartment blocks ℡0784/344359. A grey two-storey house with nine rooms, most with semadari beds, and five with bathrooms. All have box nets and ceiling fans, and the management are friendly and happy to arrange tours. To get there, follow the track from the main road between blocks #1 and #4 (the numbers are painted on the side). BB ❹

**Pemba Crown Hotel** Bomani St, in the centre ℡024/245 4191 or 0777/493667,

Ⓦwww.pembacrown.com. Centrally located, this new four-storey hotel is Wete's best, with eleven rooms on its top two floors, all with decent bathrooms, a/c, fans, round nets, and balconies. The staff are friendly and helpful, and there's internet access. BB ❸

**Sharook Guest House** In the centre ℡024/245 4386 or 0777/431012, Ⓔsharookguest@yahoo.com. Run by a welcoming and very helpful local family, this calm place is well used to tourists, and a bargain at the price. Rooms are large and have fans and round nets, and most also have bathrooms complete with toilet seats and paper (a rarity elsewhere). There's satellite TV in the sitting room by the entrance, and a wide choice of reliable tours. BB ❸

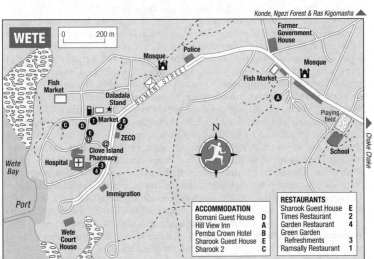

Konde, Ngezi Forest & Ras Kigomasha

**WETE**

0 — 200 m

Former Government House

Police
Mosque
Mosque
Fish Market
Fish Market
Daladala Stand
BOMANI STREET
Market
N
ZECO
Clove Island Pharmacy
Playing field
Hospital
Wete Bay
School
Immigration
Port
Wete Court House

Chake Chake

| ACCOMMODATION | | RESTAURANTS | |
|---|---|---|---|
| Bomani Guest House | D | Sharook Guest House | E |
| Hill View Inn | A | Times Restaurant | 2 |
| Pemba Crown Hotel | B | Garden Restaurant | 4 |
| Sharook Guest House | E | Green Garden | |
| Sharook 2 | C | Refreshments | 3 |
| | | Ramsally Restaurant | 1 |

**Sharook 2** 150m west of *Sharook Guest House*, same contacts. Construction on this new three-storey hotel beside a banana grove was almost complete at the time of writing, and promised much, especially the west-facing rooms on the second floor with sea views (the top floor is for dining). All rooms are large, tiled and well equipped, and all but one are en suite. BB ❹

## Eating and drinking

There's not a lot of formal choice for **eating out**, but one or two places turn up trumps if you order several hours before you intend to eat. Best of these is *Sharook Guest House* (see p.571), with a good range of very well-prepared dishes for around Tsh8000. Several basic restaurants along the main road provide cheaper meals, the best being *Times Restaurant* near *Pemba Crown Hotel*, which has a wide variety; *Garden Restaurant*, which does indeed have a garden; and *Green Garden Refreshments* (better for snacks) nearby, both at the west end of town. Near the market, the dingy-looking *Ramsally Restaurant* is reliable for *pilau* and *supu ya kuku* (chicken broth).

An often better choice are the ✻ **street food stalls** around the market and daladala stand, and along the main road near the post office. Wete's unusual speciality is **shellfish** or winkles, of which there are at least two kinds: *kombe*, having black-and-white shells, and *chaza*, with reddish ones. Grilled, they're a superb accompaniment to a filling and spicy soup based on tomatoes, potatoes and sliver-thin sticks of fried cassava. There's also goat meat *mishkaki* (which goes well with shellfish), and it's all very cheap indeed: a full bowl of soup with a skewer of meat or shells costs just Tsh300, the same as a glass of freshly pressed sugar cane juice. As with Mkoani, there are no **bars** in town, nor restaurants selling alcohol.

## Ngezi–Vumawimbi Nature Reserve (Ngezi Forest)

Until the introduction of cloves in the nineteenth century, sixty percent of Pemba was covered by indigenous forest. Nowadays, the only sizeable remnants are small patches at Ras Kiuyu and Msitu Mkuu in the northeast, and **NGEZI FOREST**, being one third of the 29-square-kilometre Ngezi–Vumawimbi Nature Reserve straddling the neck of Ras Kigomasha peninsula in the northwest.

Wilder, junglier, darker and more brooding than Jozani Forest on Unguja, Ngezi is an ecological island towered over by forty-metre-tall mvule teak trees festooned with necklaces of lianas and vines. The major attraction for naturalists is the chance of spotting the endemic **Pemba flying fox**, actually a species of fruit-eating bat (*popo*) with a wingspan up to 1.8 metres. Other mammals include the **marsh mongoose** – Pemba's only indigenous carnivore – and the endemic **Pemba vervet monkey** (or green monkey, locally called tumbili). With luck, you might also see the diminutive **Pemba blue duiker** (*chesi or paa wa Pemba*), feral pigs introduced by the Portuguese, and **Kirk's red colobus** (see p.591), introduced in 1970 when fourteen monkeys were relocated from Unguja's Jozani Forest. Another exotic species is the **Javan civet cat**, believed to have been brought to the island by traders from Southeast Asia for musk production. The ancient Indian Ocean trading links are also evidenced by the presence of several plant and tree species native to both Asia and Madagascar. The forest's **birdlife** has more than enough to interest keen twitchers, including four endemics: the threatened Russet's scops owl, the Pemba white-eye, Pemba green pigeon and the violet-breasted sunbird. So it's with good reason that locals consider the forest sacred: Ngezi contains at least six **ritual areas**, called *mizimu*, that are periodically swept clean for the benefit of the ancestral spirits who dwell there.

**Getting to Ngezi** is easiest on an organized tour: around $40 per person from Wete, or up to $60 including a couple of hours at Vumawimbi Beach. Coming by **daladala**, you can get as far as the scruffy market town of **Konde**, 4km east of the reserve (#601 from Wete, #602 from Chake Chake, #604 from Mkoani). Daladala drivers should be happy to take you straight to the gate for an extra few thousand shillings. Alternatively, you could cycle, a 36-kilometre round-trip from Wete, or less if you base yourself at *Kervan Saray Beach* (see below), who rent bicycles for Tsh10,000 a day; they also offer free lifts to the reserve gate in the morning – the walk back takes a leisurely two hours.

The office at the gate (daily 7.30am–4pm) collects a Tsh6000 **entry fee**, which includes the services of a guide, although an additional tip is appreciated. There's no charge if you're cycling or driving through to reach Ras Kigomasha peninsula. Although you can walk around Ngezi unaccompanied, it's best to take the guide, both for their knowledge and for security, as there have been muggings in the past. With advance notice, you could also go looking for flying foxes, or scout for scops owls. There are a few interesting leaflets posted on the walls inside the office but nothing to take away.

## Ras Kigomasha

Passing through Ngezi, the forest ends as suddenly as it began, giving way to scrub, patches of cultivation, a rubber plantation started by the Chinese, and a couple of fabulous and virtually deserted beaches on either side of Pemba's northernmost point, **Ras Kigomasha** ("ras" means "head"). The beach on the west side is known as **Panga ya Watoro**, curiously meaning "the knife of the refugees". To the east, **Vumawimbi** ("roaring surf") is a gently curving, four-kilometre-long bay.

**Public transport** stops at Konde, so it's best to arrange a pick up from there with one of the two hotels on the peninsula. If you're driving, be aware the road through Ngezi Forest is very muddy during and after the rains, often requiring 4WD, high clearance and ample mud-driving skills, but the road is rarely blocked completely.

**Kervan Saray Beach** Ras Kigomasha, 10km from Konde ☎0772/659805, ⊛www .kervansaraybeach.com. Set just back from the beach on the west coast, this is the base for Swahili Divers (see p.513), and is great value even for non-divers. With just twelve rooms, it's also the most intimate. Kudos accrues for the dorm, which – at $45 per person *full-board* – is a bargain. The other rooms are in huge stand-alone cottages, their enormous beds mounted on cement pedestals. Apart from diving and snorkelling ($20 if sharing a boat with divers), you can go kayaking around the mangroves of Njao Gap (initial access is by motorboat), and they're happy giving lifts to Ngezi Forest in the morning. FB dorms ❺, rooms ❻
**The Manta Resort** Ras Kigomasha, 14km from Konde ☎0777/423930 or 0777/628333, ⊛www .themantaresort.com. Near the top of the island, this relaxed and unpretentious place sits on a coral bluff

above the magical Panga ya Watoro beach, and is particularly recommended for scuba divers, given that Oxygène Pemba are based here (see p.513). Unfortunately, it's overpriced even by Zanzibar's standards: the cheapest rooms, in "The Village", are in a cluster of unremarkable if comfortable cottages with wooden floors and ceiling fans, but without much in the way of views, or privacy. Larger and with a/c are the "Garden Rooms", in a row of semi-detached bungalows (which can be combined for families), but best are the simple but stylish "Seafront Villas", built on stilts on the edge of the bluff, with floor-to-ceiling windows and west-facing verandas. There's a delightful thatched restaurant overlooking the beach, an equally lovely beach bar, a swimming pool (also with views), and a host of activities, including a spa, nature and bird walks, fishing from inflatable kayaks, and road and sea excursions. Internet access. No children under 7. FB ❾

## Hamisi ruins

Several medieval ruins lie off the road east of Konde. The most impressive, and easiest to find, are the sixteenth-century **Hamisi ruins** (also known as the

Haruni or Chwaka ruins), signposted 8km east of Konde. Tradition has it that the fortified town and palace was the seat of Harun bin Ali, a son of Muhammad bin Abdulrahman (see p.568). Tyranny appears to have been a family trait, as hinted at by Harun's nickname, Mvunja Pau: *mvunja* means destroyer, and *pau* is the pole that takes the weight of a thatched roof.

The first building you see is a small **mosque**, much of it reduced to blocks of collapsed masonry. The *mihrab* remains more or less intact, in spite of a tree root growing into it. The mosque was built for Harun's wife and gets its nickname of Msikiti Chooko ("Mosque of the Green Bean") from the ground beans or peas that were blended with the mortar to strengthen it. Some 100m southeast of the mosque are the remains of a particularly large **tomb**, surmounted by a ten-sided pillar bearing curious upside-down shield-like indents on one side. On the other side of the pillar is an incised eight-petalled floral motif, oddly off-centre. The tomb is said to be that of Harun.

Fifty metres south of here is a large **Friday mosque** that appears to be raised by a metre or so above the ground, a false impression caused by the amount of rubble covering the original floor. Its mihrab is in almost perfect condition; the five circular depressions on either side of it originally held Chinese porcelain bowls, and people still leave offerings there.

# Travel details

Daladala routes are detailed throughout this chapter. See the box on p.530 for more information on moving on from Stone Town, and p.564 for getting to Pemba.

## Ferries

**Pemba (Mkoani)** to: Dar (3–5 weekly but unreliable; 6hr or overnight); Mkoani (5–7 weekly but unreliable; 2–5hr)
**Pemba (Wete)** to: Tanga (1 weekly; 6hr).
**Stone Town** to: Dar (5–9 daily; 2–5hr).

## Flights

Airline codes used below are: CA (Coastal Aviation), RA (Regional Air), SA (Safari Airlink), TA (Tropical Air) and ZA (ZanAir). Where more than one flies to

the same destination, the airline with most frequent flights or shortest journey times is listed first. Routes marked with an asterisk need a minimum of four passengers to operate.
**Pemba** to: Dar (TA, CA, ZA: 1 daily; 40min–1hr); Zanzibar (CA, TA, ZA: 3 daily; 30min); Tanga (CA: 1 daily; 20min).
**Zanzibar (Stone Town)** to: Arusha (ZA, RA, CA: 3 daily; 1.5hr–2.5hr); Dar (CA, ZA, SA, TA: 15 daily; 20min); Kilwa* (CA: 1 daily; 2hr 10min); Mafia (CA: 1 daily; 1hr 30min); Manyara* (CA: 1 daily; 3hr 25min); Pangani* (RA: 1 daily; 30min); Pemba (ZA, CA, TA: 4 daily; 30–40min); Ruaha (CA, SA: 2 daily; 3hr); Selous (CA, SA, ZA: 4 daily; 1hr 15min); Serengeti (CA: 1 daily; 4hr 20min–6hr); Tanga (CA: 1 daily; 1hr 5min).

# Contexts

# Contexts

# History

anzania's history is the intertwining of two tales: that of the coast (including Zanzibar and Mafia), and that of the hinterland (Tanganyika). Tanganyika's written history started just five hundred years ago, and little is known of earlier times other than the rough direction of mass migrations, and what little can be gleaned from **archeological records**. In contrast, the coast's turbulent and often brutal history is well recorded, as the western Indian Ocean's **monsoon** winds and currents brought it within reach of sailors from Persia and Arabia, India and the Far East, ancient Greece, Egypt and Rome, Phoenicia, Assyria and Sumeria.

The first lasting link between Tanganyika and Zanzibar was the Zanzibari-controlled ivory and slave trade, which drew its raw materials – people and elephant tusks – from the mainland. The second link was the unification of Tanganyika and Zanzibar in 1964 to create the present **United Republic of Tanzania**. A marriage of convenience, some say, and indeed the two parties have shown little affection for one another over the course of their union. In spite of this, Tanzania continues to be held up as an example of mutual co-operation between different peoples and cultures, showing that ethnic conflict ignited by artificial national boundaries imposed by the Europeans can be overcome.

## The people of Tanzania

Mainland Tanzania has been inhabited since the dawn of mankind. Some 3.75 million years ago, a family of hominids with chimpanzee-like faces strode across an area of wet volcanic ash in **Laetoli** in Ngorongoro. At the time of their discovery in the 1970s, the fossilized footprints of these three *Australopithecus afarensis* provided the first absolute proof that our ancestors were walking upright way before anyone had imagined. Fossilized hominid remains and stone tools found at **Oldupai Gorge** nearby trace the evolution of man from those first faltering steps to the genesis of *Homo sapiens*.

Tanzania's "modern" historical record starts with a modest collection of 70,000-year-old **ostrich shell beads** unearthed in the Serengeti, which are among the **earliest man-made items** intended for something other than just survival. More beautiful, and visitable, are Tanzania's **rock paintings**, especially in the Irangi Hills. The most recent were left barely a hundred years ago, but the oldest may be a mind-boggling 30,000 years old. Given that they're all outdoors (not in caves), the thousands of paintings are miraculously well preserved, and depict a land of wild animals and everyday domestic life not so different from today.

The artists were **hunter–gatherers**, living off wild game, honey, berries, fruits, nuts and roots; most of these cultures disappeared long ago, having been either assimilated or annihilated by more powerful newcomers. Two exceptions were the **Hadzabe and Sandawe tribes** of central Tanzania. The Sandawe abandoned their ancient way of life in the 1950s, but the Hadzabe persist, albeit under immense adverse pressure (including ill-managed tourism) that looks set to extinguish their culture within the next decade. Interestingly, both tribes speak languages characterized by clicks, similar to those spoken by southern Africa's hunter-gatherers (the "San" or "Bushmen"), who also had a strong tradition of rock painting. The similarities point to the existence of a loosely linked and widely dispersed hunter-gathering culture across much of sub-Saharan Africa, before the arrival of the Bantu turned their world upside-down.

## The Bantu

Cameroon is considered to be the cradle of the ethno-linguistic group known as the **Bantu**. Nowadays spread over much of sub-Saharan Africa, the Bantu are primarily an agricultural people, and have been for thousands of years. Their success at agriculture ultimately led to overpopulation, so starting the first of several waves of **Bantu migrations** in search of fresh land. The first to reach Tanzania arrived as early as 1000 BC, with the last coming just a few centuries ago. Over time the migrants split into myriad distinct tribes, each developing their own cultures, belief systems and languages. Elements common to most Bantu societies, apart from linguistic roots, are their agricultural way of life, monotheism, and knowledge of **iron working**. Excavations in Ufipa in southwestern Tanzania, and Kagera, west of Lake Victoria, have shown that, until the European method of mass-produced steel was perfected, Tanzania's deceptively simple furnaces produced the world's highest-quality steel, fired at temperatures that were unthinkable in eighteenth-century Europe. Nowadays, Bantu-speakers comprise all but a handful of Tanzania's 129 officially recognized tribes.

## The Nilotes

Tanzania's second-largest and most traditional ethno-linguistic group are the so-called **Nilotes**, or Nilotic-speakers, and include the country's most famous tribe, the Maasai. As the academic label suggests, their origins lie in the Upper Nile valley of southern or central Sudan, from where their ancestors began fanning out, both south and west, as early as two thousand years ago. Indeed, there are compelling similarities between present-day tribes and ancient Egypt's and Sudan's "Black Pharaohs": physical traits, hairstyles, the reliance on cattle, the belief in a unique God, social structure, even language. Some theorists posit that the Nilotes are in fact one of Israel's "lost tribes", seemingly borne out by the existence of traditional Jewish communities in Ethiopia and Uganda.

**Cattle** define all Nilotic tribes, providing everything from daily sustenance (blood and milk rather than meat) to clothing and shelter, and social standing. The semi-arid nature of Nilotic terrain, however, exposed them to frequent droughts, something that has become acutely problematic in recent decades. Aggressive **territorial expansion** was the way to minimize the blows of nature, as typified by the hierarchical, quasi-militaristic form of traditional Nilotic society. The first Nilotes to enter Tanzania were presumably ancestors of central Tanzania's **Gogo** (who are now mixed with Bantu), followed by the **Barbaig**, both of whom were pushed south by the arrival of the **Maasai** some three hundred years ago. In the modern world, the nomadic lifestyle is increasingly untenable, especially as the best grazing lands – now national parks – are closed to herders. As such, some Nilotes have done the unthinkable by becoming farmers, but Nilotic traditions are amazingly resilient, as you'll be able to see at one of several cultural tourism programmes around Arusha.

## Empires of the monsoon

The first non-Africans to visit Tanzania, sometime before 2000 BC, were **Sumerian traders** from Mesopotamia, followed a millennium later by the **Phoenicians**, who used Zanzibar as a stopover en route to Sofala in Mozambique, to trade in gold. The earliest coins found in Zanzibar are over 2000 years old, and come from ancient Parthia (northeast Iran), Sassania (Iran/Iraq), Greece and Rome. Egyptian coins and a dagger have also been found, as have Roman glass beads, all proving that trading connections between East Africa and the **Mediterranean** were strong. At that time it would appear that Zanzibar and the coast were controlled by Sabaeans from the kingdom of Sheba (modern Yemen), who brought weapons, wine and wheat to exchange for ivory and other East African goods.

The sailors were carried by the **monsoon**'s winds and currents, which blow south for half the year, and north for the other. This obliged sailors to stay a while before the monsoon switched direction, and in due course **trading towns** sprouted along the coastline. The second-century *Periplus of the Erythraean Sea*, which calls the coast Azania, mentions one such place called **Rhapta**, which scholars tentatively identify with Pangani or an as yet unknown location in the Rufiji Delta. Also mentioned, two days' sail away, is the island of **Menouthias**, probably Pemba.

## The Swahili

In later centuries, the East African coast became part of a vast trading network that included China, Malaysia and Indonesia. Malay and Indonesian influence lasted from the sixth century to at least the twelfth, and the **Indonesians** are believed to have introduced coconuts, bananas, and possibly the Polynesian-style *ngalawa* outriggers still used today. Chinese presence is seen in numerous finds of coins and porcelain, and in written accounts.

The first outsiders who can be positively identified as establishing a permanent presence in East Africa were the **Persians**: by the end of the first millennium AD, they ruled a series of city-states from Somalia in the north to Mozambique in the south. According to legend, they arrived in 975 AD after the king of Shiraz dreamt that a **giant iron rat** destroyed the foundations of his palace. Taking it as a bad omen, the king set sail with his six sons in seven dhows. Separated in a storm, each went on to found a city, including Kizimkazi in Zanzibar, and Kilwa on the mainland. Whatever the truth of the tale, Persian traders were certainly well acquainted with the East African coast, which they called Zang-I-Bar ("the sea of the blacks"), hence the name Zanzibar.

The Persians were not averse to marrying Africans, and in so doing gave rise to East Africa's "Shirazi" culture. Later, intermarriage with Arabs created the **Swahili** (from the Arabic word *sahel*, meaning "coast"), whose birth coincided with an upsurge in Indian Ocean trade. **Gold** and **ivory** were the main African exports, though slaves, turtle shell, leopard skin, rhinoceros horn, indigo and timber also found ready markets. The Swahili civilization reached its peak in the fourteenth and fifteenth centuries, when its city states – especially **Kilwa** – controlled the flow of gold from the port of Sofala in Mozambique, itself controlling mines in what's now Zimbabwe, and which some scholars say were the original King Solomon's Mines.

The main legacy of Swahili civilization is its language, **Kiswahili**; essentially a Bantu tongue enriched with thousands of words borrowed from Persian and Arabic, and nowadays also Portuguese, Hindi, English and German. Over the centuries Kiswahili spread inland along trade routes, and is now the lingua franca of eastern Africa, and the official language of Tanzania and Kenya.

## The Portuguese

The growth and prosperity of the Swahili came to an abrupt end following the arrival of the **Portuguese**. The first to visit was Vasco da Gama in 1498, en route to "discovering" the ocean route to India, which would circumvent the need to trade across a series of Arab middlemen in the Middle East. Although Portuguese involvement in East Africa was initially limited to its use as a staging post, the riches of the Swahili trade quickly kindled an avaricious interest. In

1503, part of Unguja Island (Zanzibar Island) was sacked by the Portuguese captain **Ruy Lourenço Ravasco**, who exacted an annual tribute in gold from Unguja's traditional rulers, the Mwinyi Mkuu. Kilwa Kisiwani on the mainland – East Africa's most prosperous city – was sacked two years later, and within a decade the Portuguese had conquered most of the Swahili coast. However, the Portuguese presence disrupted the ancient trading network so badly that the entire region fell into decline, and formerly prosperous cities were abandoned and crumbled away.

The collapse of the trading network deterred further Portuguese interest other than maintaining a number of harbours to act as stepping stones along the route to India. This lack of attention, and increasingly stretched military resources, opened the door to a new power: **Oman**. In 1606 Pemba was taken by Omanis based in Malindi, Kenya, and in 1622 the Portuguese suffered a monumental defeat at the **Battle of Hormuz**. The defeat signalled the *de facto* ascendancy of Omani power in the region, although the Portuguese held on to Unguja until 1652, when the Omani sultanate sent a fleet at the behest of the Mwinyi Mkuu. The last Portuguese stronghold in East Africa north of Mozambique, Mombasa's Fort Jesus, fell to the new rulers in 1698.

### Zanzibar and the slave trade

Having ejected the Portuguese, Oman was swift to assert its control over East Africa. The only real threat to their sovereignty was from a rival Omani dynasty, the Mazrui family, based in Mombasa. The Mazruis seized Pemba in 1744, but were unsuccessful in their attempt to take Unguja eleven years later. In spite of the rivalry, Zanzibar's trade flourished, the key to its wealth being **slavery**, demand for which rocketed after the establishment of sugar and clove plantations in European-owned Indian Ocean territories.

The spiralling prices for slaves, and ivory, gave Zanzibar considerable economic independence from Oman. The pivotal figure was Seyyid bin Sultan bin Ahmad bin Saïd al-Busaïdi (ruled 1804–1856), **Seyyid Saïd** for short, who at the age of fifteen assassinated his cousin to become the sole ruler of the Omani empire. The sultan recognized the importance of Zanzibar and East Africa, and spent most of his reign developing and consolidating it, encouraging merchants to emigrate from Oman, and continuing incursions on the African mainland. In 1811 he opened Stone Town's notorious **slave market**, which during the following sixty years traded over a million lives. Shrewd diplomacy with the British – who were increasingly pushing for the trade's abolition – allowed Seyyid Saïd to wrest Mombasa from the Mazrui family in 1827. The sultan also cultivated trading relationships beyond the Indian Ocean: the United States opened their consulate in Stone Town in 1837, and European nations swiftly followed.

In 1841, with the entire East African coast now under his control, and backed by the Western powers, Seyyid Saïd took the unusual step of moving the **Omani capital** from Muscat to Zanzibar, beginning a short-lived but immensely prosperous golden age, bankrolled not just by ivory and slaves, but **cloves** – a shrewd introduction by Seyyid Saïd as Zanzibar accounted for four-fifths of the global output.

## Explorers and colonizers

Seyyid Saïd was succeeded by **Sultan Majid**, and after a brief power struggle between him and his brother, the Omani empire was split into two: the Arabian half centred on Muscat, and the vastly more prosperous African one centred on Zanzibar and headed by Majid.

The African half's control of the mainland trade routes made it, and the mainland port of Bagamoyo, logical bases for the European exploration of the "dark continent". The first Europeans known to have travelled through Tanzania were the German missionaries **Johann Ludwig Krapf** and **Johannes Rebmann**, who in the 1840s tried to convert several tribes to Christianity, without much success. In 1848, Krapf – who considered Africans "the fallen man, steeped in sin, living in darkness and [the] shadow of death" – moved inland to try his luck elsewhere, and became the first European to describe Mount Kilimanjaro (to the incredulity of bigwigs back home, who ridiculed the idea of a snow-capped mountain on the Equator). Hot on his heels came a train of other **explorers** and missionaries, among them such Victorian heroes as Sir Richard Francis Burton, James Augustus Grant, Joseph Thomson, Samuel White Baker and John Hanning Speke. Many of them set out to locate **the source of the Nile** (see p.398), a riddle that had baffled Europeans since Herodotus in the fifth century BC. The search for the Nile's source was not just an academic exercise or vain glory seeking: whoever controlled the Nile's headwaters would control Egypt and (from 1869) the Suez Canal.

The "riddle of the Nile" was finally solved by **John Hanning Speke**, who reached Lake Victoria in 1858, and went on to sail down the great river. The most famous explorers to have graced East Africa though are a duo whose names have become inseparable: the journalist-turned-adventurer **Henry Morton Stanley**, and the missionary-turned-explorer **David Livingstone**. Their famous "Dr Livingstone, I presume?" encounter took place in 1871 at Ujiji, on the eastern shore of Lake Tanganyika (see p.431).

Although Livingstone was careful about how he went around preaching the gospel of the Lord, he was an exception among a motley bunch of missionaries who believed that Africans were primitive and inferior and therefore in need of "civilizing". But with competition heating up between European powers for new markets and natural resources, the supposedly backward nature of the Africans and the handy excuse of wanting to stamp out the slave trade (in which Europeans had freely participated) gave them the perfect excuse to begin the conquest of the continent by force. The **partition of Africa** was rendered official in a series of conferences and treaties in the 1880s, and in 1890 Germany took nominal control of Tanganyika, while Britain grabbed Kenya, Uganda and Zanzibar.

## The German conquest of Tanganyika

The mid-1880s were a time of considerable turmoil throughout Tanganyika, with arrival of the militaristic **Ngoni tribe** in the south (see p.504), the expansion of the equally warlike Maasai in the north (see pp.356–357), and increasingly bloody incursions by Zanzibari slavers right across the country from east to west. For most tribes, this period was a disaster, but a handful managed to take advantage of the situation, most famously the **Nyamwezi**. Under the wily leadership of **Chief Mirambo** (see p.447), they took military control of portions of the trade routes, which they used to exact tributes from passing caravans. The tributes financed the purchase of arms, with which Mirambo constructed a short-lived empire between central Tanganyika and what's now Burundi, Rwanda and Uganda.

This turbulent state of affairs should have eased the **German conquest** of Tanganyika, but their problems began the instant they arrived. In 1888, coastal slave traders – who were none too appreciative of Germany's intention to wrest away control of the caravan routes, and levy taxes – rose up in arms. Led initially by a slaver named Abushiri ibn Salim al-Harthi – who gave the uprising its name, the **Abushiri War** (see p.121) – the conflict dragged on for over a year before the Germans finally crushed resistance. Having "pacified" the coast, German troops headed inland. Central Tanganyika was an easy conquest as Mirambo's empire had crumbled following the chief's death in 1884, but further south the Hehe tribe, under **Chief Mkwawa** (see p.474), were a formidable adversary, which they proved in 1891 by annihilating an attacking German force. Hehe resistance only ended in 1898 with Mkwawa's suicide, but his death signalled a mere lull in armed resistance. In 1905, frustrated by harsh German rule, a vast swathe of central and southern Tanganyika rose up once more in what became known as the **Maji Maji Uprising** (see p.173). Using scorched-earth and terror tactics, the German army (the *Schutztruppe*) took two years to crush the uprising, after which colonization proper began.

Work included the construction of a railway from Dar es Salaam to Kigoma port on Lake Tanganyika, following almost exactly the route of the most infamous of nineteenth-century slave roads. The railway arrived in Kigoma in February 1914, just before **World War I**. Although the war's main focus was Europe, the German troops posted in Tanganyika, ably led by Paul von Lettow-Vorbeck – chief architect also of the genocide perpetrated against Namibia's Herero tribe in 1904–08 – began a guerrilla-style conflict against the British based in Kenya and Zanzibar, and Belgians in Burundi and Rwanda. Lettow-Vorbeck's purpose was not to defeat the numerically superior Allied forces, but to tie down resources that might have been more productively used back in Europe. The strategy worked, and Lettow-Vorbeck's force remained undefeated until 1918, when the Armistice brought an end to the slaughter and forced his surrender.

## The British Protectorate of Zanzibar

Sultan Majid's successor, **Sultan Barghash** (ruled 1870–88), inherited vast wealth, but also an empire on its last legs. Barghash must have felt particularly ill-starred: his accession coincided with a devastating **cholera epidemic** that killed ten thousand people in Stone Town alone, and in April 1872, a **cyclone** destroyed all but one ship in Stone Town's harbour (around three hundred in all), and levelled 85 percent of Unguja's clove plantations. These disasters were compounded in 1873 when the British, backed by their all-powerful navy, forced the **abolition of the slave trade** between the mainland and Zanzibar (slavery itself only ended in 1897). Meanwhile, European plans for **the partition of Africa** proceeded at full clip, and Zanzibar's mainland possessions – with the exception of a six-kilometre coastal strip – were taken from it in 1886. Barghash was succeeded in 1888 by his son, Khalifa bin Saïd, but when he too died, just two years later, Zanzibar was declared a **British Protectorate**. The sultanate was allowed to continue in ceremonial capacity, but the real shots were called by the British – quite literally, in August 1896. Two hours after the passing of Sultan Hamad bin Thuwaini bin Saïd, the palace complex in Stone Town was seized by Khalid, a son of Barghash, who, urged on by 2500 supporters, proclaimed himself sultan. The British, who preferred Thuwaini's cousin, Hamud ibn Mohammed, issued an ultimatum that Khalid ignored. At precisely 9.02am on August 27, the **shortest war in history** began when three British warships opened fire on the palace complex. By 9.40am the British had reduced two palaces to rubble, killed five hundred people and forced the surrender of Khalid, who took refuge in the German consulate from where he fled into exile.

# The road to Independence

At the end of World War I, the British were given control of Tanganyika, though the administration remained separate from that of Zanzibar, which was nominally still a sultanate. **British rule** in Tanganyika (1919–61) was relatively benign, and merely picked up where the Germans left off: Dar es Salaam was expanded, as were agricultural towns such as Arusha and Morogoro, and the railway was extended to Mwanza on Lake Victoria. The five-decade British Protectorate over Zanzibar was similarly uneventful, the highlight being the installation of a much-needed sewerage system for Stone Town.

**World War II** was a major turning point in the history of Tanzania, and Africa. Many East African had been conscripted as soldiers and porters for the British and expected something in return – self-rule, or even independence. Opposition to colonial rule sprang up right across the continent, and with the new world order now dominated by the United States and the Soviet Union change was inevitable. In Tanganyika, the independence movement was headed by **TANU** (the Tanganyika African National Union), founded as the Tanganyika African Association in 1929. From 1954 onwards, TANU was led by **Julius Kambarage Nyerere**, a mild-mannered school-teacher from Butiama close to Lake Victoria, and graduate of Edinburgh University. Professing a peaceful path to change inspired by Mahatma Gandhi, Nyerere's open-minded and down-to-earth style won TANU widespread support, and the grudging respect of the British, who, faced with the inevitability of independence, saw in Nyerere a figure they could trust. Following a string of rigged legislative elections, in August 1960 mounting tension finally forced free elections for 71 seats of the Tanganyika Legislative Council. TANU won all but one, Nyerere became chief minister, and in that capacity led the move towards **Tanganyikan Independence**, which was proclaimed on December 9, 1961.

## Baba wa Taifa: Julius Nyerere

Tanzania's first and still much-loved president, **Julius Kambarage Nyerere**, was born in 1922 to a chief of the small Zanaki tribe in Mwitongo village, near Butiama close to the eastern shore of Lake Victoria. Nyerere was educated at Tabora Secondary School in central Tanzania and at Uganda's celebrated Makerere College, before going on to study history and economics at Edinburgh University. One of Tanganyika's first university graduates, he returned to Tanganyika in 1952 where he became leader of TANU, and succeeded in securing Tanzania's peaceful transition to Independence in 1961 (in contrast to neighbouring Kenya, whose road to freedom was long and bloody). Nyerere's unpretentious, softly spoken and light-hearted style (and wonderful smile) perfectly complemented his political vision of tolerance, courtesy, modesty and non-violence, words that could equally be applied to the nation as a whole.

Although Nyerere's economic legacy – the decade-long **Ujamaa** experiment (see p.585) – was utterly disastrous, the one unassailable achievement over his 24-year tenure as president was as nation builder. From 129 different tribes, he forged a cohesive state completely free of the divisive tribalism that has plunged many other African countries into chaos. As such, Nyerere is affectionately known to Tanzanians as **Mwalimu** ("Teacher") and **Baba wa Taifa** ("Father of the Nation").

Nyerere died of leukaemia on October 14, 1999 (now a national holiday), and is buried in the family graveyard close to the museum in Butiama (see p.410). He ranks with Nelson Mandela as one of the twentieth century's great African statesmen.

## Zanzibari Independence – and revolution

In Zanzibar the situation was more complicated, as there were effectively **two colonial overlords**: the British, who wielded political, judicial and military power, and the Omanis, who owned most of the island's resources, and whose sultans remained heads of state, in name at least.

The first rumblings of **discontent** came in 1948, when African dockers and trade unionists publicly protested against British and Arab domination. Britain eventually allowed the formation of political parties to dispute elections held in 1957. Africans were represented by the **Afro-Shirazi Party (ASP)**, while the Arab minority supported the Zanzibar Nationalist Party (ZNP). Between 1959 and 1961 a series of increasingly rigged elections gave the ZNP, in coalition with the Zanzibar and Pemba People's Party (ZPPP), disproportionate representation in the council, with the ASP consistently denied its rightful share. Heedless of the rising tension, the British instituted limited self-government in June 1963, and the following month another round of elections was held, which again saw the ASP lose, despite having polled 54 percent of the vote. Nonetheless, Britain went ahead with plans for independence, and on December 10, 1963, the **Sultanate of Zanzibar** came into being.

African resentment of the Arabs, who made up just twenty percent of the isles' population, was barely contained, and on January 12, 1964, four weeks after Independence, **John Okello**, a Ugandan migrant labourer and self-styled "Field Marshal", led six hundred armed supporters in a bloody **revolution**. In one night of terror, some twelve thousand Arabs and Indians were massacred, and all but one percent of Stone Town's non-African inhabitants fled the country. Among them was Zanzibar's last sultan, Jamshid ibn Abdullah, who ended up exiled in England. Okello was merely the spark; the real power was wielded by the ASP leader, Sheikh Abeid Amani Karume, who declared himself Prime Minister of the Revolutionary Council of the **People's Republic of Zanzibar and Pemba**.

# The United Republic of Tanzania

As President of Tanganyika, Nyerere's first moves were to promote a sense of national consciousness: Kiswahili was made the official language and was to be taught in every school, while tribal chiefdoms – a potential source of conflict – were abolished. Elections in 1962 overwhelmingly returned Nyerere as President, who in 1963 consolidated his power by declaring Tanganyika a **one-party state**.

The chaos of the Zanzibari Revolution coincided with the height of the **Cold War**, and came shortly after Nyerere had survived an army mutiny, for which he had recourse to the British marines. Feeling threatened by the possibility of extremists taking power in Zanzibar, Nyerere sought to defuse the threat through an **Act of Union** between Tanganyika and Zanzibar, which would give him the power to intervene militarily on the isles. Karume, for his part, was in a quandary, as the exodus of Arabs and Indians devastated Zanzibar's economy, and few international organizations were willing to help a left-wing regime that had come to power through such violent means. The solution was to accept Nyerere's overtures for the Union, which was signed on April 26, 1964, bringing into existence the present **United Republic of Tanzania**. Nyerere became Union president and Karume one of two vice-presidents. Zanzibar retained political and economic autonomy, including its own president and parliament, and also gained fifty of the 169 seats in the Tanzanian National Assembly. In spite of these concessions, Karume came to view the Union as a mainland plot to take over the islands, and even now – almost five decades down the road – few people on either side are happy with the marriage.

## Ujamaa

As first President of the Union, Nyerere faced huge **challenges**. Tanzania was one of the poorest countries on earth, with just twelve doctors and 120 university graduates to its name. Life expectancy was 35 years, and 85 percent of the adult population was illiterate. The outside world was willing to help, but the inevitable strings would compromise Tanzania's independence. Instead, in February 1967, at the height of an extended drought, Nyerere delivered a speech that became known as the **Arusha Declaration**, in which he laid out his vision of self-reliant, non-Marxist "African socialism": "The development of a country is brought about by people, not by money. Money, and the wealth it represents, is the result and not the basis of development… The biggest requirement is hard work. Let us go to the villages and talk to our people and see whether or not it is possible for them to work harder."

In practice, those noble ideals translated into "villagization": the resettlement of rural households, who accounted for over ninety percent of the population, into collective **Ujamaa villages** – *Ujamaa* being the Kiswahili word for brotherhood or familyhood, meaning "togetherness". Until 1972 resettlement was voluntary, and around twenty percent of the population shifted. This, however, wasn't enough, so **forcible resettlement** started and by 1977 over thirteen million people, or about eighty percent of the population, resided in some eight thousand *Ujamaa* villages.

Unfortunately, the policy was an **economic disaster**. Vast areas of formerly productive land were left untended and the communal system proved to be more fertile for corruption and embezzlement than for agriculture. Yet the policy did have its successes: access to clean water, health care and schools was vastly improved, and by the 1980s adult **literacy** had soared to over ninety percent. Equally important, throwing everyone together in the same, sinking boat, forged a strong and peaceful sense of **national identity** that completely transcended tribal lines, and created a nation of people justifiably proud of their friendly relations with each other, and with outsiders. Tanzania is one of the few African countries wholly unaffected by ethnic or religious conflict, and is unique in having a population that takes pride in both its tribal and national identity.

### Depression, collapse and conciliation

By the mid-1970s, Tanzania was in a terrible state. On the mainland, *Ujamaa* bequeathed a **wrecked economy**, and the one-party system and opposition to forced relocation meant that by 1979 Tanzania's jails contained more political prisoners than in apartheid South Africa. Over on Zanzibar, Karume, who had courted the USSR, Cuba and China for help in establishing state-run plantations, had brought about similar ruin but without any sense of unity: the isles remained, and still remain, bitterly divided, the most obvious political gulf mirroring geography, with pro-government Unguja Island and pro-opposition Pemba Island. Karume became increasingly paranoid and dictatorial. He deported Asians whom he believed were "plotting" to take over the economy, elections were banned, arbitrary arrests and human-rights abuses became commonplace and there were even allegations that Karume was behind the murder of leading politicians and businessmen. In April 1972, following two previous attempts on his life, an **assassin's bullet** finally found its mark.

Big changes came in 1977. The economic failure of *Ujamaa* was glaringly apparent, and the same year the **East African Community** between Tanzania, Kenya and Uganda, founded in 1967, was buried when rock-bottom relations with capitalist Kenya closed the border between the two countries. With both sides of the Union increasingly isolated, closer ties seemed to be the way forward. In February 1977, Zanzibar's ASP – under Karume's more moderate successor, Aboud Jumbe – merged with TANU to form the **CCM** (Chama Cha Mapinduzi – The Revolutionary Party), which remains in power today. Nyerere became chairman, and Jumbe vice-chairman.

## The Kagera War and the road to change

While relations with Kenya were sour, things were worse with **Idi Amin**'s brutal dictatorship in Uganda. Matters came to a head in October 1978, when Uganda invaded Tanzania's northwestern **Kagera Region**. Tanzania barely had an army worth the name, so it took a few months to train up a force of some fifty thousand men, who responded, assisted by armed Ugandan exiles, with a counter-attack in January 1979. Much to the surprise of seasoned military observers, they completely routed the supposedly better-trained, US-backed Ugandan army, and pushed on to Uganda's capital, Kampala, driving Idi Amin into exile. The war, although brief, was something that Tanzania could ill afford, and the estimated $500-million cost ensured further economic misery back home.

As Tanzania sank deeper into **debt** and finally resorted to international donors for aid, Nyerere found himself increasingly at odds with his socialist ideals. Far from being self-reliant, Tanzania was more dependent than ever. The economy had collapsed, agriculture barely sufficed, and the country was saddled with a crippling debt. In 1985, with the donors demanding economic reforms, **Nyerere resigned**. It was time for change.

## The multiparty era

The 1985 elections ushered in a Union government headed by the pragmatic **Ali Hassan Mwinyi**, whose ten-year tenure was characterized by the wholesale desertion of Nyerere's socialist policies. Instead, IMF-imposed capitalist reforms were the order of the day. Another condition of donor support was the scrapping of the one-party political system, so since 1995 Tanzania has been a **multiparty democracy**, with elections held every five years. On the mainland people vote for the Union parliament and presidency; on Zanzibar, there are two additional polls, one for Zanzibar's separate executive, and the other for the Zanzibari president. On the mainland, the electoral process has been smooth and, despite media bias in the run-ups, has given little reason to doubt the results, with the ruling CCM and their presidential candidates easily winning the votes (former journalist Benjamin Mkapa in 1995 and 2000, and the charismatic Jakaya Kikwete in 2005). Steady **economic improvement**, and a hopelessly divided mainland opposition, should see Kikwete and the CCM romping home to yet another victory in the next vote, scheduled for the end of 2010.

## Zanzibar's troubles

Things could not have been more different on **Zanzibar**, whose experience of multiparty politics has been marred by bitterly disputed elections, condemnation from international observers, withdrawal of foreign aid, outbursts of violence, political repression, and a whole lot of bad blood between the CCM and their formidable foes, the **Civic United Front (CUF)**. As heir to the ZNP and ZPPP, CUF favours looser ties with the mainland, even secession, and at one time rather foolishly vaunted the imposition of Islamic sharia law, which lost it the support of Western nations. Needless to say, CCM have painted their challengers as religious extremists to be kept out of power at all costs.

In 1995, CCM was declared victorious by the slenderest of margins, with 26 seats to CUF's 24. **Salmin Amour** was duly reinaugurated as Zanzibari president, responding to his critics with police harassment and arbitrary arrests, causing around ten thousand CUF supporters to flee and the European Union to cut off aid. As has become habitual with Zanzibar's embattled leaders, Amour claimed that the isles' troubles were being orchestrated by an external "plot", and only after four years of bitter wrangles did CCM and CUF agree to a Commonwealth-brokered reconciliation, known as **Muafaka** – "the Accord". For a while, *Muafaka* gave a glimmer of hope, but the 2000 elections – which saw Karume's son, **Amani Karume** – elected president, were just as divisive, as were elections in 2005, and there's little hope that the 2010 vote will be any different.

## The Union and the future

While **Mkapa's presidency** of the Union (1995–2005) was largely overshadowed by events in Zanzibar, his tenure saw a number of quiet but positive changes, continuing Mwinyi's reformist legacy. Most obvious was the further liberalization of the **economy**. The results, until the oil shock and banking crisis of 2008, were certainly impressive from a macro-economic stance: inflation was under four percent, GDP was growing by seven to ten percent annually, and per capita income had doubled to over $500 a year. But even in the pre-crash context, these figures are misleading. Per capita income had certainly increased, but only for those in work. Averaged out across all people of working age, the figure barely topped $200, with over one third of rural Tanzanians surviving on less than **a dollar a day** (the internationally accepted "poverty line"). The increase in GDP wasn't as rosy as it looked, either: a large chunk is accounted for by tourism and mining, sectors largely owned by foreign companies, with little trickle-down effect to the masses, and also heavily impacted by the global economy's troubles. Tanzania remains heavily dependent on **foreign aid**, despite China and the G8 having written off a substantial portion of the country's debts, and **corruption** has been a constant theme, even with the high-profile arrest of two former ministers in 2008.

On the positive side, one of the first fruits of debt forgiveness was an ambitious and so far successful programme to place the country back on track towards **universal primary education** (and literacy), last achieved during Nyerere's tenure. The country's woeful **infrastructure** has also been addressed: an ambitious road construction programme is well under way, and even with projects habitually finishing years behind schedule, the benefits are beginning to be felt, particularly along the north–south corridor from Dar to Mozambique, and west to Mwanza and the lake region. Internationally, Tanzania has forged closer ties with Kenya and Uganda. In 2001, the **East African Union** was resurrected, with its 27-member legislative assembly based in Arusha. The three nations also agreed on a Customs Union, the first step towards political federation, and there's little doubt that regional cooperation is the way forward, especially in these post-crash times.

# Wildlife and habitats

espite tremendous habitat losses over the last century, due to a ten-fold increase in the human population, Tanzania is one of the twelve most biodiverse nations on earth, and has almost a third of its surface area under some form of official protection, whether national parks or several types of reserve. The **species counts** don't lie: 320 types of mammals, 1200 kinds of birds, 1400 species of butterfly, 380 varieties of reptiles and amphibians, and over ten thousand distinct plant species, a quarter of which are found nowhere else.

# Habitats

Tanzania's varied **habitats** range from savanna grasslands and bushlands to woods, forests (including rainforests), lakes, rivers, swamps, mangroves and reefs.

## Savanna and semi-arid habitats

**Savanna** is either tropical grassland or lightly wooded bushland, and covers huge swaths of Tanzania, particularly in the north. Although the **grasslands** are the epitome of wild Africa, humans have long had a hand in their ecology: bush fires set by cattle herders cleared the land of scrub (and tsetse flies), and the trampling of their herds inhibited new growth, which altogether created a paradise for plains game. Over the last century, however, cattle herders – famously the Maasai – have been excluded from all but the poorest grasslands, and the ecological balance has shifted. Filling the niche formerly occupied by cattle are wildebeest, whose current population is ten times what it was in the 1950s.

Traditionally, cattle herders preferred flat terrain, and generally avoided the hilly woodlands surrounding them. In those areas, the dominant tree species are thorny **acacias**, a hardy breed perfectly capable of surviving for years without rain. Also thriving in these semi-arid woodlands are cactus-like **euphorbia**, whose corrosive sap is toxic to almost anything except rhinos.

The true **desert** around Lake Natron is drier still and plant life very limited; the few trees and bushes here are stunted, and large areas are bare stony desert with just a thin and patchy growth of desert grasses and perhaps a few bushes along seasonal watercourses.

## Woodland and forest

Roughly a third of Tanzania, particularly in the centre and south, is covered by deciduous **miombo woodland** (see p.210), *miombo* being the local name for the dominant *Brachystegia* family of trees. Despite its dry appearance for much of the year, *miombo* is heaven for big browsing mammals, including elephants, thanks in large part to the presence of **tsetse flies**, vectors for sleeping sickness. Wild animals have acquired immunity, but the disease strikes livestock and people with impunity, so infested areas are sparsely populated by humans, if at all. Parks and reserves with substantial tracts of *miombo* include Mikumi, Selous and Ruaha.

Tanzania's **rainforests** are at their most spectacular in the ancient Eastern Arc Mountains (see p.279), which is a disconnected chain of massifs that includes North and South Pare, East and West Usambara, Uluguru and Udzungwa.

A stable climate over millions of years courtesy of the western Indian Ocean monsoon, and the forests' isolation from one another (the massifs are separated by low-lying savanna and steppe) has created some of the most biodiverse habitats on earth. Unfortunately, the extent of these forests has declined massively over the last century, due to commercial logging, wood collection for making charcoal, and clearance for agriculture (leading to soil erosion). Nonetheless, the surviving forests – many now protected as forest or nature reserves – contain an extraordinary variety of life, and one place in particular – Amani Nature Reserve – fully deserves its unofficial tag of the Galapagos of Africa.

The rainforests are at their richest between 200 metres and 1500 metres above sea level. Further up, the rainforests give way to cloudy **montane forests** interspersed with grassy meadows. The main montane forests are to be found on Mount Kilimanjaro and Mount Meru, whilst for highland meadows, Kitulo National Park in southern Tanzania is sheer paradise. Beyond the tree line (around 2900m), the so-called **Afro-Alpine zone** bears strong similarities to those of other high East African mountains, and includes giant heather, protea and groundsel and desolate high-altitude tundra: see p.273 for a full description.

## Wetlands

Whilst Tanzania is for the most part semi-arid, its rugged geology has given it a number of large lakes, both freshwater and alkaline. In the far west, three of Africa's "Great Lakes" dominate the scene, ecologically as well as economically. **Lake Victoria**, in the northwest, is the world's second-largest freshwater lake, and the main source of the River Nile. Sadly, the lake has become a perfect example of catastrophic environmental damage caused by man, having been the scene of the mass extinction of hundreds of fish species in the last few decades (see p.393). Still, the lake retains its beauty, along with a good deal of avian wildlife, particularly at Rubondo Island National Park. Southwest of here, filling a deep Rift Valley fissure, is **Lake Tanganyika**, the world's second-deepest. It contains an amazing profusion of fish species, especially evolutionary marvels called cichlids. Even richer is **Lake Nyasa** (Lake Malawi) in southwestern Tanzania, another deep Rift Valley lake, which contains over four hundred cichlid species – one third of the world's total – many of which are unique. Apart from extraordinary fish life, the lakes also mark the eastern boundary of central and west African flora and fauna, and their shores contain many plant and animal species absent elsewhere in Tanzania, most famously the chimpanzees at Gombe Stream and Mahale national parks beside Lake Tanganyika.

Most of Tanzania's other inland water bodies are **soda lakes**, occupying Rift Valley depressions that over the ages have been filled with sediment, making them extremely shallow and prone to enormous fluctuations in size. Their alkalinity isn't overly conducive to wildlife, but they are important drinking points during and after the rains when the water is fresher. Their most spectacular inhabitants are lesser **flamingos**, usually in flocks of tens or even hundreds of thousands, for whom soda-loving algal blooms are the staple food – and source of their pink colour. The main soda lakes are Manyara, Natron and Eyasi, all in the north, and Rukwa, in the south.

Tanzania's few **permanent rivers** are all under increasing pressure from deforestation, unsustainable land use, and ever more erratic rains due to global warming. The main rivers, all draining into the ocean, are the Ruvuma (along the border with Mozambique), the Rufiji/Ruaha system (in the centre), and the Pangani (watered by the northern highlands, including Kilimanjaro's snowmelt). These and other permanent rivers are favourable dry-season habitats for wildlife, when the surrounding lands become too dry. Particularly rich is the Great Ruaha as it flows through Ruaha National Park, and the Rufiji as it flows through the northern part of Selous. **Seasonal rivers**, which only flow during the rains, are also known as sand rivers; permanent vegetation along their banks, and water pools in their beds during the dry seasons (which are sometimes deliberately excavated by wild animals such as elephants) are particularly good places for seeing wildlife.

Where rivers pass through flat land, **marshes and swamps** dominate. As the abode of hippos, crocodiles and birds, they're exceptionally rich in wildlife, whether in the rains when water levels are at their highest, or in the dry season, when the waters drain into permanent water pools. The best areas for seeing these habitats are Selous Game Reserve and, in the far west, Katavi National Park.

## The coast

Along with rainforests, Tanzania's richest habitats – and the most colourful – are **coral reefs**, which form a fringing barrier along much of the shore between Kenya and Mozambique, and also surround the archipelagos of Zanzibar and Mafia. Corals, which thrive in warm, shallow tropical waters, are a strange mix of microscopic animal and mineral. Growing together in colonies of trillions, they form gigantic reefs, which provide a perfect habitat for all kinds of marine life, from micro-organisms, sea cucumbers and crustaceans to a dazzling array of fish, dolphins, sea turtles and whales – all of which can be visited either by snorkelling or scuba diving; see pp.56–57 for more information.

The paradisiacal palm-backed beaches of the tourist brochures cover but a tiny fraction of Tanzania's coastline. Most of the coast is actually flanked by humid and silty **mangrove forests** (*mikoko* in Kiswahili). Highly specialized, these habitats play a vital role in coral reef ecology by acting as filters for rainwater, nurseries for fish, and by impeding coastal erosion. Although fun to travel through by boat, mangroves are not noted for faunal diversity, although they can contain unusual species of birds, and – with luck – **mudskippers**, which are fish on the evolutionary road to becoming amphibians. The mangroves themselves are uniquely adapted to their salty, waterlogged environment; for instance, many species have spiky aerial roots through which they breathe. The largest mangrove forest is in the Rufiji delta, but easier to visit are the mangrove-lined creeks of Saadani National Park, or indeed mangroves either side of most of Tanzania's beaches.

# Mammals

The majority of Tanzania's 320 **mammal species** are vegetarian; the big emblematic predators at the top of the food chain are far fewer, but are the dominant topic of conversation at game lodges.

## Chimpanzees

**Chimpanzees** live right across Africa's tropical rainforest belt, from The Gambia to Lake Tanganyika in western Tanzania, where there are several communities at both Gombe Stream and Mahale Mountains national parks. Chimpanzees are our closest living relatives, and irresistibly fascinating. Like us, they're intelligent and complex (and sometimes temperamental) social creatures which feel and share emotions, and are able to adapt to different environments and foods, pass on knowledge learned from experience and make and use simple tools, like probes for fishing ants and termites from their nests. They also hunt in a human way, use plants medicinally, raid each other's communities and sometimes descend into states of war. Their **communities** consist of fifteen to eighty individuals, headed by "alpha males", whose dominance depends not so much on physical strength as an ability to form and keep strategic alliances with other males. Chimps are endangered, their global population having dropped from two million a century ago to under 300,000, a figure that's expected to halve over the next three chimpanzee generations. The main threats are on-going habitat loss, subsistence hunting and the killing of mothers to capture infants for the pet trade, entertainment industry and – notoriously – biomedical research.

## Other primates

Apart from chimps, Tanzania has dozens of other primate species. One you'll see almost anywhere with a few trees is the small and slender **vervet monkey**, which has effortlessly adapted to humans, and their food. Away from us, they forage for fruits, leaves, insects and just about anything else small and tasty. Their main predators are leopards, and large birds such as the crowned eagle; hence the vervet's constant and nervous skyward glances. Males are distinguished by a natty set of blue genitalia; the more vibrant the colour, the higher the individual's rank.

Like chimpanzees, **baboons** are hierarchical, but you'll see them all over the place. Tanzania has two species: yellow baboons in the centre and south, and the larger olive baboons in the north. Baboons live in complex and highly territorial troops led by dominant males, in which social ties are reinforced by mutual grooming. Large males are quite capable of mauling humans, so treat them with respect – and never feed or tease baboons, or tempt them with food.

Almost as common in certain areas, notably on the coast and in lowland rainforests, are agile **blue monkeys**, whose predilection for agricultural crops makes them a pest. Other than colour, the species is very similar to smaller **red tail monkeys** (whose tails are actually orange), from whom they diverged only recently; male blue monkeys who fail to gather their own "harem" can be accepted into red tail troops, and hybrids of the two species are known.

The most arboreal of Tanzania's primates, and found all over the country, is the acrobatic **black-and-white colobus monkey**, which rarely descends to the ground, and can be distinguished by its lack of thumbs. Rare offshoots include various species of **red colobus monkey**, notably in the Udzungwa Mountains, in Zanzibar's Jozani Forest, in northwestern Selous, and at both Gombe and Mahale.

Another common primate, which you're likely to see or at least hear if you stay in a game lodge, is the diminutive **bushbaby** (galago). There are two species: the cat-sized greater galago, and the kitten-sized lesser galago. Both are very cute, with sensitive, inquisitive fingers and large eyes and ears to aid their hunt for insects and small animals. They also have ear-splitting cries (hence the name), something that may well wake you with a jolt at night.

## Rodents and hyraxes

Rodents aren't likely to make a strong impression, unless you're lucky enough to do some night game drives – or preferably walks; Tarangire and Selous are good for this. If you partake in either, you may see the bristling back end of a **crested porcupine** or the frenzied leaps of a **spring hare**, dazzled by headlights or a torch. In rural areas off the beaten track you occasionally see hunters taking home **giant rats** or **cane rats** – shy, vegetarian animals, which make good eating. Tanzania has several species of **squirrel**, the most spectacular of which are the giant forest squirrel – with its splendid bush of a tail – and the nocturnal **flying squirrel** – which actually glides, rather than flies, from tree to tree, on membranes between its outstretched limbs. The two species of **ground squirrel** – striped and unstriped – are widespread and are often seen dashing along the track in front of a safari vehicle.

The bucktoothed, furry **hyraxes**, which you're certain to see on the kopjes and around the lodges of the Serengeti, look like they should be rodents, but in fact are technically ungulates (hoofed mammals) and form a classificatory level entirely their own. Incredibly, their closest living relatives are elephants. Present-day hyraxes are pygmies compared with some of their prehistoric ancestors, which in some cases were as big as bears. Rock hyraxes live in busy, vocal colonies of twenty or thirty females and young, plus a male. Away from the lodges, they're timid in the extreme – not surprising in view of the wide range of predators targeting them.

## Cats

Tanzania's predators are some of the most exciting and easily recognizable animals you'll see. Although often portrayed as fearsome hunters, many species do a fair bit of scavenging and all are content to eat smaller fry when conditions dictate or the opportunity arises.

Of the large cats, **lions** are the easiest to find. Lazy, gregarious and large – up to 1.8 metres in length, not counting the tail, and up to a metre high at the shoulder – they rarely make much effort to hide or to move away, except on occasions when a large number of tourist vehicles intrude, or if elephants are passing through. They can be seen in nearly all the parks and reserves. Especially good photo opportunities are in the Serengeti, where they form particularly large prides; at Ngorongoro, Mikumi and Ruaha you may well also see them hunting. Normally, it's females which do the hunting (often co-operatively and at night). Surprisingly, their success rate is only about one in three attacks, so they tend to target young, old or sick animals. When they don't kill their own prey, they'll happily steal the kills of other predators.

Intensely secretive, alert and wary, **leopards** are stealth hunters, and live all across the country except in the most treeless zones. Their unmistakable call, likened to a big saw being pulled back and forth, is unforgettable. Solitary and mainly active at night, you may see them by day resting up in trees. They also sometimes survive on the outskirts of towns and villages, carefully preying on different domestic animals to avoid a routine. They tolerate nearby human habitation and rarely kill people unless provoked. For the most part, leopards live off any small animals that come their way, including small mammals, primates and birds, pouncing from an ambush and dragging the kill up into a tree where it may be consumed over several days, away from the attentions of scavengers. The spots on a leopard vary from individual to individual, but are always in the form of rosettes.

The world's fastest mammal, and commonly seen in the Serengeti, is the **cheetah**. Often confused with leopards because of their spots, once you get to know them they're easy to identify: slender, more finely spotted, and with small heads, long legs and distinctive "tears" under their eyes. Cheetahs prefer open ground where they can hunt… at speeds clocked at up to seventy miles an hour (112kph). As they hunt by day, cheetahs – or, rather, their prey – are easily spooked by humans: keep your distance and be quiet.

Other large Tanzanian cats include the part-spotted, part-striped **serval**, found in most of the parks, though its nocturnal nature means it's usually seen scavenging around lodges at night. Up to a metre long including the tail, it uses its large ears to locate and approach prey – game birds, bustards, rodents, hares, snakes or frogs – before pouncing. The heavily built grey-black **African civet** resembles a large, terrestrial genet. It was formerly kept in captivity for its musk (once a part of the raw material for perfume), which is secreted from glands near the tail. Being nocturnal, they're infrequently seen, but are predictable creatures, wending their way along the same paths at the same time night after night, preying on small animals or looking for insects and fruit. Also nocturnal but much rarer is the aggressive, tuft-eared **caracal**, a kind of lynx that favours drier zones such as Mkomazi and Tarangire.

## Other carnivores

The biggest carnivore after the lion is the **spotted hyena**; it's also, apart from the lion, the one you will most often see, especially in the Serengeti. Although considered a scavenger *par excellence*, the spotted hyena – with its distinctive sloping back, limping gait and short, broad muzzle – is also a formidable hunter, most often found where antelopes and zebras are present. In fact, their success rate at hunting, in packs and at speeds up to 50kph, is twice that of some specialized predators. Exceptionally efficient consumers, with strong teeth and jaws, spotted hyenas eat virtually every part of their prey in a matter of minutes, including bones and hide and, where habituated to humans, often steal shoes, unwashed pans and refuse from tents and villages. Although they can be seen by day, they are most often active at night – when they issue their unnerving, whooping cries. Socially, hyenas form territorial groups of up to eighty animals. These so-called clans are dominated by females, which are larger than males and compete with each other for rank. Curiously, female hyenas' genitalia are hard to distinguish from males', leading to a popular misconception that they are hermaphroditic. Not surprisingly, in view of all their attributes, the hyena is a key figure in mythology and folklore, usually as a limping, heartless bad guy, or as a symbol of duplicitous cunning. In comparison with the spotted hyena, you're not very likely to see a **striped hyena**. A usually solitary animal, it's slighter and much rarer than its spotted relative, though occasionally glimpsed very early in the morning. You have reasonable odds of seeing them at Tarangire, and at Ruaha, which marks their southernmost extent.

The unusual and rather magnificent **African hunting dogs**, also called wild dogs or "painted wolves" (in Latin, *Lycaon pictus*), have disappeared from much of their historical range in Africa. Their remaining strongholds are at Mikumi, Selous and Ruaha, and there are smaller and more endangered populations at Mkomazi and Tarangire. Canine distemper and rabies have played as big a role in their decline as human predation and habitat disruption. They are efficient pack hunters, running their prey in relays to exhaustion before tearing it apart, and live in groups of up to forty animals, with ranges of almost eight hundred square kilometres. The commonest members of the dog family in Tanzania are the **jackals**, one of the few mammalian species in which mating couples stay together for life. The black-backed or silver-backed jackal and the similar side-striped jackal can be seen just about anywhere, usually in pairs. Whilst all three will scavenge, in the main their meals are hunted birds, small mammals and insects. **Bat-eared foxes** live in burrows in the plains, and while not uncommon, are rarely seen as they're most active at dawn and dusk. Their very large ears make them unmistakable.

The unusual **honey badger** or **ratel** is related to the European badger and has a reputation for defending itself extremely fiercely. Primarily an omnivorous forager, it will tear open beehives (to which it is led by a small bird, the honey-guide), its thick, loose hide rendering it impervious to their stings. The solitary and nocturnal **genets** are reminiscent of slender, elongated black-and-white cats, with spotted coats and ringed tails. They were once domesticated around the Mediterranean, but cats proved better mouse-hunters, and in fact genets are related to mongooses. They're frequently seen after dark around national park lodges. Most species of **mongoose**, attractive animals with elongated bodies and long tails, are also tolerant of humans and, even when disturbed out in the bush, can usually be observed for some time before disappearing. Their snake-fighting reputation is greatly overplayed: in practice they are mostly social foragers, fanning out through the bush, rooting for anything edible – mostly invertebrates, eggs, lizards and frogs. The most common are the dwarf, banded and black-tipped (also called slender mongoose), the latter often seen darting across tracks as you approach. Rarer are the marsh mongoose (frequent at Gombe) and white-tailed mongoose (also at Gombe, and Serengeti).

## Elephants

Larger than their Asian cousins and rarely domesticated, African **elephants** are found throughout Tanzania, and almost all the big plains and mountain parks have their populations. These are the most engaging of animals to watch, perhaps because their interactions, behaviour patterns and personalities have so many human parallels. They lead complex, interdependent social lives, growing from helpless infancy, through self-conscious adolescence, to adulthood.

Babies are born with other cows in close attendance, after a 22-month gestation, and suckle for two to three years. Elephants' basic family units are composed of a group of related females, tightly protecting their babies and young and led by a venerable matriarch. It's the matriarch that's most likely to bluff a charge – though occasionally she may get carried away and tusk a vehicle or person. Bush mythology has it that elephants become embarrassed and ashamed after killing a human, covering the body with sticks and grass. They certainly pay much attention to the disposal of their own dead relatives, often dispersing the bones, spending time near the remains, and returning to the site for several years. Old animals die in their seventies or eighties, when their last set of teeth wears out and they can no longer feed.

Seen in the wild, elephants seem even bigger than you would imagine – you'll need little persuasion from those flapping, warning ears to back off if you're too close – but are surprisingly graceful, silent animals on their padded, carefully placed feet. In a matter of moments, a large herd can merge into the trees and disappear, its presence betrayed only by the noisy cracking of branches as they strip trees and uproot saplings. Relatively quiet they may be to our ears, but researchers have discovered that vibrations from stamping elephant feet can be picked up 50km away, and are almost certainly a form of communication, complementing their equally remarkable language of very low-frequency rumbles.

Until the 1950s, elephants inhabited almost ninety percent of Tanzania, but their range now covers just half that original area. Apart from habitat loss, elephant populations also suffered from **ivory poachers**, especially in the 1970s and 1980s, when three-quarters of the national population were massacred. The more peaceful 1990s managed to bring their Tanzanian population back to a healthy hundred thousand of which sixty thousand or so are concentrated in Selous Game Reserve. The best place to see them, though, is in Tarangire National Park, decorated by suitably Brobdingnagian baobab trees.

# Rhinos

The **rhino** is one of the world's oldest mammalian species, having appeared on earth some fifty to sixty million years ago, shortly after the demise of the dinosaurs. Nowadays, it's also one of the most critically endangered, as a result of catastrophic poaching for their valuable horns in the 1970s and 1980s, which completely wiped out the populations at Tarangire, Mikumi and Mkomazi. There are five species worldwide, the Tanzanian one being the hook-lipped or **black rhinoceros**. The name is a misnomer, having been given in counterpoint to the white rhino, where "white" was a mistranslation of the Afrikaans for "wide", referring to its lip: the white rhino's broad lip is suitable for grazing, whereas the black rhino's is adapted for browsing. Both species are actually grey.

Until the mid-1970s, black rhinos were a fairly common sight in many Tanzanian parks and reserves. In the 1960s, for example, the Selous contained over three thousand, some with long upper horns over a metre in length. Today, the Selous **population** is barely 150, accounting for three-quarters of Tanzania's total (which had started the 1960s at around ten thousand). The driving force behind the poaching, which began in earnest in the 1970s, was (and is) the high price for rhino horn on the black market. The horn is actually an agglomeration of hair, and has long been used to make status-symbol dagger handles in Arabia and an aphrodisiac medicine in Far Eastern countries. Contributing factors to the decline are their long gestation period (15–18 months), and the fact that calves remain dependent on their mothers until the age of five, when the next one comes along. The **location** and size of most surviving populations is, understandably, a closely guarded secret, and the only rhinos that can readily be visited by tourists are at Ngorongoro Crater.

# Hippos

**Hippopotamuses** are among the most impressive of Africa's creatures – lugubrious pink monsters that weigh up to three tons and measure up to four metres from their whiskered chins to their stubby tails. Despite their ungainly appearance they're highly adaptable and found wherever rivers or freshwater lakes and pools are deep enough for them to submerge and also have a surrounding of suitable grazing grass. They are supremely adapted to long periods in water, a necessity as they need to protect their hairless skin from dehydration; their pinkish colour is a natural secretion that acts as a sunblock. In the water, their clumsy feet become supple paddles, and they can remain completely submerged for six minutes, and for hours on end with just their nostrils, eyes and ears protruding. They communicate underwater with clicks, pulses, croaks and whines, and at the surface with grunts, snorts and aggressive displays of fearsome dentition. After dark, and sometimes on wet and overcast days, hippos leave the water to spend the whole night grazing, their stumpy legs carrying them up to 10km in one session.

Hippos are thought to be responsible for more human deaths in Africa than any other animal except malarial mosquitoes. Deaths mainly occur on the water, when boats accidentally steer into hippo pods, but they can be aggressive on dry land, too, especially if you're between them and water, or when they're with calves. They can run at 30kph if necessary, and their enormous bulk and steel-crunching jaws advocate extreme caution. Yet if they pass through a campground at night, nary a guy rope is twanged.

## Zebras

**Zebras** are closely related to horses and, together with wild asses, form the equid family. Burchell's zebra is the only species in Tanzania, and is found throughout the country. In Serengeti and Tarangire, zebras gather in migrating herds up to several hundred thousand strong, along with wildebeest and other grazers. Socially, they're organized into family groups of up to fifteen individuals led by a stallion. The stripes appear to be a defence mechanism for confusing predators: bunched up in a jostling herd, the confusion of stripes makes it very difficult to single out an individual to chase; the stripes are also said to confuse tsetse flies.

## Pigs

The commonest wild pig in Tanzania is the comical **warthog**. Quick of movement and nervous, warthogs are notoriously hard to photograph as they're generally on the run through the bush, often with the young in single file, tails erect like antennae, though you can catch them browsing in a kneeling position. They shelter in holes in the ground, usually old aardvark burrows, and live in family groups generally consisting of a mother and her litter of two to four piglets, or occasionally two or three females and their young. Boars join the group only to mate, and are distinguishable from sows by their longer tusks, and the warts below their eyes, which are thought to be defensive pads to protect their heads during often violent fights.

Also common but rarely seen is the nocturnal **bush pig**, which inhabits forest and dense thickets close to rivers and marshes. They're brownish in colour, resemble European boars, and weigh up to 80kg.

## Giraffes

Tanzania's national symbol, and the world's tallest mammal (up to five metres), is the **giraffe**, found wherever there are trees. The species in Tanzania is the irregularly patterned Maasai giraffe. Both sexes have horns, but can be distinguished by the shorter height of the females, and by the tufts of hair over their horns. Daylight hours are spent browsing on the leaves of trees too high for other species; acacia and combretum are favourites. Non-territorial, they gather in loose leaderless herds, with bulls testing their strength while in bachelor herds. When a female comes into oestrus, which can happen at any time of year, the dominant male mates with her. She will give birth after a gestation of approximately fourteen months. Over half of all young fall prey to lions or hyenas, however. Oddly, despite the great length of their necks, they're supported by only seven vertebrae – the same as humans.

## Buffaloes

The fearsome African or Cape **buffalo**, with its massive flattened horns and eight-hundred-kilogram bulk, is a common and much-photographed animal, closely related to the domestic cow. They live in herds of several hundred, which can swell to over a thousand in times of drought. Though untroubled by close contact with humans or vehicles, they are one of Africa's most dangerous animals when alone, when their behaviour is unpredictable. Their preferred habitat is swamp and marsh, though they have also adapted to life in highland forests. Buffaloes are often accompanied by **oxpeckers** and **cattle egrets**, which hitch rides on the backs of buffalo and other game. They have a symbiotic relationship with their hosts, feeding off parasites such as ticks and blood-sucking flies. The oxpeckers also have an alarm call that warns their hosts of danger like lurking predators.

## Plains-dwelling antelopes

Plains-dwelling antelopes are common throughout Tanzania, even outside protected areas. Large herds of white-bearded **wildebeest** or gnu are particularly associated with the Serengeti; their spectacular annual migration is described in the box on p.376. The blue wildebeest (or brindled gnu) of central and southern Tanzania lack beards and are paler in colour. The strong shoulders and comparatively puny hindquarters of both species lend them an ungainly appearance, but the light rear end is useful for their wild and erratic bucking when attacked. Calves begin walking within minutes – a necessity when predators are always on the lookout.

There are two main species of **gazelles**: **Thomson's** ("Tommies"), which can survive extremely arid conditions, and the larger **Grant's**. Both are gregarious, and often seen at roadsides. Almost as common is the **impala**, seen either in breeding herds of females, calves and one male, or in bachelor herds. They're seldom far from cover and, when panicked, the herd "explodes" in all directions, confusing predators. Only males have horns. Also putting in frequent appearances is the huge, cow-like **eland**, which weighs six hundred to nine hundred kilograms and has a distinctive dewlap. Females are reddish, males are grey; and both have corkscrew-like horns. Equally imposing is the **fringe-eared oryx**, present in small numbers throughout the country but best seen at Tarangire, and whose long straight horns may explain the unicorn myth. They live in herds of up to forty animals, and are migratory. Also plains-dwelling is the elegant **gerenuk**, an unusual browsing gazelle able to nibble from bushes standing on its hind legs (its name is Somali for "giraffe-necked"); in Tanzania, its range is restricted to the semi-arid north, around Lake Natron, Longido and Mkomazi, with a few in Tarangire.

Two more species, these favouring rocky islands rising from the plains, are the surprisingly aggressive **steinbok** which, despite a height of only 50cm, defends itself furiously against attackers (best seen at Tarangire), and the grey and shaggy **klipspringer** (Afrikaans for "stone jumper"), whose hooves are wonderfully adapted for scaling near-vertical cliffs. Like dikdiks, both are monogamous, giving birth to one offspring each year; their territory is marked by secretions from glands near the eyes. Klipspringers can easily be seen at Ruaha, Tarangire and Manyara, and sometimes in Udzungwa.

## Bushland and forest-dwelling antelopes

The rather ungainly, long-faced **hartebeest** family, with its distinctive S-shaped horns, has three representatives in Tanzania: the reddish **Liechtenstein's hartebeest** is the most common, especially in *miombo* and acacia woodland (Saadani is a good place to spot them); the paler **Coke's hartebeest**, with a longer, narrower head, is rarely found in the north; and, resembling hartebeest, the **topi**, whose males often stand sentry on top of abandoned termite mounds in the Serengeti and in Katavi. The striped **kudu** are also very localized, and their preference for dense bush makes them hard to see; your best chance is at dawn or dusk. There are two species, both browsers: **greater kudu**, with eight to ten lateral stripes, are best seen at Selous, Mikumi and Saadani; and the smaller **lesser kudu**, which has more stripes, can be seen in Mkomazi and Tarangire. Both can be seen at Ruaha. The spiralled horns of the male greater kudus can grow up to 180cm, and have long been used by local people for making musical instruments.

Other large bushland antelopes include the massive **roan antelope**, with their backward-sweeping horns, large ears and black-and-white faces, found mainly in Katavi, Ruaha and Mahale and often seen close to water in the mornings, and the related **sable antelope**, with their handsome curved and swept-back horns. Males are black with white bellies and face markings; females are all brown. They thrive in *miombo* woodland, making them regular sightings at Mikumi, Selous, Ruaha, Mahale and Katavi. There's also a lighter and smaller subspecies at Saadani on the coast. The large **bushbuck** is nocturnal, solitary and notoriously shy – a loud crashing through the undergrowth and a flash of a chestnut rump are all most people witness.

Top marks for Bambi-like features goes to **Kirk's dikdik**, a miniature antelope found all over the country. Measuring no more than 40cm in height (4kg in weight), they're most active in the morning and evening. Usually seen in mono gamous pairs (the males are horned, the females are slightly larger), their territories are marked by piles of droppings and secretions deposited on grass stems. Their name mimics their whistling alarm call when fleeing. The forest-loving **suni** antelope is even daintier, measuring up to 32cm in height, but rare and with a scattered distribution: you have very good odds on seeing them on Prison Island in Zanzibar, and a reasonable chance at Zanzibar's Jozani Forest, the Pugu Hills near Dar, in the Udzungwa Mountains and on Rubondo Island where they've been introduced. The **duikers** (Dutch for "diver", referring to their plunging into the bush) are larger – the **common duiker** is around 60cm high – though they appear smaller because of their shorter forelimbs. It's found throughout the country in many habitats, but most duikers are more choosy and prefer plenty of dense cover and thicket. Their isolation from other communities means that they've evolved into several subspecies which still confuse taxonomists: the most common family is that of the **blue duiker** (and related **Abbot's duiker**), which ranges from Mount Rungwe in the south to the world's largest population in the forests of Kilimanjaro. Rarer subspecies include the tiny **Ader's duiker** on Zanzibar (Chumbe Island and Jozani Forest); the **Pemba blue duiker** (Ngezi Forest on Pemba Island); a relict population of blue duikers on Juani Island in the Mafia archipelago; **red duikers** (Kilimanjaro and Udzungwa) and **grey duikers** (Gombe and Kilimanjaro).

## Antelopes found in or around water

Easily confused with impala, the **Bohor reedbuck** prefers long grass and reed beds near swamps, where they're easily concealed. Only males have horns; short, ringed and forward-curving. They're most easily seen in Mikumi, Selous and Ruaha, but are also present in Saadani, Katavi and Tarangire. **Mountain reedbuck**, common in Ngorongoro, are similar. The related brownish-grey **common waterbuck** has a much wider distribution; they have a distinctive white ring around their rump, and are seen in mixed herds controlled by a dominant male. Like reedbucks, they're often seen near water, in which they can seek refuge from predators. The semi-aquatic **sitatunga** is found in Tanzania only in remote corners of Lake Victoria's shoreline, notably Rubondo Island.

## Other terrestrial mammals

That much-loved dictionary leader, the **aardvark**, is one of Africa's strangest mammals, a solitary termite-eater weighing up to 70kg. Its name, Afrikaans for "earth pig", is an apt description, as it holes up during the day in large burrows, excavated with remarkable speed and energy, and emerges at night to visit termite mounds within a radius of 5km. It's most likely to be common in bush country well scattered with tall termite spires. **Ground pangolins** are equally unusual – nocturnal, scale-covered mammals, resembling armadillos and feeding on ants and termites. Under attack, they roll into a ball.

In wooded areas, insectivorous **elephant shrews** are worth looking out for, simply because they are so weird (the elephant bit refers to their trunk-like snout). They're extremely adaptable, as their habitat ranges from the semi-desert around Lake Natron to the lush forests of Amani, Gombe, Jozani and Udzungwa. Tanzania's many **bats** will usually be a mere flicker over a waterhole at twilight, or sometimes a flash across headlights. The only bats you can normally observe in any decent way are fruit bats hanging from their roosting sites by day; there are visitable roosts on Chole Island in the Mafia Archipelago, at Misali and Makoongwe islands off Pemba Island and in Pemba Island's Ngezi Forest (the endemic Pemba flying fox or Mega Bat). For more "traditional" bat viewing, visit the incredible colonies of the Amboni Caves near Tanga.

## Marine mammals

Of the three main marine mammals of the western Indian Ocean, the most common are **dolphins**, which need no introduction. They're most easily seen off Kizimkazi in Zanzibar. **Whales** pass along the coast from October to December on their vast migrations around the world's oceans, and – if you're exceptionally lucky – can be heard singing when you're diving.

The rarest of all of Tanzania's mammals, rarer even than the rhino, is the **dugong** (also called manatee or sea cow), something like a cross between a seal and a walrus and which, like other marine mammals such as dolphins and whales, was at some point along its evolutionary safari lured back into the sea. In more recent times, it acted as an unlikely lure for sailors, being the prototype for the original mermaid. The legend probably had something to do with the dugong's habit of floating around on its back, letting a pair of bobbing and rather ample breasts work their magic on the mariners of yore. Their only known breeding ground in Tanzanian waters lies between the mainland and Mafia Archipelago, but hunting and the use of *jarife* shark nets has brought them close to extinction in East Africa.

# Reptiles and amphibians

The **Nile crocodile** can reach six metres or more in length. You'll see them, log-like, on the sandy shores of most of Tanzania's rivers and lakes. Although they mostly live off fish, they are also dangerous opportunists, seizing the unwary with disconcerting speed. Once caught, either by the mouth or after being tossed into the water by a flick of their powerful tails, the victim is spun underwater to drown it, before massive jaws make short work of the carcass.

Tanzania has many species of **snakes**, some of them quite common, but your chances of seeing a wild specimen are remote. In Tanzania, as all over Africa, snakes are both revered and reviled and, while they frequently have symbolic significance for local people that is quite often forgotten in the rush to hack them to bits when found. All in all, snakes have a very hard time surviving in Tanzania: their turnover is high but their speed of exit from the scene when humans show up is remarkable. If you want to see them, wear boots and walk softly. If you want to avoid them completely, tread firmly and they'll flee on detecting your vibrations. The exception is the **puff adder**, which relies on camouflage to get within striking distance of prey, but will only bite when threatened (or stood on); around ten percent of its bites are fatal. Other common **poisonous species** include black mambas (fast, agile and arboreal; properly called black-mouthed mambas), the boomslang, the spitting cobra and blotched forest cobra, night adder, bush snake and bush viper. Common **non-poisonous snakes** include the constricting African python (a favoured partner of the Sukuma tribe's dance societies; see p.403), the egg-eating snake and the sand boa.

**Tortoises** are quite frequently encountered on park roads in the morning or late afternoon. Some, like the leopard tortoise, can be quite large, up to 50cm in length, while the hinged tortoise (which not only retreats inside its shell but shuts the door, too) is much smaller – up to 30cm. In rocky areas, look out for the unusual pancake tortoise, a flexible-shelled species that can put on quite a turn of speed but, when cornered in its fissure in the rocks, will inflate to wedge itself inextricably to avoid capture. Terrapins or turtles of several species are common in ponds and slow-flowing streams.

Tanzania is also home to five of the world's seven species of **marine turtle** (green, hawksbill, loggerhead, leatherback and olive ridley), which have been around for some ninty million years. It's not unusual to see them from boats during snorkelling trips, but their populations have declined drastically, and all three nesting species – the olive ridley, green, and hawksbill – are now endangered.

**Lizards** are common everywhere, harmless, often colourful and always amusing to watch. The commonest are **rock agamas**, the males often seen in courting "plumage", with brilliant orange heads and blue bodies, ducking and bobbing at each other. They live in loose colonies often near human habitation; one hotel may have hundreds, its neighbours none. The biggest lizards, **Nile monitors**, grow to nearly 2m in length and are often seen near water. From a distance, as they race off, they look like speeding baby crocodiles. The other common monitor, the smaller **Savanna monitor**, is less handsomely marked and often well camouflaged in its favoured bushy habitat.

A large, docile lizard you may come across is the **plated lizard**, an intelligent, mild-mannered reptile often found around coastal hotels, looking for scraps from the kitchen or pool terrace. At night on the coast, the translucent little aliens on the ceiling are **geckos**, catching moths and other insects. Their gravity-defying agility is due to countless microscopic hairs on their padded toes, whose adhesiveness functions at an atomic level. By day, their minuscule relatives the day geckos (velvet grey and yellow), patrol coastal walls. In the highlands you may come across prehistoric-looking three-horned **Jackson's chameleons** creeping through the foliage, and there are several other species, most also in the highlands.

Night is usually the best time for spotting **amphibians**, though unless you make an effort to track down the perpetrators of the frog chorus down by the lodge water pump, you'll probably only come across the odd toad. There are, however, dozens of species of frogs and tree frogs, including the diminutive and unique Kihansi spray toad, whose discovery in the spray at the bottom of a waterfall in 1996 scuppered the profitability of a hydroelectric dam in the Southern Highlands, which now has to divert part of its flow to keep the toads moist.

# Birds

Tanzania's wide variety of habitats and altitudinal ranges gives it one of Africa's highest counts of **bird species**, with around 1200 recorded so far, representing 75 families. Nearly eighty percent are thought to breed in the country. Of the **migratory species**, most arrive towards the end of the year, coinciding with the northern hemisphere's winter. Many are familiar British summer visitors, such as swallows, nightingales and whitethroats, which have to negotiate or skirt the inhospitable Sahara. The scale of the migration is mind-boggling: around six *billion* birds annually.

The following sections detail some of the more frequently seen and easily identified species. For a full list, consult ⓦ www.tanzaniabirdatlas.com, or get hold of a dedicated birding guidebook (see p.610). Also useful is the African Bird Club ⓦ www.africanbirdclub.org, which publishes an excellent bulletin, and occasional monographs and itineraries as well. For **practical advice**, see "Birding" in Basics on p.55.

## Large walking birds

Several species of large, terrestrial (or partly terrestrial) birds are regularly seen on safari. The flightless **ostrich** is found in dry, open plains and semi-desert in the far north, namely Tarangire, Ngorongoro, Serengeti, and around Lake Natron. At up to 2.5m high, it's the world's biggest bird, and one of the fastest runners when need be, too. The females are neutral in colour, but courting males wow the dames with their hairless pink necks and thighs. Contrary to popular belief, they don't bury their heads in the sand, but do hide them in their plumage while resting.

The large, long-tailed **secretary bird** is also easily identified, and gets its name from its head quills, which resemble pens propped behind ears, although its "bestockinged" legs and sashaying gait are suggestive, too. It's often seen in dry, open bush and wooded country, usually in pairs, and feeds on beetles, grasshoppers, reptiles and rodents. Similarly distinctive, as well as elegant, is the **crowned crane**, its head topped with a halo-like array of yellow plumes. They're often seen feeding on cultivated fields or in marshy areas; Lake Victoria is a good place.

Another common species is the **ground hornbill**. This impressive creature lives in open country and is the largest hornbill by far, black with red face and wattles, bearing a distinct resemblance to a turkey. It's not uncommon to come across pairs, or sometimes groups, of ground hornbills, trailing through the scrub on the lookout for small animals. They nest among rocks or in tree stumps. The Maasai say their calls resemble humans talking. Also commonly seen is the world's heaviest flying bird, albeit one that prefers spending its time on the ground: the greyish-brown **Kori bustard**, whose males average 12kg – and heaviest top 20kg.

Not really walking birds, but usually seen in flocks on the ground before scattering ahead of your advance in a low swooping flight, are several species of **guinea fowl**. These game birds have rather comical and brightly coloured heads, and a luxurious covering of royal blue feathers, often spotted white.

## Flamingos and ibises

Many visitors are astounded by their first sight of **flamingos** – a sea of pink on a soda-encrusted Rift Valley lake (Natron and Manyara are the best places). There are two species in Tanzania: the greater flamingo, and the much more common lesser flamingo, which can seen in flocks of tens and sometimes hundreds of thousands. The **lesser flamingo** is smaller, pinker and with a darker bill than its greater relative. The Rift Valley population – which only nests at Lake Natron – numbers several million, and is one of only three groups in Africa. Flocks can leave or arrive at an area in a very short period of time, the movements depending on all sorts of factors including the water's alkalinity and the presence of algal blooms, so sighting big flocks is impossible to predict. Lesser flamingos feed by filtering suspended aquatic food, mainly blue-green diatom algae that occur in huge concentrations on the shallow soda lakes of the Rift Valley. **Greater flamingos** may occur in their thousands but are considerably fewer in number than the lesser, and are bottom feeders, filtering small invertebrates as well as algae. Although greaters tend to be less nomadic than their relatives, they are more likely to move away from the Rift Valley lakes to smaller water bodies and even the coast.

The most widely distributed ibis species (stork-like birds with down-curved bills) is the **sacred ibis**, which occurs near water and human settlements. It has a white body with black head and neck, and black tips to the wings. Also frequently encountered is the **hadada ibis**, a bird of wooded streams, cultivated areas and parks in northern Tanzania. It's brown with a green-bronze sheen to the wings, and calls noisily in flight.

## Water birds

Most large bodies of water, apart from the extremely saline lakes, support several migratory species of **ducks, geese, herons, storks** and **egrets**. The commonest large heron is the black-headed species, which can sometimes be found far from water. Mainly grey with a black head and legs, the black heron can be seen "umbrella-fishing" along coastal creeks and marsh shores: it cloaks its head with its wings while fishing, which is thought to cut down surface reflection from the water, allowing the bird to see its prey more easily. The **hammerkop** or hammer-headed stork is a brown, heron-like bird with a sturdy bill and mane of brown feathers, which gives it a top-heavy, slightly prehistoric appearance in flight, like a miniature pterodactyl. Hammerkops are widespread near water and build large, conspicuous nests that are often taken over by other animals, including owls, geese, ducks, monitor lizards or snakes. Another common stork is the **saddlebill**, sporting an elegant red bill with a yellow "saddle" and black banding.

## Birds of prey and carrion eaters

Tanzania abounds with **birds of prey** (raptors) – kites, vultures, eagles, harriers, hawks and falcons. Altogether, over a hundred species have been recorded in the country, several of which are difficult to miss. Two raptors particularly associated with East Africa are the **bateleur**, an acrobatic eagle readily identified by its silver wings, black body and stumpy proportions; and the ineffably elegant black-and-white **African fish eagle**, often found perched in trees overlooking water.

Six species of **vulture** range over the plains and bushlands of Tanzania and are often seen soaring in search of a carcass. All the species can occur together, and birds may travel vast distances to feed. The main differences are in feeding behaviour: the lappet-faced vulture, for example, pulls open carcasses; the African white-backed feeds mainly on internal organs; and the hooded vulture picks the bones. The **marabou stork** is another easy one to spot – large and exceptionally ugly, up to 1.2m in height and with a bald head, long pointed funnel-like beak and dangling, pink throat pouch. The marabou flies with its head and neck retracted (unlike other storks) and is often seen in dry areas, including towns, where it feeds on small animals, carrion and refuse. If you're lucky, you'll see them roosting in trees.

## Go-away birds and turacos

These distinctive, related families are found only in Africa. Medium-sized and with long tails, most **go-away birds** and **turacos** have short rounded wings. They are not excellent fliers, but are very agile in their movements along branches and through vegetation. Many species are colourful and display a crest. Turacos are generally green or violet in colour, and all are confined to thickly wooded and forest areas. Open-country species, such as the widely distributed and common white-bellied **go-away bird** (go-aways are named after their call), are white or grey in colour.

## Hornbills

Named for their long, heavy bills, surmounted by a casque or bony helmet, **hornbills** generally have black and white plumage. Their flight consists of a series of alternate flaps and glides. When in flight, hornbills may be heard before they are seen, the beaten wings making a "whooshing" noise as air rushes through the flight feathers. Many species have bare areas of skin on the face and throat and around the eyes, with the bill and the casque often brightly coloured, their colours changing with the age of the bird. Most hornbills are omnivorous, but tend largely to eat fruit. Several species are common open-country birds, including the silvery-cheeked and red-billed hornbills. Hornbills have interesting breeding habits: the male generally incarcerates the female in a hollow tree, leaving a hole through which he feeds her while she incubates the eggs and rears the young. The unusual ground hornbill is covered on p.601 under "Large walking birds".

## Rollers, shrikes and kingfishers

A family of very colourful and noticeable birds of the African bush, **rollers** perch on exposed bushes and telegraph wires. They take their name from their impressive courtship flights – a fast dive with a rolling and rocking motion, accompanied by raucous calls. Many have a sky-blue underbody and sandy-coloured back; long tail streamers are a distinctive feature of several species. The **lilac-breasted roller** is common and conspicuous.

**Shrikes** are found throughout Tanzania. Fierce hunters with sharply hooked bills, they habitually sit on prominent perches, and take insects, reptiles and small birds. Particularly rare is the **Uluguru bush-shrike**, found only in the Uluguru Mountains.

There are around a dozen species of colourful **kingfishers** found in Tanzania, ranging in size from the tiny **African pygmy kingfisher**, which feeds on insects and is generally found near water, to the **giant kingfisher**, a shy fish-eating species of wooded streams in the west of the country. Several species eat insects rather than fish and they can often be seen perched high in trees or on open posts in the bush where they wait to pounce on passing prey. One of the more common is the **malachite kingfisher**, which stays true to its roots by catching small fish: it swallows its prey head first after killing it by whacking it against branches.

## Sunbirds, starlings, whydahs and weavers

**Sunbirds** are bright, active birds, feeding on nectar from flowering plants. Over forty species have been recorded across Tanzania, though many are confined to discrete types of habitat. Males are brightly coloured and usually identifiable, but many of the drabber females require very careful observation to identify them. A particularly rare species is the black and iridescent-green **Amani sunbird**, which can be seen in small flocks at Amani Nature Reserve.

The glorious orange and blue **starlings**, which are a common feature of bushland habitats – usually seen feeding on the ground – belong to one of three species. The **superb starling** is the most widespread, found everywhere from remote national parks to gardens in Arusha, and often quite tame. It can be identified by the white band above its orange breast.

Related to finches are **whydahs**, also called widowbirds – a name that derives from their black plumage, and prodigiously long tails that resemble mourning hats worn in Victorian times. Possibly not entirely unrelated is that they're also brood parasites, depositing their eggs in the nests of other birds. Males perform a strange bouncing display flight to attract females.

**Weavers** are among Tanzania's most widespread birds. Males tend to be easy to spot, as most have bright yellow or yellow-and-black plumage, but females are sparrow-like. The various species are distinguished by range, preferred habitat, and by the shape and size of their extraordinary woven nests, which, as weavers live in colonies, can completely change the appearance of a tree. Rare species popular with birders include the unique **Kilombero weaver** in central Tanzania's Kilombero floodplain; the **Usambara weaver** in the Usambara Mountains; and the rufous-tailed weaver, for which the best odds are in Tarangire.

Adapted from the *Rough Guide to Kenya* by Richard Trillo,
with additional material from Tony Stones and Tony Pinchuck

# Books

T
here's woefully little published about Tanzania other than superficial **coffee-table tomes** waxing lyrically about wildlife or the Maasai. Locally produced books are mostly in Kiswahili, a notable exception being the output of Zanzibar's Gallery Publications (Ⓦwww.gallery-publications .net). A handful of other English-language works trickle onto the market each year, mostly self-published collections of fables and proverbs – snap them up wherever you can, as specific titles are often impossible to obtain elsewhere.

Tanzanian **bookshops** are mentioned in the "Listings" sections trailing our town accounts; the best ones are in Dar and Stone Town. Gift shops in larger beach hotels and safari lodges usually stock small selections of more touristy titles. Many of the books reviewed below can be bought **online** (try Amazon), or through Ⓦwww.africabookcentre.com. Books marked 🖈 are particularly recommended.

## Travel and general accounts

🖈 **Peter Matthiessen** *The Tree Where Man Was Born* (Harvill, UK/NAL-Dutton, US). Wanderings and musings of the Zen-thinking polymath in Kenya and northern Tanzania. Enthralling for its detail on nature, society, culture and prehistory, this beautifully written book is a gentle, appetizing introduction to the land and its people.

🖈 **George Monbiot** *No Man's Land* (Picador, UK). A journey through Kenya and Tanzania providing shocking expos of Maasai dispossession and a major criticism of the wildlife conservation movement.

**Shiva Naipaul** *North of South* (Penguin, UK). A fine but caustic account of Naipaul's travels in Kenya, Tanganyika and Zambia. Always readable and sometimes hilarious, the insights make up for the occasionally angst-ridden social commentary and some passages that widely miss the mark.

## Coffee-table books

🖈 **Mitsuaki Iwago** *Serengeti* (Thames and Hudson, UK/ Chronicle, US). Simply the best volume of wildlife photography ever assembled.

**Javed Jafferji** *Images of Zanzibar* (Gallery, Zanzibar). Superb photos by Zanzibar's leading photographer.

🖈 **Javed Jafferji & Graham Mercer** *Tanzania: African Eden* (Gallery, Zanzibar). A brochure in book form but stunningly beautiful, with many photos taken from the air.

**Javed Jafferji & Gemma Pitcher** *Safari Living*; *Zanzibar Style*; *Recipes from the Bush*; and *Zanzibar Style: Recipes* (all Gallery, Zanzibar). Four volumes of stylish eye-candy that should find favour with homemakers.

# History

Little of non-academic nature has been written about the history of mainland Tanzania; most of what's available covers Zanzibar and the Swahili coast. Nineteenth-century works, including those reviewed below, are almost all in the public domain, and can be found **online** for free: there's a list at ⓦwww .bluegecko.org/tanzania.

**Heinrich Brode** *Tippu Tip & the Story of his Career* (Gallery, Zanzibar). The semi-autobiographical story of East Africa's most notorious slave trader.

🏃 **Richard Hall** *Empires of the Monsoon* (HarperCollins, UK). A majestic sweep across the history of the western Indian Ocean.

**Christopher Hibbert** *Africa Explored: Europeans in the Dark Continent 1769–1889* (Penguin, UK). An entertaining read, devoted in large part to the "discovery" of East and Central Africa.

🏃 **John Iliffe** *A Modern History of Tanganyika*; *Africans: the History of a Continent* (both Cambridge UP, UK). The former is the definitive textbook for mainland Tanzania; the latter gives a general overview.

🏃 **I.N. Kimambo & A.J. Temu** (eds) *A History of Tanzania* (Kapsel, Tanzania). A comprehensive round-up from various authors, and the only one widely available in Tanzania. Ends at *Ujamaa* (1967).

**Alan Moorehead** *The White Nile* (Penguin, UK/Harper Perennial, US). A riveting Anglo-centric account of the search for the Nile's source, good for a quick portrayal of nineteenth-century explorers' attitudes.

**Thomas Pakenham** *The Scramble for Africa* (Abacus, UK/Harper

Perennial, US). Elegantly written and exhaustive treatment of a nasty subject; it can seem a bit Eurocentric, but what do you expect from a book about the world's biggest land grab?

**Kevin Patience** *Zanzibar: Slavery and the Royal Navy; Zanzibar and The Bububu Railway; Zanzibar and the Loss of HMS Pegasus; Zanzibar and the Shortest War in History; Königsberg – A German East African Raider* (all self-published, ⓦwww.zanzibar .net/zanzibar/zanzibar_books). Short, informative and well-researched reads. Most are available in Zanzibar or Dar.

**Emily Ruete** *Memoirs of an Arabian Princess from Zanzibar* (Gallery, Zanzibar). The extraordinary (true) tale of Princess Salme, who eloped in the 1860s with a German merchant.

**Abdul Sheriff** *Slaves, Spices and Ivory in Zanzibar* (James Currey, UK/Ohio University, US). Covers the immensely profitable eighteenth- and nineteenth-century slave trade. Abdul Sheriff is also editor of *Zanzibar under Colonial Rule* (James Currey, UK) and *Historical Zanzibar – Romance of the Ages* (HSP, UK).

**Gideon S. Were & Derek A. Wilson** *East Africa through a Thousand Years* (Evans Brothers, Kenya/UK). An authoritative round up, including the cultures and traditions of several tribes.

## Explorers' accounts

**Richard Francis Burton** *The Lake Regions of Central Africa* (Narrative Press, US); *Zanzibar; City, Island and Coast* (Adamant Media, US), and other titles. Entertaining but extremely bigoted accounts of the explorer's adventures, also amusing for the jealous scorn he heaped on his estranged companion, Speke, who really did discover the source of the Nile.

🏃 **Martin Dugard** *Into Africa: The Epic Adventures of Stanley and Livingstone* (Broadway, US). A compelling, blow-by-blow retelling of the explorers' travels before and after their famous meeting, relying heavily on their own accounts.

**Henry Morton Stanley** *Autobiography of…* (Narrative Press, US). Typical self-aggrandizement by the famous, and famously bombastic, explorer. His best-seller, *How I Found Livingstone* (Epaulet, US), needs no explanation.

**Joseph Thomson** *Through Masai Land* (Rediscovery Books). This 1885 blockbuster was the originator of "Maasai-itis". To his credit, Thomson was one of few explorers to prefer the power of friendly relations to that of the gun.

# Tanzania's people

Aside from glossy and usually superficial coffee-table splashes on the Maasai, decent material on any of Tanzania's tribes is difficult to come by, and there's no general overview.

**James de Vere Allen** *Swahili Origins* (Nkuki na Nyota, Tanzania). Masterful treatment of a potentially thorny question: exactly who, are the Swahili?

🏃 **Jakob Janssen Dannholz** *Lute – The Curse and the Blessing* (private publication, Germany). Written almost a century ago by a German missionary, this is still the best work on Pare culture and society, both for content, and in its approachable and non-judgemental style. Available in Mbaga, Tanzania.

**Gregory H. Maddox (ed)** *The Gogo: History, Customs and Traditions* (M.E. Sharpe, UK/US). Covers most facets of central Tanzania's Gogo tribe, including very detailed histories of separate clans, and song transcriptions.

🏃 **Sarah Mirza & Margaret Strobel** *Three Swahili Women* (Indiana UP, UK/US). Born between 1890 and 1920 into different social backgrounds, these biographies of three women document enormous changes from the most important of neglected viewpoints.

**David Read** *Barefoot over the Serengeti* (self-published, Kenya). No colonial rose-tint here – the author tells of his early Kenyan childhood and later upbringing in northern Tanzania with his Maasai friend, all in a refreshingly matter-of-fact way, making it a useful resource for Maasai culture, too.

**Frans Wijsen & Ralph Tanner** *Seeking a Good Life* (Paulines, Kenya). Religion and society among the Sukuma of northern Tanzania, with a Christian undertone.

# The arts

Anon *Tribute to George Lilanga* (East African Movies, Tanzania). Gorgeously illustrated tome collecting many works by one of Tanzania's leading Tingatinga painters.

🏃 **Busara Promotions** *Busara: Promoting East African Music – the First Five Years* (Gallery, Zanzibar). Clunky title, great content: reflecting the diversity of the annual Sauti za Busara festival, this is a collection of intelligent and enthusiastic articles, interviews and bios, with great pictures too.

**Manfred Ewel & Anne Outwater** (eds) *From Ritual to Modern Art: Tradition and Modernity in Tanzanian Sculpture* (Mkuki na Nyota, Tanzania). Authoritative and scholarly essays on all aspects of Tanzanian sculpture, illustrated in black-and-white.

🏃 **Yves Goscinny** (ed) *East African Biennale* (Tanzanian Publishers, Tanzania); and *Art in Tanzania* (East African Movies, Tanzania). Gloriously illustrated catalogues for the East African Biennale (formerly "Art in Tanzania"): fantastic and inspiring stuff, from Tingatinga to the brilliant woodcarvings of Bagamoyo's artists.

**Uwe Rau & Mwalim A. Mwalim** *The Doors of Zanzibar* (Gallery, Zanzibar/HSP, UK). Glossy treatment of those beautiful old carved doors and frames.

🏃 **Ali Saleh, Fiona McGain & Kawthar Buwayhid** *Bi Kidude: Tales of a living legend* (Gallery, Zanzibar). Brilliant, intense and loving hagiography of the great Zanzibari singer, compiled from various interviews.

## Fiction

Tanzanian novels in English are rare animals indeed, as most popular fiction is written in Kiswahili and books go out of print quickly. The same applies to poetry and folk tales. Strangely, you're more likely to find Tanzanian fiction in Nairobi's bookshops.

**A.M. Hokororo** *Salma's Spirit* (Nkuki na Nyota, Tanzania). Boy meets girl, except the girl has been dead for three years … An interesting window into the Tanzanian conception of life after death, and witchcraft.

🏃 **Aniceti Kitereza** *Mr Myombekere and His Wife Bugonoka. Their Son Ntulanalwo and Daughter Bulihwali* (Nkuki na Nyota, Tanzania). First published in 1945, this epic novel from Lake Victoria's Ukerewe Island tells the story of a couple's deepening devotion to one

another despite the social stigma of infertility. Superbly translated by Gabriel Ruhumbika, a descendant of Kitereza, the descriptions of local life remain as fresh as ever.

**Shaaban Robert** (tr. Clement Ndulute) *The Poetry of Shaaban Robert* (Dar es Salaam UP, Tanzania). The only English translation of works by Tanzania's foremost poet and writer, with the Kiswahili original on facing pages: a great tool if you're learning the language.

### Oral traditions and proverbs

Oral traditions (orature) are one of the jewels of Africa, encapsulating every aspect of myth, morals and reality with ogres, strange worlds and lots of talking animals symbolizing virtues and vices – hare is cunning, hyena greedy and stupid, elephant powerful but gullible, and lion a show-off. Anthologies of transcribed stories are extremely thin on the ground, so buy what you can.

**George Bateman** *Zanzibar Tales: Told by the Natives of East Africa* (Gallery, Zanzibar). A delightful collection of fables and legends first published in 1908.

**A.C. Hollis** *Masai Myths, Tales and Riddles* (Dover, US). Collected and translated over a century ago, this is a very welcome reprint of a superb work. Time has done little to dampen Hollis's evident enthusiasm and respect.

**Naomi Kipury** *Oral literature of the Maasai* (East African Educational Publishers, Kenya). A lovely selection of transcribed narratives, proverbs, songs and poetry.

**Jan Knappert** *Myths & Legends of the Swahili* (East African Educational Publishers, Tanzania). An entertaining selection of tales similar to stories told across the Muslim world, with strong echoes of the *Arabian Nights*.

**Joseph M. Mbele** *Matengo Folktales* (Infinity Publishing, US). Ably translated tales from Lake Nyasa featuring that lovable trickster the hare, and ever-hungry monsters.

**Amir A. Mohamed** *Zanzibar Ghost Stories* (Good Luck, Zanzibar). Weird and wonderful tales from the isles.

**O. Mtuweta H. Tesha** *Famous Chagga Stories* (Twenty First Century Enterprises, Tanzania). A short but sweet collection from Tanzania's most prosperous tribe.

# Guidebooks and field guides

Helpful **guidebooks** to individual national parks are published by TANAPA in Tanzania, and can be bought locally, and at the park gates. There's also a series of guidebooks for Ngorongoro published by the Ngorongoro Conservation Area Authority.

## Mammals

**Richard Estes & Daniel Otte** *The Safari Companion: A Guide to Watching African Mammals* (Chelsea Green Pub Co, UK). Reliable, beautifully illustrated by Otte, and especially detailed on social behaviour, this is one you'll love consulting on safari. Even more detailed but impractical in the field is Estes' *The Behavior Guide to African Mammals* (California UP, US).

**David Hosking & Martin Withers** *Wildlife of Kenya, Tanzania and Uganda* (Collins, UK). A handy pocket guide for first-timers, with colour photos, is readily available in Tanzania. Covers 475 species, including birds and reptiles.

**Jonathan Kingdon** *The Kingdon Field Guide to African Mammals* (Princeton UP, US). Probably the most respected guide, illustrated with drawings and paintings (most of them good), and covering all of continental Africa. It's not too handy on safari, however: for that, get the condensed *Kingdon Pocket Guide to African Mammals* (also Princeton).

Chris & Tilde Stuart *Field Guide to the Mammals of Southern Africa* (Struik, South Africa). Comprehensive coverage, with hundreds of distribution maps and photos, and a decent selection of smaller mammals, too, including bats.

## Birds

Ber van Perlo *Birds of Eastern Africa* (Princeton, US). Lightweight, compact and comprehensive, but with small illustrations and little in the way of descriptive text.

🏃 Terry Stevenson & John Fanshawe *Birds of East Africa* (Helm, UK). Pick of the bunch for ease of use in the field, with distribution maps in the text itself.

Dale Zimmerman, David Pearson & Donald Turner *A Field Guide to the Birds of Kenya and Northern Tanzania* (Helm, UK). A hefty book with unmatched coverage so long as you're not straying beyond the northern circuit.

## Scuba diving and snorkelling

Helmut Debelius *Indian Ocean Reef Guide* (IKAN, Germany). Debelius is a prolific and highly regarded author of marine guides. This catch-all, ranging from East Africa to Thailand, includes over one thousand (superb) photos. Also worth getting are Debelius' and Rudie Kuiter's more specialist IKAN publications, including the weirdly enchanting *Nudibranchs of the World*.

🏃 Anton Koornhof *The Dive Sites of Kenya and Tanzania* (New Holland, UK). A slim and dated but recommended practical guide, especially useful for first-timers, and snorkellers as well.

🏃 Matthew Richmond (ed) *A Field Guide to the Seashores of Eastern Africa and the Western Indian Ocean Islands*. The underwater bible, covering the most common species together with geology, biology, tides, even local culture and fishing techniques. Too big to take with you, though.

# Music

With almost 130 tribes, and an open attitude to foreign influences, Tanzania presents a rich **musical panorama**. On the coast, Arabia and India express themselves through the eclectic blend that is Swahili Taarab, while on the mainland Cuban rhythms underlie the brassy sounds of Dar es Salaam's ever-popular dance bands. The other major musical current, and a huge commercial hit across East Africa, is Bongo Flava, Tanzania's remarkably successful rap scene. The other genre of note, musically often far more sophisticated than the others but now sadly disappearing, is *ngoma* – the catch-all for countless flavours of traditional tribal music.

## Traditional music

Music, songs and dance played, and in parts still play, a vital role in traditional culture, not least in providing a sense of continuity from the past to the present, as can be seen in the Kiswahili name for traditional music, **ngoma ya kiasili** – "music of the ancestors". Traditional music is also a cohesive force: *ngomas* involve everyone present, whether as singers, dancers, instrumentalists, or in combination. Often drum-based, *ngoma* (which also means drum) tends to keep to its roots, giving each tribe's output a distinctive quality. The **lyrics**, typically poetry making full use of riddles, proverbs and metaphors, change according to the occasion, and are used to transmit all kinds of information, from family histories and advice to youngsters, to informing newlyweds of the pains and joys of married life, and perhaps seeking the intervention of spirits to bring rain to parched and dusty lands.

Unfortunately, traditional music is **disappearing** as rapidly as the cultures from which it sprung, so it's only in particularly remote areas (untouched by missionaries) where you're likely to come across really traditional music, or festivities. Nonetheless, even the most "developed" tribes, such as the Chagga, still have a soft spot for *ngoma* for events including weddings and baptisms, meaning that so as long you're reasonably adventurous and inquisitive in your travels, you should be able to witness something more authentic than the medleys performed in tourist hotels. Two **traditional festivals** at which music is a constant companion are **Mwaka Kogwa** at Makunduchi on Zanzibar (p.541), which celebrates the Persian New Year, and the Sukuma tribe's often comical **Bulabo festival** at Bujora near Mwanza (see p.403), which is rooted in a nineteenth-century squabble between rival witchdoctors. In southern Tanzania, there's also a fun neo-traditional festival designed to keep the old music alive, Mtwara's **MaKuYa Festival**, held every August (p.186).

If you can't coincide with these festivals, and don't have time to hunt down the real thing, there is one easy way of at least getting to *hear* traditional music. Though the *Ujamaa* period of the 1960s and 1970s destroyed a good deal of the old ways, it also limited airtime for non-Tanzanian music, with the result that sound engineers from Radio Tanzania Dar es Salaam (RTD) set off to record traditional music. The result is a priceless **archive** housed at their headquarters in Dar (see p.108), of which over a hundred recordings – covering almost as many tribes – are for sale.

## Technique and meaning

"Call and refrain" is Tanzania's predominant traditional musical style, where a soloist is responded to by a chorus, but far more interesting – often brilliantly so – is the **hypnotic quality** characteristic of the musical traditions of Nilotic cattle-herding tribes, and among the more traditional of the Bantu-speakers.

Among the semi-nomadic Nilotes, **multipart polyphony** is the main theme, where each singer or player performs only part of a rhythm (which they're free to embellish, with some restrictions), and which, combined, create an complex overlay of different rhythms, giving rise to what's been dubbed "micropolyphony" (which does funny things to your head) and would be impossible to achieve were there fewer performers, or were everyone playing or singing the same thing. The vibrant, growling throat singing of **Maasai warriors** (*morani*) is a perfect illustration, and were the complexity of the whole not enough, the buzzing of vocal chords is quite entrancing to the singers themselves. The songs are usually competitive, expressed through the singers leaping as high as they can, or bragging about killing a lion or rustling cattle. The **Gogo** (who are actually half Bantu) are equally genial with polyrhythms, more instrumental than vocal, blending orchestras of *marimba ya mkono* "thumb pianos" with single-stringed *zeze* fiddles and sensuously caressing voices to mesmerising effect (for more on their music, see p.231).

Some Bantu-speaking tribes also possess extraordinary musical talents, including the matrilineal **Luguru**, whose ever so subtle transitions between voices and flutes are simply mind-bending. On the east side of Lake Victoria, lyres are the favoured instruments. The **Kuria** tribe, straddling the Kenyan border, play the *litungu* (or *iritungu*), Africa's largest and weirdest-sounding lyre, whose deep, resonant buzzing provides the hypnotic impetus. Their neighbours, the **Luo**, play the smaller but no less gratifying *nyatiti*, an eight-stringed affair whose resonator the performer also taps using a ring on his toe. In southern Tanzania there are several more excellent musical traditions. The **Makonde** are famed for their insistent drumming (by all-women groups, too), which accompanies the unique *sindimba* stilt dance and other dances using masks – such masquerades are almost completely absent elsewhere in Tanzania. The other big musical area is Lake Nyasa, especially Mbamba Bay, where the **Nyasa** (or Nyanja) compete in a series of musical contests (*mashindano*) held in the "dance season" that follows the harvest after the long rains. The music is quite unlike anything else in Tanzania, with weirdly rasping pipes accompanied by big drums.

All wonderful stuff, but there's a serious purpose to these trance-inducing sounds. **Strident rhythms** in the agricultural work songs of the Luo and Kuria, for instance, keep fatigue at bay, whilst the intended effects of the ethereal rhythms and intricate harmonies of ritual dances can transport not just the living into a mental limbo, but the spirits of the deceased, too. An astonishing shifting of senses and dimensions can be conjured up at funerals to enable the living to bid farewell to the recently departed, or at initiation time for young men of warrior age, enabling them to come into direct contact with their proud ancestors. The concept underlying all these ideas is **continuity**, the idea that a person is never completely "dead" until forgotten by the living – a crucial concept for understanding the origin and development of many traditional African societies.

# Popular music

The heart of Tanzania's live music scene is Dar es Salaam, where dozens of **dance bands** as well as **Modern Taarab** orchestras perform in an ever-changing rota in bars and clubs in the suburbs; some of these bands also tour other towns and cities. As might be expected, **Kwaya** (meaning "choir") can be heard every Sunday in church. To catch other genres, your best bet would be to coincide with a **festival**. Of the contemporary ones, the best, attracting an extraordinary variety and quality of performers from around the Indian Ocean as well as Africa, is Zanzibar's **Sauti za Busara**, held in February (p.529). Also boasting big names is the **Zanzibar International Film Festival**, in July (p.529), whilst Dar's **B-Connected Festival** in May (p.105) is the place for the latest hip-hop and Bongo Flava.

## Dance bands

For most people, Tanzania's most enjoyable music is *muziki wa dansi* or *muziki wa jazzi* – **dance music**. It's the longest-established form of popular music in the country, having started in the 1930s when gramophone records were becoming all the rage. **Latin rhythms**, as filtered through the lens of Congo's enormously successful Afro-Cuban dance bands, have had an incredibly pervasive influence on the scene ever since its inception, and styles such as rumba, cha-cha-cha, salsa, soukous, kwasa kwasa, ndombolo and mayemu are recognized everywhere.

The Congolese style reached its apogee in the 1970s, after a number of musicians fled their war-torn country to establish a flurry of extremely popular bands in East Africa. Greatest of the lot, gathering the cream of Congo's expatriate musicians, was Tanzania's **Maquis du Zaïre**, which later became **Orchestre Maquis Original**. But after the death of their charismatic lead singer and saxophonist Chinyama Chiaza, in 1985, the band began to disintegrate. Many of its musicians went off to form their own bands, of which there's only one survivor, **Kilimanjaro Band**, whose arrangements include rhythms borrowed from traditional Tanzanian *ngomas*. Although the Congolese period was dominated by big bands (no relation to US or European "Big Bands"), an individual immigrant that made it big was **Remmy Ongala**, much admired for his powerful political and social lyrics, and driving guitar riffs, although his fan base has diminished since he become a born-again Christian.

These days, dance band line-ups commonly include several electric guitars and basses, drums, synthesizers, a brass section, a lead singer (usually also a guitarist), and female dancers whose stage antics may leave little to the imagination. Band sizes can be large – anything up to thirty members – a necessity given the almost nightly performances, and all-too-frequent defections of musicians to rival bands. Most bands are known by at least two names: their proper name, and their **mtindo**, or dance style.

### Contemporary dance bands

A throwback to traditional *ngomas* and their competing dance societies is the habit of Tanzanian dance bands to come in **rival pairs**. In the early 1980s, Orchestra Safari Sound sparred with Maquis, and at the start of this millennium African Stars was pitted against African Revolution. But the most enduring – and endearing – rivalry is between Dar es Salaam's longest-established bands, both immensely popular across the generations, and reason enough to prolong your stay in Dar in order to see them live. The oldest, nicknamed *Baba wa*

*Muzuki* ("Father of Music"), are **Msondo Ngoma,** founded in 1964 as NUTA Jazz (the initials of the trade union that funded them). In 1977 they became JUWATA Jazz and, more recently, OTTU Jazz. After splitting from the Organization of Tanzanian Trade Unions in 2007, they adopted their *mtindo* dance style as their official name: *msondo* being a drum or dance associated with girls' initiations. Musically, Msondo's output is dominated by supremely fluid guitar licks and rough, brassy horns, and, although the vocals can get lost at times, it's the most danceable live music you'll hear. Msondo's big rivals, favouring tight, upbeat, cohesive rhythms, blissful harmonies and famously poetic lyrics, are **DDC Mlimani Park Orchestra,** better known by their dance-style name, "Sikinde", and who have been going strong since 1978 when a number of JUWATA's musicians defected.

For a long time, keeping tabs on Tanzania's dance bands was simple enough, but over the last few years a welter of name changes, splits, mergers and other shenanigans have confused even the most avid fans. Most popular these days, and almost as danceable as Msondo Ngoma and DDC Mlimani (if not as melodic), are a quartet of shamelessly Congolese-style bands complete with raunchy, butt-swivelling dancing girls: **FM Academia** (also known as "Wazee wa Ngwasuma" and, by detractors, as "Wazee ya Bling Bling"); **Vibration Sound** (formerly Twanga Chipolopolo, African Revolution and Tam Tam); the pleasingly guitar-rich **Mchinga Generation** (formerly Mchinga Sound, also known as "Wana Kipepeo"); and, composed almost entirely of Congolese musicians, **Akudo Impact** (also called "Vijana wa Masauti" and by their *mtindo*, "Pekecha Pekecha"). All of them play heady, noisy blends of whatever rhythms and styles are currently making waves in Kinshasa.

Sitting halfway in style between the classic laid-back sounds of Msondo Ngoma and DDC Mlimani, and the brash Congolese imitators, are **African Stars** (or Twanga Pepeta International; their manager can't seem to decide), and **Diamond Musica International** (also known as Vijana Classic; formerly Diamond Sound and Vijana Jazz), who you're more likely to see on tour than the others.

## Taarab and Kidumbak

**Taarab** is the quintessential music of the Swahili coast, from Somalia in the north to Mozambique in the south. It's actually barely a century old, but has roots stretching way back to pre-Islamic Arabia, Persia and India – a quixotic synthesis easily discernible in its sound. The soloist – in Zanzibar usually female – sings with a high-pitched and distinctly Arabian nasal twang, and is accompanied by an orchestra of up to fifty musicians, often dressed in full European-style dinner suits (the word "taarab" derives from the Arabic for "civilized"). The main instruments are cellos and violins (*fidla*), Arabic lutes (*udi*), the Egyptian *qanun* (a 72-string trapezoid zither), reed clarinets (*zumari*; picture a snake-charmer's pipe), and sometimes drums (*ngoma*). Contemporary Taarab orchestras also feature accordions (*kodian*), trumpets (*tarumbeta*), electric guitars and synthesizers, with the latter replacing almost all instruments in so-called **Modern Taarab** groups, lending them a distinctly "Sonic the Hedgehog goes to Bollywood" kind of sound. No coincidence, as Modern Taarab is heavily influenced by Indian movie scores.

The cost of hiring a full Taarab orchestra means it's usually only performed at weddings and other large **social gatherings**, when the poetic lyrics – composed in Kiswahili and laced with Arabic – come into their own. Dealing with love, jealousy and relationships, they're often specially composed, and some songs, called *mipasho*, are specifically requested by one person to criticize or

## The doyennes of Taarab

Over the century or so that Taarab has been around, two Zanzibari stars have stood out from the firmament. The first was the hugely influential **Siti Bint Saad**, Zanzibar's first female Taarab singer and also the first to perform in Kiswahili rather than Arabic. In so doing, she did more than anyone else to popularize Taarab across the social spectrum, reaching the peak of her fame in the 1930s and 1940s, when her voice became synonymous with Swahili culture.

Equally beloved, and still going strong after a career spanning an amazing eight decades, is the all-drinking, all-smoking and all-conquering **Bi Kidude** (real name Fatuma Binti Baraka), who began her career in the 1920s under the tutelage of Siti Bint Saad. Like her mentor, Bi Kidude was not afraid to broach controversial topics in her songs, including the abuse of women, and as her fame grew, she did away with the veil that she and Siti Bint Saad had been obliged to wear for public performances. Old age has done absolutely nothing to temper her independence, or her verve: she has experimented with jazz/dance fusion, has graciously collaborated with various Bongo Flava stars, and has also popularized drum-based *Unyago* (which she plays in "hobby horse" style), whose **sexually explicit** lyrics were traditionally reserved for getting girls up to speed at their initiation ceremonies. With her deep, bluesy and mesmerizing (if not exactly pretty) voice, the "little granny", her nickname, is a true giant among African musicians.

upbraid another. Although the "accused" is never named, his or her identity is easily guessed by the parties involved. Taarab is danced almost entirely by women, who shuffle along in a conga while shaking their bottoms in a rippling movement called *kukata kiuno*, meaning "to cut the waist" – it looks lazy, but drives men crazy.

The more traditional Taarab orchestras are in Stone Town, the main ones being **Ikhwani Safaa** (Malindi Taarab), founded in 1905, and **Culture Music Club** (Mila na Utamaduni), the largest and most successful, who began life in the Afro-Shirazi Party in the years before Independence. In **Dar es Salaam**, the big orchestras are the synthesiser-heavy Jahazi Modern Taarab, Zanzibar Stars Modern Taarab, and East African Melody.

The cheaper alternative to a Taarab orchestra is the more percussive and dance-friendly **Kidumbak**, unkindly dubbed Kitaarab ("small Taarab") by some, on account of its traditional role as a proving ground for musicians. The usual Kidumbak ensemble consists of just four or five musicians, and includes drums (*dumbak*), and a peculiar bass made from a tea chest, both instruments giving a far more African flavour than "pure" Taarab. **Makame Faki**, also known as "Sauti ya Zege" (gravel voice) is the main exponent, and performs regularly in Stone Town.

## Rap (and Bongo Flava)

Tanzanian rap and hip-hop have taken the country, and East Africa, by storm. The most popular genre, propelled by ample airtime, is a fusion of rap and R&B known as **Bongo Flava** (*bongo*, meaning "brains", being the nickname for Dar es Salaam and, nowadays, Tanzania). Bongo Flava's massive success single-handedly revived Tanzania's recording industry, but the commercial focus is often quite obvious, not least when songs are penned in English, and there are also rather a lot of proponents merely mimicking what's on MTV or on Africa's Channel O, rarely straying beyond mushy love songs or equally vapid "ghetto" posturing. At its best, though, Bongo Flava can be mind-bendingly inventive in its use of samples and computer-generated riffs, and equally inspired in the rhythms of their raps.

The most popular acts change on a quasi-monthly basis: you can listen to the latest, and a heap more besides, on the internet: see p.618 for websites. Currently finding favour and actually worth listening to are **Mwanafalsafa** ("Philosopher") who's more socially committed than his Gangsta style suggests; the similarly "hard" **Fid Q**, with witty lyrics and a musically more eclectic offering than most; the slick, R&B-leaning **Chid Benz**; and **Mwana FA**, for some especially lush backing tracks. A handful of older acts also remain popular, the better ones including the cheerfully upbeat **"Sir" Juma Nature**, **Mr Nice** (known for comic lyrics and sampling classic *muziki ya jazzi*), and – rapping since 1994 (then as part of Hard Blasters) – **Professor Jay**, who sits comfortably in the rapidly narrowing no man's land between Bongo Flava and purer hip-hop (see below). If you're into the history of Bongo Flava, the "granddaddies" were **Kwanza Unit** (early 1990s), **Mr II** (aka Sugu or 2Proud, now in the US), and, for Bongo Flava's R&B roots, **Afro Reign** circa 1995/96.

All boys so far, but the few girls in Bongo Flava aren't to be outdone, although, as you might guess, the sexy, sassy, soul diva stereotypes hang thick – essentially Tanzanian takes on Mariah Carey. The best of these, with a smooth and almost "girl band" sound, is **Dataz**. More fun, however, and musically varied, are **Ray C**, for whom Modern Taarab is a favoured theme; and the raunchy **Lady Jaydee**, who favours R&B but whose broad musical palette has seen her collaborate with many other Bongo Flava stars as well as jazz bands, *ngoma* groups, and even Zanzibar's nonagenarian wonder Bi Kidude.

Far less commercial and more likely to be performed in Kiswahili is **hip-hop**, whose lyrics typically broach thorny social issues such as poverty, AIDS, politics and identity. Sometimes performing with no backing at all, some hip-hop artists have experimented with traditional music crossovers, with some inspiring results. Worth seeking out are the gravelly voiced **Kikosi cha Mizinga**, some great crossover riffs from **Watengwa**, and **X-Plastaz**'s Maasai rap.

## Reggae

Whilst popular, **reggae** is woefully under-represented, historically because of government crackdowns on "subversive" ganja-smoking types, and nowadays as it's simply been eclipsed by Bongo Flava. The official distrust of reggae started in Nyerere's time. The story goes that during the celebrations for Zimbabwe's Independence in 1980, Nyerere refused to shake hands with Bob Marley. Come evening, Marley's rendition of *Africa Unite* was persuasion enough, and Nyerere got on stage to make amends, to huge applause. The government gave up hassling Rastas in 1995. **Jhikoman** is the most active performer; also well regarded is **Roots & Culture**, founded in 1983 by Jah Kimbute. **Ras Nas** is the other star.

## Kwaya

With its roots steeped in American gospel and European hymns, **Kwaya** ("choir") is perhaps the least Tanzanian of the popular music styles, though if the blaring wattage from mobile tape vendors is any indication, *Kwaya* cassettes far outsell any other genre. The best make superb use of traditional *ngoma* rhythms, vocal power and instruments; the worst, which sadly is a lot of them, use quite awful synthesized loops – no fun if you're stuck on a bus blasting it out. Each *Kwaya* belongs to a church; Sunday Mass is the time and place for catching it live, with luck peppered with fiery admonitions from a crazed preacher.

# Discography

Not to toot our own horn, but one of the best compilations for a bit of everything is the *Rough Guide to the Music of Tanzania* (World Music Network). It, and the following CDs, are found easily enough on the internet (⊛www.stern smusic.com has a particularly good selection), but keep looking while you're in Tanzania, as most recordings – especially on tape – never make it out of the country. A great place to start is RTD in Dar es Salaam (see p.108), which has several hundred different cassettes of dance band classics and traditional *ngoma*.

## Traditional music

**Gogo** Hukwe Zawose, *Chibite* (RealWorld); Master Musicians of Tanzania, *Mateso* (Triple Earth); *Chants des Wagogo et des Kuria* (Inedit); *Musiques rituelles Gogo* (VDE-Gallo).

**Maasai** *Music of the Maasai* (⊛www.laleyio.com); *Maasai Warrior Chants* and *Namayana* (both ⊛www .aangserian.org.uk).

**Rangi** *Rhythms of the Rangi* (⊛www .aangserian.org.uk).

**Sukuma** *Tanzania: Music of the Farmer Composers of Sukumaland* (Multicultural Media).

**Various tribes** *East Africa: Ceremonial & Folk Music* (Nonesuch); *Tanzania Instruments 1950* (Sharp Wood); *Tanzania Vocals 1950* (Sharp Wood).

**Zanzibar** Imani Ngoma Troupe: *BAPE*, Songs and Dances from Zanzibar (Felmay).

## Dance music

**African Stars (Twanga Pepeta)** *Mtaa wa Kwanza* (ASET); *Password* (ASET).

**African Revolution** *Maisha Kitendawili* (ASET).

**Bana Maquis** *Leila* (Dakar Sound).

**DDC Mlimani Park Orchestra** *Sikinde* (World Music Network); *Sungi* (Popular African Music).

**Mbaraka Mwinshehe/Morogoro Jazz Band** *Masimango* (Dizim).

**FM Academia** *Dunia Kigeugeu* (Ujamaa Records).

**Msondo Ngoma (OTTU Jazz Band)** OTTU Jazz Band *Piga Ua* (Ujamaa Records); *The Best of Msondo Ngoma* (Ujamaa Records).

**Remmy Ongala & Orchestre Super Matimila** *Songs for the Poor Man* (Real World/Womad); *The Kershaw Sessions* (Strange Roots); *Sema* (Womad Select).

**Various artists** *Dada Kidawa, Sister Kidawa* – Classic Tanzanian Hits from the 1960s (Original Music); *The Tanzania Sound* (Original Music); and *Musiki wa Dansi: Afropop Hits from Tanzania* (World Music Network/ Africassette).

## Taarab and Kidumbak

**Bi Kidude** Zanzibar (RetroAfric); *Machozi ya Huba: Bi Kidude*, Zanzibar 2003 (HeartBeat Records, Zanzibar); *Zanzibara 4: The Diva of Zanzibari* (Buda).

**Culture Musical Club** Taarab 1 & 4: The Music of Zanzibar (Globestyle); *Spices of Zanzibar* (Network Medien); *Bashraf: Taarab Instrumentals from Zanzibar* (Dizim);

Waridi, Scents of Zanzibar (Jahazi Media/EMI).

**Ikhwani Safaa** Taarab 2: The Music of Zanzibar (Globestyle); Zanzibara 1: A Hundred Years of Taarab in Zanzibar (Buda).

**Makame Faki** Various Zanzibar-published CDs, and, with Kidumbak

Kalcha group, *Ng'ambo – The Other Side of Zanzibar* (Dizim).

**Various artists** Music from Tanzania and Zanzibar (3 vols, Caprice); Poetry and Languid Charm (Topic/BLSA); Soul & Rhythm: Zanzibar (2 CDs, Jahazi Media/EMI); Zanzibar: Music of Celebration (Topic).

## Bongo Flava and Hip-Hop

**Kwanza Unit** *Kwanzanians* (Madunia/RAHH).

**Lady Jaydee** *Machozi* (Benchmark); *Binti* (Smooth Vibes); *Moto* (Smooth Vibes).

**Mr II** *Bongo Flava* (Kwetu Entertainment); *Sugu* (Social Misfit).

**Mwanafalsafa** *Unanitega* (Mawingu Records).

**Professor Jay** Machozi, Jasho na Damu (GMC); Mapinduzi halisi (GMC).

**Ray C** *Na wewe milele…* (GMC Wasanii).

**X-Plastaz** *Maasai Hip Hop* (OutHere Records, ⓦwww.xplastaz.com).

**Various artists** Bongo Flava – Swahili rap from Tanzania (OutHere Records).

# Online resources

ⓦ**www.africanhiphop.com** News and reviews of rap and hip-hop across the continent, plus two-hour webcasts (and archive) at ⓦafricanhiphopradio.com.

ⓦ**www.afropop.org** Lots of good features on Tanzanian music.

ⓦ**www.babkubwa.com** Up-to-date articles in English, plus music streams and links to downloads.

ⓦ**www.bluegecko.org/kenya** Principally Kenya, this site includes dozens of traditional recordings from the Luo, Maasai, Kuria, Makonde and Digo.

ⓦ**www.bongoradio.com** Chicago-based Tanzanian internet radio station.

ⓦ**www.busaramusic.org** Organizers of Zanzibar's foot-hopping Sauti za Busara festival. Click through to the database for performer bios.

ⓦ**www.eastafricantube.com** Heaps of music and video clips, mainly Bongo Flava, making this *the* place to get attuned to the latest.

ⓦ**www.natari.com** An amazing resource from a cassette fanatic, with many sound clips (mostly from the heyday of the dance bands), and some tapes for sale, too.

ⓦ**www.the-real-africa.com** Hundreds of contemporary videos from Tanzania, plus thousands from elsewhere around Africa.

# Language

# Language

# Kiswahili

**K**iswahili is the glue that binds Tanzania together. It's essentially a Bantu tongue, enriched by thousands of loan words, primarily Persian and Arabic, but also Hindi, Portuguese, German and English. English is widely spoken in touristic areas, but elsewhere you'll need to learn the basics. Don't worry about getting things wrong: people will be delighted (and no doubt amused) to hear you try.

A recommended **book** is the *Rough Guide Swahili Phrasebook*. There's also an excellent **online dictionary** at Ⓦwww.kamusiproject.org. For **language courses** and tuition, see this book's Index.

## Pronunciation

Kiswahili is **pronounced exactly as it's written**, with the stress nearly always on the penultimate syllable. Where an apostrophe precedes a vowel (eg *ng'ombe*, cattle), the vowel is accentuated, something like a gulp.

A as in appetite

AO sounds like "ow!"

B as in bedbug

CH as in China, but often sounds like "dj"

D as in dunderhead

DH like a cross between dhow and thou

DJ as in ginger

E between the "e" in bed and "i" in bid

F as in fan

G as in guide

GH at the back of the throat, like a growl; nearly an "r"

H as in harmless

I as in happy

J as in jug

K as in kiosk

KH as in a growling loch

L as in lullaby. Often pronounced "r"

M as in munch; preceding a consonant, it's one syllable, eg mnazi (coconut), "mna-zi"

N as in nonsense; preceding a consonant, it gives a nasal quality

NG as in bang

O as in orange

P as in paper

Q Same as K

R as in rough, or rolled. Often pronounced "l"

S as in silly

T as in Tanzania!

TH as in thanks

U has no English equivalent; it's the "ou" in a properly pronounced French vous

V as in victory

W as in wobbly

Y as in you

Z as in Zanzibar!

# Words and phrases

## Greetings and general conversation

Tourists are greeted with Jambo or, more correctly, Hujambo ("Things"). If you don't speak Kiswahili the reply is also *Jambo*, but if you want to make an effort, reply with Sijambo and continue with one of the following:

| | |
|---|---|
| News? | Habari? |
| Your news? | Habari gani? |
| What news? | Habari yako? |
| Good morning | Habari za asubuhi |
| How's work? | Habari za kazi? |
| How was the trip? | Habari za safari? |
| How's the day? | Habari za leo? |

Reply with:

| | |
|---|---|
| good/very good | Mzuri/Mzuri sana |
| clean or pure | Safi |
| not bad | Sibaya |

I show my respect Shikamoo or Shikamooni (when greeting several). Said to elders on the mainland, usually qualified by a title, eg Shikamoo, bibi, for an old woman (reply with Marahaba)

| | |
|---|---|
| Peace | Salaam, Salamu or Salama |
| Reply with | Salaam, Salamu or Salama |

### Kiswahili proverbs

The ability to pepper conversation with appropriate **proverbs** (*methali*) is much admired in Africa, and Tanzania is no exception, the pithier sayings even finding their way onto *kangas* worn by women, to express sentiments that might be taboo if spoken aloud. You might find some of the following useful yourself.

**Asifuye mvuwa imemnyea** He who praises rain has been rained on.

**Atangaye na jua hujuwa** He who wanders around by day a lot, learns a lot.

**Fadhila ya punda ni mateke** The gratitude of a donkey is a kick.

**Fumbo mfumbe mjinga mwerevu huliangua** Put a riddle to a fool, a clever person will solve it.

**Haba na haba, hujaza kibaba** Little and little, fills the measure.

**Haraka haraka haina baraka** Hurry hurry has no blessings.

**Heri kufa macho kuliko kufa moyo** Better to lose your eyes than your heart.

**Heri kujikwa kidole kuliko ulimi** Better to stumble with toe than tongue.

**Kila ndege huruka na mbawa zake** Every bird flies with its own wings.

**Kizuri chajiuza kibaya chajitembeza** A good thing sells itself, a bad one advertises itself.

**Maji ya kifufu ni bahari ya chungu** Water in a coconut shell is like an ocean to an ant.

**Mchumia juani, hilla kivulini** He who earns his living in the sun, eats in the shade.

**Mgeni ni kuku mweupe** A stranger is like a white fowl (noticeable)

**Mjinga akierevuka mwerevu yupo mashakani** When a fool becomes enlightened, the wise man is in trouble.

**Moyo wa kupenda hauna subira** A heart deep in love has no patience.

**Mwenye pupa hadiriki kula tamu** A hasty person misses the sweet things.

**Nazi mbovu harabu ya nzima** A rotten coconut in a heap spoils its neighbours.

**Penye nia ipo njia** Where there's a will there's a way.

**Ukipenda boga penda na ua lake** If you love a pumpkin also love its flower.

**Ulimi unauma kuliko meno** The tongue hurts more than the teeth.

**Usisa firie Nyota ya Mwenzio** Don't set sail using somebody else's star.

| | |
|---|---|
| Good morning/ good evening | Subalkheri/ Masalkheri (used in Zanzibar) |
| What's up? | Vipi? or Mambo? or Mambo Vipi? |
| Reply with cool (slang) | Poa, Bomba, Fresh or Gado |
| Hello?! (said on knocking or entering) | Hodi?! reply with welcome Karibu or Karibuni if replying to several |
| What is your name? | Jina lako nini? |
| My name is... | Jina langu... |
| Where are you from? | Unatoka wapi? |
| I am from... | Ninatoka... |
| May I take your picture? | Ninakwenda kupiga picha? |

## Titles

Use the following freely in greetings, and don't be afraid of calling an old lady you've never met before "grandmother" – it's a compliment.

| | |
|---|---|
| friend | rafiki |
| child | mtoto, *pl* watoto |
| mother/father | mama/baba (also an older person) |
| sister/brother | dada/kaka (also someone your age) |
| grandmother/ grandfather | bibi/babu (also an elderly person) |
| mister | bwana (lit. "master") |
| relative | ndugu (also figurative) |
| sir | mzee, *pl* wazee (respectful) |
| teacher | mwalimu (also anyone intelligent) |

## Nationalities

| | |
|---|---|
| Australia; Australian | Australia; Mwaustralia, *pl* Waaustralia |
| Canada; Canadian | Kanada; Mkanada, *pl* Wakanada |
| England; English | Uingereza; Mwingereza, *pl* Waingereza |
| Ireland; Irish | Ayalandi; Mwayalandi, *pl* Waayalandi |
| New Zealand; New Zealander | Nyuzilandi; Mnyuzilandi, *pl* Wanyuzilandi |
| Scotland; Scottish | Uskoti; Mskoti, *pl* Waskoti |
| South Africa; South African | Afrika Kusini; Mwafrika Kusini, *pl* Waafrika Kusini |
| United States; American | Marekani; Mmarekani, *pl* Wamarekani |
| Wales; Welsh | Welisi; Mwelisi, *pl* Wawelisi |

## Basic words and phrases

| | |
|---|---|
| please | tafadhali |
| thank you | asante (asanteni when speaking to several), or ushukuru, or, on Zanzibar, shukrani |
| yes/no | ndio/la (or hapana as an adverb) |
| none, there isn't | hakuna or hamna |
| maybe | labda |
| here/there | hapa/hapo |
| this or these | hii |
| my or mine | yangu for friend(s) or family (eg mama yangu, my mother); langu (*pl* yangu) for possessions (eg jina langu, my name); changu (*pl* vyangu) for objects (eg kitanda changu, my bed; vitabu vyangu, my books) |
| Really? | Kweli? |
| bad luck | bahati mbaya |
| I'm sorry (to sympathise) | pole (usually pole sana I'm very sorry) |
| I'm sorry (to apologise) | samahani |
| Excuse me (make room) | samahani kidogo |
| And the same to you | Na wewe pia |
| God willing | Mungu akipenda or (Muslim) Inshallah |
| OK | sawa or sawasawa |
| No problem | Hakuna matata, Hamna shida, or Wasiwasi |

| good, pretty, tasty, excellent | zuri |
| bad | baya |
| big/small | kubwa/dogo |
| a lot/a little | ingi/akali |
| fast/slow | epesi/pole |
| difficult/easy | zito/epesi |
| clean | safi |

### Farewells

| Goodbye | Kwaheri ("with blessings"; Kwaherini speaking to several) |
| Good night | Usiku mwema (when leaving) |

## Getting around

| car or vehicle/ passenger vehicle | gari/gari ya abiria |
| bus/taxi/daladala/ rickshaw/train | basi/teksi/daladala/ bajaji/treni |
| bicycle/scooter/ motorbike | baisikeli/pikipiki/ motobaiki |
| driver/mechanic/ petrol/oil | dereva/fundi/petroli/ mafuta |
| boat/ferry/ passenger boat | boti/meli/meli ya abiria |
| dhow | jahazi (large), mashua (smaller), ngalawa (outrigger) |
| canoe | mtumbwi |
| plane | ndege |
| on foot | kwa miguu |
| bus stop/taxi rank | kituo cha basi/kituo cha teksi |
| train station | stesheni |
| port/crossing place (for a ferry) | bandari/kivuko |
| airport | uwanja wa ndege (lit. "stadium of birds") |
| Where is the bus station? | Kiko wapi kituo cha basi? |
| Where are you going? | Unaenda wapi? |
| Is this the bus to... | Hii ni basi kwenda... |
| When is the first/last next bus to... | Basi la kwanza/ mwisho/jingine la kwenda…saangapi? |
| When will we arrive? | Tutafika saa ngapi? |

| Sleep well | Lala salama |
| Come back again | Rudi tena |
| We shall meet again | Tutaonana |

### Language difficulties

| I don't understand | Sifahamu |
| Sorry, I don't understand Kiswahili | Samahani, sifahamu Kiswahili |
| My Kiswahili is very bad | Kiswahili changu ni kibaya sana |
| Could you repeat that? | Sema tena? |
| Do you speak English? | Unasema Kiingereza? |
| How do you say... in Kiswahili? | Unasemaje kwa Kiswahili…? |

| ticket | tikiti |
| I'd like one ticket to... | Naomba tiketi moja ya kwenda… |
| one-way/return | kwenda tu/kwenda na kurudi |

### Directions

| Where is...? | Iko wapi...? |
| Where does this road go? | Njia hii inakwenda wapi? |
| the junction for... | njia panda ya… |
| left/right | kushoto/kulia |
| up/down | juu/chini |
| north/east/south /west | kaskazini/mashariki/ kusini/magharibi |
| straight ahead | moja kwa moja |
| keep going | twende tu |
| just there | palepale |
| wait (or be patient) | subiri |
| highway or road | barabara |
| street | mtaa |
| road or path | njia |
| roundabout | kiplefti ("keep left", from old English road signs!) |
| Can I walk? | Naweza kwenda kwa miguu? |
| slowly/carefully | pole pole/taratibu |
| quickly | haraka |
| Stop! | Simama! |

| | | | | |
|---|---|---|---|---|
| How many kilometres? | Kilometa ngapi? | | The car has broken down | Gari imevunjika |
| I'm going to… | Ninaenda… | | Safe journey | Safari njema |
| Let's go! | Twende! | | | |
| I want to get off here | Nataka kushuka hapa | | | |

## Numbers, time and dates

| | | | | |
|---|---|---|---|---|
| ¼ | robo | | quarter to ten | saa kumi kasa robo |
| ½ | nusu | | half past ten | saa kumi na nusu |
| 1 | moja | | dawn/morning/midday | alfajiri/asubuhi/adhuhuri |
| 2 | mbili | | afternoon/evening /night | mchana/jioni /usiku |
| 3 | tatu | | now/right now | sasa/sasa hivi |
| 4 | nne | | not yet/later | bado/baadaye |
| 5 | tano | | | |
| 6 | sita | | | |
| 7 | saba | | | |
| 8 | nane | | | |
| 9 | tisa | | | |
| 10 | kumi | | | |

### Days and weeks

| | | | | |
|---|---|---|---|---|
| 11 | kumi na moja | | every day/every week | kila siku/kila wiki |
| 12 | kumi na mbili | | Which day? | Siku gani? |
| 20 | ishirini | | today/tomorrow/ in two days | leo/kesho/kesho kutwa |
| 21 | ishirini na moja | | yesterday/several days ago | jana/majuzi |
| 30 | thelathini | | Monday | Jumatatu |
| 40 | arbaini | | Tuesday | Jumanne |
| 50 | hamsini | | Wednesday | Jumatano |
| 60 | sitini | | Thursday | Alhamisi |
| 70 | sabaini | | Friday | Ijumaa |
| 80 | themanini | | Saturday | Jumamosi |
| 90 | tisini | | Sunday | Jumapili |

### Months

| | | | | |
|---|---|---|---|---|
| 100 | mia or mia moja | | this month/this year | mwezi huu/mwaka huu |
| 121 | mia moja na ishirini na moja | | January | Januari |
| 200 | mia mbili | | February | Februari |
| 1000 | elfu or elfu moja | | March | Machi |
| 2000 | elfu mbili | | April | Aprili |
| 1,000,000 | milioni | | May | Mei |

### Time

| | | | | |
|---|---|---|---|---|
| hour(s)/minutes | saa/dakika | | June | Juni |
| What time?/What time is it now? | Saa ngapi?/Saa ngapi sasa hivi? | | July | Julai |
| ten o'clock | saa kumi | | August | Agosti |
| ten o'clock exactly | saa kumi kamili | | September | Septemba |
| quarter past ten | saa kumi na robo | | October | Oktoba |
| | | | November | Novemba |
| | | | December | Desemba |

## Accommodation

| | | | |
|---|---|---|---|
| hotel | hotel, nyumba ya wageni, nyumba ya kulala, or gesti | I want a room for two/three nights | Nataka kukaa kwa usiku mbili/tatu |
| campsite | uwanja wa kambi | Where's the bathroom/toilet? | Bafu/choo kiko wapi? |
| Where can I stay? | Naweza kukaa wapi? | hot water/cold water | maji moto/maji baridi |
| Can I stay here? | Naweza kukaa hapa? | bed | kitanda, pl vitanda; two beds vitanda viwili |
| reception | mapokezi | | |
| room | chumba, pl vyumba; | | |
| bedroom | chumba cha kulala | bedsheet/pillow | shiti/mto |
| room with bathroom | chumba selfu, chumba kwa bafu or chumba self containa | towel | taulo |
| | | mosquito net | chandarua |
| | | table and chair | kiti na meza |
| | | television | televisheni |
| room sharing bathroom | chumba siselfu or chumba common | candle | mshumaa |
| | | key | funguo or msingi |
| | | laundry | ufuaji |
| I'd like to see a room | Napenda kuona chumba | firewood | kuni |

## Security

| | | | |
|---|---|---|---|
| security guard | askari | thief | mwizi |
| danger | hatari (seen on signs) | police/officer | polisi/afisa |
| guard dog | mbwa mkali | | |

## Health

| | | | |
|---|---|---|---|
| I'm ill | Mimi ni mgonjwa | medicine | dawa (Western: dawa baridi; traditional: dawa kali) |
| doctor/dentist /hospital | daktari/daktari wa meno/hospitali | | |
| pharmacy | duka la madawa (or dispensari) | pills | vidonge |
| | | I'm allergic to... | Nina mzio wa... |
| pain/fever/nausea/ headache | umivo or umo/homa/ kichefuchefu/ maumivu ya kichwa | mosquito repellent | dawa ya mbu |
| | | razor/soap /toothpaste | sembe/sabuni/dawa ya meno |

## Shopping

| | | | |
|---|---|---|---|
| money/shilling/dollar | pesa/shilingi/dola | May I have/I want/ Give me... | Naomba/Nataka/ Nipe... |
| credit card/travellers' cheques | kadi ya benki/hundi ya msafiri | | |
| bank | benki | I don't want... | Sitaki... |
| shop | duka (eg duka la vitabu, bookshop) | I don't want to do business | Sitaki biashara |
| | | What's the price? | Pesa ngapi?, Bei gani? or Shilingi ngapi? (pronounced "shilingapi") |
| receipt | risiti | | |
| bag | mfuko | | |
| What is this? | Nini hii? | | |
| Do you have... | Kuna... | That's very expensive/cheap | Ni ghali/rahisi sana |

| Do you have something cheaper? | Una chochote kilicho rahisi zaidi? | Can you reduce the price? | Utapunguza tena kidogo? |
| Do you accept dollars? | Mnakubali dola? | OK, that's fine | Haya, sawa |

## Animals (*wanyama*)

| aardvark | mhanga, *pl* wahanga | elephant shrew | sengi |
| aardwolf | fisi mdogo, *pl* fisi wadogo | fish | samaki |
| | | frog | chura, *pl* vyura |
| baboon | nyani | gazelle | swala granti (Grant's), tomi (Thomson's) |
| bat | popo, *pl* mapopo | | |
| bat-eared fox | mbweha masikio | genet | kanu |
| bee | nyuki | gerenuk | swala twiga |
| bird | ndege | giraffe | twiga |
| blue monkey | nyabu | goat | mbuzi |
| buffalo | nyati or mbogo | Guinea fowl | kanga |
| bushbaby (galago) | komba | hare | sungura |
| bushbuck | kulungu or mbawala | hartebeest | kongoni |
| bush pig | nguruwe mwitu | hippopotamus | kiboko, *pl* viboko |
| butterfly | kipepeo, *pl* vipepeo | horse | farasi |
| cane rat | ndezi | hyena | fisi madoa (spotted), fisi miraba (striped) |
| caracal | simba mangu | | |
| cat | paka | impala | swala pala |
| cow, cattle | ng'ombe or gombe, *pl* magombe | insect | dudu, *pl* madudu |
| | | jackal | bweha |
| chameleon | kinyonga, *pl* vinyonga | klipspringer | mbuzi mawe |
| | | kudu | tandala mkubwa (greater), tandala mdogo (lesser) |
| cheetah | duma | | |
| chicken | kuku | | |
| chimpanzee | sokwe | leopard | chui |
| civet | fungo | lion | simba |
| colobus monkey | mbega | lizard | mjusi, *pl* mijusi |
| crocodile | mamba | mongoose | nguchiro |
| dikdik | digidigi or dika | monkey | tumbili |
| dog | mbwa | monitor lizard | kenge |
| dog (wild, or African hunting) | mbwa mwitu | oribi | kasia, *pl* makasia |
| | | oryx | choroa |
| dolphin | pomboo, *pl* mapomboo | ostrich | mbuni |
| | | otter | fisi maji |
| donkey, ass | punda | pangolin | kakakuona |
| duck | bata, *pl* mabata | pig | nguruwe |
| dugong (manatee) | nguva | porcupine | nungu or nungunungu |
| duiker | nysa (common), mindi (Abbot's), funo or kiduku (red; *pl* viduku), paa (blue) | rat | panya |
| | | ratel (honey badger) | nyegere |
| | | reedbuck | tohe |
| | | rhinoceros | kifaru, *pl* vifaru |
| eland | mpofu or mbungu | roan antelope | kirongo, *pl* virongo |
| elephant | tembo or ndovu | rock hyrax | pimbi or wibari |

| | |
|---|---|
| sable antelope | palahala |
| safari ant | siafu |
| serval | mondo |
| shark | papa |
| sheep | kondoo |
| snake | nyoka |
| spring hare | kamendegere |
| squirrel | kindi or chindi |
| steinbok, grysbok | dondoo or dondoro |
| topi | nyamera |
| tortoise | kobe, *pl* makobe |
| tree hyrax | pelele or perere |

| | |
|---|---|
| turtle | kasa kikoshi (Olive Ridley), kasa mwamba (Hawksbill), kasa uziwa (Green) |
| vervet monkey | ngedere |
| warthog | ngiri or gwasi, *pl* magwasi |
| waterbuck | kuro |
| whale | nyangumi |
| wild dog | mbwa mwitu |
| wildebeest | nyumbu |
| zebra | punda milia |

## Eating and drinking

| | |
|---|---|
| food | chakula |
| restaurant | hoteli (mgahawa is a very basic one) |
| street food vendor | mama lisha ("feeding lady"; also baba lisha) |
| breakfast/lunch /dinner | chakula cha asubuhi/ chakula cha mchana/chakula cha jioni |
| table/chair | meza/kiti |
| knife/fork/spoon | kisu/uma/kijiko |
| plate | sahani |
| glass/cup/bottle /sachet | bilauri (or glasi)/ kikombe/chupa/ kiroba |
| a piece of… | kipande cha… |
| half (portion) | nusu |
| mixture | mchanganyiko (or nusu nusu for half-half) |

| | |
|---|---|
| enough! | tosha! or basi! |
| roast/boiled/stewed/ fried/mashed | kuchoma/kuchemsha/ rosti/kukaanga/ kuponda |
| Is there any…? | Iko…? or Kuna…? |
| I am hungry | Ninasikia njaa |
| I am thirsty | Nina kiu |
| Do you serve food? | Kuna huduma ya chakula? |
| I don't eat meat | Mimi sili nyama |
| hot/cold | moto/baridi |
| Enjoy your meal! | Karibu chakula! or Kufurahia chakula! |
| Good food! | Chakula kizuri! or Chakula kitamu! |
| Cheers! | Maisha marefu! ("Long life!"); Maisha mazuri! ("Life is good!"); Afya! ("Health!") |
| I'd like the bill | Lete bili tafadhali |

# Menu reader

Except in basic places whose menus are chalked up on blackboards (if they have more than one dish), menus tend to have English translations, or are simple couplets (rice/chips/*ugali*/chapati/*pilau* with beef/goat/fish/prawns/beans): once you learn the words for the basic staples, you're on your way. Particularly notable dishes are mentioned in Basics (see pp.39–41) but there are some things that aren't immediately obvious.

## Basics

| | |
|---|---|
| achali/kachumbari/ kiungo cha embe | pickle/pickled onion/ mango relish |
| adesi or dengu | lentils |
| chumvi | salt |
| haradali/kechap | mustard/ketchup |
| jibini or chisi | cheese |
| korosho/karanga | cashew/peanuts |
| mafuta | oil |
| maharage or kunde | beans |
| mahindi | corn (maize) |
| mayai... | eggs |
| ... ya kuvuruga/ kukaanga/ kuchemsha | scrambled/fried/ boiled |
| mkate | bread |
| mtama | millet |
| muhogo | cassava |
| pilipili manga | pepper |
| pilipili or pilipili hoho | chilli |
| shelisheli | breadfruit |
| siki | vinegar |
| sukari | sugar |
| wali | rice |

## Meat (*nyama*)

| | |
|---|---|
| figo | kidney |
| firigisi | gizzards |
| maini | liver |
| nyama ya ... | Used to describe the type of meat |
| ...bata | ...duck |
| ...bata mzinga | ...goose |
| ...kondoo | ...mutton |
| ...kuku | ...chicken |
| ...mbuzi | ...goat |
| ...ng'ombe | ...beef |
| ...nguruwe (or kiti moto) | ...pork |
| steki | steak |
| ulimi | tongue |
| utumbo | tripe |

## Fish (*samaki*) and seafood

| | |
|---|---|
| changu | bream |
| chewa | rock cod |
| kaa | crab |
| kamba | prawns |
| kamba mtii (or kamba kochi) | lobster |
| kolekole or nguru | kingfish |
| pweza/ngisi | octopus/squid |
| sangara | Nile perch |

## Vegetables (*mboga*)

| | |
|---|---|
| biringani; small bitter ones are nyanya chungu ("bitter tomato"), also called ngogwe aubergine (eggplant) | |
| boga | pumpkin |
| kabichi | cabbage |
| karoti | carrots |
| kisamvu | cassava leaves |
| matembere or mabamia | okra (lady's fingers) |
| mbaazi or pizi | peas |
| mchicha | spinach |
| nyanya | tomatoes |
| pilipili mboga or pombo | sweet pepper green leaves (generic) |
| saladi | salad |
| tango | cucumber |
| uyoga | mushrooms |
| viazi | potatoes |
| viazi vitamu | sweet potatoes |
| vitunguu | onions |

## Herbs and spices (viungo vya chakula)

| | |
|---|---|
| giligilani | coriander |
| hiliki | cardamom |
| jira | cumin |
| karafuu | cloves |
| kungumanga | nutmeg |
| manjano | turmeric |
| mchaichai | lemon grass |
| mdalasini | cinnamon |
| mrehani | sweet basil |
| simsim | sesame |
| tangawizi | ginger |

## Fruit (tunda, pl matunda)

| | |
|---|---|
| embe | mango |
| fenesi | jackfruit |
| limao | lemon |
| machungwa | orange |
| mchekwa, mtopetope or mtomoko | custard apple |
| mishmishi | apricot |
| mua | sugar cane |
| nanasi | pineapple |
| nazi (dafu for drinking) | coconut |
| ndimu | lime |
| ndizi | banana |
| papai | papaya (pawpaw) |
| pasheni | passion fruit |
| pea | avocado |
| pera | guava |
| shokishoki | lychee |
| stafeli | soursop |
| tende | dates |
| tikiti | watermelon |
| tunda la kizungu or tofaa | apple |
| ukwaju | tamarind |
| zabibu | grapes |

## Drinks (kinywaji, pl vinywaji)

| | |
|---|---|
| barafu | ice |
| bia (also pombe, busa) | beer |
| buli la chai/kahawa | pot of tea/coffee |
| chai | tea |
| chai rangi/maziwa/ masala/ tagawizi | black tea/milky/ spiced/ginger |
| juisi/juisi ya matunda | juice/fruit juice |
| kahawa | coffee |
| kokoa iliyo moto | hot chocolate |
| maji/maji ya kunywa | water/drinking water |
| maziwa/mtindi (or maziwa mgando) | milk/buttermilk |
| tuwi | coconut milk |
| yenye barafu/ yasiyokuwa barafu | with ice/without ice |

## Dishes and snacks

| | |
|---|---|
| andazi | doughnut (rarely sweet) |
| ashikrimu | ice cream |
| biriani | highly spiced dish of meat and rice |
| biskuti | biscuits |
| chipsi | chips |
| chipsi mayai | chip omelette |
| chop | several possibilities, all with an oily deep-fried batter: hard-boiled egg (egg chop), a short cylinder of meat and other stuff, or even a rib of mutton or chicken leg (chicken lollipop) |
| halua | an aromatic, super-sticky, super-sweet glob of cooked wheat gluten |
| kababu | fried meatball |
| katlesi or kachori | minced meat wrapped in mashed potato |
| keki | cake (eg keki ya matunda, fruit cake) |
| kitumbua | deep-fried rice cake |
| kiwanda | omelette |
| mahindi | maize cob |
| mantabali | "Zanzibari pizza", supposedly stuffed chapati but can be almost anything |
| matoke | banana stew |
| mchuzi (eg mchuzi wa nazi coconut sauce) | stew, sauce or curry |

| | | | |
|---|---|---|---|
| **mishkaki** or **mishikaki** | a little skewer of grilled meat, usually beef or goat | **supu** | literally soup, in local places this is a spicy broth (usually goat or beef, *supu ya mbuzi/ng'ombe*) served with lemon and chilli, and eaten at breakfast along with chapatis. *Supu ya makongoro* is with animal hooves, *supu ya utumbo* is with intestines |
| **mtori** | a light banana soup (Moshi and westwards) | | |
| **nyama choma** | char-grilled meat (goat is best), traditionally accompanied by grilled bananas (*ndizi*) and chilli | | |
| **pilau** | rice spiced with cardamom, cinnamon, cloves and pepper, and whatever else comes to hand | | |
| | | **ugali** | Tanzania's staple, a stodgy cornmeal polenta usually served with a small bowl of stewed fish, meat or vegetables |
| **pweza na nazi** | octopus simmered in coconut sauce – a Zanzibari favourite | | |
| **sambusa** | samosa (triangle of pastry, usually stuffed with minced meat, onion and pepper, sometimes just potato) | **uji** | porridge; traditionally made from finger millet (*uji wa ulezi*) |

# Glossary

**Afrika ya Mashariki** East Africa

**askari** security guard or soldier

**banda**, *pl* **mabanda** any kind of hut, usually rectangular and with a sloping thatched roof

**bao** a chess-like board game

**baraza** stone bench, a sitting or meeting place

**boma** Maasai village; also colonial-era headquarters (from British Overseas Management Administration)

**boriti** mangrove poles used in building

**buibui** the black cover-all cloak and veil of Muslim women

**chai** a bribe (literally "tea")

**choo** toilet (gents **wanaume**, ladies **wanawake**)

**chuo kikuu** university

**imamu** Imam, a mosque's prayer-leader

**fly catcher** tourist tout (called **papasi** on Zanzibar)

**jengo**, *pl* **majenjo** building

**kabila**, *pl* **makabila** tribe

**kanga** or **khanga** printed cotton sheet incorporating a proverb, worn by women

**kanisa** church

**kanzu** man's long robe (Muslim areas)

**kaskazi** northeast monsoon (Dec–March)

**kitabu** book

**kitenge**, *pl* **vitenge** double-paned cotton cloth

**kofia** man's embroidered cap (Muslim areas)

**kopje** a low, eroded granite outcrop, a feature of the Serengeti

**korongo** ditch or ravine

**kusi** southwest monsoon (June–Sept)

**makuti** palm-leaf thatch, used for roofing

**malaya** prostitute (easily confused with *malaika*, angel…)

**mbuga** black cotton soil, impassable by motor vehicles in rains

**mgahawa** small restaurant

**mihrab** prayer niche set in a mosque's *qibla*, the wall facing Mecca

**msikiti** mosque

**mtaa** ward or neighbourhood; street

**Mungu** God

**murram** red clay and gravel road

**mzungu**, *pl* **wazungu** European or white person

**ngoma** dance, drum, music, celebration (*ngoma ya kiasili* traditional music)

**panga** machete or knife

**posta** post office

**rondavel** round hut or cottage, often thatched

**safari** any journey

**semadari** traditional Zanzibari four-poster bed

**serikali** government

**shamba** farm

**shisha** water pipe

**shuka** red robe worn by Maasai men

**shule** school (mainland)

**simu** telephone

**skuli** school (Zanzibar)

**soko, soko kuu** market, main market

**tembe** flat-roofed hut, common in central Tanzania

**ubalozi** embassy, consulate

**utalii** tourism

# Small print and
# Index

# A Rough Guide to Rough Guides

Published in 1982, the first Rough Guide – to Greece – was a student scheme that became a publishing phenomenon. Mark Ellingham, a recent graduate in English from Bristol University, had been travelling in Greece the previous summer and couldn't find the right guidebook. With a small group of friends he wrote his own guide, combining a highly contemporary, journalistic style with a thoroughly practical approach to travellers' needs.

The immediate success of the book spawned a series that rapidly covered dozens of destinations. And, in addition to impecunious backpackers, Rough Guides soon acquired a much broader and older readership that relished the guides' wit and inquisitiveness as much as their enthusiastic, critical approach and value-for-money ethos.

These days, Rough Guides include recommendations from shoestring to luxury and cover more than 200 destinations around the globe, including almost every country in the Americas and Europe, more than half of Africa and most of Asia and Australasia. Our ever-growing team of authors and photographers is spread all over the world, particularly in Europe, the US and Australia.

In the early 1990s, Rough Guides branched out of travel, with the publication of Rough Guides to World Music, Classical Music and the Internet. All three have become benchmark titles in their fields, spearheading the publication of a wide range of books under the Rough Guide name.

Including the travel series, Rough Guides now number more than 350 titles, covering: phrasebooks, waterproof maps, music guides from Opera to Heavy Metal, reference works as diverse as Conspiracy Theories and Shakespeare, and popular culture books from iPods to Poker. Rough Guides also produce a series of more than 120 World Music CDs in partnership with World Music Network.

Visit www.roughguides.com to see our latest publications.

Rough Guide travel images are available for commercial licensing at www.roughguidespictures.com

# Rough Guide credits

**Text editors**: Edward Aves, Róisín Cameron and
Amanda Howard
**Layout**: Sachin Gupta
**Cartography**: Deshpal Dabas
**Picture editor**: Michelle Bhatia
**Production**: Rebecca Short
**Proofreader**: Stewart Wild
**Cover design**: Chloë Roberts
**Photographer**: Suzanne Porter
**Editorial**: Ruth Blackmore, Andy Turner, Keith
Drew, Alice Park, Lucy White, Jo Kirby, James
Smart, Natasha Foges, Emma Traynor, Emma
Gibbs, Kathryn Lane, Monica Woods, Mani
Ramaswamy, Harry Wilson, Lucy Cowie, Lara
Kavanagh, Alison Roberts, Joe Staines, Peter
Buckley, Matthew Milton, Tracy Hopkins, Ruth
Tidball; **Delhi** Madhavi Singh, Karen D'Souza,
Lubna Shaheen
**Design & Pictures**: **London** Scott Stickland,
Dan May, Diana Jarvis, Mark Thomas, Nicole
Newman, Sarah Cummins, Emily Taylor;
**Delhi** Umesh Aggarwal, Ajay Verma, Jessica
Subramaniam, Ankur Guha, Pradeep Thapliyal,
Sachin Tanwar, Anita Singh, Nikhil Agarwal
**Production**: Vicky Baldwin

**Cartography**: **London** Maxine Repath, Ed
Wright, Katie Lloyd-Jones; **Delhi** Rajesh
Chhibber, Ashutosh Bharti, Rajesh Mishra,
Animesh Pathak, Jasbir Sandhu, Karobi Gogoi,
Alakananda Bhattacharya, Swati Handoo
**Online**: **London** George Atwell, Faye Hellon,
Jeanette Angell, Fergus Day, Justine Bright, Clare
Bryson, Aine Fearon, Adrian Low, Ezgi Celebi,
Amber Bloomfield; **Delhi** Amit Verma, Rahul Kumar,
Narender Kumar, Ravi Yadav, Debojit Borah,
Rakesh Kumar, Ganesh Sharma, Shisir Basumatari
**Marketing & Publicity**: **London** Liz Statham,
Niki Hanmer, Louise Maher, Jess Carter, Vanessa
Godden, Vivienne Watton, Anna Paynton, Rachel
Sprackett, Libby Jellie, Laura Vipond, Vanessa
McDonald; **New York** Katy Ball, Judi Powers,
Nancy Lambert; **Delhi** Ragini Govind
**Manager India**: Punita Singh
**Reference Director**: Andrew Lockett
**Operations Manager**: Helen Atkinson
**PA to Publishing Director**: Nicola Henderson
**Publishing Director**: Martin Dunford
**Commercial Manager**: Gino Magnotta
**Managing Director**: John Duhigg

**SMALL PRINT**

# Publishing information

This third edition published January 2010 by
**Rough Guides Ltd**,
80 Strand, London WC2R 0RL
14 Local Shopping Centre, Panchsheel Park,
New Delhi 110017, India
**Distributed by the Penguin Group**
Penguin Books Ltd,
80 Strand, London WC2R 0RL
Penguin Group (USA)
375 Hudson Street, NY 10014, USA
Penguin Group (Australia)
250 Camberwell Road, Camberwell,
Victoria 3124, Australia
Penguin Group (Canada)
195 Harry Walker Parkway N, Newmarket, ON,
L3Y 7B3 Canada
Penguin Group (NZ)
67 Apollo Drive, Mairangi Bay, Auckland 1310,
New Zealand
Cover concept by Peter Dyer.

Typeset in Bembo and Helvetica to an original
design by Henry Iles.
Printed in Singapore
© Jens Finke, 2010
Maps © Rough Guides
No part of this book may be reproduced in any
form without permission from the publisher except
for the quotation of brief passages in reviews.
648pp includes index
A catalogue record for this book is available from
the British Library
ISBN: 978-1-84836-075-4
The publishers and authors have done their best
to ensure the accuracy and currency of all the
information in **The Rough Guide to Tanzania**,
however, they can accept no responsibility for
any loss, injury, or inconvenience sustained by
any traveller as a result of information or advice
contained in the guide.

1   3   5   7   9   8   6   4   2

# Help us update

We've gone to a lot of effort to ensure that the
third edition of **The Rough Guide to Tanzania**
is accurate and up-to-date. However, things
change – places get "discovered", opening hours
are notoriously fickle, restaurants and rooms raise
prices or lower standards. If you feel we've got it
wrong or left something out, we'd like to know,
and if you can remember the address, the price,
the hours, the phone number, so much the better.

Please send your comments with the subject
line "**Rough Guide Tanzania Update**" to ©mail
@roughguides.com. We'll credit all contributions
and send a copy of the next edition (or any other
Rough Guide if you prefer) for the very best
emails.
Have your questions answered and tell others
about your trip at ®www.roughguides.com

# Acknowledgements

**Jens Finke** I would like to thank the following very nice people who went out of their way to help me in Tanzania:

Elly Amani, Annette (Tulia Beach), Alex Balfour, Rob & Jeanann Barbour, David Barker, Rudolf Blauth, Michelle Bragg, Mwinyi Haji Boko Bwanga, Christian Chilcott, Immaculate Diyamett (TTB), Danielle & Jean Dominique, Mark Evans, Jane Fox, Gobba in Mbeya, Tara Guthrie, Whitney Hall, Farid Hamid, Andy and Susie Hart and indeed everyone at Neema Crafts, Olav Holten, Peter Junior, Wim and Kerstin at Kasa Divers, Rachel Kessi, David Kimera, Massimo Lancelotti, Alban Lutambi, Francesca Marty, Devota Mdachi (TTB), Rajab Mdaki, Haji Khamis Mdungi, Andrew Mjawa, Godwill Mkunda, Meja Mkundah, Flo Montgomery, Oscar Ngalay Mosha, John Mugenfi, Victor Mugisa, Paul Nnyiti (WCST), Niko Ntinda, Hannes Potgieter, Gilly Roberts, Corodius Sawe, Leonie Schollmeyer, Rodgers Shelukindo, and Farhat Jah (Raf), Emma and Stu at Swahili Divers. Back home, special thanks go to Maria Helena for her endless patience and good humour in weathering the oft tenebrous Rough Guide storms, and to my quartet of eagle-eyed editors: Edward Aves, Keith Drew, Amanda Howard and Róisín Cameron.

**Henry Stedman** I would like to thank Karen Valenti at KPAP, everyone at Shidolya and TK, and Simon and James at East African Safaris

# Readers' letters

Thanks to all the readers who have taken the time to write in with comments and suggestions (and apologies if we've inadvertently omitted or misspelt anyone's name):

Sunita Abraham, Nassor S. Ali, Ron and Ruth Alkema, Genevieve Anderson, Kevin Barnes, Debi Basu, Bob Beams, Abbey Beck, Robert and Julia Belcher, Beth and Hai (Texas), Ben Botha, Lyn Brayshaw, Sarah Carroll, Neil Cave, Johanna Court-Brown, Gemma Crespi, Nancy Cutinha, Jan Dodd, Donna Duggan, Maria Eneqvist, Seth Falconer, Blathnaid Ni Fhatharta, Bruce Fox, Gabriel Glöckler, Michael Godfrey, Hok Goei, Richard Grubb, Charlotta and Heribert Heck, Catriona Helliwell, Andy Hemingway, Nick Hepworth, Suzanne Heuts, Kik van den Heuvel, Mairi Hutchison, Tom Ingvarson, Faryl Kaye, Sarah Kennedy, Gijsbert Koren, Esther Leenders, Issa Machano, Fiona Mackay, Hannah Manson and friends, Alfred Massawe, Lilia McGonigle, Haji Khamisi Mdungi, Luigi Meloncelli, Jan Messing, Ben Miller, Saori Miura, Mwinjuma Muharami, Ron and Viv Moon, Liam Murray, Peggy Novak, Graham Openshaw, Wendy Paton, Helen Peeks, Mayte Penelas, Manuel Duran Pereira, Andrea Perlo, Will Phillips, Simon Pleasance, Caroline Porter, Suzanne Porter, John Ragatz, Lisa Rajan, Jan van de Ree, Patricia Rhodes, Martin Rievers, Denys, Gilly & Jane Roberts, Corodius Sawe, Gillian Shaw, Ernie Skelly, Ove Slyngen, Ben Smith, Glen Spurrell, Joshua Switzky, Andrew Talks, Vivian Unterweger, Christel de Valk, Paul Wadden, Charlene West, Adam Williams, Randall Wood, Colin and Jane Woodhams, Fronza Woods.

## Photo credits

All photos © Rough Guides except the following:

SMALL PRINT

p.152 Gereza Fort, Kilwa Kisiwani © Ariadne Van Zandbergen/Alamy

p.158 Turtle © Darryl Leniuk/Masterfile

p.170 Mosque, Kilwa Kisiwani, Tanzania © Jason Gallier/Alamy

p.191 Makonde carver © Zute Lightfoot/Alamy

p.214 Giraffe, Mikumi National Park © Graeme Miller/Alamy

p.225 Blue monkey, Udzungwa Mountains National Park © MJ Photography/Alamy

p.248 Elephants and Mount Kilimanjaro © Dan Kite/iStock

p.262 Hiking to Barafu Camp, Mount Kilimanjaro © WorldFoto/Alamy

p.336 Wildebeest migration, Ngorongoro Crater © Keith Drew

p.352 Pelicans, Lake Manyara National Park © Superstock

p.358 Masaai © Tanzanian Tourist Board

p.377 Young lions, Serengeti © John Pitcher /iStock

p.390 Bismarck rock, Lake Victoria © De Agostini/World Illustrated/Photoshot

p.419 Egyptian goose and chicks, Rubondo Island © Peter Arnold Inc./Alamy

p.424 Hippo Katuma River, Katavi National Park © Joe McDaniel/iStock

p.434 Boarding MV *Liemba*, Lake Tanganyika © Karsten Wrobel/Alamy

p.445 Chimpanzees, Mahale National Park © Nigel Pavitt/John Warburton-Lee/Alamy

p.464 Isimila, Iringa © Travel Ink/Alamy

p.470 Playing *bao*, Iringa © Andy Aitchison /CORBIS

p.480 Baobab tree, Ruaha National Park © Jon Arnold Images Ltd/Alamy

p.498 Matema Beach, Lake Nyasa © Ariadne Van Zandbergen/Alamy

# Index

Map entries are in colour.

www.roughguides.com

# Map symbols

maps are listed in the full index using coloured text

## Regional Maps

▪▪▪▪ International boundary
▪▪▪ Chapter division boundary
▪▪▪▪ Disputed boundary
▬▬ Motorways
═══ Major tarred road
─── Minor tarred road
─── Untarred road
········· 4 wheel drive
····· Footpath
▬▬ Railway
─── Coastline/river
─ ─ Ferry route
▬▬ Wall
✈ International airport
✈ Domestic airport
♦ Point of interest
▲ Mountain peak
⛰ Mountain range
◉ Crater
Gorge
Reef rocks
Hill shading
Waterfall
Spring
⌣ Bridge
Viewpoint
⌂ Cave
∴ Ruins
Lighthouse
Church
Δ Campsite
Hut
Ranger post
⊠–⊠ Gate
Picnic site

♦ Museum
National park/nature reserve
Glacier
Swamp
Mangrove swamp
Coral reef
Beach

## Town Maps

═══ Tarred roads
═════ Untarred roads
ⓘ Information office
⊠ Post office
🕒 Telephone office
@ Internet access
⊙ Statue
🅿 Parking
★ Transport stop
⊞ Hospital
Swimming pool
Mosque
Sikh temple
Hindu temple
Petrol station
Toilets
Coconut plantation
Mango tree
Building
Church
Market
Stadium
Christian cemetery
Muslim cemetery
Park

# The last word ...

The vast majority of visitors to Tanzania and Zanzibar arrange and book their whole trip in advance. The best lodges and guesthouses are heavily over-demanded for much of the year. Turning up on the doorstep is simply not an option, you need to book well ahead of time. Transport too needs to be pre-planned, with overland safari companies running short of decent vehicles and internal airlines often operating at maximum capacity. Add to that the complexity of linking all these components together and you start to understand exactly why even the most hardened independent travellers suddenly find themselves booking through a travel agent.

The good news is that the safari world, Tanzania and Zanzibar in particular, are serviced by some exceptional specialist travel companies, staffed by people with genuine enthusiasm, in depth knowledge and real first hand experience of travelling and working in Africa. These guys should be able to take the hard labour out of trip planning, get you deeper under the skin of the place and even deliver the whole thing at a lower price than if you had booked all the elements individually.

One of the leading companies involved in putting together tailormade safaris to this area is Africa Travel Resource, which specialises in innovative and off the beaten track trips to suit a broad range of budgets. Whether or not you ultimately end up arranging your trip with them, it may well be worth taking a good look at their website www.africatravelresource.com, which has for some time been widely regarded as the leading internet resource for travel to Tanzania and Zanzibar.

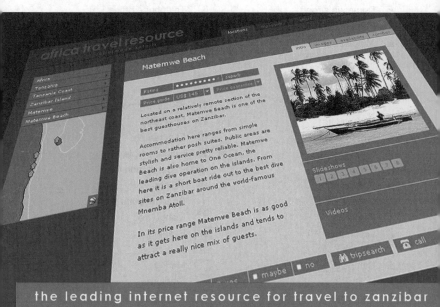